Special Edition

Using
Windows® 98,
Second Edition

SETTING UP A
WINDOWS 98 NETWORK

1. Right-click Network Neighborhood and select Properties.
2. Make sure the configuration tab is selected, and click the Add button. You will see the Select Network Component Type dialog box (see Figure 1).

At this point, Windows 98 will inform you that it is building a Driver Information Base. When that process is complete, you will see the Select Network Adapters dialog box. Scroll down the list of manufacturers on the left side of the dialog box to select the appropriate one, and then select the specific network adapter from the list on the right (see Figure 2).

After rebooting your system, you can go to the Device Manager to determine whether the card has been installed properly.

Planning and Implementing the Transport Layer

When you have finished setting up your physical connection, you must install a protocol that both systems will use to communicate with one another. By installing a like protocol, you enable the computers to talk to each other. In this fashion, protocols are much like our languages. Just as two individuals must speak the same language to communicate, so must two computers. For two computers to "talk" to one another, they too must first agree on a common language. This common language is the *protocol*.

To install a protocol, follow these steps:

1. From the Start menu choose Settings, Control Panel, and then double-click the Network icon.

2. The Network dialog box appears. On the Configuration tab, choose Add. The Select Network Component Type dialog box appears (see Figure 3).

Figure 3

Choose a protocol from the Network Component Type list.

3. Choose Protocol, and then click Add. The Select Network Protocol dialog box appears. Choose Microsoft from the Manufacturers list.

The next step is to choose the protocol from the Network Protocols list. For our purposes, assume a workgroup environment in which communication to NetWare systems is not a requirement. In this case, the two protocols that a Windows 98 network will utilize are NetBEUI and TCP/IP. All other protocols in the list relate to different operating system environments. Although NetBEUI and TCP/IP will both work equally well for our purposes, they are quite different to configure:

■ **NetBEUI**—For a home network using Windows 98, the easiest protocol to set up is NetBEUI. With NetBEUI, there is no further configuration beyond the installation of the protocol. After this is done, the systems running NetBEUI will be able to communicate with one another. NetBEUI uses broadcasts across the physical network to send information from one computer to another. With broadcasts, the sending computer transmits information to all computers on a network but uses the destination computer's name, technically called the NetBios name, to identify the computer being transmitted to. This is like calling out to someone in a crowd by yelling their name. Everyone within ear shot will hear you calling them, but only the person being called by name will respond and communicate back to you.

To use NetBEUI when this is finished, simply choose this protocol on both (or all) systems on your home network and proceed to enable your Windows 98 environment to share resources (files, folders, and printers). (Sharing resources is addressed later in this booklet.) If you are using a router, be sure it is capable of forwarding broadcasts.

■ **TCP/IP**—If you feel adventurous, you may choose to use TCP/IP as your protocol. TCP/IP is capable of transmitting in a point-to-point fashion. That means that, unlike NetBEUI, which broadcasts to everyone just to find one recipient, TCP/IP uses a special IP address that uniquely identifies a computer from the rest of the network. By using IP addresses, one computer can send a message directly to another, instead of having to call out to everyone on the network to find them. You can think of an IP address as a ZIP+4 and the Network card address (called a MAC address) as the street number. If you have a ZIP+4 on a letter, the carrier knows exactly which block you live on in your area. When he gets to your street, he looks at the street number to find the exact location of your house. By using TCP/IP, you can potentially minimize the broadcast traffic on your network by directing it instead of sending it everywhere in search of its intended recipient. In a Windows 98 environment, this protocol will require a bit of configuration before it will work smoothly. As is the case with all transport protocols, you first must configure the protocol before moving on to sharing resources.

After you have decided which protocol you want to use for your home network (NetBEUI or TCP/IP), choose it from the Network Protocols list and click OK. Windows 98 will install your new protocol. If you are asked to reboot, do so.

If you choose TCP/IP, the protocol will have to be configured with an IP address. If you are not prompted to o so during the protocol's installation, you can configure it after you reboot your system. To do so, from the Start menu choose Settings, Control Panel, and then double-click the Network icon. The Network dialog box appears.

On the Configuration tab, choose the TCP/IP protocol that refers to your network adapter (see Figure 4).

Figure 4

Choose the TCP/IP protocol that references your network adapter.

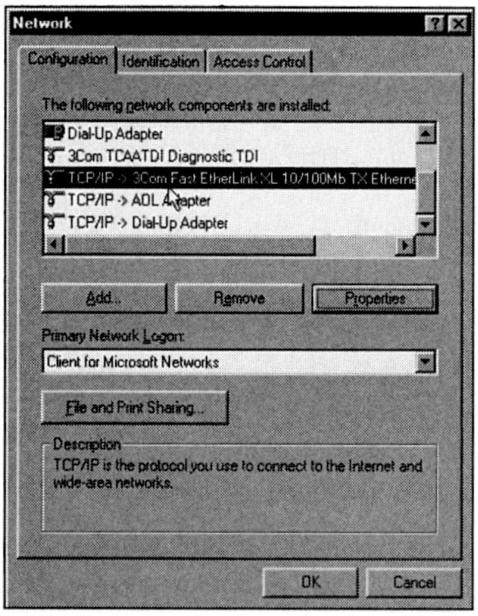

Click properties and choose the IP Address tab. Here, you will enter an IP address to uniquely identify your computer on your home network. IP addresses are four sets of numbers separated by a period, such as 192.168.1.1. Although you can choose any address, some ranges are specifically set aside for private use in the home or office:

- 10.0.0.0 through 10.255.255.255—All must begin with 10.*something.* For example, 10.200.50.95 is acceptable, 11.200.50.95 is not. The subnet mask for this address is 255.0.0.0.
- 172.16.0.0 through 172.31.255.255—All must begin with 172.16–31.*something.* For example, 172.28.1.1 is acceptable, 172.200.1.1 is not. The subnet mask for this address is 255.255.0.0.
- 192.168.0.0 through 192.168.255.255—All must begin with 192.168.*something.* For example, 192.168.1.1 is acceptable, 192.164.1.1 is not. The subnet mask for this address is 255.255.255.0.

As long as you use the same range of numbers for all your computers, they will be capable of communicating with each other. For example, if you choose the first range, an acceptable IP address would be 10.1.1.1. The next computer on your network should be 10.1.1.2, the next 10.1.1.3, and so on.

After you have entered an IP address for your protocol, your system will restart. To test whether the IP address is working properly, open a command prompt, type `ipconfig`, and press Enter. The IP address you entered should appear for your network adapter. To test whether the IP address is working properly, open a command prompt, type `ping` and the IP address of your computer, and press Enter. You should get a reply.

Next, test another computer on your network by typing `ping` and the IP address of another computer, and press Enter. Again, you should get a reply. If there is no reply, follow the steps carefully from the physical setup all the way back to the transport setup and test again.

Planning and Implementing the Application Layer

After you have set up your physical and transport layers, you are ready to set up Windows 98 to share resources with the other computers through the Application layer.

1. From the Start menu choose Settings, Control Panel, and then double-click the Network icon.
2. The Network dialog box appears. Choose the Identification tab. In the Workgroup box, make sure all computers are in the same workgroup. If any are different, rename them so they are the same on all the computers.
3. Select the Configuration tab. Select the File and Print Sharing button. The File and Print Sharing dialog box appears.
4. Click the first check box to give others on the network access to your files. Click the second check box to give others on the network access to your printers. Click OK, and then click OK again. You will be asked to restart your system. Click OK.

When Windows restarts, you can enable a folder (not files alone, however) or a printer to be shared. The steps are the same for folders or printers with only slightly different choices. For this example, I'll choose a folder with files you want to share.

1. Right-click the folder. Choose Sharing from the menu.
2. In the Shared Info Properties dialog box, click the Shared As check box to select it (see Figure 5).

Figure 5
Share resources with restrictions by setting access passwords.

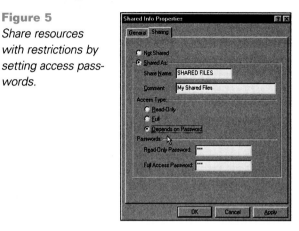

3. Next, give a name to your shared folder to identify it to others on the network. You also can add comments to further identify the resource.
4. For a folder, you can choose whether to give Full control to others or Read-Only permission. Or, you can set a password for each type of access and give different levels of control based on the associated password. For example, based on the password you give him or her, let your spouse have Full Access to a shared folder but give your kids Read-Only or no permission.

    If sharing a printer, you will not have different levels of access, but you can set a password to allow its use by someone or not.
5. When you are finished, click OK. The folder or printer will appear with a hand icon under it to indicate that your computer is sharing it.

When you have completed all these steps, use Network Neighborhood to browse to a computer. You should see any shared folders or printers in the window for that computer. Click the shared folder or printer on the other computer to use it as a resource without leaving your chair.

You have now successfully set up and tested your network and shared resources. Good luck and have fun!

Special Edition
Using
Windows® 98,
Second Edition

Ed Bott

Ron Person, et al.

A Division of Macmillan USA
201 W. 103rd Street
Indianapolis, Indiana 46290

CONTENTS AT A GLANCE

SPECIAL EDITION USING WINDOWS® 98, SECOND EDITION

International Standard Book Number: 0-7897-2203-8

Library of Congress Catalog Card Number: 99-067443

Printed in the United States of America

First Printing: December 1999

01   00   4   3

TRADEMARKS

WARNING AND DISCLAIMER

Associate Publisher
Jim Minatel

Acquistions Editor
Tracy Williams

Development Editors
Mark Cierzniack
Jill Hayden

Managing Editor
Lisa Wilson

Project Editor
Tonya Simpson

Copy Editor
June Waldman

Indexer
Aamir Burki

Proofreaders
Billy Fields
Bob LaRoche

Technical Editor
Bill Bruns

Team Coordinator
Vicki Harding

Media Developer
Andrea Duvall

Interior Designer
Ruth Harvey

Cover Designers
Dan Armstrong
Ruth Harvey

Copy Writer
Eric Borgert

Layout
Darin Crone
Ayanna Lacey
Daniela Raderstorf
Mark Walchle

CONTENTS

ABOUT THE AUTHORS

Dean Andrews is a freelance writer living in Boston. After receiving a bachelor degree in computer science from the University of California at Berkeley, he worked as software developer at IBM and was a systems consultant to small businesses in the San Francisco bay area. In 1991, he joined the computer press and has worked on staff at *InfoWorld*, as a senior test developer, and *PC World*, as the manager of usability testing. Now, as a freelancer writer, he frequently contributes to a variety of publications including *PC World*, *Macworld*, and Boston.com, the online hub of the *Boston Globe*. Mr. Andrews also is a contributing author in *Peter Norton's Guide to Upgrading and Repairing PCs* and *Windows 98 Installation and Configuration Handbook*.

Ty Belknap has been in the computer industry for more than six years, working as a hardware technician, technical support advisor, and software support engineer. He helped launch the Windows 95 help desk for Microsoft and vowed to "never do it again." He currently is a support engineer for a government agency in Washington state. He is spending his free time obtaining his MCSE, and currently holds MCPs in Windows 95 and Networking Essentials. Ty can be reached by email at wrldbuld@blarg.net.

Ed Bott is a bestselling author and award-winning computer journalist with more than 12 years experience in the personal computer industry. As senior contributing editor of *PC Computing* magazine, he is responsible for the magazine's extensive coverage of Windows 95/98, Windows NT, and Microsoft Office. He also writes the magazine's monthly "NT Update" column. From 1991 until 1993, he was editor of *PC Computing*, and for three years before that he was managing editor of *PC World* magazine. Ed has written eight books for Que Publishing, including *Special Edition Using Office 2000*, *Using Windows 95 with Internet Explorer 4, Special Edition*, and *Using Office 97*, both published in 1998.

Ed is a two-time winner of the Computer Press Award, most recently for *PC Computing*'s annual Windows SuperGuide, a collection of tips, tricks, and advice for users of Windows 95, Windows 98, and Windows NT. For his work on the sixth annual edition of the Windows SuperGuide, published in 1997, Ed and co-author Woody Leonhard earned the prestigious Jesse H. Neal Award of the American Business Press, sometimes referred to as "the Pulitzer Prize of the business press." He lives in Redmond, Washington, with his wife, Judy Merrill, and two incredibly smart and affectionate cats, Katy and Bianca.

Phil Callihan is the WAN Administrator at the National Center for Manufacturing Sciences (NCMS), a research and development consortium based in Ann Arbor, Michigan. Phil has six years of experience with Microsoft products and holds both the MSCE and MCT certifications from Microsoft. In addition to his employment at NCMS, he works as consultant and performs training in Microsoft Networking and Internet technologies. He is a 1993 graduate of the University of Michigan. Phil lives in Ann Arbor, Michigan with his wife Lisa and their dog Tribble. Phil can be reached on the Internet at philc@ncms.org and on his home page (http://mis.ncms.org/philc/phil.htm).

Michael Desmond is a senior associate editor at *PC World* magazine and author of *Peter Norton's Guide to Upgrading and Repairing PCs*. He is also president of the Computer Press Assocation, an organization of working editors, writers, and producers covering computing issues and the industry. He is a contributor to both the Special and Platinum Editions of *Using Windows 98* and was co-author of *Platinum Edition: Using Windows 95*. Michael lives in Vermont with his wife, Anne, and two sons, Kevin and Patrick.

Theresa Hadden, MCSE, MCT, has more than 10 years of System Administration experience using Novell, UNIX, and Windows NT. She is presently teaching in the MCSE program at a local college where she teaches core courses and Internet products, both in the classroom and via the Internet. In addition, she does consulting for organizations with Windows NT and Novell networks. She is actively involved in the design and implementation of online courses that include instructor access utilizing audio conferencing via the Internet. She is the mother of two sons and lives in New Mexico.

Jerry Honeycutt provides business-oriented technical leadership to the Internet community and software development industry. He has served companies such as The Travelers, IBM, Nielsen North America, IRM, Howard Systems International, and NCR. Jerry has participated in the industry since before the days of Microsoft Windows 1.0, and is completely hooked on Windows 95 and the Internet.

Jerry is the author of *Using the Internet with Windows 95*, *Windows 95 Registry & Customization Handbook*, *Special Edition Using the Windows 95 Registry*, *VBScript by Example*, *Special Edition Using the Internet 3E*, *Using the Internet 2E*, and *Windows NT and Windows 95 Registry and Customization Handbook* published by Que. He has been printed in *Computer Language* magazine and is a regular speaker at the Windows World and Comdex trade shows on topics related to software development, Windows 95, and the Internet.

Feel free to contact Jerry on the Internet at `jerry@honeycutt.com` or visit his Web site at `http://rampages.onramp.net/~jerry`.

Grant King is a software developer, author, and attorney who lives in Atlanta with his wife, Nancy, and daughter, Elizabeth. He has been either the lead author or a contributing author on several books and articles relating to 32-bit Windows operating systems and software development. He also maintains The Windows Mill, a Web site devoted to news about Windows 95, Windows 98, and Windows NT. Grant received his B.A. from The University of the South and his J.D. from Georgia State University College of Law where he graduated *magna cum laude*. His email address is `ggking3@mindspring.com`.

Curtis Knight is a senior quality assurance analyst, technical writer, and technical editor. Curtis lives in Vancouver, Washington. By day he works in Symantec Corporation's Beaverton, Oregon development site. At night he is a freelance writer and technical editor for Macmillan Computer Publishing.

Curtis' overall computer industry experience includes MIS, technical support, data recovery, quality assurance, technical writing, and technical editing. Like most computer professionals, he is his family's personal computer consultant. He is currently training his 11-year-old son to take over the family consulting responsibilities.

Dan Logan is an award-winning freelance writer, book publisher, technical writer, and journalist from Cambria, California. He has contributed to several computer books, including Que's *Using PCs*. He has also published a regional book, the *Computer Resource Guide: San Luis Obispo and Santa Maria*, and is publisher of a regional Web site and newsletter called the Tri-tip Computer News (`http://www.thegrid.net/dlogan`). Dan's articles have appeared in more than 40 magazines and newspapers, including the *Los Angeles Times* and *San Francisco Chronicle*. He is on the board of directors of Softec, the Central Coast Software and Technology Association.

Larry Passo is a Principal Systems Engineer for QuickStart Technologies, a Microsoft Solution Provider Partner and Authorized Technical Education Center, at their headquarters in Newport Beach, California. With more than 20 years of experience in the computer industry as a software developer, design engineer, and network specialist, Larry holds certifications as both a Microsoft Certified Systems Engineer and as a Microsoft Certified Trainer. He provides advanced-level consulting and training for a variety of Microsoft operating systems and the Microsoft BackOffice family of products and is a contributing writer for *Microsoft Certified Professional* magazine. Larry and his wife, Debra, live in Irvine, California.

Ron Person has written more than 20 books for Que Corporation, including the best-selling original editions of *Special Edition Using Microsoft Word 97* and *Special Edition Using Microsoft Excel 97*. He was lead author for the original editions of the best-selling *Special Edition Using Windows 95* and *Platinum Edition Using Windows 95*. He has an M.S. in Physics from Ohio State University and an M.B.A. from Hardin-Simmons University. Ron was one of Microsoft's original Consulting Partners and Microsoft Solution Providers.

James Portanova, CNE, is a self-employed computer programmer and consultant who has earned a CTIA A+ certified technician rating. He owns Network Consulting Services, which specifies, installs, configures, maintains, and troubleshoots local area networks for small- to medium-sized business and professional clients. He is also the owner of Hot Properties Software, the programming and reselling arm of his business.

James earned a B.A. in English and Philosophy from Adelphi University in Garden City, New York in 1976.

He is the author of the 1996 "Career Focus" feature article for *LAN Times*. James is currently involved in completing the requirements for the MCSE+Internet track.

Lisa Porter works as a systems engineer and database programmer with Triad Systems, Inc. in Dayton, Ohio. She holds a certification as an MCSE and is a Microsoft Certified Trainer. She has more than 10 years experience in programming and has been working with the Microsoft Windows environments for the past seven years. She consults through the business that she and her husband, Michael Porter, own. Her network engineering knowledge, combined with her programming experience, gives her exceptional troubleshooting skills in a variety of systems environments. When she is not working, she enjoys spending time with her husband and the rest of the "family," consisting of their basset hound, cat, and her horse. Lisa can be reached by email at `lporter@triadsysinc.com`.

Michael E. Porter is a systems consultant for Triad Systems in Dayton, Ohio. Mike earned a Bachelor of Science Degree from Miami University in Oxford, Ohio and a Master of Business Administration with a concentration in MIS from the University of Dayton.

Mike is also a senior instructor with Learning Tree International focusing on Microsoft operating systems, TCP/IP, and systems security. Mike has more than 14 years of systems and networking experience as NetWare systems administrator, NT administrator, and UNIX systems integrator. Mike currently holds an MCSE and is in the process of completing the CNX designation. He and his wife, Lisa, live in Oakwood, Ohio with their basset hound, Hank.

Paul Sanna has been using PCs for almost 10 years, and he has been using Windows NT since its first Beta program. Paul is a project manager in the development department of Hyperion Software, Stamford, Connecticut, where he works on the company's line of client/server financial accounting software. He has co-authored three books on Windows 95, *Understanding Windows 95*, *Inside Windows 95* (New Riders), and *The Windows Installation and Configuration Handbook* (Que). He has a degree in English from Boston University. Paul lives in Bethel, Connecticut, with his wife, Andrea, his twin daughters, Rachel and Allison, and their new sister, Victoria. He can be reached on the Internet at psanna@ix.netcom.com.

Rob Tidrow is a writer, Web site designer, trainer, and president of Tidrow Communications, Inc., a firm specializing in content creation and delivery. Rob has authored or co-authored more than 25 books on a wide variety of computer topics, including Windows 95, Netscape Communicator 4, Windows NT, and Microsoft Internet Information Server 4.0. He authored *Windows 95 Registry Troubleshooting*, *Windows NT Registry Troubleshooting*, *Implementing and Supporting Windows 95*, all published by New Riders, and *Windows 95 Installation and Configuration Handbook*, published by Que. He is also contributing author to *Special Edition Using Microsoft Office 97*, *Inside Windows 95, Deluxe Edition*, *Platinum Edition Using Windows 95*, *Inside the World Wide Web*, and *Windows 95 for Network Administrators*, all published by Macmillan Computer Publishing. He lives in Indianapolis, Indiana with his wife, Tammy, and their two sons, Adam and Wesley. You can reach him on the Internet at rtidrow@iquest.net.

John West is a managing consultant at IntelliNet Corporation (www.intelli.net), based in Atlanta, Georgia. IntelliNet is a Microsoft Solution Provider Partner and ATEC, specializing in infrastructure planning, deployment, and support. John is an MCSE, MCSD, MCT, and CNE. When he's not designing large NT-based network deployments, he enjoys creating Web sites with ASP and programming with Visual Basic. He likes to write programs that help administer and monitor the networks he's implementing. To relax, he enjoys boating at Lake Lanier and hanging out with his friends from church. Contact John at johnw@intelli.net.

Craig Zacker has been employed as a network administrator, a technical writer and editor, a Webmaster, a technical support engineer and supervisor, a courseware developer, and a freelance network consultant. He now spends most of his time tinkering with computers and writing about them. His previous credits for Que include *Special Edition Using NetWare 4.1*, *Platinum Edition Using Windows 95*, *Windows NT 4.0 Workstation Advanced Technical Reference*, and *Upgrading and Repairing Networks*, among others. He can be reached at `craigz@tiac.net`.

DEDICATION

To Judy, for her love and patience, and to Katy and Bianca, who have taught me the meaning of happiness.

TELL US WHAT YOU THINK!

As the reader of this book, *you* are our most important critic and commentator. We value your opinion and want to know what we're doing right, what we could do better, what areas you'd like to see us publish in, and any other words of wisdom you're willing to pass our way.

As an Associate Publisher for Que, I welcome your comments. You can fax, email, or write me directly to let me know what you did or didn't like about this book—as well as what we can do to make our books stronger.

Please note that I cannot help you with technical problems related to the topic of this book, and that due to the high volume of mail I receive, I might not be able to reply to every message.

When you write, please be sure to include this book's title and author as well as your name and phone or fax number. I will carefully review your comments and share them with the author and editors who worked on the book.

Fax:	317-581-4666
Email:	opsys@mcp.com
Mail:	Associate Publisher
	Que
	201 West 103rd Street
	Indianapolis, IN 46290 USA

INTRODUCTION

As an upgrade to the best-selling software package in history, Windows 98 had a tough act to follow. The original release of Windows 95 revolutionized the computer industry, and today Windows is the undisputed standard for personal computing. Buying a PC without Windows is virtually impossible, and thousands of productivity programs, utilities, and games assume your PC is running Windows.

Windows 98 and Windows 98, Second Edition don't look dramatically different from Windows 95, but under the hood they're packed with changes that make computing and communication easier. The same is true with this book: *Special Edition Using Windows 98, Second Edition* adheres to the same high standards as its best-selling predecessors, but between the covers the content is updated to represent all the upgrades Microsoft has added to create Windows 98, Second Edition. Microsoft has included Internet Explorer 5 with the Windows 98, Second Edition package, and we've updated this volume to help you work effortlessly and productively with its new features and capabilities.

It doesn't matter how you use Windows 98 and Internet Explorer. If your family shares a home computer for work and play, you'll find plenty of help here. If you dial in to a local Internet service provider, we can help you make smoother, faster connections. We've also included detailed information that can help you integrate your computer into a business network, whether your business is a simple storefront or a far-flung multinational corporation.

HOW TO USE THIS BOOK

This book was designed and written expressly for intermediate and advanced Windows users who understand the importance of keeping up with advances in technology. *Special Edition Using Windows 98, Second Edition* contains detailed information about every aspect of Windows 98 and Windows 98, Second Edition, including setup, customization, troubleshooting, and networking. You'll find complete coverage of Internet Explorer 5 here as well, from basic Web browsing to advanced security topics. *Special Edition Using Windows 98, Second Edition* also includes step-by-step instructions on how to find and install online updates.

Special Edition Using Windows 98, Second Edition is a comprehensive reference that makes it easy for you to accomplish any task quickly and effectively. To help organize this enormous breadth of coverage, we've divided the book into seven parts, beginning with the essentials and progressing to more specialized or advanced subjects.

PART I, "GETTING STARTED"

This part covers the absolute essentials of Windows 98 and Internet Explorer 4 and 5. Pay particular attention to Chapter 1, "What's New in Windows 98," which includes an overview of significant new features in Windows 98, Second Edition including Internet Explorer 5. You will find the basics of starting and quitting Windows as well as controlling the operating system to help you accomplish your tasks. Windows 98, Second Edition also includes a new HTML-based help system; you'll find details about the changes in Chapter 4, "Getting Help."

PART II, "WORKING WITH FILES AND FOLDERS"

Windows 98 completely replaces the original Windows Explorer with a single browser window that lets you manage files, folders, and Web pages in the same window. Read Chapter 5, "An Overview of the Windows Interface," for step-by-step instructions on how to configure the new Windows interface, including the controversial Active Desktop. This section also introduces Windows 98's new set of file-management tools. You'll learn basic and advanced techniques for programs, files, and folders, whether they're stored on a local disk or on a corporate network. You'll also find detailed information to help you customize the new Explorer and manage associations between data files and programs. Should you convert existing drives to the FAT32 file system? Chapter 9, "Working with Disks and Drives," demystifies this important new feature.

PART III, "WORKING WITH APPLICATIONS"

Literally tens of thousands of applications are available for Windows 98. Collectively, they give you the power to organize your thoughts, communicate with other people, run a business of any size, and even create your own custom applications. This section covers the essentials of installing, running, and managing applications[md]including 32-bit Windows programs as well as older 16-bit Windows and MS-DOS programs. You'll also find details about applets included with Windows itself. And you'll learn how to make any application work well with local and network printers.

PART IV, "CONFIGURING AND CUSTOMIZING WINDOWS"

Windows owes a large measure of its enormous popularity to its impressive flexibility. This section exhaustively details how you can modify Windows 98 to suit your personal preferences. Add new hardware, reconfigure existing peripherals, set multimedia options, and troubleshoot your system. Customize the Active desktop, Start menu, and taskbar. Change the colors, fonts, and background images to make Windows more visually appealing. Reset the many system-level options that help define how Windows works, from which keyboard layout and language you prefer to which sounds play in response to system events.

PART V, "WINDOWS INTERNET SERVICES"

In just a few years, the Internet has evolved into a crucial source of information for tens of millions of people, and increasingly it's a major force in banking, commerce, and stock trading. This comprehensive section details all of Windows 98's Internet-related features. It covers every aspect of Internet connectivity, from setting up a dial-up connection, to configuring TCP/IP options, to downloading files from FTP servers. If you have questions about the World Wide Web, email, newsgroups, or Internet security, you'll find the answers here.

PART VI, "WINDOWS NETWORK SERVICES"

Even a two-person office can benefit from the capability of Windows to communicate and share files over a network. This section covers the full range of network topics: setting up a simple workgroup; sharing resources on a small network; setting up Windows 98 as a client on larger networks with Novell NetWare and Windows NT servers. This section also covers Windows 98's Personal Web Server, which lets you turn any Windows 98 PC into a full-featured Web host for use on a corporate network; it's also ideal for staging a personal Web site that you plan to upload to an Internet service provider.

PART VII, "APPENDIXES"

If you're upgrading from Windows 95, look here for details on how you can make sure your system includes the most recent patches and updates.

SPECIAL FEATURES IN THE BOOK

Que has more than a decade of experience writing and developing the most successful computer books available. With that experience, we've learned what special features help readers the most. Look for them throughout the book to enhance your learning experience.

NOTES

Notes present interesting or useful information that isn't necessarily essential to the discussion. This secondary track of information enhances your understanding of Windows, but you can safely skip notes and not be in danger of missing crucial information. Notes look like this:

> **Note**
>
> Be careful not to add too much to your taskbar. If you do, you might find yourself spending more time searching your taskbar than it would take to just browse to the file, application, or shortcut the old-fashioned way.
>
> To gain maximum benefit from toolbars and Quick Launch, implement them only for those programs you use frequently. If you access a file or program once a week or less, think twice before establishing a toolbar or Quick Launch icon.

TIPS

Tips present short advice on quick or often overlooked procedures. These include shortcuts that save you time. A Tip looks like this:

> **Tip #0**
>
> Select multiple items on the desktop by clicking on the desktop and dragging the selection rectangle that displays so that it surrounds the items. Release to select all objects within the rectangle.

CAUTIONS

Cautions warn you about potential problems that a procedure might cause, unexpected results, and mistakes to avoid.

> **Caution**
>
> When the Task Scheduler brings up the Backup utility, you must run the proper backup job. The Task Scheduler runs only the Backup utility; it doesn't perform the actual backup.

TROUBLESHOOTING

No matter how carefully you follow the steps in the book, you eventually come across something that just doesn't work the way you think it should. Troubleshooting sections anticipate these common errors or hidden pitfalls and present solutions. A Troubleshooting section looks like this:

 If you use the Windows Setup feature to add new components and find that it simultaneously removes other components, read "Uninstalling Components" in the "Troubleshooting" section near the end of this chapter.

Near the end of each chapter you will find the Troubleshooting section, which answers all the troubleshooting questions for that chapter.

CROSS REFERENCES

Throughout the book, you see references to other sections and pages in the book (like the one that follows this paragraph). These cross references point you to related topics and discussions in other parts of the book. They also point to Internet references where you can find out additional information about topics.

→ **See** "Creating Custom Web Views," **p. 134.**

→ **See** "Managing Buttons on a Toolbar," **p. 329.**

CONVENTIONS

In addition to these special features, several conventions are used in this book to make it easier to read and understand. These conventions include the following.

UNDERLINED HOTKEYS, OR MNEMONICS

In this book, hotkeys appear underlined like they appear onscreen. In Windows, many menus, commands, buttons, and other options have these hotkeys. To use a hotkey shortcut, press Alt and the key for the underlined character. For example, to choose the Properties button, press Alt and then R.

SHORTCUT KEY COMBINATIONS

In this book, shortcut key combinations are joined with plus signs (+). For example, Ctrl+V means hold down the Ctrl key and then press the V key.

MENU COMMANDS

Instructions for choosing menu commands have this form:

Choose File, New.

This example means open the File menu and select New, which is one way to open a new file.

Instructions involving the Windows 98 Start menu are an exception. When you are to choose something through the Start menu, the form is as follows:

Open the Start menu and choose Programs, Accessories, WordPad.

In this case, you open the WordPad word processing accessory. Notice that in the Start menu you simply drag the mouse pointer and point at the option or command you want to choose (even through a whole series of submenus); you don't need to click anything.

This book also has the following typeface enhancements to indicate special text:

Typeface	Description
Italic	Italic is used to indicate terms and variables in commands or addresses.
MYFILE.DOC	Filenames and directories are set in all caps to distinguish them from regular text, as in MYFILE.DOC.
`Monospace`	Mono indicates screen messages, code listings, and command samples. It also indicates text you type, as well as Internet addresses and other locators in the online world.
<u>Underline</u>	Underline indicates keyboard hotkeys. For example, to choose the Properties button, Press Alt and then R.

GETTING STARTED

CHAPTER 1

WHAT'S NEW IN WINDOWS 98

In this chapter

FASTER, SMARTER, EASIER: ARCHITECTURAL IMPROVEMENTS IN WINDOWS 98

The new release of Windows 98, Windows 98 Second Edition, goes beyond the original Windows 98 product. Since the release of the original Windows 98, many improvements have been implemented. For example, Windows 98 Second Edition adds new hardware support and improved online capabilities that include the use of enhanced Internet browsing, conferencing, and multimedia technologies. The real emphasis is on greater Internet accessibility with the goal of providing a faster and easier way to take advantage of all that the Internet has to offer. Windows 98 Second Edition includes Internet Explorer 5.0, Microsoft's popular browser software. Release 5.0 of Internet Explorer provides breakthroughs in Web performance, usability, and flexibility.

Of the many changes that define Windows 98 Second Edition, the most prominent is the roll of Internet Explorer 5.0. It is tightly integrated into Windows 98, with no need to upgrade from Explorer 4.0 to 5.0 in an additional operation. And Windows 98 also does a superb job of getting the most out of all the new types of hardware and software that have sprung up over the last four years.

- Windows 98 Second Edition is the ultimate maintenance release. It includes numerous updates, bug fixes, and usability modifications that make the product better than ever.

- In all, Windows 98 contains drivers for more than 1,200 new devices, and virtually all of them support Plug and Play for simplified setup. *Plug and Play* is a technology that allows the operating system to automatically detect and configure a newly installed device. Some categories of hardware supported in Windows 98 didn't even exist when Windows 95 first hit store shelves. Most significant of all are peripherals that use the universal serial bus (USB).

  Universal serial bus technology (USB) allows multiple devices, such as keyboards, scanners, and digital video cameras, to be hot-swapped; that is, you do not have to turn off the PC to add or remove a device, and you do not have to reboot for the operating system to recognize the device. You can plug just about any type of device into a *USB* port, including mice, keyboards, modems, scanners, digital cameras, speakers, telephones, and more. This technology makes your PC incredibly more flexible and does away with the need for serial and parallel ports, IRQs, and other configuration hassles.

→ **See** *Chapter 21, "Configuring Hardware," and Chapter 22, "Adding New Hardware to Windows 98," for details on how to install new device drivers and configure peripherals.*

- Whether you upgrade an existing copy of Windows 95 or install Windows 98 on a new PC, you'll notice significant changes in Windows 98. The new Setup program is dramatically streamlined compared with its Windows 95 equivalent. You answer a few questions at the start, and then—because it's capable of restarting automatically—the Setup program runs unattended.

- Compared to Windows 95, Windows 98 is generally faster, although you might notice that some tasks take longer than they would on the same system running Windows 95.

In particular, startup and shutdown should go more quickly, especially on new systems. Most of the key system files, including networking components like Windows Sockets services and Transmission Control Protocol/Internet Protocol (TCP/IP), have also been tuned for performance. And on large networks you'll notice completely new options, including support for *Point-to-Point Tunneling Protocol* and *NetWare Directory Services*.

- One of the most significant weaknesses in the original retail release of Windows 95 was its dependence on the old 16-bit file allocation table *(FAT; page 11, 21, 155)* format. That restriction becomes particularly painful when you add a hard drive greater than 2GB because FAT16 forces you to create multiple partitions even if you don't require them. Microsoft fixed those problems with the introduction of the FAT32 disk format in OEM Service Release 2 of Windows 95. Windows 98 has all these features and more, including a new tool you can use during an upgrade: a utility that quickly converts your existing data to the new format.

→ To learn more about converting existing FAT volumes, **see** Chapter 9, "Working with Disks and Drives."

- Notebook users will see improved power management features, enhancements in the way Windows works with PC cards, and support for the latest infrared devices.

→ To reach your notebook's full potential, **see** Chapter 25, "Special Features for Notebook Users."

- And if you have a dial-up Internet connection, you'll find substantial improvements in the Dial-Up Networking features, including a simplified wizard for creating connections and support for *multilink* connections, which use two phone lines for faster data transfers.

→ If you can't wait to get a connection to the Internet, **see** Chapter 26, "Establishing a Dial-Up Internet Connection," for details.

How Windows and the Web Work Together

If you've grown accustomed to the Windows 95 interface, you'll see some changes in Windows 98. The Windows Desktop Update, first introduced with Internet Explorer 4.0 and standard in Windows 98, adds hundreds of improvements to the tools and techniques you use to manage files, folders, and programs in Windows. Most of the changes are simple refinements, but if you're willing to turn on some of the new options, you can radically change the way Windows works.

→ For a full description of the changes to the Windows interface, including its many options, **see** Chapter 5, "An Overview of the Windows Interface."

For example, you can add your own shortcuts to the new Quick Launch toolbar—just to the right of the Start button—to make it easier to get started with your favorite programs. The Start menu is also improved. Most notably, you can now reorganize items on the Programs menu by dragging them directly from one place to another.

Windows 95 offered the Windows Explorer for file management and a separate Internet Explorer for Web browsing. Internet Explorer 4.0 brought the two Explorers into a single window, and Windows 98 incorporates that feature. If you prefer to browse files and folders with the single-click navigation techniques of Internet Explorer, you can configure Windows to work that way. And you can use HTML templates to view any or all of your folders so that they look and act like Web pages.

→ Why would you want to treat your files like Web pages? **See** Chapter 8, "Managing Files Using Web View," for a description of some of the benefits.

When you use Windows 98, you have ready access to the Web. A new Favorites option on the Start menu, for example, lets you jump quickly to your favorite Web sites. And if you turn on the *Active Desktop*, you can embed live HTML components (such as news or stock tickers, with Java, Active X, or JavaScript) or even entire Web pages on the Windows desktop.

→ For a full discussion of the Active Desktop, **see** Chapter 30, "Web Subscriptions and the Active Desktop."

A NEW WAY TO EXPLORE THE INTERNET

If you've used Netscape Navigator or previous versions of Internet Explorer, you're already familiar with the basic concepts of Web browsing. Windows 98 includes the full suite of Internet applications Microsoft introduced with Internet Explorer 4.0. You'll find much more than just a Web browser.

INTERNET EXPLORER 4.0 AND 5.0: OFFLINE BROWSING AND WEB SUBSCRIPTIONS

The single biggest objection to the Internet (at least for users with ordinary dial-up connections) is that it's too slow. Internet Explorer 4.0 and the recently released Internet Explorer 5.0 address that concern by letting you set up Web subscriptions, which you can use to download individual pages or entire Web sites at regular intervals. Then, when you tell Internet Explorer 4.0 or 5.0 that you'd like to work offline, you can browse the stored pages without dialing up and waiting for them to download.

Finding information on the Internet is easier with Internet Explorer 4.0 and 5.0 than it was with earlier browsers, and new tools enable you to organize that information more intelligently, too.

→ To learn how to set your home page and speed up your Web connections, **see** Chapter 27, "Web Browsing with Internet Explorer 5.0."

STAY IN TOUCH WITH OUTLOOK EXPRESS MAIL AND NEWS

With Windows 98, Microsoft officially replaces the Windows 95–vintage Exchange Inbox with a new Internet-standard email program called Outlook Express. The new mail client software is easy to set up, easy to use, and easy to customize. If you receive large volumes of email, you'll appreciate the Inbox Assistant, which lets you define rules the software can use to automatically manage messages for you. Outlook Express also acts as a reader for accessing Internet news servers, like those that offer support for Microsoft products.

→ To learn the full benefits and use of this Internet-standard email program, **see** Chapter 31, "Using Outlook Express."

WEB EDITING AND PUBLISHING TOOLS

Windows 98 won't let you set up a Web site that can compete with Yahoo!, but the product does include basic tools you can use to create Web pages. FrontPage Express is a graphical Web-page editor that incorporates a subset of the features in Microsoft's award-winning FrontPage program.

→ To learn more about creating your own Web page, **see** Chapter 32, "Creating Web Pages with FrontPage Express."

PART
I
CH
1

AN OPERATING SYSTEM THAT MAINTAINS ITSELF

Maintaining the health of your PC is like visiting the dentist: Even highly motivated PC users do irksome maintenance chores less often than they should. Windows 98 can't supply extra motivation, but it does include software that automates some of the more unpleasant tasks. Most notable is the Tune-Up Wizard, which regularly scans local hard disks for errors, *defragments* disks, and cleans up unneeded files—all without requiring any work from you.

And if you've ever tried to use Windows 95 to troubleshoot a hardware or software problem, you've probably experienced information overload. With Windows 98, the new System Information tool consolidates a wealth of data—about system resources, hardware, components, and running tasks—in a single location. This well-organized window is also a launching pad for other troubleshooting tools, such as the System File Checker (which undoes the damage when a crucial file becomes corrupted) and the Registry Checker (which automatically backs up your database of system settings for quick recovery in the event of trouble). And whenever Microsoft issues a Windows patch, you can install it automatically by clicking the Windows Update icon.

→ For a more detailed explanation of the System Information tool, **see** Chapter 23, "Maintaining and Troubleshooting Your System."

WINDOWS 98 AT HOME

If you've installed Windows 98 at home, you're probably expecting your PC to work hard and play hard. For game players, there's *DirectX5 (page 13)* and *MMX (page 13)* support, two technologies that make multimedia more appealing. In addition, the broadcast architecture components let you watch TV on your PC (if you have compatible hardware, of course).

→ Chapter 19, "Setting Up Windows 98 Multimedia," explains how DirectX and MMX technology boost the performance of the latest gaming software.

Are you concerned about setting up a single PC that every member of the family can use? The Family Logon option lets you create custom desktops for everyone, and you can use Internet Explorer 5.0's Content Advisor to block access to Web sites that contain violence, pornography, or other material you deem undesirable.

→ For details on how to block undesirable Web content, **see** "Controlling Access to Undesirable Content," **p. 632**

WINDOWS 98 IN THE OFFICE

In a corporate setting, you're most likely to be concerned with getting Windows 98 to work smoothly with an existing network. From an administrator's viewpoint, Windows 98 doesn't look dramatically different from Windows 95—although it's smoother in operation. However, you'll find support for many more network cards, for example, and you'll find it easier to connect with Windows NT or NetWare networks. And Windows 98 also makes it easier than it used to be to configure a TCP/IP connection (the default protocol in Windows 98).

→ If you need more details on implementing Windows 98 in a networked environment, **see** Chapter 34, "Configuring Windows Network Components," and Chapter 36, "Setting Up a Simple Windows Network."

CHAPTER 2

STARTING AND QUITTING WINDOWS 98

In this chapter

STARTING WINDOWS

After you install Windows, you can start it by simply turning on your computer. In most cases, computers start directly into Windows 98. If your computer requires a real-mode (16-bit) driver, you might see a DOS-like text screen as the drivers load. (Windows 98 has many new drivers, but real-mode drivers might be required for hardware that does not have a Windows 98 32-bit driver. These real-mode drivers are the ones used by Windows 3.x or DOS.) Also, if your Windows has multiple configurations installed—for example, to work with different hardware configurations—then a text screen prompts you to choose between the configurations. After you make your choice, Windows starts.

⚠ *If you're having trouble with the initial reboot of Windows 98 just after installation, see "Startup and Reboot Problems" in the "Troubleshooting" section at the end of this chapter.*

For a faster startup, press the Esc key during startup of Windows 98 to bypass the Windows 98 logo. To permanently bypass the logo, use Notepad or WordPad to edit the MSDOS.SYS file. Add LOGO=0 to the Options section. To see the logo on startup, just change the 0 to 1. (MSDOS.SYS is located in the root of the startup drive and has Hidden, Read-Only, and System attributes. To edit MSDOS.SYS, use the File, Properties command in the Windows Explorer to clear the file's Read-Only attribute.) Another benefit of eliminating the logo is that you can see what's going on in the background, such as the loading of drivers enumerated in the CONFIG.SYS and AUTOEXEC.BAT files.

Tip #1	If you are dual booting between Windows 98 and Windows NT, the boot sequence is a bit different. As the system boots, the user is presented with a screen that enables the user to toggle up and down with the arrow keys to select the desired operating system. What the user sees displayed is the contents of a BOOT.INI file located in the system partition of the drive, for example, C:\ BOOT.INI. You may choose to edit the file to customize what is displayed onscreen. The easiest and safest way to customize the screen display is to use the System icon in the Windows NT control panel and select the default operating system to load. This graphical user interface (GUI) tool is used to edit the BOOT.INI file. Or you can really learn about the BOOT.INI file by editing it directly. To do so, you must remove the file's System, Read-Only, and Hidden attributes. You can then use Notepad to edit the file.

LOGGING ON TO WINDOWS

When Windows starts, it might display a dialog box that contains your name and an edit box for your password. Windows uses the name and the password from the logon dialog box for several purposes:

- Windows matches the name against a user profile. The user profile tells Windows which configuration of desktop and software settings to use.
- If the computer is connected to a network, Windows logs you on to the network using the name and the password. (If the computer is connected to a network, an additional field will be displayed in the dialog box for the domain or server name.)

After logon is complete, the Windows 98 desktop displays with the My Computer, Recycle Bin, Network Neighborhood, and perhaps additional icons. When you initially start Windows, it displays a Welcome to Windows 98 screen. You can close this screen by selecting the very small check box in the lower-left corner of the Welcome screen; that way, you won't have to deal with the pesky screen whenever you start Windows 98. If you ever want to rerun the Welcome screen, click Start, Run; and type `Welcome` in the edit box; and click OK.

Starting Windows with Your Custom Profile or Network Password

Windows can assign unique Windows settings and network capabilities to each username and password. In some cases—for example, if you are sharing a computer—you might want to shut down Windows and log on as a different user. In those cases you don't have to completely shut down Windows. To log on as a different user without shutting down, follow these steps:

1. Click Start, Log Off *username*.
2. Click Yes in response to `Are You Sure You Want to Log Off?`. An Enter Windows Password dialog box displays.
3. Enter the new User Name and Password.
4. Click OK.

If multiple user profiles are on your Windows 98 system, you might not be able to tell which desktop you're using currently. To know who and where you are at all times, create a unique folder on the desktop of each profile. Name the folder to indicate the logon name, for example, `This is Mary's Desktop`. If you provide this information for each configuration, a glance at this empty folder's title tells you which desktop you are currently working on. In addition, you can place a text file in the folder that enumerates the settings for this desktop profile.

Tip #2　Another way to find out who you are logged on as is to click the Start button—the second choice up from the bottom is Log Off [username].

→ For more information about setting up a Windows network and logging on in different networked environments, **see** "An Administrator's Guide to Windows Networking," **p. 764** and "Choosing Your Primary Network Logon," **p. 792.**

Disabling the Password Dialog Box

If you are not using the logon dialog box to enter a network password or to load custom settings, you might as well avoid seeing it each time you start Windows. To prevent the logon dialog box from displaying, follow this procedure:

1. Right-click the Network Neighborhood icon on the desktop; then click Properties.
2. Click the Configuration tab and then the Primary Network Logon pull-down list. Select Windows Logon. Click OK.

3. Click No when Windows prompts you to restart the computer.

4. Click Start, Settings, Control Panel to open the Control Panel.

5. Open the Passwords icon.

6. Click the User Profiles tab; then select the All Users of this Computer Use the Same Preferences and Desktop Settings option.

7. Click the Change Passwords tab; then click the Change Windows Password button. Enter blank passwords. Click OK to close the Change Windows Passwords dialog box. Click Close to close the Passwords Properties dialog box.

Tip #3

If the system is ever connected to a network, you will have to enable this feature. A network connection to an authentication server, such as Windows NT, allows for the user's profile to be stored centrally. Whenever the user logs on to a Windows 98 system anywhere in the network, the logon specific profile is downloaded. This great feature benefits both administrators and users. For the administrator of the system, all user profiles can be managed on a single server, and users have the freedom to "roam" the network, log on at any Windows 98 system, and have their desktop available.

CONTROLLING PROGRAMS AND DOCUMENTS WHEN WINDOWS STARTS

You can define how Windows applications and documents open on startup. By defining which applications or documents automatically open and whether windows are full-screen or windowed, you can help set up an easy-to-use system for novice computer users.

RUNNING PROGRAMS AND DOCUMENTS ON STARTUP

Windows can start programs or open documents in the appropriate program when it starts. Windows starts all program or document files or shortcuts located in the Windows\Start Menu\Programs\StartUp folder. Instead of manually creating or moving files into this folder, use the following method to create shortcuts in the StartUp folder.

To specify programs or documents that you want Windows to run at startup, follow these steps:

1. Right-click in a gray area on the taskbar; then click Properties.

2. Click the Start Menu Programs tab (see Figure 2.1).

3. Click Add; then click Browse.

4. Select the program or document you want to open on startup. Select All Files from the Files of Type list if you need to see documents. Click Open.

5. Click Next.

6. Select the StartUp folder; then click Next.

7. Accept the default title for the program or type a new title in the Select a Name for the Shortcut text box. The name you enter is displayed in the Startup menu.

8. Click Finish.

9. Repeat steps 3 through 8 to add more programs or documents to the StartUp folder, or click OK if you are finished.

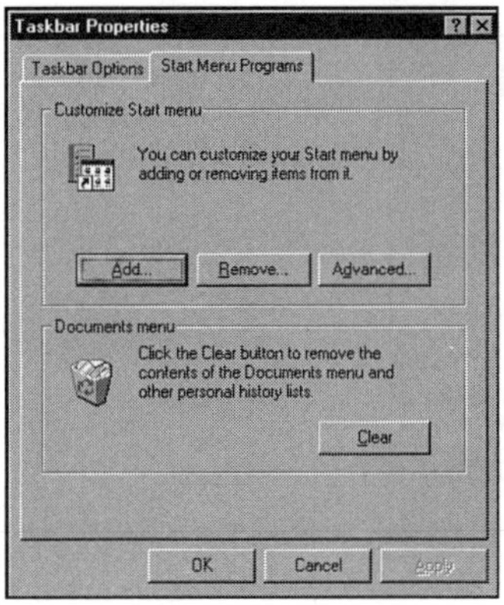

Figure 2.1
Use the Start Menu Programs tab to specify programs to run at startup.

> **Note**
>
> If you frequently change the programs or documents that you want to run on startup, make the StartUp folder accessible as a shortcut on the desktop so you can drag shortcuts to program or document files in and out of it. Don't drag the actual program or document file to the StartUp folder because you might delete the actual file during later changes to the StartUp folder.

If you want folders to open on your desktop when Windows starts, use the right mouse button to drag a folder into the Windows\Start Menu\Programs\StartUp folder. Click Create Shortcut(s) Here from the context menu.

→ To become more proficient using shortcuts, **see** "Using Shortcuts," **p.102**.

SPECIFYING HOW PROGRAMS, DOCUMENTS, AND FOLDERS DISPLAY

You can control whether programs, documents, or folders start in a normal window, are minimized to the Taskbar, or are maximized. To control how they are displayed when Windows starts, follow these steps:

1. Add the program, document, or folder to the StartUp folder, as described in the section "Running Programs and Documents on Startup." (If you manually drag a file into the StartUp folder, use a right-drag and create a shortcut rather than leaving the actual file in the StartUp folder.)

2. Open the StartUp folder in either My Computer or Explorer. The StartUp folder is located in Windows\Start Menu\Programs\StartUp.

3. Right-click the shortcut for the item you added to StartUp; then click Properties.

4. Click the Shortcut tab. (This tab is only available for shortcuts. You cannot change this property in a program, document, or folder's properties.)

5. Select one of the three options—Normal Window, Minimized, or Maximized—from the <u>R</u>un drop-down list (see Figure 2.2).

Figure 2.2
Use the Shortcut Properties page to specify how a program or document is displayed on startup.

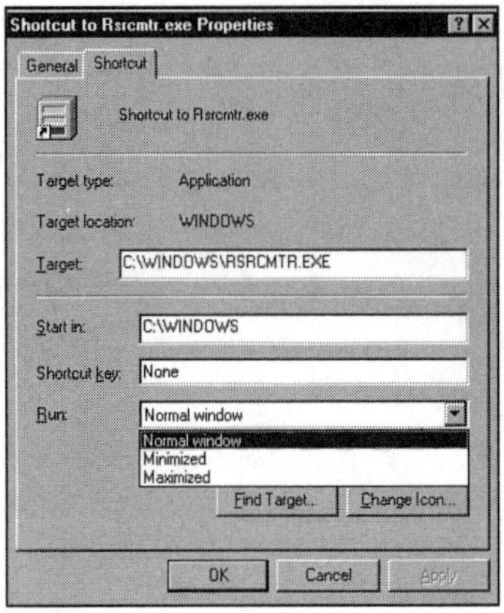

6. Click OK.

 If you're having trouble getting Windows to start correctly, see "Startup and Reboot Problems" in the "Troubleshooting" section at the end of this chapter.

→ The Windows Explorer interface is your main tool for accessing files and folders. To get a closer look at Explorer, **see** "Using Windows Explorer to View Files and Folders," **p. 80**.

To prevent programs, documents, and folders from opening on startup, hold down the Shift key while Windows is starting (after you enter your logon username and password). Release the Shift key after the desktop is displayed.

REMOVING PROGRAMS, DOCUMENTS, AND FOLDERS FROM STARTUP

To remove a program or document from the StartUp folder, you can delete the shortcuts from the StartUp folder or follow these steps:

1. Right-click a gray area of the Taskbar; then click <u>P</u>roperties.

2. Click the Start Menu Programs tab.

3. Click <u>R</u>emove.

4. Open the StartUp folder and select the program, document, or folder you want to remove.

5. Click <u>R</u>emove. Return to step 4 to remove more if necessary.

6. Choose Close.

PROTECTING YOURSELF WITH A STARTUP DISK

A startup disk can help you recover data from your hard disk when Windows will not start. The startup disk starts your computer in DOS mode even when Windows will not start. You can then use DOS commands, such as COPY, to copy or access important data files.

If you didn't take advantage of the opportunity to create a startup disk during Windows 98 installation, you can create a startup disk at any time. Always make multiple startup disks and test them to make sure they give you access to your hard drive.

To create a startup disk, follow these steps:

1. Open the Add/Remove Programs option in the Control Panel.
2. Click the Startup Disk tab.
3. Insert a disk into the A: drive. Any contents on the disk are deleted.
4. Choose Create Disk and follow the instructions as they are displayed onscreen.

    To create the startup disk, you must have your original Windows program disks (or CD-ROM) because the startup disk boot files are copied from the source disks to be sure of their integrity.

5. Click OK.

Make at least two copies of your startup disk. Keep one accessible and the other in a safe location.

Caution

A startup disk created for a FAT16 version of Windows 98 does not give you access to the data on a hard drive formatted for FAT32. If you did not create a startup disk with the appropriate *FAT (pages 11, 21, 155)* system, you might be able to use a startup disk created from another computer that has the same FAT system.

The Windows 98 startup disk includes drivers for common CD-ROMs and creates a RAM disk on which it unpacks many useful DOS tools/commands from a CAB file included on the disk.

To start using the startup disk, insert it in the A: drive and reboot the computer. The computer should restart and show the A: prompt in DOS. You can now use DOS commands to copy files from the hard drive, replace corrupted Windows files, or reinstall a disk-based version of Windows.

If you have the available disk space, a convenient way of always having access to the Windows installation and driver files is to copy all the CAB files from your Windows installation CD-ROM onto your hard disk. After booting from the startup disk, go to the appropriate directory and run SETUP. When installing new hardware, point Windows to this directory when it asks for the installation disk.

CREATING A STARTUP DISK FROM DOS

If you cannot boot into Windows 98 but are able to start your computer into a command prompt, you have the option of creating a Windows 98 startup disk from MS-DOS. To do so, you must be able to boot into a fully functional DOS environment with access to the system's hard drive.

To create a Windows 98 startup disk from MS-DOS, follow these steps:

1. Restart your computer, press and hold down the Ctrl key until the Windows 98 Startup menu appears, and then choose Command Prompt Only from the Startup menu.

2. Insert a blank, formatted floppy disk into the A: drive.

3. Type the following commands, pressing Enter after each command:
   ```
   cd windows\command
   smartdrv.exe
   bootdisk a:
   ```

4. Follow the onscreen instructions to finish making the startup disk.

> **Note**
>
> SMARTDRV.EXE is not a required file in creating a Windows 98 startup disk. It is used only to speed the creation of the disk.

STARTING WINDOWS AFTER TECHNICAL PROBLEMS OCCUR

Windows is guaranteed to fail occasionally. These failures and their recovery are handled more automatically in Windows 98 than in previous versions of Windows.

CHECKING FOR DRIVE ERRORS WITH SCANDISK

Should Windows be shut down incorrectly or if errors on your hard disk are detected, Windows automatically runs *ScanDisk*, a program that checks for invalid filenames, file and folder name-length errors, magnetic surface errors on the drive, and more. If you start your computer and ScanDisk begins running, usually your best option is to let it run using its default settings. You can run ScanDisk at any time to manually check your hard drive.

If you want control over how ScanDisk runs, you can edit the MSDOS.SYS file as follows:

1. Make a copy of the MSDOS.SYS file with a name like MSDOS.BAK. The file is located in C:\.

2. Use Notepad or WordPad to open MSDOS.SYS.

3. Edit the AutoScan line in the [Options] section to change ScanDisk's startup behavior:

   `AutoScan=0`   Disables ScanDisk on startup.

AutoScan=1   Default; Windows startup pauses, giving you the chance to stop it. If not stopped, ScanDisk runs automatically.

AutoScan=2   ScanDisk runs automatically when needed without pausing for operator intervention.

4. Save MSDOS.SYS as a text file back to its original location.

→ For more helpful information on maintaining and troubleshooting your Windows 98 system, **see** "Using ScanDisk to Prevent and Repair Damage," **p. 459**.

Starting Windows in Safe Mode or an Alternative Mode

If Windows has difficulty starting, you must start it in one of its diagnostic modes. In most troubleshooting situations, you should start in Safe mode. In *Safe mode*, Windows uses basic default settings that restart Windows with minimal functionality. For example, if a video adapter driver is incorrect or becomes corrupted, Windows restarts in Safe mode using a default driver, standard VGA, that provides minimum functionality. In this case, Safe mode enables you to see Windows so you can use the Control Panel or the Device Manager to correct the problem.

⚠ *If you're having trouble with a video adapter driver while setting up Windows 98, **see** "Video Adapter Driver Conflict During Setup" in the "Troubleshooting" section at the end of this chapter.*

When Windows starts in Safe mode, a message informs you that Windows is running in Safe mode and that some of your devices might not be available. The words *Safe mode* are displayed at each corner of the screen.

The default Safe mode settings use a generic VGA monitor driver, the standard Microsoft mouse driver, and the minimum device drivers necessary to start Windows. When you start Windows with the default settings, you cannot access CD-ROM drives, printers, modems, or other external hardware devices. One of the Safe modes allows networking.

While you are in Safe mode, you can click Start, Settings, Control Panel and reset drivers or system settings.

→ For help on troubleshooting hardware and driver problems, **see** the section "Troubleshooting Common Problems" in Chapter 23. You can also find help in the various chapters on installing hardware drivers.

To start Windows in a different mode, follow these steps:

1. Turn on the computer.

2. Hold down the Ctrl key as soon as the memory tests are complete. Continue holding it down as Windows starts.

3. The Windows 98 Startup Menu displays different starting modes. If you do not press a key within 30 seconds, Windows continues startup with the default selection. Press an up or down arrow key to prevent automatic startup.

   The Microsoft Windows 98 Startup menu offers choices that reflect the configuration of your system. You might see some or all of the following choices:

   • Normal

   • Logged (\BOOTLOG.TXT)

- Safe mode
- Safe mode with network support
- Step-by-step confirmation
- Command prompt only
- Safe mode command prompt only
- Previous version of MS-DOS

4. Select the mode in which you want to start; then press Enter.

To skip the Windows 98 Startup menu and start directly in a mode, start your computer and hold down one of the key combinations shown in the following table while Windows is starting:

Operating Mode	Key Combination	Actions
Windows 98 in Safe mode without networking	F5	Loads HIMEM.SYS and IFSHLP.SYS, loads DoubleSpace or DriveSpace if present, and then runs Windows 98 WIN.COM. Starts in Safe mode.
Windows 98 in Safe mode with minimum Processes the network functions	F6	Loads HIMEM.SYS and IFSHLP.SYS. Registry, loads COMMAND.COM, loads DoubleSpace or DriveSpace if present, runs Windows 98 WIN.COM, loads network drivers, and runs NETSTART.BAT.
DOS command prompt	Shift+F5	Loads COMMAND.COM.
Step-by-step	Shift+F8	Gives you Yes or No decision over each Windows 98 startup action such as loading drivers.

→ To learn strategies for keeping up Windows 98 and adding new hardware on the computer, **see** "Keeping Windows 98 Up-to-Date," **p. 448** and "Using the Add New Hardware Wizard," **p. 434.**

USING STEP-BY-STEP MODE TO TEST STARTUP INTERACTIVELY

Interactively test each action in the boot process by following the procedure mentioned in the section "Starting Windows in Safe Mode or an Alternative Mode" and selecting Step-by-Step Confirmation. This mode provides an onscreen display for each action as Windows loads. You must type a Y (Yes) or N (No) for each action. You can boot Windows 98 but bypass suspect drivers by responding with N.

Tip #4	If you boot into a DOS prompt and attempt to start Windows 98 by using the /d:n switch (by typing win /d:n) Windows 98 might appear to start in Safe mode with network support, but in reality you have no network connectivity. The notable feature here is that Windows 95 supported this command. The only fix here is not to start Windows 98 in Safe mode with network support with the /d:n switch. Microsoft has confirmed that this problem exists in Windows 98.

MANAGING WINDOWS AFTER AN APPLICATION FAILURE

Windows 98 continuously polls applications to see whether they are running and responding. When an application fails to respond, Windows 98 displays a dialog box in which you can click the End Task button to close the application. You lose all changes to data in the application since the last time you saved. Click Cancel to return to the application.

If the application misuses memory or has a fatal error that causes the application to fail, other applications usually are not involved. When an application fails to respond—for example, clicks or keystrokes get no response—press Ctrl+Alt+Delete to display the Close Program dialog box.

The application that has trouble shows the phrase [Not Responding]. To continue working in Windows on your other applications, you must shut down this application. Select the application and click End Task. If you click Shut Down or press Ctrl+Alt+Delete again, all applications and Windows 98 shut down.

CONTROLLING SYSTEM, MONITOR, AND DISK POWER WITH POWER MANAGEMENT

Power management reduces the power consumption of your PC or its components. Power management is not just an issue for battery-operated laptop computers; the unnecessary power consumption by the huge number of PCs not only wastes money and resources but also increases pollution. As a user, you benefit by having your computer restart very quickly in the same way that you left it. All of these power management methods are available only if your computer and its components are built to support Windows power management.

Power management works three ways:

Automatic power management	You set your PC to turn off the monitor and hard disk automatically after a specified idle time.
Standby	You put your computer on standby rather than shutting it down. Active applications and documents are stored in memory.
Hibernate	You hibernate your computer for overnight or longer stretches of time. Active applications and documents are stored to disk.

AUTOMATIC POWER MANAGEMENT FOR MONITORS

You can set your monitor to turn off after a specified time of inactivity on your computer. Your monitor must be designed to take advantage of Windows power management for this feature to work. To set the length of inactive time before the monitor is shut off, follow these steps:

1. Open the Power Management option in the Control Panel.

2. Click the Power Schemes tab shown in Figure 2.3.

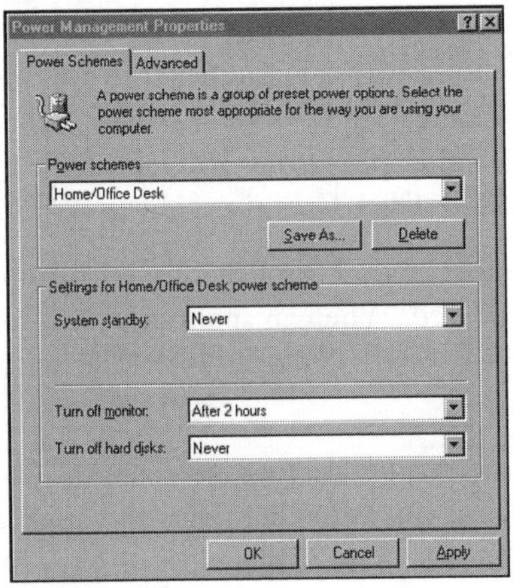

Figure 2.3
Use the Power Schemes tab to specify how long devices are inactive before being turned off or put on standby.

3. If you have previously defined a scheme for power management, select it from the Power Schemes drop-down list.

4. From the Turn Off Monitor drop-down list, select how long the computer can be inactive before the monitor is turned off. Select a time that is less than the System Standby time.

5. If you want to save this time under your scheme name, click Save As, enter a name, and then click OK.

6. Click OK in the Power Management Properties dialog box.

SETTING THE ELAPSED TIME TO AUTOMATIC STANDBY

If you're backand forth and up and down from your desk a lot, you can save power by setting your computer to go automatically to standby after a period of inactivity. Your computer must be designed to take advantage of Windows power management for this feature to work. To set the length of inactive time before standby, follow these steps:

1. Open the Power Management option in the Control Panel.

2. Click the Power Schemes tab shown in Figure 2.3.

3. If you have a scheme previously defined for working on your desktop system, select the scheme from the Power Schemes drop-down list.

4. Select from the System Standby list how long the computer can be inactive before going into standby.

5. If you want to save this standby time under your scheme name, click Save As, enter a name, and then click OK.

6. Click OK in the Power Management Properties dialog box.

PUTTING YOUR COMPUTER ON STANDBY

If you plan to leave your computer for a short time, you might want to put it on standby. Standby conserves energy by turning off drive motors and the monitor. Power remains to memory so your work and Windows are maintained just as you left them. When you turn the computer's power switch on, the hard drive spins back up to speed, and the monitor comes back on. Windows and applications do not have to be loaded because they are already in memory. With the standby option, your computer comes on significantly faster than if you had used the Shut Down command. Of course, you wouldn't want to put your computer on standby if you are in the middle of a file download from another system.

To put your computer on standby, click Start, Shut Down and then click Stand By in the Shut Down Windows dialog box. To restore the computer from standby, turn it on again as you would if it had been shut down. In most cases this means turning on the computer's power switch.

If the computer loses power completely while it is in standby, you will lose any unsaved work or settings in memory. If you are concerned about losing work, save your documents before going to standby. All in all, this feature has a cost associated with it that can make it unattractive to use.

HIBERNATING YOUR COMPUTER

Putting your computer in *hibernation* saves everything in memory to your hard disk and then turns off all power. Restarting your computer from hibernation is not as fast as restoring from standby, but when your computer restarts, all programs, documents, windows, and settings are just as you left them when you shut down. Use hibernation when you will be leaving your computer for long periods of time, such as overnight or weekends. The computer and its components must have been built to take advantage of Windows power management.

To put your computer in hibernation, follow this procedure:

1. Open the Power Management option in the Control Panel.

2. Click the Hibernate tab. If there is no Hibernate tab, your computer does not support hibernation. Click the check box.

3. If you are using a portable computer, click the Advanced tab. Click either When I Press the Power Button on My Computer or When I Close the Lid of My Computer; then click Hibernate.

4. Turn off your computer.

PASSWORD PROTECTING WHILE IN STANDBY OR HIBERNATION

If you have confidential information on your computer, you won't want to reveal that information to someone who restores power to your computer from standby or hibernation. To password protect your computer while it's in standby or hibernation, follow these steps:

1. Open the Power Management option in the Control Panel.

2. Click the Advanced tab.

3. Select Prompt for Password when Computer Goes off Standby.

FILE SYSTEM CONSIDERATIONS WHEN DUAL BOOTING WITH WINDOWS NT

Windows 98 operates in a multiboot system in the same way as previous versions of Windows, Windows NT, and DOS operated. A few provisos involve the *FAT32* file system that might have been installed with Windows 98 or Windows 95 OSR2.

You cannot multiboot to another operating system if the C: drive is a FAT32 file system. Other file systems are not able to access files on a partition formatted as FAT32. The older operating systems, such as DOS and previous versions of Windows and Windows NT, do not recognize the FAT32 file system. Some utilities enable Windows NT to access a FAT32 volume. See the end-of-chapter section "Secrets of Mastering the Windows 98 Environment" for more information.

If you want to use Windows 98 in a multiboot system, format the C: drive as a FAT16 file system. You can have other partitions formatted in FAT32, but DOS and versions of Windows or Windows NT prior to release 5.0 do not recognize files on the FAT32 partition.

→ For more information on the different types of file systems and how to deploy them **see** "Choosing a File System," **p. 155** and "Converting a FAT16 Drive to FAT32," **p.160.**

SHUTTING DOWN WINDOWS

Windows now has multiple methods of turning off your computer. To shut down your computer, click Start, Shut Down, and then click one of the following choices:

Stand By	To conserve power and restore application, documents, and settings quickly when restarting
Shut Down	To turn off power and be prompted to save documents
Restart	To reload and restart Windows
Restart in MS-DOS Mode	To shut down Windows and restart with a DOS prompt

TROUBLESHOOTING

STARTUP AND REBOOT PROBLEMS

After putting some applications in the StartUp folder so they would run on startup, Windows fails to start correctly.

To see whether the applications in the StartUp folder are causing the problem, hold down the Shift key during startup. (If you hold down the Shift key during initial startup, Windows goes into Safe mode.) This step prevents applications in startup from starting. If Windows starts correctly, then a problem exists with one of the applications. Remove all the applications from the folder and then put each back, one at a time, until you find the offending application.

WINDOWS 98 HANGS DURING FIRST REBOOT

When installing Windows 98, the Windows 98 Setup might fail to respond, or "hang," during the first reboot.

In most cases this behavior occurs because the video adapter driver is incorrect or configured improperly or because a program on your computer might not be completely compatible with Windows 98.

VIDEO ADAPTER DRIVER CONFLICT DURING SETUP

You're having trouble with a video adapter driver while setting up Windows 98.

If you have a video adapter driver conflict, you must start your computer in Safe mode and then run Setup. To start Windows 98 in Safe mode, restart your computer, press and hold down the Ctrl key, and then choose Safe Mode from the Startup menu. To change the video adapter driver to the standard video graphics adapter (VGA) follow these steps:

1. Click Start, point to Settings, click Control Panel, and then double-click Display.
2. Click the Settings tab, and then click Advanced.
3. Click the Adapter tab, and then click Change.
4. Click Next, click Display a List of All the Drivers in a Specific Location, So You Can Select the Driver You Want, and then click Next.
5. Click Show All Devices.
6. In the Manufacturers box, click Standard Display Types.
7. In the Models box, click Standard Display Adapter (VGA), click OK, and then click Next.
8. Click Next, click Next, and then click Finish.
9. Click Close, click Close, and then click Yes to restart your computer.

At this point, run Windows 98 Setup again. If you get through the Windows 98 Setup, take the time to check the adapter manufacturer's Web site to determine whether an updated driver is available.

SECRETS OF MASTERING THE WINDOWS 98 ENVIRONMENT: ACCESSING FAT32 VOLUMES ON A DUAL-BOOT SYSTEM

FAT32 is a file system driver that enables Windows NT to access FAT32 formatted partitions. You should not convert the boot partition, the first partition on the system to FAT32. Windows NT boots from this partition. And Windows NT cannot boot from a FAT32 partition.

The optimum disk configuration for multiboot systems is to format the first partition, the partition containing the boot files for the operating systems, FAT. FAT allows access to the boot files during system startup for DOS, Windows 98, and Windows NT. User and mission-critical data can then be stored on additional partitions on the system running FAT32.

When using the *FAT32* utility you are accessing preexisting FAT32 drives. You cannot create or convert FAT32 partitions from within Windows NT. If you plan to set up a multiboot system, it is best to do so from scratch. The first step is to partition a fresh drive, preferably a low-level, formatted, small computer system interface (SCSI) drive. Partition the drive with the first partition formatted FAT16, and one or more remaining partitions formatted FAT32. The first partition must be as large as you can make it to accommodate all system files for both Windows 98 and Windows NT as well as the all-important virtual memory swap or page files each operating system (OS) uses. The rest of the drive space can be partitioned as necessary for data storage. After FAT32 is installed, the FAT32 volumes are accessed as read-only while running Windows NT. Given this limitation, this type of configuration is most suitable in systems in which the Windows 98 operating system is the one used most often or as the "desktop OS." The *FAT32* utility can be accessed from the Sysinternals Web site at `http://www.sysinternals.com`.

CHAPTER 3

NAVIGATING AND CONTROLLING WINDOWS

In this chapter

BASIC ELEMENTS OF THE WINDOWS 98 INTERFACE

Each graphical element in a Windows screen causes some effect when clicked. To run Windows effectively, you should know the name and function of each element.

The Windows desktop in Figure 3.1 contains multiple application windows. The figure identifies the parts of a typical Windows 98 screen.

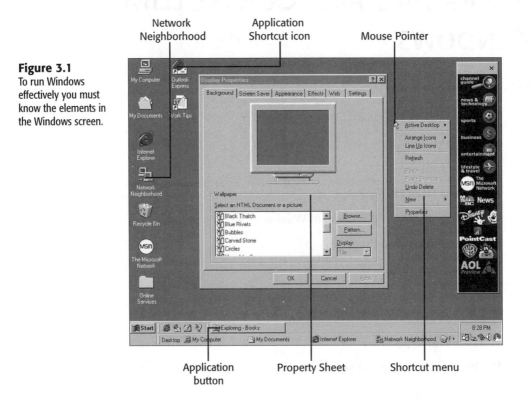

Figure 3.1
To run Windows effectively you must know the elements in the Windows screen.

PROGRAM AND DOCUMENT SHORTCUT ICONS

You can place on the desktop *shortcut* icons that point to program or document files. Clicking an icon starts the program or opens the document in the appropriate application. By modifying the shortcut's properties, you can control how the program's window opens.

→ To learn about saving time by organizing access to your files, **see** "Using Shortcuts," **p. 102.**

FOLDER ICONS

Clicking a shortcut icon that points to a folder opens the folder into a window. A folder shortcut also acts as conduit to the actual folder. For example, dragging and dropping a file from Windows Explorer onto a folder shortcut places that file into the folder the shortcut points to.

→ To learn about creating, renaming, and deleting shortcuts, **see** "Using Shortcuts," **p. 102.**

DESKTOP

The Windows desktop covers the entire screen and lies under all icons, windows, and objects. It is the container for shortcut icons, the taskbar, desktop toolbars, and program windows. When the desktop displays active content such as a Web site or Channel bars, it is known as the *Active Desktop*.

→ To find out more about how to configure your desktop to match your work environment, **see** "Creating Custom Web Views," **p. 134** and "Managing Buttons on a Toolbar," **p. 329.**

ACTIVE DESKTOP

The Windows desktop becomes the Active Desktop when it displays active content such as Web components or links to Web data or an Active Channel. The Active Desktop can contain hyperlinks that open programs, documents, or Web sites. It also can display information that frequently updates through an Internet or intranet connection.

→ For more information on determining the type of Windows desktop that best fits your needs, **see** "Classic or Web? Choosing a Navigation Style," **p. 68** To really add some excitement to your desktop, you can create and use a Web page as your desktop; **see** "Adding Web Content to the Active Desktop," **p. 636.**

MY COMPUTER

The My Computer shortcut gives you access to all the resources in your computer, hard drives, CD-ROMs, Control Panel, printers, and so forth. The My Computer window displays the same resources as the left pane of Windows Explorer.

→ For more details on using My Computer and enjoying a simple, uncluttered view of the resources on your system, **see** "Two Views of Windows Explorer," **p. 78.**

Tip #5	If you don't use My Computer to get to your resources and you are viewing your desktop as a Web page, then you are in luck. With Windows 98 you can modify or even hide the icons on your desktop. Simply follow these steps:
	1. On the Start menu, point to Settings and then click Control Panel.
	2. Double-click the Display icon.
	3. Click the Effects tab.
	4. In the Desktop icons section, select the icon you want to change and then click Change Icon.
	5. Select the icon you want to use or click Browse to look for icons in a different location.
	6. To remove desktop icons, select the Hide Icons When the Desktop Is Viewed as a Web Page check box.

NETWORK NEIGHBORHOOD

If you are connected to a network, click Network Neighborhood to open an Explorer Window displaying all available network resources. You can connect or disconnect from network drives, find computers on the network, or use network resources such as shared folders and files.

➔ As with any other icon in Explorer view, Network Neighborhood can be expanded to list systems on the network and their shares. **See** "Using Explorer with Shared Resources on a Network," **p.122.**

START

Click Start to display a menu of programs, documents, and Windows tools. All Windows features are available through Start or from one of its submenus. Start is displayed at the left end of a horizontal taskbar or the top of a vertical taskbar.

➔ To learn two different ways to add items to the Start menu, **see** "Adding and Removing Programs in the Start Menu," **p. 330.**

TASKBAR

The taskbar is easily accessed to display all programs currently open and running. Click a program button in the taskbar to activate the window containing that program. The taskbar is movable and can be relocated or resized to anywhere onscreen. You can hide the taskbar so that it displays only when the pointer touches the screen edge containing the taskbar.

⚠ *If you're having trouble viewing the taskbar while running certain applications, see "Obscuring the Taskbar" in the "Troubleshooting" section at the end of this chapter.*

➔ To place the taskbar in a more convenient location on the desktop or resize the taskbar, **see** "Resizing the Taskbar," **p. 323.**

CHANNEL GUIDE

The channel guide is displayed both on the Active Desktop and in Internet Explorer. It gives you easy access to specialized Web sites that can send information to your browser at predefined times. Web sites that use a channel include a navigation map that enables you to find information more quickly.

➔ For details on subscribing to Active Channels and managing the Channel bar, **see** "Managing the Channel Bar," **p. 653.**

DESKTOP TOOLBARS

Desktop toolbars give you quick access to frequently used programs, documents, folders, and hyperlinks; clicking a button on a toolbar opens that program, document, folder, or Web site. Toolbars are more accessible than desktop shortcuts because you can move and resize folders as well as hide them against the side of a screen. When you move the mouse pointer against that side of the screen, the toolbar is displayed, ready for use.

➔ If you think you have too many toolbars or one that is too big, **see** "Managing Buttons on a Toolbar," **p. 329.**

SHORTCUT MENUS

Shortcut menus display menus that contain the most appropriate actions for the item on which you right-click. These menus are real time-savers.

PROPERTY SHEETS

Resources in Windows such as the desktop, printers, shortcut icons, disks, folders, and so on, have associated property sheets. These property sheets display fixed and changeable characteristics (properties) about the item. Display property sheets through a menu selection or by right- clicking the item and then clicking Properties.

USING THE MOUSE

Nearly all actions in Windows and Windows programs can be controlled with the mouse. Most people, after they become familiar with Windows, use a combination of mouse actions, reserving a few keystroke combinations for frequently repeated commands.

Tip #6	Windows 98 can be configured to use the Web style single-click with a mouse rather than the classic style double-click to complete some Windows actions. Learn about these two styles in the following sections.

DRAGGING ITEMS WITH A MOUSE

Dragging with a mouse selects multiple text characters or moves graphic objects such as windows. Dragging is the same whether you have single- or double-click selected. Place the mouse pointer over a movable object, such as a file icon; then press and hold down the left mouse button. Continue holding down the button as you move the mouse. The object moves with the mouse pointer. When you have positioned the object where you want it, release the mouse button to drop the object.

Tip #7	Select multiple items on the desktop by clicking on the desktop and dragging the selection rectangle that displays so that it surrounds the items. Release to select all objects within the rectangle.

RIGHT-CLICKING TO DISPLAY SHORTCUT MENUS

Most objects in Windows and Windows programs have a shortcut menu associated with them. This shortcut menu contains frequently used commands appropriate to the selected item. For example, the shortcut menu that displays when you right-click selected text includes the commands Cut, Copy, and Paste.

In some situations, such as dragging a file onto the desktop, you can drag using the right mouse button. When you release the right mouse button, a shortcut menu gives you the choices of Move Here, Copy Here, and Create Shortcut(s) Here. You can also hold down the Shift key as you right-click a file or folder to get a menu that lists every available command.

ACTIVATING WITH CLASSIC STYLE (DOUBLE-CLICK METHODS)

When Windows is configured in classic style, a single click selects an item, such as a file, folder, or shortcut, and a double-click activates it. You can select adjacent (contiguous) files by clicking the first file in a list and then holding the Shift key as you click the last file you want to select. All files between the first click and Shift+click are selected. To select multiple nonadjacent files, click the first file; then hold down the Ctrl key as you click additional files in the same folder. Ctrl+click a selected file to deselect it.

ACTIVATING WITH WEB STYLE (SINGLE-CLICK METHOD)

Changing Windows 98 to use a Web style of navigation makes the mouse work on the desktop or in Windows and Internet Explorer as it does on Web pages. A single click activates an item. For example, a single click on a desktop icon opens the icon's program or document.

Note

If you have just switched to the Web style, you might find yourself occasionally opening more files and folders than you want. For example, you might open a folder in the Explorer's right pane the old way, with a double-click, only to find that you've activated a program or document. What has happened is that the first click opened the folder and the second click activated a file or program.

To select a single desktop item, or a file or folder in Explorer, move the pointer over the item and pause. The focus, highlighting, moves to that item.

To select multiple adjacent items on the desktop or in Explorer, move the pointer over the first item and pause until it is selected. Do not click. Hold down the Shift key and move the pointer smoothly until it is over the last item you want to select; then pause. All items between the first and last are selected.

To select nonadjacent items on the desktop or in Explorer, move the pointer over the first item and pause until it is selected. Do not click. Hold down the Ctrl key and smoothly move the pointer over the next item to select and pause until that item is selected (see Figure 3.2). Continue the process of holding the Ctrl key, moving, and pausing until each nonadjacent item is selected.

Figure 3.2
Select nonadjacent items by pausing the pointer over items as you hold down Ctrl.

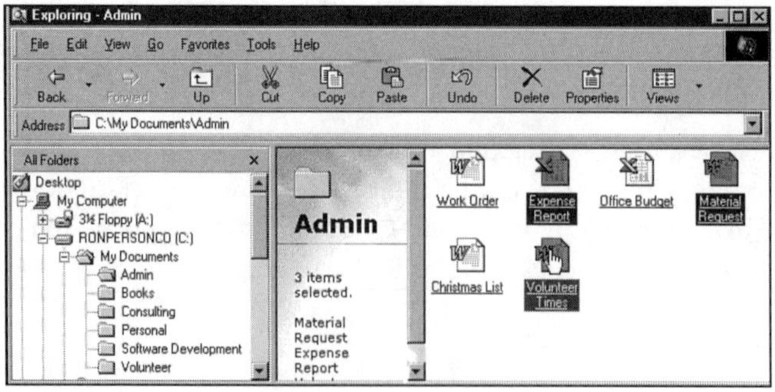

Activate or run multiple selected items by right-clicking one of the items and selecting Open or another appropriate command from the shortcut menu.

USING THE MICROSOFT INTELLIMOUSE

Microsoft released the IntelliMouse coincidentally with the release of Office 97. This new mouse has a small wheel between the left and right mouse buttons. Rolling the wheel with your index finger enables you to scroll without using scrollbars, pan in any direction, zoom documents using different magnifications, expand/collapse outlines, and drill down or up in worksheet data. The features available depend on the program.

Tip #8	Older applications can also take advantage of the IntelliMouse wheel. All you need to do is load the IntelliMouse software drivers.

Holding down the IntelliMouse wheel button, located between the mouse buttons, in combination with the Ctrl or Shift keys gives you access to the features and commands listed in Table 3.1.

TABLE 3.1   INTELLIMOUSE ACTIONS

Roll wheel	Scroll up in a window by rolling the wheel forward. Scroll down in a window by rolling the wheel down.
Drag wheel	Pan any direction in a window by holding down the wheel button as you move the mouse in any direction. The entire document moves in any direction.
Ctrl+wheel roll	Zoom a document to greater or lesser magnification by holding down the Ctrl key as you roll the wheel forward or backward.
Shift+wheel roll	Expand or collapse data structures like outlines or worksheet drilldowns by holding down the Shift key as you roll the wheel forward or backward.

Tip #9	If you ever have a problem with a context menu remaining onscreen when you roll the IntelliMouse wheel to close the menu, the problem is not with the mouse. The operating system controls the opening and closing of context menus but does so based on a predefined set of recognizable mouse or keyboard actions. The operating system does not recognize the rolling IntelliMouse wheel as an action designed to close the context menu. If you encounter this problem, you can close the context menu by pressing the Esc key or by using the left mouse button to select something other than the context menu.

USING THE KEYBOARD

Table 3.2 shows the keyboard shortcuts that can save you time as you become proficient in Windows. A few of these keystrokes, such as F1 for Help, Alt+Tab to switch between applications, and F2 to edit selected text should be part of everyone's skill set. Some keyboards, such as the Microsoft Natural Keyboard, include a *Windows key* and an *application key* that give quick access to certain predefined functions.

TABLE 3.2   UNIVERSAL WINDOWS SHORTCUT KEYS

Topic	Description	Key Combination
Close, Program	Exit active program	Alt+F4
Close, Document Window	Close the active document window	Ctrl+F4
Help	Display Windows Help	Windows+F1
Help	Display Help for the selected item in a dialog box	F1
Menu, Document's System	Display document system menu to control program window	Alt+hyphen
Menu, Program	Activate menu bar	F10
Menu, Program's System	Display program system menu to control program window	Alt+Spacebar
Menu, Select Menu	Select from the active menu bar the menu containing the underlined letter	Alt+*underlined letter*
Menu, Shortcut	Display shortcut menu for selected item	Shift+F10 or Application key
Menu, Start	Display Start menu	Ctrl+Esc or Windows
Command, Cut	Cut selected item	Ctrl+X
Command, Copy	Copy selected item	Ctrl+C
Command, Paste	Paste item from the Clipboard at current insertion point	Ctrl+V
Command, Delete	Delete selected item	Delete key
Command, Delete	Delete selected item from the desktop without Recycle Bin	Shift+Delete
Command, Find: All Files	Display Find: All Files dialog box when desktop is active	F3 or Windows+F
Command, Find: Computer	Display Find: Computer dialog box when desktop is active	Ctrl+Windows+F

Topic	Description	Key Combination
Command, Minimize	Minimize all windows	Windows+M
Command, Minimize or Restore	Minimize or restore all windows	Windows+D
Command, Properties	Display properties of selected item on desktop	Alt+Enter
Command, Refresh	Refresh all window contents	F5
Command, Rename	Rename selected item	F2
Command, Run	Display Run dialog box	Windows+R
Command, Select All	Select all items when desktop is active	Ctrl+A
Command, System Properties	Display System Properties dialog box	Windows+Break
Command, Undo	Undo last effect of last command	Ctrl+Z
Command, Undo Minimize	Undo minimizing all windows	Shift+Windows+M
Switch, Document Window	Activate the next document window	Ctrl+F6
Switch, Program Window	Activate the next application window	Alt+Tab
Switch, Program	Activate taskbar and cycle through buttons	Windows+Tab

PART

I

CH

3

USING MENUS AND DIALOG BOXES

The Windows system of graphical menus and dialog boxes reduces the learning curve and increases skill retention. Menus are displayed in the same location in all programs and display groups of commands by functional category. Dialog boxes present a unified way of defining an object's properties or modifying a command's operation. The operating techniques for menus and dialog boxes are the same for all Windows applications.

CHOOSING MENUS AND COMMANDS

The menu bar, located directly under the title bar of a program, displays the menu names. Windows programs use the same menu headings for common functions (such as File, Edit, Window, and Help), which makes it easier for you to learn new applications. To open a menu, click its name with the left mouse button, or press Alt and then the underlined letter in the menu name.

Menu items, also known as commands, are displayed on each menu. Point to any menu item to select it. Click to activate the menu item or type the letter underlined in the submenu item name. If an arrow appears to the side of the menu item, a submenu opens. Click the menu item to keep the submenu open or move over the submenu item and click to activate that command. Menu items followed by an ellipsis (three dots) display a dialog box with additional options.

USING COMMON DIALOG BOXES TO OPEN AND SAVE DOCUMENTS

Most programs designed for Windows 95 and Windows 98 have a few dialog boxes in common. The two most frequently used common dialog boxes are Save As and Open. Figure 3.3 shows an Open dialog box from WordPad. The Save As dialog box is very similar.

Navigating and managing files and folders within the work area of the Open or Save As dialog box is identical to working within an Explorer window. For example, you can drag and drop files or folders, use Ctrl-drag to copy and rename files or folders, right-click for an appropriate shortcut menu, and so on.

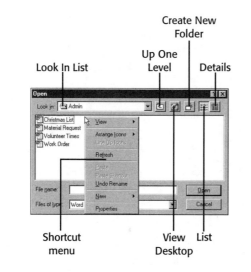

Figure 3.3
Save As and Open dialog boxes, common to many programs, have many features built in.

The common Open and Save As dialog boxes use the same techniques as Explorer windows do for navigating among folders and for moving or copying files from folder to folder. Table 3.3 lists the methods of manipulating folders.

TABLE 3.3 NAVIGATING, MOVING, AND COPYING IN COMMON DIALOG BOXES

To:	Do this:
Change drives or folders	Click Look In list
Open a folder	Activate folder
Go up a folder	Click Up One Level button or press Backspace

To:	Do this:
Create a new folder	Click Create New Folder button
Rename file or folder	Select, F2
Move file or folder	Drag
Copy file or folder	Ctrl+drag
Create shortcut	Right drag, Create Shortcut(s) Here

Tip #10

From a common Save As or Open dialog box, press F4 to display the Save In or Look In lists. Press F5 to refresh the file and folder contents of the dialog boxes.

Within the Open or Save As dialog box, you can create a new folder in thecurrently displayed folder by clicking the Create New Folder button at the top of the dialog box. The folder is displayed with its name selected. Type a new name over the selection and press Enter.

Rename a file or folder by selecting it and then pressing F2. Edit the name; then press Enter. To delete files or folders, select those you want to delete; then press Delete. Respond Yes when asked whether you want to send the file or folder to the Recycle Bin.

PART

I

CH

3

SELECTING OPTIONS FROM DIALOG BOXES

Use the controls in dialog boxes to change properties or the effect of a command. Figure 3.4 shows the Font dialog box from WordPad. Figure 3.5 shows the Word 6 tab from the Options dialog box in WordPad.

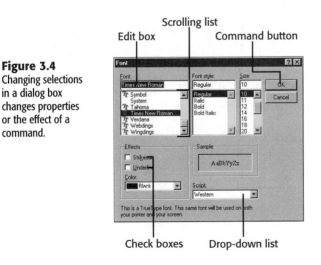

Figure 3.4
Changing selections in a dialog box changes properties or the effect of a command.

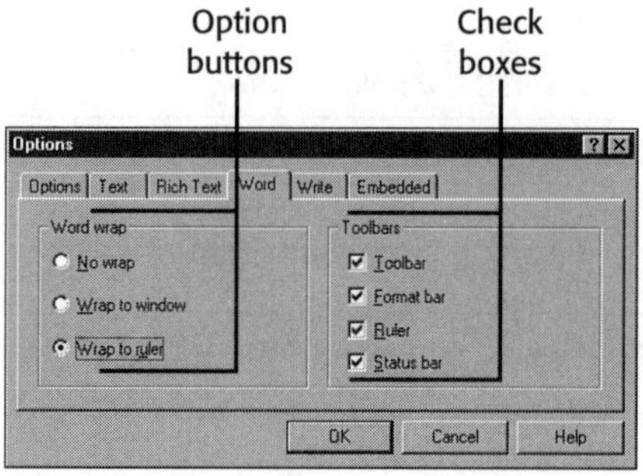

Option buttons   Check boxes

Figure 3.5
You can select one option button from a group, but you can select any number of check boxes.

USING THE MOUSE IN DIALOG BOXES

In most cases only one or two items are changed in a dialog box, and a mouse is efficient for selecting the control and clicking OK. Table 3.4 shows mouse actions in a dialog box.

TABLE 3.4   DIALOG BOX MOUSE ACTIONS

Control Type	Effect	Mouse Action
Check box	Change check box	Click
Option buttons	Select one from group	Click to select and clear others
Edit box	Edit text or number	Click and drag to select, and then type
Scrolling list	Scrolls list, then selects	Click or drag scrollbar, click item in list
Drop-down list	Select from drop-down list	Click down arrow, click item in list
Command button	Choose command button	Click

USING THE KEYBOARD IN DIALOG BOXES

If you need to change many settings in a dialog box or if using a mouse is not possible, use one of these keyboard methods. If it's too much to remember all these keystrokes, just remember Ctrl+Tab to move between tabs in a dialog box and Alt+*underlined letter* to select or clear a control. Table 3.5 shows keystrokes for operating a dialog box.

TABLE 3.5   DIALOG BOX KEYS

Effect	Keystroke
Move to next control	Tab
Move to previous control	Shift+Tab
Select next tab	Ctrl+Tab
Select previous tab	Shift+Ctrl+Tab
Acts the same as a click on the current control	Spacebar
Choose active button	Enter
Cancel dialog box	Esc
Select or clear control	Alt+*underlined letter*

Tip #11	You can cut, copy, and paste between dialog boxes or between dialog boxes and applications. Select the text; then press Ctrl+X to cut or Ctrl+C to copy. Press Ctrl+V to insert text from the Clipboard.

CONTROLLING THE SIZE AND POSITION OF WINDOWS

The taskbar's shortcut menu enables you to quickly arrange windows on the desktop. Right-click a gray area of the taskbar; then click one of the following commands to arrange all open windows:

Cascade Windows	Arrange windows in an overlapping cascade from top to bottom, left to right.
Tile Windows Horizontally	Arrange windows in horizontal strips across the full screen width. Screen height is divided evenly between windows.
Tile Windows Vertically	Arrange windows in vertical strips from screen top to bottom. Screen width is divided evenly between windows.
Undo Tile	Restore all windows to their previous locations.

PART

I

CH

3

Quickly clear the desktop of windows by right-clicking a gray area of the taskbar and then clicking Minimize All Windows.

To quickly arrange your desktop so you can work in two program windows that evenly divide the screen, right-click a gray area of the taskbar; then click Minimize All Windows. Now display only the two programs in which you want to work by clicking their buttons in the taskbar. Finally, right-click a gray area of the taskbar; then click Tile Windows Horizontally or Tile Windows Vertically.

Move a window by dragging its title. Change the size of windows by dragging a window's edge or corner.

Move a desktop icon by dragging the icon. When you manually move desktop icons, they might not align exactly. If you want all the icons to rearrange themselves in a certain order in columns at the left of the screen, make a choice from that submenu for Arrange Icons. If you want to align icons where you've placed them, you should choose Line Up Icons. If you always want them aligned along the left side whenever they are moved or when you create a new icon, click Auto Arrange. To turn off Auto Arrange, you must click the menu choice again. If you want to align icons, right-click the desktop; then click Arrange Icons. From the submenu, click one of the choices for how you want to align the icons on the desktop: by Name, by Type, by Size, or by Date. If you want desktop icons to automatically align themselves whenever they are moved, click Auto Arrange on the submenu.

CHANGING SETTINGS AND PROPERTIES

Nearly every item on the Windows desktop or within a program's contents has associated properties. Properties are characteristics inherent to an item. A property sheet for each item enables you to view and change properties. To display an item's property sheet, right-click an item; then click Properties on the shortcut menu. A property sheet similar to the Display Properties sheet in Figure 3.6 displays. Change properties by selecting, editing, or clearing entries and then clicking OK.

Figure 3.6
Property sheets enable you to view and change an item's properties.

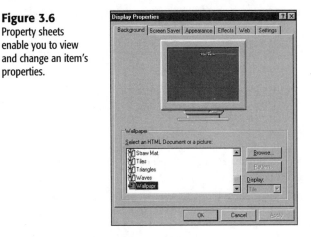

USING THE START MENU

The Start menu is the starting place for many Windows tasks. You can open the Start menu at any time, from within any program, with one mouse click. From the Start menu, you can start programs, open recently used documents, customize the look and feel of Windows, find files and folders, get Help, and shut down your computer.

STARTING A PROGRAM

To start a program from the Start menu, click Start. Point to Programs. The Program menu then is displayed to the right. Point to the program you want to start, as shown in Figure 3.7, and click. You can keep any of these menus open by clicking once on the menu. If you do not click, the menu closes when the pointer moves away.

If the program you want to start is not displayed in the Start menu, point to an appropriate folder on the Start menu to see the programs within the folder. If you have moved the taskbar, you might not see the taskbar and Start button at the bottom of your screen. If you see a gray line at one edge of the screen, move the pointer to that edge to display the taskbar.

Tip #12

If you want to move the taskbar to a more convenient location on the desktop, all you must do is single-click on an open gray space on taskbar, continue to hold down on the left mouse button and drag the toolbar to either the top or side of the screen.

Figure 3.7
Open the menu
that contains the
program you want
to start and then
click the program.

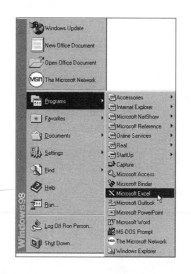

When you open a program, a button for the program appears in the taskbar. These buttons tell you which programs are open. Quickly activate the window for one of these programs by clicking on its button.

→ If you want to customize the items available for selection on the start menu, **see** Adding and Removing Programs in the Start Menu," **p. 330.**

OPENING A RECENTLY USED DOCUMENT

Clicking the Documents command on the Start menu displays your most recently opened documents. When you choose this command, the Documents submenu is displayed with a listing of the files that you have worked on recently. To open a document in this list, simply click on it. Windows then automatically starts the associated application, if it is not already running, and opens the document.

After a while, the Documents menu can become quite long and contain documents that you no longer are working with. To clear the list, right-click a blank area of the taskbar and choose Properties. Select the Start Menu Programs tab on the Taskbar Properties dialog box; then click the Clear button.

USING THE TASKBAR

The taskbar resides at an edge of the screen, usually the bottom, and displays all programs currently open and running. Switch between programs by clicking a program button on the taskbar.

Tip #13	If you are a lover of the keyboard and a former Windows 3.x user, you can still press Alt+Tab to cycle between programs without using the mouse or taskbar.

USING TOOLBARS

Toolbars reside on the taskbar and provide quick access to applications and other resources. In addition to the four default toolbars, you can create custom toolbars that contain buttons for programs, files, folders, and hyperlinks. Figure 3.8 shows the four built-in toolbars.

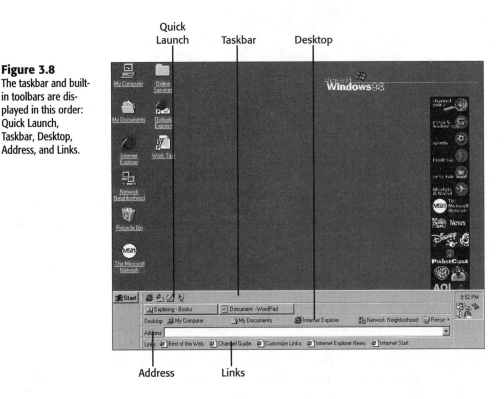

Figure 3.8
The taskbar and built-in toolbars are displayed in this order: Quick Launch, Taskbar, Desktop, Address, and Links.

To display a built-in toolbar, right-click in a gray area of the taskbar or a toolbar, click Toolbars, and then click the name of the toolbar. To remove a toolbar, right-click the toolbar title; then click Close. You cannot close the taskbar. The toolbars are described in Table 3.6.

TABLE 3.6   BUILT-IN TOOLBAR DESCRIPTIONS

Toolbar	Description
Address	Displays hyperlinks you enter to Web or local items
Link	Displays hyperlinks to Web sites: Best of the Web, Microsoft, Product News, Today's Links, and Web Gallery
Desktop	Displays a button for each item on the desktop
Quick Launch	Shows desktop, displays channels, launches Internet Explorer, launches Mail

Move a toolbar by dragging the move handle at its left corner. Dragging a toolbar to midscreen creates a toolbar window. To resize and manipulate toolbar windows, use normal window techniques.

Tip #14	If you want to get rid of the Office Shortcut bar and have a more versatile tool to work with, the new Windows 98 Quick Launch bar is a flexible and handy alternative. It's located just to the right of the Start button on the taskbar. You can place buttons on it in any order and put it anywhere you want on your desktop.

PART

I

CH

3

WORKING WITH APPLICATIONS

Windows enables you to run more than one program at a time. Each program is displayed in its own window or as an item on the taskbar. The term *active* describes the window that is receiving input. The active window is usually the top program window. The active window's title bar is a different color than that of inactive windows.

Figure 3.9 shows two program windows. The active window contains multiple documents. The taskbar at the bottom of the screen displays the programs that are running. The button for the active program is highlighted on the taskbar.

→ To find out how to install Windows 98 applications, including legacy 16-bit applications, **see** "Installing Windows Applications," **p. 197.**

SCROLLING IN A DOCUMENT

Document windows containing contents larger than the window display scrollbars. A vertical scrollbar displays along the right edge and a horizontal scrollbar along the bottom edge.

Figure 3.9
This active program window contains multiple document windows.

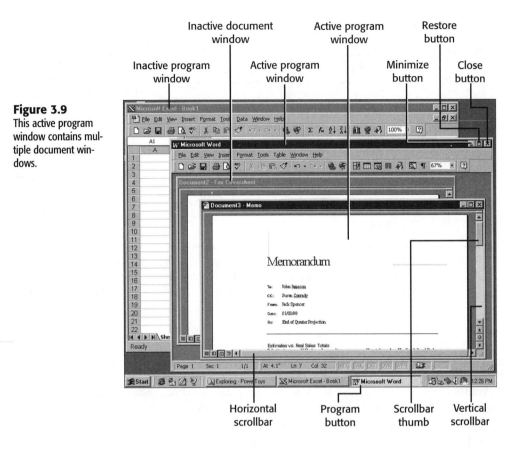

In most programs you can move through document contents by using the mouse with the actions shown in Table 3.7.

TABLE 3.7   SCROLLING WITH MOUSE ACTIONS

Movement	Mouse Action
Scroll by smallest increments	Click arrowheads at ends of scrollbar
Scroll by screens	Click in scrollbar
Scroll to edge of document	Drag thumb in scrollbar to appropriate end of scrollbar

In most programs you can move through document contents by using the keyboard with the actions shown in Table 3.8.

TABLE 3.8   SCROLLING WITH KEYSTROKES

Movement	Keystroke
Scroll up/down by line	Up/down arrow key
Scroll left/right by character	Right/left arrow key
Scroll left/right by word	Ctrl+right/left arrow key
Scroll to beginning of line	Home
Scroll to end of line	End
Scroll up/down by screen	Page Up/Page Down

SELECTING TEXT AND OBJECTS

Select text by dragging across the text. Select words by dragging across or double-clicking the word. You can also select entire paragraphs by triple clicking on them.

Select objects by clicking on them. On the Windows desktop and in most programs, you can select multiple items by clicking on the first object and then holding Shift or Ctrl as you click other objects.

Select multiple adjacent objects on the desktop by dragging the pointer diagonally across the objects you want to select. A selection rectangle is displayed as you drag. Objects within or touching the selection rectangle are selected when you release the mouse button.

Select text with the keyboard by holding down the Shift key as you move. Select words by holding the Shift and Ctrl key as you press an arrow key.

USING SIMPLE EDITING TECHNIQUES

Edit text with a mouse by clicking within text to position the insertion point and then typing. Replace text by selecting it and then typing.

Edit text with the keyboard by moving the insertion point to where you want to insert text and then typing. Replace text by selecting it and then typing. Delete selected text by pressing the Delete key.

COPYING AND MOVING

Use menu commands or mouse actions to copy or move selected items. Cut a selected item from its current location by choosing Edit, Cut (Ctrl+X). Copy a selected item by choosing Edit, Copy (Ctrl+C). Paste the cut or copied item by moving the insertion point to the desired location and then choosing Edit, Paste (Ctrl+V).

PART

I

CH

3

To move a selected item with the mouse, drag the selected item to its new location; then release. To copy a selected item, hold down the Ctrl key as you drag the item.

Tip #15	Ctrl+C and Ctrl+V are two of the most useful commands in your arsenal. Regardless of the text environment, you can copy and subsequently paste the text into any document or work. These commands are especially useful for copying materials into Word from a CD-ROM.

➜ For more details on sharing data among programs, including how the Clipboard works in this process, **see** "Understanding the Data-Sharing Capabilities of Windows 98," **p. 224.**

SWITCHING BETWEEN DOCUMENT WINDOWS

Activate a document window by clicking on a portion of the window. If you cannot see the inactive window to click on it, then click Window, and click on the document name you want active. In some programs you can cycle between document windows by pressing Ctrl+F6.

CLOSING A DOCUMENT WINDOW

Close a document window by first activating the document and then clicking File, Close or clicking the Close button for the document window. If the document has been modified since the last time it was saved, you are asked whether you want to save the document. If you click Yes, the document is saved with its current name.

QUITTING WINDOWS APPLICATIONS

Most Windows applications use the same procedure for quitting. To quit a Windows application, follow these steps:

1. Activate the application by clicking the application's window or by pressing Alt+Tab until the window is active.

2. Click File, Exit; press Alt+F4; or click the Close button for the program window.

If the application contains documents that you have modified since the last time that you saved them, the application prompts you to save your changes before the application quits.

WORKING WITH THE ACTIVE DESKTOP

The *Active Desktop* in Windows 98 can change the way you work and think. Instead of working from a Windows desktop containing static folders and icons, you can work from the Webtop, a desktop that displays dynamic information, which changes to meet your needs. The Active Desktop can show you static or changing information from your local PC, your network, or the Web.

The Active Desktop is one of the most important aspects of the Webtop metaphor. In Windows 95, the desktop displays static information such as shortcut icons to start programs or open folders as well as a picture or pattern as a background. The Active Desktop in Windows 98 makes your desktop a display and work area for constantly changing information. For example, your Active Desktop can contain live Web pages, ActiveX components, and Java applets. This feature enables you to see changes to information that might be important to your work and life, such as currency or stock market changes as well as local weather or news bulletins specific to your interests.

You can turn the Active Desktop on or off and customize it to fit your needs. You can use any HTML page as your Active Desktop. That is, your Active Desktop can display information such as the following:

- Any graphic or text that displays in a Web page
- Web links to favorite sites such as finance, sports, lifestyle, or weather
- Continually updating Web pages from favorite sites
- Information pushed to your active desktop from channel vendors
- ActiveX components or Java applets that run as applications in the Active Desktop
- Help information or company bulletins that change frequently

PART

I

CH

3

Tip #16	You might encounter a couple of quirks when using the Active Desktop. First, when you open the Display Properties dialog box, the Web tab is missing. Second, when you right-click the desktop, the Active Desktop command is missing. This behavior can occur if you are using the *TweakUI* program and the Active Desktop Enabled feature is not enabled through the program.
	If you are not familiar with the program, Tweak UI is included with Microsoft Windows 98 Power Toys and is located on the Windows 98 CD-ROM in the Tools\Reskit\Powertoy folder. TweakUI is a productivity tool that enables advanced users to modify some of the settings for the Windows User Interface. Some TweakUI options are also available in other configuration screens, and some options are unique to TweakUI.
	TweakUI offers configuration options for many items including mouse devices, Explorer, the desktop, My Computer, and networks. For more information, see the program's help file.

→ For additional information on modifying your desktop, **see** "Customizing the Windows Display," **p. 332** (Ch 17) and "Displaying Objects on the Active Desktop," **p. 638**.

→ To really soup up your desktop, try turning it into a Web page. **See** "Using an HTML Page as Your Desktop," **p. 637**.

TROUBLESHOOTING

OBSCURING THE TASKBAR

The windows of some programs written for older versions of Windows cover the taskbar, so it is difficult to switch between applications or click the Start button.

Even when you can't see the taskbar, you can switch between applications by holding down the Alt key and pressing Tab. A bar is displayed with icons for each application. Press Tab until the application you want is selected; then release both keys.

To display the taskbar and open the Start menu at the same time, press Ctrl+Esc.

SECRETS OF MASTERING THE WINDOWS 98 ENVIRONMENT: USING WINDOWSWITCHER

WindowSwitcher is a neat little tool that enables you to go back and forth between all open documents, workbooks, and any other Windows-based applications. When more than one document, workbook, or presentation is open, WindowSwitcher displays the inactive windows as a series of buttons on the taskbar. These handy shortcuts save a lot of time because the user doesn't have to go to the specific application's Window menu to switch over to one of the other inactive (but open) windows; just click the window's button on the taskbar or press Alt+Tab. WindowSwitcher automatically activates that window. WindowSwitcher displays the captions and appropriate icons of the inactive windows in the taskbar and remembers up to 10 windows in each application. If a caption is too large to display on the taskbar, simply hold the mouse pointer over the button and a ToolTip displays the full caption.

CHAPTER **4**

GETTING HELP

In this chapter

UNDERSTANDING HELP

Beginners and experts alike occasionally need help operating Windows or one of its applications. The Help system in Windows 98 is new, but you will find it very easy to use. It includes access to help files on your local drive, links to resources on the Web, access to Microsoft support engineers, and a Windows Update Manager that keeps your software and drivers current. This chapter also contains a brief description of the WinHelp system used in Windows 95 and earlier Windows applications.

Windows 98 Help uses the new HTML Help engine created by Microsoft. The HTML Help engine displays HTML pages containing help information. With this help engine, Windows 98 can look locally, on your network, or on the Internet for help files or other types of assistance programs. Although HTML Help displays HTML pages, you will not find a large collection of HTML Help files on your system. The HTML Help engine accesses HTML files that have been compressed into one or more files, thereby preserving disk space.

Windows applications existing when Windows 98 was released use the WinHelp system that was available in Windows 95.

GETTING HELP FROM WINDOWS HELP FILES

You start Windows 98 Help by clicking Start, <u>H</u>elp. Figure 4.1 shows the Help window that appears. The help shown uses the HTML Help engine.

Figure 4.1
Windows 98 Help uses the HTML Help engine to produce clean and simple displays.

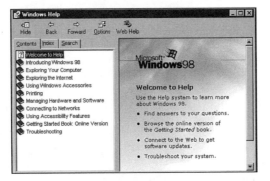

 Note

To start Help from within a Windows application, you can press the F1 key. Windows then displays help information for the active application or window.

NAVIGATING THE CONTENTS PANE

The Contents tab, the left pane shown in Figure 4.1, lists Windows 98 help topics by category. The contents pane of the Help window displays the books and pages with their topic titles. The right pane displays the contents of the page that's selected in the left pane.

Categories in the left pane appear as books. You can open a book to see additional categories or help pages it contains. Figure 4.2 shows the Contents tab with a book expanded to multiple levels and a page selected from the book. To expand or close a book, click in the left pane on the book or its topic title.

⚠ *If you ever have any problems with the book icon changing its appearance, you are not alone. For a detailed discussion of the problem, see "The Book Icon Changing Appearance" in the "Troubleshooting" section at the end of this chapter.*

Help Hide
(Show) Button

Figure 4.2
Expand books see their topical contents.

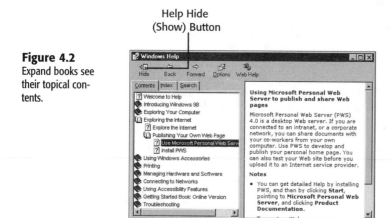

You can change the widths of the panes by dragging the vertical bar between the panes to the left or right. To completely hide the left pane, click the Hide button in the toolbar. While the topic list is hidden, the Hide button is replaced by a Show button. Click the Show button to redisplay the topic list pane.

JUMPING TO A RELATED HELP TOPIC

Some help topics contain hyperlinks to related topics. These hyperlinks appear underlined as you would expect in a Web browser. To display a page of related information or a list of related topics, click the hyperlink. To return to the original page, click the Back button located on the toolbar.

SEARCHING BY TOPIC ON THE INDEX PAGE

If you aren't sure of how to describe the topic on which you need help, use the Index tab. The Index tab, shown in Figure 4.3, enables you to find the help you need by scanning for appropriate words or phrases. The Index tab is visible when the left pane is shown.

Suppose you want to find information on a feature called NetWatcher. As you can see in the figure, you would type the word netwatcher and then click Display. A Topics Found window appears showing all topics containing this keyword. Choose one of the topics listed, such as Using Net Watcher to Monitor Shared Resources Use. In the right pane, the Help system displays how to use NetWatcher to monitor shared resources.

PART

I

CH

4

You can search through the list by scrolling or by typing a keyword or phrase in the edit box at the top of the list. When you find a word or phrase that seems to be appropriate, click on it.

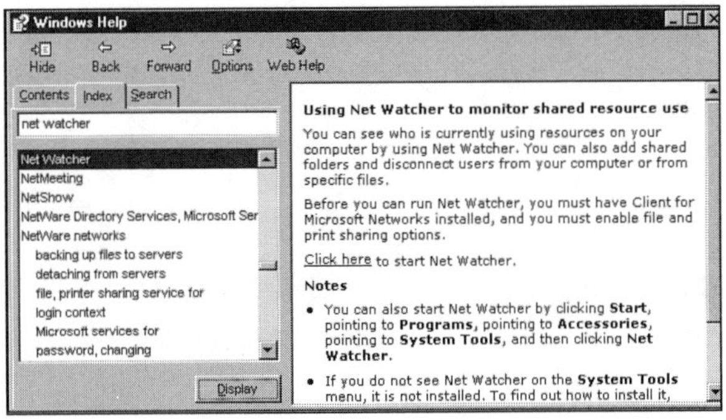

Figure 4.3
The Index tab displays phrases describing helpful topics.

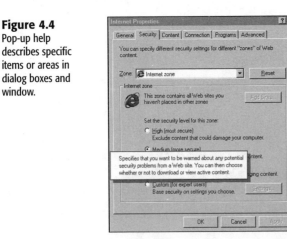

In some cases, when you click <u>D</u>isplay, the Topics Found window appears, showing a list of subcategories that further differentiate your choice. Just choose the topic most related to what you want. Help appears in the right pane of the Help window.

If you aren't sure what you are looking for, scroll through the index looking for related topics. Choose a related topic and then check the right pane to see whether the topic contains a hyperlink to a more specific topic that fits your needs.

GETTING HELP ON THE ACTIVE DIALOG BOX

 If you are faced with a dialog box or window that contains an item you need help with, look for a question mark button in the upper-right corner of the dialog box or window. Click the question mark button and then click the item in the dialog box or window about which you want information. A pop-up window like that shown in Figure 4.4 shows you information about the item. When you finish reading the information, click to close the pop-up window.

Figure 4.4
Pop-up help describes specific items or areas in dialog boxes and window.

FINDING HELP WITH A KEYWORD

If you know a word that describes the topic you need help on, click the Search tab. To find all topics that contain your word, type the word in the text box at the top of the right pane and then click List Topics. Help displays a list of topics that contain this word, as shown in Figure 4.5.

Multiple topics usually appear in the Topic list. Click the topic that looks most helpful and then click Display to see the help information in the right pane.

Figure 4.5
Help displays a list of topics that contain the word you type in the text box.

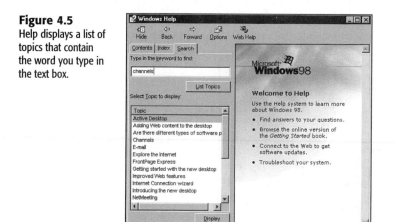

PRINTING A HELP TOPIC

If you have a large display area, you might want to display the application in which you are working and the Help window side by side. However, if your display area is smaller or if you want to create a written reminder, you might want to print a page of help so you can refer to it as you work.

To print any displayed page, either right-click the topic shown in the contents pane and choose Print, or click in the right pane and choose Print.

PART

I

CH

4

Tip #17

One of the handiest pieces of information that you can print or copy from help is a list of an application's shortcut keys. If you didn't get a shortcut keystroke template for your application, look in the application's help contents for a topic similar to Keyboard Shortcuts. Copy these topics by selecting them and pressing Ctrl+C. Then paste (Ctrl+V) them into a word processor, reorganize them, and print them. Alternatively, you can print the topics directly from help. You can then copy the contents at a reduced size and paste them onto 3-by-5 cards.

USING WINDOWS 95 HELP

Windows 95 and applications designed for Windows 95 use the WinHelp engine to create a help system that is slightly different from Windows 98 HTML Help. Even if you use Windows 98, you will probably continue to see and use help based on the WinHelp engine because it is used with Windows 95–compatible applications. Figure 4.6 shows the Windows 95 Help system's Contents tab for Microsoft Word 97. It is similar to the Contents tab in Windows 98 Help. However, Windows 95 Help has only a single pane. The Index and Search tabs function similarly to those in HTML Help, but they also disappear when you select a help selection.

Figure 4.6
Windows 95–based help systems are similar to those of Windows 98, but the tabs and topics disappear and are replaced by specific help contents you choose.

If you compare Figure 4.1 with Figure 4.6, you see that the HTML Help in Figure 4.1 displays the procedural steps or help information in a window to the side of the help topic. Because the Contents or Index list in Windows 98 Help remains open in the left pane, you can easily see the context of a procedure and related help. However, in Windows 95 Help, the Contents, Index, and Search tabs disappear when a Help window appears.

Another significant difference between the two types of help is that Windows 98 Help is displayed in a browser. Therefore, it can run scripting languages, supports Dynamic HTML, and contains links to Internet and intranet sites. This feature enables Windows 98 Help to be more active and to link users to current information and downloadable files.

ADDING CUSTOM NOTES TO HELP TOPICS

You can annotate your own notes to help topics in Windows 95 Help. You might want to use annotations to describe a topic in greater detail, to document information related to tasks you do, or to add a function-related tip. When a Windows 95 help topic has an annotation, a Paper Clip icon appears next to it.

To create an annotation, follow these steps:

1. Display the topic that you want to annotate.

2. Click the <u>O</u>ptions button and then choose <u>A</u>nnotate. The Annotate dialog box, a small notepad, appears.

3. Type the notes that you want to save regarding this help topic.

4. Click the <u>S</u>ave button.

To read the annotation to a topic, just click the Paper Clip icon. To remove an annotation, click the Paper Clip icon and then choose <u>D</u>elete from the Annotate dialog box.

COPYING HELP INFORMATION TO ANOTHER APPLICATION

You can create a collection of help topics from Windows 95 Help by copying the help information and pasting the data into another Windows application such as a word processor document file.

→ To get up and running on moving or copying data, **see** "Cutting, Copying, and Pasting Data," **p. 224.**

To copy the contents of a Windows 95 Help window, click the Options button, and then click Copy. Then, use normal Windows paste procedures to paste the data into another application.

PART

I

CH

4

Tip #18

To copy portions of text in the help screens of Windows 98 or Windows 95 Help windows, drag across the text to select it and then press Ctrl+C. Paste it into the new location by using the paste procedure appropriate to the receiving application. If you are not sure of the appropriate procedure, press Ctrl+V to paste the selection.

FINDING HELP ON THE WEB

The Web offers a wide range of resources that are available to help you with Windows 98. Windows 98 has built-in links to some of these resources. To display these links, click Start, and choose Programs, Accessories, Welcome to Windows. You will see links to numerous resources, including Microsoft's Web site and Microsoft Technical Support.

USING THE MICROSOFT SUPPORT PAGE

If you have an Internet browser installed, you can connect to the Windows Support Web page shown in Figure 4.7. Click the Support Online hyperlink to display the Microsoft Technical Support page shown in Figure 4.8. From this page, you can search for support or answers by product and by keyword. This page also displays tabs that link you to frequently asked questions, phone numbers, and support options. If you want to go there directly in your browser, enter the uniform resource locator (URL) for Microsoft's Support page at www.microsoft.com/support.

Figure 4.7
Microsoft's Support page contains links to help, tips, and troubleshooting for Microsoft products.

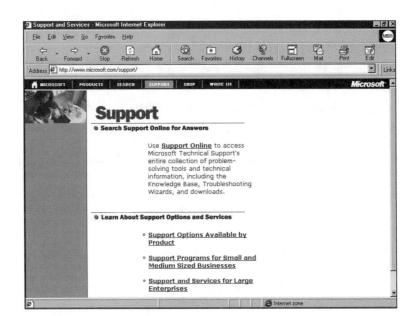

Figure 4.8
From the Microsoft Technical Support page, you can search for support or answers by product and by keyword.

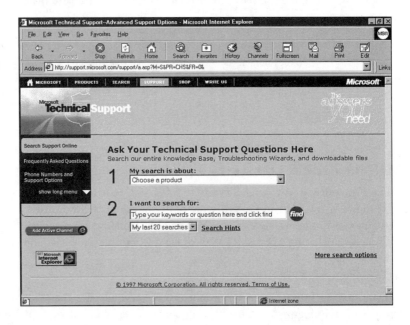

Within the Windows Support page, you will find many hyperlinks to helpful resources. Some of the most valuable resources are covered in the other sections of this book.

→ To find out more about Internet Explorer, **see** "What Is Internet Explorer 5.0?," **p. 556** and "Navigating Internet Explorer," **p. 562.**

LOOKING FOR FAQs

Many bulletin boards and Web sites maintain lists of frequently asked questions (FAQs) about the site's topic. In most cases involving generic problems, you should look through the FAQ lists on Microsoft's Support page before you do a search through the Knowledge Base. To access Windows FAQs from the Support page, go to the main support page at www.microsoft.com/support and click the Frequently Asked Questions link. A page similar to Figure 4.9 appears. Select the product and topic you want and then click the Find button.

Figure 4.9
A FAQ list contains answers to the site's most common questions.

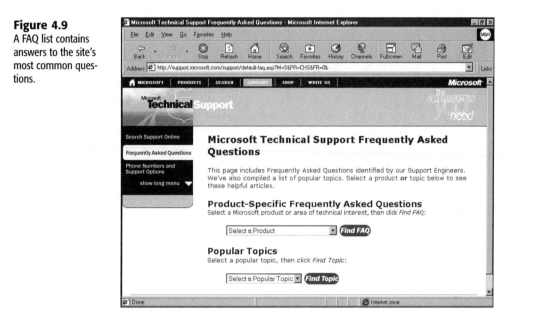

PART
I

CH

4

REPORTING PROBLEMS TO ONLINE SUPPORT ENGINEERS

Sometimes, you try and try only to finally realize that you're not getting closer to solving the computer problem you face. That's when it's time to call in the professionals. For a fee, you can submit a technical problem to Microsoft's technical support engineers. To do so, go to the Microsoft Support Web page and click the Phone Numbers and Support options. Follow the instructions to register for online support. Microsoft gives no-charge support for 90 days. After that period, you can subscribe to fee-based support options.

Tip #19

When you initiate a support call with a Microsoft technical support person, make sure to ask for an incident number. That number serves as a reference just in case the problem wasn't resolved. If you have to call back to further discuss the problem, the incident number allows the Microsoft technician to pick up the issue where you left off. Be careful to never "close" a support incident until you are fully satisfied that the issue has been resolved.

CONSULTING THE HARDWARE COMPATIBILITY LIST

If you have difficulty getting Windows 98 to recognize or properly run a hardware device, you will probably want to examine the *Hardware Compatibility List (HCL)*. It contains a list of computer systems and peripherals that have been tested by the Microsoft Windows Hardware Quality Labs. To see this list, access the Microsoft Support Web page and select Windows 98 from the My Search Is About list. In the I Want to Search For box, type `Hardware Compatibility List`. Then, click the Find button to access a page containing hardware compatibility information.

Tip #20	Some devices and their drivers on the HCL are more compatible than others. By "more compatible" I mean they are easier to install either through *Plug and Play (page xxx)* or manually. A good rule of thumb when you are deciding on a hardware purchase is to ask around to find others who are running similar devices and components; get their opinions on what works and how well. It isn't always a good idea to be on the "bleeding edge of technology," but you can safely and wisely stay with the most recent tried-and-true hardware on the "leading edge."

GETTING ANSWERS FROM TECHNET

One of the most valuable resources of technical knowledge on Windows and Windows applications is TechNet. TechNet is a compilation of troubleshooting procedures, technical papers, product descriptions, product announcements, drivers, and so on. TechNet is a paid subscription service that sends you three CDs each month with more than 150,000 pages of technical information, 14 Resource Kits, Service Packs, the KnowledgeBase, and the software library containing the latest drivers and patches. It also includes a full-text search engine to help you find what you need. Most of the materials found on TechNet can also be accessed, albeit much more slowly, online at Microsoft's Web site.

To learn more about subscribing to TechNet, click the Web Resources link on the Windows 98 Help page and then click the TechNet hyperlink on the Windows Support Web page.

To subscribe to the TechNet CD-ROM, contact Microsoft at

Microsoft TechNet
One Microsoft Way
Redmond, WA 98052-6399
FAX: 206-936-7329, Attn: TechNet
Voice: 800-344-2121
Internet: technet@microsoft.com
Web: www.microsoft.com/technet

GETTING PEER SUPPORT THROUGH NEWSGROUPS

Newsgroups provide you with an online area in which you can post technical questions and get responses from your peers. As you can see from the few newsgroups listed in the left pane of Figure 4.10, newsgroups cover a wide range of topics including Microsoft products. You can access newsgroups with most Internet newsreader software. You must configure your newsreader for Microsoft's news server at msnews.microsoft.com. If you are using Internet Explorer 4, the newsgroup reader was configured for Microsoft's news service when you installed Internet Explorer 4 and Windows 98.

Figure 4.10
Subscribing to Microsoft's news service gives you access to a wide range of topics.

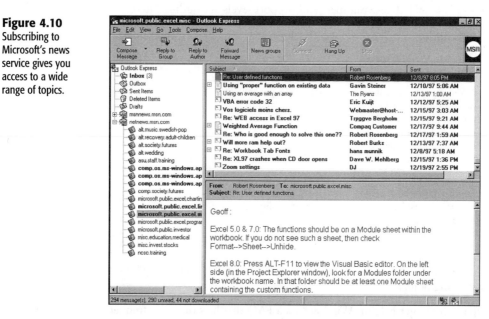

PART

I

CH

4

Caution

Although you can gain valuable real-world information through newsgroups, you must be cautious. Unless the most valuable professional (MVP) who monitors the newsgroup answers your question, your peer might give you a completely wrong answer. Also, some newsgroups are filled with extraneous conversations that veer away from the newsgroup's topic.

Newsgroups are monitored by MVPs. These professional consultants and trainers are very conscientious and hard working. They are volunteers and are paid only in professional recognition and their desire to help others, so help them out. Be careful of advice from respondents who are strangers to you. Although they mean well, they might not be well informed.

→ Learn more in "Setting Default Mail and News Clients," **p. 579.**

FINDING HELP, SUPPORT, AND RESOURCES

Even though local and online help is readily accessible, you might find it more comforting to talk with a person who guides you through troubleshooting. Or maybe you find books to be a less expensive yet very informative way of learning.

GETTING TELEPHONE SUPPORT

For customer service and product upgrade information, call 800-426-9400. At the time this book was published, Microsoft offered three methods of support for Windows with live support personnel. These numbers and support levels are outlined here:

Description	Type	Telephone
Support for 90 days from your first support call.	Free. Initial 90-day support.	425-635-7000
$35 charge to a credit card until the specific problem is resolved. Make sure you keep the charge code ID and incident ID assigned by Microsoft.	$35 per incident charged to a credit card.	800-936-5700
$35 charge to a telephone number until the specific problem is resolved. Incident ID is assigned by Microsoft.	$35 per incident charged to telephone.	900-555-2000

This support is available Monday through Friday, 6:00 a.m. to 6:00 p.m. Pacific time, excluding holidays.

You also can get help on Windows via a FAQ that lists the most frequently asked questions and their answers. To get answers from FastTips, call 800-936-4200.

Microsoft also supports a stable of service providers who can give you or your company help on Windows. A list of service providers follows.

Name	Description	Support Options	Telephone
Sitel	Technical services	Wide range of services available	800-363-5448
Corporate Software	Corporate support	Windows 95 support and training	617-440-1000
Unisys Corporation	Support for home users and businesses	$35 per incident $2.95 per minute Prepaid callbacks	900-555-5454 800-757-8324 800-863-0436

CONSULTANTS AND TRAINING

Microsoft Certified Solution Providers and Certified Trainers are consultants and trainers certified by Microsoft to work with or train on Microsoft products. They are independent consultants who have met the strict qualifying requirements imposed by Microsoft.

You can find the Microsoft Certified Solution Providers and training centers in your area by calling 800-SOL-PROV.

Tip #21

Que is the publisher of *Platinum Edition Using Windows 98* and of the *Special Edition Using* series of books. To order books or catalogs or to get additional information, please call Macmillan Computer Publishing at

317-581-3500

800-428-5331

Or point your browser to

`http://www.mcp.com/`

TROUBLESHOOTING

THE BOOK ICON CHANGING APPEARANCE

When I click a Book icon in the left pane on the Contents tab to open the help topic, and subsequently press the plus-sign key on the numeric keypad, my book icon changes appearance.

The icon is displayed with a red mark and mysteriously cycles through different icons ending up as a Folder icon as you press the plus-sign key. This issue is an onscreen problem only and does not affect the functionality of help. As a workaround for this problem, press the minus-sign key on the numeric keypad to cycle the icon back to the Book icon. Of course, you can quit and restart help.

CHAPTER 5

AN OVERVIEW OF THE WINDOWS INTERFACE

In this chapter

Introducing the Windows Desktop Update

When Microsoft introduced Internet Explorer 4.0 (IE4), the company didn't just offer a Web browser: The complete IE4 package included an optional component called the Windows Desktop Update, which made radical changes to the interface that debuted in the original version of Windows 95.

With Windows 98 the Windows Desktop Update is no longer an option, but instead, is an integral part of the new operating system. Windows 98 also ships with Internet Explorer 5.0 (IE5), which is discussed in Chapter 27, "Web Browsing with Internet Explorer 4.0." If you're familiar with the original Windows 95 interface and haven't previously used IE4 or IE5, you'll notice the following interface changes when you install Windows 98:

- An enhanced taskbar, which includes a new Quick Launch toolbar and changes the way taskbar buttons work
- An enhanced Start menu, with a new menu item for Web Favorites, new options on the Find menu, and the capability to edit or rearrange program shortcuts directly
- New folder and desktop options, including a choice of single-click or double-click navigation
- Many, many small improvements to the original Windows interface, which collectively make file management more productive
- The Web View option with which you can display the contents of drives and folders as part of a customizable Web page
- The optional Active Desktop setting, which enables you to add Web pages and HTML components to the Windows desktop

→ For detailed information about the Active Desktop, **see** Chapter 30, "Web Subscriptions and the Active Desktop."

> **Note**
>
> Because the names are so similar, it's easy to confuse the Windows Desktop Update and the Active Desktop. In fact, even some Microsoft marketing pieces use the two names interchangeably. The two are not the same, however; in fact, the Active Desktop is one small part of the Windows Desktop Update.

Classic or Web? Choosing a Navigation Style

With the Windows Desktop Update installed, you have several important interface choices to make. To see the available options, open My Computer or an Explorer window and choose View, Folder Options. Click the General tab to see the dialog box shown in Figure 5.1.

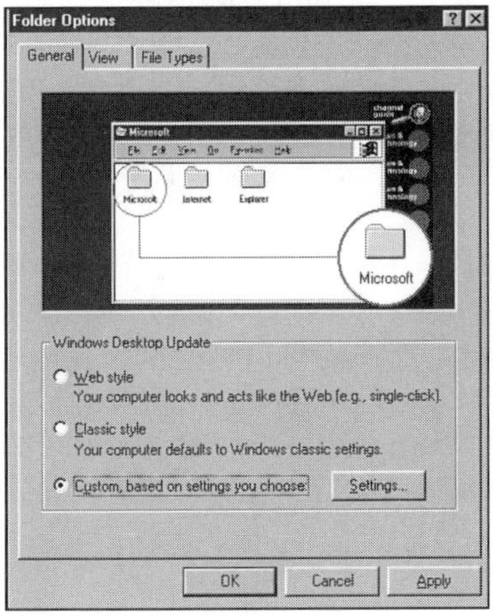

Figure 5.1
Choose your interface: the Classic Windows style, one that resembles a Web browser, or one that combines the two.

If the Folder Options choice is unavailable, see "Finding Folder Options in Explorer" in the "Troubleshooting" section at the end of this chapter.

Choose one of the following three interface options:

- Web Style—This style sets the Windows desktop and folder options to resemble your Web browser. Icons are underlined, like hyperlinks on a Web page. You point at icons to select them and single-click to open folders and launch programs.

- Classic Style—This interface resembles the original Windows 95 interface. As in Windows 95, you single-click to select icons and double-click to open folders and launch programs.

- Custom Based on Settings You Choose—With the Custom option, you can mix and match interface options. After you choose this option, click the Settings button to choose from four options in the Custom Settings dialog box, shown in Figure 5.2.

The following sections provide details on the options in the Custom Settings dialog box.

PART

I

CH

5

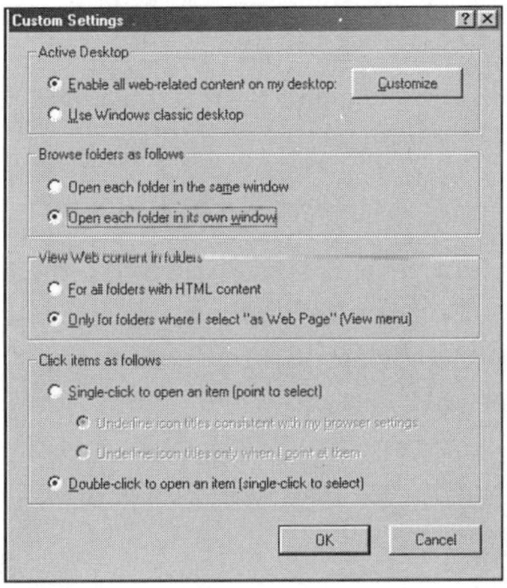

Figure 5.2
Choose any combination of these options to create your own custom interface.

Tip #22

> Although the Custom Settings dialog box looks daunting, it actually follows a simple organi-zation. Each option includes two choices. If you choose the top item in each list, you end up with Web style; choose the bottom option in all four cases, and you end up with Classic style.

TURNING ON THE ACTIVE DESKTOP

Choosing the option labeled Enable All Web-Related Content on My Desktop has the same effect as checking the Active Desktop's View As Web Page option: Both turn on the Active Desktop. Clicking the Customize button takes you to the Web tab of the Display Properties dialog box. Choosing Use Windows Classic Desktop turns off the Active Desktop.

→ For a full discussion of your Active Desktop options, **see** "Offline Favorites and the Active Desktop" **p. 635.**

CHOOSING A BROWSING STYLE

In the Classic style Windows interface (Open Each Folder in Its Own Window), the origi-nal window remains open when you display the contents of a new drive or folder. If you drill down through multiple folders and subfolders, you end up with a screen full of windows. Choose the Web style interface (Open Each Folder in the Same Window) to display the contents of each new drive or folder in the same window you started with, replacing the existing contents.

→ To find out more about which browsing style is right for you, **see** "Two Views of Windows Explorer," **p. 78.**

VIEWING WEB CONTENT IN FOLDERS

Thanks to the Windows Desktop Update, Explorer lets you view any folder as a Web page, using a standard folder template or a custom HTML page you create. Web view adds a ban-ner to the top-left side of the Folder window and an information pane below it; the file list appears on the right side of the window. Choose the top option (For All Folders with HTML Content) to use Web view with all folders; choose the bottom option (Only for Folders Where I Select "as Web Page" [View Menu]) if you want to selectively turn on Web view.

→ For a full discussion of Web view, including details on how to create your own custom HTML folder templates, **see** Chapter 8, "Managing Files Using Web View."

SINGLE-CLICK OR DOUBLE-CLICK?

The most important interface choice you must make is how to use the mouse to select icons and open folders or launch programs. By default, Windows 98 takes a conservative approach, preserving the familiar double-click style introduced in the original Windows 95 interface. To change this option, choose Web style or open the Custom Settings dialog box and choose Single-click to Open an Item (Point to Select). The first time you choose this option, the Single-Click warning dialog box, shown in Figure 5.3, appears.

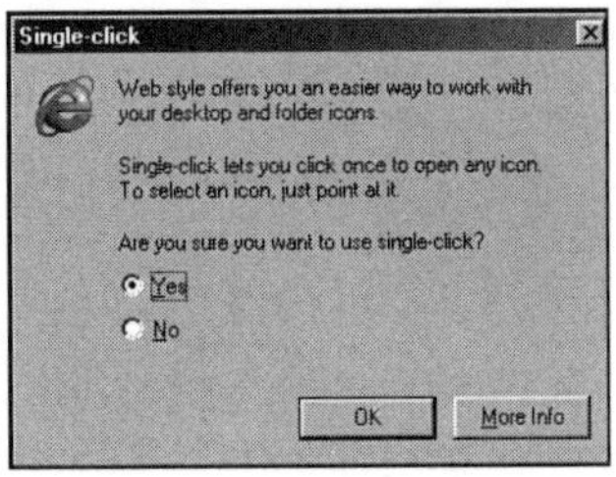

Figure 5.3
Because the single-click interface is a radical change, Windows asks you to confirm your choice when you select it.

Why the warning? Because when you choose the Web style interface, you change the way Windows handles some of its most basic tasks. Table 5.1 presents a side-by-side comparison of how you deal with files and folders in the two navigation styles.

TABLE 5.1   WEB STYLE VERSUS CLASSIC STYLE

Task	Web Style	Classic Style
Select an icon	Point to the icon.	Click the icon.
Open an icon	Click the icon.	Double-click the icon.
Select a group of adjacent icons	Point to the first icon, press and hold down the Shift key, and point to the last icon.	Click the first icon, press and hold down the Shift key, and click the last icon.
Select multiple icons	Hold down the Ctrl key and point to individual icons.	Hold down the Ctrl key and click individual icons.
Drag and drop	Point to an icon, press and hold down the mouse button, and drag icon to a new location (same as Classic style).	Point to an icon, press and hold down the mouse button, and drag icon to a new location.

PART

I

CH

5

Tip #23

As the table shows, there are some decided differences between using the mouse and using the keyboard to choose multiple files and folders. Even as a seasoned Windows operator, I find the Web style difficult to manage when the task of choosing multiple files or folders to move or copy becomes necessary. With the Web style, the tendency to select unwanted files or folders that happen to be in close proximity to the desired ones becomes a frustration to even the most nimble of fingers. You could deliberately arrange your files and folders to minimize the possibility of this occurrence, but that takes more time and effort than it's usually worth. My advice is to choose a custom setting where the two styles can be joined to suit your particular needs. (Chapter 6, "Managing Files with My Computer and Windows Explorer," includes a detailed discussion of how to integrate the two.)

If you've chosen the single-click option, but Windows ignores you when you adjust the option to under-line icons only when you point at them, see "Forcing Classic Style" in the "Troubleshooting" section at the end of this chapter.

CUSTOMIZING OTHER FOLDER OPTIONS

Installing the Windows Desktop Update adds an assorted group of advanced folder options as well. To adjust these settings, choose View, Folder Options and then click the View tab of the Folder Options dialog box. The advanced folder options are listed at the bottom of the dialog box, as shown in Figure 5.4. Table 5.2 outlines the effects of the various settings.

Figure 5.4
These are the default settings for advanced folder options.

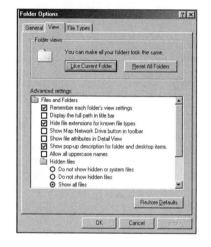

TABLE 5.2   ADVANCED FOLDER OPTIONS

Option	Effect when Checked
Remember Each Folder's View Settings	Saves the icon view of folder windows; also saves size and position when you use the multiwindow browsing option. Does not apply to two-pane Explorer windows.
Display the Full Path in Title Bar	Shows full DOS-style path (for example, C:\Windows\System) in folder windows. This option is handy when comparing subfolders with identical names in different parts of the Explorer tree.
Hide File Extensions for Known File Types	Uncheck this box to show all file extensions, even when the file type is registered.

Option	Effect when Checked
Show Map Network Drive Button in Toolbar	Adds two buttons to the Standard toolbar. Check this option if you regularly assign drive letters to shared network folders.
Show File Attributes in Details View	Adds a column at the far right of Details view.
Show Pop-Up Description for Folder and Desktop Items	Displays ScreenTips when you point to My Computer and other desktop items; experienced users should not check this box.
Allow All Uppercase Names	Normally, Windows capitalizes only the first letter of all filenames (for example, Abc). Remove the check from this box to allow file and folder names to consist of all uppercase letters (such as ABC).
Hidden Files	Choose whether to display hidden and/or system files.

→ For more help with folder option settings, **see** "Changing the Appearance of a Folder's Contents," **p. 84** and "Associating Files with Programs," **p. 108.**

TROUBLESHOOTING

FINDING FOLDER OPTIONS IN EXPLORER

I've opened Explorer, but I can't find the Folder Options choice on the View menu.

You're probably viewing a Web page in the Explorer window, in which case the View menu offers an Internet Options choice instead. Click in the Address bar, type C:\, and press Enter. The Folder Options command should now appear on the View menu.

FORCING CLASSIC STYLE

Windows ignores my underline choices.

When you choose the single-click option in the Custom Settings dialog box, you also have the choice to underline all icon titles (as Internet Explorer does) or to underline icons only when you point at them. If you've selected the top choice in all four sections of the Custom Settings dialog box, Windows shifts your choice to Web style and ignores your underlining preferences. The only way to force Explorer to accept this change is to select the bottom (Classic) choice in one of the first three sections of this dialog box.

WORKING WITH FILES AND FOLDERS

CHAPTER **6**

MANAGING FILES WITH MY COMPUTER AND WINDOWS EXPLORER

In this chapter

TWO VIEWS OF WINDOWS EXPLORER

The most basic building block of Windows is the icon. Every object you work with—including files and folders, drives and network servers, programs, printers, and shortcuts to Web pages—has its own icon. Program icons are as distinctive as product logos; data files use standard icons that help you group related files easily; system objects use icons that are intended to illustrate their main function. And they're all organized into folders and subfolders in a strict hierarchy.

Most often when you view or manage icons and folders, you use a program called Windows Explorer in one of its two views. Right-click a drive or folder icon, and shortcut menus let you choose between the two faces of Explorer: Click <u>O</u>pen, and the contents of the drive or folder you selected appear in a simple window; choose <u>E</u>xplore, and you see a more complex view, with one pane that shows all the resources available to you and another that displays the selected folder's contents. After they learn how Explorer works, most Windows users incorporate both views into their working style.

VIEWING RESOURCES IN MY COMPUTER

For a simple, uncluttered view of all the resources on your computer, find the My Computer icon on the desktop and open it. The resulting window looks something like the one shown in Figure 6.1.

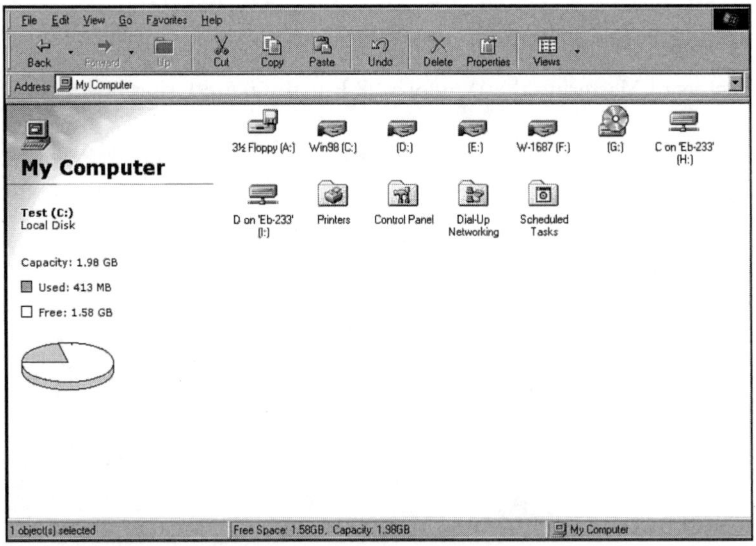

Figure 6.1
The My Computer window offers a simple way to view local resources, including drives, printers, and other hardware.

Microsoft's interface designers created My Computer as the primary file management interface for novice users, but even Windows experts find it ideally suited for some file management tasks. Because the My Computer window displays the amount of free disk space, for example, it's a convenient way to see at a glance how much total storage is available on your system.

Tip #24

To see the maximum amount of information about drives in the My Computer window, choose View, Details. Click the Free Space heading to sort drives in order of available storage space.

BROWSING THE CONTENTS OF A FOLDER

Unlike Windows Explorer, which displays the outline-style hierarchy of all drives and folders on your system, the My Computer window displays the contents of one folder at a time. To view the contents of drives and folders from the My Computer window, open a drive icon, then a folder within that drive, and then a folder within that folder. Keep drilling down in this fashion until you find the folder you're looking for.

The two easiest ways to go back up through the hierarchy of folders are to press the Backspace key and to click the Up button on the Standard toolbar. (If the toolbar is hidden, choose View, Toolbars, Standard Buttons to make it visible.)

What happens to the current folder window when you open a drive or folder icon from the My Computer window? If you've chosen the *Web style* interface, the contents of the folder you selected replace the contents of the current window, so you're always working with a single window. If you've selected the *classic style* interface, on the other hand, the My Computer window remains open and a new drive or folder window appears. For each folder you open, you see a new folder window (see Figure 6.2).

Up button

Figure 6.2
Opening a folder window shows this simple view of the folder's contents.

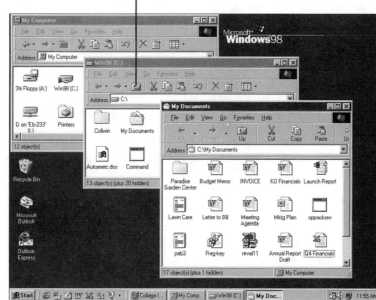

PART

II

CH

6

The multiple-window option (classic style) creates unnecessary and confusing clutter when you delve several folders deep. But sometimes you want to open two or more windows at once so you can move or copy icons from one folder to another. Windows lets you specify whether each new folder will use the same window or will open in a separate window. To adjust the default behavior of folder windows, you use the Custom settings in the Windows Desktop Update.

→ To change the way your folders look and behave, **see** "Customizing Other Folder Options," **p. 72.**

Tip #25

> Another option for viewing multiple folders or drives, even with the Open Each Folder in the Same Window option set, is to start anew from the My Computer icon (or from a short-cut on the desktop to a specific location). This approach is handy if you want to use drag and drop along with the tidier view of one window per browse request to copy data from one location to another. After you have browsed to your desired file or folder location in one window, double-click on My Computer to open a second Browse window. This window does not affect the open window already showing the desired file or folder. The second instance of the Browse window behaves the same as the first with each level of browsing replacing the contents in the already open window. You can repeat this process as many times as necessary to locate all the files and folders you want to copy. Then, simply drag each file or folder to its new location and drop it in.

The settings you choose in the Folder Options dialog box determine whether a new folder window replaces the current window or opens a new one. You can also hold down the Ctrl key and double-click on a folder or drive icon to override the default setting at any time. If the default is the single-window option, this step opens a new window; if your default is to open a new window, this step replaces the contents of the current window. Note that this option requires you to hold down Ctrl and double-click even if you've chosen the Web style single-click option.

Note

> When you view the contents of a floppy disk, Windows does not automatically update the display when you change disks. Likewise, if another user adds, renames, or deletes files in a shared network folder, these changes do not automatically appear in an open window on your system. Under these conditions, you need to *refresh* the display to see the most up-to-date contents. In Windows Explorer, point to the icon for the drive or folder and click to refresh the window. Alternatively, you can choose View, Refresh or press F5.

USING WINDOWS EXPLORER TO VIEW FILES AND FOLDERS

When you right-click on a drive or folder icon and choose Explore from the shortcut menu, Windows opens the two-paned view of Explorer, which comprises a tree-style All Folders pane on the left and a contents pane on the right. The title bar contains the word *Exploring*, followed by the currently selected drive or folder. As the example in Figure 6.3 shows, the left pane includes every available resource, including local and network drives, system folders, and even Internet shortcuts.

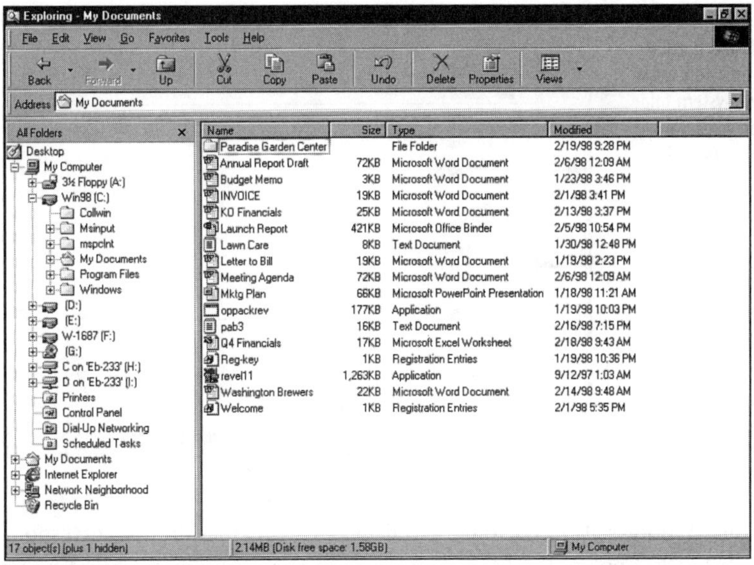

Figure 6.3
Windows Explorer provides these two panes in which you can quickly navigate through local, network, and Internet resources.

Tip #26

Here are some common ways to open Windows Explorer. Open the Start menu and choose Programs, Windows Explorer. Right-click on the Start button or the My Computer icon and choose Explore. Type `Explorer` in the Run dialog box or at an MS-DOS prompt. Create a shortcut on the desktop or on the Quick Launch bar.

As noted earlier, the two-pane Explorer uses the same program code as the single-pane folder window, adding only the All Folders pane. When you use the Explore command to open a new window, you can show or hide the All Folders pane by choosing View, Explorer Bar, All Folders. This technique lets you quickly switch between Internet pages, folder windows, and Explorer windows. Curiously, if you start with a folder window onscreen or if you start by opening an Internet shortcut, the All Folders pane is not available.

UNDERSTANDING THE EXPLORER HIERARCHY

When you use the two-pane Explorer view, it's easy to see the organization of drives, folders, and system resources in the All Folders pane. If the Address bar is visible, you can see a compact version of the same tree in a folder window. Click the arrow at the right of the Address bar to see a drop-down list like the one shown in Figure 6.4.

If you've used MS-DOS or earlier versions of Windows, the hierarchy of a local drive is easy to understand: Each drive can contain one or more folders, starting with the root folder. Windows and Windows applications create folders to store program and data files, and you can create folders within folders to keep your files organized. In the case of data and program files, folders and subfolders are directly equivalent to MS-DOS directories and subdirectories.

PART

II

CH

6

Figure 6.4
The Address bar lets you jump to different drives or system folders even when the All Folders pane is hidden.

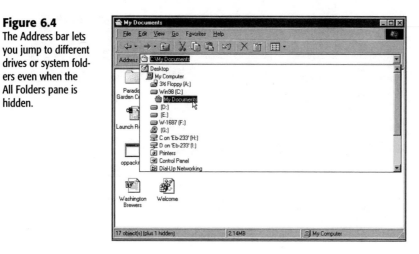

But Windows also uses folders to display objects that do not correspond to directories on a hard disk. Look at the All Folders pane or the drop-down list in the Address bar, and you'll see that Explorer organizes available resources within a consistent hierarchy. The Desktop icon is always at the top of the list. It includes the following objects:

- *My Computer* displays icons for all local drives, any shared network drives that have been mapped to a drive letter, and the Printers, Control Panel, Scheduled Tasks, and Dial-Up Networking folders.

- *Network Neighborhood* shows icons for all servers and workstations in your network.

- *Internet Explorer* displays shortcuts for Web pages you've added to the Active Desktop, as well as pages you've browsed recently.

- *Recycle Bin* shows files you've deleted recently.

- *My Documents* points to the folder where you store personal documents. On a single-user system, the default folder is C:\My Documents; on a system with multiple user profiles, this folder is located elsewhere.

- Any folders you create on the desktop appear at the bottom of the All Folders pane and the drop-down Address list.

Tip #27

If you have set up custom profiles for individual users of your computer, you can create folders, files, and shortcuts that appear on the desktop or Start menu. You'll find the All Users folder within the Windows folder; any objects you create in the desktop or Start Menu folders here are visible to anyone who logs on to the computer.

USING EXPLORER MENUS AND TOOLBARS

When you browse files and folders using Explorer, you have access to a consistent set of menus and toolbar buttons. When you select system folders, additional menu choices and buttons appear to reflect special options available in those folders. For example, when you view the contents of the Subscriptions folder, two new toolbar buttons let you update subscriptions; in addition, Briefcase folders add menu choices and toolbar buttons that let you synchronize files.

→ For a detailed description on how to get the most out of the Briefcase, **see** "Using the Briefcase to Keep Files in Sync," **p. 515.**

NAVIGATING THROUGH THE EXPLORER HIERARCHY

With the help of Windows Explorer, it's easy to display the contents of any drive or folder. When you click on an icon in the All Folders pane, the contents of that folder appear in the right pane.

By default, each branch of the tree-style listing in the All Folders pane is collapsed when you first open the two-pane Explorer view; all you see are the top-level icons for drives and system folders. A plus sign to the left of an icon means additional folders are beneath it. Click the plus sign to expand that branch and see additional folders. When you expand the folder listing, the plus sign becomes a minus sign. Click the minus sign to collapse that branch again. Figure 6.5 shows a typical display with the contents of the Accessories folder visible in the right pane.

⚠ If a disappearing plus sign is giving you trouble, see "The Disappearing Plus Sign" in the "Troubleshooting" section at the end of this chapter for more information.

Figure 6.5
Click the plus sign to expand a branch of the tree; click the minus sign to collapse the list again.

PART

II

CH

6

To display the contents of a different folder, select its icon in the All Folders pane. As you move from folder to folder, you can use the Back and Forward buttons to quickly return to folders you visited previously.

You can also use the keyboard to navigate through file and folder listings in Explorer. Here's a partial listing of useful keyboard shortcuts:

- Use the Tab key (or F6) to move from pane to pane. When you press Tab, the selection moves from the All Folders pane to the contents pane, then to the Address bar, then back to the All Folders pane, and so on.

- When the focus is in the All Folders pane, you can press the up and down arrows to move through the list of folders without expanding collapsed branches. The contents of the selected icon automatically appear in the right pane as you move through the list.

- To move to the parent of the currently selected folder, press the Backspace key.

- To expand a collapsed folder, select its icon and press the right-arrow key or the plus (+) key on the numeric keypad. Use the minus (–) key on the numeric keypad to collapse a branch.

- To quickly move to the Address bar and open the drop-down list of top-level icons, press F4.

- Press the star (*) key on the numeric keypad to expand all branches of the currently selected icon.

Caution

Be careful when using the star (*) key shortcut! Pressing this key when the Desktop or Network Neighborhood icon is selected might cause extremely long delays as Explorer checks the contents of every available network drive.

CHANGING THE APPEARANCE OF A FOLDER'S CONTENTS

Display options let you control how icons appear in an Explorer window. You can choose the size, arrangement, and order of icons, and you can also specify whether Explorer should show or hide system files. The options described in this section work the same way in folder windows and in the contents pane of Windows Explorer.

ICONS, LIST, OR DETAILS: CHOOSING A VIEW

Windows lets you choose from four icon arrangements when displaying the contents of a folder. Each view has advantages and disadvantages under given circumstances. To apply a new view to the folder currently displayed, choose View and then select one of the following choices:

- *Large Icons* view displays full-size icons (32 pixels on each side), which help you easily distinguish between different types of icons. A label appears along the bottom of each icon. You can position icons anywhere within the folder. This view is most practical for folders that contain few icons, such as My Computer; it's an impractical choice when you want to find a small number of files in a folder that contains hundreds of icons.

- *Small Icons* view displays icons that are one-fourth the size of those in the Large Icons view (making them 16 pixels on each side). A label appears to the right of each icon. Initially, Small Icons view arranges icons in rows from left to right, but you can move the icons anywhere within the folder. This view is useful when you want to select a large number of icons in one motion.

- *List* view uses the same size icons and labels that Small Icons view does. In List view, however, Windows arranges icons in columns, starting at the top left of the contents window; when the column reaches the bottom of the window, Windows starts a new column to the right. You cannot rearrange the position of icons in this view.

- *Details* view enables you to see the maximum information about objects in any window. From left to right, each row in this view includes the file's icon, name, size, type, and the date the file was last modified. Note that these details change slightly for different types of windows; the My Computer window, for example, shows the total size and amount of free space in the last two columns. You cannot move or reposition icons in Details view.

The Views button on the Standard toolbar lets you cycle through all four views for the current folder. Each time you click, the view changes to the next option. Alternatively, you can use the drop-down arrow at the right of the Views button to choose a view.

Tip #28	Thumbnail view displays a file as an image. For example, available image files appear in the Explorer window as miniature versions of the actual image.
	You will not see this option by default. To enable this special view, you must enable the Thumbnail option for the specific folder holding the image files. To do so, right-click on the folder, choose Properties, check the Enable Thumbnail View check box, and then click OK. Then open the folder whose properties you enabled, select View from the menu bar, and choose Thumbnails.
	Thumbnail view is a fast way to view your available image files without wasting time loading each image into the appropriate application for viewing. However, this view causes some performance issues because the system index created for the thumbnails takes up space and memory resources. Even a folder with only five or six image files can easily create an index file of a megabyte or more.

PART

II

CH

6

ARRANGING FILE AND FOLDER ICONS

When you Small Icons view, Windows lets you move icons anywhere within the folder. You can cluster your favorite icons in one location and move the others to a far corner, for example, or just rearrange the order in which the icons appear. Two options let you control the arrangement of icons within a folder.

If you prefer to have all your icons lined up neatly at all times, choose View, Arrange Icons, Auto Arrange. A check mark appears next to this menu choice to indicate that it is in use with the current folder. You can still move icons into any order you want, but other icons will shift position to make room for the icons you move. When you resize a folder window with this option turned on, the rows of icons automatically reposition so that you can see them properly within the window.

If you prefer to arrange icons yourself but you want them to snap into position along an imaginary grid, rearrange the icons and then choose View, Line Up Icons. This option allows you to leave empty spaces within the folder window. If you resize the window, some icons may no longer be visible; you'll need to use the scrollbars to view them.

Caution

These icon-arranging options apply to the Windows desktop as well. Right-click on any empty desktop area and choose Line Up Icons to straighten the display of icons on the desktop. Avoid checking the Auto Arrange option on the Windows desktop, however. Most users prefer to position desktop icons in predictable locations; letting Windows automatically arrange desktop icons lines them up in columns, from top to bottom and left to right, without regard for wallpaper and Active Desktop items. That arrangement can make it difficult to work with desktop icons.

SORTING FILES AND FOLDERS

Windows lets you sort the contents of any folder by using one of four menu choices. These options work the same in folder windows and in the contents pane of an Explorer window.

To sort files within a folder, follow these steps:

1. Display the contents of the folder.
2. Choose View, Arrange Icons; or right-click in any empty space within the contents pane and choose Arrange Icons from the shortcut menu.
3. Choose one of the following options from the submenu:

   - By Name—Sorts in ascending alphabetical order by filename, with folders grouped at the top of the list.
   - By Type—Sorts in ascending alphabetical order by file type (note that this option does not sort by file extension; Windows uses the registered name of the File Type to determine sort order).
   - By Size—Sorts folders first in ascending alphabetical order by name and then arranges files by size, with the smallest files at the top of the list.
   - By Date—Sorts folders by date in descending order and then sorts files the same way; in both cases, newest files appear at the top of the list.

By far the easiest way to sort files and folders is to switch to Details view. When you click on the column headings in Details view, Windows sorts the folder's contents by the column you selected. Click again to sort in reverse order—something you cannot do in any other view.

SAVING FOLDER DISPLAY OPTIONS

When you use the two-pane Windows Explorer, the view options you choose apply to all folders you display in the contents pane. If you choose Large Icons view for one folder, all folders are displayed in that view until you choose a different view.

When you use folder windows, however, Windows lets you save separate view options for each folder. As you move from folder to folder, the view changes to reflect the settings you last used. If you prefer to set all folder windows to a single view, follow these steps:

1. Open any folder window and choose View. Select Large Icons, Small Icons, List, or Details. If you want to use Web view for all folders, choose View, As Web Page.

2. Choose View, Folder Options and then click on the View tab. You'll see the dialog box shown in Figure 6.6.

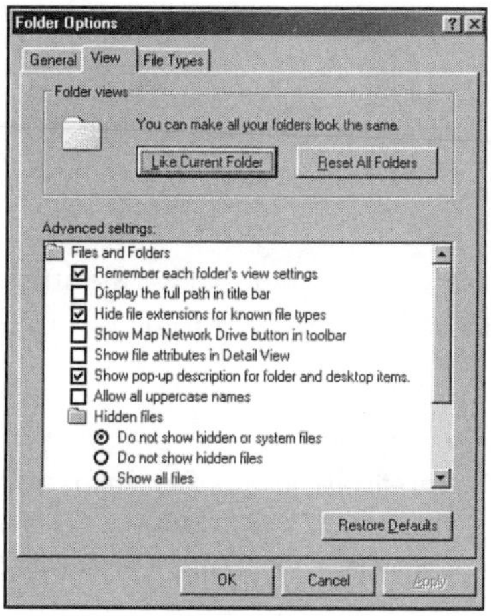

Figure 6.6
Choose a view you want to use for all folder windows.

3. In the Folder Views area, click the button labeled Like Current Folder.
4. When you see the confirmation dialog box, click Yes.
5. Click OK to save your changes.

Note that using this option does not save the sort order for windows, nor does it save toolbar settings.

To restore folder windows to their default view settings, choose View, Folder Options; click the View tab; and click the button labeled Reset All Folders. This step restores the My Computer, Control Panel, Fonts, and other system folders to their default, Large Icons view.

DISPLAYING OR HIDING CERTAIN FILE TYPES

You can set four special attributes for all files and folders you create under MS-DOS or Windows. Using these settings, you can prevent inadvertent damage to important files. To

PART

II

CH

6

see the assigned attributes for a given file or folder, select its icon and choose Properties from the shortcut menu. Click the General tab to see the current settings for the following four attributes:

Attribute	Description
Read-only	Prevents changes to files and folders. Note that setting a folder's read-only attribute does not prevent changes to the files within that folder.
Hidden	Prevents the display of files using Windows Explorer or the MS-DOS DIR command.
Archive	Marks files that have been changed since they were last backed up. The MS-DOS XCOPY command and most backup programs use the Archive attributes to perform partial backups.
System	Prevents the display of files and folders required by the system.

Note

Windows 98 sets the read-only attribute on a number of system folders, including the Windows and My Documents folders.

For the most part, Windows and Windows applications adjust file attributes automatically. The one reason you might want to manually adjust file attributes is to set a crucial work-group file as read-only.

Caution

Setting the Read-only or System attribute for an object doesn't make it impossible to delete that file or folder; those settings only add a warning dialog box to the process. If the file is truly important, make sure to store a backup copy in a safe location.

Windows hides a tremendous number of files by default. Why? To prevent accidental changes or deletions that can cause the system to stop working properly. Look at the left side of the status bar in any Explorer window to see how many hidden files are in the current folder.

If you're confident that you can work with hidden and system files without causing your computer to crash, you can adjust Explorer's options to display those files. Follow these steps:

1. Open Windows Explorer or any folder window and choose View, Folder Options.
2. Click on the View tab. In the Advanced Settings box, find the entry labeled Hidden Files.
3. Select the Show All Files option, as shown in Figure 6.7.

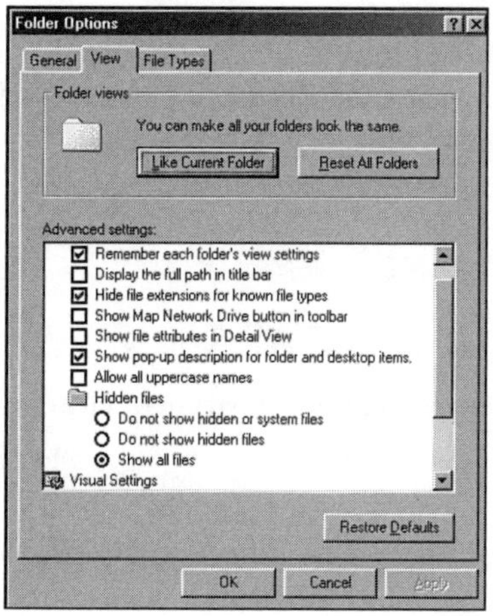

Figure 6.7
Use this option to make hidden and system files visible.

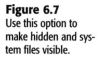

4. Click OK to save your changes and close the Folder Options dialog box.

If you choose to make hidden files visible, you'll be able to easily distinguish them in Explorer windows. In Explorer, hidden files appear as grayed-out icons. (You might have to press F5 or choose View, Refresh to make these files appear.)

> **Caution**
>
> Windows usually has a good reason for setting some files as hidden or system. If you need to change that attribute, just do it temporarily (to edit MSDOS.SYS, for example). Be sure to change the attribute back when you're finished.

If you use the menus or the Ctrl+A keyboard shortcut to select all files in a folder that contains hidden files, Windows displays a warning message like the one in Figure 6.8. You cannot manage hidden files from Explorer unless you make them visible.

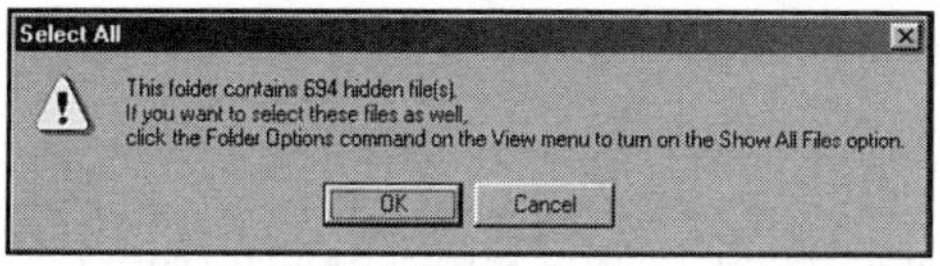

Figure 6.8
Before you can select all the files in this folder, you must make hidden files visible.

PART

II

CH

6

You can use Explorer to change the Read-only, Hidden, and Archive attributes of a file or folder. To do so, right-click on the icon, choose Properties, and check or uncheck the appropriate box. Explorer does not allow you to change a file's System attribute, however. If you must perform that task, open an MS-DOS Prompt window and issue the command ATTRIB -S *filename*. For more information about the ATTRIB command, type ATTRIB /? at the MS-DOS prompt.

Tip #29

Do you want to see information about file attributes every time you switch to Details view? Open Explorer and choose View, Folder Options. Then, click the View tab and scroll through the list of Advanced Settings. Check the option labeled Show File Attributes in Details View and click OK.

CUSTOMIZING EXPLORER'S APPEARANCE

Like most parts of Windows, Explorer contains a wide array of customization options.

CHANGING THE WIDTH OF PANES

To change the proportions of the two panes when using Windows Explorer, point to the vertical dividing line between the panes. When the pointer changes to a two-headed arrow, click and drag in either direction. Release the mouse button when the panes are the desired sizes.

CHANGING THE WIDTH OF COLUMNS

In Details view, Windows uses columns to display information about files, folders, and system objects. To change the width of columns, point to the dividing line between column headings. When the pointer changes to a two-headed arrow, click and drag in either direction. You can also double-click on the dividing line to the right of a column heading to automatically resize that column to match the widest entry it contains.

 If you notice a problem with missing columns when you switch to details view, see "Missing Columns in Details View" in the "Troubleshooting" section at the end of this chapter for more information.

SHOWING AND HIDING THE STATUS BAR

The status bar shows important information about the number and size of objects in the current folder, and it works the same in folder windows and in the two-pane Explorer view. To show or hide this screen element, choose View, Status Bar. A check mark next to the menu choice means the status bar should appear at the bottom of the window.

SHOWING AND HIDING TOOLBARS

By default, the Address bar and the Standard Buttons toolbar (with text labels) appear when you open the two-pane version of Explorer. You can use both screen elements with folder windows as well. To show or hide either element, choose View, Toolbars and then check or uncheck the Standard Buttons and Address Bar menu choices.

You cannot customize the buttons on these toolbars, but if you want maximum room to work with files and folders, you can hide the text labels on the Standard Buttons toolbar. To do so, choose View, Toolbars and then remove the check mark from the Text Labels menu choice. Figure 6.9 shows a screen in which the text labels for the toolbar buttons are not displayed.

Figure 6.9
To conserve Explorer space, hide the text labels that normally appear under the toolbar buttons.

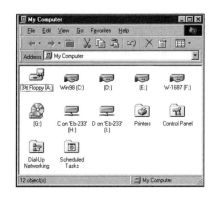

OPENING EXPLORER AT SPECIFIC FOLDERS OR FILES

The full two-pane Explorer view can be overwhelming, particularly when you just want to reorganize files among a handful of subfolders in a single location. The solution is to create shortcuts for each task. It's possible to launch a copy of Explorer that opens at the location where you want to work. Even better is to restrict the display of objects in the left pane so that it includes only the drives or folders with which you want to work.

If you create a shortcut with only the command explorer, the default two-pane Windows Explorer opens, with all resources visible in the All Folders pane. To reduce the clutter, you must use command-line switches along with the Explorer command. Specifically, follow the command with the /e switch to force it to open in two-pane mode (use /n to specify a single-pane window instead). Normally, Explorer uses Desktop as the root of the All Folders pane, but you can specify any drive or folder to fill this role. When you do, the display becomes much less confusing. Use the /root, object switch to restrict the scope of the All Folders pane to the object you specify. In place of object, substitute the name of a network server (in Universal Naming Convention [UNC] format), a local drive, or a folder.

 For a detailed explanation of all the options you can use when creating an Explorer shortcut, read the Microsoft Knowledge Base article "Command-Line Switches for Windows Explorer." You'll find it at

http://support.microsoft.com/support/kb/articles/q130/5/10.asp

To open a two-pane Explorer window that includes only files and folders on drive C:, for example, follow these steps:

1. Right-click on any empty desktop space and choose New, Shortcut. The Create Shortcut Wizard appears.
2. In the Command Line text box, enter the following command (spacing and punctuation are crucial):
   ```
   explorer /e,/root,c:\
   ```
3. Click Next and then name the shortcut Explore Drive C.
4. Click Finish. The shortcut appears on the desktop.
5. Open the shortcut to verify that it works. You can move or copy the shortcut to another location if you want.

MANAGING FILES AND FOLDERS

Although many Windows applications offer basic file management functions, Explorer is the tool you'll use most often to organize your files. Regardless of which view you choose, Explorer allows you to create new folders, copy and move files between folders, delete files, and rename files.

SELECTING FILES AND FOLDERS

Before you can perform any action on an object, you must select the object. The procedures for selecting files, folders, and other icons depend on the folder and desktop options you've chosen. If you've chosen the classic style (double-click) interface, you click on an icon to select it. If you've chosen the Web style (single-click) interface, on the other hand, simply point at a file to select it. Objects change color to indicate that you've selected them.

Tip #30	Use the Display Properties dialog box to adjust the color of selected items.
	→ **See** "Customizing the Windows Desktop," **p. 336.**

To select multiple icons that are adjacent to one another in a folder window or on the desktop, select the first icon, hold down the Shift key, and then select the last icon. All the icons between the two are also selected. To select multiple icons that are not adjacent to one another, select the first one, hold down the Ctrl key, and select all additional icons. To deselect an icon, continue holding down the Ctrl key and select it again.

You can also use marquee selection to quickly select a group of adjacent files with the mouse. To use this technique, draw an imaginary rectangle around the group of files (see Figure 6.10). Specifically, point to one corner of the rectangle, hold down the left mouse button, and drag the selection to the opposite corner. This technique works with all icon views.

You can also use the keyboard to select multiple icons. In a two-pane Explorer window, press Tab to move the focus into the right contents pane. Then, use the arrow keys to move through the list to the first item you want to select. To select a group of adjacent icons, hold down the Shift key and use the arrow keys to move through the list. To use the keyboard to select a group of icons that are not adjacent, select the first file, hold down the Ctrl key, and use the arrow keys to move through the list; press the Spacebar for each file you want to select.

To quickly select all the files a folder, choose Edit, Select All (or press Ctrl+A). To deselect all current selections, click on any empty space or on another object in the folder window or on the desktop.

Figure 6.10
As you draw this rectangle around a group of icons, watch the dotted line. All icons within the box are selected.

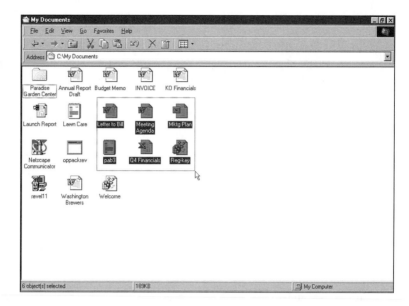

Tip #31

There's a lightning-fast way to select all but a few icons within a folder. This technique comes in handy when you want to archive or delete most of the files in a folder yet keep a small number of items. Select the objects you plan to keep and then choose Edit, Invert Selection. You can now use any of the standard Windows techniques to move, copy, or delete the selected objects. Another option is to press Ctrl+A to highlight them all and then hold down Ctrl while you deselect the ones you want to keep.

RENAMING A FILE

To rename a file or folder, first select its icon. Then, use any of the following options to select the name for editing:

■ Press the F2 key.

■ Choose File, Rename.

■ Right-click the icon and choose Rename from the shortcut menu.

When the label text is selected, type the new name. To save the name you enter, press Enter or click on any empty space on the desktop or in a folder window.

RENAMING MULTIPLE FILES

There is no way to rename more than one file at a time using Explorer. To accomplish this task, you must open an MS-DOS Prompt window and use the REN (Rename) command.

PART
II

CH

6

To rename multiple files with long filenames, use this procedure:

1. Open the Start menu and choose Programs, MS-DOS Prompt.

2. At the MS-DOS prompt, type CD *pathname* to switch to the directory that contains the files you want to rename. You might have to repeat the command a few times to reach the correct drive and directory.

3. Type REN *oldname.ext newname.ext*. If either name contains a space, enclose the name and extension in quotation marks. Press Enter.

4. Use the ? wild card character to match any single letter in the filename; use the * wild card to substitute for any group of characters. For example, if you start with the following group of files:

   05 Sales Forecast.xls

   06 Sales Forecast.xls

   07 Sales Forecast.xls

   08 Sales Forecast.xls

Enter this command at the MS-DOS prompt to rename them in one operation:
REN "?? Sales*.*" "?? Mrktg*.*"

The result is four files named as follows:

   05 Mrktg Forecast.xls

   06 Mrktg Forecast.xls

   07 Mrktg Forecast.xls

   08 Mrktg Forecast.xl

Tip #32

Another good tip to remember when setting the Folder Options for Files and Folders View, is to clear the Hide File Extensions for Known File Types box. This option saves you if a file extension is not properly associated in the Folder Options, File Types settings or if more than one application is associated with a particular file extension (such as the .dbf file that has several different database programs associated with it). Also, this technique helps to ensure that a file is properly renamed. Without this option, renaming a file with a .{extension} causes the system to append the extension as part of the filename and as an extension for that file. For example, renaming a text file note.txt with the Hide File Extensions for Known File Types box checked causes the system to rename the file as note.txt.txt.

CREATING NEW FOLDERS

To create a new folder, follow these steps:

1. Select the icon for the drive or folder in which you plan to create the new folder.

2. Right-click on the icon or on any empty space in the contents pane and choose New, Folder.

3. The new folder has a generic name; to replace it with a more meaningful name, just start typing. When you've finished, press Enter to record the new name.

→ When naming folders, you must follow the same rules that govern long filenames. **See** "Working with Long Filenames," **p. 120.**

MOVING AND COPYING FILES AND FOLDERS

With Explorer, the easiest way to move and copy files is not always the surest. When you select one or more objects and drag them from one location to another, the results can vary dramatically. The exact effect depends on the location and the type of file. When you use Explorer to drag and drop files, one of three things happens:

- When you drag an object from one location to another on the same logical volume, Explorer *moves* the object. On local drives each logical volume uses the same drive letter, so dragging a group of icons from C:\Windows\Temp to the Windows desktop moves them to the new location.

- When you drag an object from one logical volume to another, Explorer *copies* the file. If you drag a group of icons from C:\Data and drop them on the icon for a floppy disk (A:) or a shared network folder, Explorer leaves the original files untouched and creates copies in the new location.

- When you drag a program file from one location to another, regardless of location, Explorer *creates a shortcut*, leaving the original file untouched.

Even though this default behavior is based on sound logic, the results can be confusing to novice users. Even experienced Windows users can sometimes stumble over these rules. For example, if you drag multiple program icons from a folder onto the desktop, Explorer creates a group of shortcuts; but if you select even one icon that isn't a program, Windows moves or copies instead.

The best way to predict what Explorer will do when you drag and drop icons is to examine the mouse pointer before you release the mouse button. If you see a plus sign just to the right of the pointer (see Figure 6.11), you can expect a copy; a small arrow next to the pointer means you'll get a shortcut; and a plain pointer means you're about to move the selected objects. If the pointer you see doesn't match the result you intended, press Esc before releasing the mouse button to abort the procedure.

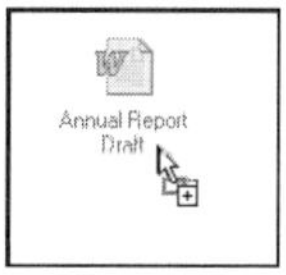

PART

II

CH

6

Figure 6.11
The small plus sign next to the mouse pointer means you're about to make a copy of this icon.

For maximum control over the results of drag-and-drop operations, select one or more objects and hold down the right mouse button as you drag. When you release the button, Windows pops up a shortcut menu like the one shown in Figure 6.12. The default action appears in bold type, but you can choose any of the three actions, or you can cancel the whole operation if you prefer.

Figure 6.12
When you hold down the right mouse button while dragging files, Windows lets you choose the result you prefer from a shortcut menu like this.

DRAGGING AND DROPPING FILES BETWEEN FOLDERS

The easiest way to move or copy files between folders is to open two folder windows and arrange them side by side. Follow this procedure to let Windows position two folder windows automatically:

1. Minimize or close all open windows. The easiest way to accomplish this task is to click the Show Desktop button on the Quick Launch toolbar.

2. Open both folder windows so that they're visible on the desktop.

3. Right-click any empty space on the taskbar and choose Tile Windows Vertically from the shortcut menu. Windows arranges both windows so that each occupies exactly half the display.

If you inadvertently left an extra window open on the desktop before attempting this procedure, right-click an empty space on the taskbar, choose Undo Tile, and try again.

To move or copy files from one folder window to another, select the icon or icons and drag them to any empty space in the destination folder.

Tip #33

To quickly copy one or more files to a floppy disk, select the icon(s) in an Explorer window, right-click, and choose Send To from the shortcut menu. Then, choose the floppy drive from the submenu.

➔ **See** "Customizing the Send To Menu," **p. 118.**

DRAGGING AND DROPPING FILES IN EXPLORER VIEW

To use the two-pane Explorer view to move or copy files, follow these steps:

1. Open Windows Explorer. In the All Folders pane (left pane), select the icon for the folder that contains the files you want to move or copy.

2. In the contents pane (right pane), select the icon or icons you want to move or copy.

3. Hold down the right mouse button and drag the icon(s) over the top of the folder icon in the left pane. If the icon for the destination folder is not visible, let the mouse pointer hover over the parent icon for a second or two; the branch expands automatically.

4. When the pointer is over the icon for the destination folder, release the mouse button.

5. Choose the appropriate action—Move, Copy, or Create Shortcut(s)—from the menu that appears.

USING CUT, COPY, AND PASTE

Explorer offers one final option for moving and copying files that doesn't involve dragging and dropping. Use the Windows Clipboard to cut, copy, and paste files between folders and drives in exactly the same way you copy text and graphics between documents. These techniques work equally well in Explorer windows, in folder windows, in email messages, and on the Windows desktop.

To use the Clipboard to copy, move, or create shortcuts, follow this procedure:

1. Select the file or files.

2. To copy a file from one folder to another, use the Copy command; to move a file, use the Cut command. Any of the following mouse or keyboard techniques will work:
   - Choose Edit, Copy or Edit, Cut.
   - Right-click on the selected icon and choose Copy or Cut.
   - Press Ctrl+C (Copy) or Ctrl+X (Cut).
   - Click the Copy or Cut button on the Explorer toolbar.

3. Display the contents of the destination folder and use any of the following commands to complete the move or copy:
   - Choose Edit, Paste.
   - Right-click on the folder icon or in the contents pane and choose Paste.
   - Right-click on the folder icon or in the contents pane and press Ctrl+V.
   - Click the Paste button on the Explorer toolbar.

COPYING DISKS

Trying to copy an entire hard disk or CD-ROM is impractical, but copying a floppy disk is ridiculously easy. Windows includes a utility that handles the whole process in two passes— one for the source (original) disk and the second for the destination (copy) disk.

PART

II

CH

6

To copy a floppy, make sure you have a formatted disk that's the same size as the original you plan to copy. Then follow these steps:

1. Insert the original disk in the floppy drive.

2. Open the My Computer window or Windows Explorer, right-click on the floppy drive icon (normally A:), and choose Copy Disk.

   If you have only one drive that handles the selected disk format, the same drive letter appears in the Copy From and Copy To areas of the dialog box. If you have more than one such drive, select the destination drive in the Copy To box; if the destination drive is a different drive, insert the destination disk in that drive.

3. The Copy Disk dialog box (Figure 6.13) appears. Click Start, and Windows reads the entire contents of the disk into memory.

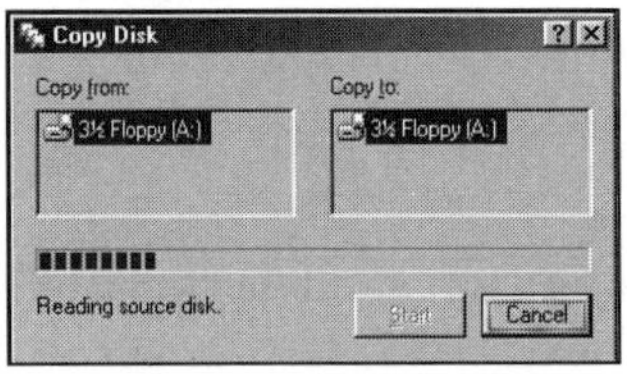

Figure 6.13
Follow the prompts to duplicate a floppy disk.

4. If you're copying from one physical drive to another, Windows handles the operation in one pass. On single-drive systems, Windows displays a prompt when the Copy From phase is complete. Remove the original disk, insert the destination disk into the drive, and click OK.

5. Windows transfers the stored data to the destination disk; if the disk requires formatting, that is done automatically. When the copy is completed, a message appears at the bottom of the Copy Disk dialog box.

6. To copy another floppy, remove the destination disk, insert another source disk, and repeat steps 3 through 5. When you've finished, click Close.

Caution

Windows automatically erases any data on a destination disk without prompting you. That can be disastrous if the destination disk contains important data. If you store important files on floppy disks, always use the write-protect tab to prevent accidental erasure.

DELETING FILES AND FOLDERS

To delete one or more files or folders, select the icons and then use any of the following techniques:

- Press the Delete key.
- Choose File, Delete from Explorer's menu bar.
- Right-click and choose Delete.

- Drag the icon(s) and drop them on the Recycle Bin icon.
- To delete files completely without using the Recycle Bin, hold down the Shift key and press the Delete key, or right-click and choose <u>D</u>elete.

Normally, when you delete one or more files or folders, Windows displays a Confirm File Delete dialog box. You can turn off the dialog box that asks whether you're sure you want to send the files to the Recycle Bin. However, when you bypass the Recycle Bin by choosing the option in the Recycle Bin properties (addressed in more detail later in this chapter), you must deal with the dialog box shown in Figure 6.14.

Figure 6.14
When you bypass the Recycle Bin, Windows forces you to deal with this dialog box.

Confirm Multiple File Delete

Are you sure you want to delete these 4 items?

Yes   No

Caution

When you delete a folder, you also delete all files and subfolders within that folder. Check the contents carefully before you trash an entire folder.

UNDOING CHANGES

In Windows you can undo the last three actions you perform when working with Windows Explorer. If you inadvertently delete a file, move it to the wrong location, or make a mistake when renaming a file or folder, click the Undo button on the Standard Buttons toolbar or press Ctrl+Z.

It's not always easy to tell exactly what Undo will accomplish, and there's no Redo option to restore your original action, either. Within an Explorer window, look at the top of the <u>E</u>dit menu to see what Windows can undo. Likely choices include <u>U</u>ndo Delete, <u>U</u>ndo Move, and <u>U</u>ndo Rename.

Tip #34

The Undo shortcuts also work if you make a mistake on the Windows desktop. If you inadvertently move or delete a desktop file by mistake, press Ctrl+Z immediately to recover.

USING THE RECYCLE BIN

The Windows Recycle Bin can't prevent every file management disaster, but it can help you recover if you accidentally delete a crucial file. When you use Windows Explorer to delete a local file, it doesn't actually disappear; instead, the Recycle Bin intercepts and stores it. The file remains there until you empty the Recycle Bin or until it is displaced by a newer deleted file. As long as that file remains in the Recycle Bin, you can recover the file intact.

Tip #35

Remember to verify that your files are actually being stored in the Recycle Bin by looking at the properties of that icon (addressed in more detail later in this chapter). In the Recycle Bin properties, you can specify whether to utilize the Recycle Bin as temporary undelete storage by choosing or not choosing the Remove Files Immediately When Deleted option.

Caution

The Recycle Bin is far from perfect, and every Windows user should be aware of its limitations. If you use a network connection to delete files on another computer, or if you delete files on a floppy disk or other removable media, those files are not saved in the Recycle Bin. Likewise, using the DEL command from an MS-DOS Prompt window removes the files permanently, without storing safe copies in the Recycle Bin. And if you overwrite a file with another file of the same name, the old file does not go into the Recycle Bin. If these limitations disturb you, check out Norton Utilities and other third-party programs, which can expand the capabilities of the Recycle Bin to cover some of these situations.

Another limitation of the Recycle Bin is that it does not save a file or group of files that exceed the available disk space specified in the Recycle Bin properties. You receive no warning about the impending permanent loss of those files or folders.

If you're having trouble emptying the Recycle Bin or changing its properties, see "The Recycle Bin Is Not Working Properly" in the "Troubleshooting" section at the end of this chapter.

RECOVERING A DELETED FILE

To recover a deleted file, open the Recycle Bin (you'll find its icon on the desktop). Browse the contents until you find the file or files you're looking for. To return the file to its original location, right-click and choose Restore from the shortcut menu. To restore the file to another location, such as the Windows desktop, drag the icon or icons to the location where you want to restore them.

CHANGING THE SIZE OF THE RECYCLE BIN

By default, the Recycle Bin sets aside 10 percent of the space on every local hard disk for storing deleted files. If your hard disk is nearly full, that may be too much; on the other hand, if you have ample disk space, you may want to reserve more space for the Recycle Bin. On systems with more than one drive, you can choose different Recycle Bin settings for each drive.

To adjust the Recycle Bin's appetite, follow these steps:

1. Right-click on the Recycle Bin icon and choose Properties from the shortcut menu. The Recycle Bin Properties dialog box appears (see Figure 6.15).

2. Each drive has its own tab in the dialog box. Use the option at the top of the Global tab to specify whether you want to configure the drives independently or to use one setting for all drives.

3. Use the slider control on the Global tab to change the percentage of disk space reserved for the Recycle Bin (adjust this setting on each of the dialog boxes for individual drives).

You can choose any setting between 0% and 100%, but the most realistic settings are between 3% and 20%.

4. To stop using the Recycle Bin completely, check the box labeled Do Not Move Files to the Recycle Bin.

5. To avoid seeing the confirmation dialog box every time you move a file to the Recycle Bin, clear the check mark from the box labeled Display Delete Confirmation Dialog Box.

6. Click OK to save your changes and close the dialog box.

Figure 6.15
The default setting is to use 10 percent of hard disk space for storing deleted files. Use this dialog box to adjust this setting.

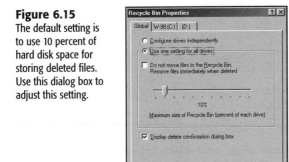

EMPTYING THE RECYCLE BIN

Under normal circumstances, you shouldn't need to delete the Recycle Bin. When it fills up, Windows automatically deletes the oldest files to make room for new files you delete. If you run short of hard disk space—when installing a new program, for example—you may need to clear out the Recycle Bin to make room. To delete all files from the Recycle Bin, right-click on its icon and choose Empty Recycle Bin.

Tip #36

Another way to empty your Recycle Bin and to clear up unnecessary or temporary files is to utilize the Windows 98 Disk Cleanup System Tool. From the Start menu, choose Programs, Accessories, System Tools, Disk Cleanup. Choose the drive you want to manage. Windows 98 displays the common temporary storage folders, such as the Recycle Bin, and the temporary Internet files on that drive and the amount of space each is using.

PREVIEWING A DOCUMENT WITH QUICK VIEW

Even the most compulsive filenaming system can't tell you exactly what's in every file on your hard drive. Using Windows Explorer, you can examine a file's name, type, size, and the date it was last modified. But to see the contents of a file, you need to open it with its associated application—or use the Windows Quick View utility to peek inside.

To view the contents of a file, right-click on the file and choose Quick View. A Quick View window like the one in Figure 6.16 appears.

Figure 6.16
Use the Quick View utility to see the contents of a file without opening it.

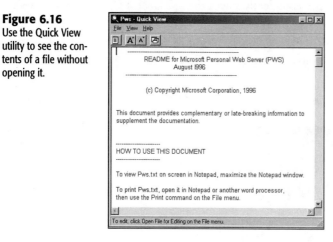

Although Quick View is useful, it's far from perfect. It supports only a limited number of file types, for example, and you can't copy the file's contents to the Windows Clipboard or print the file. The version of Quick View included with Windows 98 lets you view simple text and graphics files and those created by some word processing programs; unlike its Windows 95 predecessor, it allows you to view files created by Office 97 applications.

 If you use Quick View regularly, consider purchasing the full commercial version from its developer: Inso software. Quick View Plus adds support for hundreds of file types. It also enables you to copy text and graphics to the Windows Clipboard or send a file directly to a printer without having to open the application. For more details, go to
http://www.inso.com

USING SHORTCUTS

The files you use most often are scattered across your hard disk in a number of folders. When you set up a new program, its files go in their own folders, and you organize data files using whatever system makes most sense—by project, date, or department, for example. If you had to root through folders and subfolders every time you wanted to open a document or launch a program, you'd hardly have any time to get work done.

So, how do you maintain an orderly filing system and still keep programs and documents close at hand? The solution is to use *shortcuts*. As the name implies, a shortcut is a pointer file that allows you to access a file without moving the file or creating a copy of it. You can create a shortcut for almost any object in Windows, including programs, data files, folders, drives, Dial-Up Networking connections, printers, and Web pages. Windows uses shortcuts extensively: Every item in the Programs folder on your Start menu is a shortcut, for example, and every time you save a Web address to your Favorites folder, you create an Internet shortcut. Learning how to create and manage shortcuts is a crucial step in mastering Windows.

HOW SHORTCUTS WORK

Shortcuts are small files that contain all the information Windows needs to create a link to a *target file*. The shortcut uses the same icon as the target file, with one crucial difference: a small arrow in the lower-right corner that identifies the icon as a shortcut instead of an original.

When you right-click on a shortcut, the available menu choices are the same as if you had right-clicked on the target file. Opening the shortcut has the same effect as opening the target file.

Shortcuts are a tremendous productivity aid. If you have a document file stored six sub-folders deep, for example, you can create a shortcut icon and store it on the desktop so it's always accessible. The target file remains in its original location.

You can create many shortcuts to the same file. For your favorite programs, you might create shortcuts on the desktop, on the Start menu, and on the Quick Launch bar. Each shortcut takes up a negligible amount of disk space (typically no more than 500 bytes), even if the original file occupies several megabytes of disk space.

What happens when you attempt to launch the target file using its shortcut icon? Windows is intelligent enough to reestablish the link to the target file even if you've moved or renamed the original; to do so, it follows these steps:

1. Windows looks at the static location (the filename and path) whether the file is stored locally or on a network.
2. If that file no longer exists, Windows checks to see whether you've renamed the file, looking in the same folder for a file with the same date and time stamp but a different name.
3. If that search fails, Windows checks to see whether you moved the file, looking in all subfolders of the target folder and then searching the entire drive. (On a network location, the search extends to the highest parent directory to which you have access rights.) If you have moved the target file to a different drive, Windows won't find it and the shortcut will break.
4. If Windows can't find the target file, it tries to identify the nearest matching file and displays a dialog box like the one in Figure 6.17. Confirm the choice if it's correct; otherwise, choose No and then delete the shortcut and re-create it, using the correct file.

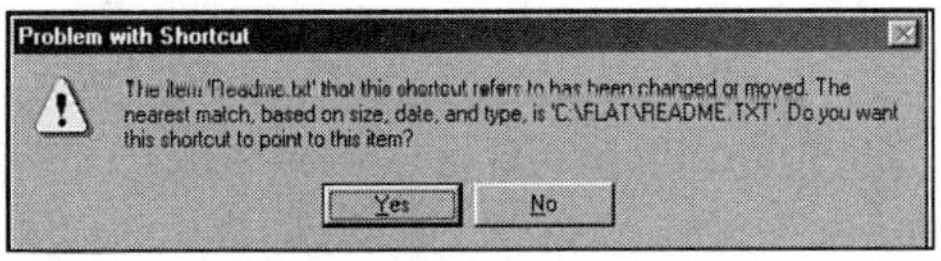

PART

II

CH

6

Figure 6.17
If Windows can't locate the target file for a shortcut, it suggests the closest matching file.

→ To find out more about creating shortcuts to the Internet, **see** "Using Internet Shortcuts," **p. 588.**

CREATING A NEW SHORTCUT

One of the most convenient ways to create a new shortcut is with the help of the Create Shortcut Wizard. Follow these steps:

1. Right-click on an empty space on the Windows desktop and choose New, Shortcut. The Create Shortcut dialog box shown in Figure 6.18 appears.

Figure 6.18
Creating a new shortcut is a two step process with this wizard.

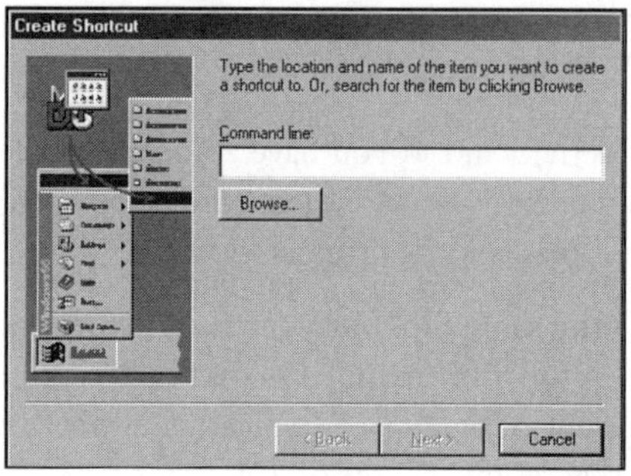

2. Click the Browse button and select the document or program file from the Browse list. To create a shortcut to a drive or folder, you must type its name directly in the Command Line text box. Include the full path if necessary. Then click Next.

3. Give the shortcut a descriptive name and click Finish. Test the shortcut to make sure it works correctly.

You can also create a shortcut from an icon. Select the icon in an Explorer window, hold down the right mouse button, and drag the icon to the desktop or another folder. Choose Create Shortcut(s) Here from the menu that pops up.

Tip #37	The easiest way to create a shortcut is to right-drag the program icon to the place where you want the shortcut to be.

RENAMING A SHORTCUT

To modify the name that appears under a shortcut icon, right-click the icon and choose Rename. (This technique works with shortcuts on the Programs menu and Quick Launch folder as well.) The pointer changes to an I beam, and the entire name is selected. Begin typing to completely replace the name or click to position the insertion point where you want to add or change text. After you edit the name, press Enter or click on an empty portion of the desktop or taskbar to register the change. Note that changing the name of a shortcut does not affect the target file.

DELETING A SHORTCUT

To delete a shortcut, use any of the techniques described earlier in this chapter. When you delete a shortcut, you remove only the link to the target file. The target file itself remains intact in its original location.

SETTING THE PROPERTIES FOR A SHORTCUT ICON

To change the appearance and behavior of a shortcut icon, right-click on the shortcut icon and choose Properties. The General tab of the properties sheet includes basic information, such as the shortcut's name and when it was created. Click the Shortcut tab to change the link between the shortcut and its target file. Using the options on the Shortcut tab (see Figure 6.19), you can make the following adjustments:

- To associate a different file with the shortcut, click in the Target box and type the filename, including its full path.

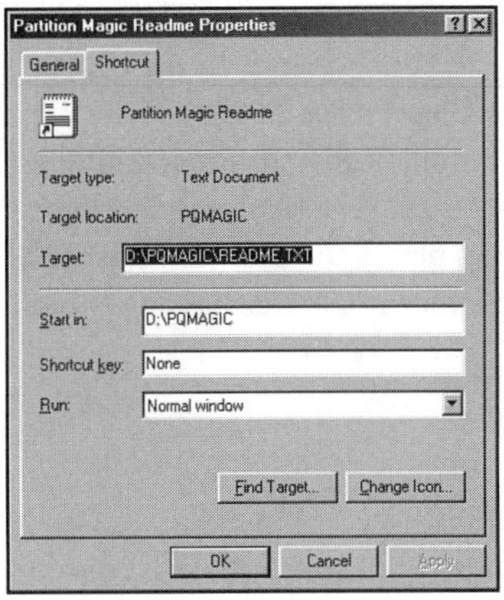

Figure 6.19
The shortcut's properties sheet lets you change the target file, startup folder, shortcut key, and icon used by a shortcut.

- To specify a startup folder, click in the Start In box and enter the name of the folder, including its full path. (This setting is most useful for programs.)
- To define a keyboard shortcut, click in the Shortcut Key box and then press the specific key combination you want to use. The shortcut key must consist of a letter or a number plus any two of the following three keys: Ctrl, Alt, and Shift. (If you simply press a letter or number, Windows defaults to Ctrl+Alt+*key*.) You can also use any function key (F1–F12) with or without the Ctrl, Alt, and Shift keys. You cannot use Esc, Enter, Tab, the Spacebar, Print Screen, or Backspace. To clear the Shortcut Key box, click in the box and press the Spacebar.

PART
II

CH
6

> **Caution**
>
> Shortcut keys you create take precedence over other access keys in Windows. Be careful that you don't inadvertently redefine a systemwide key combination or one that you use in other Windows applications.

- Indicate whether you want the document or application to run minimized, maximized, or in a window.
- Change the icon that appears with the shortcut.

TROUBLESHOOTING

THE RECYCLE BIN IS NOT WORKING PROPERLY

In some situations, you might find that when you right-click the Recycle Bin, you can neither empty the Recycle Bin nor access the icon's Properties. Also, without your direction to do so, the files are bypassing the Recycle Bin and being permanently deleted. This problem may arise when you have a fixed hard disk that is marked as a removable drive.

THE DISAPPEARING PLUS SIGN

I see a plus sign to the left of a drive icon, but when I click the icon, the plus sign disappears.

Windows is behaving exactly as designed. When you open the two-pane Explorer view, Windows checks the contents of all local hard drives and adds the plus sign if it detects subfolders. However, Windows does not automatically check for subfolders on removable drives (such as floppy disks) or network connections because doing so might slow down the performance of your system. Instead, Windows places the plus sign next to each of those icons and waits until you select the icon to see whether the folder has any subfolders. If there are none, Windows removes the plus sign, as you've seen.

MISSING COLUMNS IN DETAILS VIEW

One or more columns are missing when I switch to Details view.

You might have resized a column to zero width, which makes it disappear from view. To restore the default column widths, click anywhere in the contents pane, hold down the Ctrl key, and press the + key on the numeric keypad.

SECRETS OF MASTERING THE WINDOWS 98 ENVIRONMENT: USING POWERDESK UTILITIES

To really jazz up your Windows 98 system, try PowerDesk Utilities 98. It is a complete and totally integrated set of tools specifically designed to help you get more out of the Windows 98 desktop. The core utility of PowerDesk Utilities 98 is PowerDesk, a powerful file manager for Windows 98. PowerDesk provides seamless access to all PowerDesk Utilities features and can be used from anywhere in Windows.

PowerDesk Utilities also includes a zip utility that supports all popular types of compressed files. Zip files appear as normal Windows folders, so you can view, unzip, and zip files with ease right from PowerDesk or Windows Explorer. In addition, a special preview window utility allows you to click on a file to see its contents in a special "preview" window. The viewer is fast and powerful, with support for more than 80 types of files.

CHAPTER **7**

ADVANCED FILE MANAGEMENT TECHNIQUES

In this chapter

ASSOCIATING FILES WITH PROGRAMS

When you attempt to open an icon, Windows checks the file's extension against a database of registered file types to determine what action to take. A registered file type can have multiple actions (open and print, for example), all of which are available on the right-click shortcut menus. Windows uses the default action when you launch the icon. If Windows does not recognize the file type, it offers a dialog box and lets you choose which application to use with the file you've selected.

File extensions have been around since the very first version of DOS. Beginning with the first release of Windows 95, Microsoft began tracking file types as well. File types are inextricably linked to file extensions, but the relationship isn't always easy to understand. Here are the essential facts you need to know:

- File types typically have friendly names (HTML Document), whereas extensions are typically three or four letters (.HTM or .HTML). The support for four-letter extensions is for compatibility with UNIX systems on the Internet.

- File types are listed in their own column when you choose Details view in Windows Explorer. You can also inspect a file's properties to see which file type is associated with it. Extensions for registered file types are hidden by default; extensions for unregistered file types are always visible in the Explorer list.

- Every file type has an associated icon, which appears when you view files of that type in Windows Explorer or a folder window.

- Every unique file extension is associated with one and only one file type at a time. After you install Microsoft Word, for example, Windows associates the .DOC extension with the Microsoft Word Document file type.

- A file type, on the other hand, can be associated with multiple extensions. The HTML Document file type works with both .HTM and .HTML extensions, for example, and files of the JPEG Image file type can end with the extension .JPE, .JPEG, or .JPG.

- As the previous examples illustrate, a file extension can be more than three letters long.

- Windows common dialog boxes (File Open and File Save As) include a drop-down list that lets you choose a file type; Windows adds the default extension for the file type automatically when you save a document.

- A Windows filename can contain more than one period. Windows defines the extension as all characters that appear after the last period in the filename.

Most application programs handle the details of registering file types and associations when you install them. Creating a file type manually and editing an existing file type are cumbersome and difficult processes best reserved for expert users as a last resort.

⚠ *If you are trying to open a file of one extension type and are getting the wrong file type, see "Problems with File Extensions" in the "Troubleshooting" section at the end of this chapter.*

→ For more information on working with file associations, **see** "Managing File Associations," **p. 203.**

Tip #38

> One thing to keep in mind when several applications are running on your Windows 98 system is that a single file extension can have multiple applications associated with it. A good example of this situation is a database file with a .DBF extension. This file could be a dBASE file, a FoxPro file, or even an Act! file. The most recently loaded application takes possession of the .DBF files and is the application that launches when the file is accessed through Explorer. A good clue that this has indeed happened is that the application fails to recognize the actual file upon opening and gives the following (or similar) error: `Unrecognized file or format. Cannot open.` When you have established that the wrong application is associated with the file, you must view the file associations and either change the association or use an alternative method to temporarily launch an application for that particular file. (These methods are detailed shortly in this chapter.)

VIEWING FILE ASSOCIATIONS

To see a list of all registered file types, open Windows Explorer or any folder window (including My Computer). Choose View, Folder Options and then click the File Types tab. Windows displays a list like the one in Figure 7.1.

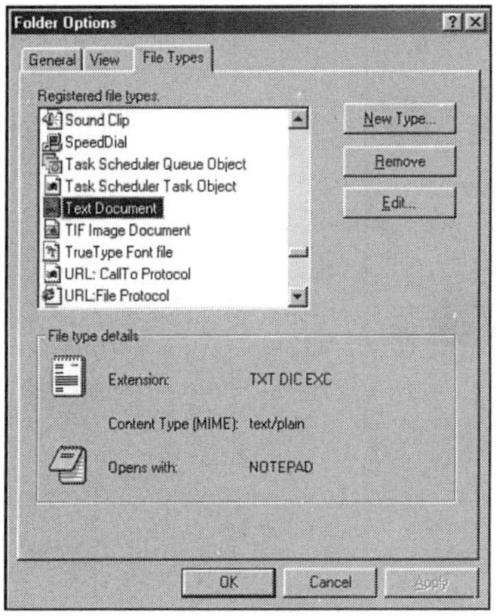

Figure 7.1
Use this list of registered file types to see which applications are associated with the various file types.

The list is arranged in alphabetical order by file type. As you scroll through the list, note that the details in the dialog box change. For each entry in the list, you can view the registered file extensions, MIME details, and the name of the associated application.

Caution

> Multipurpose Internet mail extensions (MIME) are the standards that define how browsers and mail software should handle file attachments. Do not adjust these settings in the File Types dialog box unless you are certain the changes will produce the correct result. Unnecessary tinkering with these settings can cause your mail and Web pages to be unreadable.

PART
II

CH
7

CHANGING FILE ASSOCIATIONS

Windows enables you to associate only one program with each action for each file type. In most cases, if two applications claim the right to edit or open a given file type, the one you installed most recently will claim that file type as its own. If a newly installed program "hijacks" a file type in that way, you might want to restore the association with the older application. You have two options for doing so:

■ Reinstall the original program—The setup process typically edits the Windows Registry and adjusts file associations. If the setup program was written correctly, you will not lose any custom settings or data.

■ Edit the file type directly—To change the associated program to the one you prefer, follow these steps:

1. Open Windows Explorer or any folder window (including My Computer) and choose View, Folder Options. Click on the File Types tab.

2. Select the file type you want to change and click the Edit button. The Edit File Type dialog box appears (see Figure 7.2).

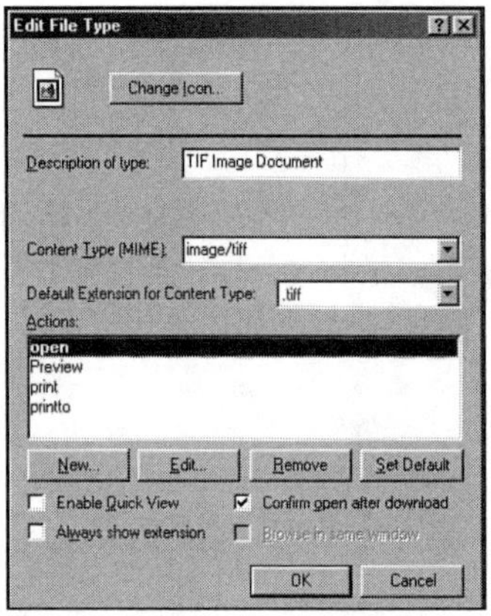

Figure 7.2
Use caution when manually editing file types. Entering a wrong setting in this dialog box can hinder your ability to work with common document types.

3. Select an entry from the Actions list—the default action is in bold type—and click the Edit button. The dialog box shown in Figure 7.3 appears.

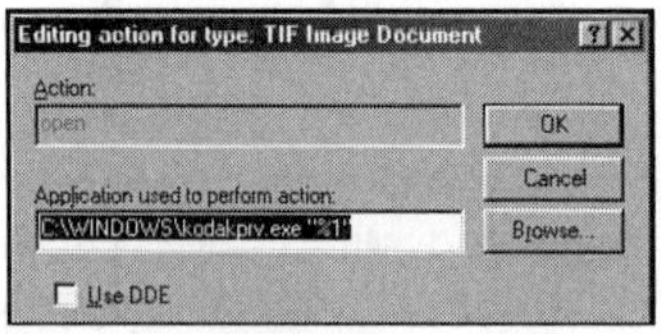

Figure 7.3
Change the program listed here to adjust how Windows works with a given file type.

Caution

Note that some actions require dynamic data exchange (DDE), an extremely complex process that passes information between programs; if you see these options listed, exit this dialog box and don't attempt to edit the action by hand.

4. Click the Browse button. In the dialog box that appears, find and select the executable (EXE) file for the program you want to use with the selected action; then click Open.

5. The filename you selected now appears in the Application Used to Perform Action text box. Click OK to close the Editing Action dialog box and save your change.

6. Repeat steps 3 through 5 for other actions you want to change. When you finish, click OK to close the Edit File Type dialog box. Then click OK again to close the Folder Options dialog box.

Three options in the Edit File Type dialog box are worth noting here:

- Set Default—Choose an action and click the Set Default button to make that action the default action for the file type. The previous default action still appears as a choice on right-click shortcut menus.

- Enable Quick View—Check this box to control whether you see a Quick View choice on the shortcut menu for the selected file type.

→ The Quick View utility is a real time-saver. For more details on how to use this tool, **see** "Previewing a Document with Quick View," **p. 101.**

- Always Show Extension—Check this box to display the file's extension in all Explorer and folder windows. This setting is useful if you regularly change the extensions of certain types of documents (such as RTF documents created by Office 97 and Office 2000) but don't want to clutter the Explorer window with other extensions.

Caution

It's possible to completely eliminate a file type or an action associated with a file type. Generally, however, such a drastic step is not recommended. The settings for each file type take up a trivial amount of space in the Windows Registry, and removing a file type can cause installed programs to fail.

USING AN ALTERNATIVE PROGRAM TO OPEN A REGISTERED FILE TYPE

You might have several programs at your disposal with which you can view or edit a particular type of file. For example, FrontPage Express and Microsoft Word both allow you to edit HTML files. Unfortunately, Windows forces you to associate one and only one program with the default action for each registered file type. However, you can override that default decision at any time and choose which program you want to use for a given file icon. To do so, follow these steps:

1. Select the document icon, hold down the Shift key, and right-click. The shortcut menu that appears includes a new Open With choice that's not found on the default menu.

PART
II
CH
7

2. Choose Open With from the shortcut menu, and the dialog box shown in Figure 7.4 appears.

Figure 7.4
Use this dialog box to open a document with the application of your choice instead of the default program.

3. Scroll through the list and find the program you want to use. Note that the list shows only the short names of executable files (Winword, for example), not the long names of the applications (Microsoft Word).

4. If the program appears in the list, select its entry. If you can't find its entry, click the Other button, browse for the program's executable file, and then click Open.

5. Before you click OK, note the check box labeled Always Use This Program to Open This Type of File. By default, this box is unchecked. Do *not* add a check mark unless you want to change the program associated with the Open action for this type of file.

6. Click OK to open the document.

OPENING AN UNRECOGNIZED FILE TYPE

When you attempt to open the icon for an unrecognized file type, Windows displays an Open With dialog box similar to the one shown in Figure 7.4. Two crucial differences between this dialog box and the one that appears when you hold down the Shift key and click a recognized file type enable you to quickly create a new file type for the unrecognized type.

- This Open With dialog box includes a text box at the top. Enter the name of the new file type there.

- By default, the box labeled Always Use This Program to Open This Type of File is checked. Remove this check mark if you don't want to create a new file type.

If you accidentally create a new file type from this dialog box, you can easily remove that file type. Open the Folder Options dialog box, click the File Types tab, select the newly created file type, and click the Remove button.

FINDING FILES

A hard disk with a capacity measured in gigabytes can hold tens of thousands of files in hundreds or even thousands of folders. So you shouldn't be surprised if you occasionally lose track of one or more of those files. Fortunately, Windows includes a handy utility that lets you hunt down misplaced files, even if you can't remember the file's exact name. You can search for a portion of the name, or you can search for some other detail, such as the size and type of the file, the date it was created, or a fragment of text within the file.

FINDING A FILE OR FOLDER BY NAME

To begin searching for a file on a local disk or on a shared network drive, click the Start button and choose Find, Files or Folders. (If Windows Explorer is open, choose Tools, Find, Files or Folders.) Windows displays a dialog box like the one in Figure 7.5.

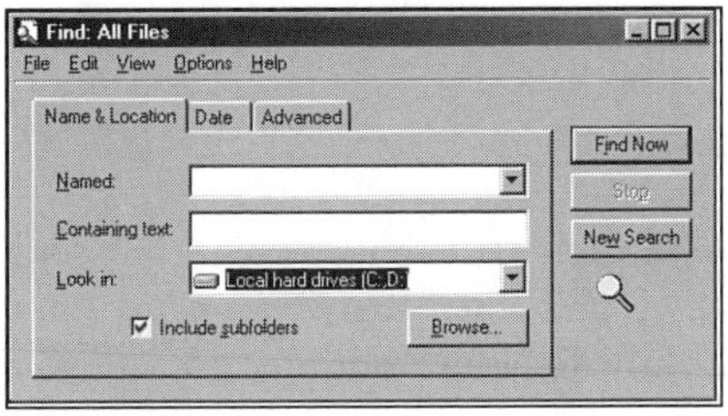

Figure 7.5
Use the Find utility to search for any file—anywhere on your computer or across a network.

The most common type of search is to look for a file when you remember all or part of the name. Here's how:

1. Click in the box labeled Named and enter all or part of the filename. (The file extension is not necessary.)

Tip #39

DOS-style *wildcards* (* and ?) are not required in the Named box, but they can be extremely useful in helping you reduce the number of matches. For example, if you enter the letter *b*, Windows returns all files that include that letter anywhere in the name. On the other hand, a search for *b** finds only files that begin with *b*, and a search for *b???.** returns only files that begin with the letter *b* and contain exactly four characters, not counting the extension.

2. Tell Windows which drives and folders you want to look in. If you opened Find from Windows Explorer, the Look In box includes the name of the currently selected drive or folder; if not, this entry shows the location you specified when you last used Find. Enter a folder name directly (C:\Data, for example) or click the Browse button to choose a folder name from a dialog box or use the drop-down list to select any of the following default locations:

    The Windows desktop

    The My Documents folder

    Document Folders, which includes My Documents and the Desktop folder

    Any local drive

Any mapped network drive

All local hard drives

My Computer (searches all local hard drives as well as floppy and CD-ROM drives)

Tip #40	You can specify multiple locations in the Look In box. Enter the full path, including the drive letter or Universal Naming Convention (UNC) style server and share name, for each location. Separate the entries in this list with semicolons.

3. To search in all subfolders of the location you selected, place a check mark in the box labeled Include Subfolders.

4. Click Find Now to begin searching.

The more details you provide, the more restrictive the results. But don't provide too much information; if you do, you're likely to miss the file you're looking for, especially if the spelling of the filename is even slightly different from what you enter.

Windows compares the text you enter in the Named box with the name of every file and folder in the specified location, returning a result if that string of characters appears anywhere in a filename. For example, if you enter log as the search parameter, Windows turns up all files that contain the words *log*, *logo*, *catalog*, or *technology* (see Figure 7.6). A search's results appear in a pane at the bottom of the Find dialog box.

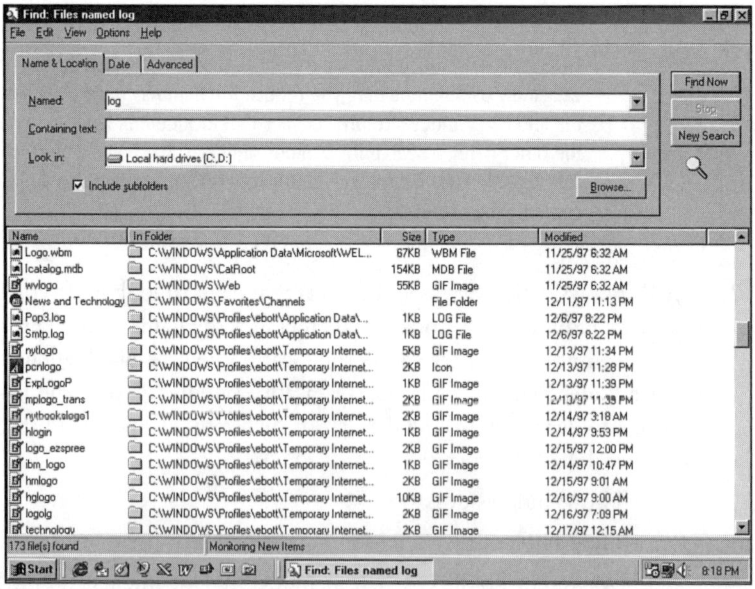

Figure 7.6
The Find utility returns all filenames that include the characters you enter. Click on any column heading to sort the results.

By default, the results list appears in Details view. However, you can right-click in the results pane and use the shortcut menu to change to a different view. You can also click on the column headings to sort results by name, size, type, the date the files were last modified, or the folder in which the files are stored. Click again to sort in reverse order.

Tip #41	After you complete a Find, look at the status bar at the bottom of the window. The message `Monitoring New Items` means that Windows continues to watch your actions and will update the results list automatically if you create, rename, move, or delete files that match the specified criteria.

ADVANCED SEARCH TECHNIQUES

The Find utility is fast and extremely effective, even when you haven't the vaguest idea what the target file is named. Advanced options let you search using other criteria.

If you have a general idea of when you created a file or when you last edited it, click the Date tab and narrow the search by date. Spinners let you specify ranges of dates by day or month. To find all files you worked with yesterday or today, for example, click the Find All Files option, choose Modified from the drop-down list, and choose the option During the Previous 1 Day(s). You can also specify a range of dates, as illustrated in Figure 7.7.

Figure 7.7
Narrow your search by entering a range of dates.

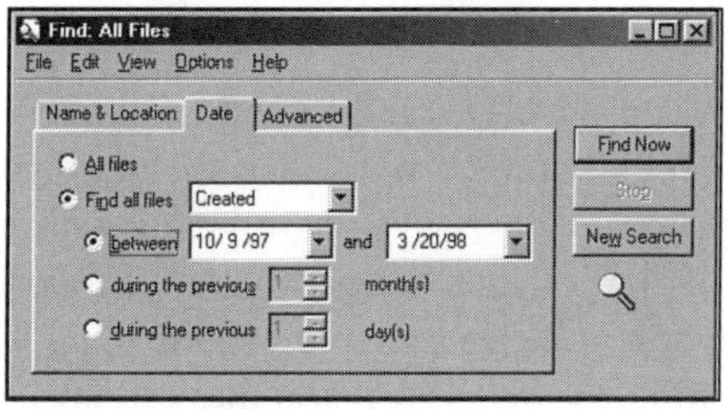

You can type dates into this dialog box, but using the built-in calendar controls that appear when you click drop-down arrows in date boxes (see Figure 7.8) is much easier. On the calendar that appears, click the month heading to produce a menu of months; click the year to reveal a spinner control that lets you quickly adjust the year.

Figure 7.8
This calendar appears automatically when you click the drop-down arrow.

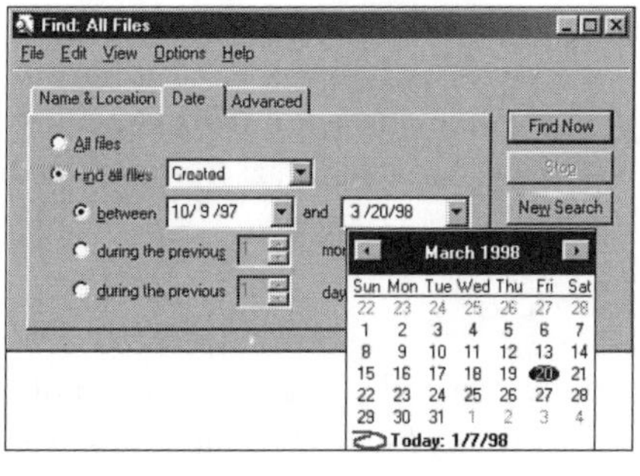

PART

II

CH

7

Click the Advanced tab to search for files by type and by size. On this tab (shown in Figure 7.9), you can select only registered file types. Because it requires you to enter size parameters in kilobytes, be sure to multiply by 1,000 when specifying megabytes.

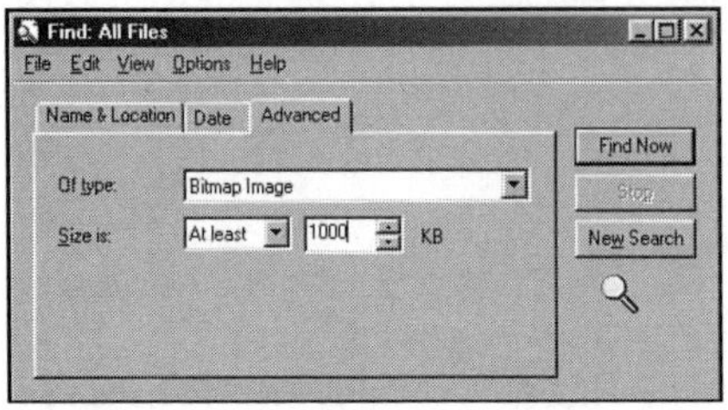

Figure 7.9
This set of search criteria lets you hunt down large graphics files.

Tip #42

Use the Find utility to organize and archive files. For example, you can search for all Microsoft Word files modified more than six months ago and then move the results to a backup location on the network. Or, you might use advanced Find parameters to search for files larger than 1MB in size. If you leave all boxes blank and check the Include Subfolders option, the resulting list includes all files on your computer, up to a maximum of 10,000. You can then sort that list to find files of a certain type or size.

With the help of the Find utility, you can also search for text within files. Obviously, it won't do you much good to search for common words like *the*, but if you remember a specific phrase that appears in a lost document, you can have Windows track down all files that contain that phrase. To look for a draft of your company's annual report, for example, click the Name & Location tab and type annual report in the Containing Text box. Click the Find Now button to begin searching. Note that text searches can take a very long time, especially on large hard disks or across a network.

Tip #43

Combine the settings from the Find dialog box to narrow your search for a specific file. For example, you might order Windows to search for a Microsoft Word document that contains the phrase *annual report* and was last modified in February 1998. With these specifics you have a good chance of finding the file you're looking for, even if you can't remember its name.

If the search didn't find the file you were looking for, modify the criteria and click the Find Now button again. Or, to clear all criteria and start from scratch, click the New Search button.

MANAGING FILES FROM THE FIND WINDOW

Because the Find dialog box is actually a specially modified version of Windows Explorer, you can use the results pane for virtually any file management task. Right-click on any icon to display a shortcut menu that includes file management options, or drag items from the results pane and drop them anywhere—in a folder window, Windows Explorer, the desktop, or an email message.

Use the File menu or right-click for these choices:

- Open
- Quick View
- Send To
- Cut and Copy (available only from the shortcut menu)
- Create Shortcut
- Delete
- Rename
- Properties

The Find utility includes an extremely powerful feature that's so well hidden even many Windows experts don't know it exists. Select any file in the results pane and choose File, Open Containing Folder. This choice, available only from the main menu and not from the right-click shortcut menus, opens a window displaying the full contents of the folder that contains the file you selected in the Find Results pane.

Tip #44	Along the same integrated Web desktop theme as the Active Desktop, Windows 98 has a link to an Internet search page through the Find option on the Start menu. This option enables you to find local files, folders, and computers on your intranet and to search the Internet as well. Thus, the Windows 98 Find option provides seamless integration of the desktop environment with the Internet. With dial-up Internet access, this option opens your default Internet connection, asks whether you want to connect, and then displays a default Internet search page with several available search engines.

SAVING AND REUSING A SEARCH

If you find yourself performing the same search regularly, save the search criteria as an icon so you can reuse it later. To save a search and use it later, follow these steps:

1. After you've completed your search, choose File, Save Search. You won't be prompted for a name or location; instead, Windows automatically creates a Saved Search icon on the desktop.
2. Close the Find window and locate the new Saved Search icon on the desktop. The icon has a descriptive name drawn from the title bar of the search. Rename the icon if you want. You can also copy or move the icon to any other location, including the Start menu.
3. To reuse a saved search, double-click its icon and click the Find Now button.

PART

II

CH

7

Caution

When you reuse a saved search, the results are not up-to-date. The Options menu in the Find dialog box includes a Save Results menu item, but checking this option might not produce the effect you expect. Save Results keeps the search results pane open, displaying the names of the files you found. The next time you use that saved search, the results pane reappears, but the contents do not reflect files you've added, deleted, or renamed since the last time you used the search. To update the list, you must click the Find Now button.

WORKING WITH COMPRESSED FILES

File compression utilities make it possible to pack large files into small spaces. Therefore, they enable you to store large numbers of files in a single archive. Windows 98 users typically encounter compressed files in one of two formats:

- CAB—Setup files for Windows 98 and other Microsoft products are stored in Cabinet format; you can recognize these files by the .CAB extension. Microsoft's Setup program processes cabinet files automatically, without requiring any utilities.

- ZIP—The Zip compression format is a widely used standard for distributing files over the Internet. Windows does not include support for Zip files.

Windows Explorer treats cabinet files as though they were folders. You can open a cabinet file, browse its contents, and copy files by simply opening a cabinet file. Windows also includes a command-line utility with which you can pull one or more compressed files out of a cabinet. This capability is useful when Windows won't boot and you need to replace a lost or corrupted system file to reinstall or repair Windows. The Extract tool also lets you list the files in a cabinet so you can determine the exact location of the file you're looking for. To see detailed instructions on this command, go to an MS-DOS prompt, type EXTRACT /?, and press Enter.

 Although many utilities let you work with Zip files, the best by far is WinZip, from Nico Mak Computing. Download the shareware version from

`http://www.winzip.com`

CUSTOMIZING THE SEND TO MENU

Whenever you right-click on a file or folder, one of the choices on the shortcut menu is Send To. Selecting this option opens a submenu containing destinations to which you can send the selected icon with one click. The result is the same as if you had selected the file and dropped it directly on a shortcut. This option enables you to move files around without having to open Explorer windows.

All the entries on the Send To submenu are shortcuts stored in the \windows\profiles\ username\sendto folder. When you install Windows 98, the Send To menu includes a relatively small number of destinations: your default floppy drive, the Windows desktop, and the My Documents folder. Programs like Microsoft Outlook, Microsoft Fax, and the Web Publishing Wizard add shortcuts to this list, as does the Windows PowerToys collection.

It's simple to add new shortcuts in the SendTo folder. When you do, the new shortcuts immediately show up on the Send To menu. You can add shortcuts to local or network folders, printers, applications (such as Notepad or WordPad), or drives. You can even create a cascading menu by creating a subfolder in the SendTo folder and then creating shortcuts in that subfolder.

Tip #45

Another method of adding shortcuts to the Sendto folder is to right-drag and copy an existing shortcut into that folder.

To customize the Send To menu, follow these steps:

1. Open the Start menu, choose Run, type sendto, and press Enter. The \Windows\SendTo folder opens.

2. Right-click on any empty space in the SendTo folder and choose New, Shortcut. Use the Shortcut Wizard to create the shortcut you want to add.

   If you prefer, you can hold down the right mouse button, drag icons into the SendTo folder, and then choose Create Shortcut(s) Here.

3. Give each shortcut a name that will be self-explanatory on the Send To menu.

4. Repeat this process for any other shortcuts you want to add.

When you finish, select an icon, right-click, and choose Send To. Windows displays an expanded menu like the one in Figure 7.10. It should include all the shortcuts you just added.

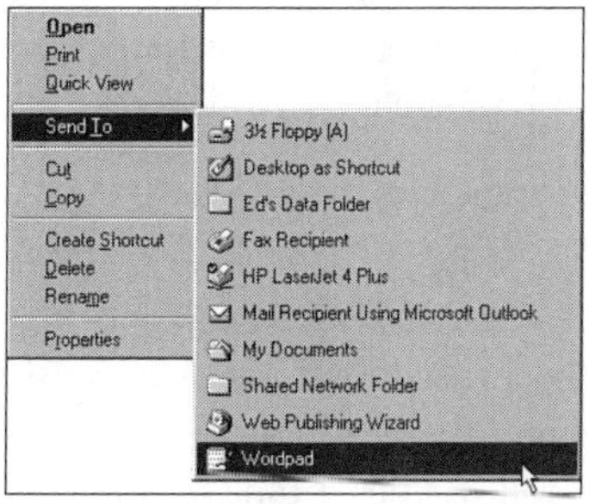

Figure 7.10
When you customize the Send To menu, you increase your one-click file management options.

Customizing the Send To menu can result in some unexpected side effects. If you plan to use this technique, be aware of these facts:

■ All shortcuts follow the Explorer rules for moving and copying. When you "send" an icon to a shortcut from a folder that is also a shortcut and on the same logical volume, you move that file; if the target is on a different drive, such as your floppy drive, you copy the file instead.

■ You can select multiple files and then choose Send To, but the results might not be what you expect. In particular, because of various undocumented program features in this and any operating system, sending multiple files to a program shortcut might not work.

■ If you add a program shortcut to the SendTo folder and then use it to open a file whose name contains a space, you might see an error message or the program might open the file using its short name instead. Again, this result seems to be a bug in the operating system. You must try this technique on a case-by-case basis.

WORKING WITH LONG FILENAMES

Windows allows you to create names for files and folders using up to 255 characters. Legal filenames can contain spaces and most special characters, including periods, commas, semicolons, parentheses, brackets ([ ]), and dollar signs. However, you are not allowed to use the following characters when naming a file or folder:

: ' " \ / * ? |

HOW WINDOWS GENERATES SHORT FILENAMES

Because Windows 98 maintains backward compatibility with older operating systems and applications, the file system automatically generates short filenames from long names you create. Although this process happens in the background, it's important to understand the rules.

When you save a file using Windows 98 or a 32-bit Windows application, Windows checks the filename you enter. If the name is a legal MS-DOS name (with no spaces or other forbidden characters), has no more than eight characters in the name, and has no more than three characters in the extension, the short filename is the same as the long filename. If the long filename contains spaces or other illegal characters or is longer than eight characters, Windows performs the following actions to create a short filename:

1. Removes all spaces and other illegal characters, as well as all periods except the rightmost one.

2. Truncates the long filename to six characters, if necessary, and appends a tilde (~) followed by a single-digit number. If this procedure duplicates an existing filename, Windows increases the number by one: ~1, ~2, ~3, and so on. If necessary, it truncates the long filename to five characters, followed by a tilde and a two-digit numeric tail.

3. Truncates the file extension to the first three characters. If the long filename does not include a period, the short filename will have no extension.

4. Changes all lowercase letters to capital letters.

> **Caution**
>
> Several books and computer magazines have published details for adjusting a Registry setting (NameNumericTail) that controls the way in which Windows automatically generates short filenames from the long filenames you create. Do not make such changes! The result can seriously affect the operation of some Windows accessories that depend on the Program Files folder. For more information on this topic, go to `http://www.microsoft.com/support/default.htm` and search for Knowledge Base article Q148594.

You cannot change the automatically generated short filename. To see the MS-DOS-compatible name for any file, right-click its icon, choose Properties, and click the General tab.

USING LONG FILENAMES WITH OLDER WINDOWS AND DOS PROGRAMS

If you use 16-bit Windows programs or the old-style Windows File Manager, long filenames are not available in common dialog boxes such as File Open and File Save As. Instead, you'll see the truncated short version of all filenames (see Figure 7.11).

Figure 7.11
When you view files using 16-bit Windows programs, you see only the short filenames, not their long equivalents.

Through a process called *tunneling*, Windows enables you to preserve long filenames even when you use older programs to edit the files. If you create a file and give it a long name using Windows or a 32-bit Windows program, and you then edit the file using a 16-bit program and save it to a short filename, Windows preserves the long filename.

WORKING WITH LONG FILENAMES AT AN MS-DOS PROMPT

When you open an MS-DOS Prompt session within Windows 98, Windows recognizes long filenames and allows you to work with them directly. By default, directory listings display the DOS-compatible short name at the left and the long name at the right, as shown in Figure 7.12.

When managing files from an MS-DOS prompt, you can use either the long or short version. If you want to display, rename, copy, or move a file whose filename contains one or more spaces, you must enclose the entire name and path in quotation marks.

PART
II

CH

7

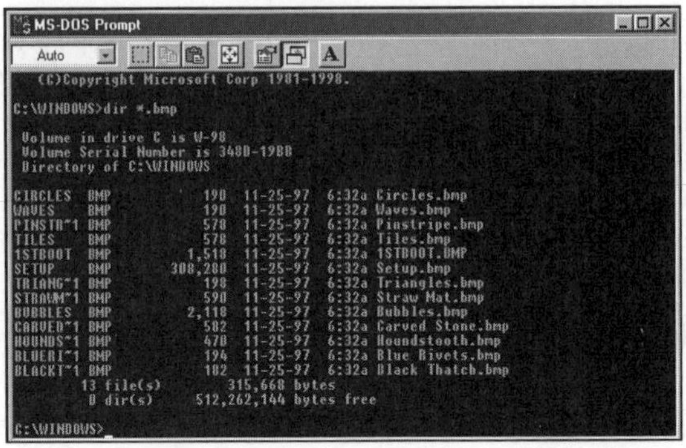

Figure 7.12
Type DIR in an MS-DOS Prompt session to see long and short filenames.

Tip #46

Some old Windows 3.x habits die hard, for example, the Winfile utility that brings up the old File Manager interface from the 3.x versions. Unfortunately, this old habit could cause you some unneeded headaches when you copy or move a file with a long filename. Winfile was left behind for backward compatibility, and the long filename is converted to an MS-DOS-compatible (short) filename in 8.3 format. For example, a file named Customers.doc is displayed as custom~1.doc after you copy or move it. When you try to open the file from a shortcut or an old file list in an application, the system does not recognize the new shorter name in place of the old Long File Name (LFN). My advice is to avoid confusing yourself and others and to start using Windows Explorer.

USING EXPLORER WITH SHARED RESOURCES ON A NETWORK

Windows Explorer lets you view and manage files and folders across a network, provided you have a working network connection and sufficient permissions. Use Network Neighborhood to view all available network resources or to map shared resources to drive letters to make them easier to work with. If you know the exact name of the shared resource, you can enter it directly into any Windows common dialog box.

USING NETWORK NEIGHBORHOOD TO VIEW SHARED RESOURCES

Icons for other computers, including Windows workstations and network servers, appear in Network Neighborhood. You'll typically see some or all of the following icon types when you open Network Neighborhood:

- Windows workstations
- Windows NT servers
- NetWare and other servers
- Windows workgroups (which in turn contain icons for other workstations)

When you open a computer icon in Network Neighborhood, you see all the named shares available on that computer. These may be individual drives, folders, printers, or fax modems. Before you can browse shared files and folders or print to a shared printer, you must have permission to use that resource.

To connect with a shared resource, follow these steps:

1. Open Windows Explorer and click Network Neighborhood.

2. Click the plus sign to the left of the computer name; available shares appear in a list below the computer icon, as in Figure 7.13.

Figure 7.13
Network Neighborhood displays all shared resources available on other workstations and servers.

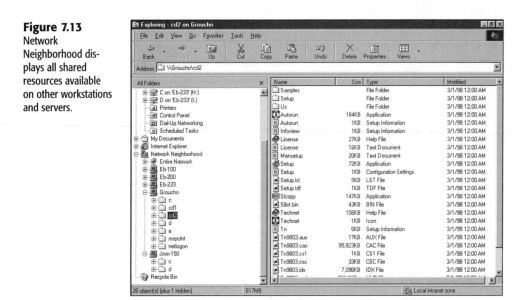

3. Select a share name from the list, and its contents appear in the right-hand pane.

4. Open a document, launch an application, or perform any other file management task as though you were working with a local file or folder.

→ For more information about sharing resources on your computer with other network users, **see** Chapter 37, "Sharing Network Resources."

Tip #47

Network Neighborhood lists only computers that have the File and Print Sharing option turned on in their Network properties. If you browse through Network Neighborhood and don't see your own computer in the list, it does not mean that you cannot access the network. If you want to add your computer to the network and share files, you can right-click the Network Neighborhood icon and choose Properties. Under the Configuration tab, click the File and Print Sharing button. Check the appropriate boxes and then click OK; Click OK again to exit the Network Neighborhood Properties dialog box. Restart your computer.

OPENING SHARED FOLDERS WITH UNC NAMES

In Windows programs and in the Start menu's Run dialog box, you can specify any file by entering its UNC pathname. To use a UNC name, you must follow this syntax:

\\computername\sharename\path

For example, if a coworker whose computer is named BillG has created a shared folder named Budget and has given you permission to access that folder, you can browse the shared files by typing \\Billg\Budget in the File Open dialog box and pressing Enter. You can also create a shortcut to a shared network drive or folder by using the UNC name of the resource.

 If you are experiencing problems connecting to a Windows NT system and can verify that you have a connection to the, see "Troubleshooting Connections to Windows NT Systems" in the "Troubleshooting" section at the end of this chapter.

MAPPING A NETWORK DRIVE

Drive mapping, as the name implies, lets you assign a virtual drive letter to a shared network resource. When you map a network drive, you refer to it by drive letter, just as though it were a local drive on your own computer.

You might want to map drive letters for two reasons. First, it makes working with files more convenient; instead of browsing through Network Neighborhood, you can simply choose a drive letter from the Drives drop-down list in a common dialog box. Second, some older programs (and even some components of Windows 98) do not allow you to browse network resources directly; in such cases, the only way to access a shared file or folder is to first map it to a drive letter.

To map a shared drive or folder, follow these steps:

1. Open Network Neighborhood in a folder window or Windows Explorer and then open the server or workstation icon to display available shared resources on that computer.

2. Right-click the share icon and choose Map Network Drive from the shortcut menu. The Map Network Drive dialog box shown in Figure 7.14 appears.

Figure 7.14
Mapping a shared folder to a drive letter is the only way to use network resources with some programs.

3. Select an available drive letter from the Drive drop-down list.

4. If you want Windows to automatically reestablish the drive mapping every time you start your computer, check the box labeled Reconnect at Logon. If you want the mapping to be temporary, remove the check from this box.

5. Click OK to map the drive to the selected letter. The mapped drive letter is available in all common dialog boxes. You can also display the drive's contents directly by typing the drive letter and a colon in the Run dialog box (available via the Start menu).

Note

All mapped drives appear in the My Computer window alongside the icons for local drives. The label for a mapped drive includes the share name, server name, and drive letter.

To remove a drive mapping, follow these steps:

1. Right-click the Network Neighborhood icon and choose <u>D</u>isconnect Network Drive. A list of mapped drives appears.

2. Choose the mapped drive from the <u>D</u>rive list.

3. Click OK to disconnect. You will not see a confirmation dialog before disconnecting.

FINDING A COMPUTER ON YOUR NETWORK

Large networks can include hundreds of computers across different domains and workgroups. On large networks, just opening Network Neighborhood and displaying all the icons in it can take minutes. To find a specific computer without browsing through the entire network, follow these steps:

1. Click the Start button and choose <u>F</u>ind, <u>C</u>omputer. The Find Computer dialog box appears (see Figure 7.15).

Figure 7.15
To avoid long delays when you open Network Neighborhood, search for a computer name instead.

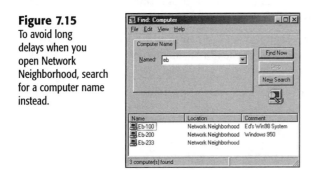

2. In the <u>N</u>amed box, enter all or part of the computer name you're searching for.

3. Click the F<u>i</u>nd Now button. A list of matching computer names appears in the results pane at the bottom of the dialog box.

Tip #48

Right-click a computer name and choose P<u>r</u>operties to see more information about the computer, including the name of the workgroup or domain it belongs to and the operating system it uses.

MANAGING FILES FROM AN MS-DOS PROMPT

You can do certain things from an MS-DOS prompt that you can't do any other way, and for some people an MS-DOS session is the most efficient way to work. By using the DIR command and MS-DOS wildcards, for example, you can quickly display a filtered list of files within a given folder and redirect the output to a text file. In addition, the MS-DOS prompt offers the only way to use wildcards to quickly rename a group of files and is the fastest way to change the extension (and thus the file type) of some types of documents without having to adjust Windows Explorer preferences.

Tip #49

To see command-line switches for DIR and other MS-DOS commands, type the particular command followed by /? at the MS-DOS prompt. If the instructions scroll off the top of the screen before you can read them, add ¦ MORE to the end of the command.

STARTING AN MS-DOS PROMPT SESSION

To open an MS-DOS Prompt session within Windows, open the Start menu and choose Programs, MS-DOS Prompt.

Note that an MS-DOS Prompt session behaves differently from the command prompt that appears when you restart your computer in MS-DOS mode. Here are some key differences:

- The MS-DOS Prompt session allows you to work with long filenames. In MS-DOS mode, you see only the short 8.3-style names.

- The MS-DOS Prompt session can run in a window or in full-screen mode. When you start in MS-DOS mode, on the other hand, you are limited to full-screen display.

- All network resources are available to an MS-DOS Prompt session; accessing those resources in MS-DOS mode requires that you load real-mode network drivers.

- You can launch any Windows or MS-DOS program or batch file from the MS-DOS Prompt window. When you restart in MS-DOS mode, you can run MS-DOS programs only.

Tip #50

To switch between a windowed MS-DOS Prompt and a full-screen display, press Alt+Enter.

To close an MS-DOS Prompt window, type EXIT at the prompt and press Enter.

USING THE WINDOWS CLIPBOARD WITH THE MS-DOS PROMPT

You must use a special set of procedures for copying text to and from an MS-DOS Prompt window. These procedures are particularly useful when you need to copy a lengthy filename, complete with its full path. Follow these steps:

1. Open an MS-DOS Prompt window. If the MS-DOS Prompt session opens in full-screen mode, press Alt+Enter to force it into a window.

2. Click the Control-menu icon at the far left of the title bar to open the pull-down Control menu shown in Figure 7.16.

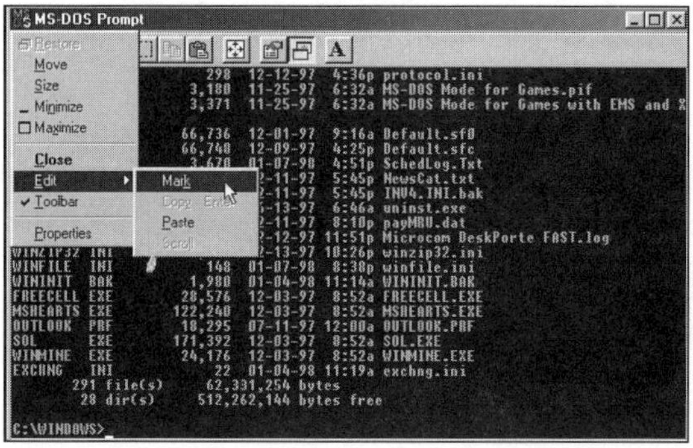

Figure 7.16
Use this pull-down menu to cut, copy, and paste text between an MS-DOS window and the Windows Clipboard.

3. Choose the <u>E</u>dit command, and a cascading menu appears to the right.

4. To copy part or all of the screen, choose Mar<u>k</u>. This option switches the mouse pointer into Mark mode, which enables you to select any rectangular portion of the MS-DOS screen.

5. Mark the section you want to copy and then press Enter. Whatever you marked is copied to the Windows Clipboard; you can then paste the text into the MS-DOS window or into any Windows program.

6. To paste text from the Clipboard into your MS-DOS window, position the insertion point at the desired location in your DOS screen. Click the Control-menu icon on the title bar and choose <u>E</u>dit, <u>P</u>aste from the pull-down menu.

→ For more information on using the Clipboard to move and exchange data, **see** "Using the Windows Clipboard to Exchange Data," **p. 224.**

USING UNC PATHNAMES IN AN MS-DOS PROMPT WINDOW

In Windows programs and in the Start menu's Run dialog box, you can specify any file by using its UNC pathname. However, an MS-DOS Prompt window does not recognize UNC names. To list or manage shared files across the network from an MS-DOS Prompt session, you must first map the share to a drive letter. Use the procedures outlined earlier in this chapter to do so.

To map a drive letter at the MS-DOS prompt, type NET USE *driveletter:* *servername**sharename* (substitute the appropriate drive letter, server name, and share name). For more details about this command, type NET USE /? and press Enter.

PART

II

CH

7

TROUBLESHOOTING

PROBLEMS WITH FILE EXTENSIONS

My document appears to have the correct extension, but when I try to open it, the wrong application launches.

One possible reason for this problem is that you or another user tried to add or change the file extension manually by adding a period and the extension. If the Hide File Extensions for Known File Types box is not checked, the associated program added its own (hidden) extension as well, resulting in a filename such as Letter.doc.rtf. To see the full name, including extensions, choose View, Folder Options; click the View tab; and remove the check mark from the box next to the option labeled Hide File Extensions for Known File Types. The file extension is now visible and editable.

TROUBLESHOOTING CONNECTIONS TO WINDOWS NT SYSTEMS

When I attempt to connect to a shared drive or folder on a Windows NT server, I'm asked to supply a password for \\servername\IPC$. What's the problem?

Your computer has successfully created an interprocess communication (IPC) connection with the Windows NT resource, but the Windows NT domain controller does not recognize your username and password. You must log off and log on again, using an account that is valid on the domain.

SECRETS OF MASTERING THE WINDOWS 98 ENVIRONMENT: ADVANCED FILE MANAGEMENT USING WINZIP

WinZip is a handy utility that enables you to compress files and subsequently archive them for easy, space-efficient access. A file archive is a file that contains other files, and Zip files are one of the most common types of archive format. Normally, to save space in the storage of the archive, the files in an archive are compressed. When creating an archive, WinZip uses the term *add* to mean "compress files and add them to an archive." After archiving the files, you can extract them. *Extract* means to "decompress" the files that make up an archive. The extraction process creates separate files on a designated disk or storage device.

You can create a new archive while using the WinZip GUI tool and selecting New Archive from either the WinZip File pull-down menu or the New toolbar button. This activates the New Archive dialog box. The entire process is very simple with the New Archive dialog box.

Start by typing the name of the archive you want to create, not the names of the files you want to compress. The New Archive dialog box works like a standard Windows file management dialog box, so you can choose the drive and folder where you want to create the archive. The names of any existing archives on the selected drive and folder are listed to help you choose a name that is not already in use. Usually, after creating an archive, you will want to add files to the archive. Verify that the Add Dialog check box is checked to automatically activate the Add dialog box. You can find out more about WinZip at
`http://www.winzip.com.`

CHAPTER **8**

MANAGING FILES USING WEB VIEW

In this chapter

WHAT IS WEB VIEW?

Windows 98 incorporates a single Explorer window that lets you shift effortlessly between local files and pages on the Web. So why not go the next step and view your files and folders as Web pages?

Ordinarily, Explorer displays files, folders, and other system objects as icons in a window. You can choose between large and small icons, or you can arrange them in a list or in a column-oriented Details view. A separate Web view option, independent of the icon arrangement you've chosen, enables you to add Web-style information panels around the display of icons.

When you turn on Web view, Explorer uses HTML templates to customize your view of files and folders. You see more information at a glance, and for a modest investment of programming time, you can even create custom views that make it easier for other users to navigate through folders. With Web view turned on, an ordinary folder display changes to resemble the one in Figure 8.1.

Figure 8.1
When you choose Web view, Explorer displays extra information about the current folder and files within it.

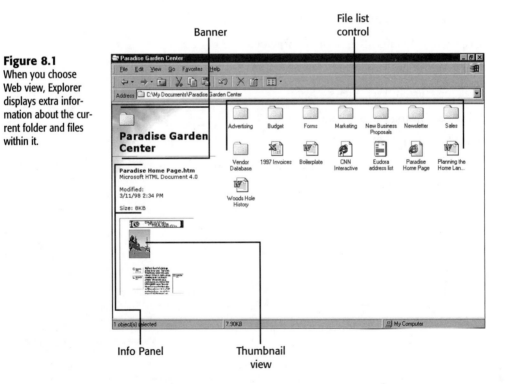

The default Web view includes four standard elements:

- A banner identifies the title of the current folder.
- An info panel displays details about the folder and the currently selected file(s).

- Thumbnail images of certain file types appear below the contents pane, making it easier to identify the file's contents at a glance.
- The file list is contained in an ActiveX control embedded within the Folder window.

Web view works in Folder windows and in the contents pane of a two-pane Explorer window.

USING WEB VIEW WITH FOLDERS

If you've selected Web style navigation, Web view is turned on for all folders by default. If you've selected Classic style navigation, Web view is disabled for all folders by default. With custom settings, you can choose whether to enable or disable Web view by default.

→ To find out more about setting your navigation options, **see** "Classic or Web? Choosing a Navigation Style," **p. 68.**

Regardless of the global settings, you can turn Web view on or off for any folder. The Web view menu choice is a toggle: If Web view is on, choose <u>V</u>iew, As <u>W</u>eb Page to restore the current Folder window to a normal Explorer view.

Setting this option for one Folder window does not have any effect on other Folder windows. However, if you turn on Web view using the two-pane Explorer view, your preferences apply to all folders you view in the current Explorer window.

DISPLAYING THUMBNAILS AND FILE INFORMATION

When you choose Web view and select any file, the info panel at the left side of the window displays that file's name, its file type, the date it was last modified, and its size. If you select a Folder icon, the info panel shows the name only.

When you select multiple files, the info panel displays a different set of details: a count of the number of items you've selected, the total combined size of the selected files (useful if you're planning to move or copy files to another folder), and a column listing the name of each selected file (see Figure 8.2).

Below the info panel, the default Web view template includes a thumbnail image of certain file types. Only a handful of file formats appear as thumbnails in Web view. Those that do include Document files; Bitmap, GIF, and JPEG images; and Web pages in HTML format (if the page is stored locally or in your browser's cache). If you create a document with one of the applications in the Standard edition of Microsoft Office 97 and Office 2000, you can see detailed information about the file, along with a thumbnail image of the document.

Figure 8.2
When you select multiple documents in Web view, you see these summary details in the info pane.

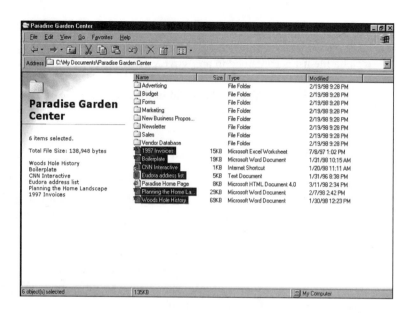

If you're an Office 97 or Office 2000 user, taking advantage of Web view requires some extra effort. By default, Word and Excel files do not display thumbnail images unless you choose File, Properties, click the Summary tab, and check the box labeled Save Preview Picture. Similarly, the info panel displays the name of the author and other file properties, but only if you go out of your way to add that information in the Summary dialog box.

Can you turn on thumbnails for a given file type? Unfortunately, the answer is no. In theory, any application can add thumbnail support if the developer integrates its file formats with the WebViewFolderContents object; that's the ActiveX control that adds Web view capabilities to the Windows Explorer. If an application includes this feature, it should appear automatically, without extra effort on your part.

 If you are having problems viewing thumbnails, see "Problems with the Thumbnail View" in the "Troubleshooting" section at the end of this chapter.

Don't confuse the thumbnail image in Web view with the Folder view option of displaying files as thumbnails. When you want to display files as thumbnails, you must first check the Enable Thumbnail View box for the folder. The Thumbnail option does not become available in the View menu until you have enabled the folder. The Thumbnail option displays the files as images (the compatible image files appear in the Explorer window as miniature versions of the actual image) and cannot be used with the Web view. The Thumbnail option adds a hidden file (Thumbs.db), which takes up disk space indexing the images, and adds some overhead to the system memory while being utilized.

You can also preview documents such as Excel spreadsheets or a Word document by opening the document; choosing File from the pull down menu, selecting Properties; checking Save Preview Picture under the Summary tab; and saving the document. Any documents with this option checked display a miniature version of the first page of text.

USING WEB VIEW WITH SYSTEM FOLDERS

A handful of system folders use custom Web view templates. When you display the My Computer folder in Web view, for example, a display like the one in Figure 8.3 appears.

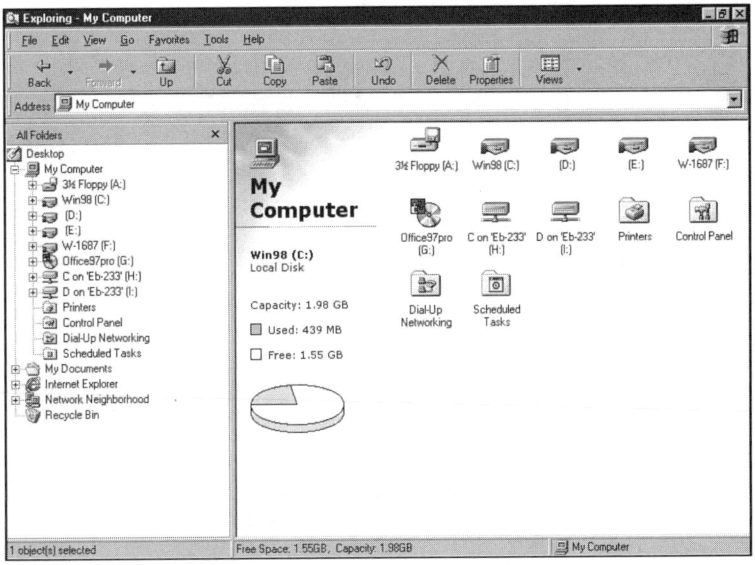

Figure 8.3
You see detailed drive information when you turn on Web view in the My Computer folder.

> **Caution**
>
> Although it's easy to forget this fact, the Windows desktop is just another Explorer folder, minus the window borders, menus, and toolbars. When you turn on the Active Desktop and display Web content on the desktop, you've actually told Windows to display the desktop folder in Web view. IE4 automatically generates a custom Web view template, called DESKTOP.HTT, every time you customize your Active Desktop settings. Although it's theoretically possible to find this template and edit it manually, doing so is not recommended.

Other system folders have custom Web view templates, including the Control Paneland Printers folders. Table 8.1 lists the built-in Web view templates in a typical Windows 98 installation. All of these templates are stored in the Windows\Web folder.

TABLE 8.1   BUILT-IN WEB VIEW TEMPLATES

Template File	Description
CONTROLP.HTT	Displays help text in the Info panel when you select individual Control Panel icons. Includes hyperlinks to two Microsoft Web pages.
FOLDER.HTT	The default template Windows uses when you customize Web view options for a folder. Editing this file does not change folders you have already customized.

TABLE 8.1   CONTINUED

Template File	Description
DESKMOVR.HTT	Provides support for Active Desktop objects. Do not edit this file.
MYCOMP.HTT	Displays information about selected local and network drives in My Computer; also displays help text for system folders.
PRINTERS.HTT	Offers instructions for setting up a new printer; selecting the printer icon displays the number of messages in the print queue.
SAFEMODE.HTT	Contains information and troubleshooting links for resolving problems when the Active Desktop crashes.
DIALUP.HTT	Displays information to help you use the Dial-Up Networking folder.
NETHOOD.HTT	Provides an explanation of the contents of the Network Neighborhood.
RECYCLE.HTT	Includes JavaScript links that let you empty the Recycle Bin or restore all its contents at once.
SCHEDULE.HTT	Explains how the Scheduled Tasks folder works.

Caution

Before editing any of the default templates in the Windows\Web folder, be sure to create backup copies so you can recover the original HTML files if you want to start over.

CREATING CUSTOM WEB VIEWS

There's no particular magic to Web view. When you display a folder's contents and choose View, As Web Page, you instruct Explorer to look in the current folder for two files:

- DESKTOP.INI lists shell objects that allow the folder to interpret HTML code and display files in a defined region within the folder. It also includes pointers to custom HTML templates and/or background images for the folder. If this file does not exist in the current folder, Explorer uses default settings.

- FOLDER.HTT is a hypertext template file that defines scripts, objects, and HTML code that allow files to be displayed. If this file does not exist in the current folder, Explorer uses the default file in the Windows\Web folder. You can customize this template file, and you can use a file with a different name by specifying it in DESKTOP.INI.

Windows also includes a wizard that lets you customize the look of a folder by editing the Web view template.

Caution

You cannot force users to open a folder in Web view. If you've designed a custom Web page to help other users of your PC navigate in a particular folder or to simplify file access for co-workers on a network, your work will pay off only if they choose to use Web view. If they access the custom folder with a version of Windows that does not include the Windows Desktop Update, they cannot view your changes.

USING THE WEB VIEW WIZARD

To customize the appearance of a folder in Web view, choose View, Customize This Folder. That action launches the wizard that appears in Figure 8.4. Note that, as wizards go, this one is fairly crude.

Figure 8.4
Use this wizard to edit the Web view template or add a background graphic to a folder.

When you choose the option Create or Edit an HTML Document, the wizard launches Notepad and loads the hypertext template specified in DESKTOP.INI. If you are using the wizard for the first time in a given folder, the wizard copies the FOLDER.HTT template file from the Windows\Web folder. When you finish editing the file in Notepad, you can close the Customize This Folder dialog box and return to the folder to see your changes.

The second option, Choose a Background Picture, enables you to add a background graphic behind the file list control on the Web view folder. You can use any file in any standard graphic format, including Bitmap, JPEG, or GIF. To see how this process works, start the Customize This Folder Wizard and follow these steps:

1. Select Choose a Background Picture. Click the Next button.

2. The next dialog box (see Figure 8.5) displays a list of graphics files from the \Windows folder. Click the Browse button to choose a different folder if necessary.

3. As you click on graphics files in the list, the contents of the file appear in the Preview window at the left of the dialog box. If the graphic is small, Windows tiles the image to fill the preview box.

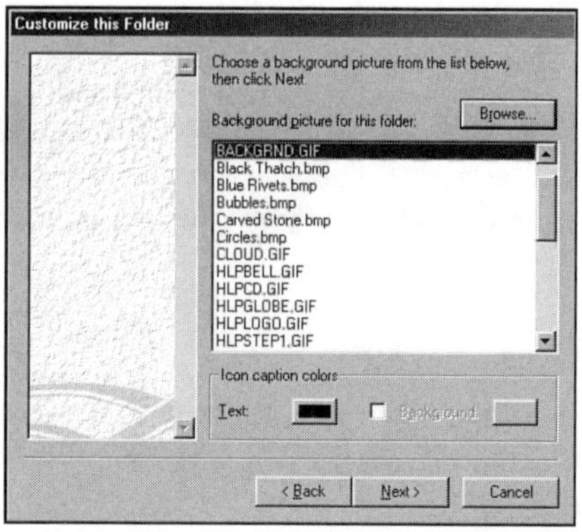

Figure 8.5
Choose a background image to appear behind the file list control in Web view. Pick a light image that won't obscure icons.

4. When you've selected an appropriate graphics file, click the Text button to choose a contrasting color for the icon labels that appear on top of the graphic. You might also want to check the Background check box and adjust the color that is to appear behind the icon labels.

5. Click Next to record your changes; then, click Finish to close the wizard. You might have to press F5 to refresh the folder's contents and see your changes.

Tip #53

If you must use a graphic behind the file list control, choose a light image, preferably in a shade of gray. Dark or detailed images such as photographs can make it difficult to see icons in the file list.

EDITING A HYPERTEXT TEMPLATE

To edit a hypertext template, you need to be fluent in HTML—and you won't be able to fall back on the WYSIWYG editor in FrontPage Express. By default, when you choose to customize the hypertext template file for a folder, Windows dumps you into the most rudimentary HTML editor imaginable: Notepad.

→ To learn about editing in Notepad, **see** "Using Notepad," **p. 292.**

Some sections of FOLDER.HTT are strictly for Web experts. Don't edit the scripts that display file information, for example, unless you're sure you know what you're doing. But even an inexperienced editor can safely add hyperlinks to the default folder template.

Note

Future updates to Windows and Internet Explorer might include more complex templates for customizing folders. In that case, you might need to adjust the instructions that follow to deal with the revised HTML code.

The default folder template includes a section where you can add your own hypertext links to Web pages or files. (Open Control Panel and turn on Web view to see examples of these links.) To customize this section, use the Customize This Folder Wizard to open FOLDER.HTT for editing in Notepad. Then, follow these steps:

1. Choose <u>S</u>earch and enter the following text in the Fi<u>n</u>d What text box:

   A FEW LINKS OF YOUR OWN

   Then, click Fi<u>n</u>d Next.

2. The HTML code in this section includes two sample URLs. Replace the samples with your own link, and replace the link text (Custom Link 1 and Custom Link 2) with your own label.

3. To create additional links, copy the two lines that follow the first sample link and paste them below the second sample. Repeat for any additional links and then customize as in step 2.

4. Delete the comment tags above and below the links to make them visible in Web view. When you finish, the code should look like the sample shown in Figure 8.6.

Figure 8.6
Edit the hypertext template to add links that appear in Web view. Note that links can include Web pages, folders, or file-names.

5. Close Notepad, saving the file with the default name. Then, press F5 to refresh the Folder view and see the links in place.

REMOVING CUSTOM WEB VIEW SETTINGS

If you've customized a folder's Web view template and you're not happy with the results, use the wizard to delete your changes and start over. The procedure is simple:

1. Choose <u>V</u>iew, <u>C</u>ustomize This Folder.

2. Select the <u>R</u>emove Customization option and then click the <u>N</u>ext button.

3. A dialog box appears, warning you that you're about to delete FOLDER.HTT and remove custom settings from DESKTOP.INI. Click <u>N</u>ext to continue.

4. Click Finish to close the wizard. You'll see the default Web view settings for the current folder.

Advanced Customization Options

A skilled HTML author can perform an unlimited amount of customization. As you learned earlier, you can create your own hypertext template file, giving it any name. Store it in the folder you want to customize, open DESKTOP.INI, and enter the name of your custom HTML file after the `PersistentMoniker=` entry.

Tip #54

Remember, bothDESKTOP.INI and FOLDER.HTT are hidden files. To edit either one without using the wizard, you may need to adjust Explorer's options to show hidden files.

➔ **See** "Changing the Appearance of a Folder's Contents," **p. 84.**

Although most users specify an HTML file in DESKTOP.INI, you have the option of calling out a Web page in this file. This option is not officially supported, but it works just the same. You can point a folder to a page on the Internet or your intranet. The effect is a bit baffling: Although the Address bar displays the name of the folder, the Explorer window shows the Web page listed in DESKTOP.INI.

To use the file list control in a custom Web page, open the default FOLDER.HTT file and copy the file list code to the Clipboard. Then, paste the code into your custom HTML document. Look for this block of code:

```
<object
classid="clsid:1820FED0-473E-11D0-A96C-00C04FD705A2">
</object>
```

You also might have to add a Position statement to place the control where you want it to appear on the page.

Troubleshooting

Problems with the Thumbnail View

I've turned on Web view, but I can't see a thumbnail view in some folders.

The Folder window you're using may be too small. Maximize the folder and see whether thumbnails appear. When you restore the drive or folder to a window, try resizing it, watching the changes in Web view as the window decreases in size. The banner along the top becomes more compact, and the thumbnail viewer goes away when the window reaches a certain size.

SECRETS OF MASTERING THE WINDOWS 98 ENVIRONMENT: CREATE AND CUSTOMIZE A USER-DEFINED TOOLBAR IN WINDOWS 98

One neat feature many users don't know about is the ability to create a custom toolbar with their favorite shortcuts and folders. The nice thing about this feature is that it allows further integration between the Web style interface and the Classic interface available in the Folder Options dialog box. Your custom toolbar can be displayed on the taskbar or as a free-form toolbar on the desktop.

To create your user-defined toolbar:

1. Create a new folder to hold the contents of your new toolbar. (To create a folder, right-click on the desktop, choose New, click Folder, type a name for the folder such as `Mary's Toolbar`, and then press Enter.

2. Copy the items you want on your toolbar to the folder you made in step 1. Include shortcuts, frequently accessed folders, even shortcuts to Web pages.

3. Right-click the taskbar (where your Start menu resides), Choose Toolbars, click New Toolbar.

4. Browse to the folder you created in step 1, choose the new folder, and then click OK.

5. Restart your computer.(Your new toolbar is visible before you restart your computer; however, the toolbar creation process is not complete until you restart.)

To customize or close your new toolbar, right-click the toolbar and choose the appropriate selection from the menu. You may want to remove the folder name label associated with your toolbar by right-clicking your toolbar and then clicking Show Text to remove the check mark.

To add an item to your custom toolbar, drag the item to the toolbar or add the new item to your custom toolbar folder. To remove an item, drag it off the toolbar or remove it from your custom toolbar folder.

To make your custom toolbar a free-form toolbar on the desktop, click on the left portion of the custom toolbar on the taskbar and drag it to a new location on your desktop. This feature is a great way to organize and manage shortcuts and folders without cluttering the desktop with free-standing shortcuts. It's also a great way to organize multiple users on one PC by giving each user a custom toolbar of shortcuts that he or she can drag and drop to any desired location.

CHAPTER **9**

WORKING WITH DISKS AND DRIVES

In this chapter

One of the oldest relics of DOS that has been retained in Windows 98 is the way that the operating system handles its local disk storage. The *File Allocation Table (FAT)* file system and the use of drive letters to represent the disk drives installed in the computer are unchanged from earlier versions of DOS.

However, Windows 98 has not stood idle in this respect. The capacity of hard disk drives has grown more rapidly than virtually any other area of computing technology. Also, new types of storage devices, such as CD-ROM and removable cartridge drives, are becoming standard equipment on new systems. Windows 98 supports today's large capacity drives, as well as a wide range of other storage devices.

> **Note**
>
> This chapter assumes that the hardware in your system has already been correctly installed and configured and is ready to access.
>
> → For help on installing hardware in your system, **see** "Using the Add New Hardware Wizard," **p. 434.**
>
> → For information on hardware configuration, **see** "How Windows 98 Works with Hardware," **p. 418.**
>
> → If you are having problems accessing disk drives or other devices, **see** "Troubleshooting Common Problems," **p. 470.**

WINDOWS 98 AND LOCAL MEDIA

The steady rise in capacity and sophistication of the local storage devices in the typical PC has forced operating systems to change to keep up with the technology. Most new systems today are equipped with a CD-ROM drive in addition to the standard floppy and hard disk drives. Many are also shipping with a removable cartridge drive, usually an Iomega zip drive, as standard equipment.

In addition, the capacity of the typical hard disk drive has skyrocketed to the point at which drives holding from 2 to 6 gigabytes or more are common, even on entry-level machines. Windows 98 supports a wide array of storage devices, and yet it maintains the familiar drive access paradigms at the Windows command line and in the graphical interface.

FLOPPY DRIVES

The floppy disk drive was the original storage medium for the personal computer. At one time most users ran their applications directly from floppies; the lucky users had a second floppy drive on which to store their data. Today, as a software distribution medium, the floppy disk is virtually obsolete because of its limited capacity and the size of current applications.

As a case in point, the core Windows 98 installation files would require more than 70 floppy disks, and even that number would be higher if Microsoft didn't use a special format to store 1.7 megabytes on each disk. When compared to a single CD-ROM that can store much more data and be produced much more cheaply, the choice is obvious.

As demonstrated by Microsoft, the physical disk can be formatted to a greater capacity, but the format is a proprietary read-only one that is designed primarily to inhibit the copying of disks. IBM introduced a 2.88-megabyte floppy disk drive standard in 1991, but like many IBM innovations, it never caught on with other manufacturers.

All DOS and Windows operating systems reserve the drive letters A: and B: for floppy disk drives. Today, floppy drives serve primarily as an alternative boot device in case of a hard drive failure. Most systems are configured to boot from the floppy if a disk is present in the drive, which is why the Windows 98 installation process requires that you create an emergency startup disk.

→ Chapter 2, "Starting and Quitting Windows 98," contains more information on creating a startup disk.

HARD DISK DRIVES

Hard diskdrives are, of course, the core of a PC's data storage subsystem. Hard drives usually offer the greatest capacity and the highest speed of any storage medium in the machine. To keep up with ever larger applications and data files, hard drives have had to become faster and more capacious at an incredible rate. At the same time, the price of hard disk storage has plummeted: A 1-gigabyte drive that sold for $2000 in the early 1990s can now be had for less than $200.

This need for increasingly larger hard drives has resulted in serious inefficiencies when they are used with legacy file systems such as FAT16, which was originally developed for use with DOS. Windows 98 addresses these problems with a new file system, FAT32, that makes it possible to use large hard disk drives more efficiently.

The large capacityof today's drives and the limitations imposed by existing file systems often make it necessary for users to divide hard disk drives into separate partitions. A *partition* is a portion of a hard disk that is devoted to exclusive use by a specific file system. When you create multiple partitions on a single disk and all are compatible with Windows 98, the operating system uses a different drive letter to access each partition.

> **Note**
>
> In a technical sense, a hard disk storage device consists of the disk itself, which takes the form of a stack of platters, and the drive that spins the platters and moves the heads to the appropriate position. However, DOS and Windows users commonly use the word *drive* to refer to a logical drive, represented by a letter that the operating system assigns to a partition as it is accessed. Thus, you might hear people refer to the physical device as a *hard disk* or as a *hard drive*, meaning that although a unit has only one mechanical drive, that unit may in fact have several partitions and, therefore, several logical drives.

You can also create partitions for different file systems on the same disk. You can, for example, create one FAT32 partition for use with Windows 98 and another *NT File System (NTFS)* partition for use with Windows NT. However, to access a partition, you must load an operating system that supports its file system. In this example each operating system can access its own partition but not the other partition because Windows NT doesn't natively support FAT32 and Windows 98 doesn't support NTFS. If you used FAT16 instead of FAT32, however, Windows NT could access both partitions.

When a partition is not supported by an operating system, it is effectively invisible. In the example just presented, each operating system mounts its own partition as the C: drive, no matter where each partition is physically located on the disk. Each operating system has its own function or utility for creating partitions on hard drives. NetWare, OS/2, and other operating systems have their own file systems.

CD-ROM DRIVES

In a very short time, theCD-ROM drive has become an almost ubiquitous part of the average PC configuration. Because most applications and operating systems are now distributed on CD, a CD-ROM drive is essential on a standalone system. On business networks, CD-ROM drives tend to be less prevalent because software can be installed and distributed over the network.

Originally, CD-ROM drives were limited to use with a small computer system interface (SCSI) subsystem, which made them more costly and difficult to configure. However, the adoption of the *enhanced integrated drive electronics (EIDE)* interface has enabled CD-ROM drives to share the host adapter used by the EIDE hard drives that are typically found in desktop PCs.

For a CD-ROM drive to operate on an EIDE interface, the device must be supported by the system basic input/output system *(BIOS) (page xxx)*, just like the hard disk and floppy drives. This support allows the CD-ROM to be used as a boot device, simplifying the installation of operating systems onto new systems.

Note

For older systems that do not have BIOS support for EIDE devices, you can purchase an expansion card that effectively replaces the system BIOS and permits the connect of additional devices such as CD-ROM drives.

When Windows 98 detects a CD-ROM drive on the system during the installation process, it accesses the disk using the next available drive letter after the floppy drive and hard disk partitions. You can access files on the CD-ROM using Windows Explorer or the My Computer window just as you would access files on a floppy or a hard drive—except of course that the CD-ROM is a read-only medium.

Note

Writeable CD-ROM drives are now available at reasonable prices, along with software that enables you to write to the disk by dragging and dropping files in Windows Explorer. These are known as *write-once/read-many, or WORM*, devices. In addition, rewriteable CD-ROM drives are now on the market, but the disks that they create are not readable by standard read-only drives.

REMOVABLE CARTRIDGE DRIVES

Although the technology has been available for many years, rewriteable, removable, magneto-optical cartridge drives are becoming increasingly popular options on desktop PCs. Many desktop systems aimed at the home consumer market now include a cartridge drive as standard equipment.

The Iomega zip drive is rapidly becoming a *de facto* standard for removable data storage. To their advantage, the drive and the media are both inexpensive, their proliferation makes it easy for users to exchange files, and their 100-megabyte capacity makes them a more practical alternative than floppy disks.

PART
II
CH
9

Iomega also produces higher-capacity cartridge drives, such as the JAZ drive, available inboth 1-gigabyte and 2-gigabyte versions. These devices rival hard drives in terms of speed and flexibility. Cartridge drives can use the EIDE, SCSI, or USB interface to connect to the system. Models that connect through the computer's parallel port are especially easy to move from system to system.

Like the other drive types discussed in this section, Windows 98 accesses cartridge drives with a standard drive letter. Larger capacity drives, such as the JAZ, even support the creation of multiple partitions, enabling you to use them just like hard disk drives.

However, using multiple partitions on removable media can cause a rearrangement of the system's assigned drive letters, depending on how many partitions exist on a particular cartridge. The drive letter of a CD-ROM mounted after a removable drive changes, for example, depends on the number of DOS partitions on the cartridge that is currently loaded. You can avoid this problem by configuring Windows 98 to permanently assign drive letters to specific devices. To do so, open the System Control Panel and select the Device Manager tab. Open the Properties dialog box for the removable device, click the Settings tab, and select a range of drive letters. After you reboot the system, those letters will never be assigned to another device.

DVD DRIVES

Various manufacturers continue to develop new types of storage devices for use with PCs, hoping to see their product become a standard in the way the zip drive has. The most promising of these devices is the *DVD* drive.

Originally named the *Digital Video Disk*, the device is now often called the *Digital Video Display Disk* because of its adaptation for use on computers. The DVD medium looks just like a CD-ROM except that the former has two sides, and each side can have two separate layers. By adjusting the focus of the laser that reads the disk, the device can read a separate data stream on each of the layers on each side. This technology increases the potential capacity of the disk enormously.

DVD was originally intended as a read-only video transport medium. It used *MPEG-2* compression to store more than two hours of video plus high-quality audio and other material on a single disk. Movies are already becoming available on DVD, and many PC vendors are offering the drives on their high-end systems.

As a data storage medium, DVD has great potential for use in the PC world, but it's still too early to gauge its success. A ratified standard does not yet exist for the technology, and a recordable version of DVD is currently in development, which could end up replacing the read-only version in general use.

Tip #55	The Windows 98 DVD Players are designed to work with the Windows 98 decoder drivers. To add or remove the DVD Player, a supported DVD decoder adapter must be installed and detected by the operating system.
	After a supported DVD decoder adapter is detected and the Windows 98 drivers are installed, a shortcut for DVD Player is added to the Entertainment menu, and the option to add or remove DVD Player becomes available under Multimedia on the Windows Setup tab in the Add/Remove Programs tool. After installation the DVD Player software can be removed and reinstalled without having to reinstall the decoder drivers.

UNDERSTANDING DISK PARTITIONS

To view, create, and manage a disk drive's DOS partition table in Windows 98, you use a program called *FDISK*. FDISK is a command-line utility inherited from DOS that has changed little in appearance over the years. The primary difference in the Windows 98 version of FDISK is its capability to create partitions using the new FAT32 file system.

Note

FAT32 was actually introduced in the OEM Service Release 2 of Windows 95, but Windows 98 fully integrates it into the operating system by enabling you to convert existing FAT16 partitions to FAT32.

Under Windows 98, no matter which FAT file system you use, the partitions that FDISK creates on a disk drive are referred to as DOS partitions. FDISK creates a partition table on the drive in the *master partition boot sector*, which is the first sector on the drive. This table lists the locations of the other *partition boot sectors* on the drive. Each partition boot sector precedes the section of the disk that has been allocated for that partition.

Each partition boot sector contains information that defines the size and nature of a particular partition. The partition boot sectors and the master partition boot sector are strictly DOS conventions. Other non-DOS file systems create their own partitions and have their own methods of allocating space on a drive.

Note

All Windows 98 hard disks and some types of removable disks have a master partition boot sector and one or more partition boot sectors. Floppy disks, however, do not have these and, as a result, cannot contain multiple partitions.

Since DOS 3.3, it has been possible to create multiple DOS partitions on a single hard disk. The first partition that you create is called the *primary DOS partition*, and any others are called *extended DOS partitions*. In contrast, some other file systems (such as NetWare's) allow you to create only one partition of that type per disk.

As long as it has sufficient capacity, you can use one hard disk drive to boot several different operating systems, each of which uses its own file system. You can create DOS partitions of any size, leaving unallocated space on the disk, and then use the partitioning utility from another operating system to create partitions for a different file system in that empty space.

Each area of a hard disk that is allocated as a DOS partition by the partition boot sectors begins with a *DOS volume boot sector*. After you make a particular DOS partition *active* (or bootable) with FDISK and you install the DOS, Windows 95, or Windows 98 system files on it, the system BIOS passes control of the machine to that partition's DOS volume boot sector each time the system starts. Then, the code in the DOS volume boot sector runs and attempts to load the system file IO.SYS from the root directory of the partition. If IO.SYS is not found, the boot fails.

Note

Because floppy disks have no partition boot sectors, the DOS volume boot sector always goes on the first sectors of the disk. That enables the floppy to function as a boot device just like a hard drive. The system BIOS is the item that determines whether control of the machine should pass to the floppy drive or to the active partition on the hard disk.

USING FDISK

To create DOS partitions on a hard disk, you must run the FDISK utility from the DOS command prompt. You can run FDISK from a Windows 98 DOS session, but only if you do not intend to work with the currently active partition. Obviously, if you destroy the partition containing the system files and operating system the computer is currently using, the system will halt as soon as you exit FDISK.

After you create a partition, exit FDISK, and reboot the system, you will find that the system has assigned a drive letter to the new partition. You can switch to that drive letter from the DOS prompt, but you cannot read from it or write to it because the drive has not yet been formatted. You must use the FORMAT utility from the command line, Windows Explorer, or the My Computer window to format the drive before you can use it to store data.

In most cases the best way to run FDISK is from a boot floppy so that you can continue to access the machine even if the hard disk has no partitions. You can create a Windows 98 startup disk by launching Add/Remove Programs from the Control Panel, selecting the Startup Disk tab (see Figure 9.1), and following the instructions you find there.

Figure 9.1
A Windows 98
startup disk contains
all the tools you need
to boot the system
and partition and to
format its hard disks.

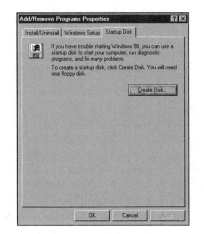

The Windows 98 startup disk includes the system files needed to boot the computer to the DOS prompt, as well as the FDISK and FORMAT utilities you need to prepare the hard disk for a full Windows 98 installation.

If your system contains a hard disk drive with a capacity greater than 512 megabytes, Windows displays the following message when you run FDISK:

```
Your computer has a disk larger than 512 MB. This version of Windows
includes improved support for large disks, resulting in more efficient
use of disk space on large drives, and allowing disks over 2 GB to be
formatted as a single drive.

IMPORTANT: If you enable large disk support and create any new drives on this
disk, you will not be able to access the new drive(s) using other operating
systems, including some versions of Windows 95 and Windows NT, as well as
earlier versions of Windows and MS-DOS. In addition, disk utilities that
were not designed explicitly for the FAT32 file system will not be able
to work with this disk. If you need to access this disk with other operating
systems or older disk utilities, do not enable large drive support.

Do you wish to enable large disk support (Y/N)..........? [N]
```

Your response to this question determines whether or not FDISK will create FAT32 partitions on your hard disks. Under normal circumstances, drives with a capacity of less than 512 megabytes cannot use FAT32. On the other hand, if you have a large capacity drive and want to create a partition larger than 2 gigabytes, you must use FAT32. Otherwise, see "Choosing a File System," later in this chapter, for information that can help you decide whether or not you should use FAT32. This initial screen is the only indicator that the Windows 98 version of FDISK provides support for FAT32. The screens that follow are the same, whether or not you enable large-disk support.

The main FDISK screen displays the following information:

```
                    Microsoft Windows 98
                  Fixed Disk Setup Program
```

```
                    (C)Copyright Microsoft Corp. 1983 - 1998

                              FDISK Options

      Current fixed disk drive: 1

      Choose one of the following:

      1. Create DOS partition or Logical DOS Drive
      2. Set active partition
      3. Delete partition or Logical DOS Drive
      4. Display partition information
      5. Change current fixed disk drive

      Enter choice: [1]
```

The following sections provide details about each FDISK option.

CREATING PARTITIONS

Whenyou select the Create DOS Partition or Logical DOS Drive option, FDISK presents
the following options for creating a new partition on the selected hard disk:

```
Create DOS Partition or Logical DOS Drive

   Current fixed disk drive: 1

   Choose one of the following:

   1. Create Primary DOS Partition
   2. Create Extended DOS Partition
   3. Create Logical DOS Drive(s) in the Extended DOS Partition

   Enter choice: [1]
```

If the disk currently has no DOS partitions, you must first create a primary DOS partition.
If the disk already has a primary DOS partitionand still has unallocated space, you can create an extended DOS partition. Finally, if the disk already has an extended DOS partition
and you want to divide it into two drive letters, you can create logical DOS drives in the
extended partition.

When you create a new partition, FDISK first asks you whether you want to use all the
space available on the disk and make the partition active. This setting enables you to create
the most common partition configuration in one step. If you say no, you are prompted to
specify the size of the new partition in megabytes. Alternatively, you can specify a size as a
percentage of the available free space by including the percent symbol (%) after the value.

FDISK also prompts you to specify a volume label for the partition. This label can contain
up to 11 numbers or letters used to identify the partition. Windows Explorer and the My
Computer window display the volume label along with the drive letter for each local drive
on the system.

Tip #56

Another dual-booting issue between Windows 98 and Windows NT may occur when Windows 98 is installed as the primary desktop operating system and you decide to load Windows NT as the secondary operating system. During the installation of Windows NT, Setup might not correctly detect partitions created and formatted by Windows 98 Fdisk.exe. This situation develops when the partition created is larger than 8 gigabytes. The only real solution is to plan ahead and restrict partition size to less that 8 gigabytes.

MAKING A PARTITION ACTIVE

After you create a partition on your system's first or only hard disk, you will probably want to make that partition active so the system can boot from it. When you choose the Set Active Partition option, you are prompted to select the partition to hold the system boot files. Only one DOS partition on your computer can be active.

Making a partition active does not in itself make the disk bootable. It only means that the BIOS turns over control of the system to that partition at boot time. To make the disk bootable, you must also place the system boot files on that partition by formatting the drive with the system files option or by using the SYS utility.

DELETING PARTITIONS

If you select the Delete Partition or Logical DOS Drive option from FDISK's main screen, Windows displays a list of the partitions and logical drives on the selected disk. This list includes all the DOS partition types, as well as partitions created by other file systems (which are identified as non-DOS partitions).

Deleting a partition is always a big step that should cause you to stop and carefully consider your actions. Deleting a partition destroys all the data that is currently stored there and, in the case of an active partition, the system boot files as well. FDISK repeatedly prompts you to confirm your actions before it deletes the partition, including a requirement that you enter the volume name of the partition to be deleted. This safeguard virtually ensures that entering a random series of accidental keystrokes cannot cause you to lose your data.

Obviously, you must back up any important data before you delete the partition in which the data resides. You also need a means of booting your system after the partition is gone. If you delete the active partition, you must have a boot floppy disk, such as a Windows 98 startup disk, to restart the system.

Caution

Many of the personal computers sold today use a small non-DOS partition to store a configuration program for the system BIOS. This program is activated when you press a particular key combination during the system boot process (the exact key combination depends on the BIOS manufacturer). Be sure not to delete this partition unless you are certain that you have the configuration program on some other medium. Otherwise, you might be unable to access the information in the BIOS.

DISPLAYING PARTITION INFORMATION

When you choose the Display Partition Information option, you see a list of all the partitions on the selected disk. The list should look similar to this one:

```
Display Partition Information

Current fixed disk drive: 1

Partition  Status   Type    Volume Label  Mbytes  System  Usage
   C: 1       A     PRI DOS   DRIVE1        2014   FAT32   100%

Total disk space is  2014 Mbytes (1 Mbyte = 1048576 bytes)
```

This example shows that fixed disk drive 1 contains a single 2,014-megabyte partition that constitutes 100% of the space on the disk. This partition is a primary DOS partition that has been set as active and uses the FAT32 file system. FDISK has assigned the drive letter C: and the volume label DRIVE1 to this partition.

FDISK is a program that many people look upon with fear and trepidation because of the catastrophic damage that can result from accidental or improper use. The Display Partition Information option is totally safe, however, because none of the controls on this screen can affect the state of the disk.

CHANGING THE CURRENT FIXED DISK DRIVE

FDISK offers the Change Current Fixed Disk Drive option on its main screen only after detecting more than one supported disk drive in the system. FDISK can address only one drive at a time and defaults to the first drive in the system BIOS. To manage the partitions on the system's other disks, you must first use this option to select the desired drive.

Selecting the option displays a list similar to the following list that outlines the disk drives in the system along with their disk numbers, partitions, drive letters, sizes, and the percentage of the disk occupied by each:

```
Change Current Fixed Disk Drive

   Disk   Drv   Mbytes   Free   Usage
    1            2014            100%
           C:    2014
    2            2014      2     100%
           D:    2012
```

To change to another disk, you select it by specifying the disk number shown in the first column. When you select another disk drive, it becomes the default for all other FDISK functions until you change the disk drive again or exit the program. Most of the other screens contain a line that specifies the number of the disk that the program is currently addressing.

FORMATTING DISKS

When you create one or more DOS partitions on a hard disk, you must format them before you can use them to store data. The formatting process divides a partition into clusters. A *cluster* is a logical unit that represents the smallest amount of disk space that can be allocated at one time. A disk-formatting program determines the size of the clusters to be created, based on the size of the partition, and creates an entry in the FAT for each cluster. Windows 98 includes the character-based real-mode FORMAT program inherited from DOS, as well as protected-mode GUI alternatives in Windows Explorer and the My Computer window.

Tip #57	You must reboot your system after creating a partition and before formatting it. The Windows 98 version of FDISK does not reboot the system automatically after it creates a partition, as some previous versions do.

FORMATTING FROM THE COMMAND LINE

The Windows 98 FORMAT.EXE program operates from the DOS command line and provides more options than the GUI formatting utility does. The program has all the switches from previous versions of the utility that were included with DOS, although many of these switches are obsolete unless you are using older floppy disk types. Despite the program's similarity to previous versions, however, it is imperative that you use the Windows 98 FORMAT program on disks with FAT32 partitions.

The syntax for FORMAT is as follows:

```
FORMAT drive: [/V:label][/S][/B][/Q][/C]
```

These are the switches:

drive:	The variable *drive* is replaced by the drive letter of the disk to be formatted.
/V[:label]	The /V switch specifies the volume label that is to be assigned to the disk being formatted, where *label* is replaced by a string of up to eleven characters.
/S	The /S switch causes the program to write the system boot files to the specified disk after the formatting process.
/B	The /B switch causes the program to reserve sufficient space on the formatted disk for the later addition of system boot files.
/Q	The /Q switch causes the program to perform a quick format on the selected disk by overwriting its FAT table. This removes all references in the FAT table to the existing files on the disk, but does not check the clusters for damage. You can perform a quick format only on a disk that has already been formatted.
/C	The /C switch causes the program to test the clusters on the disk that have already been marked as "bad" by a previous format.

In most cases, no switches are needed with FORMAT except for a drive letter and possibly /S to create a boot disk. Other switches for FORMAT, which are now seldom needed, are appended to the syntax in this order:

```
[/F:size][/T:tracks][/N:sectors][/1][/4][/8]
```

Those switches function as described here:

/F:size	The /F switch specifies capacity of the floppy disk to be formatted, where size is replaced by a value in kilobytes or megabytes, such as 160, 180, 320, 360, 720, 1.2, 1.44, or 2.88). This switch is not needed when formatting standard 1.44-megabyte 3.5-inch floppies.
/T:tracks	The /T switch enables you to specify the number of tracks on each side of the floppy disk to be formatted.
/N:sectors	The /N switch enables you to specify the number of sectors on each track of the floppy disk to be formatted.
/1	The /1 switch causes the program to format one side of a floppy disk.
/4	The /4 switch causes the program to format a 5.25-inch 360K floppy disk in a 1.2-megabyte high-density drive.
/8	The /8 switch causes the program to format a floppy disk with eight sectors per track.

PART II
CH
9

In addition, an undocumented switch for the Windows 98 version of FORMAT enables you to specify the cluster size used to format a given partition. When you run FORMAT with the /Z:n switch, where n multiplied by 512 represents the cluster size in bytes, you can override the cluster size that is normally determined by the size of the partition.

Caution

The /Z switch is a powerful option that is not recommended for use on production systems without extensive testing. The switch does not override the 65,536 cluster limit on FAT16 drives, so it should generally be used only with FAT32. Specifying a smaller than normal cluster size may reduce the amount of disk space wasted by partially filled clusters, but it can also create enormously large FATs that severely affect the performance of the file system.

GUI FORMATTING

Windows 98 also includes a GUI-based formatting utility. To access it, right-click on a drive letter in Windows Explorer or the My Computer window and select Format from the context menu. Windows displays the dialog box shown in Figure 9.2.

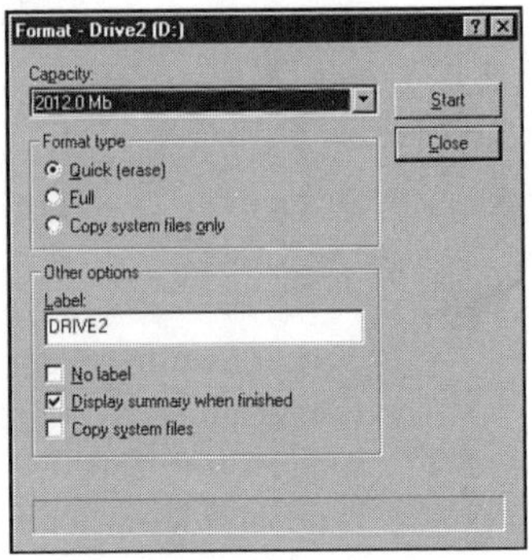

Figure 9.2
The Windows 98 GUI disk-formatting utility provides access to the same major options found in the command-line FORMAT program.

In the Format dialog box, you can select the capacity of the disk to be formatted and the type of format (quick, full, full with system files, or system files only). You can also specify a volume label for the disk. The utility does not allow you to format the hard disk drive where the Windows 98 operating system files are stored and prompts you to confirm your actions before it destroys any files on a disk that has already been formatted.

CREATING A BOOTABLE DISK

When you elect to include the system files during a format by using the /S switch with the FORMAT program or by activating the Copy System Files check box in the Format dialog box, the following boot files are written to the disk after the formatting process is complete:

- IO.SYS—Primary Windows 98 boot file
- MSDOS.SYS—Windows 98 operating system configuration file
- DRVSPACE.BIN—DriveSpace compression support files
- COMMAND.COM—Windows 98 command processor

The first three files are flagged with the system attribute, which you must remove before you can delete them. COMMAND.COM functions as a normal executable and is launched whenever you open a DOS session from the Windows 98 GUI. Together, these four files occupy 393,728 bytes, which is a substantial amount of space on a floppy disk. Unlike the boot sector and the FATs, which reside outside the disk area that is visible to the operating system, the system boot files are visible and can be manipulated by conventional means. However, such manipulation can damage the disk's capability to boot the system.

During boot time, the system BIOS in nearly all PCs is configured to check the first floppy drive for the presence of a disk containing system boot files. Therefore, you can use any floppy disk containing those files to boot the system by inserting it into the A: drive. On a hard disk drive, however, the mere presence of the system boot files on the disk is not sufficient to boot the system. You must also configure the partition containing those files to be active, as detailed in the section "Making a Partition Active," earlier in this chapter.

CHOOSING A FILE SYSTEM

In addition to its partition boot sector and its DOS volume boot sector, each DOS partition also contains two copies of its *FAT (pages 11, 21, 155)*. TheFAT is a matrix that correlates the files and folders stored in the partition with their physical locations on the hard disk. Two consecutive copies of the FAT are stored in the disk area before each partition. Like the boot sectors, the FATs are stored outside the disk area that is visible to the file system.

Note

Although the data structures that make up a partition's boot sectors and FAT tables cannot be displayed or manipulated by the standard Windows 98 file management utilities like Windows Explorer, they are not inaccessible. Many products on the market address disk devices directly instead of through the file system. These products, called *disk editors* or *sector editors*, enable advanced users to manipulate the data in a disk's boot sectors and FATs directly. You should know, however, that with these tools, you can easily and irreparably damage the data on a disk drive. In many cases, professionals use them in a last-ditch effort to recover the data on a drive that has already been damaged by an attempt to manually repair a FAT.

When files are written to a disk, they do not necessarily occupy a contiguous space equivalent to the size of the file. Instead, the files are broken up into *clusters* of a given size (sometimes called *allocation units*), which may be scattered all over the partition. As a result, the FAT is not a list of files and their locations as much as it is a list of the clusters in the partition and their contents. Whenever you accessa file on a given partition, Windows 98 accesses the directory entry for that file, which contains the starting cluster. This cluster points to the entry in the FAT representing the next cluster in the chain. Each successive cluster then points to the next until the entire file is read.

Each entry in the FAT is a 12-, 16-, or 32-bit hexadecimal number, the size of which is determined by the FDISK program—even though FORMAT actually creates the entries. All floppy disks and hard disk volumes smaller than 16 megabytes use 12-bit FAT entries. Hard disks and removable disks with volumes that are 16 megabytes or larger typically use 16-bit entries, but a volume larger than 512 megabytes can now use the Windows 98 FAT32 file system and 32-bit FAT entries.

The size of the clusters on a given partition is determined during its creation by the size of the partition that you specify in the FDISK program. The intent is to strike a balance between the number of clusters listed in the FAT and the size of those clusters. This need for balance is the source of the FAT file system's biggest problem—a problem that is addressed by the new FAT32 file system. FAT32 does not completely resolve the problem, but it does provide a greater flexibility of solutions.

Obviously, the smaller the clusters on a partition, the more clusters that partition can hold. The more clusters on a partition, the larger the FAT table must be and the longer it takes for the operating system to search the table for the information it needs to access a file. On the contrary, when you create larger clusters, the FAT table becomes smaller and more manageable, but you also increase the amount of disk space wasted by clusters that are only partially filled.

CLUSTER SIZE AND SLACK SPACE

A file canbe of almost any size, but Windows 98 splits the file into a series of uniform clusters when writing the file to disk. The result is that the last cluster is almost never an exact fit. The tail end of the file is written to the last cluster, and the remainder of that cluster stays empty (see Figure 9.3). This slack space is wasted as long as the file remains on the disk.

Figure 9.3
Because the FAT file system divides the disk into clusters of uniform size, disk space is wasted whenever a cluster is not completely filled with data.

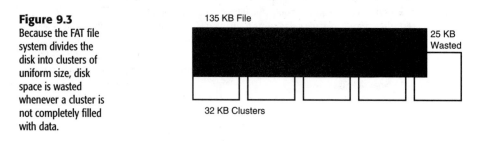

135 KB File

25 KB Wasted

32 KB Clusters

How much partition space is wasted is determined by the relationship between the size of the clusters and the size of the files. If, for example, you have large files and small clusters, relatively little space is wasted. However, the combination of small files and large clusters (a more common occurrence) produces the exact opposite effect. For example, when you store a large number of 10-kilobyte files on a partition with 32-kilobyte clusters, more than two-thirds of the allocated disk space is wasted.

FAT16 AND HARD DISK EXPANSION

Although theproblem of disk space being wasted by partially filled clusters is as old as the FAT file system, it was exacerbated to an alarming degree by the ever-increasing capacity of the typical hard disk drive. As disks and the partitions on them grow larger, the cluster size must also grow to prevent the FAT from becoming too big. FDISK uses the following cluster sizes for FAT16 partitions of various sizes:

Partition Size	Cluster Size
128MB	2KB
256MB	4KB
512MB	8KB
1GB	16KB
2GB	32KB

Because the FAT16 file system can support only 65,526 clusters, the largest partition it can support is just under 2 gigabytes. (65,526 32-kilobyte clusters equals 2,096,832 kilobytes or 2,047.6875 megabytes.)

> **Caution**
>
> FDISK uses the literal definitions of kilobyte and megabyte. That is, 1 kilobyte equals 1,024 bytes, and 1 megabyte equals 1,024 kilobytes or 1,048,576 bytes. Some hardware vendors have been known to make their drive capacities seem larger by defining a kilobyte as 1,000 bytes and a megabyte as 1,000 kilobytes or 1,000,000 bytes. Be sure to take this possibility into account when you are trying to create partitions with a particular cluster size.

INTRODUCING FAT32

When you purchase a new PC today, it is not uncommon for the machine to be equipped with a hard disk drive holding 6 or 8 gigabytes or more. The primary reason for FAT32's existence is to prevent users from having to divide a device that large into three or more separate partitions. FAT32 can support drives holding up to 2 terabytes of data (1 terabyte equals 1,024 gigabytes) and single files up to nearly 4 gigabytes, so it is likely to remain a viable tool for some time to come.

At the same time, FAT32 eliminates the file allocation table's 65,536 cluster limit, making it possible to use smaller clusters than FAT16 partitions of the same size can use. This practice results in many more clusters and a larger FAT, but FAT32 can also dramatically reduce the amount of space wasted by partially filled clusters. FAT32 partitions of various sizes use the following default cluster sizes:

Partition Size	Cluster Size
Less than 260MB	512 bytes
260MB–8GB	4KB
8GB–16GB	8KB
16GB–32GB	16KB
Greater than 32GB	32KB

Thus, with most of the hard disk drives on the market today, you can create a single FAT32 partition that uses 4-kilobyte clusters. The FAT for a 2-gigabyte drive would therefore contain 524,288 entries using FAT32, as opposed to 65,536 entries with FAT16. This might seem like a great increase in FAT processing overhead, but hard drive speeds have also increased significantly since FAT16 was developed. In most cases, converting a FAT16 drive to FAT32 does not bring about a palpable decrease in performance; some systems might even experience a notable increase in performance. In nearly every case, however, a FAT32 conversion reclaims a significant amount of disk space, often as much as 10% to 20% of the disk's capacity, although results vary widely and depend on the size of the files.

DUPLICATE FATS

FAT32 alsoincludes other improvements besides larger partitions and smaller clusters. Since its inception, the FAT file system has always used two identical file allocation tables for each partition. The two FATs are written consecutively in a contiguous area of the disk just before the beginning of the partition itself. During normal operations, the operating system updates the second FAT by copying data from the first on a regular basis.

FAT16, however, takes very little advantage of this redundancy. A FAT16 file system will use the second copy of the FAT if damaged disk sectors prevent access to the first copy, but does not access the second copy of the data if the first simply becomes corrupted. In fact, the file system is far more likely to continue to update the second FAT, overwriting it with the corrupted data from the first copy. Some third-party disk utilities can take advantage of the second FAT and use it to repair the first, but only if they perform the repair operation before the second FAT has been damaged, too.

FAT32 takes greater advantage of the two FAT copies. In any situation in which the file system finds the data in the primary copy of the FAT to be unreadable, it switches to the secondary FAT, which then becomes the primary. This approach is in direct contrast to FAT16, in which the first FAT is always the primary. In addition, FAT32 provides greater control over the FAT mirroring process. The file system can temporarily disable the process by which the data from one FAT is replicated to the other.

The modification in the behavior of the FATs results in a greater degree of fault tolerance—without the need to interrupt system operations and apply third-party utilities.

FAT32 AND SMALL PARTITIONS

Despite the first entry in the cluster size table (shown earlier, in the section "Introducing FAT32"), the Windows 98 FDISK utility in its default configuration does not create FAT32 partitions smaller than 512 megabytes. Indeed, when it detects a drive smaller than 512 megabytes, it does not even present the option to enable support for large drives.

However, certain third-party products on the market, such as Partition Magic 3.0, enable you to convert FAT16 partitions smaller than 512 megabytes to FAT32. In addition, an undocumented switch for FDISK enables you to create new FAT32 partitions smaller than 512 megabytes. By running FDISK with the /FPRMT parameter, you can specify a FAT32 partition size smaller than 512 megabytes.

Caution

FDISK's /FPRMT parameter has not been rigorously tested and should not be used on disks containing vital data. Because hard disk drives smaller than 512 megabytes are becoming an increasingly rare sight, the compatibility of these drives with FAT32 should not be a major issue. In addition, because a 512-megabyte drive with a FAT16 partition already uses 8-kilobyte clusters, the savings realized by FAT32 are not as dramatic as they would be on a larger drive.

FAT32 TOOLS

After you enable large-disk support in FDISK, the rest of the program functions identically with both FAT16 and FAT32 partitions. To verify that a partition you have created is using FAT32, you can either use the Display Partition Information option on FDISK's main screen or right-click a drive letter in Windows Explorer or the My Computer window and choose Properties from the context menu. In either case, the display should show the selected drive as using the FAT32 file system (see Figure 9.4).

Figure 9.4
The Properties dialog box for a hard disk drive identifies the file system that was used to create the partition.

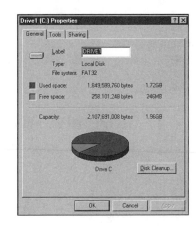

Because FAT32 operates at the file system level, it does not have compatibility problems with most applications (whether they are shrink-wrapped or custom written). The sole exception to this is a type of application that addresses the storage devices directly, such as disk utilities and some antivirus products.

> **Caution**
>
> Disk tools designed for use with the FAT16 file system, such as sector editors, disk repair tools, and defragmenters, should absolutely not be used on FAT32 drives. These tools have the potential to cause serious damage, including the loss of data, to the partition.

Windows 98 includes new versions of ScanDisk and Defrag, in both real and protected mode, that are designed to work with FAT32. If you are familiar with the functionality of ScanDisk, you'll easily understand how converting a FAT16 drive to FAT32 affects the program's diagnostic process. Whereas the examination of the FATs on a FAT16 drive takes only a few seconds, the larger tables on a FAT32 drive of the same size take longer because of the greater number of entries.

Although the Windows 98 disk utilities are certainly adequate, many users have come to rely on the greater functionality provided by third-party disk-repair and utility products. The manufacturers of these tools have by now released versions of their products that support FAT32 drives. Be sure, however, to verify that a disk utility supports the new file system before you actually use it. Otherwise, you might cause irreparable damage.

FAT32 DRAWBACKS

The primary drawback of FAT32 is unquestionably its incompatibility with previous versions of the DOS and Windows operating systems. FAT32 was originally released as part of the OEM Service Release 2 of Windows 95, but the original Windows 95 release cannot access FAT32 partitions. Likewise, all previous DOS versions and all versions of Windows NT are incompatible with FAT32. Microsoft plans to add support for the file system to the Windows 2000 release, but a FAT32 drive will not be able to serve as a boot device for a Windows 2000 system.

Because of this incompatibility, you cannot configure a system to dual boot Windows 98 and Windows NT or Windows 3.1, using a FAT32 drive to store both operating systems. You can, however, create separate partitions for the two file systems and boot each one from its own drive.

CONVERTING A FAT16 DRIVE TO FAT32

When Microsoft released the FAT32 file system as part of the Windows 95 OEM Service Release 2 product, the only way to use the new system was to delete the existing partitions on a disk drive and create new ones. Obviously, this process resulted in the loss of all of the data and, therefore, the need for a complete backup-and-restore procedure. Windows 98 remedies this problem by providing a FAT32 Conversion Wizard that enables you to preserve your data while gaining the advantages (and disadvantages) of the new file system. You access the wizard by selecting Drive Converter (FAT32) from the Start menu's Programs/Accessories/System Tools group.

The wizard provides information about the new file system and the possible consequences of the conversion. After you select a drive to be converted (see Figure 9.5), the wizard scans the drive for applications that might cause problems with FAT32 and then gives you the chance to remove them before proceeding. The wizard also gives you the opportunity to back up your data with Microsoft Backup and warns you repeatedly about the consequences of your actions, requesting your confirmation before proceeding.

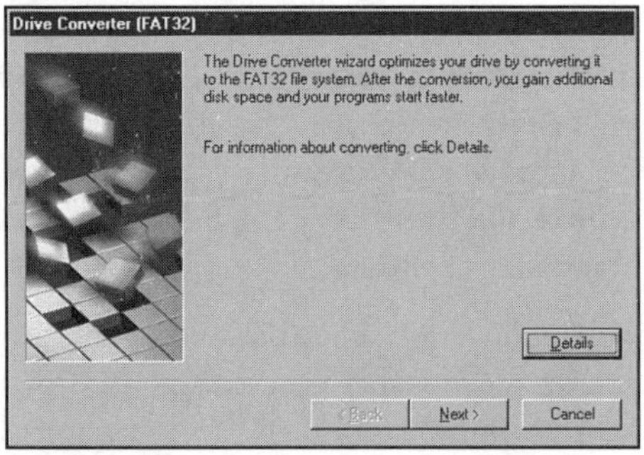

Figure 9.5
The Windows 98 FAT32 converter implements the new file system on selected drives without the need for repartitioning or reformatting.

→ For more of the details on protecting yourself through file backup, **see** "Backing Up Files," **p.186**.

The actual conversion is a DOS process. After you complete the wizard's information and configuration screens, it reboots your system to the DOS prompt. Because the converter must manipulate the existing data on the drive as it creates new clusters, the process can take many times longer than it would to partition and format an empty drive. The length of the conversion process is, of course, dependent on the number and size of the files on your drive, as well as the speed of the device itself. It is not uncommon for FAT32 conversions to take several hours.

The FAT32 conversion is a one-way trip. When it is complete, you cannot return to FAT16 without repartitioning your drive. Therefore, you must carefully consider whether FAT32 is for you before proceeding. If you ever boot your system with operating systems other than Windows 95 OSR2 and Windows 98, be aware that you will not be able to access your FAT32 partitions. In the same way, the Windows 98 DriveSpace compression and disk hibernation features do not function on FAT32 drives.

And, as with any major operation of this type, backups are essential. Make sure that you have a restorable copy of the data before you begin. You should also take whatever steps are possible to ensure that the conversion process completes without interruption. A power failure during the operation might not be avoidable, but you can use common sense precautions like connecting the system to an uninterruptible power supply (UPS) if possible and not converting your disks during a thunderstorm.

COPYING FILES, FOLDERS, AND DISKS

When you havepartitioned and formatted your disks, you can use the standard Windows 98 disk tools to store and manage your files, regardless of which file system you have elected to use. From the drive displays in Windows Explorer and the My Computer window, you can copy files, directories, and entire disks by dragging and dropping them onto other drives or directories.

By default, when you drag a file or directory to another location on the same logical drive, Windows 98 moves that file or directory, deleting it from its original location. When you drag a file or directory to a location on a logical separate drive, Windows 98 copies the file or directory, leaving the original in place.

In addition to the Windows 98 graphical file management tools, you can also use the traditional DOS COPY and XCOPY programs. COPY is an internal DOS command that's designed to copy one or more files to a new location on the same or a different drive. XCOPY is also a holdover from DOS, but it is an external program that's used to copy entire directory trees.

The syntax for COPY is as follows:

```
COPY [/A:[[-]rhsda] /C /E /H /K /M /N /P /Q /R /S /T /U /V /X /Z]
 source[+]...[destination]
```

These are the parameters and switches:

source	The *source* variable is replaced with one or more filenames. Standard DOS wildcards are permitted. If the filenames are separated by plus signs (+), the files are joined into a single destination file.
destination	The *destination* variable is replaced with the name of the file, directory, or DOS device to which the *source* is to be copied. When the *destination* is omitted, the *source* is copied to the current default directory.
/A:[-]rhsda	Copies the source files flagged with the attributes specified after the /A:. If /A is used but no attributes are specified, all files are copied, regardless of attributes.
/C	Copies a file only if a duplicate file in the destination directory is older than the source file.
/E	Suppresses the display of nonfatal error messages during the copy process.
/H	Copies files flagged with the hidden and system attributes. Normally, COPY ignores files with these attributes.
/K	Causes the copied files to retain the DOS read-only attribute if it is present in the source files.
/M	Copies only files that are flagged with the archive attribute.
/N	Parses the COPY command for testing without actually performing the copy.
/P	Prompts the user for confirmation of each file copied.
/Q	Suppresses the display of filenames and totals during the copy process.
/R	Prompts the user for a confirmation before overwriting files in the destination directory. (By default, COPY silently overwrites files.)
/S	Parses the subdirectories of the source for files to be copied, creating identical subdirectories at the destination as needed.
/T	Displays the total number of files that have been copied, but suppresses the display of individual filenames during the copy process.
/U	Copies files that are newer than files of the same name in the destination directory as well as files that don't exist at the destination at all. The /C switch does not copy files that don't exist at the destination.
/V	Verifies that the data copied to the destination directory is readable.

/X	Removes the archive attribute from the source files after they are successfully copied.
/Z	Causes COPY to overwrite a read-only file of the same name in the destination directory.

The syntax for XCOPY is as follows:

```
XCOPY source [destination] [/A /C /D[:date] /E /F /H /I /K /L /M /N /P
/Q /R /S /T /U /W /Y /-Y
```

source	The *source* variable is replaced with the name of the file or directory to be copied. Standard DOS wildcards are permitted.
destination	The *destination* variable is replaced with the name of the file or directory to which the *source* is to be copied.
/A	Copies only the source files that are flagged with the archive attribute, without changing the attribute at the source.
/C	Continues the copy process after encountering errors.
/D[:date]	Copies only the files with a date more recent than that specified by the *date* variable. If no date is specified, only source files newer than the destination files are copied.
/E	Creates all subdirectories found at the source to the destination directory, even empty ones.
/F	Displays the complete pathnames of files and directories as they are copied.
/H	Copies files flagged with the hidden and system attributes in addition to all other files.
/I	Assumes that a nonexistent destination is a directory when copying multiple files. By default, XCOPY prompts the user to identify a nonexistent destination as a file or directory.
/K	Maintains the attributes of the source files in the destination directory.
/L	Parses the XCOPY command and displays the files to be copied without actually performing the operation.
/M	Copies only the source files that are flagged with the archive attribute and then removes the attribute at the source.
/N	Copies files to the destination using DOS 8.3 filenames.
/P	Prompts the user for a confirmation before copying each file.
/Q	Suppresses the display of filenames during the copy process.
/R	Overwrites destination files flagged with the read-only attribute.
/S	Copies all subdirectories of the source to the destination except empty ones.

PART

II

CH

9

/T	Creates the directory structure of the source in the destination directory but does *not* copy files or empty directories.
/U	Overwrites olderfiles in the destination directory.
/W	Prompts the user to press a key before beginning the copy process.
/Y	Overwrites files that already exist in the destination directory without confirmation.
/-Y	Prompts the user for a confirmation before overwriting files that already exist in the destination directory.

UNDERSTANDING DISK COMPRESSION

Windows 98 includes DriveSpace 3, a disk compression product that can increase the capacity of your disk drives by 50% to 100%. As with many Windows 98 optional features, however, you should carefully consider whether using DriveSpace on your system is a good idea.

Unlike static compression programs such as PKZIP, DriveSpace compresses files automatically as they are saved to your drive and then decompresses them on-the-fly when you request access to them. Naturally, this step introduces an additional level of processing overhead that can diminish the overall performance of your system.

Compression programs function by scanning files for redundant bit patterns and replacing them with codes that take up less space than the patterns themselves. The degree of compression the program achieves is based on the nature of the files being compressed. If, for example, you apply DriveSpace to a drive that contains mostly ZIP and GIF files, you will see little gain because these file formats are already compressed and cannot be reduced.

Bitmap and database files, on the other hand, contain a large number of redundant bit patterns and often can be reduced to one fifth of their original size or smaller. Executables and dynamic link libraries typically fall between these two extremes, compressing at a ratio of approximately 2:1.

DriveSpace also can save disk space, even when you choose to create a new drive without actually compressing the files. Instead of using the standard FAT16 cluster size, which can be as large as 32 kilobytes, DriveSpace breaks files into 512-byte pieces to minimize the wasted space caused by partially filled clusters.

DriveSpace 3 is a new version of the DriveSpace program that was included in Windows 95. Originally released as part of the Windows 95 Plus! product, this new version can create compressed volumes up to 2 gigabytes in size, whereas the Windows 95 version of DriveSpace was limited to 512-megabyte volumes.

TO COMPRESS OR NOT TO COMPRESS

Dynamic compression technology has been around for several years, and at one time it was a sound method for improving the economy of PC data storage. Today, the value of disk compression has decreased—for several reasons. First, the price of hard disk storage has plummeted in recent years, to the point at which a new 2-gigabyte drive can be had for 1/10 the price of a slower model five years ago. Therefore, simply purchasing additional storage for your system might be more economical than reducing your productivity by adding compression.

Second, you can improve the storage efficiency of your hard disk drives without the aid of compression by using the FAT32 file system included with Windows 98. The gains you realize with FAT32 are not as great as those you can achieve with DriveSpace, but your system's performance is not degraded as much either.

Caution

DriveSpace compression is not compatible with the FAT32 file system. If you have any plans to use FAT32, you should not apply DriveSpace compression to your drives.

Finally, like FAT32, DriveSpace renders the data on your compressed drives inaccessible to operating systems that do not support the technology. If you ever plan toboot your system with other operating systems, carefully consider whether you will need access to the files on the drives you plan to compress.

Note

DriveSpace 3 can read disks that have been compressed with the earlier DriveSpace versions included with MS-DOS 6.22 and Windows 95, as well as disks that use the DoubleSpace technology that was part of earlier MS-DOS versions. If you want, you can upgrade these older drives to DriveSpace 3 to take advantage of its additional features. However, the compatibility is one-way: The earlier compression products cannot read disks compressed with DriveSpace 3.

HOW DRIVESPACE 3 DISK COMPRESSION WORKS

When you compressthe C: drive on your system with DriveSpace, you end up with a C: drive that can hold 50% to 100% more data than it could before. But what you are seeing is not really a drive at all. During the compression process, DriveSpace creates a file on your drive called DRVSPACE.000. This file is called a *compressed volume file*, or CVF. It is the CVF that actually contains your compressed data.

When you view the contents of your C: drive after the compression process is complete, you are actually viewing the contents of the CVF, which exists as a file on your physical disk drive that's flagged with the read-only, hidden, and system attributes. You will also find that DriveSpace has added another drive letter to your system. This new drive is your original disk, now called the *host drive*, with all of its data migrated to the DRVSPACE.000 file. In essence, DriveSpace creates a new virtual drive on your system and then switches the drive letters so that your data appears to be in the same place it always was.

You do not have to compress your entire drive when using DriveSpace. You can specify a part of the free space on the disk and create a new compressed drive out of that space. You can create several smaller compressed drives this way. Each one has its own CVF, called DRVSPPACE.001, DRVSPACE.002, and so forth.

You can also use DriveSpace to compress floppy disks, and the process is essentially the same as that for a hard disk drive. A new drive letter appears on the system, representing the host drive for the floppy. You continue to access the floppy disk using the A: or B: drive letter as before, but that is actually a view of the CVF. The floppy can hold more data as a result of the compression, but it cannot be read by a system that doesn't have DriveSpace3 installed.

When the compression process begins, DriveSpace creates the CVF file and begins compressing the files already stored on the disk. By moving newly compressed files to the CVF until it is full, the program clears space on the host drive, which DriveSpace uses to increase the size of the CVF. The process then repeats until all the files have been compressed and migrated. The smaller the amount of free space on the drive when the compression process begins, the more times the CVF has to be expanded and the longer it takes to complete the entire operation.

It is not possible to compress a drive that does not have any free space because DriveSpace must have room to work. A 1.44-megabyte floppy, for example, must have at least 512 kilobytes of free space to be compressed.

> **Note**
>
> You can compress floppy disks and removable cartridges just likeany other disks. However, when you insert a compressed disk into the drive after the system has been booted, you must mount the drive before you can access its files. To mount a drive, highlight the drive letter in the main DriveSpace window and select the Advanced, Mount command. You can dismount the disk in the same way.

COMPRESSING AN ENTIRE DRIVE

To compress a drive, you launch the DriveSpace application by selecting Programs, Accessories, System Tools in the Start menu. Figure 9.6 shows the DriveSpace 3 screen. This window lists the drives in your system, shows their compression status, and enables you to perform most compression operations. The display also includes any host drives created by previous compression operations. If a host drive is left with less than 2 megabytes of uncompressed free space after the compression process is complete, it is hidden from view in Windows Explorer and My Computer.

When you select a drive for compression, DriveSpace launches a wizard that walks you through the process. The wizard shows you the current state of the drive and the estimated amount of free space that will result from the compression process (see Figure 9.7).

If you click the Options button, you can select the drive letter that is assigned to the host drive, the amount of free space to be left on the host drive, and whether it should be visible in the Windows 98 file management utilities.

Figure 9.6
The DriveSpace 3 dialog box is the main control center for compression operations.

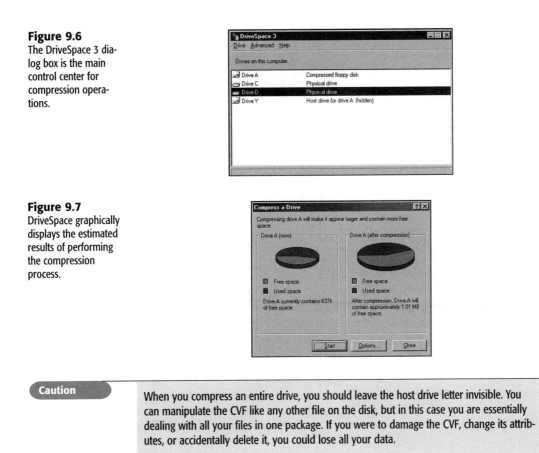

Figure 9.7
DriveSpace graphically displays the estimated results of performing the compression process.

> **Caution**
>
> When you compress an entire drive, you should leave the host drive letter invisible. You can manipulate the CVF like any other file on the disk, but in this case you are essentially dealing with all your files in one package. If you were to damage the CVF, change its attributes, or accidentally delete it, you could lose all your data.

Because DriveSpace cannot create compressed volumes larger than 2 gigabytes, it takes a different tack when faced with a hard disk drive larger than 1 gigabyte. Because the program estimates a compression ratio of 2:1, it compresses 1 gigabyte of the space on the drive, expecting to create a compressed volume of approximately 2 gigabytes. The compressed volume contains most of the existing data on the disk, and DriveSpace creates a new host drive containing free, uncompressed space.

For example, as you can see in Figure 9.8, a 2-gigabyte D: drive with 91.56 megabytes free is converted to a 2-gigabyte compressed drive (also called D:) that contains all the original data from the disk. The free space on the compressed drive increases only to 127.81 megabytes, but the host drive, X:, is left with 987.25 megabytes of free uncompressed space. You can then take that free space on the host drive and create another compressed volume that increases the total capacity of the 2-gigabyte hard disk drive to nearly 4 gigabytes.

Figure 9.8
When compressing hard disk drives larger than 1 gigabyte, DriveSpace compresses as much of the data as possible and leaves the remaining space uncompressed on the host drive.

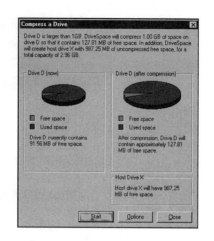

If you attempt to compress your system's boot drive or the drive on which Windows 98 is installed, DriveSpace takes steps to ensure that access to the system is still possible after the compression process and that Windows 98 performance is not too severely affected. As you pass through the screens of the Compression Wizard, DriveSpace gives you the opportunity to create or update a startup disk for your system because the compression process requires a reboot that might not be possible with your hard drive in its interim state.

> **Caution**
>
> Before beginning the compression process, DriveSpace also gives you the opportunity to back up your drive using Microsoft Backup. Whether you use this program or not, always be sure to have a viable backup before beginning a major disk operation.

⚠ *You might encounter some problems when you run the System Configuration Utility. If so, see "Problems with the System Configuration Utility" in the "Troubleshooting" section at the end of the chapter.*

COMPRESSING PART OF A DRIVE

DriveSpace 3 also adds a Compression tab to the Properties dialog box of every local drive on your computer (see Figure 9.9). From this dialog box, you can launch a full compression of the drive (which is the same operation discussed earlier in "Compressing an Entire Drive"), or you can create a new compressed drive from the free space left on the disk. Another way to access this feature is to highlight an uncompressed drive with free space on it in the DriveSpace program and then select the Advanced, Create Empty command.

The process of creating a new compressed drive is far less involved and invasive than that of compressing the existing files. In the Create New Compressed Drive dialog box (see

Figure 9.10), you specify the letter to be used for the new drive, the amount of uncompressed space to use, and the source drive for that uncompressed space. DriveSpace displays the estimated capacity of the new drive and, on your approval, creates the new CVF.

PART

II

CH

9

Figure 9.9
The Properties dialog box of every local drive has a Compression tab that displays its compression status and enables you to initiate compression operations.

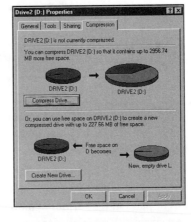

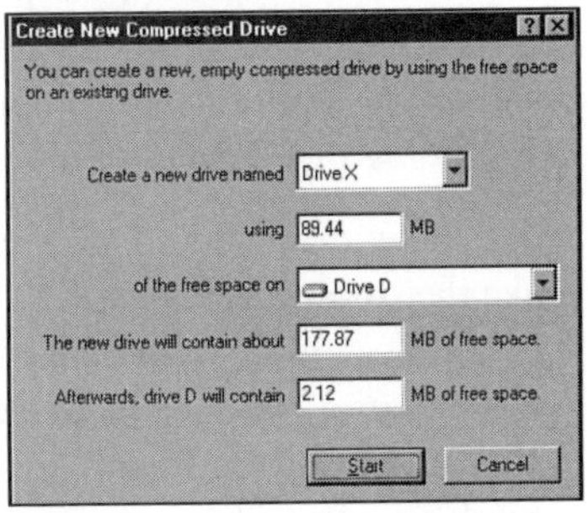

Figure 9.10
You can create new compressed volumes out of your free space by using the drive's Properties dialog box.

When you create a new compressed drive, no swapping of drive letters is necessary because the host drive still contains other data that must be accessed as before. The new CVF appears as an extra drive letter on your system, which you can access like any other disk drive.

CHANGING THE SETTINGS FOR A COMPRESSED DRIVE

You can view the current status of compressed drives on your system and manage their properties by using the DriveSpace utility. When you double-click on a compressed drive, a dialog box like that shown in Figure 9.11 appears, displaying the disk's used space, free space, and compression ratios.

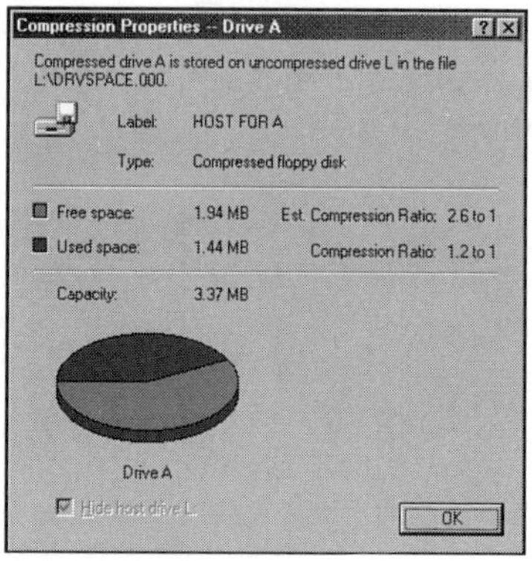

Figure 9.11
The DriveSpace utility can display the status of any currently mounted compressed drive.

CHANGING COMPRESSION RATIOS

When you are dealing with disk compression, statistics such as disk capacity are always estimates because the compression ratio for a given file is not known until it is actually compressed. The status displays in the various Windows 98 file management utilities often include an indicator of a disk's remaining free space, however. DriveSpace defaults to a 2:1 ratio in its estimates of a compressed disk's capacity. You can adjust this ratio to achieve a more realistic estimate based on the actual compression ratio of the files already on the disk and your own understanding of the types of files you will be storing on the drive.

Select the Change Ratio command from DriveSpace's Advanced menu, and Windows displays a dialog box like that shown in Figure 9.12. This dialog box shows the current actual compression ratio of the files on the disk. Beneath this current actual ratio is a slider showing the current estimated ratio, which is 2:1 by default. If you plan to store more of the same types of files that are already on the disk, you can adjust this figure to equal the actual ratio; in this case Windows 98 adjusts the estimates displayed elsewhere in the operating system. If you plan to store files you know to be highly compressible or not highly compressible, you can adjust the value accordingly. Setting the ratio to 1:1 displays the actual free space that remains available on the drive if you choose to store files that cannot be compressed at all.

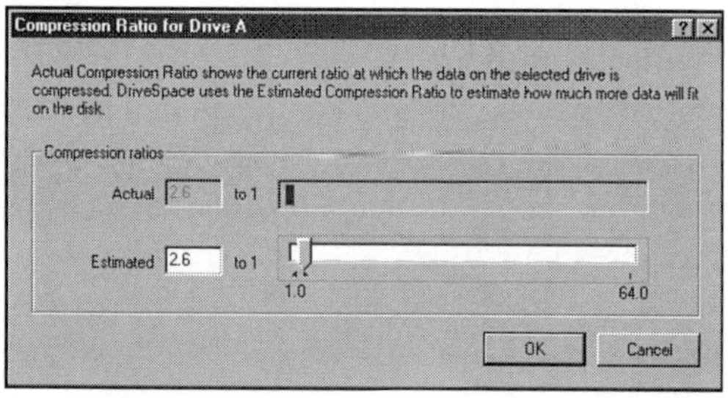

Figure 9.12
The Compression Ratio dialog box enables you to correct the Windows 98 estimates of a compressed drive's free space.

> **Note**
>
> The Change Ratio feature does not adjust the degree to which your files are compressed; it only enables you to make the Windows 98 estimates of the compressed drive's capacity more realistic.

ADJUSTING FREE SPACE

After DriveSpace creates a compressed volume, free space is usually left on both the new and the host drives. You can adjust this free space as needed, moving it to either drive, as long as the compressed drive does not exceed 2 gigabytes. To do so, choose a drive letter in the DriveSpace program and select Adjust Free Space from the Drive menu. The Adjust Free Space dialog box (see Figure 9.13) contains a slider that enables you to move space from one drive to another, changing the pie charts to display the correct proportion.

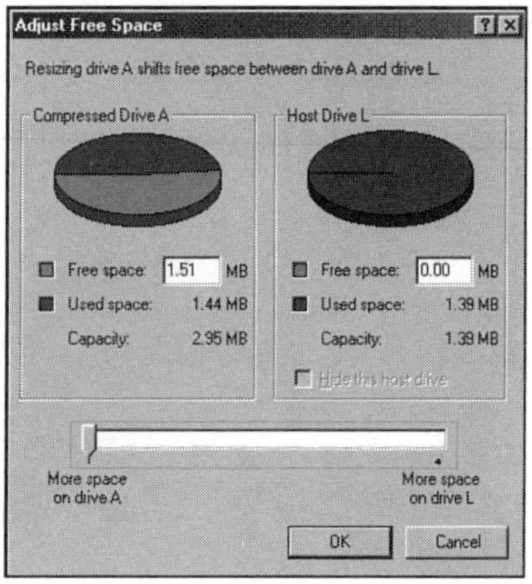

Figure 9.13
DriveSpace's Adjust Free Space feature enables you to move the remaining drive space between a compressed volume and its host drive.

CHANGING DRIVE LETTERS

Sometimes, the additional drive letters that DriveSpace creates can be confusing, especially when they are hidden and you want to use one of those letters for a network drive or some other device. You can change the letter assigned to a host drive or an empty drive by highlighting it in the DriveSpace program and selecting Change Letter from the Advanced menu.

USING THE COMPRESSION AGENT TO IMPROVE PERFORMANCE

DriveSpace provides three levels of compression that trade off disk space for system performance. By default, DriveSpace uses Standard compression. However, you can configure the system to use HiPack compression whenever new files are written to a compressed drive. To achieve the maximum possible compression, called UltraPack, you must use another utility called the Windows 98 Compression Agent.

The Compression Agent lets you initiate compression events on demand and choose the level of compression that it should apply to your drive. Unlike DriveSpace, Compression Agent does not automatically compress files on-the-fly. Instead, it takes existing compressed drives and compresses them further when you specifically instruct it to do so.

You can use Compression Agent in several different ways—to suit your work habits. You can, for example, set DriveSpace to use standard compression or even no compression, to minimize system performance degradation, and to run a nightly Compression Agent job to UltraPack your files after you finish working by using the Task Scheduler.

You can also configure the agent to UltraPack only the files that you have not accessed within a specified number of days. This setting keeps your seldom-used files at maximum compression while speeding up access to those you use frequently.

When you display the Compression page in any compressed drive's Properties dialog box, you can see a summary of the compressed files on your disk, the type of compression used, and the compression ratios achieved by each one, as shown in Figure 9.14.

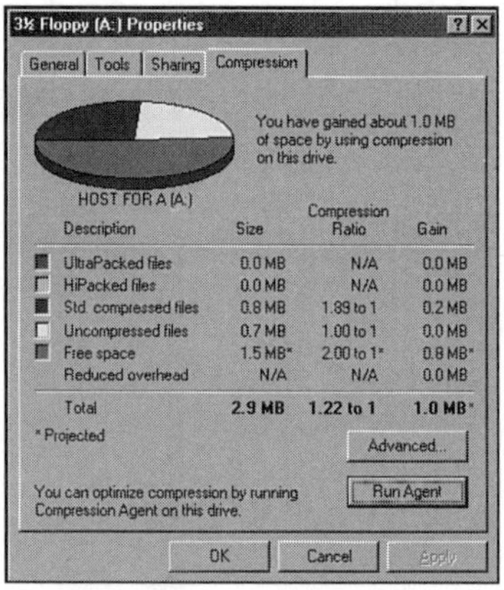

Figure 9.14
A single compressed disk can contain Standard, HiPack, and UltraPack files.

To use the Compression Agent, launch the program from the Programs, Accessories, System Tools group in the Start menu. Then, click the Settings button to see the dialog box shown in Figure 9.15. You can select the degree of compression desired, and you can access other screens that enable you to apply specific compression rules to individual files and execute compression events based on the current amount of free space on the disk.

Figure 9.15
You can use the Compression Agent to customize your system's compression behavior.

UNCOMPRESSING A DRIVESPACE VOLUME

DriveSpace enables you to return the files in a compressed volume to their uncompressed state and to delete the CVF. To do so, you highlight a drive in the DriveSpace program and select Uncompress from the Drive menu. The program displays a screen showing how much uncompressed free space will be left on the drive after the process.

Unfortunately, you are likely to have more data on the compressed drive than will fit on the same drive in its uncompressed state. The program informs you if this situation arises, letting you know how much data you must remove before the process can proceed.

DELETING A COMPRESSED DRIVE

Do not confuse the process of deleting a compressed drive with that of uncompressing it. When you highlight a drive in the DriveSpace program and select Delete from the Advanced menu, the program deletes the CVF from the host drive, destroying the data and freeing up all the disk space that data had occupied. As always, the DriveSpace program warns you of the impending data loss and requires your confirmation before it proceeds. You should use this feature only if you do not need the data on the compressed volume or you have already backed it up to another medium.

USING A CD-ROM DRIVE

CD-ROM drives have become an important component of personal computers. Most software is now distributed on CD-ROMs, and their large capacity makes them ideal for use with games and multimedia titles that require large amounts of disk space but do not warrant permanent storage on a hard disk drive.

→ Chapter 19, "Setting Up Windows 98 Multimedia," provides more information on using the Windows 98 multimedia features with CD-ROMs.

AUTOPLAY

The Autoplay feature in Windows 98 enables software developers to create CD-ROMs that automatically launch a program when they are mounted by the file system. The program can initiate the installation process for a new application or load a multimedia program that is designed to run directly from the CD-ROM.

Autoplay is made possible by the 32-bit, protected-mode device drivers that Windows 98 uses to support CD-ROMs. These drivers enable the operating system to detect the insertion of a disk into the drive. Real-mode drivers loaded from the CONFIG.SYS file do not have this capability.

When Windows 98 detects that you have inserted a disk into the CD-ROM drive, Windows mounts the disk in the file system and searches for a file called AUTORUN.INF in the root directory. This file specifies the program to be launched and the icon to be used to represent the program in Windows. A typical AUTORUN.INF file looks like this:

```
[autorun]
open=filename.exe
icon=filename.ico
```

The open= directive specifies an executable file on the CD-ROM, and the icon= directive specifies an icon file.

In your working environment, you might find that Autoplay is more of an intrusion than a help. To disable this feature, open the Properties dialog box for your CD-ROM drive in the System Control Panel, click the Settings tab, and clear the Auto Insert Notification check box.

RUNNING SOFTWARE FROM A CD-ROM

In many cases, you can save disk space on your hard drives by running applications directly from a CD-ROM. Other applications, such as games and multimedia titles, require that you do so. Some applications, such as Microsoft Office, have installation options that enable you to select how much of the software is copied to the hard disk and how much should be executed directly from the CD.

Running a program from a CD-ROM is nearly always slower than running that program from a hard disk, and you are, of course, limited to running a single application in this manner (unless your system has multiple CD-ROM drives). In some cases, however, the conservation of disk space is worth the delay—particularly if an application enables you to control which software components run from the CD. For example, you might be able toinstall the core program files of a word processor to your hard disk but run less frequently used modules (such as the grammar checker) from the CD-ROM.

IMPROVING CD-ROM PERFORMANCE

If your CD-ROM drive uses the EIDE interface, Windows 98 includes a feature that might speed up the performance of both your CD-ROM and overall system. Click the Settings tab in the drive's Properties dialog box in the System Control Panel and see whether the DMA check box is available. If you can check this box and it remains checked after you reboot the system, you are using Windows 98 bus-mastering IDE controller drivers.

Direct memory access (DMA), also called *bus mastering*, is a technique by which a device performs data transfers without utilizing the services of the main system processor. If you turn on this feature for your EIDE CD-ROM or hard disk drives, the system does not use any CPU time for drive access requests. Although bus mastering may not produce a noticeable increase in the data transfer rate for the device, it can result in a general improvement in system performance because of the reduced load on the CPU.

If, when rebooting a clean setup, your laptop is hanging with a black screen, see "Incompatible Drivers" in the "Troubleshooting" section that follows.

TROUBLESHOOTING

INCOMPATIBLE DRIVERS

After setup, my laptop opens only in Safe mode.

If you own a Toshiba Tecra or Protégé laptop, like we do, you'll be interested in knowing about a problem that may occur if you perform a *clean* installation of Windows 98 on the system. You can carry out two types of clean installations. The first type involves a disk that has been partitioned and reformatted so that you are loading the operating system from scratch. This operation is a truly clean install. The second type of clean installation is really an upgrade in which the Windows 98 system folder is in a different folder than the one in which Windows 95 is installed.

During setup in a clean installation, the second time the system starts it may just hang with a black screen. In this case, you must start the system in Safe mode. This behavior occurs because DMA is enabled by default for IDE drives in the upgrade version of Windows 98. Toshiba Tecra and Protégé computers are not compatible with the Windows 98 DMA drivers. These computers use Toshiba's own bus-mastering DMA drivers. Toshiba is presumably working on a fix for this problem.

PROBLEMS WITH THE SYSTEM CONFIGURATION UTILITY

When I attempt a Diagnostic Startup to enable the Startup menu, to disable ScanDisk after a bad shutdown, or (on a SCSI system) to disable double buffering, the effort fails.

When you use the DriveSpace utility to compress an entire hard drive, the utility swaps the drive letter assignments after the initialization of the CVF. The System Configuration utility is unaware of the drive letter swap and edits the Msdos.sys file located on the CVF instead of the Msdos.sys file on the host drive. To fix the problem, you must edit the Msdos.sys file located on the host drive. First, make the hidden host drive visible by choosing System Tools, DriveSpace. Then select the compressed drive for which the hidden drive is the host drive and modify the properties of the drive by deselecting the Hide Host Drive check box.

SECRETS OF MASTERING THE WINDOWS 98 ENVIRONMENT: HOW WIN.COM DETERMINES AN IMPROPER SHUTDOWN

The structure of the VFAT32 is such that the first 8 bytes of the table are reserved, and the last of these bytes is by default a hexadecimal 0F. The VFAT and the Windows 98 operating system work together to modify the fourth bit of this byte to be either a 1 or 0. A value of 0 indicates that the file system has actually written the data to disk, whereas a value of 1 indicates that Windows 98 was improperly shut down, possibly during a file write. During a file write, VFAT is responsible for the write to disk and clears the fourth bit to 0.

When shutting down Windows 98 in an acceptable mode, the operating system resets this bit to 1. During a subsequent reboot, the Win.com file reads the bit to determine whether the system was shut down properly. If the value of the bit reads 0, ScanDisk checks for drive errors.

CHAPTER **10**

BACKING UP YOUR DATA

In this chapter

GETTING STARTED WITH BACKUP

As experienced users are well aware, regular system backups can save you hours of frustration. In addition, if you create and follow a regular backup schedule, you will be able to recover from inadvertent corruption of the Windows 98 system Registry. Windows 98 includes a full-featured backup utility.

Note

When using help in the Backup utility, you may see references to Seagate Backup Exec because Microsoft licensed the Windows 98 Backup utility from Seagate Software, the company that makes the Backup Exec product line.

Windows 95 included a backup utility as an optional component that was available during setup. The Windows 98 version of the backup utility boasts the following improvements over the previous version:

- It is installed as a base component during Windows 98 setup.
- Improved wizard technology makes it easier to perform common tasks.
- It offers the capability to back up and restore the Windows 98 Registry.
- It works with the Windows 98 Task Scheduler so you can remind yourself to run backups.

The Windows 98 utility borrows interface elements from both previous Backup Exec versions and the Windows 95 version of Backup. The Windows 98 version of the backup utility includes these useful features:

- A graphical user interface that enables you to easily choose your backup selections.
- Support for many types of tape drives and fixed media devices.
- The ability to create backup "jobs" that target different files, allowing you to create a variety of backup strategies.
- The option to create recovery disks that can revive your personal computer after a major loss of system data.
- Password protection of backups for extra security.

The backup process is fairly straightforward. Wizards (as shown in Figure 10.1) lead you through common tasks such as backing up and restoring.

Backup also uses color-coded graphical "check marks" to indicate whether you have selected an entire folder or just specific files.

You select the files you want to back up by clicking on folders or specific files. If you select a folder, Backup backs up all the contents of that folder.

Figure 10.1
The Backup utility enables you to select entire folders or specific files to back up.

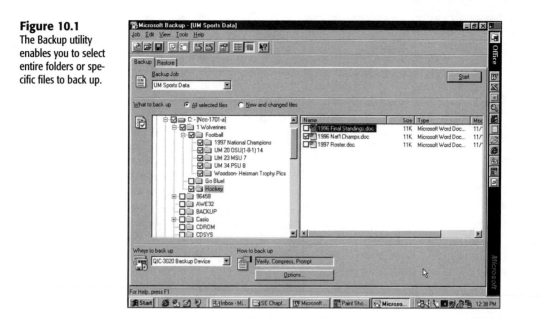

After you make your selections, you can save them for future use by creating a *backup job*. A backup job is a collection of files that you select within the Backup utility and save to a particular filename. Having created a backup job, you can quickly back up that range of files again by simply running the backup job. This routine allows you to quickly back up or restore files without selecting the files every time.

> **Note**
>
> Backup jobs also save any settings that are selected when the job is saved.

Note the different colors of the selection marks. A bright blue mark signifies that a file or entire folder has been selected (the Football folder and the 1996 Nat'l Champs Microsoft Word document, in the case of Figure 10.1). Also note that all higher-level folders that contain the 1996 Nat'l Champs document have a gray selection mark. The gray mark signifies that only a portion of the directory's contents have been selected to be a part of the backup job.

Another useful feature of the Backup utility is the capability to verify your files as you're backing them up. You should always verify your files after backing them up. To do so, you select the check box at the top of the Backup Job Options dialog box shown in Figure 10.2. The verification process double-checks to make sure that the original files match the files actually saved to your backup media. Unfortunately, this practice adds to the time it takes to run your backup job, but the peace of mind it provides is well worth the extra time.

Caution

If the verification turns up a problem, it might be time to replace the media or clean your backup device.

Figure 10.2
You can configure the Backup utility to verify files.

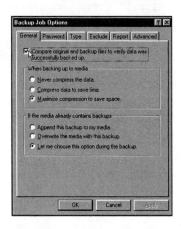

As a further safeguard for your data, you should store your backup media in a safe place—preferably at an offsite facility specializing in the archiving of data. For a monthly fee, these specialty providers maintain your backup media in an environmentally controlled area. You can even contract some providers to pick up the backups at your location. If this practice isn't cost-effective for you, find a place at home that is dry and easy to get to, in case of an emergency, for your data storage.

Tip #58

When deciding where to store backups, consider these potential dangers: electrical interference, temperature variations, and theft. Balance these factors with convenience. Also, make and follow a schedule for rotating your tapes between your computer and your storage area.

The restore process is very similar to the backup process. The Backup utility reads the catalog of files that have been saved on the backup media and allows you to choose the files you want to restore. You can restore the files to their original locations or to other locations altogether.

PREPARING A BACKUP STRATEGY

Many users don't create an overall backup strategy until it's too late. A realistic strategy should take into account available backup hardware, how much time you're willing to devote to backups, and ultimately how much work you're willing to lose given a worst-case scenario.

CHOOSING A BACKUP FORMAT

You can perform several kinds of backups. Table 10.1 outlines the four main types.

TABLE 10.1   TYPES OF FILE BACKUPS

Type	Description
Full Backup	Backs up every file selected. Marks files as having been backed up.
Incremental	Backs up every file created or changed since the last full or differential backup. Marks only files that have been created or changed since the previous backup as having been backed up.
Differential	Backs up every file created or changed since the last full or differential backup. Does not mark files as having been backed up.
Copy	This type of backup simply copies all files and folders without marking files as having been backed up.

<table>
<tr><td>Tip #59</td><td>Suppose you want to back up all your data without interrupting your normal backup schedule. For example, you might want to send an entire set of data to another person. Because the Copy backup method does not mark files, it is the quickest way to go with the least interruption.</td></tr>
</table>

To configure the backup type, select the Options button from the Backup utility main screen and then click the Type tab to see the options shown in Figure 10.3.

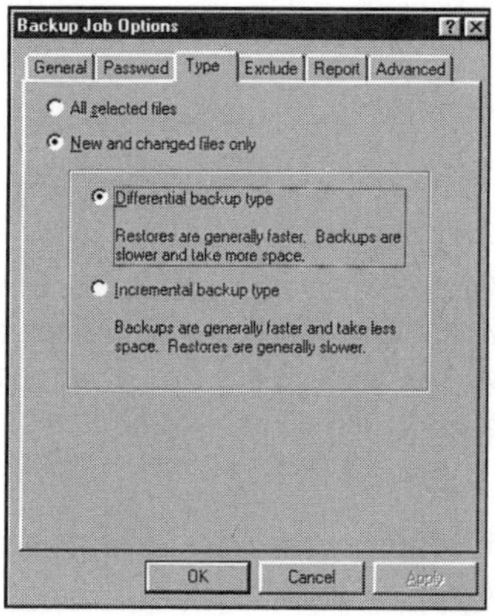

Figure 10.3
Choose the type of backup you want to perform in the Backup Job Options dialog box.

If you select the All Selected Files option, Backup performs a full backup of every file on your system. Backups and restores will be somewhat slow due to the volume of data to be processed.

If you select the New and Changed Files Only option, you also need to choose either the differential or incremental backup option. A differential backup saves new or changed files

PART

II

CH

10

to your backup device and doesn't mark them as having been backed up. For example, if you create a file on Monday, perform a differential backup that night, and then perform another differential backup on Tuesday, whether you have changed the file or not it is backed up on both days. An incremental backup saves every file created or changed since the last full or differential backup and marks the files as having been backed up. Using the previous example, if you create a file on Monday and perform an incremental backup that night, the file is backed up and marked as having been backed up. If you perform another incremental backup on Tuesday, the file is not backed up unless it has changed (been edited) since the Monday-night backup. Consequently, subsequent incremental backups take less time to run because only new or changed files are backed up.

Note

On a more technical level, a backup marker, or archive bit, is set on a file to indicate that the file has been backed up. An incremental backup marks the archive attribute, whereas the differential does not.

CREATING A SCHEDULE

Try to be realistic when creating your backup schedule. In a perfect world, all personal computers would have lightning-fast, multiple-gig backup units that would allow everyone to do full-system backups every day in a matter of seconds. But the reality is that system backups take time. On newer computer systems that have gigs of disk space, a full backup can take many hours. The following might be a good backup schedule for a moderately used home computer:

Full-System Backup (everything)	Once every other month, alternating sets
Data Backup (user files)	Once a month, alternating sets

Tip #60

The idea of *alternating sets* comes from that annoying tendency of Murphy's Law to intervene when you need to restore important data. By alternating sets (set A & set B, set 1 & set 2, or whatever you choose), you ensure that you don't overwrite a good backup with a bad one. Multiple sets also help prevent loss of data due to tape failure or other mishap.

If you create a lot of files or create very large and detailed documents, the following schedule may be necessary:

Full-System Backup (everything)	Once a month, alternating sets
Data Backup (user files)	Every day, alternating sets

Full-system backups are recommended with some amount of frequency for all systems. However, the frequency of data backups for heavy users has increased from monthly to daily. These recommendations are meant as guidelines only. Each user should create a schedule of system and data backups that makes the most sense for his or her particular situation.

DECIDING WHICH FILES TO BACK UP

A backup strategy mostly depends on how you use your computer and ultimately depends on how much data you are willing to lose in the event of a disaster.

For many users, system data changes infrequently, only during an operating system or application upgrade, for example. As a safeguard, you should back up your entire system before performing any major upgrade. For most users, personal data is much more important than application data. It's much easier to reinstall an application than to re-create personal data.

Organizing your user files into folders in a common location can facilitate backup and restore procedures. Backing up one folder and its contents is much easier than searching through all your subdirectories for a particular file.

Assuming that all your personal files are in one directory, you need to decide how often to back up that directory. The advantage of backing up only data files is that these files are usually small compared to system data files. If you change data only once or twice a week, you might want to do data backups weekly or monthly. If you frequently change documents, on the other hand, you might want to back up your data more often.

When deciding which files to back up, you should consider the priority of the following kinds of data:

- Files important to your system (operating system, Registry, and application files)
- Files that are important to you (personal documents and data)

Always maintain a good reliable system backup. Because this data doesn't normally change very often, you usually must perform a full-system backup relatively infrequently: monthly or every other month. Although you should back up your user data more often, those backups tend to be smaller than system backups and take less time.

CHOOSING THE RIGHT BACKUP DEVICE

During the last few years, backup devices have become an economical option for many computer users. Many types of devices, with varying degrees of capability, are now available. When choosing a backup device, make sure it can fulfill the needs of your overall backup strategy.

CHOOSING THE RIGHT BACKUP MEDIUM

Many hardware options are available for backing up the data on your personal computer. Here are a few questions to ask when purchasing a unit:

- How much data do I need to back up? Backup units vary greatly in capacity and speed.

- Will my backup tapes be read by machines other than mine? If so, you need to get a tape device that uses tapes of the same type the other computers use.

- How expensive is the backup media? You need more than one cartridge to implement a reliable system of backups, so the cost of the backup media is significant.

You have many choices when you decide to back up your data. Tape drives are the most common devices, but other options are available, depending on your specific needs and budgets:

- Tape drives—These are the most common backup choice, and they come in a wide variety of shapes, sizes, and prices. Many tape drives offer high capacity and good speed and are the best way for most users to back up gigabytes of data.

- Removable storage devices—These devices are being used more and more in certain applications. They are fast, reliable, and easy to use and install. Unfortunately, most do not have the capacity of tape drives.

- Compact disk (CD) writers—These devices have been dropping in price and are now being used for archival purposes. The media is inexpensive (around $2 for a CD) but has limited storage (around 650 megabytes). One advantage of this medium is that machines are more likely to have CD drives than to have tape devices, which gives you more options when you want to restore data. Unfortunately, the small capacity of the media and the Write Once Read Many (WORM) nature of CDs make this option impractical for most users. CD-R technology, which allows you to record and erase compact disks, might make this approach more feasible in the future, but capacity will always be a shortcoming.

- Network drives—This is a great solution—as long as your network resources have the capacity to handle the size of your backup file. Most network resources are backed up at the server level as well, offering even more safety for your data. The downside of saving your backups to the network is that you might not have enough storage space to perform a full backup. Check with your system administrator to ensure that you have the resources available on the network to handle your backup (.QIC) files and to schedule a time for your backup that won't saturate the network during peak usage time.

- Floppy disks—Use floppy disks only as a last resort. They are very unreliable for backups. In addition, this approach is time-consuming and slow. Friends don't let friends do critical backups on floppy disks.

INSTALLING AND CONFIGURING A TAPE DRIVE

To install a tape drive, follow these steps:

1. Read any setup directions that come with your tape drive for specific instructions on installing your device.

2. Turn off your computer and install your tape drive according to the directions that come with it.

3. Turn on your computer and boot Windows 98.

4. If your device supports Plug and Play, the system will detect it and install the proper drivers (best-case scenario).

   If Windows 98 does not detect your tape device on bootup, open the Start menu and select Settings, Control Panel, Add New Hardware. The Add New Hardware Wizard takes you through the steps for detecting and installing the software that runs your tape drive.

Tip #61	Microsoft Backup saves files in QIC format. QIC stands for Quarter-Inch Cartridge, which is a popular type of standardized tape cartridge used for tape backups. Microsoft Backup can be used with tape units that adhere to the following standards: QIC-40 low density, QIC-80 high density, and QIC-117. Even if you back up your files directly to disk instead of to tape, the file is saved in QIC format. Before purchasing a backup unit, always check to make sure that it is on the Windows 98 hardware compatibility list (HCL).

Microsoft Backup supports parallel, IDE/ATAPI, some USB, and SCSI backup devices. These devices range from external units that easily connect to your parallel port to internal devices that require varying degrees of knowledge for installation. Before you buy a tape drive, make sure you have the interface required to connect it. Windows 98 supports the following vendors: Conner, Exabyte, HP/Colorado, Iomega, Micro Solutions, Seagate, Tandberg, WangDAT, and Wangtek.

Tip #62	If you have Hewlett-Packard's (HP) Colorado Backup for Windows 95 program and try to run it in Windows 98, Colorado Backup does not detect your tape drive. An interesting twist to this problem is that the tape drive is listed in the Device Manager. This problem occurs when Microsoft Backup is currently installed on a system. To correct this situation, uninstall Microsoft Backup and reinstall Colorado backup.

FORMATTING AND ERASING TAPES

You usually have to format a new tape before you can use it to perform a backup. To format or erase a tape, follow these steps:

1. Insert the tape into your tape drive.

2. Select Tools, Media, Format. The program displays a message warning you that format-ting erases any data on the tape and may take up to 30 minutes to complete.

Tip #63 | Not all media must be formatted. Some non-QIC formats are formatted automatically dur-ing the backup process.

BACKING UP FILES

If you perform consistent backups, you will have the tools you need to recover from both minor mistakes and major computer disasters. The first place to begin is to perform a backup of your entire system.

PERFORMING A FULL-SYSTEM BACKUP WITH THE BACKUP WIZARD

To perform a full-system backup, follow these steps:

1. To start the Backup utility, open the Start menu and choose Programs, Accessories, System Tools, Backup. After the splash screen appears, the Backup Wizard begins, ready to help configure your backup procedure (see Figure 10.4).

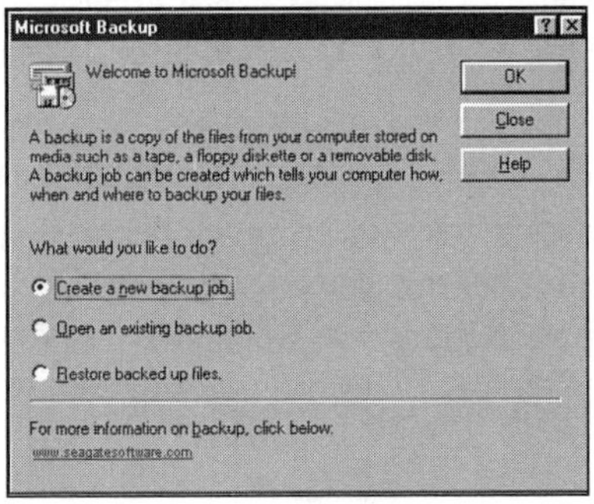

Figure 10.4
The Backup Wizard opens immediately when you execute the Backup program.

2. Select the Create a New Backup Job option and click OK.
3. In the next dialog box, select Back Up My Computer and click Next.
4. Select All Selected Files. Then click Next to continue.
5. In the dialog box that appears, indicate where you want to save your backup and click Next to Continue.

Tip #64 | Using a second drive ensures that if your system experiences a hard drive failure, you will still be able to recover your backed up data for a restore.

6. Next, you specifyhow you want to perform your backup. The following choices are available: Compare Original and Backup Files to Verify Data Was Successfully Backed Up (highly recommended) and Compress the Backup Data to Save Space (also recommended). Click Next.

7. The final screen of the Backup Wizard (shown in Figure 10.5) allows you to name your backup job, view your previous selections, and most important, actually Start execution of the backup job. Enter a name for your backup job in the text box. Be sure to give the job a name that sufficiently describes what the backup does. This name appears in a drop-down box in the Backup program from now on, and a good descriptive name will cut down on confusion later.

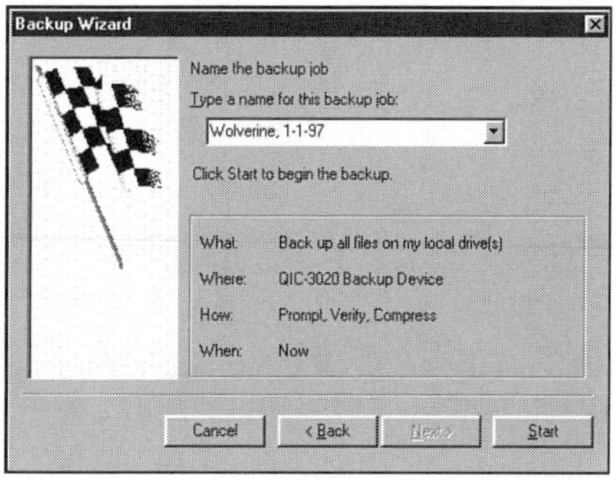

Figure 10.5
The final screen of the Backup Wizard lets you view your choices before executing your backup job.

PART

II

CH

10

8. Click Start to begin your backup. As the backup job runs, you can monitor its progress onscreen. The Backup Progress screen keeps you updated, providing such useful information as the number of files being backed up and the estimated time the procedure will take (see Figure 10.6).

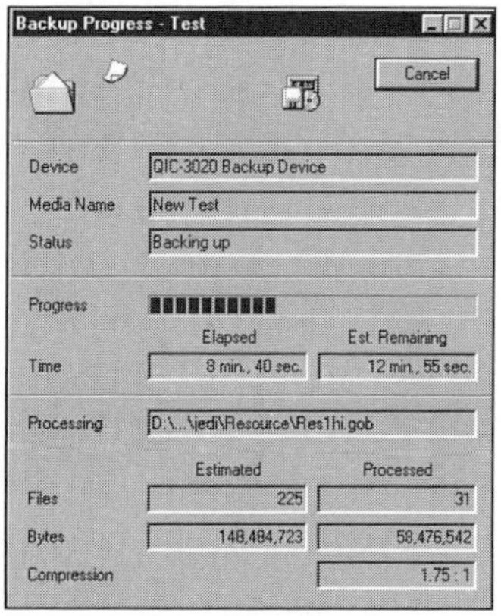

Figure 10.6
As the Backup job executes, a status screen provides you with updated information.

ENSURING THAT THE REGISTRY GETS BACKED UP CORRECTLY

The Windows 98 System Registry files are crucial to reviving your system in the event of a major hardware failure. There are two ways to back up these critical files. The first is with REGEDIT.EXE, which is covered in Chapter 24, "Working with the Windows Registry." The second is to use the Backup utility.

When using the Backup utility, you have to take only a few steps to ensure that the System Registry is backed up properly. Use the following steps:

1. Select Tools, Preferences. The Preferences dialog box shown in Figure 10.7 appears.

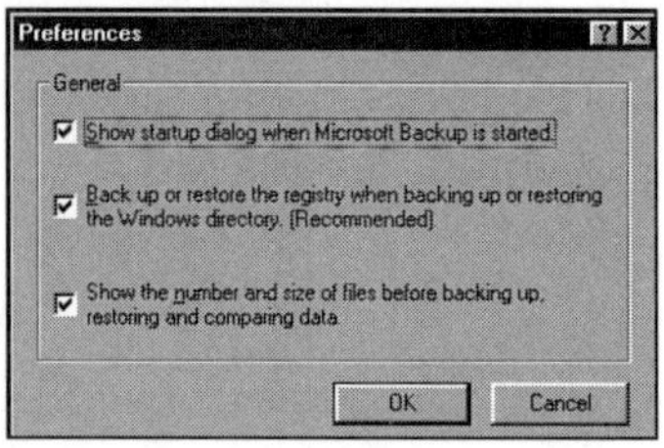

Figure 10.7
The first step to ensure that you back up the all-important Registry.

2. Check the box labeled Back Up or Restore System Registry When Backing Up or Restoring the Windows Directory. Then click OK.

3. Near the bottom of the Backup utility screen, click the Options button.

4. In the Backup Job Options dialog box (see Figure 10.8), select the Advanced tab. Check the Back Up Windows Registry box and click OK.

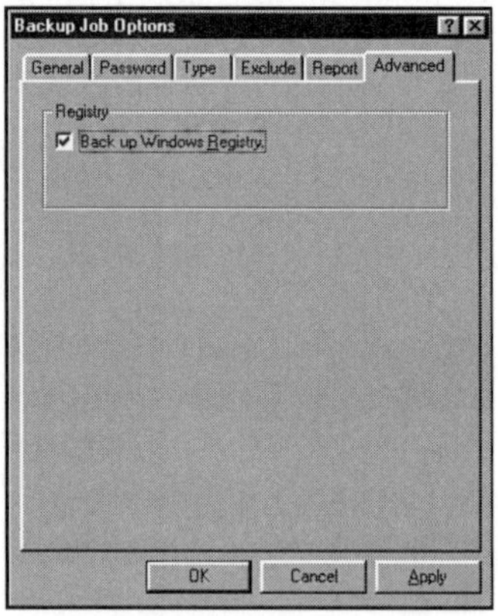

Figure 10.8
The second step to ensure that you back up the Registry.

After you complete the steps, the Registry will be backed up whenever you back up the Windows directory.

⚠ *If you are having some trouble backing up the Registry, see "Problems Backing Up the Registry" in the "Troubleshooting" section at the end of this chapter.*

SELECTING FOLDERS AND FILE TYPES FOR PARTIAL BACKUPS

As you learned earlier in the chapter, you can select specific folders to back up. You select them in the What to Back Up section of the opening Backup screen. A bright blue check marks files or entire directories for backup. A gray check mark signifies that only a portion of a directory is selected for backup.

When you're selecting files, you also have the option of excluding certain file types from being backed up. This option might come in handy, for example, if you do not want to back up temporary files or browser cache files.

To prevent a certain file type from being backed up, follow these steps:

1. At the bottom of the opening Backup window, click the Options button. The Backup Job Options dialog box appears.

2. Select the Exclude tab and then click the Add button. The Add Exclude dialog box appears (see Figure 10.9).

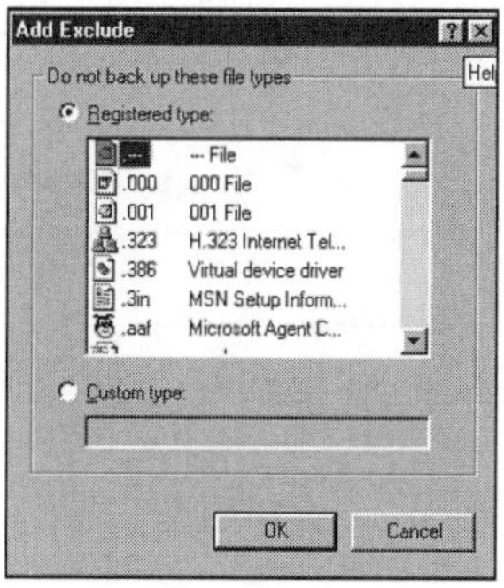

Figure 10.9
The Backup utility gives you the option of excluding certain file types from being backed up.

3. Scroll through the Registered Type list to see whether the files you want to exclude are already a registered type. If the file type is not listed, click the Custom Type option and enter the file extension that you want to filter in the text box.

4. All file types listed in this box are ignored during backup procedures. When you finish making your selection, click OK.

RUNNING A SAVED BACKUP JOB

To run a saved backup job, follow these steps:

1. Click on the Backup tab of the main Backup utility screen.

2. From the Backup Job drop-down list, select the saved backup job you want to execute.

3. Insert the tape on which you want to save your data.

4. Click the Start button to execute the job.

SCHEDULING BACKUPS WITH THE TASK SCHEDULER

A handy feature of Windows 98 is that it enables you to schedule mundane tasks to automatically execute on a regular basis. You can take advantage of this feature to remind you to perform backups.

To schedule the Task Scheduler to remind you when to perform your backups, follow these steps:

1. Click on My Computer on the Windows 98 desktop.
2. Select the Scheduled Task folder.
3. Click the Add Scheduled Task icon to start the Add Scheduled Task Wizard. Click Next to continue.
4. The wizard prompts you to select a program to schedule a task from. Select Backup and then click Next.
5. Enter a name for the task and specify an execution frequency.
6. Select the date and time you want this task to begin.
7. Click the Finish button to complete the scheduling of this task.

At the time you selected, the Backup utility will execute. You can then select the backup job you want to run.

Caution

When the Task Scheduler brings up the Backup utility, you have to run the proper backup job. The Task Scheduler runs the Backup utility for you but doesn't perform the actual backup.

CHANGING BACKUP SETTINGS AND OPTIONS

It's simple to change your backup settings and options. Follow these steps:

1. From the Backup Job drop-down box, select the name of the backup job you want to change.
2. Make any changes you want to the file selections, options, and so on.
3. When you finish making changes, open the Job menu and select Save.

RESTORING BACKED UP FILES

The Windows 98 Backup utility enables you to recover anything from a single file to your entire system.

RESTORING A FULL BACKUP

Hard drive failures and system crashes are among the most difficult problems computer users face. Media degradation, power surges, and simple human error can cause complete system failures. Persistent system crashes can be just as vexing to diagnose and troubleshoot.

Whatever the reason, it is sometimes necessary to completely restore your system. The Windows 98 Backup utility provides a solution for these problems.

RESTORING FILES TO THEIR ORIGINAL LOCATIONS

To restore files to their original locations, follow these steps:

1. Insert the tape that contains the backup you want to restore.
2. Select the Restore tab from the Backup utility's main program window. Click the Refresh button.
3. In the dialog box that appears, select the backup set from which you want to restore. Check the box next to the backup set you want and click OK.
4. In the What to Restore section, select the files you want to restore by checking the appropriate boxes.
5. In the Where to Restore drop-down box, select Original Location.
6. Click the Start button
7. A window appears, updating you on the status of the restore procedure. When the process is finished, a dialog box appears with the message `Operation Completed`. Click OK to finish.

PART

II

CH

10

RESTORING FILES TO A NEW LOCATION

To restore files to a new location, follow these steps:

1. Insert the tape that contains the backup you want to restore.
2. Select the Restore tab from the Backup utility's main program window. Click the Refresh button.
3. In the dialog box that appears, select the backup set from which you want to restore. Check the box next to the one you want and click OK.
4. In the What to Restore section, select the files you want to restore by checking the appropriate boxes.
5. In the Where to Restore drop-down box, select Alternate Location.
6. A selection box appears below the Where to Restore drop-down box. Select an alternative location to which you want to restore your files.
7. Click the Start button.
8. A window appears, updating youon the status of the restore procedure. When the restore process is finished, a dialog box appears with the message `Operation Completed`. Click OK to finish.

CHANGING RESTORE SETTINGS AND OPTIONS

To change the restore options, select the Restore tab from the Backup utility's main program window and then select the Options button. In the Restore Options dialog box, the General tab displays the rules the Backup utility uses when restoring files (such as what to do if the files being restored have the same names as files that already exist at the restore location).

Tip #64	If you plan to restore the Registry from your backups, make sure to select the Restore Windows Registry box on the Advanced tab of the Restore Options dialog box.

TROUBLESHOOTING

PROBLEMS BACKING UP THE REGISTRY

Why am I having problems restoring a Registry backup?

A problem when you configure Microsoft Backup to back up your Registry can result in not backing up the Registry at all. This situation can occur if you are not backing up the Windows folder and if all the files you are backing up are on a drive other than the boot drive.

This problem occurs because several Registry references depend on device drivers and dynamic link library (DLL) files located in the Windows folder. The Registry cannot be backed up and restored properly without the corresponding Windows folder.

To avoid this problem when you want to back up the Registry, always back up the Windows folder and always back up at least one file on the boot drive.

SECRETS OF MASTERING THE WINDOWS 98 ENVIRONMENT: USING REPORTS FOR BACKUP AND RESTORE

If you are experiencing problems with backup or restore operations, you might want to generate a type of log called a report. The report is designed to give you a better indication as to why the operation is failing. You also have the option of printing a report. Here's a sample report:

```
Start Job Report
    Job Name: File Backup
    File Backup Job Started - 10/25/98 10:14:12PM
    Processed File Count: 1
    Total Bytes Before Compression: 722,944
    Operation Completed - Yes
    File Backup Job Ended - 10/25/98 1:18:12PM
End Job Report
```

To configure the report options, follow these steps:

1. Start Microsoft Backup and then click the Close button in the Welcome to Microsoft Backup window.
2. Click the Options button and then click the Report tab.

To view or print a report, follow these steps:

1. Click the Tools menu and then click Reports.
2. Click either View or Print.

You can look at the history of the backup and restore operations in the Report.txt file. The file is located in the System\Program Files\Accessories\Backup\Reports\ directory. You can open this simple text file with Notepad.

CHAPTER 11

INSTALLING AND MANAGING APPLICATIONS

In this chapter

Understanding How Windows Runs Applications

Windows applications into two general categories: 32-bit applications (designed for Windows NT, Windows 95, and Windows 98) and 16-bit applications (designed for Windows 3.1 and lower versions). This chapter discusses how Windows 98 runs these programs. The last part of the chapter describes how to work with DOS applications in Windows 98.

Support for 32-Bit Windows Applications

Many, but not all, of the benefits of using Windows 98 result from its support for 32-bit applications. The following list outlines the advantages of working with Windows 98:

- Support for long filenames (up to 255 characters). If adapted, 16-bit applications can use long filenames.
- More efficient memory addressing.
- The capability to run each 32-bit application in its own memory space and isolate other applications if an application crashes.
- Preemptive multitasking and multithreading, allowing more efficient sharing of CPU time than with cooperative multitasking.
- Greater availability of system resources, allowing you to run more applications, create more windows, use more fonts, and so on, without running out of system resources.
- Support for Windows 3.1 applications. Although Windows 3.1 applications do not gain the benefits of a 32-bit application, they do benefit from the advantages Windows 98 derives from 32-bit device drivers and improved printing throughput due to multitasking at the operating system level.
- Improved support for MS-DOS applications.

→ To find out more about filename length in a DOS environment, **see** "Working with Long Filenames," **p. 120.**

Support for MS-DOS and 16-Bit Windows Applications

Windows 98 can run applications designed specifically for Windows 95 and Windows 98, as well as most older Windows 3.1 applications, DOS-based applications, and applications designed for Windows NT. Windows 98 does not require the traditional CONFIG.SYS, AUTOEXEC.BAT, and INI files for configuration information. However, for backward compatibility, Windows 98 can use settings from INI files and can maintain its own versions of CONFIG.SYS and AUTOEXEC.BAT to support loading real-mode device drivers.

What the Designed for Windows Logo Really Means

The Designed for Windows 95 logo program has evolved into the Designed for Windows 2000 and Windows 98 logo program. In the early days of the Windows logo program, the requirements were relatively permissive, but the program has continually been reevaluated and revised. Microsoft has added many new requirements to better serve users who are looking for software that is designed to take full advantage of the Windows 98 and Windows NT operating environments and that is fully compatible with other Windows applications. To acquire the logo, the application must be submitted for testing by an independent, third-party testing firm (VeriTest).

The basic concept behind the logo program is to provide users with a means for selecting software that has been tested for compatibility and functionality on both the Windows 98 and Windows 2000 platforms. The application has to conform to a series of criteria that ensure that the application takes full advantage of the Windows 98/Windows 2000 technology and that it is compatible with other Windows software.

 For in-depth information and specifications for the logo program and to download the "Designed for Windows Logo" handbook, visit the following Web site:

`http://msdn.microsoft.com/winlogo/default.asp`

Caution

Beware of software that claims to be "Windows compatible" and that displays a logo to this effect. Be sure your applications have the genuine Designed for Windows NT and Windows 98 logo.

PART

II

CH

11

INSTALLING WINDOWS APPLICATIONS

Most Windows 98 (and Windows 95) applications are easily installed using the setup programs that come with these applications. Installing DOS-based applications is a different matter and often not as simple. This subject is covered in a later section, "Working with MS-DOS Applications."

→ To better manage your work environment, **see** "Adding and Removing Programs in the Start Menu," **p. 330.**

INSTALLING WINDOWS 98 APPLICATIONS

The basic technique for installing Windows 98 applications consists of running the Setup (or Install) program for the application and following the prompts. The Setup program takes care of all the installation details. You can start the Setup program from the Run command on the Start menu.

Tip #65

For the most part, all Windows 98 applications install with a SETUP.EXE file. However, DOS applications are more likely to use the INSTALL.EXE or INSTALL.BAT files.

Another way to install an application is to use the Install Programs Wizard accessible via the Add/Remove Programs icon in the Control Panel. The Add/Remove Programs dialog box provides a common starting point for adding and removing Windows applications and Windows system components and accessories.

To use the Install Programs Wizardto install a Windows application, follow these steps:

1. Open the Start menu and choose Settings, Control Panel.

2. In the Control Panel window, use the Add/Remove Programs icon to open the Add/Remove Programs Properties sheet shown in Figure 11.1.

Figure 11.1
The Add/Remove Programs Properties dialog box is used to add and remove applications.

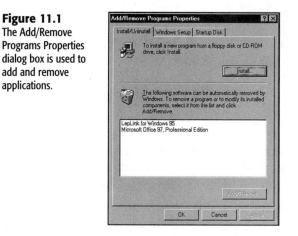

3. Choose Install to start the Install Program Wizard.

4. When the Install Program from Floppy Disk or CD-ROM dialog box is displayed, insert the first floppy disk or compact disc in the appropriate drive and choose Next.

5. The wizard searches the disk's root directory for an installation program (usually named SETUP.EXE or INSTALL.EXE) and displays the command line in the Run Installation Program dialog box.

6. If the wizard fails to find the Setup program (perhaps because it is in a subdirectory) or you want to run a different Setup program (perhaps from a network drive), you can choose Browse and select a different file in the Browse dialog box. Choose Open to insert the selected file name in the wizard.

7. When the correct command line for the Setup program is displayed in the Run Installation Program dialog box, choose Finish to start the Setup program and begin the application installation.

Tip #66

If you have a problem getting an application to run properly after installing it directly with its SETUP.EXE program, using the Add/Remove Programs icon in the Control Panel for the install may remedy the problem. If the program is not listed, it probably must be installed from its own setup location; in this case, you cannot use the Add/Remove Programs feature. If neither of these work you will have to contact the vendor of the program for additional help.

INSTALLING 16-BIT WINDOWS APPLICATIONS

Windows 98 features full backward compatibility with 16-bit Windows 3.1 applications, enabling you to install and use your Windows 3.1 applications in Windows 98 without modification.

If you encounter a compatibility problem with a legacy application—an older application designed for a previous version of DOS or Windows—running in Windows 98, check with the application's developer for a patch or workaround for the problem. In some cases, perhaps the only solution is an upgrade to a new Windows 95 or Windows 98 version of the application.

You install Windows 3.1 applications in Windows 98 the same way that you do in Windows 3.1. You simply insert the first disk of the program's installation disks in your floppy disk or CD-ROM drives, run the Setup program, using the Run command on the Start menu, and follow the prompts and instructions.

> **Caution**
>
> Save a copyof your AUTOEXEC.BAT and CONFIG.SYS files before installing any new DOS or Windows 3.x application. After you install a Windows 3.x or DOS application, it is a good idea to check your AUTOEXEC.BAT files to see if any unnecessary programs or configuration lines were added. For example, some applications add a line that loads SHARE.EXE or SMARTDRV.EXE, neither of which are needed in Windows 98. These programs not only waste memory but also might cause problems on your system if they are loaded.

PART

II

CH

11

Of course, the Setup program for a legacy application will be tailored to Windows 3.1 instead of Windows 98. For example, the installation program usually offers to create Program Manager groups and update INI files. Windows 98 intercepts Program Manager updates and automatically converts them to Start menu shortcuts. Windows 98 also transfers WIN.INI and SYSTEM.INI entries into the Registry.

WHAT IF THERE'S NO SETUP PROGRAM?

You might occasionally encounter a Windows application that does not include a Setup program. Installation for small utilities, for example, usually consists of copying a couple of files to your hard disk and adding a shortcut to your Start menu to launch the application. You should find instructions for installing the application in an accompanying manual or README file.

ORGANIZING THE PROGRAMS MENU

When you install an application, the installation process creates a new item on the Programs menu. Although this item displays automatically, you can modify it. For example, items on the Programs menu can be removed, reorganized, or renamed. Although you can modify the Programs menu by using the same procedure that customizes the Start menu, described in Chapter 17, "Customizing the Look and Feel of Windows," you have greater flexibility if you use the following technique to directly modify the folders and shortcuts on which the Programs menu is based.

→ Because you use the Start menu to initiate much of what you do in Windows 98, it's never too early to learn more about customizing it. **See** "Adding and Removing Programs in the Start Menu," **p. 330.**

The Programs menu is a reflection of the contents of a Programs folder. You can find this folder under Windows, Start Menu if you are the only person using the computer. If the computer has multiple user profiles, the appropriate Programs folder for a specific user is found under Windows, Profiles, *username*, Start Menu.

A simple way to make sure you are modifying the correct Programs menu is to log on to Windows with the username whose Programs menu you want to change. Right-click in the gray area of the taskbar and choose Properties. Select the Start Menu Programs tab; then click the Advanced button. This sequence displays an Explorer window that is restricted to the appropriate Start menu. You can modify and reorganize the Start menu or Programs menu by modifying folders and shortcuts in this Explorer.

To work on the Programs menu only, open and select the Programs folder in the left Explorer pane. The folder hierarchy and shortcut names you see displayed in the right pane are used to create the Programs menu. Modifying the folders and shortcut names modifies the Programs menu. Use normal Explorer techniques for modifying folders and files.

Create new submenus under the Programs menu by creating new folders in the right pane. Drag and drop program shortcuts into these folders to reorganize them. Delete folders you do not want, but make sure you first remove shortcut icons you want to retain.

Change Program menu item names by selecting the folder or file, pressing F2, and editing or typing a new name. Reorder files and folders by renaming them. Windows sorts the folder and shortcut names in alphanumeric order to decide the order in which they display on the Programs menu. To reorganize the Programs menu, change the names to give the sort order you want. For example, if you want Microsoft Word to appear in the menu before Microsoft Excel and you want their names shortened, change the shortcut names to *1 Word* and *2 Excel*. Another way to open the Programs menu is by right-clicking the Start button and choosing Open.

WORKING WITH PROGRAM SHORTCUTS

In Chapter 6, "Managing Files with My Computer and Windows Explorer," you learned how to create *shortcuts* to your files and programs. This section introduces some more advanced techniques for working with shortcuts.

STARTING PROGRAMS ON STARTUP

If you routinely keep some programs open because you use them throughout the day, you can have Windows 98 start these programs automatically when you start Windows. To do so, you simply create a shortcut for the program in a special folder called the StartUp folder. The StartUp folder is located in the Programs folder on the Start menu.

To create a shortcut for a program in the StartUp folder, follow these steps:

1. Open the Start menu and choose Settings, Taskbar & Start Menu.
2. Select the Start Menu Programs tab.
3. Choose Add and then Browse.
4. Locate the program you want to add to the StartUp folder in the Browse dialog box (see Figure 11.2).

Figure 11.2
Use the Browse dialog box to locate the program you want to add to the StartUp folder.

5. Select the program and choose Open (or double-click the program).

   The pathname for the selected program is displayed in the Command Line text box of the Create Shortcut dialog box.
6. Choose Next and select the StartUp folder in the Select Program Folder dialog box (see Figure 11.3).

PART

II

CH

11

Figure 11.3
Select the StartUp folder as the destination for the shortcut.

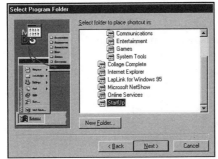

7. Type the name you want to appear in the Start menu in the text box and choose Finish.
8. Choose OK to close the Taskbar Properties dialog box.

Now, whenever you start Windows, the application you added to the Start menu starts automatically.

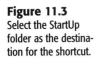

Tip #67	You can also organize the startup programs into one batch file instead, and then add the batch file to your StartUp folder. This approach saves time if you ever have to add or remove programs from the StartUp folder. Instead of managing each separate file, you can edit your batch file.

SPECIFYING HOW A SHORTCUT STARTS A PROGRAM

When you have created a shortcut for an application, you can customize the shortcut by using its Properties sheet. For example, when you create a shortcut for an application in the StartUp folder, as described in the preceding section, you can specify whether the application should start in a normal or a maximized window or be minimized as an icon on the taskbar. You can also add command-line parameters to the command line for the application, specify a folder for the application to start in, and assign a shortcut key for starting the application from the keyboard.

To customize a shortcut, follow these steps:

1. Locate the shortcut in My Computer or Windows Explorer.

2. Right-click the shortcut and choose Properties from the shortcut menu.

3. Select the Shortcut tab (see Figure 11.4).

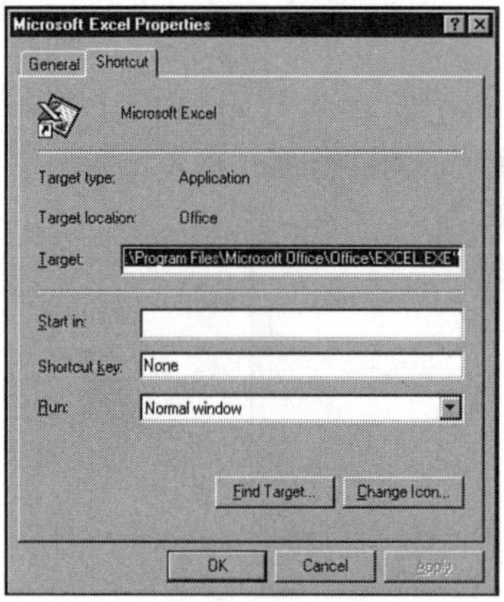

Figure 11.4
You can customize a shortcut using the Shortcut tab in the shortcut's property sheet.

4. To add a parameter to a command line, click in the Target text box, press End to move to the end of the command line, and enter a space. Type in the command-line parameter you want to add.

For example, to start an application and open a document within that application, type in the path and filename for the document you want to open at the end of the application's command line, as shown in Figure 11.5.

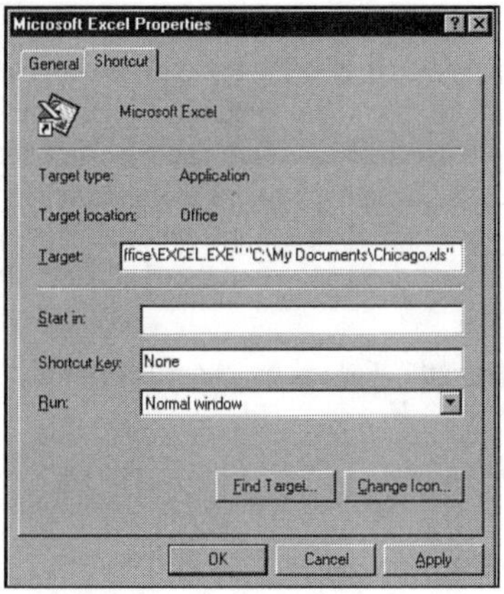

Figure 11.5
You can add command-line parameters to the command line for an application's shortcut.

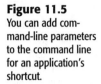

5. Specify a folder for the application to start from in the Start In text box.

   With some applications, you need to start the application in a folder that contains files related to the application.

6. Assign a keyboard shortcut for starting the application in the Shortcut Key text box.

   Keyboard shortcuts use a combination of Ctrl+Alt+*character.* You cannot use the Esc, Enter, Tab, spacebar, Print Screen, or Backspace keys.

   Shortcut keys defined in a Windows application take precedence over shortcut keys defined for a shortcut. Be sure to use a unique keyboard shortcut.

7. Specify whether you want the application to run in a normal window, in a maximized window, or minimized as an icon.

8. Choose OK.

PART

II

CH

11

MANAGING FILE ASSOCIATIONS

Recall that in Windows 3.x, you can associate a file extension with an application. For example, you can associate the .DOC extension that Microsoft Word adds to files to Word, so that when you choose a file with the .DOC extension, the file is opened in Word.

In Windows 98 you can define a *file type*, associate it with a file extension, and then associate any number of *actions* with the file type. Again, using Word as an example, you can define the Microsoft Word Document file type and then define one or more actions associated with that file type. The default action can be executed by choosing a file with the .DOC extension in Windows Explorer or in a folder window or by right-clicking a .DOC file and choosing the default action from the top of the shortcut menu that is displayed.

Other actions that you define and associate with a file type appear in the shortcut menu when you right-click a file of that type. When Microsoft Word for Windows is installed, for example, the Print command is automatically associated with the Word Document file type, so you can right-click a Word file and choose Print from the shortcut menu. The document is opened in Word, printed, and then closed.

Tip #68

You can also associate multiple file types to the same extension. This practice may be helpful if you have both Microsoft Word and WordPad applications on your computer. This approach is also helpful if you use .DBF extension database files, for example, with dBASE, FoxPro, and Act!. To associate multiple applications to the same file extension, first decide which default application to use (that is, determine which application will apply 80% of the time). The following example associates Microsoft Word and WordPad to the .DOC extension.

1. Open My Computer. From the View menu, choose Folder Options and then choose the File Types tab.

2. Find Microsoft Word Document in the Registered File Types list and click on the Edit button.

3. Under Actions, click on the New button.

4. In the Action box, type Open with WordPad in the Application Used to Perform Action box, browse to the location of WORDPAD.EXE, or type the full path to WORDPAD.EXE, enclosed in quotation marks.

5. Click OK and then click Close All until you are back at the My Computer window.

Now if you double-click a .DOC file, it still opens with Microsoft Word, but if you right-click a .DOC file, the shortcut menu appears with the option to Open with WordPad. Choose Open with WordPad on that menu. You have successfully associated two applications to the same file extension!

HOW APPLICATIONS REGISTER FILE TYPES

All file types and their actions are registered in the Windows Registry. This information is stored in the HKEY_CLASSES_ROOT key of the Registry. If you are experienced in working in the Registry using REGEDIT, you can add and edit file types directly in the Registry.

→ If you just can't wait to get your hands on the "nerve center" of Windows 98, **see** "Understanding the Windows Registry," **p. 479.**

REGISTERING A NEW FILE TYPE

Many applications automatically register a file type when you install them. In some cases, however, you might want to register a file type for an extension that is not already associated with an application.

To register a new file type, follow these steps:

1. In Windows Explorer, choose <u>V</u>iew, Folder <u>O</u>ptions.

2. Click the File Types tab of the Options dialog box (see Figure. 11.6).

3. Choose the <u>N</u>ew Type button.

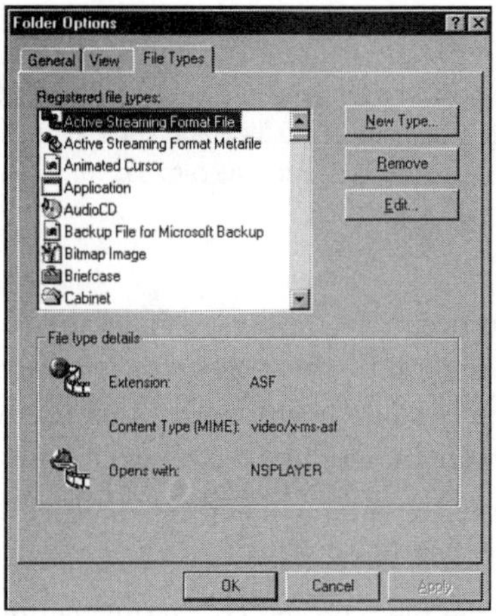

Figure 11.6
Register and modify
file types on the File
Types page of the
Options dialog box.

4. Enter a description of the file type in the <u>D</u>escription of Type text box.

   This description appears in the Registered File <u>T</u>ypes list on the File Types page of the Options dialog box. For example, if you want to use Microsoft Word to open WordPerfect files that use the extension .WPD, you could use the description WordPerfect Document, as shown in Figure 11.7.

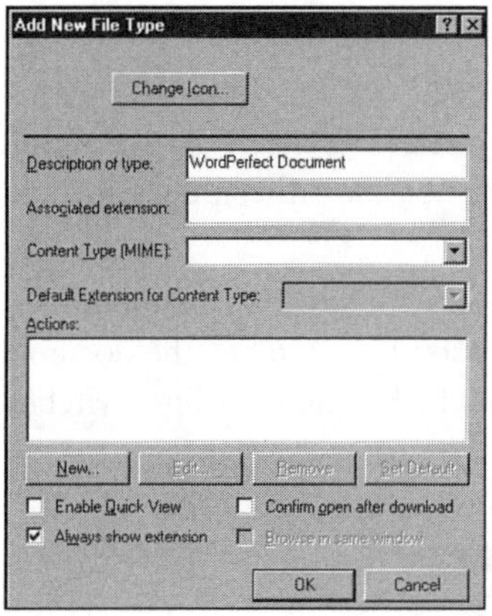

Figure 11.7
Enter the information
for a new file type in
the Add New File Type
dialog box.

5. Enter the file extension to be associated with this file type in the Asso<u>c</u>iated Extension text box. This entry is the three-letter file extension associated with DOS-based files. In this example, you would enter WPD.

6. Select the type of file from the Content <u>T</u>ype (MIME) list. This list shows all the installed applications in the Registry.

7. To specify an action to be performed on this file type by its associated program or to add a shortcut menu item for this file type, skip step 8 and continue with the next procedure to specify an action.

8. Click OK twice.

> **Note**
>
> Multipurpose Internet mail extensions (MIME) is a standard for defining different types of file attachments for email delivered over the Internet. The goal of MIME is to allow multiple types of data—such as text, video and audio files, and application files—to be gathered together in an email message and transferred successfully from sender to recipient even if they are using different email applications.

You can specify the type of action that occurs on a file type when the file is chosen. The action you specify also appears as an item on the file type's shortcut menu and on the File menu when that file is selected. This procedure begins with either the Add New File Type or Edit File Type dialog box open. To create actions for a new file type, follow the preceding procedure through step 7; then continue here. To edit an existing file type, select the file type from the Registered File Types list and click Edit.

To simultaneously specify actions for the file type and create shortcut menu items, follow these steps:

1. Click New to add a new action to the file type in the New Action dialog box.

   The action is actually a custom command that is displayed on the shortcut menu when you right-click the file.

2. Type an action, for example, Open in Word, in the Actions text box.

   Your entry appears as an item on the shortcut menu for this file type. You can type anything, but commands usually start with a verb. If you want the command to have an accelerator key, precede that letter with an ampersand (&).

3. Enter or select the application to be used to perform the action in the Application Used to Perform Action text box. If you do not know the application's path, use the Browse button to select the application.

   Some applications have command-line switches you can append to the end of the command line to control how the application behaves. See the documentation or online help for your application to find out which command-line switches are available.

   Figure 11.8 shows the completed New Action dialog box.

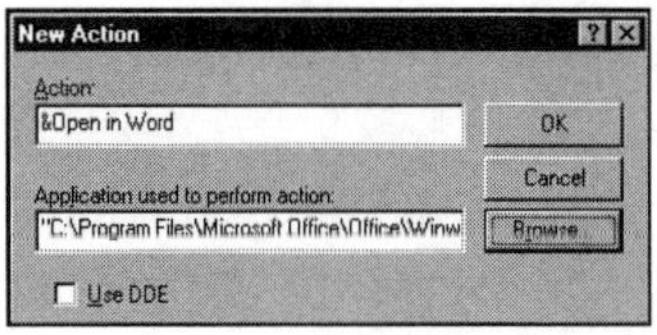

Figure 11.8
Designate a shortcut menu action and the program used to perform that action in the New Action dialog box.

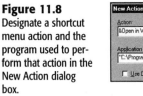

4. Select the Use DDE check box if the program uses *dynamic data exchange (DDE)* and add the DDE statements for this action. This option is rarely used.

   See the next section, "Understanding DDE Settings," for more information on using DDE statements to communicate with an application.

5. Choose OK.

6. If you have more than one action listed in the <u>A</u>ctions box, select the one you want to be the default action and choose the <u>S</u>et Default button.

   The default action is the one that is performed when you double-click a file of this type in Explorer or a folder window.

7. Select the appropriate check boxes for the file type. Choose from the following:

Enable <u>Q</u>uick View	Quick View allows you to view a file without opening it.
Al<u>w</u>ays Show Extension	Always displays the MS-DOS extension even when the Hide File Extension option has been chosen.
Confirm <u>O</u>pen After Download	Request confirmation before opening files after downloading them from the Internet.

8. Choose Close twice.

→ Quick View is a real time-saver. To get a head start on saving time with this feature, **see** "Previewing a Document with Quick View," **p. 101.**

UNDERSTANDING DDE SETTINGS

If the application you use to create a file type and define an action uses DDE, you can use DDE statements to exercise more control over the actions carried out by the application. *DDE* statements are messages that are passed to the application to tell it which actions to carry out.

Figure 11.9 illustrates the use of DDE statements in the definition of the Print action for the Microsoft Excel Worksheet type. The first DDE statement in the <u>D</u>DE Message text box is the command passed to Microsoft Excel to specify which action to take when the Print command is selected from the shortcut menu for an Excel Worksheet:

```
[open("%1")][print()][close()]
```

This DDE statement tells Excel to open the selected file, print the file with the default print options, and then close the worksheet.

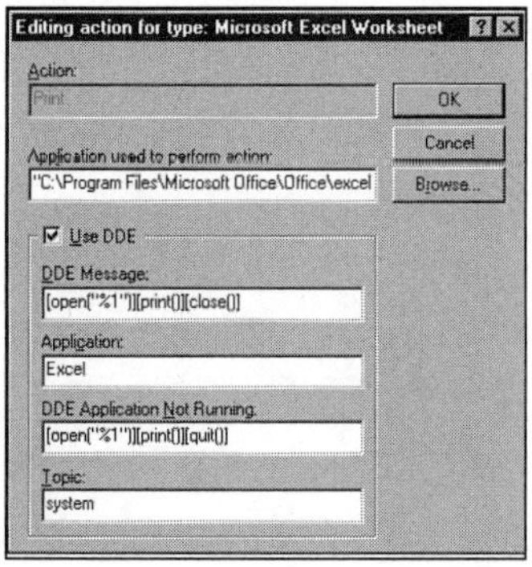

Figure 11.9
You can use DDE statements to control the actions associated with a registered file type.

PART
II

CH
11

The entry in the Application box is the string used to start a DDE exchange with the specified program. If this box is left empty, the command that is displayed in the Application Used to Perform Action text box is used.

The following DDE statement appears in the DDE Application Not Running box:

```
[open("%1")][print()][quit()]
```

This statement starts Excel, prints the selected file, and then exits Excel.

These two simple examples illustrate how useful DDE statements can be. By specifying two different statements in the DDE Message and DDE Applications Not Running boxes, you can control the behavior of Excel when you select the Print command from the shortcut menu. When Excel is already opened, the file you select is opened in that session of Excel (that is, another session of Excel is not started), printed, and then closed. The running session of Excel is not terminated.

When Excel is not already open, on the other hand, and you select the Print command, Excel is started, the selected file is opened and printed, and then Excel isshut down.

CHANGING THE ICON FOR A FILE TYPE OR OTHER OBJECT

You can change the icon used to designate a file type, drive, folder, and other objects on your computer. To change the icon used for a particular file type or object, follow these steps:

1. In Windows Explorer, choose View, Folder Options.
2. Choose the File Types tab to display the File Types page of the Options dialog box (refer to Figure 11.6).
3. Select the file type or other object whose icon you want to change in the Registered File Types list.
4. Choose the Edit button.
5. Choose the Change Icon button to display the Change Icon dialog box.
6. Select a new icon from the Current Icon scrolling list.

   The name of the file containing the icons currently shown is listed in the File Name text box. You can use the Browse button to search for a new file containing different icons. Figure 11.10 shows the selection of icons in the Moricons.dll file, which is located in the Windows folder on your hard drive.
7. Choose OK and then Close twice.

Figure 11.10
Use the Change Icon dialog box to select a new icon for a file type or other type of object.

WORKING WITH MS-DOS APPLICATIONS

Although Windows 98 is designed to shield the user from the often-confusing world of the command line, AUTOEXEC.BAT, CONFIG.SYS, and memory-management practices, Windows 98 offers surprisingly rich support for those users who still desire or need to work in the MS-DOS environment. Windows 98 offers extensive control over MS-DOS application environments, allowing you to fine-tune your MS-DOS sessions to optimize performance.

Many MS-DOS applications run under Windows 98 without any modifications. In some cases you need to modify the setup for the application for it to run in Windows. For applications that won't run at all under Windows 98, a special mode helps you run them quickly and easily from within Windows and then automatically returns you to your Windows session when you're finished.

PART

II

CH

11

INSTALLING AND UNINSTALLING MS-DOS APPLICATIONS

Installing MS-DOS applications is a straightforward procedure. Simply locate and run the installation program for the application. The installation program creates a storage area for the application, copies the files to it, and performs the additional operating system configuration chores that might be necessary for successful operation. You might have to handle some of the steps yourself. Look for the documentation for the manual program installation instructions in the program folder. Often, this file is a simple text file labeled README.TXT or INSTALL.TXT.

You can also run the installation program for an MS-DOS application from the MS-DOS prompt. Running the installation program from an MS-DOS prompt is just like doing it on a machine that's running only MS-DOS. Follow these steps to begin:

1. Open a new MS-DOS session from the Start menu.
2. At the MS-DOS prompt, enter the command to start the installation program (for example, `a:\install.exe`) and press Enter.
3. When the installation program is finished, close the MS-DOS session manually or run the application if you want.

Some MS-DOS applications don't have installation programs. This practice is most common with shareware applications or small utility programs.

To install your application manually, follow these simple steps:

1. Open a new MS-DOS session from the Start menu.

2. At the MS-DOS prompt, enter the command to create a folder for your program (for example, md c:\myprog) and press Enter.

3. Enter the command to copy the program to the new folder, such as xcopy a:*.* c:\myprog. MS-DOS copies the files to the new folder.

You might need to alter the preceding routine slightly if your application comes as a compressed archive (such as a Zip file or an ARJ file). Usually, all that is required is an additional step for decompression after the files are copied.

CONFIGURING YOUR MS-DOS APPLICATION

Your MS-DOS applications are very likely to run fine without any reconfiguration. Preset configurations for the most popular MS-DOS applications are stored in Windows, and in many cases these configurations work perfectly. However, if your MS-DOS application doesn't run properly (or at all), you can modify many settings by using the Properties sheet to control how your MS-DOS application runs. To display the Edit Properties sheet, click the Properties button in the toolbar of the MS-DOS window.

GENERAL PROPERTIES

The General properties page is primarily informational, with minimal controls other than file attributes (see Figure 11.11).

Figure 11.11
The General properties page gives you most of the basic information about the file and easy access to control of the file attributes. Context-sensitive help is available at any time from the ? tool in the upper-right corner.

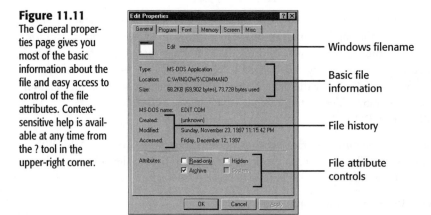

Windows filename

Basic file information

File history

File attribute controls

The only real controls exposed in the General properties page are the file attribute settings. These settings are used mainly to protect documents (by setting the read-only attribute), and you shouldn't alter them unless you have a specific reason.

PROGRAM PROPERTIES

The Program properties page gives you control over the basic environment your application starts with (see Figure 11.12).

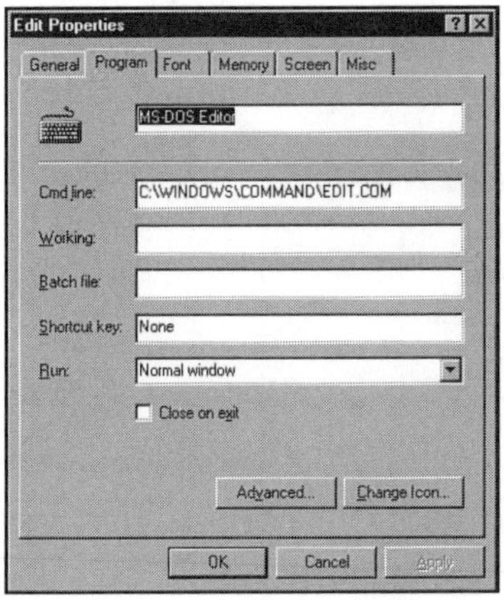

Figure 11.12
The Program properties page enables you to alter the variables used to name and start the application.

Choosing the Advanced button in the Program properties page opens the Advanced Program Settings dialog box, shown in Figure 11.13.

Senses application requirements for real-mode support

Keeps MS-DOS programs from reacting to the Windows environment

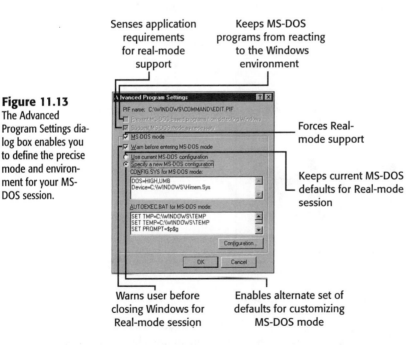

Figure 11.13
The Advanced Program Settings dialog box enables you to define the precise mode and environment for your MS-DOS session.

Forces Real-mode support

Keeps current MS-DOS defaults for Real-mode session

Warns user before closing Windows for Real-mode session

Enables alternate set of defaults for customizing MS-DOS mode

If you must run your application in MS-DOS mode, here's where you can enable it. You can even set up custom CONFIG.SYS and AUTOEXEC.BAT values for your session. If you click the Specify a New MS-DOS Configuration option, you can edit the special CONFIG.SYS and AUTOEXEC.BAT values right in this dialog box.

If you click the Configuration button, you see the dialog box displayed in Figure 11.14.

The settings under the Advanced Program Settings dialog box should be altered only if your MS-DOS application simply won't run in a standard session with the default settings. For that matter, don't even enable MS-DOS mode unless your application demands it.

→ If you are from the "old school" or just want to learn more about working with DOS, **see** "Using MS-DOS Mode," **p. 215.**

Figure 11.14
The Select MS-DOS Mode Configuration Options dialog box lets you control expanded memory, disk caching, disk access, and command-line editing.

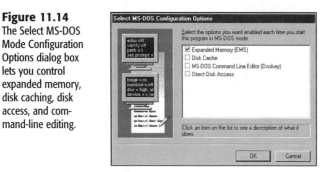

FONT PROPERTIES

The Font properties page is primarily informational, with minimal controls other than file attributes (see Figure 11.15). It works just like the Font list control on the MS-DOS session toolbar.

Figure 11.15
The Font properties page lets you choose the font type and size and gives you both a window and font preview.

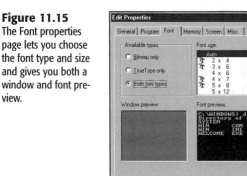

MEMORY PROPERTIES

The Memory properties page makes simple work of the traditional maze of MS-DOS memory management routines (see Figure 11.16). With a few mouse clicks, you can configure your application memory precisely as needed.

Enables protection
for session memory
range

Figure 11.16
The Memory proper-
ties page vastly sim-
plifies this formerly
arcane management
issue.

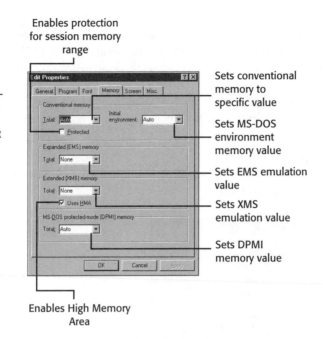

Sets conventional
memory to
specific value

Sets MS-DOS
environment
memory value

Sets EMS emulation
value

Sets XMS
emulation value

Sets DPMI
memory value

Enables High Memory
Area

If your application works without altering these values, *do not change them.* If your application doesn't work with the default settings, consult the documentation for your application
to determine what the appropriate settings are. Then you can alter the values in this dialog
box. Proceeding in any other way, unless you have considerable experience with the techniques involved, can severely inhibit the performance of your system.

SCREEN PROPERTIES

The Screen properties page lets you control the appearance of the MS-DOS session (see
Figure 11.17).

Figure 11.17
The Screen properties
page gives you control
of the size, type, and
performance of the
MS-DOS interface.

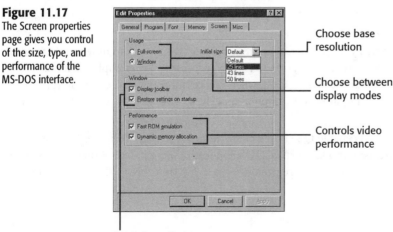

Choose base
resolution

Choose between
display modes

Controls video
performance

Controls toolbar usage

You might find that certain MS-DOS programs (especially those running in Graphics mode) respond poorly to the video emulation used in windowed mode. If so, try defeating the performance defaults by clearing the Fast ROM Emulation and Dynamic Memory Allocation options. Fast ROM Emulation tells the Windows 98 display driver to mimic the video hardware to help display MS-DOS programs faster. Dynamic Memory Allocation releases display memory to other programs when the MS-DOS session isn't using it. If you experience strange display problems with your MS-DOS programs, try changing these settings.

MISCELLANEOUS PROPERTIES

The Misc properties page covers the remaining configuration items that don't fit under the other categories (see Figure 11.18).

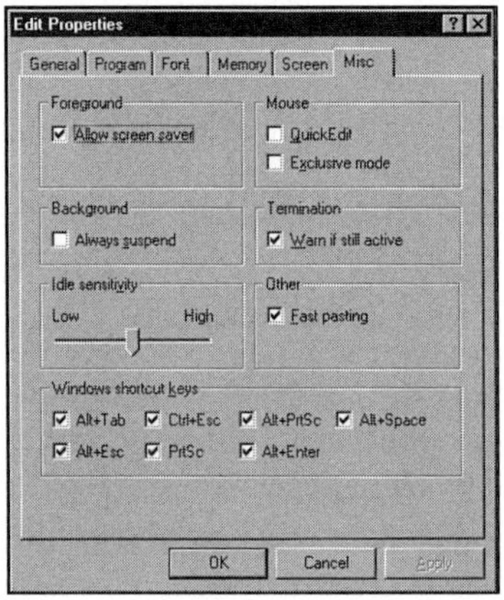

Figure 11.18
The Misc properties page controls screen saver, mouse, background operation, program termination, shortcut key, and editing options.

- The Allow Screen Saver check box lets your default Windows screen saver operate even if your MS-DOS session has the foreground.

- The Always Suspend item freezes your MS-DOS application when you bring another application (either MS-DOS or Windows) to the foreground. If you have an application that must perform time-sensitive operations (such as a communications program), make sure to disable this option.

- Idle Sensitivity tells your MS-DOS program to yield the system to other applications if it really isn't doing anything important. A word processor, for example, won't have a problem letting go of the system clock when you're not using it. A communications program, however, might need to respond quickly, so you want to set its idle sensitivity to Low.

- The Mouse controls enable QuickEdit mode (letting you mark text using just the mouse) and Exclusive mode (the MS-DOS application has control of the mouse cursor when the application is in the foreground, even if you try to move the mouse out of the MS-DOS window).

- The <u>W</u>arn If Still Active item in the Termination box tells Windows to notify you before the MS-DOS session is closed. It's really best to leave this enabled unless you are absolutely certain that the MS-DOS program will never, ever have open data files when you close it.

- The <u>F</u>ast Pasting setting simply tells Windows that your MS-DOS program can handle a raw data stream dump from the Windows Clipboard. Some MS-DOS programs clog at full speed, so if you paste to your MS-DOS application and you consistently lose characters, turn off this setting.

- The Windows Shortcut <u>K</u>eys item allows you to override the standard quick navigation aids built into the Windows environment, just for your MS-DOS session (some MS-DOS programs think they can get away with using the same keys, and something has to give—Windows!). By default, Windows "owns" these shortcuts, but you can lend them to your MS-DOS application by clearing them here.

USING MS-DOS MODE

Although you can run most DOS applications without any difficulties from within Windows, you might have problems with some poorly designed MS-DOS applications; some MS-DOS applications demand total control over system resources and access hardware directly.

Windows 98 accommodates a poorly behaved application to the best of its capability, via *MS-DOS mode*. This mode is the equivalent of Real mode present in older versions of Windows, with some improvements.

MS-DOS mode works by giving the errant MS-DOS application the entire system for the duration of the session. Windows removes itself from memory, leaving only a small "stub" loader in preparation for its return to control of your system.

Before you decide to enable MS-DOS mode for an application, try these other options:

- Confirm that you've optimized the MS-DOS session settings for that application. Check the program's documentation for special memory requirements or other unusual needs. You might be able to adjust the MS-DOS support in Windows to make the application work in a standard MS-DOS session.

- Try running the application in Full screen mode, using the Alt+Enter key sequence.

If either of the preceding methods works, you will have a faster, more convenient alternative to the DOS window, that provides the full benefit of Windows multitasking and other features, all of which disappear during the MS-DOS mode session.

Whenever possible, Windows 98 determines that an application needs to run in MS-DOS mode and automatically closes down all other applications and switches to this mode. Unless you specify otherwise, Windows warns you when it is about to switch to MS-DOS mode.

PART

II

CH

11

In some cases, you might have to manually configure an application to run in MS-DOS mode. If you try to run such an application, an error message tells you that you can't run the application in Windows. In this case, you should manually configure the application to run in MS-DOS mode, using the following steps:

1. If you haven't created a shortcut for the application, create one now. You must use a shortcut to modify the settings of a DOS application.
2. Right-click the shortcut for the application and choose Properties.
3. Select the Program tab and choose Advanced to display the Advanced Program Settings dialog box.
4. Select the Prevent MS-DOS–based Programs from Detecting Windows option.
5. Choose OK.

Click the shortcut icon to try running the application. If the application still doesn't run, follow these steps:

1. Open the Advanced Program Settings dialog box again, as in steps 2–3 in the preceding task.
2. Select the MS-DOS Mode option.
3. Choose OK.

Try running the application again. If it still doesn't run, you have to modify the configuration for the MS-DOS mode, using the following steps:

1. Open the Advanced Program Settings dialog box.
2. Select the Specify a New MS-DOS Configuration option. The dialog box is displayed, as shown Figure 11.19.

   Selecting this option allows you to override the default settings for the MS-DOS mode session.

Figure 11.19
Windows enables you to override the default settings for MS-DOS mode support. You can even run a special CONFIG.SYS and AUTOEXEC.BAT file for each application.

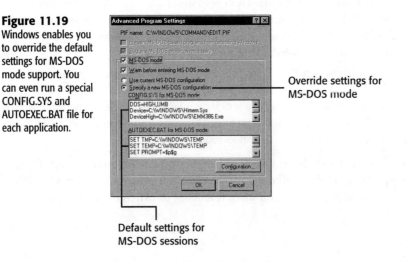

Override settings for MS-DOS mode

Default settings for MS-DOS sessions

3. Modify the lines in the CONFIG.SYS for MS-DOS mode and AUTOEXEC.BAT for MS-DOS mode windows as needed to allow this application to run.

   The changes you make here affect this application only. In this way you can customize each application that must run in MS-DOS mode.

4. If necessary, choose the Configuration button, select from the options in the Select MS-DOS Configuration Options dialog box, and choose OK.

   Be aware that when you choose from among the options in this dialog box, you remove the entries that already appear in the CONFIG.SYS and AUTOEXEC.BAT text boxes.

> **Caution**
>
> Use the Direct Disk Access option with great care. It is possible for an MS-DOS application to destroy long filename support when you select this option.

5. Choose OK twice to close the dialog boxes.

> **Tip #69**
>
> If Windows 98 does not restart after you quit the MS-DOS program running in MS-DOS mode, type `win /w` at the command prompt to restart Windows.
>
> You might also want to add that line in the custom AUTOEXEC.BAT file for your MS-DOS program so that Windows starts properly after you exit from the MS-DOS program.

 If you are having problems with your MS-DOS applications, see the section titled "Running MS-DOS-Based Programs" in the "Troubleshooting" section at the end of the chapter.

PART

II

CH

11

REMOVING APPLICATIONS

When you install a Windows application, not only do you copy the application's files into its own folder, but in most cases numerous other support files are copied into the Windows folder and the Windows Registry file is modified as well. For this reason, uninstalling an application can be a complex procedure. Fortunately, many application Setup programs now offer an uninstall option to automate the process when you need to remove the application from your system. The Add/Remove Programs Properties sheet has an uninstall feature that can help with this process.

UNINSTALLING APPLICATIONS AUTOMATICALLY

To uninstall an application automatically, start by opening the Control Panel and choosing the Add/Remove Programs icon to open the Add/Remove Programs Properties sheet—the same sheet you used to install the application (see Figure 11.20). Only applications that provide uninstall programs specifically designed to work with Windows 98 are displayed in the list of applications that Windows 98 can remove automatically.

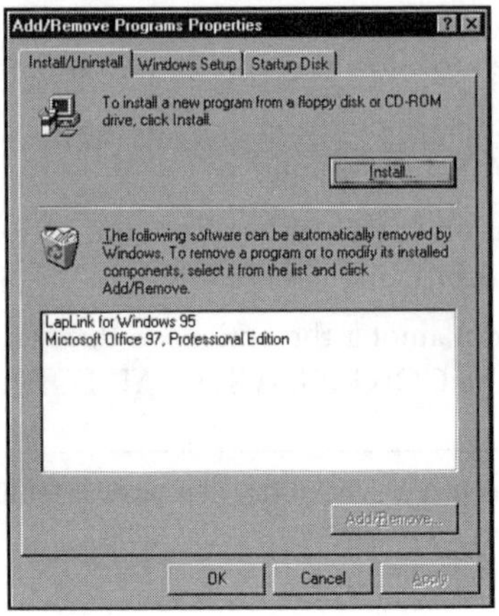

Figure 11.20
In the Add/Remove
Programs Properties
sheet, you can
remove applications
as well as install
them.

To remove an application, select it from the list of applications in the lower portion of the dialog box and choose Remove. After you confirm that you want to remove the program, Windows runs the selected application's uninstall program.

REMOVING MS-DOS APPLICATIONS

If you decide to remove an MS-DOS application from your computer, follow these steps:

1. Locate the application folder in Windows Explorer or My Computer.

2. Check to make sure no data files are in the folder (or subfolders in the folder).

3. Drag the folder to the Recycle Bin or press Del and choose Yes.

→ For more information about removing files and folders in Windows 98, see "Deleting Files and Folders," **p. 98.**

TROUBLESHOOTING

RUNNING MS-DOS PROGRAMS IN WINDOWS 98

When I double-click an MS-DOS program icon, I receive the following error message:
```
This program cannot be run due to restrictions in effect on this computer.
Please contact your system administrator.
```

This same behavior occurs if you type the name and path of the program from the Run command on the Start menu and then click OK.

With so many people working on a network these days, unforeseen issues can arise. This particular error occurs if you are connected to a network server and the network administrator has set a system policy using System Policy Editor (POLEDIT.EXE) that has disabled your ability to use the MS-DOS prompt. The administrator may not have been aware that when the MS-DOS prompt was disabled through a system policy, it also disabled all MS-DOS programs that may have been available in Windows.

This behavior can also occur if System Policy Editor on a local computer has disabled the MS-DOS prompt through a Registry edit.

To resolve this problem, you can do one of two things:

You can edit the Registry using System Policy Editor (POLEDIT.EXE) or Registry Editor (REGEDIT.EXE) if you have the permission to do so. Or, contact your system administrator and request that he or she enable the MS-DOS prompt if possible.

If the first method is not an option, then you may be able to work around this problem by restarting your computer in MS-DOS mode to specifically run your MS-DOS programs. However, the system administrator might also have set a policy to disable single-mode MS-DOS programs, and you might not be able to run your programs in MS-DOS mode either.

SECRETS OF MASTERING THE WINDOWS 98 ENVIRONMENT: KEEPING WINDOWS 3.X SETTINGS FOR APPLICATIONS

If you decide to upgrade from Windows 3.x by placing Windows 98 in the Windows 3.*x* directory, you don't have to reinstall all of your applications. The Windows 98 Setup program automatically adds information about the currently installed Windows 3.x applications to the Windows 98 Registry. The Setup program also converts existing Program Manager groups and adds them to the Programs menu on the Start menu.

If you choose to install Windows 98 in a different directory, you have to reinstall all Windows-based applications to ensure that they will function properly while running in the Windows 98 environment. Copying .GRP and .INI files from your previous \Windows directory, though a valiant effort, is not enough to run applications under Windows 98.

WORKING WITH APPLICATIONS

CHAPTER 12

SHARING DATA BETWEEN APPLICATIONS

In this chapter

UNDERSTANDING THE DATA-SHARING CAPABILITIES OF WINDOWS 98

Windows 98 enables you to share date in three ways. At the simplest level, you can transfer data from one application to another by using the Clipboard to copy and paste. When you exchange data with this method, no link is established between the source and destination documents.

The second way to share data between applications is to establish a link between the source and destination applications. Windows 98 and many Windows applications support *object linking and embedding (OLE)*, a technology that lets you use data from a source or *server application* in one or more other destination or *client applications*. If you link data and then update the source data, the destination data is automatically updated also. For example, you can have a live data feed of stock prices continually update an Excel worksheet.

A third way to share data, which also uses the OLE technology, is to embed data. You can use object linking and embedding to create *compound documents*, documents that use data embedded from other applications. The difference between embedding an object in a document and cutting and pasting or linking data is that you can edit the embedded object without leaving the application it's in. For example, you can edit an Excel chart from within a Word document.

USING THE WINDOWS CLIPBOARD TO EXCHANGE DATA

The simplest way to exchange data from one location to another, whether it is within an application or between applications, is to use the Windows 98 Clipboard. The Clipboard is an application that you use to temporarily store data you are exchanging from one location to another. You *cut* or *copy* data to the Clipboard and then *paste* the data from the Clipboard into a document. The data remains in the Clipboard until you cut or copy new data to the Clipboard or remove it manually, so you can paste the data into a document as many times as you like.

CUTTING, COPYING, AND PASTING DATA

The most common method for transferring data via the Clipboard is to use the menu commands that are found in most Windows applications. The Cut, Copy, and Paste commands are usually found in the Edit menu. Note the distinction between cutting and copying. When you cut data from a document, that original data is *moved* to the Clipboard and no longer appears in its original location. When you copy data from a document, a copy of the data is placed on the Clipboard, and the original data remains intact where it was.

To cut or copy data from one location to another, follow these steps:

1. Select the data in the source document that you want to cut or copy to another document (or another location in the same document), as shown in Figure 12.1.

Figure 12.1
Select the data you want to cut or copy in the source document.

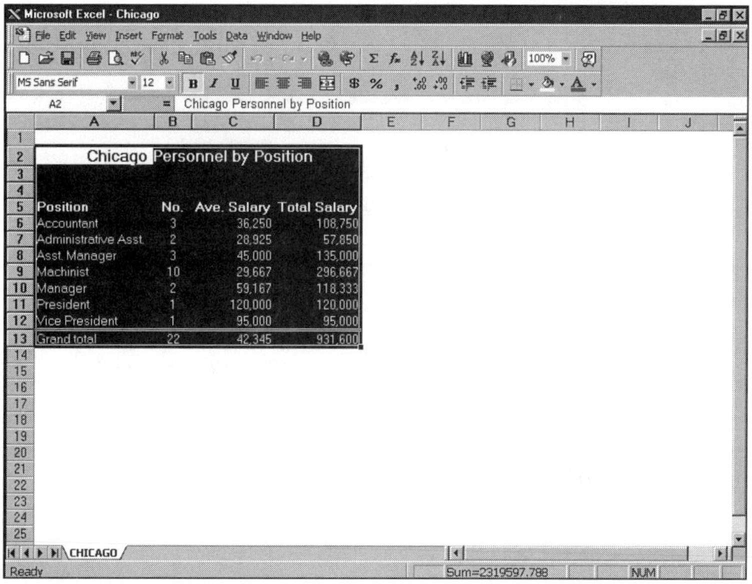

2. Choose <u>E</u>dit, Cu<u>t</u> or press Ctrl+X to cut (move) the data to the Clipboard.

   or

   Choose <u>E</u>dit, <u>C</u>opy or press Ctrl+C to copy the data to the Clipboard.

3. Place the insertion point at the point in the destination document where you want to paste the data.

   If you are working with a document in another application, open that application and the destination document and place the insertion point where you want the data.

4. Choose <u>E</u>dit, <u>P</u>aste or press Ctrl+V to paste the data from the Clipboard into the destination document. Figure 12.2 shows data from an Excel worksheet pasted into a Word document.

Many applications have Cut, Copy, and Paste buttons on a toolbar that you can use instead of the menu commands. Your application might also have shortcut menus that you can display by right-clicking the selected text. The shortcut menu has the Cu<u>t</u>, <u>C</u>opy, and <u>P</u>aste commands.

PART

III

CH

12

Tip #70

Quick View Plus is an add-on product for Windows 98 created by Inso Corporation. Quick View Plus enhances the Quick View feature that comes with Windows 98 in several ways. These include the capabilities to preview many more types of files and to copy and paste information from a file that you are viewing. This feature allows you to view a file created by an application you don't have on your computer and then to copy and paste information from that file into another document.

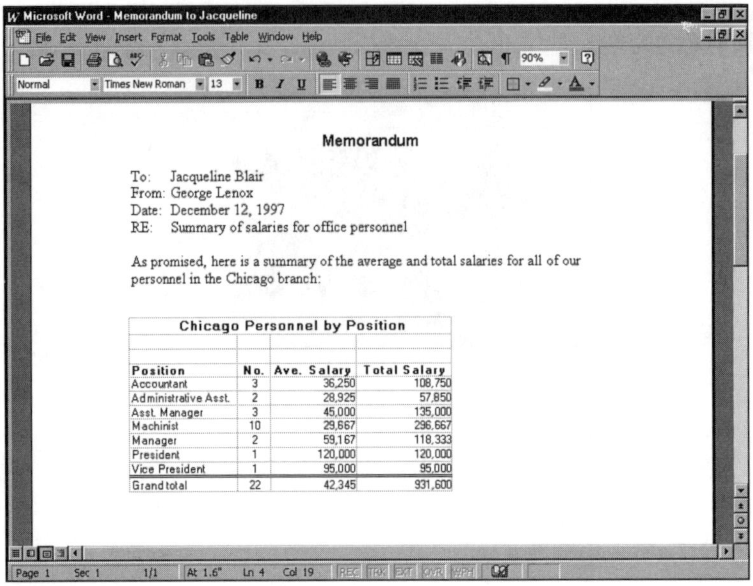

Figure 12.2
A data table from an Excel worksheet has been pasted into a Word document.

USING DRAG-AND-DROP EDITING TO MOVE OR COPY INFORMATION

A second method for exchanging information is to use the mouse to drag and drop selected information, which can be text, graphics, or data, from one location to another. When you drag and drop information, the information is not stored in the Clipboard. The information moves directly from one location to another. In this section, you learn how to drag and drop information within an application. In the section "Creating Compound Documents," later in this chapter, you learn how to drag and drop objects from one application into another.

To use the drag-and-drop method, you must be working with an application that supports it. The applications in the Microsoft Office suite support it, for example, as does WordPad. Check the documentation or online help for your application to find out whether it supports drag-and-drop editing.

To copy information with drag-and-drop editing, follow these steps:

1. Open the application and then the document that contains the text you want to move or copy.

2. Select the text you want to move or copy.

3. To *move* the text, position the mouse pointer over the selected area and drag the text. The mouse pointer changes as you drag.

   To *copy* the text, hold down the Ctrl key and then drag the selected text. A plus sign (+) appears next to the mouse pointer.

   Until you release the mouse button to drop the text, you can press or release the Ctrl button to change between copying and moving the selection.

4. Drag the text to the position in the document where you want to place it. The vertical bar indicates the position of the new text.

5. Release the mouse button to complete the move or copy procedure, and the text appears in the new location.

Some applications, such as Word for Windows, allow you to use drag-and-drop editing to move or copy text between two documents. To do so, make sure you can see both documents onscreen at the same time and then drag the item from one document to another using the preceding steps.

USING KEYBOARD SHORTCUTS

Keyboard shortcuts work the same as menu commands but are quicker to execute while typing. Table 12.1 shows the keyboard shortcuts that are common to all Windows 98 applications.

TABLE 12.1   CUT, COPY, AND PASTE KEYBOARD SHORTCUTS

Action	Shortcut Keys
Cut	Ctrl+X or Shift+Delete
Copy	Ctrl+C or Ctrl+Insert
Paste	Ctrl+V or Shift+Insert

COPYING INFORMATION TO A DIALOG BOX

You can use the keyboard shortcuts for cutting, copying, and pasting if you want to transfer information to a dialog box. You can use the keyboard shortcuts, for example, to copy the name and address information from a letter into the Envelopes and Labels dialog box in Word so you don't have to retype it.

To copy information from a document into a dialog box, follow these steps:

1. Select the information in the document that you want to copy into the dialog box.

2. Choose Edit, Copy or press Ctrl+C.

3. Open the dialog box into which you want to copy the information.

4. Place the insertion point in the text box into which you want to copy the data.

5. Press Ctrl+V to insert the text from the Clipboard. Figure 12.3 shows the Contact dialog box in Microsoft Outlook in which a recipient's address has been pasted into the Address text box.

When you are in a dialog box, you can't use the Edit menu or the toolbar buttons, which is why you need to make use of the keyboard shortcuts. You can reverse the previous procedure to copy data from a dialog box into a document: Select the data in the dialog box; press Ctrl+C to copy it to the Clipboard; and then use the menu, keyboard, or toolbar technique to paste the information into a document.

PART

III

CH

12

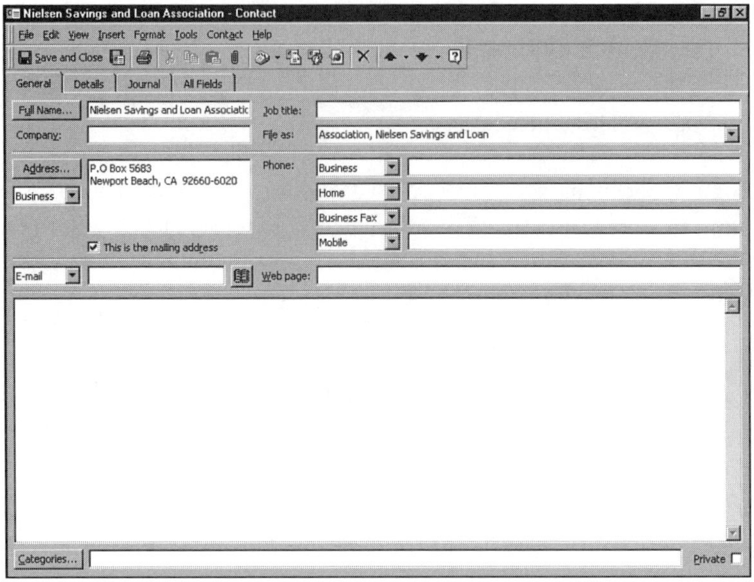

Figure 12.3
Paste the information into the text box in the dialog box.

CAPTURING SCREENS WITH THE CLIPBOARD

Windows has the built-in capability to capture screens. You won't be able to crop, rotate, scale, or perform other operations on the screen image, as you can with many of the screen-capturing applications that are available. But if your needs are simple, you can use the Clipboard to capture an image of your screen. The captured image is stored in the Clipboard in bitmap format.

To capture the entire screen and paste it into a document, follow these steps:

1. Set up the screen to appear as you want it in the screen image.
2. Press Print Screen to capture the entire screen using the screen resolution currently set for the display. The screen image is stored in the Clipboard.

   To capture just the contents of the active window, press the Alt+Print Screen keys.
3. Open the document in which you want to insert the image and place the insertion point where you want the image to appear.
4. Choose Edit, Paste or press Ctrl+V. Windows 98 pastes the screen image into the document in bitmap format.

Tip #71

Remember that the Clipboard does not stack cut or copied information. Therefore, if you have used a Windows or keyboard command to cut or copy an item to the Clipboard, doing so again without specifically saving the last Clipboard item overwrites the last item saved. When you finally go to paste the cut or copied item in another location, only the most recently cut or copied item appears in the paste.

⚠ *If you are working with Digital Video Display (DVD) images and trying to use the Print Screen key, you may run into some problems. For more information on how to handle this situation, see "Using the Print Screen Key" in the "Troubleshooting" section at the end of this chapter.*

VIEWING AND CHANGING CLIPBOARD DATA

You can view the contents of the Clipboard from the Clipboard Viewer. To open the Clipboard Viewer, choose Start, Programs, Accessories, System Tools, Clipboard Viewer. The last data that you cut or copied to the Clipboard appears in the Clipboard Viewer. If the Clipboard Viewer isn't listed in your Accessories menu, start the Add New Programs utility in Control Panel; choose the Windows Setup tab, System Tools; and install the Clipboard Viewer.

SAVING THE CONTENTS OF THE CLIPBOARD

Data you copy to the Clipboard is lost when you cut or copy new data or shut down Windows. If you want to reuse that data at a later time, you can save the contents of the Clipboard as a file. To save data that's in the Clipboard Viewer, follow these steps:

1. In the Clipboard Viewer, choose File, Save As to open the Save As dialog box.
2. Type a filename in the File Name text box (the Clipboard Viewer automatically appends the .CLP extension).
3. Click OK.

To open a Clipboard file that you have saved, follow these steps:

1. In the Clipboard Viewer, choose File, Open to open the Open dialog box.
2. In the File Name list box, select the file you want to open. If necessary, select the file location from the Folders list box.
3. Click OK.

If you currently have something stored in the Clipboard, the Clear Clipboard message asks whether you want to clear the contents of the Clipboard. Choose Yes to replace the current contents with the data in the .CLP file. Choose No if you don't want to clear the contents of the Clipboard.

VIEWING TEXT IN THE CLIPBOARD VIEWER

The Clipboard Viewer lets you view the Clipboard contents in different file formats. The Clipboard stores information in multiple formats so you can transfer information between programs that use different formats.

On the Display menu, you have several options for viewing the contents. The Display menu shows only the formats that are available for the current data in the Clipboard. All other formats are grayed out.

PART

III

CH

12

The most common formats are

- Text—Displays the contents in unformatted text, using the current Windows system font.

- Rich Text Format—Displays the contents in Rich Text Format (RTF). RTF retains any character formatting, such as font and font style.

- Original Equipment Manufacturer (OEM) Text—Displays the contents in the unformatted OEM character set. You usually use this option when you copy text from the Clipboard to DOS applications.

To view the contents in another format, follow these steps:

1. In the Clipboard Viewer, select the Display menu and choose a format. The Clipboard Viewer changes to reflect your choice.

2. To return to the original format, choose Display, Auto.

VIEWING A PICTURE IN THE CLIPBOARD VIEWER

The Display menu's Picture option enables you to view a picture or formatted text that you cut or copy to the Clipboard. The formatted text shows all the characterizations you add to the text, such as color, fonts, and other formatting. To use the Picture option in the Clipboard Viewer, follow these steps:

1. Cut or copy a picture to the Clipboard (from Paint, for example). If you want to view formatted text, open a document in WordPad or a similar application and cut or copy formatted text to the Clipboard.

2. Open the Clipboard Viewer.

3. Choose Display, Picture to see the item that you copied or cut to the Clipboard.

EXCHANGING DATA BETWEEN WINDOWS AND DOS

You are not limited to sharing data between Windows applications. If you are still using DOS applications in the Windows environment, you can use the Clipboard to exchange information, including text and graphics, from Windows to DOS, from DOS to Windows, and between DOS applications. You can even transfer text from the MS-DOS command prompt to the document.

To exchange data from a DOS application to a Windows application, follow these steps:

1. Open the DOS application. The DOS application should be in a window, not in the full screen.

2. Open the Control menu and choose <u>E</u>dit, Mar<u>k</u> or click the Mark button on the toolbar. A blinking cursor appears in the upper-left corner of the DOS window, indicating that you are in the Marking mode.

3. Click in the location where you want to start marking, hold down the left mouse button, and drag a box around the text or graphics that you want to copy.

or

To use the keyboard to mark the text, hold down the Shift key and use the arrow keys to mark the text.

4. Choose <u>E</u>dit, <u>C</u>opy or press Enter or click the Copy button on the toolbar. The selection is copied to the Clipboard.

5. Open the document in the Windows application in which you want to insert the Clipboard contents.

6. Place the insertion point where you want to insert the Clipboard contents.

7. Choose <u>E</u>dit, <u>P</u>aste or press Ctrl+C or click the Copy button on the toolbar.

Figure 12.4 shows a block of text selected in the MS-DOS Editor and the <u>E</u>dit, <u>C</u>opy command in the Control menu. In Figure 12.5, the selected text from the MS-DOS Editor document has been pasted into a Word document.

Figure 12.4
You can mark text in a DOS application and copy it to the Clipboard by using the commands in the Control menu or the tools on the toolbar...

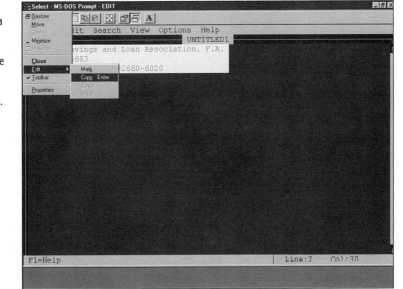

PART

III

Cн

12

Text that was
copied from the
MS-DOS Editor

Figure 12.5
...and paste the text
into another applica-
tion.

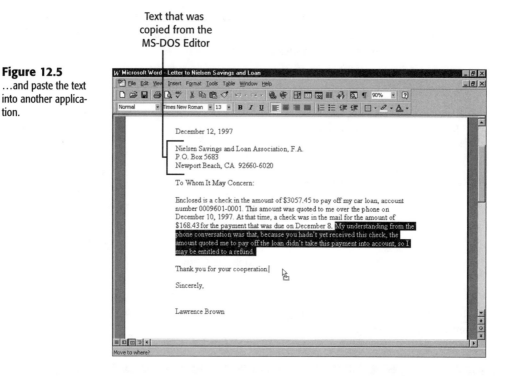

You can also copy data from a Windows application into a DOS application. However, any formatting that has been applied to the Windows data is lost when it is pasted into the DOS application.

To copy data from a Windows application to a DOS application, follow these steps:

1. In the Windows application, open the document that contains the information you want to copy.

2. Select the information and choose <u>E</u>dit, <u>C</u>opy or press Ctrl+C or click the Copy button on the toolbar. The selection is copied to the Clipboard.

3. Open the DOS application. The DOS application should be in a window, not in the full screen.

4. Place the cursor in the location where you want to insert the contents of the Clipboard.

5. Open the Control menu and choose <u>E</u>dit, <u>P</u>aste or click the Paste button on the tool-bar. The contents of the Clipboard are inserted into the DOS document.

USING FILE CONVERTERS TO IMPORT FILES

In some cases you might want to import an entire file from one application into another application instead of just copying and pasting part of a document. Many Windows applications have built-in *file converters* that enable you to convert a file of one format into the format of the application in which you are working. In many cases the file converter preserves the formatting of the original document. For example, you can import a WordPerfect document into Word for Windows and preserve many of the formatting enhancements.

To open and convert a file from one application into another application, follow these steps:

1. Open the application into which you want to import the file.
2. Choose File, Open and locate the folder in which the file you want to convert is stored. You might have to choose All Files from the Files of Type (or equivalent) list box because the file you are converting probably doesn't use the same filename extension as files created by your application.
3. From the list of files, select the file you want to convert.
4. Click Open.

If the application has the correct conversion filter, the file is converted and opened in the application. You may need to fix some of the formatting if it was lost in the conversion process. If your application was unable to convert the file, it may be that you didn't install the necessary converter when you installed the application. Check the documentation for your application to see which converters are included and run the Setup program again if necessary to install the required converter.

Tip #72

RTF files have become the common language for exchanging files between word processors. You can preserve much of the formatting you apply to a document if you save it as an RTF file. If you don't have the correct converter for exchanging a file from one application to another, try turning the document into an RTF file and importing it into the receiving application.

LINKING DATA

The two techniques that you have learned so far place static copies of selected data in a new location. There is no link between the data in the source and destination documents.

A more sophisticated way to exchange data in Windows 98 is through linking. Before the arrival of the OLE standard, dynamic data exchange (DDE) was the technology used to link data. Now, OLE offers both linking and embedding. With OLE, you can create links from one document or file to another document or file. These links can be between documents that are created in the same application (such as Word) or documents that are created in different applications (such as Word and Excel). After you establish a link, you can update the linked information automatically by editing the original source of the information. This means you can use data in various places but update it in only one place.

You can set up a *link* only between two applications (or two documents) that support OLE. The application that requests data is called the *client* application. The other application, called the *server* application, responds to the client application's request by supplying the requested data. When you change the data in the client application, Windows 98 automatically changes the data in the server application. The advantage to exchanging data by links is that data is kept up-to-date in both the client and server applications.

One example of how you can use data linking is to create a report in Microsoft Word that includes a data table linked to a worksheet in Excel. As you update the data in the Excel worksheet, the table in the Word report document is automatically updated so your reports always reflect the latest data. Using this approach, you don't have to re-create a new report each time your data changes. Figure 12.6 shows a data table in Excel that is linked to a document in Word (which is shown in Figure 12.7). The difference between the table in Figure 12.7 and the one shown in Figure 12.2 is that this table is linked to the data in the Excel worksheet; when you change the data in the Excel worksheet, the table in the Word document is automatically updated.

Tip #73

One important thing to know before you choose to link an object in Windows is that if you plan to distribute your file, the client machines that will use your file with the linked object must also have the application installed that runs the linked file. For example, if you link an Excel spreadsheet in a Word document and then send that document plus the accompanying spreadsheet to another computer, the receiving computer must also have Excel. If you embed the same spreadsheet, a runtime version of the application necessary to run that file format is also embedded in the file. As you might have guessed, linked files can save a lot of space when sharing an object, such as a graph of company sales, by keeping only one copy of the object that is available to all other documents. But first, always be sure that your recipient has the applications necessary to support your links.

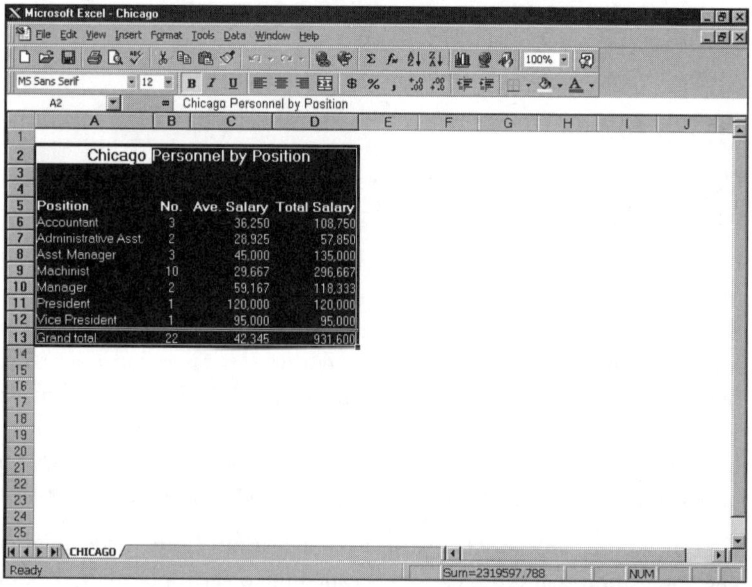

Figure 12.6
Data from an Excel spreadsheet can be linked to a Word document.

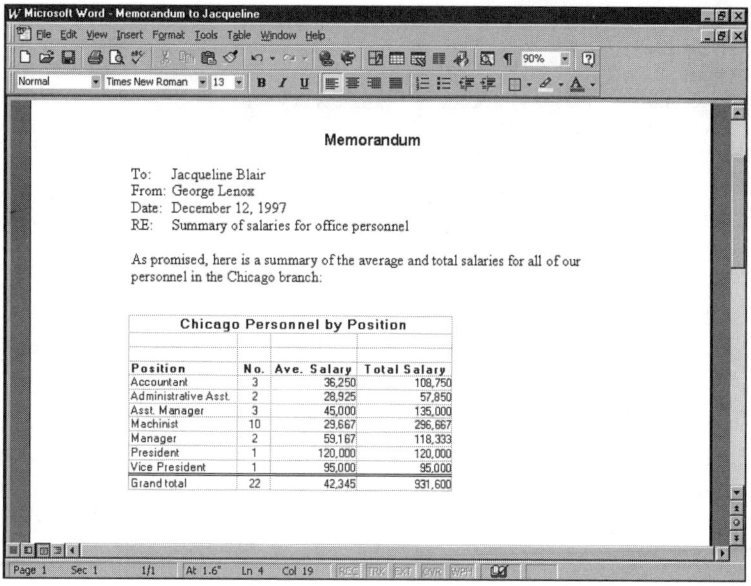

Figure 12.7
Any changes you
make in the Excel
worksheet are
reflected in the
table in the Word
document.

Windows 98 provides two ways to use linking: interactively and through a macro language. The simplest way to link data uses the copy and paste techniques you learned earlier in this chapter with a few important differences. Instead of the Paste command, you use either the Paste Special or Paste Link command. These commands enable you to set up the link between the source and destination documents.

The second method involves creating a macro in the application's macro language to automate data transfer or to store data in a programming variable that can then be used by another Office application. This method isn't discussed in this book. See *Special Edition Using Visual Basic for Applications*, published by Que, for more information on creating links using a macro language.

To set up a link between two applications, follow these steps:

1. Open the source document and select the data you want to link to a destination document (refer to Figure 12.6).

2. Choose Edit, Copy or press Ctrl+C to copy the selected data to the Clipboard.

3. In the destination application, open the document to which you want to link the data.

4. Choose Edit, Paste Special, and the Paste Special dialog box appears. Figure 12.8 shows the Paste Special dialog box in Microsoft Word.

5. Select the Paste Link option. If you don't select this option, the data is pasted into the destination document without linking.

6. Depending on the type of data you are working with, make an appropriate selection in the As dialog box. For example, to paste data from an Excel worksheet into a Word document, you would select the Formatted Text (RTF) option.

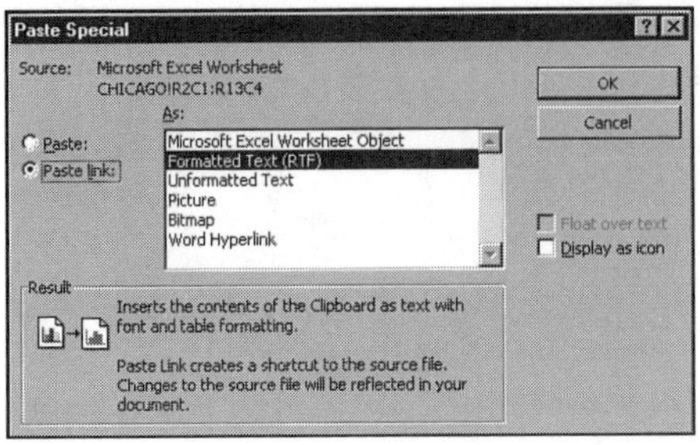

Figure 12.8
Use the Paste Special dialog box to set up the link between the source and destination documents.

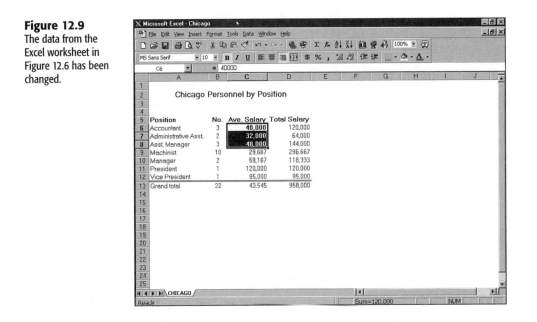

7. Click OK. The data is inserted into the destination document. (Refer to Figure 12.7, which shows the Excel data from Figure 12.6 inserted into a Word document.)

After a link is established, whenever you change data in the source document, the data is automatically updated in the destination document. Figure 12.9 shows the Excel worksheet from Figure 12.6 with some of the data changed. Figure 12.10 shows the table in the Word document from Figure 12.7 as it reflects these changes.

Figure 12.9
The data from the Excel worksheet in Figure 12.6 has been changed.

Caution

If you change the name or path of your client or server document, you must reestablish your links. You should make a habit of changing or creating filenames and directories for your documents before you create links. Otherwise, your data links will be broken, and your data will no longer be updated automatically.

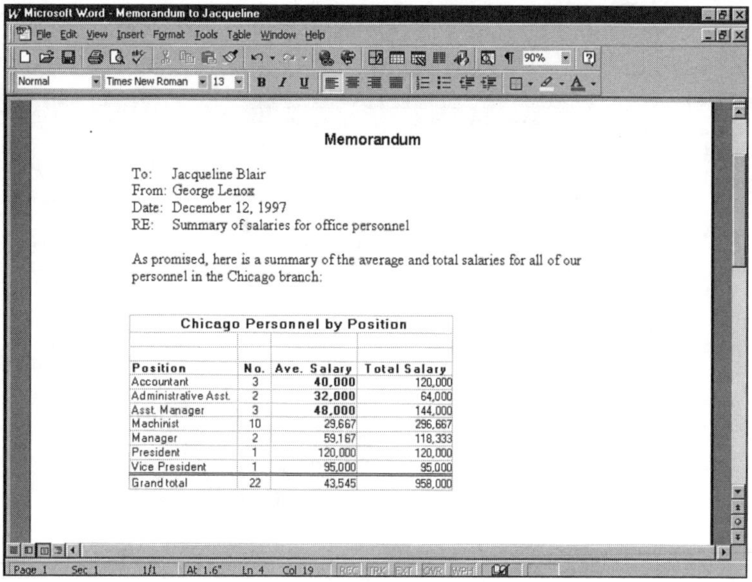

Figure 12.10
The table in the Word document is automatically updated to reflect the changes in the Excel worksheet.

CREATING COMPOUND DOCUMENTS

In this section you will learn how to create compound documents. *Compound documents* are documents you create using multiple types of data pulled in from various applications. The technology used to create compound documents is Microsoft's OLE.

The basic building blocks of a compound document are *objects*. Objects are embedded into the *container* or *client* application, which contains one or more embedded objects. For example, you can embed a graphics object from a graphics application and a data table from an Excel worksheet into a Word document, which acts as the container for the objects. An application that supplies an object is referred to as a *server* application. The server application provides OLE services to the client application.

The major difference between a document created from OLE objects and one created by using the simple copy and paste and linking techniques that use the Clipboard is that you can edit embedded objects without leaving the client application. If you use copy and paste, you have to edit the information in the source application and repeat the copy-and-paste procedure to update the client. And even if you link data, you have to open the source application to edit the linked data.

In an OLE compound document, you simply double-click the object you want to edit, and the menus and toolbars of the object's original application temporarily replace those of the client application. Figure 12.11 shows an Excel object in a Word document. Notice that the Word menus and toolbars have been replaced with Excel's menus and toolbars so that you can edit the object *in place*. When you finish editing the object, you click outside the object to restore the client application's menus and toolbars.

You're still in Word...   ...but these are Excel
                                            menus and tools.

Figure 12.11
You can edit an Excel
chart in Word by using
OLE 2.0 capabilities.

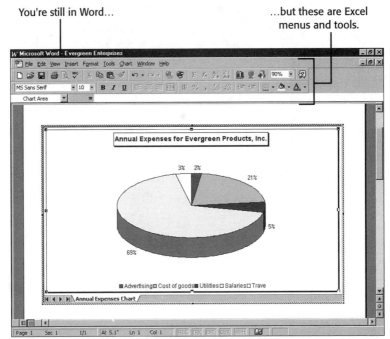

In some cases, when you double-click an object, the source application of the object opens in a separate window instead of the source's menu and toolbars appearing over those of the client. In such cases, you edit the object in its original application and then return to the compound document.

Tip #74

Typically, if the object is embedded and its source application is not available, it utilizes in-place editing from within the main document. If the object is a linked file or if the embedded file has its source application available, then a separate window opens for the object's source application.

Like linked data, embedded objects can be updated dynamically whenever the source data changes. One of the main benefits of using OLE applications is that you can take advantage of the strengths of several applications, each of which excels at what it does, to create a single document. For example, you can use your favorite graphics application to produce the graphics for a document, use your spreadsheet application to analyze and summarize your data, and use your word processor to create a professional-looking document. OLE enables you to pull all these pieces together into one document and then edit and update information as needed.

It is important to understand the differences between linking and embedding data. When you link information, the information is stored in the source document. The destination document contains only the code needed to locate the information in the source document.

Conversely, embedded information is actually stored in the destination document, and the OLE code points to the source *application* instead of the source *file*. This approach enables you to access the source application's tools for editing.

EMBEDDING INFORMATION IN YOUR DOCUMENTS

You can embed information from one document into another by using either the menu commands or drag-and-drop editing. When you use the menu commands, you have the option of linking or not linking the object with its source. When you drag and drop an object, the object is not linked to its source.

To use the menu commands to embed an object from one document to another, follow these steps:

1. Select the information in the source document.
2. Choose Edit, Copy or press Ctrl+C.
3. Open the destination application and document.
4. Choose Edit, Paste Special to display the Paste Special dialog box.
5. Select the object from the As list.
6. Select either the Paste or Paste Link option.

   If you select Paste, the object is embedded but *is not* linked to the source document. When you double-click the object, the menus and toolbars for the source application appear, allowing you to edit in place.

   If you select Paste Link, the object *is* linked to the source document. When you double-click the object, the original document opens and the information you linked is selected.
7. Click OK, and the information is inserted into the destination document as an object, as shown in Figure 12.12.

When you click the embedded object, square handles appear at the corners and ends, surrounding the object. You can drag these handles to resize the object.

You can also use drag-and-drop editing to embed an object. OLE 2.0-compliant applications fully support this feature, enabling you to drag an object from one application and drop it in another application.

To drag and drop information from one application to another, follow these steps:

1. Open the source and destination applications and arrange their windows side by side.
2. In the source document, select the information you want to embed.
3. To move the object from the source to the destination, drag the selected object and drop it at the desired location in the destination document.

   To copy the object, hold down the Ctrl key as you drag and drop it into the destination document. A plus sign appears next to the mouse pointer when you hold down the Ctrl key. Don't release the Ctrl key until after you release the mouse button.

PART

III

CH

12

Figure 12.12
A Microsoft Excel table inserted as an object in a Word document. Notice the handles around the object when it is selected.

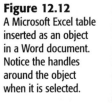

Tip #75

If you accidentally move data that you want to copy from one application to another with the drag-and-drop technique, switch back to the *source* application and choose Edit, Undo to restore the information in the source document. The object in the destination document is not affected.

When you drag and drop information from one application to another, you do not have the option of linking the embedded object to its source. Use the menu method described earlier to link an embedded object.

If the application you want to drop an object in is minimized or is hidden by other applications, you can drag the object over the application's button on the taskbar and pause for a few seconds. The application window then appears. In the application window, drop the object at the desired location in the application.

Note

When you drag and drop information from one application to another, the information is embedded as an object in the destination document if the data types for the two applications are different. If the data type is the same, the information is inserted in its native format. When you drag and drop a range of cells from Excel to a Word document, for example, the data is inserted as an object. When you drag a text selection from Word to Excel, on the other hand, the selection is inserted as straight text because a cell can accept text. To insert a text selection as an object, you must use the Edit, Copy and Edit, Paste Special commands.

INSERTING A NEW OBJECT INTO YOUR DOCUMENT

If you want to use the features of another application in your compound documents, you can choose Insert, Object and select an application from the provided list. Many applications now support this feature of OLE 2.0, including the standard Microsoft Office applications, the applications that come with Windows 98 (for example, Paint and WordPad), and other Windows 98 applications.

Some Windows applications come with small applications that can be used only from within the main application. Microsoft Office 97 comes with several smaller applications that support OLE, as you can see in Table 12.2. When you install Microsoft Office on your system, these applications are installed in a centralized location that allows many Office applications to access them easily. The WordPad application, which comes with Windows 98, can embed many types of objects, some of which are listed in the table.

TABLE 12.2   OFFICE 97 APPLICATIONS THAT SUPPORT OLE

Application	Use
Microsoft Clip Gallery	Inserts clip-art pictures
Microsoft Map	Inserts a map showing different levels associated with data
Microsoft Equation	Creates mathematical expressions
Microsoft Graph	Inserts charts from data in a Word table
Microsoft Organization Chart	Creates organizational charts
Microsoft Word Picture	Inserts a picture and the tools associated with the Word drawing toolbar
Microsoft WordArt	Creates logos and other special text effects

To insert an object from another application into a document, follow these steps:

1. In the destination document, place the insertion point where you want to insert the object.

2. Choose Insert, Object. The Object dialog box appears (see Figure 12.13).

Figure 12.13
The Object dialog box lists applications you can use to insert objects in a document.

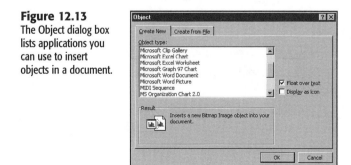

PART

III

CH

12

3. Select the <u>C</u>reate New tab and then select an application from the <u>O</u>bject Type list.

4. If you want to display the object as an icon, select the Displ<u>a</u>y as Icon check box.

5. Click OK. Depending on the applications you are working with, either a separate window for the application appears within the document, or the menu bar and toolbars change to those of the source application (as shown in Figure 12.14). In this figure, notice that although the title bar displays Microsoft Word, the menu and toolbars are those of Excel. Likewise, the object displays the worksheet and scrollbars of Excel.

Figure 12.14
Some applications permit in-place editing: The menu bar and toolbars for the source application appear when you insert an object from that application.

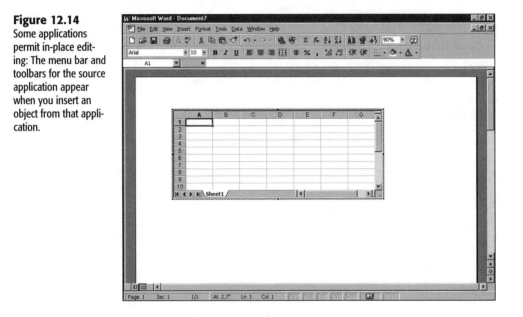

6. Create the object by using the application's menus and toolbars.

7. When you finish creating the object, return to the document in one of two ways:

   If a separate window appeared for the application, choose <u>F</u>ile, E<u>x</u>it.

   If in-place editing was enabled, click outside the object to restore the destination application's menus and toolbars.

EDITING AN EMBEDDED OBJECT

Regardless of which method you use to embed information into your document, you can edit the embedded object with the tools of the source application. To edit the object, follow these steps:

1. Click the object. Handles appear around the object, and the status bar tells you to double-click the object.

2. Double-click the object. Depending on the source and destination applications, either a separate window for the program appears or the current window's toolbar and menu bar change to those of the source application.

3. Edit the object by using the source application's toolbar and menus.

4. When you finish editing the object, exit the object. If you launched a separate window for the application, choose File, Exit. If you stayed in your destination document, click outside the object.

Tip #76

Embedding objects, especially graphic files, significantly increases the size of the document as a whole. Thus, embedding an object is a good choice for information that seldom changes and is not useful to someone else in another venue (that is, it is not likely to be a file that needs to be shared through another application or document). Embedding is also appropriate if the recipient of your file might not have the source application needed to edit the object. Use the linking functionality when the linked object is able to be physically shared or if you know the recipient will have the source application necessary to open the object.

CREATING DOCUMENT SHORTCUTS

Document shortcuts enable you to quickly navigate to a particular location in a document. You can, for example, create a document shortcut on the desktop to a cell in an Excel worksheet so that you can open Excel and the target worksheet from the shortcut, and the cell will be selected. You can create a shortcut to a location or selection in any OLE 2.0-compliant application. You can keep these shortcuts on the desktop, or you can place them in a folder on the desktop if you don't want to clutter up your desktop with shortcuts. Using folders to store your document shortcuts also can help you organize them.

You might use document shortcuts to save time, for example, if you're spending a lot of time navigating from one location to another in a particular document. To reduce navigation, you can create document shortcuts to key locations in the document. You can then collect all the shortcuts for a document into a folder so that it becomes a computerized table of contents that streamlines navigation.

To create a document shortcut, follow these steps:

1. Make a selection in the document (select cells in a worksheet or text in a word processing document).

2. Drag and drop the selection onto the desktop by using the right mouse button.

3. From the shortcut menu that appears when you release the mouse button, choose Create Document Shortcut Here.

When you choose a desktop shortcut, the document opens to the original selection. You can move the shortcut to a folder that you create on the desktop.

> **Note**
>
> Not all OLE-compliant applications allow you to use drag-and-drop editing to create document shortcuts. In such cases, you can create a document shortcut by making a selection; choosing Edit, Copy; right-clicking the desktop; and choosing Paste Shortcut from the menu.

CREATING DOCUMENT SCRAPS

You also can create document scraps on your desktop. *Scraps* are pieces of information from any OLE document that you store on your desktop or in a folder. At any time you can drag a scrap into a document in any OLE application to insert it as an embedded object. You can use the scrap as many times as you like and in as many documents as you like.

To create a scrap, follow these steps:

1. Select the information from which you want to create a scrap.
2. Drag the selection to the desktop or to a folder.

A scrap consisting of the selected information is created. If you choose the scrap, the information in the scrap is displayed in the application in which it was created. You can drag and drop the scrap into any OLE document to embed it as an object in the document.

Use scraps to create pseudo-sticky notes on your desktop. If you want to save a bit of information on your desktop so you won't forget it, open WordPad (open the Start menu and choose Programs, Accessories, WordPad); type the note; select the text; and drag it to the desktop. You don't have to save the WordPad file. The name of the scrap that appears on the desktop is taken from the first sentence of the scrap text. However, you can rename the scrap to give it a more useful name. To read the note, simply choose the scrap.

Another way to use scraps to increase your productivity is to store boilerplate text that you use over and over again as scraps. Suppose, for example, that you have several standard paragraphs you use repeatedly in contracts. You can create a scrap for each paragraph. Then, whenever you are creating a new contract and you need one of the paragraphs, you can drag a copy of the scrap into your document. To keep your desktop from getting cluttered with scraps, organize them in folders that you create on your desktop.

Tip #77

> You can drag a copy of a desktop scrap into an email message created from Outlook Express, which is OLE compliant. This technique is a very handy way to quickly send text from a document or cells from a worksheet to a client or co-worker.
>
> → **See** Chapter 31, "Using Outlook Express," to learn how to use Outlook Express to send email.

CREATING WEB LINKS IN DOCUMENTS

In Chapter 27, "Web Browsing with Internet Explorer 5.0," you learn how to create shortcuts on your desktop to sites on the Internet. This approach is useful if you routinely access certain sites and want to be able to access them more quickly by double-clicking a shortcut. You also can embed these shortcuts into any OLE document so that you can access these sites from within the document. Imagine distributing a document to your colleagues loaded with shortcuts to useful sites on the Internet. All they have to do is open the document and choose the shortcuts.

To embed an Internet shortcut in a document, drag and drop the shortcut from the desktop into the document. You can then choose that shortcut to sign on to the Internet and go directly to that site.

TROUBLESHOOTING

USING THE PRINT SCREEN KEY

I cannot use the Print Screen key to copy a DVD image.

If you attempt to cut or copy an image of a DVD movie by pressing the Print Screen key, only a blue or black box appears to be pasted into the document. The explanation is twofold:

- A DVD data stream is decoded and then redirected back to your video adapter. The video stream is sent directly from the video adapter to the DVD decoder card and then directly to the monitor as an overlay. This process bypasses slower portions of the computer's subsystem to improve playback time. Because the DVD data stream does not actually pass through the Windows subsystem and thus does not leave a residue in the system that can be captured, you capture only the playback area in which the movie is displayed, which is empty.

- This situation is also a function of DVD security. Making the capture of the DVD data stream difficult discourages people from illegally copying DVD movies.

SECRETS OF MASTERING THE WINDOWS 98 ENVIRONMENT: USING QUICK VIEW

Quick View enables you to view files in most popular file formats without having to open the application in which the file was created. As a time-saver, Quick View is really handy for looking at attachments sent in email messages or for browsing files on a network.

Another nice feature of Quick View is that it enables you to drag and drop a file from Windows Explorer or the desktop into an open Quick View window. If, by chance, the extension of the file is not associated with a known application, the Open With dialog box is displayed so that you can determine whether to view the file in the Quick View window or to open the selected file with the appropriate application.

Be sure to preset the default Open command for any file type that you display with Quick View. To do so, choose View, Options from the Windows Explorer menu and set the default Open command. This practice helps users who often work with and view a certain type of file type but do not have the particular application installed locally on their systems. Quick View also enables you to assign extensions to applications and to view files with those extensions in a specific file format.

You can customize the Quick View window in the following ways:

- Viewing files in Standard view or Page view, in both Landscape and Portrait modes.
- Viewing files in different fonts and font sizes.
- Rotating bitmap files so documents such as fax messages are oriented correctly.

CHAPTER 13

PRINTING

In this chapter

USING THE PRINTERS FOLDER

One of the most basic uses for a computer is to print out documents. Although as a society we are moving towards the goal of decreasing the amount of paper we generate, in many cases you will still find the need to print material from your computer to preserve it or share it with other people. To print letters, graphs, pictures, or other such items, you must install a printer on your computer and understand some of the basics of managing any printers used by your computer. This chapter shows you how to fully use the printing features found in Windows 98.

The printer settings for your computer are stored in the Printers folder. The usual way to access the Printers folder is to click on the Start button, select Settings, and then choose Printers. This sequence opens the Printers folder, as shown in Figure 13.1.

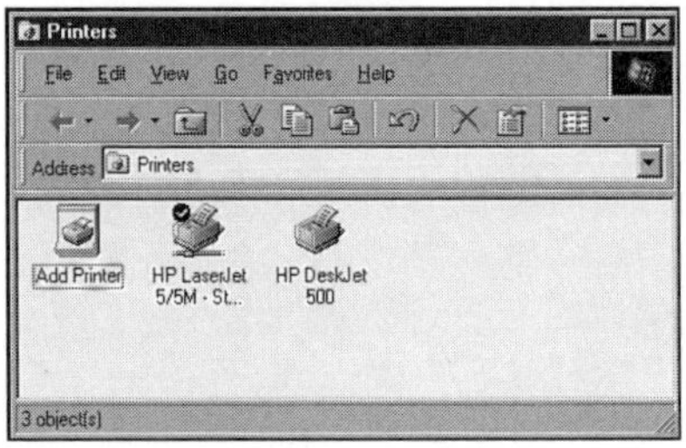

Figure 13.1
The Printers folder provides a central place from which to manage all your local and network printers. Note in this example that the HP LaserJet 5 is a network printer and is also shown as the default printer.

You can also access the Printers folder by any of the following methods:

- Selecting Printers from the Control Panel
- Opening My Computer and choosing Printers
- Clicking on Printers in the left pane of Windows NT Explorer

The Printers folder contains icons for adding a printer as well as for any printers you have installed on your computer. If you have any other devices or software that use a printer driver, such as a fax modem, an icon representing the printer driver for that device also appears in this folder.

DEFAULT PRINTER

Although you might have more than one printer installed on your computer, only one printer can be defined as the default printer; however, you can change this setting at any time. The printer set as the default printer is automatically selected each time you print a document.

You can easily tell which printer is set as the default by looking at the printer icons in the Printers folder. As shown in Figure 13.1, the default printer has a check mark in the upper-left portion of its icon.

When you install the first printer on your computer, it is automatically installed as the default printer. Unless you change the default setting, the first printer you install on your computer remains as the default, even if you later add printers to the Printers folder.

If you want to select a different printer as the default, right-click on that printer's icon in the Printers folder and choose Set as Default. The check mark moves to the selected printer's icon, and that printer is now set as the default printer.

| Tip #78 | Another handy feature in Windows is the capability to set up a fax program as a printer. Doing so makes the task of preparing a document to be faxed very user friendly. For example, if you have created a cover page and a document and you want to fax it through your modem's fax software, simply use the Print window (discussed later in this chapter) to choose the fax software's print device. The fax software typically prompts you for any necessary information and voila, you have a simple and professional way to send a fax anywhere—all from your desktop. |

Printer Properties

A printer's properties are the detailed settings for that printer and are contained in the corresponding Properties page. You can access a printer's Properties page by either of the following methods from within the Printers folder:

- Right-clicking on the printer's icon and choosing Properties
- Clicking on the printer's icon with the left mouse button and then selecting Properties from the File pull-down menu

Because the Properties page for a printer is directly related to the functions exposed through the printer's driver, the Properties page looks somewhat different from printer to printer. Thus, the Properties page for your printer might not be identical to the Properties page in Figure 13.2.

Figure 13.2
The Properties page for a printer contains multiple tabs, each with various options you can set for that printer.

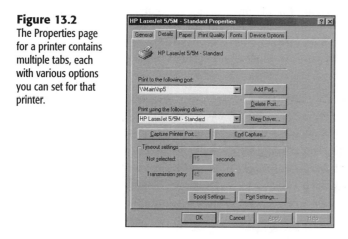

PART

III

CH

13

INSTALLING A LOCAL PRINTER

For installation purposes, Windows 98 distinguishes between local and network printers. A local printer is one that is physically connected to your computer via a cable, whereas a network printer is physically attached to another computer but is available for use by your computer through your network connection.

Before you attempt to set up a local printer on your computer, you first must make sure that you can connect to that printer from your computer. Some of the things you must check are

- Which port the printer needs to be plugged in to
- Whether the printer is physically connected to the computer properly
- Whether the printer is turned on; Windows 98 can't detect a printer that's not turned on
- The exact make and model of that printer, for example, HP DeskJet 500

PLUG AND PLAY

In an effort to make it easier for you to install printers and other hardware on your computer, Microsoft has worked with hardware manufacturers to develop the *Plug and Play (page 430)* standard. Through the use of Plug and Play support, Windows 98 can automatically detect hardware attached to your computer and install the appropriate drivers without any intervention on your part.

Assuming that your printer is Plug-and-Play compliant, installing it is as easy as turning on your attached printer and booting into Windows 98. Plug and Play can install your printer either during the Windows 98 installation process or at any time thereafter when you want to add a printer.

In either event, when Windows 98 loads, it should automatically detect that the printer has been added to your computer. It then brings up a dialog box that informs you of this fact. After identifying the printer, Windows 98 attempts to install the correct driver for that printer. At this point, Windows might prompt you to insert the Windows 98 CD-ROM and begin to look for the driver on that disc. If the driver did not come with Windows 98 or if you have an updated driver that you want to install instead, simply insert the driver disk from your hardware manufacturer into a disk drive and direct Windows 98 to that drive.

For this process to work properly, you have to make sure that the printer you want to add complies with the Plug-and-Play standard. If you are purchasing the printer in a store, look for the Designed for Windows 98 logo on the printer box. This logo indicates that the printer has undergone hardware-compatibility testing to make sure that it is fully compatible with Windows 98, including Plug and Play. Because Plug and Play was also supported in Windows 95, the printer should also be fully compatible with Windows 98 if the logo indicates that the printer was designed for Windows 95. One more thing to be aware of is that you need a bidirectional printer cable, which most printer cables are these days.

If your printer is an older model or if it came packaged with your computer, you might not be able to tell whether it supports Plug and Play. If Windows 98 does not automatically recognize your printer, you must manually add it to your computer configuration through the Add Printer Wizard.

USING THE ADD PRINTER WIZARD

If your printer does not support Plug and Play, you can manually install the printer on your computer by using the Add Printer Wizard. Open the Printers folder and double-click on the Add Printer icon. After the Add Printer Wizard window appears, click on the Next button to begin using the wizard.

Select the radio button for Local Printer and click the Next button (see Figure 13.3). You are then asked to choose the manufacturer and printer model for your printer. First select the manufacturer by scrolling down to the name (or abbreviation) for your printer's manufacturer in the left pane of this page of the wizard. Select that name by clicking on it, and a list of all available printers from that manufacturer appears in the right pane. Select your printer's model by clicking on its name in the right pane.

Figure 13.3
The Add Printer Wizard helps you set up a printer on your computer.

Tip #79

When the Add Printer Wizard prompts you to choose a printer manufacturer and model, you can quickly skip to your hardware manufacturer's printer listings by pressing the first letter of the manufacturer's name. Thus, if you press the letter *E*, the list scrolls down and selects Epson, thereby automatically opening the available printer selections for Epson printers from which you can choose.

Unless your printer is a very recent model, Windows 98 probably already has the correct driver. In fact, Windows 98 includes drivers for more than 1,000 printers. However, if your printer does not appear on the list, you must click on the Have Disk button and insert a disk containing your printer's drivers into the floppy disk or CD-ROM drive. These drivers should have been supplied to you on disk when you bought your computer. After you indicate the drive on which Windows 98 should look, it then reads the disk you have inserted and lists any available printer drivers found on that disk. Note that the driver might be in a subdirectory on the disk, so you should check the documentation that came with your printer if you are unable to locate the driver. If you are still unable to locate the driver, you must contact the printer's manufacturer to obtain a Windows 98 driver for your printer (a Windows 95 driver should also work).

After you have selected the correct manufacturer and printer model for your printer, click on the Next button. You are then asked to choose the port on which you want to install the printer (see Figure 13.4). This entry is the hardware port to which you have attached the printer to your computer. In most cases the correct port is LPT1, although you might need to check with your computer's manufacturer or the documentation that came with your computer to determine which port you should select.

Figure 13.4
To install the printer correctly, you must select the port to which your printer is attached.

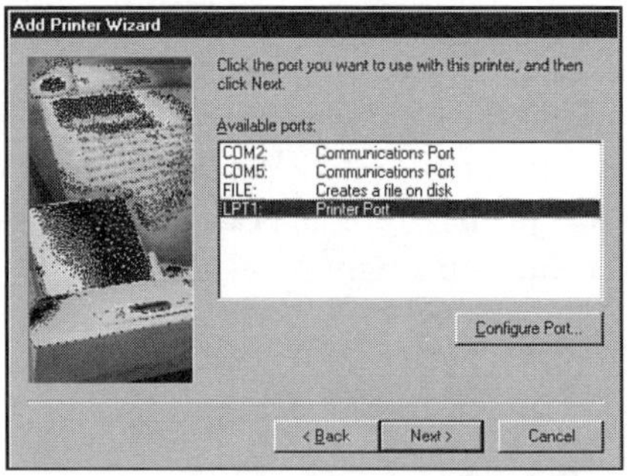

As part of the process of selecting a port, you can also configure the port, such as by having Windows 98 check the status of the port each time before it prints. If you want to change these settings, click on the Configure Port button found on this page of the Add Printer Wizard.

After selecting a port for your printer, you are asked to choose a name for the printer (see Figure 13.5). In most cases, the default, which is usually the brand and model number, will suffice. However, if you plan to share this computer with other people on a network, you might want a more descriptive name, such as "7th Floor Laser Printer."

Figure 13.5
You must provide a name for your printer that distinguishes it from other printers on your computer or the network.

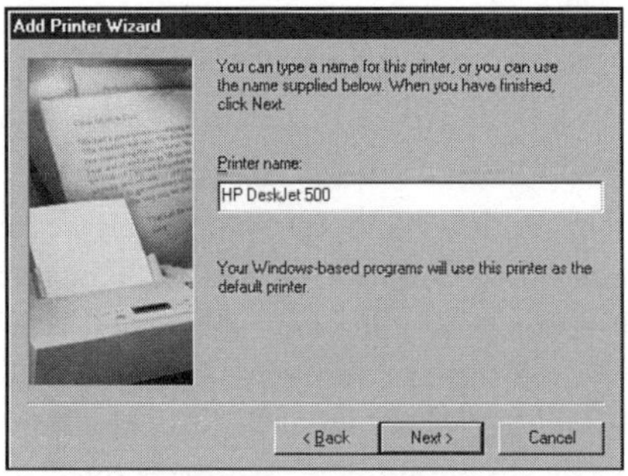

You then come to the last page of the Add Printer Wizard, where you are asked if you want to print a test page. Microsoft recommends that you print a test page when you install a printer. If you have not installed this printer on your computer before, take this opportunity to make sure that everything is working correctly. Simply choose the Yes radio button, which is selected by default, and a test page prints as soon as your printer has been installed.

After you click on the Finish button, Windows 98 installs and configures the printer for use on your computer. Unless the drivers for this printer have previously been added to your computer, perhaps, for example, you previously installed this type of printer, a dialog box appears asking you to insert the Windows 98 CD-ROM. After you put the CD-ROM into the drive and click on the OK button, the printer driver and any other necessary files are copied to your computer. After this process has ended, an icon for your printer appears in the Printers folder. If this printer is the only one installed on your computer, the printer is automatically selected as the default printer.

If you made it through all of these steps without incident, you are finished. Congratulations! You have just successfully installed your printer in Windows 98. If you must install a network printer, you will find that the steps needed to make that installation are virtually the same as installing a local printer.

⚠ *Various basic problems can confront you in the configuration and implementation of printers. For more information on these problems, see "Help with Basic Printer Problems" and "Printer Installation Issues" in the "Troubleshooting" section at the end of this chapter.*

SETTING UP A NETWORK PRINTER

Setting up a network printer in Windows 98 can be as easy as connecting to a local printer, thanks in part to Microsoft's Point and Print process. This process usually enables you to automatically install the correct network printer driver without having to have the Windows 98 CD-ROM or other disk containing the printer driver. Through Point and Print, when you use the Add Printer Wizard to add a network printer, Windows 98 is often able to download the printer driver from the computer or server to which the printer is attached.

Before attempting to set up a network printer on your computer, you first must know how to connect to the printer. Some of the information you must know is

■ The name that the printer and its attached computer or server (if applicable) uses on the network

■ Whether the printer is set up for sharing over the network

■ The exact model of that printer, for example, HP LaserJet 5

PART

III

CH

13

Tip #80

When you attempt to connect to a network printer manually, (for example, with a `Net Use` command), keep in mind that the printer name in the Printers folder on the local system is not necessarily the share name you need to connect to that printer. To find the share

continues

continued

> name for a printer, right-click the printer you want to connect to and select Sharing; then notice the box labeled Share Name. This entry is the printer's "name" on the network and is the name you use when attempting to connect to that network printer.

CONNECTING TO THE NETWORK

To install a network printer on your computer, you first must be connected to the network. If you have not already established a network connection with your computer, refer to Chapter 37, "Sharing Network Resources," before attempting to connect to and install a network printer. You might also need to check with your network administrator to make sure that you have permission to access that printer because the printer may refuse your connection if you do not have permission.

While you are connected to the network, open the Printers folder and double-click on the Add Printer icon. The Add Printer Wizard then appears. Select the radio button for Network Printer and click the Next button.

You are then asked to supply the location of the printer on the network. If you already know the name of the printer and it's attached computer on the network, you can simply type the name into the field on this screen, as shown in Figure 13.6. Note that you must supply the Universal Naming Convention (UNC) path for the location of the printer, such as *computername**printername* where *computername* is the name of the computer to which the printer is attached and *printername* is the name of the printer. Thus, in Figure 13.6, Main is the name of the computer on the network to which the printer hp5 is attached.

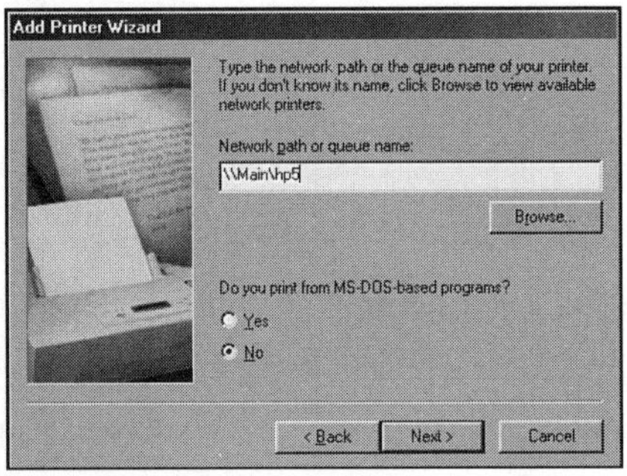

Figure 13.6
You must tell the Add Printer Wizard the location of the computer that you want to install on the network.

If you are not sure of the exact name of the computer and printer on the network, click on the Browse button. A separate window (see Figure 13.7) now lists all other computers on the network that have shared printers.

Click on the plus sign to the left of any computer listed in this window to expand the view to show all shared printers attached to that computer. Click on the OK button after you have selected the printer you want to add.

Figure 13.7
The Browse window enables you to select from all available shared printers on the network.

Note

You can choose to install only a single printer each time you run the Add Printer Wizard. If you want to install more than one printer on your computer, you have to add the printers one at a time. After adding the first printer, you can then add printers one by one. This rule applies to both local and network printers.

Before you move to the next window in the Add Printer Wizard, be sure to check the correct radio button indicating whether you want to print from MS-DOS programs. If you select Yes and click on the Next button, the next window of the wizard asks you to capture a printer port for these MS-DOS programs. Even though this shared network printer is not physically attached to your computer, MS-DOS programs often need to believe that they are printing to a local port. By choosing a port to capture for this purpose, when MS-DOS programs attempt to print to this port, Windows 98 automatically redirects the print job to the network printer.

As with local printers, the Add Printer Wizard asks whether you want to print a test page. Select the Yes radio button if you want to see whether your connection to the network printer is working properly. After you have decided whether you want to print a test page, press the Finish button to install the printer on your computer.

After you have selected the network printer you want to install and have finished with the Add Printer Wizard, Windows 98 connects to that printer to determine its exact type. After determining the printer's make and model, Windows 98 checks the computer for a correct version of that printer's driver. If Windows finds the driver, the printer should install correctly and you are finished adding this printer to the Printers folder. In most cases, however, Windows 98 either downloads the correct driver to your computer or prompts you to insert a disk containing the driver into one of your disk drives.

The next section considers what happens when Windows 98 can download the printer driver to your computer. Then, the section titled "Installing Printer Drivers from Disk" explains what happens when Windows 98 cannot download the driver.

PART

III

Cʜ

13

Tip #81

Although you can use the Add Printer Wizard to add a printer to your computer, an easier way is to open Network Neighborhood and browse for the printer (you will probably first have to double-click on the icon for the computer to which the printer is attached). After you find the printer, right-click on the printer's icon and choose Install. This step opens the Add Printer Wizard but skips several windows, thus making it easier and quicker to add a network printer.

POINT AND PRINT

When you are finished with the Add Printer Wizard, Windows 98 attempts to install the printer driver from the computer to which the printer is attached (if applicable). In many cases, if the shared printer is set up correctly on the computer to which it is attached, Windows 98 can download the printer driver from that computer and install it on your computer. This feature is known as *Point and Print*.

If this process works correctly on your computer, a dialog box tells you that Windows 98 has found the proper driver on the remote computer and is installing the driver on your computer. Then, you can connect to and use that printer.

For the Point and Print feature to work properly, the computer to which the shared printer is attached must be running Windows 98, Windows NT Server, or be a Novell NetWare server. Note, however, that this feature does not always work properly, and as such you may still have to install the printer driver from either the Windows 98 CD-ROM or the printer driver disk supplied by the manufacturer.

INSTALLING PRINTER DRIVERS FROM DISK

If you are unable to install the driver for your printer through the Point and Print feature described in the previous section, you must use the Windows 98 CD-ROM or another disk with the appropriate driver to provide Windows 98 with the printer driver. After Windows 98 installs the printer driver, an icon for the printer appears in the Printers folder.

Tip #82

If you are having any trouble installing a printer driver or getting the manufacturer's version or the Windows 98 version of the driver to set up your printer properly, try to contact the manufacturer. Most printer vendors have a Web site where you can get the most recent version of the printer driver for your version of Windows. Even a printer, new out of the box, can have an outdated printer driver because system demands often change more frequently than printer models do.

PRINTING FROM APPLICATIONS

After you have installed one or more printers on your computer, you can print from within any application. In Windows 98, when you print from a Windows application, you can change a number of the printer's configurations within the application itself for the print job you are processing. Windows 98 also includes a print spooler that enables you to get back to work while the operating system processes the print job in the background.

CHANGING CONFIGURATIONS

In most Windows applications, you can print the document you are working on by pressing a toolbar button or by selecting Print from the File pull-down menu. After you tell the application to print the document, you usually see a window that enables you to change any needed settings for that print job. Note that although you don't always see this window when you choose a Print button on a toolbar, you should usually see a Print window if you use the pull-down menu.

Figure 13.8 shows the Print window as it appears in the Windows 98 WordPad application. This window shows the relevant information on the selected printer, such as the printer's name and its current status. If you want to change from the default printer to a different printer, just choose the other printer that you want from the drop-down box next to Name. Instead of printing the entire document, you can select one or more pages for printing by entering that information into the Print range frame. To fax your document, choose the appropriate fax print device in the pull-down menu.

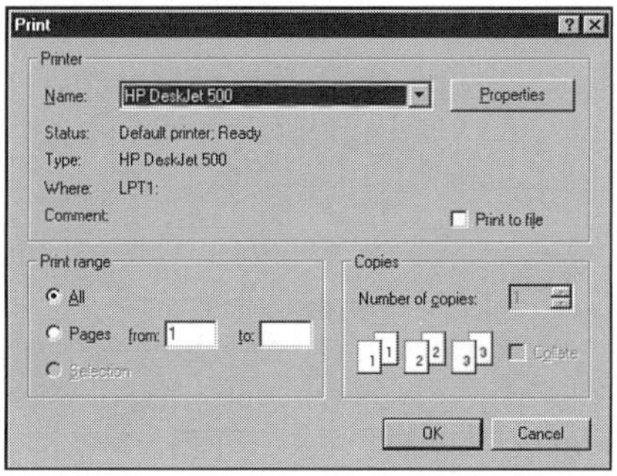

Figure 13.8
When printing from within applications, you can change your printer settings to best match the needs of your print job.

If you click the Properties button, a separate window appears that contains many of the same properties settings available for this printer in the Printers folder. From this window, you can set the printer resolution, change the paper size, alter the way the document is printed (such as from portrait to landscape), and fine-tune other properties settings. After changing the printer settings, click on the OK button to return to the main Print window and print the document.

Note that the Print window includes an option to print to a file rather than to the selected printer. If you choose this option by selecting the Print to File check box, Windows does not save the file as a text file, but rather saves the printer output into a data file, as opposed to sending it to the printer right away. Unless you want to save this raw printer data for some reason, you probably do not want to use this Print to File feature. If you want to save the file rather than print it, you should choose either Save or Save As from the File pull-down menu.

PART
III

CH
13

SPOOLING

Windows 98 includes a 32-bit print *spooler* that supports preemptive multithreading and multitasking, thereby enabling you to get back to work more quickly after you initiate a print job. Before print spoolers were incorporated into the operating system, when you printed a document in an application, you often had to wait until the entire document had been printed before you could return to work in that application. However, with Windows 98, when you tell an application to print a document, the print spooler takes over and accepts the print job in place of the actual printing device to which you have directed the document.

Thus, the print spooler effectively acts as an intermediary that receives the print job on behalf of the printer and temporarily stores the job on your hard disk. When the application finishes sending either part or all of the print job to the spooler (depending on the print spooler options you have chosen for your printer), the application is freed up to continue with other work, and the print spooler begins feeding the print job data to the printer in the background.

By default, the print spooler begins feeding print data to the printer after it has received the first page of data from the application. However, if you want to return control to the application more quickly, you can adjust the print spooler properties so that it does not begin printing until the spooler receives the entire document. To change these and other print spooler settings, you must reconfigure the properties for each printer on which you want to make these changes. To do so, right-click on the printer's icon in the Printers folder and choose Properties. Then, select the Details tab and choose the Spool Settings button.

In this window (see Figure 13.9), you can change the default settings by instructing Windows 98 to wait until the last page is spooled before sending the document to the printer. This setting shortens the time it takes to return control to the application that is printing the document. Alternatively, if you are having printing problems and want to see whether the print spooler is causing the problem, select the related radio button to have all applications print directly to the printer. However, this option usually prevents you from working in the application until the printer has finished printing the document.

Tip #83

If you are using a network printer in a Windows NT environment, you shouldn't try to have the application print directly to the printer (thus bypassing the spooler) because spooling actually occurs on both the client and the server. In a normal operation, the client machine spools the document into a manageable format and then sends that information to the server to be spooled until the network printer is available. By bypassing the spooling feature entirely, you create more network traffic and a possibility that the job may not reach the printer before it times out. This situation causes your system to freeze, and your documents are not printed. Also, because the job is not prepared before it reaches the printer, the possibility of a mismatched driver could cause the sent document to print incorrectly, often sending hundreds of garbled pages out of the printer.

Figure 13.9
You can change the spool settings for the print spooler on a printer if you want to return control to an application more quickly or if you must troubleshoot printing problems.

In this same window, you also see that you can choose between the *EMF (enhanced metafile printing)* and *RAW* spool data formats. Normally, you want to use the default setting for your printer to help ensure error-free printing. Using EMF usually returns control to the application more quickly than using the RAW data format does because the latter must be generated by the printer driver. If the default for your printer is RAW, try using EMF to speed up the printing process in your application. However, because some applications do not support EMF, if you experience problems, you should switch back to the RAW format.

After a print job has been sent to the spooler, a Printer icon appears in the system tray indicating that Windows 98 is processing the print job. If you click on this icon, a window opens for that printer from which you can get additional information about the status of the print job. For more information about managing print jobs through this Printer window, see the next section on managing print jobs.

MANAGING PRINT JOBS

Through the process of sending documents to your local or network printer, instances will arise when you must cancel a print job or simply find out what other documents are waiting to be printed. To view the status of a printer, you can open the Printer window for that device. If you are in the process of printing a document from your computer, you can click on the Printer icon in the system tray to bring up the window for that printer. You can also open that printer's window by double-clicking on its icon in the Printers folder. Note that although the first method might display only print jobs created by your computer, the latter method should display all pending print jobs, including those from any other users on your network.

When you open a Printer window, all currently pending documents for that printer are displayed (see Figure 13.10). The pending print jobs are shown in their order in the print queue. The print job at the top of the print queue is the document currently being printed. Any documents below that are printed in descending order.

PART

III

CH

13

Tip #84

Don't be alarmed if you cannot see your spooled document in the Printer window. Today's printers achieve faster processing times by utilizing their internal memory. This practice allows jobs to be held in memory on the printer and thus empties out the spooler, even though the job has not yet begun to print or is not yet finished printing. This technology is especially popular on network printers designed to handle large jobs and heavy print traffic. Unfortunately, this approach also gives you less time to catch a mistake while it can still be managed in the printer's spooled jobs.

Figure 13.10
The Printer window shows all print jobs currently pending on a printer and enables you to delete or pause any of your pending jobs.

By right-clicking on any of the pending print jobs, you can choose to either pause or cancel that job. When you pause a print job, it is skipped over when its place in the queue comes up. Although you can exercise control over your own documents, usually you cannot pause or cancel other people's print jobs unless you have administrative privileges on that printer.

In addition to pausing or canceling print jobs, you can purge all pending documents by selecting that option from the Printer pull-down menu, subject to the security restrictions discussed earlier regarding other users' documents. You can also change any of the properties for the selected printer by choosing Properties from the Printer pull-down menu.

SPECIAL PRINTING CONSIDERATIONS

Although we have already discussed most of the main printing features in Windows 98, a number of other areas are worth considering. In this section we look at how to print

- By dragging and dropping a file onto a printer's icon
- A file from any disk drive through Windows Explorer
- Frames in HTML documents viewed in Internet Explorer
- From within MS-DOS applications
- Documents containing color graphics
- When your printer is unavailable
- With multiple types of paper configurations

DRAG-AND-DROP PRINTING

Although you normally print a document from within an application in which you are working, you can also print a document without being in an application. You do so by dragging and dropping the document onto a Printer icon. One way to drag and drop is to create a shortcut for one or more of your installed printers on your desktop. Then, you can print documents by dragging them from the desktop or any window and dropping them onto the printer shortcut.

To create a desktop shortcut for one of your installed printers, open the Printers folder. With either your left or right mouse button, select the printer's icon from the folder and drag it to the desktop. When you release the mouse button, a shortcut for the printer is created. If you prefer not to create a desktop shortcut for the printer, you can drag and drop documents onto the printer's icon in the Printers folder.

When you drag and drop a document onto a printer's icon, Windows 98 opens the related application, prints the document within the program, and then closes that application. Because Windows 98 looks for a program that has previously been associated with that type of file to open an application and print the document, you must have previously installed a program on your computer that is registered for handling that file type. Thus, if you want to print a document created in Microsoft Excel, you must have Excel loaded on your computer because Windows 98 looks for an application associated with that file extension (in this case, files having a .XLS or other Excel-related extension). Another option is to use the Excel Viewer, which enables you to view and print Excel worksheets, but not make changes to them.

PRINTING FILES FROM DISK

In addition to printing files by dragging and dropping them onto printer icons, you can print directly from disk. In most cases, printing from disk is the quickest way to print a document without having to open the application yourself.

To print a file directly from disk, simply select the file from within Windows Explorer. The file can be located on any floppy drive, hard drive, or network drive to which you have access. Right-click on the file and choose Print. The printing process is identical to that in drag-and-drop printing. Thus, Windows 98 opens the application associated with that type of file, prints the file within that application, and then closes the application automatically.

PART
III
CH
13

| Tip #85 | It is usually a good idea to open a document and use Print Preview on the File menu before sending the document to the printer. Spreadsheet applications, in particular, send more pages than you may have bargained for, even though the information is actually only one page long. You can adopt many strategies to avoid this problem, such as diligently setting a print area in spreadsheet applications, but it is still a good idea to check before you make a mistake you will regret. |

PRINTING FRAMES IN INTERNET EXPLORER

Although the Print window that appears when you are printing from an application is normally consistent from program to program, one difference occurs when you print a document that contains multiple frames from within Internet Explorer. A Web page that contains multiple frames may appear as a single page but is actually made up of multiple pages within a single frameset. Each frame is a separate document that can be printed out through your computer.

When you print a page containing multiple frames, the Print window has options not found when printing from other applications (see Figure 13.11). From this window, you can print the selected frame (which usually is the main, or largest, frame), all frames individually, or the frameset as it appears on your screen. You can also specify whether to print all linked documents, in which case Internet Explorer prints all pages for which hyperlinks appear on the page you are printing, or to print a table containing links for these documents.

Figure 13.11
When printing an HTML document containing multiple frames, you have several options regarding which frames to print.

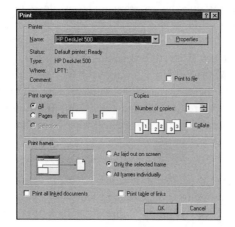

→ For further information on printing within Internet Explorer, **see** Chapter 28, "Finding, Organizing, and Saving Web-Based Information."

PRINTING FROM MS-DOS APPLICATIONS

Although most applications you run on your computer are probably written for Windows, you might have a few MS-DOS applications from which you will need to print. Windows 98 fully supports printing from MS-DOS applications, although you do not get the full benefits found in printing from Windows applications, such as *EMF* spooling. All print jobs created by MS-DOS applications are intercepted by the 32-bit print spooler prior to being sent to the printer, resulting in a quicker return of control to the application.

PRINTING IN COLOR

One problem encountered when printing color graphics is that the color displayed on your monitor might not match the color generated by the printer. To help alleviate this problem,

Microsoft has included support for *Image Color Matching (ICM)* in Windows 98. Although Windows 95 supports ICM 1.0, Windows 98 supports the newer ICM 2.0, which includes a number of technical improvements. The result is a better correlation between the colors as they appear on your monitor and those generated by your color printer. Because ICM is supported on multiple platforms, the images you create in Windows 98 applications should appear virtually the same on computers that are running other ICM 2.0–compliant operating systems.

OFFLINE PRINTING

If you use a laptop computer or if your printer is available only via a network connection, you are a good candidate for using the offline printing feature in Windows 98. With a laptop computer, you may not always be physically connected to your printer, such as when you are working on a document on an airplane. Similarly, if you work in a networked environment, you may at times not be able to print because of problems connecting to the printer over the network. As the name implies, offline printing enables you to generate print jobs when you are not connected to a printer and to print them at a later time.

Note

Offline printing works only for portable and networked computers and also requires the use of the print spooler supplied with Windows 98. If you have configured the printer not to use print spooling, you have to enable this feature to put your printer into offline mode. Because offline printing is not supported for local printers, if you want to stop printing on a local printer, right-click on the printer's icon in the Printers folder and choose the Pause Printing command.

To use offline printing, open the Printers folder and select the printer you want to use offline. Right-click on the printer's icon and choose Use Printer Offline, at which point a check mark appears next to this choice. Any print jobs you generate are held in the queue until you instruct Windows 98 to actually print these jobs. When you want to print the stored jobs, right-click on the printer's icon and deselect the Use Printer Offline option.

Tip #86

If you are using a desktop computer that is connected to a network printer and the network connection is interrupted for any reason, the printer automatically goes offline. As a confirmation of this, you should immediately check your printer's log to see whether the printer has gone offline before you resubmit your print jobs. Also, if you have resubmitted and the print jobs are spooled in the Offline Printer window, be sure to remove any duplicates before you restore the printer. When the printer is online, the network printer may process many of the duplicate jobs before you can manage them in your spooler.

If your laptop is configured to be used with a docking station, when you boot your computer, Windows 98 automatically selects offline printing if it detects that you are not connected to the docking station. If you later boot your laptop while being docked, the offline printing feature is turned off and any stored print jobs are sent to your printer.

MANAGING PAPER

By changing the properties for a printer, you can select the paper size, the paper tray the printer should use, and other such settings as determined by the capabilities of your printer. The properties can be changed at any time either from the Printers folder or from within any application.

To change the printer paper properties from within an application, select Print from the File pull-down menu and then click on the Properties button. You can also access these properties by right-clicking on the printer's icon in the Printers folder and choosing Properties. In either event, a Properties page similar (but probably not identical) to that shown in Figure 13.12 appears (this example is from the WordPad application).

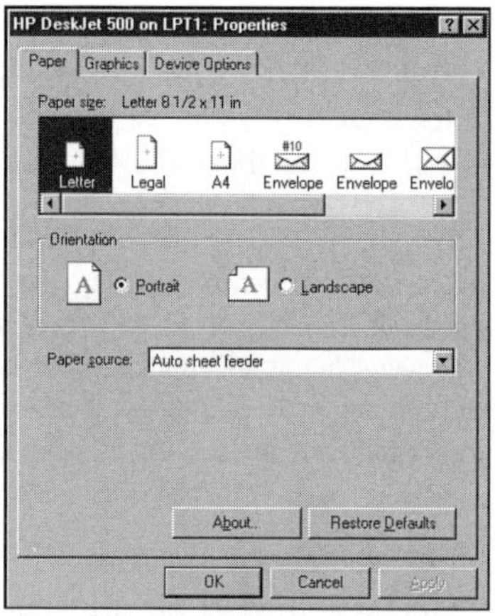

Figure 13.12
You can change a printer's paper configurations to best match the needs of the document you are printing.

After the Properties page appears, click on the Paper tab. From here you can select the size of the paper on which you are printing as well as the layout of the print job, that is, landscape or portrait. If your printer has multiple trays, an envelope holder, or other paper sources, you can also change the paper source on this part of the printer's Properties page. As mentioned previously, because the properties page appears differently from printer to printer, the display for your printer will likely appear somewhat differently than that shown in Figure 13.12.

CONFIGURING A PRINTER FOR MULTIPLE USES

With Windows 98 you can set up multiple virtual printers, each of which points to a single physical printer. This practice enables you to create one configuration for high-quality graphics printing, one for landscape (as opposed to portrait) printing, or any other configurations you want. Each configuration can be saved as a separate printer, even though all the configurations point to a single printing device.

To have the operating system configure additional printers for this purpose, use the Add Printer Wizard to go through the same process that you used to install the printer previously, but this time give the printer a slightly different name. Thus, you might name one printer High graphics and another Landscape.

When you install each of these printers, the Add Printer Wizard tells you that a driver for this type of printer is already installed on your computer. The wizard then asks whether you want to keep the existing driver or install this new one. Unless you have a version of the driver on a disk that is newer than the Windows 98 CD-ROM, keep the existing driver.

After you have finished using the Add Printer Wizard, a new icon appears for this printer. Right-click on its icon and choose Properties. Configure the printer according to its new name. Thus, for the Landscape printer example, select the option to use landscape printing rather than portrait.

Your new virtual printers are also available for use within your applications. Thus, when you want to print a job in landscape format, choose the Landscape printer rather than your main printer. This technique gives you a quick and easy way to print in this format without having to change the printer's properties each time.

REMOVING PRINTERS

Although the focus of this chapter has involved installing and managing printers, you might need to remove installed printers and related devices from your computer. For example, if you buy a new printer and give the old one away, you would have no reason to keep the old printer's driver on your computer.

To remove a printer and its related drivers from your computer, open the Printers folder. Right-click on the printer's icon and choose Delete. Windows 98 then asks you to confirm that you want to remove that printer from your computer. Click on the Yes button to remove the printer.

During the process of removing the printer, a dialog box asks whether you also want to remove the files that the printer used—that is, the driver and any other related files needed for use by that particular printer. If you think that you might use that printer in the future, you can choose No to keep these files on your computer. By doing so, you can avoid installing the files from the Windows 98 CD-ROM the next time you add the printer to your computer. Otherwise, choose Yes to remove all the files associated with this printer from your computer. When the process is complete, the printer's icon is removed from the Printers folder.

TROUBLESHOOTING

HELP WITH BASIC PRINTER PROBLEMS

The help files that come with Windows 98 include several Troubleshooters, which are wizardlike guides to helping you solve common print errors that might occur. If you experience a printing problem in Windows 98 and are not able to fix it on your own, you should try the Print Troubleshooter before seeking technical support.

To start the Print Troubleshooter, click on the Start button and select Help. In the Help window, double-click on the Troubleshooting book icon and then again on the Windows 98 Troubleshooters icon. This item expands to show a list of Troubleshooters from which you can select. Click on Print in this listing to open the Windows 98 Print Troubleshooter in the right pane of this window, as shown in Figure 13.13.

Figure 13.13
The Print Troubleshooter can help solve many of the most common printing problems in Windows 98.

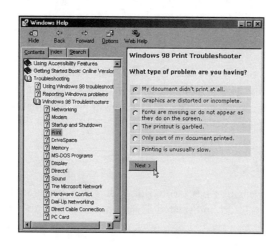

To use the Troubleshooter, select the radio button for the type of problem that is closest to that which you are experiencing. Then press the Next button and proceed through the steps. If there is no Troubleshooter for your particular problem or if the Troubleshooter does not fully solve the problem, you might need to contact either your printer manufacturer or Microsoft by using the Windows Update tool located off the Start button. This tool connects you to the site http://windowsupdate.microsoft.com/.

PRINTER INSTALLATION ISSUES

You might run into several problems during a printer installation in Windows 98. The first issue is not finding any printers listed in the Print dialog box. If you are unable to select a specific model because no list appears, verify that the printer INF file exists. This file, Msprint*x*.inf, is in the Windows INF directory and contains the information displayed in the Manufacturer and Model lists. If the file is missing, you must either run Setup again or copy the file from another Windows 98 system.

The second issue is a file-copy error that occurs during the installation of a printer. If you get an error during the file-copy operation while using the Add Printer Wizard, the wizard displays error-specific information. This information includes the source and destination paths and filenames being copied when the error occurred. To continue the installation, you must verify the location of the specified files and try again.

SECRETS OF MASTERING THE WINDOWS 98 ENVIRONMENT: TWO USEFUL PRINTING UTILITIES

Although Windows 98 doesn't come with the best operating system printing features to date, in keeping with Microsoft's encouragement of third-party utilities, here are a couple of good ones.

InternetPrint, by Nadio, Inc., is a universal printer driver that enables you to send documents to remote printers over the Internet. InternetPrint functions as a printer driver and is called from within a running application. The criterion to determine whether InternetPrint will work for you is simple: If you can print a particular document from within an application to your local printer, then you can use InternetPrint to send the document to a remote printer. InternetPrint works with documents that contain any combination of text, graphics, and images. This utility can be found at `http://softseek.com/Utilities/File_Printing/`.

Directory Printer for Windows, by Glenn Alcott, addresses a need that many GUI operating systems have overlooked. Namely, Directory Printer creates printouts of filenames stored on your system.

Directory Printer is a comprehensive tool that enables you to print a simple list of files in a directory or folder; to determine the format (single, double, or quad column); and to specify which file attribute information to include, as well as the sort order, the print font, the file types, and the number of subfolders. The output organizes files by folder and gives you the total number of files and number of bytes used. This utility can be found at `http://www.qualityimage.com/`.

CHAPTER **14**

Using Windows Accessories

In this chapter

Windows 98 comes with several accessory applications, ranging from very simple applications, such as Calculator and Notepad, to more powerful applications such as WordPad (a word processor) and HyperTerminal (a communications tool). Table 14.1 describes the accessories that come with Windows 98 and tells you where to look to find out more about them. This chapter explains how to use the following Windows 98 tools: Calculator, HyperTerminal, and Phone Dialer.

TABLE 14.1 WINDOWS 98 ACCESSORIES

Accessory	Description
Calculator	Used to perform calculations onscreen as you would on a desktop calculator. (Covered in this chapter.)
Imaging	Used to view, annotate, print, manage, store, and share images that have been created from faxes, scanned documents, or computerized images. (Covered in Chapter 16, "Using Paint and Imaging.")
Notepad	A simple text editor that you can use to create and edit text files. (Covered in Chapter 15, "Using Notepad and WordPad.")
Paint	An easy-to-learn graphics application that you can use to create and modify graphics images. (Covered in Chapter 16, "Using Paint and Imaging.")
WordPad	A word processing application used to enter, edit, and format documents. (Covered in Chapter 15, "Using Notepad and WordPad.")
Character Map	Used to insert special characters in your documents. (Covered in Chapter 18, "Working with Fonts.")
Dial-Up Networking	Used to connect your computer to another computer or a network using your modem. (Covered in Chapter 38, "Remote Access with Dial-Up Networking.")
Direct Cable Connection	Used to connect to another computer using a cable. (Covered in Chapter 25, "Special Features for Notebook Users.")
HyperTerminal	A communications application used to work online with your computer. (Covered in this chapter.)
Phone Dialer	A tool for storing and automatically dialing phone numbers from your computer. (Covered in this chapter.)
CD Player	Used to play music CDs on your computer. (Covered in Chapter 19, "Setting Up Windows 98 Multimedia.")
DVD Player	Used to play DVD discs from your DVD drive. (Covered in Chapter 20, "Using Windows to Play Games and Watch TV.")
Media Player	Used to play multimedia files (video, audio, and animation). (Covered in Chapter 19, "Setting Up Windows 98 Multimedia.")

Accessory	Description
Sound Recorder	Used to record digital sound files on your computer. (Covered in Chapter 19, "Setting Up Windows 98 Multimedia.")
Games	Four games—FreeCell, Hearts, Minesweeper, and Solitaire—for your entertainment. (Discussed briefly in this chapter.)

ADDING WINDOWS ACCESSORIES

The Add/Remove Programs icon in Control Panel enables you to install and remove Windows components and accessories, as well as applications. If you opted not to install a particular Windows 98 accessory when you installed Windows but you change your mind later, you can use the Windows Setup feature to add or remove a Windows component. To do so, follow these steps:

1. Open the Start menu and choose Settings, Control Panel.

2. Open the Add/Remove Programs Properties sheet by using the Add/Remove Programs icon.

3. Select the Windows Setup tab to display a list of Windows components as shown in Figure 14.1.

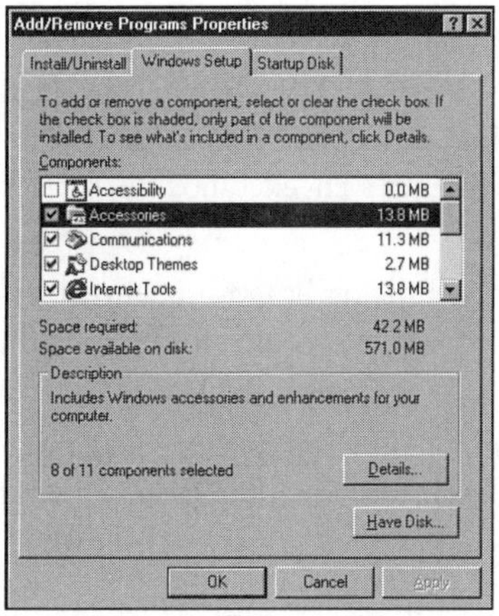

Figure 14.1
The Windows Setup tab of the Add/Remove Programs Properties sheet lets you add and remove various components of Windows.

In the Components list box, a check mark next to an item indicates that the component is already installed on your system. If the check box is gray, the Windows component has more than one subcomponent, and some (but not all) of the subcomponents are currently installed. For example, in Figure 14.2 only some of the subcomponents (Calculator and Games) of the Accessories component are installed. To see what's included in a component, choose Details.

PART

III

CH

14

4. Select a component in the Components list box. The Description box in the lower portion of the dialog box displays a description of that component and tells you how many of the available subcomponents are selected.

5. If the component you selected consists of more than one subcomponent, choose Details to open a dialog box listing the subcomponents. (For example, Figure 14.2 shows the Accessories dialog box listing the subcomponents of the main Accessories component.) In some cases, a subcomponent has additional subcomponents, which you can view by choosing Details again.

Figure 14.2
The Accessories dialog box lists a component's parts. By choosing Details, you can narrow your selections.

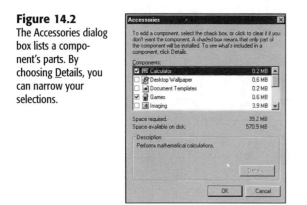

6. Mark a component for installation or removal by clicking the check box beside that item in the Components list. Adding a check mark to a blank check box marks that item for installation. Conversely, clearing a checked box instructs Windows to uninstall that component.

7. If you're selecting subcomponents in a dialog box you opened by choosing a Details button, click OK to close that dialog box and return to the Add/Remove Programs Properties sheet.

8. When the check marks in the Components lists specify the components that you want for your Windows system, choose Apply in the Add/Remove Programs Properties sheet. You'll need to supply the Windows Setup disks or CD when prompted.

If when you add new components, Windows automatically removes others, see "Adding Components" in the "Troubleshooting" section at the end of this chapter.

CALCULATING WITH CALCULATOR

Like a calculator you keep in a desk drawer, the Windows Calculator is small but saves you time by performing all the calculations common to a standard calculator. The Windows Calculator, however, has added advantages: You can keep this calculator onscreen alongside other applications, and you can copy numbers between it and other applications.

The Standard Windows Calculator, shown in Figure 14.3, works so much like a pocket calculator that you need little help getting started. The *keypad*, the onscreen representation, contains familiar number *keys*, along with memory and simple math keys. A display window just above the keypad shows the numbers you enter and the results of calculations. If your computational needs are more advanced, you can choose a different view of the calculator, the Scientific view (see Figure 14.4).

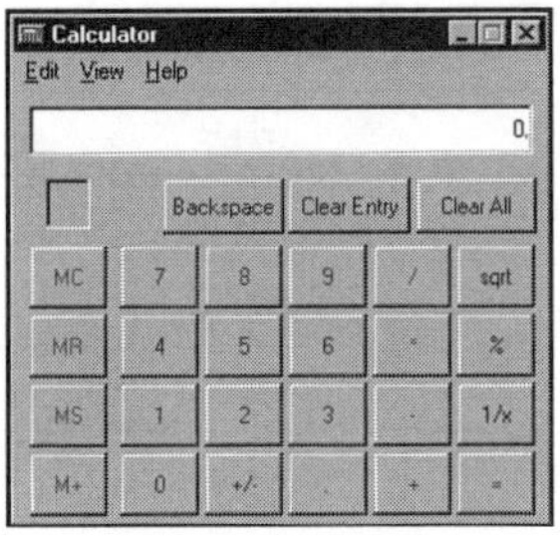

Figure 14.3
The Standard Calculator works like a pocket calculator.

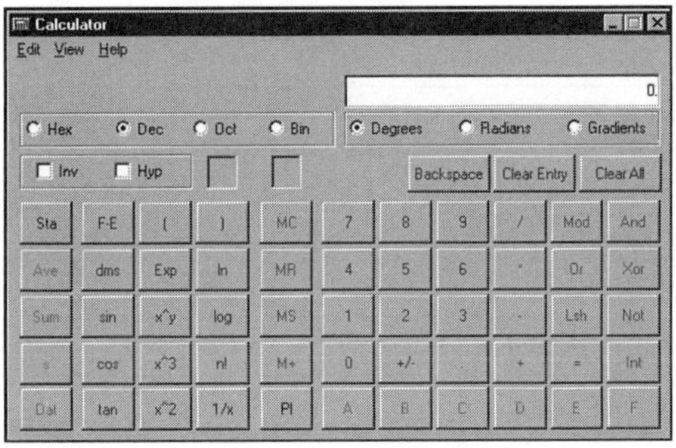

Figure 14.4
Choose the Scientific Calculator view if your needs are more advanced.

To display the Windows Calculator, open the Start menu and choose Programs, Accessories, Calculator. The Calculator opens in the same view (Standard or Scientific) in which it was displayed the last time it was used.

To close the Calculator, click the Close button in the title bar. If you use the Calculator frequently, however, don't close it; click the Minimize button to minimize the Calculator to a button on the taskbar.

The Calculator has only three menus: Edit, View, and Help. The Edit menu contains two simple commands for copying and pasting; the View menu switches between the Standard and Scientific views; and the Help menu is the same as it is in all Windows accessories.

OPERATING THE CALCULATOR

To use the Calculator with the mouse, just click the appropriate numbers and sign keys, the way you would press buttons on a desk calculator. Numbers appear in the display window as you select them, and the results appear after the calculations are performed.

To enter numbers from the keyboard, use either the numbers across the top of the keyboard or those on the numeric keypad (you must first press the Num Lock key if the Num Lock feature is not enabled). To calculate, press the keys on the keyboard that match the Calculator keys. Table 14.2 shows the Calculator keys for the keyboard.

TABLE 14.2 KEYBOARD EQUIVALENTS FOR THE CALCULATOR

Calculator Key	Function	Keyboard Key
MC	Clear memory	Ctrl+L
MR	Display memory	Ctrl+R
M+	Add to memory	Ctrl+P
MS	Store value in memory	Ctrl+M
CE	Delete displayed value	Del
Back	Delete last digit in displayed value	Backspace
+/–	Change sign	F9
/	Divide	/
*	Multiply	*
–	Subtract	–
+	Add	+
sqrt	Square root	@
%	Percent	%
1/x	Calculate reciprocal	R
C	Clear	Esc
=	Equals	= or Enter

Note

To calculate a percentage, treat the % key like an equal sign. For example, to calculate 15% of 80, type 80*15%. After you press the % key, the Calculator displays the result (in this case, 12).

You can use the Calculator's memory to total the results of several calculations. The memory holds a single number, which starts as zero. You can add to, display, or clear this number, or you can store another number in memory.

COPYING NUMBERS BETWEEN THE CALCULATOR AND OTHER APPLICATIONS

When working with many numbers or complex numbers, you make fewer mistakes if you copy the Calculator results into other applications instead of retyping the result. To copy a number from the Calculator into another application, follow these steps:

1. In the Calculator display window, perform the math calculations required to display the number.

2. Choose Edit, Copy, or press Ctrl+C.

3. Activate the application in which you want to place the calculated number.

4. Position the insertion point in the newly opened application where you want the number copied.

5. From the newly opened application, choose Edit, Paste, or press Ctrl+V.

You can also copy and paste a number from another application into the Calculator, perform calculations with the number, and then copy the result back into the application. A number pasted into the Calculator erases the number currently shown in the display window.

To copy a number from another application into the Calculator, select the number in the application and choose Edit, Copy. Then activate the Calculator and choose Edit, Paste.

If you paste a formula in the Calculator, you can choose the equal (=) button to see the result. For example, if you copy 5+5 from WordPad, paste the calculation into the Calculator, and then choose the = key, the resulting number 10 appears. If you paste a function, such as @ for square root, the Calculator performs the function on the number displayed. If, for example, you copy @ from a letter in WordPad and paste it into Calculator when the display shows the number 25, the result 5 appears.

Numbers and most operators (such as + and –) work fine when pasted into the Calculator display, but the Calculator interprets some characters as commands. The following chart lists the characters the Calculator interprets as commands:

Character	Interpreted As
:c	Clears memory
:e	Lets you enter scientific notation in decimal mode; also the number E in hexadecimal mode
:m	Stores the current value in memory
:p	Adds the displayed value to the number in memory
:q	Clears the current calculation
:r	Displays the value in memory
\	Works like the Dat button (in the Scientific calculator)

USING THE SCIENTIFIC CALCULATOR

If you have ever written an equation wider than a sheet of paper, you're a good candidate for using the Scientific Calculator. The Scientific Calculator is a special view of the Calculator.

To display the Scientific Calculator, activate the Calculator and choose View, Scientific.

The Scientific Calculator works the same as the Standard Calculator but adds many advanced functions. You can work in one of four number systems: hexadecimal, decimal, octal, or binary. You can perform statistical calculations, such as averages and statistical deviations. You also can calculate sines, cosines, tangents, powers, logarithms, squares, and cubes. These specialized functions aren't described here but are well documented in the Calculator's Help command.

→ For a more detailed explanation of how to access and use the Help command, **see** "Getting Help from Windows Help Files," **p. 54.**

USING HYPERTERMINAL

HyperTerminal is a Windows accessory that enables you to connect your computer to another PC or online service. HyperTerminal is a full-featured communications tool that greatly simplifies getting online. With HyperTerminal you can connect to a friend's computer, a university, an Internet service provider, or even CompuServe.

Before the existence of graphical interfaces to online services such as CompuServe and The Microsoft Network, most communications tools were character-oriented. For example, students all over the world used terminal emulation programs to connect to their schools' computers. They typically used VT100 terminal emulation to make their PCs behave like any other display terminal on the system.

If you can use the graphical communications tools mentioned here, why do you need a character-oriented tool such as HyperTerminal? The reason is that most bulletin boards, Internet shell accounts, and university connections are still character-oriented. Most bulletin boards do not provide a graphical interface. HyperTerminal does the following:

- Makes the focal point of your activities the connections you create (documents), which allows you to dial or configure a connection without loading HyperTerminal first
- Automatically detects the terminal-emulation mode and communications parameters of the remote computer
- Fully integrates with TAPI and the centralized modem configuration, which provides Windows 98 applications with a single interface to your modem for dialing, answering, configuration, and more
- Supports several popular terminal-emulation modes and file transfer protocols, such as VT100, VT52, and Kermit
- Enables you to greatly customize each of your connections

WHAT YOU CAN AND CAN'T DO WITH HYPERTERMINAL

HyperTerminal is a communications tool with many uses. The following list describes many tasks you can perform with HyperTerminal:

- Connect to another computer and exchange files
- Connect to an online service (such as CompuServe) that supports one of HyperTerminal's terminal-emulation modes

- Connect to a school's computer using VT100
- Connect to an Internet service provider using a shell account and even access the World Wide Web using Lynx

Although HyperTerminal is a useful communications tool, it is not the only tool you will need for your communications activities. The following list describes some activities you can't do and refers you to other chapters in this book:

- Connect to another network.

→ If you need to connect your computer to another network, **see** Chapter 26, "Establishing a Dial-Up Internet Connection" **p. 521.**

- Graphically connect to the Internet World Wide Web. Although many service providers provide Lynx, a character-oriented Web browsing tool, you need a graphical browsing tool to take full advantage of the Web.

→ For help getting started with the Internet Explorer graphical browsing tool, **see** Chapter 27, "Web Browsing with Internet Explorer 5.0," **p. 555.**

⚠ *If you're having trouble with the screen contents of a HyperTerminal connection, see "Determining the Correct Terminal Emulation" in the "Troubleshooting" section at the end of this chapter.*

→ If you need to learn more about a RAS, **see** "Connecting to a Remote Access Server," **p. 850.**

Creating a New Connection

When you installed Windows, you were given the option of installing HyperTerminal as one of your accessories. If you did not install HyperTerminal or if you removed it from the Start menu, you can install it at any time by selecting Install/Remove Applications from Control Panel. To load HyperTerminal, open the Start menu and choose Programs, Accessories, HyperTerminal. If you have not yet configured your modem, Windows prompts you to set it up the first time you run HyperTerminal.

Figure 14.5 shows the HyperTerminal folder. By default, each connection that you create appears in this folder as an icon.

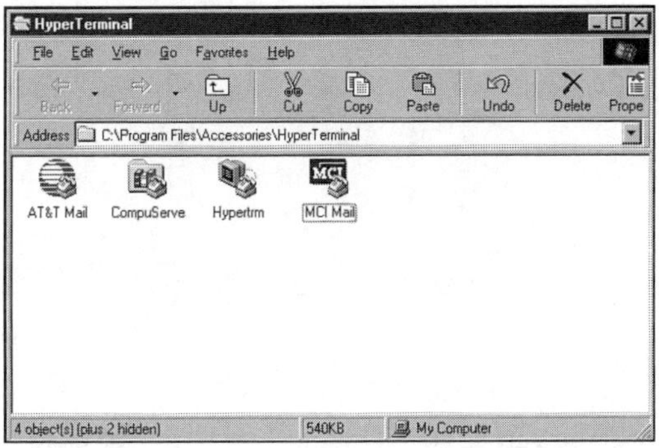

Figure 14.5
Choose Hypertrm to create a new HyperTerminal connection or choose another icon to open an existing connection.

→ To configure your modem for use with HyperTerminal, **see** "Configuring a Modem," **p. 425.**

Before you can connect with HyperTerminal, you need to create a new connection. To do so, follow these steps:

1. Choose the Hypertrm icon in the HyperTerminal folder.

   If HyperTerminal is already loaded, choose File, New or click the New button on the toolbar. HyperTerminal prompts you for a new connection description.

2. In the Connection Description dialog box, shown in Figure 14.6, type a descriptive name for your new connection, select an icon, and click OK. HyperTerminal then displays the Phone Number dialog box.

Figure 14.6
Create a new connection and select an icon to help you identify it later.

3. Type the phone number for your new connection. Then verify the country code, area code, and modem choice and click OK. HyperTerminal displays the Connect dialog box, shown in Figure 14.7.

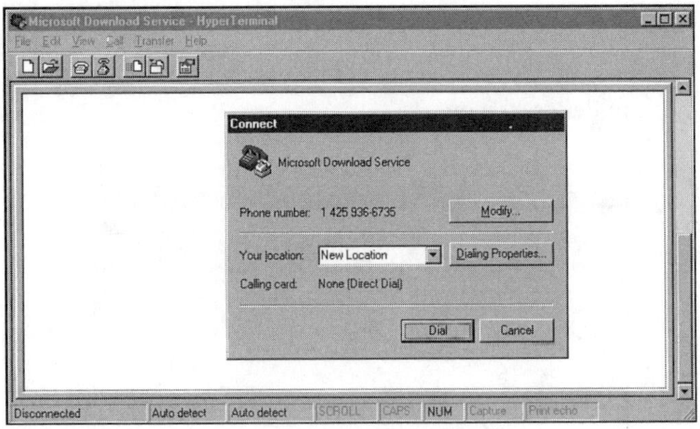

Figure 14.7
After you set up the connection, simply click Dial to begin.

4. Select your location (usually Default Location) and click Dial if you want to establish your new connection. You can choose Dialing Properties to change the default location, the outside line access, and other dialing properties.

Figure 14.8 shows the entire HyperTerminal window with a session in progress. Most of HyperTerminal's features are available on the toolbar. To see what a toolbar button's function is, hold the mouse pointer over the tool for a few seconds, and a tooltip appears.

Figure 14.8
After establishing a connection to the remote computer, you interact with it just like a display terminal on the system. Click the scrollbar to review previously displayed text.

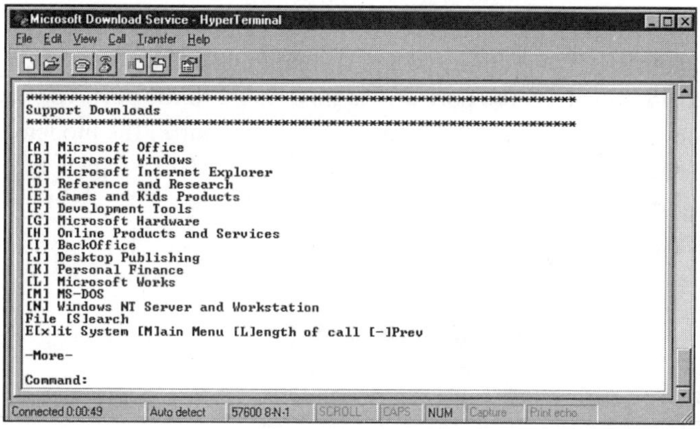

To save your new connection, choose File, Save As. HyperTerminal prompts you for a filename. If you want your connections to show up in the HyperTerminal folder, accept the default path. If you quit HyperTerminal without saving your new connection, HyperTerminal prompts you for a filename.

To hang up, choose Call, Disconnect or click the Disconnect button on the toolbar.

USING AN EXISTING CONNECTION

The next time you want to use the connection you previously created, it appears in the HyperTerminal folder. To establish this connection, choose the icon in the folder and click Dial.

If HyperTerminal is already running, choose File, Open or click the Open button on the toolbar.

CHANGING A CONNECTION SETUP

It is easy to change the properties for a connection after you create it. You can change the connection's icon, name, country code, area code, phone number, and modem in the connection's properties sheet (see Figure 14.9).

To change the properties of your connection, follow these steps:

1. Choose File, Properties or click the Properties button on the toolbar.

   You can change the HyperTerminal Properties sheet without even running HyperTerminal. To do so, right-click the connection you want to change in the HyperTerminal folder and then choose Properties.

PART

III

CH

14

2. Choose Change Icon, select another icon from the list, and change the connection name.

3. Select a country code.

4. Type the area code and phone number. (If you select the default location when you dial, Windows does not dial the area code if it matches your default area code.)

5. Select a modem. Windows displays the modems you currently have installed or enables you to go directly to the port. If you go directly to the port, you can bypass the Windows 98 modem configuration so you can control the modem directly. For normal use, select a configured modem so that you can take advantage of centralized modem configuration.

6. Click OK to save your settings.

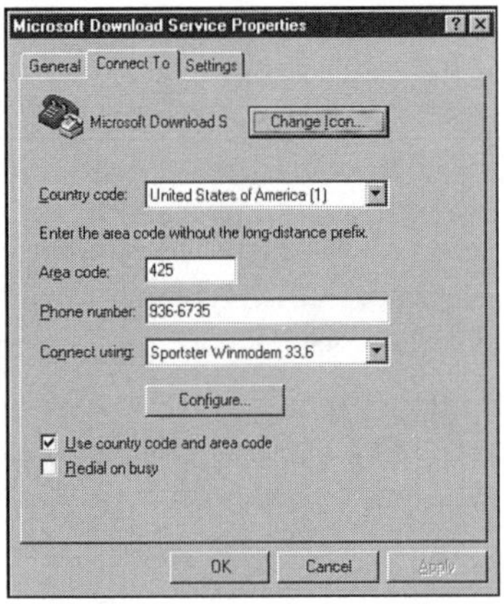

Figure 14.9
Change the icon, name, phone number, and modem to use for this connection. Click OK to permanently save your settings.

CONFIGURING THE CONNECTION SETTINGS

The Settings tab of the properties sheet enables you to change the terminal properties of HyperTerminal. For example, you can change the terminal-emulation mode. Figure 14.10 shows the Settings tab of this sheet. Table 14.3 describes each terminal emulation available in HyperTerminal.

TABLE 14.3 TERMINAL EMULATION SUPPORTED BY HYPERTERMINAL

Protocol	Description
ANSI	A popular generic terminal emulation, supported by most UNIX systems, that provides full-screen emulation.
Auto Detect	A system that automatically determines which terminal emulation the remote computer is using.
Minitel	An emulation primarily used in France.

Protocol	Description
TTY	Actually, the absence of any terminal emulation. TTY simply displays all the characters it receives on the display.
Viewdata	An emulation primarily used in the United Kingdom.
VT100	The workhorse of terminal emulations. Many remote systems such as UNIX use this.
VT52	A predecessor to VT100 that provides full-screen terminal emulation on remote systems that support it.

Figure 14.10
Use the Settings tab of the properties sheet to change the terminal emulation and other useful settings.

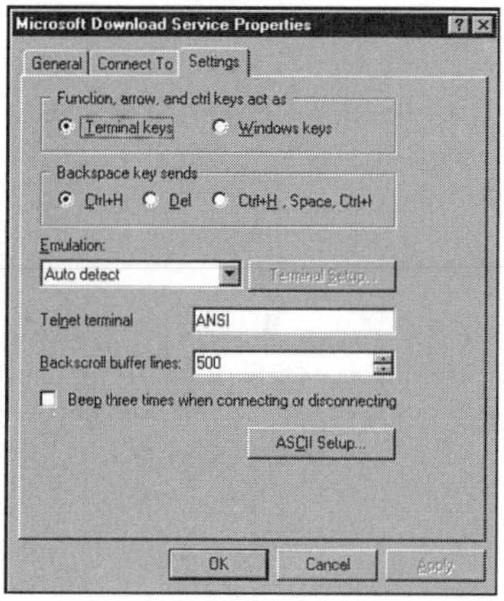

To change the settings for this connection, follow these steps:

1. Choose File, Properties or click the Properties button on the toolbar. (Alternatively, right-click a connection document in the HyperTerminal folder and choose Properties.)

2. On the Settings tab, choose Terminal Keys or Windows Keys.

    Terminal Keys sends function keys F1 through F12 and arrow keys to the remote computer instead of acting on them in Windows; Windows Keys causes Windows to act on those function keys. For example, if you choose Terminal Keys and press F1, the key is sent to the host and the host responds to it. If you choose Windows Keys and press F1, Windows responds to the key by displaying Help.

3. In the Backspace Key Sends box, select Del or Ctrl+H, Ctrl+}. This selection determines which character is sent to the remote computer when you press the Backspace key.

4. Set Emulation to the terminal emulation you want. HyperTerminal must be using the same terminal emulation the host computer is using.

    If you set Emulation to Auto Detect, HyperTerminal automatically determines which emulation the host is using and configures itself appropriately. Use this setting for normal situations.

PART

III

CH

14

5. Enter the number of lines you want in the Backscroll Buffer Lines box. In the HyperTerminal main window, the current screen is displayed with a white background. If you press Page Up or use the scrollbar to scroll backward, you see previously displayed text with a gray background. The default value for Backscroll Buffer Lines is 500 lines, which allows you to review about 20 screens and doesn't consume a large amount of memory.

6. Turn on Beep Three Times When Connecting or Disconnecting if you want to be notified when you are making or breaking a connection.

7. Optionally, click the ASCII Setup button and set the options for how text files are to be sent and received. Figure 14.11 shows the ASCII Setup dialog box, and Table 14.4 describes each option.

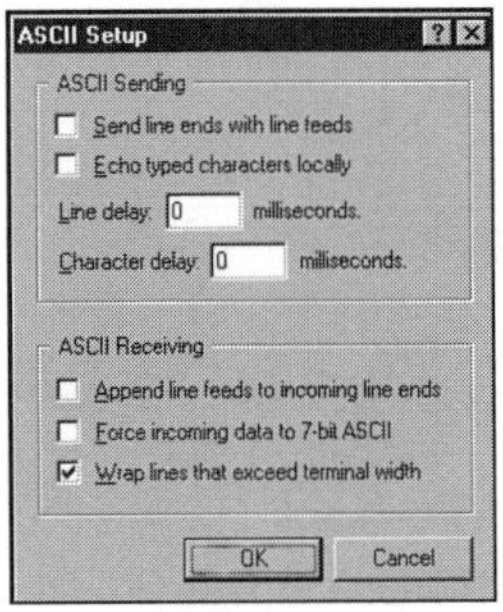

Figure 14.11
Use the ASCII Setup dialog box to configure how ASCII files will be sent and received. For example, you can choose to send line feeds with line ends.

TABLE 14.4   ASCII SETUP OPTIONS

Option	Description
Send Line Ends with Line Feeds	Attaches a line feed to the end of every line that HyperTerminal sends. Turn on this option if the remote computer requires it or if you turned on Echo Typed Characters Locally. Pressing Enter moves you to the beginning of the current line instead of starting a new line.
Echo Typed Characters Locally	Displays each character you type on the keyboard instead of depending on the host to echo each character. Turn on this option if you can't see the characters you type. If you see each character twice (ssuucchh aass tthhiiss), turn off this option.
Line Delay	Sets how much time to delay between lines. Increasing the amount of time between lines allows the remote computer time to get ready for the next line. Increase this setting in increments of 100 milliseconds if the remote computer frequently loses portions of each line.
Character Delay	Sets how much time to delay between characters. Increasing the amount of time between characters allows the remote computer time to get ready for the next character. Increase this setting in increments of 5 milliseconds if the remote computer randomly loses characters.

Option	Description
Append Line Feeds to Incoming Line Ends	Attaches a line feed to lines received. Turn on this option if the lines you receive from the host computer are displayed one on top of another.
Force Incoming Data to 7-bit ASCII	Changes 8-bit characters to 7 bit. Turn on this option if HyperTerminal displays unrecognizable symbols. This option forces HyperTerminal to stick with readable characters.
Wrap Lines That Exceed Terminal Width	Turns word wrapping on or off. Turn on this option if you want lines that are longer than the terminal width to be continued on the followingline.

Tip #87

You can also set HyperTerminal to receive a connection from another computer. To set up HyperTerminal to answer an incoming call, follow these steps:

1. From the Start menu, choose Programs, Accessories, Communications, HyperTerminal.
2. Double-click the Hypertrm.exe icon. You are prompted to create a connection name, such as Incoming, to answer incoming calls.
3. Enter information for this connection, including a phone number. The phone number is not actually used for this connection, so any seven numbers will do, and then click OK. When HyperTerminal prompts you to connect, click Cancel.
4. On the File menu, click Properties and select the Settings tab.
5. Click ASCII Setup and configure how ASCII files should be received. Click OK and OK again to return to HyperTerminal.
6. Wait for the incoming call. When you see the command "ring" or you hear the phone ring, type the answer command for your modem. On most modems the answer command is ATA. If your modem supports automatic answering mode, you can type the command ATS0=1 to allow the modem to answer the incoming call automatically. (If you don't know whether your modem supports this feature, contact the modem manufacturer.)

EXCHANGING FILES WITH THE REMOTE COMPUTER

You can easily exchange files with another computer by using HyperTerminal. For example, you may want to download a program update from the bulletin board of your favorite software vendor. You also can download public domain software from a variety of bulletin board systems (BBSs) around the country.

Caution

Before you run a program downloaded from a remote computer on your own computer, run the download through a virus scan program to make sure that it's not infected. Otherwise, severe and irreparable damage may occur to your programs and data files if you download a virus.

PART

III

CH

14

You might be asked to upload a data file to a vendor's bulletin board so that the vendor can help you fix a problem. HyperTerminal can also upload files.

DOWNLOADING FILES

Before you begin downloading a file, you must make sure that you have a connection with a host computer, as described in the previous section "Using an Existing Connection."

The procedure for starting a download varies between bulletin boards and other host computers; follow the instructions given to you online. When you do start, make a note of the file transfer protocol you select on the host. HyperTerminal supports several popular file transfer protocols, described in Table 14.5.

TABLE 14.5   FILE TRANSFER PROTOCOLS SUPPORTED BY HYPERTERMINAL

Protocol	Description
Xmodem	Xmodem is an error-correcting protocol supported by virtually every communications program and online service. It is slower than the other protocols.
1K Xmodem	1K Xmodem is faster than Xmodem, transferring files in 1,024-byte blocks as opposed to the slower 128-byte blocks in regular Xmodem. Otherwise, the two protocols are similar.
Ymodem	Many bulletin board systems offer Ymodem, which is another name for 1K Xmodem.
Ymodem-G	Similar to Ymodem, Ymodem-G implements hardware error control. It is more reliable than the first three protocols. However, to use Ymodem-G, your hardware must support hardware error control.
Zmodem	Zmodem is preferred by most bulletin board users because it is the fastest protocol of those listed. Zmodem is reliable, too, because it continues a valid download even if it's interrupted and because it adjusts its block sizes during the download to accommodate bad telephone lines. Zmodem has two other features that make it stand out from the rest. First, the host can initiate the download (you do nothing beyond step 1). Second, you can download multiple files at one time using Zmodem. The host computer initiates a download for each file you select.
Kermit	Kermit is extremely slow when used in the context of HyperTerminal and should not be used if one of the other protocols is available. Kermit is a protocol left over from VAX computers and mainframes.

To download a file from a host computer, follow these steps:

1. Follow the online instructions to start the download process on the bulletin board or host computer. Remember to note which file transfer protocol you select.

2. If you selected Zmodem as the protocol, you are done. The host computer initiates the file transfer with HyperTerminal.

   If you selected any other protocol, choose Transfer, Receive File or click the Receive toolbar button. The Receive File dialog box appears (see Figure 14.12).

3. Enter a folder name or choose Browse to select a folder from a dialog box. Then select a protocol to use for downloading the file. The protocol you use should match the protocol you chose (or the system chosen for you) on the host computer.

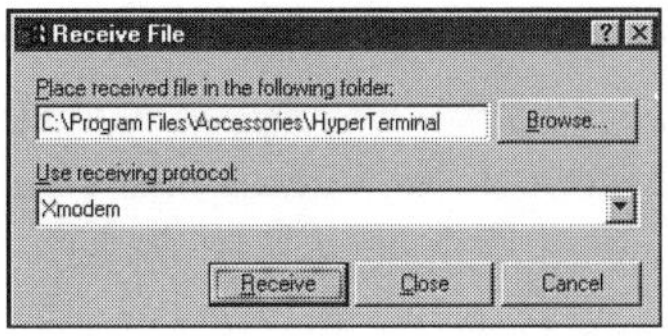

Figure 14.12
Tell HyperTerminal where you want to store the file and then click Receive to begin the download.

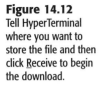

4. Click Receive, type a filename, and click OK. HyperTerminal starts your download. Figure 14.13 shows the dialog box that displays the status of your download. (You might see a different dialog box, depending on the protocol you chose.)

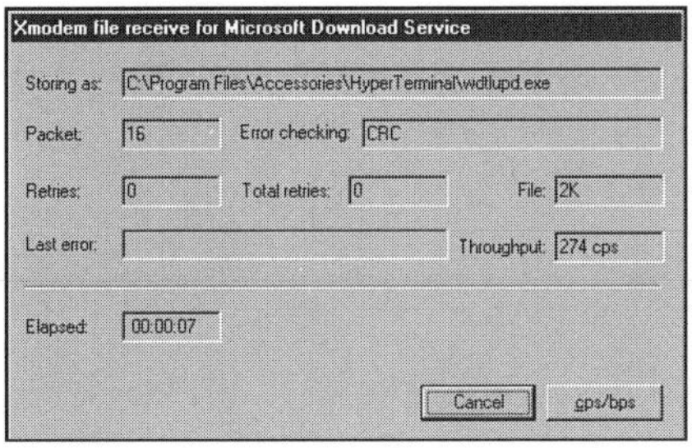

Figure 14.13
This dialog box shows the status of your download, including the filename and time elapsed. The dialog box might be different, depending on which protocol you used for the download.

UPLOADING BINARY FILES

You can upload both binary and text files. Binary files include bitmaps, programs, and word processing documents that contain more than just readable text. For example, a program file contains code and program data that is not readable. On the other hand, text files contain characters that are easy to read. This section describes how to upload a binary file.

→ To learn how to upload text files, **see** "Uploading Text Files," later in this chapter.

Before you begin uploading a binary file, you must establish the connection to the host computer as outlined in "Using an Existing Connection." Then, to upload a binary file to a host computer, follow these steps:

1. Follow the onscreen instructions to initiate the upload on the bulletin board or host computer. The host displays a message indicating that it's waiting for you to start uploading.

> **Note**
>
> If you are using Zmodem, you might not need to start the upload on the host computer. Zmodem can initiate the upload on the host for you. To try initiating the upload from your computer, skip step 1. However, if the host computer doesn't understand how to initiate an upload this way, you have to start over from step 1.

2. Choose Transfer, Send File or click the Send button on the toolbar. HyperTerminal displays a dialog box similar to the one shown in Figure 14.12 in the preceding section, "Downloading Files."

PART

III

CH

14

3. Enter a filename or choose <u>B</u>rowse to select a file from a dialog box.

4. Select a protocol to use for uploading the file. The protocol you use should match the protocol you chose (or the system chosen for you) on the host computer.

5. HyperTerminal starts the upload to the host computer. It shows the status of your upload in a dialog box similar to the one shown in Figure 14.13.

 If you're having trouble using Ymodem-G as a transfer protocol, see the "Transfer Protocols" section at the end of this chapter.

 If you're still having trouble uploading or downloading files, see "Transfer Protocols" in the "Troubleshooting" section at the end of this chapter.

UPLOADING TEXT FILES

Before you begin uploading a text file, make sure you're connected to a host computer, as described in the earlier section "Using an Existing Connection." Then, to upload a text file to a host computer, follow these steps:

1. Start the upload on the bulletin board or host computer. The host displays a message indicating that it's waiting for you to start the upload.

2. Choose <u>T</u>ransfer, Send <u>T</u>ext File. HyperTerminal prompts you for a text filename.

Caution

Don't try to use this procedure to upload a binary file. You might think that the file transfers okay, but the remote computer will receive a file with garbage in it.

3. Enter a filename or click <u>B</u>rowse to select a file from a dialog box.

4. Click <u>O</u>pen. HyperTerminal starts uploading the text file to the host computer. Note that you do not see a dialog box showing the status of the upload.

Note

HyperTerminal was developed by Hilgraeve Inc. for Microsoft Windows 98. Hilgraeve also produces a full-featured communications application called HyperACCESS. To find out more about HyperACCESS and to download a trial version of the software, visit the Hilgraeve Web site at `http://www.hilgraeve.com`.

WORKING WITH PHONE DIALER

Phone Dialer is a handy accessory built into Windows 98 that remembers up to eight phone numbers and that you can use as a speed dialer. Although this feature may seem a bit redundant if you already have a speed dialer built into your existing phone, Phone Dialer is very easy to program and change, and it can do the more intricate dialing needed to navigate voice-mail systems and make credit card calls. It can even keep a log of your outgoing and incoming calls. To access Phone Dialer, open the Start menu and choose Programs, Accessories, Phone Dialer (see Figure 14.14).

Figure 14.14
Use Phone Dialer to
make calls with your
modem.

ADDING PHONE DIALER ENTRIES

When you start Phone Dialer, it doesn't have any speed-dial entries set. Your first task is to add names and phone numbers to the eight blank dial memories. Choose any blank entry and enter the name and number you want to save (see Figure 14.15). You can choose a button by clicking it or by pressing Alt+ the number that appears next to the button.

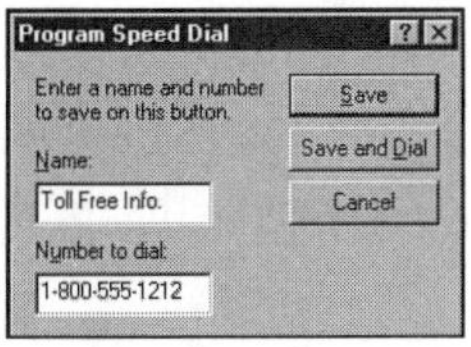

Figure 14.15
You can enter a short
name for each Phone
Dialer entry.

Both the Save and the Save and Dial buttons are now available. You can click the Save and Dial button to immediately dial the number of your new entry, or you can use the Save button to program your speed-dial entry and exit the dialog box.

Tip #88	If you want to enter a phone number that contains letters (555-FOOD or 1-800-555-SNOW), put quotation marks (") around the letters, as in 1-800-555-"SNOW".

After you have entered and saved your number, choosing the speed-dial entry immediately starts the phone dialing process and opens the dialog box shown in Figure 14.16. While waiting for your call to be answered, you can type a description of the call as you would like it to appear in the phone log.

Choose the Hang Up button if you want to abort the call immediately. The Change Options button gives you a chance to stop the call and redial with a number you type into the Number to Redial field. This feature allows you to specify exactly what you want the modem to dial, ignoring any properties (such as your calling card number) set in the Dialing Properties sheet. After typing your number, choose the Redial button to dial your new entry. If you choose the Dialing Properties button, any changes you made in the

PART

III

CH

14

Number to Redial text box are discarded, and your original speed-dial number appears with your current Dialing properties applied to it.

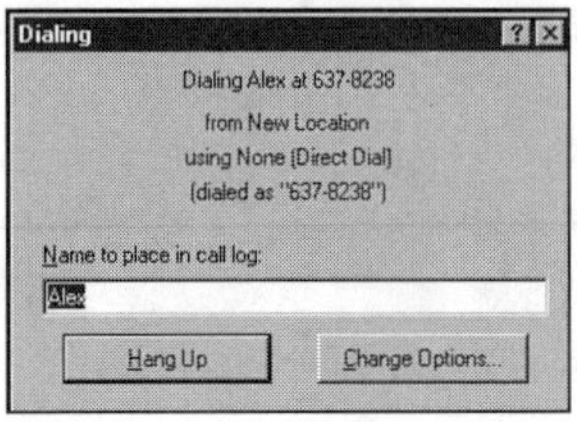

Figure 14.16
Enter a log entry while the phone is dialing.

USING COMPLEX PHONE NUMBER SEQUENCES

The convenience of voice mail has produced an annoying side effect: All those voice menus prompting you to "Press one to leave a message, Press two to talk with an operator" can drive you crazy and waste a lot of your time. Likewise, credit cards and various long-distance carriers require us to use dozens of numbers and procedures to make connections. However, a few built-in extras in your modem can handle things like credit card dialing, long-distance service connections, and navigation through many voice-mail hierarchies:

- To wait for the prompts within a voice-mail system, you can use the comma (,) to insert a 2-second pause within your dialing sequence. Use more than one comma for a longer pause.
- If you need to wait for a secondary dial tone, enter the letter W.
- If you need to wait for silence on the line, you can insert the @ sign.
- If you are making a credit card call and need to wait for the tone from your long-distance carrier, insert a dollar sign ($) followed by your card number.
- You can use the * and # characters within the phone number to make those voice-mail menu selections.

For example, let's say you want to make a personal long-distance call from your office and charge it to your AT&T calling card. You know that your company's long-distance carrier is MCI, so you'll have to access the AT&T network to get the cheapest rates. Here's how to build your Phone Dialer sequence:

1. Type a 9 followed by a W to access the outside line and wait for the dial tone.
2. Type the AT&T network access code, 10"ATT", followed by a zero (0) to start the credit card call.
3. Type the phone number you're trying to reach, such as 205-555-3161
4. To wait for AT&T to give its signal for you to enter your calling card number, type $.
5. Type in your credit card number, such as 314-555-2222-4321.

Together, all these pieces of your dialing sequence would read:

9W10"ATT"0(205)-555-3161$314-555-222-4321

That number is a definite candidate for saving in Phone Dialer!

USING THE PHONE DIALER LOG

Phone Dialer comes with a log in which it keeps a record of your outgoing and incoming calls (see Figure 14.17). Each time you connect a phone call, Phone Dialer places an entry in this text file. You can use the Edit menu commands to cut, copy, and delete from this log, and you can redial an entry in your log by double-clicking the entry or by selecting Log, Dial.

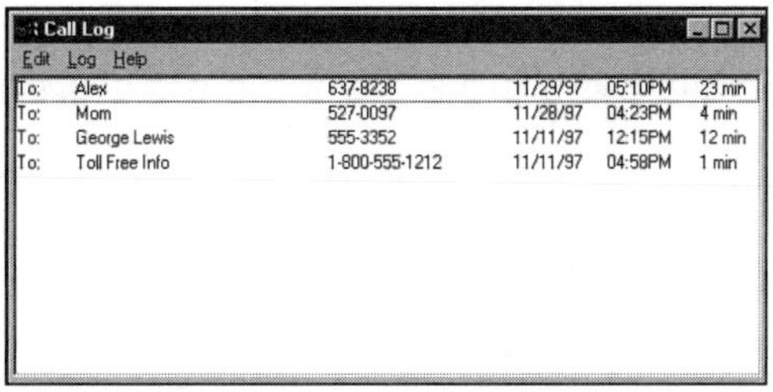

Figure 14.17
You can use log entries to redial or copy and paste into other documents.

PLAYING GAMES

Windows 98 includes four games for your diversionary pleasure: FreeCell, Hearts, Minesweeper, and the classic Solitaire. To start a game, open the Start menu and choose Programs, Accessories, Games. Then select the game you want to play from the Games submenu.

If you don't see any games, they weren't installed when you installed Windows. See "Adding Windows Accessories" (earlier in this chapter) to find out how to add the games by using your Windows 98 installation CD-ROM or disks.

After you open a game, use the Help topics to learn the objective and rules of the games and to get some tips on strategy. If you are connected to a network, check out Hearts, which you can play with others who are connected to your network.

TROUBLESHOOTING

DETERMINING THE CORRECT TERMINAL EMULATION

I connected to a service fine, but all I see onscreen is garbage—usually at the bottom of the screen.

Choose File, Properties to display the properties sheet for your connection. Then click the Settings tab and set Emulation to Auto Detect. HyperTerminal automatically determines which terminal emulation your service uses.

ADDING COMPONENTS

Windows removes other components when I add new ones.

If you clear a check box for a component that was checked, you are telling Windows to remove the component, not install it, when you run Windows Setup. This situation can be confusing the first time you run Setup again to add new components. Do not remove the check marks for the components that are already installed unless you want to uninstall them.

TRANSFER PROTOCOLS

I'm trying to use Ymodem-G as the transfer protocol, but it doesn't work.

Your modem probably doesn't support hardware error control. Try using Ymodem instead.

I still can't download or upload a file.

Make sure that you are selecting the exact same transfer protocol the host computer is using. If you continue to have difficulty, contact the sysop (system operator) of the remote computer.

SECRETS OF MASTERING THE WINDOWS 98 ENVIRONMENT: A LITTLE-KNOWN TIP ABOUT USING PHONE DIALER AND CALL WAITING

Phone Dialer does not dial the code to disable call waiting, even though the This Location Has Call Waiting. To Disable It, Dial *<Code>* option for Dialing Properties on the Tools menu is checked and filled in properly. Even though this setting is available as an option in the Dialing Properties off the Tools menu, Phone Dialer does not acknowledge the setting. To properly disable call waiting, you must manually add the appropriate code as a prefix to the number being dialed. For example, if the number you are dialing is 555-1212, you would manually enter the call-waiting code, such as *70, with the number being dialed. So, in this example, you would type `*70, 555-1212` in the Number to Dial dialog box. The comma after the code allows a pause after the prefix is dialed to give the system enough time to disable the call waiting before the number is dialed.

CHAPTER 15

USING NOTEPAD AND WORDPAD

In this chapter

USING NOTEPAD

Notepad is a miniature text editor. Just as you use a notepad on your desk, you can use Notepad to take notes onscreen while working in other Windows applications. Notepad uses little memory and is useful for editing text you want to copy into a Windows or DOS application that lacks editing capability.

Notepad retrieves and saves files in text format. This feature makes Notepad a convenient editor for creating and altering text-based files. Because Notepad stores files in text format, almost all word processing applications can retrieve Notepad files. However, if you want to format your documents, you need a true word processor.

→ To learn how to use the word processor that comes with Windows 98, **see** "Creating Documents in WordPad," later in this chapter.

STARTING NOTEPAD

To start Notepad, open the Start menu and choose Programs, Accessories, Notepad. Notepad starts up and displays a blank document in the Notepad window (see Figure 15.1). You can begin typing.

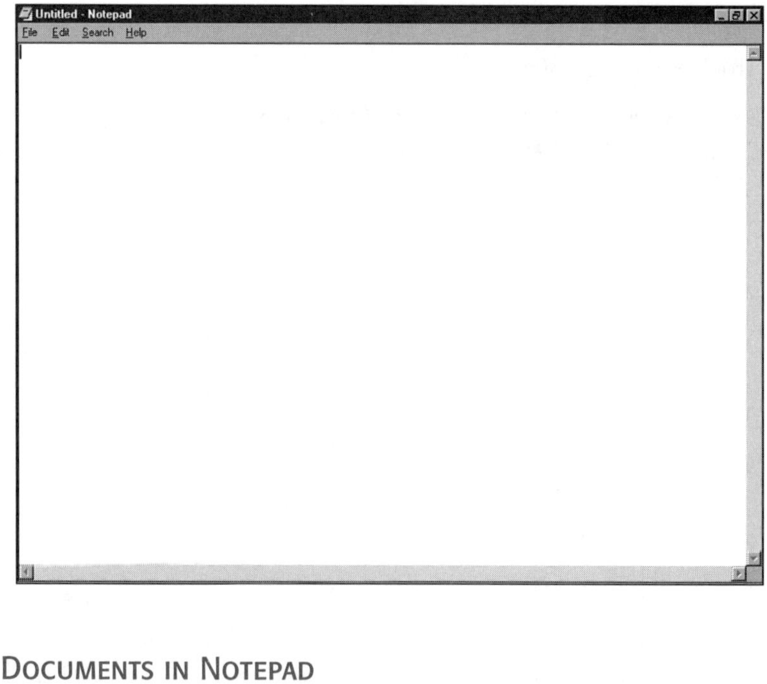

Figure 15.1
The initial blank
Notepad file is ready
for text.

WORKING WITH DOCUMENTS IN NOTEPAD

Unlike most word processing applications, Notepad doesn't, by default, wrap text to the following line. You must choose Edit, Word Wrap to activate this feature.

You can move the insertion point by using either the mouse or the keyboard. You select and edit text in Notepad the same way you select and edit text in WordPad. See "Selecting and Editing Text" later in the chapter for details.

Limited formatting is available from the File, Page Setup command. You can change margins and add a header or footer, but you cannot format characters or paragraphs in any way. You also can use the spacebar and the Tab and Backspace keys to align text. Tab stops are preset at every eight characters.

With the commands on Notepad's Edit menu, you can cut, copy, and move text from one place in a file to another. Text that you cut or copy is stored in the Clipboard. When you paste text, the contents of the Clipboard are copied from the Clipboard to the document at the location of the insertion point.

→ To learn more about cutting. moving, and copying text, **see** "Using Simple Editing Techniques," **p. 49** (Chapter 3) and "Copying and Moving," **p. 49.**

CREATING A TIME-LOG FILE WITH NOTEPAD

By typing a simple entry (.LOG) at the top of a Notepad document, you can have Notepad enter the current time and date at the end of a document each time you open the file. This feature might be convenient if you have to take phone messages or calculate the time spent on a project. Note that you must enter the text .LOG on the first line of the document, and you must use uppercase. As an alternative, you can choose Edit, Time/Date or press F5 to insert the current time and date at the location of the insertion point.

Tip #89	Notepad can open binary files, but WordPad cannot. Although most of what you see when you open a binary file is unreadable, you can sometimes find helpful information in the header of the binary file. You can also use Notepad to quickly edit system files previously edited with QBASIC. These system files include AUTOEXEC.BAT and CONFIG.SYS. In fact, Notepad is a great tool to use if you want to create small custom batch files for your computer. Simply type the command-line text in Notepad and then save the file as a .bat file. For example, if you want to connect to network shares when you start your computer, use successive net use commands and then simply add the custom .bat file to your Startup folder. Connecting in this manner is faster than waiting for the browser to initialize in Network Neighborhood.
	These are good reasons to keep Notepad on your computer even if WordPad is more suitable for most tasks.

CREATING DOCUMENTS IN WORDPAD

WordPad, the word processor that comes with Windows 98, can perform most basic word processing tasks. Although WordPad is not nearly as powerful and versatile as a full-featured word processing application (such as Word 2000), it is much more powerful than Notepad, the text editor that comes with Windows 98. Notepad is great for editing simple text files, such as AUTOEXEC.BAT, CONFIG.SYS, or any of the *INI* files (an INI file contains system or application configuration information) but is limited to working with files smaller than 50K and cannot format text. With WordPad you can perform all the basic editing tasks, such as cutting and pasting text and finding and replacing words and phrases. You can also format characters, paragraphs, and documents. In addition, WordPad is *OLE (pages 296-298)* compliant, which means you can share data, including graphics, with other OLE-compliant applications. However, WordPad does not have many of the features found in advanced word processors, such as a spell checker, tables, headers and footers, and mail merge.

CREATING A NEW DOCUMENT IN WORDPAD

WordPad resides in the Accessories submenu of the Start menu. To start WordPad, open the Start menu and choose Programs, Accessories, WordPad. The WordPad window appears, as shown in Figure 15.2. When you open WordPad, you are presented with a blank document. You might see different screen elements than those shown in Figure 15.2, depending on which elements you have been added or removed by using the View menu.

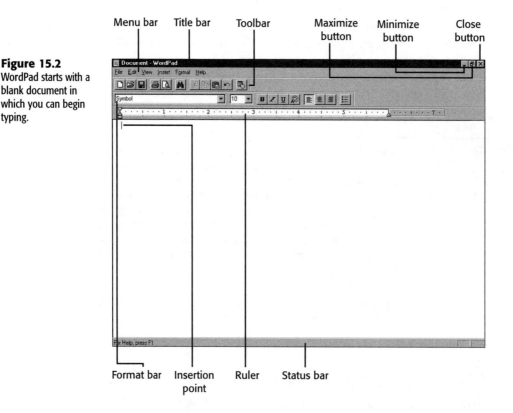

Figure 15.2
WordPad starts with a blank document in which you can begin typing.

To create a new document in WordPad, follow these steps:

1. Choose File, New or click the New button on the toolbar to display the New dialog box (see Figure 15.3).

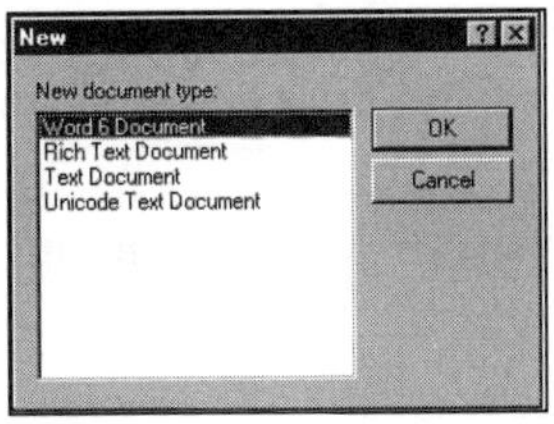

Figure 15.3
Select one of the four document types when you create a new document.

2. Select the type of document you want to create:

- Word 6 Document—This document type can be opened in Word 6, Microsoft Word 95, Microsoft Word 97, and Word 2000.

- Rich Text Document—This format (RTF) is compatible with several word processing programs and includes fonts, tabs, and character formatting.

- Text Document—This format includes only simple text characters with no formatting and is useful for creating batch files.

- Unicode Text Document—A universal character standard that uses a double-byte character set containing more than 38,000 characters, including characters for most of the major languages.

3. Click OK.

Tip #90	There might be times when you attempt to use WordPad to save a Unicode text document as a text document or an MS-DOS-format text document, but the document remains in Unicode format and becomes unidentifiable garbled text in the new format. In this case, you must select and copy the Unicode text from the original document and paste it to a new blank WordPad document. Then save the file in the desired format. Now your new file should work properly.

If you already have a document open, WordPad prompts you to save changes to that document if it has unsaved changes, and then WordPad closes that document. You can work on only one document at a time in WordPad because it does not support the Multiple Document Interface (MDI) standard.

You can enter and edit text in a WordPad document just as you would in any word processor, using the standard keys for moving around the document and deleting text. See "Selecting and Editing Text" later in the chapter for details.

Because WordPad is an *OLE (page xxx)* 2-compliant application, you can insert objects from other OLE applications into a WordPad document, or you can insert all or part of a WordPad document into another OLE application. You can, for example, insert a graphic created in Windows Paint as an object into a WordPad document and then double-click the Paint object and edit the graphic in place. When you do so, the WordPad menus and toolbars are replaced with the Paint menus and toolbars while you edit the object. You also can use the Insert, Object command or the drag-and-drop method for exchanging information with other OLE applications.

→ To learn more about the specifics of OLE, **see** "Creating Compound Documents," **p. 237.**

OPENING WORDPAD DOCUMENTS

To open an existing WordPad document, follow these steps:

 1. Choose File, Open, the toolbar. The Open dialog box appears (see Figure 15.4).

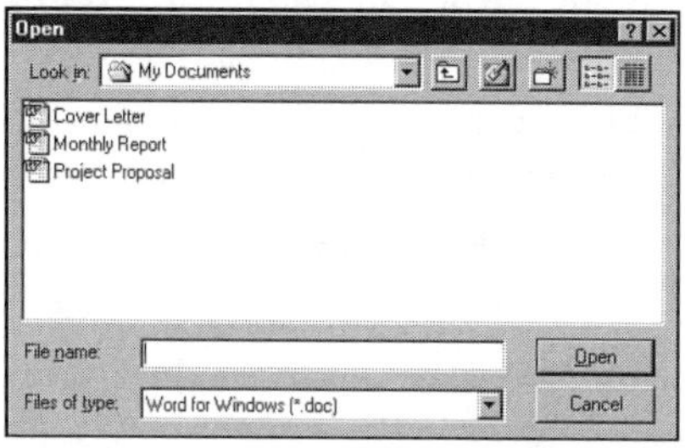

Figure 15.4
Use the Open dialog box to locate and open WordPad documents.

2. Navigate to the disk and folder where the file you want to open is located.

3. Select the type of files you want to list from the Files of Type box.

4. Select the file you want to open and choose Open, or double-click the filename.

If you're confused about why a file saved in WordPad has a .DOC extension, see "Saving Documents" in the "Troubleshooting" section at the end of this chapter.

SAVING WORDPAD DOCUMENTS

To save a document in WordPad, follow these steps:

 1. Choose File, Save As or click the Save button in the toolbar to display the Save As dialog box (see Figure 15.5).

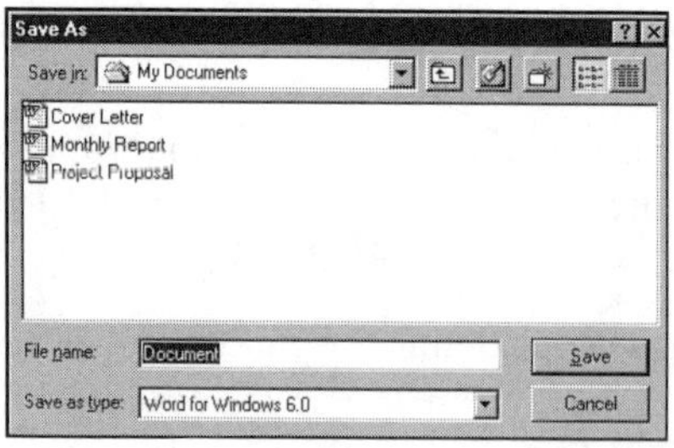

Figure 15.5
The Save As dialog box enables you to save a file in any drive, folder, or format you want.

2. Select the drive and folder where you want to save the file.

3. Type the name for the file in the File Name text box.

4. Select a format from the Save as Type list if you want to save the file in a format other than WordPad.

5. Click Save or press Enter.

After you have saved a file for the first time, you can resave that file by choosing File, Save or by clicking the Save button in the toolbar.

If you're having problems with saving WordPad documents to a disk while in WordPad, see "Saving Documents" in the "Troubleshooting" section at the end of this chapter.

USING WORDPAD TO CREATE AND EDIT SYSTEM, BATCH, AND TEXT FILES

WordPad is very useful for creating and editing .TXT and system files (that is, files with the extensions .BAT, .SYS, .INI, and so on), especially when the file in question is too large for Notepad. When you open a .SYS, .INI, .BAT, or .TXT file in WordPad, edit or view it, and then resave it, the file is saved with its original file extension. This feature eliminates the possibility of inadvertently saving a system file with the wrong extension, as can happen in a regular word processing program. In addition, WordPad provides more features (such as the Replace command) for editing your files than does Notepad.

To create a new text file in WordPad, choose File, New and select Text Document in the New dialog box. When you save the document, it is given the .TXT extension automatically. If necessary, change the extension (for example, to .BAT for a DOS batch file).

Tip #91	Create a shortcut for WordPad in the SendTo folder so you can quickly open any file with WordPad from Explorer or a Folder window.

→ To make the Send To process more efficient, **see** "Customizing the Send To Menu," **p. 118.**

You can change the association for .TXT files so that they open in WordPad instead of Notepad when you open them from Explorer or My Computer. To change the association, follow these steps:

1. Choose View, Folder Options in Explorer or My Computer and select the File Types tab.

2. Select Text Document from the Registered File Types list and then click Edit.

3. In the Actions list of the Edit File Type dialog box, select Open. Then click Edit.

4. Choose the Browse button. Then locate and select WORDPAD.EXE, which is located in the Program Files\Accessories folder.

5. Click OK and make sure that .txt is selected in the Default Extension for Content list.

6. Click Close twice.

CREATING POST-IT NOTES ON YOUR DESKTOP

Because WordPad is an *OLE (pages 296-298)* 2-compliant application, you can drag and drop selected portions of a WordPad document into other OLE applications or onto the desktop.

When you drag a selection onto the desktop, you create a scrap; double-click the icon for the scrap, and WordPad opens to display the information in the scrap. You can use these scraps as electronic Post-It notes to secure to your desktop bits of information you might otherwise lose track of.

If you create desktop notes frequently, such as while you're on the phone, you can add WordPad to your StartUp folder so that it is immediately available, or you can simply create a shortcut on the desktop to WordPad. To create a note on your desktop, follow these steps:

1. Open WordPad and create the note.

2. Select the note and drag and drop it on the desktop. The scrap appears as a desktop icon, labeled with the first few words of the note. The data is saved as a file in the desktop folder.

You can rename the scrap if you want. Note also that you don't have to save the note in WordPad. Whenever you double-click the Scrap icon, the note opens in WordPad. If you open the scrap and make changes, the changes are automatically saved to the scrap when you close WordPad.

SELECTING AND EDITING TEXT

WordPad uses standard editing techniques, as found in most word processors. You can place the insertion point wherever you want to add text and begin typing. To delete characters, press Backspace (to delete characters to the left) or Delete (to delete characters to the right).

When you must work with larger blocks of text, such as words, sentences, or paragraphs, you can use your mouse to select the text with one of the techniques listed in Table 15.1.

TABLE 15.1 MOUSE TECHNIQUES FOR SELECTING TEXT

Selection	Action
One word	Double-click the word.
Several words	Double-click the first word and drag to the end of the last word.
Any amount of text	Hold down the mouse button and drag from the beginning to the end of the text.
Between two points	Move the insertion point to the beginning, click, move to the second point, press and hold down Shift, and click at the second point.
One line	Click the selection bar (white space) to the left of the line.
Several lines	Hold down the mouse button and drag up or down in the selection bar.
Paragraph	Double-click in the selection bar (blank area) to the left of the paragraph.
Entire document	Press Ctrl and click in the selection bar.

To select text with the keyboard, position the insertion point at the beginning of the text you want to select, hold down the Shift key, and use the arrow keys to move the insertion point to the end of the text. To move the selection a word at a time, hold down the Shift and Ctrl keys as you press the arrow keys. You can select all the way to the end of a line by pressing the Shift and End keys.

After you have selected a block of text, you can delete it by using the Delete or Backspace key. To move or copy the selected text, use the Edit, Cut or Edit, Copy keys, as described in the next section. If you start typing when text is selected, whatever you type replaces the selected text.

MOVING AND COPYING TEXT

You can move or copy text by using either the menu commands or the mouse. To move or copy text with the menu commands, follow these steps:

1. Use one of the techniques described in the preceding section to select the text you want to move or copy.
2. Choose Edit, Cut or press Ctrl+X or click the Cut button on the toolbar.

   Alternatively, choose Edit, Copy or press Ctrl+C or click the Copy button on the toolbar.

3. Position the insertion point where you want to move or copy the text.
4. Choose Edit, Paste or press Ctrl+V or click the Paste button on the toolbar.

To move or copy text with the mouse, follow these steps:

1. Select the text you want to move or copy.
2. Point to the text with the mouse, hold down the mouse button, and drag the insertion point to the location where you want to move or copy the text.

   If you are copying the text, hold down the Ctrl key as you drag the text. A plus sign appears next to the mouse pointer, indicating that the text will be copied.

3. Release the mouse button.

WordPad is an OLE-compliant application, which means you can also drag text from a WordPad document into documents in other OLE-compliant applications. To simplify this operation, place the two application windows side by side before you move or copy the text.

FINDING AND REPLACING TEXT

WordPad has Find and Replace commands that enable you to find a string of text, and if you want, to replace the found text with new text.

To find a string of text, follow these steps:

1. Choose Edit, Find or press Ctrl+F. The Find dialog box appears (see Figure 15.6).

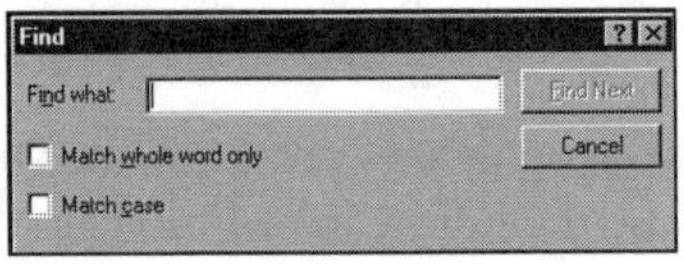

Figure 15.6
Use the Find dialog box to search a document for a string of text.

2. In the Find What text box, type the text string you want to find.

    (Optional) Select the Match Whole Word Only option to find text that exactly matches the text you typed in the Find What text box.

    (Optional) Select the Match Case option to find text that has the same case structure as the text you typed in the Find What text box.

3. Choose Find Next to find and select the first occurrence of the text.

4. Choose Find Next again to select the next occurrence of the text.

5. When you find the text you're looking for, click Cancel or press Esc.

Even after you close the Find dialog box, you can repeat the last find operation by choosing Edit, Find Next or by pressing F3.

To find and replace a text string, follow these steps:

1. Choose Edit, Replace to display the Replace dialog box (see Figure 15.7).

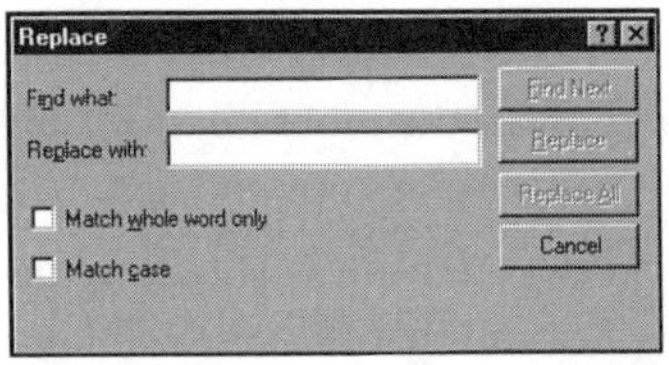

Figure 15.7
You can search for a text string and replace it with new text using the Replace dialog box.

2. Type the text you want to replace in the Find What text box.

3. Type the text you want to insert in the Replace With text box.

4. Choose Find Next to locate the first occurrence of the text you typed in the Find What text box.

5. If you want to replace this text with the text in the Replace With text box, click Replace.

    or

    If you don't want to replace this text with the new text, click Find Next again to locate the next occurrence of the text.

6. To automatically replace all occurrences of the text in the Find What text box with the text in the Replace With text box, choose Replace All.

7. When you finish replacing text, click Cancel or press Esc.

FORMATTING IN WORDPAD

WordPad enables you to format characters, paragraphs, and documents. At the character level, you can select a font, a point size, and character attributes (such as bold and italic). At the paragraph level, you can align text to the left, right, or center. You can also specify the left, right, and first-line indents for a paragraph. At the document level, you can set the margins, change the orientation of the document (either portrait or landscape), and specify the paper size and which tray of your printer is used.

FORMATTING CHARACTERS

You can use either the menu or the Format bar to format characters. To format text you have already typed, select the text first and then choose the formatting. To format text you are about to enter, position the insertion point where you will enter the text and then choose the formatting.

To format characters with the menu commands, follow these steps:

1. Choose Format, Font to open the Font dialog box (see Figure 15.8).

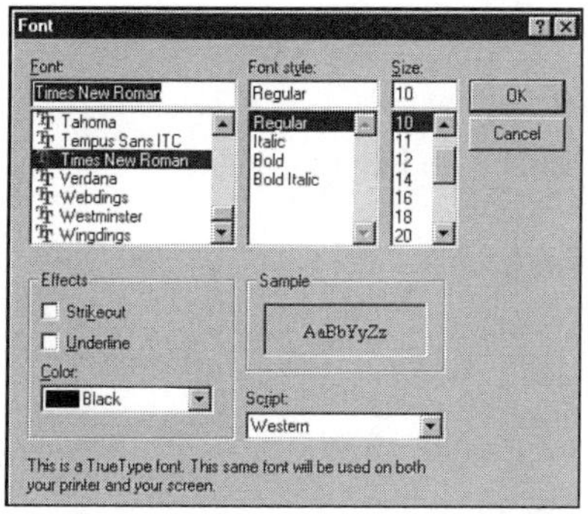

Figure 15.8
Select character formatting in the Font dialog box.

2. Select a font from the Font list box, a font style from the Font Style list box, and a point size from the Size list box. To preview your selections, look in the Sample box.

   (Optional) You can also select the Strikeout and Underline effects in the Effects box, and you can select a font color from the Color list.

3. When you finish making your selections, click OK.

You can make the same formatting selections from the Format bar. If the Format bar is not visible, choose View, Format Bar to display it. You can also toggle the font effects (bold, italic, and underline) on and off from the keyboard. Press Ctrl+B for bold, press Ctrl+I for italic, and press Ctrl+U for underline.

Tip #92	A strange quirk you might encounter in WordPad occurs when you create a document with a 12-point font size. When the document is saved and reopened, the font may change to WordPad's default 10-point font size. Apparently, if you begin any document and use a 12-point font size before you use another font size in a WordPad document, such as when you set the font from the start of your document, the 12-point font size is lost when you save the document. The only way to change the font to 12-point before printing is to choose Select All from the Edit menu, change the font back to 12-point, and then print the document. When the document is saved and closed, it again reverts to the default 10-point font size. This quirk does not occur with other font sizes. So, for an easy work around, use an alternative font size.

FORMATTING PARAGRAPHS

In WordPad you can adjust the text alignment and indentation of paragraphs. To format a paragraph, place the insertion point in the paragraph you want to format and then make your formatting selections. If you want to format more than one paragraph, select all the paragraphs you want to format. You can use either the menu commands or the Format bar and ruler to make your paragraph formatting selections.

To use the menu to format paragraphs, follow these steps:

1. Select the paragraphs you want to format.
2. Choose Format, Paragraph to display the Paragraph dialog box (see Figure 15.9).

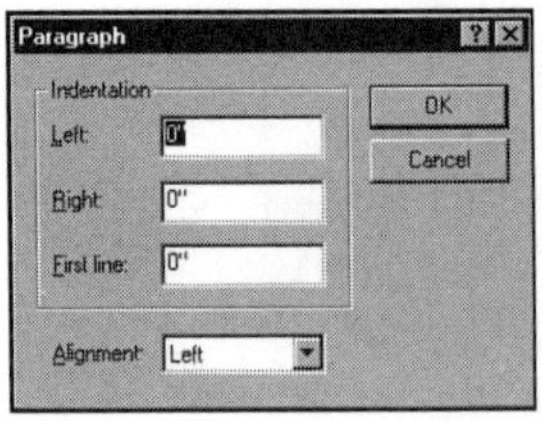

Figure 15.9
Adjust the alignment and indentation for paragraphs in the Paragraph dialog box.

3. Specify the indentation settings in the Left, Right, and First Line text boxes.

   Because WordPad uses both proportionally spaced fonts and fonts of different sizes, it uses inches, not number of characters, to measure indentations and margins. Make sure you enter your settings in inches.
4. Select a paragraph alignment from the Alignment list.
5. When you finish making your selections, click OK.

To use the ruler to set indentations, follow these steps:

1. Choose View, Ruler if the ruler is not displayed.

2. Select the paragraph or paragraphs you want to change.

3. Drag the indent markers on the ruler to the desired settings.

You can also use the Format bar to change paragraph alignment. Select the paragraph or paragraphs you want to change and then click the Align Left, Center, or Align Right button on the toolbar.

CREATING A BULLETED LIST

WordPad enables you to add bullets to a list of items. To create a bulleted list, first type the items in the list. Each item should be a separate paragraph. Then select all the paragraphs and choose Format, Bullet Style to add the bullets. You can remove bullets by selecting the bulleted items and choosing Format, Bulleted Style again. If you press Enter at the end of a bulleted item to start a new paragraph, the new paragraph is also bulleted.

FORMATTING A DOCUMENT

Document formatting affects the appearance of an entire document. When you set the margins for a document, for example, those settings affect every page of the document.

To change the document formatting, follow these steps:

1. Choose File, Page Setup to display the Page Setup dialog box (see Figure 15.10).

Figure 15.10
Use the Page Setup dialog box to change the margins, orientation, and paper size for a document.

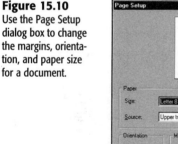

2. Enter the settings for the margins (in inches) in the Left, Right, Top, and Bottom text boxes.

3. Select either Portrait or Landscape orientation.

4. Select a paper size from the Size list.

5. If necessary, make a different selection from the Source list.

6. Click OK to put your changes into effect.

SETTING TABS

By default, WordPad has tab settings every 1/2 inch. You can also set custom tabs from either the menu or the ruler. WordPad uses only left-aligned tabs.

To set a custom tab with the menu, follow these steps:

1. Select the paragraph in which you want to set the custom tabs.

2. Choose Format, Tabs to display the Tabs dialog box (see Figure 15.11).

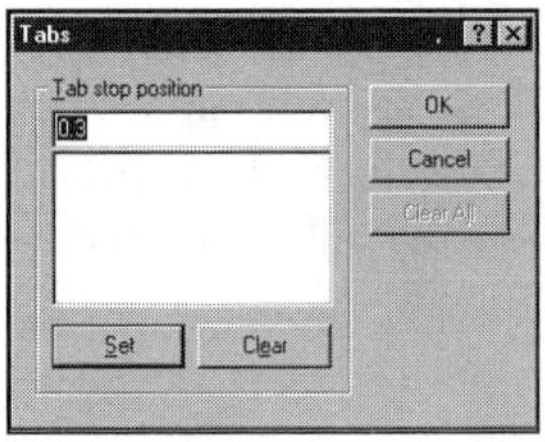

Figure 15.11
Set custom tabs in the
Tabs dialog box.

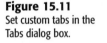

3. Enter the setting for the custom tab in the text box (in inches).

4. Choose Set.

5. Repeat steps 3 and 4 to set up additional custom tabs.

6. To clear a tab, select it in the list of tabs and choose Clear.

7. When you finish settings tabs, click OK.

To set a custom tab with the ruler, select the paragraph in which you want to set custom tabs and then click on the ruler wherever you want to set a tab. You can move an existing tab by dragging it along the ruler with the mouse. To remove a tab, drag it off the ruler.

PRINTING A WORDPAD DOCUMENT

Printing a document with WordPad is very easy. You can preview a document to see exactly how it will appear on the printed page before you actually print the document, which saves you time and paper. Choose File, Print Preview to preview a document. Figure 15.12 shows the Print Preview window.

To zoom in for a close-up view of the document, click the magnifying glass on the area of the document you want to see up close or choose the Zoom In button. To zoom back out, click again or choose Zoom Out. Choose Close to close the Print Preview window.

To print a document, follow these steps:

Figure 15.12
Save time and paper by previewing your document before you print it.

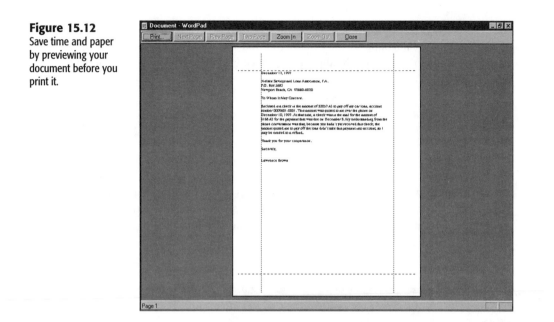

1. Choose File, Print or click the Print button in the toolbar to display the Print dialog box (see Figure 15.13).

Figure 15.13
Make your selections for printing a document in the Print dialog box.

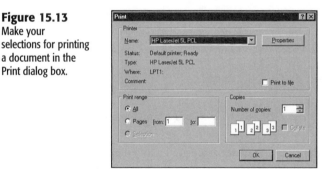

2. Select a printer from the Name list.

   After you make this selection, you do not have to do it again for printing other documents unless you want to change printers.

3. In the Print Range box, indicate what you want to print:

   Select All to print the entire document, or select Pages and specify a range of pages in the From and To text boxes. WordPad does not enable you to print a block of selected text.

4. To print the document to a file instead of to a printer, select the Print to File box. When you start the print job, you are prompted for a filename and location.

5. Specify the number of copies you want to print in the Number of <u>C</u>opies box.

   WordPad does not support the collating option when you specify multiple copies. However, your printer might allow you to specify collation from its control panel.

6. Click OK.

 If you're having problems with printing selected blocks of text or multiple or collated copies while in WordPad, see "Printing in WordPad" in the "Troubleshooting" section at the end of this chapter.

CHANGING WORDPAD SETTINGS

You can change several of WordPad's default settings in the Options dialog box (shown in Figure 15.14). Your choices, available on each of the six tabs, include setting the measurement units, determining how word wrap operates, and presetting the toolbars that are displayed. To change any of these settings, choose <u>V</u>iew, <u>O</u>ptions; select the tab you want; make your selections; and click OK.

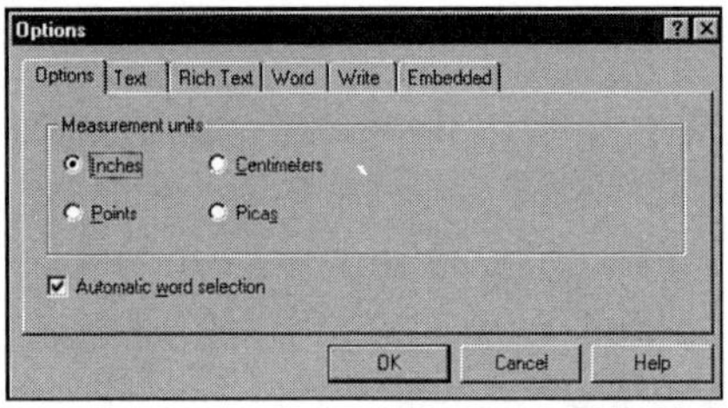

Figure 15.14
You can customize some of WordPad's default settings in the Options dialog box.

TROUBLESHOOTING

SAVING DOCUMENTS

WordPad appends the filename with the .DOC extension when I try to save a file in WordPad with a nondefault extension.

When you save a file with an extension that is not associated with an application in the Registry, WordPad appends the default .DOC extension to the filename. In Notepad, the default extension .TXT is appended to the filename. To avoid this problem, enclose the filename in quotation marks.

I cannot save a document to a floppy disk using WordPad.

This situation can occur if your floppy disk doesn't have enough free space to save the desired document. The system reacts in one of three ways:

- The document does not get saved, but no error message appears. This scenario occurs if the file is only slightly larger than the space available; for example, a 10KB file is attempting to copy to a disk with only 9KB of free space.
- The system hangs. This scenario occurs if the file is several bytes larger than the space available; for example, a 12KB file is attempting to copy to a disk with only 9KB of free space.

- An error message stating either An unexpected error occurred while writing a:\<filename.doc> or Unknown error writing to drive a: <filename.doc> is displayed. This scenario occurs if the file is much larger than the space available; for example, a 20KB file is attempting to copy to a disk with only 9KB of free space.

The only solution to this problem is to free up space on your floppy disk.

PRINTING IN WORDPAD

I am unable to print multiple or collated copies from WordPad. Why are these features unavailable in the File Print dialog box?

WordPad does not support multiple or collated printing. Unless these features are supported with the printer driver for your particular printer, you cannot print multiple or collated copies from WordPad.

The Selection option is unavailable in the File Print dialog box when I try to print just the WordPad text selection.

Although this option is shown in the File Print dialog box, WordPad does not support the capability to print selected text. To work around this limitation, you can copy the text to a new WordPad document and print that document.

SECRETS OF MASTERING THE WINDOWS 98 ENVIRONMENT: HOW TO CREATE A WORDPAD TEMPLATE

You can create a template file in WordPad to be used over and over again as a time-saver. To create a template file in WordPad follow these simple steps:

1. Open a new file in WordPad.
2. Make any changes you want to the file that is to be part of the template; for example, the font size, font style, and margin settings you want to use. When you are working in WordPad, to change the default font, you must type some text into the template and then assign the font.
3. Save the file with a name that easily identifies the template, such as Document Arial TEMPLATE.TPL.
4. Double-click My Computer.
5. On the View menu, click Options.
6. On the File Types tab, click the New Type button.
7. Type a description of the template in the Description of Type box.
8. In the Associated Extension box, type tpl.
9. Click the New button.
10. In the Action box, type open.
11. In the Application Used to Perform Action box, enter the complete path for WordPad.
12. Click OK until the Options dialog box closes.

When you double-click a file with a .tpl extension, the file opens in WordPad.

CHAPTER 16

USING PAINT AND IMAGING

In this chapter

EDITING GRAPHICS IN WINDOWS

Windows 98 gives you two capable graphic file editors, Windows Paint and Imaging for Windows. Windows Paint is simple and easy to use, but it also might be as powerful a graphics application as you will ever need for creating and modifying bitmap (BMP) as well as GIF and JPEG graphics used on Web pages.

Imaging for Windows enables you to open, modify, and annotate a wide range of graphic file formats including TIFF, BMP, PCX, JPEG, GIF, fax documents, and more. With Imaging for Windows, you can add annotations to documents, highlight areas or text, rotate or magnify, and combine individual documents into a single multipage document. Imaging includes the capability to control scanners.

USING WINDOWS PAINT

When you must make simple modifications to a BMP, GIF, or JPEG image, you might want to choose Windows Paint. It's quick to learn yet has a full set of basic bitmap drawing tools.

STARTING WINDOWS PAINT

To start Paint, click Start, Programs, Accessories, Paint. Paint starts up and opens a new, empty Paint file (see Figure 16.1).

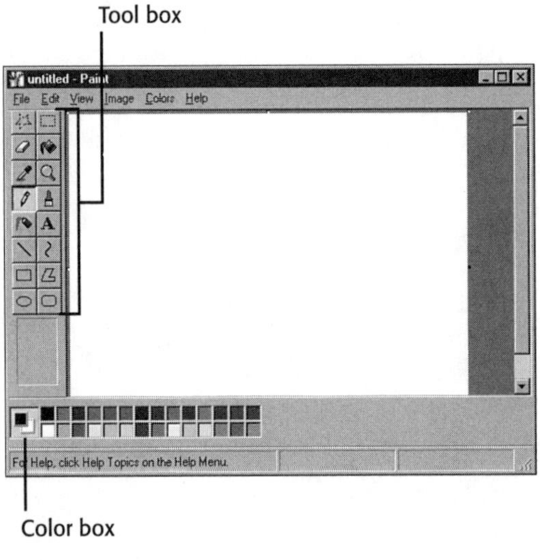

Figure 16.1
When you start Paint, a new file opens.

Tool box

Color box

To open a previously saved Paint file, click File, Open. Double-click the file in the Open dialog box.

VIEWING IMAGES IN PAINT

Use different levels of magnification to examine your drawing more closely or to paint and modify an image at the smallest, or pixel, level. Use the View, Zoom or View, View Bitmap commands or the Magnifier tool to magnify an image so you can work on fine details. When an image is magnified, you can edit the individual pixels in letters or the drawing.

The larger magnifications of the picture display the *pixels*, or tiny squares of color, which make up your painting. Paint with any of the tools you use in normal magnification.

To change the view, follow these steps:

1. Click View, Zoom.
2. Click Normal Size (Ctrl+Page Up), Large Size (Ctrl+Page Down), or Custom. If you select Custom, the Custom Zoom dialog box is displayed. Select 100%, 200%, 400%, 600%, or 800%; then click OK.
3. Use the scrollbars to display the part of the painting you want to see.

To zoom back out to regular editing view, choose View, Zoom; then click Normal Size, or click the Magnifier tool and then click in the picture.

Tip #93

Windows 98 does not include support for .pcx files in Paint. If you want to view or edit a .pcx file, you must use Microsoft Imaging for Windows. To start Imaging, from the Start menu choose Programs, Accessories, Imaging.

EDITING A GRAPHICS FILE

Because Paint is a bitmap graphics application, the shapes you create are painted onscreen in one layer. Although you can't layer objects, you can select portions and move, rotate, stretch, and change colors. As an aid for Web graphics, you also can make graphics backgrounds transparent so a Web page background shows through.

As you edit, be aware that completed objects cannot be edited, only erased or painted over and replaced. You can edit any object while creating it, but not after you complete the object. To remove an object you have just drawn, click Edit, Undo.

When you reach a stage in your drawing that momentarily satisfies you, save the drawing with a unique name. This step enables you to return to previous stages. When the drawing is finished, erase the unneeded files.

USING THE PAINT TOOLBOX

The Paint toolbox includes tools for selecting areas, airbrushing, typing text, erasing, filling, brushing, drawing curves or straight lines, and drawing filled or unfilled shapes. Most of the tools operate using a similar process, as described in the following steps.

PART
III

CH
16

To create or modify an image, you first must select the appropriate tool. If the tool uses a color, you must also select a color. Figure 16.2 shows the individual tools in the toolbox located on the left side of the screen.

Figure 16.2
Paint's toolbox provides the tools you need to create and modify a picture.

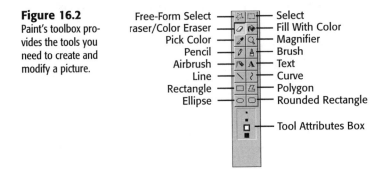

Free-Form Select ——— Select
raser/Color Eraser ——— Fill With Color
Pick Color ——— Magnifier
Pencil ——— Brush
Airbrush ——— Text
Line ——— Curve
Rectangle ——— Polygon
Ellipse ——— Rounded Rectangle

——— Tool Attributes Box

The color box offers foreground and background color choices. At the left end of the color box (see Figure 16.3) is a box overlaying a box. The top box is the foreground color; the bottom box is the background color. When you draw with the left mouse button, the line is in the foreground color and the background color fills the object. Drawing with the right mouse button reverses the use of foreground and background colors.

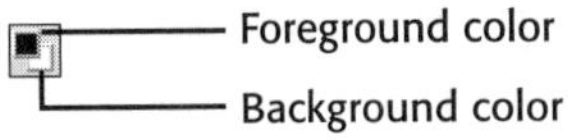

Figure 16.3
Choose foreground and background colors from the color box.

——— Foreground color
——— Background color

To select a tool or foreground color, click the left mouse button on the tool or color. Select a background color by right-clicking on a color.

To draw with the tools from the toolbox, follow these steps:

1. Click the tool you want to use.
2. Position the pointer where you want to begin drawing; then, press and hold down the mouse button as you draw with the mouse.
3. Release the mouse button to stop drawing.

 If you notice a trail of black dots as you move the Brush tool across the canvas, see "Printing Attributes" in the "Troubleshooting" section at the end of this chapter.

The exceptions to this process are as follows:

- The Text tool, which you click to position the insertion point; then you type the text
- The Paint Fill tool, which works by pointing and clicking

- The Curve tool, which works by dragging a line and then clicking to the side of the line to create an arc

- The Polygon tool, which requires a click at each vertex of the polygon

USING SIMPLE TOOLS

The toolbox tools listed in Table 16.1 use simple procedures for operation. Tools not in this table are described in subsequent sections. Drawing with the left mouse button down uses the foreground color. Drawing with the right mouse button down uses the background color.

PART

III

CH

16

TABLE 16.1 SIMPLE TOOLS

Function	Tool Name	Description
Select a rectangle	Select	Click the tool; then select an area by dragging a rectangular box.
Erase under tool	Erase	Click the tool; then select the eraser size at the bottom of the toolbox. Drag with the left mouse button to erase. Background color is used to erase.
Fill interior of connected borders with color	Fill with Color	Click the tool. Left-click inside shape to fill with foreground color. Right-click for background color.
Pick color from picture for use with a drawing tool	Pick Color	Click the tool; then click color in the picture for use with drawing tool.
Magnify the picture to work at pixel levels	Magnifier	Click the tool; then click magnification value at bottom of the toolbox. Use any tools while magnified.
Draw free-form lines	Pencil	Click the tool; then drag to draw a one-pixel-wide, free-form line.
Draw with variable-width brush	Brush	Click the tool; then select from the brush shapes at the bottom of the toolbox. Drag to paint.
Paint with patterns of dots of varying density	Airbrush	Click the tool; then select a sprayer size at the bottom of the toolbox. Select a color. Click or drag to spray. Hold the tool in one position longer to spray more densely.
Draw a straight line	Line	Click the tool; then select a line width at the bottom of the toolbox. Drag the mouse to draw a straight line. Cancel the line that you're drawing by clicking the right mouse button before you release the left mouse button. Draw vertical, horizontal, or 45-degree angles by holding the Shift key.

continues

TABLE 16.1   CONTINUED

Function	Tool Name	Description
Draw rectangle or square borders or filled shapes	Rectangle	Click the tool; then click the Border Only, Border and Fill, or Fill Only icon at the bottom of the toolbox. Drag to draw a rectangle. Border size is the last line size selected. Hold Shift to draw squares.
Draw an oval or circle	Ellipse	Click the tool; then click the Border Only, Border and Fill, or Fill Only icon at the bottom of the toolbox. Drag to draw an oval. Border size is the last line size selected. Hold the Shift to draw a circle.
Draw a rectangle with rounded corners	Rounded Rectangle	Click the tool; then click the Border Only, Border and Fill, or Fill Only icon at the bottom of the toolbox. Drag to draw a rectangle with rounded corners. Border size is the last line size selected. Hold the Shift to draw a square with rounded corners.

SELECTING A FREE-FORM AREA

The Free-Form Select tool enables you to select an area of any shape by drawing a free-form boundary around the area. Click the Free-Form Select tool and two additional icons are displayed in the toolbox. From these two, select either the Opaque (includes the background) tool or the Transparent (omits the background) tool at the bottom of the toolbox. Draw any shape to enclose the area to be selected. If you make a mistake while using the Free-Form Select tool, click the left mouse button outside the cutout area to cancel the selection.

ADDING TEXT TO A PICTURE

Use the Text tool to add text to your painting. Click the Text tool and, in the tool attributes box below the toolbox, select Opaque (the background color fills the text box behind the text) or Transparent (the picture appears behind the text). Next, in the picture area, drag to determine the size of the text box. The text toolbar is displayed, as shown in Figure 16.4. If the toolbar does not appear, click View, Text Toolbar to display it. Select a font; a point size; and bold, italic, or underline. A button is available to orient text vertically or horizontally. Click in the text box and type.

Tip #94

If your painting includes a lot of text, you might find editing easier if you type the text in a word processor, select and copy it, and then paste it into Paint.

Figure 16.4
Type text in the text
box and format with
the Text toolbar.

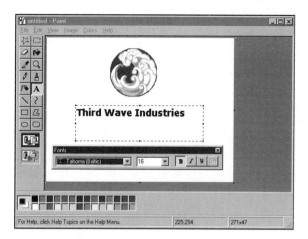

DRAWING CURVES

 The Curve tool draws a curve. To draw a curve, follow these steps:

1. Click the Curve tool.

2. Select a line width from the tool attributes box.

3. Drag to draw a straight line. Release the mouse button at the end of the line.

4. Move the pointer to the side of the line; then drag the pointer to pull a curve in the line.

5. When you've achieved the arc you want, release the mouse button.

6. Click in the same spot to freeze the curve; to create an S-shaped curve, click on the other side of the line and repeat the process.

DRAWING OBJECTS WITH MANY SIDES (POLYGONS)

The Polygon tool draws a multisided shape. Each side on the shape is a straight line. To draw a polygon, follow these steps:

1. Click the Polygon tool; then click the Border Only, Border and Fill, or Fill Only icon in the tool attribute box.

2. Click and drag to draw the first side of the polygon. As with the Line tool, you can use the Shift key to draw a straight line segment oriented in 45-degree increments.

3. Release the mouse button and click at the next corner of the polygon. Continue to click at each of the remaining corners until the next-to-last corner.

4. Double-click at the next-to-last corner. Paint automatically draws the last connecting line that finishes the polygon.

CHOOSING A FILE FORMAT

To save a Paint file, click File, Save As. Type the name in the File Name text box; then, click the Save As Type box to select one of the following file formats:

Format	File Extension Assigned
Monochrome bitmap	BMP
16-color bitmap	BMP
256-color bitmap	BMP
24-bit bitmap	BMP
JPEG	JPG, JPEG
GIF	GIF

Finally, click Save.

Tip #95	If you plan to save or send a lot of your paint creations, I suggest saving the file in the JPEG format. JPEG images use compression that can significantly reduce the large file sizes usually associated with graphic color images. As you use Paint and Imaging more and more, the graphic files you use will take up a lot of space on your hard drive. Also, if you plan to send a picture to a friend or relative, the file size and the line-speed connection on the network or on the Internet determines how long your file takes to actually send and be received.

Tip #96	If you are planning to send a picture across a network or the Internet, I recommend using a higher level of compression. Doing so results in a lower image quality, however; if image quality is not a factor, a higher level of compression saves time and money for both the sender and the recipient. A lower level of compression results in higher image quality, but the file is not as small. Use the compression setting when you are trying to save space on your hard drive. Remember, bitmaps have no compression, so using JPEG, instead of BMP, with any amount of compression saves space on your hard drive and makes your friends happier to receive your pictures over the Internet.

USING IMAGING

Windows 98 includes free imaging software provided by Kodak called Imaging for Windows. Imaging for Windows can be used to view, annotate, print, manage, store, and share images that have been created from faxes, scanned documents, or computerized images. If you have a scanner, you can scan documents into Imaging for Windows.

You can annotate stored documents with graphics, highlights, and text. Imaging for Windows even includes predefined or custom "rubber stamps" that can be stamped on an image. Documents can be passed on to others as a file. The imaging software is OLE-compatible, so you can select and then drag documents from the imaging software and drop them into applications such as Microsoft Word, Exchange, or Lotus Notes. Double-clicking on an embedded image of a document activates the image and switches the application's menus and toolbars to those of the Imaging for Windows software.

Imaging for Windows reads many file formats, for example, AWD (Fax), BMP, PCX/DCX, JPG, XIF, GIF, WIFF, and TIF. The software stores documents in an industry-standard multipage TIF 6.0, AWD (Microsoft FAX), or BMP (bitmap) format.

STARTING IMAGING

Open Imaging for Windows by clicking Start, Programs, Accessories and then selecting Imaging. Imaging opens with a blank new document. By default, AWD and TIF files open when the files are opened from an Explorer window.

Imaging for Windows runs either in a Read Only mode to preview images or in an Editing mode. If you want editable files to open in the Imaging Preview mode so they cannot be edited, choose Tools, General Options and click the Preview button in the General Options dialog box.

Tip #97	If the title bar for a document shows (Read Only), the document is in a format that Image cannot edit. Save the document to TIF, AWD (Fax), or BMP formats if you want to edit it.

MODIFYING IMAGES

Imaging for Windows includes several tools to help you modify images, although you should not consider it a graphics-editing application. If you are modifying images, you might want to display the Imaging and Annotation toolbars by choosing View, Toolbars and selecting these two toolbars. From the Page menu or the Imaging toolbar, you can rotate an image in 90-degree increments clockwise or counterclockwise.

The Annotation menu or toolbar enables you to draw freehand lines and rectangles, highlight areas, create text boxes, and stamp with rubber stamps. The annotations you make are objects. Objects remain distinct and editable from the picture background. You can select an object with the Annotation Selection arrow and move, copy, or delete the object. Saving the file in TIF format enables you to make further changes to the objects when you reopen the file. Saving to BMP or AWD format freezes the annotations.

INSERTING AND APPENDING IMAGES INTO A MULTIPAGE DOCUMENT

Build a multipage document by opening a new document or opening one of the documents to be contained (see Figure 16.5). To insert a document before the current document, choose Page, Insert. If you want to insert a scanned image, choose Scan Page from the submenu, which will activate your scanner's scanning software. To insert an image from an existing file, choose Existing Page and select the file from the Open dialog box.

Figure 16.5
Construct and view multipage documents in Imaging for Windows.

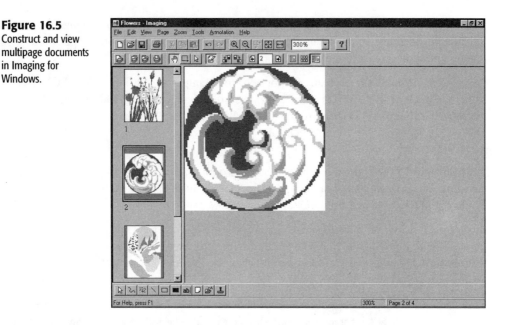

If you want to insert an image at the end of a multipage document, choose Page, Append and then choose either Scan Page or Existing Page from the submenu, depending on the source of the file you want to append.

WORKING WITH SCANNED IMAGES OR DIGITAL PHOTOS

Use Imaging for Windows to scan documents and images directly. Before you can scan a document, you must install your scanner; then click File, Select Scanner. Select the scanner you want and choose OK. After you have selected a scanner, you can scan a new document by clicking File, Scan New. The control window for your scanner or digital camera is displayed. Follow the procedure described for your scanner or digital camera.

Imaging for Windows works with TWAIN-compliant scanners and digital cameras. If your scanner or camera does not work with Imaging for Windows, check to make sure the scanner is TWAIN-compliant and is correctly installed.

VIEWING AND ANNOTATING FAX FILES

Use Imaging for Windows to collect and annotate fax documents such as the one shown in Figure 16.6. You also can create a multipage fax document from separate fax documents or image files, as described in the preceding section "Working with Scanned Images or Digital Photos."

Add comments to a fax image by annotating the image with a text overlay or by drawing on it. To annotate an image with a drawing, highlight, text, note, or rubber stamp, choose the type of annotation you want from the Annotation menu. The highlighter draws with a color over the fax image. When the file is saved to an AWD format, the highlight color changes to black-and-white shading.

Figure 16.6
View, annotate, and aggregate fax documents.

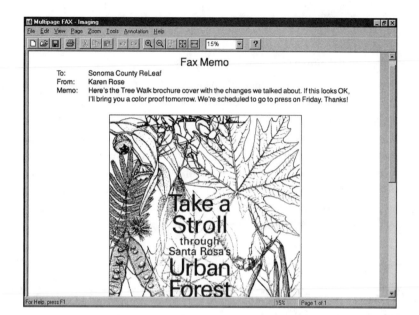

Tip #98

Make multipage documents easier to browse by choosing View, Page and Thumbnails. This option displays the thumbnails in a scrollable left pane and the full image of the selected thumbnail in the right pane, as shown in Figure 16.5.

CHOOSING A FILE FORMAT

The file format in which you save your work affects changes you have made to the document or image. The default format for new files is TIF although you can select AWD (Fax) or BMP format from the New Blank Document dialog box. When you create the new document, you can also specify the color depth, compression, resolution, and size.

If you create a TIF file, a variety of color palettes are available and you can use compression to reduce the file size. AWD files are limited to black and white, and compression is automatic. If you annotate an AWD file, the annotation becomes a permanent part of the file when saved. BMP files can have different color palettes, but they are limited to a single page and cannot be compressed.

Tip #99

Change a file type by opening the file and then resaving it with the new file type. The new file is limited by the color palette, size, and compression options available to the new file type.

TROUBLESHOOTING

PRINTING ATTRIBUTES

When I create a new image with the Microsoft Paint Brush tool, black dots sometimes trail the Brush tool as I move it across the canvas. Why?

This condition can occur when you have enabled the Black and White option in the Image menu's Attributes dialog box. To prevent this problem, create black-and-white images using the color image Attribute but using only black and white. When you create the new image with the Paint tool, the image is in color by default and the problem is averted. Alternatively, if you are working with a premade image, you can modify an existing black and white image by changing its Attribute to color and then editing the image with black-and-white as your color choices.

SECRETS OF MASTERING THE WINDOWS 98 ENVIRONMENT: USING PAINT TO GET A LISTING OF FILES AND FOLDERS

If you're not using a third-party utility, getting a printout of a list of files or folders on your system might be a bit of a challenge. In Windows 98 you can use Paint to obtain a listing of your files or folders by copying an image of a My Computer or Windows Explorer window to the Clipboard. Then, you can paste the image into an image-editing program, like Paint, and print the image.

To use Paint to create and print an image of a listing of files or folders, follow these steps:

1. In My Computer or Windows Explorer, open the folder you want to print and then press Alt+Print Screen to copy an image of the active window to the Clipboard.
2. Click Start, point to Programs, point to Accessories, and then click Paint.
3. On the Edit menu, click Paste and then click Yes to display the image.
4. On the File menu, click Print.

CHAPTER 17

CUSTOMIZING THE LOOK AND FEEL OF WINDOWS

In this chapter

ESTABLISHING CUSTOM SETTINGS FOR EACH USER

Windows 98 enables you to create a profile for each user of the computer. Your user profile contains your individual customizations to Windows 98. This means that when you log on to the system, the settings you established for yourself are still there. When your co-workers log on, their settings are still there also.

Tip #100

> As you read through this chapter, remember that when you are told to click on a file or folder and then click the OK or Open buttons, it is often possible to simply double-click the file or folder to finish the task.

If more than one person uses your computer, you should set up user profiles before you begin implementing any of the customizations in this chapter. That way, when other people log on to the computer, they will be able to make their own customizations to Windows 98 without affecting one another's settings.

To establish user profiles, follow these steps:

1. Open Control Panel and activate Users. When you see the dialog box in Figure 17.1, click the Next button to continue.

Figure 17.1
Activate Users from Control Panel and click Next to begin setting up a new user profile.

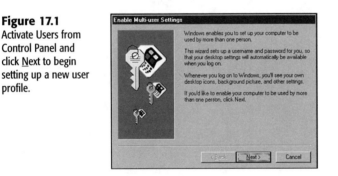

2. In the Add User dialog box, type a username into the User name text box, and click Next to continue.

3. In the Enter New Password dialog box, type a password into the Password text box and press the Tab key to move the insertion point to the Confirm password text box. Retype the identical password in the Confirm password text box and click Next to continue.

4. In the Personalized Items Settings dialog box, check the items you want to customize. For example, if you want a separate My Documents folder for this user, check the My Documents Folder check box. If you want this user to have a custom Start menu, check the Start Menu check box.

You also must decide whether to tell Windows 98 to create a copy of each of these items or create new ones with default settings. Creating new items for each user saves disk space if the new user doesn't make very many changes to Windows 98 settings.

When you've finished making your choices, click <u>N</u>ext to continue.

5. When the Ready to Finish dialog box displays, click <u>F</u>inish to continue. Windows sets up the new user profile and prompts you to reboot the computer.

To set up more profiles, run Users from Control Panel again to repeat this setup routine for each new user.

Tip #101

> Be careful when using custom profiles on your computer. When this option is enabled and multiple user profiles are in use, a new program, not in the original profile template, appears only in the profile of the user who installed that program.

 If the User Profiles option is disabled and now your custom icons are missing from the desktop or the Start menu, see "Disabled or Lost Profiles" in the "Troubleshooting" section at the end of the chapter.

PART

III

CH

17

RESIZING THE TASKBAR

Occasionally, you might want to resize the taskbar. For example, if your system has enough memory to allow several applications to be open simultaneously, the taskbar can become so cluttered that the icons are too small to tell which is which. In this case, resizing the taskbar can help you read the icon text.

Another reason to resize the taskbar is that with all the customization features implemented in Windows 98, the taskbar can contain numerous toolbars and Quick Launch icons. Resizing the taskbar makes it easier to find the elements you need to work with.

Note

> Be careful not to add too much to your taskbar. If you do, you might find yourself spending more time searching your taskbar than it would take to just browse to the file, application, or shortcut the old-fashioned way.
>
> To gain maximum benefit from toolbars and Quick Launch, implement them only for programs you use frequently. If you access a file or program once a week or less, think twice before establishing a toolbar or Quick Launch icon.

To resize the taskbar, move the mouse pointer over the inside edge of the taskbar until it becomes a double-headed arrow. Drag the edge of the taskbar until it is the size you want. (It is possible to size it as large as one-half the screen area.) Now release the mouse button.

MOVING THE TASKBAR

By default, Windows places the taskbar at the bottom of the screen. If you prefer the taskbar in a different position, you can move it to any of the four edges of the screen. For example, photographers often need to drag the taskbar to one side of the screen to allow more vertical desktop real estate when working with a vertically formatted photograph.

To move the taskbar, point to a blank area of it and use the left mouse button to drag it where you want it.

USING THE NEW TASKBAR FEATURES

When you right-click on a blank area of the taskbar, a shortcut menu (often called a *context menu*) pops up. The main purpose of this menu is to give you access to taskbar customization. The menu also has options for rearranging the open windows on your desktop.

The first item on the taskbar's shortcut menu is toolbars. Toolbars contains a menu with three options: Desktop, Quick Launch, and New Toolbar.

Figure 17.2 shows the taskbar with two additional toolbars.

Figure 17.2
The taskbar can become cluttered quickly. This taskbar has two additional toolbars: Address and Desktop.

- Address—Use the Address toolbar to access files and Web pages right from the taskbar. You use this toolbar exactly as you use the one in your favorite Web browser.

- Links—Remember the Links toolbar right next to the Address toolbar in Internet Explorer? This is the same toolbar. You don't have to open Internet Explorer to access these links.

- Desktop—When you select Desktop, the Desktop toolbar is added to the taskbar. The Desktop toolbar contains all the folders, files, and shortcuts on your desktop. Use the small arrows on the left and right ends of the toolbar to scroll through the icons.

  This toolbar can be a major advantage if you normally maximize the window of the application you're currently working with and your taskbar is set to be visible at all times. The Always on Top setting for the taskbar is covered later in this section.

■ Quick Launch—By default, the Quick Launch toolbar appears just to the right of the Start button on the taskbar. When you install Windows, Setup automatically places four useful icons in the Quick Launch toolbar: Internet Explorer, Mail, Show Desktop, and View Channels. The Quick Launch toolbar provides one-click access to your most commonly used applications.

To add your own shortcuts to the Quick Launch toolbar, drag the file or shortcut to the Quick Launch toolbar, and a shortcut is created for your application or file.

Table 17.1 describes the four buttons added to Quick Launch during the Windows install.

TABLE 17.1   BUILT-IN DESKTOP TOOLBARS

Toolbar Name	Description
Internet Explorer	Yep, you guessed it, this button is a shortcut to Internet Explorer.
Mail	The Mail button is a shortcut to Microsoft's contact manager Outlook Express. Outlook Express is included with Internet Explorer 4.x.
Show Desktop	This button is probably the most useful of the four buttons that Windows places on the Quick Launch toolbar. If your desktop becomes cluttered with open application windows or if your current Application window is maximized and you need to get to your desktop, click the Show Desktop icon to automatically minimize all your windows. Click the icon again, and all your windows are restored to the previous state and position.
View Channels	When you click this button, you get a full screen browser to view your channels. If you have not set up your Internet access, the Internet Connection Wizard guides you through the setup.

→ To enable a wizard to help you set up an Internet connection, **see** "Using the Internet Connection Wizard," **p. 522.**

PART

III

CH

17

CREATING TOOLBARS WITH FREQUENTLY USED FOLDERS AND WEB PAGES

Windows 98 provides you with a quick and simple way to establish your own custom toolbars for your most often used files and folders. In a nutshell, it creates a toolbar that contains shortcuts to all the files and subfolders within the folder you select.

To create a custom toolbar follow these steps:

1. Select Toolbars, New Toolbar from the taskbar shortcut menu.

2. The New Toolbar dialog box pops up. This dialog box provides a Windows Explorer style view of your system.

3. Navigate to the folder you want to convert to a toolbar and click the OK button. The folder is now represented in a toolbar.

Tip #102

> If you are comfortable using My Briefcase, it is an excellent candidate for addition to the custom toolbar. That way you can quickly synchronize documents that you work on while away from your PC.

You can also create a toolbar for your favorite Web pages. If you have a permanent Internet connection (generally through your local area network at the office), you can create a toolbar that displays a Web page. You can create a Web page toolbar even if you use a dial-up connection to the Internet, but the toolbar is not quite as useful.

To create a Web page toolbar, follow these steps:

1. Point Internet Explorer to the Web page you want to display.
2. Right-click the taskbar, point to Toolbars, and select New Toolbar.
3. In the New Toolbar dialog box, scroll down to Internet Explorer and click the plus sign to expand it.
4. Select the Web page you want; then click the OK button to create the new toolbar and to close the New Toolbar dialog box. A new toolbar is displayed on your taskbar.

Tip #103

> At the taskbar's default size you can see only one line of your Web page at a time. To see more of your Web page on your new toolbar, you can either use the spinner buttons at the right or resize the taskbar. See the section "Resizing the Taskbar" earlier in this chapter for details.
>
> To remove a custom toolbar, right-click the taskbar or a toolbar, point to Toolbars, and click on the toolbar you want to remove.

ARRANGING YOUR OPEN WINDOWS

The taskbar context menu contains four options for rearranging the windows on your desktop. Can't make sense of what's open? Desktop too cluttered? Don't want to close any applications? No worries; this section will help you get a handle on the mess.

These options are accessed by right-clicking on the taskbar:

■ Cascade Windows—When you select this option, all open windows are displayed in a cascading arrangement beginning in the upper-left corner of the screen and going toward the lower-right corner.

■ Tile Windows Horizontally—When you select this option, your windows are tiled from left to right, top to bottom in alphabetical order.

■ Tile Windows Vertically—To arrange your windows from top to bottom, left to right in alphabetical order, select this option.

■ Minimize All Windows—If you need to minimize all open windows, select this option. This effect is similar but not identical to the Show Desktop button in the Quick

Launch toolbar. The difference is that Show Desktop is a toggle that also restores your windows to their previous size. Minimize All Windows is not a toggle. You have to restore your windows one at a time.

- Changing Taskbar Options—You have several options available for giving your taskbar an attitude adjustment. These adjustments are made from the Taskbar Properties dialog box.

Right-clicking the taskbar and selecting Properties is the quickest way to access the Taskbar Properties dialog box. Figure 17.3 shows the Taskbar Properties dialog box.

Figure 17.3
With the Taskbar Properties dialog box, you select the options you want and click the OK button.

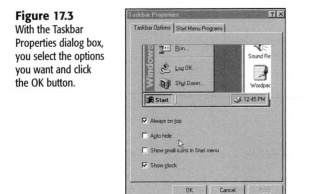

Taskbar Properties can also be accessed through Start, Settings, Taskbar.

Table 17.2 describes the four options available for customizing the taskbar.

TABLE 17.2   TASKBAR OPTIONS TAB

Check Box	Description
Always on Top	When you check this box, your taskbar is always visible, even when you maximize a window.
Auto Hide	When you check this box, your taskbar changes to a very thin line. To make the taskbar visible again, simply point to the thin line.
Shows Small Icons in Start Menu	If you check this box, the icons and Start menu are slightly smaller and the Windows logo down the left side of the menu is removed. To see the difference, watch the Preview window as you check and uncheck this box.
Show Clock	Check this box to make the clock visible in the system tray, which appears to the far right of the taskbar. To remove the clock from the system tray, uncheck the box.

If you check both Always on Top and Auto Hide, you can maximize your Application window and still have easy access to the taskbar any time by pointing to the edge of the screen where your taskbar is.

Tip #104	One nice feature of custom toolbars is the capability to separate them from the taskbar and display them separately on your desktop, either floating or anchored to any top, bottom, or side. Simply drag the custom toolbar off of the taskbar and onto the desktop.

SETTING THE DATE AND TIME

To change the date and time on your computer, follow these steps:

1. Double-click the clock in the taskbar. The Date/Time Properties dialog box is displayed as shown in Figure 17.4.

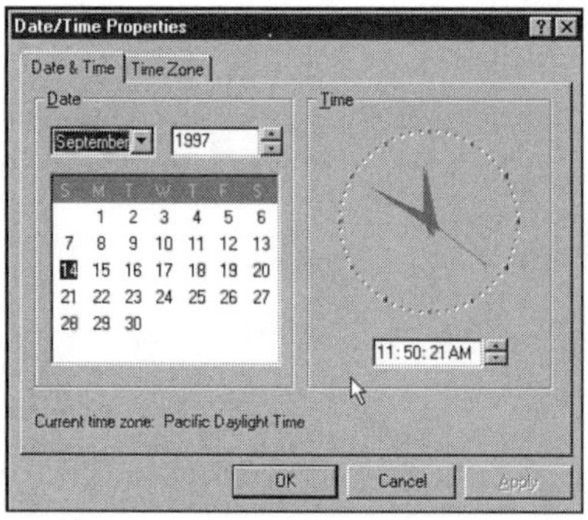

Figure 17.4
Double-click the clock to bring up the Date/Time Properties dialog box.

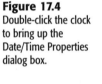

2. The dialog box is divided into two sections: date and time. To change the month, click the down arrow to the right of the month list box. Click the month you want from the drop-down list.

3. To change the year, either highlight the text in the year text box and type the year directly or use the spinner buttons to advance one year at a time up or down.

4. Select the day of the month by clicking in the calendar box.

5. The time section shows an analog clock and a digital clock in a text box. The time is changed using the digital clock text box. This text box is divided into four fields: hour, min., seconds, and a.m./p.m. To change the time, place the insertion point in the field you need to change, and use the spinner buttons to the right of the text box to increment or decrement the field. You can also type directly into the fields. For example, if the current time reads 11:00:00pm and you need to change it to 3:00:00pm, simply use your mouse to highlight the 11 and type the number 3.

Changing the Time Zone

After adjusting the date and time, double-check the current time zone display at the bottom of the Date and Time tab. If it displays the wrong time zone, select the Time Zone tab in the Date/Time Properties dialog box.

This tab displays a world map and a drop-down list box from which you can select the proper time zone. To select the time zone, click the down arrow at the right side of the Time Zone drop-down list box. Select the proper time zone from the list and click Apply.

Also at the bottom of this tab is a check box titled Automatically Adjust Clock for Daylight Saving Changes. If you check this box, Windows automatically adjusts for daylight savings time twice a year. If you live in an area where daylight savings time is not in effect, such as Indianapolis, make sure this box is not checked.

When you're finished, click the OK button to close the Date/Time Properties dialog box. Your changes are applied when you click the OK button. Alternatively, click Apply after making your changes; then close the dialog box.

PART

III

CH

17

Managing Buttons on a Toolbar

Now that you've been experimenting with the taskbar, you might have too many toolbars, or one or more of them might be too big. This section explains some taskbar management techniques.

Resizing Toolbars

When you have too many toolbars, you can't see everything. To get around this problem, you can resize your toolbars, shrinking those that you don't need to see and expanding the others.

To resize a toolbar, point to the small vertical bar at the left edge of the toolbar; drag left to expand it, right to make it smaller. When you resize a toolbar, the toolbar to the left of it expands or contracts automatically.

Removing Toolbars

If you got carried away with those custom toolbars and you want to get rid of some, right-click the taskbar or the title of one of the toolbars, point to Toolbars, and click the toolbar you want to remove.

Removing Buttons from the Quick Launch Bar

The buttons on your Quick Launch bar are just fancy shortcuts. To remove a button from the Quick Launch bar, right-click it and choose Delete from the context menu.

HIDING TEXT AND TITLES ON THE CUSTOM AND DESKTOP TOOLBARS

Another way to reduce the size of your toolbars is to tell Windows not to display the text for each icon.

To hide icon text, right-click the toolbar title and click Show Text to remove the check mark. To hide the toolbar title, right-click the toolbar title and click Show Title to remove the check mark.

REMOVING TOOLBARS

Figure 17.5 shows the context menu for a Quick Launch button.

Figure 17.5
The context menu for a Quick Launch button; to remove the button, click Delete.

ADDING AND REMOVING PROGRAMS IN THE START MENU

You can use two approaches to add items to the Start menu: placing it manually in the Start Menu folder in the Windows directory or by using the wizard. If you prefer to use the wizard approach, follow these steps.

> **Note**
>
> The Start menu is actually a folder on your hard disk, located in the Windows directory. Any files or shortcuts you place in \Windows\Start Menu\ show up in your Start menu.

1. Right-click a blank area of the taskbar and select Properties.
2. Select the Start Menu Programs tab.
3. Click the Add button. This step starts the Create Shortcut Wizard (see Figure 17.6).

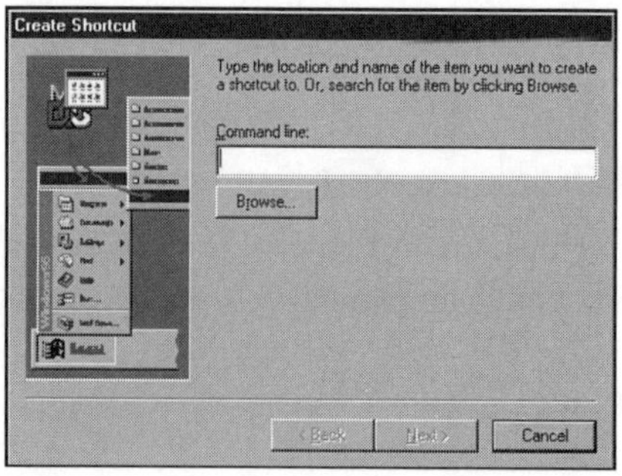

Figure 17.6
Click the Add button from the Start Menu Programs tab to start the Shortcut Wizard. Type the path to the document or program or click Browse to search for it. Then click Next.

4. The first dialog box in this wizard asks for the command line of the executable file for the program. If you know the path and filename of the executable for the application, type it into the Command Line text box. If you don't know the path and filename, you can click the Browse button to open the Browse dialog box. Find the executable name and click the Open button.

   When the path and filename for the executable are displayed correctly in the Command Line text box, click the Next button.

5. Windows displays the Select Program Folder dialog box, which is a tree-style view of your Start menu. You can select an existing folder, or you can click the New Folder button to create a new folder. If you decide to create a new folder, Windows displays a new folder with the name program group (1), highlighted in Rename mode. Type a new name for the folder and press Enter.

6. When you've selected a folder or created a new one, click the Next button.

7. The Select a Title for the Program dialog box is displayed. In the Select a Name for the Shortcut text box, type an intuitive name for your new shortcut.

8. Click the Finish button.

9. Now, check the Start menu to make sure it works properly. If it does, close the Taskbar Properties dialog box with the OK button.

To remove a program shortcut from the Start menu, follow these steps:

1. Right-click a blank area of the taskbar and select Properties.

2. Select the Start Menu Programs tab.

3. Click the Remove button. The Remove Shortcuts/Folders dialog box is displayed.

4. Navigate to the shortcut you want to remove and click the Close button.

5. Now, go to the Start menu to make sure the shortcut was removed properly. If it was, close the Taskbar Properties dialog box with the OK button.

PART

III

CH

17

Tip #105

You can remove an entire folder from the shortcut menu by selecting the folder. When you select a folder name, all shortcuts and folders under that folder are removed from the Start menu.

If you prefer to use Windows Explorer to create and remove folders and shortcuts for the Start menu, click the Advanced button. The Advanced button launches Explorer and takes you directly to the Start Menu folder. From here, simply create new folders and shortcuts the same way you would any other folder on your hard drive.

CLEARING THE DOCUMENTS LIST IN THE START MENU

Windows 98 maintains a history of the documents you've accessed. You can access these documents by clicking Start, Documents and selecting the document you need to access.

Clearing the list is useful if you have accumulated several documents in the Documents history that you no longer access frequently or that don't exist anymore.

To empty the Documents menu, follow these steps:

1. Right-click a blank area of the taskbar and select P_roperties.
2. Select the Start Menu Programs tab.
3. Click the Clear button in the Documents Menu section at the bottom of the page.

CUSTOMIZING THE WINDOWS DISPLAY

Today's video cards and monitors give you a wide choice of resolutions and color schemes. This section shows you how to adjust the display to your needs.

USING DESKTOP THEMES

One of the coolest customization features of the Microsoft Windows 95 Plus Pack now comes as standard with Windows 98. You can use Desktop Themes to customize wallpaper, screen savers, mouse pointers (animated cursors), and many other elements of your Windows display. Some elements of the Desktop Themes include custom icons for My Computer, Network Neighborhood, and Recycle Bin; custom sounds for system functions; and even custom mouse pointers and color schemes.

Microsoft includes all the themes from the original Plus Pack as well as a few new ones, or you can create and save your own themes by either mixing existing elements or using your own sounds, wallpaper, animated cursors, and so on.

You can access Desktop Themes from Control Panel. Select a theme from the Theme drop-down list and proceed to customize as you wish.

CHANGING THE SCREEN RESOLUTION

Screen resolution is a measure of the density of the pixels displayed. More pixels mean finer detail. One side effect of high resolution is that everything appears smaller. The advantages are more content on the screen, and you get more detail.

To adjust the screen resolution, follow these steps:

1. From the Display Properties dialog box shown in Figure 17.7, select the Settings tab. The top portion of this page contains one or more icons that represent your monitor(s). Multiple monitors are covered later in the chapter.
2. If more than one monitor is attached to the computer, click the monitor you want to adjust.
3. Click the down arrow at the right of the S_creen Area drop-down list box and select the resolution you want.
4. Click A_pply.

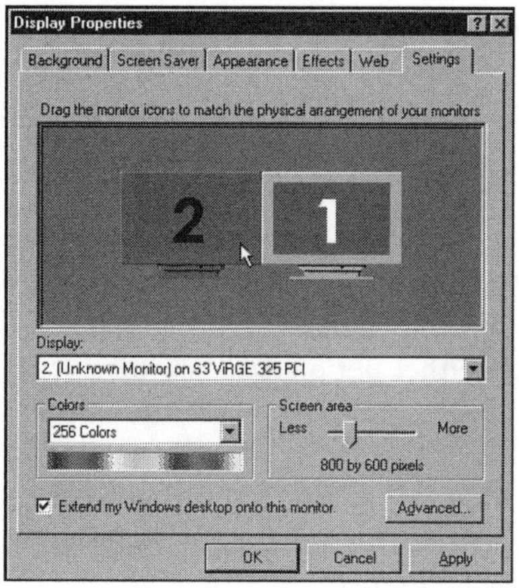

Figure 17.7
Right-click the desktop and select Properties to make changes to your display. To change screen resolution, select the Settings tab.

5. Click the OK button.

6. The resolution changes, and Windows displays a confirmation dialog box. If you're happy with the display, click the OK button within 15 seconds. If the display is unreadable, wait 15 seconds and Windows will restore the settings to the previous resolution.

CHANGING THE NUMBER OF COLORS AVAILABLE TO YOUR MONITOR

The Color palette box in the Display Properties dialog box allows you to determine the number of colors your applications and Windows send to the monitor. The number of colors available depends on several factors: the quality of the video card, the quality of the video driver, and the amount of video RAM available. The combination of these factors determines which color palette and video resolution combinations are available.

To change the number of colors available, follow this procedure:

1. From the Display Properties dialog box, select the Settings tab. The top portion of this page contains one or more icons that represent your monitor(s). Multiple monitors are covered in the section "Configuring Multiple Monitors."

2. If more than one monitor is attached to the computer, click the monitor you want to adjust.

3. Click the down arrow to the right of the Color drop-down list and select the number of colors you want your applications and Windows to display.

> **Note**
>
> Remember that 3D graphics require more video RAM than 2D graphics do. Therefore, depending on the selected resolution, your 3D graphics might not use the number of colors you choose here. In this case, your 3D graphics will be a bit on the ugly side until you choose a lower resolution.

→ Changing your resolution is covered in the previous section, "Changing the Screen Resolution."

4. If you choose a color palette too high for the resolution selected in the <u>S</u>creen Area section, Windows decrements the resolution to the highest resolution that can be used with the color palette you select. Experiment until you find an acceptable combination.

CHANGING FONT SIZES

By default, Windows uses a font size of 96 dots per inch. This setting is referred to as Small Fonts, or Normal size. Large Fonts is 125 percent of Normal size, or 120 dots per inch. You can also specify a custom font size if neither option is satisfactory.

To change your font size, follow these steps:

1. From the Display Properties dialog box, select the Settings tab. The top portion of this page contains one or more icons that represent your monitor(s). Multiple monitors are covered in the section "Configuring Multiple Monitors."

2. If more than one monitor is attached to the computer, click the monitor you want to adjust.

3. Click the <u>A</u>dvanced button. This step brings up a property sheet for your video adapter.

4. On the General tab, click the down arrow to the right of the <u>F</u>ont Size drop-down list box and select Small Fonts, Large Fonts, or Other.

5. If you selected either small or large, click the OK button to apply the changes, and close the dialog box.

6. If you want to specify a custom font size, select Other.

7. In the Custom font size dialog box, you can select from a drop-down list in the <u>S</u>cale fonts to Be ___% of Normal Size drop-down list or type the scale you want directly into the box. The minimum scale is 20%. If you type something smaller into the box, Windows will change it for you to 20%.

8. The scale sample is displayed in the sample box and states the pixels (dots) per inch. You can also drag to the scale you want by clicking anywhere within the ruler and dragging left or right to decrease or increase the font scaling.

9. When you find the scale you want, click the OK button.

10. When you finish making your adjustments, click the OK button to apply the settings and close the Display Properties dialog box.

ADJUSTING THE REFRESH RATE

To adjust the refresh rate for your video adapter, follow these steps:

1. From the Display Properties dialog box, select the Settings tab. The top portion of this page contains one or more icons that represent your monitor(s). Multiple monitors are covered in the section "Configuring Multiple Monitors."

2. If more than one monitor is attached to the computer, click the monitor you want to adjust.

3. Click the Advanced button. This step brings up a property sheet for your video adapter.

4. At the bottom of the Adapter tab is a drop-down list called Refresh Rate. Most adapters only have two settings available: Adapter Default and Optimal. Some list specific refresh rates measured in Hz. In this case you want to pick the highest refresh rate for your monitor and resolution.

   Generally, you want to set the refresh rate to optimal, especially if you're having trouble with screen flicker.

Tip #106

If you ever find that you have adjusted your video settings to a point where you can no longer use the display to navigate through Windows, there is still a way to regain your display without rebuilding your computer. Restart Windows 98 and press (and hold) F8 after the initial boot screen passes (with the BIOS Setup option) but before Windows 98 loads. The system Start menu will appear and give you several startup options, such as Normal, Command Prompt, and Safe Mode. Choose Safe Mode. After you have successfully booted to Safe Mode, from the Start menu, choose Control Panel. Click the Display icon and then select the Settings tab. Choose Advanced, Change. The Upgrade Device Driver Wizard is displayed. Click Next and follow the instructions to reinstall the original video device driver configuration.

PART

III

CH

17

CONFIGURING MULTIPLE MONITORS

This section shows you how to use a dual-monitor setup. This text assumes a setup of two monitors and does not give details on hardware installation.

→ For more details on how to use a second monitor with Windows 98, **see** "Adding a Second Display," **p. 445.**

For details on changing resolution, refresh rate, and color settings for each monitor, refer to the appropriate sections in this chapter.

Windows 98 supports up to eight monitors. Each must have its own PCI VGA video adapter. Monitors are numbered from 1 through 8, but four PCI slots is about all you get with most systems.

Setting up Windows to work with your monitors is very simple when you have the hardware installed. Follow these steps:

1. From the Display Properties dialog box, select the Settings tab. The top portion of this page contains one or more icons that represent your monitors. The icons are squares containing large digits representing the number of the monitor.

2. Click once on monitor 2. In the bottom-left corner of the Settings page, click the I Want to Use This Monitor check box.

3. By default, monitor 2 is assumed to be on the left side. You can move the icons around to better represent the physical setup of your monitors. If your main monitor is on the right side, simply move the icons around with the mouse until they represent the actual positioning of your two monitors. You can even arrange them in a vertical or diagonal arrangement.

4. The positioning of the icons is significant because it determines how you access each monitor.

5. When you have the icons arranged, click the OK button.

That takes care of getting your second display ready to use. Now let's see how to use it.

The secondary display becomes an extension of your desktop. Therefore, it does not have its own taskbar. In fact, nothing is on the secondary display until you put something there.

Getting objects to the other monitor is very easy. All you do is drag the object to the other monitor. If your secondary monitor is to the left, just drag the object off the left side of your primary monitor.

Tip #107	If you want to work with Netscape and Internet Explorer at the same time, drag one to the other monitor. You can even drag the taskbar to the other monitor to get it out of your way.

CUSTOMIZING THE WINDOWS DESKTOP

You can customize your desktop so it has a look and feel that reflects your personality and how you work.

This section shows you how to create your own color schemes, put a nice nature photo on your desktop, and add texture to your desktop background.

USING EXISTING COLOR SCHEMES

To use an existing color scheme, follow these steps:

1. In the Display Properties dialog box, select the Appearance tab.

2. The top half of the Appearance tab shows the various elements of the desktop and your application windows that can be modified. This Preview window shows the effect of the currently selected colors for each component or scheme.

3. To select an existing scheme, click down or to the right of the Scheme list box and select a scheme from the list. The effects of the scheme are displayed in the Preview window.

4. If one of these schemes is suitable, select it and click Apply. The new color scheme is applied immediately. If you like what you see, click the OK button to close the dialog box.

CREATING CUSTOM COLOR AND TEXT SCHEMES

If none of these schemes are appropriate and you want to change only a few elements, follow these steps to create your own color scheme:

1. Click the down arrow to the right of the Item drop-down list box and select the element you want to change.

2. Click the Color button to display the color palette. If you see the color you want, select it. If the color you want is not there, select Other to display a larger color palette and the Custom Colors dialog box. Select an existing color or create your own and click the OK button.

3. When you've finished making color changes, click Apply to see what the changes will really look like. If you don't like them, switch back to the Windows standard color scheme and start over, or modify the colors you don't like. When you get the colors you want, click the OK button.

   Some elements can also be resized. If a particular element can be resized, the Size box is no longer grayed.

Tip #108

If you find a scheme that is very close to what you want, you can select that scheme, change the colors of the few items you want to change, and then use the Save As button to give the new scheme the name.

4. To change the fonts, click the down arrow to the right of the Font drop-down list box; then select the desired font from the drop-down list.

5. To change the font size, either select from the existing lists by clicking the Size text box or highlight the contents of the Size text box and type the font size directly into the box.

6. To change the color of the font, click the down arrow in the color box to display the color palette and then click on the color you want to use. Click the Other button to create a custom color or to select from a larger color palette.

7. To the right of the Color Palette button are the Font Style and Italics buttons. These are toggle buttons. If the button is depressed, that font style is turned on. To turn it off, simply click the button again.

8. When you have selected all the colors, fonts, and sizes you need, click the Save As button. This step brings up the Save Scheme dialog box. In the Save Color Scheme As text box, type the name you want to give to your new color scheme; then click the OK button.

Tip #109

Be sure your color scheme does not make the text on your desktop or in your folders "unseeable" by giving the text a color that does not contrast enough with the chosen background colors.

WALLPAPERING YOUR DESKTOP WITH A GRAPHIC

Would you prefer to display a graphic or even a photo on your desktop instead of that blasé background? No problem; here's how:

1. From the Display Properties dialog box, select the Background tab. The top half of this property page is a graphic representation of your monitor/desktop. When you select wallpaper from the Wallpaper list, Windows displays a preview of the wallpaper there. Figure 17.8 shows the Background tab with a photo of Mount St. Helens selected as the wallpaper.

Figure 17.8
Right-click the desktop and select Properties. Use the Background tab to change the wallpaper and pattern for your desktop.

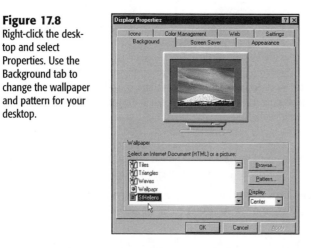

2. Scroll through the items in the Select an Internet Document (HTML) or a Picture box and click the one you want to use.

   If the graphic you want to use for your wallpaper is not visible in the Wallpaper list, click the Browse button and navigate to the location of your bitmap or HTML file. Select the file you want and click the Open button.

Tip #110

> To get your own files to show up in the Wallpaper list, simply copy them to the Windows folder. The next time you go to the Display Properties dialog box, your Custom wallpaper will show up in the Wallpaper list.

3. Most wallpaper bitmaps are very small and can be tiled to create a wallpaper effect. In the lower-right corner of the Background property sheet is the Display drop-down list. Click the down arrow to the right of this list box to display the list. Select either Tiled or Center. If you choose Center, only one copy of the bitmap is displayed directly in the center of your desktop. Center is the recommended method for displaying photographs and HTML files.

Tip #111	You can also use Paint to display a custom creation or a ready-made bitmap; then choose Set as Wallpaper from the File menu.

CHANGING THE BACKGROUND PATTERN

To change the background pattern:

1. Select (None) in the Wallpaper list.

2. Click the Pattern button to display the Pattern dialog box.

3. Click on the pattern you want to display. See the effect in the Preview window to the right of the Pattern list.

4. To modify the pattern, click the Edit Pattern button. This displays the pattern, which allows you to modify the pattern to your liking. When you're finished editing the pattern, click the Change button to view the sample. If the sample is satisfactory, click Done.

5. Click the OK button to return to the Display Properties dialog box.

6. Click Apply to see the changes. If you like the changes, click the OK button.

PART

III

CH

17

CHANGING DESKTOP ICONS

Want to change those system icons on the desktop? Follow these steps:

1. From the Display Properties dialog box, select the Effects tab. In the Desktop Icons box, Windows displays the system icons that can be changed, including an option to use large icons.

2. In the Desktop Icons box, click the icon you want to change, and then click the Change Icon button. This step opens the Change Icon dialog box.

3. By default the icons reside in explorer.exe. Scroll to the right and left until you find the icon you want and click on it. Then click the OK button to close the dialog box. Windows displays the changes in the Desktop Icons box.

4. If none of these icons suit your fancy, you can select another file to choose icons from by clicking the Browse button. This step opens a standard Windows Browse dialog box. In the Files of Type drop-down list, select the file type you want to search for. Navigate the directory of the file you want to search.

   Icons are small images embedded inside files. Generally, the icon for a particular application is embedded inside the executable file. Some of these icons have a .DLL extension and some have an .ICO extension, but virtually any file can contain an icon. In fact, the executable files of most Windows applications (.EXE or .COM) contain their own icon, which is the icon Windows uses by default.

   Some .DLL files and most .ICO files are nothing more than a large collection of files. Shell32.dll is such a file. You can find Shell32.dll in the Windows directory.

The two check boxes in the Visual Settings area are self-explanatory. To turn on a feature, click to place a check in the check box. To disable the feature, remove the check mark.

- Use Large Icons simply displays larger versions of the icons.
- Show Icons Using All Possible Colors uses the maximum number of colors in the icons, depending on the color palette you have set for your display.

USING THE SCREEN SAVER

Many of the Windows NT screen savers have been included in Windows 98. This gives you a much broader and more interesting selection of screen savers than previous versions of Windows.

Experiment with the individual setting for each screen saver and make changes often to keep your computer a little more interesting.

Tip #112	Be wary of highly animated screen savers or wallpaper, especially those you can download from the World Wide Web. They tend to cause Kernel32 exceptions, which force you to reboot your system and could cause you to lose any unsaved work. This problem is especially likely to occur if you rarely shut down your system.

PROTECTING YOUR COMPUTER WITH A SCREEN SAVER PASSWORD

If you don't want someone walking up to your computer and snooping around while you're getting coffee, follow these steps to set up password protection:

1. From the Display Properties dialog box, select the Screen Saver tab.
2. Click the down arrow to the right of the Screen Saver list box and select a screen saver if one isn't already selected.
3. Click the Password Protected check box.
4. Click the Change button. This step opens the Change Password dialog box.
5. In the New Password text box, type the new password you want to use; then press the Tab key to move to be Confirm New Password text box. Retype your new password and click the OK button.
6. Windows displays a dialog box in the middle of the screen telling you that your password has been successfully changed. Click the OK button. If the two passwords don't match, Windows tells you to type them again.

USING YOUR DISPLAY'S ENERGY-SAVING FEATURE

The IBM XT (with the Intel 8086 processor) and its clones had a 100-watt power supply. Thus, at its peak usage, the XT used about the same power as a 100-watt light bulb. And the then-popular CGA monitor also used very little power, less than a television set.

With all the modern computing power and high-resolution video and other components now available, systems today use three to five times more power than they did in the 1980s.

Energy Star includes several Environmental Protection Agency (EPA) programs that set standards for energy efficiency. These standards are implemented in most modern computer hardware and office equipment.

 The EPA has complete information on the Energy Star programs on its Web site:

`http://www.epa.gov/appdstar/esoe/es_office.html`

To take full advantage of the power-saving features of an Energy Star–compliant monitor, follow these steps:

1. From the Display Properties dialog box, select the Settings tab.

2. You will see the property sheet for your video adapter. Select the Monitor tab. Table 17.3 describes the options on the Monitor page.

TABLE 17.3   POWER-SAVING FEATURES

Option Name	Description
Monitor Is Energy Star Compliant	If your monitor is Energy Star compliant, check this box. Most ES-compliant monitors have two power-indicator lights on the front: yellow to indicate power has been reduced and green to indicate Full power mode. Sometimes, one light changes colors.
Automatically Detect Plug and Play Monitors	If your monitor is Plug-and-Play–compatible, check this box. Windows detects the power-saver features of the monitor and uses the appropriate software.
Reset Display on Suspend/Resume	Most adapters don't need to reset the display after a suspend. If your display is working properly, ignore this setting. Some monitors flicker during a reset. If the flicker bothers you, try unchecking this box.

Remember that you can also use your computer's CMOS settings to make your hard drive spin down when it's not in use. Refer to your BIOS manufacturer's documentation for information on adjusting these settings. Remember that if you are connected to a network and your hard drive spins down, your computer disconnects from the network and changes to any open files are lost.

CHANGING THE SCREEN SAVER AND SCREEN SAVER SETTINGS

To select a new screen saver, follow these steps:

1. Click the down arrow next to the Screen Saver drop-down list and select the screen saver you want. The screen saver you select appears in the Preview area.

2. Click the Settings button to change the behavior and appearance. The types of settings vary with each screen saver. Experiment with the different settings; you can preview settings you have selected by clicking the Preview button.

Tip #113

The best way to use the preview is to use the Alt+V keyboard shortcut. Often, after you click on the Preview button and you release the mouse, you inadvertently move the mouse slightly. The slightest mouse movement turns off this screen saver preview. If you use the keyboard shortcut, you won't accidentally move the mouse before you're finished previewing.

3. To display customized text, select Scrolling Marquee or 3D Text from the Screen Saver list and click the Settings button. Type the text you want to display onscreen and experiment with the other adjustments.

Changing the Sounds Related to Windows Events

Windows 98 associates different sounds with each event. For example, if an error occurs, the default sound is a chime. You can change this setting so that a different sound bite plays for any particular event. In fact, you can record your own sounds if you have a microphone for your sound card. For instance, you can record a WAV file that says, "An error has occurred." This kind of customization is great for sight-impaired users.

Only sound files in the WAV format can be associated with Windows events. WAV files have the extension .WAV. For your own WAV files to show up in the Name drop-down box, you must store them in the Media folder under the Windows folder; for example, c:\windows\media\My sound.wav.

Sound America is an excellent Internet source for WAV files. The Sound America Web site has literally thousands of sound files, most of which are WAV format. They are free for the downloading, and most of them are less than 100KB in size.

The Web site address is http://www.soundamerica.com.

To change the sound associated with a Windows event, follow these steps:

1. From Control Panel, select the Sounds icon. The Sounds Properties dialog box is displayed.

2. In the Events box, select the event you want to change the association for. If a Speaker icon appears to the left of the event, a sound is already associated with that event. Otherwise, no sound has been associated with that event (see Figure 17.9).

3. In the Name drop-down list box, select the sound file you want to associate with this event. To associate a WAV file that is not in the Media folder, click the Browse button, navigate to the location of that file, and select from the Browse dialog box.

4. To preview the sound, click the right arrow to the right of the Preview icon.

Figure 17.9
Sounds Properties
dialog box.

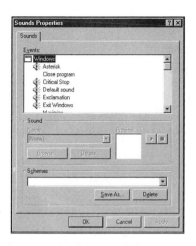

Tip #114

Windows also supplies several preset schemes that you can select from the Schemes drop-down list box. Click the down arrow to the right of the Schemes drop-down list to select the scheme you want to use.

5. When you finish making your custom sound associations, you can save this sound scheme with a unique name. Click the Save As button, type a name for the new sound scheme into the Save This Sound Scheme As text box, and click the OK button.

Tip #115

One very practical use for this feature is to find or record an intuitive or unique sound to associate with New Mail Notification. This way, when new mail comes in, you get something more than just a chime.

Now you will know right away when you receive a new email message, and you can check to see whether it's the important one you've been waiting for all day. Of course, your email program must support this feature.

CUSTOMIZING MOUSE AND KEYBOARD SETTINGS

You can customize the behavior of the mouse and keyboard to make them work exactly the way you want them.

From Control Panel, select mouse. You'll see the Mouse Properties dialog box. Table 17.4 describes the options in the Buttons tab in the Mouse Properties dialog box.

TABLE 17. 4   MOUSE PROPERTIES—BUTTONS TAB

Option Name	Description
Button Configuration	To configure your mouse for left-handed use, click the Left-handed radio button. This option reverses the functionality of the left and right mouse buttons.
Double-click Speed	To adjust the double-click speed, move the slider bar in the Double-click Speed section of the Buttons tab. Double-click the Jack-in-the-box in the Test area to test the new speed setting.

MOUSE POINTERS AND ANIMATED CURSORS

The appearance of the mouse pointer depends on the task you are doing. The normal pointer is a white arrow pointing up and slightly left. If the computer is busy, such as when loading an application, the mouse pointer becomes an hourglass. This icon indicates that no other processing can occur until the current process is finished. If a process is working in the background, the mouse pointer becomes a combination of an arrow and an hourglass.

Windows provides several other mouse pointer schemes. To select a different scheme, click the down arrow to the right of the Scheme drop-down list. Select the pointer scheme you want to use.

Caution

One thing to note is that animated pointers suck the life out of a computer. If your computer seems sluggish after installing these pointers, that's why.

To create your own scheme of mouse pointers, select the pointer you want to change and click the Browse button. This opens a dialog box showing the contents of the Cursors folder under Windows (c:\windows\cursors).

If you select a particular scheme but you want to use the Windows default for a few of the pointers, select the pointer you want to change and click the Use Default button.

When you finish creating your pointer scheme, click the Save As button, type the new name in the Save This Cursor Scheme As text box, and click the OK button.

CALIBRATING MOUSE MOVEMENT

The Motion tab gives you the following options:

- Pointer Speed sets the speed the pointer moves across the screen when you move the mouse. Move the slider to the left to slow down mouse movement and to the right to speed up mouse movement.

- Pointer Trail displays mouse trails. Click the Show Pointer Trails check box. Adjust the length of the pointer trail with the slider bar below the check box. Kids love this feature. If you don't like the mouse trails, try not to let your kids find out about this option.

- Working with the IntelliMouse: Microsoft has developed a great alternative to the three-button mouse. The IntelliMouse has a left and right mouse button with a small wheel-button combination in between. To take full advantage of the wheel, your application must specifically support the mouse wheel. The wheel button behaves differently in each application. Table 17.5 describes the functions of the wheel button in Word 97.

TABLE 17.5   FUNCTIONS OF THE INTELLIMOUSE WHEEL BUTTON

Action	Effect
Single click	This activates a scrolling feature. The scroll box in the vertical scrollbar changes appearance, and the pointer changes to a dot with an arrow above and below it when the pointer is directly over the scroll box. If the pointer is above or below the scroll box, one of the arrows disappears and the page begins to scroll in that direction. The farther the pointer is from the center of the Document window, the faster the document scrolls.
Click and hold	The pointer changes to a dot with an arrow above and below. When you move the pointer up, the bottom arrow goes away and the document scrolls up. The reverse is true if you move the pointer down. A "ghost" pointer is visible at the position the pointer was in when you pressed the wheel. The farther the pointer is from the ghost pointer, the faster the document scrolls.
Spin without click	The document scrolls up or down three lines at a time.
Hold left button and spin	The text is highlighted as if you were doing a drag operation with the mouse.

PART

III

CH

17

MAKING WINDOWS ACCESSIBLE FOR THE HEARING, SIGHT, AND MOVEMENT IMPAIRED

The Accessibility Options are indispensable for computer users with disabilities. Microsoft has done a fantastic job here. Many of these features are also useful for nonimpaired users as well. Even if you don't think you need any of these features, take a glance through them; you might be surprised at what you can do!

To open the Accessibility Properties sheet, double-click Accessibility Options in Control Panel. Windows opens the dialog box shown in Figure 17.10.

Figure 17.10
You can run
Accessibility Options
from Control Panel.

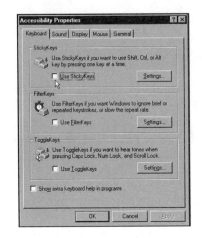

KEYBOARD TAB

The keyboard tab has three features:

- StickyKeys makes it easier to use multiple key combinations that include the Shift, Alt, and Ctrl keys. These keys are called modifier keys. For example, Shift+F10 activates the shortcut menu. When StickyKeys is enabled, you can press and release the Shift key and then press and release the F10 key to get the same effect (see Figure 17.11).

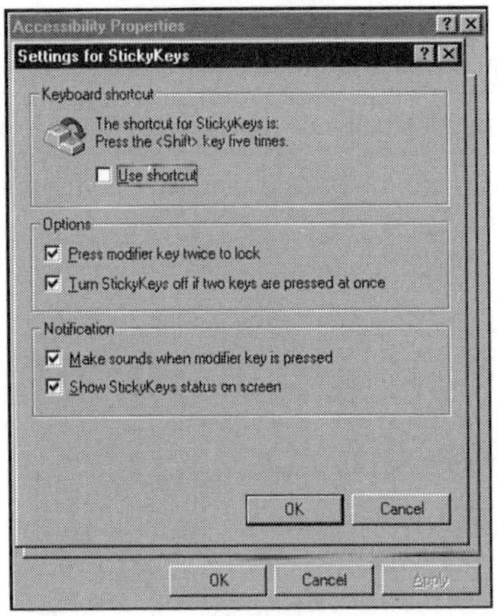

Figure 17.11
StickyKeys Settings
dialog box.

- FilterKeys tells Windows to ignore repeated keystrokes (see Figure 17.12).
- ToggleKeys gives audio feedback whenever Caps Lock, Num Lock, or Scroll Lock are pressed. To activate this feature, press the Num Lock key for five seconds, click the Settings button, and check the Use Shortcut box.

Figure 17.12
FilterKeys Settings
dialog box.

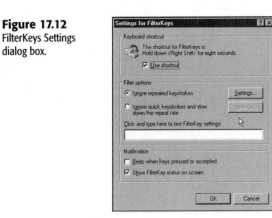

SOUND TAB

The Sound tab contains two visual feedback features: SoundSentry and ShowSounds.

- SoundSentry tells Windows to give visual feedback when normally only audio feedback would occur. The Settings button allows you to select the type of visual feedback.

- ShowSounds tells your applications to give visual feedback when they would normally give audio feedback only.

DISPLAY TAB

The Display tab feature forces your applications to use the color scheme specified in the Settings dialog box (click the Settings button).

In the Settings dialog box, you can check the Use Shortcut box to enable the left Alt+left Shift+Print Screen keyboard shortcut to enable the feature.

In the High Contrast Color Scheme section, you can specify which scheme to use.

MOUSEKEYS

MouseKeys enables you to use the arrow keys and the numeric keypad to control your mouse pointer. Click the Settings button to fine-tune this feature.

GENERAL TAB

The General tab enables you to make a few global adjustments to Accessibility Options.

- Automatic Reset tells Windows to turn off all Accessibility Options after a specified time of inactivity.

- Notification provides two options for giving visual and audio feedback when features are turned on or off. This setting helps avoid accidentally toggling features on and off.

- SerialKey Devices is used when special input devices are attached to any of the serial ports. Use the Settings button to tell Windows what port the device is plugged into.

USING THE WINDOWS "POWER TOYS" COLLECTION

Windows Power Toys is a collection of small utility programs developed for Windows 95. Some of them have been built into Windows 98, such as the taskbar tools that enable you to single click for a view of the desktop or any other shortcut you want. Many other Power Toys, such as Cabview, are not built in but are still useful and are worth installing.

For example, the AutoPlay Extender provides AutoPlay capabilities for CD-ROMs that don't have AutoPlay support.

Cabview is a tool for viewing and extracting files from cabinet archives. An updated Cabview.dll is now included in the Windows 98 install. Installing the older version of Cabview from Power Toys is not recommended. CAB, short for cabinet, is a file archive format for distributing software and was implemented with the original release of Windows 95.

Thirteen Power Toys are available; a readme.txt file explains the functionality of each one.

> **Caution**
>
> Remember that Microsoft does not provide support for these utilities, and they were originally designed for Windows 95. Some of them might not work properly under Windows 98. Carefully read all documentation available before using any of the Power Toys.

You can download the Power Toys from Microsoft's Web site at

`http://www.microsoft.com/windows95/downloads/contents/wutoys/`
`➥w95pwrtoysset/default.asp`

TROUBLESHOOTING

DISABLED OR LOST PROFILES

The user profile is disabled, and my custom icons are missing.

When user profiles are disabled, Windows 98 returns to using the profile that existed before you enabled the User Profiles option. Any custom settings created by users after the user profiles option was enabled are lost.

If the user profiles still exist in user-specific folders, you can access these profiles to regain your lost settings as follows:

1. From Windows Explorer, open the Windows directory and then browse to the Profiles folder.
2. Open the folder that has your logon name.
3. The Desktop folder in the user-specific folder contains the custom shortcuts you created. Drag the shortcuts from the Desktop folder to the Windows 98 desktop. The user-specific folder also contains a Start Menu folder. Similarly, drag the custom Start

Menu items from the profile Start Menu folder to the Start Menu folder that Windows 98 is currently using.

You have now reclaimed your desktop and Start menu without having to start from scratch.

SECRETS OF MASTERING THE WINDOWS 98 ENVIRONMENT: CUSTOMIZING A SINGLE DESKTOP FOR MULTIPLE USERS

If you share a computer with one or more people at home or at work, you can set up a different desktop configuration, or user profile, for each user.

Subsequently, each person is greeted with his or her own customized settings upon logging on to Windows. These settings include the desktop settings, programs, Start menu, and Favorites. Assigning a unique profile of work environment settings to each computer user immunizes each person from profile changes made by other users in a separate logon. Of course, the first step in using profiles is to set up a unique username and password for each person. To set up user profiles, follow these steps:

1. Click the Start button, point to Settings, and then click Control Panel. The Control Panel window appears.
2. Double-click Users. The Enable Multi-User Settings Wizard starts.
3. Follow the wizard's instructions.
4. Repeat this process to create personalized settings for each user.

PART **IV**

CONFIGURING AND CUSTOMIZING WINDOWS

CHAPTER **18**

WORKING WITH FONTS

In this chapter

UNDERSTANDING FONTS

Windows 98 provides several fonts that enable you to vary the look of your onscreen and printed text. A *font* is a set of characters in a single style defined by size, weight, and other features. Fonts are often members of type faces (type families) that are variations on that same style, for example Arial, Arial Black, Arial Bold, Arial Bold Italic, and Arial Italic. The Arial font is shown in Figure 18.1.

Figure 18.1
The Windows 98 Arial font of the Arial type family.

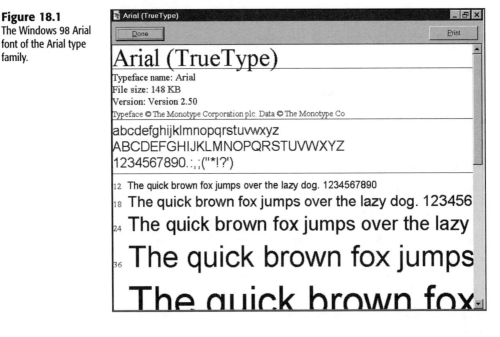

There are two general categories of fonts: bitmap and scalable. Bitmapped (raster) fonts are tailored to the pixels on a monitor or the dots of ink put down by a printer. These fonts are fixed in size; they can be enlarged or reduced, but their edges become jagged in the process.

Bitmapped fonts look best in the sizes in which they were created. At even multiples of their original size, they might scale well, but in other sizes, or rotated, the likelihood is that the image quality will suffer. Generally, bitmapped fonts should not be enlarged.

Scalable fonts, originally developed for high-end computers and printers, allow you to change the size of the font while retaining the characters' proportions and without causing the edges of the letters to become jagged.

Windows 98 uses Microsoft TrueType fonts, which are scalable. Every character in a TrueType font is stored as an outline that is used in the creation of every size of that character. The TrueType font file also contains all the other data it needs to produce an image, including the rules (hints) for fine-tuning the outline of the character at any given size. When the image has been sized, Windows rasterizes it to produce the image best suited to the capabilities of the monitor or printer even if they are low-resolution devices. Hinting is needed on low-resolution monitors and printers, including VGA monitors and 300dpi laser printers.

INSTALLING AND REMOVING FONTS

Windows 98 comes with a collection of TrueType and bitmap fonts (see Table 18.1). These are installed in the Fonts folder (c:\windows\fonts). TrueType fonts have the extension .TTF, whereas bitmap fonts have .FON extensions (see Figure 18.2). You can add more fonts to the system or remove many of them. You can install roughly 1,000 TrueType fonts in Windows 98. (The number is limited by the file size limits for the Registry key and the graphics device interface.)

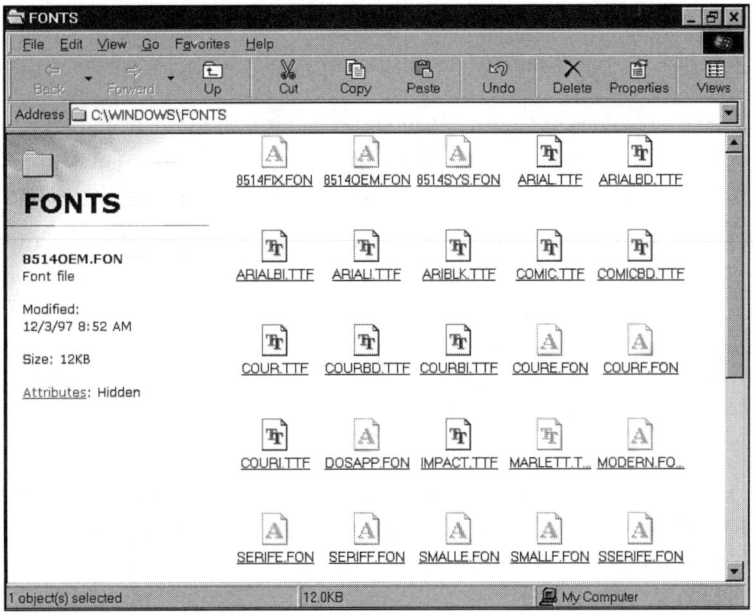

Figure 18.2
When you view font files as large icons, TrueType fonts display a TrueType icon.

Windows ships with many fonts that serve special purposes. Windows uses a small number of system fonts to create its own screens (see Table 18.1). Deleting these fonts can cause glitches on your Windows screens or prevent you from booting Windows. OEM fonts support older equipment installed on the system. And the fixed-width fonts provide compatibility with older versions of Windows.

Windows 98 also supplies a few vector fonts. *Vector fonts* are a type of scalable font typically used with plotters and high-resolution output devices. Modern.fon is a vector font.

PART

IV

CH

18

TABLE 18.1   SPECIALIZED FONTS SUPPLIED WITH WINDOWS 98

Font Filename	Description
VGASYS.FON	VGA (640×480) resolution system font
VGAOEM.FON	VGA (640×480) resolution terminal font

continues

TABLE 18.1   CONTINUED

Font Filename	Description
VGAFIX.FON	VGA (640×480) resolution monospaced system font
8514SYS.FON	8514/a (1024×768) resolution system font
8514OEM.FON	8514/a (1024×768) resolution terminal font
8514FIX.FON	8514/a (1024×768) resolution monospaced system font
VGA850.FON	VGA (640×480) resolution terminal font (International)

PREVIEWING FONTS

The Fonts folder in Control Panel works a bit differently from other folders. You can preview the system fonts and TrueType fonts in the Fonts folder from the Windows 98 font viewer. To see the fonts that come with Windows 98, follow these steps:

1. Click on Start, point to Settings, activate Control Panel, and activate Fonts.

2. Point to the font you want to preview and activate.

Note

Keep in mind that the term *activate* means to click if the *Web desktop* is enabled and double-click if it isn't.

You can use this procedure to preview a font file even if it is located in another folder. Font files need not be in the Fonts folder. New printer fonts can be installed when you install a new printer; these new fonts won't be placed in the Fonts folder, but they will show up with the fonts listed in Windows programs, such as Word for Windows.

Table 18.2 is a list of the TrueType fonts that come with Windows 98. These fonts are available as both screen and printer fonts.

TABLE 18.2   ADDITIONAL FONTS SUPPLIED WITH WINDOWS 98ARIAL

Arial Black
Arial Bold
Arial Bold Italic
Arial Italic
Comic Sans MS
Comic Sans MS Bold
Courier New
Courier New Bold
Courier New Bold Italic

Courier 10,12,15 (VGA resolution)

Courier 10,12,15 (8514/a resolution)

Courier New Italic

Non-Windows Application Font

Impact

Marlett

Modern

MS Sans Serif 8,10,12,14,18,24

MS Serif 8,10,12,14,18,24

Small Fonts (VGA resolution)

Small Fonts (8514/a resolution)

Symbol

Symbol 8,10,12,14,18,24

Tahoma

Tahoma Bold

Times New Roman

Times New Roman Bold

Times New Roman Bold Italic

Times New Roman Italic

Verdana

Verdana Bold

Verdana Bold Italic

Verdana Italic

Webdings

WingDings

PART

IV

CH

18

ADDING NEW FONTS

There are hundreds of fonts available that you can purchase or find free on the Internet. However, new fonts must be installed, not simply copied into the Fonts folder, for Windows and Windows applications to recognize them.

To add a font to the Fonts folder, follow these steps:

1. Click on Start, point to Settings, activate Control Panel, and activate Fonts.

2. Activate the File menu; then activate Install New Font.

3. Activate the drive; then activate the folder with the font you want.

4. Activate the font you want to add.

> **Note**
>
> If you want to add more than one font, press and hold the Ctrl key while activating the font files you want to add.

If you are on a network, you can add fonts from a network drive without using your computer's disk space. Follow these steps:

1. Activate <u>F</u>ile; then activate <u>I</u>nstall New Font.

2. In the Add Fonts dialog box, be sure the Copy fonts to Fonts folder check box is not checked. This option is available only when you install TrueType or raster fonts from the Install New Font command.

3. Choose OK.

 Microsoft periodically makes more TrueType fonts available for no charge at `http://www.microsoft.com/typography/free.htm`

PRINTING A FONT SAMPLE

To print a sample of a font, follow this procedure:

1. Click on Start, point to <u>S</u>ettings, activate <u>C</u>ontrol Panel, and activate Fonts.

2. Point to the font you want to print; then activate it.

3. Choose Print on the font sample page.

> **Note**
>
> If you want to choose more than one font, press and hold the Ctrl key; then activate each font you want.

LOOKING AT FONT FILE PROPERTIES

Using the Windows 98 font utility, you can look at useful information about the font file on the Properties sheet. Follow these steps:

1. Click on Start, point to <u>S</u>ettings, activate <u>C</u>ontrol Panel, and activate Fonts.

2. Point to the font and right-click.

3. Point to P<u>r</u>operties and activate.

The Properties sheet for a TrueType font has a single tab called General (see Figure 18.3) that shows the font file name, type of file, location, size, attributes, and other information.

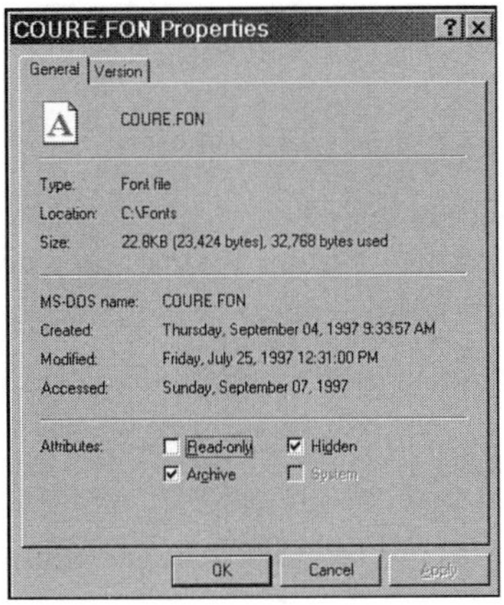

Figure 18.3
The General tab shows the font file name, type of file, location size, and other information.

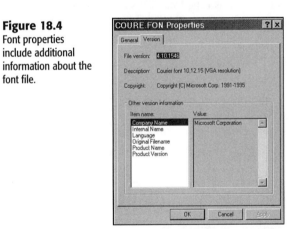

For other types of font files such as .FON files, the Properties sheet also shows a Version tab (see Figure 18.4), which gives additional information about the font file, including the file version, description, copyright, and other version information such as company name, internal name, language, original filename, and product version.

Figure 18.4
Font properties include additional information about the font file.

DELETING A FONT

Many users do not need dozens or hundreds of fonts. If you don't use many fonts and would rather have more disk space, you can delete many of the fonts. To uninstall a font and delete it to the Recycle Bin, follow these steps:

1. Click on Start, point to Settings, activate Control Panel, and activate Fonts.

2. Activate the font icon or font file you want to delete.

3. Activate File and activate Delete.

Note

If you want to delete more than one font, press and hold the Ctrl key while activating each font.

If you want to uninstall a TrueType font without deleting it from your hard drive, you must create a folder in which to keep a copy of the font file. To uninstall a TrueType font without deleting it (the font information remains in the Registry), follow these steps:

1. Click on Start, activate Programs, and activate Windows Explorer.

2. Create a new folder for copies of the TrueType font files.

3. Copy the fonts you want to remove from the Fonts folder to the new folder.

4. Follow the procedure for deleting a font described in the previous section.

When you want to reinstall a font you removed, follow these steps:

1. Click on Start, point to Settings, activate Control Panel, and activate Fonts.

2. Activate the File menu; then activate Install New Font.

3. Activate the drive; then activate the folder with the font you want.

4. Select the Copy Fonts to Fonts Folder option so the font file is copied rather than moved. Activate the font you want to install. Choose OK.

USING FONTS IN APPLICATIONS

When a font is installed, Windows 98 applications can access it. Figures 18.5 and 18.6 show the font dialog boxes for WordPad and Word. To access the Font dialog box from within the application, follow these steps:

1. Point to Format on the menu bar and activate.

2. Point to Font and activate.

3. Activate the font you want to use.

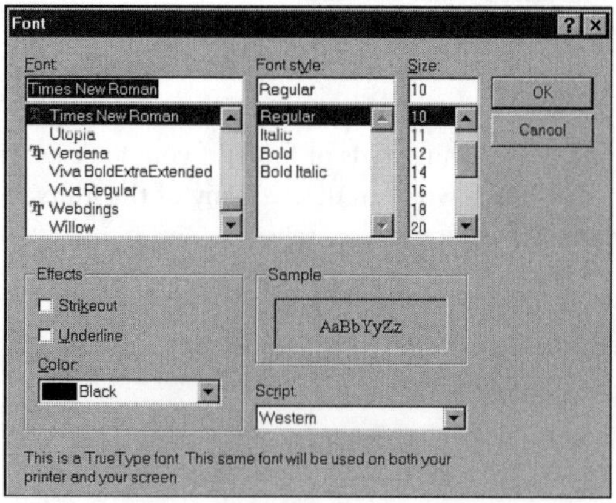

Figure 18.5
The Font Access configuration dialog box in WordPad.

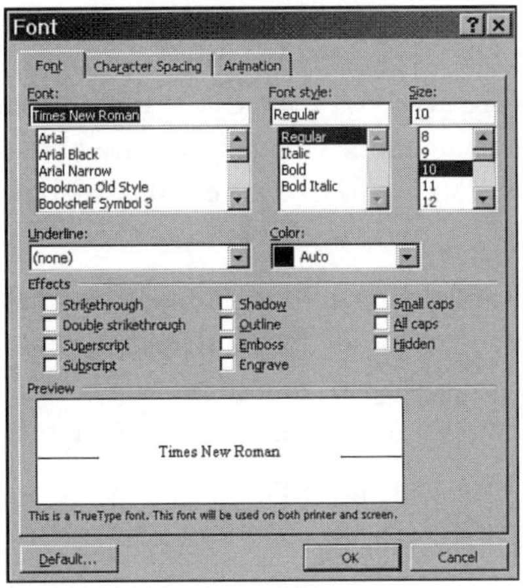

Figure 18.6
The Font Access dialog box in Microsoft Word 97.

 Microsoft maintains an informative Typography page at `http://www.microsoft.com/typography/`. Here, you can find details on the development of TrueType, free TrueType fonts and utilities, developer information, descriptions of the features of TrueType and OpenType, and links to other typography-related sites.

MANAGING FONTS

If you do a lot of document design and use a variety of fonts, you spend a fair amount of time installing and previewing fonts, printing out font samples, and studying font file properties. The Windows 98 applet for managing fonts gives you the tools to perform these tasks—and to sort the available fonts by their similarity to a specified font.

SORTING BY FONT SIMILARITY

To sort the fonts in the Fonts folder according to their similarity to a specified font, follow these steps:

1. Click on Start, point to Settings, activate Control Panel, and activate Fonts.

2. Activate the View menu and then activate List Fonts by Similarity.

3. Activate a font. The fonts will be listed in their order of similarity to the chosen font.

The fonts are sorted as very similar, fairly similar, or not similar. If no PANOSE information is available on a font (PANOSE is a widely used typeface matching system that identifies fonts with a 10-digit number), that is noted.

USING THIRD-PARTY FONT MANAGEMENT SOFTWARE

Although the Windows 98 font manager handles many tasks, third-party font management software can provide more extensive capabilities if you must manage large numbers of fonts. For example, some third-party font managers group fonts into sets that suit your work habits, activating or deactivating a font or sets of fonts as you need them.

Adobe Type Manager (ATM) Deluxe version 4.5 from Adobe Systems allows you to manage not only Windows TrueType fonts but also Adobe PostScript Type 1 scalable fonts. (Earlier versions of ATM didn't work with TrueType files; TrueType fonts, although in some instances appearing very much like their Adobe counterparts, are not the same and do not share the same file formats.) People who use fonts a lot often have Type 1 fonts in their collections. Adobe sells more than 2,000 Type 1 typefaces.

ATM (see Figure 18.7) has other useful features. It can simulate fonts that a document calls for but aren't on your computer. It automatically loads an inactive font into Windows when a document calls for it. It can use antialiasing to smooth the edges of Type 1 fonts. And it has a multiple master feature that you can use to create your own typefaces.

You can find an overview of Adobe Type Manager Deluxe 4.5 at

http://www.adobe.com/prodindex/atm/main.html

Figure 18.7
The Adobe Type Manager Control Panel enables you to manage Windows TrueType fonts and Adobe PostScript Type 1 scalable fonts.

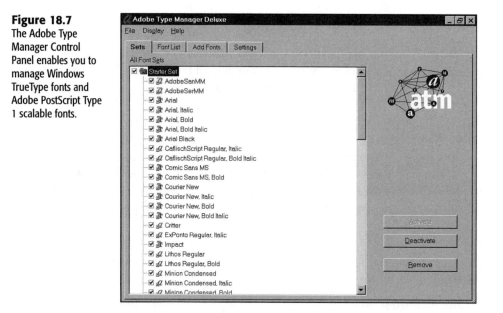

Bitstream Font Navigator, Agfa Font Manager, and FontMinder are some other popular font managers. FontMinder was created by Ares Software Corporation, but Adobe purchased the program from Ares in 1996, and some of its features, in particular the capability to automatically activate sets of fonts when a given application is launched, might be incorporated into ATM in the future.

USING OTHER FONT TECHNOLOGIES

With Microsoft TrueType and Adobe's Type 1 fonts, you might have all the font power you need. However, other font technologies such as Bitstream TrueDoc, Monotype ESQ, and Adobe's Type 3 format can extend the range of typefaces available to you.

A narrow market of print professionals uses Adobe Type 3 fonts. Type 3 fonts come in both scalable and bitmapped fonts, but they don't use hinting. The Type 3 format was designed to produce high-quality output on high-end PostScript-capable printers and service bureau image setters that have hardware for interpreting PostScript commands. Type 3 fonts make use of the full set of PostScript PDL capabilities.

MAKING FONTS LOOK THEIR BEST ON THE SCREEN

Bitmapped fonts are best used at their design sizes. Enlarging bitmapped fonts produces jagged edges ("jaggies"). And how the font looks onscreen also depends on the resolution capabilities of the monitor and graphics card. At lower resolutions, instead of smooth lines or smooth curves, you might see jagged edges on the characters in your display or print output. Jaggies appear when the monitor or printer doesn't have the resolution to display a smooth line.

Font smoothing or antialiasing makes the edges of characters appear smoother. To turn on font smoothing in Windows 98, follow this procedure:

1. Click on Start, point to Settings, activate Control Panel, and activate Fonts.
2. Activate View, Folder Options, View.
3. Check the box titled Smooth Edges of Screen Fonts.
4. Choose OK.

If your text still doesn't appear smooth enough for your purposes, you might need to purchase a monitor and graphics card capable of higher resolutions.

PART

IV

CH

18

MATCHING SCREEN FONTS WITH PRINTED OUTPUT

One of the computer user's most frustrating problems develops when the printed page coming out of the printer doesn't match what is seen onscreen. Fonts are among the likely culprits for this problem. If the printer doesn't have access to the same font shown onscreen, the font that is substituted is likely to have minute differences that are enough to throw off spacing.

How do you make sure the screen and printer fonts are the same? Windows applications using TrueType download the fonts to the printer, so the printer and screen display use the same fonts.

Although in most cases you want the same screen and printer fonts, in some situations you might want to use screen fonts in your document that your printer cannot print. This behavior is useful if the document will be printed on another printer or be used by a service bureau on an image setter. In this case you can select fonts that you know are supported by the other printer or service bureau, and you can see onscreen how your document will look, even though you can't obtain an accurate printout from your own printer.

Tip #116

Keep in mind that most Windows TrueType and Adobe PS fonts are licensed and copy-righted, and they can't legally be copied to a disk or across a network unless covered by the license.

The appearance of the text and graphics on a page printed on a laser printer is controlled through a page description language (PDL). The two standard page description languages are Adobe's PostScript and Hewlett-Packard's Printer Control Language (PCL). PCL and PostScript printers run under Windows 98. Windows 98 uses a 32-bit universal printer driver that works with the printer-specific drivers supplied by printer manufacturers for their machines.

Hewlett-Packard (HP) was one of the pioneers in laser printer development for personal computers. The Hewlett-Packard LaserJet series is the standard for laser printers, and other manufacturers adopt a subset of the PCL commands in their printer drivers for some degree of HP compatibility.

PostScript became the standard for desktop publishing because service bureaus have used it for years with their image setters to produce camera-ready copy. Users' familiarity with PostScript has helped it retain its dominant position despite competition from HP and TrueType.

Your printer can be configured using the Windows 98 Printer Properties screen. The Windows 98 Printer Properties screen gives you useful information about your printer's configuration and enables you to control its operation. Each printer has its own configuration options, and these vary widely among printers (see Figure 18.8).

To use the Printer Properties screen, follow these steps:

1. Click on Start, point to Settings, and activate Control Panel.
2. Select Printers.
3. Right-click on the PostScript printer you will be using.
4. Activate Properties.

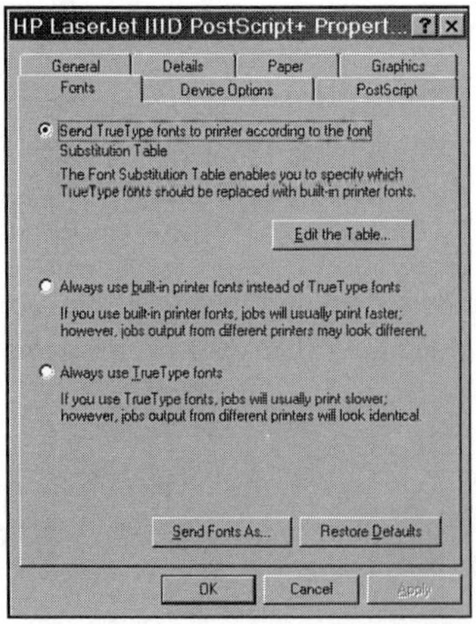

Figure 18.8
The Fonts tab on this Printer Properties screen shows the choices available on an HP LaserJet PostScript printer.

Printers come with resident fonts, some with more, some with less, depending on the model. A resident font is a font permanently stored in a printer's read-only memory. You can also add fonts by inserting font cartridges designed for the printer or by downloading soft fonts from the computer.

Some laser printers have slots that accept font cartridges, which are read-only memory boards loaded with a collection of fonts. Font cartridges have the advantage of not using computer or printer memory.

Printers can also take advantage of soft fonts. A *soft font* is one that is downloaded from the computer to the printer's random access memory (RAM; it is also referred to as a *download-able font*). The TrueType fonts that come with Windows 98 are soft fonts. Soft fonts use both disk space and printer memory. If you don't have enough memory in your printer to handle your printing needs (including a set of soft fonts), look into installing more RAM; on most laser printers you can increase the amount of RAM. Soft fonts must be downloaded to the printer and that takes time, but when they are downloaded, subsequent print jobs print faster.

To force the use of TrueType fonts on a PostScript printer, follow these steps:

1. Click on Start, point to Settings, and activate Control Panel.
2. Select Printers.
3. Right-click on the PostScript printer you will be using.
4. Activate Properties.
5. Choose the Fonts tab.
6. Choose the Always Use TrueType Fonts button.
7. Choose OK.

PART

IV

CH

18

USING THE CHARACTER MAP

The computer's keyboard offers only a worm's-eye view of the characters available to the user. To present what is actually available to users in a particular font, Windows 98 uses a character map (see Figure 18.9).

To insert a character from the character map, follow this procedure:

1. Click on Start, Programs, Accessories, Character Map.
2. Double-click on the character you want. (Continue to hold the mouse button down if you want to see the character magnified.)
3. Activate Copy.
4. Return to your application.
5. Place the cursor where you want to insert the character and then paste.

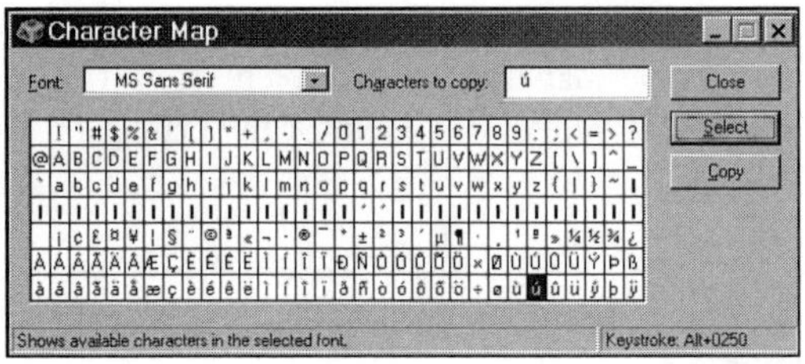

Figure 18.9
In the lower-right corner of the window, the character map for MS Sans Serif shows the keystroke shortcut for the character.

Various keyboard shortcuts allow you to insert extended ASCII characters in your documents. These shortcuts eliminate your having to keep returning to the character map. You can create a document with your most frequently used keyboard shortcuts or create macros for them in your Windows applications.

Figure 18.9 shows the keystroke combination for the character ú. To use the keystroke shortcut to a character, follow these steps:

1. Place the cursor where you want to insert the character.
2. Press Num Lock.
3. Press and hold the Alt key.
4. Using the numeric keypad on the keyboard, type the four digits for the character you want to insert.
5. Release the Alt key. The character is displayed at the insertion point.

USING WINGDINGS, SYMBOLS, AND OTHER UNCONVENTIONAL FONTS

To give you a taste of the plethora of distinctive fonts beyond those that come with Windows 98, Windows includes three TrueType fonts of signs and symbols. Wingdings.ttf is an array of pointers and borders that can be used to dress up a document. Symbol.ttf is a collection of characters including the uppercase and lowercase Greek alphabets for mathematical and scientific notation and common business use. And the recently developed Webdings.ttf typeface reflects the growing interest in the Internet with a selection of characters for Web designers; these font images move more quickly across the Internet than graphics files will.

USING FONTS ON THE WEB

The Internet has expanded the concept of document publishing. In its early days, the Internet used only a limited number of fonts. But with the introduction of the graphically oriented World Wide Web and the spreading recognition of the Internet's possibilities, users demanded greater typeface options than the Internet was capable of providing.

Typeface limitations revived the old problem of making onscreen and printed output look the same. Widespread efforts are being made to overcome the typeface limitations inherent in existing HTML specifications. The World Wide Web Consortium, an organization founded to develop common protocols for the evolution of the Web, has identified the following typeface-related needs that must be addressed to give users greater flexibility in their use of fonts on the Internet or on intranets:

A font format that supports resolution independence, kerning, and ligatures

A mechanism for downloading fonts and converting them to the platform format

An inventory of fonts available over the Internet, and copyright protection and payment schemes for those fonts

A means for addressing, naming, and matching fonts on the Web

 For information and discussion of developments regarding fonts and the World Web Wide, visit the World Wide Web Consortium's Fonts and the Web page at http://www.w3.org/Fonts/. You can find a mailing list for font/Web issues at www-font; subscribe by sending the word *subscribe* to www-font-request@w3.org.

EMBEDDING TRUETYPE FONTS

To overcome the problem of disrupted document formatting due to changed fonts, font vendors are incorporating font embedding technology that allows you to embed the needed fonts in the document file.

Windows 98 supports TrueType font embedding. Four levels of font embedding exist, and the TrueType font vendor builds the embedding level into the font. The embedding levels include the following:

1. Restricted license—No embedding allowed.
2. Print and preview—Document must be opened as read-only. Fonts must be installed temporarily on the remote system.
3. Editable—The selected font can be viewed on the monitor and printed, and the host document can be edited but must be installed temporarily on the remote system.
4. Installable—The embedded fonts can be viewed, printed, edited, and permanently installed on another computer and used in other applications.

Tip #117

A useful tool for embedding is Microsoft's font properties extension for Windows. Download the free self-extracting file ttftext.exe from http://www.microsoft.com/typography/property/property.htm. When the software is installed, the font properties extension (see Figure 18.10) adds tabs to the Properties screen to give you additional information about a font. Activating the Embedding tab tells you the embedding level of the font.

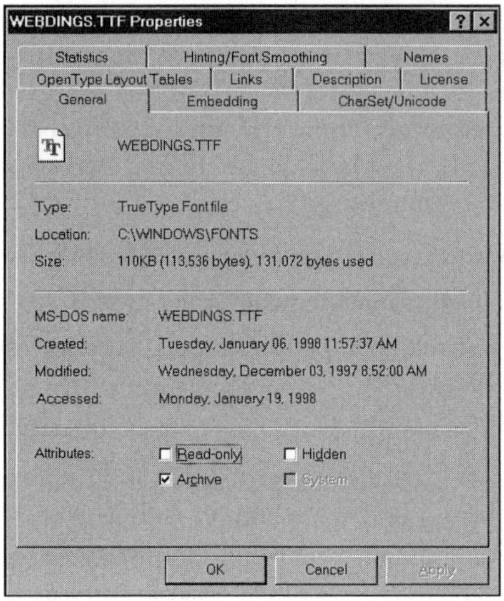

Figure 18.10
You can install the Font Properties extension applet for more information about your font files.

To save a file with embedded fonts in a Windows application such as Microsoft Word 97, follow these steps:

1. In the Document window, choose File, Save As.

2. Select Options.

3. Select Embed TrueType fonts.

4. Choose OK.

MOVING TO OPENTYPE FONTS

OpenType is a new format initiative by Microsoft and Adobe, aimed at making it easier for users to use and organize sets of TrueType and PostScript Type 1 fonts onscreen and in print. An OpenType font can have TrueType outlines, Type 1 outlines, or both. Type 1 files can be rasterized by a Type 1 rasterizer or converted to TrueType data for rasterization.

The OpenType format enables Web page designers to use high-quality fonts in their online documents. The new format should also reduce download times.

DEALING WITH INTERNATIONAL CHARACTER SETS

Windows 98 offers multilanguage support. Windows 98 supports Greek; Turkish; and the Baltic, Central European, and Cyrillic language groups. With this support enabled, you can view documents written in these scripts. With multilanguage support installed, a 652-character set is available in the Arial, Courier New, and Times Roman fonts.

To install the multilanguage support, follow this procedure:

1. Click on Start, point to Settings, activate Control Panel, and select Add/Remove Programs.

2. Choose the Windows Setup tab, check Multilanguage Support, and then activate Details.

3. Place check marks next to the languages you want to include.

4. Choose OK and then choose OK again to restart your computer and make the changes take effect.

If you want to write or edit documents in any of these languages, you must add keyboard support for the language. To do so, follow these steps:

1. Click on Start, point to Settings, activate Control Panel, and select Keyboard.

2. Select the Language tab and then activate Add.

3. Select the languages you want.

4. Check the Enable Indicator on taskbar box.

When you have installed multilanguage and keyboard support, the language indicator is displayed on the taskbar. You can choose a toggle (Left Alt+Shift or Ctrl+Shift) to switch between two language scripts. The taskbar shows the language currently active (see Figure 18.11).

PART

IV

CH

18

Figure 18.11
The active language (in this example, EN for English) is displayed on the Windows 98 taskbar.

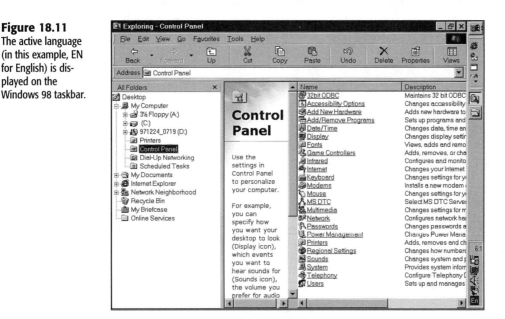

Windows 98 supports other languages such as Japanese, Chinese, Korean, and Arabic, but you must buy a language-specific version of the program to do so. These versions also support the pan-European language groups.

Secrets of Mastering the Windows 98 Environment: Working with Multilanguage Content

If you are working with multilanguage content in your documents, any Win32 application that supports "international services" automatically activates the correct fonts and corresponding keyboard layouts. This feature facilitates editing language-specific text within a document.

Most Win32-based applications can determine the language used in a document by marking the text with a language-specific identifier. Then the application is able to use the spell checker, thesaurus, hyphenation engine, and grammar checker that are specific to the language being checked.

To use the multilanguage font capabilities in Windows 98, follow these steps:

1. Install multilanguage support under Windows 98 (described earlier).
2. Make sure your application uses the Win32 NLS API. You can check the documentation that came with the application for more information.
3. Use the application's dialog boxes to set the font attributes and indicate the language attributes of selected text.

CHAPTER 19

SETTING UP WINDOWS 98 MULTIMEDIA

In this chapter

INTRODUCING ACTIVEMOVIE

Windows 98 extends and improves the video-handling talents found in Windows 95. The old Media Player applet is still on hand to play back video files, but the new video workhorse is ActiveMovie. This up-to-date facility provides a one-stop shop for popular video formats.

UNDERSTANDING THE VIDEO PROPERTIES DIALOG BOX

You can instantly find information on any video file by right-clicking its icon and selecting Properties from the shortcut menu. The Properties dialog box includes three tabs: General, Details, and Preview. The General tab contains information such as file size and dates.

You find useful information in the Details sheet, as shown in Figure 19.1. In addition to the runtime of the video clip, the Details sheet contains information on the audio and video encoding schemes used to create the file—potentially very useful information if you're trying to get optimal performance. The Video format section includes helpful data on the pixel resolution of the captured video, as well as the frame rate and data rate.

Figure 19.1
Detailed information about frame rates, playback data rates, and capture resolutions can help you troubleshoot video playback problems.

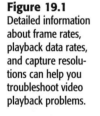

Click the Preview tab, and you can view the selected video clip directly from the Properties dialog box. Click the Play button. The slider bar control, which scrolls to the right as the video plays, lets you jump to any portion of the clip. To stop the clip, click the Stop button.

 If you are having problems playing video files, see "Problems Playing Video Files" in the "Troubleshooting" section at the end of this chapter.

PLAYING VIDEO FILES

Windows 98 provides two applets for playing back digital video clips. They are

- ActiveMovie control
- Media Player

New to Windows 98 is the ActiveMovie control. This applet takes over the video-handling duties from the venerable Media Player and adds greater file support and better performance, though you can still use Media Player to view files with the .AVI extension.

The easiest way to play a video clip in Windows 98 is to launch it directly from Windows 98 Explorer by selecting the icon. The ActiveMovie player launches, and the video begins playing after a brief pause.

PLAYING VIDEO FILES FROM ACTIVEMOVIE

To use the ActiveMovie control to play a video, do the following:

1. Open the ActiveMovie control from the Windows 98 Start menu by clicking Start, Programs, Accessories, Entertainment, ActiveMovie Control.
2. In the Open dialog box, select Movie Files from the Files of Type drop-down control.
3. Navigate to the directory that contains the file you want to play. Any files with valid video file extensions (.AVI, .MPG) appear in the dialog box.
4. Click the Open button. The ActiveMovie control appears.

Tip #118

If the ActiveMovie player is already open, you can play back videos by dragging and dropping the desired file's icon onto the ActiveMovie window.

PART

IV

CH

19

5. Click the Play button. The video clip begins playing.
6. To stop playback, click the Stop button.

PLAYING VIDEO FILES FROM MEDIA PLAYER

To play your video clips from the Media Player, do the following:

1. Open the Media Player applet from the Windows 98 Start menu by clicking Start, Programs, Accessories, Entertainment, Media Player.
2. Select File, Open to go to the Open dialog box.
3. Click the Files of Type drop-down control and select Video (*.avi).
4. Navigate to the directory that contains the file you want to play. All files with the .AVI file extension appear in the dialog box.

Tip #119

You can launch files from the Device menu. Click Device and then select the media type from the numbered list. The Open dialog box then appears, displaying only files matching the selected type.

5. Click the Open button. The filename appears in the window bar of the Media Player.

6. Click the Play button. The AVI file begins playing. The slider control advances as the file plays.

7. To stop the file, click the Stop button.

WORKING WITH ACTIVEMOVIE VIDEO

In addition to providing support for many video file formats beyond AVI, ActiveMovie provides useful tool controls to customize video playback.

OPEN AN ACTIVEMOVIE FILE

You can load a video file into ActiveMovie by dragging and dropping any recognized video file type, including AVI and MPEG, onto the Application window. The file takes a few seconds to load, during which time the application bar displays something like the following:

```
Demo.avi (Opening)
```

After it's loaded, ActiveMovie displays file information in the Interface window:

■ The total file runtime is shown at the left.

■ The current position in the file is displayed in large characters in the center, as measured in either frames or seconds. (The word frame or time appears directly below the number to identify the unit of measure.)

PLAY AN ACTIVEMOVIE FILE

To play a file, do any of the following:

■ Double-click anywhere on the information display or the Video window.

■ Right-click anywhere on the information display or Video window and select Run from the context menu.

■ Click the Play control button at the bottom of the window.

EXPLORE THE PROPERTIES RESOURCE

You can optimize video playback by right-clicking the ActiveMovie display interface and selecting Properties from the context menu. The ActiveMovie Control Properties window includes four tabs:

- Playback—Selects the section of the clip to play back and sets the clip to rewind or keep playing upon reaching the end.
- Movie Size—Sets the size of the Video playback window.
- Controls—Customizes ActiveMovie interface elements.
- Advanced—Provides information on ActiveMovie filters.

USING THE PLAYBACK SHEET

The Playback Properties sheet provides useful tools for controlling the way the open audio file plays, as shown in Figure 19.2.

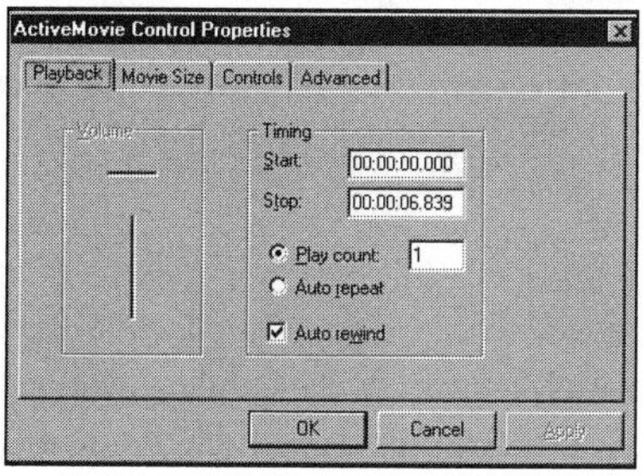

Figure 19.2
Select a section of the file to play or make a file play over a specific number of times from the Playback sheet.

The slider bars in the Volume area are grayed out, but you can still tweak your video clips from the Timing area of the Playback sheet by doing the following:

- Enter a time value into the Start and Stop text boxes to constrain playback to a desired portion of the audio file.

> **Note**
>
> The format of the Start and Stop boxes depends on whether you have selected a time-based or frame-based display of the video clip duration. For precise work, frame values are generally more convenient to use than are time values.

- To play a file over a specific number of times, activate the Play Count radio button and enter the desired value in the text box.
- To play a file over continuously until interrupted, click the Auto Repeat radio button.
- To automatically reset the file to the beginning after it plays, check the Auto Rewind check box.

USING THE MOVIE SIZE SHEET

The Movie Size sheet lets you set the size of the Playback window for the open file. Click the Select the Movie Size drop-down list item to see the following size options:

- Original Size—Playback window is the same size as that at which the original video was captured.

- Double Original Size—Doubles the height and width of the original captured video.

- 1/16 of Screen Size—Plays in a window that is 1/16 the size of the current display area.

- 1/4 of Screen Size—Plays in a window that is one-fourth the size of the current display area.

- 1/2 of Screen Size—Plays in a window that is half the size of the current display area.

- Maximized—Plays in a standard Playback window that occupies the entire display.

Caution

> Playing video at expanded resolutions can reduce frame rates and result in jerky playback, as the central processing unit (CPU) and graphics card struggle to output the increased number of graphics pixels. A doubled Video window, for example, contains four times the graphics information of a video played at native resolution (two times the height plus two times the width yields a four-times increase in pixels).

Like the Maximized option, checking the Run Full Screen check box causes the open video file to expand to the size of the display. However, this mode does not run in a standard Playback window; instead, all the other elements on the display are disabled to allow the video playback to take over the screen. For systems with older graphics cards, this dedicated Video playback mode can help boost the playback frame rate of full-screen video clips.

USING THE CONTROLS SHEET

The Controls sheet gives you access to interface controls for playing files:

- Check the Display Panel check box to show the file information box.

- Check the Control Panel check box to display the VCR-like control buttons and the Trackbar slider bar.

- Inside the Control Panel area, check any of the Position controls, Selection controls, and Trackbar check boxes to make the appropriate controls available on the ActiveMovie interface.

- From the Colors area, you can customize the ActiveMovie display panel by selecting colors from the Foreground and Background Color buttons.

WORKING WITH MEDIA PLAYER VIDEO

With its improved performance, wider file support, and enhanced features for developers, ActiveMovie is the video playback tool for Windows 98. Still, Microsoft has kept the Media Player applet around for those who want to use it. After a file is loaded into Media Player, you can access a number of controls from the menu bar.

WORKING WITH THE OPTIONS DIALOG BOX

The Options dialog box lets you control how video clips play back. To open the Options dialog box, click Edit, Options. You can do the following from the Options dialog box:

- Check the Auto Rewind check box to set the file back to the beginning after it stops playing.

- Check the Auto Repeat check box to have the video play until stopped by the user.

The OLE Object area, shown in Figure 19.3, contains tools for customizing playback of video files within external applications, such as word processors or spreadsheets:

Figure 19.3
You can customize the playback of video files inside other applications by using the Media Player's Options dialog box.

PART

IV

Сн

19

- Check the Control Bar on Playback check box to have VCR-like control buttons appear beneath the embedded Video window inside documents. Enter the name you want to appear with embedded clips in the Caption text box.

- Check the Border Around Object check box to have a thin border appear around the embedded video image.

- Check the Play in Client Document check box to have the video clip play in its window without invoking the Media Player interface.

- Check the Dither Picture to VGA Colors check box to use the basic 16-color palette in the Playback window.

> **Note**
> The dither control should be used only with systems with very limited graphics resources, such as graphics boards that cannot support 16-bit color output. Dithering to the limited VGA palette results in very poor color reproduction, making many video clips unusable.

Working with the Selection Dialog Box

Click Edit, Selection to go to the Selection dialog box. From here, you can demarcate a portion of the file to be played back or to be sent to another application.

- Click All to select the entire audio file; then, you can copy the entire file for pasting elsewhere.
- Click None to clear any existing selection.
- Click From to enter the start point (measured in minutes:seconds:tenths) of the selected area. Enter the endpoint in the To box or enter the length of the desired selection in the Size box.

Note

The position information in the From, To, and Size boxes appears as either number of frames or in amount of time (minutes:seconds:tenths), depending on which format (either frames or time) you select from the Scale menu item.

Working with the Device Menu

You also find useful tools in the Device menu:

- To open files from the Device menu, simply click the desired file type, which appears in a numbered list. The Open dialog box is constrained to files with the extension matching the type you selected.
- To launch the Windows 98 Volume Control applet, click Device, Volume Control.

→ To learn more about the Volume Control applet, **see** "Working with the Volume Control Tool," later in this chapter.

Using the Video Properties Dialog Box

Click Properties under the Device menu to go to the Video Properties dialog box. Here, you can set the size of the Playback window for the open file, as shown in Figure 19.4. A representation of a monitor with a Video window serves as a guide to let you preview the size of the Video window. Click the Window drop-down list item to see the following size options:

Caution

As with ActiveMovie, expanding the Video window can impair system performance.

Figure 19.4
The Video Properties dialog box previews the size of the adjusted Video window.

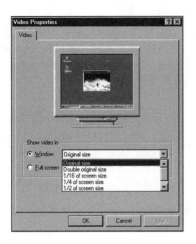

The Full Screen radio button sets the video file to play back at the full size of the display. However, this mode does not run in a standard Playback window; instead, all the other elements on the display are disabled to allow the video playback to take over the screen. For systems with older graphics cards, this dedicated Video playback mode can help boost the playback frame rate of full-screen video clips.

WORKING WITH VIDEO IN THE WINDOWS 98 DEVICE MANAGER

The Windows 98 Device Manager provides access to all hardware settings. Here, you can examine the graphics settings that may be affecting video playback. To access graphics controls under the Device Manager, do the following:

1. Click Start, Settings, Control Panel and then click the System icon.

2. Click the Device Manager tab.

3. Click the (+) symbol next to the item called Display Adapters. The name of the currently loaded driver appears beneath the entry.

4. Select the device that appears and select Properties.

The Properties dialog box features three tabs: General, Driver, and Resources. The General sheet provides basic information, such as the manufacturer of the device driver and the hardware it is tailored for.

Click the Resources tab, and you find the standard resource interface for Windows 98 hardware. The display lets you view and adjust memory address settings for the graphics adapter.

PART

IV

CH

19

Note

You are unlikely to use this facility to fix conflicts with the display hardware because any such conflict would render the display inoperable. However, you might be able to cross-reference the address information provided with that shown in another device's Resource sheet. This technique is useful for determining which devices are in conflict.

A welcome new feature of Windows 98 is the addition of the Driver sheet. Two buttons appear at the bottom of the sheet. The Driver File Details button lets you view the actual driver files used to operate the graphics adapter. More interesting is the Upgrade Driver button, which launches the Windows 98 automated hardware update scheme. To automatically upgrade your graphics adapter driver (see Figure 19.5), do the following:

1. Click Start, Settings, Control Panel and then click the System icon.
2. Click the Device Manager tab.
3. Click the (+) symbol next to the item called Display adapters. The name of the currently loaded driver appears beneath the entry.
4. Select the device that appears and select Properties.
5. Click the Driver tab and click the Upgrade Driver button.
6. Click the Next button.
7. Click the top radio button to search for a newer driver and click Next.
8. Activate the appropriate check boxes to find the newest driver software. In most cases, you will want to check the Microsoft Windows Update check box to check Microsoft's Internet-based index of driver updates.
9. The Internet Download Agent launches, connecting you to the Internet and taking you to the appropriate driver site.
10. Follow the instructions to download the device driver software and install it on your system. You must restart your PC after you are finished.

⚠ *If you are experiencing graphics problems, see "Resolving Graphics Problems" in the "Troubleshooting" section at the end of the chapter.*

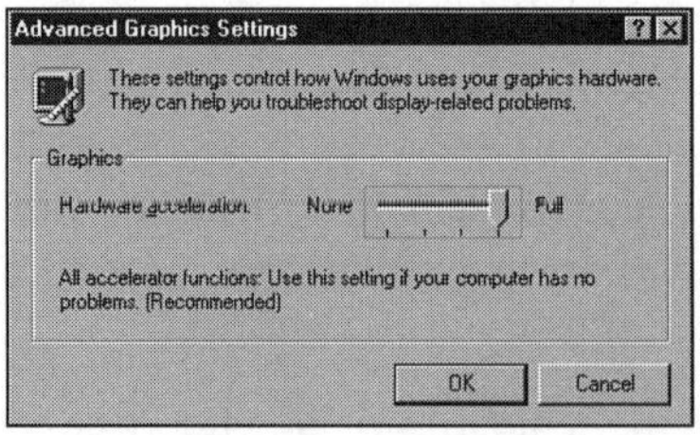

Figure 19.5
The Advanced Graphics Settings dialog box lets you incrementally turn off hardware acceleration features to improve stability.

WORKING WITH THE MULTIMEDIA PROPERTIES CONTROLS

The Multimedia Properties dialog box, found in the Control Panel, provides access to a variety of multimedia settings under Windows 98. To open the Multimedia Properties dialog box, click Start, Settings, Control Panel. Click the Multimedia icon, and the Properties dialog box appears.

Five tabs are arrayed across the top of the Multimedia Properties dialog box. Two of these directly affect video playback:

- Video—Lets you size Video playback windows.
- Advanced—Provides access to driver and configuration settings for all audio, video, and other multimedia devices.

USING THE VIDEO SHEET

The Video sheet of the Multimedia Properties dialog box provides the same Video window size controls found in both the ActiveMovie and Media Player applets. When you select a window size option, the image of the display updates to show a facsimile of what the clip will look like. Click the Window drop-down list item, and you see the following options:

- Original Size—Playback window is the same size as that at which the original video was captured.
- Double Original Size—Doubles the height and width of the original captured video.
- 1/16 of Screen Size—Plays in a window that is 1/16 the size of the current display area.
- 1/4 of Screen Size—Plays in a window that is one-fourth the size of the current display area.
- 1/2 of Screen Size—Plays in a window that is half the size of the current display area.
- Maximized—Plays in a standard Playback window that occupies the entire display.

PART
IV

CH
19

The Full Screen radio button sets the video file to play back at the full size of the display. However, this mode does not run in a standard Playback window; instead, all the other elements on the display are disabled to allow the video playback to take over the screen. For systems with older graphics cards, this dedicated Video playback mode can help boost the playback frame rate of full-screen video clips.

WORKING WITH THE DEVICES SHEET

The Devices sheet of the Multimedia Properties dialog box gives you access to drivers and hardware configurations for video devices and other multimedia components. The sheet provides a list of multimedia components under the Multimedia Drivers heading. To view the installed devices for a given component, click the (+) symbol next to the item.

When it comes to video controls, the most important stop is the entry called Video Compression Codecs. Here, you find a laundry list of video compression/decompression drivers, as shown in Figure 19.6, which allow the ActiveMovie and Media Player applets to recognize and play back digital video files.

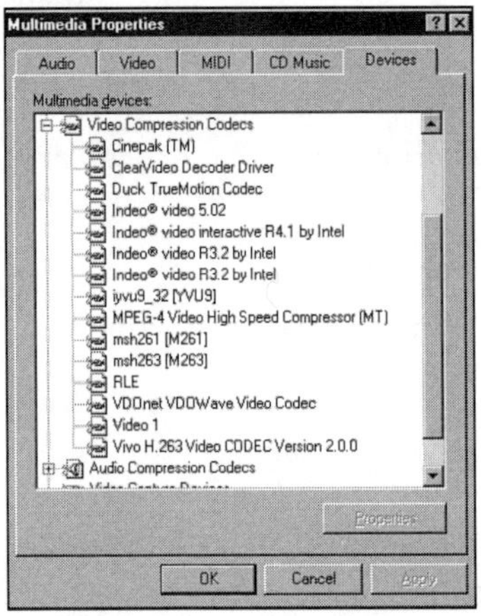

Figure 19.6

More codecs than you can shake a stick at: The Devices tab lets you see what types of video files your PC is equipped to handle.

You can view the controls and properties associated with each codec by selecting an item and clicking the Properties button. The Properties dialog box also lets you remove the selected codec. Some codec property boxes also include a Settings button, which may simply provide a splash screen showing the vendor and date—such as with the Cinepak codecs—or may provide controls for managing compression settings.

Also under the Devices tab is a heading for Video Capture devices. Here, you find driver entries for video capture cards, parallel port cameras (such as Connectix's QuickCam), and other video input devices. Individual configuration options for these devices—which are provided by the vendor—may be available from the Devices sheet by using the Settings tab. If you do not have a capture device installed, the Video Capture Device item does not contain any underlying entries.

INTRODUCING DVD VIDEO

One of the most significant advances in PC-based multimedia is the *Digital Video Display*, or *DVD*. Based on 5.25-inch discs that look identical to CD-ROMs, DVD-ROM can store up to 4.7GB on a single side. Down the road, enhanced DVD-ROM discs will be able to nearly double the amount of data on each side. The standard also allows for two-sided discs, meaning that DVD-ROM discs will eventually hold as much as 17GB of data—perfect for broadcast-quality, high-resolution video.

In fact, DVD uses the same MPEG-2 video format seen in Direct Satellite Services (DSS) such as DirecTV, USSB, and PrimeStar. The problem is that MPEG-2 video is very complex, requiring hardware-based decompression to provide smooth playback of the broadcast-quality video. Although fast MMX-enhanced PCs can play MPEG-2 video, hardware is needed to make it acceptable for viewing.

Windows 98 provides support for DVD-ROM drives and hardware, including components for handling MPEG-2 video and AC-3 surround sound audio. However, you must make sure that you have the proper drivers to operate the DVD-ROM drive and the add-in board. Check with your vendor.

USING AUDIO TOOLS IN WINDOWS

Windows 98 provides a variety of tools to let you play, edit, and create audio files. In addition to maintaining the familiar Windows 95 tools, Windows 98 introduces new tools, such as the ActiveMovie control.

PC-based audio comes in two forms: wave audio and musical instrument digital interface (MIDI). Wave audio, or WAV files, are digital representations of analog sound. When you record speech or music to the hard disk, for example, the resulting file is a wave audio file.

MIDI files use a series of commands to tell the PC sound hardware what notes and instruments to play. This makes for smaller files, but you are limited by the library of instruments available to your hardware and software.

UNDERSTANDING THE AUDIO PROPERTIES DIALOG BOX

PART
IV

CH
19

You can find information on any audio file by right-clicking any WAV or MIDI file icon and selecting the Properties item from the shortcut menu. The Properties sheet for WAV and MIDI files displays key information on the size, length, and format of the file. The General sheet displays file size and type information. Click the Details tab for useful information such as the encoding scheme used to create a WAV file, as well as the duration of WAV and MIDI files (see Figure 19.7). You can sample both WAV and MIDI files from the Preview sheet of the Properties dialog box by clicking the Play button on the sheet. The clip plays directly from the sheet.

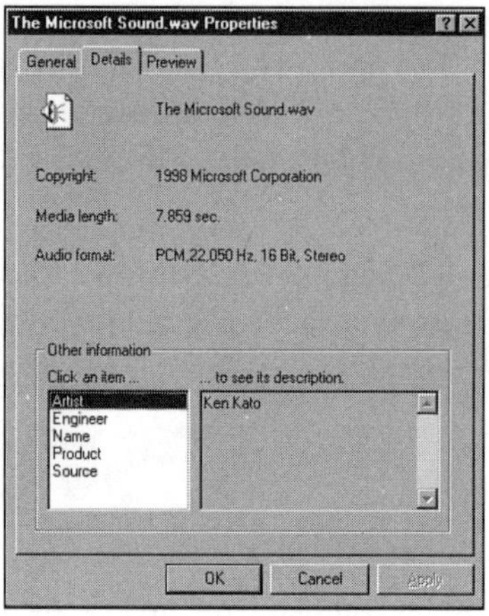

Figure 19.7
From the Details tab, you can check useful information such as the encoding format of WAV files and the overall runtime of the audio clip.

PLAYING AUDIO FILES

Windows 98 provides several ways to play back wave audio files, including the following:

- ActiveMovie control
- Sound Recorder
- Media Player

Both the Media Player and Sound Recorder are unchanged from Windows 95. The ActiveMovie control, however, is new and is an important resource for handling audio.

The easiest way to play a WAV or MIDI file in Windows 98 is to launch it directly from Windows 98 Explorer. For MIDI files, the ActiveMovie player launches, and the file begins playing immediately. For WAV files, the Sound Recorder applet launches. In both cases, the applet closes as soon as the file finishes playing.

PLAYING AUDIO FILES FROM ACTIVEMOVIE

To play an audio file using the ActiveMovie control, do the following:

1. Open the ActiveMovie control from the Windows 98 Start menu by clicking Start, Programs, Accessories, Multimedia, ActiveMovie Control.
2. In the Open dialog box, select Audio Files from the Files of Type drop-down control.
3. Navigate to the directory that contains the file you want to play. Any files with valid audio file extensions (.WAV, .MID) appear in the dialog box.
4. Click the Open button. The ActiveMovie control appears.

Tip #120

If the ActiveMovie player is already open, you can play audio files by dragging and dropping the desired file's icon onto the ActiveMovie window.

5. Click the Play button. The WAV or MIDI file begins playing, as shown in Figure 19.8.

Figure 19.8
A position bar and time display prompt you during playback of files under ActiveMovie.

6. To stop the file, click the Stop button.

PLAYING AUDIO FILES FROM SOUND RECORDER

You can also play wave audio files from the Windows 98 Sound Recorder. Follow these steps:

1. Open the Sound Recorder applet from the Windows 98 Start menu by clicking Start, Programs, Accessories, Entertainment, Sound Recorder.

2. Select File, Open and navigate to the WAV file to be played from the Open dialog box.

3. Click the Open button.

4. The Sound Recorder interface reappears. Click the Play button to hear the sound file.

5. Click the Stop button to stop playing the file.

PLAYING AUDIO FILES FROM MEDIA PLAYER

To play audio files from the Windows 98 Media Player, do the following:

1. Open the Media Player applet from the Windows 98 Start menu by clicking Start, Programs, Accessories, Entertainment, Media Player.

2. Select File, Open to go to the Open dialog box.

3. Click the Files of Type drop-down control and select either Sound (*.wav) or MIDI Sequencer (*.mid; *.rmi).

4. Navigate to the directory that contains the file you want to play. All files with the selected audio file extension appear in the dialog box.

PART
IV

CH
19

Tip #121

You can launch files from the Device menu. Click Device and then select the media type from the numbered list. The Open dialog box then appears, displaying only files matching the selected type.

---

5. Click the Open button. The filename appears in the window bar of the Media Player.

6. Click the Play button. The WAV or MIDI file begins playing. The slider control advances as the file plays.

7. To stop the file, click the Stop button.

PLAYING AUDIO CDs

Like Windows 95, Windows 98 lets you play audio CDs in your CD-ROM drive by using the CD Player applet, shown in Figure 19.9. To play CDs, do the following:

Figure 19.9
The CD Player applet provides all the functions of a standard audio CD player.

1. Open the CD Player applet from the Windows 98 Start menu by clicking Start, Programs, Accessories, Multimedia, CD Player.
2. Place an audio CD into the CD-ROM drive.
3. Click the Play button just to the right of the information display screen.
4. Jump to the previous or next track by clicking the Back or Forward buttons.
5. To reverse or fast forward within a track, click the appropriate Reverse and Fast Forward buttons until you reach the desired point in the song.
6. To stop play, click the Stop button. Or, click the Pause button to keep your place in the current track.
7. Eject the audio CD by clicking the Eject/Load button.

WORKING WITH THE WINDOWS 98 SOUND RECORDER

If you want to record or edit WAV files in Windows 98, use the Sound Recorder applet. This section introduces you to Windows 98 audio editing and recording.

When you open a file in Sound Recorder, you see a visual representation of the audio file, including a status bar that indicates how far along in the file you are. The buttons beneath the slider bar control operations such as fast forward and rewind, similar to a tape recorder. Position shows the current point in the audio file, and Length tells you the complete duration of the file in seconds.

The File menu contains a number of familiar options, including facilities for saving audio files. The Revert command lets you undo edits.

Recording WAV Files with Sound Recorder

If you want to record a WAV audio file, the only option within Windows 98 is the Sound Recorder applet. To record an audio file, do the following:

1. Open the Sound Recorder by clicking Start, Programs, Accessories, Entertainment, Sound Recorder.
2. To begin recording, click the red Record button.
3. When you are done recording, click the Stop button.
4. Prepare to save the file by clicking File, Save As.
5. Click the Change button in the Save As dialog box.
6. In the Sound Selection dialog box, set the audio quality for the file. You can select telephone, radio, or CD quality settings from the Name drop-down box, or you can fine-tune the file encoding by selecting from the Format and Attributes drop-down boxes.
7. Click OK and then click Save to save the file to the desired subdirectory.

Editing WAV Files

Sound Recorder provides some useful editing tools that let you enhance existing WAV files. These capabilities can be accessed from the application menus.

- Insert a WAV file within another WAV file—Go to the point in the open file where you want to insert a file and click Edit, InsertFile. From the Insert File dialog box, select the file you want to insert.
- Mix two sound files together—With the initial WAV file open, click Edit, Mix with File. From the Mix with File dialog box, select the file you want to mix with the original WAV file.
- Delete part of a WAV file—To shave a portion off the front or back of an open WAV file, go to the desired point in the file and click Edit. Select either Delete Before Current Position or Delete After Current Position. The file now begins or ends at the selected point.
- Adjust volume and speed—From the Effects menu, click IncreaseVolume (by 25%) or DecreaseVolume to make the file play back louder or quieter. To speed or slow the rate of playback, click Effects, Increase Speed (by 100%) or Decrease Speed.
- Reverse playback of the file—To play the open WAV file from back to front, click Effects, Reverse.
- Add an echo—Click Effects, Add Echo to include an echo effect in the sound file.

PART
IV

CH
19

Saving WAV Files

When you save WAV files in Sound Recorder, you can set the compression and audio format to best suit your needs. Although recordings of your favorite CDs require high-fidelity digital playback, simple sound effects and speech clips can use formats that consume less space. Click File, Save As; and in the Save As dialog box click the Change button. The Sound Selection dialog box lets you set the compression format and bit rate and depth of the WAV file.

From the Name drop-down control, select from one of three options, as shown in Figure 19.10.

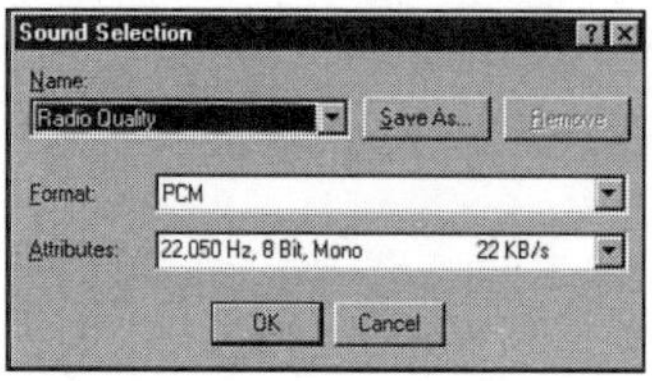

Figure 19.10
The Sound Selection dialog lets you select from precooked audio formats, or you can roll customized schemes of your own.

- CD Quality—16-bit, 44.1kHz, stereo
- Radio Quality—8-bit, 22.05kHz, mono
- Telephone Quality—8-bit, 11.025kHz, mono

The CD Quality option is best for recorded music or any clip that requires the most precise playback. Radio Quality is a good compromise for music or speech clips because it conserves disk space while keeping much of the audio fidelity. Telephone Quality minimizes file sizes but results in limited audio quality.

WORKING WITH ACTIVEMOVIE AUDIO

You can use ActiveMovie to play WAV and MIDI files. In both cases, the new applet gives you a number of controls to let you customize playback.

OPEN AN ACTIVEMOVIE FILE

You can load a file into ActiveMovie by dragging and dropping a WAV or MIDI file onto the Application window. The file takes a few seconds to load, during which time the application bar displays something like

```
Canyon.mid (Opening)
```

After a file is loaded into ActiveMovie, file information appears in the black window:

- The total file runtime appears at the left.
- The current position in the file appears in large characters in the center (the word time appears directly below it).

PLAY AN ACTIVEMOVIE FILE

To play a file, do any of the following:

- Double-click anywhere on the black window.
- Right-click anywhere on the black window and select Run from the context menu that appears.
- Click the Play control button at the bottom of the window.

EXPLORE THE PROPERTIES RESOURCE

You can optimize audio playback by right-clicking the ActiveMovie display interface and selecting Properties from the context menu. The ActiveMovie Control Properties window includes four tabs:

- Playback—Controls volume and playback selection.
- Movie Size—Sets the size of the video playback window.
- Controls—Customizes ActiveMovie interface elements.
- Advanced—Provides information on ActiveMovie filters.

Of these, Playback and Controls are important for audio playback.

USING PLAYBACK PROPERTIES

The Playback Properties sheet provides useful tools for controlling the way the open audio file plays, as shown in Figure 19.11.

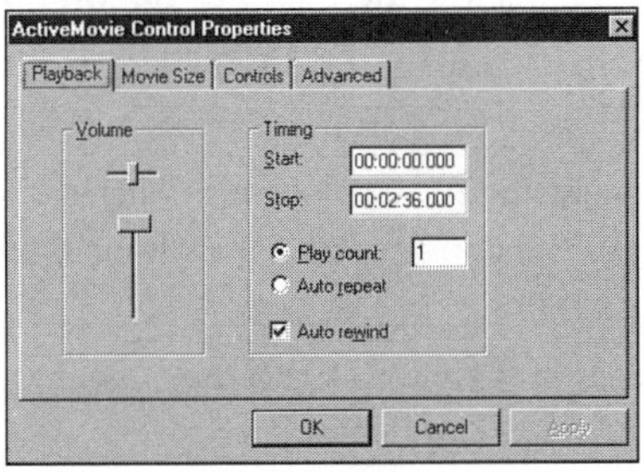

Figure 19.11
Volume and Timing controls let you customize playback of audio files.

Slider bars located in the Volume area on the left side of the Playback sheet control volume and balance:

- Slide the vertical slider bar up or down to increase or decrease playback volume.
- Slide the horizontal slider bar to the left to increase output on the left speaker or to the right to increase output on the right speaker.

In the Timing area, you can do the following:

- Enter a time value into the Start and Stop text boxes to constrain playback to a desired portion of the audio file.

- To play a file a specific number of times, enter the desired value into the Play Count text box.

- To play a file continuously until stopped, click the Auto Repeat radio button.

- To automatically reset the file to the beginning after it plays, check the Auto Rewind check box.

USING CONTROLS PROPERTIES

The Controls Properties sheet gives you access to interface controls for playing files, as shown in Figure 19.12.

Figure 19.12
You can slim down the ActiveMovie interface by turning off many of the VCR-like control elements on the display. You can even tweak the colors.

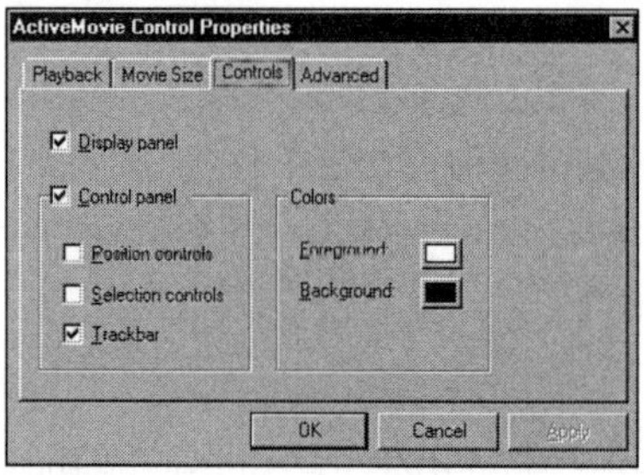

- Check the Display Panel check box to show the file information box.

- Check the Control Panel check box to display the VCR-like control buttons and the Trackbar slider bar.

- Inside the Control Panel area, check any of the Position controls, Selection controls, and Trackbar check boxes to make the appropriate controls available on the ActiveMovie interface.

- From the Colors area, you can customize the ActiveMovie display panel by selecting colors from the Foreground and Background color buttons.

WORKING WITH MEDIA PLAYER AUDIO

In Windows 98, ActiveMovie replaces the Media Player applet, but the program is still available if you want to use it. After a file is loaded into Media Player, you can access a number of controls from the menu bar.

WORKING WITH THE OPTIONS DIALOG BOX

The Options dialog box lets you control how audio files play back. To open the Options dialog box, click Edit, Options. You can do the following from the Options dialog box:

- Check the Auto Rewind check box to set the file back to the beginning after it stops playing.
- Check the Auto Repeat check box to have the file play continuously until stopped by the user.

The OLE Object area contains tools for customizing playback of audio files within separate applications:

- Check the Control Bar on Playback check box to display VCR-like control buttons audio clips embedded into documents. Enter the name you want to appear with embedded clips into the Caption text box.
- Check the Border Around Object check box to add a thin border around the embedded audio file icon.
- Check the Play in Client Document check box to have the audio clip play without invoking the Media Player interface.

You can also find useful tools in the Device menu:

- To open files from the Device menu, simply click the desired file type, which appears in a numbered list. The Open dialog box is constrained to files with the extension matching the type you selected.
- To launch the Windows 98 Volume Control applet, click Device, Volume Control.

→ For more on the Volume Control applet, **see** "Working with the Volume Control Tool," later in this chapter.

- Click Device, Properties to access the MCI Waveform Device Setup. Here, you can adjust the size of the WAV audio buffer by sliding the horizontal scrollbar to the left or right, as shown in Figure 19.13.

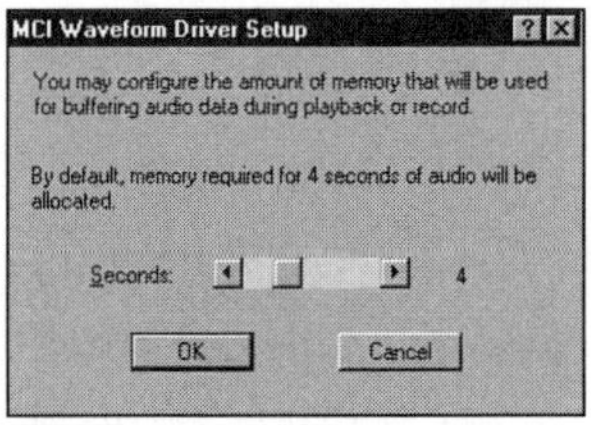

Figure 19.13
Avoid choppy audio playback by increasing the memory buffer in the MCI Waveform Driver Setup dialog box.

PART
IV

CH
19

WORKING WITH THE SELECTION DIALOG BOX

Click Edit, Selection to go to the Selection dialog box. From here, you can demarcate a portion of the file to be copied to the Windows 98 Clipboard.

- Click All to select the entire audio file, allowing you to copy the entire file for pasting elsewhere.

- Click None to clear any existing selection.

- Click From to enter the start point (measured in minutes:seconds:tenths) of the selected area. Enter the endpoint in the To box or enter the length of the desired selection in the Size box.

USING THE CD PLAYER

The CD Player lets you create custom play lists by entering information about the currently loaded CD and then setting up the list of tracks you want to play. When the audio CD is later loaded, Windows 98 recognizes the unique bit pattern of the disc and calls up the information you entered. Other features are also available for tweaking playback.

CREATING A CUSTOM PLAY LIST

To create a custom play list for a loaded audio CD, do the following from the CD Player: Disc Settings dialog box shown in Figure 19.14:

Figure 19.14
The Play List feature is one of the most powerful options offered by the CD Player.

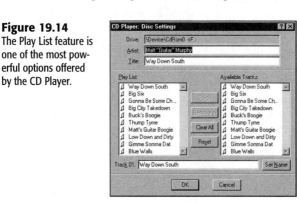

1. Click Disc, Edit Play List to bring up the CD Player: Disc Settings dialog box.

2. Enter the album's artist and title in the Artist and Title text boxes.

3. To name the album tracks, select a track in the Available Tracks scroll box and enter the song title in the Track text box. Click Set Name. Repeat for each track.

4. To build a play list, first select any tracks in the Play List scroll box you want to remove and click the Remove button.

Tip #122	You can select multiple tracks at once by holding down the Ctrl key while clicking on tracks. To select a range of continuous items, click on a track, hold down the Shift key, and then click the end track of the group. All the tracks from the first to last item are selected.

5. To reorder tracks, click the desired track and wait until the note icon appears above the selected item. Drag the item so that the position arrow to the left of the Play List scroll box points above the track you want to move to, and then release the mouse button.

6. You can restore any deleted tracks to the Play List scroll box by selecting the track in the Available Tracks scroll box and clicking the Add button.

TOURING THE CD PLAYER

The CD Player provides a lot of controls in its compact interface, matching the functionality of dedicated CD players.

In the View menu, you find the following capabilities:

- Toolbar hides and displays icons that let you set play lists, change the information display view, and adjust play rules.

- Disc/Track Info hides and displays the Artist, Title, and Track drop-down controls.

- Status Bar hides and displays text at the bottom of the applet showing total play time of the CD as well as the play time of the selected track. The status bar also provides information about icons on the toolbar.

- The Track Time Elapsed, Track Time Remaining, and Disc Time Remaining items determine which information appears in the main Display window of the CD Player applet.

- The Volume Control item launches the Windows 98 Volume Control applet.

In the Options menu, you find the following capabilities:

- The Random Order, Continuous Play, and Intro Play items let you determine how the CD Player moves through the tracks on the installed audio CD.

- The Preferences item reveals the Preferences dialog box where you can adjust the appearance of the display, limit the intro play length, and specify other options, as shown in Figure 19.15.

PART

IV

CH

19

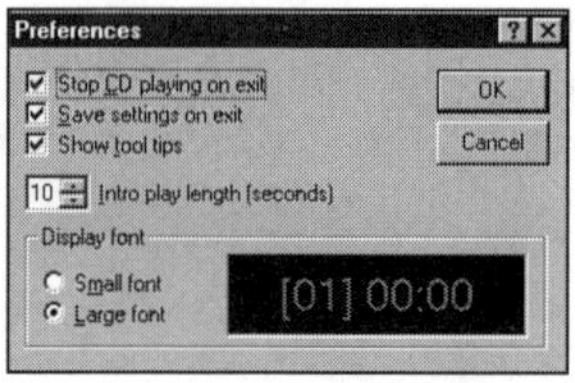

Figure 19.15
Use the Preferences
dialog box to tweak
the CD Player inter-
face and behavior.

WORKING WITH THE VOLUME CONTROL TOOL

Windows 98 provides a one-stop shop for tweaking the level and balance settings for your
sound card's various inputs and outputs. Not only can you adjust overall volume, you can
also adjust the volume and balance of individual inputs and outputs, including WAV and
MIDI audio output, and CD audio playback.

You can access the Volume Control in the following ways:

- Double-click the Speaker icon on the Windows 98 taskbar.

Tip #123

The easiest way to adjust volume is to click the Speaker icon on the taskbar. A small slider
bar control lets you adjust the volume level or mute the audio altogether. The small control
disappears after you click on any other area of the screen.

- Launch the applet from the Start button by clicking Start, Programs, Accessories,
  Entertainment, Volume Control.
- Launch the applet from the Media Player by clicking Device, Volume Control.

The Volume Control (shown in Figure 19.16) provides controls for playback and recording
operation, as well as for specific audio applications such as voice recognition. Each audio
component is represented with a horizontal slider bar to adjust balance and a vertical slider
to adjust volume. A check box allows you to turn a given component on or off.

Figure 19.16
The Windows 98
Volume Control is the
master control for set-
ting balance and
volume settings.

AVAILABLE CONTROLS

The default view for the Volume Control is for playback devices. The components that appear are listed in Table 19.1.

TABLE 19.1 COMPONENT SUPPORT IN THE VOLUME CONTROL TOOL

Control Name	Operation	What It Does
Volume Control	Playback	All audio output
Line-in	Playback, Record	Audio originating from the sound board's line-in port
Microphone	Playback, Record	Audio captured by the microphone
CD	Playback, Record	Audio played from the CD-ROM drive's analog out port
MIDI	Playback	Playback of MIDI files
Wave	Playback	Playback of wave files
Record Control	Record	All audio input
Voice Commands	Other	Voice input from microphone

ACCESSING VOLUME CONTROL CAPABILITIES

To access the volume control settings for playback, record, or other applications, click Options, Properties and then click the desired radio button in the Adjust Volume For area of the Properties dialog box.

In the Show the Following Volume Controls scrolling box, select the check box items you want to display in the Volume Control. Deselecting an item causes it to not be displayed when the Volume Control is launched.

If you have more than one audio device installed in your PC, you can select which device to work with. Select the desired device from the Mixer Device drop-down list.

WORKING WITH AUDIO IN THE WINDOWS 98 DEVICE MANAGER

If you want to tinker with hardware under Windows 98, you need to know your way around the Device Manager. To access audio controls under the Device Manager, do the following:

1. Click Start, Settings, Control Panel, and click the System icon.
2. Click the Device Manager tab.
3. Click the (+) symbol next to the item called Sound, Video and Game Controllers. An entry for your audio hardware appears, as shown in Figure 19.17.

PART

IV

CH

19

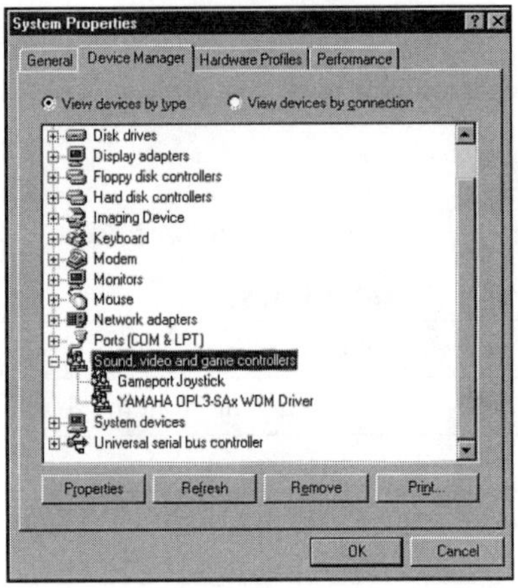

Figure 19.17
Click the Sound, Video and Game Controllers item, and the audio hardware installed on the computer appears.

4. Select the audio device that appears and select Properties.

The Properties dialog box features three tabs: General, Driver, and Resources.

INSIDE THE GENERAL SHEET

The General sheet identifies the manufacturer and model of the selected device, as well as information on any conflicts in the Device status area. It also lets you tailor the device for use by a specific system profile.

INSIDE THE DRIVER SHEET

The Driver sheet lets you view information about the device drivers used to run the selected hardware. To check which driver files are loaded for the device, click the Driver File Details button and browse the Driver Files scrolling text box on the page that appears.

An intriguing new feature is the automated driver update facility in Windows 98. To update your audio drivers, do the following:

1. Click the Update Driver button from the Driver sheet, and the Upgrade Device Driver Wizard is launched.
2. Click the Next button.
3. Select the top radio button to search for a more recent driver and click Next.
4. Tell Windows 98 where to look for the new drivers. Click the appropriate check box to have Windows 98 search the floppy drive, the CD-ROM drive, a subdirectory on the hard disk, or the Internet.
5. Click Next to begin searching the selected areas and download the new driver.

INSIDE THE RESOURCES SHEET

Finally, the Resources sheet lets you change the hardware resources for the audio device, including IRQ, DMA, and base I/O address settings. The Conflicting Device list text box at the bottom of the sheet prompts you if a hardware device conflict is present. If so, you can adjust the resource settings of a device by doing the following:

1. Uncheck the Use Automatic Settings check box.
2. Select the desired resource item in the Resource Type list and click the Change Setting button.
3. Enter the desired resource setting. You can also use the spinner controls to advance or decrease the number.
4. Click OK twice to make the new settings take effect.

WORKING WITH THE MULTIMEDIA PROPERTIES CONTROLS

The Multimedia Properties box, found in the Control Panel, is ground zero for managing multimedia settings in Windows 98. Here, you find resources for handling audio drivers and hardware, as well as for compression schemes used in saving files. To open the Multimedia Properties box, click Start, Settings, Control Panel. Select the Multimedia icon, and the Properties box appears.

Five tabs are arrayed across the top of the Multimedia Properties box.

- Audio—Provides record and playback line level controls, as well as record-quality settings.
- Video—Lets you size Video playback windows.
- MIDI—Provides controls for adding and configuring additional MIDI devices such as keyboards.
- CD Music—Controls volume of audio CD playback through the CD-ROM drive's analog out port.
- Advanced—Provides access to driver and configuration settings for all audio, video, and other multimedia devices.

PART

IV

CH

19

USING THE AUDIO SHEET

The Audio sheet of the Multimedia Properties box is divided into two sections: Playback and Recording. Each lets you adjust overall volume-level settings. What's more, Windows 98 adds intriguing controls over audio playback and recording.

CONTROLLING AUDIO PLAYBACK SETTINGS

You can select the audio playback device to control by picking it from the Preferred Device pick list. To change settings for the device, click the Advanced Properties button.

The Speakers sheet, shown in Figure 19.18, lets you configure Windows 98 for your particular speaker setup. The large image depicting a PC with speakers changes to reflect your selection. Click OK to let the new settings take effect.

Figure 19.18
The Speakers sheet of the Advanced Audio Properties dialog box lets you tweak audio playback to suit your speakers.

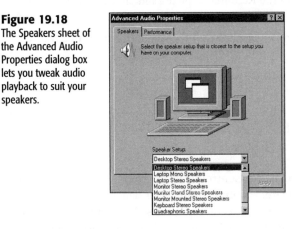

To tweak audio playback to your system's performance, click the Performance tab. The Hardware Acceleration slider bar enables Windows 98 to use more of the available hardware features and memory in the audio playback. If you experience problems with playback, try to move the slider to the left. Deactivating acceleration features can help eliminate conflicts.

The Sample Rate Conversion Quality slider bar determines how much processing power the PC applies to creating realistic audio playback. If your system is very fast, move this slider to the right. You should enjoy better audio without an unacceptable loss of performance. To return to the original settings, click the Restore Defaults button.

CUSTOMIZING WAVE AUDIO RECORDING PROFILES

As with playback, you can adjust settings for audio recording. Select the recording device from the Preferred Device pick list and click the Advanced Properties button to go to the Advanced Audio Properties sheet.

Here, you find only a Performance tab, which looks identical to that for audio playback described earlier. Moving the Hardware Acceleration and the Sample Rate Conversion Quality slider bars lets you trade audio quality for smoother performance and better stability. To return to the original settings, click the Restore Defaults button.

USING THE MIDI SHEET

The MIDI sheet of the Multimedia Properties dialog box lets you configure and install MIDI devices such as keyboards and MIDI-capable sound cards. By default, the Single Instrument radio button is active, denoting the primary MIDI device on the sound board.

CREATE A CUSTOM MIDI SCHEME

If external MIDI devices are attached to your PC, you can create a custom configuration to employ them. To create a custom configuration, do the following:

1. Click the Custom Configuration radio button.
2. Click the Configure button.
3. In the MIDI Configuration dialog box, select the desired channel and click the Change button.
4. In the Change MIDI Instrument dialog box, select the desired MIDI device in the Instrument drop-down control and click OK.
5. To assign the new configuration a name, click the Save As button (or simply click OK to make the changed settings your default configuration).
6. Enter a name for the new MIDI scheme and click OK. Click OK again to return to the MIDI sheet.

When your custom MIDI scheme is selected, the assigned device plays when the corresponding channel is called up in a MIDI score.

ADD A MIDI DEVICE

You can also use the Multimedia Properties dialog box to install a new MIDI device, such as a keyboard. To add a new device, do the following:

1. From the MIDI sheet on the Multimedia Properties dialog box, click the Add New Instrument button.
2. In the MIDI Installation Wizard box, select the MIDI port the device will be connected to and click Next.
3. Install the disk with the device's MIDI definition into drive A: and click Browse.
4. Select the appropriate IDF file from the Open dialog box and click Open.
5. Click the Next button.
6. In the Instrument Name text box, enter a name for the new device and click Finish.

ADJUSTING AUDIO CD PLAYBACK

The CD Music sheet lets you set the volume of playback for the audio CDs played in CD-ROM drives. This sheet also lets you manage multiple CD-ROM drives and deal with different audio formats coming from the drives. Here are the controls you can access from the CD Music sheet:

PART

IV

CH

19

- The CD-ROM drive drop-down list lets you select the drive to configure (allowing you to work with more than one drive).

- If your CD-ROM sends audio CD music over the system bus, select the Digital CD Playback Enable check box to get enhanced audio CD playback.

- Adjust the volume of the selected CD-ROM drive by moving the Headphone slider bar left or right.

WORKING WITH THE DEVICES SHEET

The Devices sheet of the Multimedia Properties dialog box provides access to drivers and hardware configurations for audio devices and other multimedia components. This sheet provides a list of multimedia components under the Multimedia Drivers heading. To view the installed devices for a given component, click the (+) symbol next to the item, as shown in Figure 19.19.

Figure 19.19
The Devices sheet of the Multimedia Properties dialog box provides access to a host of audio devices and controls.

You can view the controls and properties associated with each device by selecting an item and clicking the Properties button. From the Properties dialog box of each component, you can deactivate or remove the device. Some device property boxes also include a Settings button, which takes you to the corresponding control for the hardware.

In addition to wave and MIDI devices, the Devices sheet includes a roster of items under the Audio Compression Codecs item. These compression drivers let Windows 98 save sound files in compact format and are listed in order of priority. Higher-priority codecs are more likely to be used by applications than are lower-priority codecs. You can change the priority by selecting a codec, clicking the Properties button, and selecting a new priority number in the Change Priority From drop-down control, as shown in Figure 19.20.

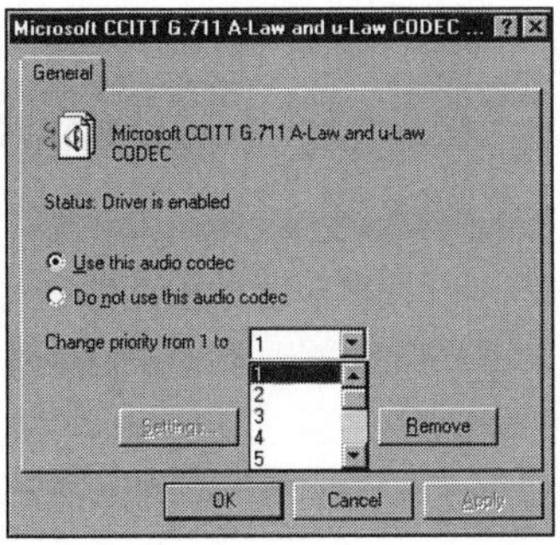

Figure 19.20
Tell Windows 98 how to compress audio files from the Codec Properties dialog box.

TROUBLESHOOTING

PROBLEMS PLAYING VIDEO FILES

I'm having problems with my video playback.

If a video file fails to play or suffers from jerky playback, use the Properties dialog box to check the encoding. If the file was encoded at a resolution higher than 320×240 pixels or if the file uses 16-bit or 24-bit color, your system may require an upgrade to handle the playback. If the file does not play, check to see which codec is identified in the Properties dialog box. You may need to install the proper video playback driver for your system to recognize the video format.

RESOLVING GRAPHICS PROBLEMS

I'm having display-related problems.

Onscreen problems manifest themselves in a variety of ways. One of the main causes of these problems occurs when memory becomes scarce. If you have the amount of memory being allocated to the graphics driver and its programs set too high to aid in graphics acceleration, system performance can suffer dramatically. Naturally, the severity of the problem is relative to the number and size of programs running on your system. Common types of display problems range from the system not responding or locking up, to a specific program erroring out, to the mouse pointer freezing. You resolve graphics problems by turning off acceleration features within your graphics card. From the System Properties sheet, click the Performance tab and click the Graphics button. If the Hardware Acceleration slider bar is set all the way to the right, as shown in Figure 19.5, drag the control a step to the left and click OK. Click Yes when Windows 98 prompts you to restart. If the problems continue, you can repeat the process, further disabling acceleration features that may be causing the problem.

SECRETS OF MASTERING THE WINDOWS 98 ENVIRONMENT: MAKING THE RIGHT HARDWARE CHOICE FOR MULTIMEDIA SUPPORT

Make sure to select a computer that is balanced in all phases of hardware. In other words, the system should have sufficient processor speed, RAM, and disk subsystem performance to meet the hardware demands of multimedia applications.

In multimedia systems a balance of the various hardware components is very important, particularly with regard to the disk subsystem. Multimedia playback places heavy demands on the CD-ROM (for reading data), on the hard disk (for writing data), on the CPU (for decompressing data), and on the video and audio subsystems (for playback). Just having a fast CPU is not enough for a high-performance multimedia system. In fact, a fast CPU and a subpar disk subsystem actually cause a bottleneck at the disk subsystem, leaving the CPU in an idle state as it waits for program instructions to be retrieved from disk. So, don't hesitate to spend a little extra on the disk subsystem; you should purchase either a small computer system interface (SCSI) or an Enhanced Integrated Development Environment (EIDE) supported device.

A multimedia system has specialized hardware requirements. For a multimedia system, the graphics, video, and audio subsystems are designed to optimize the capabilities of software that uses Microsoft DirectX interfaces. The Direct X technology is hardware intense.

The ideal multimedia system should be able to handle the following tasks with little or no perceptible performance degradation:

- Run game software, including the latest titles, with the most complex, realistic graphics and audio.

- Run the most up-to-date educational software titles, which deploy full-screen video and interactive animation.

- Participate on the Internet in real-time fashion. That is, support and provide enhanced Web communications capabilities with animated Web sites, chat rooms, and so on.

- Provide high-performance support for personal communications over the Internet through multimedia email, Internet audio phone, and video phone.

- Provide connectivity support to typical consumer-electronics devices. For example, provide home theater surround audio such as Dolby Digital (AC-3) for games and DVD movies.

CHAPTER 20

USING WINDOWS TO PLAY GAMES AND WATCH TV

In this chapter

WINDOWS AND ARCADE-STYLE GAMES

Windows 98 helps turn PCs into true entertainment centers. Games, professional-quality video playback, and TV broadcasts are all supported within Windows 98. This chapter introduces you to some of the most advanced and intriguing capabilities of Windows 98.

Gaming is big business, and Microsoft knows it. But until very recently, the vast majority of games were developed to play directly on DOS, inviting a raft of compatibility and resource problems for those who played them. Windows 98 includes a set of refined technologies and features designed to lure both game developers and game players to the new operating system.

WHAT IS DIRECTX?

At the core of this effort is a set of technologies called DirectX. This set of device drivers, Application Programming Interfaces (APIs), and Windows 98 components enable a broad range of gaming applications, from rapid-fire screen updates to responsive and reliable input device operation. For users, the benefits are immediate. Games install and play more reliably and benefit from accelerating hardware like 3D graphics cards and sound boards. What's more, they can even run side by side with mundane applications such as spreadsheets and word processors.

DirectX includes the following components:

- DirectDraw and DirectVideo—Boosts performance of 2D and 3D graphics for all applications
- Direct3D—Enables standard 3D graphics handling and acceleration
- DirectSound and DirectSound 3D—Provides a standard for managing audio, including positional 3D audio for producing the effect of surround sound on two speakers
- DirectInput—Controls input devices such as joysticks and game pads
- DirectPlay—Provides standard tools for multiplayer gaming over phone lines, networks, and serial cables

These components provide a series of common interfaces to the hardware on your PC. Game makers simply write code to the appropriate DirectX components and move on to making their games work well. Windows 98 and the DirectX components then handle the task of making things happen behind the scenes. The result: vastly improved compatibility with all types of hardware.

> **Note**
>
> Older DOS and Windows games not written for DirectX still run fine on your DirectX-equipped PC; they just lack access to performance-enhancing shortcuts and acceleration. Games that use an older version of DirectX, such as DirectX 2.0 or 3.0, enjoy some performance benefits but might not be able to take full advantage of all available features.

PERFORMANCE ISSUES

Just as important, DirectX enables much improved performance under Windows 98. One reason game makers wrote software to DOS was because the simple operating system—with its direct access to hardware devices—allowed developers to squeeze every ounce of performance out of systems. Windows 98, by contrast, uses thick layers of code to ensure compatibility, with the predictable result of slowing performance.

DirectX provides a shortcut for developers. Although Microsoft still foists strict standards to maintain compatibility, DirectX lets developers send commands directly to graphics hardware, audio components, and other areas of the PC. The streamlined approach results in higher frame rates and more responsive play, as shown in Figure 20.1

In addition, the common set of gaming functions means that chip makers can design hardware to accelerate DirectX-based games. For example, games that use Direct3D to create 3D graphics are able to gain a performance benefit from a wide range of Direct3D-aware graphics cards. These cards take the performance burden off the CPU, allowing other areas of the game to become more responsive.

Tip #124

The trend in most types of controllers is to integrate a processor of varying capacity into the card. This provides a two-fold benefit. First, this on-board processor can provide a significant increase in the performance of the device itself. Additionally, the overall system performance improves also because the main CPU of the computer can spend more time taking care of other chores.

Figure 20.1
Fast-action, 3D games like Quake II were impossible to create under Windows until DirectX APIs provided a standard way for developers to get top performance for demanding titles and games.

INSTALLING DIRECTX

So you want DirectX; how can you tell it is installed on your PC? Actually, Windows 98 comes with the full suite of DirectX software already installed. However, Microsoft is constantly updating the DirectX set, so you might need to install a new version down the road. There are two ways to get DirectX:

- Download from Microsoft's Web site at www.microsoft.com/directx
- Load as part of the installation routine of a new CD-ROM-based game or multimedia title

If an updated DirectX version comes with a game or other software product you install, you are prompted to install the new version during the process. If you download the files from Microsoft, however, you need to launch the installation manually. The easiest method is to

1. Find the file DXSETUP.EXE in the directory where you originally downloaded the file.
2. Launch DXSETUP.EXE and follow the instructions that appear onscreen.
3. Restart your system after the installation routine is complete.

Caution

When DirectX installs, it examines your graphics card drivers to see whether the drivers have been registered with Microsoft as approved DirectX drivers. In some cases, the installation might prompt you to overwrite the existing drivers with the generic DirectX drivers included with the update. In some cases, this step can fix compatibility problems caused by incompatible drivers; but in other instances, it can disable key features of your graphics card. If you recently downloaded graphics card drivers and are happy with their performance, click the No button when the prompt appears. You can always install the approved DirectX drivers later, should problems develop.

Tip #125

You don't want to install the Microsoft Windows 95 version of DirectX 6.0 on a Windows 98-based computer. If you do so, you see the following error message: Your operating system is Windows 98. To install DirectX on Windows 98, please select DirectX 6 from the Windows Update Web site (see earlier in the chapter).

If you are running an older version of DirectX and are having problems with your video and sound cards, see "Video and Sound Card Problems with Earlier Versions of DirectX" in the "Troubleshooting" section at the end of this chapter.

CONFIGURING JOYSTICKS AND OTHER GAME CONTROLLERS

Setting up joysticks was no picnic with DOS-based games. Most games supported only a few models, and calibration and setup usually had to happen outside the game itself. So if you noticed problems with response, you had to quit the game, enter a setup program, and restart the game—potentially a long process.

Windows 98 provides a standard applet interface for setting up joysticks and other devices. If you need to change controller settings, the game simply calls up the applet, which does all the real work. Best of all, you never have to close the game itself; it can stay active in the background (paused, of course) while you update your hardware settings.

INSTALLING A JOYSTICK OR GAME CONTROLLER

To set up a new game controller under Windows 98, do the following:

1. Click Start, Settings, Control Panel, and select the Game Controllers icon.

2. In the General sheet of the Game Controllers dialog box, click the Add button.

3. Select the specific device type in the Game Controllers scrolling list box and click OK, as shown in Figure 20.2.

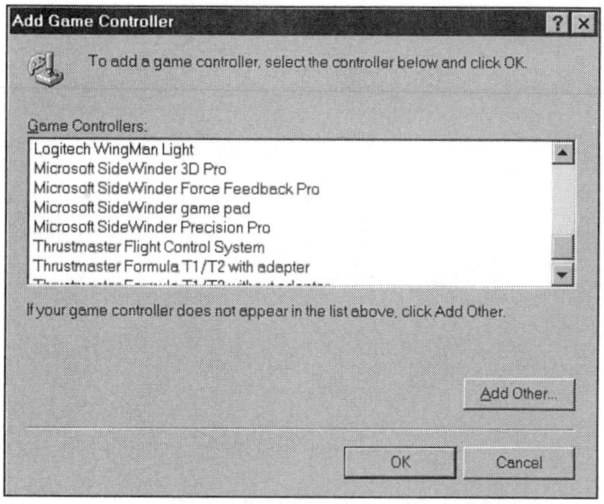

Figure 20.2
The Add Game Controller list box includes support for popular joysticks, game pads, throttles, and steering wheels.

4. If your device is not listed, click the Add Other button and click the Have Disk button at the following dialog box to install new device drivers.

5. The new device should be listed in the General sheet, with an entry of OK under the Status column.

6. The new device is now installed. Click OK to finish the installation.

PART

IV

CH

20

Tip #126

If you have an older or unsupported joystick, don't despair. Windows 98 keeps a database of generic joystick types—defined by the number of buttons and other controls—you can select from. In addition, most joysticks support emulation modes matching that of popular products from CH and Thrustmaster. Find out your joystick's preferred emulation and load the matching controller model; you should enjoy better performance.

CONFIGURING A JOYSTICK OR GAME CONTROLLER

To change the settings of an installed game controller, do the following:

1. Click Start, Settings, Control Panel, and select the Game Controllers icon.

2. In the General sheet of the Game Controllers dialog box, select the device you want to adjust in the Game Controllers scrolling list box and click Properties.

3. In the Test sheet, shown in Figure 20.3, a graphics depiction of the device provides a visual response when you push buttons or other controls. This step lets you determine whether all the controls are working normally.

Figure 20.3
The Test sheet lets you learn about your game input device's controls and make sure they are all working properly.

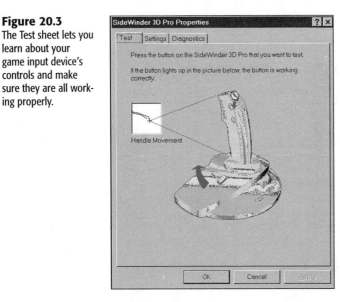

4. Click the Settings tab to see whether all features are enabled. Click the appropriate check boxes next to the identified feature to enable or disable the specific control.

5. Click the OK button to let any changes take effect.

Note

Until about a year ago, almost all joysticks used an analog signal to communicate positions to the PC. The problem with these "dumb" joysticks is that the CPU must constantly check the game port to see what the joystick is reporting—even if nothing has changed. Game makers say this process can sap 15% to 20% of your CPU time, a major drag when fast frame rates spell the difference between success and defeat. New digital joysticks from Microsoft, Logitech, CH, and other vendors send updates directly to the CPU, freeing your system to do other tasks and improving the precision and responsiveness of the device. If you are on the market for a new stick, consider going with a digital model.

USING WEBTV FOR WINDOWS

The WebTV for Windows software turns a properly equipped PC into a functioning television set. This feature allows you to view TV programming side by side with your applications, as well as to browse TV listings and capture video and images. You need to have a TV tuner card installed in your PC to pick up broadcasts, and an Internet connection is useful for downloading the latest TV listings and schedules.

To install the WebTV for Windows software, do the following:

1. Click Start, Settings, Control Panel and select the Add/Remove Software icon.
2. Click the Windows Setup tab. Wait a moment while Setup searches for installed components.
3. In the Components box, scroll down to the WebTV for Windows item and click the box to the left so that a check appears in the box.
4. Click OK.
5. If the Windows 98 CD-ROM is not already in the drive, insert it when prompted. You will have to restart your system once or twice before all the changes take effect.
6. When the software is installed, a small television icon appears on the taskbar, in the group next to the Start button.

To watch a program, simply launch the WebTV for Windows application and go to the channel you want. Use one of the following methods to launch WebTV for Windows:

- Click the TV icon in the left side of the Windows 98 taskbar.
- Click Start, Programs, Accessories, Entertainment, WebTV for Windows.

USING THE PROGRAM GUIDE

WebTV for Windows launches to the Program Guide, which displays the available channels in the main window. Use the scrollbar on the right side to browse through the channels; use the scrollbar across the bottom to see what is on at different times during the day. A timeline across the top of the window shows the time of day for the programs being displayed.

Just above the display window, you can set the Program Guide to display programming for a specific date, time of day, or subset of channels, as shown in Figure 20.4. Clicking these reduces the amount of data displayed in the window, making it easier to find the program you want.

PART

IV

CH

20

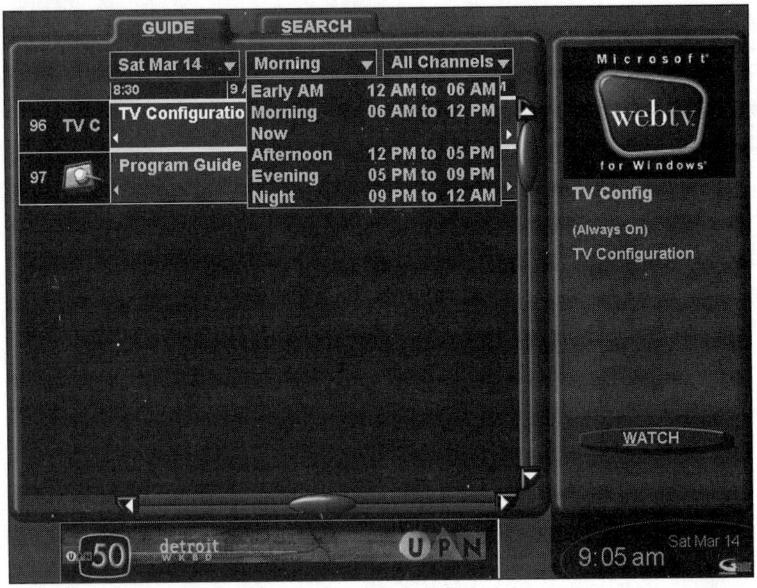

Figure 20.4
The Program Guide
can overwhelm you
with choices. Use one
of the useful filters to
limit the information.

In addition, you can search for specific programming by clicking the Search tab at the top of the Program Guide window. A list of programming categories appears along the left side while the window in the center displays the results of your searches. You can click on one of the categories to see all the programs fitting that definition, or you can enter text into the Search box at the lower left to look for a specific word or description. Just enter the text and click the Search button at the bottom to see the results in the main window.

You can further winnow your searches from the pick list controls at the top of the screen, shown in Figure 20.5. The control on the left lets you filter by days or by programs being broadcast at the moment. The control on the right lets you sort the resulting search by time or by title.

To view a program, simply select it from the results window. If the program is on, the WebTV application tunes to the appropriate channel and displays it.

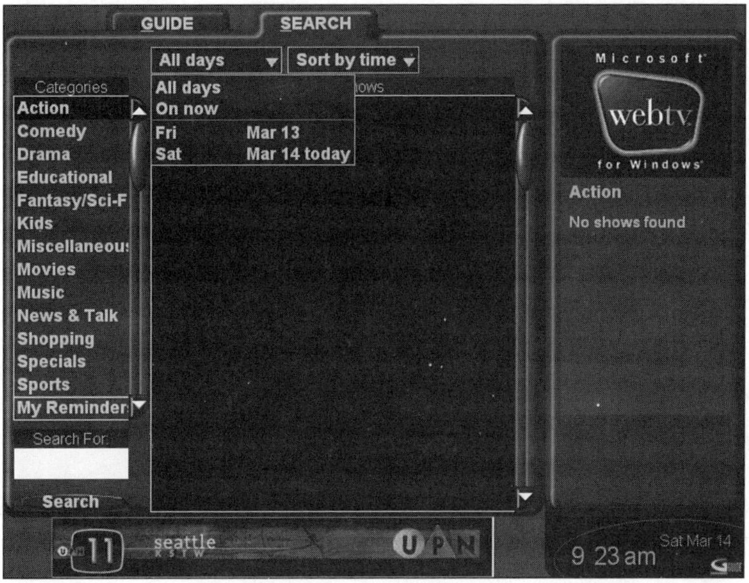

Figure 20.5
The useful Search screen lets you search for programs by category, text string, and time of day.

CHANGING CHANNELS

There are several ways to select a channel to view under WebTV for Windows. For most methods, you must access the TV toolbar, which runs across the top of the WebTV screen. To evoke the TV toolbar, shown in Figure 20.6, press F10 or the Alt key. To change the channel, do one of the following:

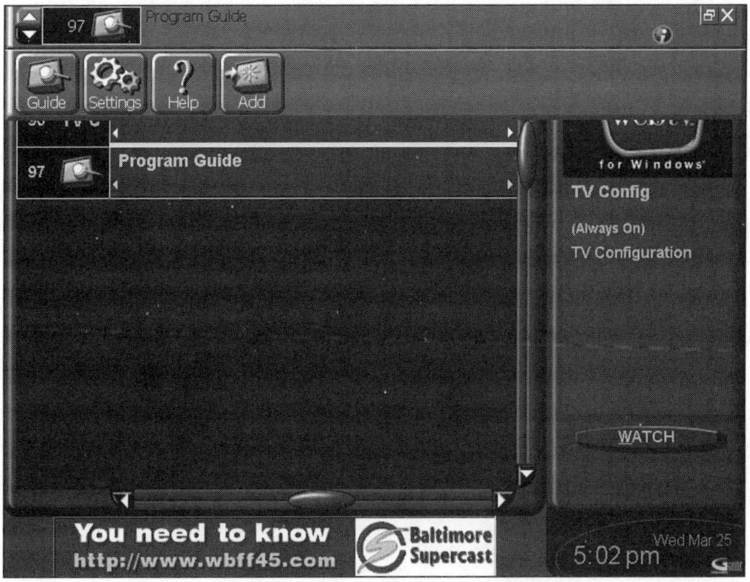

Figure 20.6
The TV toolbar enables you to change channels, adjust settings, and add or remove custom channels.

- Click the arrows on the spinner control in the left corner of the TV toolbar, which appears across the top of the screen.

- Enter the number in the channel control on the TV toolbar by dragging the cursor over the current entry and typing the new channel over it. Press Enter to go to the channel.

- Click one of the preselected channel icons on the TV toolbar.

- You can also use a remote control (provided your system supports one) to enter channel changes.

FULL SCREEN OR WINDOW?

By default, WebTV for Windows launches in Full Screen mode, meaning you cannot see your other programs while watching TV. To adjust WebTV for Windows to take up only part of the screen, do the following:

1. Press F10 or Alt to invoke the TV toolbar.

2. Click the small double-box icon that appears in the upper-right corner of the TV toolbar. (Be sure not to click the X icon by accident. That closes WebTV!)

3. The WebTV screen shrinks to take up a portion of the screen. Move the icon so that it hovers above a corner of the window and turns into a double arrow.

4. Click the corner and drag the window to the desired shape and size. Repeat on the other corner if necessary.

OTHER TV OPTIONS

WebTV for Windows mates its broadcast capabilities with some of the best features of the PC. For example, if a broadcaster embeds data signals in the broadcast, you can display running text, graphics, and other information alongside the program. A football broadcast, for example, might display the scoring statistics of a team that has just taken the field.

You can tell whether a particular broadcast is enhanced if WebTV for Windows places a blue icon next to the entry in the TV Guide window. A red circle icon indicates that the programming is not enhanced. The icons also appear for programs shown on the TV toolbar banner.

By default, WebTV enables the enhanced content; you must turn it off if you want to simply view the broadcast. To turn off the enhancements on a broadcast, do the following:

1. Press F10 or Alt to invoke the TV toolbar.

2. Click the blue icon that appears on the far-right side of the TV toolbar banner.

3. In the context menu that drops down, click the Enhancements item (it should have a check mark next to it).

4. The enhancements are now disabled. To enable this feature, click the blue icon again and click the Enhancements item.

WebTV for Windows also supports closed captioning, displaying running text of dialog along the bottom of the screen. You can even have WebTV look for specific words in the text stream—for example, President Clinton—and have the program take an action, such as turning up the volume.

To turn on Closed Captioning, do the following:

1. Press F10 or Alt to bring up the TV toolbar.
2. Click the Settings icon.
3. In the Settings dialog box, click the <u>S</u>how closed captioning check box. A check should now appear in the box.
4. Click OK.

USING DVD PLAYERS WITH WINDOWS

DVD is a major improvement to the multimedia and data storing capabilities of desktop PCs. DVD-ROM discs, which look identical to CD-ROM media, can hold up to 17GB of data—more than 30 times that stored on a CD-ROM disc. In addition, DVD-ROM provides vastly improved audio and visual quality (see Figure 20.7) from PC-based digital video.

Figure 20.7
High-quality MPEG-2 digital video delivers professional-quality video playback to the PC. In fact, it's the same format used by direct broadcast satellite providers like DirecTV.

Video-enabled DVD-ROM titles generally require two new hardware components:

- A DVD-ROM drive—An optical disk drive, very similar in appearance to a CD-ROM drive, that can read both DVD-ROM and CD-ROM discs
- A decoder board—A PCI add-in card that includes hardware for decoding compressed MPEG-2 video and audio for playback on the PC

INSTALLING THE DVD COMPONENTS OF WINDOWS

If your PC has the necessary DVD hardware, Windows 98 allows you to immediately take advantage of the features. In some cases, however, you must manually install the DVD components of the Windows 98 operating system. Follow these steps:

1. Click Start, Settings, Control Panel and then select the Add/Remove Software icon.
2. Click the Windows Setup tab. Wait a moment while Windows 98 reviews its configuration.
3. Scroll down the Components list box until you find the Multimedia entry.
4. Click the Details button to bring up the list of available Multimedia components.
5. Click the box next to the DVD Player item so that a check mark appears in the box.
6. Click OK, and click OK again to have Windows 98 install the software.
7. Insert the Windows 98 CD-ROM if prompted. Restart the PC to have the changes take effect.

USING THE DVD PLAYER SOFTWARE

In general, most DVD-ROM drive kits come with their own player software, like that shown in Figure 20.8. Likewise, many DVD-ROM-based games and titles play video and audio within the confines of their own interface. In these cases, you don't need to access the Windows 98 DVD Player software. In fact, the interface provided with your DVD-ROM drive and kit generally offers more features than the player included with Windows 98. However, the DVD Player is useful to browse through DVD-ROM discs and to play back selected MPEG video clips.

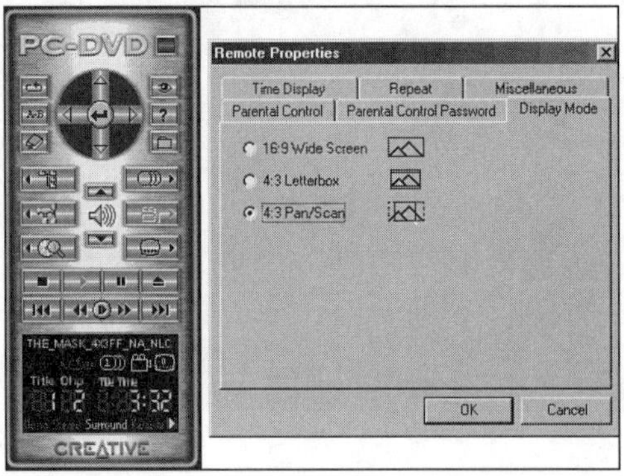

Figure 20.8
Creative Labs uses a remote-control-like interface to switch tracks, play video, and control playback settings. The capability to display either letterbox or standard TV format video is just one of DVD's useful features.

To open the DVD Player, click Start, Programs, Applications, Accessories, Entertainment. Click DVD Player. The player application loads.

The DVD Player applet offers a concise interface to browse content on DVD-ROM discs. A simple VCR metaphor lets you select among available video tracks, with familiar push buttons used to play, advance, pause, and rewind the video. A window displays the video track, elapsed time, time remaining, and other information for each track. Users can also access letter-box format, closed captioning, and subtitling, provided they are available on the disc.

TROUBLESHOOTING

VIDEO AND SOUND CARD PROBLEMS WITH EARLIER VERSIONS OF DIRECTX

Can I install DirectX 2.0 on a Windows 98 system?

You will run into trouble if you attempt to install Microsoft DirectX 2.0 or a program that includes DirectX 2.0 on a Windows 98 system. Doing so may disable your video adapter or sound card. DirectX 2.0 is not compatible with Windows 98. If you find yourself in this situation, you can install a DirectX 5.0 video adapter and sound card driver from the Windows 98 CD-ROM. The following steps describe how to install a video driver. Installing a sound card drive is an almost identical process. To install a video driver, follow these steps:

1. Click Start, point to Settings, click Control Panel, and then double-click Display.
2. On the Settings tab, click Advanced.
3. On the Adapter tab, click Change, click Next, click Display a List of All the Drivers in a Specific Location, So You Can Select the Driver You Want, click Next, and then click Have Disk.
4. Insert the Windows 98 CD-ROM into the CD-ROM drive. If the Windows 98 screen appears, click Cancel and then click Browse. If the Windows 98 screen does not appear, click Browse.
5. In the Drivers\Display folder on the Windows 98 CD-ROM, double-click the appropriate folder for your video adapter, click OK, and then click OK again.
6. Click the appropriate video adapter driver, click Next, click Next again, click Finish, and then click Yes to restart your computer.

If a driver for your video adapter isn't on the Windows 98 CD-ROM, you should probably be able to download and install the latest version of DirectX from the sound card manufacturer's Web site.

If an updated driver is not available from the manufacturer, the latest version of DirectX may include one. To view the list of video and audio drivers included with the latest version of DirectX, go to the Microsoft Web site. If your card is listed on the Web site, it is supported by the latest update of DirectX. So you merely update your installation of DirectX to remedy the problem. To access the site, point your browser to `http://www.microsoft.com/directx/overview/hardware/default.asp`.

CHAPTER **21**

CONFIGURING HARDWARE

In this chapter

HOW WINDOWS 98 WORKS WITH HARDWARE

Windows 98 doesn't radically change the way things were handled under Windows 95, but it does include some useful new tools and tweaks. At the center of all hardware, however, is Windows 98 Plug and Play (PnP) technology, the combination of software and hardware that allows the operating system to automatically manage devices.

For PnP to work, your peripherals, system BIOS, and the Windows 98 operating system (see what these terms mean below) must all incorporate PnP technology. When Windows 98 starts, the operating system and the PC go through a series of steps to establish configurations, arbitrate conflicts, and record changes.

- System BIOS (basic input/output system)—The system BIOS is the low-level code that boots your system, detects the hard disk, and manages basic operations. PnP systems employ a specifically tuned BIOS that has the intelligence to detect hardware and manage configuration changes.

Note
To see whether your BIOS is PnP-compliant, look for the BIOS information on your monitor at the beginning of the boot process. As part of the initial screen when you start your computer, a text message identifying the type of BIOS and version number should mention PnP. You can also check the Windows 98 Device Manager through the Control Panel, System Icon, Device Manager tab for a PnP BIOS listing.

- Windows 98 operating system— Windows 98 interacts with the system BIOS and the installed hardware and keeps track of hardware resources.

- Hardware peripherals—Adapter cards and other peripherals must incorporate PnP circuitry to provide automated configuration. PCI add-in cards, by definition, are PnP-compliant, whereas Industry Standard Architecture (ISA) cards must be specifically designed for the feature. External peripherals such as modems and printers can be PnP as well.

Tip #127
Always turn off the computer when adding or removing any device inside the system. Having a Plug and Play BIOS doesn't absolve the user, or installer, from having common sense.

- Device drivers—The final piece of the PnP puzzle is the device driver. Peripherals must use dynamic drivers (called VxDs) that allow configurations to be changed on-the-fly. You can usually get the latest driver versions from the peripheral manufacturer.

These components all come together to eliminate the need for the user to tell each peripheral exactly which resources it can access. Windows 98 assigns interrupt request (IRQ), DMA, and I/O address settings based on the overall picture that PnP provides.

Although Windows 98 makes things easy, you must be knowledgeable about the resources your devices need. This information enables you to diagnose and fix simple conflicts without having to resort to time-consuming or costly repair services. IRQs are the most critical of the system resources, if only because nearly all devices need them.

IRQ numbers enable hardware devices to get the CPU's attention. A PC has 14 IRQs, but not all are actually available to your peripherals. In fact, as PCs incorporate more and more devices, IRQs have become increasingly scarce, which sometimes results in failed installations and conflicts. Table 21.1 lists the IRQs and their most common uses. As you can see, only about a third of these may be available, and often even those are occupied.

TABLE 21.1   COUNTING IRQS

IRQ Number	Application
2	Cascade from IRQ9
3	Available (or second COM port)
4	COM1, COM3
5	Available (or second printer port, LPT2)
6	Floppy disk controller
7	Printer port (LPT1)
8	System clock
9	Graphics adapter
10	Available
11	Available
12	Mouse (PS/2 systems)
13	Math coprocessor (if applicable)
14	Hard drive controller
15	Available

WALKING THROUGH PLUG AND PLAY

Each time you boot the system, a series of steps launches the PnP process. All the hardware on the system is checked at boot time. If new hardware has been installed, the PnP system detects it and takes the appropriate steps.

The following list details the steps that Windows 98 goes through during system startup:

1. The system BIOS identifies the devices on the motherboard (including the type of bus), as well as external devices such as disk drives, keyboard, and video display and other adapter cards, that are required for the boot process.

2. The system BIOS determines the resource requirements (IRQ, DMA, I/O, and memory address) for each boot device. The BIOS also determines which devices are older devices with fixed resource requirements and which are PnP devices with flexible resource requirements. Notice that some devices don't require all four resource types.

3. Windows 98 allocates the remaining resources, after allowing for older resource assignments to each PnP device. If many older and PnP devices are in use, Windows 98 may have to perform many iterations of the allocation process, changing the resource assignments of the PnP devices each time to eliminate all resource conflicts.

4. Windows 98 creates a final system configuration and stores the resource allocation data for this configuration in the registration database (the Registry).

5. Windows 98 searches the Windows\System folder to find the required driver for the device. If the device driver is missing, a dialog box asks you to insert into drive A: the manufacturer's floppy disk containing the driver software. Windows 98 loads the driver into memory and then completes its startup operations.

Notice that Windows 98 makes educated guesses about the identity and resource requirements of older devices. The operating system features a large database of resource settings for older devices, which enables the system to detect and configure itself to a variety of existing hardware. However, the detection process is not perfect, and it forces dynamic PnP peripherals to be configured around the static settings of older hardware.

INSTALLING DEVICE DRIVERS

Device drivers are a critical part of hardware configuration. This software acts as a bridge between your hardware and the Windows 98 operating system, enabling the two to talk to each other. Drivers not only enable features but also enhance performance and fix bugs and conflicts. For this reason, users should always keep an eye out for improved versions of driver software for their hardware. Devices most affected by device driver updates include graphics cards, sound cards, scanners, printers, and video capture devices.

Windows 98 makes it easy to install new driver software, via the Update Device Driver Wizard. Simply follow these steps:

1. Click Start, Settings, Control Panel and then select the System icon.

2. Click the Device Manager tab to display the list of device types available to your PC (see Figure 21.1).

Figure 21.1
The Device Manager lets you browse among device types to access properties for specific hardware.

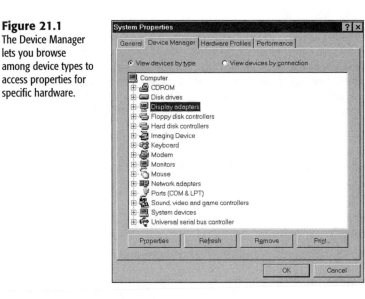

3. In the scrolling list box, click the plus sign next to the hardware category you want to work with.

4. Double-click the specific device item that appears, and Windows displays the Properties dialog box for that item.

5. Click the Driver tab and then click the Update Driver button shown in Figure 21.2.

Figure 21.2
The Update Driver button, found in the Device Properties dialog box of many devices, makes it easy to search out the latest driver versions available on the Web.

6. The Update Device Driver Wizard launches. Click Next.

7. Click the top radio button to tell Windows 98 to search for a new driver. Click Next.

8. Tell Windows 98 where to look for the new driver. If you want to try to find the latest version on the Web, make sure the Microsoft Windows Update check box is checked.

Windows 98 searches the selected locations for a new driver. Again, you can often find the most recent versions by searching Microsoft's Web-based index of device drivers.

PART

IV

CH

21

Tip #128

Windows 98 might carry you off to Microsoft's approved driver index, but you might find more recent—if unapproved—drivers at the manufacturer's Web site. Finding these drivers won't happen automatically, however. You must use your Web browser to go to the vendor's site, find the appropriate driver files, and download them to an empty directory on your hard disk. If the file is compressed (using PK Zip or some other utility), you must expand it as well. Then use the Update feature to browse over to the directory containing the files and install from there.

9. Windows 98 tells you if it finds a more recent driver. If you want to install the software, click Next.

10. After the driver is installed, you must reboot your system.

MANAGING OLDER (NON-PNP) HARDWARE

Managing non-PnP hardware is more complicated than managing PnP devices. These older devices lack the capability to be dynamically configured by Windows 98, and they may be difficult to detect during setup. In addition, PnP device installations must be able to work around existing older devices already in the system.

Because of the large number of older non-PnP devices in the market, the Windows 98 Plug and Play capability is designed to work with them. Windows 98 includes a large database of hardware devices that provides information on the preferred settings for hundreds of such devices.

Older adapter cards use one of the following two methods for setting device resources:

■ Mechanical jumpers—Mechanical jumpers create a short circuit between two pins of a multipin header. Jumpers are commonly used to designate resource values for sound cards and must be set to match the resource settings of Windows 98. If the jumper settings do not match those set in Windows 98, the device will not operate.

■ Nonvolatile memory (NVM)—Nonvolatile memory—such as electrically erasable, programmable read-only memory (EEPROM)—retains data when you turn off your PC's power. Network adapter cards and sound cards commonly use NVM. Usually, you must run a setup program for the card to match the board settings to those of the operating system.

⚠ *If you're having trouble getting Windows to recognize an external modem, see "Windows 98 Doesn't Recognize My External Modem" in the "Troubleshooting" section at the end of this chapter.*

OLDER DEVICE DETECTION DURING WINDOWS 98 SETUP

When you run the Windows 98 Setup program, the operating system attempts to detect all the hardware devices in your PC, including older devices such as ISA sound cards and network adapters. The operating system then installs 32-bit protected mode drivers for peripherals for which updated drivers are available. However, Windows 98 often keeps references to real-mode (16-bit) device drivers in the CONFIG.SYS and AUTOEXEC.BAT files, which are used when the system runs DOS software in DOS-only mode.

If Windows can't identify an older device, you need to install the device manually. See the manufacturer's instructions for installation.

CHANGING SETTINGS AFTER A DEVICE IS INSTALLED

If the resource values for a newly installed device are incorrect or if you receive a `Resource Conflict` message, you need to stop the detection process and do the following:

1. Click Start, Settings, Control Panel and then double-click the System icon to open the Control Panel's System Properties sheet.

2. Click the Device Manager tab. If an exclamation point is superimposed on the new device's icon, that device is experiencing a resource conflict with other hardware.

3. Double-click the entry for the new card to display the properties sheet for the device.

4. In the Resource Settings list box, select the resource whose value you need to change and click the Change Settings button (see Figure 21.3).

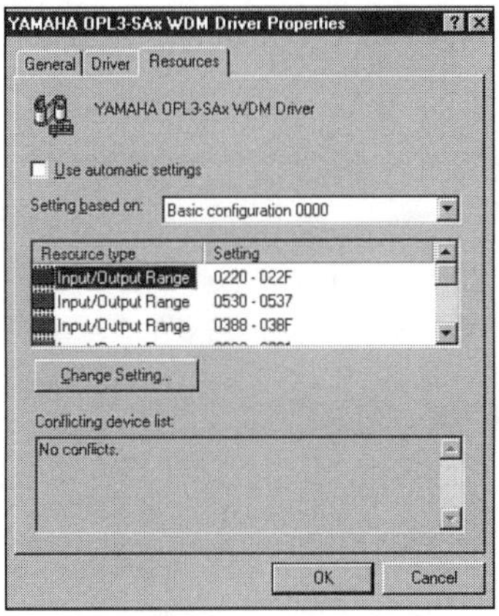

Figure 21.3
The Resources tab enables you to override the automatic settings in Windows 98 to work around IRQ, address, and DMA conflicts.

5. Use the spinner controls to adjust the number in the Value box to match the number that's preset on the device hardware.

   If a conflict with an existing card occurs, the card with the conflicting resource is identified in the Conflict Information text box. When you find a value setting that displays the `No Devices Are Conflicting` message in the Conflict Information text box, stick with that setting.

6. Make the corresponding change in the card by using the jumpers or via software.

7. After making all the changes necessary to eliminate resource conflicts, click OK to close the resource's edit dialog box. Then, click OK to close the properties sheet for the specific device.

PART
IV

CH
21

8. Click OK to close the System Properties sheet.

9. Windows prompts you to restart the system. Shut down and restart Windows 98 to put your new settings into effect.

Tip #129	When you make multiple configuration changes, it can take Windows two or more restarts to sort out the situation. If you run across problems with the installed device after finishing the process, don't give up too easily. Try rebooting the system—from a cold boot, just to be sure—one or two times.

INSPECTING HARDWARE PROPERTIES WITH DEVICE MANAGER

The Windows 98 Device Manager is ground zero for managing resources and controlling devices. You can access this useful facility from the Windows 98 Control Panel by clicking Start, Settings, Control Panel and then selecting the Systems icon. From the System Properties dialog box, choose the Device Manager tab. (Or you can simply right-click the My Computer icon on the desktop, choose Properties from the context menu, and click the Device Manager tab to access its interface.)

When you get to the Device Manager, you will see a scrolling list box. To see the resources for any hardware device, follow these steps:

1. Click the plus symbol next to the category of hardware you want to examine (see Figure 21.4).

Figure 21.4
Clicking the plus (+) sign next to a device category reveals the installed hardware.

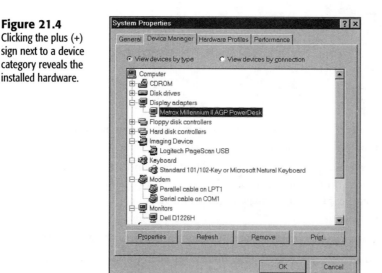

2. Select the specific device from the expanded tree-and-branch listing and click Properties. The Properties dialog box for that device appears.

3. Depending on the device, you can change system resources, update driver software, and alter settings from this dialog box. Make any necessary changes.

4. To put your changes into effect, click the OK button in the Properties dialog box.

CONFIGURING A MODEM

Modems are among the most frequently updated peripherals, in part because of the rapid advance in communication data rates. In addition, many users have several dial-in routines set up for calling into various services or locations, which can require additional tweaking of the hardware. Fortunately, Windows 98 provides a sensible standard interface for adjusting modem settings.

To access modem controls, click Start, Settings, Control Panel and then select the Modems icon. The Modem Properties dialog box appears.

Tip #130	If you want to see how well your modem is working and its connection speed, launch the System Monitor by clicking Start, Programs, Accessories, System Tools, System Monitor. In the System Monitor dialog box, click Edit, Add Item. From the Category list, choose the Dial Up Adapter entry. Then click the Connection Speed item and click OK. A System Monitor chart reports the bit rate of the modem.

GENERAL PROPERTIES

When you open the Modem Properties dialog box, the General page appears first. You can have one or more modems set up under Windows 98, and they appear in the main window of this dialog box. To change settings on a particular modem, select the desired device in the main window and click the Properties button.

In the General sheet of the dialog box that appears, you can assign the modem a new COM port address. Simply click the Port drop-down button and select the desired address. This control is often useful when your modem is conflicting with a mouse or another modem; switching to a free COM port enables the modem to work properly.

The Speaker Volume slider bar appears just below the Port control. This control lets you adjust volume so that the sound of dialing and connecting is not too loud to live with, yet remains loud enough to hear in case there is a problem.

Finally, the Maximum Speed drop-down list enables you to set the serial port to accept a desired data rate. In general, try to give yourself a little head room because modem compression can boost data rates above that of the reported connection rate. A setting of 57,600 or 115,200 is recommended.

PART
IV
CH
21

CONNECTION PROPERTIES

The Connection page of the Modem Properties dialog box lets you adjust settings that allow your modem to speak the language of other modems. If your modem is working (if you can hear it dial numbers) but fails to connect, changing some of the settings on this page might resolve the problem.

CONNECTION PREFERENCES

The first stop is the Connection Preferences area, where you can adjust the data bit, stop bit, and parity values of your modem. In general, you should assume that the following default values will work for the named controls:

> Data bit:
>
> Parity: None
>
> Stop bits:

If you continue to have problems, check with the Internet service provider (ISP) or provider on the other end to see whether the provider uses these values.

CALL PREFERENCES

The Call Preferences area enables you to customize calling behavior. It provides the following controls:

- Wait for Dial Tone Before Dialing—Avoids dialing if someone else is on the line. Uncheck this option if you have a call messaging service that notifies you by using a stuttered dial tone.
- Cancel the Call If Not Connected Within xxx—Keeps your modem from indefinitely hogging the phone line if a connection is not made. The default value is 60 seconds; just be sure to allow enough time for the connection to be made.
- Disconnect a Call If Idle for More Than xxx—When this option is activated, Windows 98 hangs up if no modem activity is detected in the number of minutes specified in the text box.

ADVANCED SETTINGS

You'll also find some less-important controls by clicking the Advanced button. From the dialog box that appears, you can turn hardware compression on and off and take control of default error-checking modes.

The Port button takes you to the Advanced Port Settings dialog box. Two slider bars let you commit more or less memory to storing bits coming into or going out of the modem. Moving the slider controls all the way to the right can help speed performance and avoid buffer overruns that can result in lost data.

RESOLVING CONFLICTS

When it comes to resolving conflicts, the Device Manager is again the best place to start. Problems often occur when hardware devices try to grab the same system resource; however, incompatible hardware may also be the culprit.

USING THE DEVICE MANAGER FOR CONFLICTS

If a device is conflicting, you will see an indication on the Device Manager page of the System Properties dialog box. An exclamation point next to a device, as shown in Figure 21.5, means that a conflict has been detected.

Figure 21.5
Windows 98 eases troubleshooting by pointing out device conflicts in the Device Manager.

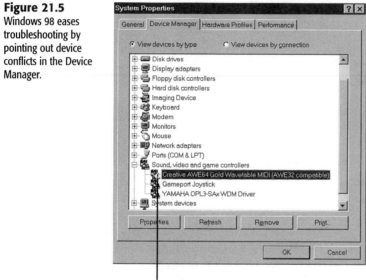

The exclamation
point

You can alter the settings for the offending device by double-clicking the highlighted item and clicking the Resource tab of the device's properties dialog box.

When a conflict exists, it is described in the Conflicting Device list box at the bottom of the sheet. To resolve the conflict, do the following:

1. Uncheck the Use Automatic Settings check box.
2. In the scrolling list box in the center of the dialog box, scroll to the desired item and double-click it.
3. Use the spinner control that appears to assign a new setting for the resource. Click OK.
4. Click OK again to put the changes into effect. You usually have to restart the system.

PART

IV

CH

21

TWEAKING PERFORMANCE LEVELS

Problems can also occur when hardware such as graphics and audio accelerators don't properly support advanced features. Windows 98 lets you troubleshoot these problems by selectively turning off individual features until you find a profile that works properly.

To scale back graphics acceleration features, follow these steps:

1. Click Start, Settings, Control Panel and select the System icon.
2. Click the Performance tab and then click the Graphics button to display the Hardware Acceleration slider bar shown in Figure 21.6.

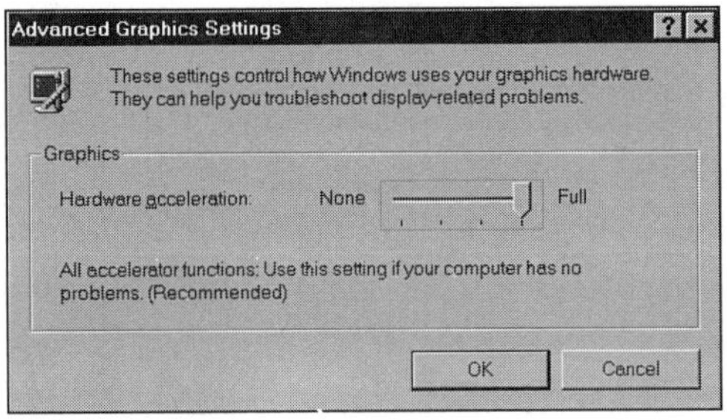

Figure 21.6
Adjusting the Hardware Acceleration control might help alleviate problems related to your graphics card.

![Advanced Graphics Settings dialog box. Text reads: "These settings control how Windows uses your graphics hardware. They can help you troubleshoot display-related problems." Graphics section with "Hardware acceleration:" slider from None to Full. "All accelerator functions: Use this setting if your computer has no problems. (Recommended)" OK and Cancel buttons.]

3. Drag the Hardware Acceleration slider bar to the left one notch and click OK.
4. Click Yes when Windows 98 tells you to restart the system. If the problem disappears, you know your graphics hardware is not able to effectively provide full capabilities.

> **Note** 
>
>
>
> You can also access this control from the Windows 98 Control Panel by selecting the Display icon, clicking the Settings tab, and then clicking the Advanced button. In the dialog box that comes up, click the Performance tab, and the same control appears.

You can tweak audio capabilities in much the same way. If you are experiencing audio problems, try disabling some of the hardware acceleration in an effort to ferret out a problem.

1. From the Windows 98 Control Panel, select the Multimedia tab.
2. In the Audio sheet, click the Advanced Properties button.
3. Click the Performance tab to display the audio performance controls shown in Figure 21.7.

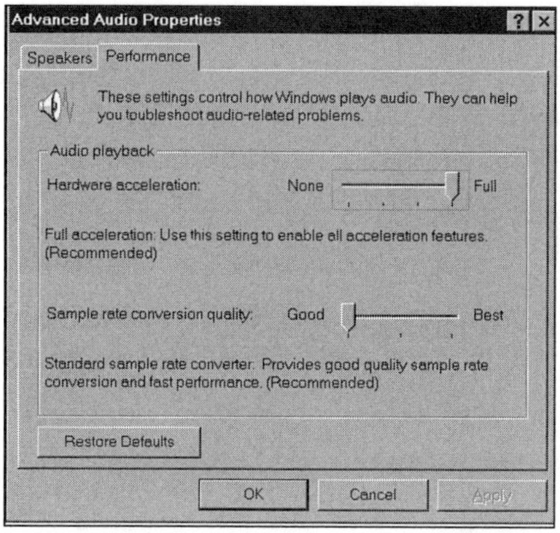

Figure 21.7
The Performance tab lets you adjust the sample rate of audio data to achieve higher-quality results or to alleviate hardware-related problems.

4. Drag the Hardware Acceleration slider bar to the left one notch to disable part of the audio acceleration capabilities.

5. Click OK, and then click Yes to restart the system when prompted.

REMOVING UNNEEDED DEVICE DRIVERS

Sometimes, problems can occur if the driver for a previously removed device has not been uninstalled. You can remove the device driver from Windows 98's Device Manager list by following these steps:

1. Click Start, Settings, Control Panel and then double-click the System icon.

2. Click the Device Manager tab and double-click the icon for the hardware type of the device that was removed to display the installed devices. An exclamation point super-imposed on a device icon indicates a removed or inoperable device.

3. Click the list item to select the device you want to remove and then click Remove.

4. Confirm that you want to remove the device by clicking OK in the Control Device Removal message box.

If you have more than one hardware configuration, a modified version of the Confirm Device Removal message box appears. Make sure the Remove from All Configurations option button is selected; then click OK to remove the device and close the message box.

CREATING HARDWARE PROFILES

Windows 98 lets you create multiple hardware profiles—a useful feature for notebook users who need different hardware settings when they are on the road or plugged into a docking station at the office. You can create hardware profiles from the Hardware Profiles page of the System Properties dialog box, as shown in Figure 21.8.

PART
IV

CH
21

Do the following:

1. Go to the System Properties dialog box by clicking Start, Settings, Control Panel and then clicking the Systems icon.

2. Click the Hardware Profiles tab.

3. Select the hardware profile present in the list box and click the Copy button.

4. In the To text box of the Copy Profile dialog box, enter the name you want to assign to the new profile.

5. Click OK. The new entry now appears next to your default hardware profile, as shown in Figure 21.8.

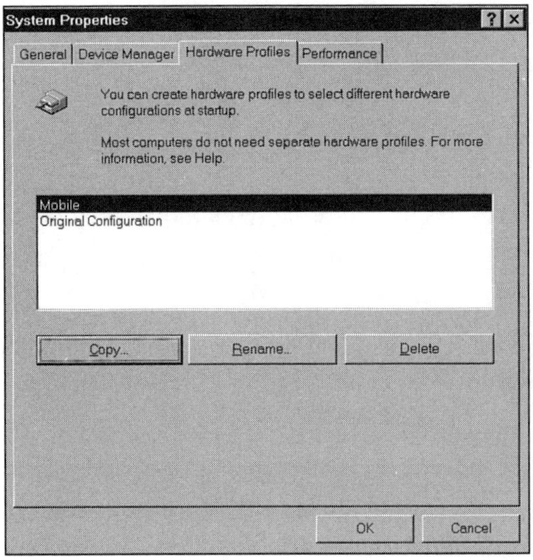

Figure 21.8
Create new hardware profiles simply by copying from an existing profile.

> **Note**
>
> The profile you create will be identical to the one you copied. To tailor the profile to meet your needs, you need to go to the Properties dialog box of each peripheral found in the Device Manager. At the bottom of the General page, you can set the device to be associated with one or all hardware profiles.

TROUBLESHOOTING

PROBLEMS WITH WINDOWS 98 RECOGNIZING EXTERNAL MODEMS

Windows 98 isn't recognizing my external modem.

If Windows 98 doesn't seem to be recognizing an external modem, the issue is with the type of adapter you are using. If you are using a 9-pin to 25-pin serial adapter, it may lack the wiring needed to pass *Plug and Play (pages 250, 430)* data to and from your PC. You need to purchase a newer adapter that allows Plug and Play to work with your external serial device.

SECRETS OF MASTERING THE WINDOWS 98 ENVIRONMENT: HOW HARDWARE PROFILES ARE SUPPORTED IN THE REGISTRY

When you configure multiple hardware profiles on a Windows 98 system, you are actually making changes to the Registry in the HKEY_CURRENT_CONFIG key. This part, or hive, of the Registry is stored in the System.dat file. The HKEY_CURRENT_CONFIG key includes a pointer to the current system configuration. This information is stored in the collection of configurations located in HKEY_LOCAL_MACHINE \Config\000x, which contains the current hardware configuration of the system. The number x refers to the configuration number. So if you have a docked and an undocked mode for your portable computer, you would have a separate subkey for each configuration: 0001 and 0002.

Under the \Config\000x subkey, you see the system's hardware configuration information. For example, the Display subkey specifies screen fonts and screen settings, such as resolution. The Enum subkey contains subkeys that specify Plug and Play BIOS, and the System subkey contains subkeys that list available printers. You can use this information to verify whether a specific type of device is installed on your system. Chapter 24, "Working with the Windows Registry," takes a closer look at the Registry.

CHAPTER **22**

ADDING NEW HARDWARE TO WINDOWS 98

In this chapter

USING THE ADD NEW HARDWARE WIZARD

Installing new hardware under Windows 98 is eased by the use of Plug and Play (PnP) technology and the Add New Hardware Wizard. Most hardware sold today provides Plug and Play capability; in addition, most systems sold over the past few years comply with PnP. The result: easier hardware installations.

Not sure whether your system is PnP-compatible? The following components must be in place for PnP to work with your installations:

- A Plug and Play BIOS (see Figure 22.1)
- A Plug and Play operating system, such as Windows 98 or Windows
- Plug and Play-compliant hardware devices, including adapter cards

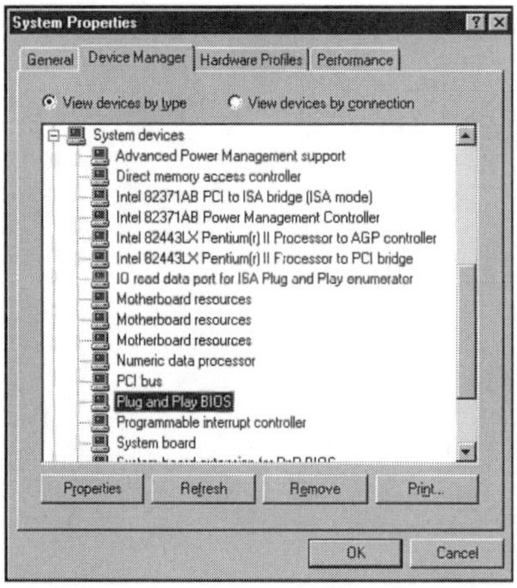

Figure 22.1
The Windows 98 Device Manager indicates whether your system's BIOS is PnP-compliant.

If you have a working PnP-compliant system, hardware installations should go much more smoothly. Even when Windows 98 doesn't get it right—which does happen occasionally— the intuitive onscreen guides help prompt you as to what to do.

The Add New Hardware Wizard provides a user-friendly interface for hardware installation procedures. Several things can happen to launch the wizard, including these:

- Windows 98 detects a new hardware device during operation.
- Windows 98 detects a new hardware device during boot up.

- The user selects the Add New Hardware icon from the Windows 98 Control Panel.

INSTALLING PLUG AND PLAY HARDWARE

Regardless of how the wizard is invoked, it provides a consistent step-by-step approach. The following steps represent a typical sequence of events that occur when the Windows 98 Add New Hardware Wizard detects a new device at start up.

1. Windows 98 tells you that new hardware has been detected. After a period of time, the Message Building Driver database appears. A timeline in the dialog box shows the progress of the update.

2. The Add New Hardware Wizard dialog box prompts you to tell Windows 98 where to find drivers for the new device. Click the Next button to continue.

3. Windows 98 recommends that you search for new drivers; click the top radio button to do so. If you know exactly where the drivers are located, click the bottom radio button to display a list of all drivers located in a certain area. Click Next.

4. Tell Windows 98 where to search by checking the drives and locations to search. If you have checked either the CD-ROM or floppy disk, make sure the media with the drivers is in the appropriate drive.

5. When Windows finds the appropriate .INF file, you are prompted to install it by clicking Next.

Note

If Windows 98 can't find the required device driver file in the expected location, you are prompted to browse for the necessary files.

6. When the driver installation is complete, click the Finish button. You may be prompted to restart Windows 98.

Tip #131

By default, the Add New Hardware Wizard often asks you to insert the Windows 98 CD-ROM. But depending on the age of your Windows 98 disc, you may find newer drivers included with the hardware itself. As a general rule, you should use the newest drivers you can when installing new products. In fact, it is a good idea to check the manufacturer's or Microsoft's Web site and download the newest driver available before installing any hardware.

Caution

Installing new hardware involves making changes to the Windows 98 Registry, the central configuration database that is vital to your system's operation. Before you install a new device, you should back up your Registry settings. Open the Registry by clicking Start, Run. Type Regedit in the text box and click OK. In the Registry Editor, select the My Computer icon at the top of the list on the left, click the Registry menu item, and then click Export Registry File. Save the file to a desired location (such as to a floppy disk) by using the Export Registry File dialog box. Also give your exported Registry file a name. If your existing Registry becomes corrupt following an installation, you can fix the problem by using your old, working Registry from your hard drive or floppy disk. An even better idea is to back up the entire Windows directory, which ensures that you can return your operating system to its native state should the installation overwrite or corrupt any key system files.

→ For more details on backing up the Windows 98 Registry, **see** "Backing Up the Windows Registry," **page 491.**

USING THE ADD NEW HARDWARE WIZARD FOR UNDETECTED DEVICES

What do you do if the wizard fails to properly detect your newly installed card? You need to intervene and manually tell Windows 98 what you are installing. But the wizard's consistent interface does help guide you. Follow these steps:

1. Follow steps 1 through 5 in the preceding section. Windows 98 prompts you by saying that it was unable to determine the new hardware device. Click Next.

2. The next dialog box offers a list of hardware device types, as shown in Figure 22.2. Select the appropriate device type and click Next.

3. In the dialog box shown in Figure 22.2, click the device's vendor in the Manufacturers list box and then click the device model in the Models list box.

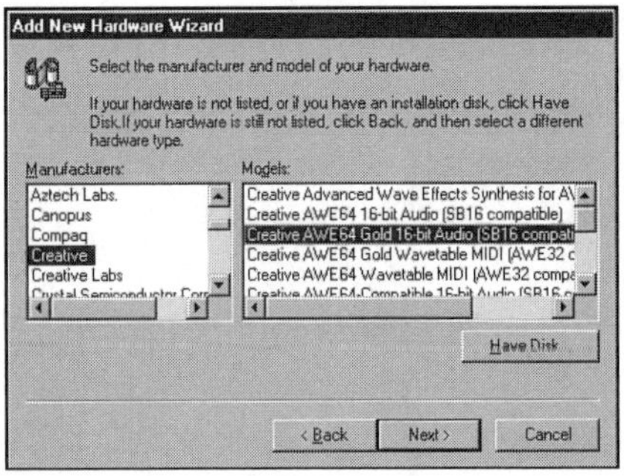

Figure 22.2
The Add New Hardware Wizard provides a comprehensive list of device types from which you can pick out your specific hardware during installation.

4. If you are loading drivers from a floppy disk or CD-ROM, click Have Disk and navigate to the appropriate INF file. The device drivers are then loaded.

5. When the driver installation is complete, a message box advises you that system settings have changed and asks whether you want to restart Windows 98. Click Restart Now so that your driver change takes effect.

ADDING INTERNAL ADAPTERS

The Windows 98 Plug and Play feature, assisted by the Add New Hardware Wizard, makes it easy to install an internal adapter card. Sound boards, graphics cards, and internal modems are all common add-in card installations.

INSTALLING AN INTERNAL ADAPTER

You must exercise caution when working inside your system. Rough handling or incorrect installations can damage delicate leads and electronics, rendering your PC inoperable. You should always unplug your system before you open the case to ensure that a power spike does not damage components during installation.

Caution

Static electricity is a real concern when you're working inside a PC case. Before you touch or handle any cards, make sure you touch one of the PC's metal supports. This action effectively grounds you and draws away any static charge you've accumulated.

To install an adapter card, do the following:

1. Shut down the PC and unplug the power cord from the back of the system box.

2. Remove the system case. Usually, this step entails unscrewing a single thumbscrew or using a Phillips head screwdriver to remove two or more screws located along the back of the case.

Note

If you own a Compaq system, you may need a Torx screwdriver for the unique screws that are used to attach Compaq cases. You can find a Torx driver at your local hardware store or at most computer stores.

3. If the system is a tower or minitower design, lay the system on its side so that the CPU and cards are pointing up. Make sure to place the PC on the ground or some other stable surface.

4. Use a Phillips head (or Torx) screwdriver to unscrew the back plate of the add-in slot you want to use. Remove the back-plate protector or the card, if a card is already installed in the slot.

5. Insert the new card into the desired slot, applying gentle, even force along the top of the card. You may have to rock the card slightly from front to back to gain entrance to the slot.

6. Make sure the card is properly seated and is level inside the slot. The card's back ports should be accessible from the back of the system.

7. Attach any necessary wires or cables to the card. Leave the case off the PC until you are sure the device is working.

Note

Some computers, including models from Compaq, actually will not boot with the cover off. If your PC fails to start, try replacing the cover and booting again.

8. Plug in the PC and start the system. Windows 98 should detect the new card and launch the Add New Hardware Wizard. Follow the instructions as outlined above.

9. After the new drivers are installed, you will probably need to shut down the system and restart. After verifying that the new device is working properly, shut down the PC and reattach the case.

> **Note**
>
> Be careful not to lose the back plates you remove when you're installing a new card. You'll want to keep them handy to cover up the open slot in the back of the chassis if you ever remove the device. Otherwise, your PC will be more susceptible to gathering dust on the motherboard and fans, which can lead to overheating. In addition, open back-plate slots, or blanks, can reduce the efficiency of airflow in the PC chassis, again inviting heating problems with fast CPUs.

INSTALLING OLDER ADAPTER CARDS

The easiest way to install a new older device in a Windows 98 system is to use the Add New Hardware Wizard's automatic detection feature to identify the new card or device. But the wizard can also determine whether you have removed a card. Autodetection is best suited for PCs that have few or no specialty adapter cards, such as sound and video capture cards.

The following steps describe the automatic detection process for installing a Creative Labs Sound Blaster AWE 32 card:

1. Set nonconflicting resource values for your new adapter card by using jumpers or, after you install the card, the card's setup program.
2. Shut down Windows 98 and turn off the power on your PC.
3. Install the new adapter card in an empty ISA slot and then make any required external connections, such as audio inputs and speaker outputs for sound cards. If you want CD audio, make sure to connect the small direct input line from the card to the CD-ROM.
4. Turn on the PC power and restart Windows 98.
5. Start Control Panel and double-click the Add New Hardware icon to start the Add New Hardware Wizard. (This step is necessary only if Windows 98 doesn't recognize the card at startup.)
6. Click Next. Then, select the Yes (Recommended) radio button in the dialog box that appears.
7. Click Next to display the wizard's boilerplate.
8. Click Next to start the detection process. After a few minutes of disk activity, the wizard advises you that the detection is complete.
9. Click Details to display what the wizard detected.
10. If the wizard does not detect your newly installed card, you must install the card manually. Click Cancel to terminate the automatic detection process.
11. Click Finish to install the required drivers from the Windows 98 CD-ROM or floppy disks. The message box indicates the expected medium. You may also consider downloading the latest, greatest driver from the manufacturer's Web site.
12. Insert the Windows 98 CD-ROM into the drive and click OK to install the drivers.
13. If Windows 98 can't find the required device driver file in the expected location, you are prompted to browse for the necessary files.

14. When the driver installation is complete, a message box advises you that system settings have changed and asks whether you want to restart Windows 98. Click Restart Now so that your driver change takes effect.

Tip #132

> If the specific device model name does not appear in the list, don't panic. Click the <u>H</u>ave Disk button below the Mo<u>d</u>els list box, and then insert the driver disk or CD-ROM provided with the hardware. Navigate to the proper drive letter, and the appropriate .INF file will appear. Click OK to load the drivers and device information into Windows 98 from the media.

UNDERSTANDING ADAPTER CARDS

Although adapter installations are relatively similar, several types of adapters are available for PCs. Depending on the age and model of your system, you will need to make sure you purchase cards that are supported in your PC's motherboard. The four most common card types are

- ISA—A low-speed bus common on PCs since their inception; at least one or two slots available on most motherboards.

- PCI—A fast 32-bit bus common on Pentium and faster PCs; generally used for graphics, network cards, and—more recently—sound boards.

- VL bus—A fast 32-bit bus common on 486 systems; generally used for graphic cards.

- AGP—A superfast 32-bit bus that runs at two to four times the speed of PCI; used exclusively for advanced graphics on Pentium II–based systems.

Two other bus types, EISA and MicroChannel, provide faster-than-ISA performance and offer Plug and Play features. However, both are aging bus designs that have fallen out of favor and are generally being replaced by PCI cards and slots.

Before you make any upgrade, you need to make sure that you buy a card that matches the available slots in your PC. A VL bus graphics card, for example, will not fit into a Pentium MMX system that features slots for ISA and PCI cards. Likewise, a new ISA sound card won't be of any use if all the ISA slots are already occupied by other necessary peripherals.

Plug and Play is also a factor. Although Windows 98 recognizes most ISA and VL bus cards, neither bus specifically requires that cards provide PnP capability. PCI and AGP, on the other hand, were designed with PnP in mind.

Note

> Owners of 486 PCs may face a bigger issue: the disappearance of VL bus-based cards. Most graphics board makers have switched their efforts to PCI and, more recently, AGP. If you have a 486 PC that you want to upgrade to handle 3D graphics and video playback, you may be out of luck. If you really want to use these applications, consider upgrading to a Pentium or faster system with PCI card slots.

INSTALLING A MODEM

Modem installations are among the most common of upgrades, if only because of the rapid-fire improvement of modem speeds to the current level of 56 kilobits per second (kbps). Although I recommend always buying the fastest modem you can reasonably afford, the final decision is a question of internal versus external design.

The main advantage of internal modems is their lower cost: They often cost $20 to $30 less than their external counterparts. Part of the savings is due to the fact that internal models don't include the power supply, plastic case, and serial cable found on external modems.

External models provide valuable flexibility. For example, a locked up signal can be fixed by toggling the external modem on and off, whereas an internal modem requires a system reboot. Likewise, informative status lights let you see whether the modem is sending and receiving bits. (However, the Windows 98 modem status applet, shown in Figure 22.3, makes this issue less of a concern.)

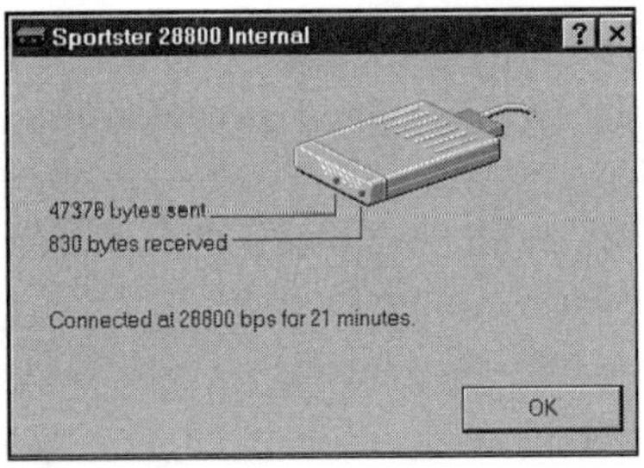

Figure 22.3
Double-click the modem light icon on the Windows 98 taskbar, and you'll see a full-fledged dialog box that shows you how much data your modem has moved.

> **Sportster 28800 Internal**
>
> 47376 bytes sent
> 830 bytes received
>
> Connected at 28800 bps for 21 minutes.
>
> OK

Installing an internal modem is the same as installing any internal adapter card. Installing an external unit simply means plugging the phone cords into the proper modem jacks, plugging in the power cable, and attaching the serial cable to the appropriate serial port on the back of your PC.

After the physical installation is complete, you must tell Windows 98 to work with the newly installed device. Do the following:

1. With the modem installed and powered on, click Start, Settings, Control Panel. Select the Modems icon.

2. In the Modems Properties dialog box, click the Add button.

3. Keep the check box unchecked and click Next to have Windows 98 detect the modem.

4. After a few moments, a final dialog box appears. Click Finish to complete the installation and return to the Modem Properties dialog box. The modem is now installed and available to your Windows applications.

INSTALLING A NEW DISK DRIVE

Windows 98 itself is large enough to motivate a hard disk upgrade, particularly given the low cost of disks with capacities in the 6GB to 18GB range. These are a few of those types of hard disks:

- Enhanced Integrated Development Environment (EIDE)—Common in PCs built within the past three years, these are the most common hard disks on the market.

- Small computer system interface (SCSI)—High-performance systems may use SCSI-based drives, which boast faster response and better multitasking features than do their EIDE cousins.

- Integrated Development Environment (IDE)—An aging standard that supports smaller disks (up to 540MB only).

The vast majority of users have EIDE hard disks for the simple reason that they are less expensive than SCSI drives yet provide capacities of 9GB and beyond.

INSTALLING A HARD DISK

To install an EIDE hard disk, you must physically mount the drive in the system. You must decide whether the disk is to be the main bootable hard disk or whether it is to serve as a second disk for your system.

If the disk drive is to be a second disk, you should connect it to the same EIDE port as the first disk, using the available second connector provided on the cable running from the motherboard to the primary disk drive. Before installing the disk, make sure the pins near the back of the drive unit are set so that the disk is configured as a slave (the boot disk is already set as the master for its EIDE port).

Tip #133	If you have an EIDE CD-ROM drive, set it as the master device on the secondary IDE channel and set the two hard disks as master and slave on the primary channel. This approach improves the performance of the CD-ROM drive and avoids possible time-out problems that can occur when the slow-response CD-ROM drive shares resources with quicker hard disks.

Proceed with the installation.

1. Power down the PC, unplug the power cord, and remove the case.
2. Locate an open internal drive bay (or an external bay if no internal ones are available). Make sure the bay matches the size of the drive, which in most cases is 3.5 inches.
3. Slide the new drive into the available bay, take care to line up the screw holes in the drive with the slots in the drive mounting.
4. Use the supplied screws to secure the drive in the drive bay. Don't overtighten the screws; turning them too far into the drive can puncture the sealed casing.

5. Plug the available connector from the primary EIDE cable into the back of the drive. Align the red stripe on the cable with the side of the drive that contains pin 1, which is usually next to the power input. (Newer systems may use a connector that is keyed with a notch in the cable connector and a corresponding tab that lines up on the port connector. Check the drive documentation carefully.)

6. Plug the power cable from the power supply into the back of the drive. The connector is shaped to fit only one way. Make sure the connection is firm.

7. When you are sure everything is seated properly and secured, plug in the PC and boot it up. The new drive should automatically appear with an incremented drive letter that is one greater than the highest used by your original disk drive. Another good idea is to set the BIOS to automatically recognize the new drive.

ADDING A SCSI DEVICE

The Small Computer System Interface (SCSI) devices may be more common in Macintosh computers than in most PCs, but the daisy-chained bus is still often found on scanners, high-performance hard disks, and other devices. Although more expensive than the popular enhanced IDE bus found on many PCs today, SCSI enjoys several key advantages:

- Higher maximum throughputs
- More efficient multitasking
- Support for both external and internal devices
- Convenient daisy-chained setup

EXPLAINING SCSI

SCSI comes in several varieties. Most new devices use either Fast SCSI or Fast and Wide SCSI, though an even faster version—Ultra SCSI—is now available for high-performance peripherals. Table 22.1 compares various SCSI types.

TABLE 22.1 THE MANY FACES OF SCSI

SCSI Type	Data Rate	Good For
SCSI	10MBps	Scanners, tape backup drives
Fast SCSI	20MBps	CD-ROM drives, hard disks
Fast and Wide SCSI	40MBps	Hard disks
Ultra SCSI	80MBps	Fast hard disks

Unlike IDE, SCSI is a daisy-chained bus, which means that peripherals are connected in a row (much like a string of Christmas lights) from a point originating at the system motherboard. Daisy chaining allows users to connect as many as seven devices from a single SCSI card or port. Each SCSI device must be assigned a unique ID number, called a SCSI ID, that Windows 98 can use to identify devices on the chain. These numbers run from 0 to 7.

Although all devices should work regardless of their assigned ID—assuming that no ID is repeated on the chain—the truth is less clear. Some SCSI devices, such as bootable hard disks, may require an ID number of 0 or 1, whereas others may have a preferred ID assignment. The result: You might have to tweak the ID assignments of the devices for all of them to work properly. Check your documentation closely for such requirements when assigning ID numbers.

INSTALLING A SCSI ADAPTER

Most PCs sold today do not include a built-in SCSI card or connector—they rely on the less-expensive enhanced IDE bus to drive devices such as hard disks and CD-ROM drives. So, if you want to add a high-performance CD-ROM drive, hard disk, scanner, or other peripheral, you may have to install a SCSI adapter card.

The process is identical to that of adding a new adapter card, which is detailed in the section "Installing an Internal Adapter," earlier in this chapter. When the Add New Hardware Wizard comes up, Windows 98 should detect both the card make and model (if it doesn't, you may have to select it manually from the list of SCSI adapters provided in the wizard). When the appropriate driver software is loaded and the system restarts, the card will be ready to host SCSI devices.

> **Note**
>
> Many SCSI adapters include a built-in floppy controller. You should check to make sure this feature is disabled to avoid a conflict with the working controller on your motherboard.

INSTALLING A SCSI DEVICE

SCSI device installations under Windows 98 resemble those for other hardware: The operating system detects the new hardware and guides you through the driver installation process. There are a few tweaks, however.

1. Shut down the PC and unplug the power cord.
2. Remove the terminator plug SCSI Out port of the last device in the SCSI daisy chain and then plug the new device's cable into the port.
3. Plug the other end of the cable into the SCSI In port on the new device. Make sure the total length of your daisy chain doesn't exceed 15 feet because devices won't behave reliably beyond that point.
4. Fit the terminator plug on the new device's SCSI Out port.
5. Select a unique SCSI ID for the new device, using the provided wheel control or other facility (usually found on the back of the device).

6. Power up the system. The Add New Hardware Wizard should detect the new device and prompt you to install drivers for the device.

7. After the drivers are installed, restart the system. The new SCSI device should be ready to go.

> **Note**
>
> SCSI termination can be tricky. If this is the first external device you are installing, you must change the termination setting on the card because it will be terminated if no external devices are present.

 If you're having trouble getting a SCSI device to work properly, see "Common Windows Problems with SCSI Devices" in the "Troubleshooting" section at the end of this chapter.

INSTALLING A USB PERIPHERAL

New to the PC landscape is the *Universal Serial Bus (USB)*, a low- to medium-speed bus designed to replace the serial, parallel, keyboard, and mouse ports on your computer. Windows 98 is the first operating system to provide full USB support, which makes it easier than ever to add external peripherals to your PC. Table 22.2 shows some of the devices served by USB:

TABLE 22.2   USB CHANGES EVERYTHING

Device Type	Devices
Input	Mice, keyboards, joysticks
Imaging	Scanners of all types
Multimedia	Video conferencing cameras, speakers, wave audio
Output	Printers, monitor controls

Like SCSI, USB lets you connect, or daisy chain, hardware devices to each other, eliminating the need to plug everything into the back of your PC. So a scanner can be hooked to your monitor, which in turn is hooked to your PC, and that spells welcome cable relief. What's more, devices such as scanners and speakers, which now require their own power plugs, can draw their power over the USB cable, reducing the number of necessary electrical plugs. USB lets you hook up a maximum of 127 devices to your PC—though few users are likely to test that limit, nor would they want to for performance reasons.

Not surprisingly, USB is a PnP bus—more so than SCSI—so devices are automatically detected by Windows 98 (see Figure 22.4). If you attach a USB scanner to your running PC, Windows 98 automatically initializes the device, allowing you to conduct scans without rebooting or going through other steps. Likewise, the operating system unloads drivers for USB devices that are unplugged. USB can't match SCSI's performance, however, because data rates top out at 12Mbps, so don't expect to see USB hard disks and CD-ROM drives.

Figure 22.4
Like any other device, USB hardware is tracked by the Windows 98 Device Manager, as shown by the Logitech PageScan USB scanner that is logged under the Imaging Device entry.

ADDING A SECOND DISPLAY

Windows 98 adds the capability to send graphics to two displays at the same time, allowing you to expand the size of your Windows 98 desktop. For example, you can view a full-screen graphics layout on one display (at high-resolution, true color) while the other shows your email or Web browser at a different graphics setting. To run multiple displays, you need at least two VGA-compatible monitors, as well as a graphics card for each display. One important note: Because the graphics cards must run on the AGP or PCI buses, the number of free slots will probably limit display support.

To run a second display, you need to install a second graphics card. This process is identical to that outlined in the section "Installing an Internal Adapter," earlier in this chapter. After the new card is installed and running, you must shut down the PC, plug in the second monitor, and restart. The original card and display boot up to the Windows 98 desktop, and the second display subsystem can be used to display desired programs.

TROUBLESHOOTING

COMMON WINDOWS PROBLEMS WITH SCSI DEVICES

I'm having trouble using a SCSI device I just set up. What could be the problem?

If you are having trouble with a SCSI device on your Windows 98 system, be sure the SCSI bus is set up and properly terminated (refer to your specific SCSI hardware documentation for details).

As can often be the case, when you add or remove a SCSI adapter, the system might not start correctly. If you are experiencing this problem, you must make sure the ends of the SCSI bus are terminated. In other words, the bus must have terminating resistor packs (or just plain terminators) installed.

Typically, you will have only internal or only external SCSI devices on your system. In this case, the ends of the bus are probably the SCSI adapter itself and the last device on the SCSI cable. However, if you have both internal and external SCSI devices, the adapter is most likely in the middle of the bus and must not have terminators installed. A problem will occur if you disconnect a device on either end of the SCSI bus that has terminators installed—for example, if you are moving an external SCSI CD-ROM drive from one machine to another. In this case, make sure you install terminators on the device that becomes the last one on the SCSI bus.

SECRETS OF MASTERING THE WINDOWS 98 ENVIRONMENT: MORE ABOUT USB TECHNOLOGY

USB uses what is called a tiered, or layered, topology that allows you to attach up to 127 devices to the bus simultaneously. USB currently supports up to five tiers. Each device can be located approximately 16 feet from its hub. There are three standard types of USB components.

The first component is the *host*, or the system to which all devices are attached (also called the *root*, the *root tier*, or the *root hub*). The host is the system that houses the motherboard or adapter card in the computer through which all USB devices are controlled. The host manages all traffic on the bus and can also function as a hub.

The second component is the *hub*. The hub provides a point, or *port*, to attach a device to the bus. Hubs are also responsible for detecting devices being attached or detached from the bus and for providing power management for devices attached to the hub. Hubs are either *bus powered* (drawing power directly from the bus) or *self powered* (drawing power from an external source). A self-powered device can be plugged into a bus-powered hub. A bus-powered hub cannot be connected to another bus-powered hub or support more than four downstream ports. A bus-powered device that draws more than 100 Milliamperes cannot be connected to a bus-powered hub.

The final USB component is the *device* itself, for example, a keyboard or mouse. The device is attached to the bus through a port. USB devices can also function as hubs. For example, a USB monitor can have ports for attaching a USB keyboard and a mouse. In this case, the monitor is also a hub.

Note When you plug a device into a particular port for the first time, Windows 98 must go through the detection and enumeration process with that device.

CHAPTER 23

MAINTAINING AND TROUBLESHOOTING YOUR SYSTEM

In this chapter

KEEPING WINDOWS 98 UP-TO-DATE

No software is perfect, whether it's an operating system, a program, or the drivers for a piece of hardware. Companies are constantly working on their products to improve performance and reliability, and the main concern today is figuring out ways to get those improvements out to people.

→ For information on service packs, patches, and updates, **see** "The Windows Update Wizard," **p. 896.**

Recognizing this concern, Microsoft combined the use of the Internet with Windows 98 to get updates out quickly and easily, using the Windows Update Wizard.

USING THE WINDOWS UPDATE WIZARD

The *Windows Update Wizard* is a database of drivers, system utilities, and other software maintained by Microsoft. This database gives you one convenient Internet site to check to see whether Windows 98 updates are available for any components of your system. However, because Microsoft owns the site, all updated drivers on the site must be approved by Microsoft, so it may not have all the drivers you are looking for.

To use the Microsoft Update Wizard to search for updates, follow these steps

1. Click Start and click the Windows Update icon. Internet Explorer comes up automatically and attempts to connect to Microsoft's Windows Update Web site shown in Figure 23.1.

Figure 23.1
The Windows Update Wizard and Web site enable you to choose new updates or locate support information.

2. Click on Update Wizard. A Registration Wizard pops up if you are using the Update Wizard for the first time (see Figure 23.2). You must fill out the registration to continue. Part of the registration is to upload your configuration files to Microsoft. You can deselect a check box so that this doesn't happen.

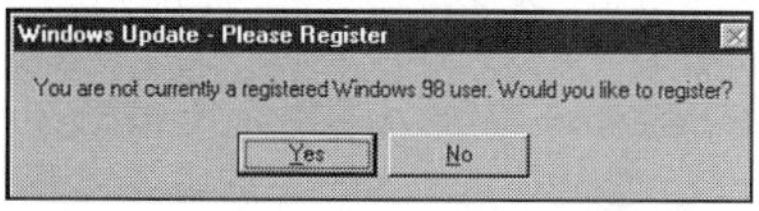

Figure 23.2
The Update Wizard does not start if you click <u>No</u>.

3. The Update Wizard Web page contains two options: Update and Restore. Click Update to scan the Internet for updated system files. A new Internet Explorer window pops up, as shown in Figure 23.3. The Update Wizard loads necessary components into your system and then scans the database for updated drivers.

Figure 23.3
When you click Product Updates, a new page is loaded with a list of updates available for download.

PART

IV

CH

23

4. As updates are found, the wizard refreshes the screen and the list of files available for update. Select a file in the list on the left to see a description of the file, size, and approximate download time on the right side of the main window.

5. Click on Install to install the file. Only one file can be installed at a time, and you might need to restart your computer after a file is installed. Let the computer restart if necessary before downloading a second update, so you know the system is still working properly.

The Update Wizard keeps track of where the new and old files are in case there's a problem. If your system crashes after you install a new file or if some functions no longer work properly, you can go back and reinstall the old files. To do so, follow these steps:

1. Open the Update Wizard and click Restore. A new Internet Explorer window pops up, and the wizard scans your system and gives you an installation history of product updates (see Figure 23.4).

Figure 23.4
View your installation history and download software updates.

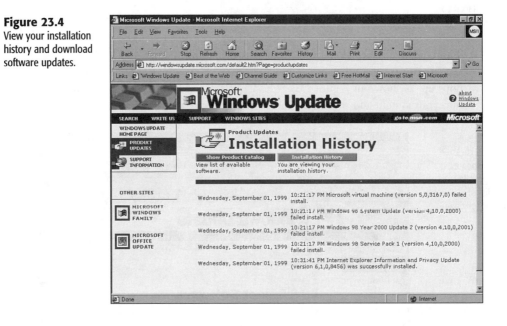

2. Select a file in the list on the left to show the description of the update.

3. You might need to restart your system if prompted.

READING YOUR REGISTRATION AND VERSION NUMBER

Your registration and version number might not seem important at first glance. But because Microsoft updates Windows 98 with patches and service packs, knowing where this information is will be helpful.

To view your current version of Windows 98 and Internet Explorer, as well as your product ID number, right-click on My Computer and select Properties. This step opens the System Properties dialog box shown in Figure 23.5.

Figure 23.5
You will find the Windows and Internet Explorer version numbers in the System Properties dialog box. Your product ID number is the first number in the Registered To area.

IMPROVING WINDOWS PERFORMANCE

The performance of Windows 98 can degrade over time as you add and remove programs and make updates to the system files. This section describes how to use the Disk Defragmenter and ScanDisk features to help keep your system working at top speed. The following subsections explain how to check performance settings, adjust virtual memory, and track system resources and provide a detailed explanation of what the Windows 98 Tune-Up Wizard is and how to use it to automate tasks.

CHECKING PERFORMANCE SETTINGS

Your computer's performance settings are vital tools in the war against problems. The main Performance page can warn you about old drivers or possible viruses and gives you an easy way to check your system resources.

Follow these steps to check your computer's performance settings:

1. Right-click My Computer.

2. Click Properties to access the system settings.

3. Choose the Performance tab at the top to view the performance settings (see Figure 23.6).

Look carefully through the main page of the Performance tab. Make sure that it lists the correct amount of memory and that the File System and Virtual Memory entries both say 32-bit. Incorrect amounts of RAM could indicate that your computer has some bad RAM chips or that you are loading an old DOS program (like Smart Drive) in your AUTOEXEC.BAT or CONFIG.SYS file.

Figure 23.6
Check the main Performance page often. Problems with your computer might show up here.

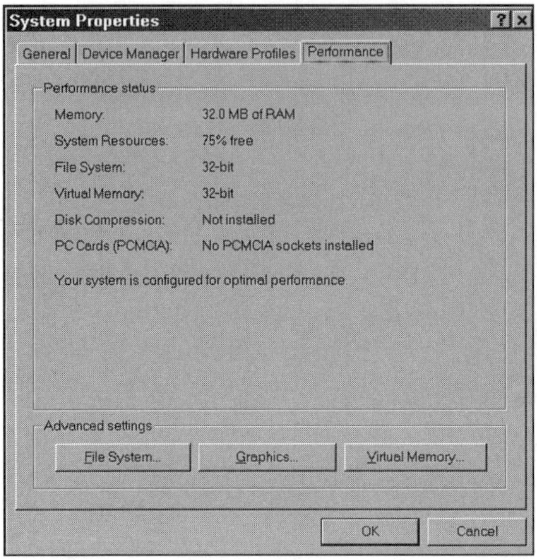

Caution

If the File System area shows some or all of your hard drives using MS-DOS Compatibility Mode Paging, you might be using an old hard disk driver or the Disable All 32 Bit Protect-Mode Disk Drivers option on the Troubleshooting tab might be checked. Use the Update Manager or contact the disk manufacturer to see whether updated drivers are available.

A virus is another potential cause of Compatibility Mode Paging. Viruses and antivirus programs are covered toward the end of this chapter.

The Performance tab gives you access to three types of advanced settings: File System, Graphics, and Virtual Memory.

FILE SYSTEM

Figure 23.7 shows the five tab options on the File System Properties dialog box: Hard Disk, Floppy Disk, CD-ROM, Removable Disk, and Troubleshooting.

Figure 23.7
Hard disk properties.

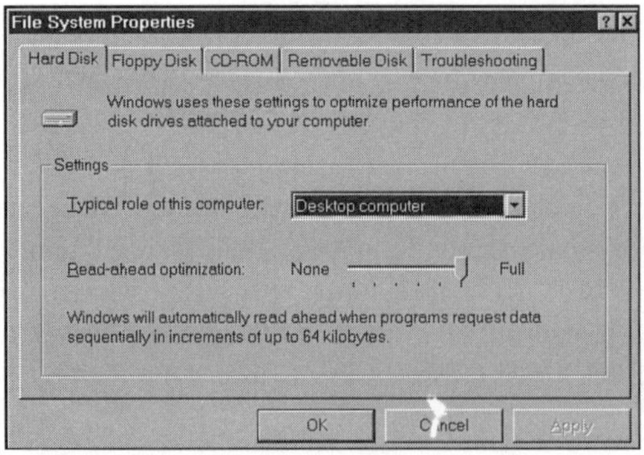

The Hard Disk tab specifies how the hard disk reads files and how the VCACHE file system works. In the Settings area, you can configure the following options:

- Typical Role of This Machine—The three options are Desktop Computer, Mobile or Docking System, and Network Computer. Laptop users should use the Mobile or Docking System option. The Network Computer option could make the system run a bit faster than the Desktop Computer option but also can cause the system to hang during shutdown or restart because the file system cache is not able to completely clear itself.

- Read-Ahead Optimization—This option should be set to Full by default, and unless your system does not shut down or restart properly, Full is the best setting. If you have trouble using the normal shutdown procedures, lower this option one step at a time to try to alleviate the problem.

PART

IV

CH

23

> **Note**
>
> VCACHE is the Windows 98 dynamic swap file. This file grows and shrinks as programs are opened and closed. The swap file, named Win386.swp, is a hidden file located on the root of your hard drive.

The Floppy Disk tab contains only one option, which enables you to have the computer search for new floppy drives every time the system is restarted. This option is good for laptop users who have removable floppy drives, but desktop users can save time by disabling it.

The CD-ROM tab configures the read-ahead buffer for your CD-ROM system. Figure 23.8 shows the two options to be configured.

- Supplemental Cache Size—Set this option to Large. The supplemental cache size is another area to lower if you are having problems shutting down or restarting your computer. If your computer hangs during shutdown, the CD-ROM cache might not be flushing itself properly.

- Optimize Access Pattern For—Choose the CD-ROM type you have. Raising the amount of the cache on smaller CD-ROM drives does not improve performance and might cause problems. Anything over a quad (4) speed CD-ROM should use the Quad-Speed or Higher setting.

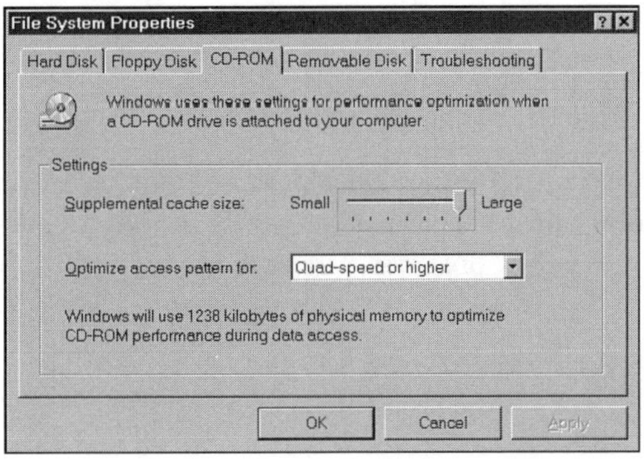

Figure 23.8
CD-ROM properties.

File System Properties

Hard Disk | Floppy Disk | CD-ROM | Removable Disk | Troubleshooting

Windows uses these settings for performance optimization when a CD-ROM drive is attached to your computer.

Settings

Supplemental cache size: Small ———|——— Large

Optimize access pattern for: Quad-speed or higher

Windows will use 1238 kilobytes of physical memory to optimize CD-ROM performance during data access.

OK   Cancel   Apply

The Removable Disk tab also contains only one option: Enable Write-Behind Caching on All Removable Disk Drives. Removable disks include devices such as zip drives, JAZ drives, and Syquest drives, and this option is a good one to check if you have a removable drive. Write-behind caching is enabled by default for your hard disks, though, so there is no reason to use this option if you don't have removable media.

Caution

If you choose to use write-behind caching on removable disks, make sure the computer is done writing to the disk before you remove it; otherwise, some information may be lost.

The Troubleshooting tab is very useful when you're working with older MS-DOS programs, especially file utility programs like Norton Utilities that weren't made for Windows 98. Figure 23.9 shows the six items on the Troubleshooting tab.

Note

Windows 98 handles file systems much like Windows 95 did, and you can use most Windows 95 file utility programs in Windows 98. If you are using FAT32, make sure the utility is FAT32-compatible.

→ For more information on FAT32, **see** "Choosing a File System," **p. 155.**

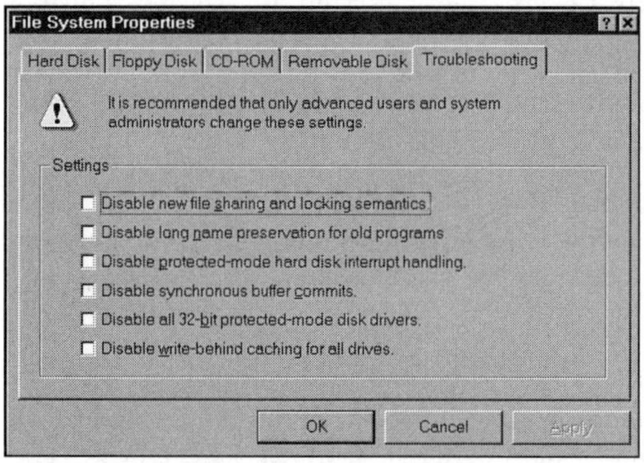

Figure 23.9
Click a check box to disable or enable an item.

Tip #134

Every time you check a box in the Troubleshooting tab, you must restart your computer.

The six options on the Troubleshooting tab are

- Disable New File Sharing and Locking Semantics—Some older MS-DOS programs cannot handle the new file-sharing capabilities of Windows. Check this box to disable Windows file sharing so older programs can work properly.

- Disable Long <u>N</u>ame Preservation for Older Programs—This box is used in conjunction with the utility LFNBK (located in the \tools\reskit\file\lfnback\ subfolder of the Windows 98 CD). LFNBK enables you to back up long filenames while using older utilities; checking this option allows the long filenames to be unlocked so LFNBK can convert long filenames to 8.3 filenames.

- Disable <u>P</u>rotected-Mode Hard Disk Interrupt Handling—Useful with older hard drives, this option lets the drive handle interrupt termination. This option should never be checked in computers with newer hard disk drives.

- Disable Synchronous Buffer <u>C</u>ommits—This option causes a write initiation of the API buffers to the hard disk but allows users to continue working before the write is completed. This will not gain you better performance, but it might cause errors and data loss if the write is not completed. Use this option only when you're troubleshooting performance problems with specific programs that may require it.

- Disable All 32-<u>B</u>it Protected-Mode Disk Drivers—Check this option if you think you are having problems writing information to the hard disk or if your computer does not start because of disk writes. Note, however, that this option causes Compatibility Mode Paging to show up in the General properties tab for all hard drives. It also slows down your system, so use this setting only for troubleshooting.

- Disable <u>W</u>rite-Behind Caching for All Drives—Here is another thing to check if your system does not shut down or restart correctly. This setting shuts off all cache options for all disk drives, including the floppy disk, and slows down your system. So it's not really a fix; it just helps you determine the source of the problem.

GRAPHICS

The Graphics button on the main Properties tab takes you to the Advanced Graphics Settings dialog box, shown in Figure 23.10.

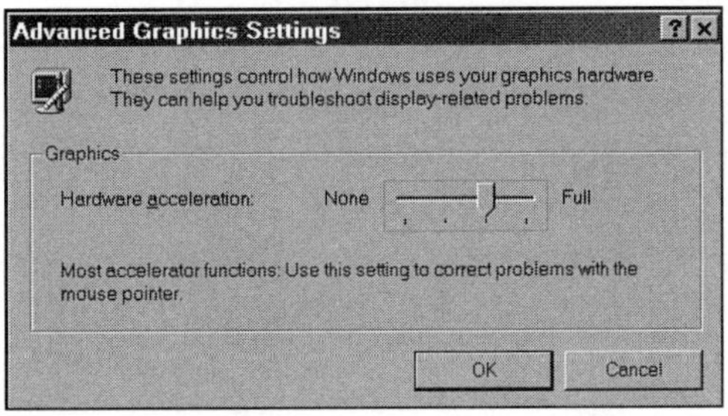

Figure 23.10
Hardware accelera-
tion can be a double-
edged sword. This
feature is not as sta-
ble as it should be.

The only option here is Hardware <u>A</u>cceleration. If you're upgrading from Windows 95, the upgrade should keep the same settings you had before. Hardware acceleration is usually a performance boost to computers, but using hardware acceleration can cause Fatal Exception errors. The text of a Fatal Exception error usually looks something like this:

```
(filename) caused a Fatal Exception error in module (filename) at:
➡0128:bfff... (more numbers)
```

The `bfff` series is the important item here. If the series of numbers starts with A, B, or C, the error could be a video problem. The first step toward correcting it is to look over the Internet or a bulletin board system to see whether new drivers are available for your video card. If your video card has the latest drivers but you are still having problems, start lowering the hardware acceleration level one step at a time. After each restart, use your computer normally to see whether the error reoccurs.

Mouse pointer problems might also be solved by lowering the Hardware Acceleration option. If your pointer disappears or if your mouse pointer seems jerky (and the mouse itself is not dirty), lower the Hardware Acceleration option one or two notches and see if that helps.

VIRTUAL MEMORY

Virtual Memory is the last option on the Performance tab (see Figure 23.11). Virtual memory allows Windows to load and run faster and more efficiently. If you restarted your computer and ran System Monitor (discussed later in this chapter), you would find that Windows has about a 6MB disk cache because the system loads virtual drivers, video drivers, the drivers to run hard disks, and more in virtual memory. In addition, every program that you load adds drivers and files to that virtual memory area.

> **Caution**
>
> Virtual memory is an integral part of Windows 98 and should never be turned off except when you're troubleshooting applicable problems.

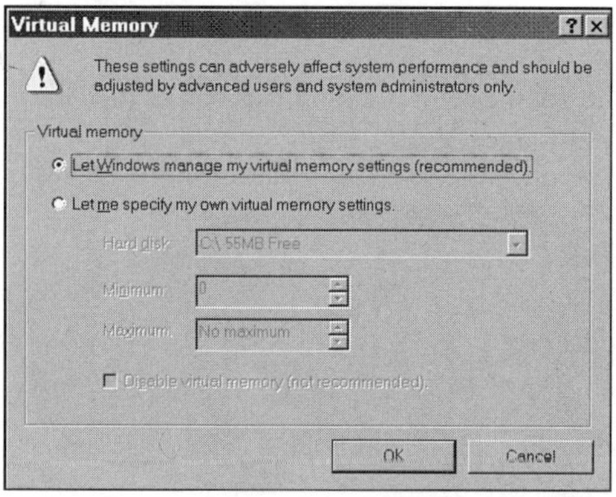

Figure 23.11
Virtual memory as the Windows 98 swap file.

The best option is to let Windows manage your virtual memory settings. Windows 98 has a dynamic swap file that grows and shrinks in size depending on what you need.

Specifying your own settings can improve performance on your computer but imposes limitations on what Windows can swap to the file from RAM. Set the minimum and maximum sizes of the swap file to the same size if you decide to specify your own settings. That step makes a permanent swap file on your hard disk that does not change size, so Windows doesn't have to manage the file. The more RAM you have, the smaller a swap file you need.

A manually created swap file should be around 20MB if you have 32MB RAM (more if you have less RAM). The recommended minimum amount for a swap file is 12MB RAM, which can be eaten up quickly.

A final option is available for disabling the swap file, but this setting will slow down your computer considerably. This setting is not recommended; you should not disable the swap file unless you are having file-related problems.

DEFRAGMENTING DISKS FOR FASTER ACCESS TO DATA

Windows 98 writes information to the hard disk drive using whatever free space there is. As programs are removed, gaps form between the files that are left on the hard disk; those gaps are then filled by new programs that are installed. This process causes *fragmentation* of the hard drive, which cannot be prevented.

As the hard disk becomes fragmented, the computer has to search many different areas to execute programs or bring up data files. This process causes a loss of performance and can cause the computer to have problems during the normal execution of programs.

Disk Defragmenter was created to alleviate these problems. The Windows 98 Disk Defragmenter searches your hard disk for files and programs that belong together and then puts them in the right spots (like organizing a filing cabinet). The new Disk Defragmenter also watches how you use your computer and puts the programs you use the most at the front of the hard disk for faster access. This step is done automatically if you check the option on the Settings submenu (detailed below), so you don't have to worry about picking and choosing which programs you might use the most.

Tip #135	Setting your screen saver to None before you start to defragment your hard disk allows the process to end faster.

To begin using Disk Defragmenter, follow these steps:

1. Click Start, Programs, Accessories, System Tools, Disk Defragmenter.
2. In the screen shown in Figure 23.12, select the drive you want to defragment.
3. Click the Settings button to open the dialog box shown in Figure 23.13.

Figure 23.12
Select the drive you
want to defragment.

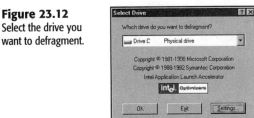

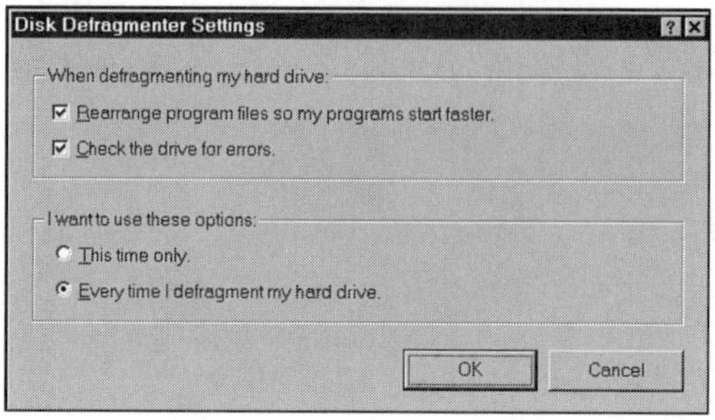

Figure 23.13
Deselect both options in the upper section for a quick defrag of your hard drive.

4. Use the following options to specify your preferences:

R̲earrange Program Files So My Programs Start Faster—This setting tells the utility to choose the programs you use the most and put them at the front of the hard disk drive. This process causes Disk Defragmenter to run slower, but your computer could show improved performance after it's done.

C̲heck the Drive for Errors—This setting tells the utility to test the sectors of the physical disk for problems. The utility might come back with a message to run ScanDisk if the error is something Disk Defragmenter can't handle. This process also causes Disk Defragmenter to run slower, but it is a good option to use if you've been having system problems.

5. If you want to save your settings, click E̲very Time I Defragment My Hard Drive. If you want to use the settings this time only, click T̲his Time Only.

6. Click OK to start the utility.

You also have the option of running Disk Defragmenter from the hard drive icon. To do so, open My Computer, right-click on a hard drive icon, and choose P̲roperties. Then, click the Tools tab to see the screen shown in Figure 23.14. The Defragmentation Status box at the bottom tells you how long it's been since your hard drive was defragmented. Select D̲efragment Now to start the Disk Defragmenter utility.

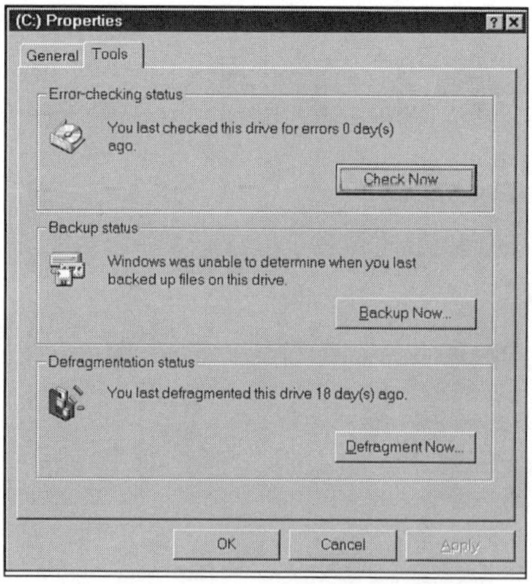

Figure 23.14
You do not have the option of changing settings when you access Disk Defragmenter in this way, but it is a quick way to defrag a specific hard drive.

USING SCANDISK TO PREVENT AND REPAIR DAMAGE

ScanDisk can search all the files on your computer, as well as the physical disk(s), for errors. When it finishes the search, ScanDisk offers you options on how to fix any errors it has found.

To start ScanDisk, click Start, Programs, Settings, System Tools, ScanDisk. The screen shown in Figure 23.15 appears. The Windows 98 version of ScanDisk is equipped to handle FAT16- and FAT32-formatted hard disks.

→ For more information on FAT16 and FAT32, **see** "Choosing a File System," **p. 155.**

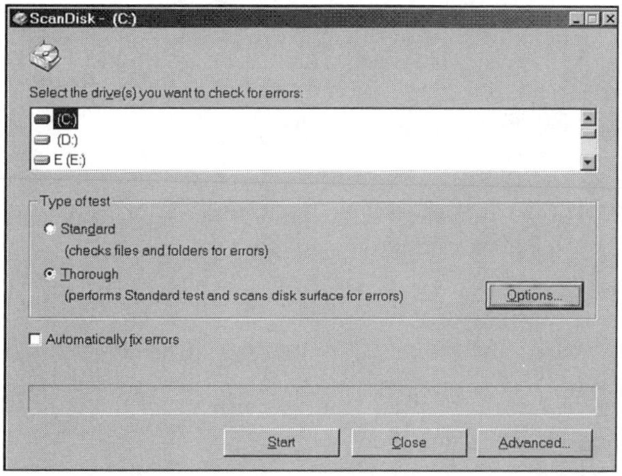

Figure 23.15
The main ScanDisk
window.

Tip #136

> You can also start ScanDisk by selecting My Computer, right-clicking on the drive you want to scan, and choosing Properties. Select the Tools tab and click the Check Now button.

The main ScanDisk window contains two options and a check box. Choose one of the following options:

■ Standard—This setting tells ScanDisk to check all files on your hard disk(s) for errors and to report any errors it finds. With this option, ScanDisk will not check the physical sectors on the hard disk(s).

■ Thorough—This setting tells ScanDisk to check all files on your hard disk(s) and to do a surface scan to check the physical disk(s) for errors. If ScanDisk finds errors on your physical disk(s), it marks the affected sectors as bad and attempts to move any information in those sectors to good sectors.

If you choose the Thorough option, you can also specify what you want ScanDisk to do by clicking on the Options button and using the options shown in Figure 23.16.

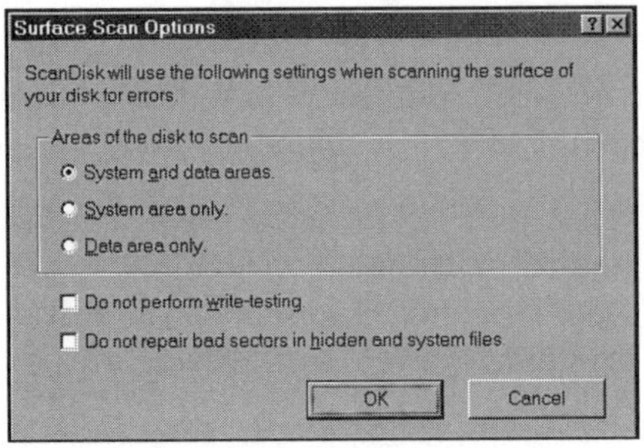

Figure 23.16
Perform a surface scan if you're having trouble installing a new program.

Caution

The files needed to run Windows reside in the System area. If your computer has a bad sector in the System area, you might not be able to restart Windows and might have to reinstall Windows from a DOS prompt.

Toward the bottom-left corner of the main ScanDisk window is the Automatically Fix Errors check box. By default, this option is not checked, and ScanDisk simply shows you each error it finds. If you check this option, ScanDisk shows you the error and gives you the following options for choosing how to deal with the error:

■ Ignore the Error and Continue—You can ignore the error if it's not serious and continue scanning the rest of the disk. ScanDisk tells you if the error is so serious that it cannot continue without fixing the error.

■ Repair the Error by—You can have ScanDisk repair the error and continue. ScanDisk asks whether you want to create an undo file. Always create one if you don't know what ScanDisk is trying to fix. You can always delete the undo file later.

■ Delete the Affected... [file, folder, etc.]—ScanDisk asks whether you want to create an undo file. It's a good idea to create an undo file just in case.

Tip #137

ScanDisk automatically fixes the error and creates an undo file if you choose to automatically fix errors.

At the bottom of the main ScanDisk screen is an Advanced button. Click the Advanced button to access these sets of options:

■ Display Summary—You can tell ScanDisk to Always Display a Summary, Never Display the Summary, or Only Give a Summary When Errors Are Found.

■ Log File—ScanDisk creates a log file called SCANDISK.LOG every time it is run. This file should be placed in the root of C:. You can choose to Replace Log, which deletes the previous log file; Append to Log, which keeps adding to the file; or No Log, which never keeps a log.

You should have a log file to keep track of errors. Use Append to Log only if you want to track errors over a period of time, though.

- Cross-Linked Files—Cross-linked files are two separate files that occupy the same space on a hard disk. This situation does not normally happen, and you may find other problems when this error comes up. The options for cross-linked files are Delete to Remove Both Files from the Hard Disk, Make Copies to Re-Copy Each File to a Different Area of the Hard Disk, and Ignore If You Want ScanDisk to Keep Searching for Other Errors Without Fixing This One. It's recommended that you make copies.

- Lost File Fragments—Generally, file fragments are created when Windows is not shut down properly. The two options are Free to Delete the File Fragments Without Viewing Them and Convert to Files to Save Them and Look at Them Later. If you choose the Convert to Files option, ScanDisk saves the fragments with an extension of .CHK in the root directory of your C: drive. You can view them with Notepad or WordPad. Most often they contain ASCII characters and can be deleted, but it's a good idea to save them if you were working on a file when Windows crashed.

- Check Files For. You have three options to choose from. Choose Invalid File Names to have ScanDisk search your hard disk for filenames that include invalid characters. Choose Invalid Dates and Times to have ScanDisk search for files that have improper dates or times associated with them. Choose Duplicate File Names to have ScanDisk search for duplicate files in the same directory.

  The latter option can slow down ScanDisk if it's searching directories with many files. In addition, if it finds duplicate files, you have the option of having ScanDisk repair the error (ScanDisk renames the files so they have different names), delete the affected files/folders, or ignore the error and continue.

- Check Host Drive First—This option is useful if you have a DriveSpace compressed drive. It tells ScanDisk to automatically check both drives for errors.

- Report MS-DOS Mode Name Length Errors—You can have ScanDisk check for filenames that are too long for MS-DOS mode to handle.

PART

IV

CH

23

Click OK to apply the Advanced option settings you've selected and return to the main ScanDisk screen.

Then click Start to run ScanDisk. ScanDisk could take a long time to run (more than half an hour if you selected the Thorough option or if the hard disk is very fragmented).

USING THE ALL-IN-ONE WINDOWS MAINTENANCE WIZARD

The Maintenance Wizard is a program that automates ScanDisk and Disk Defragmenter and clears your system of temporary files and unwanted networking components. With this wizard, you can have Windows run ScanDisk and Disk Defragmenter automatically on specific days and during specific times when you are not using your system.

To run the Windows Maintenance Wizard, click Start, Programs, Accessories, System Tools, Maintenance Wizard. The first screen you see asks whether you want to do an Express or Custom tune-up (see Figure 23.17).

Figure 23.17
Express setup is quick and easy.

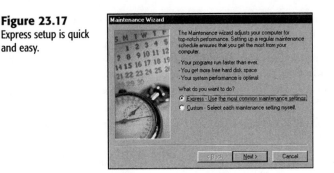

The Express method uses the most common tune-up settings and is a quick way to get the Maintenance Wizard up and running. Choose the Express setting and click Next. The next screen that appears asks what time of day you want the wizard to run. Choose your settings and click Next. Windows shows you what programs will be run. Click Finish, and you're done.

The Custom method enables you to select each maintenance setting yourself. The Custom selection allows for more flexibility but is more difficult to set up. To use the Custom setting, follow these steps:

1. Choose the Custom button and click Next. The wizard asks what time of day you want the programs to run. Choose the setting you want and click Next.

2. The Start Windows Quickly window appears. This window shows you which programs you have opening at startup. You can make Windows 98 start faster by having no programs start automatically at startup. Click Next.

3. Speed Up Programs allows you to schedule the Windows Disk Defragmenter to run on certain days at certain times. You can change when it runs by clicking Reschedule. Click Next when done.

4. In the Scan Hard Disk for Errors screen, choose the options you want. Then click Next.

5. Delete Unnecessary Files is a tricky option. Every time your computer shuts off or restarts abnormally, a temporary file is created. Many newer Windows programs make a temporary file in the case of an accidental shutdown as well. Most of the time, these temporary files are junk and can be deleted. However, if your computer freezes while you're writing an important document, you might be able to use a temporary file to restore your information.

If you do choose to delete unnecessary files, you can use the Settings button to indicate which types of files you want to delete (see Figure 23.18).

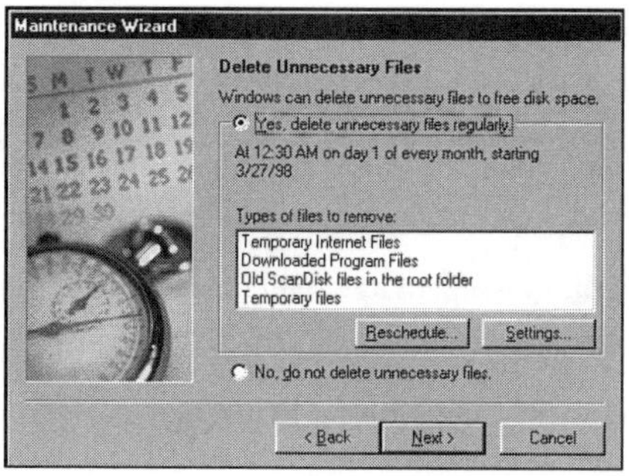

Figure 23.18
Disk Cleanup enables you to view the files that are marked for deletion.

6. The last screen confirms your choices. Your computer must be on when the scheduled choices run. Verify the information and then click Finish. This step adds Task Scheduler to the system tray on the right end of the taskbar.

KEEPING TRACK OF SYSTEM RESOURCES

During a normal day at the computer, you might find yourself opening and closing a few programs, jumping on the Internet for Web pages or to read email, and perhaps playing a game that you end up having to hide in the background. Everything you do on your computer, whether it's moving the mouse around or loading the newest game, takes *system resources*, or memory. You can reclaim resources by closing programs, but those programs don't always give back all the resources.

You can keep track of your system's resources in several easy ways:

- Right-click My Computer, select Properties, and choose the Performance tab. The System Resources line shows a percentage of your free resources. My computer becomes very slow and I'm more likely to get errors when my system goes below 75% free resources with no programs running (using 32MB of RAM). Individual systems may vary, depending on the system and the amount of RAM it has.

- Resource Meter is a good way to keep constant track of your system's resources. To use it, click Start, Programs, Accessories, System Tools and then choose Resource Meter. Resource Meter runs in the system tray of your taskbar. Hold your mouse pointer over the icon to see the free resources you have. You can also double-click the icon to bring up a bar showing your free resources.

- System Monitor is another utility that tracks system resources. Because of its size and the number of options the utility offers, we've dedicated an entire section to System Monitor. See "Using System Monitor to Detect Bottlenecks," later in this chapter.

Note

Keep in mind that Resource Meter uses system resources like all other programs do.

REPAIRING CONFIGURATION PROBLEMS

Windows 98 comes with a fantastic new utility called *System Information*. The System Information utility keeps track of all your computer's file versions, the resources your hardware is using, and the hardware and software components of your computer.

The Tools tab at the top of the utility also provides quick access to Dr. Watson, System File Checker, Registry Checker, and more.

To access the System Information utility, click Start, Programs, Accessories, System Tools, System Information.

GATHERING DETAILS WITH THE SYSTEM INFORMATION UTILITY

The Microsoft System Information utility is a great tool for use in the battle against errors. It's a one-stop utility that enables you to view the resources, system components, and software environment on your computer. You can also run System File Checker, Registry Checker, Dr. Watson, the System Configuration utility, and ScanDisk from here.

You can use the main window of the System Information utility to gather details about your computer (see Figure 23.19). This window is divided into three sections: Resources, Components, and Software Environment.

Figure 23.19
The Microsoft System Information utility enables you to make sure that Windows sees all the components in your computer.

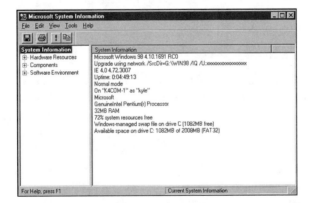

Note

This utility enables you to view your hardware settings, but you cannot change the settings from here.

→ For details on changing settings, **see** Chapter 25, "Special Features for Notebook Users."

For troubleshooting purposes, Hardware Resources is the best section to keep track of. Although the Components section and the Software Environment section have good information on Registry settings and system file versions, the Hardware Resources section contains most of the conflicts and settings needed to determine problems.

The Hardware Resources area in the left pane shows how the different hardware components on your computer are working together. The six specific types of resources you can view here are as follows:

- Conflicts/Sharing—The utility scans your computer for hardware conflicts and software-sharing violations. The right pane shows any problems it finds.

- DMA—Direct Memory Access (DMA) allows hardware devices to bypass the CPU and work directly with memory. The right pane of this window tells you which hardware device is using which DMA setting. This area is very helpful when you're adding new hardware to your computer.

> **Caution**
>
> Two hardware devices cannot use the same DMA channel. The resulting conflict would end with both devices being nonfunctional.

- Forced Hardware—Plug and Play (PnP) devices do not always play fairly. When PnP devices conflict, you can force the hardware to use specific settings. The right window pane shows you which devices are using forced settings.

- I/O—Input/output (I/O) ports are memory locations (not associated with the main memory of the computer) in which information travels between the CPU and hardware devices. Each hardware device can use several I/O ports, but no two devices can use the same I/O port.

- IRQs—When two hardware devices try to use the same IRQ, a conflict arises, and in most cases neither device works properly. IRQ conflict is the most common type of hardware conflict.

→ For more information about changing hardware settings, **see** "Inspecting Hardware Properties Using Device Manager," **p. 424** or "Using the Registry Editor," **p.485.**

→ For information on how to resolve IRQ conflicts, **see** "Resolving Conflicts," **p. 427.**

- Memory—Details the memory address that each piece of hardware uses. Again, no two devices can use the same memory address, but a single device can use several memory addresses.

From the File menu, you can choose to Export or Print any section of or the entire contents of the System Information utility. It's a good idea to print out the Resources area for reference. The information provided might come in handy if you're adding hardware, for example.

REPAIRING DAMAGED SYSTEM FILES

The System File Checker automatically scans your computer's system files and repairs any files that are damaged or corrupt. You can access System File Checker from the Microsoft System Information utility by choosing Tools, System File Checker. You don't have to have the Microsoft System Information utility running, though. Figure 23.20 shows the main screen of the System File Checker.

As an added bonus, the System File Checker includes a file extraction utility. Anyone who has ever had to manually extract files out of CAB files will love this file extraction feature. Click on the Settings button to change the default extraction settings.

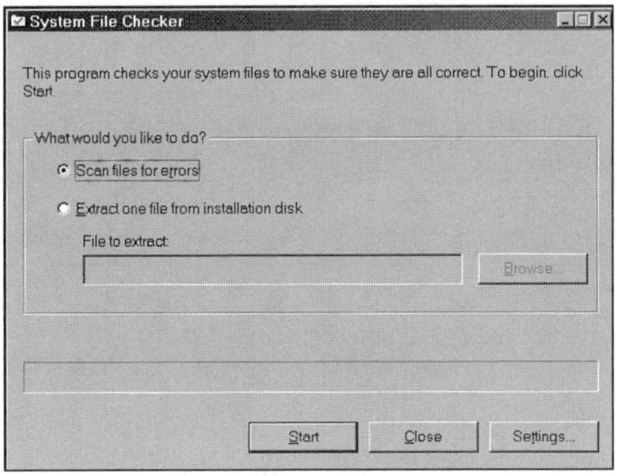

Figure 23.20
Now there's an easy way to extract files from a CD.

Follow these steps to use the file extraction feature:

1. Click the radio button to Extract One File from Installation Disk.

2. In the File to Extract box, type the filename (or you can browse your hard disk to find the file). Then click Start, and the screen shown in Figure 23.21 appears.

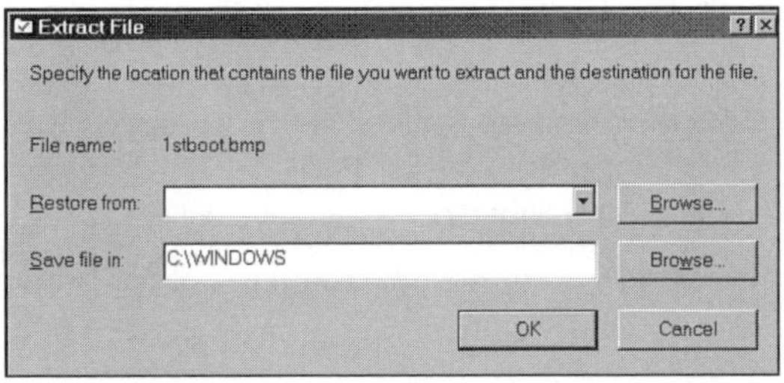

Figure 23.21
You can either type the location of the source file or click Browse to search your hard disk or the CD for the CAB files.

3. Verify the file's location (in the Restore From box) and the destination location (in the Save File In box). Use the appropriate Browse button if you need to change either one. Then click OK.

4. Windows asks whether you want to back up the current file. Doing so is a good idea if you are updating an older file because the new file might not work properly. Choose a folder to place the backup in.

   If the folder you choose does not exist, Windows asks whether you want to create it. Choose the option you want; then click OK to continue and back up the file, or click Skip to continue without backing up the file.

5. Windows should display a successful replacement message. If an error occurs, run ScanDisk to make sure there are no file problems.

SCANNING THE REGISTRY FOR ERRORS

Registry Checker is a simple yet powerful utility that's part of the Microsoft System Information utility. To start Registry Checker, first start the Microsoft System Information utility. Then follow these steps:

1. Click Tools, Registry Checker. Registry Checker automatically begins to scan the Registry for errors.

2. Registry Checker asks whether you want to back up the Registry. You should do so; having a current backup of the Registry is always good in case of future problems.

CHANGING STARTUP OPTIONS TO DIAGNOSE PROBLEMS

Microsoft's System Configuration utility is the next generation of the Safe mode feature that's used to troubleshoot problems. In the System Configuration utility, you can choose which parts of the startup process to use when restarting your computer.

To run the System Configuration utility, click Start, Run, and type `msconfig.exe` in the Run dialog box. Or, if you're in the Microsoft System Information utility, you can click Tools, System Configuration Utility. Either way, the System Troubleshooter screen shown in Figure 23.22 opens.

Figure 23.22
You can now choose startup options from within Windows.

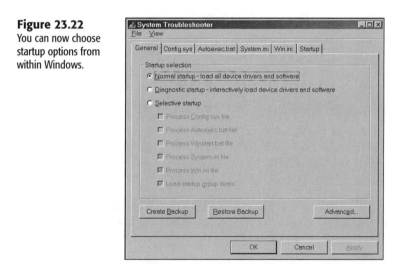

Tip #138

The System Configuration utility works in Safe mode. Use this utility to easily change startup troubleshooting options.

The Startup Selection area of the General tab offers these three startup options:

- <u>N</u>ormal Startup - Load All Device Drivers and Software—This option is selected by default. It allows your computer to start as fast as possible without loading any troubleshooting utilities.

- <u>D</u>iagnostic Startup - Interactively Load Device Drivers and Software—Select this option if you want Windows to display the Start menu each time you restart your computer. When the Start menu appears, you have 30 seconds to make your choice from among six options, which include MS-DOS mode, Safe mode, or your previous operating system. (You do not need this menu to run a step-by-step startup; that's part of the Selective Startup option.)

- <u>S</u>elective Startup—Selective Startup allows you to choose which files to load at startup. The details of using this option are outlined in the next section.

USING SELECTIVE STARTUP

Selective Startup actually offers two distinct options: using Real mode drivers and using Protected mode drivers. The Real mode drivers are CONFIG.SYS, AUTOEXEC.BAT, and WINSTART.BAT. The Protected mode drivers are WIN.INI, SYSTEM.INI, and the startup group items.

You might notice that one or more of the files listed under Selective Startup are grayed out so you can't select them. A grayed-out file is either empty or missing. Most commonly grayed out is WINSTART.BAT, which is a Real mode networking file. Because Windows handles all networking components in Protected mode, this file is usually not present. AUTOEXEC.BAT or CONFIG.SYS might be blank or missing (and, therefore, grayed out), considering Windows handles most of the startup options those files used to control.

If the AUTOEXEC.BAT, CONFIG.SYS, and WINSTART.BAT files are all grayed out, ignore the following instructions for troubleshooting using Real mode drivers. Instead, skip down to the section on troubleshooting using Protected mode drivers.

> **Caution**
>
> You should make a backup of all your files before you start the troubleshooting process. To do so, click the Create <u>B</u>ackup button at the bottom of the dialog box.

To troubleshoot your computer using Selective Startup and Real mode drivers, follow these steps:

1. Open the System Configuration utility (as described in the previous section) and click the <u>S</u>elective Startup radio button.

2. Click the boxes to place check marks next to Process <u>C</u>onfig.sys File, Process Autoe<u>x</u>ec.bat File, and Process W<u>i</u>nstart.bat File (or any of the three that are not grayed out).

3. Click the boxes to remove check marks next to Process System.ini File, Process Win.ini File, and Load Startup Group items.

4. Click OK to restart your computer.

Your system should go into a hybrid version of Safe mode. If your system freezes or encounters problems, you know that the problem resides in AUTOEXEC.BAT, CONFIG.SYS, or WINSTART.BAT. Go back through these steps and choose one file at a time until your system has the problem again. If necessary, you can view a specific file by selecting one of the tabs at the top of the System Configuration Utility dialog box. Then, you can mark out individual lines in that file until you can narrow the problem.

If you have no problems booting using Real mode drivers (or if you have no Real mode drivers to worry about), the next step is to troubleshoot the Protected mode drivers. Follow these steps:

1. Open the System Configuration utility (as described in the previous section) and click the Selective Startup radio button.

2. Click the boxes to place check marks next to Process System.ini File, Process Win.ini File, and Load Startup Group Items. (Load Startup Group Items may be grayed out; this is not a problem.)

3. Click the boxes to remove check marks next to Process Config.sys File, Process Autoexec.bat File, and Process Winstart.bat File.

4. Click OK to restart your computer.

Your computer should boot into Normal mode Windows. If your system freezes or has problems, you know that the problem resides in SYSTEM.INI, WIN.INI, or the startup groups. Repeat the troubleshooting steps and choose one file at a time until your system has the problem again. If necessary, you can view a specific file by selecting one of the tabs at the top of the System Configuration Utility dialog box. Then, you can mark out individual lines in that file until you can narrow the problem.

TRACKING SYSTEM CRASHES WITH DR. WATSON

Windows 98 comes with a new version of Dr. Watson to help track system crashes. Dr. Watson is loaded with Windows 98 but has no associated icons. To get Dr. Watson up and running, follow these steps:

1. Click Start, Run.

2. Type c:\windows\drwatson.exe (assuming that Windows 98 is loaded in the WINDOWS folder of drive C:). A new icon appears in the system tray at the right end of the taskbar.

3. Double-click the Dr. Watson icon in the system tray. Dr. Watson opens and takes a "snapshot" of your system.

With Dr. Watson running, you can easily keep track of any errors that occur. Dr. Watson intercepts each error and takes a snapshot of what your system is doing at the time the error occurs. Figure 23.23 shows one of Dr. Watson's snapshots.

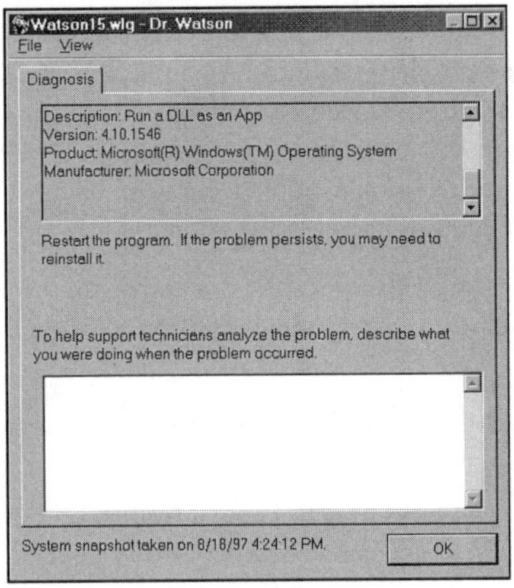

Figure 23.23
The Diagnosis window of Dr. Watson shows you which program or file caused the error.

To keep track of the errors, click in the white section on the bottom of the screen and type a description of what you were doing at the time the error occurred. Click File, Save to save your report. This information will be a big help if you end up calling technical support.

TROUBLESHOOTING COMMON PROBLEMS

Windows 98 comes with 13 troubleshooters to help with common problems. By using these troubleshooters in combination with the tools described earlier in this chapter, you should have a good basis for troubleshooting Windows 98.

The 13 troubleshooters cover the following topics:

Networking (which includes the Dial-Up Networking and Direct Cable Connection troubleshooters)

Modem	Display
Startup and Shutdown	DirectX
Print	Sound
DriveSpace	The Microsoft Network
Memory	Hardware Conflict
MS-DOS Programs	PC Card

To access any of them, click Start, Help. On the Contents tab, select Troubleshooting and then Windows 98 Troubleshooters (see Figure 23.24).

Each troubleshooter has options to choose from and gives advice on whether you should contact technical support. Each step is written in plain English so it's easy to understand.

Figure 23.24
Each troubleshooter provides a series of steps to guide you through testing different components of your computer.

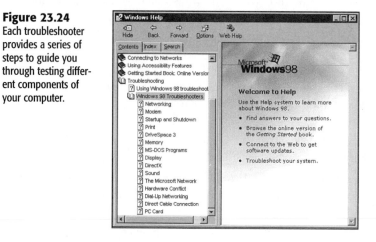

The following list describes the 13 troubleshooters:

- Network Troubleshooter—Whether you are hooking up a network adapter, logging on to a Microsoft or Novell network, or trying to use Network Neighborhood, this troubleshooter has a vast array of steps that can help you solve your problem. The LAN Troubleshooter seems to be the most detailed of all the network troubleshooting wizards. It is well done and contains a lot of good information.

- Modem Troubleshooter—The Modem Troubleshooter goes far beyond just getting your modem to work. It also helps with problems such as setting up the dialing properties, working with communications programs, figuring out a missing dial tone, connecting to the Internet, and dealing with problems related to Web pages. This troubleshooter is a great tool for the Net surfer.

- Startup and Shutdown Troubleshooter—Startup and shutdown problems are the hardest problems to work with. The computer is doing so many things during these times that it's almost impossible to figure out what failed. This troubleshooter details many important areas to look at when dealing with startup and shutdown problems. Use this troubleshooter in combination with the System Configuration utility to fix the problem.

- Print Troubleshooter—This is an expanded wizard from the Windows 95 version. It goes into greater detail on specific problems and offers a larger assortment of possible fixes.

- DriveSpace Troubleshooter—This detailed wizard covers editing the SCANDISK.INI file to allow for compressed drives and unattended scanning. It deals mostly with mounting drives that are having problems, but it also addresses some specific errors.

- Memory Troubleshooter—A very basic wizard, the Memory Troubleshooter mostly deals with simple problems, such as having too many applications open at one time or not having enough available hard disk space. This troubleshooter is a good tool for addressing basic memory problems, but it provides no in-depth information on the pesky errors that pop up from time to time.

If you want to take the guess work out of diagnosing memory problems see "Using System Monitor to Diagnose Memory Problems" in the "Troubleshooting" section at the end of this chapter.

- MS-DOS Programs Troubleshooter—This troubleshooter helps you configure MS-DOS–based programs to work in the Windows 98 environment (so you don't have to restart in MS-DOS mode).

- Display Troubleshooter—A detailed area for display problems, this troubleshooter deals with many errors that might occur and what you can do to alleviate them.

- DirectX Troubleshooter—DirectX is a relatively new component to the Windows environment. It is constantly being updated and revised, which this troubleshooter takes into account.

- Sound Troubleshooter—This troubleshooter goes in-depth on configuring sound cards and figuring out sound options, and it offers suggestions for fixing warbling sound. You'll find good coverage of CD audio drivers as well.

- The Microsoft Network Troubleshooter—This item is a lightweight troubleshooter for MSN. It covers the basics for getting up and running on the Internet, where you can get more help from the online community.

- Hardware Conflict Troubleshooter—This troubleshooter leads you through the basics of working with the Windows 98 Device Manager, providing explanations of the different types of conflicts and ways to resolve them.

- PC Card Troubleshooter—Laptop users with PC Card services will appreciate the detail this troubleshooter goes into about fixing a service or card that has stopped working. People with desktop computers probably won't use this troubleshooter.

PROTECTING YOUR SYSTEM FROM VIRUSES WITH McAFEE VIRUSSCAN

A computer virus is a program designed to create abnormal behavior on a computer. A virus used to be defined as a "malicious" program. However, some companies are finding useful purposes for programs that are basically viruses, so not all viruses are bad these days. A vast majority still are malicious, though, and some sort of antivirus program should be on every computer.

It's a common belief that viruses come from the Internet—through shareware or freeware programs or email. The fact is, however, that the first viruses created came out before the government allowed public access to the Internet. At that time, viruses sometimes came bundled with software that was bought in stores. Even today, you could go to a store and pick out a program that's wrapped in plastic, and a virus could be on the disk (though it's less common).

Note

CD-ROMs are far less susceptible to viruses, but there is still a chance of infection if the manufacturer isn't watching closely.

Email viruses (or email "bombs," as they're sometimes called) are becoming a legend in today's world. It is impossible, however, for email to be infected with a virus. But this does not mean that you cannot get a virus from reading email. You might receive an email message with a file attached, and that file could contain a virus. For that reason, you should never have your email program automatically open attached files. Instead, use your email program to save the file to a special directory. Then, before you open the file, scan it with antivirus software.

Many brands of antivirus software are available these days, and they all seem to do a decent job. One of the best and most popular is the McAfee VirusScan program.

McAfee VirusScan comes with Windows 98 Plus! You can also download the latest McAfee VirusScan from the Internet at www.mcafee.com. Click the SETUP.EXE file to start the installation process.

After it's installed, McAfee VirusScan pretty much runs itself. But be aware of the installation options you can choose from if you do a custom installation.

Each component slows down your computer a bit because McAfee searches every applicable file for possible viruses. So, pick and choose which components you feel are most relevant in your situation. Here's what each component does:

- *Command Line Scanner* loads through the AUTOEXEC.BAT file when your computer boots. This component checks all applicable files for infection. You may want to use this component only when virus security is an extremely important issue because the software loads in Real mode and can take up valuable resources. This component might increase the time needed to boot your computer.

- *VirusScan On-Demand Scanner* should always be loaded. This component enables the user to scan the computer any time. This component also includes some added features. The system slows down only when this on-demand utility is actually running.

- *VirusScan Console* contains administration tools. You can set up automatic scanning, and you can lock it so other users can't shut off the scanning software.

- *VShield On-Access Scanner* runs in the background of Windows 98. An icon in the system tray shows you that the program is running, but no other evidence is found. VShield scans all incoming files for viruses. This component uses very few resources and usually causes no noticeable difference in performance.

- *ScreenScan* constantly scans your hard disk while your screen saver is running. The idea behind ScreenScan is sound, but the component is slow in responding when you want to access your system. Because ScreenScan runs every time the screen saver is activated and is slow to stop, this component can be burdensome.

Other antivirus programs also have custom controls. Regardless of which program you use, choose the controls carefully so you don't lose too much performance.

USING SYSTEM MONITOR TO DETECT BOTTLENECKS

System Monitor is an extensive utility that enables you to track virtually anything that accesses your CPU, hard disk, memory, and network resources. It is a great resource for determining what is causing bottlenecks in your computer.

The most common bottlenecks occur in memory (RAM) and the CPU. Follow these steps to track these two components using System Monitor:

1. Click Start, Programs, Accessories, System Tools, System Monitor. The utility comes up with nothing on the screen. For each item you want to add, use the Edit, Add Item command.

2. To check the performance of your CPU, click Edit, Add Item. Then click Kernel in the left pane, select Processor Usage (%) in the right pane, and click OK.

3. To check the performance of your computer's RAM, click Edit, Add Item. Then choose Memory Manager from the left pane, select Disk Cache Size from the right pane, and click OK.

4. Click Edit, Add Item again. Then choose Memory Manager from the left pane, select Other Memory from the right pane, and click OK.

5. In the main System Monitor window, click View, Line Charts. You should see a screen something like the one shown in Figure 23.25.

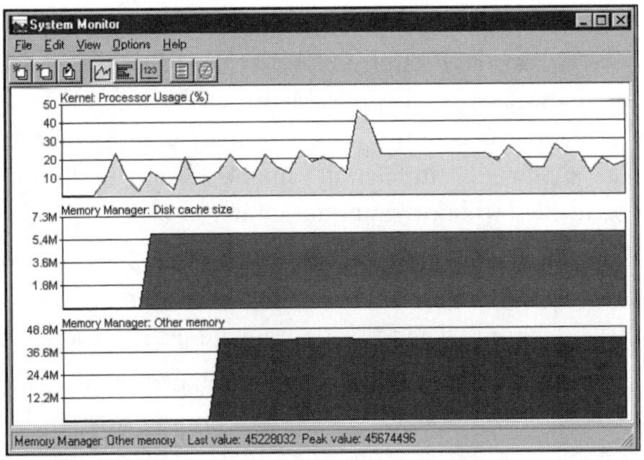

Figure 23.25
You can switch among a chart, a graph, and a numbered list in System Monitor by clicking the right three icons.

Here's an overview of the CPU and RAM performance statistics that System Monitor would display as a result of the previous procedure:

- Kernel: Processor Usage (%)—Shows approximately how much time your CPU is active. The more active time, the more likely that this is causing a bottleneck. Note that the Usage meter hits 100% every time you open a new program.

- Memory Manager: Disk Cache Size—Shows how large your disk cache is. Less memory (RAM) could indicate a larger disk cache, which means that the hard disk has to work more. Hard disks are much slower than RAM, though, so adding RAM could be a good idea if you have a large disk cache.

■ Memory Manager: Other Memory—Tracks all the tasks that your RAM is occupied with. Use this chart with the Disk Cache Size chart. If your computer has a large disk cache, it probably has a high amount of Other Memory as well. The combination of these two statistics can give you a good idea of how much memory is being swapped to the hard disk.

TROUBLESHOOTING

USING SYSTEM MONITOR TO DIAGNOSE MEMORY PROBLEMS

How can I tell if my system's poor performance is due to memory problems?

The System Monitor tool is extremely helpful in troubleshooting system performance. When it comes to system performance, memory is the most critical performance variable. The following are some basic performance issues and areas of concern with regard to monitoring memory and system performance. You can use the System Monitor for troubleshooting memory performance problems in the following situations.

With the dizzying array of applications that run in the Windows 98 environment, some might not release memory when they finish executing. If you think your system has this type of problem, monitor the value of Kernel: Threads over a period of time. This value indicates whether an application is starting threads and not releasing their resources (memory) when it closes. This condition is a real concern if an application is up and running on your system for a long period of time. Restarting your system is often the best remedy for fixing this problem.

If you suspect that your system has a lack of memory and want to confirm your suspicions, check the values for Memory Manager: Discards and Memory Manager: Page-Outs. A high value for these counters indicates a great deal of activity in RAM and disk paging. Add more RAM to solve the problem.

SECRETS OF MASTERING THE WINDOWS 98 ENVIRONMENT: HOW HARDWARE PROFILES ARE SUPPORTED IN THE REGISTRY

Virtual memory in Windows 98 is a dynamic process. Thus, as demand for memory increases, the virtual memory swap file can flex, or grow, to meet the demand. Disk resources are used efficiently because the swap file also becomes smaller as the demand for memory decreases. The Windows 98 system must have enough disk space, or "extra capacity," for the swap file to grow to an optimal size when necessary.

Because the Windows 98 swap file is dynamic, it can shrink or grow based on the operations performed on the system and based on available disk space. A dynamic swap file is usually the most efficient use of resources. A swap file can also reside on a fragmented region of a hard drive with little or no performance penalty. To get the best performance out of the swap file, make sure that the disk containing the swap file has plenty of free space so that the swap file size can shrink and grow as needed.

Normally, you should allow the system defaults to provide the best performance of virtual memory and the swap file. However, you can choose to define some additional performance settings for the swap file. For example, if you have a system with multiple physical disks, you may move the swap file location to a disk that isn't being used as much for other read and write operations. So if you have two hard drives in your system and one of the drives holds all frequently accessed user applications, move the swap file to the other, less busy drive.

To adjust the setting of the virtual memory swap file do the following:

1. In Control Panel, double-click System, click the Performance tab, and then click Virtual Memory.

2. To specify a different hard disk, click the Let Me Specify My Own Virtual Memory Settings option. Then, specify the new disk in the Hard Disk text box. Or type values (in kilobytes) in the Minimum or Maximum text box. Then click OK.

If you set the maximum swap file size in the Virtual Memory dialog box to the amount of free space currently on a drive, you will have a problem. Windows 98 operates under the assumption that it can increase the size of the swap file beyond that starting size to the maximum if more free disk space becomes available. It is always a good idea to have free space on your drive, so you should impose a fixed limit on the maximum swap file size. Make the maximum size something less than it would take to reach the capacity of the drive.

CHAPTER 24

WORKING WITH THE WINDOWS REGISTRY

In this chapter

WORDS OF WARNING: MAKE A PLAN

Working with the Registry can be risky. The worst-case scenario is that Windows 98 will no longer start. The best-case scenario is that you won't notice anything different, but on the whole, you'll probably cause certain applications or devices to behave improperly. No damage is irreparable, however, if you back up the Registry by using the methods described in this chapter.

But just to be sure you know the risks, take a look at why using the Registry Editor to edit the Registry is dangerous:

- The Registry Editor doesn't validate your changes.
- When you make a change to one value, you can easily miss related values in other parts of the Registry.
- The Registry Editor doesn't have an undo feature. As soon as you make a change, it's a done deal.

You can learn to make changes in the Registry without risking anything, and you can safely experiment with the Registry. After writing three books on the Registry (and through endless tinkering), I've made only one change that I couldn't safely recover from. You can make sure that your experience with the Registry is just as good by making a plan before you strike out to make changes.

To that end, here's a sample plan that you can change to suit your own needs:

- Back up the Registry before you make any change. You learn many techniques for backing up the Registry in this chapter. Most of them are quick and painless.
- Make only one change at a time. If you make too many changes in one sitting, you're not as likely to figure out what went wrong if Windows fails.
- Don't delete data from the Registry until you're absolutely sure of the impact. Instead, rename data so as to hide it from Windows (which has the same effect as deleting it). When you're sure that everything is okay, delete the key.
- Don't modify a Registry setting until you're sure about the impact it will have. Make a copy of the setting in a new temporary entry; then make your change. If everything works out okay, remove the temporary value. At the very least, write down the original value so that you can easily go back to it if things don't work out.
- Deleting a Registry entry can kill a system, whereas changing or modifying an entry merely causes problems of varying degrees of severity.

Tip #139

You wouldn't think the Registry would be in peril when you install a new program because you don't change any Registry settings yourself. Any time you add an application or program on your system, the Registry is updated to reflect those additions. Most applications written to run on Windows 98 should cause you no problems. However, given the unpredictability of some "rogue" applications and their possible negative effects on the Registry, you should back up the Registry before you install any new programs, particularly programs with which you're unfamiliar so that you can easily recover from a wayward Setup program's faux pas.

UNDERSTANDING THE WINDOWS REGISTRY

Windows 98 stores the entire contents of the Registry in two files: SYSTEM.DAT and USER.DAT. These are binary files that you can't view with a text editor (as you can INI files). Windows 98 also turns on the Read-only, System, and Hidden attributes of SYSTEM.DAT and USER.DAT so that you can't accidentally replace, change, or delete these files. SYSTEM.DAT contains configuration data specific to the computer on which you installed Windows 98. USER.DAT contains configuration data specific to the current user.

Take a look. SYSTEM.DAT and USER.DAT are located in C:\Windows. The location of USER.DAT will be different if you've configured the computer to use profiles, though. In that case, Windows would have created a new system folder called C:\Windows\Profiles under which you'll find a folder for each user who logs on to the machine. For example, C:\Windows\Profiles\Jerry contains my configuration data, and C:\Windows\ Profiles\Pompy contains my dog's configuration data. Each user's profile folder contains an individual copy of USER.DAT. You'll still find a default USER.DAT in C:\Windows, which Windows uses as a template for new users.

Note

Profiles enable multiple users to log on to a single computer with their own familiar settings (Start menu options, desktop configuration, and so on). You enable profiles by using the Enable Multi-Users Settings Wizard. To start the wizard, select the Users icon in the Control Panel or open the Passwords Properties dialog box by selecting the Passwords icon in the Control Panel.

UNDERSTANDING REGISTRY ENTRIES

Take a look at Figure 24.1. This figure shows you what the Windows 98 Registry looks like when viewed in the Registry Editor. In the left pane, you see all the Registry's keys. In the right pane, you see all the configuration data for the key that's selected in the left pane. Each group of configuration data in the Registry is called a *key*. Keys are very much like sections in INI files. They have names and can contain one or more bits of configuration data. Key names can be made up of any combination of alphabetical, numeric, and symbol characters, as well as spaces.

Registry keys

Figure 24.1
The Registry Editor is a simple program that packs a lot of power.

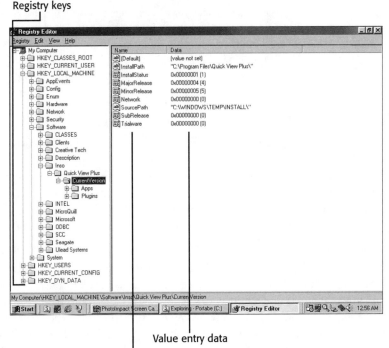

Value entry data

Value entry name

The most important difference between the Registry's keys and an INI file's sections is that a Registry key can contain other keys. That's the origin of the Registry's hierarchy. You can think of it as stuffing a stack of file folders inside another file folder. At the top of Figure 24.1 is My Computer. This entry just represents the computer whose Registry you're viewing (you can view remote computers, too). Below My Computer are the *root keys*. Each root key contains a number of *subkeys*.

Tip #140

This chapter uses the terms *key* and *subkey* interchangeably. In reality, when referring to a child key (a key underneath the key being discussed), you should call it a *subkey*.

Below subkeys are *value entries*, where Windows stores the actual configuration data. Each key can contain one or more value entries, and each value entry has three parts:

■ Name— The name can be any combination of alphabetical, numerical, and symbol characters, including spaces. The name uniquely identifies the value entry within a particular key. However, you might find the same name used in different Registry keys.

■ Data type—Whereas INI files store only string configuration data, the Registry stores a variety of data types in a value entry. Table 24.1 describes the types of data you might find in the Windows 98 Registry.

- Value Data—Value data can be up to 64KB in size in Windows 98. An important concept you need to understand is that of an empty value entry. No such animal. If Windows or some other program has never assigned a value to a value entry, the value entry contains the *null* value. Assigning a null value is very different from assigning an empty string to a value entry; an empty string is a character string that just happens to be of zero length.

TABLE 24.1   WINDOWS 98 DATA TYPES

Type	Description
String	Text, words, or phrases. The Registry always displays strings within quotes.
Binary	Binary values of unlimited size, represented as hexadecimal. (These are similar to DWORDs except are not limited to 4 bytes.)
DWORD	32-bit binary values in hexadecimal format (double words). The Registry displays a DWORD as an eight-digit (4 bytes) hexadecimal number.

PART

IV

CH

24

Note

Every key contains at least one value entry, called (Default). This chapter uses the term *default value entry* for a key. The default value entry is always a string value. Windows provides it for compatibility with the Windows 3.1 Registry and older 16-bit applications. In many cases, the default value entry doesn't contain anything at all. In other cases, a program needs to store only one value, so the default value entry is the only data stored in that key.

Tip #141

When you are viewing the Registry with the Registry Editor, you might notice that you can see keys and subkeys in the left pane, but nothing is listed in the right pane. This situation occurs even though a key or subkey is selected in the left pane and does not indicate the absence of data or values for that data and the associated key. What it does mean is that the default settings for the Registry are in place. To change or override the default settings, you need to add a data type and value data entry.

HKEY_LOCAL_MACHINE

The Windows 98 Registry contains six root keys (take another look at Figure 24.1). HKEY_LOCAL_MACHINE and HKEY_USERS are real Registry keys; the others are *aliases*. Aliases are just shortcuts to branches within HKEY_LOCAL_MACHINE or HKEY_USERS that make accessing a particular set of configuration data easier for programmers and users. Take a look at the real keys first (we cover the aliases in a bit).

HKEY_LOCAL_MACHINE contains configuration data that describes the hardware and software installed on the computer, such as device drivers, security data, and computer-specific software settings (uninstall information, for example). This information is specific to the computer itself instead of to any one user who logs on to it. The following list describes the contents of each subkey immediately under HKEY_LOCAL_MACHINE:

- Config—Config contains information about multiple hardware configurations for the computer (in other words, hardware profiles). It contains groups of individual hardware settings from which Windows 98 can choose automatically or you can choose when you start the computer. Each subkey under HKEY_LOCAL_MACHINE\Config (numbered 0001, 0002, and so on) represents an individual hardware profile. HKEY_LOCAL_MACHINE\ System\CurrentControlSet\Control\IDConfigDB contains the name and identifier of the hardware profile that Windows 98 is currently using.

- Enum—This subkey contains information about each device installed on the computer. Each subkey under HKEY_LOCAL_MACHINE\Enum represents a particular type of bus (basic input/output system, or BIOS; ESDI, PCI, PCMCIA, or SCSI, for example). Under each hardware class are one or more subkeys, which in turn contain additional subkeys that identify a single piece of hardware. The organization of this branch and its contents depends largely on the devices you install on the computer and how the manufacturer organizes its settings.

- Hardware—Windows 98 doesn't do much with this subkey because it provides hardware for compatibility with Windows NT.

- Network—This subkey contains information about the user who is currently logged on to the computer. Each time a user logs on to the computer, Windows stores details about the current network session (such as the user's logon name) in HKEY_LOCAL_MACHINE\Network\Logon.

- Security—This subkey contains information about the computer's network security provider, administrative shares (for remote administration), and public shares. Windows 98 keeps track of all the open network connections other users have on your computer in HKEY_LOCAL_MACHINE\Security\Access. You'll find a single subkey for each connection.

- Software—This subkey and the next are the heart and soul of HKEY_LOCAL_MACHINE. Programs store settings that are specific to the computer in this subkey. These programs store their settings in branches that look like HKEY_LOCAL_MACHINE\ Software*CompanyName**ProductName**Version*, where *CompanyName* is the name of the company, *ProductName* is the name of the product, and *Version* is the current version number of the product. You'll find many Windows-specific settings in this subkey, too, in HKEY_LOCAL_MACHINE\Software\Microsoft\Windows\CurrentVersion.

> **Note**
>
> The single largest branch in the Registry is HKEY_LOCAL_MACHINE\Software\Classes. This subkey describes all the associations between documents and programs, as well as information about COM objects; thus, it is very large. You can also get to this branch through the root key HKEY_CLASSES_ROOT, which is an alias for HKEY_LOCAL_MACHINE\ Software\Classes.

- System—Windows maintains *control sets*, each of which determines exactly which device drivers and services Windows loads and how it configures them when Windows starts. For example, a control set provides the various parameters Windows needs when it starts, such as the computer's name on the network and the current hardware profile. A control set also controls which device drivers and file systems Windows loads and provides the parameters Windows needs to configure each driver.

The Windows 98 Configuration Manager

The Configuration Manager is the heart of Plug and Play. It is responsible for managing the configuration process on the computer. It identifies each bus on your computer (PCI, SCSI, ISA) and all the devices on each bus. It also notes the configuration of each device, making sure that each device is using unique resources (IRQ and I/O address).

To do its job, the Configuration Manager works with three key components: bus enumerators, arbitrators, and device drivers. Here's a summary of the purpose of each component:

Bus enumerators	Bus enumerators are responsible for building the *hardware tree*. They query each device or each device driver for configuration information.
Arbitrators	Arbitrators assign resources to each device in the hardware tree. That is, they dole out IRQs, I/O addresses, and such, to each device.
Device drivers	The Configuration Manager loads a device driver for each device in the hardware tree and communicates the device's configuration to the driver.

PART

IV

CH

24

HKEY_USERS

HKEY_USERS contains the user-specific configuration data for the computer. That is, Windows stores configuration data for each user that logs on to the computer in a subkey under HKEY_USERS. If you haven't configured the computer to use profiles, all you'll find is a single subkey called .DEFAULT. The following list describes what you'll find in HKEY_USERS\.DEFAULT or within each user's subkey:

■ AppEvents—AppEvents contains associations between the sounds Windows produces and events generated by Windows and other programs. Under AppEvents, you'll find two subkeys: EventLabels, which describes each sound event, and Schemes\Apps, which assigns sound files to each event.

■ Control Panel—Control Panel contains settings that the user can change from the Control Panel (such as Display and Accessibility Options). Many of the settings in Control Panel are migrated from the Windows 3.1 WIN.INI and CONTROL.INI files.

■ InstallLocationsMRU—This subkey contains the last several paths from which you've installed Windows extensions. Every time you double-click the Add/Remove Programs icon in the Control Panel and click the Have Disk button on the Windows Setup tab to install an extension, Windows 98 records the path of the INF file in InstallLocationsMRU.

■ Keyboard Layout—Keyboard Layout defines the language used for the current keyboard layout. You change these values by clicking the Keyboard icon in the Control Panel.

- Network—Windows 98 stores persistent network connections in HKEY_CURRENT_USER\Network\Persistent. Each subkey represents a mapped drive letter (D, E, F, and so on). Under each drive letter's subkey, you'll find a handful of value entries—such as Provider Name, RemotePath, and UserName—that describe the connection.

- Software—Software is by far the most interesting subkey in this branch. It contains software settings that are specific to each user. Windows stores each user's desktop preferences under this subkey. In addition, each program installed on the computer installs user-specific preferences in this subkey. This subkey is organized just like the similarly named subkey in HKEY_LOCAL_MACHINE.

Note

The Registry has an order of precedence. Windows or other programs often store duplicate data in both HKEY_USERS and HKEY_LOCAL_MACHINE. In such cases, the configuration data stored in HKEY_USERS has precedence over the data stored in HKEY_LOCAL_MACHINE. Windows uses this approach so that individual user preferences will override computer-specific settings.

ALIASES

Even though the Registry Editor does show six root keys, there are really only two: HKEY_LOCAL_MACHINE and HKEY_USERS. The remaining root keys are really just aliases that refer to *branches* (entire portions of the Registry beginning with a particular key) within the other two root keys. In other words, aliases are a bit like shortcuts in Explorer: If you change a value in one of the aliases, that value is actually changed in either HKEY_LOCAL_MACHINE or HKEY_USERS.

Here's more information about each alias:

- HKEY_CLASSES_ROOT—An alias for HKEY_LOCAL_MACHINE\Software\CLASSES, which contains the associations between file types and programs.

- HKEY_CURRENT_USER—An alias for a branch in HKEY_USERS that contains the configuration data for the user who is currently logged on. Normally, HKEY_CURRENT_USER points to HKEY_CURRENT_USER\.DEFAULT.

- HKEY_CURRENT_CONFIG—An alias for HKEY_LOCAL_MACHINE\Config*Profile*, where *Profile* is one of 0001, 0002, and so on. It contains the current hardware configuration for the computer.

- HKEY_DYN_DATA—An entry that contains dynamic information about the current status of the computer. HKEY_DYN_DATA isn't really an alias, but it is totally dynamic and is not permanently stored on disk.

Note

When you export the Registry to a REG file, the file contains entries found only in HKEY_LOCAL_MACHINE and HKEY_USERS. That's because exporting the aliases is redundant.

Abbreviations for Root Keys

Many publications (but not this one) use abbreviations for the root keys. The following table gives the abbreviation used for each root key:

Root Key	Abbreviation
HKEY_CLASSES_ROOT	HKCR
HKEY_CURRENT_USER	HKCU
HKEY_LOCAL_MACHINE	HKLM
HKEY_USERS	HKU
HKEY_CURRENT_CONFIG	HKCC
HKEY_DYN_DATA	HKDD

USING THE REGISTRY EDITOR

REGEDIT might not be on your Start menu but is probably in your Windows folder (C:\Windows). The filename is REGEDIT.EXE. To open it, choose Start, Programs, Run. Then type regedit and click OK. The REGEDIT window pops up. If you want, you can drag REGEDIT.EXE from your Windows folder to the Start button to create a shortcut (see Figure 24.2).

Figure 24.2
The Regedit icon.

 If your system is part of a large, networked environment, you may not have sufficient privileges on your system to edit the Registry. For more information, see "Problems Making Changes to the Registry" in the "Troubleshooting" section at the end of the chapter.

Caution

Preventing user access to the Registry Editor requires the cooperation of the program that the user is using to edit the Registry. REGEDIT cooperates. Other programs probably won't. Thus, in Windows 98 you can't be sure that a user doesn't have access to the Registry.

SEARCHING FOR KEYS AND VALUE ENTRIES

When you search the Registry, REGEDIT looks for keys, value names, and value data that match the text you specify. In other words, REGEDIT searches by using the name of each key, the name of each value entry, and the actual data from each value entry. You can use the search feature to find entries relating to a specific product, to find all the entries that contain a reference to a file on your computer, or to locate entries related to a particular hardware device.

Here's how to search the Registry:

1. Choose <u>E</u>dit, <u>F</u>ind from the main menu, and REGEDIT displays the Find dialog box shown in Figure 24.3.

Tip #142

If you select any item in REGEDIT's left pane and start typing the name of a Registry key, REGEDIT moves to the key that best matches what you've typed thus far. For example, expand HKEY_CLASSES_ROOT. Then press the period (.), and REGEDIT selects .386; press b, and REGEDIT selects .bat; press m, and REGEDIT selects .bmp. Note that if you pause between keystrokes, REGEDIT starts your *incremental search* over with the next key you type.

Figure 24.3
Use these options to search for an item in the Registry.

2. Type the text for which you want to search. If you're searching for a number, try both the decimal and hexadecimal notations because both formats are common in the Registry.

3. In the Look At section, deselect the parts of the Registry in which you don't want REGEDIT to search: <u>K</u>eys, <u>V</u>alues, and/or <u>D</u>ata.

4. Click <u>F</u>ind Next, and REGEDIT searches for a match. This step can sometimes take quite a while (up to a few minutes on slower machines). If REGEDIT finds a matching key, it selects that key in the left pane. If REGEDIT finds a matching value entry, it opens the key that contains the value entry in the left pane and selects the value entry in the right pane.

5. If the result isn't exactly what you had in mind, press F3 to repeat the search. When REGEDIT reaches the bottom of the Registry, a dialog box tells you that the search is over.

Tip #143

If the left pane isn't big enough to easily tell which key REGEDIT found, look at REGEDIT's status bar to see the full name of the key. Alternatively, you can drag the window divider to the right to make more space in the left pane.

RENAMING A KEY OR VALUE ENTRY

Sometimes you have a really good reason to rename a key or value entry: to hide an entry from Windows while you test a change. Well, that's easy enough. Renaming a key or value entry in REGEDIT is similar to renaming a file in Windows Explorer except that you can't rename the REGEDIT item by clicking on the name. Instead, you select the key or value entry that you want to rename; choose Edit, Rename; type over the name or change it; and then press Enter.

| Tip #144 | You can also rename a key or value entry by selecting it and pressing F2. |

CHANGING AN ENTRY'S VALUE

As a user, changing a value entry's setting is probably the number one activity you'll do with REGEDIT. You might want to personalize your desktop, for example, or you might need to adjust a Transmission Control Protocol/Internet Protocol (TCP/IP) setting to work better with your network.

Here's how to change a value entry:

1. Double-click a value entry in the right pane to open the Edit dialog box. Remember that each value entry can be a string, DWORD, or binary data. The exact dialog box depends on the type of data stored in the value. Figures 24.4, 24.5, and 24.6 show you what each dialog box looks like.

2. Change the value and then click OK to save your changes.

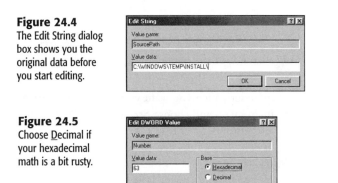

Figure 24.4
The Edit String dialog box shows you the original data before you start editing.

Figure 24.5
Choose Decimal if your hexadecimal math is a bit rusty.

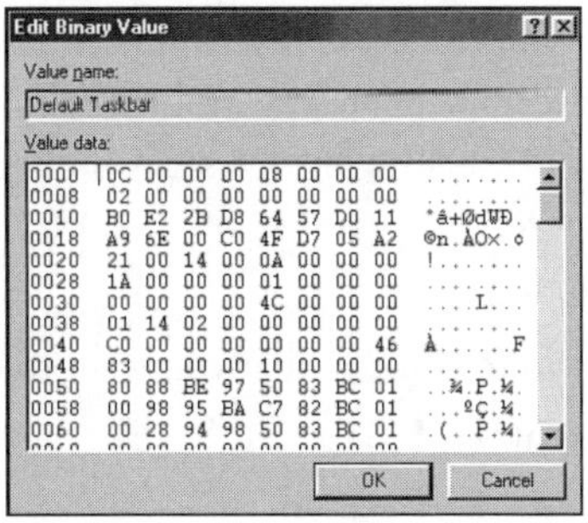

Figure 24.6
You can use the Windows calculator (in Scientific mode) to convert decimal values to hexadecimal values for use in this dialog box.

Tip #145

Protect yourself when changing value data. Note the name of the value entry that you want to change and then rename it with some obscure name that Windows won't recognize such as MyValue. Then, create a new Registry key with the name you assigned (as described in the section "Creating a New Key or Value Entry") and set its value to what you want. This way, you can always restore the original setting by deleting the value entry you created and renaming the value entry you saved with its original name.

Changes that you make to the Registry might not be reflected immediately in Windows or the programs that are currently running. The only way to make sure is to close REGEDIT and restart Windows or the affected program.

To restart Windows 98 quickly, choose Shut Down from the Start menu. In the Shut Down Windows dialog box, select Restart the Computer and then hold down the Shift key and click OK. Windows 98 restarts without rebooting your computer.

CREATING A NEW KEY OR VALUE ENTRY

Creating a new key or value entry is generally harmless—and equally useless unless, of course, you know for sure that either Windows or another program will use your new key. For example, the Microsoft Knowledge Base might instruct you to create a new Registry key to fix a problem. That's useful. Creating a new key out of thin air is pretty useless, however.

To create a new key or value entry, do one of the following:

- New key—Select the existing key under which you want your new subkey to appear. Choose Edit, New, Key from the main menu; type the name of your key; and press Enter.

- New value entry—Select the existing key under which you want your new value entry to appear. Choose Edit, New from the main menu and choose String Value, Binary Value, or DWORD Value from the resulting submenu. Then, type the name of your new value entry and press Enter. You can edit your key as described in the section "Changing an Entry's Value" earlier in this chapter.

DELETING A KEY OR VALUE ENTRY

Be very careful about deleting keys and value entries from your Registry. You'll likely prevent Windows from working properly if you carelessly delete keys or value entries from the Registry. If you don't know for sure what will happen or if you haven't been instructed to do so, *don't delete anything*. However, if you do need to delete a key or value entry, use these steps:

1. Highlight the key or value entry you want to delete.
2. Press Delete, and REGEDIT asks you to confirm that you want to delete the item.
3. Click Yes to delete the key or value entry.

Tip #146

> Before deleting a key, rename it with some obscure name such as MyNukedKey. This step hides the key from Windows and your applications. Then, restart your computer. If everything works okay, go ahead and delete the key.

IMPORTING AND EXPORTING REGISTRY ENTRIES

There are two ways you can work with the Registry. You can work with it in its current form (SYSTEM.DAT and USER.DAT in Windows 98) by using REGEDIT. Or, you can export it to a text file (REG file) and edit it with your favorite text editor, such as WordPad (the file is too big for Notepad). If you export your Registry to a text file, you can use your editor's search-and-replace features to make massive changes to it. Be careful, however, because you can inadvertently change a value you don't mean to change.

Aside from editing the Registry with a text editor, exporting the Registry to a text file has a more practical purpose. You're not limited to exporting your entire Registry. You can export a specific key and all its subkeys and value entries (the branch). Thus, you can export a tiny part of the Registry for the following purposes:

- Backing up—You can export a branch of the Registry in which you're making many changes. If you get confused or if things get out of hand, you can import that file back into the Registry to restore your settings.
- Sharing—You can export a key or a branch that contains a cool Registry hack. Then, share that REG file with your friends so they can implement the same hack by importing the text file you provided (all they have to do is double-click the file).

To export your entire Registry or just a specific branch, perform the following steps:

1. In the left pane of the window, select the key that represents the branch you want to export. (If you're exporting the entire Registry, you can skip this step.)
2. Choose Registry, Export Registry File from the main menu. REGEDIT displays the Export Registry File dialog box shown in Figure 24.7.

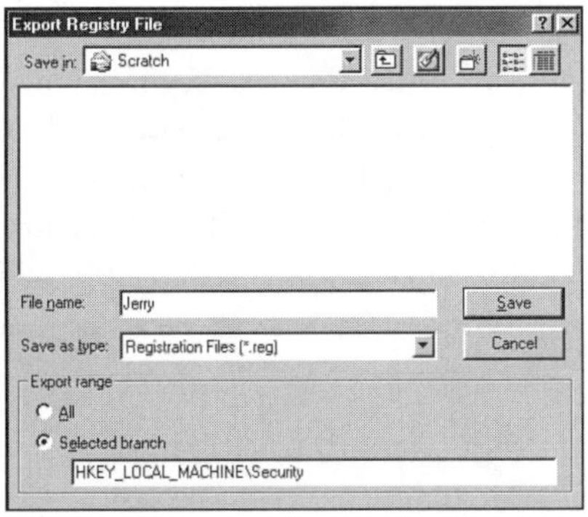

PART
IV

CH
24

Figure 24.7
You can export a branch of the Registry or the whole thing.

3. If you're exporting the entire Registry, select <u>A</u>ll in the Export Range section. Otherwise, select S<u>e</u>lected Branch, and REGEDIT automatically fills in the key you selected in step 1.

4. In the File <u>N</u>ame text box, type the name of the file into which you want to export the Registry. If you don't add a file extension, REGEDIT uses the default file extension (.REG).

5. Click <u>S</u>ave.

The resulting file looks very much like a classic INI file. To see the file, open it in Notepad: Right-click the REG file and choose <u>E</u>dit. (Notepad offers to open the file in WordPad if it's larger than 64KB.) The first line always contains REGEDIT4, which identifies the file as a REGEDIT file. The remainder of the file contains the keys and value entries REGEDIT exported. Figure 24.8 shows what exported Registry entries look like in a text file.

Figure 24.8
A Registry export file looks a lot like an INI file.

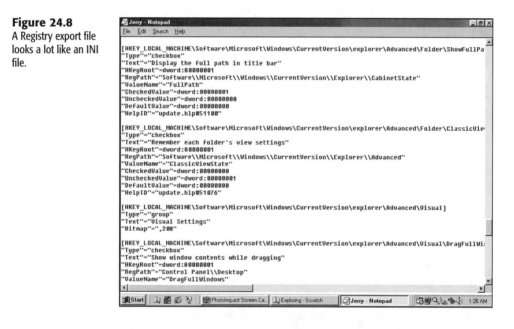

The file is split into multiple sections, with each Registry key in its own section. The name of the key is shown in brackets. It is the fully qualified name of that key in the Registry file (in other words, you see the entire name of the branch including the name of the root key). Each value entry for a key is listed in that key's section. The value entry's name appears in quotation marks, except for default value entries, which REGEDIT indicates with the at sign (@). The appearance of the value entry's data depends on its type, as shown in Table 24.2.

TABLE 24.2   FORMATS FOR STRING, DWORD, AND HEX DATA

Type	Example
String	"This is a string value"
DWORD	DWORD:00000001
HEX	HEX:FF 00 FF 00 FF 00 FF 00 FF 00 FF 00

After you've made changes to your exported file, you might want to import it back into the Registry. In Windows Explorer, right-click an exported Registry file and choose Merge. Windows updates your Registry.

Caution

Be careful not to accidentally double-click a REG file. If you do, Windows automatically merges it with the Registry because merge is the default action for the REG file type.

PART

IV

CH

24

BACKING UP THE WINDOWS REGISTRY

You'll find comfort in knowing that Windows 98 automatically backs up the Registry for you. Once each day, Windows 98 uses the Windows Registry Checker (SCANREGW.EXE in C:\Windows) to back up the Registry to CAB files you find in C:\Windows\Sysbckup. The first backup is named RB000.CAB, the second is RB001.CAB, and so on. The file with the highest number is the most recent backup file; thus, RB004.CAB is a more recent backup than RB002.CAB.

Right-click one of the CAB files, presumably the most recent, and choose View to examine its contents. You'll find four files in it: SYSTEM.DAT, SYSTEM.INI, USER.DAT, and WIN.INI. By default, Windows Registry Checker keeps only five backup copies of the Registry, but you can increase that number by changing the MaxBackupCopies entry in SCANREG.INI to a higher number, perhaps 10.

You can also force Windows Registry Checker to make additional backup copies of the Registry after making the daily backup. Here's how:

1. Run SCANREGW.EXE (located in C:\Windows). After scanning the Registry for errors, the Windows Registry Checker asks whether you want to make another backup copy of the Registry.

2. Click Yes, and Windows Registry Checker backs up the Registry to another CAB file in C:\Windows\Sysbckup. A dialog box tells you when Windows Registry Checker is finished.

3. Click OK to close the Windows Registry Checker.

Windows Registry Checker is the preferred method for backing up the Registry. However, alternative methods might suit your needs better; you learn about those methods in the following sections.

Create a Startup Disk

If you're in a pinch and can't start Windows 98, you'll be very glad that you created a *startup disk*. This disk gets your computer going when it won't start from the hard drive. You'll also find a handful of utilities on the disk that you might be able to use to fix your computer. Here's how to create the startup disk:

1. Double-click the Add/Remove Programs icon in the Control Panel.

2. In the Add/Remove Programs Properties dialog box, click the Startup Disk tab.

3. Click the Create Disk button and follow the onscreen instructions. Windows 98 will likely ask you for your Windows 98 CD-ROM (or disks).

4. When Windows 98 finishes creating your startup disk, click OK to close the Add/Remove Programs Properties dialog box.

5. Label your emergency startup disk and keep it in a safe place just in case you encounter problems starting Windows 98.

Windows 98 places several generic CD-ROM drivers on the startup disk, along with a RAM disk driver to which Windows 98 unloads a CAB file containing some handy utilities. If the drivers you require are not among them, you may have to copy the 16-bit DOS drivers to the disk. Then, create a CONFIG.SYS and AUTOEXEC.BAT that loads them properly.

→ For more details on creating a startup disk, see Chapter 2, "Starting and Quitting Windows 98."

COPY THE REGISTRY FILES TO A SAFE PLACE

The absolute easiest way to back up the contents of the Registry is to copy the files that contain the Registry to a safe place. You can even do this step from Windows 98 Explorer, as explained here:

1. Create a folder on your computer to hold the backup copy of the Registry (C:\Windows\Registry, for example).

2. Make sure that you can view hidden files in Windows 98 Explorer (remember that SYSTEM.DAT and USER.DAT are hidden files). To make hidden files visible, choose View, Options from the main menu, select Show All Files, and click OK.

3. Copy SYSTEM.DAT from C:\Windows to the backup folder.

4. Copy USER.DAT or your own personal profile folder from C:\Windows to the backup folder.

5. Restore the Windows 98 Explorer window so that it hides those system files: Choose View, Options from the main menu, select Hide Files of These Types, and click OK.

If you would rather copy these files more or less automatically, you can create a batch file that does the same thing. Then, all you have to do is execute the batch file to copy SYSTEM.DAT and USER.DAT to a safe place.

The following batch file copies both files (SYSTEM.DAT and USER.DAT). The batch file uses the Xcopy command with the /H and /R switches. The /H switch copies files with the Hidden and System attributes. You use this switch in lieu of changing the files' attributes with the attrib command. The /R switch replaces read-only files. That way, Xcopy can write over previous backup copies of the Registry. %WinDir% expands to the location of your Windows folder when the batch file runs.

```
xcopy %WinDir%\system.dat %WinDir%\Registry\ /H /R
xcopy %WinDir%\user.dat %WinDir%\Registry\ /H /R
```

> **Note**
>
> If you configured Windows 98 to use user profiles, you need to tweak this batch file to make it correctly back up your USER.DAT and USER.DA0 files. In particular, you need to change the second line so that it copies these files from your profile folder instead of from the Windows folder. You can also enhance this batch file so that it copies USER.DAT and USER.DA0 files for all users on the computer by copying the second line for each user.

BACK UP YOUR SYSTEM WITH A TAPE DRIVE

Windows 98 comes with a tape backup utility that you can use as part of your regular backup strategy. Although Windows 98 Setup doesn't install this utility by default, you can use the Add/Remove Programs icon in the Control Panel to install the backup program. After you install it, choose Start, Programs, Accessories, System Tools, Backup to run it.

By default, *Microsoft Backup* doesn't back up the Registry. Thus, to back up the Windows 98 Registry, you must perform the following steps before starting the backup:

1. Choose Job, Options from the main menu to display the Backup Job Options dialog box.

2. Click the Advanced tab, and you see the Backup Job Options dialog box shown in Figure 24.9.

Figure 24.9
By default, Microsoft Backup doesn't back up the Registry.

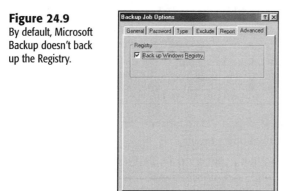

3. Select Back Up Windows Registry.
4. Click OK to save your changes.
5. Perform your backup as usual.

EXPORT THE REGISTRY WITH THE REGISTRY EDITOR

As you learned earlier in this chapter, you can export the entire contents of the Registry into a REG file (see "Importing and Exporting Registry Entries").

Caution

Don't rely on an exported copy of the Registry as your only backup. Microsoft has recorded problems that have occurred when users attempted to restore a backup using this method. For example, Windows 98 might not correctly update all Registry data.

The best use for this method is to back up only the portion of the Registry in which you're making changes. That way, if something goes wrong while you're editing the Registry, you can easily restore that branch by double-clicking the REG file.

USE THE EMERGENCY REPAIR UTILITY

The Emergency Repair Utility (ERU) is a tool that you can use to back up your important configuration files. You can back up those files to a floppy disk or to another folder on your computer. Microsoft configured the ERU to back up your most important configuration files, including

AUTOEXEC.BAT	PROTOCOL.INI
COMMAND.COM	SYSTEM.DAT
CONFIG.SYS	SYSTEM.INI
IO.SYS	USER.DAT
MSDOS.SYS	WIN.INI

You'll find the ERU on your Windows 98 CD-ROM in \Tools\Misc\ERU. Copy all four files to a folder on your computer. Then, add a shortcut to your Start menu by dragging ERU.EXE and dropping it on the Start button. After you've copied the ERU to your computer, use these steps to back up your configuration files, including the Registry:

1. Start ERU by choosing it from the Start menu or by double-clicking ERU.EXE in Windows 98 Explorer.

2. Click Next after ERU pops up. In the dialog box that appears next, choose between backing up to a floppy or backing up to another folder.

3. Choose Drive A: if you want to back up your configuration files to disk; choose Other Directory to back up your configuration files to another folder on your hard drive. Click Next to continue.

4. If you're backing up your configuration files to another folder on your computer, type the path of the folder in the space provided. Then, click Next to continue. Otherwise, insert a formatted disk in drive A: and click OK to continue. You see a list of files that ERU is backing up, as shown in Figure 24.10.

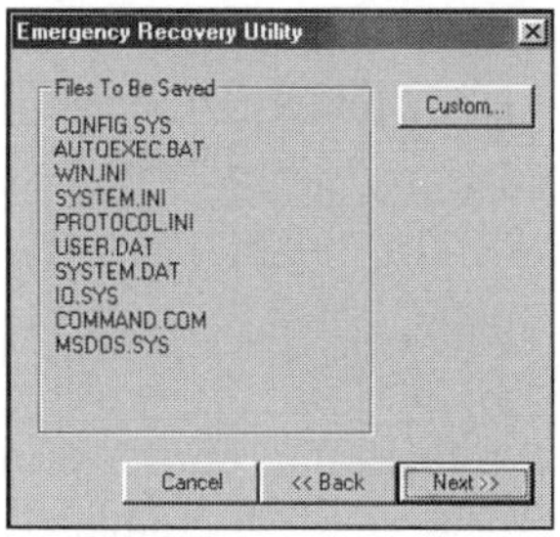

Figure 24.10
You can specify which files ERU includes in the backup.

5. Click Custom to change the files that ERU includes in the backup.

6. Click Next, and ERU backs up your configuration files into the destination you chose.

7. ERU displays a dialog box that explains how to restore your configuration settings if something bad happens to them. Click OK to close it.

RESTORING THE WINDOWS 98 REGISTRY

As you learned earlier, Windows 98 uses a utility called Windows Registry Checker to back up copies of the Registry to CAB files stored in C:\Windows\Ssybckup. You can restore any one of those backups using the Real mode version of this utility named SCANREG.EXE, which you find in C:\Windows\Command. Follow these steps:

1. Start Windows in MS-DOS mode. To do so, select Command Prompt Only from the Windows 98 boot menu. Or, choose Shut Down from the Start menu, select Restart in MS-DOS Mode, and press Enter.

2. Type `scanreg /restore` to start the Microsoft Registry Checker.

3. Select a backup from the list provided. Microsoft Registry Checker displays the date, status, and filename of each backup. Ideally, you should pick the most recent backup; however, if you know the most recent one doesn't work, pick the next most recent backup.

4. Press Enter, and Microsoft Registry Checker restores the backup to your computer.

5. Press Enter to restart your computer.

Although using Microsoft Registry Checker is the preferred method for restoring the Registry, you can use other methods. The sections that follow describe methods for restoring the alternative backups you learned about in the previous sections.

RESTORE YOUR COPY OF THE REGISTRY FILES

Did you make a backup copy of SYSTEM.DAT and USER.DAT? If so, you can easily restore those files and continue with business. Here's how:

1. Make sure that you can view hidden files in Windows 98 Explorer. To make hidden files visible, choose View, Options from the main menu, select Show All Files, and click OK.

2. Copy your backup copy of SYSTEM.DAT to C:\Windows.

3. Copy USER.DAT or your own personal profile folder to C:\Windows.

4. Restore the Windows 98 Explorer window so that it hides those system files: Choose View, Options from the main menu, select Hide Files of These Types, and click OK.

5. Restart your computer.

If you prefer, you can create a batch file that automatically restores your backup copies of SYSTEM.DAT and USER.DAT. Then, all you have to do is double-click the batch file to restore them.

The following batch file restores your backup files. It uses the Xcopy command with the /H and /R switches. The /H switch copies hidden and system files. The /R switch replaces read-only files. That way, Xcopy can overwrite the current copy of SYSTEM.DAT and USER.DAT. %WinDir% expands to the location of your Windows folder when the batch file runs.

```
Xcopy %WinDir%\Registry\System.dat %WinDir%\System.dat /R /H
Xcopy %WinDir%\Registry\User.dat %WinDir%\User.dat /R /H
```

Note

If you've configured Windows 98 for multiple user profiles, you'll need to tweak this batch file to make it correctly restore USER.DAT. In particular, you need to change the second line so that it restores the backup copy into your profile folder.

RESTORE YOUR SYSTEM FROM A TAPE DRIVE

If you used the Windows 98 tape backup utility (Microsoft Backup) to back up the Registry, you can easily (if not quickly) restore the Registry to the state it was in when you last backed up your computer. You must use the following steps to instruct Windows 98 to restore the Registry:

1. Choose Job, Options from the main menu and click the Advanced tab.

2. Select Restore the Registry.

3. Click OK to save your changes.

4. Continue restoring the backup as usual.

Note

Using Microsoft Backup to back up and restore the Registry is a method better suited for a full backup. That is, if you restore the Registry from a backup tape, you should also restore the entire system from the same tape. Doing so ensures that the files on your computer match the settings found in the Registry. If you restore just the Registry from an older tape, chances are good that your computer won't work correctly because the configuration data in the Registry doesn't match the remaining files on your computer.

IMPORT AN EXPORTED COPY OF THE REGISTRY

Earlier in this chapter, you learned how to export the Registry into a REG file. You can't import this file while Windows 98 is running, however, because the Registry Editor can't replace keys that are open. You need to start your computer to the DOS prompt, and then use the Registry Editor in Real mode to import the Registry. Follow these steps:

1. Start Windows in MS-DOS mode. To do so, select Command Prompt Only from the Windows 98 boot menu. Or choose Shut Down from the Start menu, select Restart in MS-DOS Mode, and press Enter.

2. Type `regedit /L:system /R:user regfile` at the DOS prompt where *system* is the path and filename of SYSTEM.DAT and *user* is the path and filename of USER.DAT. (Normally, *user* points to C:\Windows\USER.DAT, but if you're using profiles, it might point to a USER.DAT file within a profile folder in C:\Windows\Profiles.) *regfile* is the path and filename of the REG file containing the backup.

3. Restart your computer.

> **Note**
>
> This method is better suited to restoring backups containing small portions of the Registry. For instance, you can back up a single branch in which you're making changes. If you make a mistake, you can restore that single branch, without affecting other parts of the Registry.

USE THE EMERGENCY REPAIR UTILITY

The ERU is a tool that backs up all of your important configuration files, including the Registry. You learned how to back up the Registry with the ERU earlier in this chapter. Here's how to restore your configuration files from the backup:

1. Start your computer to the DOS prompt.

2. Change to the folder to which you backed up your configuration files. If you backed up your configuration files to a disk, put that disk in the drive and change to it.

3. Run ERD.EXE. It's mixed in with all the backup copies of your configuration files.

4. Select the files that you want to recover. Use the arrow keys to highlight a configuration file and then press the Enter key to select it.

5. After selecting the configuration files you want to recover, select Start Recovery and press the Enter key.

RESTORE SYSTEM.1ST

If all else fails, you'll find one more backup copy of the Registry on your computer. SYSTEM.1ST is a read-only, hidden, system file in the root folder of your boot drive. This file is a backup copy of SYSTEM.DAT that Windows 98 made after you successfully installed and started Windows 98. It contains no custom settings and no information added by the programs you've installed. The only thing this file does for you is get your machine running again if nothing else works.

Here's how to restore SYSTEM.1ST:

1. Start your computer to the DOS prompt.

2. Copy your C:\SYSTEM.DAT file to C:\Windows\SYSTEM.DAT. At the DOS prompt, type Xcopy C:\system.1st C:\windows\system.dat /H /R. Then press Enter.

3. Restart your computer.

> **Caution**
>
> Use this method as a last resort only. After you've restored SYSTEM.1ST, all the configuration changes you've made to your computer since you first installed Windows 98 will be gone.

The Windows 98 Registry Versus Windows 95 and NT

You will see little or no difference between the Windows 98 and Windows 95 Registries. The organization is the same, and the Registry Editor is the same. Inside the Registry is a different story, however. Microsoft has optimized the code and data structures that implement the Registry so that it performs much faster. The only thing you might notice is how much faster the Registry works.

The Windows 98 and Windows NT 4.0 Registries, in many ways, are very similar. However, you should be aware of the following major differences between HKEY_CLASSES_ROOT and HKEY_USERS:

- Windows NT 4.0 stores the Registry in hives, whereas Windows 95 stores the Registry in two binary files.

- Windows NT 4.0 implements full security for the Registry hives and for each individual key in the Registry. Windows 95 provides little security.

- The structure of HKEY_LOCAL_MACHINE\System is very different in Windows 95 and Windows NT 4.0.

- Windows NT 4.0 provides an additional Registry Editor that takes advantage of security and the different types of data you can store in a value.

To learn more about the differences between the Windows 98 and Windows NT 4.0 Registries, take a look at Macmillan's own *Windows 95 and Windows NT 4.0 Registry & Customization Handbook*.

TROUBLESHOOTING

PROBLEMS MAKING CHANGES TO THE REGISTRY

I see REGEDIT.EXE in my Windows folder, but either I can't run the program or it won't let me change anything in the Registry.

If you're using a computer in a networked environment, your system administrator might have disabled REGEDIT.EXE. You'll have to plead your case for access to REGEDIT.EXE to the system administrator. Note that the system administrator can also prevent REGEDIT.EXE from being installed on your computer if you're installing Windows from the network or doing a custom installation.

SECRETS OF MASTERING THE WINDOWS 98 ENVIRONMENT: DISCOVERING MORE ABOUT YOUR CPU THROUGH THE REGISTRY

If you want to learn more about the CPU on your system, you can use the Registry Editor. Go through the following steps to open the Registry to reveal more information about the processor on your system.

To open this Registry key with REGEDIT:

1. On the Start menu, click Run.

2. Type REGEDIT and then click OK.

3. Follow this path: HKEY_LOCAL_MACHINE\Hardware\Description\ System\CentralProcessor\0.

4. Double-click VendorIdentifier and put a space between Genuine and Intel.

5. Close REGEDIT, right-click the My Computer icon, and then click Properties.

You can find more information about your system and its CPU. If you look under the Genuine Intel line, you'll see that your CPU comes from the x86 Family A Model B Stepping (version) C, where A, B, and C represent the appropriate values in your system. This information is now available in the Identifier line on the path two rows above in this entry in the Registry. Thus, you can confirm the type of processor in the system without removing the cover from the system and looking on the motherboard, or locating the documentation to the system, which you might or might not have. Of course, you can reboot your system and read about the type of CPU you have according to the system BIOS, but then a reboot might not be an option at the time.

CHAPTER **25**

SPECIAL FEATURES FOR NOTEBOOK USERS

In this chapter

SETTING UP WINDOWS ON A NOTEBOOK

During the Setup process, Windows 98 asks you to specify the type of installation you want. The choices are Typical, Portable, Compact, and Custom. To install the Windows 98 components that are useful for mobile computer hardware, select the Portable option and click Next.

Tip #147

During Windows 98 installation, you can also choose the Custom option and select the notebook components individually.

The Portable installation includes support for PC Card (formerly called PCMCIA) devices, power management tools for optimizing battery conservation, docking station compatibility, infrared transmissions, and direct cable connections for communicating with other computers. Even if you don't choose the Portable option during your installation, you can always go back and manually add these notebook-specific components through the Windows Setup tab of the Add/Remove Programs Properties dialog box (see Figure 25.1).

Figure 25.1
Add the Windows 98 notebook components manually through Windows Setup.

To manually add operating system components to your notebook, use the following procedure:

1. Open the Start menu and choose Settings, Control Panel.

2. Click on the Add/Remove Programs icon to display the Add/Remove Programs Properties dialog box.

3. Select the Windows Setup tab.

4. Double-click on a component category (such as Accessories) to bring up a list of the components under that heading. Then, put a check next to the components that you want to install.

5. Click OK to close the window for the individual category and return to the Add/Remove Programs Properties dialog box. Then, click OK again.

Here's a list of the categories that contain useful notebook components that might not already be installed:

- Accessibility—Here, you'll find the options for modifying your mouse and screen settings to enable better viewing on notebook LCD panels. These components, which were intended for use by people with physical disabilities, often prove handy for notebook computer users, too. Mouse cursor options and a screen magnification tool help you find and control your mouse even on small screens.

- Accessories—The large mouse pointers under this heading let you quickly and easily find your mouse cursor on smaller notebook displays.

- Communications—Under this heading, choose the components for Dial-Up Networking, Direct Cable Connection, and Infrared communications. Dial-Up Networking controls Internet connections via a modem. Direct Cable Connection lets you transfer data from your notebook to another computer over a cable. And Infrared lets you send and receive to other computers or devices (such as printers) that have an Infrared (IR) port.

- Systems Tools—Use the Disk Compression tools in this category to make efficient use of your notebook's hard drive space. Generally, notebook hard drives offer less space than desktop drives offer. Compressing data allows you to pack more information into a smaller drive.

CONFIGURING A NOTEBOOK DOCKING STATION

Docking stations provide an expandable platform for notebook computers. For travel, an undocked notebook contains the bare minimum of components needed to get the job done—thus keeping weight down. But a docked station brings a notebook's flexibility up to that of a desktop computer in terms of card slots, drives, and devices.

Windows 98 supports *hot-docking*, which means you can dock or undock a notebook without worrying about whether the notebook's power is on or off. The operating system automatically recognizes the added components of the docking station and sets up access to them. It also autoloads any needed software drivers.

To undock a notebook while Windows 98 is running, open the Start menu and choose Eject PC. Windows 98 resets the configuration parameters of the notebook and then asks you to remove the notebook from the docking station.

CREATING AND MODIFYING HARDWARE PROFILES

Windows 98 lets you set up multiple hardware profiles for different hardware configurations of your computer. When you install the operating system on a notebook, Windows 98 sets up one hardware profile automatically for you. Then, when Windows 98 detects a major change in hardware, such as when you dock the notebook, it creates a second hardware profile for you. When you boot the PC, the operating system checks to see whether the PC is docked and then uses the appropriate profile.

If you want to modify a hardware profile or create a new one, use the following procedure:

1. Open the Start menu and choose Settings, Control Panel.

2. Double-click the System icon to display the System Properties dialog box.

3. Click the Hardware Profiles tab to display the Hardware Profiles page.

4. Select the hardware profile you want to use as the basis for your new profile and then click Copy. Windows 98 displays a Copy Profile dialog box in which you can edit the name for your new hardware profile (see Figure 25.2).

Figure 25.2
Edit the name for your new hardware profile.

5. Enter a name for your new hardware profile and then click OK. The new hardware profile appears in the Hardware Profile list.

In some cases you might want to modify a hardware profile—if Windows 98 fails to properly detect your hardware configuration, for example. You can manually adjust the hardware profile.

To manually adjust a hardware profile, use the following procedure:

1. Open the Control Panel and double-click on the System icon. Then, click the Device Manager tab to display the Device Manager page.

2. Select the hardware device that you want to add or remove from a particular profile. Then, choose Properties to display the General page of the appropriate properties sheet.

3. At the bottom of the device's General page is a Device Usage list that defines which profiles should use this device (see Figure 25.3). To remove the device from the current profile, check Disable in This Hardware Profile. To add the device to the current hardware profile, make sure this box is not checked.

4. Click OK to apply the changes.

When you power on the system, Windows 98 automatically detects the hardware profile you are using and applies the appropriate hardware profile. If your hardware profiles are so similar that Windows 98 cannot determine which one to use, Windows 98 displays a list of available profiles and prompts you to select the profile you want.

WORKING WITH DIFFERENT CONFIGURATIONS

In Windows 98 you can store different configurations for the same set of hardware devices. You could, for example, run your notebook's video graphics adapter at 640×480 resolution when you don't have an external monitor attached, but set up a profile for using 800×600 resolution when you do have the monitor attached.

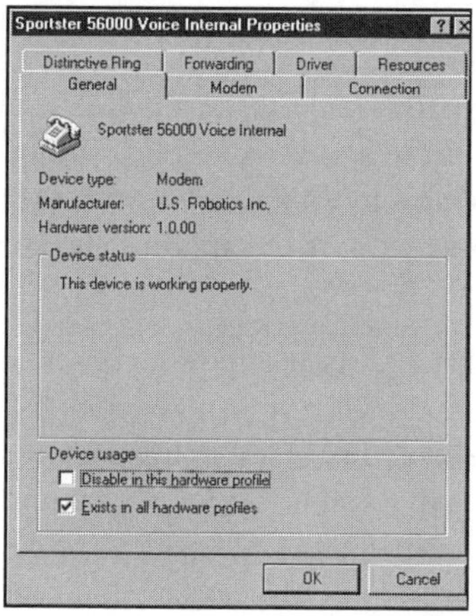

Figure 25.3
Use the Device Usage list to add or remove hardware from a profile.

To configure a new profile with the same hardware set, first start Windows 98 by using the hardware profile in which you want to make changes. To change the resolution for use with an external monitor, for example, select the hardware profile you use when you have the monitor attached. Then, change the settings for your new resolution. These changes are saved in the current hardware profile only; the other hardware profiles are unaffected.

PART

IV

CH

25

UNDERSTANDING POWER MANAGEMENT

New portable and desktop PCs feature power management capabilities that let you specify schemes for conserving power (and battery life) by shutting down devices (such as hard disks, CD-ROMs, parallel and serial ports, and so on) after a specified time of inactivity. Windows 98 takes advantage of these new hardware designs and offers a software control for power management schemes under the Power Management object of the Control Panel.

Tip #148

To use the Windows 98 power management features, your PC must support power management through its BIOS. Read your PC's documentation to find out whether the machine supports power management and to determine how to enable the capability in the BIOS.

Over the last few years, the computer industry has hammered out several specifications for PC power management. The original specification was called Advanced Power Management (APM) 1.0, and it defined interactions among a PC's hardware, *BIOS (page 144)*, and software that let the PC operate at different levels of power consumption including full power, sleep, and standby. Subsequent revisions of APM added the capability to manage the power consumption of PC Card devices and portables with multiple batteries, as well as other features.

The very latest PC power management scheme, which is supported by newer computers, is called Advanced Configuration and Power Interface (ACPI) 1.0. ACPI supports the fine-tuned management of a wide variety of hardware devices, as well as a new feature called OnNow, which enables a computer to start in just a few seconds without going through the normal boot process and to restore programs to where you last left them. Windows 98 supports both APM and ACPI on computers that have the appropriate BIOS and hardware for these power conservation schemes.

For notebook computers, the most important aspect of power conservation is extended battery life. By setting power management options for your notebook's hardware under Windows 98, you can operate your notebook for several hours on batteries without being connected to an electrical outlet. Devices that can be set for power conservation under Windows 98 include hard disk drives; monitors and LCD panels; serial, parallel, and USB ports; CD-ROM drives; DVD-ROM drives; PC Card devices; and keyboards, mice, and joysticks.

CONFIGURING POWER MANAGEMENT OPTIONS

The Power Management icon in the Control Panel gives you access to controls for setting your desired level of power management on your notebook or desktop system. Windows 98 automatically checks to see which type of power management schemes your PC supports and then displays a list of devices (on the Power Management properties sheet) that can be set for different power conservation levels.

To modify the settings for your PC's power management, use the following procedure:

1. Open the Start menu and choose Settings, Control Panel.
2. Double-click on the Power Management icon to display the Power Management Properties dialog box (see Figure 25.4).

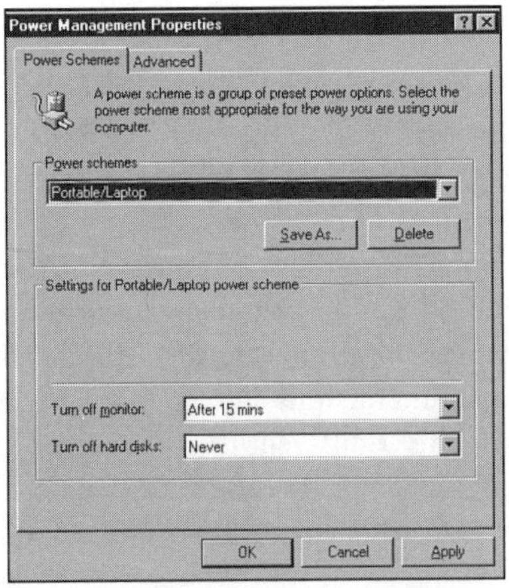

Figure 25.4
Use the Power Management Properties dialog box to control the power management settings.

3. In the Power Schemes box, choose the name of your power management scheme. The default names are Portable/Laptop and Home/Office Desk. The Settings box displays the complete list of PC devices that support power management.

4. In the Settings for Portable/Laptop Power Scheme box, pick the power conservation settings for each device.

   Use the two drop-down lists to indicate what kind of action you want to take place and how long the system should wait before performing that action. For example, with the settings shown in Figure 25.4, after 15 minutes Windows 98 turns off the monitor to conserve power. If you never want a particular device to power down, choose Never in the Turn Off Hard Disks field.

5. Click Apply to put your new settings into effect.

6. Click OK to close the Power Management Properties dialog box.

In some cases you might want to create a new power scheme. When your notebook is docked, for example, you'll probably want to use different power management settings than when it's not docked.

To create a new power scheme, use the following procedure:

1. Open the Control Panel and double-click on the Power Management icon.

2. Choose the settings for the individual devices as described in the preceding procedure.

3. In the Power Schemes box, click the Save As button to display the Save Scheme dialog box.

Note

If you want to display the Power Meter on the Windows 98 taskbar, check that option on the Advanced tab of the Power Management Properties dialog box.

PART

IV

CH

25

USING PC CARD DEVICES

Almost all notebook computers now come with credit card–size PC Card slots for quickly adding or removing devices. A wide variety of devices can be found on PC Cards including network adapters, hard drives, SCSI adapters, modems, sound cards, video capture cards, and so forth. Windows 98 works with the PC Card controller on your notebook to activate these devices. As with docking stations, Windows 98 lets you insert and remove PC Cards on-the-fly (called hot-swapping) without rebooting the PC.

PC Card devices enable you to quickly expand the capability of your notebook without sacrificing the small size and travel weight of the base notebook platform. Notebooks come with two or three PC Card slots, so sometimes PC Card manufacturer's put two or more functions on one PC Card (such as a modem and a network adapter). Windows 98 improves over Windows 95 in the handling of multifunction PC Cards by automatically recognizing the individual functions of these types of cards. Windows 98 lets you configure and enable the functions separately.

Note

In the past, the PC Card data path was limited to 16 bits. Newer PC Card controllers support PC Card32 (Cardbus), which expands the data path for PC Cards to 32 bits. Windows 98 supports PC Card32, which allows for high-bandwidth data transfer to and from PC Card devices. PC Card devices that require this type of bandwidth include video capture cards and 10/100Mbs networking cards.

REAL MODE VERSUS PROTECTED MODE PC CARD DRIVERS

If your computer has PC Card slots, Windows 98 automatically recognizes and loads the PC Card components of the operating system during the operating system installation. During the installation, Windows 98 preserves any existing PC Card support software so as not to accidentally disable any PC Card devices. Your pre-Windows 98 PC Cards might use Real mode drivers, but Windows 98 requires a 32-bit Protected mode driver for any card that will be supported via the Plug and Play architecture. Plug and Play PC Card support allows Windows 98 to maximize performance, dynamically load drivers, and stay aware of the insertion and removal of PC Card devices. Fortunately, Windows 98 provides two tools that help you transition from Real mode to Protected mode drivers: PC Card Wizard and the PC Card Troubleshooter.

To enable 32-bit PC Card support, activate the PC Card Wizard. To start the PC Card Wizard, use the following procedure:

1. Open the Start menu and choose Settings, Control Panel.
2. Double-click on the PC Card (PCMCIA) icon. The first time you click on this icon, Windows 98 displays the PC Card (PCMCIA) Wizard.
3. Choose No and then Next to inform the wizard that you are not setting up Windows 98 from a network server. (If your Windows 98 installation disk is on a network server or a CD-ROM device connected through a PC Card adapter, choose Yes and then Next.)
4. If Windows 98 detects any existing Real mode PC Card drivers, it displays a dialog box asking whether you want to review the changes before Windows disables the drivers. If you want the wizard to automatically remove the drivers, choose No and click Next. If you want to view and verify the deletion of the Real mode drivers, choose Yes and click Next.
5. If you selected Yes in step 4, the wizard displays a set of dialog boxes that show the device entries for CONFIG.SYS, AUTOEXEC.BAT, and SYSTEM.INI that it will delete. If you want to save any of these entries, click on it to deselect it and then click Next.
6. After removing the Real mode drivers (if any), the wizard displays the final dialog box and asks you to click Finish to complete the process and enable 32-bit PC Card support. Click Finish, and Windows 98 restarts so that the changes can take effect.

If you're having any difficulty getting a particular PC Card to work, invoke the PC Card Troubleshooter. The PC Card Troubleshooter asks questions about your problem and makes suggestions on possible fixes.

To activate the PC Card Troubleshooter, use the following procedure:

1. Open the Start menu and choose Help to display the Windows Help screen.

2. On the Contents tab, click Troubleshooting. Then, choose Windows 98 Troubleshooters from the expanded list of troubleshooters.

3. Click on PC Card to activate the PC Card Troubleshooter (see Figure 25.5).

Figure 25.5
Use the PC Card Troubleshooter for help with PC Card devices.

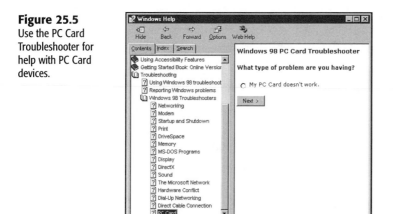

INSTALLING PC CARD DEVICES

After you have enabled 32-bit PC Card support, Windows 98 can usually install PC Card devices automatically. When you insert a modem card, for example, Windows 98 detects the new card and automatically installs the new drivers for it. If your PC Card is not recognized automatically, you must manually install support for it.

To manually install a PC Card device other than a modem or network adapter, use the following procedure:

1. Insert the new PC Card into an appropriate slot. (Read the card's documentation and your system's documentation to determine whether to use a specific slot.)

2. Open the Control Panel and choose the Add New Hardware object to start the Add New Hardware Wizard. Then, click Next.

3. Choose Yes and then Next to enable the wizard to automatically detect your new PC Card device.

4. If it is unable to detect the new device, the wizard displays a hardware selection dialog box. Choose the type of device you are installing and click Next.

5. Answer the questions regarding your problem and click Next to continue with the troubleshooting session.

6. Select the manufacturer of the device you are installing from the Manufacturer's list. Then choose the model of the device from the Model list on the right. If you cannot find your particular device or if your device includes a driver disk, click Have Disk and then follow the onscreen instructions for installing the driver.

7. Click OK to complete the new hardware installation process.

PROPER TECHNIQUE FOR REMOVING OR INSERTING PC CARD DEVICES

Before you remove a PC Card device, you should shut it down. Choose the PC Card object in the Control Panel to display the Windows 98 PC Card Properties dialog box. There, you'll find the list of active PC Cards and their sockets.

To shut down a device, select the device from the list on the Socket Status page and click on Stop. Windows 98 shuts down the device and lists the socket as empty. Then, you can physically remove the card from the PC Card slot.

To insert a new device, you don't need to follow any procedure. Simply insert the device into an appropriate PC Card slot, and Windows 98 automatically starts services for it.

USING DIAL-UP NETWORKING ON A NOTEBOOK

With the *Dial-Up Networking* (pages 852-854) capabilities of Windows 98, you can access other computers, a LAN, or even the Internet and World Wide Web through an Internet service provider (ISP). This section covers the notebook-specific techniques of setting up locations, connecting to a remote system, accessing ISPs, and autodialing.

→ For additional information on connecting to remote systems, **see** "Managing Dial-Up Networking Connections," **p. 537.**

LOCATION SETUP

Windows 98 provides an easy way to set up your location, which is particularly useful if you're traveling with your notebook. For example, you can quickly connect to remote locations while staying in a hotel by modifying the Telephony location setting in the Control Panel.

To modify your location setting, use the following procedure:

1. Open the Start menu and choose Settings, Control Panel.

2. Choose the Telephony object. The first time you choose this object, Windows 98 asks you to select your Country/Region from a list and enter the area code of your home base. Do that, and then click Next to display the Dialing Properties dialog box.

3. In the I Am Dialing From box, enter a name for your new location (such as Hotel). Then, choose your new Country/Region, Area Code, any codes necessary for accessing an outside line, and your calling card information.

4. When you finish, choose <u>N</u>ew. Windows 98 displays a message box, informing you that your new location was created.

You can use your new Dial-Up Connections as you normally would at home, but now you are dialing from a different location.

CONNECTING TO A REMOTE SYSTEM

Using the Dial-Up Networking connection, you can access remote systems, such as your business's Windows NT server, from any location. Simply double-click on your desktop's My Computer object and choose the Dial-Up Networking object. If you've already set up access to your remote system, it is listed among the objects in the Dial-Up Networking window. If you haven't already set up your connection, choose the Make a New Connection object, and the wizard will walk you through the steps. You'll end up with a Connect To dialog box similar to the one shown in Figure 25.6.

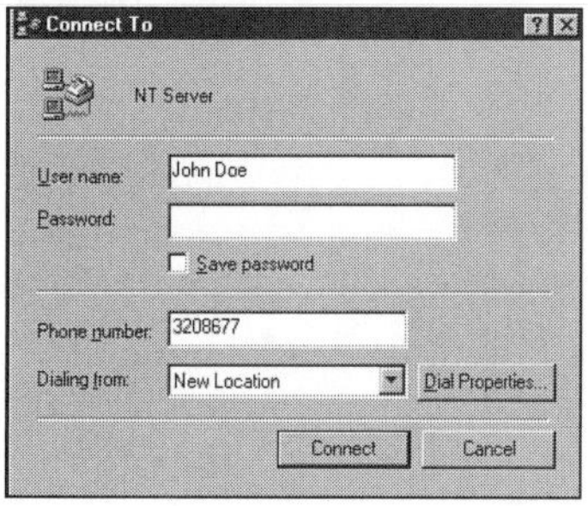

Figure 25.6
Verify your remote connection settings before choosing Connect.

Verify the User Name, Password, and Phone Number settings, and then choose Connect. If you have trouble connecting, confirm these settings with your system administrator. Also double-check your location parameters (as described in the preceding section, "Location Setup"). After you've established a connection, you can share files and data with the remote computer as you normally would.

USING A DIAL-UP NETWORKING SCRIPT

Some Internet service providers don't support Microsoft Challenge Handshake Authentication Protocol (MS CHAP), so you must enter your username and password each time you access their service. Fortunately, Windows 98 supplies scripting tools for Dial-Up Networking so that you can automate this process.

You can find details of the scripting language in the SCRIPT.DOC file that's located in your program files directory (usually under C:\Windows). In this file are instructions and examples for building a script that works with your service's login screens. After you build a script, you need to assign it to a Dial-Up Networking connection.

ASSIGNING A SCRIPT TO A DIAL-UP NETWORKING CONNECTION

After building a script, you must associate it with the Connection icon that you've already defined. Use the following procedure to assign a script to a Dial-Up Networking Connection icon:

1. Double-click the My Computer icon on your desktop and then choose the Dial-Up Networking icon.

2. In the Dial-Up Networking folder, highlight the dial-up icon to which you want to assign your new script.

3. From the Dial-Up Networking window, select File, Properties. Windows 98 displays a Dial-Up Networking properties sheet.

4. Choose the Scripting tab to show the script assignment page of this connection. It will be similar to the one shown in Figure 25.7.

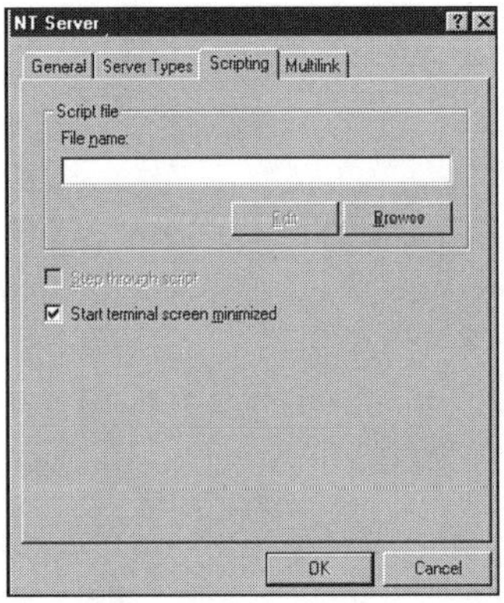

Figure 25.7
Use the Scripting tab of a Dial-Up Networking properties sheet to assign a script to a connection.

5. In the File Name text box, enter the name and path of your script. (Use the Browse button to find it if you don't remember the exact location.)

6. If you want to check each step of the script, click to put a check mark in the Step Through Script box.

7. Click OK to complete the process.

Your object now has a script assigned to it that runs each time you activate that Dial-Up Networking connection.

SHARING RESOURCES VIA A DIRECT CABLE CONNECTION

With Direct Cable Connection, Windows 98 allows you to share files and resources (such as a printer) with another computer through either a cable or wireless infrared port connecting the two systems. If both PCs do not feature infrared ports, you must, of course, provide your own serial or parallel cable to attach the PCs. After you make the connection, you can quickly access or transfer files back and forth.

Under Direct Cable connection, one PC acts as the host (or server), and the other PC assumes the role of guest (or client). The host PC is the gateway that enables the guest PC to access a network to which the host is attached. In Windows 98 the host can act as a gateway for NetBEUI and IPX/SPX network protocols, as well as for TCP/IP networks.

SETTING UP DIRECT CABLE CONNECTION

Windows 98 automatically installs the Direct Cable Connection components unless you tell it not to with a custom installation. If, for some reason, Direct Cable Connection is not installed on your PC, you can install it from the Windows 98 installation disc. Use the following procedure to install Direct Cable Connection from the installation disc:

1. Open the Start menu and choose Settings, Control Panel.

2. Choose the Add/Remove Programs object, and then select the Windows Setup tab.

3. In the Components list, double-click on the Communications component to display the communications tools of Windows 98.

4. Click to put a check mark in the Direct Cable Connection box. (If a check is already there, this utility is already installed on your PC.)

5. Click OK, and Windows installs Direct Cable Connection.

Next, you must attach the two computers with a cable or use infrared ports. Check the documentation of both PCs to determine whether they offer infrared ports. Otherwise, locate either a serial or parallel port cable and use it to connect the two systems.

For best performance results, use a parallel port cable. Modern parallel ports can be set to different modes under a computer's BIOS. These settings are usually classified as standard bidirectional, enhanced parallel port (EPP), and enhanced capabilities port (ECP). For the fastest data transfer, set both computers to use either EPP or ECP mode for the parallel ports.

The final step involves setting one of the computers as the host and the other as the guest. Those procedures are outlined in the next two sections.

SETTING UP THE HOST

Again in Direct Cable Connection, you need to set up one computer as the host and the other as the guest. First set up the host computer. To do so, use the following procedure:

1. Open the Start menu and choose Programs, Accessories, Communications, Direct Cable Connection. Windows 98 asks whether you are setting up the host or the guest.

2. Select the Host option, and then click Next. Windows 98 then asks you to choose the port to use for Direct Cable Connection.

PART

IV

CH

25

3. Choose the port you want to use for your connection. If you are planning to use an infrared port, choose Install New Ports and follow the instructions for selecting your infrared device. Otherwise, click Next.

4. Windows 98 then asks whether you want to enable file and print sharing with the guest. If so, choose File and Print Sharing and follow the instructions. Otherwise, click Next.

5. Windows 98 asks whether you want to password protect the host to prevent unauthorized access. To enable password protection, put a check mark next to Use Password Protection (as shown in Figure 25.8). Then, choose Set Password to enter the password the guest computer must use to access the host.

6. Click Finish to complete the setup.

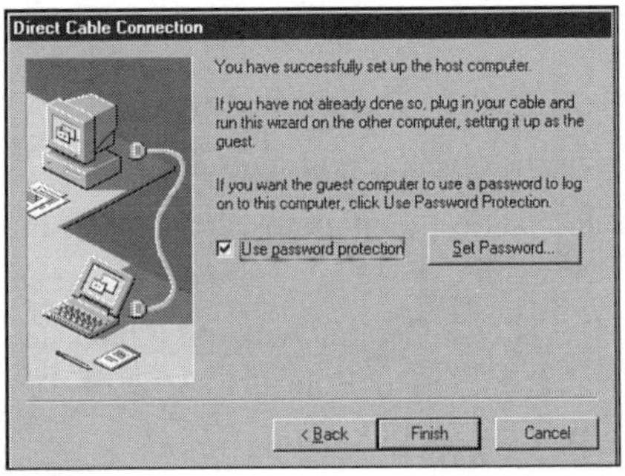

Figure 25.8
Check Use Password Protection to restrict access to the host.

SETTING UP THE GUEST

After you've configured the host, use the following procedure to set up the guest:

1. Open the Start menu and choose Programs, Accessories, Communications, Direct Cable Connection.

2. In the Direct Cable Connection dialog box, choose Guest and then Next.

3. Choose the port for the guest, and then click Next.

4. Click Finish to complete the setup.

USING THE DIRECT CABLE CONNECTION

After setup, you need to start the Direct Cable Connection software on both the host and guest computers before you can begin sharing resources. First, start the host computer by opening the Start menu and choosing Accessories, Communications, Direct Cable Connection. If the settings in the resulting dialog box are correct, choose Listen to set the host in the mode to communicate with a guest. If you want to change any of the settings, choose Change and make your changes.

Then, start the Direct Cable Connection on the guest computer. To do so, open the Start menu and choose Accessories, Communications, Direct Cable Connection. The dialog box that appears is similar to the one that starts the host except that now the Listen button is a

Connect button. Choose Connect to activate the Direct Cable Connection so you can begin sharing resources.

USING THE BRIEFCASE TO KEEP FILES IN SYNC

Most notebook PC users work on a desktop system as well. Many times users must transfer files back and forth between their notebook computer and their desktop computer. Someone who takes a notebook while traveling, for example, often finds the need to keep these two sets of files synchronized so that he or she doesn't lose valuable work. Windows 98 supplies a Briefcase feature to help users track and synchronize files shared between PCs.

Here is a typical scenario using Briefcase:

1. You create a Briefcase on your notebook PC.
2. Using Direct Cable Connection, you copy one or more files to the Briefcase over a network or from a desktop.
3. You modify and update the Briefcase files while traveling with your notebook.
4. While you are away from your office, a colleague modifies the same files on your desktop system.
5. When you return to the office you reconnect the notebook and desktop via a network connection or Direct Cable Connection. Then, you open the Briefcase on your notebook.
6. You use the Briefcase to determine which files have been modified and which are the most current versions. You also use the Briefcase to transfer updated files back and forth between the systems.

In essence, the Briefcase is an ordinary folder that has shell extensions and hidden database files that track file changes for files within the Briefcase folder. Windows 98 creates one Briefcase folder on your desktop during the installation process. However, you might find that creating several small Briefcases where you need them might be more manageable. Additionally, using Briefcases on floppy disks isn't really recommended—even though the Windows documentation says you can—because of the limited space available on floppies.

CREATING A BRIEFCASE

Again, Windows 98 automatically creates a Briefcase called My Briefcase on your desktop during installation. But you might prefer to create new Briefcases that relate to individual projects. To create a Briefcase, use the following procedure:

1. Determine where you want to create your new Briefcase. You can specify the desktop or a folder on any available drive.
2. To create a new Briefcase on the desktop, simply right-click on the desktop, choose New, and then choose Briefcase. To create a new Briefcase on your hard drive, start Windows Explorer, select the folder in which you want to store the new Briefcase, and

PART
IV

CH
25

then choose File, New, Briefcase from the Explorer menu. Windows 98 adds a new Briefcase object to the location you have specified.

3. To change the name of the new Briefcase folder, right-click on the folder and choose Rename. Enter the new name for your Briefcase and press Enter.

ADDING FILES AND FOLDERS TO A BRIEFCASE

You can use standard file move and copy techniques to add files to a Briefcase. Simply open the folder (through My Computer, for example) where the files reside and drag them into the Briefcase folder. If you hold down the Ctrl key while dragging, the files are copied. If you hold down the Shift key, the files are moved.

You can also use Windows Explorer to copy or move files to a Briefcase. By right-clicking on a file, you can send it to a Briefcase. Specifically, you right-click on the file or files you want to send and choose Send To. From the list of files that appears, choose your Briefcase folder. Windows 98 then copies the files you specified.

Caution

Be careful not to place one Briefcase inside another Briefcase. You cannot drag and drop a file into a Briefcase that is in another Briefcase.

Tip #149

If you right-drag a file to a Briefcase folder, a box displays your options: Choose Move Here to move the file or Make Sync Copy to copy the file.

SYNCHRONIZING FILES

Synchronizing files is the key feature of the Briefcase. After you work with shared files remotely on your notebook, save them back to the Briefcase folder.

To do so, reconnect the two computers that you're sharing files between, open the Briefcase, and choose Update All from the controls at the top of the window. Windows 98 displays a dialog box similar to the one shown in Figure 25.9.

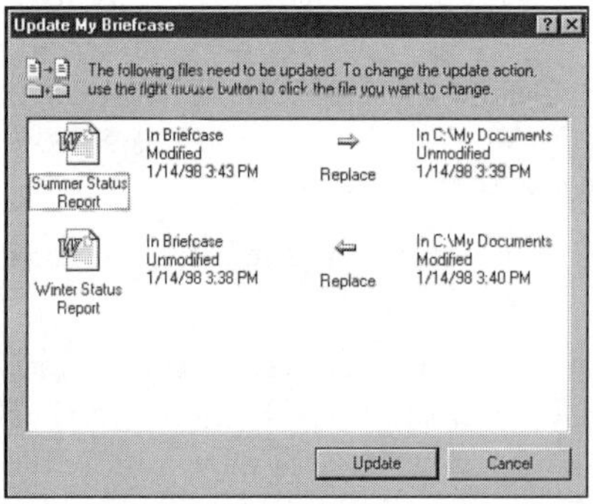

Figure 25.9
The briefcase displays how the files have been modified.

The Briefcase dialog box shows you when the files were last updated on each machine and which is the more recent version. If the actions suggested in the dialog box are appropriate, choose Update; Briefcase then performs those actions. If an action is not appropriate, right-click on the action to change it. Windows 98 displays your action options. If you just want to check the status but do not need to synchronize the files, choose Cancel in this window.

If you prefer to update individual files, select each file by clicking on it (or hold down the Ctrl key and click on a group of files). Then, choose Update Selection from the controls at the top of the Briefcase menu. Only the files you selected appear in the update list.

For the most effective use of Briefcase, update files across a network or Direct Cable Connection. Using a floppy disk is usually incredibly slow.

SPLITTING SYNC COPIES FROM ORIGINALS

In some cases, you may want to disassociate a Briefcase file from the original file. For example, you might need to generate two different reports from the same base file. If you do, you need to "split" the file in the Briefcase (the sync copy) from the original file. To do so, highlight the file within the Briefcase and choose Briefcase, Split from Original. Windows 98 changes the entry for that file in the status column to Orphan.

Another way to split a sync copy from an original file is by using the file's properties sheet. Right-click on the Briefcase file you want to split and choose Properties to display the file's properties sheet. Choose the Update Status tab to see the file's synchronization status. Windows displays a dialog box similar to the one shown in Figure 25.10. Click Split from Original to remove the link between the files.

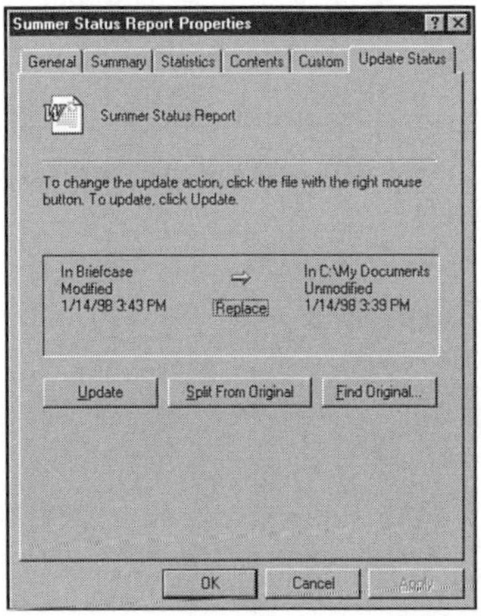

PART
IV

CH
25

Figure 25.10
You can also split a sync copy from an original via the file's properties sheet.

USING INFRARED CONNECTIONS

Infrared light is below the spectrum of red light and is not visible to the human eye. Recently, the use of this light spectrum has moved beyond the world of television and VCR remote controls and into the realm of computers. New infrared (IR) ports on computers allow wireless connections between computers and devices. Windows 98 supplies software supporting IR ports on notebooks and desktops. Although IR ports are still not a common communication medium for computers and computer peripherals, the very latest computers do ship with these ports. On a computer with an IR port, Windows 98 lets you share files and resources, communicate to networks, and even print to other computers and peripherals with IR ports.

Unless Windows 98 finds an IR port on your PC during the installation process, it will not install the IR component of the operating system. If, for some reason, your computer features an IR port but Windows 98 did not install the IR software, you can load the software manually from the installation disc.

Use the following procedure to install the Infrared component of Windows 98:

1. Open the Start menu and choose Settings, Control Panel.

2. Choose Add/Remove Programs and then choose the Windows Setup tab of the Add/Remove Programs Properties dialog box.

3. From the Components list, choose Communications, and then choose Details. Put a check next to the Infrared component and click OK. If the Infrared check box is already checked, the IR software is already installed on your computer.

⚠️ *If you are having some problems with your infrared connection, see "Basic Problems with Infrared Transmissions" in the "Troubleshooting" section at the end of the chapter.*

SETTING UP AN INFRARED PORT

After you install the software, you must set up your IR port. Windows 98 provides a wizard to help you through the process. To set up an IR port, use the following procedure:

1. Open the Start menu and choose Settings, Control Panel.

2. Choose the Infrared icon in the Control Panel. Windows 98 displays the Add Infrared Device Wizard, shown in Figure 25.11.

Figure 25.11
Use the Infrared Device Wizard to set up an IR port.

3. Click Next to display the manufacturer's list of IR devices.

4. If you have driver software for the IR port that arrived with your computer, choose Have Disk. Otherwise, pick the manufacturer's name from the list on the left and then choose the model name of your IR device.

5. Windows 98 asks you to verify your selection. If it's correct, click Next. Otherwise, choose Back to return to the preceding screen.

6. The next dialog box asks you to confirm the port to which your IR device is attached. If that information is correct, click Next. Otherwise, choose Back to return to the preceding screen.

7. Click Finish to complete your IR port setup.

After your IR port is installed, you can use it in place of a serial or parallel cable for a Direct Cable Connection. Read the "Using the Direct Cable Connection" section of this chapter for instructions on setting up an IR port for Direct Cable Connection.

TROUBLESHOOTING

BASIC PROBLEMS WITH INFRARED TRANSMISSIONS

I have installed the infrared component correctly but still have no infrared connection.

If you are having problems with your infrared connection, check these basic areas as you troubleshoot.

First determine whether the distance between infrared adapters is correct. If you think that distance is the problem, try moving the devices closer together or farther apart. The devices cannot be more than 3 feet apart, and some devices work best if kept at least 6 inches apart. Make sure that there is no interference or an obstruction between the devices.

Also check the alignment between the infrared adapters. Infrared devices produce an arc of infrared light. This arc is typically between 15 and 30 degrees. Attempt to realign the devices so that they fall within this arc.

Always look for a problem with interference. Infrared transmission is very susceptible to interference. For example, direct sunlight contains infrared light and can cause degradation of the infrared signal that is transmitted between devices.

SECRETS OF MASTERING THE WINDOWS 98 ENVIRONMENT: INSTALLING PC CARDS AND COM PORT ASSIGNMENTS

Installing a communications device, such as a PC Card, causes Windows 98 to automatically assign a communications port (COM port). This process uses the base I/O port addresses as displayed in the following list:

- COM1 at 3F8 (input/output range)
- COM2 at 2F8
- COM3 at 3E8
- COM4 at 2E8

If you are attempting to install a device that has a "nonstandard base address" or if all four of the standard ports have already been assigned, Windows 98 automatically assigns the modem to the next available COM port. For example, if COM1 through COM4 are already assigned, COM5 port is the next available port.

If you are running legacy 16-bit Windows 3.1 applications, those applications may not be configured to access ports higher than COM4. In this case, you must adjust the base address in Device Manager, in the System option in Control Panel, or remove other devices to free up a COM port with a lower number.

Another interesting issue develops if you are running devices that are not Plug and Play compliant. You might have to change the resource settings for their communications ports. This step can be done through the Device Manager.

CHAPTER 26

ESTABLISHING A DIAL-UP INTERNET CONNECTION

In this chapter

USING THE INTERNET CONNECTION WIZARD

If you can't access the Internet through an office network, look for one of the literally thousands of independent service providers and online services scattered throughout the world that will gladly give you a dial-up account—for the right price, of course. Windows 98 supplies all the software you need to make a fast, reliable Internet connection. All you need to add is a modem or other connecting device.

The first time you open the Internet icon on the desktop, you launch the Internet Connection Wizard (see Figure 26.1). After you run through this initial setup routine, when you click the Internet icon, the Internet Explorer program starts.

Figure 26.1
These three options are just a small sampling of what you can do with the Internet Connection Wizard.

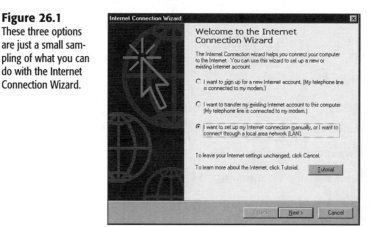

The Internet Connection Wizard is a remarkably versatile piece of software. After you get past the initial explanatory screen, you have three choices:

- You can sign up for a new Internet account. The Internet Connection Wizard offers a referral list of Internet service providers (ISPs) in your area.

- You can set up an existing Internet account for access through Windows 98, either over the phone or through a network.

- You can tell the Internet Connection Wizard to use your existing Internet connection. If you're comfortable with TCP/IP and networking, this is a reasonable choice.

The Internet Connection Wizard doesn't have to be just a one-time deal. You can make the wizard reappear at any time by following these steps:

1. Right-click on the Internet Explorer icon on the desktop.
2. Choose Properties, and then click the Connections tab. The dialog box shown in Figure 26.2 appears.

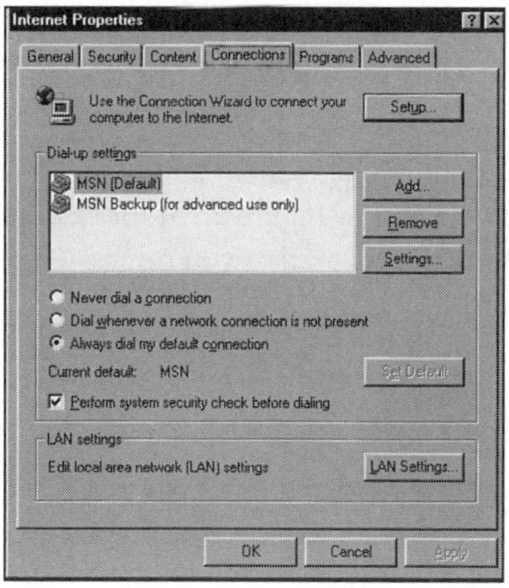

Figure 26.2
Want to use the
Internet Connection
Wizard again? Click
the Setup button on
this dialog box.

3. Click the Setup button.

Don't underestimate the Internet Connection Wizard. Although it's easy to stereotype it as a tool for beginners, this wizard is useful for experts as well, and it handles nearly every imaginable task when it comes to setting up and managing Internet connections. Because of the sheer number of choices available when you run the Internet Connection Wizard, trying to explain or illustrate every step would be pointless (and probably impossible). But here is a partial list of what you can use it for:

- Install and configure a modem (or set up a LAN connection for Internet access instead).
- Adjust the dialing settings you use, including the local area code and the prefixes you use to access outside lines.
- Create and edit Dial-Up Networking connection icons for one-button access to the Internet.
- Adjust advanced Internet settings.
- Enter and edit account information you use to connect with an ISP.

PART
IV

CH
26

> **Note**
>
> If you have not yet installed Dial-Up Networking, the Internet Connection Wizard installs these system services automatically. You need your original Windows CD-ROM or disks, and you need to restart the computer to complete the installation.

INSTALLING AND CONFIGURING A MODEM

There are two obvious prerequisites to any dial-up connection: You need a modem (or another type of connecting device, such as an ISDN adapter), and you need a phone line. If you haven't set up a modem previously, the Internet Connection Wizard includes a series of steps that automatically install the correct drivers and configure your modem. You can also use the Modems option in Control Panel to add a new modem or to configure an existing one.

Although most dial-up connections use only one modem at a time, you can install multiple communication devices. The system depicted in Figure 26.3, for example, includes an analog modem and an ISDN adapter. Note, however, that you can assign only one device to each Dial-Up Networking connection.

Figure 26.3
This system includes two communication devices: a 3Com ISDN adapter and a Microcom analog modem. Both are available for dial-up connections.

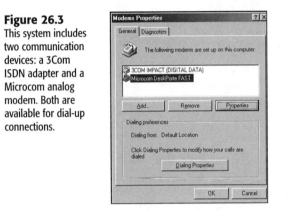

➔ For instructions specific to installing a modem, **see** "Installing a Modem," **p. 440.**

ADDING A NEW ANALOG MODEM

Windows 98 does a super job of identifying and configuring the correct modem type from a list of hundreds of choices. If your modem is Plug and Play-compatible, Windows should detect it automatically, install the correct drivers, and configure all relevant settings. For modems that don't take advantage of *Plug and Play (pages 250, 430, 524-525)* detection, you might have to do the installation and configuration duties manually.

> **Note**
>
> PC Card modems for mobile computers require different installation procedures. Chapter 25 provides step-by-step instructions.

➔ To learn more about installing and using PC Cards, **see** "Using PC Card Devices," **p.507.**

To add a new modem, follow these steps:

1. Open the Modems icon in Control Panel.
2. If you have not previously set up a modem on this system, the Install New Modem Wizard appears. If you are adding a new modem, click the Add button.

3. In the Install New Modem dialog box, click the Next button to allow Windows to detect your modem and proceed to step 4. If you've downloaded a driver or if the manufacturer supplied a driver on disk, and you're certain that this driver is more up-to-date than the built-in Windows drivers, select the option to skip detection, click Next, and skip to step 5.

4. If Windows detected your modem properly, click Finish to install the driver. Skip over all additional steps.

   If Windows did not correctly detect your modem, click the Change button and proceed to step 5.

5. If you bypassed the detection process or if Windows did not correctly detect your modem, Windows displays a list of available modem drivers. Choose the modem manufacturer from the list on the left and the model name from the list of modems on the right. If you have an updated Windows 95 or Windows 98 driver, click the Have Disk button and specify the location of the driver.

6. Select the port to which the modem is attached. Most desktop PCs have two serial ports (COM1 and COM2), and a mouse may be attached to one; Windows does not list a serial port if the mouse is attached to it. If you have multiple free serial ports, Windows should detect the correct one. You might need to check the system documentation or the label on the physical port to verify which port the modem is using.

7. Click Finish to install the driver and configure the modem.

PART
IV

CH
26

Tip #150

If you can't find a compatible Windows 95 or Windows 98 driver for your modem, select (Standard Modem Types) from the top of the Manufacturers list and choose the generic model that most closely matches your modem's speed. Although you will lose any advanced features included with your modem, you should be able to send and receive data at the modem's rated speed.

CONFIGURING AN ANALOG MODEM

After you install drivers for an analog modem, it should be configured correctly. Still, it can't hurt to double-check settings to guarantee that the device is properly set up for maximum performance. Several nested dialog boxes include options for adjusting drivers, connection speeds, port assignments, and hardware-specific connection settings, including control over the volume of the modem's built-in speaker.

To set basic modem options, open the Modems icon in Control Panel, select the modem whose settings you want to adjust, and click Properties. A dialog box like the one shown in Figure 26.4 appears. Click the General tab.

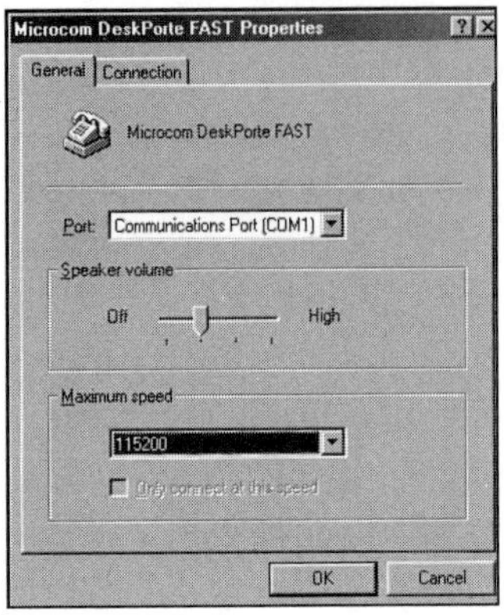

Figure 26.4
Use the General tab to adjust the volume of the modem's internal speaker. (Confusingly, the Maximum Speed setting does not control modem-to-modem speeds.)

Three basic options are available here:

- Port—This dialog box displays the port the modem is configured to use. To switch the modem to another port, use the Port drop-down list.

- Speaker Volume—This option enables you to adjust the modem's speaker. The slider control uses four positions: Off, Low, Medium, and High (from left to right). For most circumstances, the Low setting is the best because it enables you to hear the dial tone and handshaking sounds so that you know to retry a connection when your modem and the one at the other end are not communicating.

- Maximum Speed—Don't be confused by the Maximum Speed control at the bottom of this dialog box. This setting controls the internal speed at which your computer communicates with the modem, and on most Pentium-class computers, that speed is invariably faster than the transmission speed of the modem itself. Previous versions of Windows typically set this value too low. On most Pentium PCs, you can safely set the port speed to 115,200bps. Reduce this setting only if you experience persistent data errors when sending and receiving. Avoid the check box labeled Only Connect at This Speed.

To set general connection options, click the Connection tab. You'll see a dialog box like the one shown in Figure 26.5.

You can adjust the following settings here:

- Connection Preferences—The Connection preferences section at the top of the dialog box specifies settings for data bits, parity, and stop bits. These settings are typically used for direct modem-to-modem communications rather than TCP/IP connections that use the Internet-standard Point-to-Point Protocol (PPP) or Serial Line Interface Protocol (SLIP). You should not have to adjust these settings for Internet access.

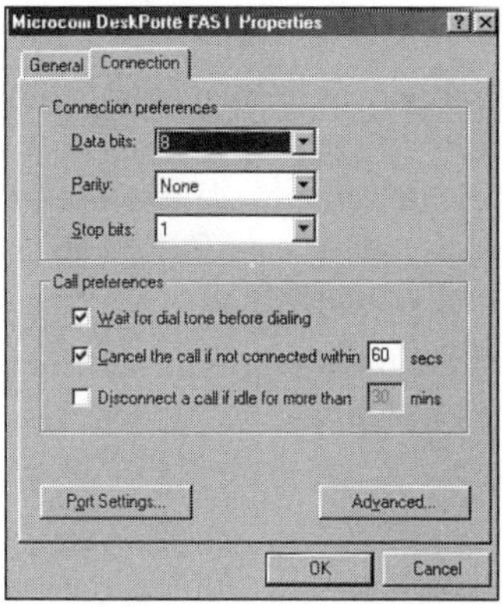

Figure 26.5
Avoid the temptation to tinker with these connection settings. For most circumstances, the default settings work best.

- Call Preferences—Note the check mark in front of the box labeled Wait for Dial Tone Before Dialing. If your phone system uses a dial tone that differs from the standard U.S. dial tone, Windows mistakenly believes the line is dead and refuses to dial until you clear this box. Likewise, voice-mail systems that alter the normal dial tone to a "stutter" signal can confuse Windows unless you clear this box.

  If you choose the option Cancel the Call If Not Connected Within *XX* Secs, you must enter a value for a number of seconds in the box. The 60-second timeout is sufficient for most domestic calls. If some of your dial-up connections routinely require lengthy connect times, you should increase this value to avoid timeout errors.

  The Disconnect a Call If Idle for More Than *XX* Mins option lets you specify the amount of time the connection can be idle before Windows disconnects automatically. This setting is appropriate only for modem-to-modem connections; for Internet connections, use the timeout settings defined by the Internet Explorer Connection Manager.

PART

IV

CH

26

Finally, you can set hardware-specific options that control the basic functioning of your modem. Click the Advanced button to see the dialog box shown in Figure 26.6.

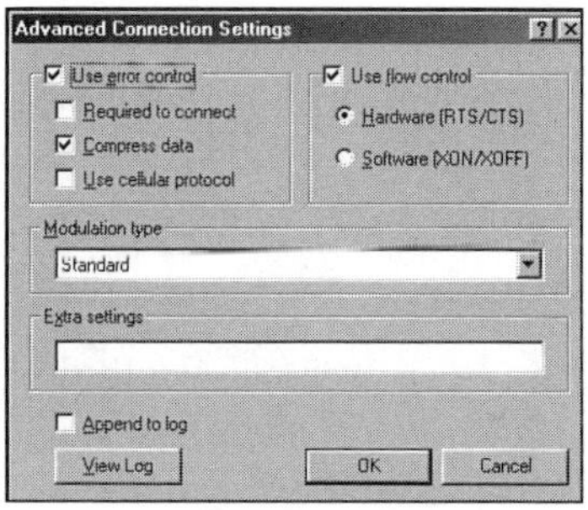

Figure 26.6
Adjust these advanced connection settings only if you understand the consequences of your actions. Unnecessary tinkering here can actually reduce data transmission speeds.

Four advanced options are available in this dialog box:

- Use Error Control—Error control options reduce the likelihood of noisy phone lines causing data corruption. Most modern modems support both data compression and error control. The modem information file should set these options for your specific modem. The Use Cellular Protocol box enables the MNP10 error control protocol, which can be used with some (but not all) cellular modems.

- Use Flow Control—Flow control governs the integrity of the connection. By default, Windows 98 enables hardware flow control, and most modern modems support this mode for best performance. Software flow control should never be used for an Internet connection.

- Modulation Type—Do not change modulation types unless the manufacturer of your modem specifically recommends that you do so.

- Extra Settings—If necessary, click in the Extra Settings box and add AT commands that enable or disable a particular feature of your modem or adapter. For example, S0=5 tells your modem to answer automatically after five rings. Check your modem documentation for AT commands applicable to your hardware.

Zoom Telephonics offers a comprehensive source of information about modem technology and the AT command set. You can browse its listings at

`http://www.modems.com`

CONFIGURING AN ISDN ADAPTER

Most home and small-office dial-up connections use conventional analog lines. In some areas, you can use the Integrated Services Digital Network (ISDN) to establish high-speed digital connections. Compared with analog lines, ISDN circuits offer significant advantages:

- Connection times are practically instantaneous, for example, unlike on analog lines that require 20 seconds or more to establish a connection.

- Transmission speeds are typically two to five times faster than on most analog modems.

- The connection is digital from end to end, which means you won't lose data because of noise on the line—something that can't be said for the typical analog connection.

- A typical ISDN configuration includes two digital data channels and one analog data port; this technology enables you to plug in a conventional telephone or modem and talk or send data over an analog connection while simultaneously sending and receiving data on a digital channel.

ISDN technology has its share of disadvantages as well. Generally, these lines cost more—sometimes many times more than an analog line. Not all ISPs support ISDN, and those that do often charge a premium as well. And finally, configuring an ISDN connection can be a nightmare, and the technology is difficult and filled with jargon.

ISDN hardware comes in all shapes and sizes, and every piece of hardware uses a different setup routine. Some devices install as network adapters, others as modems, and still others as routers on a network. When you choose an ISDN device from the Add Hardware option in Control Panel, Windows installs the ISDN Wizard. This tool allows you to configure the technical details of your ISDN line, as shown in Figure 26.7.

Tip #151

You can connect up to eight devices to a single ISDN line. These devices can be a mix of all types. For example, network routers and bridges, ISDN fax machines, ISDN telephones, and standard analog telephone devices can be connected to a single ISDN line.

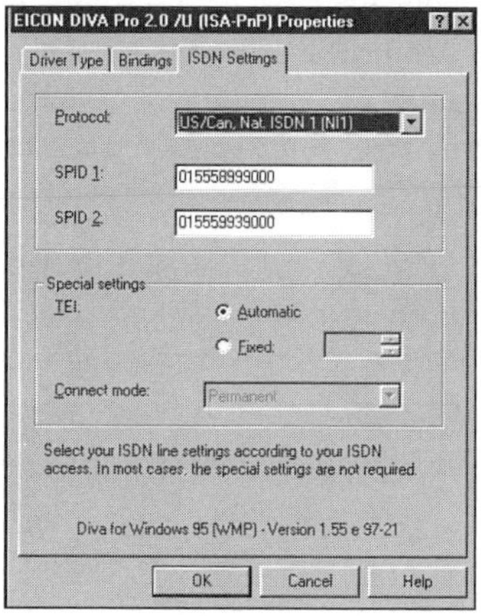

Figure 26.7
Although some ISDN adapters emulate modems, this device from Eicon Systems looks like a network card to Windows 98.

For more information about ISDN technology, check out Dan Kegel's detailed Web page at
`http://www.alumni.caltech.edu/~dank/isdn/`

For details on how to order ISDN service, plus links to updates of the ISDN software for Windows 98, try Microsoft's Get ISDN page:
`http://www.microsoft.com/windows/getisdn/about.htm`

Although the ISDN Configuration Wizard makes setup somewhat easier than it used to be, the process is still complex. When connecting an ISDN line, you must get detailed instructions from the manufacturer of the adapter and from the phone company—and then follow those instructions to the letter. At a minimum, you need to know the service provider IDs (SPIDs), the telephone numbers for each channel, and the switch type used in the telephone company office. Some ISDN hardware includes a utility that enables you to upload this information directly to the adapter.

PART

IV

CH

26

Tip #152	After you successfully install your ISDN adapter, it appears as a choice in the Internet Connection Wizard and the Dial-Up Networking Wizard.

OTHER HIGH-SPEED ACCESS OPTIONS

Telephone companies are no longer the only sources of access to the Internet. An increasing number of high-speed alternatives to traditional dial-up access use different types of wires—and in some cases no wires at all.

Hughes Network systems, for example, sells a small satellite dish called DirecDuo that provides Internet access at speeds of up to 400Kbps as well as several hundred channels of TV programming. Not to be outdone, many phone companies are rolling out systems that use Digital Subscriber Line (DSL) technology to provide Internet access at speeds in excess of 1MB per second while allowing you to use the same line for voice calls. And some cable TV companies now offer Internet access over the same cable you use to receive television signals.

Depending on the system configuration, these solutions can deliver data at speeds of up to 10MB per second, roughly on a par with local area network performance. Although Windows 98 does not offer built-in support for any of these cutting-cdge technologies, third parties offer hardware and Windows drivers that work well. If you plan to use any of these services, be sure to ask the provider for detailed instructions on how to access the service from Windows 98.

CONFIGURING A CONNECTION TO AN EXISTING INTERNET ACCOUNT

Windows 98 uses a service called Dial-Up Networking (DUN) to connect your system to the Internet over telephone lines. The Internet Connection Wizard automatically installs Dial-Up Networking if necessary. Individual connection icons within the Dial-Up Networking folder contain all the information you need to connect with the Internet. You'll find the Dial-Up Networking folder in the My Computer window. To open this system folder from the Start menu, click Start and choose Programs, Accessories, Dial-Up Networking.

If you already have an account with an ISP, the wizard's step-by-step procedures can help you create a Dial-Up Networking connection with a minimum of clicking and typing. The default settings assume you're making a standard PPP connection, with IP address and DNS (Domain Name Server) settings assigned dynamically. Follow these steps:

1. Start the Internet Connection Wizard and choose the option to set up a connection manually, or I Want to Connect Through a LAN. Click Next to continue.

2. Choose the option to connect using your phone line and click Next.

3. Enter the dial-in phone number of your Internet service provider. You can adjust advanced settings for the connection by clicking on the Advanced button. For standard PPP connections for which you don't need to specify an IP address or DNS servers, select No and click Next. (See the next section, "Adjusting Advanced Settings," for more information on when and how to adjust the advanced settings.) Click Next when you are ready to move on.

4. Enter your username and password and click Next.

5. Give the connection a descriptive name, as in Figure 26.8, and click Next.

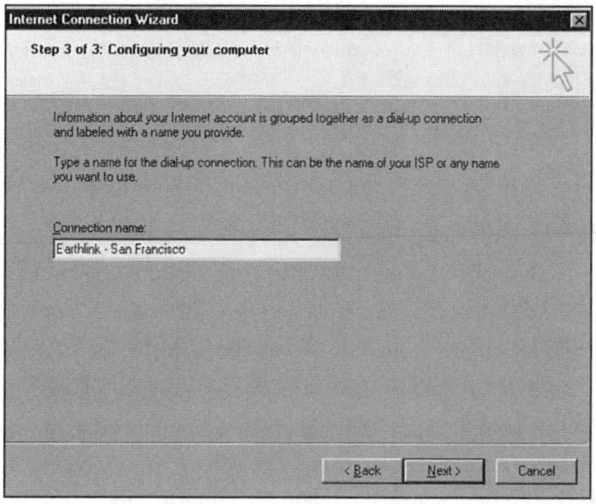

Figure 26.8
The default connection icon uses a generic name. You can add location info to make the icon's purpose easier to identify.

6. If you need to set up mail and news accounts or a directory server, the wizard provides separate steps to help with each of these tasks. (See Chapter 31, "Using Outlook Express," for instructions on setting up these accounts.) When you reach the end of the wizard, click Finish to create the Dial-Up Networking connection icon.

ADJUSTING ADVANCED SETTINGS

As you saw in step 7 of the previous procedure, the Internet Connection Wizard includes an option for adjusting advanced connection settings. If your Internet service provider uses a SLIP connection or requires scripting or if you need to enter a fixed IP address and specify addresses for DNS servers, select Yes in the Advanced Settings dialog box (see Figure 26.9) and fill in the four boxes that follow.

Advanced settings include the following:

- Connection Type—Choose PPP or SLIP connection.
- Logon Procedure—Either select the manual option to bring up a Terminal window when connecting or specify a logon script.

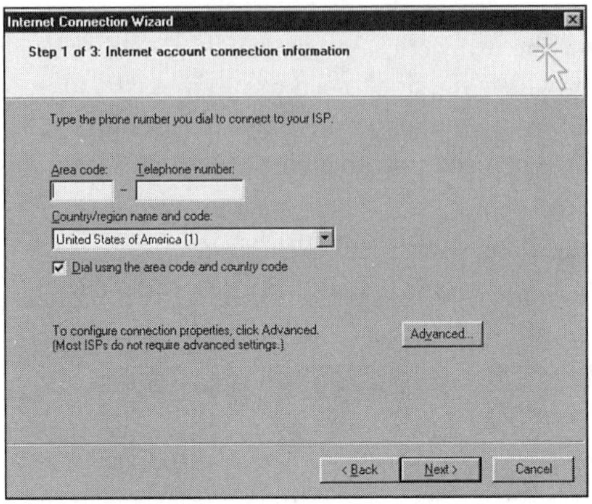

Figure 26.9
When you select the
Advanced button, the
Internet Connection
Wizard takes a brief
detour into advanced
configuration options.

- IP Address—If your ISP provides a fixed IP address, enter it here.
- DNS Server Address—If your ISP requires you to specify primary and backup name
  servers, enter their IP addresses here.

Tip #153

These Advanced settings are useful if you have multiple dial-up accounts (a corporate dial-up server and a personal account with an ISP, for example). Create a separate Dial-Up Networking icon for each account, and then individually adjust the IP address and other settings for each connection icon.

USING MULTILINK OPTIONS FOR FASTER CONNECTIONS

Most dial-up Internet connections are simple one-modem, one-line propositions, and transmission speed is limited by the slower of the two modems at the ends of the connection. Under specialized circumstances, though, you can use two or more connecting devices to increase the speed of a dial-up connection. These so-called *multilink connections* require the following conditions:

- You must have multiple devices to bind together into a single virtual connection.
- Each device requires its own driver software.
- Each device needs access to a separate analog phone line or a channel on an ISDN line.
- The dial-up server at the other end of the connection must support multilink PPP connections.

The most common use of multilink connections is to join two 56KB or 64KB channels on an ISDN line to create a 112KB or 128KB connection.

To enable multilink options on an existing connection, follow these steps:

1. Open the Dial-Up Networking folder, right-click on the connection icon you want to modify, and choose Properties from the shortcut menu.

2. Click the Multilink tab. The dialog box shown in Figure 26.10 appears.

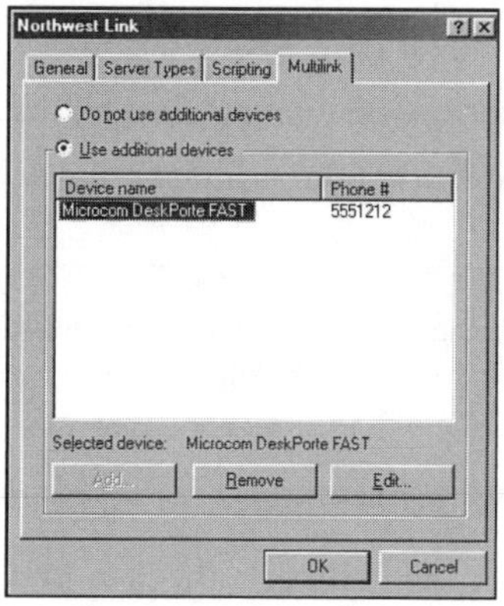

Figure 26.10
If your ISP supports multilink PPP, use these settings to combine two modems to create a faster virtual connection.

3. Select the Use Additional Devices option, and the grayed-out buttons at the bottom of the dialog box become available.

4. Click the Add button and choose a modem or ISDN adapter from the drop-down list. If no choices are available, click Cancel and set up your additional hardware. Then continue.

5. Enter a separate phone number for the additional device if required. The hardware documentation and service provider can supply more details about your specific configuration.

6. Select any entry in the list and use the Remove or Edit button to modify the entry.

7. Click OK to save your changes.

Tip #154

If you are using ISDN, make sure that the ISDN card is dual channel. If it is not, you cannot use multilink.

CREATING AND EDITING LOGON SCRIPTS

Today, most commercial ISPs use logon servers that communicate easily with Windows Dial-Up Networking connections. Some older providers or noncommercial dial-up sites, however, might require additional keyboard input that the Windows connection can't provide. In such cases, you must create a logon script for use with the Dial-Up Networking connection. When you open a connection icon whose configuration details include a script, Windows opens a Terminal window and sends the additional commands. The script might operate unattended in the background, or it might stop and require that you make an entry in the Terminal window.

Script files are simple text files that end in the extension .SCP. You'll find these four general-purpose scripts in the Program Files\Accessories folder:

- CIS.SCP establishes a PPP connection with CompuServe.
- PPPMENU.SCP logs on to a server that uses text menus.
- SLIP.SCP establishes a SLIP connection with a remote host machine.
- SLIPMENU.SCP establishes a SLIP connection on a menu-based host.

Tip #155

Some scripts require editing before use. If so, the prudent approach is to back up the script file you plan to modify before you make any changes.

To assign a script to a connection icon, follow these steps:

1. Open the Dial-Up Networking folder, right-click on the icon, and choose Properties from the shortcut menu.

2. Click the Scripting tab. The dialog box shown in Figure 26.11 appears.

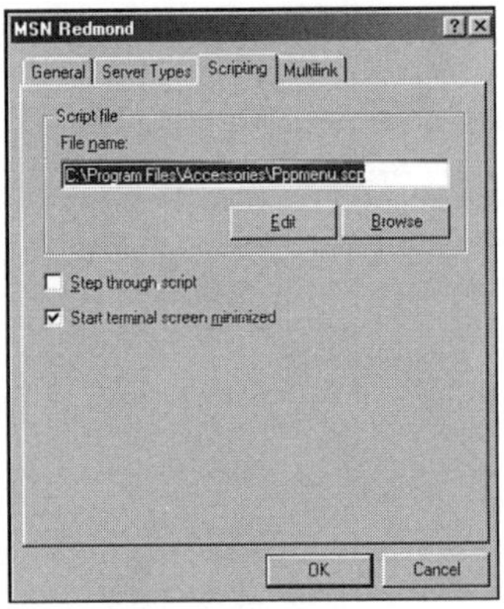

Figure 26.11
Choose a logon script from this dialog box. Then, click the Edit button to open Notepad and edit the script.

3. Click the Browse button and navigate to the Accessories folder. Select a script from the list and click Open.

4. If you need to modify the script, click the Edit button. The script opens in Notepad. Make any necessary changes and save your changes before closing the Editing window.

5. To avoid being distracted by the script as it runs, check the Start Terminal Screen Minimized box.

6. To tell Windows that you want the script to pause after each step so you can see where modifications are needed, check the Step Through Script box.

7. Click OK to save your changes.

When you open a Dial-Up Networking connection with a script attached, the Terminal window appears. If you selected the Step Through Script option, Windows also displays the Automated Script Test window (see Figure 26.12).

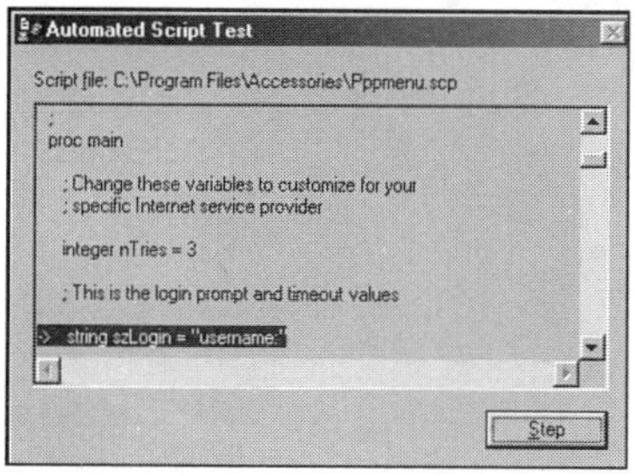

Figure 26.12
Use the step option to walk through a logon script one step at a time for debugging purposes.

Normally, the terminal window doesn't accept keyboard input. If you need to respond to a prompt, check the Allow Keyboard Input box. When the script has finished processing, you might need to click Continue to complete the connection.

Note

For detailed documentation of the dial-up scripting language, look in the Windows folder for a file named SCRIPT.DOC.

SETTING UP A NEW ACCOUNT WITH AN ISP

The top option on the Internet Connection Wizard lets you choose an ISP and set up a new Internet account. Although you can research available ISPs and sign up for an account on your own, this wizard offers a quick, hassle-free way to change service providers or set up a new account.

Using the wizard is a straightforward process. You specify the country you live in, the area (or city) code, and any necessary dialing instructions. The wizard installs a handful of required software components, including support for TCP/IP and Dial-Up Networking. During the setup and configuration process, the wizard may restart your system one or more times. Although the wizard manages the details of shutting down and restarting, you have to respond to dialog boxes like the one in Figure 26.13 to move the installation process along.

Eventually, the wizard makes two phone calls. The first is to Microsoft's Internet Referral Service, which uses your area (or city) code and the first three digits of your phone number to identify Windows 98-compatible ISPs available in your area and language. Because Microsoft regularly updates the roster of eligible service providers, the exact choices you see will vary; the list should resemble the one shown in Figure 26.14.

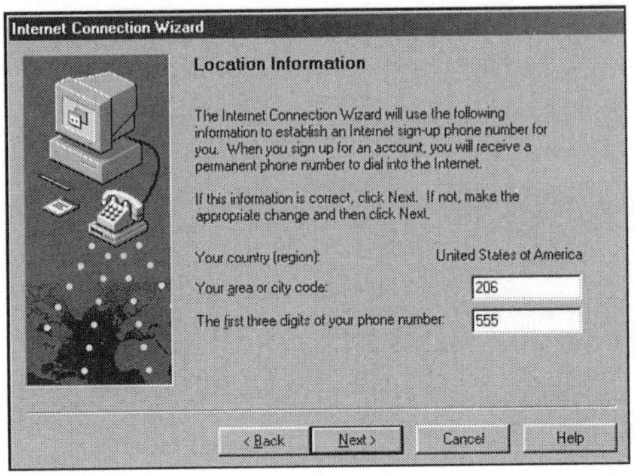

Figure 26.13
The Internet
Connection Wizard's
automatic signup
option requires
almost no interven-
tion except for input
in this dialog box.

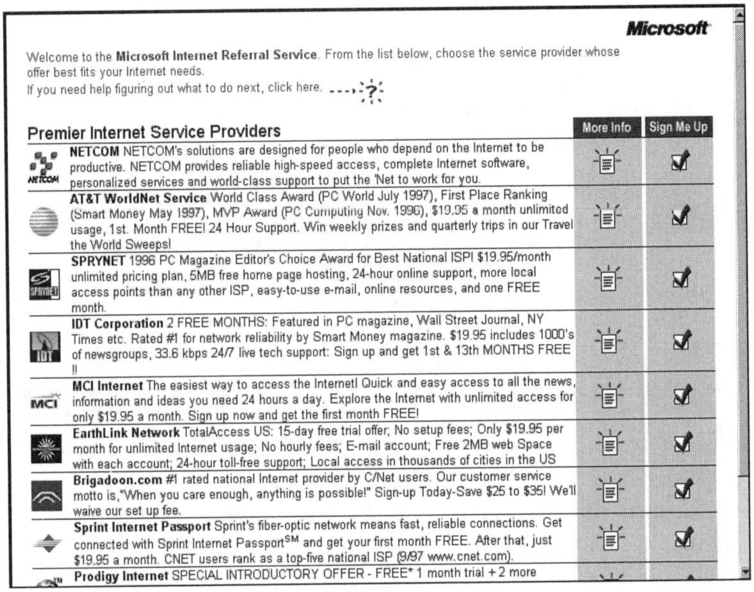

Internet Connection Wizard

Location Information

The Internet Connection Wizard will use the following information to establish an Internet sign-up phone number for you. When you sign up for an account, you will receive a permanent phone number to dial into the Internet.

If this information is correct, click Next. If not, make the appropriate change and then click Next.

Your country (region): United States of America

Your area or city code: 206

The first three digits of your phone number: 555

< Back   Next >   Cancel   Help

Figure 26.14
The Microsoft Internet
Referral Service gen-
erates a list of avail-
able ISPs just for you,
based on your loca-
tion and operating
system.

Microsoft

Welcome to the **Microsoft Internet Referral Service**. From the list below, choose the service provider whose offer best fits your Internet needs.
If you need help figuring out what to do next, click here.

Premier Internet Service Providers	More Info	Sign Me Up
NETCOM NETCOM's solutions are designed for people who depend on the Internet to be productive. NETCOM provides reliable high-speed access, complete Internet software, personalized services and world-class support to put the 'Net to work for you.		
AT&T WorldNet Service World Class Award (PC World July 1997), First Place Ranking (Smart Money May 1997), MVP Award (PC Computing Nov. 1996), $19.95 a month unlimited usage, 1st. Month FREE! 24 Hour Support. Win weekly prizes and quarterly trips in our Travel the World Sweeps!		
SPRYNET 1996 PC Magazine Editor's Choice Award for Best National ISP! $19.95/month unlimited pricing plan, 5MB free home page hosting, 24-hour online support, more local access points than any other ISP, easy-to-use e-mail, online resources, and one FREE month.		
IDT Corporation 2 FREE MONTHS: Featured in PC magazine, Wall Street Journal, NY Times etc. Rated #1 for network reliability by Smart Money magazine. $19.95 includes 1000's of newsgroups, 33.6 kbps 24/7 live tech support: Sign up and get 1st & 13th MONTHS FREE !!		
MCI Internet The easiest way to access the Internet! Quick and easy access to all the news, information and ideas you need 24 hours a day. Explore the Internet with unlimited access for only $19.95 a month. Sign up now and get the first month FREE!		
EarthLink Network TotalAccess US: 15-day free trial offer; No setup fees; Only $19.95 per month for unlimited Internet usage; No hourly fees; E-mail account; Free 2MB web Space with each account; 24-hour toll-free support; Local access in thousands of cities in the US		
Brigadoon.com #1 rated national Internet provider by C/Net users. Our customer service motto is,"When you care enough, anything is possible!" Sign-up Today-Save $25 to $35! We'll waive our set up fee.		
Sprint Internet Passport Sprint's fiber-optic network means fast, reliable connections. Get connected with Sprint Internet Passport[SM] and get your first month FREE. After that, just $19.95 a month. CNET users rank as a top-five national ISP (9/97 www.cnet.com).		
Prodigy Internet SPECIAL INTRODUCTORY OFFER - FREE* 1 month trial + 2 more		

If the summary information isn't enough to help you decide, click the More Info icon to the right of a listing for extra details about that company's services. When you're ready to choose, click the Sign Me Up icon to the right of the entry you want. The Internet Connection Wizard makes a second phone call, this one to the provider you've chosen.

Each provider's sign-up procedure is special, but in general you must supply your name, address, and credit card information. The wizard takes care of all remaining details, includ-ing setting up Dial-Up Networking connection icons and installing any necessary access software.

MANAGING DIAL-UP NETWORKING CONNECTIONS

Windows stores every connection icon you create in the Dial-Up Networking folder. Although you can make copies and shortcuts for use elsewhere, the only way to create or manage these icons is to open the Dial-Up Networking folder (see Figure 26.15). You'll find it in the My Computer folder or inside the Accessories folder on the Start menu.

> **Note**
>
> Believe it or not, some Microsoft documentation calls these icons *connectoids*.

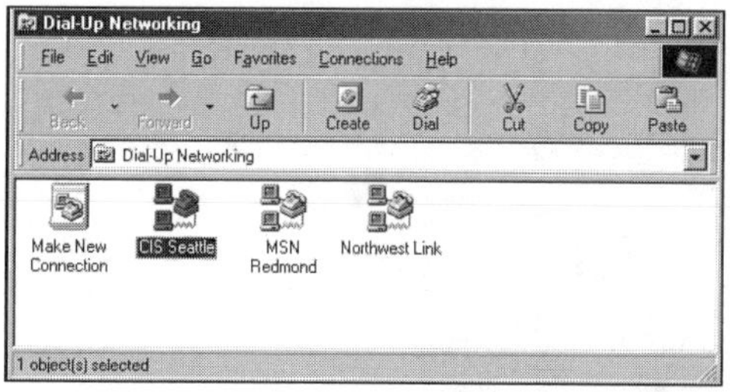

Figure 26.15
Open the Dial-Up Networking folder to create or manage your connection icons. Note the additional Create and Dial icons in the toolbar.

Like the Desktop, Control Panel, and Printers folders, the Dial-Up Networking folder is a special system folder and doesn't have a corresponding MS-DOS-style directory. To make this folder more accessible, open the My Computer window and drag the Dial-Up Networking icon onto the Quick Launch bar or drag the icon onto the Start button to create a shortcut at the top of the Start menu.

ADDING A NEW DIAL-UP NETWORKING CONNECTION

As you've seen, the Internet Connection Wizard creates connection icons as part of the process of configuring your Internet connection. If you're comfortable working directly with connection icons, you can create them from scratch by using a two-step wizard accessible from the Dial-Up Networking folder. Follow these steps:

1. Open the Dial-Up Networking folder and open the Make New Connection icon.

2. In the Make New Connection Wizard, give the connection a name and select a modem or other communication device. Then click Next.

3. Enter the area (or city) code, country code, and phone number of the server you want to dial. Click Next.

4. Click Finish to save the connection in the Dial-Up Networking folder, where you can edit it later.

PART

IV

CH

26

Caution

Although this wizard provides a quick way to create a Dial-Up Networking icon, the default settings almost always require editing. For example, by default these connections use three different protocols; most Internet connections need only TCP/IP.

ADJUSTING THE PROPERTIES OF AN EXISTING CONNECTION ICON

Regardless of how you create a Dial-Up Networking connection icon, you can change its properties at any time. Open the Dial-Up Networking folder, select an icon, right-click the icon, and choose Properties. You'll see a multiple-tab dialog box like the one in Figure 26.16.

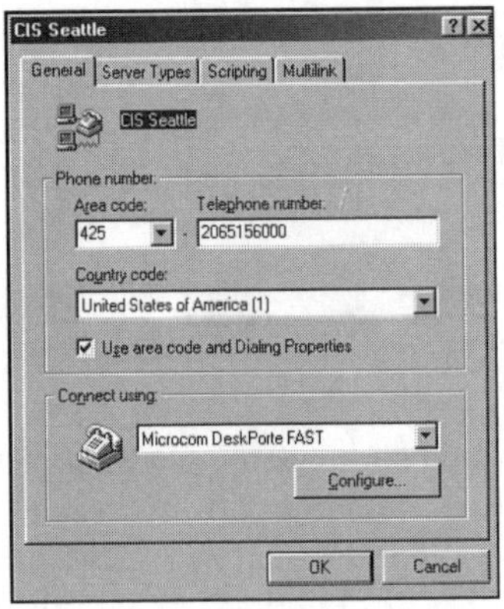

Figure 26.16
Use this dialog box to change the phone number or modem associated with a connection.

On the General tab, you can adjust the area code, country code, and phone number for any connection. You can also change the modem or other connecting device you use for the connection.

Click the Server Types tab to adjust properties specific to the server with which you plan to connect. Figure 26.17 shows the choices available.

If you're having trouble connecting to a RAS (Remote Access Server) server, see "Problems Connecting to the Remote Server" in the "Troubleshooting" section at the end of this chapter.

The Type of Dial-Up Server drop-down list contains five choices. You'll select PPP in most cases. If you're dialing into a UNIX server with a shell account, however, you might need to choose SLIP or CSLIP.

Note

PPP stands for Point-to-Point Protocol. *SLIP* is short for Serial Line Interface Protocol. PPP has largely replaced SLIP as the standard method of remotely accessing Internet service providers, thanks to its better error-checking features and its capability to handle automatic logons.

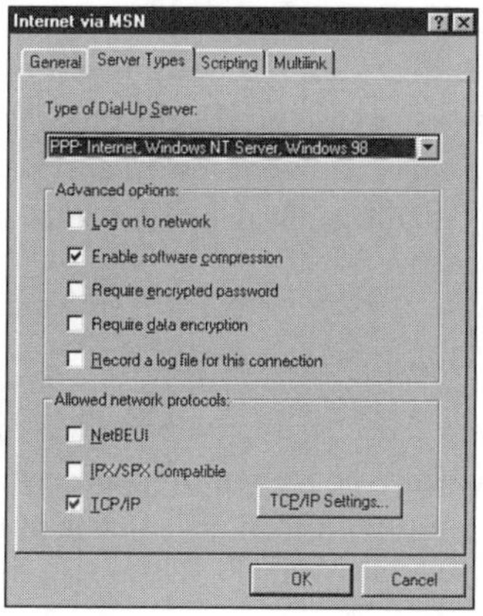

Figure 26.17
If your ISP uses any
nonstandard settings,
you need to adjust
them here.

Unless your ISP recommends that you change settings in the Advanced options area, leave that section alone; the defaults are correct for standard PPP connections. For example, most ISPs support Password Authentication Protocol (PAP) or the Challenge-Handshake Authentication Protocol (CHAP). If you check the Require Encrypted Password box, you won't be able to log on.

For Internet access, you can improve performance by clearing the check marks in front of NetBEUI and IPX/SPX in the list of Allowed Network Protocols. TCP/IP is the only protocol you need for Internet access.

→ To find out how to configure different protocols to be used with RAS, **see** "Connecting to a Remote Access Server," **p. 850.**

Finally, click the TCP/IP Settings button to check the configuration details of your connection. You'll see a dialog box like the one in Figure 26.18.

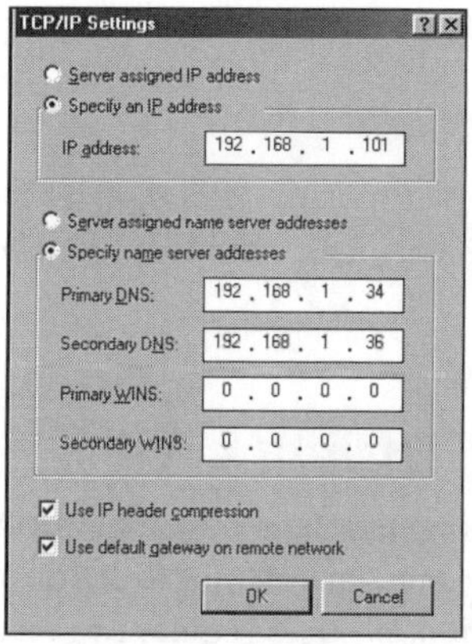

Figure 26.18
If your ISP has
assigned you a static
IP address, enter it
here, along with the
addresses of DNS
servers.

The default settings for a Dial-Up Networking connection assume you're dialing into a network that assigns you an IP address automatically each time you connect, without requiring you to specify DNS servers. On networks that use static IP addresses, you manually fill in your IP address and the addresses of DNS servers. For access to an ISP, leave the WINS server entries blank and don't change the default gateway or IP header compression unless your ISP specifically recommends it.

CREATING A SHORTCUT TO A DIAL-UP CONNECTION ICON

Although connection icons can exist only in the Dial-Up Networking folder, you can create shortcuts to those icons and use them anywhere you want. To place a shortcut on the desktop, open the Dial-Up Networking folder, select an icon, right-click it, and choose Create Shortcut. You can also right-drag a connection icon to any folder or onto the Start menu and choose Create Shortcut(s) Here from the menu that appears when you release the icon.

MOVING OR COPYING CONNECTION ICONS

Right-clicking a connection icon does not produce Cut, Copy, or Paste menus. But you can share these icons with other users or copy them to other machines if you know the undocumented technique. When you drag a connection icon out of the Dial-Up Networking folder and drop it in any legal location, including the desktop or a mail message, Windows creates a special Dial-Up Networking Exported File, which has the .DUN extension.

These exported files resemble shortcuts but behave differently. There's no shortcut arrow, for example. In addition, when you right-click a Dial-Up Networking Exported File icon and choose Properties, you see an abbreviated properties sheet in place of the normal shortcut information. But if you drop one of these files in the Dial-Up Networking folder of another machine running Windows 95 (with Dial-Up Networking version 1.1 or later) or Windows 98, the file works just as though you'd created the connection from scratch. This technique is excellent for quickly giving other users access to Dial-Up Networking without forcing them to go through the process of creating a connection icon from scratch.

RENAMING AND DELETING CONNECTION ICONS

To rename a connection, open the Dial-Up Networking folder, select the icon, right-click, and choose Rename. To delete a connection icon, select the icon, right-click, and choose Delete.

USING LOCATIONS TO CONTROL DIAL-UP CONNECTIONS

Each time you use a Dial-Up Networking connection icon, you have the option of specifying which *location* you want to dial from. Settings for each location include the area (or city) code for that location, calling card information, prefixes required to reach an outside line or to dial long distance, and much more. Locations are especially useful for owners of portable PCs: By simply selecting a location entry from a list, you can tell Windows to dial the access number for your ISP's server when you're at home but to use a dialing prefix, area code, and calling card number when you're on a business trip in another city.

Even if you always dial in from your home or office, you can still take advantage of multiple locations—especially if your Dial-Up Networking calls sometimes incur long-distance or toll charges or if your telephone company requires special dialing procedures for nearby area codes.

To set up dialing locations for the first time, use the Telephony option in Control Panel. To adjust dialing options on-the-fly when you're making a dial-up connection, click the Dial Properties button to the right of the phone number in the Connect To dialog box. And if you've opened the Modems option in Control Panel, you can click the Dialing Properties button on the bottom of the General tab. Regardless of which technique you use, you'll see a dialog box like the one in Figure 26.19.

Figure 26.19
You can use dialing locations to define dialing prefixes and area code preferences or to bill your calls to a telephone credit card.

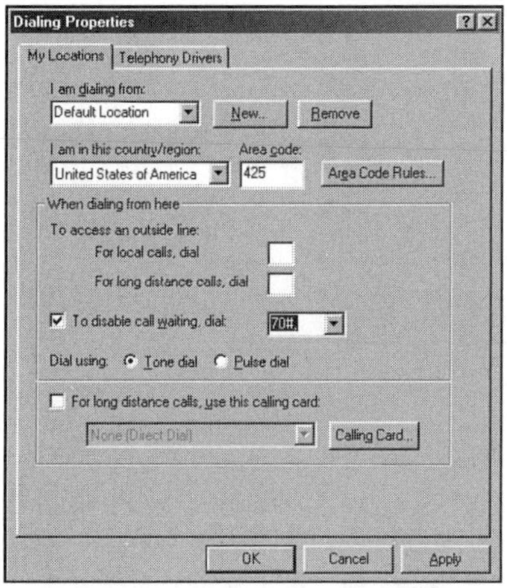

> **Note**
>
> Why are dialing settings grouped under the Telephony icon? All 32-bit Windows communications programs use a common feature set called the Telephony Application Programming Interface, or TAPI for short. Programs that use TAPI can detect when another TAPI-aware program wants to use a phone line, which makes it easier for the two programs to share a single line gracefully. A simple TAPI function lets them use centrally defined dialing settings as well.

If your ISP has multiple access numbers and you sometimes get a busy signal on your local number, you might want to call a number outside your area code. To that end, you can set up a location that lets you charge the daytime calls to a less expensive long-distance provider with a telephone credit card.

Follow these steps to set up a new location called Credit Card Call from Home:

1. Use the Telephony option in Control Panel to open the Dialing Properties dialog box.

2. Click the New button, and then click OK in the message box that confirms you've created a new location.

3. Note that the text in the box labeled I Am Dialing From is selected. Start typing to replace the default location name with a descriptive entry, such as Credit Card from Home.

4. Check the box labeled For Long Distance Calls, Use This Calling Card.

5. Select your calling card number from the drop-down list. If you're using a prepaid card or if your telephone card isn't in the list, select None (Direct Dial).

6. Click the Calling Card button, and the dialog box shown in Figure 26.20 appears.

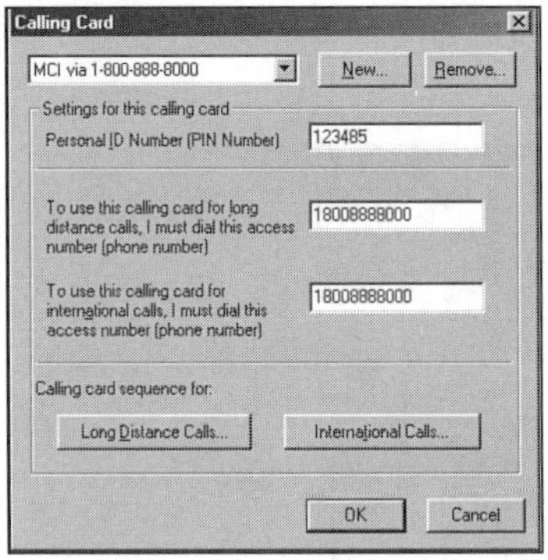

Figure 26.20
Use the Calling Card dialog box to set up access options for a telephone calling card.

7. If you're creating a new card type, click the New button and give the entry a name. Enter your PIN (if required) and enter or verify access numbers for long-distance and international calls.

8. Click the Long Distance Calls button. The dialog box shown in Figure 26.21 appears, with suggested default settings for your call. Make a note of the sequence of steps your long-distance company requires for you to make a call with your calling card and then use the drop-down lists to add or edit those steps here.

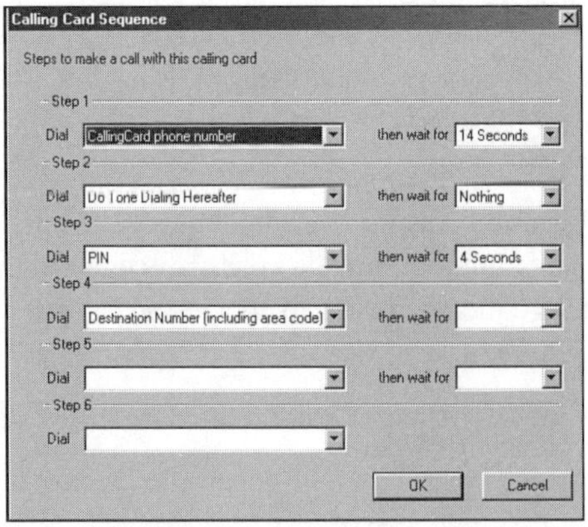

Figure 26.21
Although this dialog box looks daunting, it's remarkably effective for scripting calls you make with a calling card.

9. Click OK to save this sequence and repeat the process for international calls if necessary.

10. Click OK to save your dialing settings.

Now, whenever you want to use a telephone calling card to call a Dial-Up Networking connection, just select the appropriate location in the Connect To box. Windows automatically punches in the correct sequence of tones.

Tip #156

> Because Telephony locations work with all TAPI applications, you can use these same calling card settings with the Windows 98 Phone Dialer (found in the Accessories group) and other communication programs as well.

Another good use of dialing options, at least for residents of the United States, is to help cope with the explosion of new area codes over the past few years. At one time, people dialed all local calls direct and dialed 1 plus the area code and number for long distance. No more. Today, most large metropolitan areas have been partitioned into smaller zones, each with its own area code. As a result, some local calls demand an area code, but others don't. No firm set of rules dictates when you dial 1.

The version of Dial-Up Networking that debuted in Windows 95 worked well enough but fell down completely on this job. Windows 98 vastly improves your ability to deal with non-standard area codes and dialing configurations. To adjust these options, open the Dialing Properties dialog box and click the Area Code Rules button. Windows displays the Area Code Rules dialog box shown in Figure 26.22.

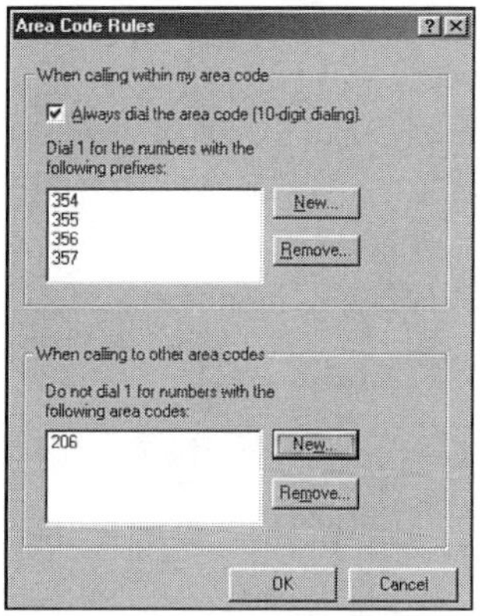

Figure 26.22
Have local dialing rules changed for you? Use these advanced area code options to tell Windows exactly how to dial.

Use the options at the top of the dialog box to specify dialing rules for prefixes within your own area code. The bottom options specify how to handle nearby area codes.

Tip #157

> Would you prefer to not use dialing properties at all? When you create a Dial-Up Networking connection icon, clear the check mark from the box labeled Use Area Code and Dialing Properties. Then enter the phone number exactly as you'd like Windows to dial it, complete with any prefixes, area codes and city or country codes, and calling card numbers.

USING THE MICROSOFT NETWORK FOR INTERNET ACCESS

Although it started out with the launch of Windows 95 as an online service competing with America Online and CompuServe, today The Microsoft Network (MSN) is a curious hybrid. Though partly an entertainment medium with "channels" of content ranging from the Disney Blast to Microsoft Investor, it's also a low-cost ISP with worldwide coverage and a variety of access plans.

Naturally, Microsoft makes it easy to install the MSN access software and to sign up for a trial account. Look on the Windows desktop for an icon called Setup MSN Internet Access. If you choose this option, it will load nearly 4MB of software and call a Microsoft server to establish your account. Although MSN uses many of the same components as Windows 98 (most notably Internet Explorer 4.0), MSN also adds its own distinctive touches, including a custom Connection Manager.

A typical MSN setup makes these changes to your system:

- MSN's Connection Manager replaces the Internet Explorer dialer.
- MSN automatically configures email and news accounts with the username you choose at startup.
- The icon in Outlook Express and Internet Explorer changes from the stylized Explorer logo to MSN's logo.
- An additional icon appears in the taskbar's notification area when you're connected to MSN. Right-click on that icon for a cascading menu with access to all of MSN's services.

In addition, MSN makes other subtle changes throughout the operating system, including installing and configuring a handful of multimedia players.

Tip #158

> If you use MSN to access the Internet but aren't fond of its interface, you can have the best of both worlds. When you install MSN, it adds a connection icon to the Dial-Up Networking folder. Use that icon to connect, and you'll bypass all of the MSN interface changes. Even if you uninstall the MSN software completely, you can still access your MSN account with this connection icon. If you do so, for your username, enter MSN/username (include the slash but substitute your username) and dial your local MSN access number.

USING OTHER ONLINE SERVICES

Increasingly, online services resemble ISPs both in the services they offer and the rates they charge. When you open the Online Services folder on the Windows desktop, you have access to shortcuts with which you can connect to America Online (AOL), AT&T WorldNet, CompuServe (which is now owned by AOL), and Prodigy Internet.

The icons in the desktop folder are shortcuts to much larger setup files stored on the Windows 98 CD-ROM. You can use these icons to open a new account or to enable access to an existing account with one of these services.

For more details about each of the online services, including technical support numbers, see the text file in the Online Services folder.

CONNECTING TO THE INTERNET

After you've created a Dial-Up Networking icon that contains your connection settings, you can establish a connection by using any of these three methods:

- Open the Dial-Up Networking folder and use that icon to manually connect to the Internet. This option gives you maximum control over when and how you connect to the Internet.

- Set up Internet Explorer to automatically open a Dial-Up Networking connection whenever you attempt to access a Web page. By default, this option requires you to respond to a confirmation dialog box before actually dialing. This option is appropriate if you use a single line for voice and data calls.

- Use advanced settings in the Dial-Up Networking folder to make a hands-free connection that doesn't require confirmation from you whenever you attempt to access any Internet resource. This option is best if you have a dedicated data line and don't want any interruptions from Windows.

PART

IV

CH

26

MAKING A MANUAL CONNECTION

To connect to the Internet manually, follow these steps:

1. Select the connection icon and open it. A dialog box like the one shown in Figure 26.23 appears.

2. Check your username and enter a password if necessary. To store the password for reuse, check the Save Password box.

3. Check the entry in the Phone Number box. If the format is incorrect, choose a new location or edit the number to include the required prefixes.

4. Click the Connect button. Windows opens a modem connection and attempts to dial the number. You'll see a series of status messages, like the one in Figure 26.24, as the connection proceeds.

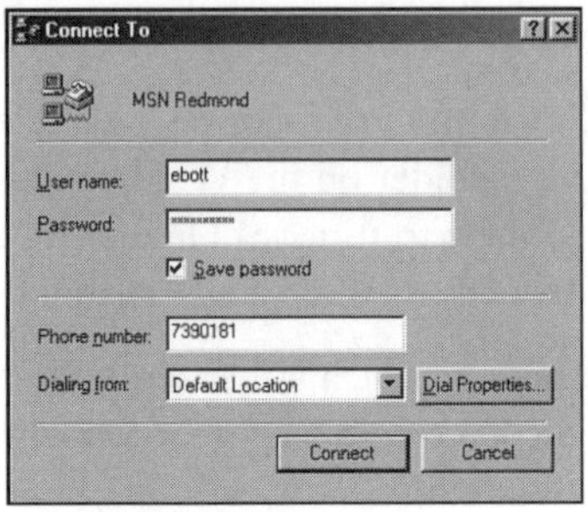

Figure 26.23
Regardless of the settings you defined for the connection icon, this dialog box lets you temporarily change the phone number, username, location, and other settings.

Figure 26.24
Status messages like this can help you identify problems when making an Internet connection.

After you successfully complete the connection, you'll see an informational dialog box like the one in Figure 26.25. At the same time, a Dial-Up Networking icon appears in the notification area to the right of the taskbar.

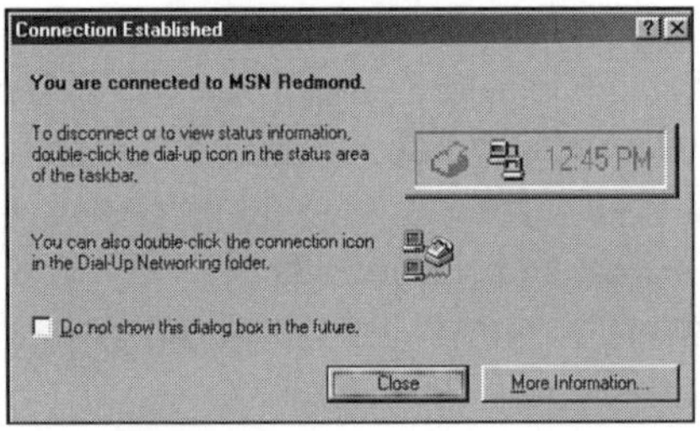

Figure 26.25
If you'd prefer not to see this dialog box after every completed connection, check the option just above the Close button.

MONITORING CONNECTION STATUS

Whenever you have an open connection to the Internet, you can check its status in a variety of ways. For example, you can double-click the icon in the notification area, or you can right-click and choose Status to see the total time this connection has been open and the total number of bytes you've received and sent (see Figure 26.26).

Tip #159

To see status information at a glance without opening a dialog box, simply point to the icon in the notification area. After a few seconds, a ScreenTip will appear.

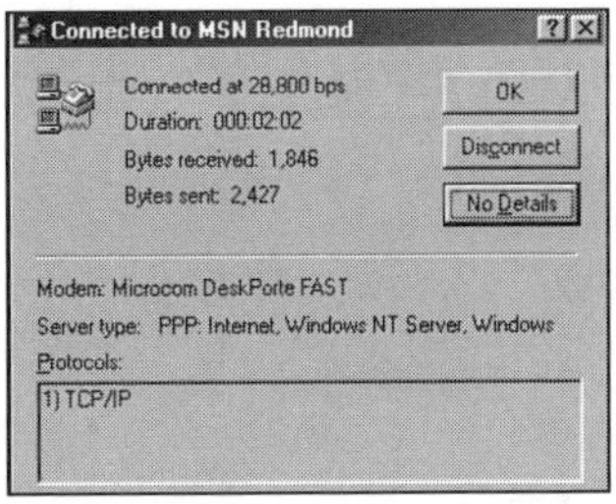

Figure 26.26
To eliminate the display of connection information in the bottom of this status dialog box, click the No Details button.

CLOSING YOUR INTERNET CONNECTION

When you've finished working with your Internet connection, you have three options for closing it:

- Right-click the icon in the notification area and choose Disconnect.

- Right-click the connection icon in the Dial-Up Networking folder and choose Disconnect. (Note that the same menu is available if you right-click on a shortcut to a connection icon.) This technique is useful if the taskbar icon is not available for some reason.

- If the connection status dialog box is open, click the Disconnect button.

CONNECTING (AND DISCONNECTING) AUTOMATICALLY

Internet Explorer includes a component called Connection Manager, which can automatically establish an Internet connection whenever you attempt to access a Web page. You can configure Connection Manager to pause for confirmation or to dial automatically.

> **Note**
>
> Connection Manager does not work with other Internet programs. If you want Outlook Express to dial automatically each time you check your mail, you'll have to set up separate dialing options from that program. See Chapter 32, "Creating Web Pages with FrontPage Express," for details on how to set up an automatic mail and news connection.

To set up Connection Manager, open the Internet Options dialog box and click the Connection tab. Choose the option labeled Connect to the Internet Using a Modem and then click the Settings button. The Dial-Up Settings dialog box shown in Figure 26.27 appears.

After you configure all Connection Manager options, click OK to close the Dial-Up Settings dialog box and then click OK again to close the Internet Options dialog box. Then open Internet Explorer and try to access a Web page. If you don't have an open Internet connection, you'll see a Connect To dialog box like the one in Figure 26.28.

PART
IV

CH
26

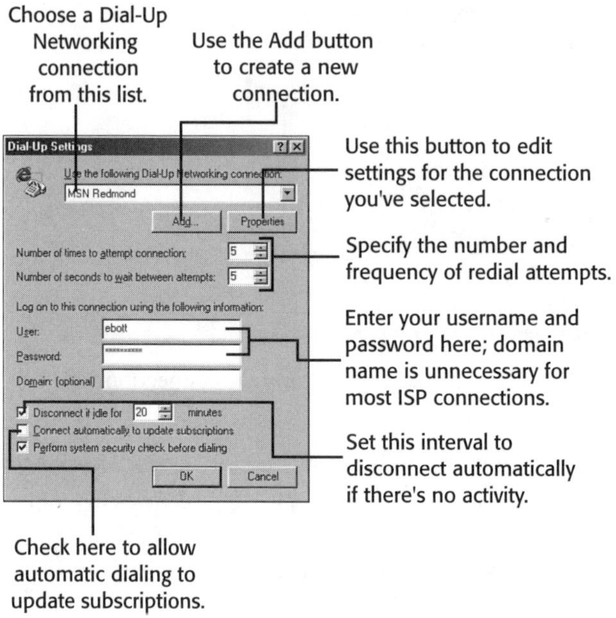

Choose a Dial-Up
Networking
connection
from this list.

Use the Add button
to create a new
connection.

Figure 26.27
Internet Explorer can
handle the dialing
duties, but you have
to specify these
options first.

Use this button to edit
settings for the connection
you've selected.

Specify the number and
frequency of redial attempts.

Enter your username and
password here; domain
name is unnecessary for
most ISP connections.

Set this interval to
disconnect automatically
if there's no activity.

Check here to allow
automatic dialing to
update subscriptions.

Figure 26.28
By default,
Connection Manager
prompts you before
trying to make a dial-
up connection.

Here are some tips for getting maximum benefit out of Connection Manager:

- Check the <u>S</u>ave Password box to store your password in the Windows cache. Remove the check from this box if you don't want other users to be able to access your Internet account.

- If you see the Connection Manager dialog box but you're not ready to connect, click the Work <u>O</u>ffline button.

- Check the box labeled <u>C</u>onnect Automatically If You Have a Dedicated Data Line, and you won't need to confirm your action each time you dial.

The Disconnect If <u>I</u>dle option automatically closes your dial-up connection if there's been no activity for the amount of time you specify. The default value is 20 minutes, but you can reset the idle time to any value between 3 and 59 minutes.

If you're working with a Web page when the idle timer expires, Internet Explorer won't suddenly close the connection. Instead, you'll see an Auto Disconnect warning dialog box like the one shown in Figure 26.29. You have 30 seconds to respond before Connection Manager shuts down access to the Internet.

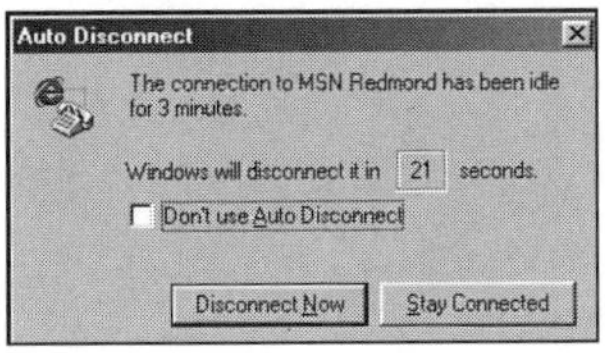

Figure 26.29
You'll receive fair warning before Connection Manager shuts down an open connection.

The Auto Disconnect dialog box gives you these options:

■ Click the Disconnect Now button to close the connection immediately.

■ Click the Stay Connected button to reset the timer and continue working with Internet Explorer.

■ Check the Don't Use Auto Disconnect box to disable this feature until you reset it. (This step has the same effect as clearing the check box in the Dial-Up Settings dialog box.)

Caution

Some sites can keep an Internet connection open indefinitely. For example, stock tickers that automatically refresh every few minutes keep your connection from hanging up, as do sites that deliver streaming data such as RealAudio. Don't expect Internet Explorer to disconnect automatically if you leave one of these pages open and then walk away from your computer.

PART

IV

CH

26

MAKING A HANDS-FREE MANUAL CONNECTION

If you prefer not to use the Connection Manager, open the Internet Options dialog box and configure *Internet Explorer* to connect via a local area network. With this setting you have to connect manually by using a Dial-Up Networking connection icon before attempting to access a Web page. To turn this procedure into a single-click process, follow these steps:

1. Open the Dial-Up Networking folder.

2. Open the connection icon you want to automate, and then enter your username and password. Check the Save Password box.

3. Click Connect. When the status dialog box appears, click Cancel to abort the connection and return to the Dial-Up Networking folder.

4. Choose Connections, Settings.

5. Clear the check marks in front of the boxes labeled Prompt for Information Before Dialing and Show a Confirmation Dialog After Connected, as shown in Figure 26.30.

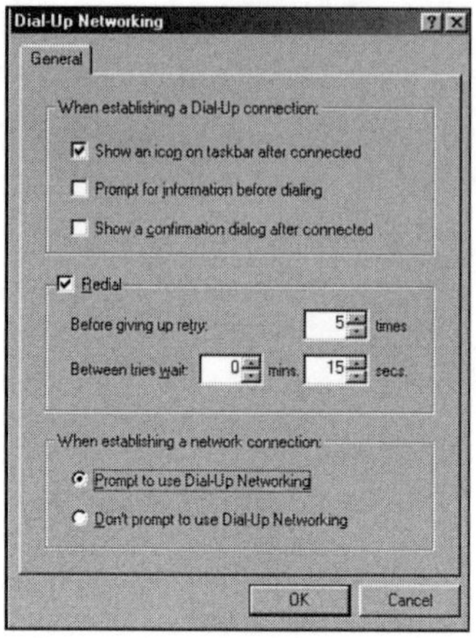

Figure 26.30
Use these settings to
bypass all dialog
boxes when you click
on a connection icon.

6. Check the Redial box and set automatic retry options if desired.

7. Click OK to save your changes.

TROUBLESHOOTING

PROBLEMS CONNECTING TO THE REMOTE SERVER

I am unable to establish a connection to the RAS.

If you are having problems connecting to a remote server, make sure that your system and the remote system are using the same protocol, such as TCP/IP. If both systems are using TCP/IP, make sure the TCP/IP configuration on both systems is configured properly. That means the IP address, subnet mask, and default gateway on both the client and the server are correct. On the client side, you may also have to edit the routing table to indicate a specific network or host to receive packets.

SECRETS OF MASTERING THE WINDOWS 98 ENVIRONMENT: SETTING UP YOUR SYSTEM TO USE DNS

The Internet uses DNS to resolve, or translate, computer and fully qualified domain names (FQDNs), such as www.mcp.com, into IP addresses. A DNS server maintains a database, which is really a flat text file maintained by a DNS administrator, that maps domain names to IP addresses. As with most types of file systems, DNS organizes the FQDNs in a hierarchical fashion with a corresponding IP address mapping.

Most ISPs dynamically assign IP addresses for DNS servers to their clients on demand. If yours does not or if you have a direct connection to the Internet, you must configure your system to point to a DNS server. In this case, and assuming you have Microsoft TCP/IP installed on your system, these settings are configured in the TCP/IP Settings dialog box in Dial-Up Networking. You need to know the IP address of your local DNS server for this method to work.

Follow these steps to configure your system to point to a DNS server:

1. In Dial-Up Networking, right-click the connection you have defined for the Internet, and then click Properties.

2. In the connection's properties sheet, click Server Types, and then click TCP/IP Settings.

3. In the TCP/IP Settings dialog box, select the Specify an IP Address option and type your IP address.

4. Select the Specify Name Server Addresses option, and then type the IP address of the DNS server in the Primary DNS dialog box.

WINDOWS INTERNET SERVICE

CHAPTER 27

WEB BROWSING WITH INTERNET EXPLORER 5.0

In this chapter

WHAT IS INTERNET EXPLORER 5.0?

Internet Explorer 5.0 (IE5) delivers all the basic functionality you've come to expect from a Web browser. It lets you gather information from servers located on your company's intranet or on the World Wide Web. It displays text and graphics in richly formatted pages, runs scripts, accesses databases, and downloads files. With the help of IE5, you can establish secure, encrypted sessions with distant servers so that you can safely exchange confidential information, such as your credit card number, without fear that it will be intercepted by a third party.

Note

For maximum security, you must download the 128-bit encryption patch or the updated IE5 version, which includes this feature, from Microsoft's Web site.

IE5 also helps you protect your computer. IE5 uses the concept of security zones, for example, to tightly restrict the ability of unknown Web servers to interact with local computers and network resources. With one set of security settings for your local intranet, another for trusted sites, and another for the Internet at large, you can automatically download files from local servers but control downloads from external sites.

Using subscriptions, you can transfer Web-based information automatically to a desktop or notebook PC and then view those pages even when you're not connected to the Internet.

Internet Explorer 5.0 looks much like Internet Explorer 4.0 (IE4) but has a bit more functionality as you will see as this chapter progresses. You can use the versatile Explorer bar—a simple frame that locks in place along the left edge of the Browser window—to organize your Favorites list, search for information on the Web, or browse pages stored in your local cache. Because the browser shares code with Windows Explorer, you can display the contents of a folder on your local PC or network and then jump to a Web site in the same window. Dozens of configuration options make the interface more comfortable.

To open Internet Explorer and display your home page, click the Internet icon on the desktop or the Quick Launch bar. Figure 27.1 shows the default Browser window.

Note

When you run Internet Explorer 5 via the Microsoft Network Service (MSN), the MSN logo appears in the top-right corner of the browser.

The Uniform Resource Locator for the current page appears in this Address bar

You can hide the Quick Links bar or move it to another location at the top of the browser window

The Standard toolbar gives you one-click access to frequently used tasks

Explorer bars help you find information and revisit favorite web pages

Figure 27.1
The Internet Explorer interface includes these basic navigational elements.

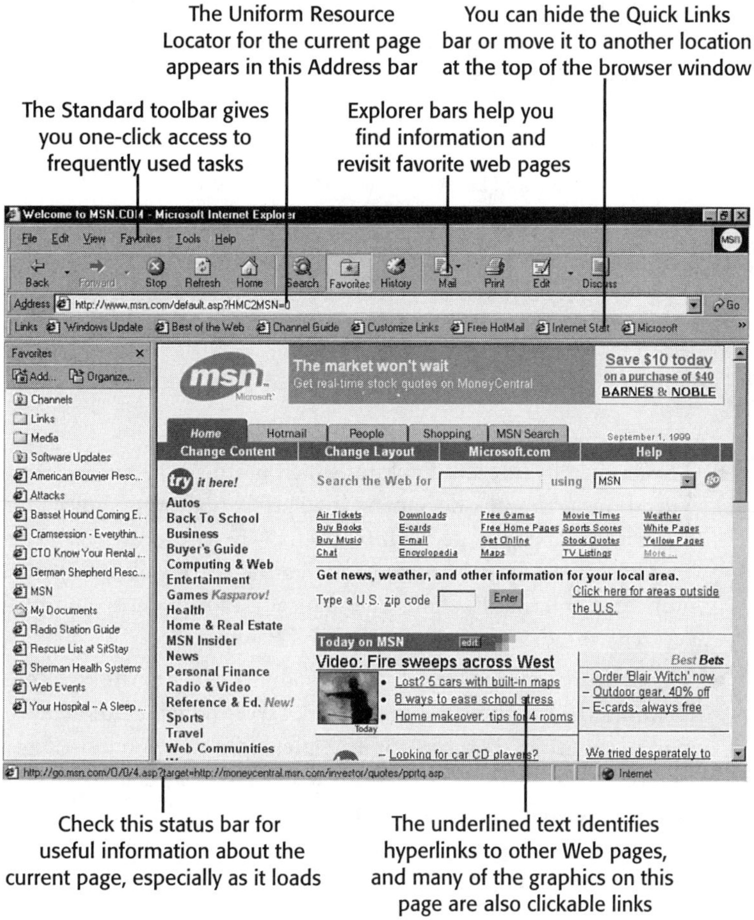

Check this status bar for useful information about the current page, especially as it loads

The underlined text identifies hyperlinks to other Web pages, and many of the graphics on this page are also clickable links

DECODING UNIFORM RESOURCE LOCATORS

Before you can open a Web page, you have to specify its location, either by clicking on a shortcut or link that points to the file or by entering its full name and path in the Address bar. For a *Hypertext Markup Language*, or *HTML*, document stored on your local PC or a network server, use the familiar [drive]:\filename or \\server-name\sharename\filename syntax. For Web pages stored on a Web server on the Internet, you need to specify a *Uniform Resource Locator*, or *URL*.

PART
V
CH
27

Note

Some otherwise credible sources insist that *URL* actually stands for Universal Resource Locator, but the organizations that set Internet standards agree that *U* is for *Uniform*. Opinion is evenly divided on whether to pronounce the term "earl" or spell out the letters *U-R-L*.

As Figure 27.2 shows, each URL contains three essential pieces of information that help Internet Explorer find and retrieve information from the Internet. (Some optional types of information, including port numbers and query parameters, may also be part of a URL.)

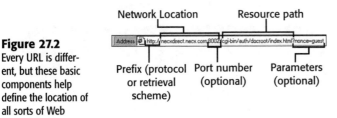

Figure 27.2
Every URL is different, but these basic components help define the location of all sorts of Web resources.

- The prefix tells Internet Explorer which protocol or retrieval scheme to use when transferring the document. The prefix is always followed by a colon. Standard Web pages use the http: prefix, whereas secure Web pages use https:. The URL for a file stored on a File Transfer Protocol (FTP) server uses the prefix ftp:. Internet Explorer automatically adds the http: and ftp: prefixes if you type an otherwise valid Web or FTP address.

- The network location, which appears immediately to the right of the prefix, identifies the Internet host or network server on which the document is stored: www.microsoft.com, for example. Note that you must separate the prefix from network location in URLs with two forward slashes. This part of a URL may also include a username and password for connecting with resources on servers that require you to log on. If the server requires a connection over a nonstandard Transmission Control Protocol (TCP) port number, you can add a colon and the port information at the end of this entry.

- The resource path defines the exact location of the Web page or other resource on the specified server, including path, filename, and extension. This entry begins with the first forward slash after the network location. If the URL doesn't include the name of a page in the resource path, most Web servers load a page called default.htm or index.htm. Two special characters define parameters that appear after the path: ? indicates query information to be passed to a Web server, and # identifies a specific location on the page.

Tip #160

> To display a blank page in your Web browser, use the URL about:blank. Also, you can use the Internet Explorer window with Windows Explorer to browse for files and folders by choosing the File menu and selecting Open. Windows then gives you the option to browse through your system and displays the results in an Explorer window.

You can type a surprising number of prefixes in the Address bar. Each uses its own protocol or retrieval method to gather information. For a detailed listing of most generally used URL prefixes, see Table 27.1.

TABLE 27.1   LEGAL URL PREFIXES

Prefix	Description
`about:`	Displays internal information about the browser. IE5 uses this prefix to display some error messages, including `about:NavigationCanceled`.
`file:`	Opens a local or network file. Used in other browsers but not required with IE5 when the Windows Desktop Update is installed.
`ftp:`	Connects with a server running the File Transfer Protocol.
`gopher:`	Connects with a server running the Gopher or Gopher+ Protocol.
`http:`	Retrieves information from Web servers using Hypertext Transfer Protocol.
`https:`	Creates a connection with a secure Web server and then encrypts all page requests and retrieved information over Secure Hypertext Transfer Protocol.
`mailto:`	Launches the default email client and begins composing a message to the address named in the URL.
`news:`	Connects with a Usenet news server using the default news reader.
`nntp:`	Connects with a Usenet news server using the NNTP access.
`res:`	Resource within a binary file; IE5 uses information with DLL files to display some help information.
`telnet:`	Launches the system's default Telnet client to create an interactive session with a remote host computer.
`wais:`	Connects with Wide Area Information Servers that contain large databases.

WORKING WITH WEB PAGES

The basic building blocks of the World Wide Web are simple text documents written in HTML. To communicate with the Web server on which a given page is stored, your browser uses *Hypertext Transfer Protocol*, or *HTTP*.

Every time you open an HTML document, Internet Explorer interprets the formatting tags and other coded instructions in that document and displays the fully formatted results in your Browser window. A single Web page may contain text, graphics, links to other pages and to downloadable files, and embedded objects, such as ActiveX controls and Java applets. When you load that Web page, it might in turn load dozens of additional linked files, especially graphics images.

→ For more information on securing your system and limiting what ActiveX and Java programs can accomplish, **see** "Restricting ActiveX Controls," **p. 621** and "Limiting Java Applets," **p. 626.**

HTML pages can incorporate scripts that cause specific actions to take place in response to a trigger event; for example, clicking a button to submit data from a Web-based form for processing by a Web server. Dynamic HTML instructions let the contents of the Browser window change as you work with the page.

PART

V

CH

27

To see the underlying HTML code for the current Web page, choose View, Source. Internet Explorer uses its basic text editor, Notepad, to display HTML source, as shown in Figure 27.3.

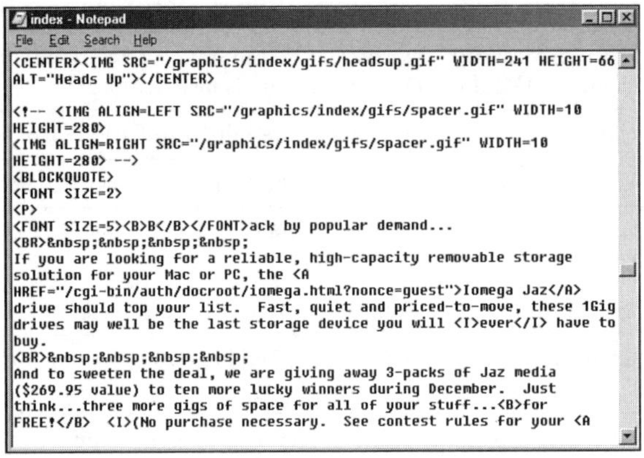

Figure 27.3
Because HTML documents are strictly text, you can view the underlying source code in the bare-bones Notepad editor.

```
index - Notepad
File  Edit  Search  Help
<CENTER><IMG SRC="/graphics/index/gifs/headsup.gif" WIDTH=241 HEIGHT=66
ALT="Heads Up"></CENTER>

<!-- <IMG ALIGN=LEFT SRC="/graphics/index/gifs/spacer.gif" WIDTH=10
HEIGHT=280>
<IMG ALIGN=RIGHT SRC="/graphics/index/gifs/spacer.gif" WIDTH=10
HEIGHT=280> -->
<BLOCKQUOTE>
<FONT SIZE=2>
<P>
<FONT SIZE=5><B>B</B></FONT>ack by popular demand...
<BR>    
If you are looking for a reliable, high-capacity removable storage
solution for your Mac or PC, the <A
HREF="/cgi-bin/auth/docroot/iomega.html?nonce=guest">Iomega Jaz</A>
drive should top your list.  Fast, quiet and priced-to-move, these 1Gig
drives may well be the last storage device you will <I>ever</I> have to
buy.
<BR>    
And to sweeten the deal, we are giving away 3-packs of Jaz media
($269.95 value) to ten more lucky winners during December.  Just
think...three more gigs of space for all of your stuff...<B>for
FREE!</B>  <I>(No purchase necessary. See contest rules for your <A
```

Tip #161

FrontPage Express (page 631) adds an Edit button to the Internet Explorer toolbar. When you install Microsoft's full-strength Web page editor, FrontPage, it takes over this function. Click the Edit button to begin editing the current Web page. To choose another text editor, click on the down arrow next to the Edit button for a list of alternative editors.

WORKING WITH HYPERLINKS

Hyperlinks are HTML shortcuts that activate with a single click. Clicking a link has the same effect as typing its URL into the browser's Address bar. The specific action depends on the prefix: A link with the http: prefix, for example, allows you to jump from page to page. Other prefixes typically found in links carry out specific actions: A link can allow you to begin executing a script (javascript:), download a file (ftp:), begin composing a mail message (mailto:), or open Outlook Express to read a linked newsgroup message (news:).

On a Web page, the clickable portion of a hyperlink can take several forms. Text links appear in color (blue, by default) and are underlined. A Web page designer can change the look of a text link and can also attach a link to a picture or button on the screen. Internet Explorer changes the shape of the pointer when it passes over a link. To see additional information about a link, look in the status bar or inspect the link's properties. Some Web pages, such as the one in Figure 27.4, include pop-up help text for the image under the pointer; the status bar shows where the link will take you.

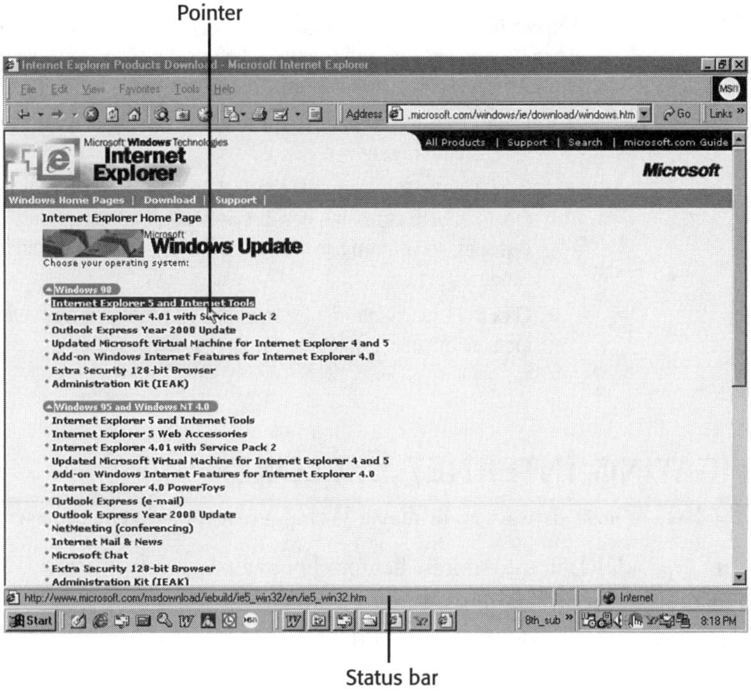

Pointer

Figure 27.4
The pop-up ScreenTip and the status bar offer helpful information about this link; you can also right-click to inspect its properties.

Status bar

⚠ *If you're having trouble connecting to a link because the linked page doesn't open properly, see "Clicking a Linked Page That Doesn't Open Properly" in the "Troubleshooting" section at the end of this chapter.*

To copy the underlying URL in text format from a link to the Windows Clipboard, right-click on the link and choose Copy Shortcut. For a link that's attached to a graphic, choose Copy only if you want to copy the image itself to the Clipboard.

Normally, clicking on a link replaces the page displayed in the current window. To open the linked page in its own window without affecting the current page, right-click on the link and choose Open in New Window.

STARTING INTERNET EXPLORER

The browser window opens automatically when you click on a hyperlink or an Internet shortcut. To open Internet Explorer and go directly to your home page, use the Internet Explorer icon on the desktop or on the Quick Launch bar.

PART
V

CH
27

Tip #1001

You can have two or more browser windows open at one time—a technique that's handy when you're gathering and comparing information from multiple sources. To open a new browser window, use any of these three techniques:

- Choose File, New, Window. The new window displays the same contents as the current browser window.

- Press Ctrl+N. This keyboard shortcut has the same effect as using the File menu. In both cases, the new browser window "remembers" previously visited sites, so you can use the Back button just as you would in the original window.

- Click the Launch Internet Explorer Browser button in the Quick Launch toolbar. The new window opens to your home page.

Navigating Internet Explorer

You have at least six ways to display a Web page in the current browser window:

- Type a URL in the Address bar, or choose a previously entered URL from the drop-down list, and press Enter.

- Type a URL in the Run box on the Start menu.

- Click a link on an HTML page.

- Open an Internet shortcut on the desktop, in a folder, in the Favorites list, or in a mail message.

- Click a shortcut on the Links bar.

- Use the Back and Forward buttons, the File menu, or the History list to return to previously viewed pages.

Tip #1001

When using IE5 and adding a Web page to your Favorites, select Make Available Offline to store the most recently viewed version for offline use. IE5 allows you to easily create, move, rename, or delete folders or files from Favorites with the Organize button. Right-click a Favorite to see options, such as printing.

Using the Address Bar

You can click in the Address bar and painstakingly type a full URL to jump to a particular Web page, but IE5 includes several shortcut features that reduce the amount of typing required for most Web addresses.

You don't need to start with a prefix when you enter the address of a valid Internet host. For example, when you type

```
www.microsoft.com
```

the browser automatically adds the `http://` prefix. If the address you enter begins with ftp, the browser adds the `ftp://` prefix.

Caution

You should be aware of an important distinction between the forward slashes used in URLs and the backslashes used in local files and in Universal Naming Convention (UNC) names that refer to network resources. If you type `\\servername` in the Address bar, you see a list of all the shared resources available on a network server, whereas `//servername` jumps to the default HTML page on the Web server with that name.

If you type a single word that doesn't match the name of a local Web server, Internet Explorer automatically tries other addresses based on that name, using the common Web prefix www and standard top-level domains: `.com`, `.edu`, and `.org`. To tell Internet Explorer to automatically add www to the beginning and com to the end of the name you typed, press Ctrl+Enter.

USING AUTOCOMPLETE TO FILL IN THE BLANKS

As you move from page to page, Internet Explorer keeps track of the URL for every page you visit. Each time you begin to type in the Address bar, Internet Explorer checks the History list and attempts to complete the entry for you, suggesting the first address that matches the characters you've just typed. You can see the results of the AutoComplete feature in Figure 27.5. Note that the characters you type appear on a plain white background, and the suggested completion is highlighted.

Figure 27.5
The AutoComplete feature suggests the first address that begins with the characters you've typed.

When the AutoComplete feature makes a suggestion, Internet Explorer scans the list of addresses you've entered previously, in alphabetical order, and then chooses the first matching address. If you type www.m, for example, www.matrox.com might be the first suggestion. To accept the completed address, just press Enter.

If the suggested address isn't the one you want, you have two alternatives. If you continue typing, Internet Explorer revises its suggestion based on the new text you type. In the preceding example, if you type i so that the Address bar reads www.mi, Internet Explorer might suggest www.microsoft.com.

What do you do if dozens of pages in your History list begin with the same domain name? After AutoComplete makes its first suggestion, use the down arrow to cycle through every entry in your history list that begins with that string of text. When you reach the right address, press Enter to load that page.

You can simply ignore AutoComplete suggestions and continue typing the address. If you find the feature more confusing than helpful, follow these steps to turn off AutoComplete:

1. Choose View, Internet Options.

2. Click the Advanced tab.

3. Clear the check mark from the box labeled Use AutoComplete.

4. Click OK to close the dialog box and save your changes.

Tip #164	With IE5 you can list your History sites by date visited, site name, number of visits, or order you visited today. You can use the History feature with the search tool to find keywords on any of the pages you visited.

NAVIGATING WITH THE MOUSE

Click the Back button to jump to pages you've previously visited and then click the Forward button to return. When you right-click on either button (or use the arrow at the right), a list of the nine most recent pages appears, as shown in Figure 27.6.

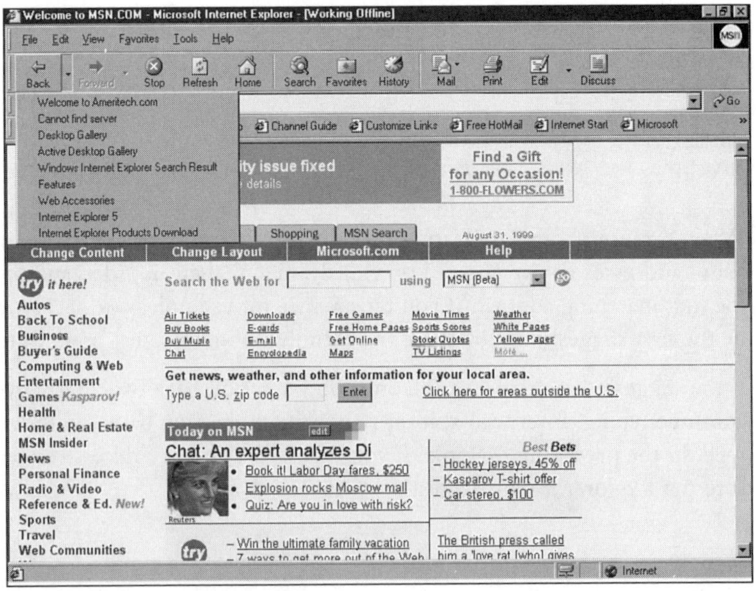

Figure 27.6
Right-click or use the drop-down arrow for a faster alternative to repeatedly clicking the Back or Forward button.

If you own a Microsoft IntelliMouse, use the wheel (located between the buttons) to take advantage of four navigational shortcuts:

- Hold down the Shift key and roll the wheel downward to return to the previously viewed page; hold down Shift and move the wheel up to go forward again.

- Roll the wheel up or down to scroll three lines at a time through a Web page (the Advanced tab of the Internet Options dialog box lets you adjust this setting).

- Hold down the wheel button and move the mouse in any direction to scroll. Release the wheel button to stop scrolling.

- Click the wheel to turn on continuous scrolling. Move the pointer, and the page scrolls automatically in that direction, like a TelePrompTer. The farther you move the pointer, the faster the page scrolls. To resume normal scrolling, click the wheel again or press Esc.

Tip #165

Nearly every object on a Web page is accessible via shortcut menus. Right-click to inspect properties, copy or print an image, or add a page to your Favorites list, for example.

→ To better surf the Web and get to the places you like the most, **see** "Using the Favorites Folder to Organize Your Favorite Web Sites," **p. 588.**

WORKING WITH FRAME-BASED PAGES

Frames are an effective way for clever designers to make Web pages more usable. Unlike ordinary pages, which fill the browser window from border to border, frame-based pages split the window into two or more zones, each with its own underlying HTML code and navigation controls. The most common use of frames is to add a table of links along one side of the browser window with pages displayed in the frame on the other side; because the frame containing the list of links is always visible, it's easy to quickly move through the site without constantly hitting the Back button. Not surprisingly, Microsoft's developer pages (see Figure 27.7) make good use of frames.

Working with frames takes practice. The Back and Forward buttons, for example, don't let you navigate within a frame. To move back and forth within a frame, you have to select the frame itself, right-click, and then click the Back or Forward menu choices. Likewise, to view the source code for a frame, you need to right-click in the area of interest and choose View Source from the shortcut menu. When you save or copy a frame-based page, make sure to select the portion of the document you want and not just the small master document that contains pointers to the frames.

→ For more about printing a frame-based page, **see** "Arranging Frames on the Printed Page," **p. 601.**

PART

V

CH

27

Figure 27.7
Look carefully, and you can see four frames in this page. In addition to the obvious navigation area at left, two frames appear along the top. The main browser window is a frame with its own scrollbar.

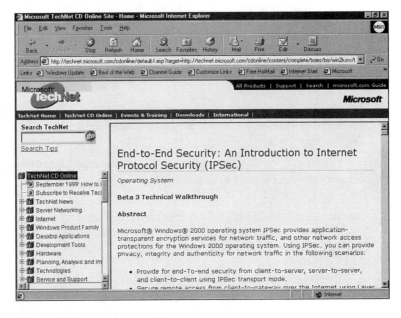

NAVIGATING WITH THE KEYBOARD

For most people, most of the time, the mouse is the best tool for navigating with Internet Explorer. But the Web browser also offers superb keyboard support, which is important for users who have physical disabilities that make it difficult or impossible to use a mouse. Keyboard shortcuts are also a useful way to accelerate Web access for skilled typists who prefer to keep their hands on the keyboard while they work.

Most of the movement keys in IE5 work as they do elsewhere in Windows. Home and End go to the top and bottom of the current page, for example. The Up and Down arrow keys move through the page, and the Page Up and Page Down keys move up and down in bigger jumps.

You can use shortcut keys to choose commands and view documents. Many of the pull-down menus include pointers to keyboard alternatives. The following table lists the most useful keyboard shortcuts in Internet Explorer.

To Do This	Press This
Go to the next page	Alt+Right Arrow
Go to the previous page	Alt+Left Arrow, Backspace
Display a shortcut menu for a link or object	Shift+F10
Move forward between frames	Ctrl+Tab
Move back between frames	Shift+Ctrl+Tab

To Do This	Press This
Move to the next link on a page	Tab
Move to the previous link on a page	Shift+Tab
Activate the currently selected link	Enter
Refresh the current page	F5
Stop downloading a page	Esc
Open a new location	Ctrl+O
Open a new browser window	Ctrl+N
Save the current page	Ctrl+S
Print the current page or active frame	Ctrl+P

Tip #166

With IE5 you can click on the Go button (see Figure 27.8) rather than press the Enter key after you type a URL in the Address bar.

Figure 27.8
Use the Go button in IE5 to load the Web page for the URL you have chosen.

USING IMAGEMAPS

One popular navigational aid on some Web pages is the imagemap. Instead of assigning links to a series of graphics objects or buttons, a Web designer can create links to specific coordinates of a single large image. The imagemap in Figure 27.9, for example, lets you jump to linked pages using a map of Houston, Texas. How do you know when you're working with an imagemap? Watch the status bar at the bottom of the browser window as the mouse passes over the image; if you see coordinates, as in this figure, an imagemap is under the pointer.

Imagemaps are clever and useful jumping-off points on Web sites. Their only drawback is that they require the use of the mouse; there's no way to use an imagemap with the keyboard.

PART

V

CH

27

Figure 27.9
The coordinates at the end of the URL in the status bar are your tip-off that this site is using an imagemap for navigation.

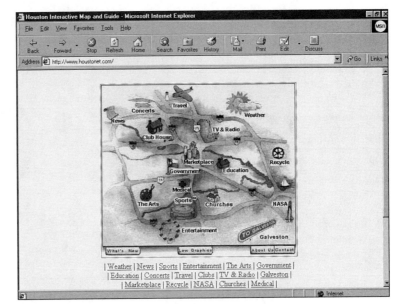

GATHERING INFORMATION FROM THE STATUS BAR

Each time your browser makes a connection with a Web server, valuable information appears on the status bar along the bottom of the screen. The status bar (see Figure 27.10) shows the following:

- The status of the current download—look for an hourglass over a globe as a page loads and a full-page icon when the download is complete.

- The status of objects currently loading, including linked graphics, ActiveX components, and Java applets. This area also counts down the number of items that have not yet been downloaded.

- Point to a link to see its associated URL in the status bar; use the Advanced tab of the Internet Options dialog box to switch between full URLs (http://www.microsoft.com/default.asp) and friendly names (Shortcut to default.asp at www.microsoft.com).

- A blue progress bar shows what percentage of the entire page has been loaded.

- Look for a padlock icon to indicate when you're viewing a page over a secure connection or using international language support; when you print a page, you see a printer icon here.

- The security zone for the current page appears at the far right of the status bar.

→ For more about Internet security, **see** "Establishing and Maintaining Internet Security Zones," **p. 616.**

Figure 27.10
You can find important information about the status of the current page here.

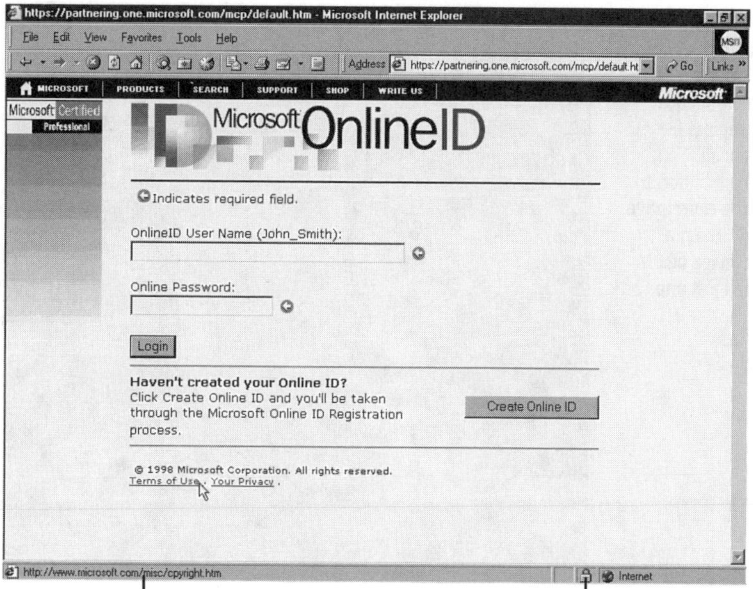

Status bar   Security icon

Want to quickly adjust Internet Explorer security options? Double-click on the status bar; that shortcut has the same effect as choosing Tools, Internet Options, Security from the pull-down menu.

STOPPING DOWNLOADS AND RELOADING PAGES

Web pages don't load properly for many reasons, but the most common is too much traffic on the server you're trying to reach or on one leg of the connection between your browser and the remote server. Click the Stop button (or press Esc) to immediately stop a download. Take this step if you're certain the page you requested has stalled or is unavailable and you don't want to wait for the browser to time out. Stopping a download can also be a time-saving tactic if the page contains many bulky graphics elements and you can already see the link you want to follow or the section you want to read.

The Refresh button is especially valuable when viewing frequently updated pages, such as weather information, traffic maps, or stock quotes, to guarantee that the version you see is the most recent and not a stale copy from the Internet Explorer cache. You should also click the Refresh button when a download fails in the middle of a page or when one or more objects on a page fail to load, as in the example in Figure 27.11.

PART
V

CH
27

Figure 27.11
The empty box with the X (lower left of the screen) means that a graphics file failed to load. Click the Refresh button to reload the entire page or right-click on a specific image box to download just one image.

Tip #168

You don't have to refresh the entire page if a small portion of the page failed to load. Look for a red X or broken image icon, indicating a linked file that failed to load. To refresh just that portion of the page, right-click and choose S̲how Picture.

SETTING YOUR HOME PAGE

Every time you start Internet Explorer, it loads the page you designate as your home page. By default, Microsoft takes you to home.microsoft.com from where you can follow links to assemble a home page based on your own interests. You can designate any Web page as your home page; if you're connected to a company intranet, you may prefer to set a local page on your intranet to load automatically at startup.

To reset your home page, load the page you want to use; then choose V̲iew, Internet O̲ptions; and click on the General tab (see Figure 27.12). Click Use C̲urrent to set the current page as your home page. Click Use D̲efault to restore the default Microsoft home page. Click Use B̲lank to replace the home page with a blank page that loads instantly.

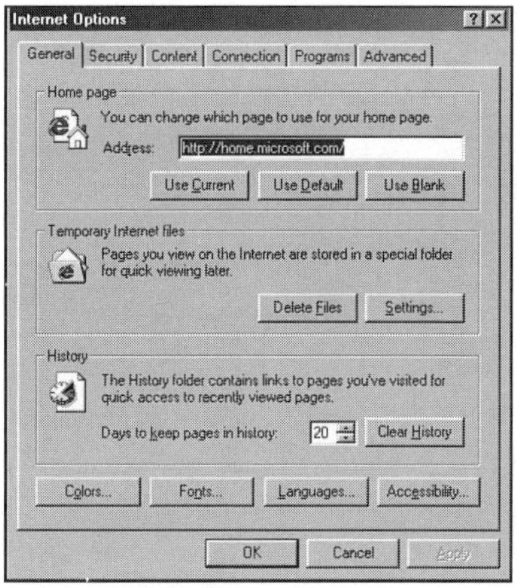

Figure 27.12
Choose your preferred home page and then use the Internet Options dialog box to designate that page to run every time you start Internet Explorer.

Tip #169

When choosing a home page, make sure it's readily accessible to avoid delays when you start your browser. Better yet, use FrontPage Express to construct your own home page, with links to favorite sites inside your intranet and on the World Wide Web. See Chapter 32, "Creating Web Pages with FrontPage Express," for more details on how to use FrontPage Express.

INCREASING THE SIZE OF THE BROWSER WINDOW

Pieces of the Internet Explorer interface can get in the way of data, especially on displays running at low resolutions, but you can make more space available for data in the browser window. Most methods for doing so involve hiding, rearranging, or reconfiguring these optional interface elements.

The simplest way to reclaim space for data is to hide the toolbars and status bar. To hide the status bar, choose View and click Status Bar; to eliminate one or more of the three built-in toolbars, right-click on the menu bar and remove the check marks from Standard Buttons, Address Bar, or Links.

You can also rearrange the three toolbars, placing them side by side or one on top of the other. You can even position any toolbar alongside the menu bar. To move a toolbar, click on the raised handle at the left and then drag the toolbar to its new position. Drag the same handle from right to left to adjust the width of the toolbar.

Want to shrink the oversize buttons on the browser window? Choose View, Internet Options; click on the Advanced tab; and check the option to use the smaller Microsoft Office-style buttons instead; next choose View, Toolbars and clear the check mark from Text Labels. The results should resemble what you see in Figure 27.13.

PART

V

CH

27

Figure 27.13
These smaller buttons, without labels, fit comfortably alongside the Address bar to make room for more data in the browser window.

To configure Internet Explorer for the absolute maximum viewing area, load any page and then click the Full Screen button. This view, shown in Figure 27.14, hides the title bar, menu bar, Address bar, and Links bar. The Standard buttons toolbar shrinks to its smallest setting and even the minimize and close buttons in the upper-right corner adjust their size and position.

Figure 27.14
Click the Full Screen button to expand the Internet Explorer browser window to its maximum size.

Tip #170

If you prefer the extra screen real estate you get with Full Screen view, you can configure IE5 to automatically open all Web pages this way. You can also configure IE5's channels to appear by default in Full Screen view. To set up either option, choose View, Internet Options; click the Advanced tab; and check the box labeled Launch Browser in Full Screen Window or Launch Channels in Full Screen Window.

In Full Screen view, right-clicking on the toolbar lets you add the menu bar, Address bar, or Links bar to the same row. The Auto Hide choice on the same shortcut menu lets every last piece of the interface slide out of the way; to make the toolbar reappear, move the mouse pointer to the top edge of the screen.

To switch back to normal view, click the Full Screen button again.

ADJUSTING FONTS AND COLORS TO MAKE WEB PAGES MORE READABLE

Can you change the look of a Web page? That depends on decisions the designer of the page made when creating it. Some Web pages use only generic settings to place text on the page. Sophisticated designers, on the other hand, use Web templates called *cascading style sheets* to specify fonts, colors, spacing, and other design elements that control the look and feel of the page. You can specify the fonts and colors you prefer when viewing basic Web pages; advanced settings let you ignore style sheets as well.

The primary benefit is for people with physical disabilities that make it difficult or impossible to read the screen. To adjust any of these settings, choose View, Internet Options and then click the General tab.

Tip #171

If you're curious about how a Web designer created the specific look of a page, use the View Source option to inspect the HTML code. If you like a particular look, you might be able to copy and paste the code to adapt the design for use in your own Web page.

To adjust the default fonts, click the Fonts button. In addition to selecting from a limited assortment of options for proportional and fixed fonts, you can also change the size Internet Explorer uses for basic Web pages from its default size (Medium). Choose smaller settings to pack more information onto the screen; use larger values to make text easier to read.

Click the Colors button to change the default values for text and backgrounds on basic Web pages. By default, Internet Explorer uses the Window colors you defined for the Windows Display settings; with the Standard Windows settings, that means black text on a white page. To change the defaults, you must change that systemwide setting or click the Use Windows Colors check box and specify

PART

V

CH

27

different <u>T</u>ext and <u>B</u>ackground colors, as shown in Figure 27.15. Internet Explorer also allows you to reset the colors for links here.

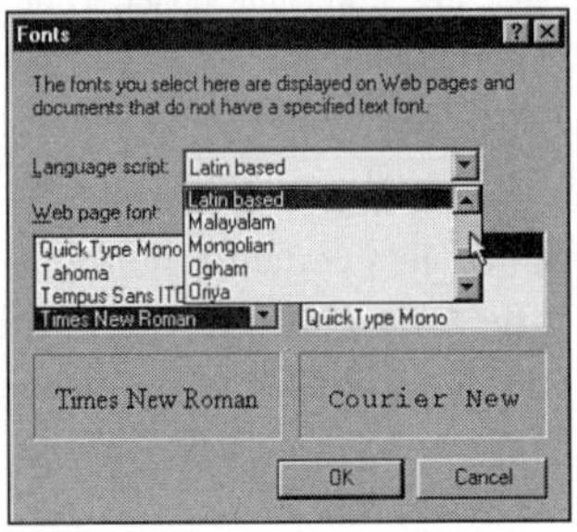

Figure 27.15
Setting alternative font choices affects only basic Web pages—those that don't use style sheets.

Changes you make to default fonts and colors do not apply to pages that use style sheets unless you make one final adjustment. Click the Acc<u>e</u>ssibility button and check the appropriate boxes to tell the browser to ignore colors, font styles, and font sizes specified in style sheets.

You can increase or decrease default font sizes exclusively for pages you open in the current session. Choose <u>V</u>iew, Fo<u>n</u>ts and select one of the five relative sizes from that menu. This change applies only when viewing pages that use standard fonts, and Internet Explorer returns to normal settings if you close and then reopen the browser window. When you adjust font sizes, be aware that pages can look odd and, in some cases, can even become unreadable. If you find yourself using this feature regularly, go to the Advanced tab on the Internet Options dialog box and check the option to add a Fonts button to the Standard toolbar.

VIEWING WEB PAGES IN OTHER LANGUAGES

Do you frequently find yourself browsing pages created in an alphabet that's not the same one used in your Windows language settings? Before Internet Explorer can display foreign-language pages, you must use the IE5 Setup program to install support for the appropriate languages. A Pan-European add-in allows most Western European languages to display correctly. Japanese, Korean, and Chinese add-ins are available as well.

→ To learn more about installing multi-language support, **see** Appendix B, "Updating Internet Explorer 5.0," **p. 887.**

After you install the additional font support, you should be able to see pages in any of those alphabets, as shown in Figure 27.16.

Figure 27.16
If you try to view foreign-language Web pages, you may see only a garbled mess (left); you need to add fonts for the extra languages to see them correctly (right).

Tip #172

> If you regularly view Web pages that are designed to display in different languages, tell IE5 which ones you prefer. Choose View, Internet Options and click the Languages button on the General tab. Add support for the appropriate languages and place your preferred language at the top of the list.

CONFIGURING INTERNET EXPLORER TO WORK WITH OTHER PROGRAMS

When you install Internet Explorer, it includes most of the capabilities you need for browsing basic Web pages and handling other types of data, such as streaming audio and video. IE5 allows you to dramatically expand its capabilities with a variety of add-in programs. Some install themselves automatically, with your permission, whereas others require you to run a separate Setup program.

INSTALLING AND USING ADD-INS AND PLUG-INS

Core components of Internet Explorer let you view text formatted with HTML as well as graphics created in supported formats, including *JPEG and GIF images (page 576)*. To view other types of data, you must install add-in programs that extend the capabilities of the basic browser. Add-ins can take several forms:

- ActiveX controls offer to install themselves automatically when needed. Depending on your security settings, Internet Explorer may refuse to install ActiveX add-ins, or you may have to click a confirming dialog box. ActiveX controls can perform a practically unlimited variety of functions; examples range from simple data-viewing panels to sophisticated analytical engines for tracking stock quotes. MSNBC's home page, shown in Figure 27.17, includes an ActiveX control that automatically turns current headlines into entries on a cascading menu, making it easier for you to navigate through the day's news.

→ **See** Chapter 19, "Setting Up Windows 98 Multimedia," for a detailed discussion of ActiveX and Java security issues.

PART
V

CH
27

Figure 27.17
This ActiveX control on MSNBC's home page enables you to browse news headlines and jump to linked pages from cascading menus.

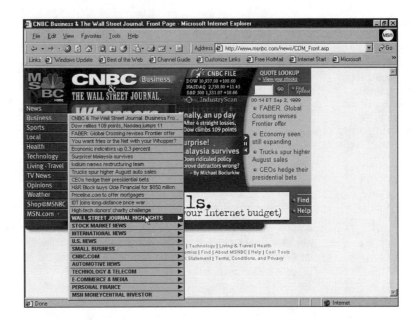

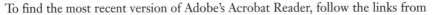

Tip #1001

There's no need to seek out ActiveX controls. Pages that require add-ins offer to install the control when you need it, and most controls download in a matter of minutes even over relatively slow connections.

■ Java applets download and run each time you access the page containing the helper program. The security settings for Java applets prohibit them from interacting with local or network resources except on the originating machine, and you can't install them permanently, as you can ActiveX controls.

■ Other add-in programs and plug-ins use standard installation routines and can often run on their own. Two must-have add-ins for Internet Explorer are RealNetworks's RealPlayer, which allows your browser to receive live audio and video broadcasts over the Internet, and Adobe's Acrobat Reader (see Figure 27.18), which lets you display and print richly formatted documents, complete with graphics, columns, and other design elements that go far beyond HTML. Both are free (in fact, RealPlayer 4.0 is included with IE5); upgrades to more powerful versions are available for a price.

 To download the most recent streaming audio and video player from RealNetworks, follow the links from

`http://www.real.com`

To find the most recent version of Adobe's Acrobat Reader, follow the links from

`http://www.adobe.com`

Figure 27.18
When you view a formatted document with the Adobe Acrobat Reader, it takes over the browser window and adds its own toolbars.

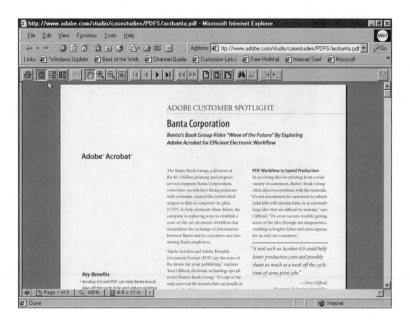

TUNING IN TO THE INTERNET WITH WINDOWS MEDIA PLAYER

One of the most intriguing uses of Internet bandwidth is to deliver so-called streaming media. Unlike conventional sound and video files, which require you to download the entire file before beginning to play it back, streaming media begins playing as soon as the first bits reach your browser. With streaming media, radio stations can "broadcast" their signals over the Internet, making it possible for sports fans, for example, to follow the exploits of their hometown heroes no matter how far they roam.

Streaming media can consist of audio, video, or both. On a normal dial-up connection at 28.8K, audio typically works well, but video signals are unbearably choppy because the pipe between server and client simply can't deliver data fast enough. Video broadcasts are more practical on company intranets, where network cables can deliver data fast enough to handle broadcast-quality signals.

Internet Explorer includes two useful streaming-media players: Real Audio Player and Windows Media Player. For video broadcasts, the Windows Media Player can function as an ActiveX control, with the viewing screen embedded in the HTML page, or it can run as a standalone application with its own menus and VCR-style controls. (See Figure 27.19 for an example of the Windows Media Player in action.)

PART

V

CH

27

Figure 27.19
With its menu bar and VCR-style controls, the Windows Media Player looks like a standard Windows application and is easy to control. If only the video window is visible, right-click to set options.

Windows Media Player includes several useful customization options. To access the Windows Media Player properties sheet, right-click on the image window or on the player controls and choose Options. You see a dialog box like the one in Figure 27.20.

Figure 27.20
Use the settings on the Advanced tab to configure Windows Media Player to work through a proxy server by choosing the streaming media available and then clicking the Change button.

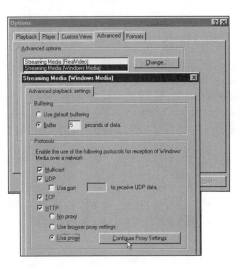

Click the Playback tab to shrink the Video window to half the normal size or expand it to double the default size. Select the Custom Views tab to choose full controls, simple controls, or none at all.

Use the options on the Advanced tab to configure Windows Media Player on a network that uses a proxy server. You need to check the documentation from the server to see which TCP and/or UDP ports are required.

Basic information appears under the clip being viewed. If you chose the Full Screen option on the View menu, press Esc to return the view to normal; the information about the clip will be visible once again. By choosing Statistics from the shortcut menu, you can view information about the current connection (see Figure 27.21). By choosing Properties, you can view details about the clip not otherwise shown in the bottom box under the clip.

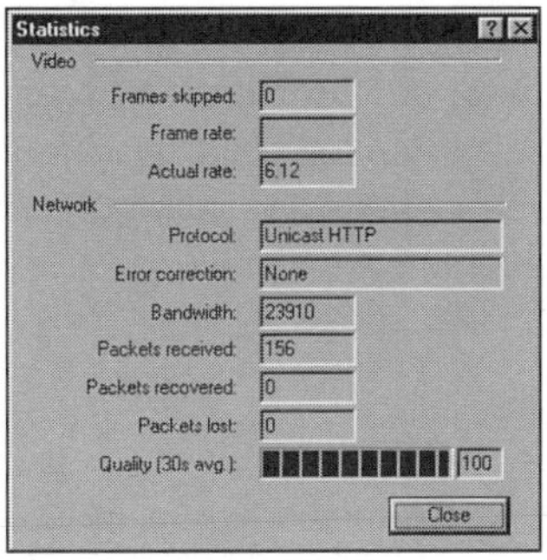

Figure 27.21
By choosing Statistics from the shortcut menu, you can view information about the current video stream and network connection.

SETTING DEFAULT MAIL AND NEWS CLIENTS

The Mail button on the Standard toolbar launches your default email program. Links that begin with the news: prefix fire up your default news reader. If you have more than one program that can work with Internet Explorer, you can control which one starts up when it's needed. To switch between Outlook 97 and Outlook Express as your default mail program, for example, choose View, Internet Options, click the Programs tab, and choose the preferred program from the drop-down lists shown in Figure 27.22.

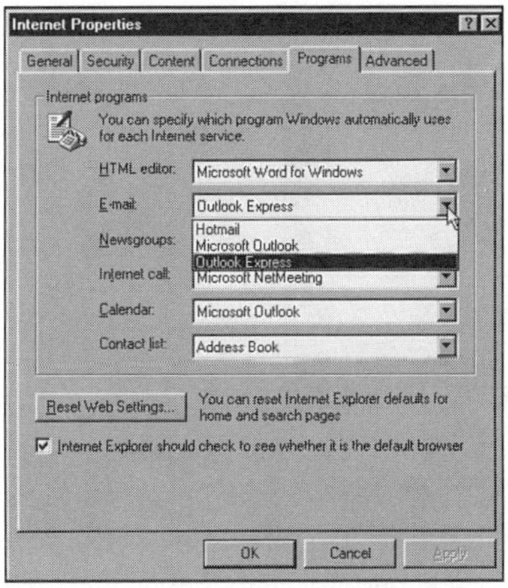

Figure 27.22
To switch from one helper program to another, use these drop-down lists. Only programs specifically written to work with Internet Explorer appear here.

PART

V

CH

27

SPEEDING UP WEB CONNECTIONS

Tuning Internet Explorer for speed and responsiveness involves inevitable trade-offs between rich content and quick results. Elaborate graphics, video clips, sound files, and other large elements add fun and extra dimensions to the Web, but waiting for those elements to download over a slow connection can become frustrating quickly.

Selectively filtering out some types of downloadable content can reduce the amount of time it takes to load a page the first time. Intelligently managing the browser's cache makes it much faster to access pages a second or subsequent time. Of course, even the most careful configurations can't overcome traffic jams on the Internet.

BROWSING WITHOUT GRAPHICS

When slow downloads are a problem, the most common culprit is a page that's overstuffed with graphics, sound, and video files, which take time to download. To turn Internet Explorer into a lightning-fast text-only browser, follow these steps:

1. Choose View, Internet Options and click on the Advanced tab.
2. Scroll down to the Multimedia branch of the tree.
3. Remove the check marks from all boxes in this section, as shown in Figure 27.23.
4. Click OK to apply your changes.

Figure 27.23
Clear all the check boxes in the Multimedia section to transform Internet Explorer into a speedy text-only browser.

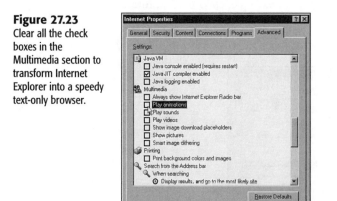

With multimedia options turned off, Internet Explorer shows generic icons, empty boxes, and simple text labels where you would normally see images. It also ignores any sound files, animations, or video clips embedded in the page. Some sites work perfectly well without images; *Fortune* magazine, for example, offers an all-text page (see Figure 27.24) that loads quickly and doesn't require any graphics images. (You can always use shortcut menus to manually request any content you've turned off.)

Figure 27.24
Who needs graphics? Even without images for its buttons, this all-text page is eminently readable, thanks to excellent labels.

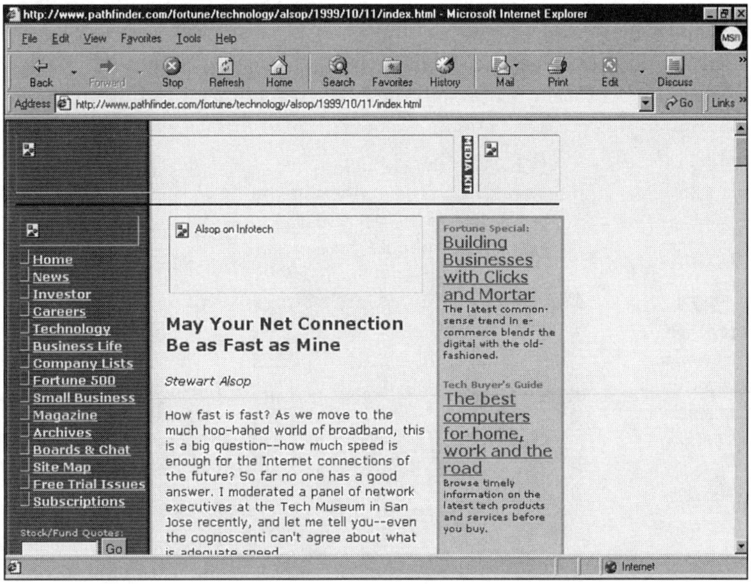

Although turning off the browser's capability to load image and multimedia files can dramatically improve performance, it can also block important information. On sites that use imagemaps as their only navigation tool, for example, there's literally no way to get around without displaying that image. To selectively show a picture after downloading the text-only page, right-click and choose Show Picture from the shortcut menu.

Tip #174

One of the most useful Internet Explorer Power Toys adds a Toggle Images button to the Standard toolbar. If you want to speed up downloads by selectively turning off the display of images, without having to continually open and close dialog boxes, this add-in is essential. You can find it at

```
http://www.microsoft.com/ie/ie40/powertoys
```

MANAGING THE BROWSER'S CACHE

With or without graphics, the best way to improve performance is to make sure the browser's cache is correctly configured. Each time you retrieve a new Web page, Internet Explorer downloads every element and stores a copy of each one in a cache directory on your hard disk. The next time you request that page, the browser first checks the cache; if it finds a copy of the page, it loads the entire document from fast local storage, dramatically increasing performance.

When the cache fills up, Internet Explorer throws out the oldest files in the cache to make room for new ones. To increase the likelihood that you'll be able to load a cached copy of a page instead of having to wait for it to reload from the Internet, adjust the size of the cache. Choose Tools, Internet Options and click the General tab (see Figure 27.25) to find all the controls you need to fine-tune the Web cache.

Checking the cache less
frequently improves performance
but increases the risk you'll
see an out-of-date page.

Figure 27.25
Give the browser cache extra working room, and you'll increase Internet Explorer's performance.

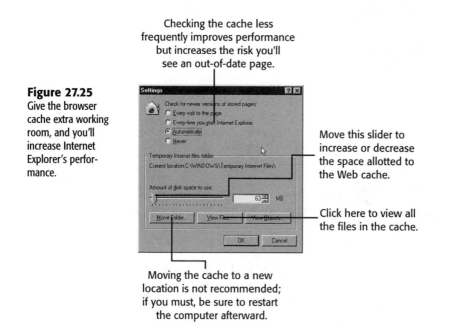

Move this slider to increase or decrease the space allotted to the Web cache.

Click here to view all the files in the cache.

Moving the cache to a new
location is not recommended;
if you must, be sure to restart
the computer afterward.

Caution

If you tell Internet Explorer that you never want to check for a more recent version of cached pages, your browser will seem remarkably faster. Beware, though: For pages that update frequently, such as news headlines or stock quotes, you have to work to see the most recent version. If you choose this setting, get in the habit of clicking the Refresh button to make sure the page is up-to-date.

When should you click the Delete Files button? This action completely empties the Temporary Internet Files folder and can have a noticeable negative impact on how fast your favorite pages load. Under ordinary circumstances, Internet Explorer manages the size of the cache by itself. You might need to clear the cache manually, though, if a corrupt cached file is causing Internet Explorer to crash, if you've run out of disk storage and you need to make room for crucial files, or if you plan to do a full system backup and you don't want to include all these cached Web files.

VIEWING CACHED FILES AND OBJECTS

Normally, you use the History Explorer bar to browse full pages stored in the browser cache. But you can also view the individual objects in the cache: HTML pages, graphics, ActiveX controls, and even cookie files. Click the View Files button in the Settings dialog box to see a full listing, like the one shown in Figure 27.26.

Figure 27.26
The Temporary Internet Files folder holds a copy of every object you've viewed in the browser recently. Right-click to open, copy, or delete any file.

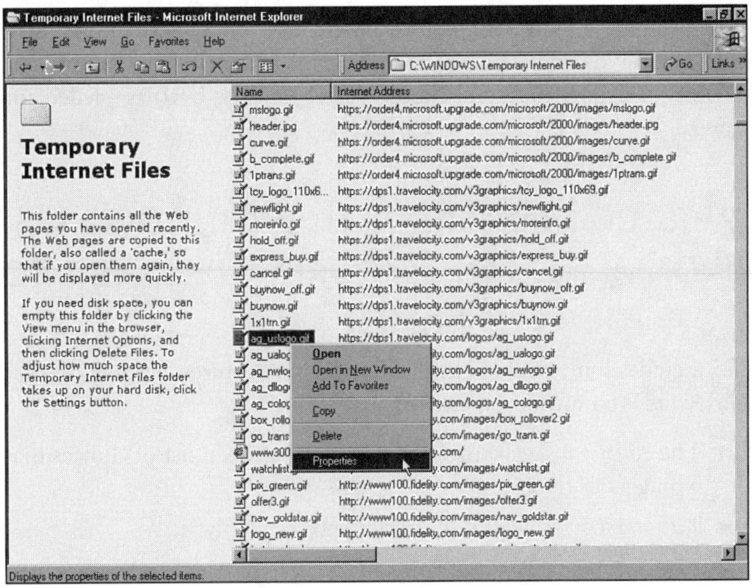

→ To get more information on cookies, **see** "How Safe Are 'Cookies'?" **p. 629.**

The Temporary Internet Files folder is unlike any other folder you'll see in Windows. Notice the column headings, for example, which track the time a file was last created. Double-click on column headings to re-sort the list—that's particularly useful for finding and deleting large files that are cluttering up the cache. Use shortcut menus to inspect the properties of stored objects and open, copy, or delete them.

PART

V

CH

27

Note

Where are cached pages really stored? Windows organizes all cached files using a maze of hidden folders inside the Temporary Internet Files folder. These folders have randomly generated cryptic names like 25NMCE84; shell extensions in Windows pull the contents of all these folders together into a single display in the Temporary Internet Files folder. Although you can use the DOS Attrib or Windows Find commands to see these files in their actual locations, avoid the temptation to move or delete these hidden objects. Use Internet Explorer's View Files button to manage them instead.

TROUBLESHOOTING

CLICKING A LINKED PAGE THAT DOESN'T OPEN PROPERLY

I click a link, but the linked page doesn't open properly.

Clicking a link most often fails because the specified page has been moved or no longer exists on that server. Another possibility is that the author omitted a crucial portion of the Web address or simply mistyped it. You can sometimes open the link (or its parent) anyway, although you may need to take several extra steps. Right-click on the link and choose Copy Shortcut. Select the entire contents of the Address bar, right-click, and choose Paste. Edit the URL as needed and press Enter.

SECRETS OF MASTERING THE WINDOWS 98 ENVIRONMENT: IE5 FEATURES DESIGNED TO MAKE LIFE ON THE WEB EASIER

IE5 includes some really beneficial automated features designed to speed and simplify your Web surfing experience.

- The *AutoComplete* feature provides a drop-down list of choices that match what you're typing as a URL.
- The *AutoCorrect* feature corrects typos as you type.
- The *AutoSearch* feature allows you to search Web results when you type a portion of a URL in the Address bar.
- The *AutoInstall* feature installs an IE5 component required by a Web page on an as-needed basis.
- The *AutoDetect* feature provides visual cues about what's accessible offline.
- The *AutoConfiguration* feature locates and connects to the appropriate proxy server on your intranet to enable you to gain access to the Internet.

Other features in IE5 include *Web accessories*. Web accessories are developed and distributed by major Web sites to work with their sites and customize aspects of your IE5 browser, such as your toolbar and menu items. This technique makes it much easier to work with a particular site. By combining Web accessories with the features in IE5 properties, you can customize your Web environment. Through Internet Explorer properties, you can choose the default search engine(s) that you want to use, and you can customize the default email client on your system and the default Web site you connect to. By using the Content Advisor, you can control sites that you or your family members are allowed to visit.

In this chapter, we discussed some of the settings you can choose and how to change them in the Internet Explorer Properties, Content, and Program tabs. Read on to Chapter 28, "Finding, Organizing, and Saving Web-Based Information," for more details on using the History bar, adding links, using the Favorites folder, and working with Web pages. Look in Chapter 29, "Internet Security," for more information on the Content Advisor and other security features in IE5.

CHAPTER **28**

FINDING, ORGANIZING, AND SAVING WEB-BASED INFORMATION

In this chapter

USING INTERNET SHORTCUTS

Regardless of where you find a Web page—on a corporate intranet or on a distant server—deep down inside it's nothing more than a document file. And just as you use conventional shortcuts to organize documents stored locally, Internet shortcuts are the most effective way to organize Web-based information. When you inspect the properties of an Internet shortcut, you see a page of settings like the one in Figure 28.1.

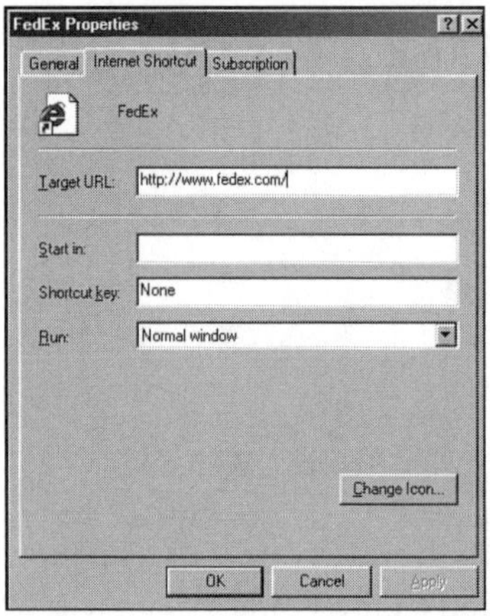

Figure 28.1
The target for an Internet shortcut is an URL rather than a local or UNC file specification.

Internet shortcuts behave just like other shortcuts. You can add Internet shortcuts to the desktop or Start menu, move them between folders, send them to other people in mail messages, or rename the shortcut without affecting the target it points to.

→ For more information on how best to use shortcuts, **see** "Using Shortcuts," **p. 102.**

If you start the Create *Shortcut (pages 32, 845)* Wizard and enter a valid URL in the Command Line box, Windows creates an Internet shortcut. You can drag that shortcut into the browser window or the Address bar to open the target page or drop the shortcut into the Favorites folder or Links bar to make the page more readily accessible.

Tip #175

Creating a shortcut that points to the Web page you're currently viewing in the browser window is easy. Just choose File, Send, Shortcut to Desktop. When the shortcut is on your desktop, you can rename the shortcut, modify its properties, move it to another folder, or send it to a friend or coworker in an email message.

USING THE FAVORITES FOLDER TO ORGANIZE YOUR FAVORITE WEB SITES

If you've used a Web browser before, you're already familiar with the concept of saving pointers to Web sites you visit frequently. Netscape Navigator calls them bookmarks, and prior versions of Internet Explorer saved shortcuts to Web pages in a Favorites folder.

Internet Explorer 5.0 (IE5) also lets you collect Internet shortcuts in a Favorites folder, but the user interface for working with Favorites is dramatically different.

Tip #176	If you had a copy of Netscape Navigator installed when you upgraded to Windows 98, all your Netscape bookmarks are now available in the Favorites folder. This conversion is a one-time process, however; new Navigator bookmarks you create after installing Windows 98 are not saved in the Favorites folder.

Click the Favorites button to open the Favorites Explorer bar; this frame along the left border pushes the main browser window to the right. When you choose an entry from the Favorites list, the page you selected appears in the browser window, as in Figure 28.2.

Figure 28.2
Click on a shortcut in the Explorer bar at left, and the target page appears in the browser window at the right. Arrows at the top and bottom of the Favorites list let you scroll to additional entries.

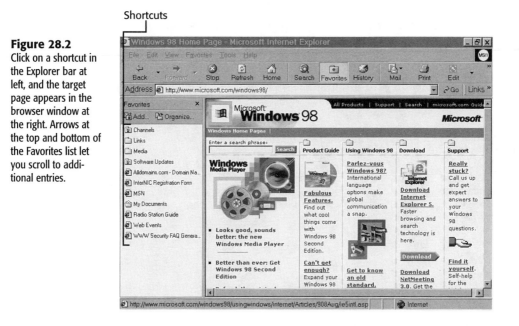

Note	When you run IE5 via the Microsoft Network Service (MSN), the MSN logo appears in the top-right corner of the IE5 browser.

The Favorites folder is located within the Windows folder; if you've enabled multiuser settings, each user with a profile on the computer gets a personal Favorites folder. The contents of the Favorites list appear in alphabetical order on the pull-down Favorites menu and in the Explorer bar. To reorder the shortcuts in the Favorites menu, drag any entry to a new position by holding down the mouse button instead of clicking.

PART
V

CH

28

Tip #177

Although the Favorites folder is most useful with Internet shortcuts, you can move any object there, including files, folders, and shortcuts to documents or programs. Clicking on a document or program shortcut in the Explorer bar usually launches the associated application in its own window.

ADDING A WEB PAGE TO THE FAVORITES FOLDER

To add the current page to the Favorites list, use one of these two techniques:

- Drag the page icon from the left of the Address bar and drop it into the Favorites Explorer bar.
- If the Explorer bar is not visible, choose Favorites, Add to Favorites.

You can also use shortcut menus to create new entries in the Favorites folder. Follow this simple procedure:

1. Right-click on any blank space or text in the current page.
2. Choose Add to Favorites from the shortcut menu; you'll see a dialog box like the one in Figure 28.3.

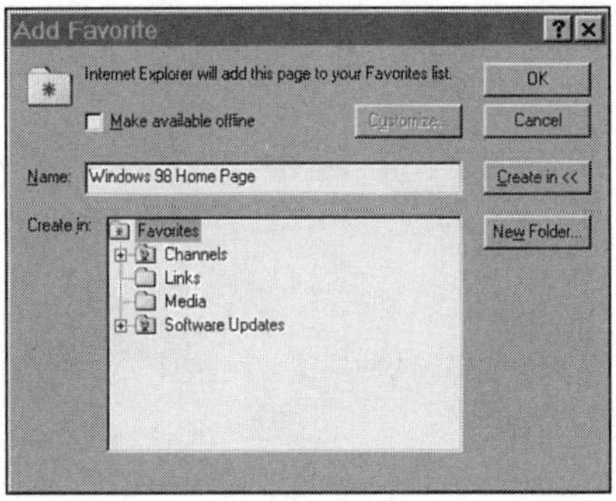

Figure 28.3
When you create a new entry in the Favorites folder, give it a new name if necessary to help you identify the page later.

3. Give the shortcut a descriptive name, if you want, or use the default page title.
4. Click the Create In button and choose a subfolder in the Favorites list.
5. Click OK to create the new shortcut and close the dialog box.

Tip #178

If the current page contains a link to a page you'd like to add to your Favorites folder, you can use the same technique without having to open the page. Point to the link, right-click, and then follow the steps outlined earlier.

When you add a Web page to your Favorites list, you also have the option to download pages automatically at scheduled intervals.

→ For more details on how to use Offline Favorites, **see** "Using Offline Favorites to Download Web Pages,"
p. 642.

DELETING AND RENAMING FAVORITES

To delete an Internet shortcut in the Favorites folder, point to the shortcut, right-click, and
choose <u>D</u>elete.

To rename an Internet shortcut, point to its entry in the list and choose Rena<u>m</u>e. Edit the
name of the shortcut and press Enter to save your changes.

USING SUBFOLDERS TO ORGANIZE FAVORITES

As you add items to the Favorites folder, the list can quickly become too long to work with
comfortably. When you reach that point, use subfolders to help organize the Favorites list.
You can create an unlimited number of subfolders in the Favorites folder, and you can even
add new folders within those subfolders.

With the Favorites Explorer bar open, it's easy to move one item at a time from folder to
folder. However, you can't use the Explorer bar to create new folders or to move more than
one shortcut at a time. For these more serious organizing tasks, choose F<u>a</u>vorites, <u>O</u>rganize
Favorites; that step opens the dialog box shown in Figure 28.4, which includes the full set of
tools you need.

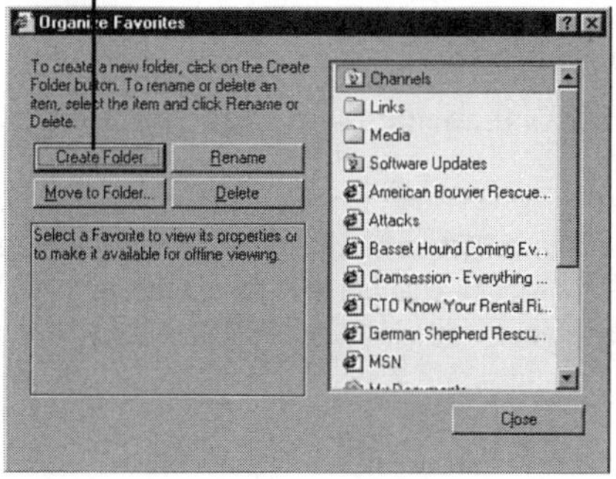

Click here to
create a new
folder

Figure 28.4
Use the buttons along
the side of this dialog
box to organize your
Favorites folder. Right-
click or use
ScreenTips to gather
more information
about a shortcut.

Moving shortcuts to a new folder is a simple process, as long as you perform the steps in the
right order. Open the Organize Favorites dialog box and do the following:

1. Click the Create Folder button; the new folder appears at the end of the current folder
   list, with a generic name selected for editing.

2. Type a name for the new folder and press Enter.

3. Select one or more shortcuts from the Favorites list and click the Mo<u>v</u>e to Folder
   button.

PART
V

CH
28

4. In the Browse for Folder dialog box, click the name of the folder you just created.

5. Click OK to make the move and click Close to return to Internet Explorer.

Tip #179

You can also drag and drop Internet shortcuts within the Organize Favorites dialog box. If your collection of Favorites is relatively small, you'll probably find it easier to rearrange shortcuts this way than by using the cumbersome procedure outlined earlier.

Folders appear in alphabetical order at the top of the Favorites Explorer bar. To see the contents of a folder, click on its entry there; the list of shortcuts in the folder appears just below the Folder icon, also in alphabetical order. Click the Folder icon again to close it.

Tip #180

For fastest access to the Favorites folder, click the Start menu. The cascading Favorites menu appears between the Programs and Documents choices.

CHANGING OR ADDING QUICK LINKS

Although the Favorites folder is a convenient way to organize Web pages, it still takes a couple of clicks and some scrolling to find a particular page. For the handful of sites you visit most frequently, use the Links toolbar instead. The shortcuts on this toolbar are never more than a click away, and you can easily arrange them for fast, convenient access.

To show or hide the Links bar, right-click on the menu bar and click Links. When you first start Internet Explorer, only five shortcuts appear on the Links bar, and they all point to pages at Microsoft. In less than five minutes, you can give the Links bar a complete makeover and give your productivity a dramatic boost in the process.

Tip #181

Do you really need all those Microsoft pages on the default Links bar? Not likely. The Customize Links button leads to a simple Help screen that tells you how to change links; after you learn the technique, you can safely delete this link.

There's no limit to the number of shortcuts you can add to the Links bar. To keep navigation simple, though, you probably want to limit the number of links to no more than 10 or 12, depending on your screen resolution. The Links bar in Figure 28.5, for example, has nine shortcuts; adding even one more would push the last link off the screen. When that happens, arrows appear at either side of the Links bar to aid in scrolling.

Figure 28.5
To squeeze the maximum number of shortcuts onto the Links bar, change long page titles to shorter labels.

To give your Links bar a makeover, follow these steps:

1. Right-click on any Links you don't plan to keep and choose <u>D</u>elete from the shortcut menu.

2. To add the current page to the Links bar, drag the icon from the left side of the Address bar and drop it alongside any existing link. The shortcut icon tells you when it's okay to drop.

3. Click the Favorites button and drag shortcuts from the Favorites folder to the Links bar.

4. To rearrange the order in which links appear, grab an icon and move it to its new location. Other links shift left or right to make room.

5. To rename a link, open the Favorites Explorer bar, click on Links, right-click on the entry you want to change, and choose Rena<u>m</u>e.

Tip #182

The width of each shortcut on the Links bar is defined by its label. The shorter the name, the more links you can use. FedEx, for example, takes up much less space than Federal Express Home Page, without sacrificing any meaning.

USING THE SEARCH BAR TO FIND INFORMATION ON THE WORLD WIDE WEB

How many pages are there on the World Wide Web? No one can say for sure, but the number is at least 50 million, probably more than 100 million, and growing every day. How do you find specific information in the billions of words and hyperlinks on all those pages? That's where search engines come in.

Internet Explorer offers easy access to several popular search engines through an Explorer bar that works much like the Favorites bar.

When you click the Search button, an Explorer bar like the one in Figure 28.6 takes over the left side of the screen.

Finding information on the Web is a two-step process. First, you have to choose a search engine that's appropriate for the type of information you're looking for. Then, you have to construct your search so the pages you're looking for appear at the top of the list.

PART

V

CH

28

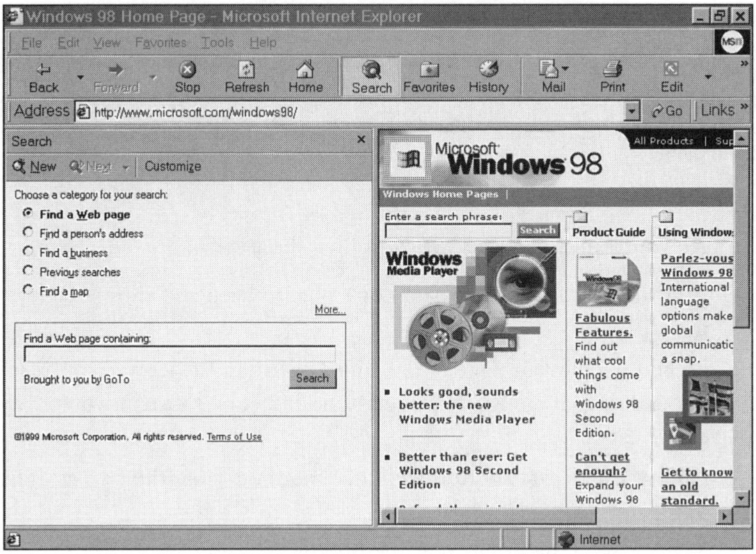

Figure 28.6
Use the default search engine and then enter the text you're looking for.

CHOOSING THE RIGHT SEARCH ENGINE

In general, search engines can be divided into two types. Category-based sites like Yahoo! organize the Internet by classification. Indexed search engines, such as Excite and AltaVista, use Web robots to gather text and create searchable databases of information. Most popular search sites now combine both techniques on their home pages.

Category searches are ideal for broad, open-ended questions, whereas indexed sites are better for finding specific facts. In either case, getting the right results takes practice and some basic understanding of how the search engine works. To avoid playing favorites, Internet Explorer picks one of its featured search engines at random every day and spotlights that choice when you click the Search button. You can accept the default or study Table 28.1 and make your own selection using the drop-down list.

TABLE 28.1   POPULAR INTERNET SEARCH ENGINES

Name	URL	Description
AOL NetFind	www.aol.com/netfind	America Online calls on a huge database of reviews to help you find people, companies, places, and information. Powered by Excite technology, it's open to non-AOL members as well.
Excite	www.excite.com	If you can't find it using Excite, it probably isn't on the Internet. Click on Channels to find information by topic or use its massive database to search the entire Web.

Name	URL	Description
Infoseek	www.infoseek.com	Enter text or click on topic links to find information. Jump to Infoseek's main page to try its impressive capability to process plain-English questions.
Lycos	www.lycos.com	One of the oldest search engines around, Lycos began as a research project at Carnegie-Mellon University. Today, it offers Yahoo!-style category lists and superb international support.
Yahoo!	www.yahoo.com	The original category-based search engine now uses AltaVista's indexing software to do keyword searches as well. Make sure you choose the correct search method before sending your request.
AltaVista	www.altavista.com	An excellent search engine that uses indexing software to perform keyword searches and searches based on category as well.

Tip #183

Don't like any of the built-in search options? Then, choose List of All Providers from the drop-down list in the Search bar. This option opens Microsoft's all-in-one search page, with links to dozens of general-purpose and specialized search sites.

PERFORMING THE SEARCH

After you've selected a search engine, follow these steps to carry out your search:

1. If you see a category that's relevant to your search, click that link. Otherwise, enter the text you're looking for in the Search box.
2. If the search engine provides any options, check them carefully. For example, do you want to search the Web, Usenet newsgroups, or both?
3. Click the button that submits your request to the search engine.
4. A list of search results appears in the Search bar, as in the example in Figure 28.7. Scroll through the list and click on any links that look promising. The page appears in the Browser window to the right of the Search bar.
5. Click on the More Results arrow at the bottom of the results list to see more entries in the results list.
6. If the search request doesn't produce the correct results, change your search or choose a different search engine and try again.

PART

V

CH

28

Figure 28.7
This search produces several matches, but the most relevant pages appear in the top 10 list on the left side of the screen. Click on the More Results arrow to move through the list 10 links at a time.

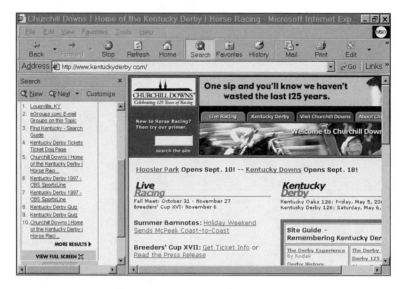

Tip #184

You don't need to click the Search button if you simply want to look for a keyword or two. If you type `find`, `go`, or `?` in the Address bar, followed by one or more words, Internet Explorer's AutoSearch feature submits your request to Yahoo! for processing, returning results in the main browser window.

If you have a favorite search engine, you can tell Internet Explorer to take you to that site instead of Yahoo! each time you use AutoSearch. To make the change, you first have to download Microsoft's Tweak UI utility, one of the unofficial Power Toys for Windows 95 and Windows 98. You can find all the Power Toys, with full instructions for their use at

```
http://www.microsoft.com/windows95/downloads/contents/wutoys/
w95pwrtoysset/
```

After installing Tweak UI, open Control Panel and start the utility; click the General tab and use the drop-down list to change the default search engine.

TIPS AND TECHNIQUES FOR MORE SUCCESSFUL SEARCHES

How can you guarantee better results when you search the Web? Try these techniques:

■ Visit the major search sites often. They regularly add new features and upgrade search interfaces. If you use only the Internet Explorer Search bar, you won't see those improvements.

■ Learn how to combine search terms using the logical operators AND, OR, and NOT to narrow the results list. Every search engine uses a slightly different syntax for these so-called Boolean queries; check the help pages at the search engine's site. The default operator is usually OR, which means if you enter two or more words, you get back any page that contains any of the words; use an ampersand, AND, or quotation marks to be more specific.

■ Don't stop at simple searches. Some search engines let you specify a range of dates to search, for example, to avoid being bombarded with stale links. Others let you specify or exclude a particular Web server. Still others let you progressively narrow a list of results by searching only in those results. Read each search engine's online instructions to see which advanced features it offers.

SAVING A SUCCESSFUL SEARCH

When you find a search that you think you'll want to reuse, follow these steps to save it:

1. Right-click anywhere in the Search bar and choose Properties.
2. Select the entire URL that appears on the General tab, then right-click, and choose Copy from the shortcut menu. Click OK to close the Properties dialog box.
3. Select the entire contents of the Address bar, right-click, and choose Paste.
4. Press Enter to load the page whose URL you just copied.
5. Create a shortcut to the current page, either on the desktop or in the Favorites folder, and provide a descriptive name.

SEARCHING FOR INFORMATION ON THE CURRENT PAGE

A Web page can consist of a single paragraph, or it can run on for tens of thousands of words. Internet Explorer's Find feature lets you search for words or phrases on the current page or within a selected frame. This feature can be extremely helpful when a search engine turns up a list of pages and you're trying to find the matching word or phrase in a specific page. To begin, press Ctrl+F and enter your text in the Find dialog box shown in Figure 28.8.

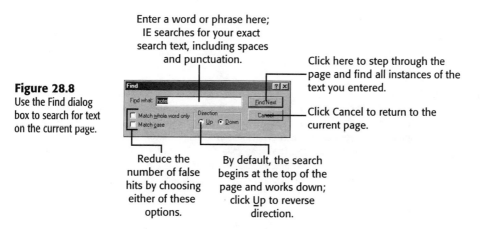

Figure 28.8
Use the Find dialog box to search for text on the current page.

Enter a word or phrase here; IE searches for your exact search text, including spaces and punctuation.

Click here to step through the page and find all instances of the text you entered.

Click Cancel to return to the current page.

Reduce the number of false hits by choosing either of these options.

By default, the search begins at the top of the page and works down; click Up to reverse direction.

PART
V

CH
28

Note that the Find dialog box searches only text that actually appears on the page; it won't look at hidden text or HTML tags in the source for the page. To search for hidden text or tags, choose View, Source and use Notepad's Search menu.

⚠️ *If you're having trouble searching for and finding text on a certain page, see "Looking for Text on Frame-Based Pages" in the "Troubleshooting" section at the end of this chapter.*

USING THE HISTORY BAR TO REVISIT WEB SITES

In addition to the cache in the Temporary Internet Files folder, Internet Explorer keeps a record of every URL you load. This History list is indispensable when you want to return to a page you visited recently but can't remember its address. If you've enabled multiple user settings on your Windows 98 PC, each user who logs in gets a private History folder.

→ For the details on History folders, **see** "Managing the Browser's Cache," **p. 581.**

 Click the History button to open an Explorer bar similar to the one in Figure 28.9. The History bar looks and acts just like the Favorites bar, snapping into position along the left edge of the browser window and pushing the main viewing window to the right.

Figure 28.9
Every time you visit a Web page, it gets an entry in this History list. If you can remember when you last viewed a page, you can narrow the search.

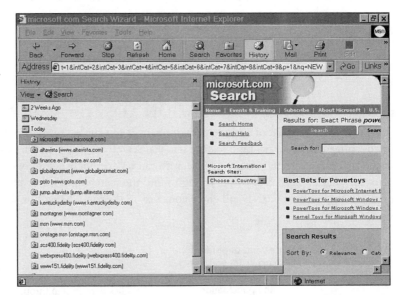

> **Note**
>
> From *Windows Explorer*, you can examine the History list by double-clicking the History icon. Individual shortcuts are not actually stored in the History folder, however; instead, Internet Explorer uses an internal database to manage the collection of shortcuts, with a single data file for each day. The entire collection is organized in one or more hidden folders. Although you can view these hidden files from a DOS prompt, there's no way to see their contents without using Explorer's system extensions.

NAVIGATING THROUGH THE HISTORY FOLDER

By default, the History folder keeps a pointer to every page you've accessed for the past 20 days. When you click the History button to open the Explorer bar, you see the list of shortcuts organized by day, with the most recent day's collection at the bottom of the list. Click on the entry for any day to see the list of shortcuts for that day, with a single entry for each resource location. Click again on any of these entries to see a shortcut for each page within that domain. When you click on an Internet shortcut in the History list, Internet Explorer loads the page in the browser window at the right. To view the history of pages before or after the 20-day default, go to Tools from the pull-down menu and select Internet Options. From the History section on the General tab, use the spinning number tool to change the number of days to keep the history of Web sites. Select a number between 0 and 999.

Tip #185	Choosing 0 as the number of days to keep the history of Web sites will clear the History list every day. However, you can still recall any page you visited earlier in the same day.

Although you cannot directly add an Internet shortcut to the History list, you can copy an entry from the History list to a variety of places: the desktop, the Start menu, the Favorites folder, or an email message, for example. Drag a shortcut from the History list to any legal destination or use the right-click menu to copy the shortcut to the Windows Clipboard.

CLEARING THE HISTORY

Internet Explorer allows you to empty the History folder completely or to delete entries one at a time. Clearing the History folder can reclaim a modest amount of disk space and make the list easier to navigate. But a more practical reason to remove items from this list is for privacy reasons—to keep another user from seeing the list of sites you've visited recently.

- To clear a single shortcut from the list, point to the shortcut, right-click, and choose Delete.

- To remove a group of shortcuts, point to the entry for a given Web location or day, right-click, and choose Delete.

- To empty all entries from the History folder, choose View, Internet Options; click the General tab; and click the Clear History button.

BROWSING THE WEB OFFLINE

Internet Explorer's cache and History folders work together exceptionally well when you choose to work offline. With the History folder visible in the Explorer bar, you can choose File, Work Offline and view any files stored in the cache, even if you have no current connection to the Internet.

When you work with Internet Explorer offline, a network icon with a red X appears in the status bar along the bottom of the browser window. Except for that indicator, you can browse pages in the History cache just as if you were working with a live Internet connection. When you point to a link that isn't cached locally, the pointer changes shape, and you see the dialog box shown in Figure 28.10. Before you can view the selected page, you must open an Internet connection.

PART

V

CH

28

Figure 28.10
The X in the status bar means you're working offline. You'll see this pointer when you attempt to access a page that isn't stored in the Web cache.

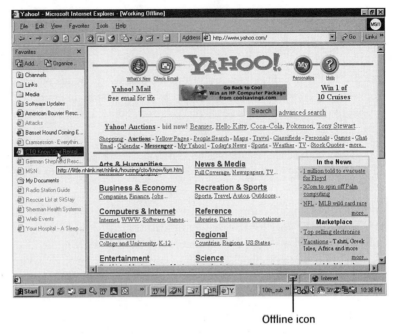

Offline icon

→ To learn more about Web cache, **see** "Using Offline Favorites to Download Web Pages," **p. 642.**

PRINTING WEB PAGES

Successfully transferring a Web page to paper can be as simple as clicking a button, although complex page designs require some preparation for best results.

To print a full Web page that doesn't include frames, click the Print button on the Standard toolbar. This action sends the current page to the printer without displaying any additional dialog boxes. Internet Explorer scales the page to fit on the standard paper size for the default printer. The entire Web document prints, complete with graphics, even if only a portion of the page is visible in the browser window.

Tip #186

By default, Internet Explorer ignores any background images or colors when printing. That behavior is by design because most of these decorations simply make printed text harder to read. To add background images or colors to printed pages, choose View, Internet Options, click the Advanced tab, and check the appropriate box in the Printing section. Be sure to reverse the process after printing.

ARRANGING FRAMES ON THE PRINTED PAGE

For more complex pages, especially those that include frames, choose File, Print (or press Ctrl+P). That step opens the Print dialog box, shown in Figure 28.11, and lets you specify how you want to arrange the page on paper.

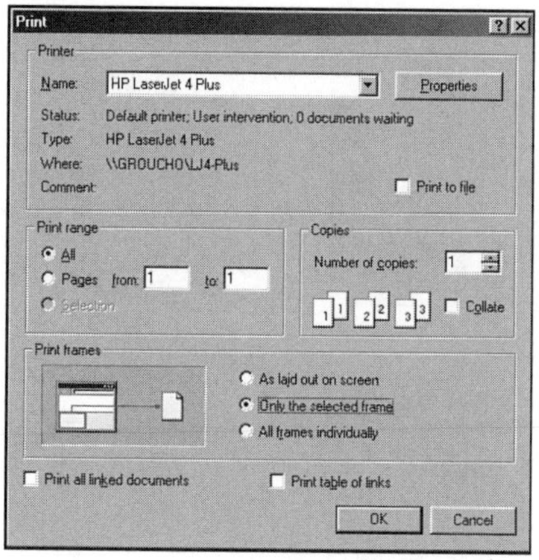

Figure 28.11
Watch the display at the left of the Print Frames box to see how a frame-based page appears when printed.

Follow these steps for maximum control over any printed page:

→ To learn about controlling print jobs, **see** Chapter 13, "Printing" for more details on configuring and using a printer.

1. Choose the area to be printed. The Selection option is grayed out unless you've selected a portion of the page.

2. Choose the number of copies to print. The default is 1.

3. Tell Internet Explorer how to deal with frames—print a single frame, print the page as it appears onscreen, or print each frame on a separate page.

4. Choose either of the two options at the bottom of the dialog box to specify whether and how linked pages will print.

5. Click OK to send the page to the printer. An icon on the status bar confirms that the page has gone to the printer.

Caution

An option at the bottom of the Print dialog box lets you print all linked documents along with the current page. Exercise this option with extreme care, because printing indiscriminately in this fashion can consume a ream of paper with a single click.

PART
V

CH
28

ADDING HEADERS AND FOOTERS TO A PRINTED WEB PAGE

To control most options that Internet Explorer applies before printing a Web page, choose File, Page Setup. By using this dialog box (shown in Figure 28.12), you can change the orientation, margins, and paper specifications for the current page. More important, though, you can specify a header and footer to print on each page.

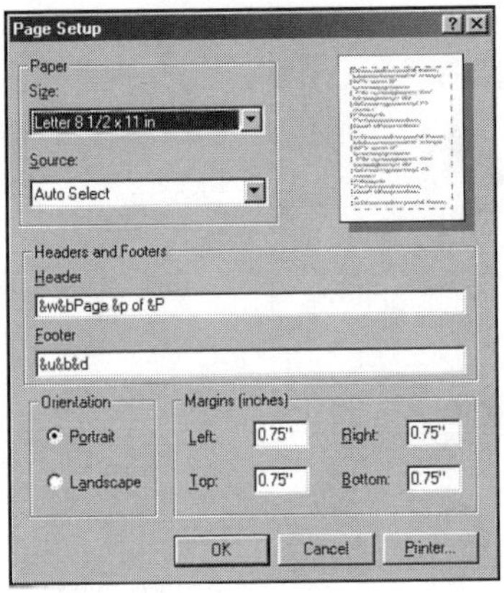

Figure 28.12
Use these formatting codes to specify a header and footer to appear on each page you print. Internet Explorer saves the format you enter here as your default.

You can enter any text as part of the header or footer; in addition, Internet Explorer uses a set of arcane codes, each prefixed by an ampersand, to add information about the current page to the header or footer. Table 28.2 lists these codes.

TABLE 28.2 CUSTOM HEADER/FOOTER VARIABLES

To Print This	Enter This Code
Window title	&w
Page address (URL)	&u
Date (short format)	&d
Date (long format)	&D
Time (default format)	&t
Time (24-hour format)	&T
Single ampersand	&&
Current page number	&p
Total number of pages	&P
Right-align following text	&btext
Center Text1, right-align Text2	&btext1&btext2

Note

If you can't remember the codes for headers and footers, click the question mark icon in the title bar of the Page Setup dialog box and point to the Header or Footer box. Watch out for a bug in the documentation, though: Any text you add after the characters &b is right-aligned, not centered, in the header or footer.

SAVING AND EDITING WEB PAGES

Only the simplest Web pages consist of a single, simple document. More often, the page you see in your browser consists of one or more HTML documents and several linked images. You cannot save all the elements on the entire page in one smooth operation. Instead, when you choose File, Save As, Internet Explorer saves the underlying HTML document and ignores any images or pages linked to that page. (You can also choose to save the current page as a plain-text document instead of an HTML-formatted page.)

To save graphics, frames, and other files linked to the current page, you must right-click on each item and choose Save Target As from the shortcut menu. Right-click on any link and use the same menu choice to save a linked page without opening it.

Tip #187

With the help of a handy Internet Explorer keyboard shortcut, you can turn any Web graphic into wallpaper for your desktop. When you find an image you'd like to install on the desktop, right-click and choose Set As Wallpaper.

→ To turn a Web graphic into wallpaper, **see** "Customizing the Windows Display," **p. 332.**

You can also edit any Web page by loading it directly from your browser into FrontPage Express. Use the Web browser to open the page you want to edit and then click the Edit button on the Standard toolbar. You can also create a shortcut to the current page, then right-click on that shortcut icon, and choose Edit.

→ If you can't wait to learn about creating Web pages and get started on your own, **see** "Creating Web Pages with FrontPage Express," **p. 711.**

DOWNLOADING FILES FROM FTP SITES

One of the most common ways to distribute files of all types over the Internet is with File Transfer Protocol (FTP) servers. Unlike Web servers, which are designed primarily to assemble hypertext documents for viewing in a browser window, FTP servers use FTP to move files between computers. Internet Explorer is capable of acting as a basic FTP client.

To connect directly to an FTP site from your Web browser, enter the name of the site in the Address bar. Because FTP servers don't include graphics support, the display you see in the browser window is as austere as the one in Figure 28.13.

PART

V

CH

28

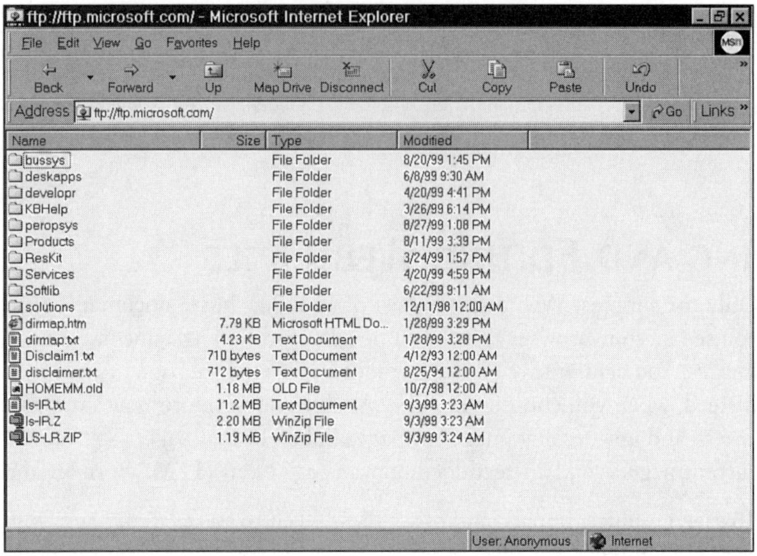

Figure 28.13
Don't expect fancy graphics or menus when you connect to an FTP site. Although this listing is plain, it's easy to find your way around.

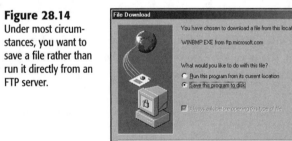

Click on any link in the FTP window to begin downloading that file. When you click on a link to a file stored on an FTP server, Internet Explorer handles the details of logging on to that server and negotiating how to transfer the file. If Internet Explorer succeeds in connecting to the FTP server, you typically see the File Download dialog box shown in Figure 28.14. Choose the Save This Program to Disk option and then designate a name and destination for the downloaded file to begin the transfer.

Figure 28.14
Under most circumstances, you want to save a file rather than run it directly from an FTP server.

Based on the size of the file and the speed of your current connection, Internet Explorer attempts to estimate the time remaining on your download. This process isn't always successful; in particular, it fails when the FTP server at the other end of the connection does not report crucial information about the file you've chosen to download. In those cases, the dialog box you see tells you how much of the file has been downloaded so far.

When you use IE5 to download a file of any sort, you see a dialog box like the one in Figure 28.15, which may include an estimate of the amount of time remaining for the file to download.

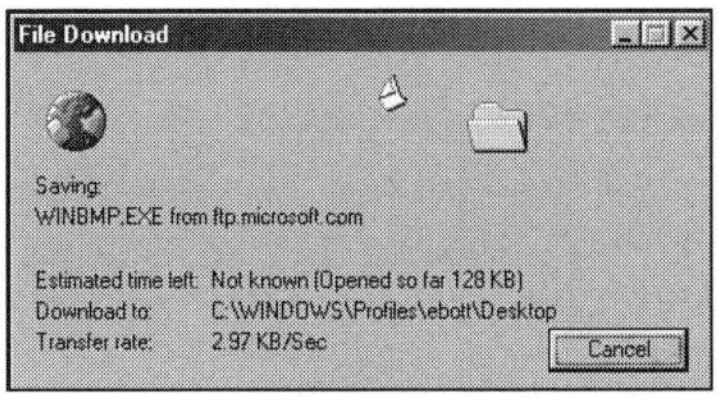

Figure 28.15
You see this progress dialog box whenever Internet Explorer downloads a file to your computer.

Tip #188

If you minimize the Download dialog box, you see the progress of your download in the label and ScreenTip of the taskbar button. You can close the browser window or switch to another page without interrupting the download.

LOGGING ON TO PASSWORD-PROTECTED FTP SERVERS

Many FTP servers allow anonymous access without a designated username and password. Microsoft, for example, uses its FTP server to freely distribute patches and updates for Windows and other products. Internet Explorer handles anonymous logons easily. Other FTP servers, however, may refuse to allow you to log on unless you enter valid account information; this practice is especially true of corporate sites intended for employees and other authorized users. Because Internet Explorer does not properly respond to password prompts from FTP servers, you have to construct a custom URL to connect to a password-protected FTP server. Click in the Address bar and enter the URL in the following format:

```
ftp://<username>:<password>@<ftp_server>/<url-path>
```

Substitute the proper username, password, and FTP server address in the preceding example.

USING THE WINDOWS 98 FTP CLIENT

Because Internet Explorer offers only the most basic FTP capabilities, it is incapable of connecting properly with some FTP servers. If you encounter such a server, use the Windows 98 command-line FTP client instead. Follow these steps to download a file from `ftp.microsoft.com`; the same techniques should work with any site:

1. Click Start and choose <u>R</u>un.

2. In the <u>O</u>pen box, type `ftp` and press Enter.

3. At the ftp> prompt, type `open ftp.microsoft.com`.

4. Enter `anonymous` as the username; although any password will suffice on an anonymous FTP server, the widely accepted custom is for you to enter your email address as the password.

5. Use the `cd` command to navigate to the proper directory and use `ls` or `dir` to list the contents of the current directory.

6. If the file you want to download is a binary (nontext) file, type `bin` and press Enter.

PART
V

CH
28

7. Type `get` *filename* to begin the download (substitute the name of the file for *filename*). To retrieve multiple files, type `mget` *filespec* (*filespec* can include wildcards, such as *.zip).

8. When your FTP session is finished, type `close` to disconnect from the server and type `quit` to close the FTP window.

For rudimentary help with FTP commands, type `help` at the FTP> prompt.

 If you use FTP regularly, invest in a full-featured FTP client like FTP Explorer. You can find this shareware product at

`http://www.ftpx.com`

TROUBLESHOOTING

LOOKING FOR TEXT ON FRAME-BASED PAGES

My search for text turned up no matches, but I'm certain the word I'm looking for is on the page.

Looking for text on frame-based pages can produce unexpected results if you're not careful. On these pages, the Find feature searches only in the current frame, not in all frames visible in the browser window. Before you open the Find dialog box and enter your search text, make sure you click in the frame in which you want to search.

SECRETS OF MASTERING THE WINDOWS 98 ENVIRONMENT: FTP COMMANDS FOR USE IN WINDOWS 98

After Microsoft TCP/IP is installed on a computer, you have a fully functional FTP client. One of the best things about using FTP to download information over the Internet is the relatively low overhead of a file transfer versus one in a Web style environment. When you are comfortable using FTP and become adept at the various commands used in the FTP environment, you will probably use it to accomplish most of your file downloads across the Internet. You can use the following FTP commands with Microsoft TCP/IP.

- **!**—Runs the specified command on the local computer.
- **?**—Displays descriptions for FTP commands. Identical to `help`.
- **append**—Appends a local file to a file on the remote computer, using the current file type setting.
- **ascii**—Sets the file transfer type to ASCII, the default.
- **bell**—Toggles a bell to ring after each file transfer command is completed. By default, the bell is off.

- `binary`—Sets the file transfer type to binary.

- `bye`—Ends the FTP session with the remote computer and exits FTP.

- `cd`—Changes the working directory on the remote computer.

- `close`—Ends the FTP session with the remote server and returns to the command interpreter.

- `debug`—Toggles debugging. When debugging is on, each command sent to the remote computer is printed, preceded by the string `--->`. By default, debugging is off.

- `delete`—Deletes files on remote computers.

- `dir`—Displays a list of a remote directory's files and subdirectories.

- `disconnect`—Disconnects from the remote computer, retaining the FTP prompt.

- `get`—Copies a remote file to the local computer, using the current file transfer type. Identical to `recv`.

- `glob`—Toggles filename globbing. *Globbing* permits the use of wildcard characters in local file- or pathnames. By default, globbing is on.

- `hash`—Toggles hash-mark (#) printing for each 2,048-byte data block transferred. By default, hash-mark printing is off.

- `help`—Displays descriptions for FTP commands.

- `lcd`—Changes the working directory on the local computer. By default, the current directory on the local computer is used.

- `literal`—Sends arguments, verbatim, to the remote FTP server. A single FTP reply code is expected in return. Identical to `quote`.

- `ls`—Displays an abbreviated list of a remote directory's files and subdirectories.

- `mdelete`—Deletes multiple files on remote computers.

- `mdir`—Displays a list of a remote directory's files and subdirectories. Allows you to specify multiple files.

- `mget`—Copies multiple remote files to the local computer, using the current file transfer type.

- `mkdir`—Creates a remote directory.

- `mls`—Displays an abbreviated list of a remote directory's files and subdirectories.

- `mput`—Copies multiple local files to the remote computer, using the current file transfer type.

- `open`—Connects to the specified FTP server.

- `prompt`—Toggles prompting. During multiple file transfers, FTP provides prompts to allow you to selectively retrieve or store files; `mget` and `mput` transfer all files if prompting is turned off. By default, prompting is on.

- `put`—Copies a local file to the remote computer, using the current file transfer type. Identical to `send`.

- `pwd`—Prints the current directory on the remote computer.

- quit—Ends the FTP session with the remote computer and exits FTP.

- quote—Sends arguments, verbatim, to the remote FTP server. A single FTP reply code is expected in return. Identical to literal.

- recv—Copies a remote file to the local computer, using the current file transfer type. Identical to get.

- remotehelp—Displays help for remote commands.

- rename—Renames remote files.

- rmdir—Deletes a remote directory.

- send—Copies a local file to the remote computer, using the current file transfer type. Identical to put.

- status—Displays the current status of FTP connections and toggles.

- trace—Toggles packet tracing; displays the route of each packet when running an FTP command.

- type—Sets or displays the file transfer type.

- user—Specifies a user to the remote computer.

- verbose—Toggles verbose mode. If on, all FTP responses are displayed; when a file transfer completes, statistics regarding the efficiency of the transfer are also displayed. By default, verbose is on.

CHAPTER **29**

INTERNET SECURITY

In this chapter

SETTING A SECURITY POLICY

By its very nature, the Internet is an insecure place. Packets of data move from machine to machine across connections that anyone with a little technical knowledge can tap into. On the Internet, simply clicking a link can download and run a program written by someone you've never met, whose motives you can't even begin to guess. When you transmit sensitive data over the Internet, it can be intercepted by complete strangers. If you run a server program, a stranger can connect directly to your computer with consequences you might not be aware of. There's no need for paranoia, but everyone who accesses the Internet should have a healthy respect for its risks.

Windows 98 and Internet Explorer 5.0 (IE5) include a broad set of security tools. Before you can properly configure these options, however, you need to establish a security policy. This policy should balance the need to protect sensitive data against the undeniable value of open access to information and the wealth of information available on the world's largest network. Different environments have different security requirements as well: With a dial-up Internet connection at home, you might not worry about the risk of break-ins, but on a corporate network, firewalls and other sophisticated security precautions are a must.

These elements should be central to any security policy:

- Authentication—When you connect to a Web site, how do you know who's really running that server? When you download and run a program, how do you know that it hasn't been tampered with or infected with a virus? When extremely sensitive information is involved, you might want to insist on secure connections guaranteed by digital certificates.

- Encryption—Certain types of data—usernames and passwords, credit card numbers, and confidential banking information, for example—are too sensitive to be sent "in the clear," where anyone who can intercept the packets can read them. For these transactions, only secure, encrypted connections are acceptable.

- Control over executable content—The Internet is filled with programs and add-ins that can expand the capabilities of your browser. Unfortunately, poorly written or malicious add-ins can carry viruses, corrupt valuable data, and even expose your network to unauthorized break-ins. On most networks, administrators try to limit the potential for damage by restricting the types of files that users can download and run.

 Microsoft publishes regular security news, advisories, and updates for Windows and Internet Explorer users; find the latest announcements at this address:

`http://www.microsoft.com/security`

CONFIGURING INTERNET EXPLORER TO USE A PROXY SERVER

With ordinary dial-up Internet connections, client machines connect directly to Web or File Transfer Protocol (FTP) servers, making it possible for a would-be hacker to break into the network. To minimize that risk, most corporate networks include a *firewall*, a secure gateway made up of one or more systems that sit between the network and the Internet at large. Firewalls restrict the ability of outsiders to connect with machines inside the network while allowing legitimate users to access resources on the Internet. This combination of hardware and software is designed to intercept and filter packets of information, letting through only those that meet strict standards of security.

Carefully isolated machines called *proxy servers* are crucial components of most corporate firewalls. When a client computer inside the firewall requests a service from the Internet— a Web page, for example, or a file on an FTP server—the proxy server intercepts the request and handles the transaction. To the server on the other end of the connection, the request looks as though it came from the proxy server; a direct (and possibly compromised) connection between it and the host machine inside the firewall is impossible.

If you want more information about firewalls? You can find links to the definitive firewalls FAQ and mailing list at

`http://www.greatcircle.com`

Before IE5 can use a proxy server, you must specify its name or IP address. Some proxies (Microsoft Proxy Server 2.0 or later, for example) can automatically configure client machines; in that case, you need to enter the name of the machine that contains the configuration files.

If you are using Internet Explorer but cannot access the security settings, see "Limited Internet Access" in the "Troubleshooting" section at the end of this chapter.

Follow these steps to set up Internet Explorer for use with a proxy server:

1. Choose Tools, Internet Options and click the Connections tab. A dialog box like the one in Figure 29.1 appears.

2. Click on the Setup button.

3. The Welcome to the Internet Connection Wizard page appears. Select the I Want to Set Up My Internet Connection Manually, or I Want to Connect Through a Local Area Network (LAN) radio button (see Figure 29.2). Click on Next.

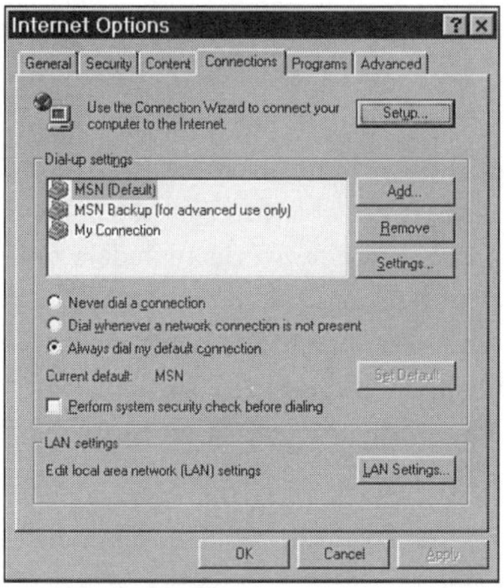

Figure 29.1
The Connections tab enables you to add and remove dial-up settings.

Figure 29.2
The Internet Connection Wizard enables you to set up with a new or existing account.

4. In the next Internet Connection Wizard window, select the I Connect Through a Local Area Network(LAN) radio button (see Figure 29.3).

5. In the next Internet Connection Wizard window, you have a choice of automatically detecting a proxy server on your LAN or manually configuring the Internet Explorer client to connect to a specific proxy server. To ensure that the proxy server is located, the recommendation is to select the proxy server manually (see Figure 29.4).

Note

When configuring a proxy server, you can use either the server's name or its IP address. The result is the same. The administrator in charge of the proxy server can supply information about your network's configuration and the appropriate IP address and port number to use if different from the default. For example, HTTP uses port number 80 by default, and FTP uses port number 21.

Figure 29.3
Choosing to connect to the Internet through a proxy server over a LAN.

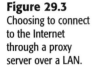

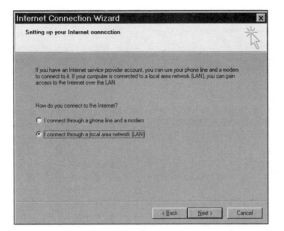

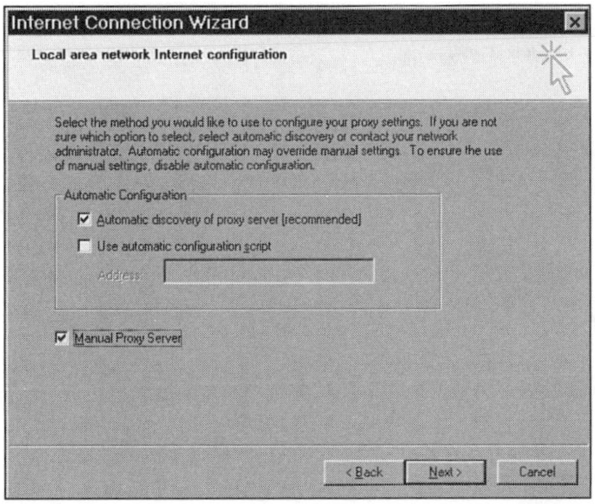

Figure 29.4
Manually configuring to a proxy server connection.

6. In the next Internet Connection Wizard window, you can select the type of service the Internet Explorer client is connecting to, the IP address of the proxy server providing the service, and the port number the service is listening on. Normally, a single proxy server provides multiple Internet services, such as HTTP or FTP (see Figure 29.5).

7. To control and limit the type and number of IP addresses the proxy server connects to on your behalf, enter the IP address or the network address of those systems in the Local Area Network Internet Configuration area. This practice helps to ensure that the proxy server doesn't attempt to route packets to the Internet when the destination is on the local network (see Figure 29.6).

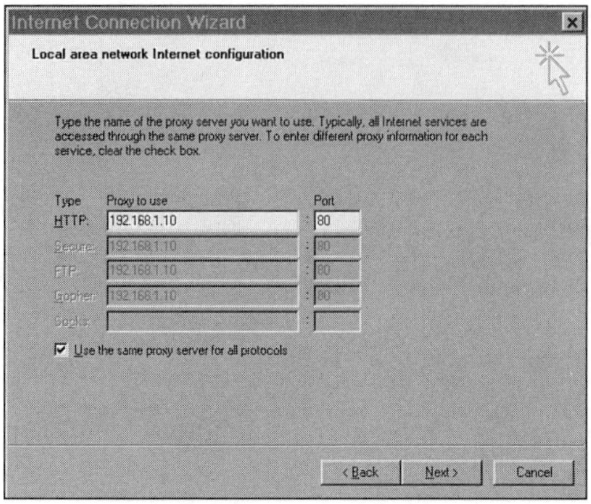

Figure 29.5
Enter proxy server information.

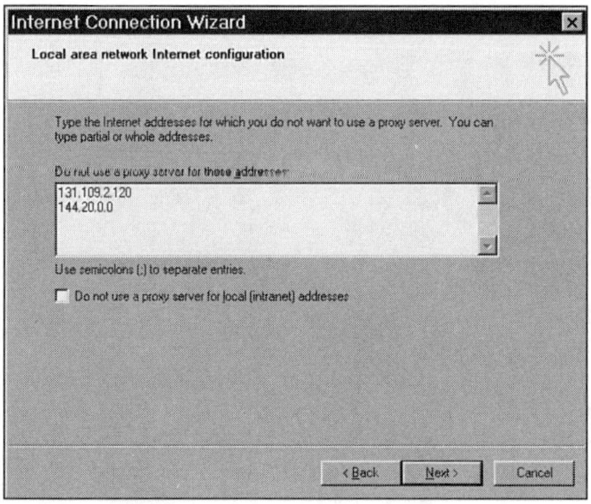

Figure 29.6
This dialog enables you to specify systems or networks you don't want the proxy server to route for you.

8. The next wizard screen asks you to set up your Internet mail account. Answer Yes or No by selecting the appropriate radio button (see Figure 29.7).

9. The next Internet Connection Wizard screen enables you to choose an existing Internet mail account or create a new one (see Figure 29.8).

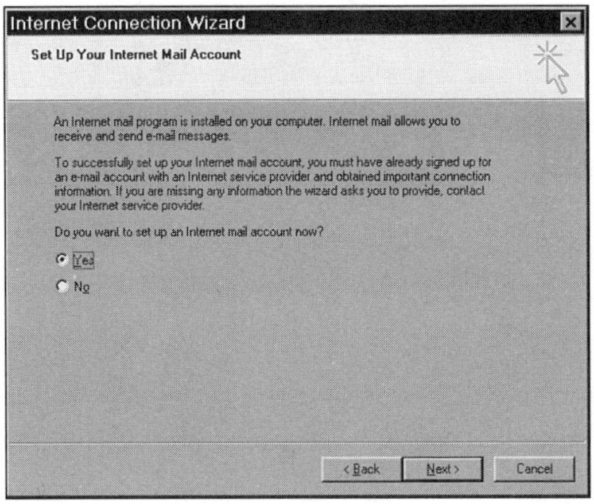

Figure 29.7
Choosing to set up an
Internet mail account.

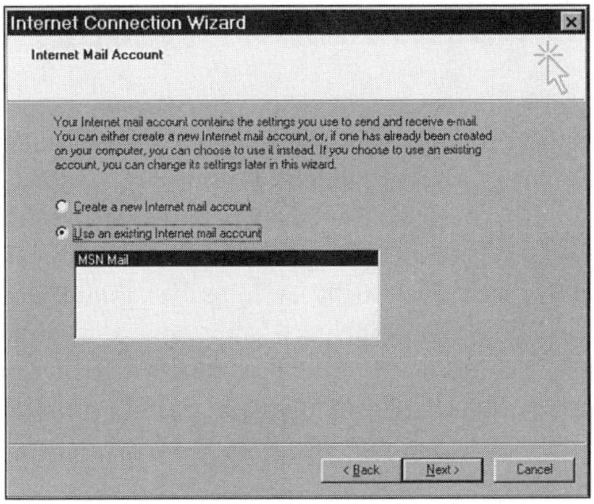

Figure 29.8
Creating or choosing
an existing Internet
mail account.

10. One of the last steps is to confirm your Internet mail account settings as shown in Figure 29.9.

11. Finish the process by telling the Internet Connection Wizard to make an Internet connection for you.

Tip #189

If your company uses a proxy server to connect to the Internet and also has an intranet of company Web sites, consider checking the Do Not Use a Proxy Server for Local (Intranet) Addresses box to speed up your local intranet connections. By checking this box, your local Web site requests are routed directly to the local intranet site on the network without being routed through the proxy server. By bypassing the proxy server, you also bypass its safety features; however, these safety features shouldn't be necessary inside the firewall on the intranet, and routing intranet requests through the proxy hurts performance without improving security.

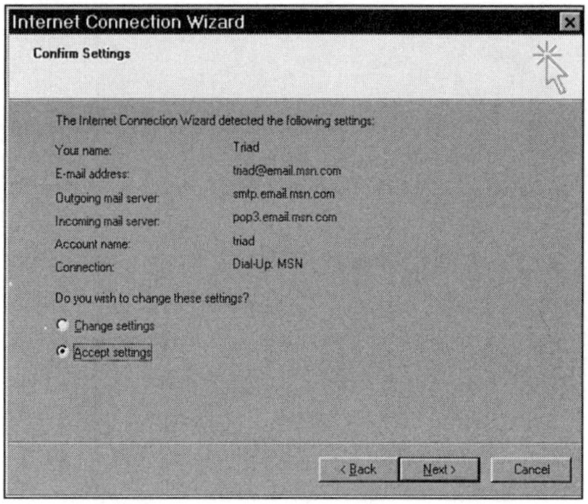

Figure 29.9
Confirming your
Internet mail account
settings.

ESTABLISHING AND MAINTAINING INTERNET SECURITY ZONES

Internet Explorer 5.0 includes dozens of security settings. If you really went overboard in trying to tighten up Internet security by applying each option to individual Web sites, you would soon discover that managing such a system would be impractical. A nice feature of IE5 is that it lets you group sites into four security zones, each with its own high, medium, medium-low, or low security settings. Initially, as Table 29.1 shows, all sites are divided into two groups: those with default locations included in the zone and those with no default locations included in the zone. As part of a comprehensive security policy, you can designate specific Web sites as trusted or restricted, giving them greater or less access to machines inside your network.

TABLE 29.1   SECURITY ZONES AT A GLANCE

Security Zone	Default Locations Included in Zone	Default Security Settings
Internet zone	All Web sites not included in other zones	Medium
Local intranet zone	Local intranet servers not included in other zones; all network paths; all sites that bypass proxy server	Medium
Trusted sites zone	None	Low
Restricted sites zone	None	High

As you use Internet Explorer to move from one address to another, the system checks to see which zone the address has been assigned to and then applies the security settings that belong to that zone. If you open a Web page on a server inside your corporate intranet, for example, you can freely download files and work with ActiveX controls or Java applets. When you switch to a page on the Internet, however, your security settings may prevent you from using any kind of active content or downloading any files.

Three built-in security levels plus a Custom option let you pick and choose security settings for a zone. Table 29.2 summarizes the security options available when you start IE5 for the first time.

TABLE 29.2 DEFAULT SECURITY LEVELS

Security Level	Default Settings
High	ActiveX controls and JavaScript disabled; Java set to highest safety level; file downloads prohibited through browser; prompt before downloading fonts or logging on to secure site.
Medium	ActiveX enabled for signed controls only, with prompt before downloading; file and font downloads permitted; Java set to medium safety level; all scripting permitted; automatic logon to secure sites.
Medium-low	This is the same as medium but without prompts before downloading. Because most content can run without prompts, be careful with this setting. It is most appropriate for sites on your intranet.
Low	Enable all ActiveX controls but prompt before using unsigned code; Java set to low safety; desktop items install automatically; file and font downloads permitted; all scripting permitted; automatic logon to secure sites.
Custom	Allows user or administrator to select security settings individually.

ADDING AN INTERNET DOMAIN TO A SECURITY ZONE

Initially, Internet Explorer has the capability to connect to every external Web site in the Internet zone. Over time, you'll identify some sites that are extremely trustworthy, such as a secure server maintained by your bank or stockbroker; on these sites, you might want to relax security settings to allow maximum access to information and resources available from that domain. Other sites, however, might earn a reputation for transferring unsafe content, including untested software or virus-infected documents. On a network, in particular, you might want to tightly restrict access to these unsafe sites.

To add the addresses for specific Web sites to a given security zone, open the Internet Properties dialog box and click on the Security tab; the dialog box shown in Figure 29.10 appears.

Figure 29.10
Adding a Web site to
the Restricted Sites
zone lets you tightly
control the site's abil-
ity to interact with
your PC and network.

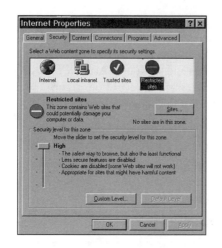

By definition, the Internet zone includes all sites not assigned to other zones; as a result, you can't add sites to that zone. Follow these steps to assign specific sites to the Trusted Sites or Restricted Sites zones:

1. Open the Internet Properties dialog box and click the Security tab.

2. Click on the Sites button.

3. Enter the IP address or fully qualified domain name of the Web site you want to include in the zone's security settings. Click the Add button.

   Be sure to include the prefix (http://, for example) but don't add any address information after the host name; Internet Explorer applies security settings to all pages on that server.

4. Repeat steps 2 and 3 to add more IP addresses or fully qualified domain names to the selected zone.

5. Click OK to close the dialog box.

Tip #190

If a Web site that appears in your Trusted Sites or Restricted Sites no longer belongs in its listed zone, you have the option of removing the site. Simply follow the same steps you used to add a site, but this time, instead of adding a Web site to the zone, remove it from the list of Web sites already present. To remove a Web server from either the Trusted Sites or Restricted Sites zone, click the Sites button, select the address from the Web Sites list, and click the Remove button. Any addresses you remove from a zone again belongs to the default Internet zone. Be sure the Internet zone security level is adequate before you remove a Web site from either the Trusted Sites or Restricted Sites zone.

Some special considerations apply when adding sites to the Trusted Sites or Local Intranet zone:

- By default, only secure sites (those with the `https://` prefix) may be added to the Trusted Sites group. To add other sites, clear the check box that reads Require <u>S</u>erver Verification (https:) for All Sites in This Zone.

- To add sites to the Local Intranet zone, you have to go through one extra dialog box, shown in Figure 29.11. Clear the middle check box if you want resources that you access without using the proxy server to fall into this group by default. Click the <u>A</u>dvanced button to add sites to the Local Intranet zone.

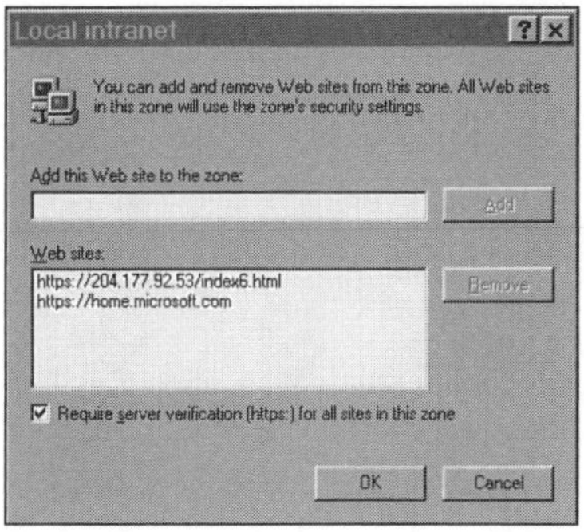

Figure 29.11
Clear one or more of these check boxes to move sites from the Local Intranet zone to the default Internet zone.

Tip #191

To verify that your Web page is reflecting the changed security zone to which you have added it, load the page and look at the status bar above the taskbar. The security zone is displayed for the page you are viewing. If this status bar does not reflect the correct zone, go through the steps again to confirm that it has indeed been added.

CHANGING SECURITY SETTINGS BY ZONE

When you first run Internet Explorer 5.0, all Internet pages have a medium security setting and all intranet pages have medium-low security settings. Both of those zones and their security settings can be modified. If your intranet is protected by a reliable firewall and you use ActiveX components developed within your company, you might want to reset security in the Local Intranet zone to low. Likewise, if you're concerned about the potential for damage from files and programs on the Internet, you can reset security for the Internet zone to high.

To assign a different security level to any of the four built-in zones, follow these steps:

1. Open the Internet Properties dialog box and click the Security tab.
2. Choose the appropriate zone from the four available at the top of the Security tab page.
3. Use the slider to configure the zone for a specific level of security by clicking the <u>H</u>igh, <u>M</u>edium, Medium-Low, or <u>L</u>ow radio button.
4. Click OK to save your new security settings.

Tip #192

When you choose the <u>H</u>igh option for the Internet zone (or use custom options to choose similar security settings), many rich content pages won't work properly.

Setting Custom Security Options

If none of the built-in security levels is quite right for the policy you've established, you can create your own collection of security settings and apply it to any of the four security zones. Instead of choosing <u>H</u>igh, <u>M</u>edium, Medium-low, or <u>L</u>ow, use Internet Explorer's <u>C</u>ustom option to step through all the security options, choosing the ones that best suit your needs. Follow these steps:

1. Open the Internet Properties dialog box and click the Security tab.

2. Choose the appropriate zone from the four available at the top of the Security tab page.

3. Click the <u>C</u>ustom Level button.

4. The Security Settings dialog box shown in Figure 29.12 appears.

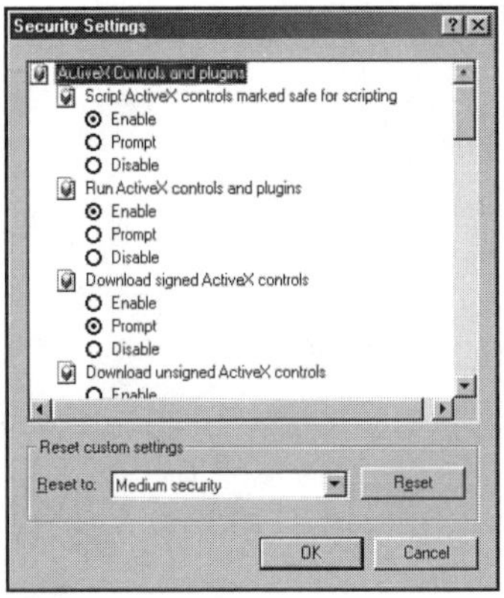

Figure 29.12
Internet Explorer includes a long list of security settings for each zone. Use context-sensitive help for a concise explanation of what each one does.

5. Scroll through the list and choose the options that best apply to your security needs. If you're not sure what an option means, right-click on the entry and choose What's This for context-sensitive help.

6. After you've finished adjusting all security settings, click OK to apply the changes to the selected zone.

Tip #193

If you have changed your security settings so many times that you are now unable to do simple browsing tasks, don't despair; just start over. To restore the default settings, open the Security Settings dialog box, choose a security level in the Reset To box, and click the <u>R</u>eset button. That step restores the custom settings to the default security settings for that level and lets you begin fresh.

RESTRICTING ACTIVEX CONTROLS

One of the most talked about features of Internet Explorer 5.0 is its support for ActiveX controls. ActiveX technology, an extension of what was known in previous versions of Windows as object linking and embedding (OLE), commonly refers to component software used across networks, including the Internet. Internet Explorer 5.0 uses ActiveX components in the browser window to display content that ordinary Hypertext Markup Language (HTML) can't handle, such as stock tickers, cascading menus, or Adobe Acrobat documents. An ActiveX chart control, for example, can take a few bits of data from a distant server and draw a chart at the speed of the local PC, instead of forcing you to wait while downloading a huge image file. The Microsoft Investor page (see Figure 29.13) offers a particularly rich example of this capability to quickly gather and manipulate data.

Figure 29.13
An ActiveX control on this page makes it possible to quickly analyze and display complex data such as stock prices.

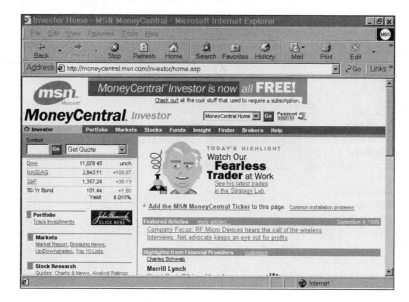

When you view a page that includes an ActiveX control, you don't need to run a setup program and restart your browser; the program simply begins downloading and then offers to install itself on your computer. That's convenient, but automatic installation also opens your computer and network to poorly written or malicious applets. Internet Explorer security options let you take control of ActiveX components and apply security settings by zone: You can completely disable all such downloads, or you can rely on digital certificates to decide which components are safe to install.

CUSTOMIZING ACTIVEX SECURITY SETTINGS

Whenever Internet Explorer encounters an ActiveX control on a Web page, it checks the current security zone and applies the security settings for that zone:

■ The default medium security settings disable any unsigned ActiveX controls and prompt you before downloading and installing those that have a valid certificate.

- The most drastic ActiveX security option completely disables any components you encounter in a given security zone, signed or not. To enable this setting in the Internet zone, set the security level to high.

- When security is set to low, the browser runs any ActiveX control. Signed controls download and install automatically; Internet Explorer prompts you before using an unsigned control.

> **Caution**
>
> Low security settings put your computer and network at risk. ActiveX controls are programs and like any executable file, they can have harmful effects to your computer if they are poorly written or if they contain viruses. The only circumstance in which we recommend this setting is in the Local Intranet zone to allow access to trusted but unsigned ActiveX controls developed by other members of your organization.

In zones where some or all ActiveX controls are disabled, Internet Explorer downloads the prohibited control but refuses to install it. Instead, you see an error message like the one in Figure 29.14.

Figure 29.14
Unless you set security options to low, you see this dialog box every time you encounter an unsigned ActiveX control. With high security, all ActiveX components are disabled.

Table 29.3 shows default ActiveX settings for each security zone. If you don't see a mix of options appropriate for your security policy, choose a zone and use Custom settings to redefine security levels.

TABLE 29.3   ACTIVEX SECURITY SETTINGS BY ZONE

Security Setting	Option	High	Medium	Medium-Low	Low
Download unsigned ActiveX controls	Prompt				X
	Disable	X		X	X
	Enable				

Security Setting	Option	High	Medium	Medium-Low	Low
Script ActiveX controls marked safe for scripting	Prompt				
	Disable				
	Enable	X	X	X	X
Initialize and script ActiveX controls not marked as safe	Prompt		X		X
	Disable	X			
	Enable				
Download signed ActiveX controls	Prompt		X		
	Disable	X			
	Enable				X
Run ActiveX controls and plug-ins	Prompt				
	Disable	X			
	Enable		X	X	X

Custom security settings offer a way to take advantage of the ActiveX controls you specifically approve while prohibiting all others. Choose the Custom security level for the Internet zone, click Settings, and enable two options: Run ActiveX Controls and *Plug-ins* and Script ActiveX Controls Marked Safe for Scripting. Disable all other ActiveX security settings. With these security settings, currently installed ActiveX controls function normally. When you encounter a new page that uses an ActiveX control, it refuses to install; you can choose to install it by temporarily resetting the security options for that zone.

USING CERTIFICATES TO IDENTIFY PEOPLE, SITES, AND PUBLISHERS

Internet Explorer uses digital certificates to verify the publisher of an ActiveX control before determining how to handle it. This feature, called Authenticode, checks the ActiveX control for the existence of an encrypted digital signature; IE5 then compares the signature against an original copy stored on a secure Web site to verify that the code has not been tampered with. Software publishers register with certifying authorities such as VeriSign, Inc., that in turn act as escrow agents to verify that the signature you're viewing is valid.

 For more information about how Authenticode uses digital signatures and certifying authorities, see

`http://www.verisign.com/developers/authenticodefaq.html`

If Internet Explorer cannot verify that the signature on the ActiveX control is valid, you see a security warning like the one in Figure 29.15. Depending on your security settings for the current zone, you might be able to install the control anyway.

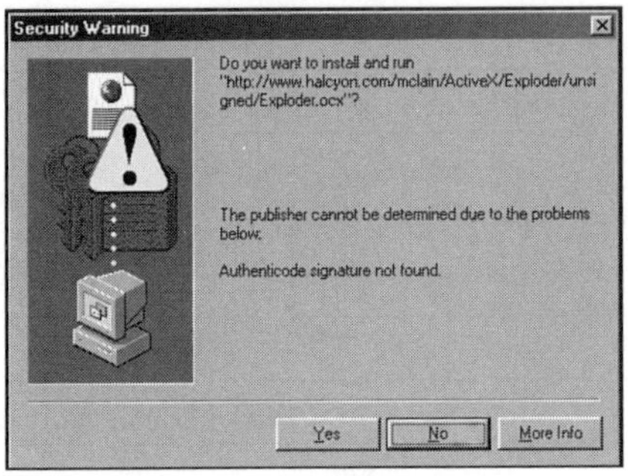

Figure 29.15
You see this warning when Internet Explorer can't verify that a certificate is valid. Click Yes to install the software anyway or No to check again later.

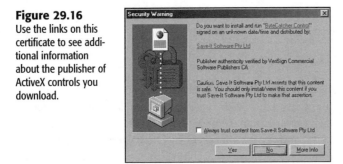

If the certifying authority verifies that the signature attached to the control is valid, and the current security zone is set to medium, you see a security warning like the one in Figure 29.16.

Figure 29.16
Use the links on this certificate to see additional information about the publisher of ActiveX controls you download.

The Security Warning dialog box confirms that the signature is valid. In addition, this dialog box offers links you can follow for more information about the publisher and gives you the option to add that publisher to a list of trusted sites:

- You can learn detailed information about the publisher gathered from its certificate. If the applet or control is requesting permission to access system resources, an additional link appears. Detailed help is available.

- You also can see additional information about the applet or control. This link typically points to a Web site run by the software publisher.

- Choose Yes to install the software and No to abort the installation.

- Check the Always Trust Content From... box to add the certificate to your list of trusted publishers. Future downloads accompanied by certificates on your trusted publishers list install automatically, without requiring your approval.

> **Note**
>
> To view and edit the full list of trusted publishers and certifying authorities (issuers of credentials), open the Internet Properties dialog box, click on the Content tab, and click on the Publishers button to view the Authenticode Security Technology dialog box. Here, you will find a list of all trusted publishers and certifying authorities.

- You also can learn general information about certificates and ActiveX security.

> **Caution**
>
> A valid certificate provides no guarantee that a signed ActiveX control is either bug free or safe. The certificate simply identifies the publisher with reasonable certainty. Based on that identification and the publisher's reputation, you can decide whether to install the software; and in the event something goes wrong, you know who to call for support.

MANAGING ACTIVEX COMPONENTS ON YOUR COMPUTER

Every time Internet Explorer adds an ActiveX control, it downloads files to the local computer and makes adjustments to the Windows Registry. However, you can't use the Control Panel's Add/Remove Programs applet (as you can with conventional programs) to remove or update Active X components; but there is a way to manage this collection. Follow these steps:

1. Open the Internet Properties dialog box and click the General tab.

2. In the box labeled *Temporary Internet Files*, click the Settings button. The Settings dialog box appears.

3. Click the View Objects button to open the Downloaded Program Files folder. You see a list of all installed ActiveX controls and Java class libraries, as shown in Figure 29.17. If you're not sure what a control does, right-click and choose Properties to see additional information.

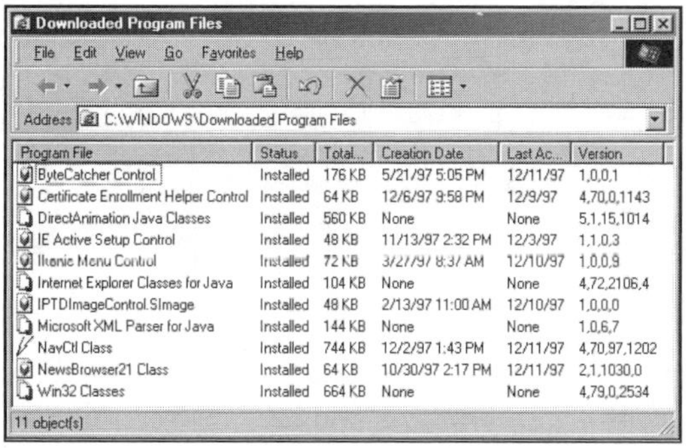

Figure 29.17
All installed ActiveX controls appear in this folder. Use the right-click shortcut menus to inspect a file's properties, update it, or remove it.

4. To delete one or more components, right-click on the entry or entries and choose Remove from the shortcut menu. This step deletes each component's executable file and clears out any Registry settings as well.

5. Close the Downloaded Program Files folder and click OK to close the Settings dialog box.

LIMITING JAVA APPLETS

Like ActiveX controls, Java applets extend the capabilities of Internet Explorer by displaying and manipulating data and images in ways that HTML can't. There's a significant difference between ActiveX and Java, though. Java applets run in a virtual machine with strict security rules. The Java Security Manager (sometimes referred to as the "sandbox") prevents applets from interacting with resources on your machine, whereas ActiveX controls are specifically designed to work with files and other applications.

Unlike ActiveX controls, Java applets are not stored on your machine. Instead, every time you access a Java-enabled page, your browser downloads the applet and runs the program in the Java virtual machine. When you've finished with the applet, it disappears from memory, and the next time you access the page you have to repeat the download. Over slow links, large Java applets can take excruciatingly long times to load, although the results can be impressive, as the example in Figure 29.18 shows.

Figure 29.18
This stock-charting page is an excellent illustration of the rich capabilities of Java applets.

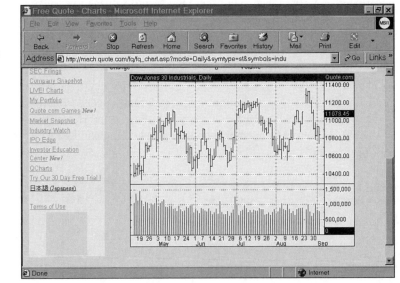

Internet Explorer's Security Settings dialog box lets you control specific aspects of the Java interface. Like ActiveX controls, Java applets also have ready-made Low, Medium, and High security options; or you can disable Java completely. A Custom option is also available, although most of its settings are meaningful only to Java developers. To adjust Java security, follow these steps:

1. Open the Internet Properties dialog box and click the Security tab.

2. Select one of the four zones at the top of the window.

3. Click the Custom Level button.

4. Scroll through the Security Settings dialog box until you reach the Java section.

5. Choose one of the five safety options.

 EarthWeb's Gamelan site is the best place on the Internet to look for Java applets and for detailed information about the Java language. You can find a link to these pages at

`http://www.developer.com/directories/directories.html`

BLOCKING DANGEROUS SCRIPTS AND UNSAFE FILE DOWNLOADS

In addition to its capability to host embedded controls and applets, Internet Explorer supports simple scripting, using JavaScript and VBScript. With the help of scripts, Web designers can create pages that calculate expressions, ask and answer questions, check data that users enter in forms, and link to other programs, including ActiveX controls and Java applets.

Although the security risks posed by most scripts are slight, Internet Explorer gives you the option to disable Active scripting as well as scripting of Java applets. You find both options in the Security Settings dialog box when you choose Custom settings.

A far more serious security risk is the browser's capability to download and run files. Although the risk of executing untrusted executable files is obvious, even document files can be dangerous. Any Microsoft Office document, for example, can include Visual Basic macros that are as powerful as any standalone program. To completely disable all file downloads, select the built-in High security option. With this setting turned on, you see a security message like the one in Figure 29.19 whenever you attempt to download a file from a Web page.

Figure 29.19
With the security level set to high, no file downloads are allowed. When you attempt to download any file, including programs and documents, you see this warning message instead.

WORKING WITH SECURE WEB SITES

When is it safe to send confidential information over the Internet? The only time you should transmit private information, such as credit card numbers and banking information, is when you can establish a secure connection using a standard security protocol called Secure Sockets Layer (SSL) over HTTP.

To make an SSL connection with IE5, the Web server must include credentials from a designated certifying authority. The URL for a secure connection uses a special prefix (`https://`), and Internet Explorer includes two important indications that you're about to connect securely: You see a warning dialog box each time you begin or end a secure connection, as well as a Padlock icon in the status bar.

After you negotiate a secure connection, every bit of data is encrypted before sending and decrypted at the receiving end; only your machine and the secure server have the keys required to decode the encrypted packets. Because of the extra processing time on either end, loading HTML pages over an SSL connection takes longer than the typical upload or download.

For more information on certificates for commercial Web servers, visit

`http://digitalid.verisign.com/server/index.html`

Although the built-in encryption capabilities of IE5 are powerful, one option can help you ensure even greater security. Because of United States government export restrictions, the default encryption software uses 40-bit keys to scramble data before transmission. That technology makes the data difficult to decode, but a determined hacker can break 40-bit encryption in relatively short order. A much more powerful version of the encryption engine uses 128-bit keys that are nearly impossible to crack; some banks and brokerage firms require the stronger encryption capabilities before you can access personal financial information online.

At this writing, the 128-bit security software is available only in the United States and Canada, although Microsoft has won permission to make this code available through banks and financial institutions overseas as well. To check which version you have, find a file called SCHANNEL.DLL, normally stored in the \Windows\System folder. Right-click on the file icon and choose Properties; then inspect the Version tab, as in Figure 29.20.

The weaker, 40-bit encryption code includes the words Export Version on the Properties tab. The stronger 128-bit security engine includes the label US and Canada Use Only. You can download the 128-bit upgrade, as long as you do so from a machine that is physically located within the United States or Canada. You can find complete download instructions for the 128-bit upgrade at

`http://www.microsoft.com/ie/`

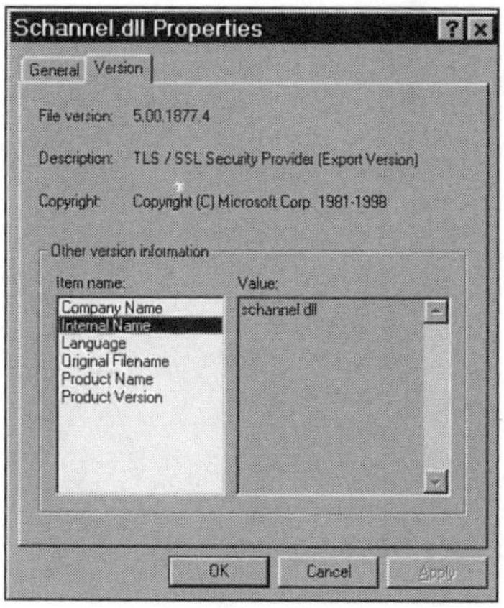

Figure 29.20
If your copy of Internet Explorer includes the Export version of this security code, your commercial transactions are not as safe as they could be.

HOW SAFE ARE COOKIES?

When you view a page in your Web browser, some servers give you more than you asked for; quietly, without your knowledge, they record information about you and your actions in a hidden file called a *cookie*. In more formal terms, these data stores are called *client-side persistent data*, and they offer a simple way for a Web server to keep track of your actions. There are dozens of legitimate uses for cookies: Commercial Web sites use them to keep track of items as you fill your online shopping basket; the *New York Times* Web site stores your username and password so you can log in automatically; still other sites deliver pages tailored to your interests, based on information you've entered in a Web-based form.

The first time you access a cookie-enabled server, the server creates a new cookie file in the Temporary Internet Files folder. That record contains the server's domain name, an expiration date, some security information, and any information the Webmaster chooses to store about the current page request. When you revisit that page (or access another page on the same site), the server can read and update information in the cookie record. Although information stored in each cookie is in plain-text format, most sites use codes, making it nearly impossible to decipher exactly what's stored there.

If you're troubled at the thought of inadvertently sharing personal information with a Web site, you can disable cookies completely, or you can direct Internet Explorer to ask your permission before setting a cookie. To control your cookie collection, follow these steps:

1. Open the Internet Properties dialog box and select the Security tab.

2. Select one of the four Web content zones, for example, the Internet zone, and click on the Custom Level button.

3. Scroll through the list of items in the Security Settings dialog box and find the Cookies item (see Figure 29.21).

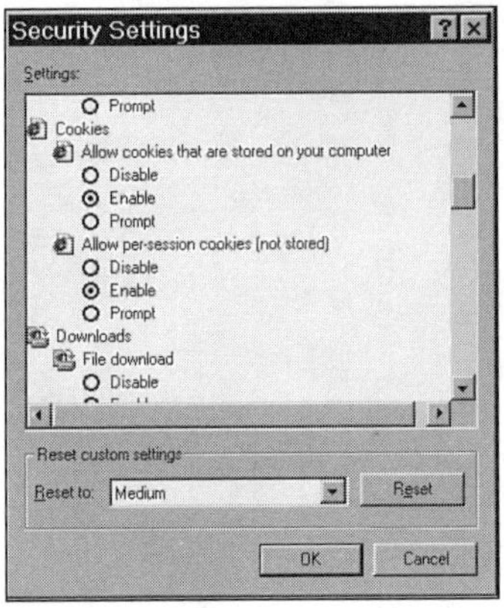

Figure 29.21
If you prefer not to share personal information with Web sites using hidden cookie files, change this default option.

4. Choose the option you prefer: Allow Cookies That Are Stored on Your Computer or Allow Per-Session Cookies (Not Stored). For either option you can choose disable, enable, or prompt.

5. Click OK to record the new security settings.

Should you be overly concerned about cookies? The privacy risks are minimal, thanks to strict security controls built into your Web browser that limit what the server can and cannot do with cookies. They can't be used to retrieve information from your hard disk or your network; in fact, a server can retrieve information only from a cookie that it or another server in its domain created. A cookie can track your movements only within a given site; it can't tell a server where you came from or where you're going next.

Many Web designers set cookies simply because that's the default for the server software they use; the information they collect gathers dust, digitally speaking. So, when you ask Internet Explorer to prompt you before accepting a cookie, be prepared for a barrage of dialog boxes like the one in Figure 29.22. Try saying no; most Web sites work properly without cookies.

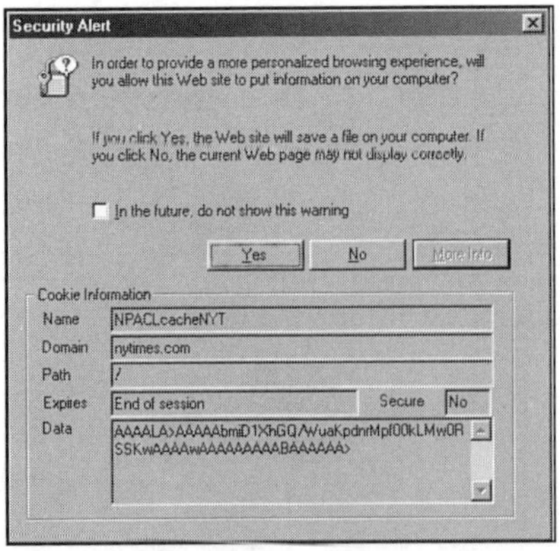

Figure 29.22
You can ask Internet Explorer to warn you before it accepts a cookie; click the More Info button to see the contents of the proposed cookie file, as shown here.

SIMPLIFYING ONLINE PURCHASES WITH MICROSOFT WALLET

IE5 enables you to conduct safe transactions over the Internet without having to reenter your credit card and address information each time. The Microsoft Wallet lets you store address and credit card information in encrypted form on your hard disk. When you encounter a Web site that allows payments from the Microsoft Wallet, you select a credit card and address from the lists you created earlier and then complete the transaction.

You can add multiple addresses and credit card entries to the Address Selector and Payment Selector lists. By entering separate home and work addresses, for example, as in Figure 29.23, you can order products and services for shipment to either address.

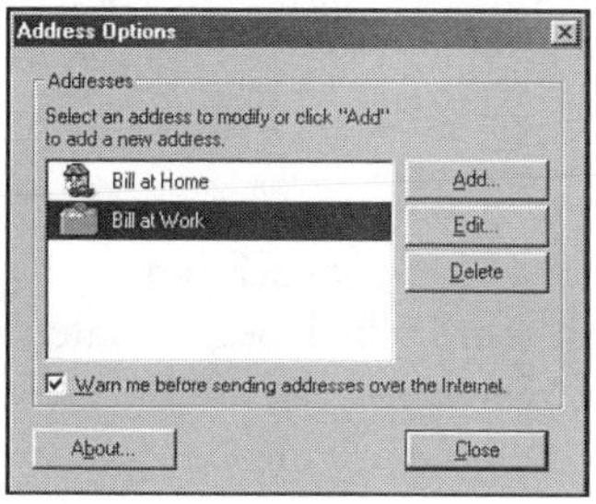

Figure 29.23
With multiple entries in the Microsoft Wallet Address Selector, you can easily tell a merchant where you want to receive goods you order over the Internet.

To add credit card information to the Payment Selector, follow these steps:

1. Choose View, Internet Options. Click the Content tab.

2. Click the Payments button to open the Payment Options dialog box.

3. Click the Add button and choose a payment method—Visa, MasterCard, American Express, or Discover—from the drop-down list.

4. Use the wizard (see Figure 29.24) to enter credit card information, select a billing address (or create a new address entry), and protect the information with a password.

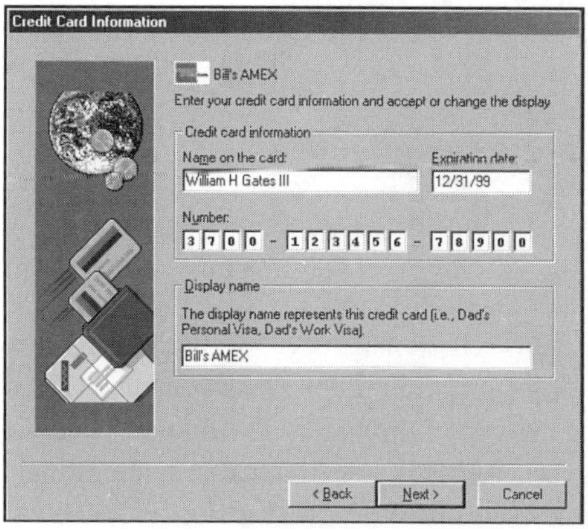

Figure 29.24
The display name you enter here identifies this card when you use the Microsoft Wallet. The following screen lets you protect this information with a password.

5. To add another credit card, repeat steps 3 and 4.

6. Click Close to exit the Payment Options dialog box.

Note that address information is not encrypted; anyone with access to your computer can view, edit, or delete this information. Credit card details, on the other hand, are password protected; if you forget your password, you have to delete the entry from the Payment Selector and then reenter the information.

CONTROLLING ACCESS TO UNDESIRABLE CONTENT

Not every site on the Internet is worth visiting. Some, in fact, are downright offensive. That situation can present a problem at home, where children run the risk of accidentally stumbling across depictions of sex, violence, and other inappropriate content. It's also potentially a problem at the office, where offensive or inappropriate content can drain productivity and expose a corporation to legal liability in the form of sexual harassment suits.

Internet Explorer includes a feature called the Content Advisor, which uses an industrywide rating system called Recreational Software Advisory Council rating service for the Internet (RSACi). This rating system can be used to restrict the types of content that can be displayed within the borders of your browser. Before you can use the Content Advisor, you have to enable it: Choose View, Internet Options, click the Content tab, and click the Enable button. You have to enter a supervisor's password before continuing. After you've handled those housekeeping chores, you see the main Content Advisor window, shown in Figure 29.25.

Figure 29.25
Use the Content Advisor's ratings system to restrict access to Web sites that contain unacceptable content.

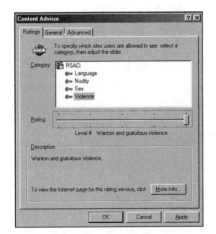

The Content Advisor interface is self-explanatory: You use slider controls to define acceptable levels of sex, violence, language, and nudity. After you click OK, only sites whose ratings match your settings are allowed in the browser window. When you implement the RSACi rating system, users can view only sites that carry some rating. Therefore, if a site does not have a RSACi rating, you cannot access that site.

To find out how to use the Content Advisor without excluding unrated pages, see "Limited Internet Access" in the "Troubleshooting" section at the end of this chapter.

Surprisingly, many adult sites adhere to the rating system, and an increasing number of mainstream business sites have added the necessary HTML tags to their sites as well. However, many mainstream business sites don't use these ratings; as a result, you probably want to avoid setting the option to restrict sites that are not rated.

TROUBLESHOOTING

LIMITED INTERNET ACCESS

I'm connected to a corporate network, and some or all the options described in this chapter are unavailable?

That's usually a sign that the network administrator has used Microsoft's Internet Explorer Administration Kit to enforce security policies from a central server. In that case, most security settings (and many other options, for that matter) are grayed out and inaccessible. See your network administrator if you need to change one of these settings.

I cannot view a Web page that has no RSACi rating.

If you cannot view a Web page or site because you have enabled the Content Advisor and the site you want to view has no RSACi rating, here's a simple solution. From Internet Explorer, Choose View, Internet Options; click the Content tab; and click the Settings button. Choose the General tab and place a check in the Users Can See Sites That Have No Rating check box. Now you can control the sites visited by employees or family members without denying them access to sites that are not rated.

CHAPTER 30

OFFLINE FAVORITES AND THE ACTIVE DESKTOP

In this chapter

ADDING WEB CONTENT TO THE ACTIVE DESKTOP

The Active Desktop represents a key change to the Windows interface. Whereas the classic Windows 95 interface uses the desktop simply as a holding area for icons, the Active Desktop treats the entire Windows desktop as if it were a Web page. You can still store icons there, but you can also add live Web pages, components written in Hypertext Markup Language (HTML), ActiveX controls, and Java applets. To see the Active Desktop in operation, look at Figure 30.1.

Figure 30.1
Add live Web content, including the headline and stock tickers shown here, to the Active Desktop.

Note

Don't confuse the Active Desktop with the Windows Desktop Update. The Windows Desktop Update, standard in Windows 98, makes sweeping changes to the Start menu, taskbar, Explorer, and other parts of the Windows interface. The Windows Desktop Update offers a number of options, including the choice of Web-style single-click navigation or the traditional double-click style. The Active Desktop is one choice in the Windows Desktop Update, but even if you choose to disable Web-based content on the desktop, the other changes in the Windows Desktop Update remain in place.

When you choose Web style as your preferred interface, the Active Desktop is automatically enabled. If you choose Classic style, on the other hand, the Active Desktop is automatically disabled, and your desktop looks and acts like Windows 95.

→ To learn more about changing the look of browsing, **see** "Choosing a Browsing Style," **p. 70**.

You can enable or disable the Active Desktop at any time, regardless of the navigation style you've chosen. Follow these steps:

1. Right-click on any empty space on the desktop and choose <u>A</u>ctive Desktop from the shortcut menu.

2. To enable or disable the Active Desktop, select the View as <u>W</u>eb Page option. A check mark appears in front of this menu choice when the Active Desktop is enabled.

3. To hide or show individual Web items, select <u>A</u>ctive Desktop, <u>C</u>ustomize My Desktop. Uncheck items on the Web tab of the Display Properties dialog box to prevent them from displaying on the Active Desktop. Restore an item's check mark to once again show it on the Active Desktop.

PART
V

CH
30

Tip #194	If you have added Web pages to your desktop and you want to take a quick look while you are still working within another application, use the Show Desktop button on the Quick Launch toolbar. Windows minimizes all applications you are running and exposes the information on your desktop.

USING AN HTML PAGE AS YOUR DESKTOP

If you're a skilled Web page designer, creating a custom page that organizes essential information and links is a trivial task. In corporate settings, using a standard HTML-based background page can be an excellent way to ensure that every user has access to the same crucial information on the intranet. Windows 98 allows you to specify an HTML page as the desktop background, just as previous versions of Windows allowed you to use a graphics image as wallpaper.

You can use any HTML editor, including *FrontPage Express (page 560)*, to create your background page. Think of this page as the base layer of the Active Desktop: Standard desktop icons sit on top of this layer, and you can add other Web elements as well. The HTML page you use as your Windows background can include hyperlinks, graphics (including a company logo), tables, HTML components, and ActiveX controls.

→ For more information on setting up your desktop, **see** "Using Backgrounds," **p. 729**.

After you create the background page, save it to local or network storage. To begin using the page as your desktop background, follow these steps:

1. Right-click on any empty space on the desktop and choose <u>P</u>roperties.

2. In the Display Properties dialog box, click the Background tab (see Figure 30.2).

3. Click the <u>B</u>rowse button to display the Browse dialog box. Select the HTML file you want to use as the desktop and then click <u>O</u>pen.

4. Click <u>A</u>pply to see your new background immediately.

5. Click OK to close the Display Properties dialog box.

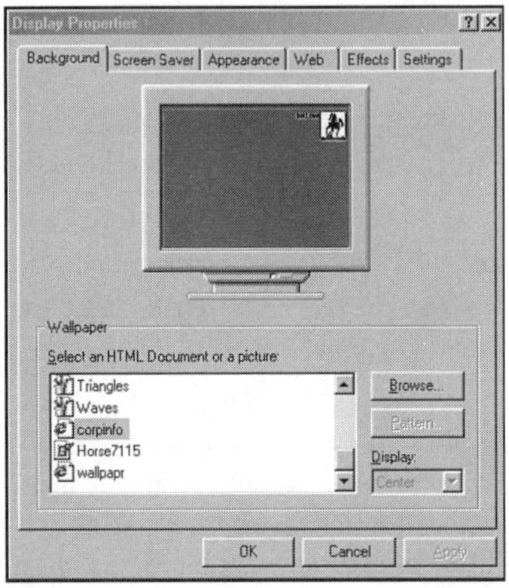

Figure 30.2
Create a custom Web page and use it in place of wallpaper to make a truly custom interface.

Tip #195

If you prefer to see only your custom background when you view the Active Desktop, open the Display Properties dialog box, click the Effects tab, and choose Hide Icons When the Desktop Is Viewed as a Web Page. To switch between the Active Desktop and the desktop icons, right-click any empty space on the desktop, choose Active Desktop from the shortcut menu, and enable or disable the View as Web Page choice.

DISPLAYING OBJECTS ON THE ACTIVE DESKTOP

Enabling the Active Desktop lets you use the Windows desktop to display a wide variety of content. You can add

- An HTML page as the Windows background; unlike wallpaper, this background can contain text, hyperlinks, images, and HTML code.
- One or more Web pages, each in its own self-contained region.
- Web components, including ActiveX controls and Java applets.
- Active Channels, which let you download prepackaged collections of Web content for offline browsing.
- Pictures, stored locally or from a Web server.

ADDING A NEW WEB PAGE TO THE ACTIVE DESKTOP

Before adding a Web page to the Active Desktop, create an Internet shortcut to the page. Then follow these steps:

1. Right-click any empty space on the desktop and choose Properties from the shortcut menu. The Display Properties dialog box appears. Select the Web tab to display the dialog box shown in Figure 30.3.

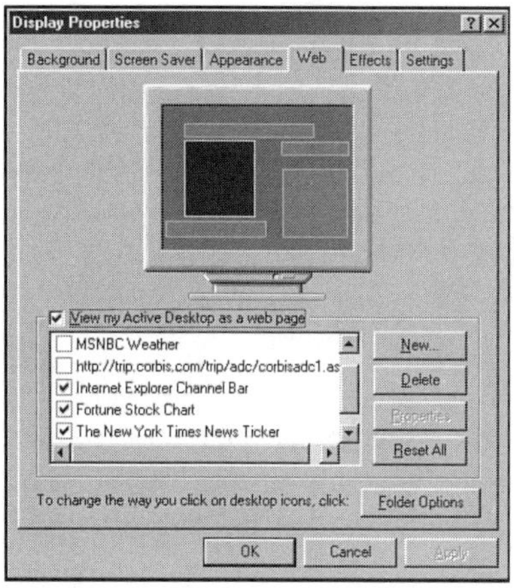

Figure 30.3
Enter a filename or Web address to add pictures or entire Web pages to your Active Desktop.

2. Click the New button. (Choose No if you're prompted to connect to Microsoft's gallery of Active Desktop components.)

3. If you know the exact filename or uniform resource locator (URL) of the item you want to add, enter it; otherwise, click the Browse button.

4. The Browse dialog box displays only files you can add to the Active Desktop—typically images and Internet shortcuts. Select the item you want to add and click Open.

5. Click OK. If you entered an Internet shortcut, you see the dialog box shown in Figure 30.4. Click the Customize Subscription button if you need to enter a password or reschedule updates. Click OK to continue.

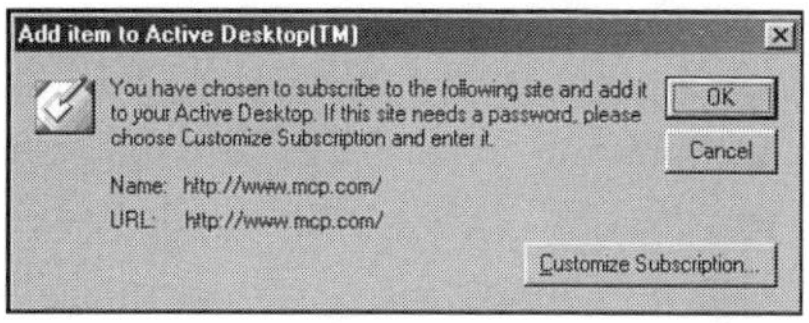

Figure 30.4
Use the Customize Subscription button to customize login and update options for Web pages on the Active Desktop.

6. The new object appears in the list at the bottom of the Web tab. Note that the screen display at the top of the dialog box shows the approximate position of each desktop item. Click Apply to display the new item and add another. Click OK to save your changes and close the dialog box.

Tip #196

If you like shortcuts, here's an easier way to add a new element to the Active Desktop: First, view the Web page or open the graphics file in the browser window; size the window so you can see a portion of the desktop. To add a Web page, hold down the right mouse

continues

continued

button and drag the icon from the left of the address onto the desktop. To add a picture to the Active Desktop, right-drag the image onto the desktop. Choose Create Active Desktop Item (or Image) Here. In fact, if you are viewing a page that has an entry link page that you want to add to your Offline Favorites, such as online banking, drag the link graphic from the page to your desktop and you will be prompted to set up a subscription. You then have the option of entering password information for the secure site. However, be sure you have a physically secure system if you choose to enter password information. Otherwise, anyone can access your personal information with one click of the mouse on your desktop.

To move or resize objects on the Active Desktop, let the mouse pointer hover over the object until a gray border appears around the object. Click on the thick bar at the top of the object and drag it to a new location. Use the borders to resize the window. Scrollbars appear if the object is larger than the window you created.

PLACING A PICTURE ON THE ACTIVE DESKTOP

The Classic Windows 95 interface lets you add one graphic, centered or tiled, as wallpaper on the Windows desktop. Using the Active Desktop, you can add multiple pictures to the desktop and rearrange them as you see fit. You can use saved image files, such as a family picture or a postcard of your favorite tropical resort. Or you can select a Web-based image that is regularly updated, such as a weather or traffic map.

Note

The Active Desktop supports three standard graphics file formats: Windows Bitmap (BMP), GIF, and JPEG File Interchange Format (JPEG). GIF and JPEG are the most common graphics formats on the Internet.

For photographs and other images that remain static, your best strategy is to create the Active Desktop item from a file stored on your local drive. Linking to a graphics file on a Web site forces the browser to try to update the file for no good reason. To save an image you find on a Web page, right-click on the image and choose Save Picture As from the shortcut menu. Give the picture a meaningful name and store it where you can find it later.

→ To find out more about saving images from Web pages, **see** "Saving and Editing Web Pages," **p. 603**.

Caution

Images and other original elements on most Web sites are protected by copyright. Displaying an image file on your personal desktop is generally considered acceptable, but reusing a copyrighted graphic on a commercial Web site without permission could land you in court.

ADDING A COMPONENT TO THE ACTIVE DESKTOP

Unlike Web pages, which sometimes have to be forced into service as an Active Desktop object, components are made for this very purpose. A component can be a simple scrap of

HTML, or it can include an ActiveX control or a Java applet. Some components are actually miniprograms you can customize to match your own preferences.

→ For more on securing against different types of Web-based applications, **see** "Restricting ActiveX Controls," **p. 621**, and "Limiting Java Applets," **p. 626**.

Microsoft's Active Desktop Gallery contains an assortment of interesting desktop components, including a useful search box, stock tickers, and several clocks. Browse the entire collection at

```
http://www.microsoft.com/ie/ie40/gallery/gal_main.htm
```

Adding a new component to your Active Desktop is simple. In most cases, the Web page designer includes an Add to Active Desktop button, like the example shown in Figure 30.5. Click this button to download and install the component.

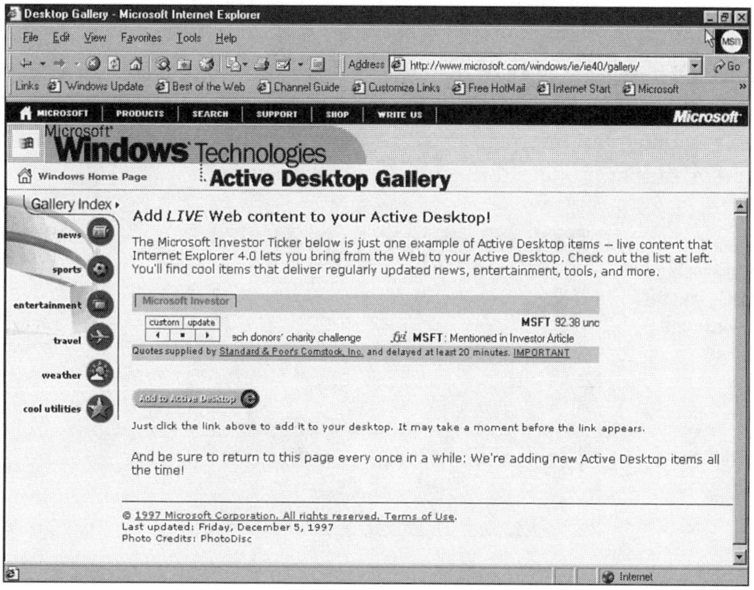

Figure 30.5
Choose a component like this stock ticker from Microsoft's gallery, and then click the Add to Active Desktop button to add the ticker to your desktop.

HIDING, REMOVING, AND EDITING OBJECTS

You don't have to display every installed component, picture, and Web site on your Active Desktop. Hide objects you use infrequently so that they remain available when you need them. To display, hide, remove, or edit objects on the Active Desktop, right-click the desktop and then choose Properties. Select the Web tab in the Display Properties dialog box.

- To hide an object, clear the check box next to its entry. The object remains in your list of installed objects.

- To remove an object from the list, select the object and click Delete. The object is permanently removed from your system.

- To adjust the subscription settings for the object, click the Properties button.

- Click OK to accept your changes.

USING OFFLINE FAVORITES TO DOWNLOAD WEB PAGES

Note

In previous versions of Internet Explorer, offline viewing was referred to as "subscribing," and Offline Favorites were called "subscriptions."

When you subscribe to a Web site by adding it to your Offline Favorites, you instruct Internet Explorer 5.0 (IE5) to regularly visit the site in search of new content. Don't let the term *subscribe* mislead you; there's no fee associated with the process. Offline Favorites are simply a way for you to automatically search for and download content from your favorite sites, without having to be online 24 hours a day, seven days a week.

If you can load a Web page into the browser window, you can subscribe to that page by adding it to your Offline Favorites. In fact, you can add it to your Favorites first, right-click on the URL in your Favorites folder, and choose Make Available Offline from the shortcut menu. This choice invokes the Offline Favorite Wizard (see Figure 30.6). This wizard will help you set up a synchronization schedule for your new Offline Favorite. You can also specify the amount of information to download from the site, although this capability is limited and might not produce the results you're expecting.

Figure 30.6
The Offline Favorite Wizard helps you set up your synchronization schedule.

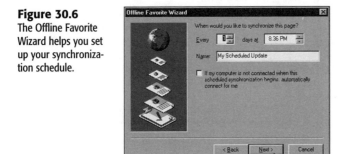

You can also subscribe to Active Channels—prepackaged collections of Web content that include a site map and a recommended schedule for updates. With the help of Channel Definition Format (CDF) files, a Webmaster can assemble just the information you need and not a page more.

Caution

With the Offline Favorite Wizard, you can instruct the browser to retrieve a given page and all pages linked to it, to a maximum depth of three pages. On Web sites that contain large collections of files, "Web crawling" can cause an unacceptable performance hit. For this reason, some sites ban WebCrawlers, and your offline browsing at these sites won't synchronize correctly.

ADDING WEB SITES AS OFFLINE FAVORITES

To add a Web site to your Offline Favorites, you start by adding it to your Favorites list. Follow these steps:

1. Open the Web page in the Browser window.

2. Choose Favorites, Add to Favorites (see Figure 30.7). Rename the shortcut, if you wish, and choose a folder. Note that the Add Favorite dialog box gives you two choices: You can simply create a shortcut in the Favorites list or you can check the Make Available Offline box to add the site as an Offline Favorite.

Figure 30.7
Check the Make Available Offline box to add a Web page to your Offline Favorites list.

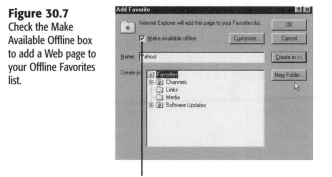

Make Available Offline box

3. Default settings download only the specified page; the update is scheduled daily at 1:00 a.m. To accept these settings, click OK and skip all remaining steps.

4. If the Web site you've selected requires a password for access or if you want to adjust any other update properties, click the Customize button. That step launches the Offline Favorite Wizard, shown in Figure 30.8.

Figure 30.8
To customize your options, follow the wizard's prompts.

5. The wizard walks you through the process of setting four subscription options (for further details on each of these options, see the following section):

- Download pages linked to the specified page. Choose a number between 1 and 3.

- Adjust the synchronization schedule IE5 uses to update this Web page. Choose daily, weekly, monthly, or custom options. To synchronize on demand, select Only When I Choose Synchronize from the Tools menu.

- Enter a username and password if the site requires it.

6. When you finish with the Offline Favorite Wizard, click Finish to add the entry to your Offline Favorites list.

MANAGING OFFLINE FAVORITES

Internet Explorer maintains your list of subscribed sites in the \Windows\ Offline Web Pages folder. Right-click on the offline Web page of your choice and choose Properties to view details, edit update schedules, remove the page from your Offline Favorites, or send email to tell you when Web site content changes (see Figure 30.9). You can even tell IE5 not to download images, sound and video, or ActiveX to save time on your updates.

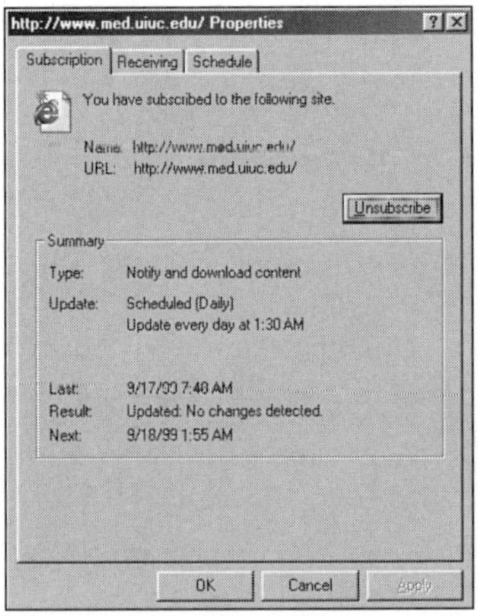

Figure 30.9
The Properties dialog box gives you a chance to edit your Offline Favorites.

CUSTOMIZING SYNCHRONIZATION SCHEDULES

By default, each Offline Favorite downloads one page, once a day, around 1:00 a.m. For most Offline Favorites, you probably want to change those defaults. Most often, you want to increase the amount of content that IE5 downloads as well as the frequency of the update schedule.

You can adjust the following options when you create the schedule, using the Offline Favorite Wizard, or you can change the schedule properties afterwards, through the Offline Web Pages folder, as discussed in the preceding section.

CONTROLLING THE SIZE AND DEPTH OF OFFLINE FAVORITES

Chances are you'll want to see more than one page for your favorite Web sites. On the front page of a newspaper like the *Los Angeles Times*, for example, you usually find links to the day's top stories. When you go to those pages, you find links to still more stories.

As part of the settings for each Offline Favorite, you can tell IE5 to follow all the links on the subscribed page. For Offline Favorites you plan to read offline, it's crucial that you enter a number large enough to gather the information you need. But it's also important to monitor the amount of material that IE5 will have to download. The number of pages needing updating can increase dramatically with each additional layer. If you don't set the right limits when setting up an Offline Favorite, the downloaded content might consume all the space in your Temporary Internet Files folder.

Tip #197	If you typically read only one portion of a Web site, don't start at the site's home page; instead, browse to the page you actually view the most and choose to add it instead. It is best to pick the site that contains any links you plan to use. On highly structured sites, this page might be deep within the site. Do the best you can to avoid pages you would not actually view or need. Also, you might not be able to directly view an Active Server Pages (ASP) page that requires dynamic input every time you access that site or a page that was created in response to a query that will change with every changed request for information.

To define exactly which pages IE5 downloads with each update, follow these steps:

1. Right-click the site's entry in the Offline Web Pages folder in the Windows directory and then choose Properties.

2. Select the Download tab. You see a dialog box like the one in Figure 30.10, with the lower option selected in the Subscription Type box.

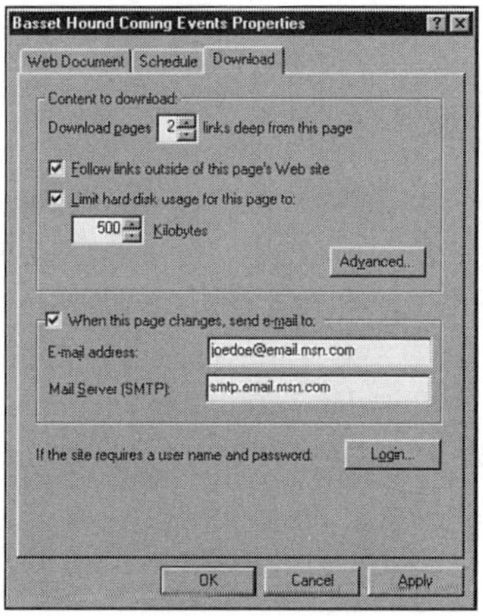

Figure 30.10
If you have selected a Favorite for offline viewing, click the Advanced button to adjust how much content to retrieve.

3. To download pages linked to the main page of your Offline Favorite, adjust the Download Linked Pages option. Enter a number between 1 and 3. To restrict the download to pages on the main site, clear the check box labeled Follow Links Outside of This Page's Web Site.

4. To restrict the total amount of content downloaded with each update, check the box Limit Hard-Disk Usage for This Page To *x* Kilobytes. Enter a limit in kilobytes (the default is 500KB).

5. Click the Advanced button. The Advanced Download Options dialog box (see Figure 30.11) appears. To further limit downloads, review the list of options in the center of the dialog box. By default, IE5 gathers image files, ActiveX controls, and Java applets, but does not retrieve sound and video files.

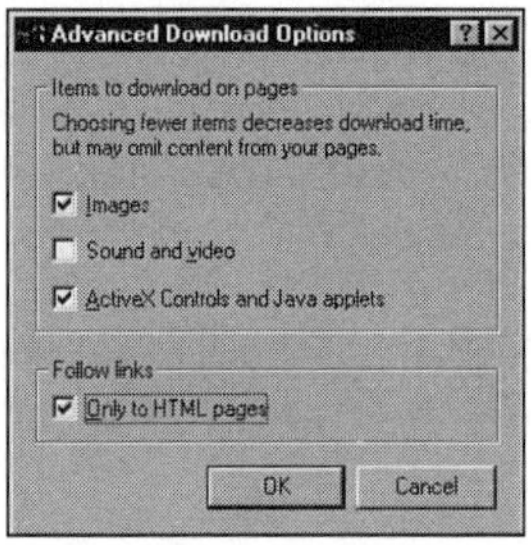

Figure 30.11
Balance these options to download the right amount of content without consuming too much disk space.

Caution

Many Web pages use images to help with navigation and to supply information. Don't restrict image downloads unless you're certain a site will be useful in text-only mode.

6. Click OK or select another tab to further customize the subscription (offline favorite update).

SPECIFYING A FORMAT FOR UPDATE NOTIFICATIONS

How do you know when a change occurs in a Web site in your Offline Favorites? Look at any Internet shortcut, on the desktop, in the Favorites bar, or in the Channel bar. A red gleam in the upper-left corner of an icon means there's new content.

If you prefer a more emphatic notice, ask IE5 to send you an email message every time it notices a change in a Web site in your Offline Favorites. The email message can be a simple notice with a hyperlink, or the message can contain a copy of the updated HTML page.

To set up email updates, follow these steps:

1. Select an entry in the Offline Web Pages folder, right-click, and choose Properties.

2. Click the Download tab.

3. Check the box labeled When This Page Changes, Send Email To. If necessary, change the address and server information.

4. Click OK to close the dialog box and save your changes.

SCHEDULING AUTOMATIC UPDATES

By default, IE5 updates your Offline Favorites once a day, at 1:00 a.m. You can adjust the update interval, or you can set the subscription for manual updates only. You can also specify whether IE5 dials your Internet connection automatically.

To adjust the update schedule, open the Offline Web Pages folder, choose Properties from the shortcut menu, and select the Schedule tab. You see a dialog box like the one in Figure 30.12.

Figure 30.12
Use these options to control how and when IE5 updates your Offline Favorite.

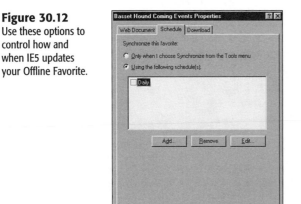

To use a regularly scheduled interval, choose the Using the Following Schedule option and select the appropriate schedule. To add a new schedule, click Add and set up a new schedule. Click the Edit button to adjust the details of the existing schedule. For example, if you subscribe to an online magazine that appears every Friday at midnight, you can tell IE5 to update your Offline Favorite each Friday morning at 5:00 a.m., before you arrive at work.

If you subscribe to a site that rarely changes or one you rarely visit, click the Schedule tab and choose the option Only When I Choose Synchronize from the Tools menu.

Tip #198

Network administrators might be horrified at the thought of thousands of users requesting Web updates on the hour. IE5 attempts to minimize that problem by randomly varying the exact time for each update by a few minutes in either direction. However, with hundreds of users trying to access the network on an hourly basis, you may decide you need to limit the available update intervals. To take maximum control over how users work with IE5, make sure you check the Internet Explorer Administrator's Kit (IEAK), available from Microsoft. IEAK integrates with Window's System Policies and enables you to restrict the choices a user has at the desktop. Conversely, if your administrator has limited your choices in this way, some of these subscription options will not be available to you. For more information about the most current release of IEAK, look here:
`http://ieak.microsoft.com/`.

You can also create a custom schedule, using a dizzying variety of options. For example, if you have a favorite business-oriented site, you can set a subscription to update once an hour, from 8:00 a.m. through 5:00 p.m., every weekday. You can update a subscription every Monday, Wednesday, and Friday. You can even specify that a site update at 9:00 a.m. on the second Tuesday of every other month. When you save a custom schedule, you can reuse the schedule with other Offline Favorites as well.

To create a custom schedule for updates, follow these steps:

1. Choose Tools, Synchronize and then click the Schedule tab.

2. Click the Add button. The Scheduled Synchronization Wizard (see Figure 30.13) starts.

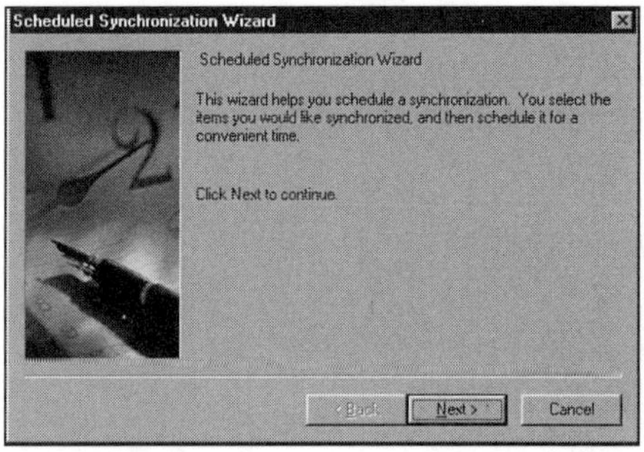

Figure 30.13
The Scheduled Synchronization Wizard helps you create a custom update schedule for your Offline Favorites.

3. Choose the Offline Favorites you want to include in this new schedule. Also, choose how you want to connect to the Internet and whether to connect automatically to complete the update.

4. Choose the day or days on which to run the update. Select Daily, Weekly, or Monthly and adjust the available options that appear to the right.

5. Choose the time or times to perform the update. Options let you repeat the update daily, weekdays, or every specified number of days. Advanced Options even let you repeat the update at intervals throughout the day.

6. Give the schedule a descriptive name and click OK.

7. Click Finish to save your changes.

UPDATING OFFLINE FAVORITES MANUALLY

IE5 lets you manually update all your Offline Favorites with the click of one button. This capability is especially useful if you are about to leave on a trip and you want to make sure your notebook computer contains the most current versions of all your Web Favorites. You can also update an individual site if you know it has new content and you don't want to wait for the next scheduled update.

To manually update all Offline Favorites, follow these steps:

1. Verify that you have a working Internet connection. If necessary, open a Dial-Up Networking connection.

2. Choose Synchronize from the Tools menu.

3. Select one or all pages that you wish to update and click Synchronize.

4. If you have a lengthy list of Offline Favorites to update, the process can take a long time. The Synchronizing dialog box (see Figure 30.14) displays the status of the operation, including any error messages that might appear. To cancel all further updates, click Stop. To skip over one site's update and proceed with the next site, click Skip. Click the Hide button to move this dialog box out of the way and continue working. You can close the Browser window or view other sites while the update process continues.

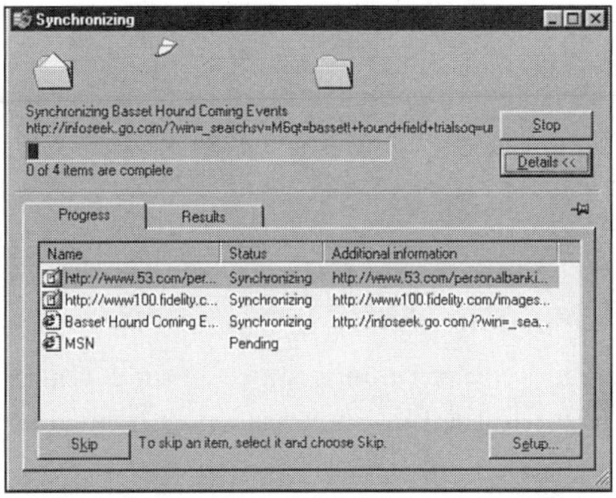

Figure 30.14
If you don't see this full status window, click the Details button.

SUBSCRIBING TO PASSWORD-PROTECTED SITES

Sites like the *Wall Street Journal* (`http://www.wsj.com`) require you to enter a username and password before browsing their sites. If you're using IE5 interactively, you can type the information directly into a login box. When you subscribe to a password-protected site, IE5 lets you include the login information so that you can get the information you're looking for automatically.

You do not have to add the specific page that includes the login screen. You can choose a page above the login screen and specify a depth of delivery that reaches below the login screen. When IE5 reaches the page that requests your user ID and password, IE5 supplies the information and continues updating the page.

To enter a username and password for use for an Offline Favorite, follow these steps:

1. If you are initially creating the subscription, click the Login button. If you are editing an existing subscription, right-click its entry in the Offline Web Pages folder in the Windows directory, and then click Properties. Click the Download tab the Login Options dialog box (see Figure 30.15).

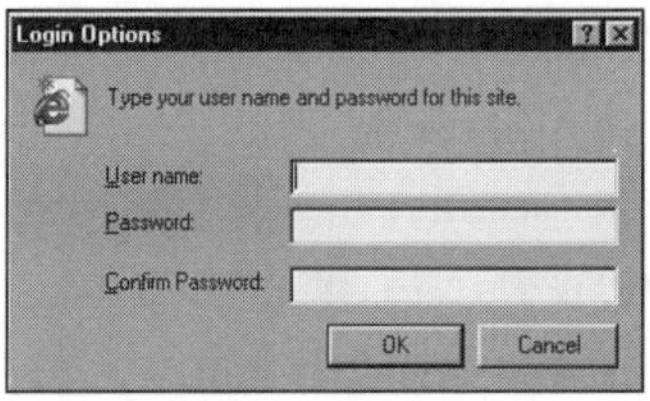

Figure 30.15
Enter login informa-
tion here for IE5 to
gain access to pass-
word-protected sites
when updating an
Offline Favorite.

2. Enter the username and password you use to gain access to the site. Make sure both entries are spelled correctly and that the case (the mix of capital and lowercase letters) is correct.

3. Click OK to return to the Download tab. Click OK again to close the dialog box and save your changes.

After setting up an update to a password-protected site, you should verify that the process works. Update the offline Web page manually; if the update fails because of an incorrect username or password, try logging in manually to make sure the site is working and the information you enter is correct. Then, edit the username and password to match those you've tested.

SPEEDING UP SUBSCRIPTION UPDATES

If you're about to hit the road and you're running short on time, you can dramatically reduce the time it takes to update all the Offline Favorites on your notebook.

Tell IE5 to concentrate on text and ignore large graphics and media files. Note that some sites use images for navigation, and at other sites images might contain important informa-tion; as a result, the pages you end up with when you use this technique might be of limited use. Still, when time is short, you can follow these steps:

1. Open the Offline Web Pages folder in your Windows directory.

2. Right-click on each site you plan to update, choose Properties, and click the Download tab.

3. Click the Advanced button to open the Advanced Download Options dialog box.

4. In the Items to Download box, clear the check mark next to the options labeled Images, Sound and Video, and ActiveX Controls and Java Applets.

5. Repeat steps 2 through 4 for each subscription you plan to update.

6. Select the group of icons to update, right-click, and choose Synchronize.

SUBSCRIBING TO ACTIVE CHANNELS

Channels are prepackaged Offline Favorites. Instead of indiscriminately delivering Web pages to your hard disk, a Webmaster can put together a collection of pages, just as a news-paper publisher assembles a daily paper. When you subscribe to an Active Channel, you download a single file, created by using the CDF. Channel files typically include multiple HTML files, graphics, a map of the Web site (including links to pages not included in the CDF file), and a publisher's recommended schedule for updates.

By default, Windows 98 adds a Channel bar to your desktop, with shortcuts to dozens of brand-name channels. Note that you don't have to subscribe to view the content in a channel.

The Channel bar contains an Internet shortcut that takes you to Microsoft's Active Channel Guide. Browse through this lengthy list by category or search for keywords by using the built-in search button. The Active Channel Guide, shown in Figure 30.16, is updated frequently.

PART
V
CH
30

Figure 30.16
Microsoft maintains this exhaustive list of channels to which you can subscribe.

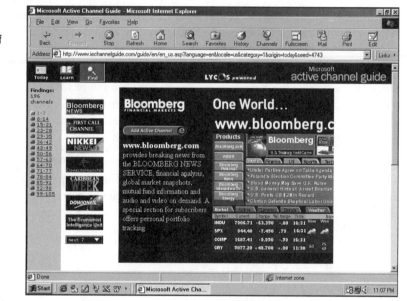

If you inadvertently delete the Channel Guide shortcut from the Channel bar, don't worry. You can find the latest list of Active Channels at

`http://windowsmedia.microsoft.com/`

ADDING A CHANNEL TO THE CHANNEL BAR

Most channels include an Add Active Channel button that enables you to add the channel's shortcut to the Channel bar. When you add a channel to the Channel bar, you typically have the option to subscribe to the channel, using the publisher's recommended schedule or a custom schedule of your choosing; if an Add This Channel button does not appear on the preview pane in the Channel Guide, right-click and choose Subscribe from the site icon at left.

VIEWING CHANNELS

When you click on a shortcut in the Channel bar on the Windows desktop, Internet Explorer opens in Full screen mode, with the Channel bar visible along the left side of the Browser window.

Although the Channel bar in the Browser window includes the same sites as its desktop counterpart, the two bars behave differently. In the browser's bar, for example, the icon for each channel is black and white until the mouse pointer passes over it. When you click on a shortcut, the channel's home page opens in the pane to the right. If the CDF file for that channel includes a site map, clicking the Channel button opens the list of available pages.

Tip #199	You can view channels as ordinary Web pages, as desktop components, or in Full screen mode. To specify whether IE5 should use Full screen mode for all channels, choose View, Internet Options, click the Advanced tab, and check the option labeled Launch Channels in Full Screen Window under the Browsing heading.

Some channels include a Screen saver view as well. You might see this option during the initial Channel setup. To enable, disable, or adjust the Channel screen saver at any time, right-click on the desktop, choose Properties, click the Screen Saver tab, and choose the Channel Screen Saver option.

→ To learn more about screen savers in channels, **see** "Using the Screen Saver," **p. 340**.

When you view a channel in Full screen mode, the Channels bar slides off the screen when you read the page; the bar reappears when you move the pointer to the left edge of the screen. If you're running at a high screen resolution, use the Pushpin icon to lock the Channels bar in place, as we've done in Figure 30.17.

BROWSING CHANNELS OFFLINE

To view Internet connection, choose File, Work Offline. Like all Offline Favorites, Active Channels share the Temporary Internet Files with pages you browse interactively. When the cache fills up, IE5 pitches the oldest pages to make way for the newest ones.

 If you are trying to Work offline, but you cannot browse the desired Web pages in this manner, see "Offline Browsing" in the "Troubleshooting" section at the end of this chapter.

→ To learn more about viewing Web pages while working offline, **see** "Browsing the Web Offline," **p. 599**.

If you encounter frequent error messages when you attempt to update or view Offline Favorites, you might have used all the available space in your Temporary Internet Files folder. To make room for more content, increase the size of the Web cache.

→ For more information on how to manage your browser's cache file, **see** "Managing the Browser's Cache," **p. 581**.

Pushpin icon

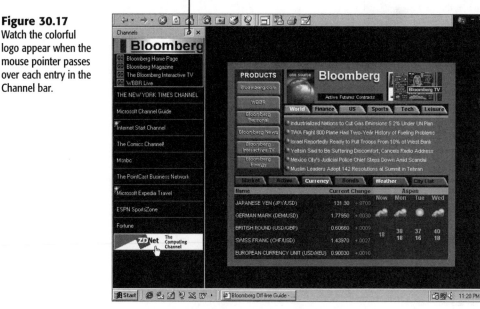

Figure 30.17
Watch the colorful logo appear when the mouse pointer passes over each entry in the Channel bar.

Note

Don't be surprised when you discover that some channels actually provide only a table of contents and links. Although these sites can give you a good idea of what's available when you go back online, you won't find enough information to justify keeping a subscription to this sort of channel.

MANAGING THE CHANNEL BAR

The Channel bar appears on the Desktop when you install Windows 98. It also appears as an Explorer bar within the Browser window when you click the Channels button.

By default, the Channel bar includes built-in shortcuts to channels delivered by some well-known companies, including Disney, America Online, and MSNBC (see Figure 30.18). In addition, shortcuts to categories—news, entertainment, and business, for example—include more shortcuts to additional channels.

Although the Channel bar initially gets a place of honor on the Windows desktop, it's really just another HTML component on the Active Desktop. That means you can customize its look and feel to suit your computing style. After you sample the selection of built-in channels and possibly subscribe to a handful, give your Channel bar a makeover, as we've done in Figure 30.19.

Figure 30.18
Out of the box, the Channel bar includes these preset selections. You can change the collection of shortcuts and rearrange the Channel bar itself.

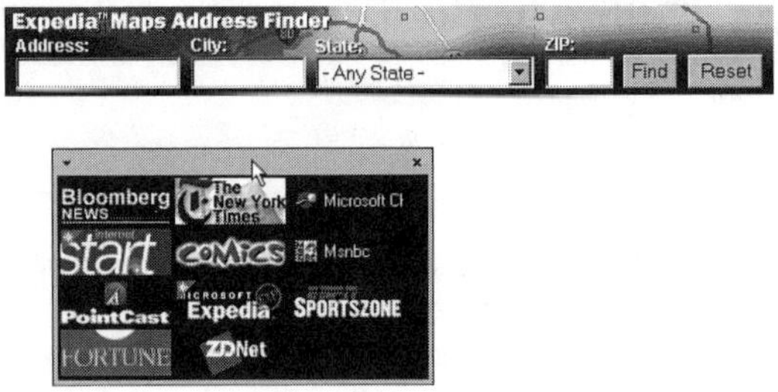

Figure 30.19
After deleting unnecessary channels and changing its size and orientation, this Channel bar looks vastly different from its default settings.

- To move the Channel bar to a different location on the desktop, click on any empty desktop space and then let the mouse pointer hover over the top of the bar until the gray sizing handle pops up. Click and drag to a new location.

- To resize the Channel bar, aim the mouse pointer at the bar and wait for a thin, gray border to appear. Click on any border and drag to change the size and orientation. Note that as the size of the bar changes, shortcuts on the bar reorder themselves automatically.

- To add or delete channels from the bar, right-click on any Channel icon and choose Delete from the shortcut menu.

Caution

Be careful before deleting any of the category icons on the Channel bar. If you've subscribed to a channel within that category, you lose easy access to the channel.

- To rearrange channels on the bar, simply drag them to the location you prefer. Other shortcuts on the bar rearrange themselves automatically.

- To remove the Channel bar from the desktop, let the mouse pointer hover over the top of the bar until the gray sizing handle pops up. Click the X in the top-right corner.

Tip #200

> The Channel bar on the desktop is identical to the one that appears in the Browser window. When you add or remove channels from one, the other changes accordingly. If you'd rather use the Windows desktop for other items, close the Channel bar there and use the Channels button on the Internet Explorer toolbar when you want to work with channels.

TROUBLESHOOTING

OFFLINE BROWSING

I'm attempting to browse a Web page offline, but IE5 cannot display the desired page.

IE5 might not be able to display a page for offline browsing if you have deleted your Temporary Internet Files. IE5 uses the Web pages that have been cached in memory and saved as Temporary Internet Files not only for faster access when you browse online but also for browsing offline. If you have recently run a disk cleanup utility, such as Disk Cleanup in Windows 98 accessories (or you recently deleted Temporary Internet Files), you may have inadvertently deleted the Web pages stored for offline browsing.

One way to prevent this situation is to make a subscription to the pages you want to browse offline and then leave the box unchecked when prompted on whether to delete all subscription content.

If you accidentally delete files you need to do offline browsing, reconnect to the page while online, disconnect from the Internet, and continue to use the Web page left in cache.

SECRETS OF MASTERING THE WINDOWS 98 ENVIRONMENT: UNINSTALLING IE5

Some actions require you to uninstall IE5 before you perform them. These actions include

- Returning to any previous version of Internet Explorer.
- Restoring a Registry (SYSTEM.DAT or USER.DAT) backup that was created in Windows 98 (or 95) before you installed IE5.
- Using a Windows NT Emergency Recovery Disk (ERD), which may have been created before you installed IE5.
- Repairing IE5 does not succeed or does not correct a problem related to IE5 or Windows 98.

Caution

> If you uninstall IE5 and Outlook Express 5, all messages created/received in the IE5 version are removed as well because of the alternative location of mail storage for Outlook Express 5.

To uninstall IE5, follow these steps:

1. Click Start, choose Settings, Control Panel.

2. In Control Panel, double-click Add/Remove Programs and then click the Install/Uninstall tab.

3. In the list of installed programs, choose Microsoft Internet Explorer 5 and then choose Add/Remove.

4. In the Internet Explorer 5 Active Setup dialog box, click Restore the Previous Installation of Internet Explorer. Then, choose Advanced to specify any additional components you want to remove.

5. Click OK. The Internet Explorer 5 Setup screen appears, and the Setup Wizard begins.

6. Click OK to restore the previous version of Internet Explorer. You are prompted to verify that you do want to restore the previous version. Click Yes to continue with the uninstall process.

7. When the uninstall is complete, you are prompted to restart your computer. Click Restart Windows to complete the uninstall of IE5.

After you uninstall IE5, the following changes may be apparent:

- Some user settings have returned to the operating system defaults.

- Any certificates obtained after you installed IE5 are missing. (If new certificates were added after installing Internet Explorer 5, a warning dialog box appears during the uninstall process, indicating that you are about to lose the certificates if you proceed. You are then given the option of continuing to uninstall or to cancel the process and manually export the new certificates to a file for later inclusion. Certificates that were obtained prior to installing Internet Explorer 5 are not removed.)

- Some components might not have been uninstalled. If additional components need to be uninstalled, you must remove them individually by using Add/Remove Programs in Control Panel.

- If you installed other programs after installing IE5, some of those programs might no longer work properly. In this case, you must reinstall the affected programs.

- Some Internet icons may remain on the toolbars in other programs, such as Microsoft Word, but may no longer work properly.

CHAPTER 31

USING OUTLOOK EXPRESS

In this chapter

SHOULD YOU SWITCH TO OUTLOOK EXPRESS?

Outlook Express, the default email client software in Windows 98, includes the basic tools you need to compose, send, and receive mail over the Internet. It uses this basic email interface for a second purpose as well: to let you read and participate in threaded discussions on Internet newsgroups. If you originally set up an email account using the email software included with Windows 95, you have an important decision to make when you upgrade: Should you stick with your old mail software, or should you switch to Outlook Express?

Starting with the first release of Windows 95, every version of Windows has included a desktop icon labeled Inbox. In the original version of Windows 95, this icon launched a program called the Exchange Inbox. Microsoft promised that this "universal inbox" would be capable of storing email from just about anywhere, as well as faxes, voice mail, and other types of data. If you've used Exchange Inbox, though, you know it's hard to configure, slow, and notoriously buggy; the fax components in particular are a usability nightmare.

In the years since the original release of Windows 95, Microsoft has updated the Exchange Inbox program slightly. The new version was renamed Windows Messaging. The update fixed several bugs (and added a few new glitches), and the new name was supposed to help dispel confusion with Microsoft Exchange Server, Microsoft's mail server package for businesses.

Although the Windows Messaging application is included with Windows 98, the Inbox icon no longer appears automatically on the desktop and Microsoft no longer recommends that you install it. The program is now officially an "orphan," replaced by the new Windows default mail program, Outlook Express. Microsoft also sells a full-featured mail package called Outlook 2000.

If you currently use Exchange Inbox or *Windows Messaging*, should you switch to Outlook Express? The answer depends on how the rest of your mail system works.

- If you have been using Exchange Inbox or Windows Messaging to gather email exclusively through industry-standard Internet mail servers, you should switch to Outlook Express. It's simple to set up, much easier to use, and does a superb job of handling Internet mail.

- If you send and receive email using a Microsoft Exchange server on a corporate network, you must use an Exchange-compatible client program. Acceptable options include the Exchange Inbox, Windows Messaging, Outlook 2000 (included with Microsoft Office 2000), or Outlook 2000. Outlook Express 5 is an option if your Exchange Server uses the *Internet Message Access Protocol (IMAP)* format or *Post Office Protocol (POP3)*.

- Microsoft Fax and another MAPI-compatible applications do not work with Outlook Express. (*MAPI* stands for *Messaging Application Program Interface*, a Microsoft standard for communication between email applications. Outlook Express supports only Simple MAPI, which allows programs like Word and Excel to use Outlook Express for sending messages.) For full MAPI compatibility, you must use an Exchange-compatible mail client.

→ To learn more about MAPI, see Appendix A,"Using Windows Messaging and Microsoft Fax," **p. 865**.

STARTING OUTLOOK EXPRESS

When you install Windows 98, you also install Outlook Express; you cannot avoid adding Outlook Express on initial setup. You, however, can uninstall the program if you decide you prefer other mail and news clients. (To uninstall Outlook Express, open the Add/Remove Programs option in the Control Panel, click the Install/Uninstall tab, choose Outlook Express 5, and click the Add/Remove button.)

A shortcut to Outlook Express 5 resides on the Quick Launch portion of the taskbar. Also, you can find Outlook Express 5 by clicking the Start button and choosing Programs. It is in the main list of folders and programs.

Outlook Express 5 imports preferences already configured by past Microsoft Mail clients and has eliminated the need to prompt you to select a location for storing data files. Outlook Express automatically stores your files under the Program Files\Outlook Express directory if you have an existing Outlook Express 4.x account and creates a folder in the root directory (that is, Windows) under Application Data\Identities*<a custom unique identifier is the label of your folder>*. This folder stores your mail and news data and manages multiple mail account files if you choose to create multiple Identities in Outlook Express (so that multiple users can access their mail through the same application without having to shut down the computer or lose an Internet connection).

→ For more information on user profiles, **see** "Establishing Custom Settings for Each User," **p. 322**.

If you want to move these data files after setting up Outlook Express for the first time, you must first use Windows Explorer to move all data folders, open the Registry Editor, find HKEY_CURRENT_USER\Software\Microsoft\Outlook Express, double-click on the Store Root value, and change that value to reflect the new location.

> **Caution**
>
> Think twice before using the Registry Editor and always make a backup. Incorrectly editing the Windows Registry can result in data loss and can cause programs not to start or not to run properly.

→ To learn about backing up and recovering the Registry, **see** "Backing Up the Windows Registry," **p. 491**.

After you configure Outlook Express, running the program takes you to the start page (see Figure 31.1), which lets you move quickly between your email, newsgroups, and contacts.

> **Tip #201**
>
> If you are comfortable with the choices available in Outlook Express, you can bypass the start page and enter directly into your inbox. Choose Tools, Options; click the General tab; and check the box labeled When Starting, Go Directly to My Inbox Folder. Now, when Outlook Express opens, it automatically opens into your inbox. This option is also available at the bottom of the Outlook Express 5 start page.

PART
V

CH
31

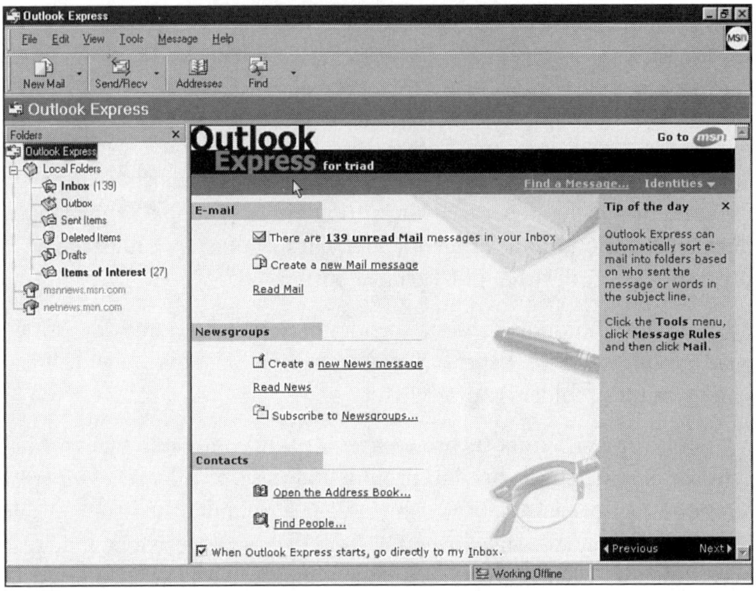

Figure 31.1
From this start page, you can jump to your email inbox, follow threaded discussions on an Internet newsgroup, or search for address information in your list of contacts.

CONFIGURING OUTLOOK EXPRESS

Before you can use Outlook Express to send and receive email, you must supply some basic configuration information. At a minimum, you have to enter the name and type of the mail server that stores and forwards your messages, along with the username and email address associated with your mail account. Before you can access newsgroups with Outlook Express, you need to enter similar configuration information, including your username and email address as well as the name of the news server you plan to use.

The *Internet Connection Wizard* handles all Outlook Express setup details, although you can also configure accounts manually. If you did not use the wizard when you first set up Internet Explorer 5.0 (IE5) or if you skipped the mail and news steps, Outlook Express 5 allows you to add new accounts by choosing Tools, Accounts and then selecting the Add button. The Add button gives you a choice between adding a new Mail, News, or Directory Services Account through an Internet Connection Wizard specific to each function.

If you receive Internet mail from multiple sources—from a corporate server and a personal account with an Internet service provider (ISP), for example—you need to establish separate Outlook Express mail accounts for each one. Each news server requires its own news account as well. There's no limit to the number of mail and news accounts you can set up in Outlook Express.

SETTING UP A DEFAULT MAIL ACCOUNT

When you start Outlook Express for the first time, the program prompts you to set up a default mail account.

Follow the wizard's prompts to enter the following information:

- Your name—This entry is the display name that appears in the From field when you send a message. Most people enter their real name; you may want to add a company affiliation or other information to help mail recipients identify you more readily.

- Your email address—When recipients reply to messages you send, their mail software uses this address.

- Mail server information—As Figure 31.2 shows, you must fill in addresses for incoming and outgoing mail servers even if a single server does both jobs. Be sure to specify the mail protocol your incoming server uses: POP3 (the default setting), or IMAP, or Hypertext Transfer Protocol (HTTP).

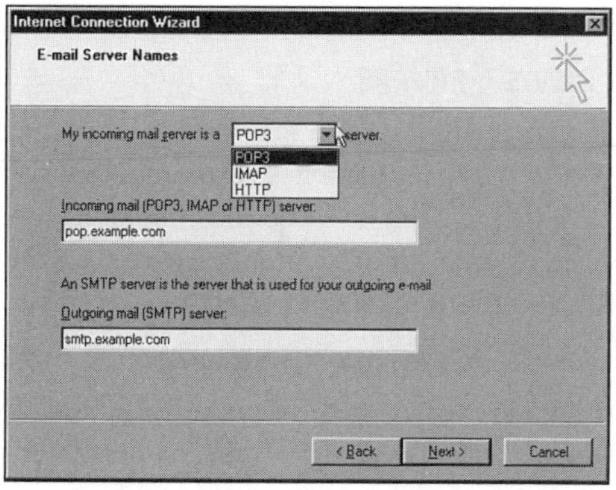

Figure 31.2
You must enter names for the servers that handle incoming and outgoing mail. In most cases, the same server handles both chores.

Note

Outlook Express supports three widely used mail standards. Most Internet service providers transfer email using servers that run *Simple Mail Transfer Protocol (SMTP)*. To download messages from an clients use version 3 of POP3. A newer standard, IMAP, is less widely used.

- Logon information—Enter the account name you use to log on to the mail server. If you enter a password in this dialog box, Outlook Express stores the password and uses it each time you check mail; for extra security, leave the Password box (shown in Figure 31.3) blank, and you are asked to enter it each time you check for mail. The Secure Password Authentication option is rarely used by Internet service providers; if you receive mail over The Microsoft Network, however, you should check this box.

To configure additional mail accounts, choose Tools, Accounts. Click the Add button, choose Mail, and the relevant portions of the Internet Connection Wizard run again.

Figure 31.3
Leave this Password box blank if you want to keep other users from accessing your mail. Outlook Express asks for your password each time you connect to the server.

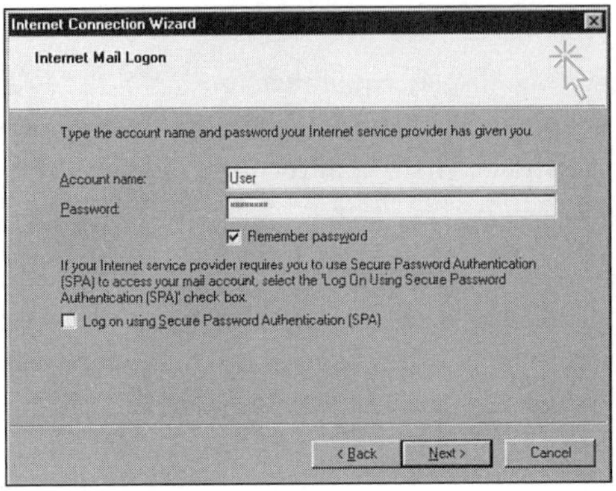

SETTING UP ONE OR MORE NEWS SERVERS

Outlook Express does more than email; it's also a full-featured news-reading client that allows you to download and read messages from newsgroup servers, post replies, and manage locally stored messages. With a few minor exceptions, the user interface is the same one you see when you send and receive mail, and the program uses the same system services to help you compose and send messages to public or private newsgroups.

→ To get better acquainted with newsgroups, **see** "How Newsgroups Work," **p. 698**.

Before you can read newsgroup messages, you must provide Outlook Express with the name of a news server to which you have access. Most ISPs offer a news feed to their customers. If your ISP's name is acme.com, for example, you'll probably find a news server at news.acme.com. The Microsoft Network provides newsgroup access on servers at msnnews.msn.com and netnews.msn.com. Microsoft's public newsgroups are available from msnews.microsoft.com. If you have access to a private news server, it might require you to log on with an account name and password.

If your ISP or corporate site does not maintain a news feed, try connecting to a public-access news server. You get what you pay for, of course; most such sites are slow and unreliable for serious news access. You can find a well-maintained list of public news servers at

http://nntp.homepage.com/public.htm

As with mail accounts, setting up a news account with the wizard is a simple fill-in-the-blanks process. The wizard appears when you choose Tools, Accounts, click the Add button, and choose News.

You must enter a name and email address for each news account. Enter the name of your news server when prompted (see Figure 31.4) and check the option at the bottom of this dialog box if the server requires you to log on with a username and password.

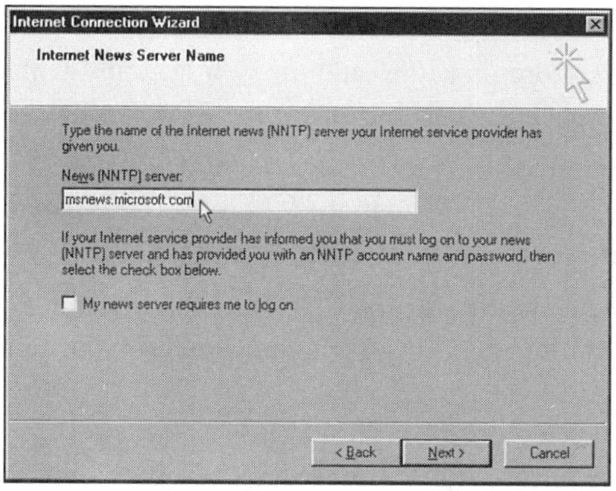

Figure 31.4
You must supply the name of a news server before accessing newsgroups with Outlook Express.

Give the account a friendly name to help identify it in the account list. The default entry is the server name, but a descriptive name like Microsoft Public Newsgroups is easier to understand than msnews.microsoft.com.

PART
V

CH

31

Tip #202

When you enter your name and email address for newsgroups, you are in fact publicizing your personal information to anyone who uses or views the same newsgroup. In fact, some experienced newsgroup participants never use their real addresses when posting because it's too easy for unscrupulous marketers to skim addresses from newsgroup participants and target them for unsolicited email, or spam. If you are concerned with this issue, put in a friendly alias instead.

MANAGING MAIL FOR MORE THAN ONE USER

On many Windows 98 computers, one user gathers mail from one or two Internet mail accounts. But Outlook Express lets you manage mail in more complex environments, with multiple users of the same computer accessing separate mail accounts through the Identity feature. Identities are managed through the Manage Identities dialog box (see Figure 31.5).

To add a new identity to your installation of Outlook Express, do the following:

1. Select Identities from the File menu. Choose Manage Identities.

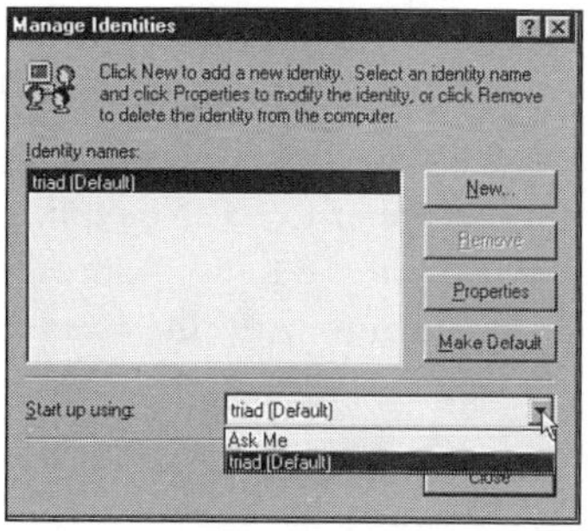

Figure 31.5
The Manage Identities dialog box enables you to add or change user information for multiple users to access the same Outlook Express 5 application without having to disconnect from the Internet. You can also choose File, Switch Identities to change accounts.

2. Click on the New button to add a new identity.

3. When Outlook Express prompts you to add the new account name, enter your new account name and then click the OK button.

4. You are asked if you want to switch to the new identity. Choose Yes to immediately set up the new account connection information. If you choose No, simply choose File, Switch Identities when you are ready to set up the new account.

5. When you select the new identity for the first time, the Internet Connection Wizard sets up your new account information to get connected to your new mail and news accounts.

You can also choose File, Identities, Add New Identity and then follow the preceding steps to add the new name and set up the new connection.

To remove an identity, select the identity in the Manage Identities dialog box list and click Remove. You must have at least one identity.

You can also change the identity that is default at startup, or let Outlook Express 5 prompt you for the user identity at each startup. To have Outlook Express prompt you at the application's start, in the Manage Identities dialog box click on the Start Up Using drop-down list and select Ask Me.

If you choose to switch identities and to log off of your current identity, Outlook Express exits and remains closed. If you choose to switch identities and choose the new identity, without logging off of your current identity, Outlook Express automatically closes the current identity and then opens the new one

ADJUSTING PROPERTIES FOR AN EXISTING MAIL OR NEWS ACCOUNT

To change the settings for a mail or news account after you set up Outlook Express, click Tools, Accounts; select the entry you want to change; and click the Properties button. The first account you create in the mail and newsgroup becomes the default account for that category. That's an important distinction because it determines which information appears onscreen when you click the Read Mail or Read News icon on the start page, and it defines which SMTP server Outlook Express uses when sending messages. To change default mail or news accounts, select the account and click the Set as Default button.

For both types of accounts, use the General tab (see Figure 31.6) to change the friendly name for the account or to edit personal information. This dialog box lets you add the name of your organization and specify a different reply-to address. For example, if you send a message using your corporate mail account but prefer to receive replies via your personal Internet mail account, enter the personal address in the Reply Address box; when recipients reply to your message, their mail software should automatically insert the preferred reply-to address.

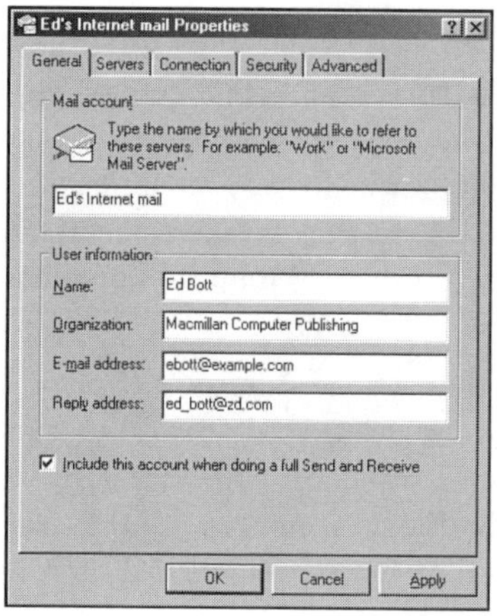

Figure 31.6
Edit the Reply Address for a mail or news account if you want to receive replies at an address other than the one from which you send messages.

The Servers tab lets you change the name or logon settings for mail and news servers. The Advanced tab lets you adjust timeout settings (sometimes necessary over very slow connections) and break apart lengthy messages (required by some mail servers running older software). Do not adjust these settings unless specifically instructed to do so by the server's administrator.

SELECTING CONNECTION OPTIONS

For each Outlook Express mail and news account, you can specify how you prefer to connect to the Internet: over a LAN, manually, or by using a modem. If your computer is permanently connected to a network with Internet access, you can set all your accounts for LAN access and be done with it. But on machines with dial-up Internet access, particularly notebook computers, you should pay close attention to these settings.

Each time you create a new account, you have a chance to specify Connection properties. To adjust these settings after you create an account, choose Tools, Accounts; select the account name; click Properties; and click on the Connection tab. You see a dialog box like the one in Figure 31.7.

Figure 31.7
This dialog box allows Outlook Express to override the default connection settings in IE5. You can choose to add a different dial-up connection to access this particular mail server.

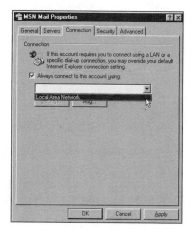

PART
V
CH
31

What's the difference between the three connection options?

- Connect using a local area network (LAN)—The LAN option assumes you have a full-time connection to the Internet through a local area network. Unless you choose to work offline, Outlook Express checks for mail every 30 minutes. To change the interval for checking mail, choose Tools, Options; click on the General tab; and change the value in the Check for New Messages Every *x* Minutes setting located in the Send/Receive Messages section.

- Connect using a specific Dial Up connection—Choose a *Dial-Up* Networking connection from the list in this dialog box or click the Add button to create a new connection. Outlook Express dials this connection whenever you attempt to access this particular mail or news server. Use this option if you do not use the IE5 dialer (for example, if you access the Web through a proxy server) but must use a dial-up connection for email.

Notebook users might want to create multiple copies of mail and news accounts, each with a different connection type, to handle different working environments. For example, you can specify a LAN connection when you're connected to the office network but use a dial-up connection to make a manual connection when you're working in a hotel room.

CHOOSING HTML OR PLAIN TEXT AS YOUR MESSAGE FORMAT

Each time you use Outlook Express to compose a message, you choose whether to use plain text only or to add graphics, colors, and rich text formatting using HTML. If most of your messages go to users of Outlook Express or other HTML-compatible mail programs, rich text formatting can make your messages livelier and more readable. With HTML formatting, your messages look and behave like Web pages; you can specify fonts and their sizes, change text colors, use paragraph styles, and control text alignment. You can add background colors and graphics, bulleted and numbered lists, and hypertext links to other Web pages.

All that fancy formatting is lost, though, if your correspondents use email software that can't interpret HTML. They'll see a plain-text version of your message along with a file attachment that they can open in a Web browser. In fact, there's a good chance they'll be annoyed when they receive your HTML messages because even a simple one-sentence message typically occupies 1K or more of disk space when translated into HTML.

Note

Users of Netscape mail products can send and receive HTML-formatted mail as well, although you might notice minor differences in the look of messages sent between Netscape and Microsoft clients.

Outlook Express lets you set separate default formats for mail and news messages, and it allows you to override those settings on individual messages. Unless you're certain that nearly all your email recipients can handle HTML attachments, your best bet is to choose plain text for mail messages. Likewise, on newsgroups where people use a variety of news reader clients, it's good manners to specify plain text as your default format.

To adjust the default settings, follow this procedure:

1. Choose Tools, Options and click the Send tab. You see the dialog box shown in Figure 31.8.

Figure 31.8
These default settings send all your mail messages in HTML format, with plain text the preferred format for news messages.

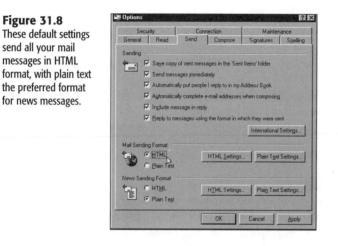

2. In the Mail Sending Format box, select HTML or Plain Text as the default format for mail messages.

3. In the News Sending Format box, select HTML or Plain Text as the default format for messages you post to newsgroups.

4. After you specify a format, the Settings button lets you specify additional formatting options. These choices are shown in Figure 31.9.

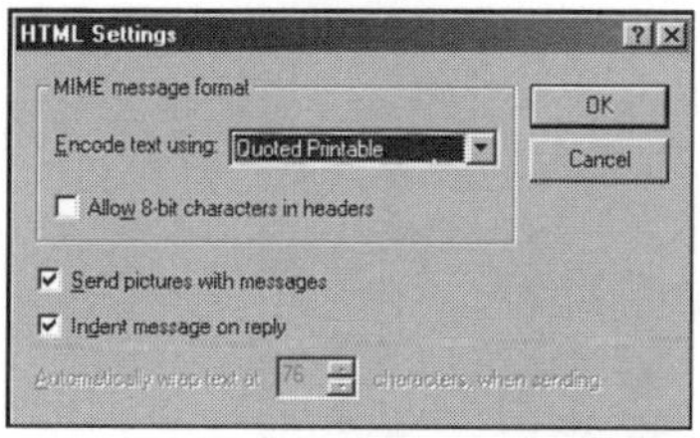

Figure 31.9
If recipients complain about stray characters (especially equal signs) in text messages, try changing text encoding from Quoted Printable to None.

For more details about the problem mentioned in Figure 31.9, see "Text Encoding" in the "Troubleshooting" section at the end of this chapter.

→ To read more about options for composing individual messages, **see** "Composing a New Message," **p. 679**.

EXCHANGING DATA WITH OTHER MAIL PROGRAMS

If you currently use another email package and plan to switch to Outlook Express, the process is simple and straightforward. Outlook Express can import address books and archived messages from the following popular mail clients:

- Eudora Pro or Eudora Light (version 3.0 or earlier)
- Netscape Mail (versions 2 or 3)
- Netscape Communicator
- Microsoft Internet Mail
- Microsoft Exchange Inbox
- Windows Messaging

In addition, you can import messages from Microsoft Outlook 2000 or Outlook 2000 and also Outlook Express 4 or 5. (See the following section for detailed instructions on how to transfer address information from Outlook 2000 to Outlook Express.)

MIGRATING FROM EXCHANGE OR OUTLOOK 2000

Do you currently use the Exchange Inbox email program that Microsoft introduced with Windows 95? In versions of Windows 95 sold after late 1996, this program might go by the name Windows Messaging. Both Exchange and Outlook 2000 use the Windows Messaging system services and the same format for messages and Personal Address Books. If you use any of these programs, Outlook Express offers to convert your messages and addresses the first time you run the program, as shown in Figure 31.10.

Figure 31.10
Switching from the older Exchange Inbox to Outlook Express can be as easy as clicking Next in this dialog box.

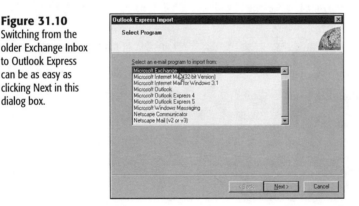

Converting data from most mail programs is a simple process, but there's one notable exception: To transfer your Contacts folder from Outlook 2000 to the Windows Address Book in Outlook Express, you need to go through a cumbersome conversion process that starts by exporting the Contacts information into an Exchange-compatible Personal Address Book (PAB). Then, you can import the PAB into Outlook Express. Follow these steps:

1. Open Outlook 2000; choose <u>F</u>ile, Impor<u>t</u> and Export; and select Export to a File. Click the <u>N</u>ext button.

2. Following the wizard's prompts, choose Comma Separated Values (Windows) from the list of export formats and then click Next. Select the Contacts folder and click <u>N</u>ext. Name the export file. Click <u>N</u>ext again. Outlook gives you the option to map any custom fields; if you have none, choose Next again and then click Finish.

3. When you click Finish, Outlook 2000 copies the information to the Comma Delimited File in the location you specified.

4. Open Outlook Express; choose <u>F</u>ile, <u>I</u>mport, Other <u>A</u>ddress Book; and select Text File (Comma Separated Values) from the list of available formats.

5. Click the <u>I</u>mport button to finish the process. Your email addresses and other contact information now appear in the Outlook Express Address Book.

RESTORING OUTLOOK EXPRESS AS THE DEFAULT MAIL CLIENT

Note that you can set up more than one mail program on a system running Windows 98. When you install another mail program, however, it might take over as the default email program that starts when you click the Mail icon on IE5's Standard toolbar or click a Mail To: hyperlink on a Web page. To restore Outlook Express as the default mail client, follow this procedure:

1. Start Outlook Express; choose <u>T</u>ools, <u>O</u>ptions; and click on the General tab.

2. Choose the button labeled This Application Is the Default Mail Handler. For news, click This Application Is the Default News Handler. Both of these items can also be set up in Internet Explorer properties, on the Programs tab. Choose Outlook Express as the default email and newsgroup program.

IMPORTING DATA FROM ANOTHER MAIL PROGRAM

When you choose <u>F</u>ile, <u>I</u>mport, Outlook Express offers a cascading menu with three additional choices. The Address Book and Messages options are self-explanatory; the third choice, Mail Account <u>S</u>ettings, lets you reuse the information (server and logon names, for example) that you've entered for one mail account when setting up another. When importing messages or addresses, Outlook Express first asks you to specify the mail program and then checks data file locations specified for that program in the Registry. If Outlook Express can't find the program on your system, a dialog box lets you specify the location.

Each import option goes through a series of dialog boxes, with slightly different choices that depend on the mail program or data type you start with. If you choose to import data from a text file with comma-separated values, for example, you have to specify which Outlook Express fields should receive each column of data in your text file. As Figure 31.11 shows, Outlook Express makes a reasonable guess at mapping fields in your text file to those in your Address Book. You can manually adjust the relationship between fields; check the box to the left of each field to include or remove it from the import operation. Click the <u>C</u>hange Mapping button, and you see a drop-down list of available Outlook Express fields.

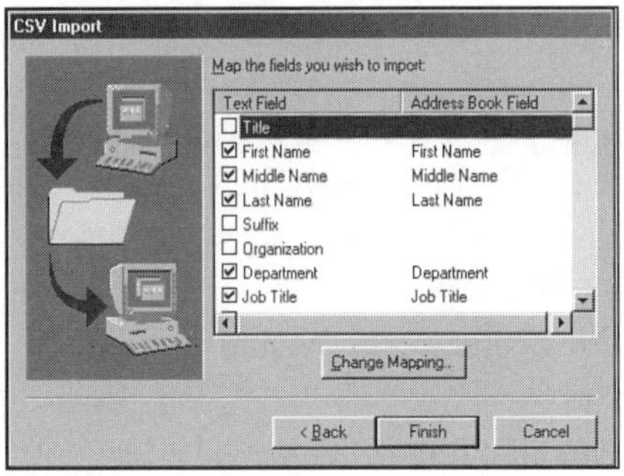

Figure 31.11
Outlook Express won't recognize the Organization label in this text file; click the Change Mapping button to tell Outlook Express that the data belongs in the Company field.

You can use the import choices to bring in messages or addresses even if your Address Book or message store already contains data. When the program detects that a record you're trying to import already exists in your Address Book, you see a dialog box like the one in Figure 31.12, at which point you can choose whether to keep the existing entry or replace it with the new data.

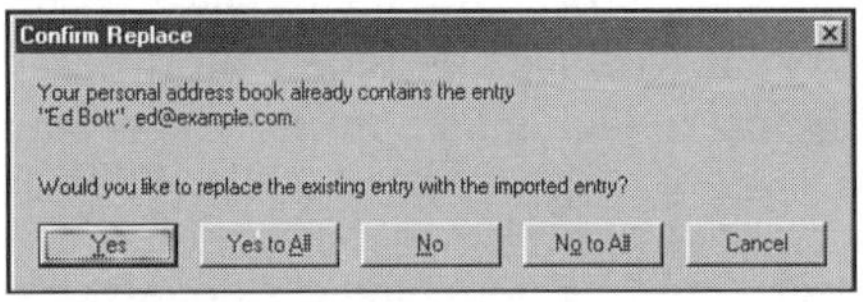

Figure 31.12
Click Yes to All to completely replace matching records in your Address Book with new data from an import file.

EXPORTING DATA TO ANOTHER PROGRAM

Unfortunately, Outlook Express isn't nearly as cooperative when it comes to moving messages and address information back to competing mail programs. When you choose File, Export from the Outlook Express menu, you can easily move information into Outlook 2000 or Microsoft Exchange. To transfer addresses into other programs, you first have to convert the information into a text file with comma-separated values and then find the corresponding import feature in the destination program. Moving messages from Outlook Express into another mail client is not easy.

READING MESSAGES IN OUTLOOK EXPRESS

When you first click the Read Mail or Read News icon on the Outlook Express main screen, you see a display much like the one in Figure 31.13.

The Folders list at the left of the screen includes the default mail folders, any additional folders you've created, all news servers you've set up, and any newsgroups to which you've subscribed. The right side of the screen includes the column-oriented message list, which shows the contents of the currently selected folder or server. Below is a preview pane that shows the contents of the currently selected message. A customizable toolbar appears at the top, and a status bar appears at the bottom of the window.

Folders list   Toolbar   Message list

Figure 31.13
The default Outlook Express layout includes the Folders list at left, the message list at top right, and a preview pane below.

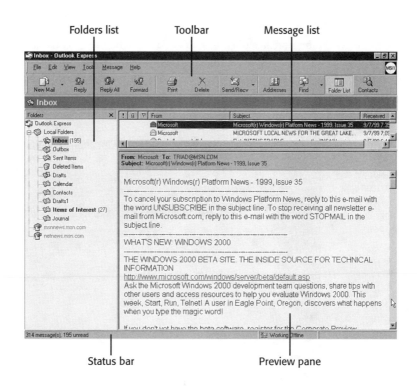

Status bar   Preview pane

Two optional parts of the Outlook Express screen—the Outlook bar and the Folder bar—are hidden by default. The message list is always visible; there's no way to make it disappear. Using a few menu choices and check boxes, though, you can show, hide, and rearrange virtually every other aspect of the Outlook Express interface.

CHANGING THE LAYOUT

To alter the basic look of Outlook Express, choose View, Layout. You see a dialog box like the one in Figure 31.14.

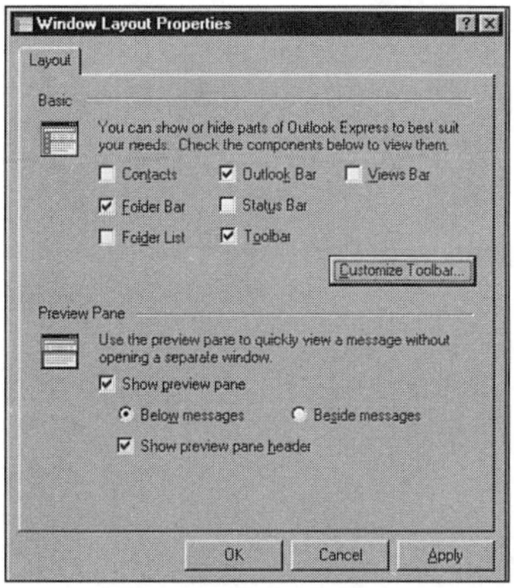

Figure 31.14
These options produce a layout that closely resembles the Outlook 2000 interface.

These settings rearrange the Outlook Express interface so that it closely resembles the Outlook 2000 interface, as shown in Figure 31.15. The Outlook bar at left shows all the default folders plus any top-level folders you create; it doesn't include icons for subfolders you create. The Outlook bar also includes icons for news servers and subscribed newsgroups. Just above the message list is the drop-down Folder bar, which shows all folders in an Explorer-style hierarchy.

Figure 31.15
The Outlook bar at left resembles the one in Outlook 2000 with one difference: You can't change the order of icons.

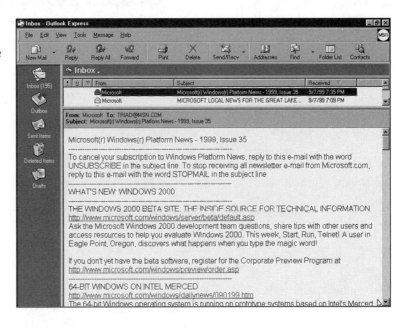

USING THE PREVIEW PANE

As you move between messages in the message list, the contents of the currently selected message appear in the preview pane. Use the layout options to change the appearance and behavior of this pane:

- To toggle the preview pane on and off, choose View, Layout and click the Use Preview Pane check box.

- To move the preview pane, choose the Below Messages or Beside Messages option.

- To show or hide the address and subject line in the preview pane, check the box labeled Show Preview Pane Header.

- To change the size of the preview pane, point to the bar between the message list and the preview pane until the mouse pointer becomes a double-headed arrow, and then click and drag.

Tip #203	When a message enters a folder in Outlook Express, such as the Inbox, each new entry in the message list appears in bold to indicate you haven't yet read it. The unread status changes when you open the message or, by default Read settings, when it has appeared in the preview pane for more than five seconds. To filter the message list so it shows only unread messages, choose View, Current View, Unread Messages. To change the setting that controls a message's read status, choose Tools, Options and then click the Read tab. Enter a different number in the Message Is Read After Being Previewed for *(number)* Seconds; alternatively, uncheck the box, and the message remains as new until it has been fully opened.

NAVIGATING THROUGH FOLDERS

After you move past the start page, the Outlook Express message list always shows the contents of the currently selected folder, newsgroup, or news server. To move from folder to folder, use one of these three techniques:

- Click on any icon in the Folders list to switch to the contents of the message list.

- If the folder bar is visible, the name of the currently selected folder, server, or newsgroup appears just above the message list. Click on that folder name to display a drop-down Folders list. The down arrow to the right of the name provides a visual clue; after you make your selection, the list snaps out of the way again.

- Click on any icon in the Outlook bar to show the contents of that location.

To view or adjust the properties of any icon, right-click on the icon and choose from the shortcut menu.

Tip #204	To quickly navigate to support on the Web, use one of the three Internet links in black at the very top of the Outlook Express start page. These links take you to the Internet Explorer Web site, Microsoft's home page, or the Outlook Express start page on the Web. The icon for the Outlook Express start page is always available at the top of bar.

SORTING THE MESSAGE LIST

To sort the contents of the message list, click on any column heading. Choose View, Columns to add or remove columns and change the order of those that are displayed. (Note that different types of objects provide different choices of columns.) Click on the border between two column headings and drag to adjust column widths.

To group mail or newsgroup messages using threads, choose View, Sort By and toggle the Group Messages by Thread setting.

OPENING INDIVIDUAL MESSAGES

Double-click on any item in the message list to open it in its own window, as shown in Figure 31.16.

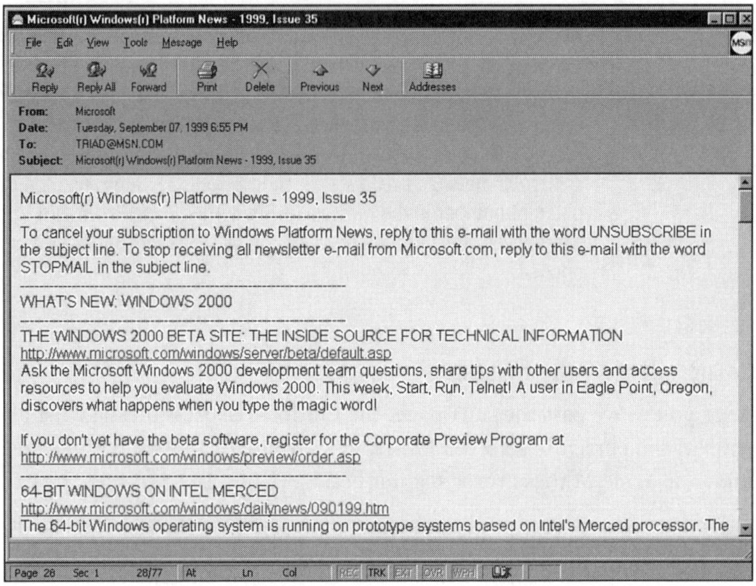

Figure 31.16
This full Message window offers more space than the preview pane. Maximize the window and use the up or down arrows to navigate without the message list.

Icons on the Message window toolbar let you save, print, or delete the current message.

To navigate through your entire message list without switching back and forth between the message list and the Message window, follow these steps:

1. Open any message in its own window. Maximize the window if you want to see as much of the message as possible without having to use the scrollbars.

2. To move to the next message in the list, click the up arrow on the toolbar. Click the down arrow to move back to the previous message

3. To move to the next unread message in the list, press Ctrl+U.

4. In threaded message lists, such as those found in newsgroups, press Ctrl+Shift+U to move to the next unread thread.

5. To move or copy a message to a folder, choose File, Move to Folder or File, Copy to Folder. To delete a message, click the Delete button on the toolbar.

CHANGING THE WAY PLAIN-TEXT MESSAGES LOOK

When you receive an HTML-formatted message, the formatting codes in the message itself control how it looks in the preview pane and in individual Message windows. If the message doesn't specify font information, Outlook Express uses default fonts and sizes to control the display of proportional fonts (used for general text) and fixed fonts (used for tabular material that must line up precisely).

When you receive a plain-text message, Outlook Express displays it using the default proportional font and the default font size. On most systems, that means plain-text messages appear in Arial, using the Medium size setting (12 point). Follow these steps to change the font and font size to improve readability or to see more text in a Message window:

1. Open any plain-text message and choose View, Fonts. Select the size you prefer from the five available choices. Note the size and close the Message window.

2. From the main Outlook Express window, choose Tools, Options.

3. Click the Read tab and then click the Fonts button in the Font Settings box.

4. To change fonts, use the Proportional Font drop-down list. (Adjusting the Fixed-Width font setting affects only HTML-formatted messages.)

5. To change to the default font size you noted earlier, use the Font Size drop-down list.

6. Click OK to save your changes. You might need to close and restart Outlook Express to see the font changes in both the preview pane and individual Message windows.

CUSTOMIZING THE OUTLOOK EXPRESS TOOLBAR

To change the look of the Outlook Express toolbar, choose View, Layout. To add, remove, and rearrange buttons, click the Customize Toolbar button; you can also open the Customize Toolbar dialog box, shown in Figure 31.17, by right-clicking on the toolbar and choosing Customize from the shortcut menu. Here, you can use the drop-down list to hide the text labels and choose small icons to dramatically reduce the amount of space the toolbar takes up.

Figure 31.17
Use the Add and Remove buttons to rearrange the toolbars for Mail and News windows.

Note the separate toolbars for Mail and News windows; therefore, you have to customize them individually. You can't customize toolbars used in Outlook Express message windows or those in the Windows Address Book.

Tip #205

If you use the Folders list regularly but don't want to sacrifice the screen real estate it demands, add the Folder List button to your toolbar. It acts as a toggle, revealing or hiding the Folders list so you can have more room for the message list and preview pane and still navigate between folders without having to wade through pull-down menus.

USING THE WINDOWS ADDRESS BOOK

Outlook Express organizes email addresses using a module called the Windows Address Book. Each contact record includes fields that allow you to track additional details about a person, including home and business addresses and phone numbers. The Windows Address Book also lets you create group records so you can send email to several individuals by entering an alias instead of a lengthy list of addresses.

Address Book information is stored in a single file with the .WAB extension. Each user profile on a machine can contain its own Address Book file, but you cannot maintain multiple address books within a single profile.

Note

Although the Windows Address Book appears to be an integrated part of Outlook Express, it's actually a separate application called WAB.EXE. If you use the Address Book frequently, you might want to create a shortcut to this program and place it on the Start menu or the Windows desktop.

To open the Windows Address Book, click the Address Book icon on the Outlook Express toolbar. As you can in any Explorer window, you can choose one of four different views for the contents of the Address Book. In the default Details view (see Figure 31.18), click on a column heading to sort the records by the values in that field; click again to sort in reverse order.

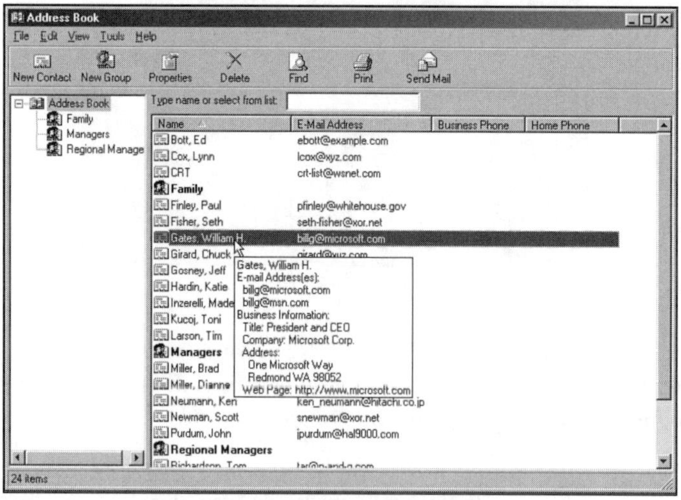

Figure 31.18
As the mouse passes over each Address Book entry, a ScreenTip displays the contents of that record.

- To open an individual record, double-click on the item, or select it and click the Properties button.
- To delete a record, select it and click the Delete button.
- To copy the text from a contact record to the Windows Clipboard, right-click the item and choose Copy from the shortcut menu.

■ To begin composing a message to a recipient whose email address is in your Windows Address Book, select the person's record and click the Send Mail button.

CREATING AND EDITING ADDRESS BOOK ENTRIES

To create a new record from scratch, click the New Contact button and begin filling in fields on the Personal tab. As Figure 31.19 shows, you can enter more than one email address for a contact. Choose one address and click the Set as Default button to tell Outlook Express to use that email address when you click the Send Mail button.

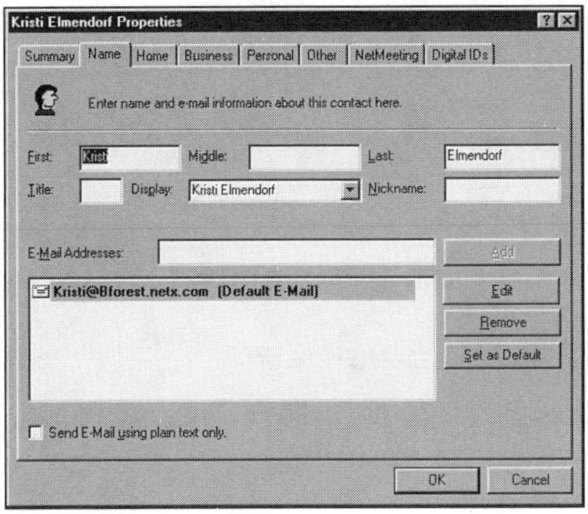

Figure 31.19
You can enter multiple email addresses in a contact record: personal and business addresses, for example.

Tip #206

Note as you enter information in the First, Middle, and Last fields that the value in the Display field automatically fills in as well. This field is what you see under the Name heading when you look at the Address list. The drop-down Display list lets you choose from several defaults, but you can enter anything you like here, including a descriptive name such as Caterer, Travel agent, or Boss. Make sure the name is descriptive enough to pick out this record when you need to send mail in the future.

CREATING MAILING GROUPS

A mailing group (also known as an alias or distribution list) lets you send messages to multiple people without having to enter each name in the message. When you enter the name of a mailing group in the address box of a message, Outlook Express substitutes the names that make up that group before sending the message. To create a mailing group, follow these steps:

1. From the File menu in Address Book, choose New Group.

2. Enter a name for the mailing group in the Group Name box. The name might be up to 255 characters long and might contain spaces and special characters.

3. Click the Select Members button. A dialog box containing names from your Address Book appears.

4. Click on a name in the list and then click the Select button to add that person's entry to the list. Continue adding names individually or hold down the Ctrl key to select more than one name at a time. Use the New Contact button to add an entry to the list.

5. When you've finished adding names to the group, click OK.

6. Add information and notes about this group in the Group Details tab, if you wish, and then click OK.

Tip #207	To simplify your mailing lists, Outlook Express lets you add group entries as well as individual names. You can use this feature to avoid having to update multiple groups. For example, you might create separate mailing groups for each department in your company: Accounting, Sales, Marketing, and so on. Then, create an All Employees list consisting of all department lists. When new employees join the company, only the department list to which they belong must be updated. Then, by association, they are included in any mailing group to which their department belongs.

To see all the groups in your Address Book, choose View, Groups List.

ADDING ADDRESS BOOK ENTRIES AUTOMATICALLY

The easiest way to create contact records in your Windows Address Book is to copy email addresses from messages you receive. Outlook Express lets you add contact records one at a time or automatically.

For one-at-a-time addressing, open a message; right-click on any name in the From, To, or CC fields; and then choose Add to Address Book from the shortcut menu, as shown in Figure 31.20.

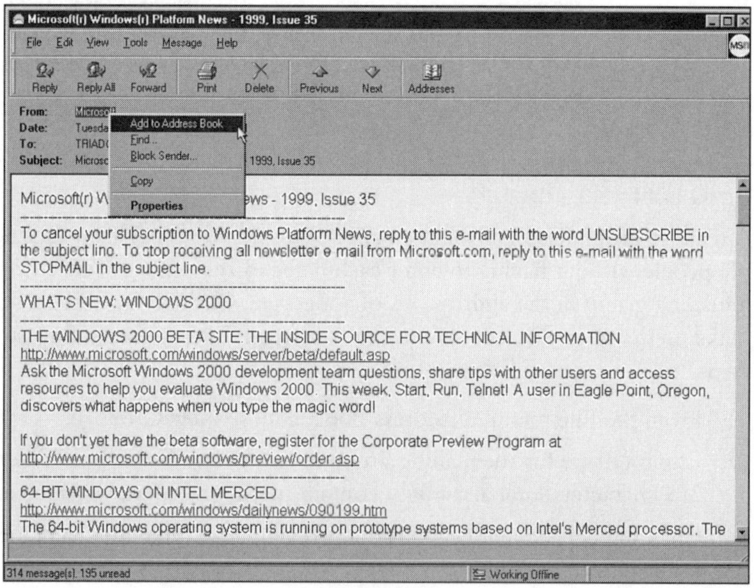

Figure 31.20
Right-click on any address and use the shortcut menu to add the name and address to your Windows Address Book.

Tip #208

If you need a better way to keep track of the email addresses of the people with whom you interact through email, let Outlook Express do it for you automatically. Choose Tools, Options; click the Send tab; and check the box labeled Automatically Put People I Reply to in My Address Book. Now, any time you reply to an email message, Outlook Express records the Reply To email address in your address book.

FINDING PEOPLE USING PUBLIC DIRECTORIES

What's the best way to find someone's email address? Copying it from an email or a business card is still the surest way to be certain your message reaches its destination. But the next best technique is to use a public directory server. When you click the Find People button on the Windows Address Book toolbar, you see a dialog box like the one in Figure 31.21.

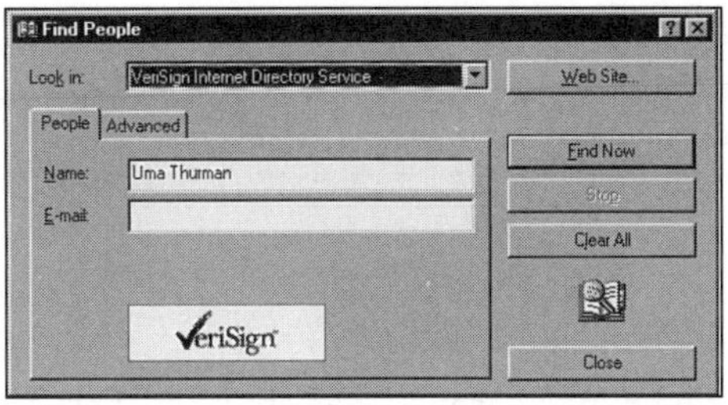

Figure 31.21
Use a public directory server to track down email addresses and add them to your Address Book.

Outlook Express gives you a choice of several public servers that use the *Lightweight Directory Access Protocol (LDAP)*, an Internet standard for exchanging directory information. Select a server in the Look In box; click in the Name box; and enter all or part of the name you're searching for. Click Find Now to begin the search.

For more information about how LDAP works, check this Web site, managed by the university where the protocol was invented:

`http://www.umich.edu/~dirsvcs/ldap/index.html`

Matching records appear in a list at the bottom of the Find People dialog box. Select a name and click the Properties button to view more information about that directory entry. Right-click and choose Send Mail to begin composing a message to that person. Click Add to Address Book to save the contact's name and address in your Windows Address Book.

COMPOSING A NEW MESSAGE

To begin a mail or news message from scratch, click the New Message button or press Ctrl+N. You see a blank New Message window like the one in Figure 31.22.

Figure 31.22
A new blank mail
message window.

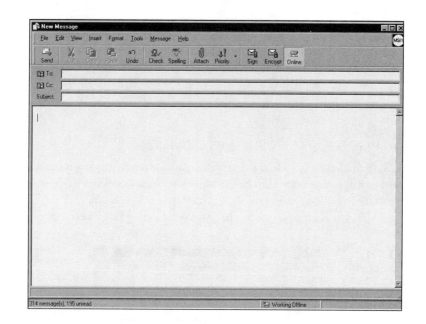

ADDRESSING A MAIL MESSAGE

Although you can simply begin typing your message within the New Message window, it's easier to start by filling out the address box. Enter the main recipients for the message on the To line and then use the Tab key to move to the Cc and Subject lines before tabbing into the body of the message.

Click the small icon in the To line or CC line to open your Windows Address Book. The Select Recipients dialog box, shown in Figure 31.23, lets you pick names from a list and add them to the address box.

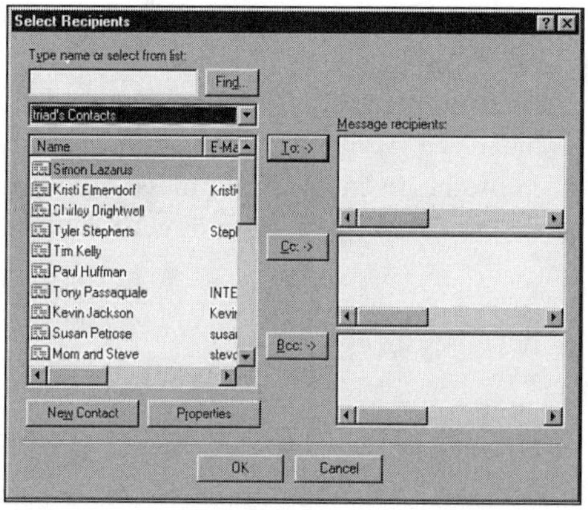

Figure 31.23
Click the small icon in
the To line or CC line
in the New Message
dialog box to open
this view of the
Windows Address
Book.

Use other buttons in the Select Recipients dialog box to create a new contact and add it to the list, to see more details about an Address Book entry. To clear a name from any of the three message recipient boxes, select the name, right-click, and choose Remove from the shortcut menu.

When you finish adding recipients, click OK to return to the New Message dialog box.

CHECKING A RECIPIENT'S ADDRESS

You don't need to use the Windows Address Book to add recipients. Simply type one or more valid email addresses in the To line and continue; be sure to separate address entries with a semicolon or comma.

If you know a name is in your Address Book, enter a few characters from the first or last name. Outlook Express fills in matching names as you type; this AutoComplete feature works almost exactly like its equivalent in Internet Explorer. When the correct name appears in the address box, press Enter to add the address and a semicolon, with the insertion point positioned for you to add another address. Press Tab to move to the next address field.

PART
V

CH

31

<table>
<tr><td>Caution</td></tr>
</table>

Check the contents of the address box carefully before sending a message. If you type even a single incorrect character here, the AutoComplete feature might insert the wrong address, and you might wind up sending a sensitive or personal message to someone other than the recipient you intended.

If you don't like this AutoComplete feature, turn it off. Choose Tools, Options; click the Send tab; and uncheck the box labeled Automatically Complete E-Mail Addresses When Composing. Even with this feature disabled, you can still enlist the help of the Address Book in completing addresses; just type a few characters from the first or last name and then click the Check Names button (see Figure 31.24). If only one Address Book entry matches the characters you typed, that entry appears in your Address box; if more than one entry matches, you have to pick the correct address from a dialog box. After Outlook Express has verified that the address is valid, Outlook Express adds a link to that address entry; you know the process was successful when you see the underline beneath each address entry.

Figure 31.24
The Check Names button returns address records that contain the characters you typed in any position.

Composing the Message

If you've chosen HTML format for your message, the Formatting toolbar appears just above the box in which you enter the message text. Use the toolbar buttons to change font and paragraph formatting, colors, and alignment. The three right-most buttons in Figure 31.25 insert a rule, a hyperlink, or a graphics image.

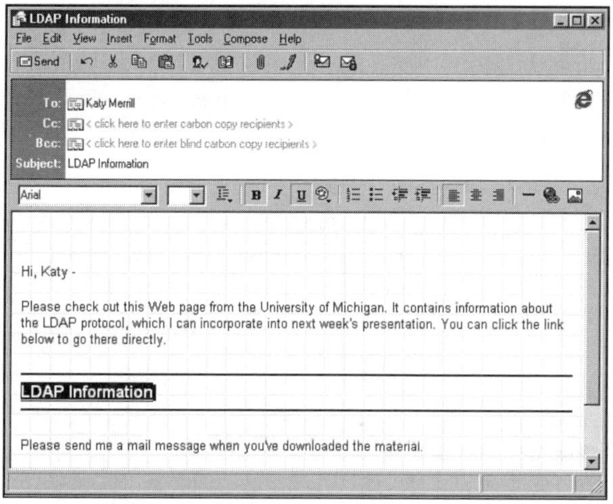

Figure 31.25
Use these formatting buttons to control the look of an HTML message. Buttons at the far right let you insert this rule and hyperlink.

The New Message window includes most of the features you expect from a formatting editor, including the ability to specify fonts, colors, and alignment; there's even a multilevel undo (press Ctrl+Z to roll back changes you've made or text you've typed).

If you are unable to use spell check on your email message, see "Borrowed Modules" in the "Troubleshooting" section at the end of this chapter.

To create a hyperlink in a message, follow these steps:

1. Select any piece of text or a graphics image.

2. Click the Insert Hyperlink button. A dialog box lets you choose from an assortment of formats, including the default http:// for Web pages, ftp:// for file locations, and mailto:// for mail links.

3. Type the URL and click OK to assign the link to the object you selected. Notice that the hyperlink appears underlined in your message.

Changing Message Formats

To change the format of a message from HTML to plain text and vice versa, choose the appropriate entry from the Format menu. You can use the General tab of a contact record to specify that an addressee always receives messages in plain text. By default, when you respond to a message, Outlook Express uses the same format as the original. When you reply to an HTML-formatted mail message, your reply uses the same format unless you specifically tell Outlook Express not to do so.

GIVING MESSAGES A CONSISTENT LOOK

When you create a message from scratch, you start with a blank slate. Your electronic messages lack basic information that you take for granted when you print correspondence on letterhead, such as your name, company name and logo, your job title, and your phone number. Outlook Express offers two features that help you apply a consistent look to your messages and supply some of this missing information.

With HTML-formatted messages, use templates called *stationery* to add background graphics, fonts, paragraph formatting, and other standard elements to mail and news messages. Use *signatures* with all kinds of messages, including text messages, to add standard information at the end of every message you create.

USING SIGNATURES

For daily use, especially in a business setting, create a standard signature to make sure important information goes out with every message you send. A signature might include your name, return email address, company affiliation, and telephone number, for example. At some companies, employees routinely add a disclaimer stating that the views expressed in email messages are personal opinions and do not represent the company.

To set up a personal signature, choose Tools, Options and click the Signatures tab. You can compose a simple text signature, like the one in Figure 31.26. You can store your signature in a text file if you prefer, or use FrontPage Express to add graphics and formatting codes, and then store the result in an HTML file. To use a file as your signature, choose the File option and specify its location.

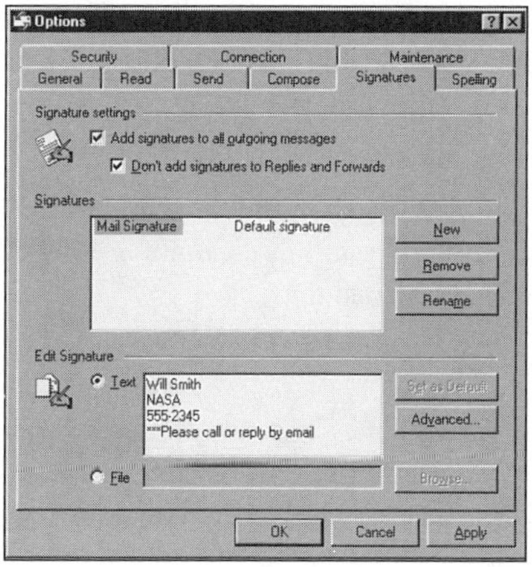

PART
V

CH
31

Figure 31.26
Netiquette dictates that signatures should be short and to the point. At four lines, this signature is long enough.

→ For more information on HTML and Front Page Express, **see** "Introducing FrontPage Express," **p. 712**.

Check boxes on the Signature tab let you specify whether you want Outlook Express to automatically add the signature to every message you create. There's also an option to skip signatures on replies and forwarded messages. Leave both check boxes blank if you prefer to add a signature to selected messages only. The Advanced button will bring up the advanced signature options, where you can set options that signatures will only be added to messages sent from certain accounts (that is, mail, news, or both).

To add a signature to a message while composing it, choose Insert, Signature on the file bar menu.

APPLYING A LOOK WITH STATIONERY

Outlook Express includes a collection of HTML templates called stationery. These starter documents typically incorporate background graphics, standard fonts, and a few styles. To see and use the sample stationery, choose Compose, New Message Using and then select an entry from the cascading menu.

Most of the sample stationery entries, built around personal themes including party invitations and greeting cards, are inappropriate for business use. But the templates might supply some ideas for stationery you can create for your own use. For example, you might use a company logo as a background graphic and add your signature in a formatted block of text set off from the main text by an HTML rule.

To modify one of the sample stationery formats, follow these steps:

1. Choose Tools, Option and select the Compose tab. In the Stationery section, check the Mail option and then click the Select button to open a list of stationery items installed on your computer.

2. Pick a format that includes the basic elements you want in your custom stationery. Use the Preview window to see what each stationery type looks like.

3. Click the Edit button to launch your default HTML editor, such as FrontPage Express or Word 2000, with the selected stationery type.

4. Add text and graphics and make any other formatting changes.

5. Save the document with a descriptive name in the same folder with the other stationery samples. (By default, these are in \Program Files\Common Files\Microsoft Shared\Stationery.) Close your HTML editor.

6. Select the stationery you just created and click OK.

To use a stationery file for all mail or news messages you compose, make sure its name is selected in the Stationery box. To compose an HTML message without using the default stationery, choose Message, New Message Using, No Stationery.

EXCHANGING ADDRESS INFORMATION WITH VCARDS

When you meet a new business contact in person, you exchange business cards. To send the digital equivalent of a business card in an email message, Outlook Express uses the vCard format. When you attach a vCard to your mail or news messages, recipients with a vCard-compatible Address Book (the Windows Address Book or Netscape Communicator, for example) can merge the attachment into their personal Address Book, creating a new record that includes all your address information.

Before you can send a vCard, you have to create a personal record in the Windows Address Book, and then tell Outlook Express to use that card as your business card. Choose Tools, Options; click the Compose tab; and go to the Business Card section to choose your card.

Caution

You can set an option in the Signature dialog box that automatically adds your electronic business card to every mail message. Think twice before you check that box, though. Your regular correspondents probably won't appreciate the extra disk space consumed by every one of those redundant business card attachments, and correspondents without a vCard-compatible address book will probably also resent the useless attachments. It's far better to selectively attach business cards by choosing Insert, Business Card.

COMPOSING A NEWS ARTICLE

Composing a message to a newsgroup uses tools that are virtually identical to those you use to create mail messages, with one major exception: Instead of picking addresses from your Windows Address Book, choose Tools, Select Newsgroups (or click the News server icon to the right of the To in the Address box). Use the dialog box like the one in Figure 31.27 to fill in one or more newsgroup names in the address box.

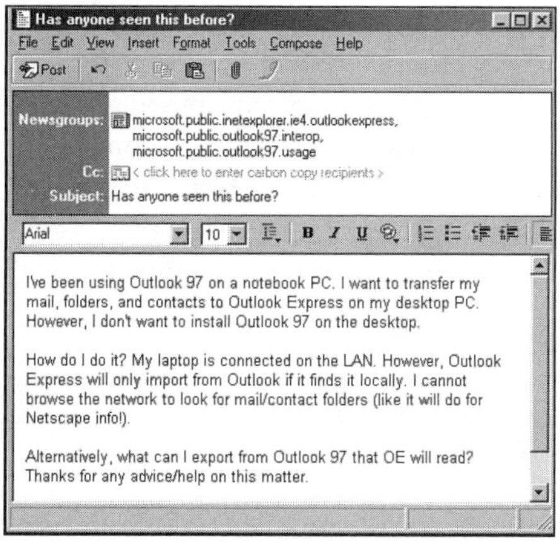

Figure 31.27
Posting the identical message to multiple newsgroups, as in this example, is generally considered bad Netiquette.

→ To learn about proper Netiquette, **see** "Working with Newsgroups," **p. 698.**

Tip #209

Before posting a question to a newsgroup, see whether the question has already been answered in a FAQ—a list of frequently asked questions. FAQs are the fastest way to get answers, and you also avoid being flamed for not reading the FAQ. The mother of all FAQs, with more than 900 files, is news.answers. There, you find information ranging from the

continues

continued

> laughably trivial (every cult TV program ever made is there, along with more information on body piercing than any human should need) to the deadly serious (you can read about a half-dozen religions or find detailed information on organ transplantation, depression support groups, and other sober topics).

SENDING YOUR MESSAGE

When you finish addressing and composing your message, you have a variety of options for actually launching it on its way:

- To send a mail message immediately using the default mail account, click the Send button.

- To post a newsgroup message immediately, click the Post button.

- To choose which mail account to use when sending a message, choose File, Send Message Using and pick the account from the cascading menu.

- To tell Outlook Express you want to choose when to send a message, choose File, Send Later.

- To save a mail message in the Drafts folder so you can work on it later, choose File, Save.

WORKING WITH FILE ATTACHMENTS

In addition to formatted text and graphics, you can attach a file to any message you compose using Outlook Express. Binary files, such as images and programs, can safely travel across the Internet, but only if you encode them into ASCII text before sending. When an incoming message includes an attachment, Outlook Express and other multipurpose Internet mail extensions (MIME) compatible mail clients are capable of converting the encoded text back into binary files.

To add a file attachment to a message you're composing, click the Paper clip icon on the toolbar. You can also attach one or more files by dragging them from an Explorer or Folder window into the Message window.

> **Caution**
>
> Not all mail client software is capable of decoding all attachment formats. If you're certain the recipient uses Outlook Express or another modern, MIME-compatible program, you should have no problem exchanging attachments. If you're not certain which mail software the recipient uses, try sending a small test attachment to verify that the process works before you send important files via email.

To view or save a file attachment in a message you've received, look for its icon:

- In the preview pane, click the Paper clip icon at the right of the preview header to see a list of attached files. Choose an item from the list to open it; you can't save an attachment from the preview pane.

- In a Message window, look for file icons in the header, under the Subject line, as shown in Figure 31.28. Double-click to open the file or use right-click shortcut menus to save the file to your local hard disk or a network location.

Figure 31.28
Right-click on its icon to open, save, or print a file attachment. When composing a message, you can also right-click to add or remove files.

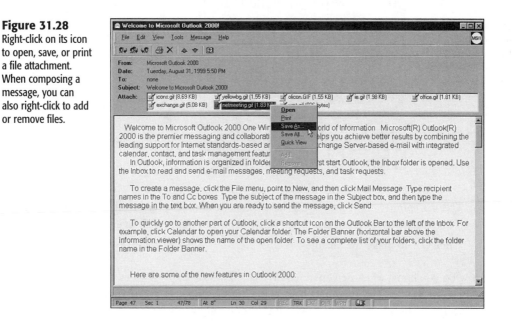

 If your attachments are not being received properly, see "Text Encoding" in the "Troubleshooting" section at the end of this chapter.

PART
V

CH
31

SENDING AND RECEIVING MAIL

Exchanging messages with a mail server is an interactive process. A mail server does not automatically send messages to your computer; to begin the transfer process, your mail client has to send a request to the server. Outlook Express can poll for mail at regular intervals, or you can send and receive messages on demand by clicking a button.

COLLECTING MAIL AUTOMATICALLY

If you have a LAN connection, Outlook Express automatically checks for new messages and sends outgoing mail every 30 minutes. To check for mail more or less frequently, follow these steps:

1. Choose Tools, Options and click the General tab. You see the dialog box shown in Figure 31.29.

2. Make sure there's a check mark in the box labeled Check for New Messages every *x* Minute(s).

Figure 31.29
On a LAN connection,
Outlook Express
checks for new mail
every 30 minutes. To
pick up messages
more frequently,
adjust this setting to 5
or 10 minutes instead.

3. Use the spinner control to adjust how often Outlook Express sends and receives mail. This number must be in the range of 1 (every minute) to 480 (every 8 hours).

4. Click OK to make the change effective.

How do you know when new mail has arrived? Outlook Express gives you two cues when you receive mail. A letter icon appears in the notification area at the right of the taskbar, and the program also plays a sound. If you find the sound disturbing, it's easy to kill the noise. Choose Tools, Options; click the General tab; and remove the check mark for that option.

You can also choose a different sound file to play when new mail arrives. Open the Control Panel and use the Sounds applet to assign a different WAV file to the New Mail Notification event.

→ If you like to "hear" your mail arrive, **see** "Changing the Sounds Related to Windows Events," **p. 342**.

Tip #210

As Outlook Express checks for mail, look in the status bar for messages that display the results of the connection and mail send/retrieve attempt. If you need more information, double-click the icon at the far right to display a dialog box with more details, including any error messages you might have received. Don't ask for too much though; most errors merely reflect the inability to log on or connect to the POP3 server.

DELIVERING THE MAIL MANUALLY

Of course, you can check for new messages any time by using the Send/Recv button. This technique works even if Outlook Express is set to check messages at regular intervals. The Send and Receive command automatically connects with every mail account and your default news account. To add or remove a server from this group, follow these steps:

1. Choose Tools, Accounts and select the account from the list.

2. Click the Properties button to display the account's property sheet.

3. Click on the General tab and check or uncheck the setting labeled Include This Account... (the exact wording is different for mail and news accounts). A check mark means Outlook Express automatically checks for messages when you click the Send/Recv button.

4. Click OK to make the change effective and then close the Accounts dialog box.

If you have multiple mail providers and you want to connect with only one of them, regardless of the default settings, choose Tools, Send and Receive from the file bar menu. Outlook Express presents a cascading menu that lets you choose which mail providers you want to connect with.

CHECKING THE MAIL WHEN YOU'RE OUT OF THE OFFICE

Outlook Express lets you file and save all the messages you send and receive. But what happens when you need to read your email from a machine other than the one you normally use? This might be the case if you normally use an office PC but occasionally check your email from home or the road. If you use the default settings, you end up with a collection of messages on different PCs.

The cure is to adjust the account settings on your "away" PC so that it downloads messages but does not delete them from the mail server. Later, when you return to the office, you can connect to the server and download all the messages, saving and filing the important ones.

You must specifically set this option for each account you intend to check. Choose Tools, Accounts; select the account; and click the Properties button. Click on the Advanced tab and then check the Delivery options shown in Figure 31.30.

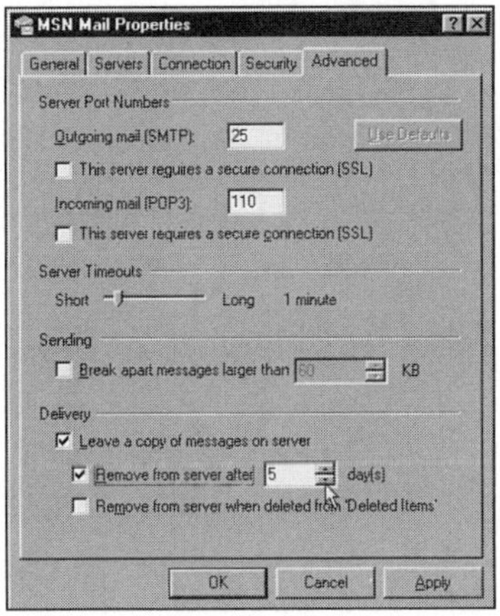

Figure 31.30
If you check your mail when you're away from the office, tell Outlook Express to leave messages on the server so you can retrieve them when you return to work.

The other two Delivery options help you avoid cluttering up the mail server by automatically deleting messages after a set number of days or when you delete them from your "away" machine.

REPLYING TO MESSAGES YOU'VE RECEIVED

The simplest way to compose a message is to reply to one you've received. The format for replies varies slightly between mail and news messages.

REPLYING TO A MAIL MESSAGE

When you select a message and click the Reply button, Outlook Express opens a New Message window, selects the same format as the message to which you're responding, fills in the To line with the sender's address from the original message, adds Re to the beginning of the original Subject line, and positions the insertion point at the top of the message. When you click the Reply to All button, Outlook Express picks up every addressee from the To and Cc lines in the original message and adds them to your new message.

By default, all replies include the full text of the original message, with a separator line between your reply and the original text. How that message appears depends on the format of your reply:

- With HTML-formatted messages, all graphics are included, and the original text is indented.

- With plain-text messages, each line of the original text begins with the > character.

Choose Tools, Options and click the Send tab to adjust these defaults, as shown in Figure 31.31.

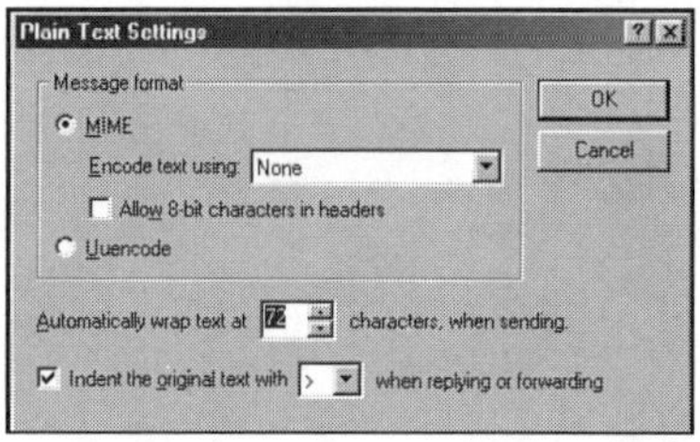

Figure 31.31
If you routinely reply to replies, lower the default text wrap to 72 characters. That setting lessens the chance that your prefix character causes lines to wrap inappropriately.

To change the default setting so all replies start with a blank message, uncheck the Include Message in Reply option.

REPLYING TO A NEWSGROUP MESSAGE

When reading newsgroup messages, you have a choice of two reply buttons. Click Reply to Group to begin composing a message to the current newsgroup; just as with a mail message, your reply includes the original posting, although the format of the separator text is different.

To reply in a private email to the person who posted the original newsgroup message, click the Reply to Author button. Although there's no Reply to All button, that option is available: Choose Compose, Reply to Newsgroup and Author to post your reply to the newsgroup *and* send a copy to the author via email.

Caution

Check the email address carefully when responding to newsgroup postings. Many newsgroup contributors deliberately corrupt the reply-to address in their messages to frustrate junk emailers. You might need to edit stray characters or words to see the real address.

FORWARDING MESSAGES

You have two choices when you forward a message you've received to another person. Select the message and click the Forward button to open a New Message window containing the original message; the message uses the same indent settings as if you had chosen to reply to the sender. Enter one or more addresses, add any comments of your own, and click the Send button.

You can also forward an email message as an attached file: Choose Compose, Forward as Attachment. That's the correct choice when you want another person to see the message exactly as you saw it, without prefix characters or other reply formatting.

PART
V

CH
31

ORGANIZING MESSAGES WITH FOLDERS

By default, Outlook Express includes five top-level mail folders. You cannot delete these basic mail folders, which perform the following crucial functions:

- All incoming messages hit the Inbox first; use the Message Rules to file or process messages automatically as they arrive.

- Mail that you've sent goes to the Outbox until the next time you exchange messages with your mail server.

- By default, a copy of every message you send goes to the Sent Items folder. To change this setting, choose Tools, Options; click the Send tab; and uncheck this option.

- When you delete a message, Outlook Express moves it to the Deleted Items folder. An option on the General tab lets you empty this folder each time you exit. By default, though, this folder stays full until you right-click on its icon and choose Empty Folder.

- The Drafts folder stores messages you've composed and saved but haven't yet sent.

Note

You can't organize newsgroup messages using mail folders, although you can drag a newsgroup message from the message list and copy the message into a mail folder.

CREATING A NEW FOLDER

You can add an unlimited number of top-level mail folders and subfolders to Outlook Express. The easiest way to create a new folder is to follow these steps:

1. If the Folders list is not visible, choose View, Layout; check the box labeled Folder List and click OK.

2. Select the folder in which you want to create the new subfolder. To create a new top-level folder, choose the Outlook Express icon at the top of the Folders list.

3. Right-click on the icon you selected and choose New Folder from the shortcut menu.

4. Enter a name for the new folder. (This dialog box also lets you use the tree at the bottom to change the location in which the new folder is created.)

5. Click OK to create the new folder.

MOVING OR COPYING MESSAGES BETWEEN FOLDERS

To move messages, drag them from the message list and drop them on the Folder icon in your Folders list. To copy messages to a folder while leaving the original file intact, hold down the Ctrl key as you drag the messages.

If you use folders extensively, use right-click shortcut menus in the Folders list to move and copy messages. As Figure 31.32 shows, these commands let you create a new folder on-the-fly. Better yet, add the Move To button to the toolbar for instant access to this dialog box.

Figure 31.32
Use the Move to Folder menu option to move messages.

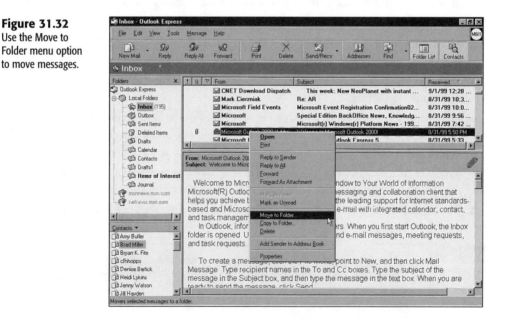

→ To create your own work environment while using Outlook Express, **see** "Customizing the Outlook Express Toolbar," **p. 675**.

Tip #211

> Adding a new top-level folder creates a matching shortcut on the Outlook bar. If you create a folder within an existing folder—under the Inbox, for example—it appears in the Folders list but not on the Outlook bar.

MOVING, RENAMING, AND DELETING FOLDERS

Open the Folders list and simply drag Folder icons to move them from one location to another. Right-click and use the shortcut menus to delete or rename a folder. You can freely move, delete, or rename any folders you create, but you can't change any of the five default mail folders.

COMPACTING FOLDERS TO REDUCE THE SIZE OF YOUR MAIL FILE

As you receive new messages and organize them into folders, the size of your mail file grows. When you move and delete messages, Outlook Express removes the messages but leaves the empty space in the mail file. Over time, this practice can cause your mail folders to waste a significant amount of space. To eliminate wasted space in a single folder, select its icon and choose File, Folder, Compact. To remove slack space from every mail folder, choose File, Folder, Compact All Folders.

PART

V

CH

31

Tip #212

> Before you compact your mail folders, it's a good idea to back up all your mail files. You may also want to export your messages and address book to another location using the File, Export menu choice. To locate the mail files, click the Start menu; choose Find, Files or Folders; and search for the data files for each folder; these files use the extension .MBX, and a matching index for each file has the same name but the .IDX extension. Folders you create go by the name Folder1.mbx, Folder2.mbx, and so on.

USING THE MESSAGE RULES TO PROCESS MAIL AUTOMATICALLY

In some busy organizations that live and die by email, workers can receive dozens or even hundreds of messages per day. Managing that torrent of messages can be a full-time job, but Outlook Express can do at least part of the work. The secret is a tool called Message Rules, which lets you define rules for Outlook Express to follow when you receive new mail.

DEFINING RULES FOR PROCESSING MAIL

To define mail rules that automate mail processing, choose Tools, Message Rules and then choose Mail from the list of options. The New Mail Rule dialog box appears, as shown in Figure 31.33.

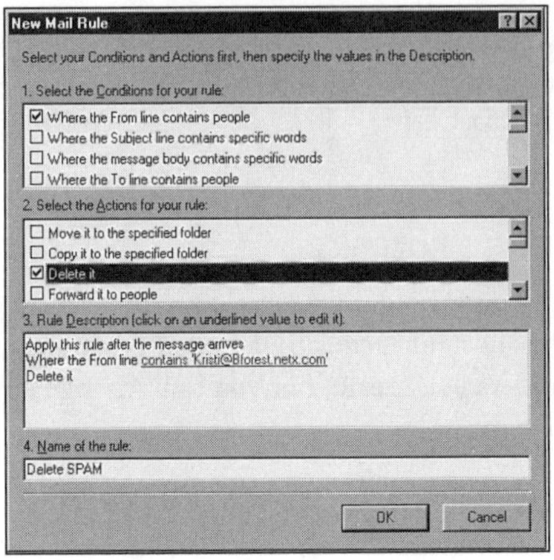

Figure 31.33
To create a mail-processing rule, define one or more criteria in the top of this dialog box and then select an action to be performed when a message meets that condition.

Each rule consists of two parts: a set of criteria and a matching action. Each time a message arrives in your Inbox, Outlook Express compares the message with the conditions defined in your Message Rules; when it finds a match, Outlook Express performs the action defined for that rule.

You can define a variety of conditions to trigger mail actions:

- Search for text in the address box, subject line, or message body.
- Look for messages that come from a specific mail account or for a message that is From, To, or CC'd to specific people.
- Look for priority or secure messages.
- Look for messages that have attachments.
- Check the size of each incoming message.
- Apply the rule to all messages.

When a message meets the conditions you define, you can order Outlook Express to move or copy it to a folder, forward it to another recipient, reply automatically with a saved message, leave the message on the server, or delete the message from the inbox or server. Other options in Outlook Express 5 include highlighting a message in a specific color, flagging it, and marking the message as read or as watched or ignored. Another option tells Outlook Express to stop processing other rules when a specific condition is met.

Figure 31.34 shows some rules you might find useful for weeding out junk mail and for helping to identify important messages:

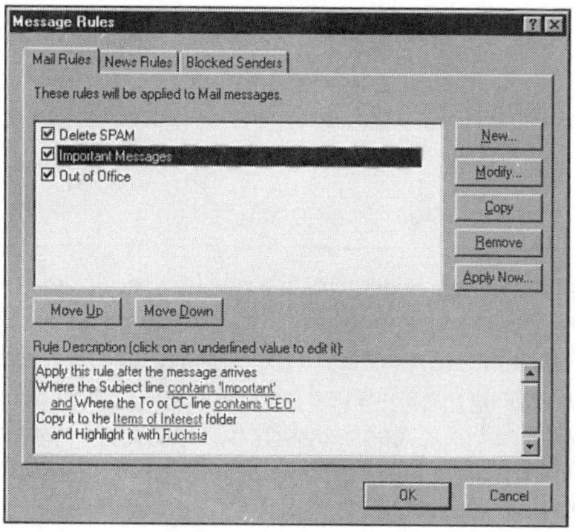

Figure 31.34
Use Message Rules to help identify important messages and eliminate junk mail.

- Automatically move mail sent by a VIP or from your company's domain (mcp.com, for example) to a special Read Me Now folder.

- Look for messages where your name is in the CC field and move them to a Read Me Later folder.

- Move messages to the Deleted Items folder if the subject contains key junk-mail phrases ("make money fast," for example) or if the message was sent by someone from whom you do not wish to receive mail (this feature is often called a "bozo filter").

Tip #213

> In Outlook Express 5 you can block a specific sender's messages with the Blocked Sender's List and the Block Sender, Message menu option. When unwanted email reaches your inbox, select the message and choose Block Sender from the Message menu list. All that sender's existing and future mail will be deleted from your mailbox automatically. You can also add people manually to your Blocked Sender's list by choosing the Block Sender tab from the Tools, Message Rules dialog box and clicking Add.

- When you're out of the office on business or on vacation, use a Message Rule to forward all your mail to an assistant and send an advisory message to the sender.

- If space on your notebook computer is tight or you have a slow Internet connection, tell Outlook Express not to download messages that are larger than a specified size—for example, 100KB.

CREATING MESSAGE RULES

Note that rules are applied in the order in which they appear in your list. If two or more conditions apply to the same message, only the first rule may be applied. This type of conflict between rules can produce effects you didn't anticipate.

- To adjust the order in which the Message Rules are applied, select a rule from the list and use the Move Up and Move Down buttons.

- To completely eliminate a rule, select it and click the Remove button.

PART

V

CH

31

- To temporarily disable a rule without eliminating it, clear the check box to the left of its entry in the list.

- To change the conditions or actions associated with a rule, select it and click the Modify button.

Tip #214	To clean up a cluttered mail folder, create a rule for specific email addresses to be moved to special folders (for example, by project, or personal versus work) or for certain messages to be deleted. When the rule appears in the Message Rules list, highlight the rule you want to apply to your existing messages and then click the Apply To button. Pick the appropriate folder from the dialog box that pops up. For example, if you want to apply the rule to messages in your inbox, choose Inbox. The Message Rules processes all the messages in the folder you select and any subfolders in it.

ENHANCING EMAIL SECURITY

By its very nature, an ordinary email message is as insecure as a postcard. It takes only the most rudimentary technical knowledge to "spoof" a message so that it appears to be coming from someone other than the actual sender. In fact, a favorite hacker trick is to send bogus mail messages that appear to have come from famous individuals such as Bill Gates. And because email travels in packets across the Internet, it's theoretically possible for anyone to intercept a transmission, read a message sent to someone else, and possibly change the contents of that message.

Outlook Express includes two features that enhance email security, although neither offers foolproof protection from a skilled and determined data thief. *Encryption* lets you encode the contents of a message so that only a recipient with a matching code key can decipher the text. A *digital signature* tacked onto the end of a message guarantees that the message originated from the sender and has not been tampered with in transit.

Before you can use either security feature, you have to acquire a digital certificate from a certifying authority and add it to Outlook Express. You also need to enable that certificate for every mail account with which you plan to use it, as shown in Figure 31.35.

To install your digital ID, follow the instructions provided by the certificate provider. The certificate includes two parts: a *public key*, which you distribute freely to others, and a *private key* that only you have access to. Anyone can encrypt a message using your public key, and after they've done so, only you can unscramble it using the private key.

SENDING A DIGITALLY SIGNED MESSAGE

To add a signature to a message, click the Digitally Sign Message button on the toolbar in the New Message window. A red icon in the lower-right corner of the address box tells you this item is a signed message.

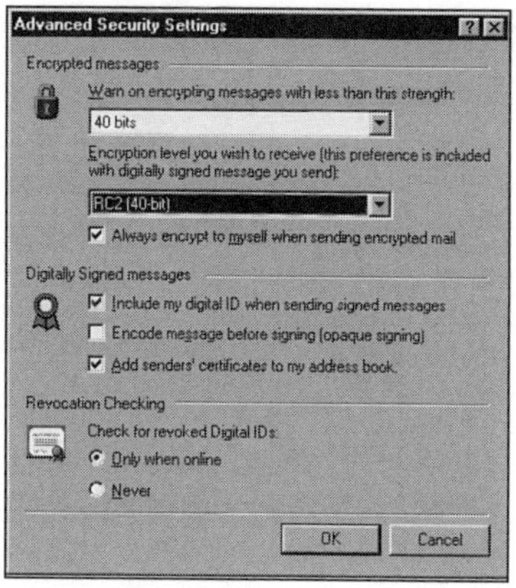

Figure 31.35
Before you can encrypt or digitally sign an email message, you need to enable a certificate like this one. Click the button at the bottom of the dialog box for more information.

> **Caution**
>
> Outlook Express includes the option to digitally sign and/or encrypt all your messages. Don't activate this feature unless you're certain that most of your correspondents use mail software that can accept digital certificates. For the overwhelming majority of email users, it's best to choose secure email options one message at a time.

ENCRYPTING A MESSAGE

To scramble a message so that only a trusted recipient can read it, click the Encrypt Message button in the New Message window. A blue padlock icon in the address box lets you know the message is encrypted. You must have a copy of the recipient's public key before you can encrypt a message to that person. (You can ask a correspondent to send you his or her public key; you can also find public keys on some directory servers and trusted Internet sites.)

 Pretty Good Privacy, Inc., has one of the best online sources of information about encryption and secure email. You can find it at

http://www.NAI.com

READING A SIGNED OR ENCRYPTED MESSAGE

Anyone can encrypt a message and send it to you, as long as the sender has a copy of your public key. When you receive the encrypted message, Outlook Express uses your private key to unscramble the text so you can read it. When you receive a digitally signed message, you see an introductory message like the one in Figure 31.36.

Figure 31.36
Outlook Express offers this help screen when you receive a digitally signed message. Note the additional information in the address header, too.

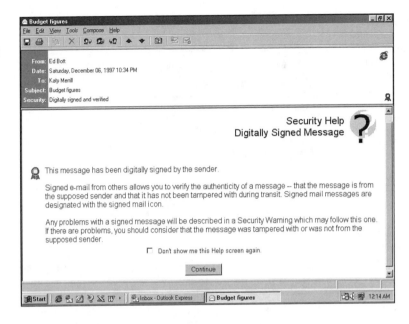

WORKING WITH NEWSGROUPS

Although newsgroup messages appear in the same window as mail messages, the mechanics of downloading and managing newsgroup messages are dramatically different from mail messages. Unlike mail messages, which are addressed directly to you, newsgroup messages are posted on public servers for all to see. You probably don't want to read every message in busy newsgroups, which can get hundreds of new messages per day.

Getting the maximum benefit from Internet newsgroups takes careful setup and management. Before you can get started, you have to identify potentially useful or interesting newsgroups.

HOW NEWSGROUPS WORK

Newsgroups are nearly as old as the Internet. They get only a fraction of the publicity that goes to the newer and flashier World Wide Web, but that doesn't mean they're less useful. On the contrary, public peer-support newsgroups can be an excellent source for quick answers to thorny software and hardware support questions. Newsgroups are also popular among hobbyists ranging from BMW enthusiasts to cat owners, and moderated newsgroups are important gathering places for computer and science professionals.

Don't be misled by the name: Newsgroups have nothing to do with the *New York Times* or CNN. They function more like public bulletin boards, organized by topic, where individuals post messages (sometimes called *articles*) that anyone with access to that group can read and reply to. Just as Web servers use HTTP to communicate, news servers use Network News Transfer Protocol (NNTP) to share information.

The oldest collection of newsgroups is called Usenet, a distributed network of servers that continually exchange messages with one another. When you post a newsgroup article to your local news server, it works its way across the network until every Usenet news server has a copy.

For the definitive description of what Usenet is and isn't, read this Web page:

`http://www.netannounce.org/news.announce.newusers/archive/usenet/what-is/part1`

Not all Usenet news servers carry all newsgroups, and it's up to the manager of a news server to decide when older messages "expire" and drop off the server. The past few years have seen a steady increase in the number of private newsgroups as corporations have recognized how easily employees can communicate through these forums.

Caution

Don't expect to find useful information in a newsgroup just because the name sounds appealing. As the Internet has grown, newsgroups have become increasingly vulnerable to spam—posts (usually commercial in nature) that are unrelated to the stated purpose of a newsgroup and simply serve to clutter the listings of articles. On some once-popular newsgroups, the only traffic these days consists of variations on chain letters and enticements to visit X-rated Web sites.

PART

V

CH

31

VIEWING THE FULL LIST OF NEWSGROUPS

The first time you connect to a news server, Outlook Express offers to download a list of all the newsgroups available there. On a well-stocked server, that can represent thousands of newsgroups. Click the Newsgroups button to view the complete list of groups available on a news server. If you've defined multiple accounts, make sure you select the correct server from the list at the left of the window, as in Figure 31.37.

Figure 31.37
To see a complete list of available newsgroups, first select a News server icon from the list at left.

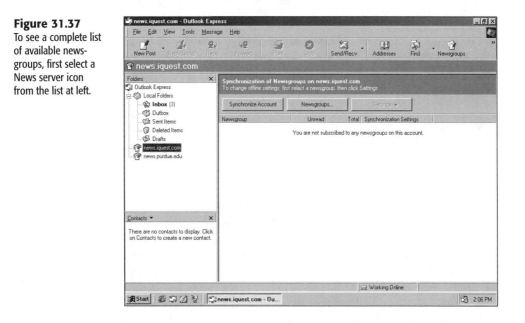

DECIPHERING A NEWSGROUP NAME

Newsgroups use a dotted naming convention like those found elsewhere on the Internet, with strict hierarchies that identify what subscribers can expect to find in each one. To read a newsgroup name, follow the hierarchy from left to right as it goes from general to specific. In Usenet newsgroups, for example, the first entry is the top-level domain. The following table lists many (but not all) of the most common top-level domains.

Top-Level Domain	Description	Sample Newsgroup
comp	General computer subjects	`comp.os.ms-windows.networking.tcp-ip`
rec	Hobbies, the arts, pop culture	`rec.music.beatles`
soc	Social issues and world culture	`soc.culture.irish`
sci	Science related, many highly specialized	`sci.space.policy`
gov	Government newsgroups	`gov.us.fed.congress.documents`
news	Newsgroup administrative issues	`news.newusers.questions`
misc	Miscellaneous, often commercial groups	`misc.taxes.moderated`

Various unofficial newsgroup hierarchies exist as well, including the infamous alt category. When people complain about pornography on the Internet, they're talking about newsgroups whose names begin with `alt.sex` and `alt.binaries.pictures.erotica`.

There are also local newsgroups, whose top-level domain identifies a geographic region (try `ba.food` for San Francisco Bay Area restaurant recommendations, or `nyc.jobs` for employment in the Big Apple), as well as private groups intended for subscribers of Internet service providers like Netcom.

Microsoft now provides its first level of technical support through newsgroups in the microsoft.* hierarchy. You can find it on `msnews.microsoft.com`, and an increasing number of Internet service providers are replicating the Microsoft news feed to their own news servers.

FINDING A SPECIFIC NEWSGROUP

Microsoft's public news servers include nearly 600 separate groups. Some well-stocked Usenet news servers have more than 15,000 distinct newsgroups. Instead of scrolling through the full Newsgroups list to find relevant ones, use the text box at the top of the dialog box to show only groups whose names contain certain letters or words. If you're looking for information about Outlook Express, for example, type the word sport to see a filtered list like the one in Figure 31.38.

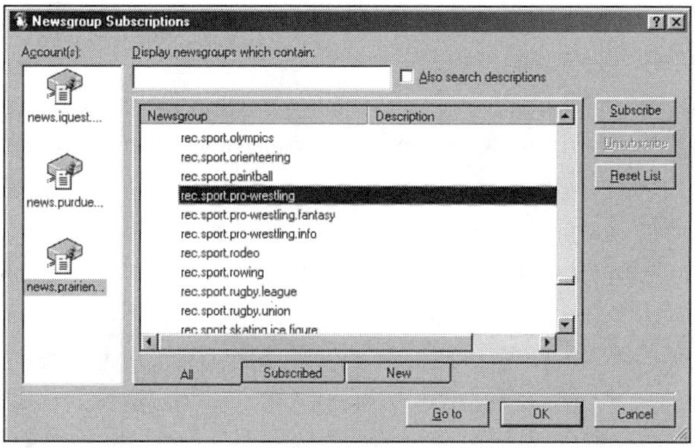

Figure 31.38
After you find the newsgroup you're looking for, double-click on its name to add it to your list of subscribed groups.

 You can't use Outlook Express to search the contents of a newsgroup for specific information. However, Web-based news archives like Deja News can search newsgroups for messages and threads that match your interests; if you find a wealth of information in a particular newsgroup, use Outlook Express to go there directly. You can find Deja News at

`http://www.deja.com`

REFRESHING THE LIST OF NEWSGROUPS

On Usenet servers in particular, new groups appear and old ones disappear regularly. If you suspect that new groups are available on a server, follow these steps:

1. Select the News server icon in the Folders list.
2. Click the Newsgroups button to show the list of all newsgroups.
3. Click the Reset List button to update the master list. This operation may take some time, especially over a slow Internet connection.
4. After you refresh the list, click the New tab along the bottom of the Newsgroups list to see only new groups.

MANAGING NEWSGROUP SUBSCRIPTIONS

Don't be confused by the buttons to the right of the Newsgroups list. Subscribing to a newsgroup doesn't cost anything, and it doesn't require you to send any information about yourself to a news server. (There's also no connection with Web subscriptions.) In Outlook Express, subscriptions are simply a way of managing the Newsgroups list to show only your favorite groups.

Follow these steps to manage your newsgroup subscriptions:

1. Select the News server icon in the Folders list and then click the Newsgroups button.
2. Click the All tab at the bottom of the dialog box to see the full list of newsgroups.
3. Select at least one name from the list; to select more than one name at a time, hold down the Ctrl key as you click.

4. Use the Subscribe button to add a newsgroup to your personal list. An icon appears to the left of the newsgroup name.

5. Use the Unsubscribe button to remove a newsgroup from your personal list. (You can also double-click on an entry in the Newsgroups list to toggle the subscribed icon.)

6. Click the Subscribed tab at the bottom of the Newsgroups list to see only the list of newsgroups you've selected. Icons for all subscribed newsgroups appear under the News server icon in your Folders list, as shown in Figure 31.39.

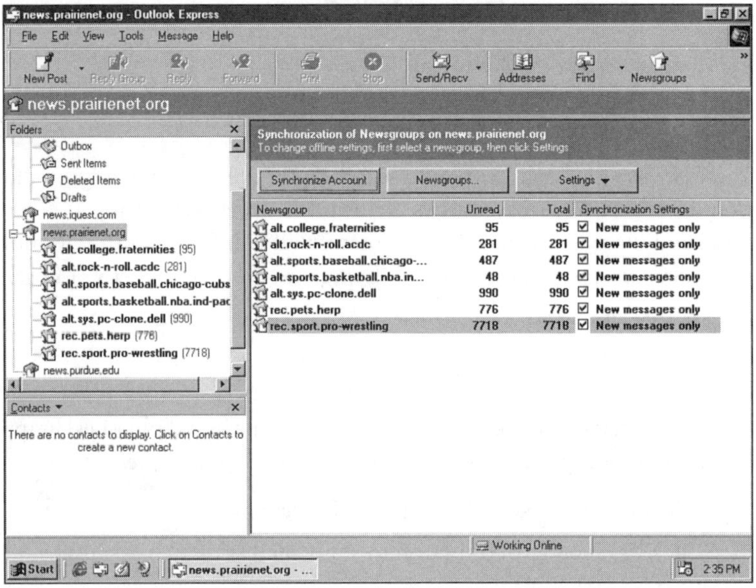

Figure 31.39
When you select a news server in the Folders list at left, the list at the right shows only newsgroups to which you've subscribed.

Tip #215

If you want to see the contents of a newsgroup but do not necessarily want to subscribe to it, select a name from the Newsgroups list and then click the Go to button to open the newsgroup. Use the Tools menu to manage subscriptions for the newsgroup you're currently viewing.

DOWNLOADING AND READING NEWSGROUP MESSAGES

Before you can read the messages in a newsgroup, you have to download them from the server to your computer. That process is not as straightforward as it sounds. For starters, you can't tell from the Newsgroups list how many messages are currently available for each newsgroup. Some obscure groups generate only a handful of messages, but popular groups might contain thousands of messages at one time, with some containing binary attachments or graphics files that occupy significant amounts of disk space. Downloading every message without first checking the newsgroup's contents is clearly a bad idea.

To make newsgroup traffic more manageable, Outlook Express distinguishes between message headers and bodies. Regardless of the size of the message itself, the header contains only the subject line, the author's name, and the message size. By default, when you open a newsgroup for the first time, Outlook Express connects with the server and asks it to transfer the 300 most recent subject headers.

Look at the status bar to see how many headers were left on the server. To download more headers, choose Tools, Get Next 300 Headers. Outlook Express always chooses the most recent headers that have not yet been downloaded.

Tip #216	If you want to see more or fewer titles than you are currently receiving, adjust the number of headers Outlook Express retrieves on each pass. By default, Outlook Express downloads 300 headers at a time. To increase or decrease this amount, choose Tools, Options and then click the Read tab. Edit the number shown in the Download *(number)* Headers at a Time option.

NAVIGATING THROUGH NEWSGROUPS

The window in which you read news messages works much the same as the Mail window, with a single notable exception: Outlook Express organizes news messages so you can follow a discussion that might take place over days or even weeks.

Newsgroups facilitate *threaded conversations*, in which one user posts a message and others reply to that message. News servers keep track of the links between original posts, replies, and replies to replies. By default, Outlook Express maintains these threads, regardless of the sort order you've chosen for messages in a given newsgroup. These messages remain grouped even when the reply title begins with the Re prefix.

Replies to a message are indented below the original message, and replies to replies are indented another level. To see all the messages in a thread, click the plus sign to the left of the message header that begins the thread. To collapse the thread so you see only the first header, click the minus sign to the left of the thread.

Navigating through threads with the keyboard is fast and easy. Use the up and down arrows to move through the list of messages. In the default view, where all message threads are collapsed, the up and down arrows move from thread to thread. To work with threads from the keyboard, use the right arrow to expand and the left arrow to collapse each thread.

If messages are not grouped properly, choose View, Sort By, Group Messages by Thread.

READING MESSAGES ONLINE

As long as the connection between Outlook Express and the news server is active, you can read messages by opening a Message window or by using the preview pane. When you select a header, Outlook Express automatically retrieves that message from the server and adds it to your file. When you double-click to open a Message window, or if you keep the preview pane open for more than five seconds, the header text changes from bold to normal type and the page icon changes from a full page to a torn page, indicating that you've read the message (see Figure 31.40).

Figure 31.40
Note the different icons in this list: Downloaded messages show as a full page, and the page is torn in half after reading.

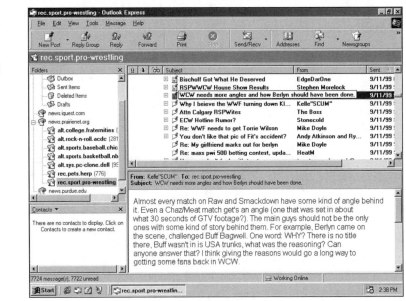

If you prefer to keep your connection open while you scroll through the headers and retrieve only those messages that look most interesting, choose Tools, Options; click the Read tab; and clear the check mark from the box labeled Automatically Show News Messages in the Preview Pane. With this option set, you must select a header and tap the space bar to retrieve a message.

WORKING OFFLINE FOR MAXIMUM EFFICIENCY

The most efficient way to work with large newsgroups is offline. Outlook Express lets you download a batch of headers, scroll through the list, and mark the ones you want to download. The next time you connect to the server, Outlook Express retrieves the marked messages, which you can read anytime.

Follow these steps to work offline:

1. Choose File, Work Offline.

2. When you see a message header you'd like to read, mark it for retrieval. You can use the right-click shortcut menu, but it's easier to select one or more message headers and press Ctrl+M.

3. To select an entire thread for retrieval, make sure the thread is collapsed, with a plus sign visible to the left. Select the first message in the thread and press Ctrl+M. The icon to the left of a message header that has been marked for retrieval changes, as Figure 31.41 shows.

Figure 31.41
The tiny arrow to the left of some headers means they've been marked for retrieval the next time you connect with the news server.

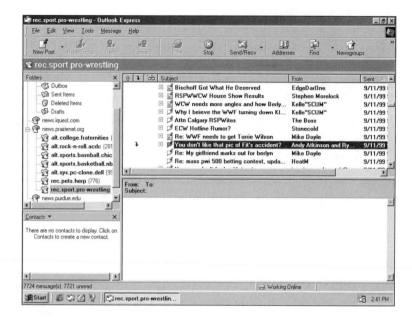

4. To remove marks, select one or more marked messages and choose Tools, Mark for Retrieval, Unmark.

5. To go online again, choose File and clear the check mark from the Work Offline choice.

6. To retrieve all marked messages, choose Tools, Download This Newsgroup. In the dialog box that appears, check the option labeled Get Messages Marked for Download, as shown in Figure 31.42.

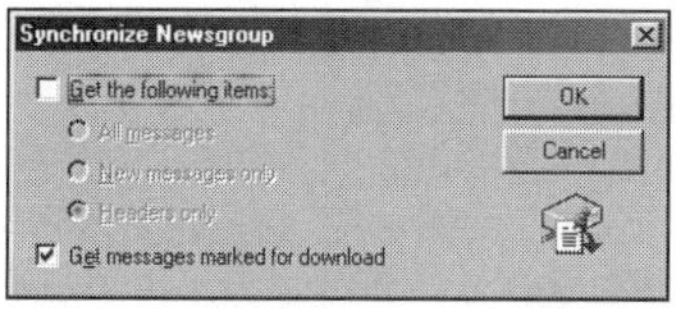

Figure 31.42
Check the option at the bottom of this dialog box to retrieve messages whose headers you've marked.

REESTABLISHING CONNECTIONS WITH A NEWS SERVER

Unless you set up your news account to hang up immediately after downloading messages or headers, the connection remains active while you work with messages and headers. By default, Outlook Express disconnects from the server after a minute of inactivity; when that happens, the text in the status bar changes.

If you're using a dial-up connection, you might need to redial at this point. Click the Connect button or choose File, Connect to redial the server. If you're connected through a LAN, you can reestablish the connection by pressing the Refresh key, F5.

USING FILTERS TO MAKE THE NEWS MORE READABLE

After a while, the sheer bulk of downloaded headers and messages from some newsgroups is overwhelming, and navigation can become nearly impossible. To cut the display down to manageable proportions, use filters to show only messages that meet specific criteria. Outlook Express includes three built-in filters, or you can create your own.

News filters are analogous to mail-processing rules created by the Message Rules. Unlike those rules, however, newsgroup filters can't move or forward messages or reply automatically on your behalf to messages.

To use a built-in filter, choose View, Current View and pick one of these choices:

- Unread Messages—Use this filter to quickly pick up new messages, especially when they're part of older threads.

- Downloaded Messages—This choice works especially well after you mark a widely scattered group of messages for offline reading.

- Replies to My Posts—For active participants in a busy newsgroup, this filter is essential.

You can also create your own filter based on one or more rules, which can be used with the built-in filters. To create the rules for your filter, choose Tools, Newsgroup Filters and then click the Add button. You see a New News Rule dialog box, as shown in Figure 31.43.

Figure 31.43
Use filters to reduce the amount of clutter in crowded newsgroups.

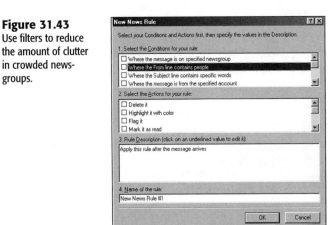

You can apply filters to a single newsgroup or server or to every server. Filters let you suppress messages from specific individuals or domains or messages with a particular keyword or phrase in the Subject line. You can also hide messages that are too old or too big.

To apply all active filters to the current display, choose View, Current View and make sure Filtered Messages is checked.

To temporarily disable a single rule, clear the check box next to its entry in the Filters list. To change the order in which rules are applied, use the Move Up and Move Down buttons.

To edit a rule, select its entry and click the <u>P</u>roperties button. To eliminate a rule permanently, click the <u>R</u>emove button.

CONTROLLING MESSAGE DOWNLOADS FOR EACH NEWSGROUP

Eventually, as you develop experience, you'll build up a list of favorite newsgroups, each with its own characteristics. Outlook Express lets you create different settings for each one, so that you can download messages and/or headers according to your preferences.

To set up each newsgroup, open the Folders list, right-click on a newsgroup entry, and choose <u>P</u>roperties. The General tab provides information about the number of messages and headers; click on the Synchronize tab (see Figure 31.44) to tell Outlook Express whether you want only headers or full messages each time you download a newsgroup.

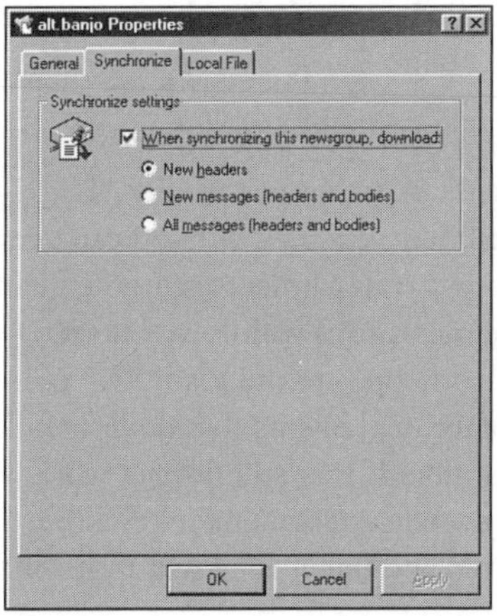

Figure 31.44
Be careful with changing Synchronize settings from the default New Headers option; downloading new or all messages on extremely active newsgroups can consume more disk space than you think.

PART

V

CH

31

After you set your preferences for each newsgroup to which you're subscribed, use one of the Download choices from the <u>T</u>ools menu to gather mail and news. Figure 31.45 shows the status screen you see if you choose Download All Messages.

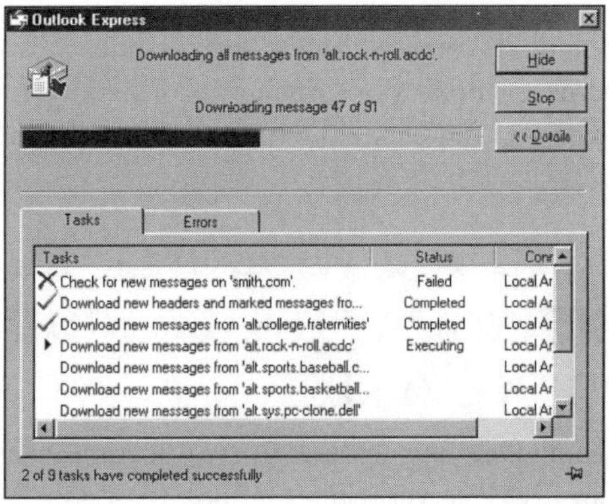

Figure 31.45
Watch this status screen for details as Outlook Express gathers mail and news from all your accounts.

TROUBLESHOOTING

TEXT ENCODING

Some recipients complain that all my paragraphs appear as a single long line or that my messages are filled with equal signs.

Mail format options control how Outlook Express encodes your messages using *Multipurpose Internet Mail Extensions (MIME)*. Quoted-Printable MIME replaces line endings and special characters (such as accented vowels) with an equal sign and an optional numeric code. This technique allows you to send some formatting information using ASCII characters. Your recipients are seeing this encoding through a mail reader that isn't fully compliant with the MIME standard. If they're unable or unwilling to switch to another mail client, choose Tools, Options; click the Send tab; and click the Settings button to the right of the mail format you've chosen. Change the Text Encoding option to None, and the problem should disappear; unfortunately, you also lose the ability to use extended ASCII characters.

My recipients report that file attachments appear as gibberish in messages they receive from me.

Your recipients are probably using a mail client that is not fully MIME-compatible, or their ISP's mail server can't process the attachments correctly. If you can't convince your recipients to change mail clients, try resending the attachment using the uuencode format instead of MIME encoding. You must send the message as plain text; choose Tools, Options; click the Send tab; and click the Settings button opposite the Plain Text option to adjust the format for outgoing attachments. Many older mail clients that don't handle MIME formatting can process uuencoded attachments just fine. If that still doesn't work, your recipients need to find a third-party program that can decode attachments: Some free and shareware programs can help convert MIME-formatted and uuencoded text to its original binary format.

→ For information on third-party free and shareware programs to unencode MIME files, **see** "Secrets of Mastering the Windows 98 Environment: Using WinZip Shareware to Decode MIME Files" at the end of this chapter.

BORROWED MODULES

I tried to check the spelling of my message, but the Tools, Spelling command was grayed out and unavailable.

Outlook Express does not include its own spell-checking module; instead, it "borrows" the spell checker from other Microsoft applications, such as Word and Works. You must install one of these applications before you can check the spelling of an Outlook Express message.

SECRETS OF MASTERING THE WINDOWS 98 ENVIRONMENT: DELETING A MESSAGE FROM AN IMAP SERVER WITH OUTLOOK EXPRESS

The Outlook Express Help topic Deleting a Message gives incorrect instructions for purging a deleted message from an IMAP server using Outlook Express.

The correct method is to first highlight the message in Outlook Express and then click the delete button. Next, you must remove any stored messages on the IMAP server by selecting Purge Deleted Messages on the Edit menu to remove the deleted messages from the folder.

SECRETS OF MASTERING THE WINDOWS 98 ENVIRONMENT: USING WINZIP SHAREWARE TO DECODE MIME FILES

From time to time, you may receive an email message with a MIME-converted attachment. This may happen when the sender's ISP uses MIME conversion to encode and compress multiple attachments sent across the Internet from its email server.

A MIME file is structured much like a Zip file. You cannot "read" it because it is actually a wrapper around a collection of files. For example, if a sender attaches two JPEGs and a letter in a *.doc format to an email message and the sender's ISP uses MIME encoding for multiple attachments, the attachment you receive will actually be a single *.mim file in which the three original files are wrapped. Before you can open either JPEG or the document, you must unwrap the MIME file with a MIME decoder.

A popular shareware application that fulfills this need is WinZip 7.0, SR-1. You can download a free evaluation copy from the WinZip Internet site: `http://www.winzip.com`. After your evaluation period is over, you can pay $29.00 to register your copy.

WinZip includes long-filename support and integration with the Windows 98 environment, making the program part of the right-click menu for any file in Windows.

I believe that WinZip is the best product on the market for the money. Unlike other decoders, such as Wincode, which deal exclusively with encoded/decoded files, this application not only decodes MIME files but also compresses, or zips, files for you to send from your computer. In fact, it has built-in support for almost all popular Internet file formats. If you have a format you are not sure of, visit the WinZip Web site and search for it. Chances are, WinZip can handle it. Other attractive WinZip features include

- A freely downloadable WinZip Internet Browser Support Add-On that allows you to download and open archives with one click using Microsoft Internet Explorer or Netscape Navigator.
- An automatic installation of most software distributed in Zip files. For example, if a Zip file contains a setup or install program, WinZip's Install feature unzips the files, runs the installation program, and cleans up temporary files.
- The WinZip Wizard, an optional feature that uses the standard and familiar wizard interface to simplify the process of unzipping and installing software distributed in Zip files. The WinZip Wizard is ideal for the rapidly growing number of PC users just learning to use Zip files.

- The Favorite Zip Folders, a feature that lets you organize Zip files into one convenient list, sorted by date. This practice makes it easier to locate all your Zip files, regardless of where they came from or where they are stored. Also, a Search facility finds any Zip files lost on your hard disk.

- The WinZip Self-Extractor Personal Edition that enables you to create files that unzip themselves. Self-extracting files are ideal for sending compressed files to others who may not own or know how to use file-compression software.

- Virus-scanner support that can be configured to work with most virus scanners.

CHAPTER 32

CREATING WEB PAGES WITH FRONTPAGE EXPRESS

In this chapter

INTRODUCING FRONTPAGE EXPRESS

Sometimes, the best way to introduce a product is to state exactly what the product is. FrontPage Express is a what-you-see-is-what-you-get (WYSIWYG) Hypertext Markup Language (HTML) page editor. Given that definition, you may be confused if you thought that FrontPage Express was a tool for building Web pages (something like Microsoft Word for the Internet). Both descriptions are accurate. FrontPage Express's sole purpose is to build pages to be viewed in a Web browser either over the Internet or over local corporate intranets. First, let's take a quick look at what HTML and WYSIWYG mean.

Like most design products today, FrontPage is a WYSIWYG product. Thus, as you build a page, you see exactly how your page will appear in a browser. This technique allows you to build Web pages quickly and accurately, without having to worry later about how your design decisions will appear in a browser.

With HTML, special character codes are inserted into the text to generate particular effects, such as bold or the appearance of a graphic, hyperlink, or a table. When a browser opens a page, the browser reads and then translates the HTML and applies its commands to the text and images you see on the screen. A few examples of HTML appear in this chapter, but fortunately, you do not have to write any HTML because FrontPage Express develops the HTML for you. As you lay out your pages in FrontPage Express, it automatically writes the HTML behind the scenes. When you save your work, FrontPage Express saves the HTML required to present the page you developed.

If you are working with a preexisting FrontPage file and are having difficulty saving the file, it may have a read-only attribute. See "Saving an HTML File" in the "Troubleshooting" section at the end of this chapter.

With that introduction to FrontPage Express and its capabilities, you are ready to use it.

LAUNCHING FRONTPAGE EXPRESS

You can launch FrontPage Express either from the Start menu or from the Internet Explorer browser. When you launch FrontPage Express from the browser, the page you were viewing is loaded directly into FrontPage Express. With this technique, FrontPage Express enables you to edit any pages you see on the World Wide Web directly at your desktop with FrontPage Express. Naturally, you won't be able to change the Web pages you're viewing (unless you are working on a Web to which you have rights), but this gives you a great way to see first-hand how real-life Web pages are built. In addition, if you are working on an existing Web, say for your company or organization, this method makes it easy to select the page you want to work on without having to attach to or access the server on which the pages are stored.

Here are the two methods you can use to launch FrontPage Express:

- To launch FrontPage Express from the Start menu, open the Start menu, choose Programs, Internet Explorer, FrontPage Express. A new blank Web page is displayed.

- To launch FrontPage Express from Internet Explorer, choose Edit, Page from the menu or click the Edit button on the Standard buttons toolbar. FrontPage Express opens, displaying the page you were viewing in the browser (see Figure 32.1).

Figure 32.1
The page you were viewing in Internet Explorer opens in FrontPage Express when you choose Edit, Page from within the browser.

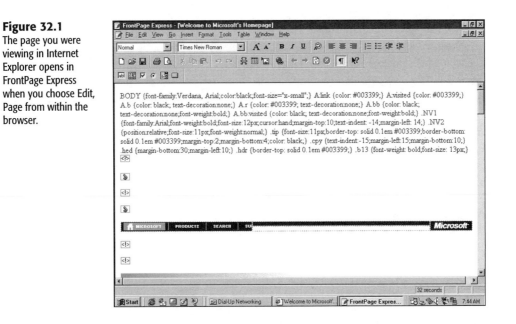

OPENING A PAGE

You can open existing pages stored locally or on an existing Web. Follow these steps to open a page:

1. Choose File, Open from the menu.

2. If you are opening a page that has not yet been published to a Web or if it is stored locally, choose the From File option. Enter the name of the file in the edit box. Use the Browse button if you need help locating the file and/or entering its name and location. Click OK.

   or

   If you are opening a page that already has been published to a Web or a page that you did not develop, choose the From Location option. Then, enter the URL and the name of the page in the edit box and click OK.

HIDING AND DISPLAYING TOOLBARS

FrontPage Express includes three toolbars. Like toolbars in other applications, the toolbars in FrontPage Express show buttons for common tasks, such as changing text size, indenting, and inserting an image. Unlike in other applications, however, you cannot modify the buttons on any of the toolbars.

Here is a description of each toolbar:

- Standard—The Standard toolbar provides many buttons you see on toolbars in other applications, such as New, Open, and Save. In addition, it offers Insert WebBot, Insert Table, and Image buttons.

- Format—The Format toolbar gives you access to most of the choices that appear on the Format menu, such as the style, font, and color selections. You use the Format toolbar to format text you have entered onto your page.

- Forms—You use the Forms toolbar when you are creating a Web page that contains standard Windows controls, such as a pushbutton or drop-down list. The Forms toolbar provides buttons with which you can add these controls to the page.

You can hide or display any of the toolbars. To display or hide a toolbar, just choose View from the menu bar and select the appropriate toolbar from the menu. If a check appears beside the toolbar name, the toolbar is already displayed. If a check does appear beside a toolbar name and you click the toolbar, it becomes hidden. Figure 32.2 shows the three FrontPage Express toolbars.

Standard Toolbar

Figure 32.2
You can display all three FrontPage Express toolbars at one time.

Forms Toolbar

Format Toolbar

SAVING YOUR WORK

At some point, you will want to save the work you have completed on your Web page. You have two choices for saving Web pages. You can save your work to a file or to an existing Web. How you originally opened the page and whether you have started a Web determine which choice you make. Here are your options:

- If your Web has not yet been started—Save your page to a file (instructions follow). You will publish your pages to a Web later.

- If your Web has been started and you are adding a new page—Save your page to the Web and be sure you provide the hyperlinks to the page. To do so, choose File, Save As; choose Location; and then supply the uniform resource locator (URL) and the name of the file.

- If you are editing a page on your Web—Just choose File, Save, and FrontPage Express updates the Web with your changes.

- If you are editing a page from a Web you don't control—You probably will not be able to save to someone else's Web. Instead, save the page to a file or save it to your own Web.

To save a page you are working on to a file, follow these steps:

1. Choose File, Save As.
2. From the Save As dialog box, choose As File.
3. Select a directory from the Save As File dialog box, enter a name for the file, and then choose Save.

CREATING WEB PAGES INSTANTLY

Almost all the information presented in this chapter helps you build Web pages by using FrontPage Express's long list of features. Luckily, FrontPage Express provides templates and wizards that remove much of the manual work that is normally involved with developing a page, such as positioning and formatting text. The list of templates and wizards appears when you choose the File, New command (see Figure 32.3).

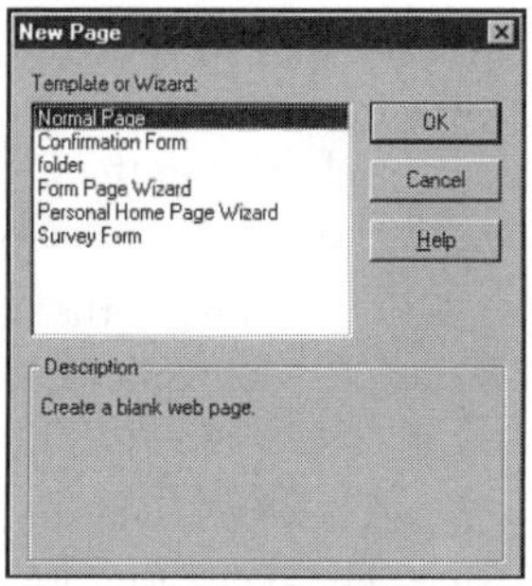

Figure 32.3
You will see a list of available templates and page wizards when you choose File, New. My list includes a custom template called folder.

PART

V

CH

32

The following sections explain how to use the templates and wizards.

USING THE PERSONAL HOME PAGE WIZARD

Many Internet service providers (ISPs) and online services host Web pages and even Web sites for their subscribers—sometimes at no additional cost. Many universities and colleges also provide this service to their students. Therefore, even someone without access to the hardware required to run a Web server can establish a presence on the Web. Many times this presence is nothing more than a personal home page with a number of links that provides an update on the life and activities of the person who posted the page.

The only requirement for this type of presence is for you to supply the content. FrontPage Express makes it easy to develop these types of pages with the Personal Home Page Wizard.

This wizard walks you through the steps required to create a personal page. When you have answered all the wizard's questions, it creates an attractive page that you can then submit to the service that is hosting your Web page. Your only work is to supply the details into the preformatted sections, which are created based on your responses to the wizard.

Here is the type of information you might supply for the Personal Home Page Wizard:

- Your employment
- Projects you're working on
- Your favorite Web sites
- Biographical information
- Your interests
- Information on how to contact you
- A form to send information or comments to you

To use the Personal Home Page Wizard, follow these steps:

1. Choose File, New from the menu. The New Page dialog box appears.
2. Select Personal Home Page Wizard from the Template or Wizard list box and then click OK. The Personal Home Page Wizard dialog appears.
3. From the Personal Home Page Wizard, select the type of content you want to include on your home page. Keep in mind that the wizard creates just one page, not a Web of linked pages. Consequently, the more items you select from the Personal Home Page Wizard, the longer your home page will be. After making your selections, click Next.
4. In the next dialog, in the Page URL box, specify the name of the page as it will be stored on the Web. In the Page Title edit box, enter the name of the page as it will appear in the browser.
5. Next, the wizard presents a series of dialog boxes in which you supply personal information that the wizard uses to build your page. The type of information it asks for depends on the choices you made in step 3. For example, if you chose to include biographical information, you are prompted to select whether to include academic information (such as the institution you attended, dates of attendance, and degree), professional information (such as your company and title), or personal information (such as important dates and milestones). Obviously, the content and number of dialog boxes depends on the types of information you want to provide. Click Next to move to the next dialog box; click Back to change the information you've already provided.
6. When the wizard has collected all the information it needs to build your page, it displays a dialog box similar to the one shown in Figure 32.4.

   This dialog box includes a list box that shows each of the major sections you're creating with the Personal Home Page Wizard. Now you have an opportunity to choose the order in which the sections appear on the page. Choose a section and then click either the Up or Down button to specify the order of the sections.

Figure 32.4
You can choose the order of sections on your personal home page.

7. Click Finish from the final dialog box, and the almost-completed page appears in a window in FrontPage Express. Review the page and replace any "instructions" that appear with the information required (see Figure 32.5).

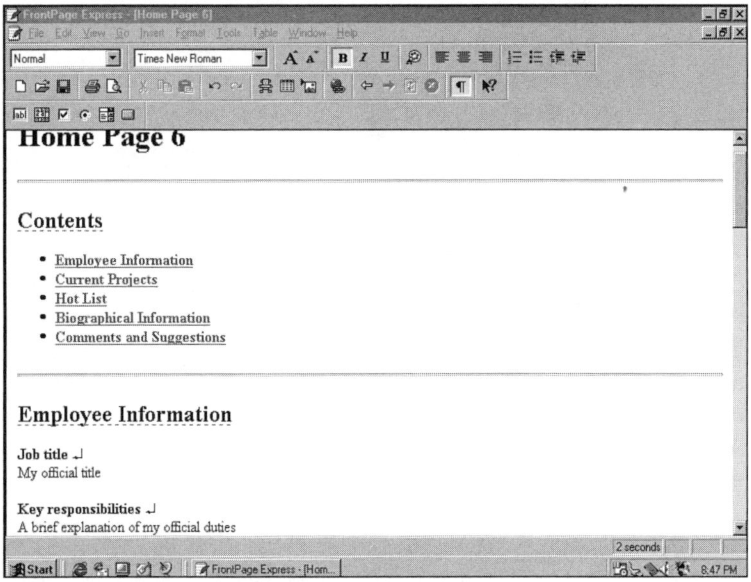

Figure 32.5
When the Personal Home Page Wizard finishes building your page, you supply some of the detailed information yourself.

USING THE FORM PAGE WIZARD

The Form Page Wizard creates a Web page that collects different types of information from the person viewing the page in a browser. For example, you might create an order form if you are selling something over the Internet, or you might create a list of questions if you are conducting a survey.

Form pages can contain many of the controls used today in Windows applications (see Figure 32.6). Controls are the onscreen elements—list boxes, buttons, check boxes, and more—that are used in Windows and in Windows application to operate the system. The Form Page Wizard automatically places on the page whichever controls are necessary to collect the information you require from the user.

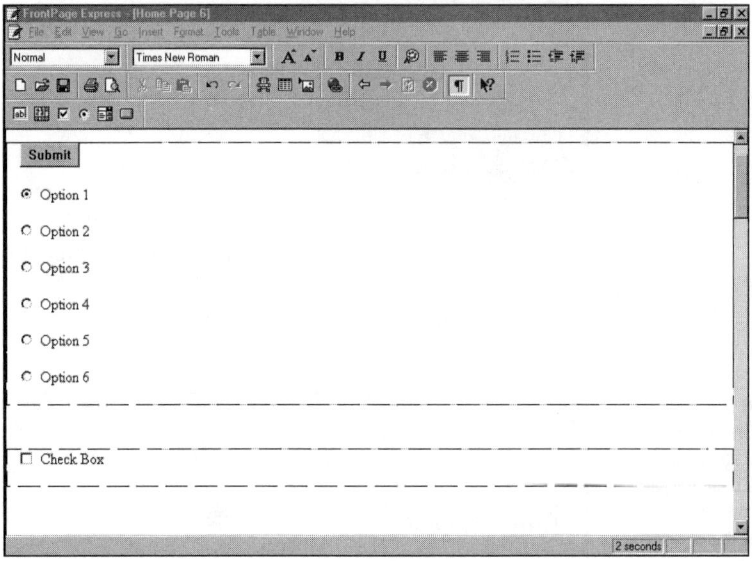

Figure 32.6
Web pages can use many of the controls used in non-Web applications.

You should understand one important point about the Form Page Wizard: Your work is not close to being done when the wizard finishes creating your form page. The wizard builds many of the controls your page requires based on your responses. However, most of the logic required to put your page to work (such as validating that a ZIP code does not contain nonnumeric values or calculating the total amount of an order) must be completed without the wizard's help. This warning is not meant to discourage you from using the wizard, though, only to inform you that the Form Page Wizard alone will not build a fully functioning form.

The following steps get you started with the Form Page Wizard.

1. Choose File, New from the menu. The New Page dialog box appears.

2. Select Form Page Wizard from the Template or Wizard list box and then click OK. The Form Page Wizard dialog box appears.

3. Click Next.

4. In the Page URL box, specify the name of the page as it will be stored on the Web. In the Page Title edit box, enter the name of the page as it will appear in the browser.

5. Click Next. If the file you specified in step 4 already exists, the wizard scans the page you specified for any content it believes to be form related. This step enables you to easily take an existing form page and modify it or to continue work on a page you've

already started. If the wizard finds any questions, it displays them in a list in the dialog box.

To add a new question to the form or to add the first question to your form if the page is new or the existing page was not a form, choose Add. The wizard displays a list of possible types of information your form can collect (see Figure 32.7).

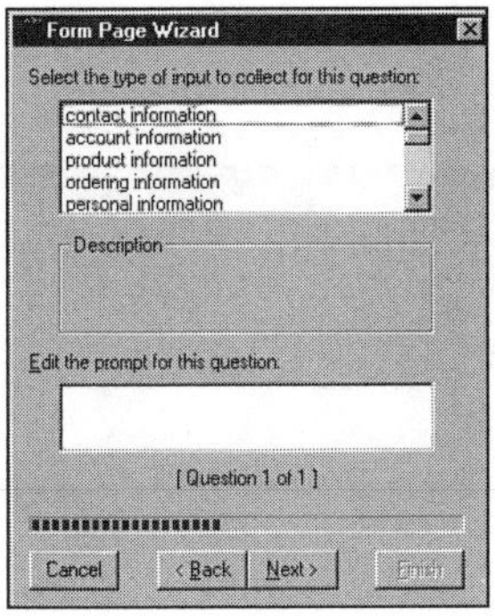

Figure 32.7
The Form Page Wizard can collect different types of information.

6. Scroll through the list and select the first type of information you want to collect on your form. Notice that when you select a particular type from the list, a note about the type appears in the Description frame beneath the list. Also notice that the prompt for the information, which will appear to the person viewing your page, appears in the edit box at the bottom of the dialog box. If you like, you can customize the prompt by editing the text in the box. When you have selected the information type you want to collect and perhaps edited the prompt, click the Add button.

7. Depending on the type of information you selected, you may be presented with another dialog box requesting more detailed information about your prompt. For example, if you select contact information in step 6, the wizard asks whether your form should request such information from the user as name, title, organization, address, and phone. Answer the prompts in the dialog box and then click Next.

8. The dialog box described in step 6 appears again. Choose the next type of information your form will request and then follow the instructions in step 7. Repeat steps 6, 7, and 8 until all the information your form will request is represented in the list box. When the list of prompts is complete, click Finish. FrontPage Express builds the page and displays it on the screen.

9. Review the page and replace any of the instructions with the information required. You can also customize many of the fields, by specifying a default value, for example. You can display the options available to any of the fields by double-clicking on the field.

USING TEMPLATES

Templates can also be used to quickly create content for the Web with FrontPage Express. The templates provided with FrontPage Express work differently than the wizards do. As you learned in the preceding section, wizards collect information and then build the page for you based on your answers. Templates do not prompt you for information. Instead, you choose the type of page you want to build from a list of templates, and then FrontPage displays a preformatted page with a series of placeholders you can replace with your own information. For example, if you base a page on the Survey Form template, you need to replace the sample questions provided by the template (such as, What is your favorite color?) with the questions you want to include in your survey. Figure 32.8 shows a new page created from the Survey Form template.

Figure 32.8
You must fill in information after creating a page from a template.

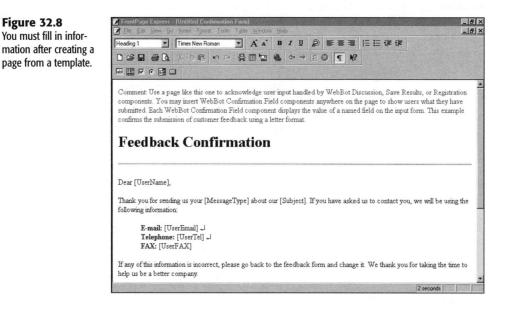

Follow these steps to create a page from a template:

1. Choose File, New from the menu. The New Page dialog box appears.
2. Select one of the templates from the list and then click OK.
3. The page appears on the screen. Review the page and replace the instructions with the information required.

FORMATTING AND POSITIONING TEXT

Entering text in FrontPage Express is very similar to entering text in any word processor. You click anywhere on the page and start entering text. You can also copy text from another application and then paste it into the Web page open in FrontPage Express. After you start entering text, you can begin formatting it, specifying text and color for the text, applying special effects, or breaking text into sections with lines, for example.

You also specify where text should appear on the page. You can specify the position and alignment of text on a line-by-line basis, or you can use built-in styles, which make it easy to apply groups of formatting commands in just one click. The next few sections cover the following formatting topics:

- Typeface, color, size, text effects
- Alignment and indent/outdent of text
- Horizontal line effects
- Bulleted and numbered lists

FORMATTING TEXT

You format text in FrontPage Express much as you do in other Windows applications. You select the text to be formatted and then make selections either from the toolbar or from choices on the Format menu.

To format text in FrontPage Express, follow these steps:

1. Select the text to be formatted.
2. Choose Format, Font from the menu.
3. To specify the typeface for the text, choose the font from the Font list.
4. To specify the style for the text, make a selection from the Font Style list. Keep in mind that the choices in the Style list depend on the font selected.
5. To specify the size of the text, make a selection from the Size list box. The choices in the Size list also depend on the font selected.
6. Apply effects such as underlining, strikethrough, or a typewriter font by selecting the appropriate check box(es) in the Effects group.
7. To select a color for the text, click the Color drop-down arrow and select a color from the list that appears. To create a color, choose Custom from the list.
8. To create a subscript or superscript effect, choose the Special Styles tab. Select the appropriate effect from the Vertical Position drop-down list and then set the amount of vertical offset from the By list.
9. Click OK.

⚠ *If you want to run your text through spell check, as you would in Microsoft Word, but can't find this feature in FrontPage Express, see "Spell Check" in the "Troubleshooting" section at the end of this chapter.*

POSITIONING TEXT

To position text in FrontPage Express, you have two options:

- Use a combination of built-in styles and indent/outdent and alignment commands.
- Use a table to lay out your page and then position text within cells.

PART

V

CH

32

The difference here is that the table option gives you more precision in placing text on the page, but this option also adds an extra layer of work and complexity. The basic rule of thumb is to use a table to lay out a page or a section of a page when graphics and text appear on the same line, such as in columns. Otherwise, the built-in styles and menu commands should suit your needs. Creating tables is covered in detail later in the chapter in the section "Creating and Editing Tables."

To use one of FrontPage Express's built-in paragraph styles and/or menu commands to position text, follow these steps:

1. Click anywhere in the paragraph to be formatted. If you want to format multiple paragraphs, select all paragraphs that will be positioned the same way.

2. To *indent* the selected paragraph(s), click the Indent button on the Format toolbar.

   To *outdent* the selected paragraph(s), click the Outdent button on the Format toolbar.

   To choose a built-in style, choose one from the drop-down list on the Format toolbar. Table 32.1 provides a short description of each FrontPage Express built-in style.

TABLE 32.1   FRONTPAGE EXPRESS BUILT-IN STYLES

Style Name	Formatting Description
Address	Italics, no indent, double-spaced
Bulleted List	Bullet, indented, single-spaced
Defined Term	Single spaced, first line left-aligned, subsequent lines indented
Definition	Single spaced, first line indented, subsequent lines further indented from first
Directory List	Same as bulleted list
Formatted	Bullet, single spaced
Heading 1	Bold, left-aligned
Heading 2	Bold, left-aligned
Heading 3	Bold, left-aligned
Heading 4	Bold, left-aligned
Heading 5	Bold, left-aligned
Heading 6	Bold, left-aligned
Menu List	Bullet, indented, double-spaced
Numbered List	Same as standard numbered list

CREATING BULLETED AND NUMBERED LISTS

You can easily add a bulleted or numbered list to your Web pages. FrontPage Express even provides a few styles of each so you can customize your lists to a certain extent. You can quickly format a list as a bulleted or numbered list from the Format toolbar, or you can make more specific choices form the Bullets and Numbering dialog box. Follow these steps:

1. Enter the list of items to be bulleted on the page. Be sure to press Enter at the end of each line.

2. Select all the paragraphs in the list.

3. To create a bulleted list, click on the Bulleted List button the Format toolbar. To create a numbered list, click the Numbered List button on the Format toolbar.

4. If you want to exert a bit more control over the appearance of the bullets or numbers, choose Format, Bullets and Numbering from the menu. Select either the Bulleted or Numbered tab, select the format, and click OK.

ADDING HORIZONTAL LINES

You can add horizontal lines anywhere on your Web page. These lines are useful for breaking your page into sections. You can specify the color, weight, alignment, and size of the line.

To add a horizontal line, follow these steps:

1. Click on the page in the location where you want the horizontal line to appear.

2. Choose Insert, Horizontal Line from the menu. A line appears on the page.

   If you are content with the appearance of the line on the page, your work is done. If you want to customize the line, continue to step 3.

3. Double-click anywhere on the line, and the Horizontal Line Properties dialog box appears (see Figure 32.9)

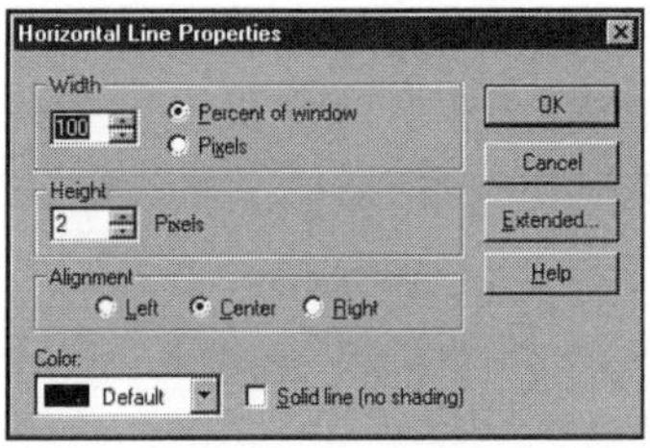

Figure 32.9
You can customize the appearance of a horizontal line on your page.

4. You can specify whether your line is a fixed length (in pixels) or whether it occupies a specific percentage of the width of your page. To specify your preference, select either Percent of Window or Pixels from the Width frame and then enter the appropriate value in the Width scrolling list box.

5. Specify the height of the line (in pixels) in the Height scrolling list box.

6. In the Alignment area, specify whether the line should be left-, center-, or right-aligned by selecting the appropriate option.

7. Select a color from the Color drop-down list.

8. To create a solid line with no shadow effect, select the Solid Line (No Shading) check box.

9. Click OK to put your changes into effect.

CREATING BOOKMARKS

A *bookmark* is a label that points to a specific location on your page. Users don't see bookmarks. A bookmark is used with hyperlinks when you want to provide a link on one page to another location on the same page. As an example, if you want to provide a link from the table of contents that appears on the top of the page to the relevant section later in the page, you would need to create a bookmark. The next section, "Inserting and Managing Hyperlinks," covers hyperlinks in detail.

Here is how you create a bookmark on your page:

1. Select the text for which to create a bookmark.

2. Choose Edit, Bookmark. The Bookmark dialog box appears (see Figure 32.10).

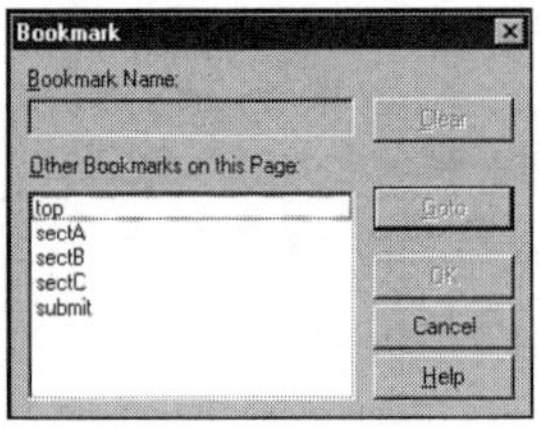

Figure 32.10
Creating a bookmark makes it easy to create a hyperlink to a specific position on a page.

3. By default, the text you selected to bookmark appears as the name of the bookmark. If this name is acceptable, click OK. If you want to specify some other text as the bookmark, enter the text in the Bookmark Name text box and then click OK.

INSERTING AND MANAGING HYPERLINKS

The capabilities of HTML allow page developers to provide links to other Web sites, and links on those Web sites to other sites, and so on. *Hyperlinks (page 725-726)* help the user navigate through the Web (or just through your site) by means of following relevant, related information. This network of links creates the Web portion of the name World Wide Web. You will most likely want to provide hyperlinks on your pages to other locations on the Web.

To add a hyperlink, follow these steps:

1. Enter the text that will be used as a link. The text might be a word, or phrase, or a name that takes the user to a specific place on the Web, or it might be the actual URL

for the location that is linked. Keep in mind that the text you want to use as a hyperlink might already have been entered. For example, you might provide a link from a word in a paragraph you entered when you first began developing the page.

> You might prefer to add hyperlinks when you have completed almost all of the other work on your page instead of worrying about the links as you develop your page. You can add hyperlinks at any time, so you might want to focus on the content of your page first and then add hyperlinks at the end.

2. Select the text you entered in step 1 (or whatever text you want to use as the link).

3. Choose Insert, Hyperlink from the menu. The Create Hyperlink dialog box appears.

   You can create a hyperlink to a page you already have open in FrontPage Express (use step 4), to a page that already exists on the Web (skip to step 5), or to a page that has not yet been created (skip to step 6).

4. To create a link to a page you have open, including the current page, choose the Open Pages tab of the Create Hyperlink dialog box (see Figure 32.11). In the Open Pages list, click on the name of the page you want to link to. Then click OK. Keep in mind that this procedure creates a link to a specific file in a specific location in a directory. If the target file is moved to another directory, the link becomes invalid.

   To create a link to a bookmark on the current open page, choose the page you are working on in the Open Pages list and then choose the appropriate bookmark from the Bookmark drop-down list.

PART

V

Сн

32

Figure 32.11
You can create a link to a page you already have open.

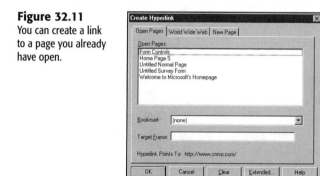

5. To create a link to an existing page on the World Wide Web, choose the World Wide Web tab (see Figure 32.12). Select the appropriate protocol from the Hyperlink Type drop-down list (more than likely, http: will be the type) and then enter the URL in the URL edit box. Click OK.

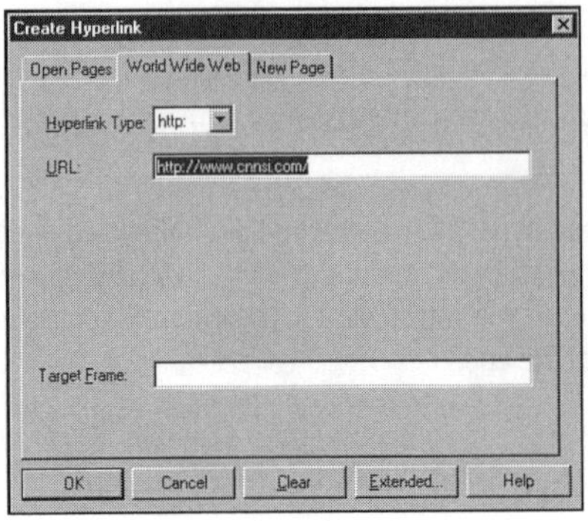

Figure 32.12
You can create a link
to any page on the
Web.

Tip #217

If you are going to add a hyperlink on your Web page, you might want to first open the desired link in Internet Explorer. Now when you choose Insert a Hyperlink, the URL of the Web page you are viewing in Internet Explorer appears in the URL dialog box of the World Wide Web tab in FrontPage Express. This method of previewing the Web page address through Internet Explorer not only eliminates any chance of mistyping the address when you create the link but also is a good way to verify that the URL is current.

6. To create a link to a new page, choose the New Page tab. Enter the title of the page to be created in the Page Title edit box and enter the filename of the page in the Page URL edit box. Click OK. The New Page dialog box (described in the earlier section "Creating Web Pages Instantly") appears. Select the type of page to be created. If you choose a page type that's based on a wizard, the appropriate wizard will be launched.

7. Click OK.

ADDING GRAPHICS

It's rare to find a Web page without at least one graphic element. You can certainly improve the appearance of your page by adding some sort of graphic. Don't worry, though, you needn't create the graphic yourself by using a drawing package. Many applications today come with dozens of clip-art images you can borrow and use on your page. For example, Microsoft Word provides a wide selection of clip art, and you can borrow any of those images for use with FrontPage Express. In addition, your local software store probably stocks a selection of graphics libraries available on CD, each of which stores thousands of images.

Your challenge as a Web page developer, then, is not to create the graphics, but rather to decide how to integrate one or more graphic element into your page. In this section, you learn how to integrate a graphic onto your page and how to manage the graphic's size. The first order of business, however, is to introduce the different types of graphics you can integrate onto your page.

Understanding Graphics Types

Many software applications available today let you draw anything from the most basic to the most complicated drawing. Some of these applications save the drawings in a specific format, which means that only applications capable of reading the format can use the graphics. Although many applications can read and write different formats, graphics for the Web usually are found in two formats: Graphical Interchange Format (GIF) and Joint Picture Experts Group (JPEG).

GIF (pronounced "jiff") is a graphics format developed by the online service CompuServe. Although several versions of the GIF file format exist, the most common one supports 256 colors. GIF is probably the most widely used format on the Web, and almost every browser and image editor supports this format.

The GIF format also supports a process known as *interlacing*. An interlaced image is displayed in the browser in stages, which enables the user to begin viewing the image much sooner than would be possible if the graphic were not interlaced. You can specify for any GIF image you include on a FrontPage Express page to be interlaced by simply checking the Interlaced option when you select the image to be loaded.

Another option that FrontPage Express supports for GIF files is *transparent images*. When an image is created, a transparent color index is selected. This color blends with the background color of the browser when the image is displayed (only if the browser supports the display of transparent images). This effect blends the focal part of the graphic—such as a picture of the author of this chapter—with the background of the browser to give the appearance of a borderless image.

JPEG images are sturdier than GIF images. JPEG (pronounced "jay-peg") was developed by the Joint Photographic Experts Group. The standard JPEG may contain up to 16 million colors. The most interesting, colorful, and detailed images you see on the Internet are most likely JPEG graphics. Considering the great resolution JPEG images provide, you may be wondering why all graphics are not JPEG format. One of the problems with JPEG images is that because of the detail they support, the file usually must be compressed when it is downloaded. And the compression process sometimes results in a loss of detail. In addition, a loss of detail sometimes occurs when a JPEG image is reduced from its original size to accommodate a specific space defined by the individual who is building the page.

Inserting the Graphic

You can insert a graphic from two different sources: from a file on your computer or network or from another site on the Web. When you insert a graphic from the Web, you are actually creating a pointer to the Web site where the graphic is located; the graphic is not actually copied to your Web site. With that in mind, you should be sure that any graphic you are referencing on another Web site will not be moved later.

Tip #218

> If you find a Web site that contains graphics you want to use in your own creations, you can easily copy it to your computer. To do so, right-click on the graphic you want to use and then select the menu choice that saves the graphic to the location you desire. That way, you have your own copy of the graphic file. Now, you can insert or edit the graphic into your creations by using the Paint and Imaging tools in Windows 98. Be sure to respect any legal issues related to using a graphic from another Web site, especially if that graphic was created by the host of the other site. You might need to pay a fee for its use.

To insert a graphic onto your Web page, follow these steps:

1. From the menu, choose Insert, Image. The Image dialog box appears (see Figure 32.13).

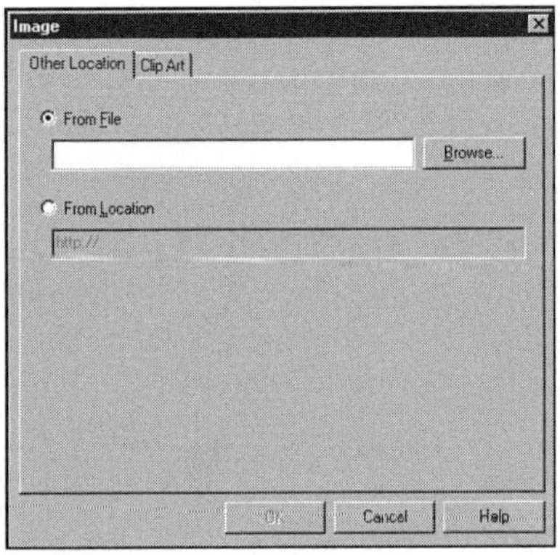

Figure 32.13
You add graphics to your page by using the Image dialog box.

2. To insert an image stored on your computer or a network resource to which your computer is attached, choose the From File option and then enter the name of the file in the edit box. Use the Browse button if you need help locating the file and/or entering its name and location.

   To insert an image stored on a Web site, choose the From Location option and then enter the URL for the site and the name of the image in the edit box.

3. Click OK, and the image appears on the screen.

MANAGING THE SIZE OF A GRAPHIC

When you insert an image into your Web page, the image occupies an area on your page that matches the image's size. In other words, if the image is 100 pixels wide by 100 pixels tall, it will occupy a 100×100-pixel area of your page at the location where you inserted it. You might want to increase or decrease the size of the graphic. You can use either of two techniques to do so:

- Select the image and then click and drag the handles that appear around the image. If you drag a handle at one of the corners of the image, you can maintain the proportional ratio of the image. If you drag a handle either horizontally or vertically, you change the horizontal or vertical aspect only.

- Double-click on the image to display the Image Properties dialog box. Choose the Appearance tab and then modify the image's size using the Width and Height scroll boxes. You can specify the image's size as a certain percentage of the page's size by choosing the In Percent option for the width, the height, or both.

Tip #219	Be sensible when deciding the size and number of graphics you want to post on your Web page. The larger the graphic, the longer it will take a Web browser to open your page. Likewise, the more graphics necessary to load for the page to be complete, the longer the user must wait to see the whole page.

ADDING A HYPERLINK TO A GRAPHIC

You might want to provide a hyperlink with a graphic on your Web page. This feature enables the user to link to another site via a graphic instead of a word or phrase.

To add a hyperlink to a graphic, follow these steps:

1. Double-click on the image to receive the hyperlink. The Image Properties dialog box appears.

2. Choose the General tab.

3. In the Location edit box in the Default Hyperlink frame, enter the URL to which the image will link.

4. Click OK.

SPECIFYING OPTIONS FOR A GRAPHIC

As described earlier, depending on the format of your graphic, you may be able to specify a number of options for it, such as whether a GIF graphic is interlaced.

To specify options for a graphic, right-click on the graphic and then choose Image Properties. The dialog box that appears contains options appropriate to the image type you selected.

USING BACKGROUNDS

You can add character to your Web pages by adding a background image or colors. When you add a background image to your page, any text or graphic you add to your page appears against that background. The size of the graphic determines how your background appears. FrontPage Express tiles the graphic across your page, which means it copies the graphic

PART

V

CH

32

across the page and down to the bottom. Therefore, if you require a broad background, such as the sky and clouds, be sure your graphic is at least 640×480 pixels. If you prefer a tiled effect, such as a company logo, almost any size is suitable.

Tip #220

An attractive effect is to present a border down the left side of the page. To create this effect, the graphic needs to be at least 1024 pixels wide, so you don't end up with a second left margin down the middle of your screen. You also might want to make sure that you don't make the graphic any taller than necessary. If the graphic requires solid colors only, then two or three pixels is all that you need. Too simple to be true? Try it. This way, you will have a nice base and border for your creation. Also, if you use a graphic that is as wide as the screen, FrontPage Express cannot wrap the image. Instead, it repeats the image down the page.

To specify a background image or color for your page, follow these steps:

1. Select File, Page Properties from the menu. The Page Properties dialog box appears. Choose the Background tab (see Figure 32.14).

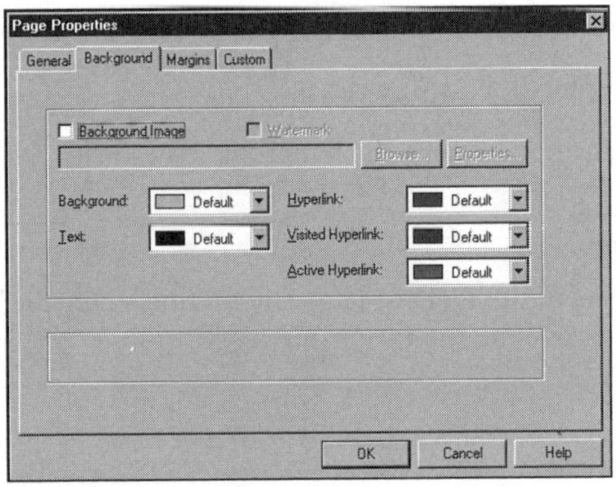

Figure 32.14
You can specify a background image and color for your page.

2. To add a background image, choose the Background Image check box and then enter the filename and location of the image in the edit box. Use the Browse button if you need help locating the file and/or entering its name and location.

3. To specify a background color for the page, select the color from the Background drop-down list.

4. Click OK.

CREATING AND EDITING TABLES

Tables are a critical component of all but the most basic Web page designs, and at some time you will probably want to create a table on a Web page you are building. The application of tables in Web pages isn't strictly to handle columns and rows. Tables make it easy to position graphics and text at any location required. By merging and splitting rows and columns, you can use tables to place graphics and text in locations that would be difficult to access using only indenting and alignment commands.

ADDING A TABLE TO A PAGE

You can add a table to your Web page from either the Standard toolbar or the menu. Using the menu enables you to specify a number of options for the table when it is created (such as cell padding and border size). When you use the toolbar to create the table, your choices are limited to the number of columns and rows. Of course, after you create a table with the toolbar, you can always select the entire table to customize it. To do so, choose Table, Table Properties from the menu.

Here are the details of the two methods for creating a table:

- Toolbar—To create a table from the toolbar, click on the Insert Table button on the Standard toolbar. Drag down to select the number of rows for your table and—*without releasing the mouse button*—drag across to select the number of columns. When you have selected the correct number of rows and columns, release the mouse button (see Figure 32.15).

- Menu—To create a table from the menu, choose Table, Insert Table. The Insert Table dialog box appears (see Figure 32.16). In the Size area, enter the number of rows and columns. Use the up and down arrow buttons in the controls to increment or decrement the current value.

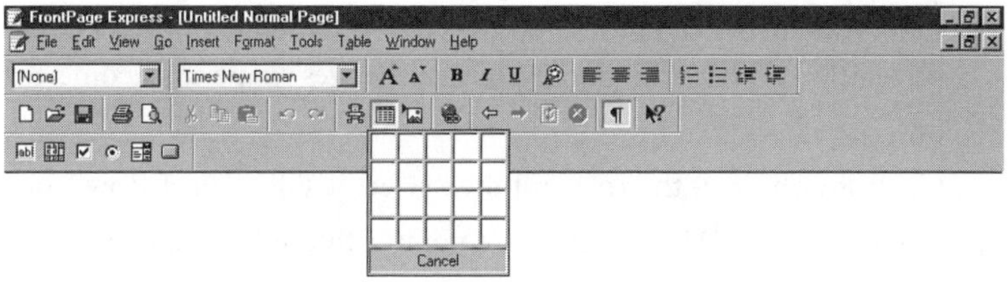

Figure 32.15
You can add a table to your page quickly by using the toolbar.

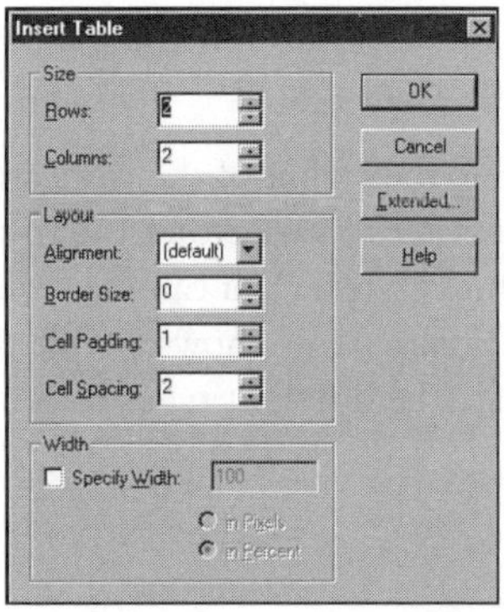

Figure 32.16
You have more options when you create a table using the Insert Table dialog box than you do when you create a table from the toolbar.

SELECTING A TABLE

After you create a table, you will probably need to customize it, possibly modifying its size or changing the column layout, for example. To customize a table in FrontPage Express, you must first select either the entire table or the component of the table you want to work with. The following list explains how to select the various components of the table.

- Entire table—Click and drag over the table until all the rows and columns are selected.

  or

  Click anywhere in the table and then select Table, Select Table from the menu.

- One cell—Move the mouse pointer towards the left edge of the cell until the pointer becomes an arrow pointing to the right. Then double-click.

  or

  Click anywhere in the cell and then choose Table, Select Cell from the menu.

- One column—Move the mouse pointer above the top border of the first row in the column. When the mouse pointer changes shape to become a darkened downward-pointing arrow, click.

  or

  Click anywhere in the column and then choose Table, Select Column from the menu.

- Range of columns—Move the mouse pointer above the top border of the first row in the first column. The mouse pointer changes shape to become a darkened downward-pointing arrow. Press and hold down the Shift key and then click and drag to select additional columns.

- One row—Move the mouse pointer to the left edge of the table, adjacent to the row to be selected. When the mouse pointer changes shape to become a darkened arrow, click.

  or

  Click anywhere in the row and then select Table, Select Row from the menu.

- Range of rows—Move the mouse pointer to the left edge of the table, adjacent to the first row to be selected. The mouse pointer changes shape to become a darkened arrow. Press and hold down the Shift key and then click and drag to select additional rows.

SPLITTING AND MERGING ROWS, COLUMNS, AND CELLS

You can use a few techniques to further define the layout of the rows and columns in your table. These techniques are useful when you want to vary either the row or height of cells with respect to other cells in the same columns or row. You can merge columns, rows, and cells together to achieve this type of effect. Figure 32.17 shows a table that uses a combination of splitting and merging to accommodate the different types of content in the table.

Figure 32.17
You can use merged and split cells to put information precisely where you want it.

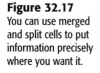

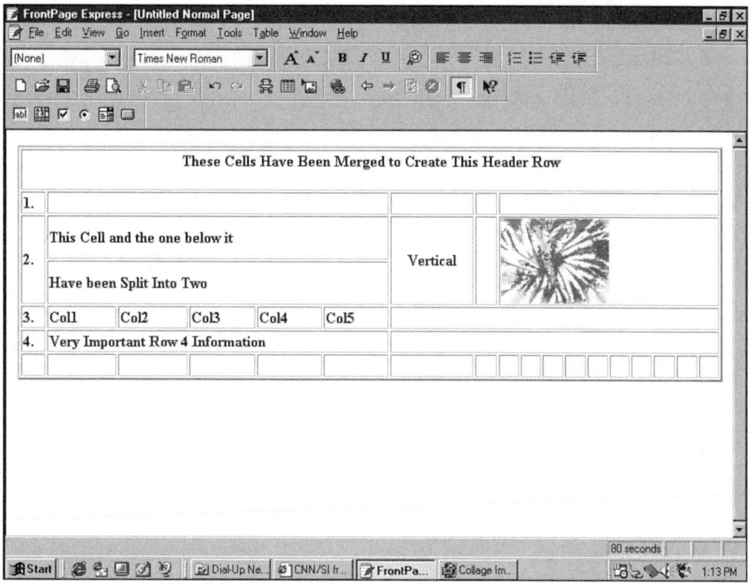

The following list outlines the techniques for splitting and merging columns, rows, and cells:

- Split a cell—Select the cell to be split and then choose Table, Split Cells from the menu. The Split Cells dialog box appears (see Figure 32.18). Choose either Split into Columns or Split into Rows. Then, specify the number of columns or rows into which the cell should be split in the Number of Columns scroll box. Click OK.

PART
V
CH
32

Figure 32.18
You can split cells into columns or rows—as many of each as you need.

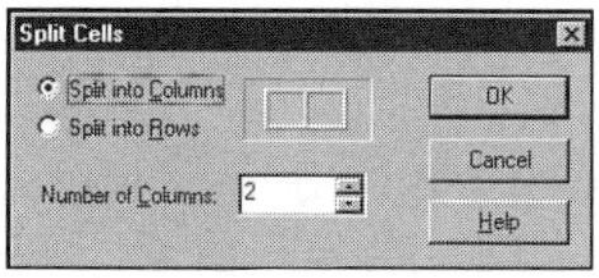

- Split all the cells in a column—Select the column and then choose Table, Split Cells from the menu. The Split Cells dialog box appears. Choose the Split into Rows option. In the Number of Rows scroll box, specify the number of rows each cell in the column should be split into. Then click OK.

- Split all the cells in a row—Select the row and then choose Table, Split Cells from the menu. The Split Cells dialog box appears. Choose the Split into Columns option. In the Number of Columns scroll box, specify the number of columns each cell in the row should be split into. Then click OK.

- Merge cells—Click and drag through the cells to be merged and then choose Table, Merge Cells from the menu.

INSERTING A TABLE WITHIN A CELL

Another method for customizing the layout of information in a table is to insert a table within a table. This approach enables you to group and lay out one set of data or content within the context of a larger table. The layout in Figure 32.19 shows a table within a table.

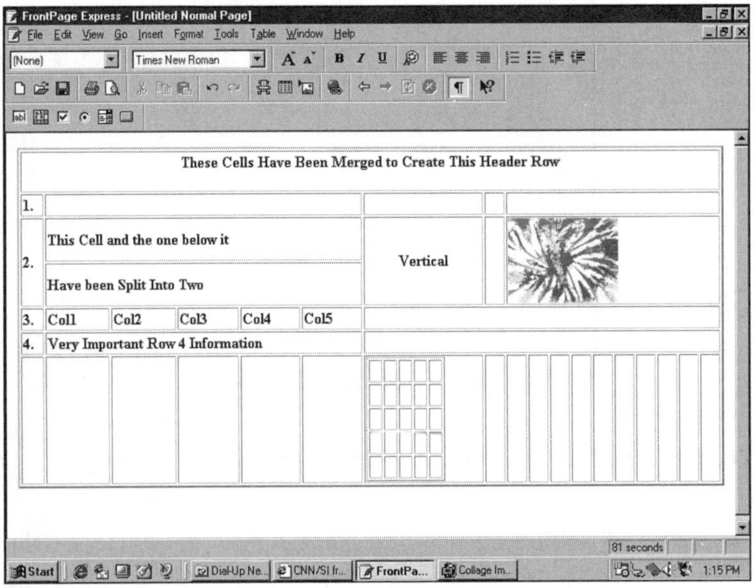

Figure 32.19
You can insert a table within another table.

To insert a table within a cell of another table, select the cell and then repeat the steps given in the earlier section "Adding a Table to a Page."

CUSTOMIZING A TABLE

In addition to merging and splitting the table and the rows, columns, and cells in your table, you can customize a number of other aspects of a table in FrontPage Express. The following list explains the options and techniques you can use to customize a table:

- Caption—You can add a caption to your table to provide the user with a quick description of the table's contents. The caption appears centered above the table, and if the table is resized or moved, the caption is automatically moved, too.

  To add a caption to your table, click anywhere in the table and then choose Table, Insert Caption from the menu. The cursor moves to the centered position over the table. Enter the caption.

- Borders—You can specify a border for the cells in your table. To do so, first select the table and then choose Table, Table Properties from the menu. Select a width for the border from the Border Size scroll box. You can also select a color for both the light portion of the shading and the heavy portion of the border shading, as well as for the border itself. Make these selections from the Custom Colors frame at the bottom of the dialog box. Then click OK.

You can also override the border settings you've applied to the entire table for just specific cells, columns, or rows. To do that, select the cells whose borders will be customized and then choose Table, Cell Properties from the menu. Make selections from the Custom Colors frame and then click OK.

- Background image/color—You can specify a cell-specific background or image. If you use a background image, the cell must be large enough to accommodate the graphic if you want the user to see all of it.

  To specify a background image or color for a cell, select the cell; choose Table, Cell Properties from the menu; and then select either a color or image from the Custom Background Frame.

- Alignment—You can specify the alignment for the contents of any or all of the cells in the table. To do so, select the components of the table for which you want to change the alignment. Choose Table, Cell Properties from the menu. In the Layout frame, specify the Horizontal and Vertical alignments for the selected cells.

- Column width/table width—You can easily specify the width of a particular column or the entire table. You specify the width either in pixels or as a percentage of the entire page.

  To specify the width for the table, select the table and then choose Table, Table Properties from the menu. Choose the Specify Width option and then select either the In Pixels or In Percent option. Enter the desired value and then click OK. To do the same for a column, choose the column and then choose Table, Cell Properties from the menu.

PART
V

CH
32

ADDING CONTENT TO A TABLE

Now that you have learned how to format and structure a table, here is a quick word on entering content for the table. To enter text and other content into a table, you use the same techniques you use to enter content directly onto the page. You click on the cell to receive the content, and then you either enter text or choose one of the options from the Insert menu to add other content, such as an image.

ADDING SOUND AND VIDEO

The appeal of a Web page can be significantly enhanced by the inclusion of multimedia content, such as sound and video. Many Web pages you can browse through today include video clips that you can view online, such as excerpts for upcoming films. Other Web sites provide background music as you browse through their pages. Integrating sound and video are simple exercises in FrontPage Express. This section explains how to integrate video and background music into your Web pages.

Tip #221	As with graphics, audio and video files also cause your page to load more slowly. Audiovisual (AVI) files are especially greedy for network bandwidth. If you incorporate AVI files into your Web creation, the user will experience a longer wait for the page to load and others on the network will also be affected as the available bandwidth is being utilized for the multimedia file transfer.

ADDING VIDEO TO A PAGE

Video is an attractive option for a Web page, and the development of video for the Web, as well as its inclusion into your Web pages, is no longer a difficult task. Specifically, new video production hardware and software tools enable you to easily develop video at the desktop. These tools even address the issue of the time it takes to download video clips. New technologies, such as *streaming* (in which the video clip and other multimedia content are played as they are downloaded) along with increased modem speeds remove almost all protestations about complicated multimedia content on the Web.

To add video to your Web page, follow these steps:

1. Choose Insert, Video from the menu. The Video dialog box appears (see Figure 32.20).

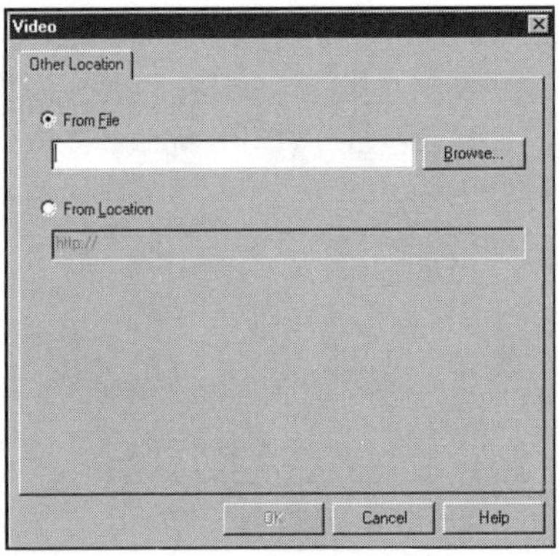

Figure 32.20
You specify the video you want to add to the page in the Insert Video dialog box.

2. Enter the name of the file containing the video content in the From File edit box. Use the Browse button if you need help locating the file and/or entering its name and location.

3. Click OK, and a block appears on the page. The block corresponds to the position on the page where the video will be played when the page is opened.

4. To customize how the video will be displayed, right-click on the block and choose Image Properties from the menu. Then, choose the Video tab (see Figure 32.21).

5. To specify that you want the video to start immediately when the page is opened, choose the On File Open check box. Alternatively, if you want the video to be started when the user's mouse passes over the video, choose the On Mouse Over option.

You can choose the number of times the video should repeat by entering a number in the Loop box. To repeat the video as long as the page is open, choose the Forever check box.

6. When you finish specifying your preferences, click OK.

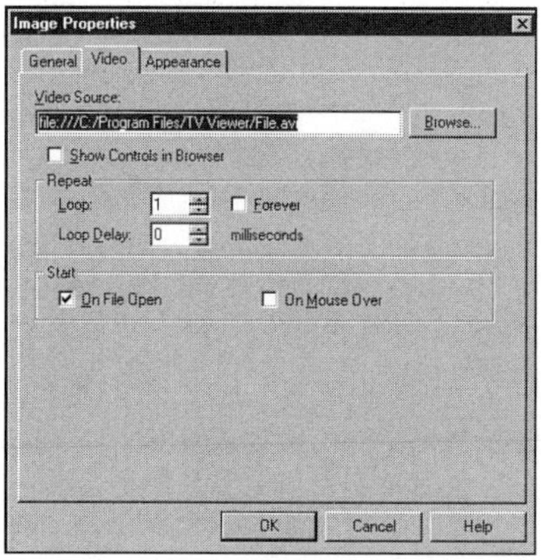

Figure 32.21
You can control how often the video runs from the Image Properties dialog box.

ADDING BACKGROUND SOUND TO A PAGE

You can add a sound to your page and play the sound automatically when the page is opened. The sound can be played once, you can specify that it should be played a certain number of times, or you can choose to have it play as long as the page is open.

To specify a background sound for your page, follow these steps:

1. Select File, Page Properties from the menu. In the Page Properties dialog box, choose the Background tab.

2. In the Location edit box, enter the name of the file with the background sound. Use the Browse button if you need help locating the file and/or entering its name and location.

3. Specify the number of times the sound should repeat by entering the number in the Loop box. To increment or decrement the value shown in the box, click the up or down button beside the control. To repeat the sound for as long as the page is open, choose the Forever check box.

4. Click OK.

PUBLISHING PAGES TO A WEB SITE

When you have created all the pages for your Web, you probably will want to publish the pages to a Web so that other users can access the pages. Simply saving the pages you've created in FrontPage Express isn't enough, however. You must publish the pages to a specific

Web so that Web server software (which is different from both FrontPage Express and your browser and must be installed separately) can process requests from users for the pages. This Web server software (on which a Web is created) must reside on a computer that browsers can access. Publishing pages to the Web involves two general steps:

1. Establishing or locating a Web site on which to publish.

2. Publishing the pages.

The next two sections cover these steps.

ESTABLISHING OR CREATING A WEB SITE

As you learned earlier in this chapter (in the section, "Using the Personal Home Page Wizard"), many ISPs host home pages for subscribers. If you plan to provide more than a single page of information, you might want to consider a host site with greater capabilities. A search of the Web will turn up dozens of companies interested in hosting your Web site for a nominal amount per month—usually less than $50.

If you have access to the server and are interested in learning the technology, Windows NT Server includes the software to host a Web site. In addition, Windows NT Workstation and Windows 98 both provide Web hosting software perfect for local Webs, such as via intranets.

PUBLISHING YOUR PAGES

Windows 98 provides the tools to publish your Web via the Web Publishing Wizard. This wizard is available from the Internet Explorer menu, which you access from the Start, Programs menu. If you do not see the Web Publishing Wizard on the menu, it probably has not been installed.

You can install the wizard from either the Windows 98 or Internet Explorer CD, or you can download it from Microsoft's site on the Internet. The wizard walks you through the steps of publishing your pages and creating a starting home page. The steps are easy to follow, and there is no requirement for in-depth Web server knowledge.

WHEN TO UPGRADE TO FRONTPAGE 2000

As you become more adept at Web page development or when your Web site development projects grow in complexity, you might consider upgrading to the full version of Microsoft FrontPage. FrontPage Express is very similar to FrontPage (especially considering that FrontPage Express is based on FrontPage), so you should run into little difficulty during the transition. Here are the main differences:

- The full version includes FrontPage Explorer, which helps to develop and manage entire Web sites made up of the pages developed with FrontPage editor.
- The full FrontPage provides clip-art samples, including video and animated samples.

- FrontPage gives you a direct link to your Web browser, which enables you to view your pages in the browser as you develop them instead of having to save and load them individually.

TROUBLESHOOTING

SAVING AN HTML FILE

When I try to save an HTML file in FrontPage Express, I receive the following error message: 13. *If I then click OK, I receive another error message, indicating that an error occurred while attempting to write the file.*

This problem can occur if you try to save a file that has Read-only attributes. To work around this problem, you must save the file with a different name, using the Save <u>A</u>s command on the File menu.

To save the file to a Web site, type the name of the file in the Page Title box and the page location in the Page Location box; then click OK. To save the file locally, choose As File, type the name of the file in the File Name box, and click Save.

SPELL CHECK

I can't find the spell check feature in FrontPage Express.

Your application is working fine. FrontPage Express does not have a spell check feature. If you want to spell check your text, write it in Word and check it there first; then cut and paste the text into FrontPage Express. The full FrontPage 2000 version has an integrated spell checker.

CHAPTER 33

COLLABORATING AND COMMUNICATING WITH NETMEETING

In this chapter

INTRODUCING NETMEETING

NetMeeting is an application that enables users to both work and play over the Internet in a collaborative fashion. By using NetMeeting, users can converse (if each has audio equipment), exchange ideas, exchange files, see what each other is working on, and even see what each other is doing (if each person has video equipment installed on his or her computer). The opportunity to collaborate and communicate over the Internet has a number of potential applications. The first section of this chapter looks at these potential applications and explains how the various components of NetMeeting work with these applications. Here's what we cover:

- How NetMeeting works
- Audio conferencing
- Video conferencing
- Application sharing and collaboration
- Sharing the Clipboard
- Using the Whiteboard
- Chatting

HOW NETMEETING WORKS

Understanding how NetMeeting works can help you make sense of the large number of components associated with the application. This short section covers a few points that can help you understand NetMeeting:

- Internet/intranet connection—You need to connect to the Internet or to your organization's intranet to use NetMeeting. If you are in a corporate organization, you probably have a connection to the Internet as part of your network. Otherwise, you must connect to the Internet via an Internet service provider.

- NetMeeting 3.01—This software enables you to collaborate and communicate as described in the chapter so far. NetMeeting is available from Microsoft's Web site for free. (Previous versions are also available with Internet Explorer 5.0 when you purchase the CD, as well as with Windows 98.)

- ILS server —For the purposes of NetMeeting users, an ILS server is nothing more than a list of NetMeeting users you can call or who can call you. Many ILS servers are available, so you must access the correct server to find a specific person (though Speed Dial, which is addressed later, can assist with this problem).

- Meeting—The meeting is the basic element in NetMeeting. If you are speaking with one person or many, you are involved in a meeting. If you are involved in a business discussion with co-workers or you are chatting about popular music and the weather, you are involved in a meeting.

AUDIO CONFERENCING

NetMeeting enables users to communicate through voice, over the Internet. Provided a computer has a sound card with a working microphone that is capable of either full-duplex or half-duplex transmission, the computer can be used to converse with someone through NetMeeting. You can also have group audio conferences through NetMeeting. When you are in NetMeeting conversations with more than one person, you can direct your audio to only one person or to all participants in the NetMeeting.

In addition, NetMeeting supports Intel's MMX technology, which means you will see improved audio performance over systems without MMX.

VIDEO CONFERENCING

Video conferencing with NetMeeting enables users to hold face-to-face meetings across the Internet (or intranet). The only requirement for video conferencing is that users have video equipment compatible with Windows 98 installed on their computer. This video equipment includes the following:

- A video capture card
- A camera

NetMeeting provides users with a number of capabilities and features for video conferencing. These features are covered in more detail, where appropriate, in later sections in this chapter:

- Switchable audio and video—When you're in a meeting with more than one person, NetMeeting allows you to easily switch to different, specific participants involved in the meeting. This way, you can direct your conversation, both the audio and video portions, to one particular person in the meeting.

- Receive images even with no video hardware—NetMeeting allows you to receive video images from other users if you do not have video capture.

- Dock and move video windows—NetMeeting makes it easy to manage the numerous windows that are displayed when you are using the application for video conferencing. You can dock both the My Video and Remote Video within the Current Call pane or allow them to float over the NetMeeting window.

- Support for H.323—NetMeeting supports the H.323 standard in audio conferencing and video conferencing, though you must first install the H.263 codec.

PART

V

CH

33

APPLICATION SHARING AND COLLABORATING

Another great feature in NetMeeting is that it enables people to share their applications over the Internet. This feature makes it easy for someone to use applications as part of their NetMeeting conversation or meeting presentation. Examples of application sharing are

- Show updated financial statistics in a spreadsheet during a NetMeeting meeting.
- Preview a presentation to a group.
- Demonstrate a software application in a sales situation.

Application sharing can be configured for one-person use, where only the person sharing the application can modify it; or application sharing can be collaborative, where any users in the meeting can also work with the application.

SHARED CLIPBOARD

The Clipboard is always available to all users in a meeting. This feature provides an easy way to share data. Any data on a NetMeeting user's Clipboard is available and is visible to other participants. Naturally, NetMeeting users must be careful that sensitive information is not on the Clipboard during a NetMeeting meeting.

WHITEBOARD WORK

NetMeeting's Whiteboard application allows users to draw ideas by using painting and drawing tools. This application is useful for drawing processes or business flows, making rough sketches of graphics ideas, or for any collaborative work that requires illustrations or rudimentary drawings.

CHATTING

NetMeeting provides a simple application for times when users do not want to or cannot communicate either by audio or video. Chat provides a vehicle for NetMeeting users to simply write each other messages. These messages can be sent to all the people in a meeting or to just one person.

FILE TRANSFERRING

You can send a file to any person involved in a meeting with you. You can select the file to send, and then continue your meeting with the recipient of the file as it is being sent, and the recipient of the file can specify a default location for all files sent via NetMeeting.

RUNNING NETMEETING

After Microsoft NetMeeting is installed, it can appear in one of two places:

- Installed with Windows 98, Second Edition—If you installed NetMeeting as part of an Internet Explorer installation with Windows 98, you start NetMeeting by opening the Start menu and choosing Accessories, Internet Tools, Microsoft NetMeeting.

■ Installed from a download—If you chose to install the newest version of NetMeeting, NetMeeting 3.01 (not available in the Windows 98 installation), by downloading NetMeeting from the Internet and then installing it, you can find NetMeeting by opening the Start menu and choosing Programs, Microsoft NetMeeting.

RUNNING NETMEETING FOR THE FIRST TIME

The first time you run NetMeeting, a number of configuration options are set. You can change any of these options at any time by choosing Tools, Options in NetMeeting. These options include

■ Personal information

■ Default directory server

■ Connection speed

■ Audio equipment configuration

The next five sections cover these options. Follow the text as you respond to the prompts in the dialog boxes that NetMeeting displays.

Figure 33.1 shows the first dialog box that appears the first time you start NetMeeting. Click Next to continue.

Figure 33.1
The first dialog box in NetMeeting describes some of the application's capabilities.

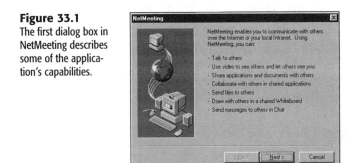

PART

V

CH

33

SPECIFYING PERSONAL INFORMATION

The second dialog box that appears when you run NetMeeting for the first time prompts you for personal information (see Figure 33.2). At the minimum, you must specify your first and last names and your email address, which you must do before you can click Next. You can also specify your location and country, as well as a general comment. Enter the information and then click Next.

Keep in mind that this information is visible to everyone who is logged on to the same directory server as you. With this in mind, the Comment field can be used to let everyone on the server know what kind of meetings you might be interested in. For example, your comment might be Business use only or Call me to test please.

Tip #222

Although you are required to enter this information, NetMeeting has no way of knowing whether the information you have entered is correct. Therefore, if you do not want to reveal your real name or email address, enter fictitious information.

Figure 33.2
The personal informa-
tion you provide is vis-
ible to all NetMeeting
users logged on to the
same directory server
as you.

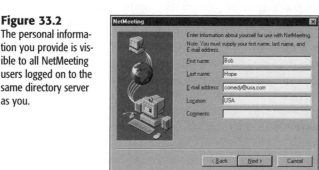

SPECIFYING A DEFAULT DIRECTORY SERVER

The dialog box shown in Figure 33.3 is next in the setup sequence. This dialog box lets you specify which directory server to automatically log on to when NetMeeting starts. A direc-
tory server keeps a list of all the people you can contact through NetMeeting who are using the same directory server. To automatically log on to the specified ILS when NetMeeting starts, click the check box next to the Log on to a Directory Server When NetMeeting Starts option. If you want to manually log on to a directory server when NetMeeting starts, leave the check box clear and click Next.

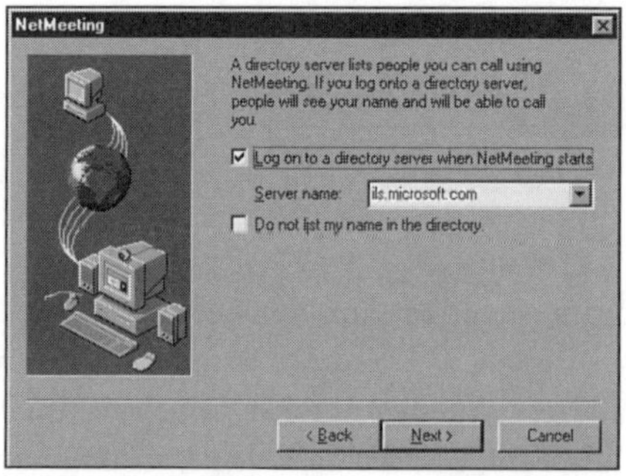

Figure 33.3
You can request to
automatically log on
to a specific ILS server
as soon as NetMeeting
starts. Also, you can
keep your information
private by checking
the Do Not List My
Name in the Directory
check box.

If you specify that you want to be logged on automatically, you must choose a directory server. Unless you know of a specific directory server, just accept the default option of ils.Microsoft.com. Click Next to continue.

DEFINING CONNECTION SPEED

You also must specify the speed of your Internet connection the first time you run NetMeeting. If you are using a modem to connect to the Internet, choose the speed, 14,000bps or 28,000bps, that is closest to the speed of your modem. If your modem is faster than 28,000bps, select that option. If you use either a local or wide area network, or an ISDN connection, to work on the Internet, then select either of those two options from the dialog box. When you have made you selection, click Next.

CONFIGURING AUDIO WITH THE AUDIO TUNING WIZARD

After NetMeeting's initial gathering of information, the Audio Tuning Wizard begins. As you know, NetMeeting can exchange audio between users. Therefore, the initial configuration process must also check for the availability and status of any audio equipment installed on your computer. These audio configuration checks and tests are collectively known as the Audio Tuning Wizard. Click Next to continue.

The Audio Tuning Wizard first determines whether the audio equipment installed on your computer works properly; then the wizard sets the volume. In the next dialog box that appears, click on the Test button. If you hear a sound, click and drag the needle on the Volume bar to a comfortable setting. When you are satisfied with the volume level, click Stop and then click Next. This step establishes the default volume level for your NetMeeting application.

Next the wizard tests your microphone. The dialog box shown in Figure 33.4 asks you to read a sentence. Read the sentence in your normal speaking voice, or at least the voice you will use when you are speaking over NetMeeting. As you read the sentence, the level of your voice is monitored, and the recording level for your computer is set. This recording level matches the loudness of your voice with the capabilities of the audio equipment installed on your computer, so your voice is always transmitted strongly and clearly. Click Next to continue and then click Finish.

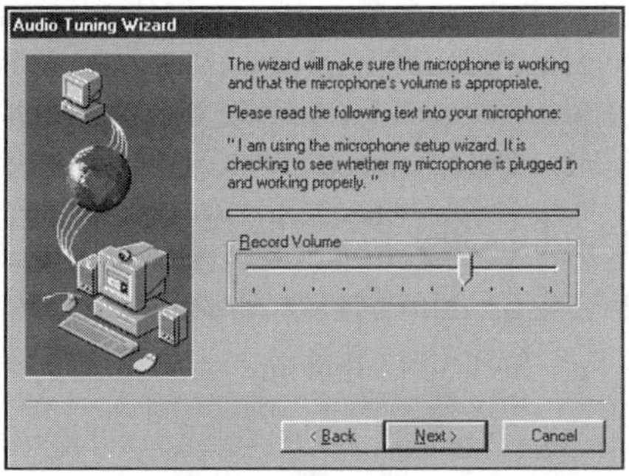

Figure 33.4
Read a sentence to test your computer's microphone.

PART
V
CH
33

After the settings for your microphone are established, the wizard's final dialog box appears. Click Next, and the Audio Tuning Wizard closes.

> **Note**
>
> You can restart the Audio Tuning Wizard at any time from NetMeeting. To do so, choose Tools, Audio Tuning Wizard.

This step marks the end of the configuration process. With NetMeeting now up and running, the next section of the chapter introduces the NetMeeting window and its components.

Tip #223

If your company's security or policy concerns prohibit the use of User Datagram Protocol (UDP) data through its firewall, you will be unable to use the NetMeeting audio and video features because audio and video streaming require dynamically assigned ports. Only secondary TCP and UDP connections support dynamically assigned ports. However, NetMeeting data-conferencing features–such as application sharing, Whiteboard, and Chat–are available because they use calls through the firewall by allowing only TCP connections on ports 522 and 1503.

NAVIGATING AND DISPLAYING INFORMATION IN NETMEETING

NetMeeting provides a large amount of information at one time. Understanding what information is presented and knowing how to see other information is important if you want to take full advantage of NetMeeting. For example, you can switch between views of the people logged on to different directory servers, or Microsoft Internet Directory, and you can also switch to a list showing people interested in chatting about the same content as you. In this section, you learn how to manipulate NetMeeting's user interface to navigate to the places you want to go and to the things you need to see.

UNDERSTANDING WHAT YOU SEE IN NETMEETING

The first step in helping you understand how to navigate and display information in NetMeeting is to identify what you see in the NetMeeting interface. Figure 33.5 points out the major components of NetMeeting. Keep in mind that the Speed Dial and History views are not shown in the figure; pictures of the views are included later in the chapter.

The following list explains the use of the major NetMeeting components:

- To place a NetMeeting call, click on the Place a Call icon.
- To end a NetMeeting call, click the End Call icon.
- To locate a person in your directories, Find Someone in a Directory
- To control the multimedia components, Start Video Adjust Audio volume

- To see the current call statistics and information, view the information in the status bar. The status bar shows the status about your current call if you are in one; otherwise, the status bar indicates that you are not currently in a call. Colorful Computer icons in the right pane of the status bar indicate a current connection to a directory server and that a call is active. To view the NetMeeting participants, look in the Current Call window above the status bar.

Figure 33.5
The NetMeeting window includes many components.

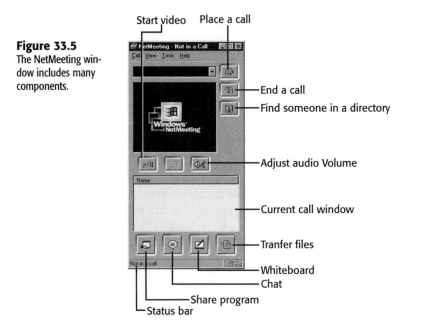

COMPLETING COMMON TASKS

The following list shows you how to complete common tasks:

- To choose the directory being used, choose Directory from the Call menu and select one of these entries: ILS, Microsoft Internet Directory, Windows Address Book, Speed Dial, or History.

- To see information about any person in any list, right-click on the entry in the list and then choose Properties from the menu that appears.

- To allow the Video windows to float over the NetMeeting window, drag the Remote Video and My Video window (only available if you have video equipment) to the left side of the screen.

- To anchor the Video windows to the right side of the NetMeeting window, drag the Remote Video and My Video window (only available if you have video equipment) to the right side of the screen.

PLACING AND RECEIVING A NETMEETING CALL

This section examines the most basic function of NetMeeting: the capability to receive and send calls and to converse by using audio or by writing messages to and receiving written messages from other NetMeeting communicators. Keep in mind as you review the information in this section that the operation of the application is much the same regardless of your computer's capabilities. You needn't do anything special if you do not have video equipment or if your audio equipment is not working properly. NetMeeting automatically manages the application and interface to match the capabilities of your computer and those who you are communicating with.

LOGGING ON TO A SERVER

You must be logged on to a directory server for participants to see your name in a directory list and to call you. By default, when NetMeeting starts, you are connected to the server specified in the Options dialog box on the General tab under Directory settings. This server is the one you specified when you ran NetMeeting for the first time, provided you specified that you be connected automatically to a server when NetMeeting begins. You can tell whether you are logged on to a server by looking at the right pane of the status bar. Two icons show the status of your connection. The single monitor/computer icon represents a current call connection when the icon is in color; a gray icon means that you do not have a current call connection. The double monitor/computer icons shows a current connection to a directory server in the same manner.

If you are not logged on to a server or if you want to log on to a server different from the one you are currently logged on to, follow these steps:

1. If you are logged on to a server already, choose Call, Log Off from *Your Server* from the menu.

2. Choose Tools, Options from the menu and then click the Directory drop-down list for a list of available directory servers.

> **Note**
>
> You can also change directory servers by choosing Call, Directory and using the Select Directory drop-down menu to pick a new directory server.

3. Select the server you want to log on to from the list and then click OK.

FINDING SOMEONE TO CALL

Finding someone to call in NetMeeting might not be as easy as finding someone to call on the telephone. Unless the person you want to call is in your Speed Dial list or in your History list, you must locate the person on one of the directory servers you have access to with your Internet connection.

To use the Microsoft Internet Directory to locate a person, choose to log on to that Directory by choosing Call, Directory. When the Directory used is the Microsoft Internet Directory, a Search window appears. You can search for other people logged on to this server by typing their first or last name, their location, email address, or their comments.

> **Note**
>
> If you plan a meeting, put a comment in your general information to help people find you, such as 4PM Event Planning. Now, participants can search for you even if they can't remember your name.

If you are already logged on to the Microsoft Internet Directory, simply select the Find Someone in a Directory icon button on the main NetMeeting interface. You can also select the Call button and then click on the Find Someone in a Directory icon button at the left corner of the Place a Call dialog box.

When you find someone you wish to communicate with, icons indicate what type of equipment is available. A camera represents video equipment, a speaker represents audio equipment, and if the computer icon has a red light in the corner, that indicates that the user is in a meeting.

Private ILS directories are still used as well. If you have an ILS on your network, choose that ILS from the directory list and the list of available accounts appears in the window below.

PLACING A CALL

Placing a call to a user is one of the simplest tasks in NetMeeting. (The tough part is locating a person to call.) When you have located a person to call in the Microsoft Internet Directory, calling is simply a matter of clicking on the person's entry. In other directories, such as History or Speed Dial, or in an ILS directory, double-click on the person's entry in the appropriate list. With these directories, you can also highlight an entry and then choose the Call button. You can also right-click on the person's entry in any list and then choose Call from the menu that appears.

PART
V
CH
33

> **Tip #224**
>
> To avoid having to look up a person in the directory who is on your network, find the IP address of that person's computer. (A person can display the IP address of a computer by typing ipconfig or winipcfg (depending on OS) at the command line.) When you know the IP of the computer you want to call, choose Call, New Call from the menu; enter the IP address; choose Using Network; and then click OK.

When you call a person, a message box shows the name of the person or computer you are calling and the status of the call (see Figure 33.6).

Figure 33.6
The Place Call dialog box shows the name or address of the computer you are trying to reach.

At this point, the person you are calling sees a message indicating that you are calling. The person can either accept your call or ignore it. If the person accepts your call, his or her name appears in the Current Call window. If the person ignores your call, a message states that your call was not accepted.

ANSWERING A CALL

You are notified in two ways when a person is trying to contact you:

- You hear the sound of a phone ringing.
- A message appears on the status bar (see Figure 33.7).

Figure 33.7
You are notified with sound and a message when you have an incoming call.

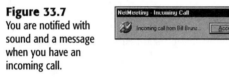

Naturally, however, there are a number of requirements for you to receive a call with NetMeeting:

1. NetMeeting must be running.
2. You must be connected to the Internet.
3. To hear the phone sound, your audio equipment, if you have it, must be working properly, and the volume must be set so that you can hear the sound.

To answer a call, click the Accept button. At that point, the caller is added to your Current Call window (see Figure 33.8). If you do not want to accept the call, click the Ignore button. A message appears on the caller's computer, indicating that you have rejected the call.

One last note about answering a call. Your name automatically appears in the directory list of the directory you are logged on to. Consequently, anyone can call you. A few options are available to keep people from bothering you:

- Use the comment field of your personal information to say Friends Only or something similar.
- Choose Call, Do Not Disturb from the menu. This setting rejects all calls.

- Choose <u>T</u>ools, <u>O</u>ptions from the menu and then click the General tab. In the Directories section, select the Do Not List My Name in the Directory option to keep your name from appearing on the directory list.

Figure 33.8
The name of the person whose call you accept is added to the list in the Current Call window.

ENDING A CALL

When you no longer want to participate in a NetMeeting meeting, simply click the End Call icon or select Hang Up from the Call menu.

HOSTING A MEETING

On certain occasions you might want to meet at a predetermined time with one or more NetMeeting users. For example, you might want to have a casual conversation or collaborate on work projects. In this case, you will want to host a NetMeeting meeting. As the host of a NetMeeting meeting, you can define who can participate by accepting or ignoring calls into the meeting.

To host a meeting with NetMeeting, from the menu, choose <u>C</u>all, Ho<u>s</u>t Meeting. A Host a Meeting dialog box requests information about the meeting you are hosting and allows you to set properties for the meeting (see Figure 33.9).

After you have input the desired settings, click OK. The NetMeeting dialog box reappears and shows your username in the Current Call pane. When you start a meeting, an icon appears beside your name in the directory list, indicating to anyone viewing the list that you are in a meeting (see Figure 33.10).

USING SPEED DIAL

Speed Dial is a feature in NetMeeting that helps you keep track of people who you communicate and collaborate with often. The Speed Dial list shows the people of your choosing

PART
V

CH

33

and whether each is logged on or not. Seeing the list of the usual people who collaborate and communicate in one place makes it easy to check on them or to connect to them without having to browse through all the directory servers.

Figure 33.9
The Host a Meeting dialog box allows you to set preferences for your meeting. You can even create a meeting password.

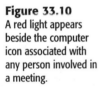

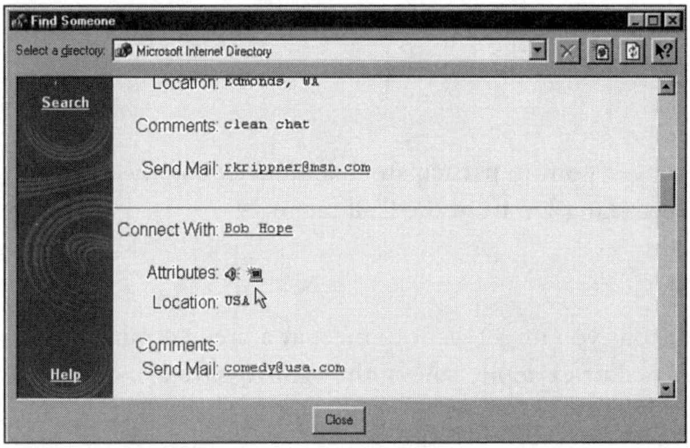

Figure 33.10
A red light appears beside the computer icon associated with any person involved in a meeting.

To display the Speed Dial list, choose Call, Directory and then choose Speed Dial from the drop-down list of available servers (see Figure 33.11).

After the Speed Dial list is displayed, you can call anyone on the list by double-clicking on a name, highlighting a name and selecting the Call button, or right-clicking on a name and choosing Call from the menu that appears.

NetMeeting provides several options to manage the Speed Dial list.

- To manually add a Speed Dial entry, choose Create Speed Dial from the Call menu. Fill in the address and whether to connect through a directory server or your network connection.

- To delete a Speed Dial entry, right-click on the name of the person to be deleted and then choose Delete from the menu that appears.

- To add a current NetMeeting participant to Speed Dial, right-click on the person to be added and choose Add to Speed Dial List.

- To add any directory entry to Speed Dial, from any directory list, right-click on the entry for the person you want to add to the Speed Dial list and then choose Add to Speed Dial List.

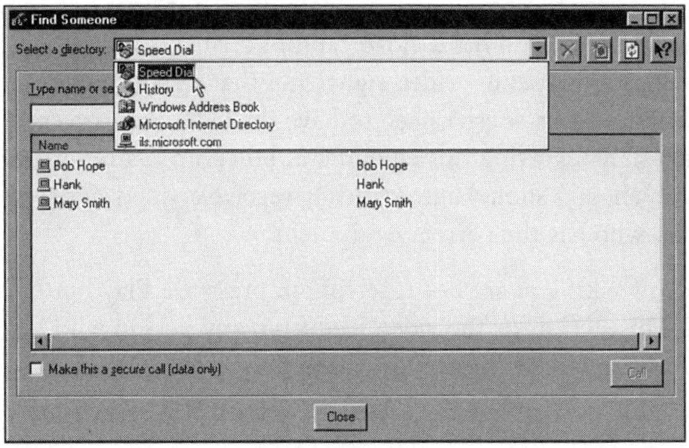

Figure 33.11
The Speed Dial list shows people you can call without identifying their server first.

COLLABORATING WITH NETMEETING

When you have connected with one or more users with NetMeeting, either by answering a call or by someone answering your call, it is time to begin collaborating and communicating. In this section, you learn how to extend NetMeeting through collaboration. Specifically, this section covers:

- Conversing with one or more users
- Using Chat to exchange written information
- Sharing applications
- Using the Whiteboard
- Transferring files

PART

V

CH

33

CONVERSING WITH OTHER USERS

The most basic way to use NetMeeting is to hold a conversation with one or more of the people in the same meeting as you. If you and the person you want to communicate with both have working audio equipment and/or video equipment, you can exchange audio and video signals.

AUDIO CONVERSATIONS

If both computers have working audio equipment, you should be able to hear the other person when he or she speaks. The volume and audio indicators flash when they pick up a signal. You can adjust any of the levels by clicking on them and then dragging either the audio or volume needles. You can also specify that these settings are handled automatically from the Audio tab of the Options dialog box. You display the dialog box by choosing Tools, Options from the menu.

VIDEO CONVERSATIONS

Video conversations depend on the video capabilities of at least one of the participants in a meeting. If at least one person has a video capture card and a camera attached to his or her computer, that person can send a video signal and that signal can be received by other members of the meeting. A user doesn't need to have the video capture card and camera to receive the video signal. Having this equipment, however, is a requirement for sending a video signal. As such, you should automatically receive a video signal when you hold a meeting with a person who has the correct equipment.

To start the video feed if you are not receiving it, press the Play button at the bottom of the Video window. This step starts the video feed from any person who has directed the feed to you. To stop receiving video, click again on the button at the bottom of the Video window.

If your computer has video equipment, the My Video window appears on your screen. Click the button at the bottom of the My Video window to see a preview of how your video will appear to others.

To start sending video, choose Tools, Video, Send.

As with the audio portion of a meeting, you can direct the video portion of the meeting to one person in the meeting. To do so, choose Tools, Switch Audio and Video and then choose the person you want to receive the signal. To stop sending video to a particular person, repeat this step.

CONFIGURING VIDEO

Several options are available to help you configure the video capabilities of your system with NetMeeting. For example, you can specify the size of the video image you send. You can also choose to receive video faster and sacrifice quality, or you can specify the opposite. These and other choices are available from the Video tab of the Options dialog box, which you display by choosing Tools, Options.

EXCHANGING IDEAS IN THE CHAT WINDOW

If you don't want to communicate with audio, video, by sharing applications, or by using the Whiteboard, or if your computer does not have the capabilities to do so, you can always communicate with Chat. The Chat feature allows you to communicate with other NetMeeting users simply by typing messages. You have available standard editing capabilities from the Edit menu, and you can even save the text of your message by using standard File Save and File Save As commands.

You can direct messages to a specific person in Chat or to all persons in Chat. The caption of the Chat windows always shows you how many people are involved in a Chat conversation. If you are in a conversation and you open the Chat window, the Chat application on the person's computer you are conversing with also opens.

To open Chat, choose Tools, Chat from the menu or click on the Chat button. Figure 33.12 shows the Chat window.

To enter a Chat message, type your message in the Message box and then press the large caption-shaped button to the right of the Message box. You have the option in Chat to send your message to everyone in the meeting or to send to one person only. To send a private message to one person, choose the person from the Send To drop-down list before sending the message.

Figure 33.12 shows how the Chat window might appear during a conversation.

Figure 33.12
Chat conversations can help debug audio and video problems and are useful when one person in a NetMeeting does not have a microphone but still needs to participate.

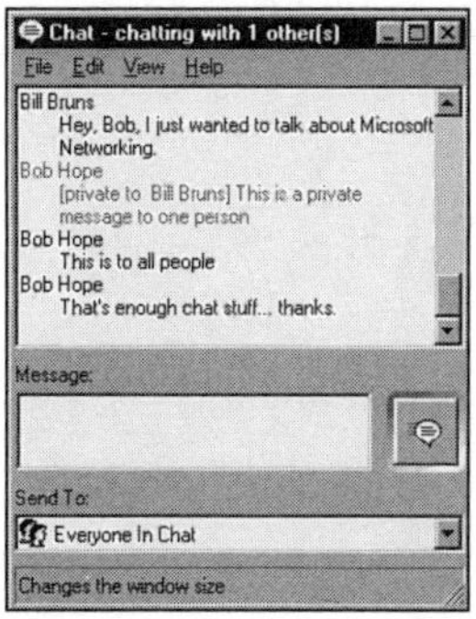

CONFIGURING CHAT

You can configure the way that Chat behaves. These choices are found on the various Chat menus. Here are some ways you can customize Chat:

- To change the font used in the Chat window, choose View, Options from the Chat window; make selections from the Fonts section of the dialog box; and then click OK.

- To change how messages are formatted in the Chat window, choose View, Options. In the Message Format section, specify how to format long messages. Make your formatting selections and then click OK.

- To specify the type of information to display with a message, choose View, Options from the Chat window and then select options from the Information Display section.

- To hide or display the status bar, choose View, Status Bar from the menu.

SHARING APPLICATIONS

As discussed in the "How NetMeeting Works" section of this chapter, you can integrate applications into your NetMeeting collaborative efforts. Consequently, you can use external

PART
V

CH

33

applications as part of your collaborative efforts with NetMeeting. By default, only the person sharing the application can use it, but you can enable users you are conversing with to also work with the application.

SHOWING YOUR WORK TO OTHER USERS

The most basic use of application sharing is to show an application on your computer to meeting participants. The only requirement for doing so, naturally, is that you have the application installed on your computer.

To show your work or application to others, follow these steps:

1. Start the application you want to share and load any document you want to share with others.

2. From the NetMeeting window and the Current Call view, select the Share Program button or choose Tools, Sharing from the menu. Notice that the list of all running applications on your computer is displayed (see Figure 33.13).

Figure 33.13
You can share any application running on your computer.

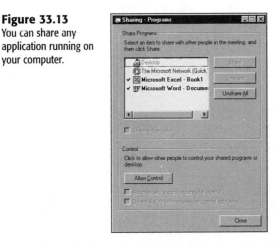

3. Select any applications you want to share. At this point, an additional item appears on the taskbars of the other meeting participants. The item appears with a hand beneath a Window icon. When people click on that item, their screen is hidden by a pattern. You must now select from the taskbar the application you want to share with the other users on your computer for them to see it The other users will not be able to use the application, and their cursors will be inoperable.

Keep in mind that they have the capability to switch to any other running application on their computer. When they switch to your shared application, however, they see it only if you are viewing it, too.

Here are two more important points related to sharing applications:

- To stop sharing an application, you can either shut down the application on your computer, or select the Share Program button in NetMeeting, reselect the application you are sharing, and select the Unshare button. The check mark beside the application you were sharing clears, indicating the application is no longer shared. To stop sharing all applications, select the Unshare All button

- You can share another application even after you make your initial selections. Select the Share Program button in NetMeeting and then select the next application you want to share. Remember, people in your meeting see only the applications you select on your computer. So you have control over how the users switch among applications.

GIVING USERS ACCESS TO THE APPLICATION

You can also give users control access to an application you have shared. This option allows one person at one time to control an application hosted on your computer. Provide this access carefully because you, in effect, are giving a remote user control over one aspect of your computer.

To allow users control over a shared application, follow these steps:

1. Start by following the steps in the preceding section, "Showing Your Work to Other Users."

2. Click on the Allow Control button. Any participant may now request control of the application from you. You can either accept or deny the request.

3. At this point, the user to whom you have given access to the application controls the application. He or she has full cursor control, and the cursor on your computer changes to a hand with the initials of the person controlling the application.

4. To take control back from the user, press the Esc key from either the application being controlled or NetMeeting.

    For the user of the application to return control, the user chooses the Prevent Control button in the Share Program dialog box.

If you are worried about users accessing your hard drive, see "Controlling Access" in the "Troubleshooting" section at the end of this chapter.

USING THE WHITEBOARD TO SKETCH YOUR THOUGHTS

NetMeeting includes a Whiteboard application. The Whiteboard application is used to share information with collaborators. By simulating the whiteboard or flipchart you would find in most corporate conference rooms, you can use NetMeeting's Whiteboard to sketch out rough ideas; draw illustrations; or create outlines, lists, or plans. You can integrate Clipboard data, as well as create multipage Whiteboard presentations.

Here is how Whiteboard works:

- When one person in the meeting starts Whiteboard, the application is launched on the computers of all other participants.

- Any changes made to the Whiteboard project are immediately displayed on the Whiteboards of all other participants.

- Whiteboard works much like any paint or drawing program. You click on different shapes and then drag and drop on the screen to draw them.

- A Whiteboard project can be saved as a Whiteboard file. To do so, choose File, Save As; give the project a name; and then click OK.

If you experience a low performance level during a NetMeeting session, see "Performance Problems" in the "Troubleshooting" section at the end of this chapter.

TRANSFERRING FILES

NetMeeting makes it easy to transfer files to people you are communicating and collaborating with. This feature makes it easy to exchange information as you hold a meeting with someone. Otherwise, you would need to leave NetMeeting to start your email program.

To send a file, follow these steps:

1. From the menu, choose Tool, File Transfer, Send a File; or right-click on the recipient's name and choose Send File from the menu that appears. The File Transfer dialog box appears.

2. Select the file to send and then click OK. The status bar at the bottom of the NetMeeting window is updated to show you the progress of the transfer.

3. While the file is being received at the recipient's computer, the dialog box shown in Figure 33.14 appears.

If you are unable to save a collaborated file to your folder, see "Sharing Files" in the "Troubleshooting" section at the end of this chapter.

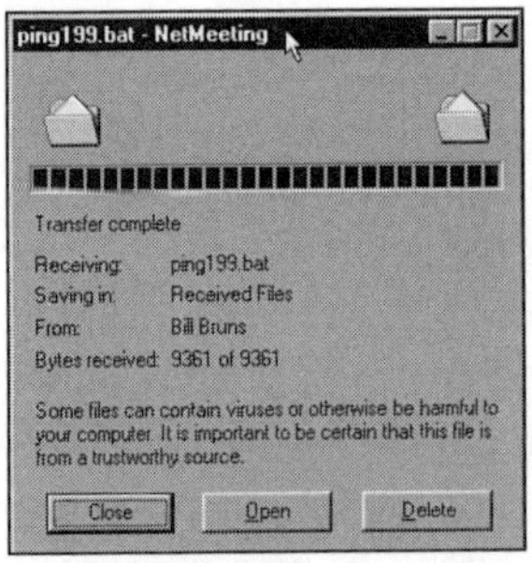

Figure 33.14
A message appears on the recipient's computer as a file is being transferred.

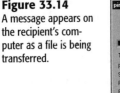

When the transfer is complete, a message also appears on the sender's machine.

Tip #225	You can also transfer a file by dragging the file's icon onto the NetMeeting Main window. When the file appears in the Main window, recipients see a standard warning dialog box that provides the following options: Open, Close, and Delete. If they accept the file, it is copied to a default destination in the C:\Program Files\NetMeeting\Received Files folder.

SPECIFYING WHERE TO STORE TRANSFERRED FILES

You can define a default location in which to store files you receive via NetMeeting. To do so, in the File Transfer dialog box, from the File menu, choose Change Folder, select the folder in which you want transferred files to be placed, and click OK.

TROUBLESHOOTING

CONTROLLING ACCESS

Can sharing a program enable other people to access my files?

When you share a program through NetMeeting and then click Start Collaborating on the Tools menu, those collaborating with you can use the program as if they were actually using your computer. When you share the program, the ability to use the program might include the ability to access your files. For example, if you can open files from your hard disk when using a program at your computer, such as opening documents in Word, chances are the other participants can also open files from your local hard disk when using the shared program from their computers.

You can minimize the amount of access participants have to your program and files by doing one or all of the following:

- To stop someone from using your shared program when you do not control the cursor, press Esc.

- To stop someone from using your shared program when you do control the cursor, click the Collaborate button in the NetMeeting main window to deselect this option.

- Never leave your computer unattended while sharing an application and collaborating.

SAVING FILES

I am unable to save files in a shared application.

File Save, File Open, and Print work only on the computer that shared the application. For each person to have a copy of the meeting file, the individual sharing the application must send copies. For instructions on how to send copies of files through NetMeeting, see the "Transferring Files" section earlier in this chapter.

PERFORMANCE PROBLEMS

When I share a program that uses many graphics, I notice a decrease in performance that increases with the number of participants in the meeting.

The performance decreases because NetMeeting intercepts calls made to the Windows graphical display interface and transmits them to the other members of the meeting. During this process, graphical resources might slow the performance noticeably, depending on the size of the files that NetMeeting must intercept and transmit.

To improve the performance in NetMeeting, consider doing one or all of the following:

- Decrease the number of participants in the meeting.
- Reduce the complexity of the graphics in the shared window, for example, by eliminating or reducing the amount of animation and/or special effects.
- Increase the speed of your network connection with a faster modem or consider isolating your meeting participants in their own network segment where outside traffic will not interfere with their own.
- Close any unused programs on your computer to increase the amount of available resources for your graphics.

SECRETS OF MASTERING THE WINDOWS 98 ENVIRONMENT: MEETING PEOPLE OVER THE WEB THROUGH ICQ

A neat site on the World Wide Web is `http://www.icq.com/products/whatisicq.html`.

Here, you will find ICQ, a site dedicated to getting people together on the Web. Besides acting as an on- and offline directory list of people, ICQ hosts private chat rooms through which you can hold a virtual meeting over the Internet. You can also use ICQ in a multiple-user mode, so groups can conduct conferences. ICQ supports a variety of popular Internet applications and serves as a universal platform from which you can launch peer-to-peer applications (such as Microsoft NetMeeting or Netscape CoolTalk).

The ICQ program runs in the background, taking up minimal memory and Net resources. While you work with other applications, ICQ alerts you when friends and associates log on, allowing you to work efficiently while maintaining a wide range of Internet functions at your fingertips. Among the functions available are Chat, email, and URL and file transfer. Every application, be it Chat, voice, message board, data conferencing, or file transfer, is done in real time. If you think ICQ might be a good tool for you, visit the site given at the beginning of this section. You'll find a wealth of information about the many features and services ICQ can provide.

CHAPTER 34

CONFIGURING WINDOWS NETWORK COMPONENTS

In this chapter

AN ADMINISTRATOR'S GUIDE TO WINDOWS NETWORKING

Windows 98 includes a comprehensive set of networking tools right out of the box. It supports peer-to-peer and client/server network configurations. Windows 98 preserves and extends the strong networking roots in Windows 95, introducing such innovations as Automatic Private Internet Protocol (IP) Addressing and the Microsoft Family Logon.

Automatic IP Addressing is intended for small, private networks using the popular (and new Windows 98 default) TCP/IP protocol suite without the need to manually configure IP addresses or configure a DHCP server.

Microsoft Family Logon lists all users who have accounts on a workstation and allows users to simply select their name from a list, instead of having to type it into a logon box.

Virtual Private Networking enables remote workers to reach their office network by "tunneling" through a public network like the Internet.

Although implementing comprehensive management and security measures still requires the use of a Windows NT, Novell NetWare, or IntranetWare Server's management capabilities, supervisors of small peer-to-peer networks should be well pleased with the surprisingly useful additions and improvements to the Window 98 arsenal of support and administrative utilities.

WINDOWS 98 NETWORK SECURITY

Windows 98 is designed primarily as a client operating system and, as such, depends on being attached to a client/server network to realize the full potential of its security features.

To gain tight control of who can access shared resources on your computer, you should use user-level access control. User-level access control allows you to grant access to your shared resources based on accounts maintained by a Windows NT domain or workgroup or a Novell NetWare server. You can control the type of access each user can have to each resource without having to assign passwords to each of your shares, as is the case if you are using share-level access control.

Both user-level and share-level access control protect the network shares on a Windows 98 computer only when they are accessed remotely. Users who bypass the startup password by clicking Cancel at the logon prompt, booting from a floppy disk, or pressing Ctrl during startup to show the Windows 98 Start menu, gain complete access to the local computer's resources. User accounts are maintained with distributed user lists and password lists, which are stored on each workstation and are easily compromised.

 If you lose or forget your password, see "Finding a Lost Password" in the "Troubleshooting" section at the end of this chapter.

Caution

Even if you use System Policy Editor to force users to log on to access a Windows 98 system, a user with an MS-DOS boot floppy can still gain full access to all local resources except for information stored on FAT32 partitions. Access to resources on a FAT32 volume requires a Win98 boot floppy.

Tip #226

If you want to protect folders and files, you have to use Windows NT Workstation and the NTFS file system.

WINDOWS 98 USER PROFILES AND THE NETWORK

Roaming profiles allow users of Windows 98 computers to have their personal user settings follow them from computer to computer by storing the user's profile on a central profile server, which copies the appropriate profile to whatever computer the user logs on to. Any user profile changes are automatically updated to the profile server.

Tip #227

Roaming profiles are based on the user's account, rather than the particular computer where the user chooses to work. Provided the logon server is properly configured, a user should be able to log on to any system in the network and access his or her profile.

Caution

Windows 98 roaming user profiles are not compatible with Windows NT roaming profiles. Windows 98 profiles and Windows NT profiles are configured differently and stored in different locations on the logon server. If your users use both types of systems, they will have different roaming profiles when they use the different systems.

Through Mandatory User Profiles, a Windows NT administrator can preconfigure any user's initial environment. Although users with Mandatory User Profiles can make modifications to their environment, these changes are not saved to the profile server and the original preferred desktop reappears the next time the user logs on to the network. This practice assures a consistent initial desktop environment across the entire network, easing support time and costs.

PART
V

CH
34

Tip #228

The only way to restrict users from making any undesired changes to their environment is to create a System Policy File with the appropriate restrictions.

ZERO ADMINISTRATION

The goal of the Zero Administration Initiative is to lower the total cost of ownership (TCO) in an organization by allowing the organization to

- Lock down desktop configurations and perform centralized management tasks.
- Efficiently install and update software on a networkwide basis.
- Monitor and control software-licensing issues.

Zero Administration specifies the use of several existing and under-development non-vendor-specific technologies to create a suite of management tools that achieve the goals stated earlier.

Technologies such as automated software installation, predefined option settings for those installs and configurations, and "push" updates across the network are all designed with Zero Administration in mind. Following is a list of some of the applications that make up the Zero Administration Initiative:

- The Microsoft Internet Explorer Administration Kit (IEAK) enables administrators to standardize and customize the Active Desktop across an organization and/or its divisions. See http://ieak.microsoft.com for more information.
- The Microsoft Systems Management Server (SMS) handles software and hardware inventory, software distribution and updates, and remote diagnostics on the network. See http://www.microsoft.com/smsmgmt/ for more information
- The Microsoft Management Console (MMC) hosts enterprise management tools from Microsoft and third-party vendors.

GETTING STARTED WITH WINDOWS 98 NETWORKING

To get started with Windows 98 networking, at a minimum you need the following:

- A null-modem cable (either serial or parallel) for use with direct cable connection software—for low-performance connectivity only
- Network adapter cards, used to connect each computer to the network cabling
- Appropriate lengths of the proper cabling and end connectors to wire each workstation to the network
- Possibly a wiring concentrator, popularly referred to as a hub, which centrally attaches each workstation to the network

Network adapter cards should be *Plug and Play*-compliant *(pages 250, 430, 524-525)* to take advantage of the Windows 98 automatic hardware configuration features. Token ring adapters are available in 4Mbps and 16Mbps speeds. Ethernet adapters are offered in 10Mbps and 100Mbps speeds. The newer 100Mbps PCI adapters are all Plug and Play-compliant.

Tip #229

While configuring your network, remember to document user account names, passwords, workgroups, computer names, and the share names of network resources

The rest of this chapter describes the basic steps of setting up a Windows 98 client on a network. The following topics are covered:

- How the Windows 98 Plug and Play features detect, install, and configure the basic components of Windows networking automatically.

- The network adapter card, your computer's connection to the networking infrastructure.

- Protocols—what they do, why they are essential to networking communication, and how to choose and configure them properly.

- How to install and configure client software. Windows 98 is designed to interoperate with most popular modern and legacy network operating systems.

- Sharing printers, files, fax modems, and access to the Internet are the main reasons networks were developed and exist at all. This chapter shows you how your computer and its resources can participate in sharing network services.

- Connecting your local area network to the Internet.

- After your network is up and running, it will require some care and attention. We give you some tips and reveal some of the secrets that professional network administrators use to keep their own networks healthier, more secure, and trouble free.

- Even the most skilled and well-informed network administrator occasionally discovers an unwelcome problem adversely affecting the network. We review some of the most common network glitches and suggest some proven solutions.

USING PLUG AND PLAY FOR AUTOMATIC NETWORK SETUP

The goal of Plug and Play is to deliver computer devices that configure themselves without manual user intervention. Generally, to install an internal Plug and Play device, all you need to do is turn off the machine, install the board, and turn the machine back on.

Windows 98 should then automatically detect the device, install the appropriate device drivers and supporting files, and configure the hardware resources, such as the following items:

- Interrupt request (IRQ) lines—Hardware lines over which peripherals send requests for service to the CPU

- Input/output (I/O) ports—Hardware paths from the hardware bus to the CPU for communication by peripheral devices

- Direct Memory Access (DMA) channels—Used by "intelligent" peripherals to directly access system memory without going through the CPU

PART

V

CH

34

To see how your computer's hardware resources are currently allocated, follow these steps:

1. In the Control Panel, open the System icon.

2. Click the Device Manager tab.

3. Highlight Computer at the top of the device tree.

4. Click Properties.

5. Toggle between the radio buttons assigned to the various resource listings, as shown in Figure 34.1.

Figure 34.1
You can view the resources used in your computer—a useful tool when installing hardware or troubleshooting problems.

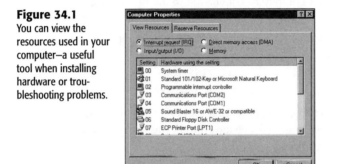

When Windows 98 detects a new device, it arbitrates among the currently installed devices that are vying for use of these limited resources. It resolves any conflicts and reassigns resources to accommodate peripherals, which might work only with certain settings.

For example, your network interface card might function properly only while using IRQ 5, whereas your sound card might be able to accept IRQs 5 or 10. In this case, if the sound card was already occupying IRQ 5 when the network card was installed in the computer, Windows might assign the sound card IRQ 10, freeing up IRQ 5 to be reassigned to the newly installed network card.

Before the development of Plug and Play, each peripheral added to a computer had to be configured in a mostly trial-and-error process. Even today, unless a system is 100% Plug and Play equipped, the user might have to do some manual tweaking to install a particular device.

The Windows 98 Plug and Play feature is especially useful in the case of network configuration. When a Windows 98 computer comes to life on an existing network connection, the Plug and Play feature

- Automatically finds and configures the network adapter
- Installs the Network Driver Interface Specification (NDIS) adapter driver
- Installs and binds any protocols that are already in use by other network adapters
- Adds client software
- Activates network services

This configuration will be completed transparently, during setup. When your Windows 98 Welcome screen comes up for the first time, if you have entered the correct logon password, you will already be connected to the network.

Another feature of Windows 98's Plug and Play for Networking is the capability to *hot-swap* laptop PCMCIA ethernet cards. When the operating system detects a new network adapter, the system automatically loads the hardware profile, which includes all the related network device drivers. Conversely, when the card is removed, the alternative profile sans network drivers is loaded.

> **Note**
>
> Some network applications and device drivers can intelligently sense when a computer is disconnected from the network and go into Offline mode. For example, a user can continue to print to a network printer while offline, and Windows spools the output to disk. When the printer becomes available, a prompt notifies the user that output is available to be printed over the network.

> **Note**
>
> To hot-swap PCMCIA network adapters and have Windows 98 automatically switch to a network-compliant profile, all running network components, including client software, adapter drivers, and network protocols, must be in full 32-bit Protected mode. Real mode 16-bit drivers are not compatible with hot-swapping.

INSTALLING AND CONFIGURING A NETWORK ADAPTER

The network adapter is your critical link to the network. It is the physical connection of your computer to the actual network cabling.

As already described in the section on Plug and Play devices, when the system is powered up again, Windows 98 detects the new hardware and the protocols running on the network wire, installs the *NDIS* drivers, and configures a Plug and Play network adapter automatically.

> **Tip #230**
>
> NDIS stands for Network Device Interface Specification. Its purpose is to serve as a standard specification for network card drivers. As long as the driver has been written to the correct NDIS standard, the card should work with any Microsoft networked operating system and supported protocol. Any network card you are planning to use should be NDIS-compliant. Currently, we are working with the NDIS 4.0 standard.

> **Caution**
>
> Although Windows 98 supports legacy network adapters, you have to make sure that they are properly configured and do not cause conflicts with other devices in your system.

If you install a legacy (a non-Plug and Play) adapter, you must take some additional steps to get it to work with your Windows 98 client. First, you should know what system resources are available to be assigned to your card. To get a resource report, do the following:

1. In the Control Panel, open the System icon.

2. Select the Device Manager tab.

3. Highlight Computer at the top of the device tree.

4. Click the Print button on the bottom right of the System Properties dialog box, shown in Figure 34.2.

Figure 34.2
Keep a copy of your system information handy. It can help when you have to troubleshoot problems.

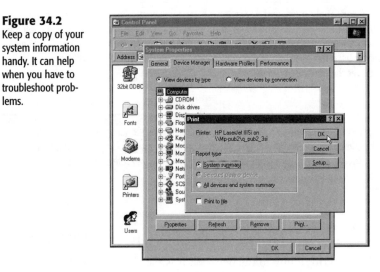

5. Select the System Summary radio button.

6. Click OK.

If you're having trouble configuring a network adapter card, see "Working Through Network Adapter Problems" in the "Troubleshooting" section at the end of this chapter.

Windows produces a concise two-page report listing all system resource assignments. The important information to notice is the IRQ summary.

Next, compare the IRQ assignments recommended in the adapter's documentation to the free resources in your current configuration. For example, if the adapter manufacturer recommends IRQ 5 or 11, check your Device Manager report to see whether any of the recommended IRQs are not being used by another device.

Note

If your adapter is the ISA bus type, it requires exclusive use of an IRQ assignment. If the adapter is a PCI bus type, it can probably dynamically share an assignment with another device already installed in the system because most recent PCI adapters are Plug and Play devices.

Configure your legacy non–Plug and Play adapter either by setting the appropriate hard-wired configuration jumpers or dip switches or by using a disk or CD-ROM–based software configuration utility. Then, install the adapter in an available expansion slot.

To configure a legacy adapter with a vendor-supplied utility, boot into DOS by holding down the Ctrl key during boot up and choosing that option from the Start menu. After you have configured the card through software, power down the computer, restart it, and then wait for Windows 98 to detect the new hardware.

Note

Whereas Windows 95 uses the F8 key to boot up into the Start menu, Windows 98 uses the Ctrl key.

Allow Windows 98 to attempt to detect your new adapter. Then confirm or change the device Windows detects in the Add New Hardware dialog box.

If Windows 98 does not autodetect the new hardware at startup, you can run the Add New Hardware Wizard from Control Panel, and once again allow Windows to search for new hardware. If Windows 98 still cannot detect your hardware, the wizard gives you the option to manually install a device; in this case click Next. Select Network Adapters from the listed Hardware types, click Next, and then specify the correct manufacturer and model. Or, if you have a driver disk, click Have Disk and specify the path to your drivers.

Make sure that the resources Windows assigns to legacy adapters match the resources previously set by jumper- or software-based configurations. If you need to change the resources that Windows 98 uses to communicate with a legacy device, you can do so by going into the Device Manager, selecting the card under Network Adapters on the device tree, clicking Properties, and then clicking on the Resources tab.

If you see any entries in the Conflicting Device list, select the Resource Type, click Set Configuration Manually, and choose the proper setting from the drop-down list. Verify that no further conflicts exist with the new settings in the Conflict Information window. Restart the computer.

Note

You might need to uncheck the Use Automatic Settings box to access the Change Setting button in the Resources dialog box.

Caution

Changing the assigned resources in Windows 98 for a hardware component automatically reconfigures Plug and Play devices only. You must change jumpers or use a vendor-supplied utility to reconfigure legacy devices.

After you restart your computer, go back into Device Manager to check that the adapter has been properly configured (see Figure 34.3). If you find a conflict, take the following steps:

1. Start Windows 98 Help from your Start menu.
2. Click on the Contents tab.
3. Select Troubleshooting.
4. Select Windows 98 Troubleshooting.
5. Select Hardware Conflict to start the Conflict Resolution Wizard.

Figure 34.3
Configuring a network adapter's resources in Device Manager.

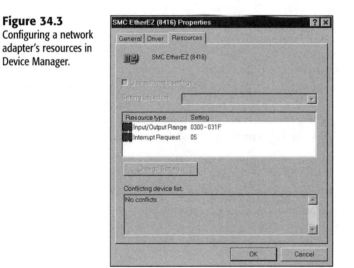

INSTALLING AND CONFIGURING NETWORK PROTOCOLS

Protocols define how communication takes place on and between networks. They stipulate the size, timing, and structure of data packets on the network. For network nodes to talk to each other, they must have at least one protocol in common.

For the three protocols that usually support local area networks (LANs), Windows 98 includes the following:

- TCP/IP—The default protocol suite on Windows 98 networks. TCP/IP is automatically bound to each detected network adapter and client. The popularity of the Internet has made TCP/IP the standard protocol in modern computer networking.

- NetBEUI—A fast, nonroutable, efficient protocol optimized for small to medium-size LANs. As a nonroutable protocol, NetBEUI functions in bridged networks, not routed ones.

- IPX/SPX Compatible Transport—A routable Novell NetWare–compatible protocol automatically installed with the Microsoft Client for NetWare. Under Windows 98, the IPX/SPX frame type and network address are automatically configured. Nodes running IPX/SPX can communicate with NetWare servers or nodes running File and Print Services for NetWare. They can also become file and print servers under NetWare themselves.

Note

In addition to the common LAN protocols, Windows 98 includes support for many newer protocols, namely

- Asynchronous Transfer Mode (ATM) Call Manager, ATM Emulated LAN, and ATM Emulation Client—For wide area networks (WANs)

- Fast Infrared Protocol—For connecting laptop computers to each other, as well as to compatible peripheral devices (such as printers)

- Microsoft 32-bit DLC—For connectivity with mainframe computers and network print devices (for example, HP JetDirect devices)

All Windows 98 protocols are 32-bit, Protected mode virtual device drivers (VxDs). In contrast to 16-bit Real mode drivers, such as those found in earlier versions of network operating systems like Artisoft's LANtastic that load in DOS prior to booting Windows, Protected mode drivers are loaded and bound entirely in Windows and therefore do not tie up conventional (the first 640KB) RAM on the workstation.

Note

Protected mode drivers are generally much faster in execution than are Real mode drivers.

For connectivity with LANs, which access or must go across internetworks, Windows 98 offers native support for multiple protocols simultaneously, either on multiple network adapters or all bound to a single network adapter.

Note

As a rule, it is wise to install and bind only those protocols required for communication across the networks you want to reach. Extraneous protocols add processing overhead to each network transmission and decrease efficiency. For example, you should unbind all but the TCP/IP protocol from a dial-up adapter that accesses the Internet because TCP/IP is the only protocol used on the Internet.

PART

V

CH

34

Network nodes need only one protocol in common to talk to each other across the network. If an additional protocol is bound to your network adapter, that protocol is ignored by other nodes on a segment that do not have that same protocol bound to their adapters.

CHOOSING A PROTOCOL AND ADJUSTING BINDINGS

To install a protocol or protocols on your network node, follow these steps:

1. In the Control Panel, open the Network icon.

2. On the Configuration tab, click the Add button.

3. In the Select Network Component Type dialog box, select Protocol and then click the Add button once more.

4. In the Select Network Protocol dialog box, select the manufacturer on the left (in this case, Microsoft) and the protocol on the right (see Figure 34.4). Click OK.

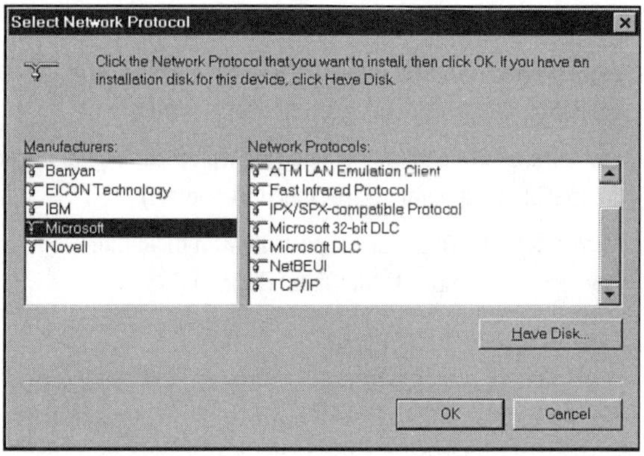

Figure 34.4
Installing a network
protocol in Network
Neighborhood.

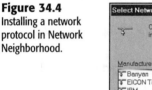

5. When you return to the Configuration tab in the Network dialog box, you can adjust the protocol bindings, which are illustrated in the Installed Components windows.

6. To deselect a binding, select it and click the Remove button.

7. To add a binding, click on the adapter listing, click Properties, choose the Bindings tab, and click the protocol you want the adapter to use.

8. Click OK to close the Network dialog box; then, restart your computer when prompted.

> **Note**
>
> For security reasons, Windows 98 prompts you to unbind TCP/IP from File and Print Services under your Dial-Up Adapter Properties page Bindings tab if that adapter will be used to access the Internet. Otherwise, other nodes on the Internet will be able to see and possibly access the resources on your node across the Internet.

CONFIGURING TCP/IP ADDRESSES

IP addresses must be unique. Ask your administrator for your address if you are on a corporate network; ask your ISP for your address if you have a dedicated connection to the Internet; use the automatic IP configuration (DHCP) in almost every other instance.

USING TCP/IP ON A PRIVATE NETWORK

On private networks (LANs that do not access the Internet) you can configure your computers with any IP addresses you want. To make the configuration of private networks easier, Windows 98 introduces Automatic IP Addressing, which automatically assigns a TCP/IP address to each host on the network when a DHCP server is not available.

Windows 98 Automatic IP Addressing uses IP network number 169.254.X.X, where the first two octets (169.254) are fixed and the last two octets are uniquely assigned to each Windows 98 computer in your network.

Caution

Nodes using Automatic IP Addressing can communicate only with their private network and cannot be seen or reached from the Internet. Automatic IP Addressing should not be used on multiple-LAN routed configurations except as a backup.

If you need to communicate with the Internet, you cannot use Automatic IP Addressing unless your network uses a proxy server to provide a connection to the Internet.

When a DHCP server is available, Windows 98 computers act as normal DHCP clients and use the dynamically assigned IP address they receive via the DHCP process.

To enable Automatic IP Addressing, follow these steps:

1. In the Control Panel, open the Network icon.
2. Click the Configuration tab.
3. Select the TCP/IP ==> Network Adapter listing.
4. Click the Properties button.
5. Click the Obtain an IP Address Automatically check box (see Figure 34.5).

PART

V

CH

34

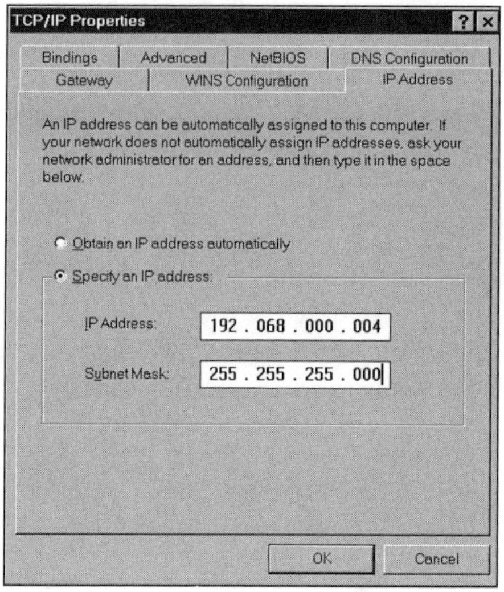

Figure 34.5
TCP/IP addressing in
Network
Neighborhood.

USING DHCP TO AUTOMATICALLY ASSIGN IP ADDRESSES

Two options are available for assigning TCP/IP addresses over a network:

- Static
- Dynamic

With static addressing, each computer is configured with one or more preselected IP addresses. Every time a computer with a static IP address is moved to a new location, or subnet, in a TCP/IP network the computer must be reconfigured with a different IP address that is appropriate for the new subnet location.

DHCP was developed to eliminate the need to manually configure and assign IP addresses across a network, which can become an administrative nightmare on large networks.

DHCP servers are configured with a range of IP addresses that are appropriate for the various parts of their network. When a computer that has been configured as a DHCP client restarts, it is assigned an IP address by any available DHCP server. Microsoft supplies a DHCP server capability only with Windows NT Server.

Note

Because DHCP is an industry standard, your network can use a DHCP server that operates on any operating system, including NetWare, UNIX, or OS/2. You can also purchase third-party DHCP server software that runs on Windows 98.

You can use the Windows 98 utility WINIPCFG to see the IP configuration parameters statically assigned to your system or assigned by the DHCP server. This utility displays the IP address, subnet mask, and gateway address (see Figure 34.6).

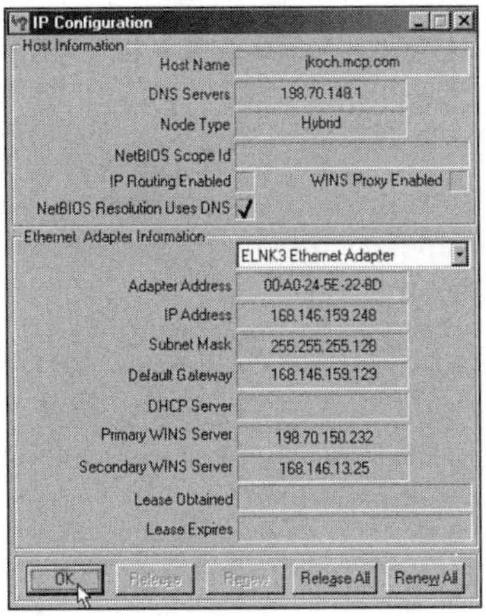

Figure 34.6
Using WINIPCFG to
show IP configuration
parameters.

The TCP/IP protocol, using DHCP, is the default in Windows 98. If a DHCP server is not available on the network when the host logs on, the host will use the last assigned address until a DHCP server comes on the network.

SETTING UP NETBEUI

No configuration options are available for the NetBEUI protocol.

SETTING UP THE IPX/SPX COMPATIBLE PROTOCOL

To configure the IPX/SPX protocol (assuming that the IPX/SPX Compatible Transport Protocol has already been installed), follow these steps:

1. In the Control Panel, open the Network Icon.
2. Select the IPX/SPX ==> Network Adapter listing in the Network Component window.
3. Click on Properties.
4. Click the Advanced tab.
5. Select the property you want to configure.
6. Use the drop-down bar under the Value field to specify the value for that IPX/SPX property.
7. Click OK twice.

PART

V

CH

34

Note   Windows 98 will automatically configure the IPX/SPX frame type and network address.

INSTALLING AND CONFIGURING CLIENT SOFTWARE

Before a computer can share its own resources or connect to other computers' resources across a network, compatible client software must be installed on each of these computers. The basic purpose of client software is the redirection of requests by a local computer to access the shared resources of remote computers and servers on the network. The client software is often referred to as the "Redirector."

To the user at the computer attached to a network, remote resources (either files or printers) look and behave like locally connected resources. But the client software behind the scenes redirects file requests over the network to the remote resources. When the client software is configured correctly, this activity is transparent to the user.

The Client for Microsoft Networks is automatically installed by Windows 98 Setup if it finds a previous version during a Windows upgrade or if a network adapter is found during the Setup program's hardware detection phase. This client supports the entire Microsoft family of products, including Windows NT, Windows 95, Windows for Workgroups (WFW), LAN Manager, and the MS-DOS add-on for WFWG.

Windows 98 can support multiple Protected-mode, 32-bit clients simultaneously but only one 16-bit Real mode client at a time.

If you need to manually install the Client for Microsoft Networks, follow these steps:

1. Open the Network icon in the Control Panel.
2. Click the Add button.
3. In the Select Network Component Type dialog box, double-click the Client listing and click the Add button.
4. In the Select Network Client dialog box, select Microsoft in the Manufacturers list and Client for Microsoft Networks in the Network Clients list.
5. Click OK.

After a client is installed, you can set the primary network logon. In the Network dialog box, open the drop-down list under Primary Network Logon. The exact choices depend on which clients are installed.

- Microsoft Family Logon is appropriate for workstations in a home environment where security is not an important consideration.
- Windows Logon is appropriate for workstations not connected to Windows NT or NetWare networks.
- Client for Microsoft Networks should be chosen for workstations that will log on to and be validated by Windows NT domains or workgroups.
- Client for NetWare Networks should be chosen for workstations that will log on to and be validated by a Novell NetWare or IntranetWare server.

To log on to a Windows NT network, a corresponding user account with username and password must already exist in the domain for that user. In addition, the Client for Microsoft Networks must specify a logon to a Windows NT domain.

The first time you log on to Windows 98, you are prompted to log on separately for each network client. If your password for Windows 98 is the same, or made the same, as the other client logons, you are automatically logged on to all the other networks simultaneously, with just one logon box, each time Windows 98 starts.

To enable logon validation for Client for Microsoft Networks, follow these steps:

1. In the Control Panel, open the Network icon.

2. Select Client for Microsoft Networks and click the Properties button.

3. Select the Log on to Windows NT Domain check box (see Figure 34.7).

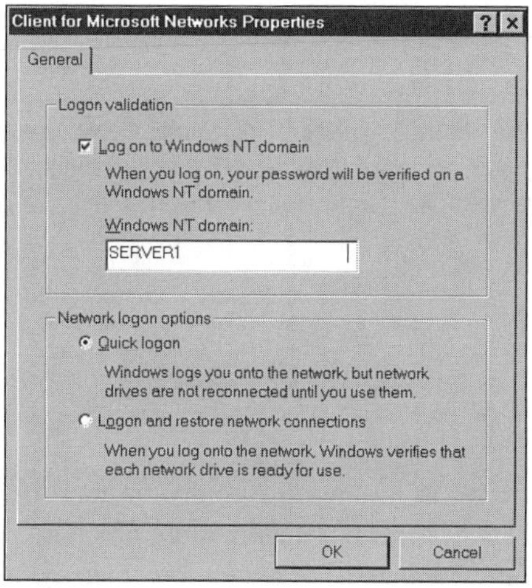

Figure 34.7
Client for Microsoft
Networks Properties
in Network
Neighborhood.

4. Enter the domain name where your user account resides in the Domain field.

5. If you prefer to verify each shared network resource, such as remote drives and printers, when you log on, click the Logon and Restore Network Connections button in the Network Logon Options section. Otherwise, click Quick Logon. The Quick Logon option allows you to log on without connecting to available resources until you actually attempt to access them and, as the name implies, is much faster than choosing to restore the network connections at logon.

6. Click OK.

7. Click OK again to close the Network dialog box.

Computers communicating over a network must have unique computer names and must have at least one protocol in common, bound to the same type of client component. (See the section titled "Installing and Configuring Network Protocols" earlier in this chapter.)

PART

V

CH

34

To check the network settings, follow these steps:

1. In the Control Panel, open the Network icon.
2. Click on the Identification tab.
3. Make sure that the Computer Name field is unique to the network.
4. Make sure the workgroup name specified is identical to the workgroup name used by all other computers in the workgroup.
5. Click on the Configuration tab.
6. In the network components display, select the Protocol ==> Network Adapter listing (for example, TCP/IP ==> 3Com EtherLink III) and click Properties.
7. Select the Bindings tab. Click to select the check box next to the client you will use to log on to the network.
8. Click OK.
9. Click OK again to close the Network dialog box.

| Tip #231 | If you specify the name of the Windows NT domain as the workgroup name under the Identification tab, the names of the Windows NT computers in the domain appear beside the names of the Windows 98 computers in your workgroup. |

If you're having problems connecting to network resources, see "Common Network Problems" in the "Troubleshooting" section at the end of this chapter.

MANAGING A WINDOWS NETWORK

Network management is a very active topic among administrators today. Companies are looking for ways to make their networks more reliable, more efficient, and less costly to support. We have already touched on several areas of network management in this chapter, such as user profiles, share-level versus user-level resource access, and the Zero Administration Initiative. Although this chapter can't address every network management issue, it does consider some of the remote administration tools included with Windows 98, which are

- Net Watcher—Allows network administrators to manage remote resources
- System Policy Editor—Creates System Policy files that can enforce settings on the various users and computers in your network

NET WATCHER

Net Watcher allows the administrator of a Windows 98 network to perform the following services on remote computers without ever leaving his or her desk computer:

- View current network connections.
- Disconnect users from the network or network resources.
- Monitor what resources are being shared on the network and by whom.
- Activate, deactivate, and modify resource shares.

To connect to a remote computer from the Net Watcher application, the remote computer must have both file- and printer-sharing services and remote administration services enabled. If your computer is running share-level security, you can connect only to other remote computers running share-level security. If your computer is running user-level security, you can connect to any other remote computers running file- and printer-sharing services.

Net Watcher has three views:

- By Connections View shows the currently connected users.
- By Shared Folders View shows shared resources. This view also includes any printer shares on the remote computer (see Figure 34.8).
- By Open Files View shows open files.

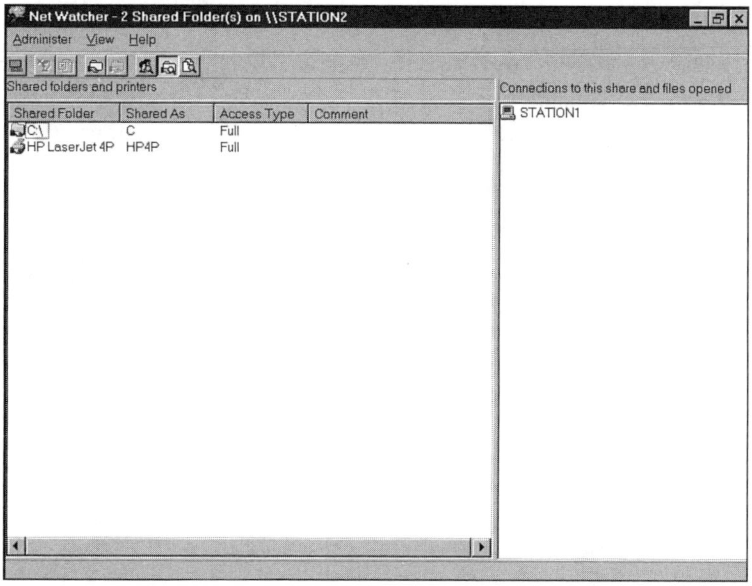

Figure 34.8
Net Watcher utility showing shared folders.

To connect to a remote computer from Net Watcher, follow these steps:

1. Go to Programs/Accessories/System Tools in the Start menu and choose Net Watcher.
2. From the Administer menu, click Select Server.
3. Enter the name of the Windows 98 system that you want to monitor and click OK.
4. Enter the correct Remote Administration password for the remote computer.

Tip #1001	You can also run Net Watcher from Network Neighborhood by right-clicking on a remote computer, selecting the Tools tab, and clicking the Net Watcher button.

To share a resource on a remote computer while using Net Watcher, follow these steps:

1. Select By Shared Folders on the View menu.
2. Select Add Shared Folder from the Administer menu.
3. Type the resource path of the drive you want to share in the Enter Path box.
4. Click OK.

SYSTEM POLICY EDITOR

The goal of system policies is to centralize the administration of all network users and computers. Implementation of system policies requires the use of a centralized Windows NT domain or NetWare server and user-level security. A single policy file located on Windows NT primary domain controllers or Novell NetWare servers controls the system policies for each user and computer. System Policy Editor is the tool that creates the policy file for a network (see Figure 34.9).

Figure 34.9
System Policy Editor
showing network
policies.

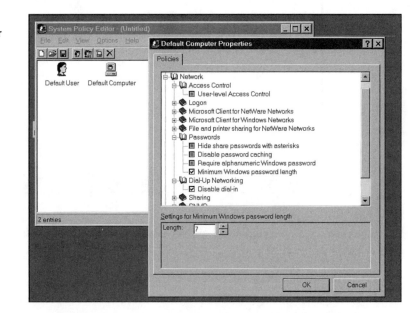

To use System Policy Editor, the Remote Registry Service must be running on the remote computer. To install the Remote Registry Service, follow these steps:

1. In the Control Panel, open the Network icon.
2. Click on the Add button.

3. Select Service and click the <u>A</u>dd button.

4. Click on <u>H</u>ave Disk and browse to the \tools\reskit\netadmin\remotreg folder on the Windows 98 CD-ROM. Click OK twice.

5. Select Remote Registry Service.

6. Click OK twice to close.

7. Reboot your computer when prompted.

An administrator can use the System Policy Editor to

- Modify the desktop.
- Remove or restrict access to items such as the Settings folder on the Start menu.
- Modify the capabilities of Control Panel applets.
- Enable or disable resource sharing.
- Hide the Network Neighborhood.
- Disable password caching (which also disables Quick Logons to resources in the Client for Microsoft Networks).
- Prevent modification of the desktop environment.

To install the System Policy Editor in Windows 98, follow these steps:

1. In the Control Panel, open Add/Remove Programs.

2. Click on the Windows Setup tab.

3. Click on the <u>H</u>ave Disk button.

4. Browse to the \tools\reskit\netadmin\poledit folder on the Windows 98 CD-ROM.

5. Click OK twice and click the check box next to System Policy Editor.

6. Click <u>I</u>nstall.

7. Click OK to close the Add/Remove Programs Properties box; there is no need to reboot your computer.

System Policy settings can be applied to groups as well as individuals. Also, default policies can be applied to users and computers or to specific computers, groups, and users. To create policies for Internet Explorer and the Active Desktop, use the Internet Explorer Administration Kit.

PART

V

CH

34

Caution

The System Policy Editor is a very powerful tool and should be used only with knowledge and extreme caution. Each item in the settings tree has three possible states: enabled, disabled, and unchanged. Accidental changes made to the remote computer's Registry can cause "unexpected results" that usually require a complete reinstallation of Windows 98.

REMOTE ADMINISTRATION SERVICES

Remote Administration Services enable network administrators to manage remote resources, shares, and Registries and to modify the desktop environment and configuration.

Both user-level security and Remote Administration Services must be enabled on each computer managed by Remote Administration Services. The computers must have at least one protocol in common.

To enable Remote Administration Services on a Windows 98 computer, follow these steps:

1. In the Control Panel, open the Passwords icon.
2. Click the Remote Administration tab.
3. Click the check box next to Enable Remote Administration of This Server.
4. If your system uses user-level security, click the Add button and specify from a Browse list which users are authorized to access this computer with Remote Administration Services. If your system uses share-level security, enter and confirm the password that should control access to your system.
5. Click OK.

Tip #1001   When both file and printer sharing and user-level security are enabled on a Windows 98 computer, remote administration is automatically enabled.

TROUBLESHOOTING

COMMON NETWORK TROUBLESHOOTING METHODOLOGY

Why can't I access the network?

When network problems occur, the best approach to troubleshooting is to start with the most obvious and likely causes of the problem, like a disconnected cable, and work up to the less obvious ones, like an incorrect IP address.

Try to determine when the problem first occurred and what, if anything, might have changed just prior to the first appearance of the problem.

- What specifically is not working now that was working before?
- When did the problem start?
- Is the system plugged in and powered on? Are all components receiving power?
- Does the user who cannot access a network drive or printer have the security permissions to do so?
- Have any exposed network cable segments recently been stepped on, twisted, bent, or relocated? Cable problems are a very common cause of network downtime.
- What might have changed about the system or configuration since the last time it worked properly?

- Was new hardware or software installed recently? Go back and retrace the steps taken during the installation. The problem could turn out to be an incorrect or outdated software version or a connector that was knocked loose during a component upgrade.

- Were any hardware or operating system error messages displayed on the monitor just before the problem occurred?

- Can the problem be reproduced? If so, you might be able to trace the problem to a misbehaving utility program or incompatible device driver.

- Do the applications related to the problem maintain any kind of activity or error log? If so, the log might contain valuable information that can point to a possible cause of the problem.

Most hardware and software vendors maintain a problem database of some kind on their Web sites. The Microsoft Knowledge Base is one of the most comprehensive in the industry. It is available 24 hours a day to anyone with an Internet connection and browser software. You can enter keywords or Boolean search terms to locate technical support documents that might relate to your precise problem.

COMMON NETWORK PROBLEMS

Why can't I connect to a remote computer?

The following are two different scenarios in which you cannot access a remote computer:

- If you cannot find the computer you are looking for in Network Neighborhood, make sure that you are logged on to the correct workgroup. Check the Identification tab in Network Neighborhood to see how you have identified your system and its workgroup or domain to the network.

- If you can log on to your computer but are not able to connect to the other resources on the network, check your protocol bindings in Network Neighborhood. You can share resources only with computers that have at least one common protocol with your computer.

FINDING A LOST PASSWORD

I lost my password. How can I reset it?

If you lose your password on a Windows 98 peer network, look for the file named *USERNAME*.PWL (where *USERNAME* is your logon name) in the \Windows folder. Erase that file, restart Windows, and the system will prompt you for a new password.

Tip #234

This method works only with a Windows 98 password. It does not help you with a lost password on either a Windows NT or NetWare network. You need the help of your network administrator if you lose or forget a password in that type of environment.

WORKING THROUGH NETWORK ADAPTER PROBLEMS

I installed a new network adapter but it doesn't seem to be working. How can I troubleshoot this?

If you have difficulty installing an adapter card into Windows 98 or if the card seems to be working, but you still cannot log on to the network, try these proven troubleshooting ideas to find a solution:

- Open Device Manager and check for any yellow exclamation points or red Xs displayed across device listings. These symbols indicate a resource conflict or a device that has been disabled in the Windows 98 hardware database. From Windows 98 Help, start the Hardware Conflict Troubleshooter Wizard and follow the prompts to resolve the conflict.

- Check to make sure that AC power is being supplied to any 10BASE-T hubs.

- Use WINIPCFG or the Network icon in the Control Panel to check your network adapter's IP settings for accuracy.

- If attempting to log on to a Windows NT domain, check that your Client for Microsoft Networks is configured to log on to the domain and that the domain name is properly specified in the Client Properties box.

- Legacy adapter cards sometimes cannot be configured under Windows 98 if their hard-coded settings conflict with the resources Windows 98 is attempting to assign to them. See the section "Installing and Configuring a Network Adapter" earlier in the chapter for instructions on how to configure a legacy adapter card under Windows 98.

- Check thinnet (10BASE-2) coaxial cabling runs for kinks and sharp bends around corners. Avoid running thinnet past fluorescent ceiling fixtures because they can cause interference that disturbs network transmissions.

- Check cable lengths between segments and overall network distance according to cable specifications. Excessive cable lengths is especially a problem with custom cable runs prepared from bulk connectors and wiring.

- Replace the terminators on 10BASE-2 cable ends. Oxidation and other contaminants can prevent a clean contact between the terminator and its T connector.

- Finally, if all else fails, try a different network adapter in that computer. Some computers have been known to work with one card in a batch and reject a nearly identical card, even from the same manufacturer.

OTHER PROBLEMS

An excellent idea is to record all incidences of problems, along with their discovered causes and their solutions, in a network journal.

Maintain up-to-date records that include a schematic of your network with a thorough hardware and software inventory. Record dates and times that software and hardware components have been added, removed, and updated, along with a record of users at each workstation. Good records are very valuable resources to have when trying to track down the possible causes of a problem.

A new feature of Windows 98, the System Configuration utility, is a useful tool for isolating startup problems. This utility is easier to use, and much less prone to error, than the old SYSEDIT utility it replaces.

Through a graphical user interface, you can selectively add and remove individual components of the Windows 98 startup files, including the AUTOEXEC.BAT, CONFIG.SYS, SYSTEM.INI, and WIN.INI files.

To launch the System Configuration utility, run MSCONFIG in the Start menu's Run box.

The System Information utility provides information on devices, components, and drivers. It keeps a history log of the system and can provide reports of changes to the system and the dates of the changes. The System Information utility is run from the \Accessories\System Tools folder on the Start menu.

Another new tool helpful in tracking down system problems is System File Checker, which automatically checks the Windows 98 system files for corruption. It can be run from the Tools menu inside the *System Information utility (page 465)*.

Scanreg (DOS version) and Scanregw (Windows version) run automatically each time Windows 98 boots up. It checks and backs up the Registry. It can also run inside the System Information utility.

SECRETS OF MASTERING THE WINDOWS 98 ENVIRONMENT: HOW TO DISABLE THE USE OF AUTOMATIC PRIVATE IP ADDRESSING

You might be in a situation in which you do not want your DHCP clients to use automatic private IP addressing. In this case you first need to determine whether or not automatic IP addressing is currently enabled on the client system.

To do so, click Start, click Run, type winipcfg, and select More Info. The next screen displays your IP address and other TCP/IP configuration information. Examine the box immediately beneath your adapter address (48-bit address expressed in hexadecimal). If the name in the box is IP Autoconfiguration Address and the IP address is in the 169.254.x.x range, automatic private IP addressing is enabled. Conversely if the name in the box is IP Address, then automatic private IP addressing is not currently in use.

If you have determined that automatic private IP addressing is being used, you can disable this feature in one of following ways:

- You can manually configure the TCP/IP address by entering a predefined IP address and other associated information into the appropriates boxes.
- You can disable automatic private IP addressing (but still leave DHCP intact) through a careful edit of the Registry.

To disable automatic private IP addressing but not DHCP, you must add the IPAutoconfigurationEnabled Registry entry with a value of DWORD 0x0 to the Registry in the following location:

`HKEY_LOCAL_MACHINE\System\CurrentControlSet\Services\VxD\DHCP`

After using the Registry Editor to add this entry, you must shut down and restart the system.

PART VI

WINDOWS NETWORK SERVICES

CHAPTER 35

CONNECTING TO AN EXISTING NETWORK

In this chapter

CHOOSING YOUR PRIMARY NETWORK LOGON

Windows 98 provides the mechanisms to connect to different types of providers on a network. In this chapter, you learn how to set up your Windows 98 workstation to connect to Microsoft Windows NT servers and workstations, to Novell NetWare servers, and to other Microsoft Windows 98 machines. After you are connected, you'll be able to access shared files and printers. You also learn how to use some of the services provided by Microsoft and Novell. One service they provide is the capability to secure your shared resources by using their native security account databases.

Because Windows 98 provides connectivity with many different network providers, at some point you might need to select a provider to connect to when you log on to your workstation. For example, you might work in a company that uses Microsoft Windows NT servers as a corporate standard. However, your department might have a Novell NetWare server with resources you need to access as well. Or, you might have a laptop on which you want to log on to Windows NT when you're connected locally, but you might want to bypass the logon when you're on the road. You can choose one provider to be your primary network logon. Common choices include Windows Logon, Windows Family Logon, Client for Microsoft Networks, Client for NetWare Networks, and NetWare Client 32.

Your primary network logon is the first provider for which you want to get a logon prompt when you begin working. Logon scripts and other tasks are executed based on your selected primary network logon. The logon script of your selected primary network logon runs last. This sequence is actually a good thing. A vital function of logon scripts is to provide consistent drive mappings to resources from your network provider. By having your primary provider's script run last, you ensure that the drive mappings for it overwrite any previously assigned mappings from your nonprimary providers. The exception is when you have Client for Microsoft Networks installed. In this case, the Windows NT logon script always runs first.

To select your primary network logon, follow these steps:

1. Run Control Panel.
2. Double-click on the Network icon.
3. Choose your primary network logon from the Primary Network Logon drop-down box as shown in Figure 35.1.

Figure 35.1
You can select your
primary network
logon from any net-
work providers set up
on your workstation.

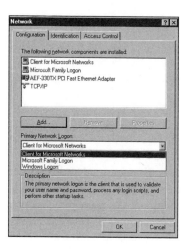

SELECTING WINDOWS LOGON

Windows Logon is the default choice for your primary network logon when you have no
network connectivity installed or when you have no network providers to connect to. When
Windows Logon is the primary network logon, you are prompted to log on to the workstation
with the prompt shown in Figure 35.2.

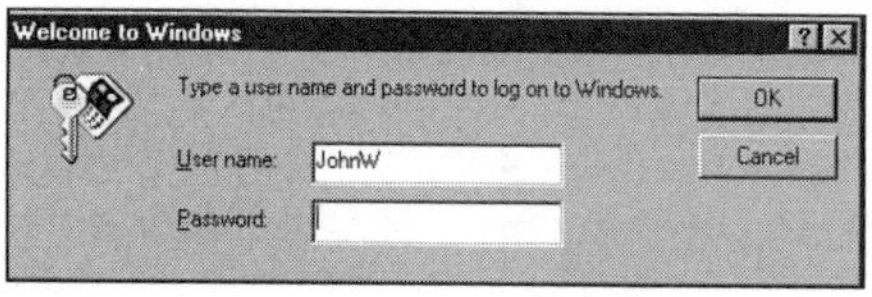

Figure 35.2
The Windows Logon
dialog box.

Windows Logon is Windows 98's built-in security. When you log on at the Windows
Logon prompt, Microsoft remembers the username and password you provide. The reasons
Windows 98 enables you to log on and identify yourself to the workstation itself are as
follows:

- Windows 98 can save each user's settings individually. These settings include Internet
favorites, Start menu items, desktop preferences, and application settings. For instance,
if you share your workstation with other members of your household, you probably
want different desktop settings than your kids do, unless you, too, enjoy staring at
Barney!

→ **See** Chapter 17, "Customizing the Look and Feel of Windows," for more information.

- Windows 98 employs password caching. Password caching makes it less cumbersome to
remember passwords you might have for various services, such as network providers,
secure Web sites, and custom applications you run. Simply select Save This Password
in Your Password List, shown in Figure 35.3.

PART
VI
CH
35

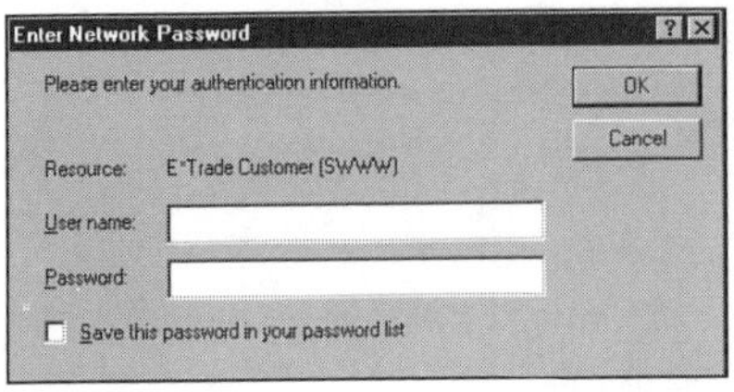

Figure 35.3
With password caching, Windows 98 can remember passwords to various services you use.

Windows 98 saves your passwords in an encrypted password cache file named with the username and secured with the password you entered at the Windows Logon dialog box. Password caching is useful, for example, when you log on to Windows NT and NetWare. By having a user account with each of these network providers that is the same as your Windows 98 username, you do not have to enter three passwords. Instead, you enter only the Windows Logon password. When the logon prompts for the other providers are displayed, the password field is already filled in, allowing you to press OK to log on.

⚠ *If you are anxious about the security implications of password caching on a Windows 98 system, see "Windows 98 Password Cache" in the "Troubleshooting" section at the end of the chapter.*

- By selecting Windows Logon as your Primary Network Provider, you prevent Windows 98 from trying to establish connections with your installed network providers. For instance, if you use a laptop, you might want to set up hardware profiles (see Chapter 21, "Configuring Hardware") so that your primary network logon is Windows Logon when you're on the road. This way, you won't have to attempt to log on to and receive errors regarding a network provider to which you're not connected.

Tip #235	If you don't want to enter a Windows 98 password each time you log on, you can leave the password blank. Of course, your cache file won't be as secure, so you need to balance convenience and security. If you have assigned a password to your Windows 98 username and later want to remove the password, you can change the password to blank (which in effect removes it) after you've logged on, using the Passwords applet in Control Panel.

SELECTING WINDOWS FAMILY LOGON

Windows Family Logon is new terminology in Windows 98. Essentially, this type of logon allows users to select from a list of users when logging on to a Windows 98 system. When you install this type of client under the Network Control Panel applet and choose this client as your Primary Network Logon, you can choose which Windows 98 username you want to use to log on. For this feature to work, however, you must have previously established user profiles on your machine (see Chapter 2, "Starting and Quitting Windows 98"). To log on with Windows Family Logon as your Primary Network Logon, simply highlight your username and enter your password, as shown in Figure 35.4.

Figure 35.4
The Windows Family
Logon box.

SELECTING CLIENT FOR MICROSOFT NETWORKS

If Client for Microsoft Networks is your Primary Network Logon, then any system policies and user profiles, if they have been created by the network administrators, are downloaded to your machine from the Windows NT network. Also, any logon scripts assigned to you on the server or domain to which you connect are run.

System policies are settings specific to the workstation from which you're logging on. For example, administrators at your site might have decided to display a dialog box with a legal notice concerning unauthorized use of network resources prior to a user logging on to any workstations on the network. The use of system policies would enable them to distribute the settings for this dialog box over the network.

User profiles are those settings specific to a user or group. If your PC is configured for multiple users, you are using user profiles. However, user profiles that are downloaded from a server overwrite any existing settings you have. For example, at work you might like to use a particular graphic for your wallpaper. However, the network administrators might want everyone to use a corporate graphic as wallpaper and can configure this preference in the network-based user profiles. In this case, your PC will be configured for the corporate graphic when you log on.

SELECTING CLIENT FOR NETWARE NETWORKS

If Client for NetWare Networks is your primary network logon, system policies and user profiles can also be downloaded. They will be retrieved from your preferred server (see "Using Microsoft's Client for NetWare Networks," later in this chapter). The NetWare login script may also be configured to run.

JOINING A WINDOWS WORKGROUP

Many smaller organizations use peer-to-peer network to fulfill their file- and print-sharing needs. A peer-to-peer network consists of workstations used for day-to-day computing tasks by their users that have also been configured to make resources available to other users on a network (see Chapter 36, "Setting Up a Simple Windows Network," for more information). With peer-to-peer networks, users' workstations are grouped into logical units called workgroups. Workgroups don't affect a user's ability to get to a resource on another computer.

They affect only what a user sees by default when he or she goes to find the resource through Network Neighborhood, Explorer, or other programs in Windows 98 that allow for browsing the network.

IDENTIFYING YOUR COMPUTER

Every computer used in peer-to-peer networking must have a unique computer name. The name can be up to 15 characters long and must not include spaces. You name it by doing the following:

1. Run Control Panel.
2. Double-click on the Network icon.
3. Select the Identification tab. Figure 35.5 gives an example of this tab.
4. Fill in your computer name.

Figure 35.5
Use the Identification tab to configure your workstation naming parameters.

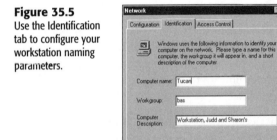

IDENTIFYING YOUR WORKGROUP

The workgroup name you provide allows you to select which workgroup of computers you are a part of when you or other users browse network resources. The name you use is arbitrary, as long as it is unique and all other computers you want to browse (share resources with) use the same name. In other words, if you name the workgroup ABC, for example, you see other computers in your default browse list that are also members of the ABC workgroup.

ADDING A COMMENT TO DESCRIBE YOUR PC

While you're at the Identification tab, be sure to describe your PC in the Computer Description text box. This information is important when your computer has file and print sharing enabled. When other users are browsing for your computer, they can see this comment if their browsing program allows them to view details, as shown in Figure 35.6.

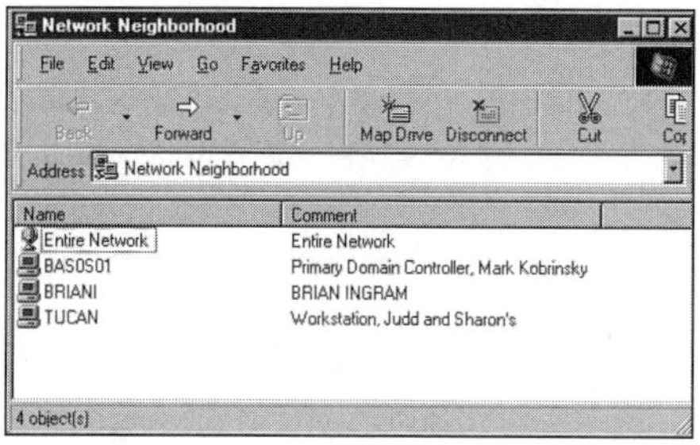

Figure 35.6
Viewing details in Network Neighborhood allows the user to see comments about the computers in the workgroup or domain.

Tip #236

Include your name in the description if your workstation name doesn't already identify you. This information enables someone who needs resources located on your computer to contact you if necessary. For example, if your workstation name is Finance and someone has a problem connecting to your workstation, he or she would know to call you if you describe your workstation as Financial Services–Jane Doe.

LOGGING ON TO A WINDOWS NT NETWORK

Windows NT, both Workstation and Server versions, is a more robust network server platform than Windows 98. With Windows NT Server especially, the platform has been designed from the ground up to be a network provider. Windows NT has several advantages over Windows 98 that make the former a better solution for file and print sharing:

- Full 32-bit Protected mode operating system—This feature increases performance and reliability.

- Integrated security account database—Users and groups are created and maintained on the Windows NT machine itself. Having an integrated security account database eliminates the need to rely on an external security provider.

- Capability to share an account database—Windows NT Servers can be placed in a common administrative and logical unit called a domain. Installing Windows NT Servers as domain controllers in a particular domain allows the security account database to be replicated to all other domain controllers in the same domain so they all have the capability to validate user account logons for that domain.

- Support for folder- and file-based security—With the use of a file system called NT File System (NTFS) on the Windows NT machine, user and group security can be assigned to individual folders and files for local and remote security, in addition to share-level security.

Microsoft Windows NT is fast becoming the dominant PC network operating system for commercial users. Even if your company isn't using it as the primary network provider, chances are that sooner or later Windows NT will be implemented in some capacity in your environment.

PART

VI

CH

35

CONNECTING TO A WINDOWS NT DOMAIN

Windows NT Servers can be organized into a logical unit called a *domain*. Each domain has one *primary domain controller (PDC)*. The PDC stores the master copy of the security account database for the domain. This database is where users, groups, and their respective settings, such as passwords and the logon script that will be run for the user, are stored. The PDC periodically synchronizes, or replicates, any changes in the security account database to the *backup domain controllers (BDCs) in the same domain*. Thus, resources such as files and printers on any of the servers can be assigned security using a single security account database. This approach helps you, the user of these resources, by making it unnecessary to have a separate user account and password for each server. The goal here is one user, one account for universal resource access.

Windows NT domains can be configured to interoperate with one other in a hierarchical fashion by using what is called a trust relationship. A trust relationship enables the administrator of one domain to assign security rights for resources to users and groups from another domain. This feature is important to you because you might log on as a user in one domain and yet need to access resources in a separate domain.

Follow these steps to configure your workstation to log on to a Windows NT domain:

1. Run Control Panel.
2. Double-click on the Network icon.
3. Set your Primary Network Logon to Client for Microsoft Networks.
4. Highlight Client for Microsoft Networks in the list of installed network components and click Properties. See Figure 35.7.

Figure 35.7
The Client for
Microsoft Networks
Properties page.

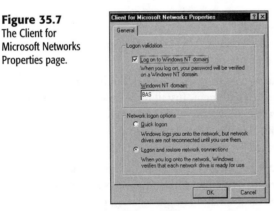

5. Check the Log on to Windows NT Domain check box.
6. Fill in the name of the domain to which you want to log on in the Windows NT Domain text box. As mentioned previously in regards to trust relationships, the domain you log on to and the domain from which you access resources might be different.

7. Select whether you want to enable Quick Logon or Logon and Restore Connections. Quick Logon displays previously mapped drives (called *persistent drive mappings*) when you browse your computer's drives; however, your workstation does not actually contact the provider of the resource to ensure that it's available until you attempt to use the drive. Logon and Restore Connections, however, tries to contact the provider as it maps the drives. This practice increases your logon time, but at least you know before you begin work that the drives really are ready for use.

Tip #237

If you're a road warrior, it would be beneficial to choose Quick Logon so that you don't get drive mapping errors when you log on to your computer while you're not connected to the network.

After you configure these settings and restart your machine, the logon dialog box appears (see Figure 35.8). After you successfully enter your username and password for the domain, your logon script runs (if your administrator has assigned you one), and any persistent drive mappings are restored as part of your roaming profile.

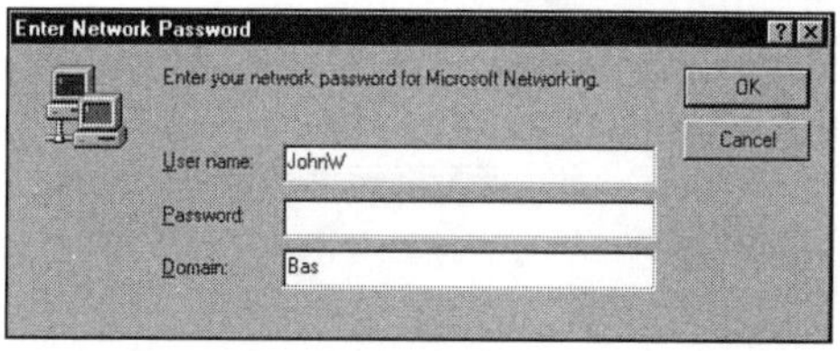

Figure 35.8
When Client for Microsoft Networks prompts you to log on, it uses the domain name you specified in the network setup.

You can also override the domain name shown in the prompt in Figure 35.8. This step is useful if you have accounts on more than one domain at your company. To override the default domain name, simply type over it with the name of another domain on your network.

Note

The workgroup name discussed previously in the section "Joining a Windows Workgroup" is also useful in a Windows NT domain environment. When you have a Windows NT domain environment, you should set the workgroup name to the name of the domain that provides most of the resources you use. For instance, if you log on to a domain called Accounts but you use resources from a trusting domain called Resources (not very original, I know), you are better off setting your workgroup name to Resources. This way, when you browse, you see the servers in the Resources domain first.

CONNECTING TO A WINDOWS NT WORKSTATION

A computer with Windows NT Workstation as its operating system has a security account database stored locally on the machine (in contrast, Windows 98 has no means to store user account information). Connecting to a Windows NT Workstation is similar to connecting to a Windows NT Server domain. However, instead of entering the domain name in the

Windows NT Domain prompt, you should enter the name of the workstation. When you log on, you are prompted for a username and password. If you do not yet have a user account in the security account database on the Windows NT Workstation, the administrator of that workstation needs to create an account for you before you can log on.

CHANGING YOUR WINDOWS NT PASSWORD

If you want to change both your Windows NT password and your Windows 98 Logon password to the same new password, follow these steps:

1. Run Control Panel.

2. Double-click on Passwords.

3. Click on Change Windows Password.

4. You are prompted to select any other passwords you want to change at the same time. Select Microsoft Networking, as shown in Figure 35.9.

Figure 35.9
When you change your Windows password, you are prompted to change other provider passwords at the same time.

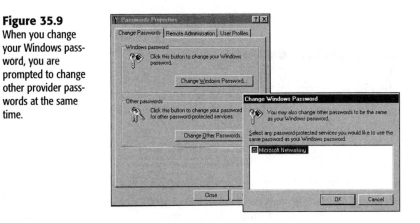

5. Enter your old Windows 98 Logon password and a new password twice for verification.

6. If your current Windows 98 Logon password and your Windows NT password are not the same, you are prompted to enter your current Windows NT password (see Figure 35.10).

7. After you've entered everything correctly, your Windows and Windows NT passwords are set to the new password you specified.

Figure 35.10
If your Windows password and Windows NT password aren't the same, you are asked to enter your current Windows NT password.

Tip #238

By keeping your Windows and Windows NT passwords the same, you won't have to remember two passwords, and you won't have to log on twice at startup. This feature is a convenience to the user but may be a security hazard to the rest of the systems on the network. Much depends on the importance of security in a particular environment.

If you don't want to keep your two passwords in sync, follow these steps:

1. Run Control Panel.
2. Double-click on Passwords.
3. Click on Change Other Passwords.
4. Select Microsoft Network and click Change.
5. Enter your old Windows NT password and a new password twice for verification.

SETTING UP USER-LEVEL ACCESS CONTROL

Windows 98 allows you to share your files and printers. This practice enables other network users to connect to your machine and access those resources remotely. You might want to limit the people who can connect to these resources. Therefore, you need some type of security on them. Windows 98 provides two security methods.

■ Share-level security—Specify a password on a resource allowing read-only, full access, or both. This type of security has limitations because everyone must use the same password and you can't limit the access by user. For this reason, Windows 98 provides user-level access.

■ User-level access—Assign rights to resources based on security information kept by a network provider. In this section, we're discussing using Windows NT as the provider. Windows NT has a security account database that contains usernames and passwords, among other information. By using user-level access on Windows 98, you can leverage these usernames to secure your resources. For instance, you might have a financial package that you want only people in the financial department to have access to. You can assign the group called LAS0Finance, to which all the financial department users belong, full rights to that package.

PART

VI

CH

35

User-level access control enables you to take advantage of security on a per user or per group basis without having to administer these users and groups. Your network administrators can worry about that!

To set up user-level access control, follow these steps:

1. Run Control Panel.

2. Double-click on the Network icon.

3. If you don't see File and Printer Sharing for Microsoft Networks in the list of networking components, click on File and Print Sharing and make the appropriate selections, depending on whether you want to share files or printers or both. You want to close the Control Panel Network applet and reboot here. After the reboot is complete, continue with step 4 at the Control Panel Network applet again.

4. After the reboot is complete, open the Control Panel Network applet again. Click on the Access Control tab (see Figure 35.11).

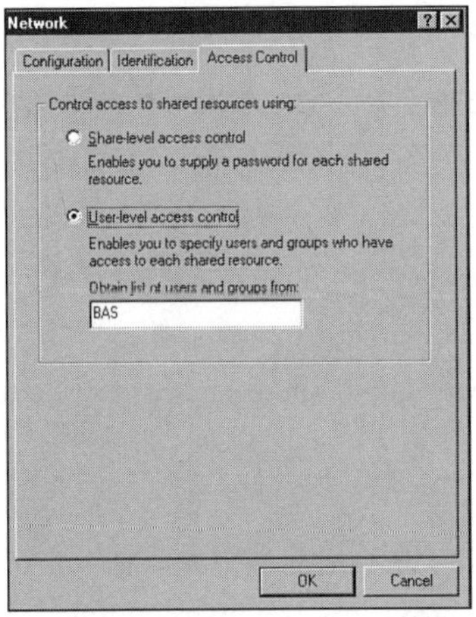

Figure 35.11
You must specify a domain from which you assign rights to users and groups.

5. Select User-Level Access Control and specify the domain to whose users and groups you will assign rights on your computer.

6. You must reboot.

After you set up user-level access control, you can assign rights to the users and groups in the domain you selected when you set up shares on your computer.

LOGGING ON TO A NETWARE NETWORK

Two versions of NetWare are still in use extensively today: version 3.x and version 4.x (the latest version is also referred to as IntranetWare). A major difference between the two versions is the directory service.

Novell version 3.x uses a type of directory service called the bindery. The bindery uses a flat model for storing account information such as usernames and passwords. Each 3.x server has a separate bindery. Therefore, if you need to access resources on more than one 3.x server, you must have an account and password for each one.

Novell version 4.x improved on this system by using a directory service called *NetWare Directory Services (NDS)*. NDS allows multiple servers to share account databases and enables you to use the same account to access all servers to which you have rights. NDS is organized into a logical hierarchical tree.

Both NetWare versions now have full native support under Windows 98 via drivers provided by Microsoft, although there are some limitations. In addition to the NetWare 4.x client Microsoft provides, NetWare also created a client for version 4.x called Client 32.

USING MICROSOFT'S CLIENT FOR NETWARE NETWORKS

The Client for NetWare Networks that comes with Windows 98 provides support for 3.x servers as well as 4.x servers with bindery emulation enabled. Bindery emulation is just what it sounds like. Even though 4.x doesn't use a bindery for directory services, Novell added the capability for it to emulate a bindery so that users who still have NetWare 3.x software support on their workstations can log on (albeit with limited functionality).

After you install the Client for NetWare Networks under the Network Control Panel applet, you need to configure the software so that you can connect to a server. Follow these steps:

1. Run Control Panel.
2. Double-click on the Network icon.
3. Set your Primary Network Logon to Client for NetWare Networks.
4. Highlight Client for NetWare Networks in the list of installed network components and click on Properties. Table 35.1 explains the options.

TABLE 35.1   CONFIGURING THE CLIENT FOR NETWARE NETWORKS OPTIONS

Option	Description
Preferred Server	The server you are prompted to log on to by default when you start Windows 98.
First Network Drive	The first drive that is used to map to resources on the NetWare server. By default, it's drive F:. If you have devices on your computer that use drive letters beyond drive E:, you should adjust this parameter so that NetWare and your devices don't try to use the same drive letters.
Enable Logon Script Processing	This check box determines whether logon scripts execute when you log on to the NetWare server. Logon scripts are created by administrators to ensure some level of consistency with the configurations of those users who connect to a server. For instance, in your organization, drive H: might always map to your home directory on the server. You should not turn off this option without contacting the network administrator first.

PART

VI

CH

35

After you configure everything and start Windows 98, you are presented with the logon prompt shown in Figure 35.12. The first time you connect, you need to ensure that your logon name is correct so that Windows 98 will remember it. After you enter the correct credentials, your NetWare logon script runs if you've enabled it as shown in Table 35.1, and you will be able to use any resources on the server.

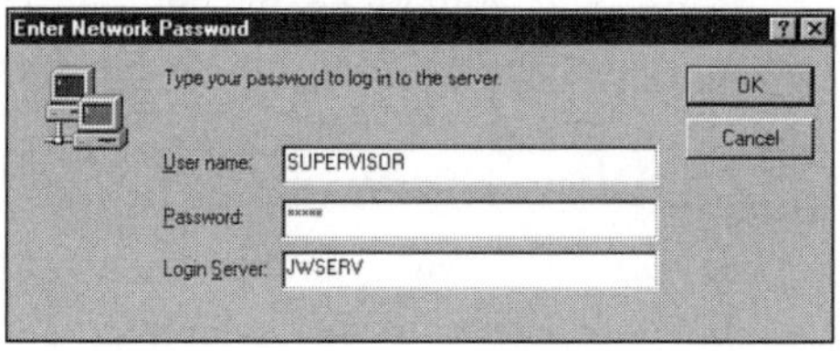

Figure 35.12
To log on to a NetWare 3.x server, or a 4.x server with bindery emulation, you simply specify your user credentials and the name of the NetWare server.

CHANGING YOUR PASSWORD WITH CLIENT FOR NETWARE NETWORKS

Microsoft's Client for NetWare Networks does not include functionality to change your password under the Control Panel Password applet. Instead, you must go to a command prompt and change it there using the Novell command Setpass. Type SETPASS and enter your old and new passwords.

USING MICROSOFT'S SERVICE FOR NETWARE DIRECTORY SERVICES

Logging on to a 4.x server with bindery emulation using the Client for Microsoft Networks has some limitations. For the fullest support of 4.x from a Microsoft-supplied client, you should use the Service for NetWare Directory Services. This client allows you to connect to the NDS tree and browse its resources. Also, the logon script in your logon context will run.

To set up your network configuration to allow connectivity to the NDS tree after you install Service for NetWare Directory Services, you need to configure the service's parameters. To do so, follow these steps:

1. Run Control Panel.
2. Double-click on the Network icon.
3. Set your Primary Network Logon to Client for NetWare Networks.
4. Highlight Service for NetWare Directory Services in the list of installed network components and click on Properties to show the configuration page (see Figure 35.13).

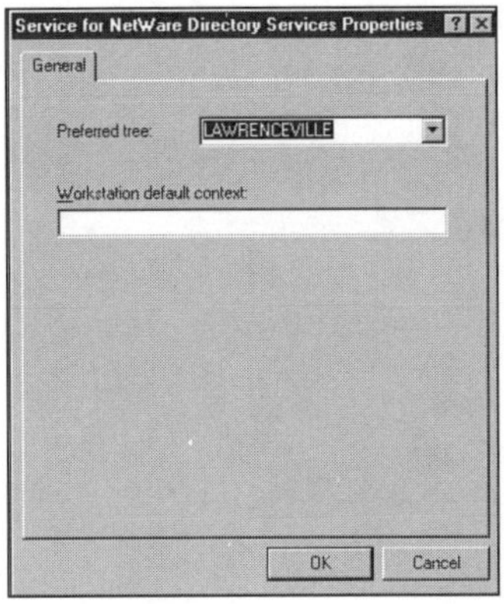

Figure 35.13
You must provide a default tree and context when setting up Service for NetWare Directory Services.

5. Enter your Preferred Tree, which is the NDS tree to which you are logging in by default. If you don't specify a Preferred Tree, NDS searches for any existing trees and prompts you to select one when you log on, as shown in Figure 35.14.

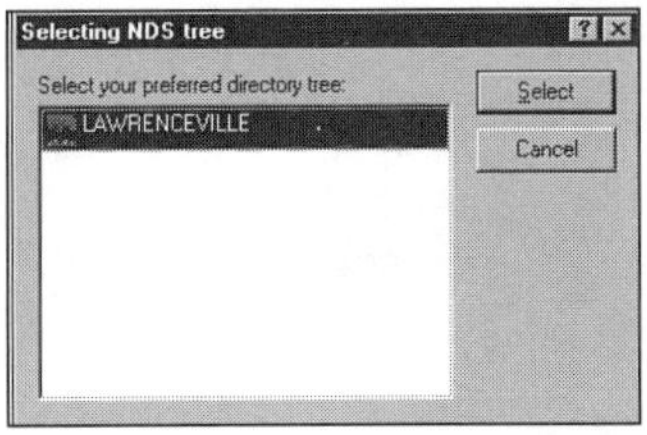

Figure 35.14
When you first log on to NDS, Service for NDS prompts you for a tree if you didn't select one under the Control Panel Network applet.

6. Enter the Workstation Default Context. Because NDS is hierarchical in nature, your account might be several levels down from the top of the tree. To make it easier to browse and refer to resources, you can set this parameter so that when you specify resources, they are assumed to be located under the context specified. For instance, the full distinguished name for your user account might be .CN=JohnD.OU=Research.O=ABCInc. If your Workstation Default Context is .OU=Research.O=ABCInc, then your logon name would be simply JohnD. When you browse, resources under this context are displayed first.

Tip #239   810 If other users want to log on to your machine but their account is located under a different context, they can still log on. They simply need to enter their fully distinguished name at the logon prompt. Their logon script will still run. The only way the Workstation Default Context affects them is that their default context when browsing and accessing resources is the one you specified in step 6.

PART

VI

CH

35

You should also specify a preferred server under Client for NetWare Networks. This step enables the workstation to make initial contact with a server in the NDS tree without having to search the network for one.

When you log on to NDS using Service for NDS, you are prompted for your username and password. Figure 35.15 shows that you can change your Workstation Default Context and Tree by clicking on the Advanced button.

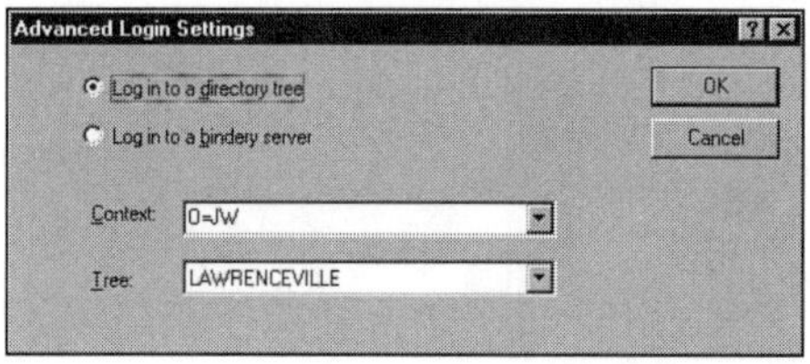

Figure 35.15

Logging on to NDS with Service for NDS. Notice that because the default context was set to O=JW, it wasn't necessary to use the fully distinguished name of .CN=Admin.O=JW. Instead, all that was required was to simply type admin.

You can use this client to log on to a 3.x server as well, by choosing Log in to a Bindery Server and specifying the server name. Figure 35.16 shows an example.

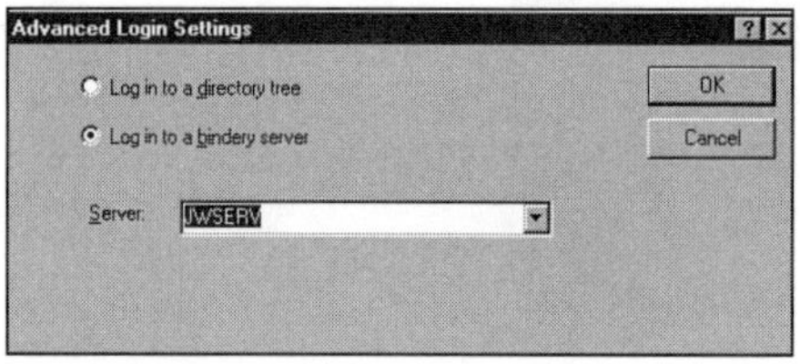

Figure 35.16

As noted on the logon screen, you cannot access the NDS tree when you log on to a bindery server.

CHANGING YOUR PASSWORD WITH SERVICE FOR NDS

You can change your password from the Control Panel Passwords applet with Service for NDS by following these steps:

1. Run Control Panel.

2. Double-click on Passwords.

3. Click on Change Other Passwords.

4. Select NDS Tree and click Change.

5. Enter your old password and your new password twice for verification.

USING NOVELL'S CLIENT 32 SOFTWARE

For the most complete support for NDS, you might want to use Novell's Client 32. In addition to providing support for all NetWare utilities, Novell's Client 32 provides granular access to many settings that allow you to totally optimize and customize the way you interface with NDS under Windows 98.

After you install Client 32, you must configure it before you can log on to the NDS tree. Follow these steps:

1. Run Control Panel.
2. Double-click on the Network icon.
3. Set your Primary Network Logon to Novell NetWare Client 32.
4. Highlight Novell NetWare Client 32 in the list of installed network components and click on Properties.
5. Fill in the properties on the Client 32 tab. Table 35.2 gives more details about these options.

TABLE 35.2   CONFIGURING CLIENT 32 OPTIONS TO ENABLE CONNECTIVITY TO NDS-BASED SERVICES

Option	Description
Preferred Server	The first server that Client 32 attempts to connect to. Entering a server name is not necessary if you specify a preferred tree, but doing so is recommended. Choosing a server eliminates the need to listen for a broadcasting server.
Preferred Tree	The tree to which you are attaching in the NDS hierarchy. If you don't specify a preferred server or preferred tree, the client looks for any broadcasting servers on the network and uses the first one that responds.
Name Context	The same as the Workstation Default Context under Microsoft's Service for NDS. It specifies the default context to be used when you log on and when you browse. It does not affect which logon script runs.
First Network Drive	The drive to which Client 32 connects resources to first. You should set this drive to a letter after F:, the default, if you have devices on your workstation such as hard drives or CD-ROM drives that use these letters.

CHANGING YOUR PASSWORD WITH NOVELL'S CLIENT 32

To change your password using Novell's Client 32, follow these steps:

1. Run Control Panel.
2. Double-click on Passwords.
3. Click on Change Other Passwords.
4. Select Novell NetWare and click Change.

PART

VI

CH

35

5. Enter your old password and your new password twice for verification.

6. Novell's Client 32 allows you to synchronize passwords for multiple accounts with which you might be attached. You can change multiple passwords at the same time by selecting the accounts in the NetWare Password Synchronization dialog box shown in Figure 35.17. The caveat is that all the accounts you want to change at the same time must have the same current password.

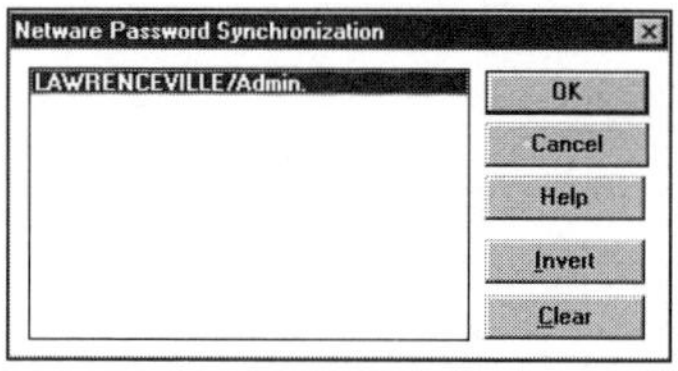

Figure 35.17
With Client 32 you can change multiple NetWare account passwords at one time.

CONFIGURING NETWARE DIRECTORY SERVICES

After you configure either Microsoft's Service for NDS or Novell's Client 32, you have support for functionality that only NDS provides. You can browse NDS trees using Network Neighborhood, Explorer, and other third party browsing tools. You can map drives to NDS volumes. You can install printers in the NDS tree. Note that you have context-sensitive options when you right-click an object.

USING NETWARE UTILITIES

Most NetWare 3.x applications should run under the 32-bit clients provided by Microsoft and Novell. The few exceptions are utilities that require support that only the VLM or NETX Real mode clients provide. In most cases, other administrative tools are available to replace these incompatible ones.

Some NDS applications cannot be used without obtaining the appropriate dynamic link libraries (DLLs) from Novell. I recommend that if you need to run NetWare utilities such as NDS Manager or NetWare Administrator for Windows 95, you use Novell's Client 32 for maximum compatibility.

SETTING UP USER-LEVEL ACCESS CONTROL

Setting up user-level access control with NetWare is very similar to setting it up with Windows NT (see the previous section, "Logging On to a Windows NT Network," for more details). The following steps show the process:

> **Note** You cannot use NetWare-based user-level security with Novell's Client 32.

1. Run Control Panel.

2. Double-click the Network icon.

3. If you don't see File and Printer Sharing for NetWare Networks in the list of networking components, click on <u>F</u>ile and Print Sharing and make the appropriate selections, depending on whether you want to share files or printers or both. Now, close the Control Panel Network applet and reboot.

4. After the reboot is complete, open the Control Panel Network applet again. Click on the Access Control tab.

5. Select User-Level Access Control and specify the NetWare server to whose users and groups you will assign rights on your computer.

6. Reboot again.

Assigning rights to NetWare users and groups is the same as assigning rights to Windows NT users and groups.

TROUBLESHOOTING

WINDOWS 98 PASSWORD CACHE

How can I stop Windows 98 from caching my password?

If you have any problems with your Windows 98 password cache or you simply don't feel comfortable with your passwords being cached, you can delete the cache file. It's located under C:\Windows. It is named with your username and the extension .PWL.

SECRETS OF MASTERING THE WINDOWS 98 ENVIRONMENT: BROWSING WITH NET COMMANDS

As an alternative to browsing for resources through the Network Neighborhood, you can use the command prompt. This method provides a way to connect to known or hidden shared resources that may not be populating the Browse list in Network Neighborhood.

You should become familiar with the basic net commands that work in the Windows networking environment. For example, you can use the net view command to perform most of the same browsing actions as Network Neighborhood or Windows Explorer.

To get help for the net view command, access the command prompt by going through the Start menu, Programs, MS-DOS Prompt. At the command prompt, type net view /?.

You can use the net use command to connect and disconnect from shared resources, such as shares and printers. Additionally, you can see all the servers that you are connected to.

To get help for the net use command, type net use ? ¦ more at the command prompt.

CHAPTER 36

SETTING UP A SIMPLE WINDOWS NETWORK

In this chapter

UNDERSTANDING NETWORKS

What is a network and why create one? A network consists of the components necessary for two or more computers to communicate. The advantages of networking include

- Monetary savings—Sharing hardware results in saving money. The most common type of hardware that is shared is a printer. Networking enables you to purchase one color printer and give everyone the ability to print to it.

- Fast access to information—You can access the needed information directly from your PC which eliminates the need for running around with a floppy disk looking for that particular memo or letter.

- Easier information management—By agreeing to store certain types of information in one location, you can always find what you need. Networks also allow for routine backup of important documents and data.

- Shared access to information—Customer information can be stored in one database so that all users can access it.

- Better communication—The use of email and group scheduling applications increases productivity.

- Improved efficiency—Networking results in improved access to a large variety of information, which means projects are completed in shorter periods of time.

A network consists of two types of components: hardware and software. The hardware components consist of various pieces of equipment that connect the computers. At a minimum, the hardware necessary to allow computers to communicate includes cables and adapter cards. Windows 98 integrates well no matter what the topology of your network.

The software required to communicate across a network includes the network operating system, a network client, and a protocol.

Windows 98 functions as a networking operating system as well as a desktop operating system. A network client allows your computer to communicate with another computer based on the type of network operating system it is using. A protocol can be thought of as the language that is spoken across your network. If two computers use different protocols, they cannot communicate.

HOW PEER-TO-PEER NETWORKS WORK

Networks can be organized either as peer-to-peer or server-based. In a peer-to-peer network, each computer acts as both a server and a client. One system has the dual capability to act as a server and to share, or provide, resources, and to connect to server-side components as a client to access resources. All information is stored on each computer. When a computer is playing the server role, it provides access to files contained on its local hard drive and on peripherals attached to the computer (such as printers, fax modems, scanners, and CD-ROM drives).

Each computer can share its resources without the need for centralized administration of these resources. Each user in a peer-to-peer network is a network administrator. This approach alleviates the need for one person to be responsible for various network administrative tasks.

The networking capabilities built into Windows 98 make it an excellent option for implementing a peer-to-peer network. As an operating system, it contains all the elements you need to allow access to local resources or to access resources located on other computers in the network. This native networking ability enables the easy sharing of local resources and access to remote resources.

Windows 98 has a point-and-click interface that permits you to browse the network to locate and access available resources. The same easy-to-use interface makes the sharing of resources extremely easy for the user. This interface alleviates the need for the user to be technically adept at network administration while still providing access to network resources.

HOW SERVER-BASED NETWORKS WORK

You can change a peer-to-peer network to a server-based network by adding a computer running the Windows NT Server operating system or a NetWare server. The basic requirements for a server-based network are

- A centralized user database, which is used to verify that the user requesting access is authorized for the level of access requested.

- Centralized repository of information. Files can be stored on one or more file servers and can be accessed by all the users on the network. This system allows for easier access to saved documents. It also makes creating backups easier because only one computer, rather than each computer in your network, needs to be backed up.

- Centralized control of resources allows the administrator to designate which users have access to stored documents and shared peripherals. It also allows for easier configuration of these resources.

In a server-based network, the burden of controlling network administrative tasks is moved from the individual user to one or more persons who are more technically proficient in network administration. This central administrative role allows for more efficient management of the network.

The client capability in Windows 98 allows it to work very well in this type of environment by providing the software necessary for user authentication, which then allows access to network resources.

PLANNING YOUR NETWORK

When you're planning your network, you need to consider several things. Here are some of the more important decisions you need to make before installing your network:

- What resources need to be shared? Do you have a small environment in which you want to share a single printer, or do you have a larger environment and the need to share multiple peripherals as well as many files and/or databases?

- How fast should your network be? Do you frequently share very large files or print large CAD or graphics files?

- How large is your network? Are you connecting only two or three computers and one printer, or will hundreds of users be accessing your network?

- How much distance will your network span? Are you creating a small network that's fully contained in one building, or do you need to connect to computers and other resources located in different cities or countries?

- Do all your computers run the same operating system, or must you connect various types of computers such as Windows and UNIX-based systems?

- Is your network small enough so that each user will be responsible for his or her own computer, or will you have one or more individuals responsible for administering your network?

Use the answers to these questions to plan your network. Items that you need to plan include its topology, what equipment you will use to connect the computers on your network, and what access method you will use. Whether or not you are creating a peer-to-peer network or a server-based network will influence your choice of operating system.

WIRING YOUR NETWORK

After determining the size of your network, you must decide on the layout and hardware components needed for installing the network. The example we are using here is a local area network (LAN) situated in a single building. The coverage of larger networks is beyond the scope of this chapter.

BUS TOPOLOGY

When planning your network, you need to consider what *topology*, or design, is the most appropriate. The topology is especially important because the largest single cost when installing a new network is the cost of running the cable.

The most basic and easiest topology to install is a bus network, which consists of two or more computers connected by coaxial cabling. Figure 36.1 illustrates a bus topology. Each computer is connected to the coaxial cable using a connector called a T-piece. The coaxial cabling must be properly terminated with a 50-ohm terminator.

Figure 36.1
A diagram of a bus
topology network.

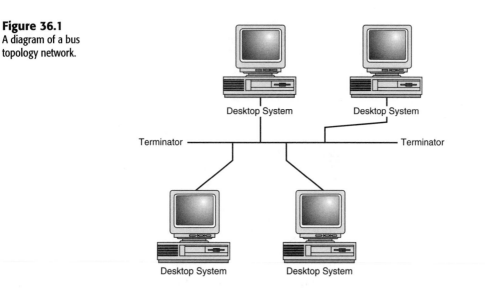

This configuration supports several computers as long as the total distance in any one segment is no greater than 185 meters. The bus topology lends itself well to installation in an area where running cabling through the walls is difficult or impossible. It is easy to expand a bus network by adding another length of cable and a T-piece.

Although this type of network is easy to install, troubleshooting can be difficult if one of the network components malfunctions. A damaged or defective cable might disrupt the entire network. Turning off your workstation, however, does not disrupt the function of the network. If you do not want to learn the ins and outs of network troubleshooting, this type of network could end up costing more in the long run.

For more information on troubleshooting a network, see "Basic Methodology for Troubleshooting Networks" in the "Troubleshooting" section at the end of this chapter.

Tip #240	With a bus topology, if you're having trouble with your network, segment your network by disconnecting the cabling in the middle. Terminate each side to identify which half is not functioning. Then continue subdividing the half that does not work until you have identified the problem component.

STAR TOPOLOGY

The next type of topology to consider is a star topology. With this configuration, a cable runs from each computer to a central piece of hardware called a *hub*. A hub can connect many computers depending on its configuration. Figure 36.2 shows a small star topology.

Figure 36.2
A cable runs from
each computer to the
hub to create a star
topology.

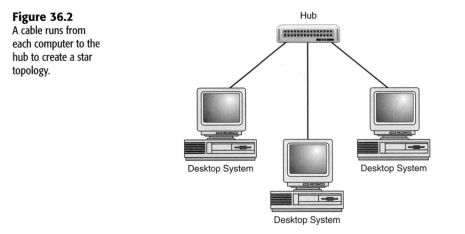

Twisted-pair wire is used for this topology; it looks a lot like telephone wire. Telephone wire
has two pairs but uses only one of them. 10BASE-T wiring uses two of the four pairs, and
100BASE-T uses all four pairs. With this arrangement, no computer can be more than 100
meters from the hub.

Tip #241	Twisted-pair wire is categorized by its speed of transmission. If you plan to expand your network, you might want to invest up front in Category 5 cable, which supports speeds up to 100Mbps. This investment will prevent you from having to rewire your network later.

This topology has the advantage of being easy to troubleshoot. A single piece of defective
cabling affects only the computer it connects. The exception is if the hub malfunctions. This
problem is referred to as a *single point of failure*. In the case of such a problem, none of the
computers attached to that hub can communicate on the network.

Initially this type of network is more expensive than a bus topology because a star topology
requires the purchase of additional equipment such as hubs. Expansion of a star topology
may require the purchase of an additional hub if no more connections are available on the
existing hub. As your network grows, the wiring can become untidy and unwieldy, especially
if you are unable to run the wiring through the walls.

Tip #242	After you decide on the topology for your network, you might want to have an expert certi- fied in the particular topology run the cable. This initial investment will save you consider- able expense later.

NETWORK ADAPTER CARD

After the cabling has been installed, you need a network adapter card for each computer in the network. This piece of hardware acts as an interpreter or interface between your computer and the network. Each card is specific for the bus type of your computer and the type of cabling you have. See the section "Configuring Your Network," later in this chapter, for more details on selecting your network adapter card.

NETWORK OPERATING SYSTEM

The network operating system controls communication between systems. Each computer must have at least a client-side operating system installed that allows for communication over the network.

Windows 98 is an excellent choice because it serves as both the network operating system and the client operating system. In addition, its user interface allows for ease of use and increased productivity. It supports a wide range of applications and has native support for mobile computing.

NETWORK PROTOCOLS

A *network protocol* is a type of software that formats data and facilitates the transport of that data over a local or wide area network. Although more than one protocol may be installed on a system, running multiple protocols increases memory demands on client computers and produces excessive network traffic. A more efficient approach is to use only the protocol or protocols necessary to communicate with other computers on your network.

Windows 98 supports three prominent network transport protocols: NetBEUI, TCP/IP, and IPX/SPX. Each of these protocols has advantages and disadvantages, as outlined here:

- NetBEUI is the smallest and easiest protocol to use because it does not require any additional configuration. The disadvantage of this protocol is that it is not routable. Consequently, it cannot communicate with a remote network. If your network is small, this selection is usually the best. Because NetBEUI is not routable, it depends entirely on broadcast transmissions, which is detrimental to network bandwidth.

Note A *router* is a device that connects different networks or network segments. Networks can be subdivided to reduce traffic and improve performance.

- IPX/SPX is generally used to communicate with a Novell NetWare server and is relatively easy to implement. This protocol is a good choice if you need to communicate across a router and do not need to access the Internet.

- TCP/IP is the protocol of choice for the Internet. It is routable, which means that it allows for communication across a large network containing one or more routers. However, it is also the most difficult of the three protocols to configure. If you do not have experience with TCP/IP, this protocol is not a good choice for a small network.

CONNECTING TWO COMPUTERS

The easiest and most common small network consists of two computers connected to each other. This setup is commonly used in small offices or home networks for the purpose of sharing a printer and/or sharing files. Three basic configurations can be used to achieve this end:

- Connection via a coaxial cable
- Connection via a crossover twisted-pair cable (see the sidebar titled "Crossover Twisted-Pair Cable")
- Connection via Direct Cable Connection using a null modem or parallel cable

The first two configurations require a network adapter card to be installed in each computer. The third option connects two computers via a cable attached to a serial or parallel port instead of a network card. The connection is made by using either a null modem or a parallel cable (not a printer cable).

USING A NETWORK ADAPTER CARD

The selection of a network adapter card depends on the type of computer it will be installed in, the type of cabling that will be used, and whether a driver is available for your operating system.

Every PC has one or two types of adapter slots. Examples of slots are PCI, ISA, EISA, VESA local bus, Micro Channel, and PC Card (PCMCIA). The network card you select must be compatible with an available slot in your computer. Refer to your PC's documentation to identify the correct type of adapter for your computer.

Tip #243
Before installing or upgrading any adapter card in your computer (such as a modem or a video card), you need to know what type of slot is available to purchase the correct type of adapter card. Most PCs sold today have a combination of PCI and ISA expansion slots.

Network cards generally allow for connection to a network in one or more ways by having the appropriate type of cable connector. A network adapter card with more than one type of connector is often referred to as a *combo* or *combination card* and generally is more expensive.

In addition to computer bus and cabling type, other issues include the type of memory the network card uses. Consult the product specifications when selecting the appropriate card for your use.

If you are using coaxial cable, the network card you select must have a BNC adapter. This type of adapter looks similar to the connector on the back of your television that is used to attach your cable. However, the one on the TV has threads and does not need a T connector. The coaxial cable is attached to a T connector, which is then attached to the network adapter card.

Caution

Never attempt to attach a coaxial cable directly to the network card. This practice results in a nonfunctioning network.

If you are using twisted-pair cable, select a network adapter card that has an RJ-45 connector. This connector looks like the connector that you use to plug your telephone wire into your telephone but is larger.

In addition to a network adapter card, you also must have software that allows your computer to communicate with the card. The software you need consists of two components:

- Network adapter card driver—This software provides for communication between your computer's operating system and the adapter card itself.

- Network protocol—This determines how the data is formatted for transport across the network. Think of it as the language that is spoken on your network.

Tip #1001

Windows 98 uses NDIS 4.0 to communicate with the network adapter card driver. This capability allows for the use of multiple protocols installed on a system operating with a single network adapter card driver. For example, running IPX/SPX to connect to a NetWare environment and TCP/IP to connect to the Internet requires only a single network card.

Before purchasing your network adapter card, make sure that a driver appropriate for your operating system is readily available. If you're using Windows 98, you'll find that drivers for the most common cards are included with the operating system. Check the hardware compatibility list that's available with the operating system or from Microsoft to ensure that you have a compatible card.

CONNECTING USING COAXIAL CABLE

After the network adapter cards have been installed in each computer, you need to attach a piece of coaxial cable. This cable must be either RG58U or RG58A/U. Although the type of cable you use for your television looks the same, it will not work.

The cabling is connected using a T-piece connector. One side of the cross bar is attached to the coaxial cable, and the other is attached to either another cable or a terminator. If it connects to a terminator, the terminator must have a 50-ohm rating. The connector is then attached to the network card. This process is repeated for each computer.

Caution

An improperly terminated network or the wrong type of cable can prevent your network from working.

CONNECTING USING TWISTED-PAIR CABLING

Although twisted-pair cabling is ordinarily used with a hub to connect computers, you can connect two computers using a special type of twisted-pair cable called a *crossover cable*. To bypass the need to use a hub, one receive pair and one send pair are crossed at one end of the cable.

Crossover Twisted-Pair Cable

Normally, when attaching the RJ45 connector to a twisted-pair cable, each of the eight wires must be connected to the same groove on each connector. That is, the wire attached to the first groove on one connector should be attached to the first groove on the other cable.

With a crossover cable, the send and receive wires need to be reversed at one end. Figure 36.3 illustrates how to reverse the wires to create a cable that connects two computers without requiring the use of a hub.

A crossover cable connects only two computers, however. If you need to connect more than two computers, you need to use a hub (see Figure 36.3).

Figure 36.3
This diagram illustrates how to cross over the wires to create a crossover cable. The numbers on the left refer to the grooves on one connector, and the numbers on the right refer to the grooves on the connector at the other end of the cable.

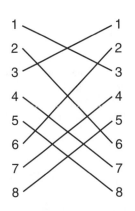

After installing the network adapter card, you just plug the crossover cable into each network card in the same manner that you plug in your telephone. If you have wired the crossover cable correctly, the two computers can communicate.

Tip #245

Unless you really enjoy wiring the ends of RJ-45 to function as a crossover cable, visit your local computer store for one off the shelf. Crossover cables are usually red to distinguish them from a straight cable.

CONFIGURING YOUR NETWORK

When the physical connections are made, use the Add New Hardware Wizard in Control Panel to detect your network adapter card. After you run the wizard, verify that the correct network components are installed. You can examine the network properties either by right-clicking on the Network Neighborhood icon and selecting Properties, or by opening the Network Applet from Control Panel.

The following three items must be installed via the Properties tab of the Network Neighborhood:

- Adapter—This item is the network card adapter.
- Protocol—This item is the language that will be used to communicate on your network.
- Client for Microsoft Networks or Client for NetWare Networks—This item is sometimes referred to as a "redirector" and allows you to communicate with other computers on your network.

The adapter should already be listed as the one that was installed using the Add New Hardware Wizard. Thanks to Windows 98 Plug and Play capabilities, no further configuration should be necessary.

Tip #246	Use the *Device Manager* to verify that the network adapter card is functioning properly and that no resource conflicts are present.

The best protocol to install when connecting only two computers is NetBEUI. Its small size and the lack of configuration requirements make it the ideal choice. All you need to do is install it.

To install NetBEUI, open the Network Properties dialog box, select Add, and then select Protocol. The Select Network Protocol dialog box appears (see Figure 36.4). Select Microsoft on the left side of the dialog box and then select NetBEUI on the right side.

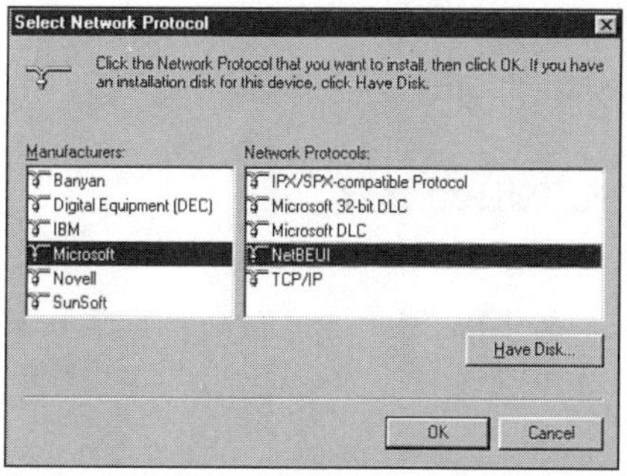

Figure 36.4
Select Microsoft from the left side of the dialog box. Select NetBEUI from the list of available protocols on the right side.

To add the Client for Microsoft Networks, click the Add button on the Configuration tab. Select Client and then click on the Add button. In the Select Network Client dialog box, select Microsoft on the left side and select Client for Microsoft Networks on the right side (see Figure 36.5).

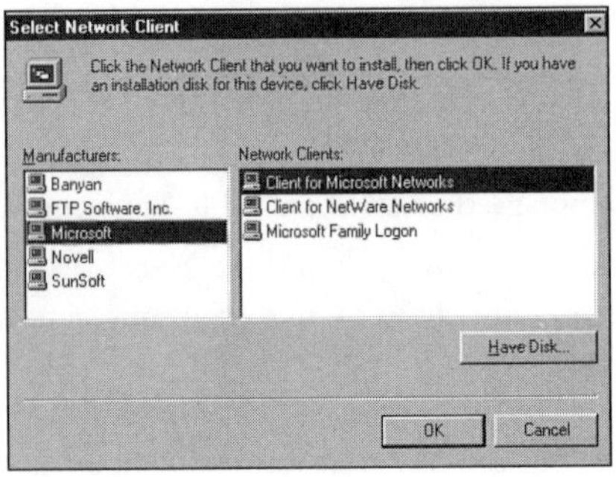

Figure 36.5
Select Microsoft on the left side and select Client for Microsoft Networks on the right side.

When you return to the Configuration tab of the Network Properties dialog box, be sure that Client for Microsoft Networks is selected in the Primary Network Logon box as shown in Figure 36.6.

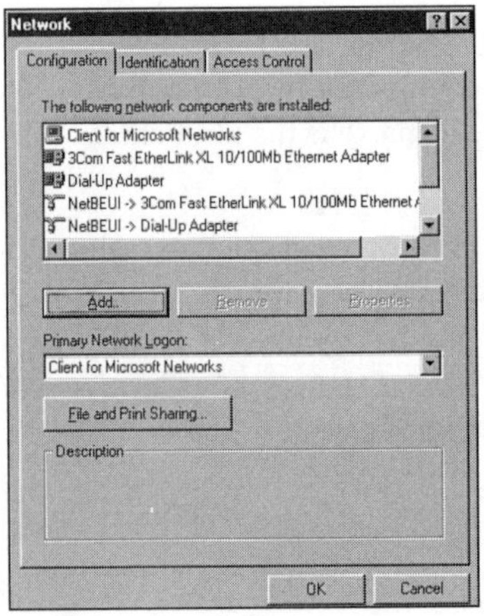

Figure 36.6
Notice that Client for Microsoft Networks appears in the Primary Network Logon box.

Next, click on File and Print Sharing. Select the appropriate check boxes to allow access to your files or to allow others to print to your printer. Then, click OK to return to the Configuration tab.

Select the Identification tab to see the options shown in Figure 36.7. Enter a name for your computer and your workgroup and then click OK.

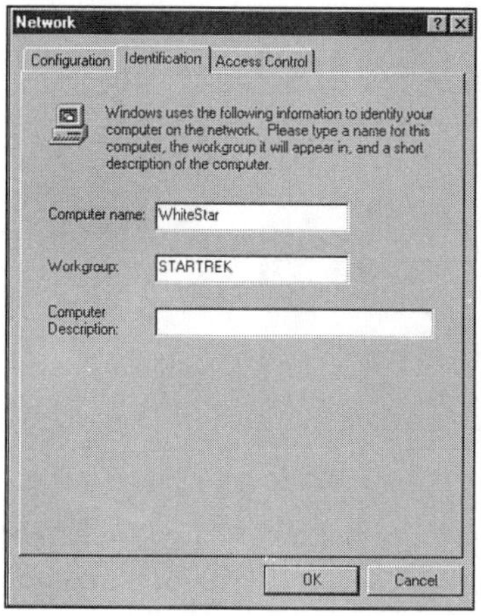

Figure 36.7
Here the computer name is WhiteStar and the workgroup name is STARTREK.

> **Note**
>
> The name you select for your computer must be a unique NetBIOS name. This name can contain up to 15 characters but cannot contain spaces or any of these characters:
>
> / \ * , . " @
>
> You should enter the same workgroup name on each computer. Although you can still communicate if the workgroup names are different, entering the same name on both computers means that they are listed as members of the same workgroup when they're viewed by someone browsing the Network Neighborhood.

USING DIRECT CABLE CONNECTION

You can avoid installing a network adapter card by connecting two computers directly, using a null modem (serial) or parallel cable attached to a serial (COM) or parallel port on each computer.

To install the Direct Cable Connection capability, run the Add/Remove Programs applet in Control Panel and click on the Windows Setup tab. In the Components list, select Communications, and then click the Details button. Select Direct Cable Connection and click OK.

After you've installed Direct Cable Connection and connected the two computers with either a serial or parallel cable, open the Start menu and choose Programs, Accessories, Direct Cable Connection. The Direct Cable Connection Wizard runs when you open Direct Cable Connection for the first time. One computer should be designated as a host and the other as a guest as shown in Figure 36.8.

Figure 36.8
Configure Direct Cable
Connection with the
wizard.

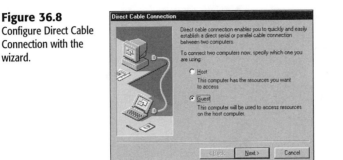

With Direct Cable Connection, you can gain access to shared folders on another computer even when your computer is not wired to a network. If the other computer is connected to a network, you can also gain access to that network.

CREATING A WORKGROUP

A *workgroup* is an organizational unit. It is a loose association of computers wherein each computer tracks and controls access to local resources. These resources may be folders located on the local hard drive or hardware devices attached directly to the computer (such as a printer). Each individual computer in the workgroup controls how access to these resources occurs.

If your network is small—fewer than 10 computers—a workgroup is an easy way to configure your network and provide access to various resources. It does not require a single individual to be designated as the administrator. Rather, each user is the administrator for his or her computer.

The disadvantages associated with a workgroup are related to its advantages. Because each user is an administrator, there is no centralized control of users or resources. As your network grows, the large number of users can result in a disorganized network. Without a centralized location for shared documents and applications, locating needed information can become difficult. The result is often lost productivity or the occurrence of duplicate versions of the same document.

Printing is one of the most common tasks performed on a network, and shared printing can lead to problems. Because the computer that is attached to the printer is acting as a print server, the additional load can cause degradation in performance. This slowdown can be a significant problem for the user working on that computer.

Tip #247

To improve performance of a computer that is extensively used as a file server, use the System option in Control Panel, Performance Tab, File System Properties, Settings and set the typical role of the computer to Network Server. If the computer is also functioning as a print server, make sure that adequate disk space is available for spooling.

→ For more information on configuring the role of a Windows 98 system, **see** the "Secrets of Mastering the Windows 98 Environment" section at the end of the chapter.

When files and folders are shared, a password is associated with the resource and the level of access that is allowed. After file sharing has been enabled, various levels of access to a resource can be defined based on passwords. These levels are Read and Full control.

Tip #248

File sharing is enabled through the File and Print Sharing button on the properties sheet for the Network Neighborhood. You can elect to share files, allow others to print to your printer, or both. You must also select Share Level Access Control on the Access Control tab.

To share a folder, right-click on it in Windows Explorer and select Properties. On the Sharing tab, select Share As. Each shared folder must have a name to identify it. A suggested name is displayed, but you can enter whatever name you want to use. The name that you enter here is displayed to any user browsing your computer across the network. Figure 36.9 shows a shared folder.

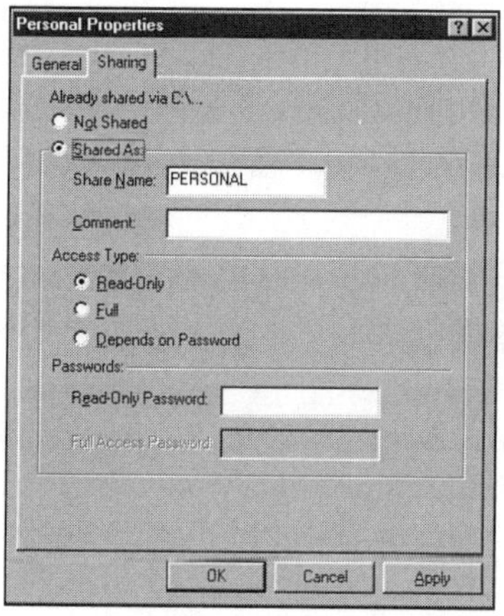

Figure 36.9
The level of access that is granted may depend on which password the user enters to access the resource.

Tip #249

As a trivial form of security, you can append the share name with a $ if you want to hide the share from users browsing your computer across the network. The share can still be accessed by anyone who knows the share's name either through mapping a drive from Network Neighborhood or with the Net Use command in the command prompt window.

You can also enter a comment to display to users as they browse your computer across the network. Use this field to identify the information that is contained in the share, which might make it easier for users to find needed information.

When you name your workgroup on the Identification tab of the Network Properties dialog box, one of two things happens. You either join an existing workgroup or create a new one. If the name you enter is an existing workgroup, the computer you are configuring becomes a member of that workgroup.

However, if you enter a name that is not the name of an existing workgroup, you create a new workgroup and that computer becomes its first member. You can then add computers to your workgroup simply by entering that workgroup's name on the Identification tab of the Network Properties dialog box of the computer you want to add to the workgroup.

SECURITY

One of the biggest problems in a peer-to-peer network that uses share-level access is the number of passwords needed to control access to resources. As more resources become available to users, they have to remember more passwords.

If a user has to keep track of multiple passwords, he or she might forget them or write them down. Either scenario prevents the security policy from doing what it is intended to do—allow access to those you want to have access and deny access to all others.

For that reason, Windows 98 offers a password caching feature that is installed by default. This feature stores passwords in a special file. When you access a password-protected resource for the first time, make sure that Save This Password in Your Password List option is checked. Your password is encrypted and then stored in a PWL file in the Windows folder.

Caution If you delete PWL files, you lose all the passwords you have stored. The next time you access a password-protected resource, you will have to retype the password.

If password caching is enabled, you can view the resources listed in the Password List File (PWL) with the Password List Editor. The editor displays only the PWL of the user who is logged on. You can disable password caching by using the System Policy Editor.

System Policy Editor

System policies provide a powerful tool for controlling how users interact with their computers and the network. One way to use system policies is to enforce specific password guidelines. These include defining the minimum password length and requiring the use of an alphanumeric logon password. System policies can also be used to disable password caching so that the user must type the password every time she or he attempts to access a shared resource.

You can use the system policy templates to define your desired policies. You can also create a new template that contains the items you want to control. Besides establishing password requirements, you can also perform the following measures:

- Control access to Control Panel

- Prevent the use of the Run command from the Start menu

- Customize the desktop

- Configure network settings

To use System Policies, you must install the System Policy Editor and the templates.

Additional policies that you can implement to improve password security include

- Instruct users not to write down passwords.

- Make sure that users know not to use obvious passwords such as the name of a spouse, child, or pet.

- Do not use dictionary words for your password.

- Use a combination of letters and numbers in mixed case; the password gOOd75doG is harder to crack than the password gooddog.

- An easy way to create a password is to combine two short words with a nonalpha-numeric character between them such as big$meal. You can also use mixed case to increase the effectiveness of your password.

You can improve the security of your network by limiting the total number of shared folders. By keeping files that require shared access in a limited number of folders, you decrease the number of passwords a user has to remember.

Disable file and print sharing on those computers that do not contain files requiring sharing. This action not only improves security, it also enhances the performance of the computer.

A Windows 98 network is easy to implement and maintain. This native functionality results in increased efficiency. It also saves you money by allowing all your users to share hardware devices such as printers.

TROUBLESHOOTING

BASIC METHODOLOGY FOR TROUBLESHOOTING NETWORKS

What must I consider when I troubleshoot a network?

If you are troubleshooting a network, you need to consider many potential variables, ranging from basic connectivity to mismatched protocols. If you can, a good practice is to examine the performance and maintenance history of the network before jumping in and trying to troubleshoot. Having a basic methodology for troubleshooting networks is a big help in developing a successful troubleshooting process.

Asking the following questions should give you a good start:

- How well did the network work before? What has been modified or changed on the network or the systems in question?

- Has any new or different network cable been removed or added? Check all cables, connections, and terminators.

- Are the network connections alive? Look at the status lights on the back of the network adapter or on the hub or switch. If you can see activity, then you have an active connection. If not, consider the cable, the network interface card in question, and even the hub or switch.

- Has a network adapter been removed or added? Can you connect to local systems but not to those on other networks?

- Which protocols are installed, and have any protocols been added or removed recently?

- Have any new network services or components been installed recently? Were they installed correctly? Always use the Microsoft System Information utility to look for problems with device conflicts. If you find conflicts, you can resolve them through Device Manager.

SECRETS OF MASTERING THE WINDOWS 98 ENVIRONMENT: SETTING THE FILE SYSTEM AND THE ROLE OF THE COMPUTER FOR OPTIMUM PERFORMANCE

With Windows 98, the characteristics of how the operating system works with the file system and the subsequent impact on disk performance are based on the role of the computer. As the user of the system, you control the configuration of how the file system is tuned to perform, including the choice of the file system and the role of the computer. Naturally, the configuration should reflect the type of work expected of the system.

For example, if your system runs many desktop applications, the performance of launching those applications depends, in part, on disk cluster size. Smaller cluster sizes give better application launch performance—the 4KB cluster size (FAT32) is best. If larger sizes are used, as in FAT16, you will experience less of a performance boost.

After you decide on which file system to use, you can determine the role of the system, or how the computer normally functions. To determine the role of the system:

1. In Control Panel, double-click System, click the Performance tab, and then click File System.

2. In the Typical Role of This Computer box, select the most common role for the computer and then click OK.

A Windows 98 system can be configured as one of the following:

- Desktop computer—This unit is a standard desktop system functioning as a client on a network or as a standalone system. This system has more than the minimum required memory and is not battery powered.

- Laptop computer—Any mobile system configured with minimal resources such as memory and disk space. Because the system is low on memory and running on battery, the disk cache is frequently flushed.

- Network server—A system that is used as a file or print server. This system is configured with more than enough memory and a larger swap file, with the system being optimized for frequent disk access.

CHAPTER 37

SHARING NETWORK RESOURCES

In this chapter

UNDERSTANDING SHARING, WINDOWS SHARES, AND SECURITY

Sharing is a critical part of almost any Windows-based network. Sharing in Windows networks means users can make resources on their computers available to other users. Without sharing, users are forced to copy the files and folders they want so that other users are free to access the network server volume. In a more specific scenario, let's say that a coworker is working with a set of files related to a project, and those files are stored in a folder on the coworker's computer. Let's also say that you need to read and possibly edit one of those files. If the person shared the folder where the files are located, you could access any of the files in the folder from your desktop as if the files were stored on your machine.

In addition to sharing folders, users can share other resources on their computers. An example of another resource a user would share is a printer. Suppose that a coworker's machine is attached to a color inkjet printer and that you need to print a color presentation. You could disconnect the color inkjet and attach it to your computer, but networking offers a better solution. Your coworker could share the computer, you could attach to it over the network, and then you could print to the printer as if it were directly attached to your computer.

UNDERSTANDING SHARES AND NETWORKS

Sharing is supported on both NetWare and Windows networks. This chapter focuses primarily on sharing in a Windows network environment. In a Windows network, the computers operate on a peer-to-peer basis, usually a mix of Windows 95, Windows 98, and Windows NT Workstation computers, or one supported by a Windows NT Server.

Keep in mind that in a peer-to-peer network, any computer that provides resources to other computers as shares is known as a server. Peer-to-peer networks usually have fewer than 10 computers. Experts usually recommend using a dedicated server to support networks with more than 10 computers. A network with a dedicated server is usually known as a client/server network.

Regardless of whether the Windows network is peer to peer or client/server, sharing works the same way. Sharing allows one user access to another user's resources. Resources capable of being shared are any of the following:

- Folders
- Files
- Removable drives
- Printers

When any resource is available over the network for users other than those running the server computer, that resource is known as a *share*. The term *share* is used throughout this chapter. When a resource is being shared, a hand appears under its icon on the screen (see Figure 37.1).

Figure 37.1
A hand appears beneath the icon of any resource that is being shared.

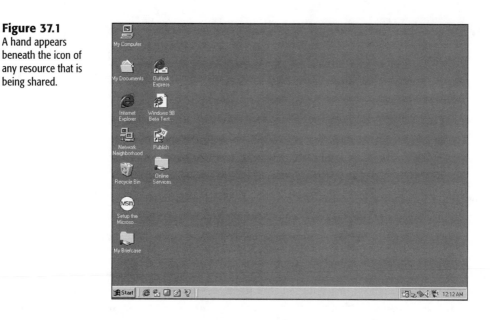

⚡ *If you're having trouble sharing resources, see "Problems with File and Printer Sharing" in the "Troubleshooting" section at the end of this chapter.*

PART

VI

CH

37

UNDERSTANDING ACCESS TYPES

Before you share a resource over the network, you need to decide what type of access you will provide. The first step in defining access to resources on your computer is to specify what kind of access scheme you will use. You have two choices for securing your computer resources in a sharing environment:

- Share-level access control
- User-level access control

The next two sections introduce these access types.

SHARE-LEVEL ACCESS CONTROL

Share-level security defines one set of rights to a specific share. For share-level access, the user defines a share for a resource; gives it a name, such as Project X Folder; and optionally secures the share with a password. The user also specifies whether people accessing the share can modify the share or just have read access. Users can access the contents of the share, in this case a folder, simply by opening the folder. Naturally, if the share is secured by a password, the user would have to supply the correct password. The most important point to keep in mind with share-level access is that all users have the same type of access to the share.

> **Note**
>
> Share-level access control applies only to remote users attempting to connect to shares on a particular system. Resource access control is not available for a locally logged-on user in Windows 98.

USER-LEVEL ACCESS CONTROL

User-level access control authenticates specific users for access to the share. This feature allows different users on the network to have individual, unique rights to each share.

User-level security requires a computer that serves as the security validation server. In other words, the network must have one computer that is a NetWare server, a Windows NT Server, or a Windows NT Workstation machine (in the absence of a Windows NT Server).

The list of users to whom you will provide access to your shared resource comes from the security validation server. In fact, when you add user access to a resource, you display the list of users with accounts on the security validation server. Although you can add users to your own machine, you cannot manage the list of users on the security validation server from Windows 98. If you want to give a user access to a share on your computer using user-level access, you must first create an account for the user on the security validation server.

CONFIGURING WINDOWS 98 FOR RESOURCE SHARING

Before any type of sharing is allowed on Windows 98, user level or share level, you must configure Windows 98 to allow sharing and to share other resources. You will not be able to access resources available for sharing on the network, nor will network users be able to access resources you have shared, without first configuring Windows 98 properly. You most likely will need to obtain the Windows 98 installation media to complete the following steps.

To configure Windows 98 for sharing, follow these steps:

1. Open the Start menu and choose Settings, Control Panel. The Control Panel folder appears.
2. Choose the Network icon.
3. Scroll through the list that appears on the Configuration tab and look for an entry named File and Printer Sharing for Microsoft Networks. If this entry already exists, skip to step 7; otherwise, continue with step 4.
4. Choose the Add button. The Select Network Component Type dialog box appears. Choose Service from the list and then choose Add. The Select Network Service dialog box appears (see Figure 37.2).

Figure 37.2
You must add the File and Printer Sharing service.

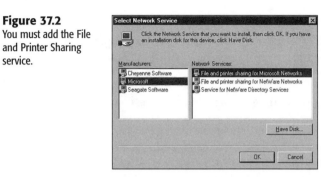

5. Choose Microsoft from the Manufacturers list and then choose File and Printer Sharing for Microsoft Networks from the Network Services list. Click OK.

6. At this point, Windows 98 installs the files it needs for file and printer sharing. You might be asked to load the Windows 98 CD-ROM or to point to a location on the network where the installation files are located. When the installation process is complete, you are returned to the Network dialog box.

7. Choose the File and Print Sharing button. The File and Print Sharing dialog box appears (see Figure 37.3).

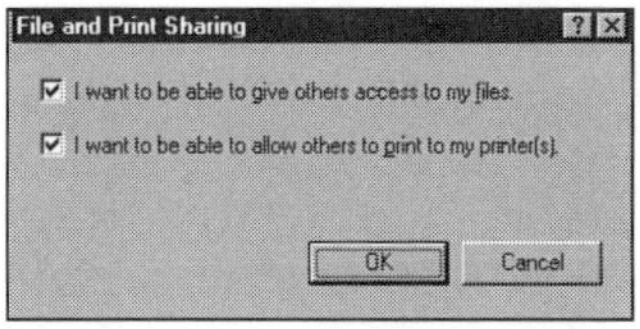

Figure 37.3
You can define whether to share files or printers or both.

8. Check both options in the dialog box and then click OK. Note that the option for printer sharing is not required for sharing files, but this step asks you to select it for use later in the chapter. Click OK from the Network dialog box. The dialog box closes, and Windows is likely to prompt you to restart your computer.

ESTABLISHING SHARE-LEVEL ACCESS TO DRIVE OR FOLDER RESOURCES

The first type of access we explore in this chapter is share-level access. This type of access is the least flexible of options, but it happens to be the easiest to administer.

CONFIGURING WINDOWS 98 FOR SHARE-LEVEL SECURITY

The first step in creating shares with share-level security is to inform Windows 98 that you want to use share-level security. Follow these steps to specify that you want to use share-level access in Windows 98:

1. Open the Start menu and choose Settings, Control Panel. The Control Panel folder appears.

2. Choose the Network icon.

3. When the Network dialog box appears, choose the Access Control tab (see Figure 37.4).

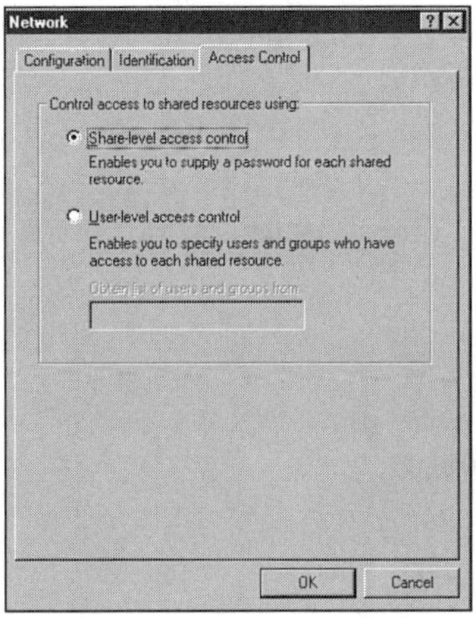

Figure 37.4
You must define what type of access scheme you will use.

4. Choose the Share-Level Access Control option and then click OK.

5. Click OK. The dialog box closes, and you are likely to be prompted to restart your system.

REVIEWING SHARE-ACCESS TYPES

When you create a share, you must specify what type of access users will have to the resource. You can assign three types of access to the resource:

- Read-Only Rights
- Full Access Rights
- Depends on Password

Read-Only Rights allow the user to view the resource, such as a file, but not change it. Full Access Rights put no restrictions on the user's access to the resource; he or she can modify the resource, rename the resource, and even delete the resource. Depends on Password means that the user is granted the rights to the share that match the password he or she enters. Because the Read-Only and Full passwords must be different, the user is granted either one set of rights or the other when the Depends on Password option is selected.

PROVIDING SHARE-LEVEL ACCESS TO A RESOURCE

It is easy to share a resource with share-level access. To do so, you simply locate the resource you want to share and then supply a name, a level of access, and a password to create the share to the resource.

To create a share with share-level access, follow these steps:

1. Right-click on the resource to which you want to provide user-level access and then choose Sharing from the menu that appears. You can create the share from wherever you can see the folder or drive, such as My Computer, the Desktop, or Windows 98 Explorer.

2. Choose the Sharing tab (see Figure 37.5).

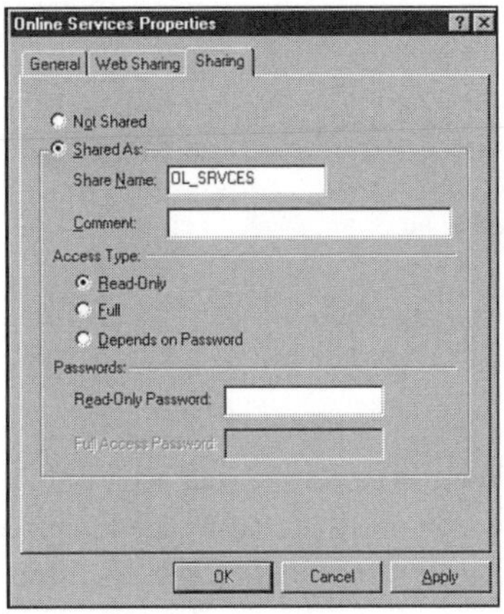

Figure 37.5
Use the Sharing tab to define a share for a resource.

3. Choose the Shared As option and then enter a name for the share in the Share Name box. This name subsequently appears to users as they browse the network and see the resources on your computer, so make it as descriptive as you can within the bounds of the 12-character limit.

4. Select one of the three Access Type options: Read-Only, Full, or Depends on Password.

Enter a password for either Read-Only or Full if you choose. If you do not specify a password, all users will have access to the share, though their rights depend on which option you chose. You are prompted to reenter the password for confirmation. If you select Depends on Password, you must enter a password for both Read-Only and Full.

5. Click OK.

REMOVING A SHARE-LEVEL ACCESS

At some point, you might want to stop sharing an existing resource on the network. To remove a share-level access, right-click on the resource you want to stop sharing and then choose Sharing from the menu that appears. Choose the Sharing tab, choose the Not Shared option, and then click OK. The share is removed.

ESTABLISHING USER-LEVEL ACCESS TO FOLDER OR DRIVE RESOURCES

In this section, you learn how to create shares to resources on your computer with user-level access. Naturally, this process has two parts:

1. Identify the resource to share.
2. Specify the users who will have access to the share and the type of access they are allowed.

This section begins by reviewing the various access types you can grant individual users and groups to shares you create.

REVIEWING USER-ACCESS TYPES

When you assign a user or a group access to a resource, you must specify what type of access that user or group has to the resource. You can assign three types of access to the resource:

- Read-Only Rights
- Full Access Rights
- Custom Access Rights

Read-Only Rights mean the user can view the resource, such as a file, but cannot change it. Full Access Rights put no restrictions on the user's access to the resource; the user can modify the resource, rename the resource, and even delete the resource. Custom Access Rights define a very specific set of actions a user or group can take with a resource. Custom Access Rights are covered in the next section.

UNDERSTANDING CUSTOM ACCESS RIGHTS

Providing a user or group with Custom Access Rights gives you the opportunity to custom build an access type for a set of users or a group with access to the resource. For example, if a user might need to change attributes for a file, but you don't want the user to delete the file, you should use Custom Access Rights to define the user's access.

When you assign Custom Access Rights for a resource to a user or group, you must individually define whether the user has the following subrights to the resource:

- Read Files
- Write to Files
- Create Files and Folders
- Delete Files
- Change File Attributes
- List Files
- Change Access Control

By turning these access rights on and off, you can create a very specialized mode of access to every resource you share.

Tip #250	When you are sharing resources on your system, a good rule of thumb is to keep the shared folder structure as simple as possible. Do not go overboard by creating different share names for the same share or creating an excessive number of separate folders to house separate files. Make every effort to create a shared folder structure based on the access level of the files in the folder and then organize the files based on type and purpose. Try to outline this structure ahead of time and implement it according to your plan.

CONFIGURING WINDOWS 98 FOR USER-LEVEL SECURITY

Now that you understand the different types of user-level access allowed in Windows 98, you need to take one more step before assigning access to shares. User-level security is not a default option in Windows 98, so you must specify that you want to use user-level security. Follow these steps:

1. Open the Start menu and choose Settings, Control Panel. The Control Panel folder appears.
2. Choose the Network icon.
3. When the Network dialog box appears, choose the Access Control tab.
4. Choose the User-Level Access Control option and then enter the name of the computer whose user list you want to use for defining access to shares on your computer. As a reminder, this computer must be a NetWare server, a Windows NT Server, or a Windows NT Workstation computer that is visible to your computer on the network.
5. Click OK. The dialog box closes, and you are likely to be prompted to restart your system.

PROVIDING USER-LEVEL ACCESS TO A RESOURCE

Defining a share with user-level access requires a few more steps than defining a share using share-level access. The first steps are the same in that you locate the resource you want to share and then give it a share name. Then the process becomes more complicated.

To create a share with user-level access control, follow these steps:

1. Right-click on the resource to which you want to provide user-level access and then choose Sharing from the menu that appears. You can create the share from wherever you can see the folder or drive, such as My Computer, the Desktop, or Windows 98 Explorer.
2. Choose the Sharing tab. The share properties page provides an area to add specific users with rights to the resource you are sharing (see Figure 37.6).

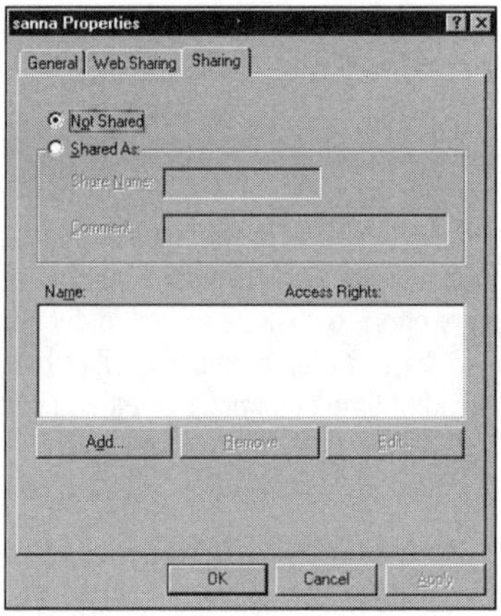

Figure 37.6
You give specific users rights to the resource you are sharing.

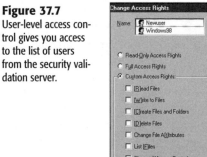

3. Click on the Shared As option and enter a name for the resource you are sharing. This name subsequently appears to users as they browse the network and see the resources on your computer, so make the name as descriptive as you can within the bounds of the 12-character limit.

4. Choose Add to begin defining user access to the resource. The Add Users dialog box appears. Notice that the list of users and groups from the computer you specified earlier in the section "Configuring Windows 98 for User-Level Security" fills the user list box (see Figure 37.7).

Figure 37.7
User-level access control gives you access to the list of users from the security validation server.

5. Click on any of the users or groups that you want to provide access for to the resource you are sharing. Then click on either the Read-Only, Full Access, or Custom button, depending on the level of access you want to grant the user or group.

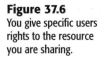 **Note**

Keep in mind that any access-level rights you provide to a group are granted to all users in the group. Before granting access to a group, be sure you know the members of the group.

6. Repeat step 5 for every user or group that you want to provide access for to the resource you are sharing. When this task is complete, click OK.

   If you defined Custom Rights for any user or group, the Change Access Rights dialog box appears (see Figure 37.8). From this dialog box, you define the specific rights for the users and/or groups listed at the top of the dialog box. Note that if you specified Custom Access Rights for more than one user or group, the rights you define in the dialog box at this point apply to each user and/or group. Choose the Custom Access Rights you want to apply to the users/groups and then click OK.

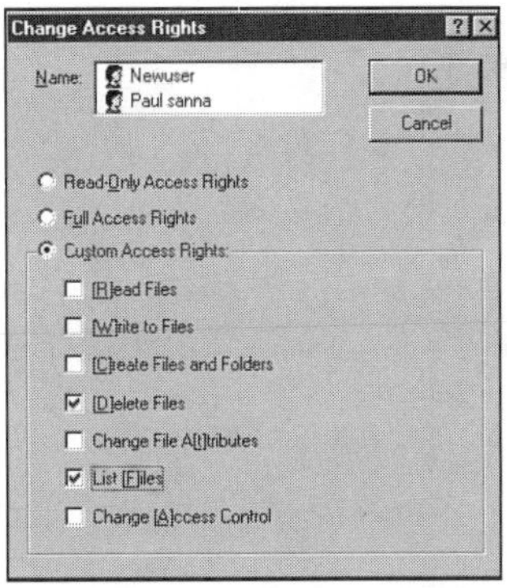

Figure 37.8
Custom Access Rights enable you to define the specific capabilities to grant to users and groups.

7. You are returned to the Properties dialog box for the resource you are sharing. Notice that the users and groups you assigned access rights to now appear in the Name box (see Figure 37.9). Click OK. This step completes the process of defining user-level access rights to a resource.

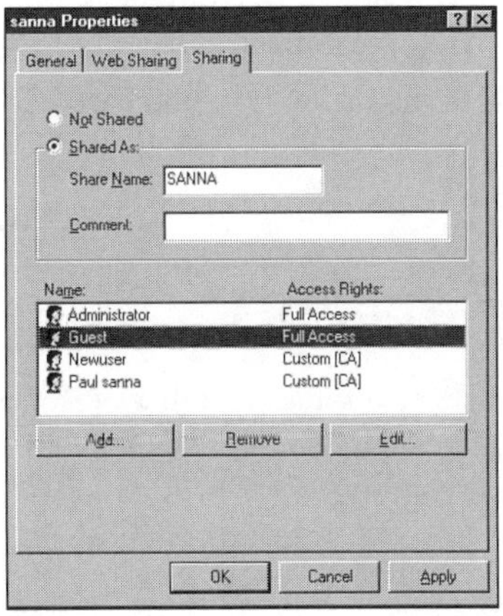

Figure 37.9
All users and groups you created access rights for appear in the Properties dialog box for the resource you are sharing.

REMOVING A USER'S RIGHTS

You might want to remove a certain user's privileges to a resource you had been sharing with that user. This action is different from removing a share for a resource, in which case all users would lose access to the resource.

To remove a user's rights to a share, follow these steps:

1. Right-click on the resource whose rights you want to change and then choose Sharing from the menu that appears.

2. Click on the user you want to remove from the name list and then click the Remove button. If more than one user or group appears in the list, a red letter *x* appears beside each name (see Figure 37.10). If only one user has access to the resource, that person is removed from the list as soon as you choose Remove.

3. Click OK.

Figure 37.10
You can see which users and/or groups you have removed from accessing the share.

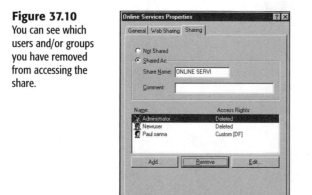

CHANGING USER-LEVEL ACCESS RIGHTS

Changing a user's or group's access rights is a simple task. To do so, right-click on the share you want to change and then choose Sharing from the menu that appears. Click on the user or group in the Name list at the bottom of the dialog box, and then choose Edit. The Change Access Rights dialog box appears (refer to Figure 37.8). Make any changes to the user's/group's rights and then click OK.

SHARING PRINTERS AND OTHER RESOURCES

So far in this chapter, we have looked at sharing folder and drive resources. Next, we look at the process for sharing other resources, such as a printer or CD-ROM drive.

SHARING PRINTERS

Sharing a printer is a fairly common task in small organizations. In typical workgroups, not everyone has a printer attached to his or her computer, but most people have a printing requirement. In these cases, sharing a printer for the workgroup is the best way to provide everyone with printing capabilities.

To share a printer attached to your computer, you follow the same steps listed earlier for sharing a file, folder, or drive option. First, though, be sure you have

- Installed the printer as you normally would at your workstation. Print a test page to be sure the printer is working properly.

- Allowed printer sharing in your Windows 98 configuration. This procedure is covered earlier in step 8 in the "Configuration Windows 98 for Resource Sharing" section of this chapter.

Note that you have to access the printer to share it from the Printers folder, which is available by opening the Start menu and choosing Settings, Printers. Also note that for user-level access rights, you can define only Full Access for each user or group you provide access for. Read-Only or Custom Rights do not apply to a printer (see Figure 37.11).

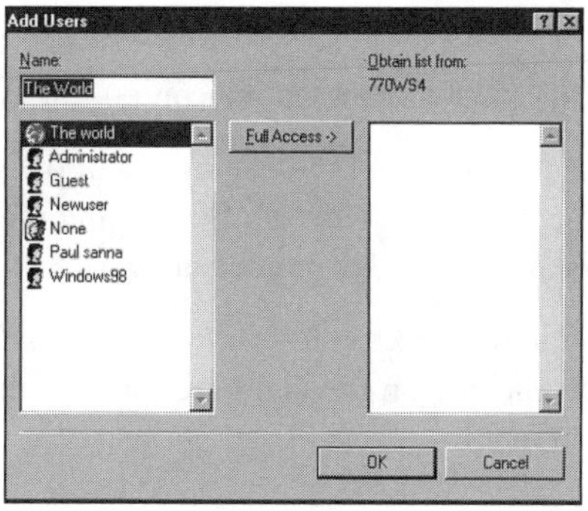

Figure 37.11
You can grant only Full Access Rights to a printer when you use user-level access rights.

SHARING CD-ROM DRIVES AND REMOVABLE DRIVES

Like sharing a hard drive, sharing a CD-ROM drive is one of the most common uses for sharing. Users who have not upgraded their computers to CD capability yet may occasionally need to access data and programs that are stored on a CD. In these cases, sharing a CD is the best way to solve the problem. The process of sharing a CD-ROM is the same as sharing a folder or drive. Here are some tips to help with defining a share to a CD-ROM drive:

- Be mindful of users accessing the CD-ROM drive on your computer. Without thinking, it would be easy to remove the CD from the drive while a sharing user is accessing the drive.

- Create Read-Only Rights to the drive. This setting keeps the user from attempting to save to the CD, in which case an annoying and difficult-to-clear error message appears.

USING SHARED FILES

So far in this chapter, you have learned how to make resources on your computer available for users on the network. In these cases, believe it or not, your computer has acted as a server on the network. Next, we look at how to play the role of the client. In this section, you learn how to access drives, files, and folders that other users have made available to you on the network.

The first step in using a shared resource is locating the computer whose resources you want to share. Locating resources is the topic of the next section.

BROWSING NETWORK NEIGHBORHOOD

Network Neighborhood is where you can see all the computers you potentially have access to. Seeing computers you can access in Network Neighborhood makes it easy to attach to their resources.

To open Network Neighborhood, just double-click on its icon on the Windows 98 desktop.

When Network Neighborhood opens, you see all the computers in the same workgroup or domain as you, as well as an icon for the entire network. By opening the entire network, you see all the domains, workgroups, trees, and servers in your network.

When you find the computer with the resources you want to share, you can view the resources available by either double-clicking on the computer or by right-clicking on it and choosing Open from the drop-down menu.

FINDING A COMPUTER ON THE NETWORK

Suppose you need to locate a computer but are unable to do so through Network Neighborhood. This situation might occur when so many computers, domains, and work-groups are listed that it is difficult to find the computer you are looking for, or perhaps the computer that you are looking for is not in your immediate area or not in your subnet. In either of these cases, you can still find a computer with Windows 98, provided you know the name of the computer.

To find a computer, be sure you are logged on to the network where you believe the computer is located. Next, open the Start menu and choose Find, Computer. The Find Computer dialog box appears.

Enter the name of the computer in the Named box and then choose Find Now. If Windows finds the computer, the Find Computer dialog box shows its location. Otherwise, Windows 98 reports that it cannot find the computer. To begin exploring the computer, you can double-click on the name of the computer in the Find Computer dialog box.

Using and Mapping Shared Drives

After you find the computer and the share you want to use, you are free to work with the share as if the resource were on your own computer. Here are some common ways to take advantage of a shared file or folder resource:

PART

VI

Ch

37

- Create a shortcut to a shared resource—Right-click on the share and then drag it to the desktop. You can use a shortcut for any kind of share. Release the mouse and choose Create *Shortcut (pages 32 and 588)* Here from the menu that appears. This way, you have direct access to the shared resource at any time, and you do not have to spend time trying to locate the host computer.

- View the contents of the share (folder only)—Double-click on the folder. To use Windows 98 Explorer to review the contents, right-click on the shared folder and then choose Explore from the menu that appears.

- Map the share to a drive letter—Right-click on the resource and then choose Map Network Drive from the menu that appears. You can use this technique for a file or drive share only. Next, choose a drive letter from the Drive drop-down list and then click OK. To make the drive mapping permanent, choose the Reconnect at Logon option before choosing OK. Mapping a drive makes it easy to refer to the share from any common dialog box. All you need to do is refer to the mapped drive letter to access the share.

Understanding UNC

Windows 98 uses a system known as the *Uniform Naming Convention (UNC)* to refer to folder and file locations on computers. This system is used with the more familiar drive letter and folders convention because, in network operations, the server name must be specified in addition to a folder name. The UNC refers to network locations. This chapter has shown you how to select resources on the network by pointing and clicking on the icon of the resource. You can also use a UNC path to select the same resources.

Here is how the UNC system works. The first part of a UNC location is the name of the computer. This computer can be a dedicated network server, or it can be a computer in a peer-to-peer network, as described in this chapter. The computer name is always preceded by two backslashes (\\). For example, to refer to the MyServer computer with a UNC command, use \\MyServer.

Normally, a specific directory location is specified as well. To map a drive to a shared directory location with a UNC command, within the command line you enumerate the entire directory hierarchy to the target directory, separating directory names with a single backslash (\). For example, to map the logical drive Z to the Very\Critical\Data directory on the MyServer computer, use the following:

```
Net use: Z: \\MyServer\Very\Critical\Data
```

Tip #251

> To share a resource with a single person and no one else, you can hide the share on the network. Hiding a share means that the share is not visible through Network Neighborhood or other browsing mechanisms such as the Net View command. To hide a share, simply append the share name with a $. For example, the share secretstuff becomes secretstuff$. Anyone wanting to connect to the share requires knowledge of the hidden share name, which you provide on an as-needed basis. To get to the hidden share, users simply enumerate the entire UNC path, including the appended $ in the command line.

One of the easiest ways to see how a UNC works is to open the Start menu and choose Run. Enter a full UNC location (computer and directories) and then click OK. The location you specified opens in a new folder window.

USING A SHARED PRINTER

The last task to look at is using a printer that another user has made available on the network and (presumably) provided access rights for. The process for adding a network printer simply involves using the Add New Printer Wizard. Be sure when the wizard starts that you specify that you are using a network computer. For more information on adding a printer to Windows 98, refer to Chapter 13, "Printing."

TROUBLESHOOTING

PROBLEMS WITH FILE AND PRINTER SHARING

Why don't I have the Sharing option on my pop-up menu?

One common problem with File and Printer Sharing for Microsoft Networks is that the Sharing command does not appear on the context-sensitive menu when you use the right mouse button to click a drive, folder, or printer. In this case, make sure to check that File and Printer Sharing for Microsoft Networks is installed. Or, if you are working in a NetWare environment, make sure that File and Printer Sharing for NetWare Networks is installed.

SECRETS OF MASTERING THE WINDOWS 98 ENVIRONMENT: USING NET WATCHER

If files and printers are shared on your system and you are responsible for managing and sharing resources on other systems in your network, then you can use the Net Watcher utility to create, add, and delete shared resources. You can use this handy utility to establish shares on remote computers and to monitor and manage connections to those shared resources. Net Watcher is really helpful when you need to know which users are connected to which shares on a particular Windows 98 system.

The Net Watcher utility comes with dedicated icons for

- Adding a shared resource or stopping a shared resource
- Displaying all shared resources, connected users, and open files
- Closing files that users have opened
- Disconnecting a user

Follow these steps to install Net Watcher:

1. Open Control Panel, double-click Add/Remove Programs, and then click the Windows Setup tab.
2. Click System Tools and then click Details.
3. Select the Net Watcher check box and then click OK.

CHAPTER **38**

REMOTE ACCESS WITH DIAL-UP NETWORKING

In this chapter

CONNECTING TO A REMOTE ACCESS SERVER

Installing Dial-Up Networking is simply the first step in connecting to remote resources via a Remote Access Server. To access remote resources, you also need to have the necessary client software and communications protocols installed.

→ For additional information on connecting to a Remote Access Server, **see** "Using the Internet Connection Wizard," **p. 522**.

By default, Windows 98 can support the following common protocols:

- TCP/IP
- NetBEUI
- IPX/SPX
- DLC

Windows 98 also ships with the following networking clients:

- Microsoft Family Logon (for Internet use)
- Client for Microsoft Networks
- Client for NetWare Networks

In addition to the integrated clients and protocols, many third-party client packages are available. A few are listed here:

- FTP software
- Telnet software
- Banyan client software
- VAX client software
- Novell's NetWare 32 client
- DEC PathWorks client

The type of network you plan to dial in to determines the combination of protocols and clients you will need. It's always a good idea to check with your network administrator.

→ To get more detailed information on network protocols in Windows 98, **see** "Installing and Configuring Network Protocols," **p. 772**.

When you install Dial-Up Networking, Windows 98 automatically configures your machine with Dial-Up Adapter, Microsoft Family Logon, and the TCP/IP protocol (see Figure 38.1). These components alone are enough to allow you to connect to the Internet successfully, but are not all that is required to dial in to a Windows NT or NetWare network. The following procedure walks you through the installation of additional network clients and/or protocols.

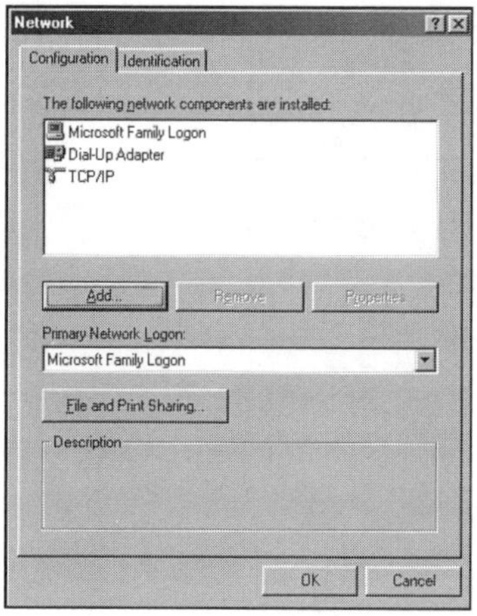

Figure 38.1
Dial-Up Adapter is
installed.

PART
VI

CH
38

1. Determine the network client/protocol combination necessary to successfully communicate on your remote network.

2. Launch your Windows 98 Network Properties by going to Control Panel and clicking on the Network shortcut, or by highlighting the Network Neighborhood shortcut on your desktop, using the right mouse button to open the drop-down menu, and choosing Properties from the available values. Either way, Windows 98 displays the Network applet.

3. To add clients or protocols, click the Add button, and Windows displays the Select Network Component Type page (see Figure 38.2).

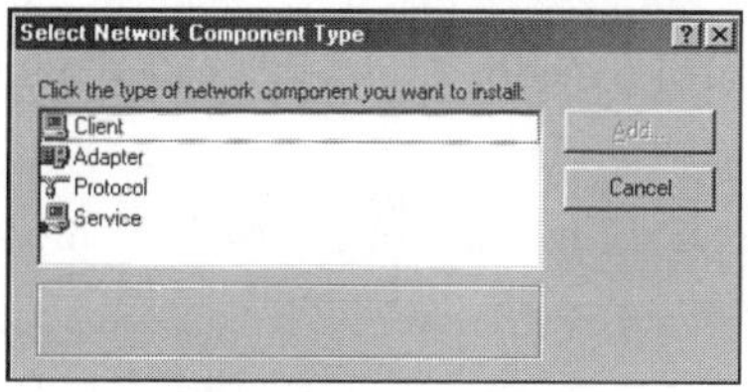

Figure 38.2
The Select Network
Component Type
page.

To add a client or protocol, highlight the appropriate choice and click Add. Components supported natively under Windows 98 are listed when you select Microsoft in the Manufacturers list, as shown in Figures 38.3 and 38.4.

4. After you've selected the appropriate network component, Windows 98 copies the necessary files to your hard drive. After all components are installed, close the Network configuration applet, and you are prompted to restart your computer. At this point, you are prepared to begin creating and managing dial-up connections.

Figure 38.3
The Select Network Protocol page.

Figure 38.4
The Select Network Client page.

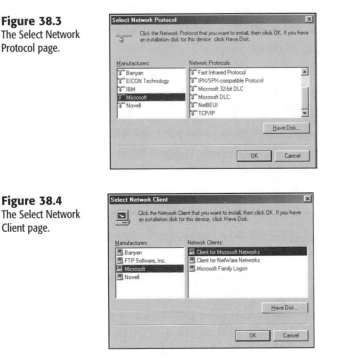

CONFIGURING TELEPHONY SETTINGS

Windows 98 offers advanced telephony settings for *Dial-Up Networking (pages 510 and 853-854)*. These settings allow you to create multiple Dial-Up profiles to be used in various situations. For example, you might be required to dial 9 to access an outside line from your office, or you might need to dial the area code for commonly called numbers when you are traveling.

Notice in Figure 38.5 that under the phone number of the ABC Company is a field labeled Dialing From. Next to this field is a button labeled Dialing Properties.

To manipulate your telephony, or dialing, properties, simply click on the Dialing Properties button to open the Dialing Properties page, shown in Figure 38.6.

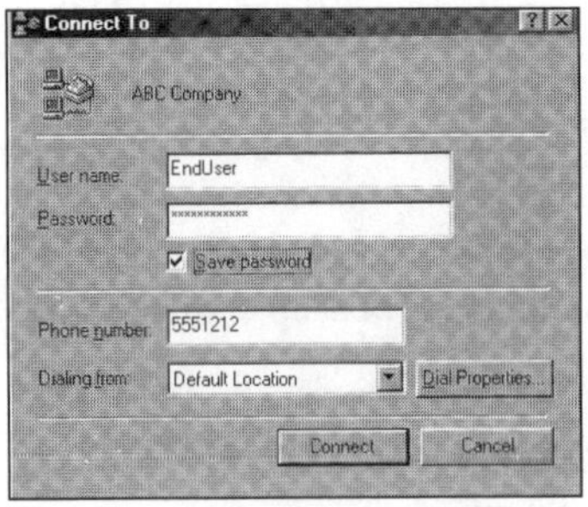

Figure 38.5
Connect to ABC Company.

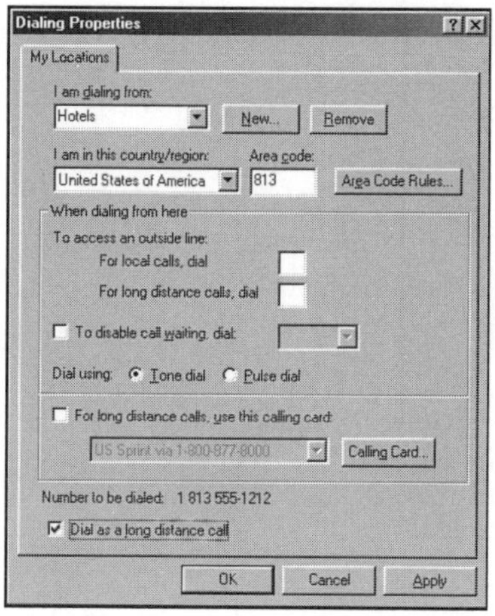

Figure 38.6
The Dialing Properties page.

This page enables you to set several dialing variables and save them as different profiles, or locations. The available variables are

- Country or region selection
- Area code selection and rules
- Outside-line access settings
- Long-distance-line access settings
- The option to disable call waiting
- The option of pulse or tone dialing
- The option to use a calling card
- The option to dial a number as a long-distance call

To create a new location, simply press the New button next to the field labeled I Am Dialing From. You are informed that your new location was created, and all settings from the previous location disappear. Follow these steps to create a new long-distance location to be used for making calling card calls from hotels:

1. Click the New button on the top of the form. In the field labeled I Am Dialing From, enter the name Hotels.

2. Do not modify the Country/Region or the Area Code settings, but instead select the Area Code Rules button. The next page is titled Area Code Rules, as shown in Figure 38.7.

3. At this point, you can set some fairly sophisticated rules; however, it is a safe assumption that you won't be staying in too many hotels within your home area code. Simply check the box next to the Always Dial the Area Code option and click OK. Windows now returns you to the main Dialing Properties page.

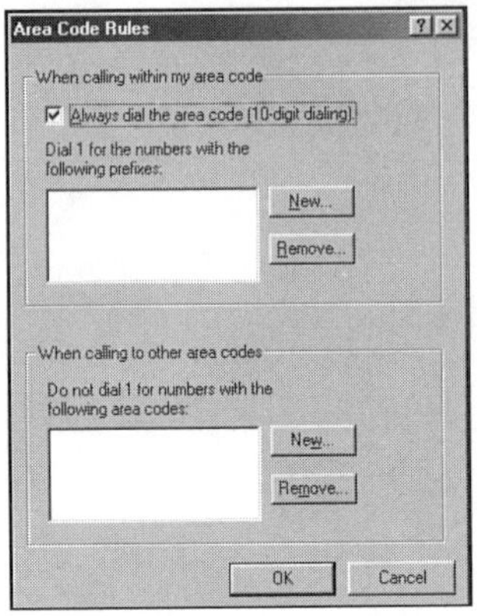

Figure 38.7
The Dialing Location Area Code Rules page.

4. Focus your attention on the When Dialing from Here section. Because most hotels require you to dial 9 to make local calls and 8 to make long-distance calls, enter 8 in the box next to the For Local Calls, Dial option and enter 9 in the For Long Distance Calls, Dial option.

5. Skip to the For Long Distance Calls, Use This Calling Card section and click on the Calling Card button. From the Calling Card page, shown in Figure 38.8, you can select your Calling Card type by using the drop-down list at the top of the page. After you select the correct card type, all default settings drop into the appropriate fields. In most cases, you simply need to enter your PIN.

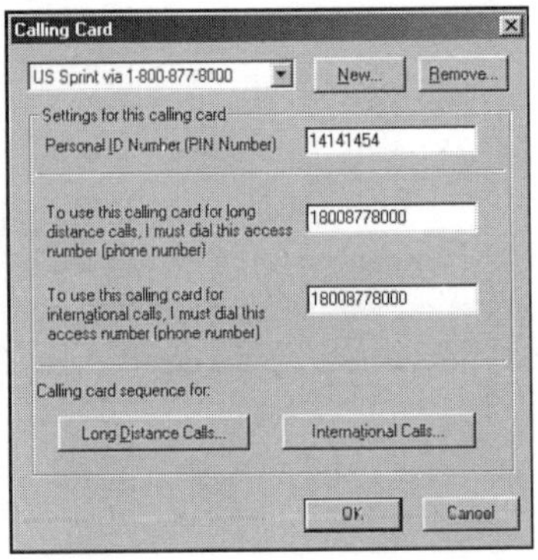

Figure 38.8
The Calling Card configuration page.

6. After your Calling Card settings are configured, click OK at the bottom of the page to return to the main Dialing Properties page. Next, because this location will always be long distance, select the Dial as a Long Distance Call check box at the bottom of the page.

7. Click Apply at the bottom of the page, and your new location is successfully created. To switch between locations, simply click the down arrow on the drop-down box located on the main Dialing page.

You can create as many location profiles as necessary and use as many calling cards as required.

USING RESOURCES VIA REMOTE ACCESS

When you dial in to a Remote Access Server and connect to the network, your workstation is essentially a normal network client with one exception: Dialing in to your network through a modem is considerably slower than when you're logged on at the office—even at today's modem speeds. Although Dial-Up Networking offers a great deal of functionality, with remote node connectivity you cannot run any sizable applications (such as Office) from the network, and you cannot transfer large amounts of data in reasonable time periods. The most effective way to use a remote node solution is to have all the applications you require resident on your Windows 98 computer and have any large documents or files on removable media. In this case, when you access your required network resources (such as a standard Word document or a Notes database), you only have to worry about passing small amounts of data back and forth across the line. Following is a list of common uses for Dial-Up Networking clients:

- Access to Microsoft Office documents or databases
- Access to Windows NT, Novell, or UNIX servers
- Access to electronic mail such as Exchange or Notes
- Access to a Notes database or an Exchange public folder
- Access to an intranet
- Access to the Internet (through a proxy server)

Dial-Up Networking is very practical for users who need access to documentation or utilities or who need to perform remote network administration. Many client/server applications such as SNA Server or Exchange work well over remote node connections. With Dial-Up Networking, you can even map drives, navigate Network Neighborhood, and browse the Internet through your network's proxy server.

<table>
<tr><td>Tip #251</td><td>If you have a connection to a RAS server but see no resources available on the system, or get an error message, make sure to check the server side of the connection. If everything is okay there, then the problem is likely to be mismatched protocols. Make sure that the Dial-Up Networking client is running a protocol that is installed on the RAS server.</td></tr>
</table>

SPECIAL CONSIDERATIONS FOR DIAL-UP CONNECTIONS

Many remote users require more than just remote node connectivity, and, likewise, many corporations have found value in providing high-performance remote solutions for their mobile workforce. Remote control applications and Windows Terminal solutions can overcome many of the performance issues seen in remote node connectivity.

PART

VI

CH

38

Remote Control

Remote control software allows users to dial in to a network utilizing Dial-Up Networking and, via specialized client software, take control of a PC on the remote network that is acting as a remote control host. After control is taken, the remote control client can manage the host workstation, run applications from the host workstation, or even provide technical support for the host workstation. Remote control software such as Reach Out, PC Anywhere, or Remotely Possible allows you to take control of and manipulate a computer with very acceptable performance by simply passing modifications to the screen across your dial-up connection. For instance, if you take control of a host workstation on your remote network and start an accounting application, the workstation does all the processing, whereas the remote control software simply passes compressed video to your workstation's remote control client. To you, it seems as if you've just launched the application on your own computer. Although remote control performance is slower than on a remote workstation, performance is very acceptable—especially if you can't access an application any other way.

Tip #252	When you want to run a program from a Dial-Up Networking client to a Remote Access Server, the program being used must be designed for that purpose. Remote control software programs are good examples of these types of programs. If your objective is to use Dial-Up Networking to occasionally run a program remotely, make sure that you purchase an application or program that supports that environment.

Windows Terminal Solutions

Remote control software is excellent for many applications; however, it is impractical to provide a remote control host workstation for a significant number of remote users. Windows Terminal Server solutions, such as Citrix Winframe or Microsoft's Windows Terminal Server (WTS), take remote control one step further. With a Windows Terminal solution, an end user can dial in to a network by using Dial-Up Networking and then use a Windows Terminal Server client to launch a Windows session from a Citrix or WTS server. This session, which is very much in the vein of a mainframe session, provides the end user with a true Windows desktop session, as well as access to almost any application at speeds approaching real-time local computing.

A Windows Terminal Server solution does not require a dedicated workstation for every remote user; instead, a single server can provide high-performance remote computing for multiple concurrent users. In addition, a Windows Terminal Server enables the network administrator to create and assign profiles to individual users or groups. For instance, the administrator can create a common profile that provides access to all common corporate applications. This profile is more than adequate for most users; however, some people might need access to secure applications. For example, the administrator could create a secure profile for accounting users that offers access to all standard applications, as well as the corporate accounting application. When users from the accounting department dial in and launch their Windows Terminal client, they have access to both the standard desktop and the accounting application. Users from other departments have access to the standard desktop only.

Windows Terminal Server solutions are evolving rather rapidly and are well worth investigation, particularly for use by employees from remote sites (such as during travel or from home).

USING A WINDOWS 98 PC AS A DIAL-UP SERVER

Windows 98 can be used as a Dial-Up Server, much like a Windows NT Server or a Windows NT workstation. To install the Windows 98 Dial-Up Server component, utilize the following procedure:

1. Go to the Control Panel and start the Add/Remove Programs applet.
2. Click on the Windows Setup tab and highlight the Communications option. Select Details, and the Communications page opens, as shown in Figure 38.9.

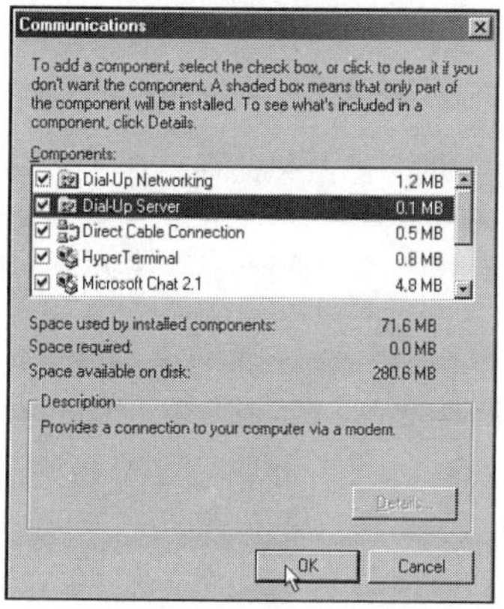

Figure 38.9
The Communications page.

3. Check the box next to the Dial-Up Server option and click OK at the bottom of the page. From the Windows Setup page, click Apply, and the appropriate files are copied to your system.
4. Restart your computer for the changes to take effect. The Dial-Up Server component is successfully installed.

After your computer restarts, you can easily configure it as a Dial-Up Server. Simply open Dial-Up Networking and go to the Connections menu. Click once for the drop-down menu and choose Dial-Up Server to access the Dial-Up Server settings page (see Figure 38.10).

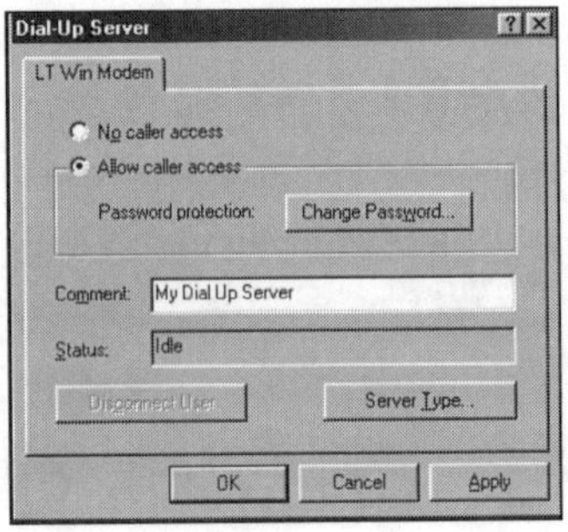

Figure 38.10
The Dial-Up Server
settings page.

Dial-Up Server configuration options are relatively simple:

- You can choose to allow or disallow caller access.
- You can require or change a password as necessary to obtain dial-up access.
- You can provide a comment for your Dial-Up Server.
- You can view the current status of your Dial-Up Server: idle or active.
- You can choose to disconnect any currently connected users.
- You can modify your server type.

All these settings, with the exception of server type modification, are self-explanatory. This option allows you to determine whether or not you want to configure your Dial-Up Server as a standard PPP server or as a Dial-Up Server that supports legacy Microsoft clients (see Figure 38.11).

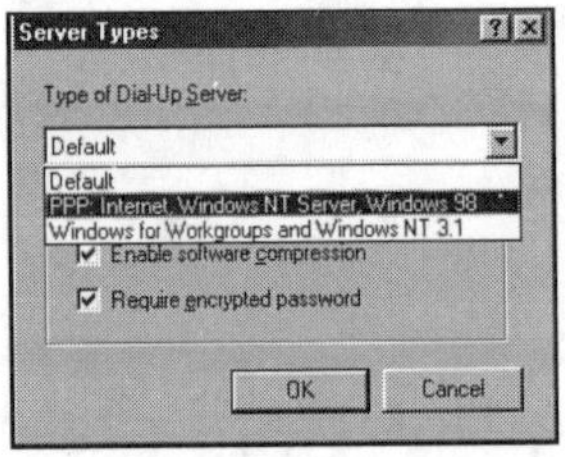

Figure 38.11
Modifying your
Dial-Up Server type.

By default, your workstation supports standard PPP connectivity, much like a Windows NT Remote Access Server; however, you can modify your server type on the Server Types page. In most cases, the default settings are the correct settings.

 If you're having trouble with your Dial-Up Networking Server not answering incoming calls, see "Checking for Hardware Problems with a Dial-Up Networking Server" in the "Troubleshooting" section at the end of this chapter.

USING PPTP TO CREATE VIRTUAL PRIVATE NETWORKS

Virtual private networking, or *VPN*, is a relatively new networking technology that allows you to access a remote network across the Internet or a network attached to the Internet via a secure encrypted connection. In Windows 98, VPN uses Point-to-Point Tunneling Protocol to create a secure tunnel to a PPTP or VPN server over Dial-Up Networking. With this technology, you can easily avoid long-distance charges when traveling or when working from a remote location. For instance, if you use a national Internet provider such as MSN or CompuServe, you normally have access to the Internet via local phone numbers no matter where you travel. If you travel to a remote location, all you need is a local access number for your ISP. After you dial your ISP, you launch a VPN connection to your corporate network across the Internet. When the connection is made successfully, you have access to all resources just as you do with traditional Dial-Up Networking.

Although VPN support is native to Windows 98, it does not install by default. To install VPN support, follow these instructions:

1. From Control Panel, open the Add/Remove Programs applet and then go to the Windows Setup page.

2. From the Windows Setup page, highlight the Communications option and select Details. The bottom Communications option is Virtual Private Networking (see Figure 38.12). Check the box next to this option and click OK at the bottom of the page.

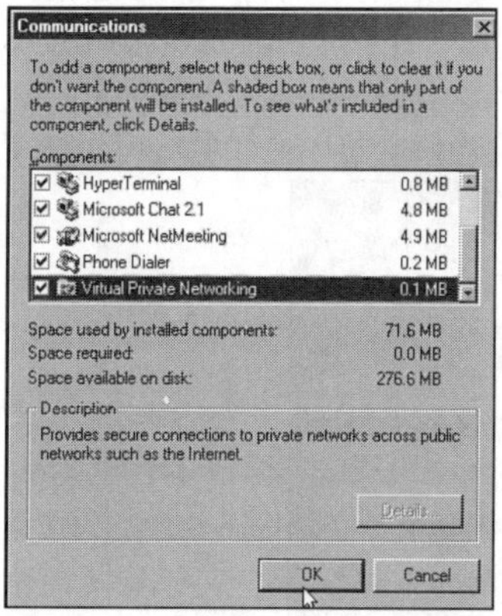

Figure 38.12
Communications options.

3. When you return to the Windows Setup page, click OK again, and all necessary files are copied.

4. Restart the computer to complete the VPN installation.

After VPN is installed on your machine, two new adapters are added to the Network properties. Figure 38.13 shows a machine with a standard Dial-Up Adapter, as well as an additional Dial-Up Adapter to provide VPN support, and the Microsoft Virtual Private Networking adapter that serves as the backbone for all VPN connections.

Figure 38.13
Network properties
with VPN support.

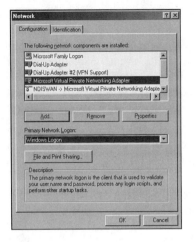

As stated earlier in this section, to make a VPN connection over Dial-Up Networking, you must first connect to the Internet or to a private network that has access to the network you want to attach to. After you make your original connection, you need to make your VPN connection. To create a VPN connection, go to your Dial-Up Networking folder and follow these steps:

1. Start the Make New Connection Wizard by clicking the Make New Connection short-cut. Then, name your connection appropriately. Next move to the field labeled Select a Device and choose Microsoft VPN Adapter from the drop-down list, as shown in Figure 38.14.

Figure 38.14
Selecting the VPN
Adapter.

2. Click Next to move to the VPN Destination window. When connecting to a remote network via VPN, you connect to a remote server much as you do when connecting to RAS. However, with VPN you're already connected to a network (or the Internet), so you simply connect to the server via its DNS name or TCP/IP address. Use this page to enter the VPN server's DNS name or its IP address, as shown in Figure 38.15.

3. After entering the host name or *TCP/IP* address, click the Next button. The next window informs you that you've successfully created your new connection. Click Finish at the bottom of the page to complete the process.

Figure 38.15
Entering the VPN
destination.

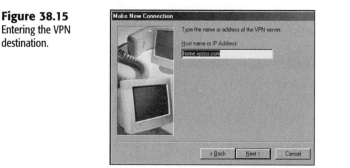

After your VPN connection is complete, you can modify its properties much as you would any other Dial-Up Networking connection. Go to the Dial-Up Networking page, highlight your VPN connection, click the right mouse button, and select Properties from the shortcut menu. You can now modify the host name or IP address or manage the server types configuration. After your VPN connection is completely configured, you're ready to connect.

TROUBLESHOOTING

CHECKING FOR HARDWARE PROBLEMS WITH A DIAL-UP NETWORKING SERVER

Why is the Dial-Up Networking Server not responding to incoming calls?

If you are having a problem with the Dial-Up Networking Server not responding to incoming calls, go through the following steps to ensure that it isn't a hardware problem.

■ If your system has an external modem, check the cable to determine whether it is connected correctly.

■ If your system has an internal modem, make sure the modem card is seated properly in its slot on the motherboard.

■ Regardless of whether your modem is internal or external, use Device Manager to check for IRQ setting conflicts and any COM port setting conflicts. Make changes if necessary.

SECRETS OF MASTERING THE WINDOWS 98 ENVIRONMENT: SECURITY AND THE WINDOWS 98 DIAL-UP SERVER

When using Dial-Up Networking, securing the resources on the server-side of the connection is always a good idea. With Windows 98, for example, you can configure a password that is required for the remote user to connect to the Windows 98 Dial-Up Server. In this case you have two choices for protecting the Windows 98 Dial-Up Server: share-level or user-level security.

When using share-level security, you assign a password on the Windows 98 Dial-Up Server. To gain access to the server, the user must furnish the password. When the secure connection is made, the user browses resources on the Windows 98 Dial-Up Server, with the resources being protected by share-level security. For this method of security to work well, the passwords required for resource access must be kept secret. Unfortunately, secrecy is difficult to maintain when the resource in question is accessed frequently. In that case, with many users having to know the password, the frequency of a security breach is greater.

User-level security is based on restricting access to a resource based on a verifiable user account provided by a Windows NT domain controller or a NetWare server. The user account databases on either of these systems is queried to authenticate the user.

PART **VII**

APPENDIXES

USING WINDOWS MESSAGING AND MICROSOFT FAX

In this chapter

READ THIS FIRST

One of the most popular communications components of Windows 98 is Microsoft Fax. To use Fax under Windows 98, you must have previously installed Fax under Windows 95. During the Windows 98 setup process, Fax is left intact. You can then use Fax to send and receive fax messages.

This appendix assumes you want to run Microsoft Fax under Windows 98, but you have not installed Windows 98 yet. You need to work through this appendix before running Windows 98 Setup, as shown in Appendix B, "Installing and Updating Windows 98." This appendix also assumes you have Windows 95 running and that Windows Messaging (formerly called Microsoft Exchange in early releases of Windows 95) is installed. If you don't have Windows Messaging installed, refer to your Windows 95 documentation.

> **Caution**
>
> If you uninstall Microsoft Fax under Windows 98, you cannot reinstall it under Windows 98. You must reinstall Windows 95, install Fax, and then upgrade to Windows 98 again.

IDENTIFYING THE FEATURES OF MICROSOFT FAX

Microsoft Fax enables you to send and receive faxes through your fax modem on your computer. You can use Microsoft Fax on a separate computer to service one user or connect it to a network to use it as a fax server in a workgroup environment.

Microsoft Fax is part of the Windows Messaging architecture and can replace any fax software you might already have installed on your computer, such as WinFax Pro. Microsoft Fax enables you to create fax messages, add cover pages, and send the messages to a fax machine or another fax modem device. Because Fax is a *Messaging Application Programming Interface (MAPI)*-compliant application, you can use other applications, such as Microsoft Word for Windows 97, to send faxes. Also, if you use Microsoft Fax to send a fax to a fax modem, you can encrypt it with a password to provide a layer of security for the document.

> **Tip #253**
>
> Microsoft Fax includes fax printer drivers so you can print to a fax modem from within any Windows application.

You also can use Microsoft Fax to receive fax messages. A message can be faxed to you by the sender calling your fax number and delivering the fax. Or, if you use fax-back services to receive technical support information, sales information, or other data, you can dial the service and have it download the document to your fax modem by using Microsoft Fax.

> **Tip #254**
>
> You can store fax messages in the Windows Messaging Inbox.

A Microsoft Fax message can be sent in two ways:

- Binary file
- Hard-copy fax

The latter option is the traditional way in which fax messages are sent and received via a fax machine, known as a Group 3 fax machine. The limitation of sending faxes this way is that the recipient cannot edit the document or use it as a binary file unless the document is scanned or keyed into a file. A *binary file* is simply a file created in an application, such as Word for Windows or Lotus 1-2-3 for Windows. Another frustrating aspect of paper faxes is that they can be difficult or impossible to read.

When you use Microsoft Fax to send a binary file to another fax modem, the recipient can view and edit the fax in the application in which it was created and modify it. This feature is handled by Microsoft Fax's *binary file transfer (BFT)* capability. BFT was originally created for the Microsoft At Work program and is now supported by Windows Messaging so that you can create a mail message and attach a binary file to it. Windows for Workgroups 3.11 and other Microsoft At Work–enabled platforms also can receive BFT messages.

One way in which you can take advantage of the BFT feature in Microsoft Fax is to use it with other applications, such as Microsoft Word for Windows. You can, for example, create a Word document and send it as a Microsoft Fax message to another user who has Microsoft Fax installed (and Word for Windows). The recipient receives the message and can read it as a Word document.

If the recipient doesn't have a fax modem card and Microsoft Fax and instead has a Group 3 fax machine, Microsoft Fax automatically prints the Word document as a printed fax image. A problem with sending files this way is the transmission speed and compression feature of the recipient's fax machine. Fax machines are much slower than fax modems, so a large binary file (such as a 50-page Word document) can take a long time to transmit and print on the recipient's fax machine. Before you send a large attached document to someone's fax machine, you might want to test this feature first.

PART

VII

APP

A

FAX MODEM REQUIREMENTS OF MICROSOFT FAX

In addition to having Windows 98 and Windows Messaging installed, you must have a fax modem installed. To use Microsoft Fax, you need the following items (these requirements are based on Microsoft recommendations readily available on its Web site at www.microsoft.com):

- A high-speed fax modem, such as a 33.6Kbps or higher fax modem
- A phone line
- A computer that meets the minimum requirements of Windows 98, but a Pentium-based computer with 32MB of RAM is recommended

When you install Microsoft Fax on a network, your system must include the following items:

- A high-speed fax modem, such as a 33.6Kbps fax modem.
- A phone line.
- At least a Pentium class computer with 32MB of RAM.
- If the computer will be used in double duty as a workstation, you should add 16MB more RAM.

Regardless of whether you set up Microsoft Fax as a standalone or networked fax service, make sure that your fax modem is compatible with Microsoft Fax.

You can use the following fax modems and fax machines with Microsoft Fax:

- Class 1 and Class 2—You need Class 1 or Class 2 fax modems to send BFT messages with attachments. These classes of fax modems also are required to use security features in Microsoft Fax.
- ITU T.30 standard— This standard is for Group 3 fax machines, which are traditional fax machines common in many business environments. Microsoft Fax converts any BFT fax messages to a T.30 nonstandard facilities (NSF) transmission to enable compatibility with these types of fax machines. (ITU stands for International Telecommunications Union.)
- ITU V.17, V.29, V.27ter standards—These types of fax machines are used for high-speed faxes up to 33.6Kbps.
- Microsoft At Work platforms—You need Windows 95, Windows for Workgroups 3.11, or another Microsoft At Work compatible platform to use Microsoft Fax. After being installed on Windows 95, Fax will work on systems that are subsequently upgraded to Windows 98.

Caution

Check the fax modem documentation to ensure that it adheres to the preceding requirements and works with Microsoft Fax. Beware that some fax modems on the market today do not work with Microsoft Fax.

If you are experiencing problems with faxing and your modem, see "Diagnosing Problems with Microsoft Fax and a Modem" in the "Troubleshooting" section at the end of this chapter.

INSTALLING MICROSOFT FAX

To configure Microsoft Fax, you first need to install the Microsoft Fax software onto your system by using the Add/Remove Programs Wizard under Windows 95. You need to have your Windows 95 installation disks or CD-ROM to add these files. Use the following steps to do this:

1. Select Start, Settings, Control Panel.

2. Double-click the Add/Remove Programs icon in Control Panel to display the Add/Remove Programs Properties sheet.

3. Click the Windows Setup page (see Figure A.1).

Figure A.1
Make sure that the Windows Setup tab is active.

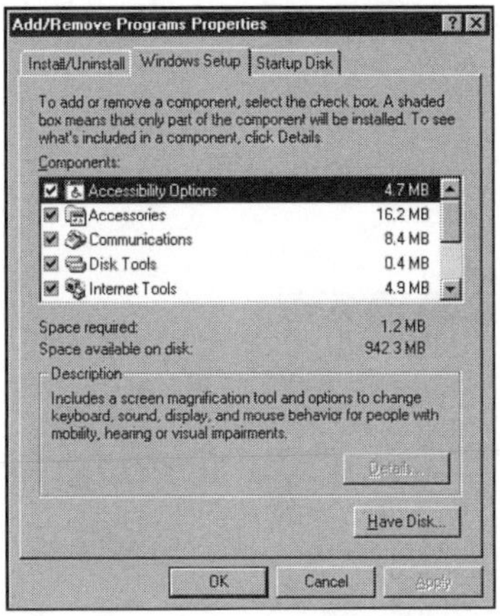

4. Scroll down the Components list box and select Microsoft Fax. Be sure not to click any other component that is already selected, or you will inadvertently remove those programs from your Windows 95 setup.

   If Windows Messaging is not installed, Windows asks whether you want to install it as you install Microsoft Fax. Click Yes.

5. Click OK.

6. When Windows 95 prompts you for a specific Windows 95 Setup disk or CD-ROM, place it in the disk drive. Windows 95 copies the files onto your hard disk and returns you to the desktop when it finishes.

Now that Microsoft Fax is on your system, you can configure Fax as a Windows Messaging information service and start sending faxes. You can configure Microsoft Fax by using either Control Panel or Windows Messaging. Just follow these steps:

1. Select Start, Settings, Control Panel. Double-click the Mail and Fax icon.

   The Windows Messaging Settings Properties sheet appears (see Figure A.2) in which you can configure the Microsoft Fax service.

Note

If you do not see this sheet, click Show Profiles on the Services page to reveal the Windows Messaging Settings profiles set up on your system. Select the Windows Messaging Settings profile and click Properties.

2. Select Microsoft Fax and click the Properties button. The Microsoft Fax Properties sheet displays (see Figure A.3).

PART

VII

APP

A

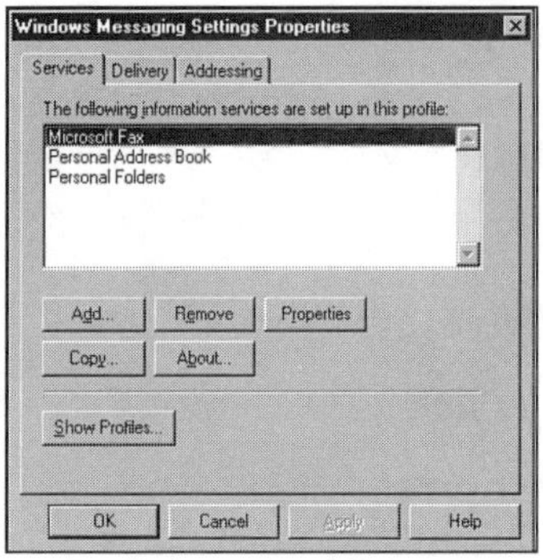

Figure A.2
The Windows
Messaging Settings
Properties sheet con-
tains all the services
you configured during
Windows 95 setup or
when configuring
Windows Messaging.

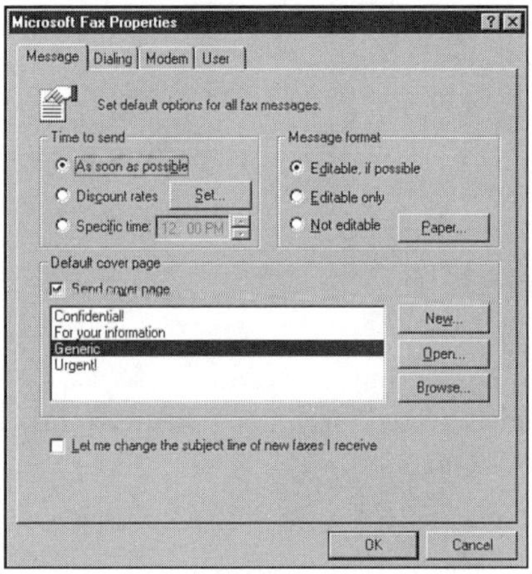

Figure A.3
The Microsoft Fax
Properties sheet
enables you to config-
ure Microsoft Fax.

3. Select the User page (see Figure A.4).

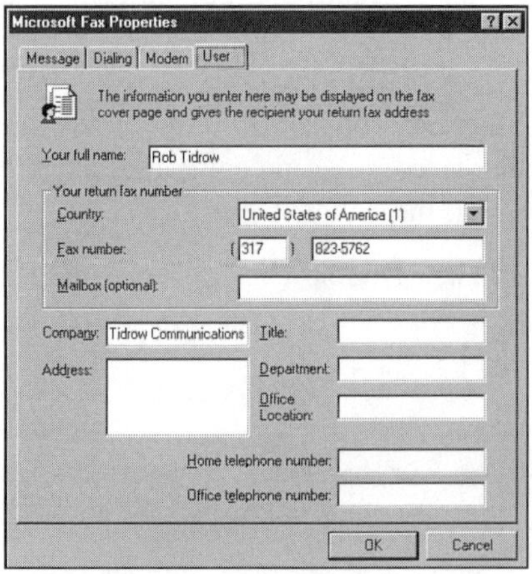

Figure A.4
Fill out the User page
so that your fax
recipients know who
you are.

4. Fill out the User sheet with the information you are asked for. For the most part, the text boxes are self-explanatory. The only text box that might need some explanation is the Mailbox (optional) item.

   The Mailbox (optional) item in the Your Return Fax Number section pertains to in-house mailboxes that you might have set up to receive fax messages. To fill in this box, type the name your administrator has assigned to you, which might be your name, email name, or some other identifier. Otherwise, leave this item blank.

Note

According to Federal Communications Commission (FCC) regulation Part 68, Section 68.318(c)(3), you must include the following items on all fax transmissions either on the top or bottom margins of all pages or on a cover page:

■ Date and time fax is sent

■ Identification of the business, "other entity," or the name of the sender

■ Telephone number of the sending fax machine

---

5. After you fill out the User page, click the Modem page to set up your fax modem to work with Microsoft Fax (see Figure A.5). If your fax modem already has been config-ured for Windows 95 (which it should be if you have an Internet or online service set up), your modem should already appear in the Available Fax Modems list.

   If your modem does not appear in the Available Fax Modems list, click the Add button. From the Add a Fax Modem dialog box, select Fax Modem and click OK. The Install New Modem Wizard helps you add the device.

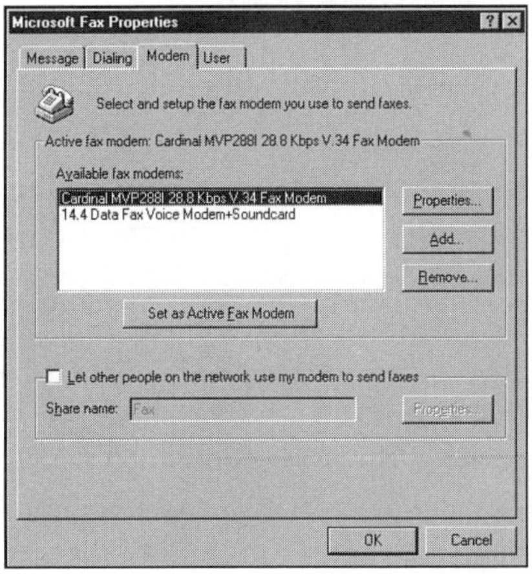

Figure A.5
You must assign a fax modem to work with Microsoft Fax from this page.

6. If more than one modem appears in this dialog box, click the modem you want to use as the default fax modem and click the Set as Active Fax Modem button.

CONFIGURING FAX MODEM OPTIONS

Microsoft Fax is a sophisticated application that you can set up to answer your phone automatically after so many rings, let you answer it manually, or not answer your phone at all (if you tend to send rather than receive most of your faxes). As part of the configuration process, you need to tell Microsoft Fax how to behave during a call, whether it's a received or delivered call. As in most other Windows components, you provide this information by configuring properties (in this case Microsoft Fax properties).

Tip #255	You also can configure these options after you've upgraded to Windows 98.

Follow these steps:

1. On the Modem page, select your fax modem in the Available Fax Modems list and click Properties. This step displays the Fax Modem Properties dialog box, as shown in Figure A.6.

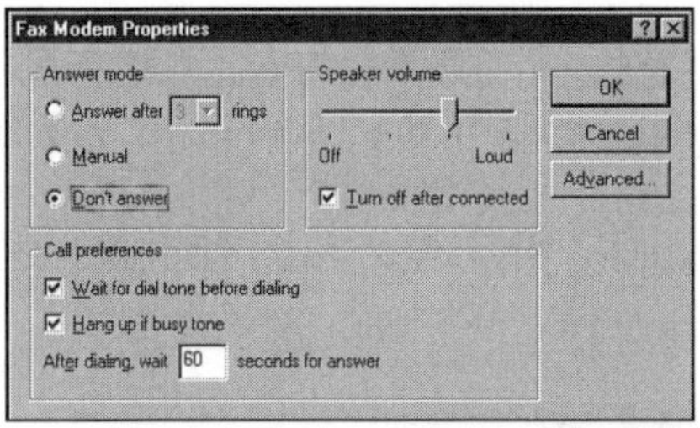

Figure A.6
Set the Microsoft Fax properties for your fax modem.

2. Set up each option, as described in the following list:

   - Answer After—Set this option to have Microsoft Fax answer a fax call after a certain number of rings. For some reason, you cannot set this value for 1 ring or for more than 10. A good number to set this to is 2 or 3.

   - Manual—Use this option if you want Microsoft Fax to display a message onscreen when a call comes in. You then answer the call manually. As a recommendation, use this option only if you have one phone line that you use for both voice and fax. Otherwise, select the Answer After option.

   - Don't Answer—Why have a fax modem if you don't want it to answer incoming faxes? The reason is that you might have to share COM ports with another device. Activate this option if your fax modem shares a port with another device, such as a mouse.

   - Speaker Volume—Set this value to about the middle of the scrollbar so that you can hear when a fax is being received. If the volume is set too high (such as Loud), your ears might start bleeding when a fax begins transmitting.

- <u>T</u>urn Off After Connected—Make sure that a check mark is in this box unless you enjoy listening to two fax devices talk to each other.

- <u>W</u>ait for Dial Tone Before Dialing—For most phone systems, this option needs to be selected to instruct Microsoft Fax to wait until a dial tone is heard before making an outgoing call.

- <u>H</u>ang Up If Busy Tone—Leave this option selected so that your fax modem doesn't stay on the line if the number you're calling is busy.

- Aft<u>e</u>r Dialing, Wait x Seconds for Answer—Many fax machines and fax modems take a few seconds to synchronize after they've been called. This option sets the number of seconds Microsoft Fax waits for the receiving machine to get in sync after it answers the call. The default is 60 seconds, which is a good starting number. Increase this number if you notice Microsoft Fax canceling calls too soon.

Tip #256	Disable the <u>T</u>urn Off After Connected option if you want to hear whether your fax transmission is still connected.

After you fill out this screen, click OK to save these configuration settings and to return to the Fax Modem Properties screen.

If you want to configure more advanced fax modem settings, click the Ad<u>v</u>anced button and read the next section. If not, skip to the "Setting Dialing Properties" section.

 If you're having trouble turning off your fax modem speaker, see "Turning Off the Fax Modem Speaker" in the "Troubleshooting" section at the end of this chapter.

CONFIGURE ADVANCED FAX MODEM SETTINGS

In the Advanced dialog box (see Figure A.7), you have the option of configuring more-sophisticated fax modem settings.

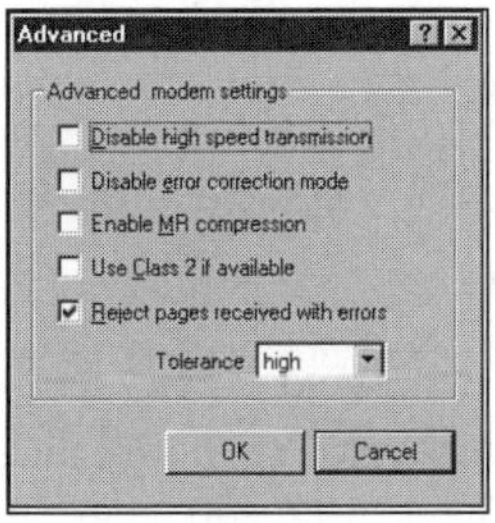

Figure A.7
Use the Advanced dialog box to troubleshoot fax modem problems that you might be experiencing.

These options are detailed in the following list:

- <u>D</u>isable High Speed Transmission—High-speed transmissions are anything over 9600bps. If your fax modem is rated for higher speeds, such as 33.6bps, you might experience transmission errors communicating with other devices. Keep this setting disabled (unchecked) unless your outgoing and incoming faxes are not being handled reliably. Select this option to slow down your transmission speeds.

■ Disable Error Correction Mode—Fax transmissions demand a great deal of cooperation between the sending fax device and the receiving fax device. You need built-in error-correction procedures to make sure that the fax you send is received properly. This option directs Microsoft Fax to send noneditable faxes, either to a fax machine or as a bitmap file, without using error correction. Keep this option disabled unless you cannot send or receive faxes reliably.

■ Enable MR Compression—Select this option to compress the faxes you send or receive to decrease the amount of time you're online. This option appears by default and is grayed out if your fax modem does not support MR compression.

Caution

Compressed faxes are more susceptible to line noise and interference. If a transmission experiences too much line noise or interference, your fax might become corrupted or your fax modem connection might be lost.

■ Use Class 2 If Available—Select this option if you have problems sending or receiving messages using a fax modem that supports Class 1 and Class 2 fax modems. The default is to leave this option disabled.

■ Reject Pages Received with Errors—Most fax transmissions have some sort of problem occur during sending or receiving. You can set Microsoft Fax to have a high tolerance (more errors can occur during transmission), medium tolerance, low tolerance, and very low tolerance (fewer errors can occur during transmission) for errors before rejecting the page being received. The default is to have a high tolerance for errors.

Caution

If you select the Use Class 2 If Available option, you cannot use error correction and you cannot send or receive editable faxes.

Click OK when these settings are ready. Click OK to return to the Modem Properties dialog box.

SETTING DIALING PROPERTIES

Now that you have Microsoft Fax set up to work with your fax modem, you need to start setting user-specific information, such as how Microsoft Fax should dial your phone. Click the Dialing tab in the Microsoft Fax Properties sheet. To begin, click the Dialing Properties button to display the My Locations page (see Figure A.8).

Note

The My Locations information might already be filled in if you set up your modem to make an outgoing call or if any of your Windows Messaging services previously dialed online services, such as the Microsoft Network.

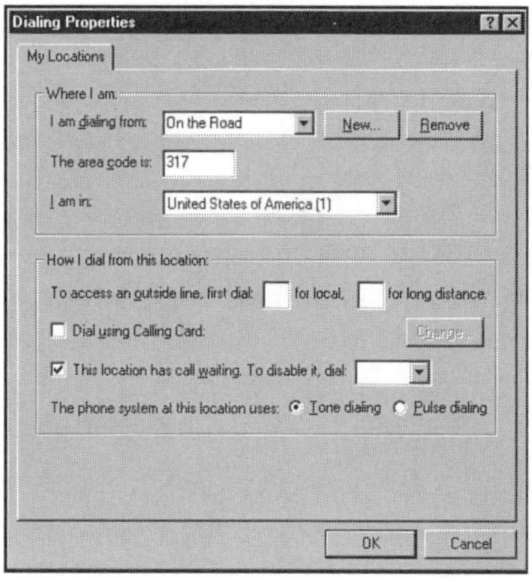

Figure A.8
Set your dialing options, such as area code, calling card numbers, and other user-specific options, in the My Locations page.

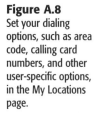

Microsoft Fax enables you to use several different configurations, depending on where you are when you send a fax. If your computer always stays in one place (such as in your office or home), you generally need to configure only one location. If, however, you use a portable PC and travel from work to home and to other places, you can configure several locations to dial with different configuration settings.

When you are in your office, for instance, you might not need to use a calling card to make a long-distance phone call to send a fax. You can set up Microsoft Fax to use a configuration that doesn't require a calling card to be entered first. On the other hand, your office phone system might require you to dial an initial number to get an outside line (such as 9). You can place this information in the Microsoft Fax configuration setting that you use from your office.

Another scenario that requires a different dialing procedure occurs when you stay in a hotel. You might always want to place any fax calls you make from a hotel room on a calling card. Set up Microsoft Fax to use your calling card number for these calls. All your configurations are saved in Windows 95 (and eventually Windows 98 when you upgrade to it) and can be retrieved each time you use Microsoft Fax.

The following steps show you how to create a new dialing location in Microsoft Fax:

1. Click the Dialing tab on the Microsoft Fax Properties sheet.
2. Click the Dialing Properties button and click New. The Create New Location dialog box appears (see Figure A.9).

Note

Windows 98 might not display the Create New Location dialog box. Instead, you just enter the new location name in the I am Dialing From drop-down box.

3. Enter a new name for the location, such as Office or On the Road. Click OK. You return to the Dialing Properties sheet (refer to Figure A.8).

PART

VII

APP

A

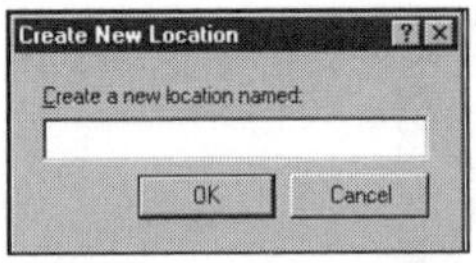

Figure A.9
Enter a name for your new location in the Create New Location dialog box.

4. In The Area Code Is text box, enter the area code from which you are calling. You might need to change or update this if you are not sure of the area code in which you are staying, such as when you are traveling.

   To tell Windows which phone numbers in your area code to dial as long distance, click the Dialing Rules button (or Area Code Rules button—this dialog box is slightly different from the one shown in Figure A.10) to display the Dialing Rules dialog box (see Figure A.10). Click the New button and enter the prefix of the phone number Windows should dial as long distance. Click OK. Click OK again to return to the Dialing Properties page.

Tip #257

If you can dial any phone numbers in other area codes as local numbers, click the New button at the bottom of the Dialing Rules dialog box. Fill out the New Area Code and Prefix dialog box. Click OK twice to return to the Dialing Properties page.

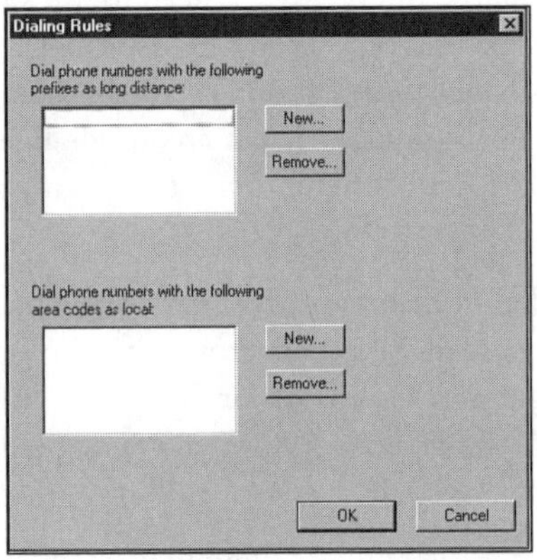

Figure A.10
For phone numbers in your area code that Windows should dial as long distance, fill out the Dialing Rules dialog box.

5. Select the country in which you are calling.

6. Enter the number (if any) you need to dial to get an outside line (such as 9) and to make a long-distance call (usually 1).

7. Click the Dial Using Calling Card for Long Distance option to enter your calling card information. Click the Change button to display the Change Calling Card dialog box (see Figure A.11). Click the drop-down list and select your card name. Fill out the Calling Card Phone Number and PIN Number fields. Click OK.

Tip #258

With Windows 98, the Calling Card dialog box might display instead of the Change Calling Card dialog box shown in Figure A.11. If the Calling Card dialog box does display, you must also fill out the PIN Number field.

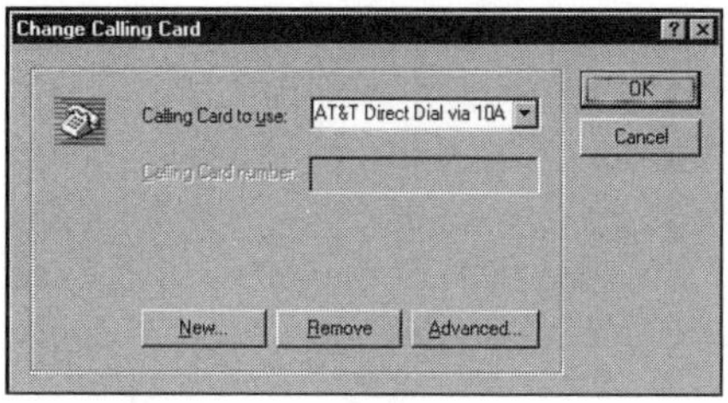

Figure A.11
Microsoft Fax can use calling card numbers to place your fax calls.

Note

To set up calling scripts for your calling card, click the Long Distance Usage or International Usage buttons to display the Calling Card dialog box. In this dialog box, select an action from the Dial drop-down box, such as Calling Card phone number. Next, select a time or tone action in the Then Wait For drop-down list, such as 10 seconds. Continue selecting actions and times to create your calling script. As you create a script, you might need to walk through the process and write down each step.

8. Check the box next to To Disable Call Waiting, Dial if your phone line uses call waiting. From the drop-down list, select the code your phone system uses to temporarily turn off call waiting. You need to obtain this code from your local phone company because each system uses a different code. Microsoft Fax provides three common codes in the drop-down list box next to this option: *70, 70#, and 1170. After you finish faxing and your fax modem hangs up, call waiting is turned back on.

Note

Most hotels use their own phone system to get outside lines, so you must enter those numbers when you know what they are.

9. Select Dial Using Tone Dial or Pulse Dial to indicate which type of phone service your phone line uses.
10. Click OK when you have this location set up. You can create as many locations as you need.

SETTING TOLL PREFIXES AND RETRY OPTIONS

Now that you have the locations set up, you need to tell Microsoft Fax which calls in your local calling area are toll calls. To do so, click the Toll Prefixes button on the Dialing page. In the Toll Prefixes dialog box (see Figure A.12), click all the numbers from the Local Phone Numbers list to the Dial 1-*xxx* First list (*xxx* is your area code) that require you to dial your area code first. Click the Add button to place numbers from the list on the left into the list on the right. Click OK when you finish with this dialog box.

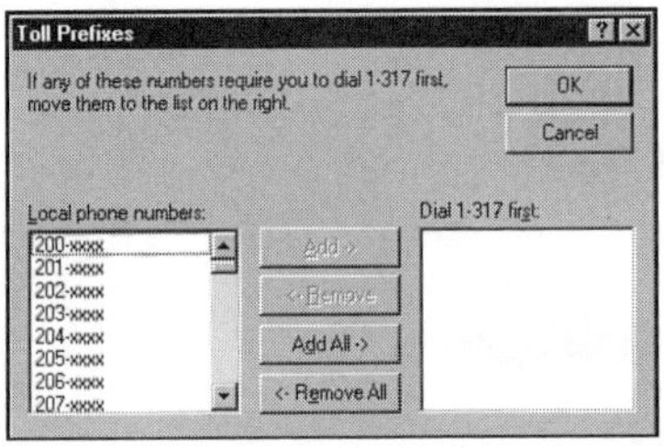

Figure A.12
Tell Microsoft Fax which prefixes in your local calling area code are long-distance calls.

Every time you call a fax number, you're not going to be lucky enough to get through. You'll get busy signals; the fax on the other side of the line won't be ready to accept your call; or, your fax modem and the recipient's fax device won't synchronize properly.

In these cases, you need Microsoft Fax to keep retrying the number you're calling. In the Dialing dialog box, set the Number of Retries option to the number of times you want Microsoft Fax to dial the number before quitting. The default is three times. You also need to tell Microsoft Fax the amount of time you want it to wait before it tries the number again. In the Time Between Retries box, set this time in minutes. The default is 2 minutes.

Now that you've taken care of the dialing options, you are ready to configure the default settings for your fax messages. Click the Message page.

CONFIGURING MESSAGE OPTIONS

The Message page (see Figure A.13) has three main areas:

- Time to Send
- Message Format
- Default Cover Page

The following sections discuss these options in detail.

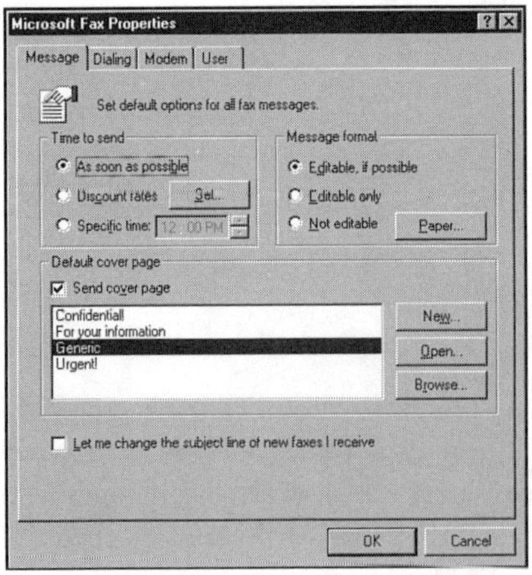

Figure A.13
Microsoft Fax lets you customize the way your default fax message looks by using settings in the Message page.

SETTING TIME TO SEND OPTIONS

You might not always want to send a fax message as soon as you create it. You might want to create a message, or several messages, and then send them at specific times, such as when you are going to lunch or when long-distance rates are lower. Microsoft Fax enables you to set the time you send fax messages in one of three ways:

- As Soon as Possible—This setting is the default; use this option to send faxes immediately after you create them.

- Discount Rates—Use this option to send your fax message(s) during predefined hours when long-distance tolls are lower. Click the Set button to set the discount rates start and end times. On the Set Discount Rates dialog box, the default discounted rate hours are set between 5 p.m. and 8 a.m. Click OK when you either set the appropriate times for your long-distance carrier or agree to keep the default settings.

- Specific Time—Set this option to an exact time to send any fax messages you have in the outbox.

CONFIGURING FAX MESSAGE FORMATS

Microsoft Fax can send fax messages in two primary formats: editable formats (as a binary file) and noneditable formats ("hard copy" faxes). Editable fax messages can be manipulated much the same as a word processing document can be changed. A Microsoft Fax editable fax can be received and edited only by a recipient who is also using Microsoft Fax. A noneditable fax can be received on a standard facsimile machine.

In the Message Format area, you set the default way in which your messages are sent. Select the Editable, If Possible option (the default) when you send faxes to both fax modems and regular fax machines. If your fax messages always must be edited by the recipient or if you want to encrypt your fax message with a password, enable the Editable Only option. (See "Setting Up Security" later in this chapter for information on using security options in Microsoft Fax.) This option sends all your fax messages as binary faxes. When using the Editable Only option, if the recipient does not have Microsoft Fax installed, the fax is not sent. Microsoft Fax places a message in your Windows Messaging Inbox folder telling you that the message was not sent.

When you're sure that your recipient doesn't have Microsoft Fax installed or if you don't want your fax to be edited, send it as Not Editable. Even if the receiving device is a fax modem, the fax message is sent as a bitmap image, so the recipient cannot directly edit the message. If, however, the user has an optical character recognition (OCR) program, he or she can export the faxed image or text as a file to edit in another application.

With the first and third options, you also can specify the type of paper used to print your fax message. Click the Paper button to display the Message Format dialog box and adjust paper settings, such as size, image quality, and orientation. For most faxes, the default settings are fine. Click OK when your paper settings are configured.

CONFIGURING DEFAULT COVER PAGES

You can opt to send a cover page with your fax message. Click the Send Cover Page option to send a cover page with all your fax messages. Microsoft Fax includes four standard cover pages you can use:

- Confidential
- For Your Information!
- Generic
- Urgent

Select a cover page that suits your needs. Generic is the default. As Microsoft Fax creates your fax message and prepares it to be sent, Fax fills in data fields on the cover page with information, such as recipient name and fax number, your name, and so on.

Tip #259	Select a cover page name and click Open to see what a cover page looks like.

Click the New button to create new cover pages from Microsoft Fax's Cover Page Editor. Use the Browse button to locate cover page files (denoted as CPE) on your computer.

CONFIGURING ONE MORE MESSAGE OPTION

One final option on the Message page is Let Me Change the Subject Line of New Faxes I Receive. Use this option to change the subject line of any faxes you receive. Because all incoming faxes are stored in the Windows Messaging Inbox, the subject (if it contains a subject) appears in the subject field there. This option gives you control over what appears in the subject field, enabling you to organize your messages as they come in. On the other hand, you must perform one more action as each fax message is received. The default is to leave this option disabled.

Click OK to save all the Microsoft Fax properties and to return to the MS Windows Messaging Setting Properties dialog box.

Congratulations! You're ready to send a fax using Microsoft Fax.

CONFIGURING A SHARED FAX MODEM

To reduce the number of fax devices and dedicated phone lines for fax services, many businesses have one centralized fax machine that everyone shares. Because of their convenience and ease of use, most people do not complain too much about walking to a fax machine to send a message or document to another fax machine. Microsoft Fax enables you to extend this sharing of fax devices by letting users in a network environment share a fax modem.

> **Note**
>
> You must have File and Printer Sharing for Microsoft Networks to share a fax modem across the network. See Chapter 21, "Configuring Hardware," for information on enabling File and Printer Sharing for Microsoft Networks.

The computer that contains the shared fax modem is called the *fax server* and is not required to be a dedicated PC. A fax server can be anyone's computer that is set up in a workgroup of other Windows 98 users. When a fax is received on the fax server, it then is routed to the recipient in the workgroup via Windows Messaging (or by attaching it as an email message using an email application such as cc:Mail).

> **Caution**
>
> Microsoft Fax cannot automatically route fax messages to workgroup recipients. They must be manually delivered to their recipients.

SETTING UP A FAX SERVER

Again, make sure that Windows Messaging is installed and that a fax modem is installed and working on the fax server before completing these steps.

Start Windows Messaging by double-clicking the Inbox icon; then perform the following steps:

1. Choose Tools, Microsoft Fax Tools, Options. The Microsoft Fax Properties sheet appears (refer to Figure A.3).
2. Click the Modem tab.
3. Click the Let Other People on the Network Use My Modem to Send Faxes option.
4. If the Select Drive dialog box appears, select the drive that the network fax will use from the drop-down list and click OK.
5. Enter the name of the shared directory in the Share Name text box.
6. Click the Properties button to configure the shared modem's properties. The NetFax dialog box appears so that you can tell Microsoft Fax the name of the shared fax modem folder (see Figure A.14). The NetFax dialog box also enables you to set up passwords for users to connect to the fax server.

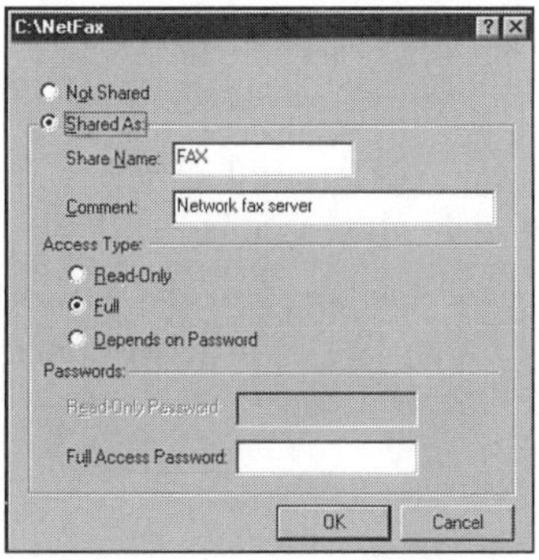

Figure A.14
Use the NetFax dialog box to set the shared fax folder and other settings for sharing a fax modem.

Note

If the Properties button does not work, switch to Control Panel and double-click the Network icon. Click the File and Print Sharing button on the Configuration page of the Network sheet. Next, select both options in the File and Print Sharing dialog box for the Microsoft network service. You then need to restart Windows 98 for these settings to take effect. These settings enable sharing on your system, so you can share the fax modem with other users in your workgroup.

7. In the Share Name field, type the name of the shared folder for the fax server. Microsoft Fax displays the name of the network fax shared directory as the default. When a user in your workgroup wants to use this folder, he or she searches for this folder on your computer on your network.

8. In the Comment field, enter a string that helps users identify the shared fax.

9. In the Access Type section, select the type of access you want users to have to the shared folder. The default is Full. Select Read-Only if you want users to read, but not modify, items in the folder. The Depends on Password option is used if you want to give different people different rights to the shared folder. You can give one password— the Read-Only Password—to some users. You then can give another password—the Full Access Password—to users who can have full access to the folder.

10. Fill out the Passwords section as necessary, based on your selections in step 9.

11. Click OK.

For users in the workgroup to access the fax server, they must know the fax server's full network name. The name is formed by joining the server's computer name (defined in the Network option in Control Panel) with the shared folder name, for example, \\RTIDROW\FAX.

SETTING UP A FAX SERVER CLIENT

In addition to configuring a fax server to share a fax modem, you must also configure the client's access to the server. The clients are those users who want to share the fax server. Start Windows Messaging on the client machine and then follow these steps:

1. From Windows Messaging, choose Tools, Microsoft Fax Tool, Options.

2. In the Microsoft Fax Properties sheet, click the Modem page.

3. In Modem properties, click the Add button to display the Add a Fax Modem dialog box (see Figure A.15).

4. In the Add a Fax Modem dialog box, select Network Fax Server and then click OK. The Connect to Network Fax Server dialog box appears, as shown in Figure A.16.

5. In the Connect to Network Fax Server dialog box, type the network name of the fax server, such as \\RTIDROW\FAX. If you do not know the network name, ask your network administrator. Click OK.

Figure A.15
The Add a Fax Modem dialog box includes the types of fax modems to which you can connect.

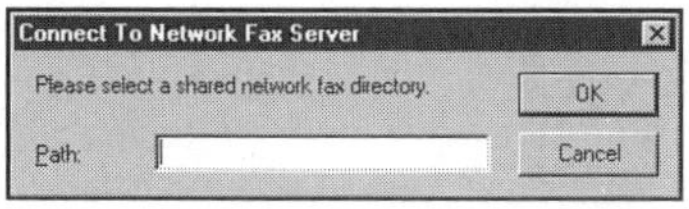

Figure A.16
To set up a client to use a shared fax server, enter the path of the shared fax server in this dialog box.

6. In the Microsoft Fax Properties dialog box, click the server name and then click the Set as Active Fax Modem button.

7. Click OK.

You might have to reboot your computer for the settings to take effect.

SETTING UP SECURITY

One of the most discussed topics in the computer industry is security. You hear about security and the Internet. You hear about LAN security. You hear about voice-mail security. Microsoft Fax enables you to securely send fax messages using public key encryption developed by one of the leaders in security, RSA Inc. Microsoft Fax also enables you to password encrypt and use digital signatures on your messages with confidence. The security features, of course, extend only to sending digital messages and files, not to printed or hard-copy faxes. These types of faxes are still subject to the eyes of anyone who happens to be walking by the fax machine when your transmission comes through.

> **Note**
>
> A *digital signature* is an electronic version of your signature. For most business transactions, such as purchase requests and employee time sheets, a signature is required to process the request. You can use a secure digital signature to "sign" requests, time sheets, and other sensitive documents.

One way to secure your fax messages is to password protect them as you send them. When you create a fax message and the Send Options for This Message dialog box appears, set the type of security you want to have for your fax message. Click the Security button to display the Message Security Options dialog box (see Figure A.17).

Tip #260

Share your password so that the recipient can open and read your fax message.

PART

VII

APP

A

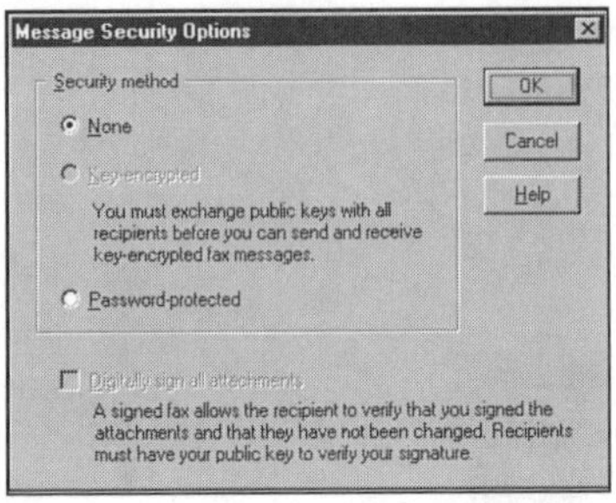

Figure A.17
You can set the type of security for your fax message in this dialog box.

If you have not set up public key encryption, you have to do so before you can use the <u>K</u>ey-Encrypted option or use a digital signature on your message. You can, however, secure the fax message with a password by choosing the <u>P</u>assword-Protected option. Figure A.18 shows the Fax Security—Password Protection dialog box that you need to fill out when you want to send a message with a password.

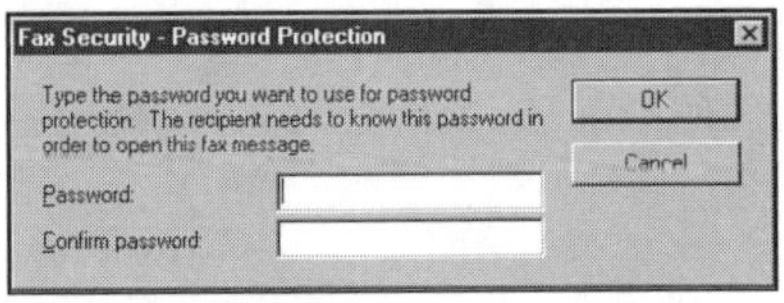

Figure A.18
To password protect your faxes, enter a password in this dialog box.

SETTING UP KEY ENCRYPTION

A *key-encrypted message* uses a public key to unlock the message for viewing. This public key is made available to your fax recipients (who must also have Microsoft Fax installed) so that only they can open your document.

You must create a public key in Windows Messaging. To do so, choose <u>T</u>ools, Microsoft Fa<u>x</u> Tools, <u>A</u>dvanced Security. The Advanced Fax Security dialog box appears (see Figure A.19). In this dialog box, if you are creating a public key for the first time, the only option you can choose is the last one, <u>N</u>ew Key Set.

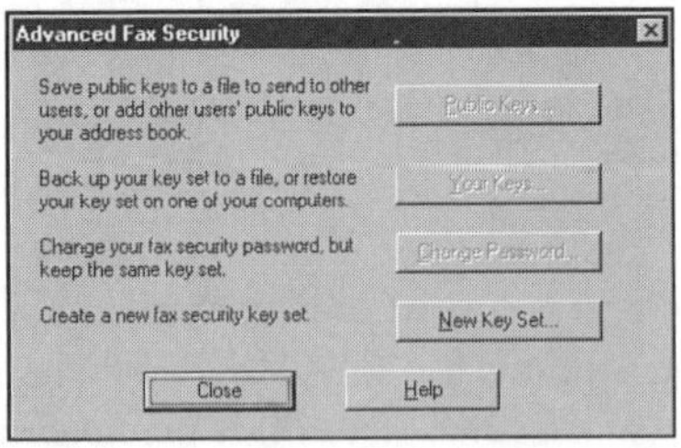

Figure A.19
Create a public key.

In the Fax Security—New Key Set dialog box, type a password in the <u>P</u>assword field and then retype it in the <u>C</u>onfirm Password field (see Figure A.20). As you would expect, the password is not displayed; only a string of ***** denotes your password. Don't forget this password; it is now your public key. Click OK to have Windows Messaging create a new public key set on your system. An information box tells you that it might take a few moments to create your key set.

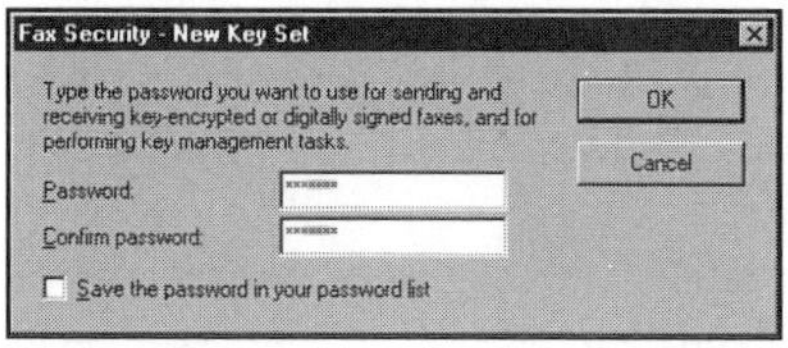

Figure A.20
You must enter a new password to create a new public key.

Sharing Public Keys

After you create a public key set, you need to distribute it to your fax recipients for them to read your key-encrypted messages. Do so by clicking the Public Keys button in the Advanced Fax Security dialog box (choose Tools, Microsoft Fax Tools, Advanced Security if you've already closed this dialog box). When the Fax Security—Managing Public Keys dialog box appears, click Save. This step saves your public key to a file so that you can send the key to other recipients.

In the Fax Security—Save Public Keys dialog box, click the name or names of the public keys you want to share. As a minimum, you should click your name here. Click OK and in the resulting window select a name and folder in which to store the keys. This file has an .AWP extension. To finish, you need to send this file to your recipients either via an attachment to a Windows Messaging message or on a floppy disk.

Receiving Public Keys

When you send your public key to a recipient, that person needs to import the AWP file into Microsoft Fax. Likewise, when you receive a public key from someone, you need to import it into your Microsoft Fax settings and add it to your address book. This step enables you to read key-encrypted messages from those users.

After you receive an AWP file from someone, store it on your system and click the Add button in the Fax Security—Managing Public Keys dialog box. Locate the filename that contains the public keys and click Open. Click the key or keys that you want to add.

Troubleshooting

Diagnosing Problems with Microsoft Fax and a Modem

Why can't Microsoft Fax open my modem for use?

To diagnose problems with a modem, you can test your fax modem by selecting Modems from Control Panel. In the Modem Properties sheet, select the Diagnostics page. In the list of ports, select the port to which your fax modem is connected. Click More Info to run a diagnostic of your fax modem. If everything is okay, you get a report of your modem's properties. If your fax modem is awaiting a call, you receive a message saying that the port is already open. You need to exit from Windows Messaging and rerun the modem diagnostics to get an accurate reading.

If you still experience problems, you need to open the Modem Properties sheet and change some of the advanced settings. You might have to experiment with these settings to find one that works for your modem. You also should make sure that you have a Microsoft Fax service set up for Windows Messaging.

TURNING OFF THE FAX MODEM SPEAKER

I don't want to hear static noise while the modems synchronize. What can I do?

If you do not want to hear the static noise while the modems synchronize, you may wish to turn off the modem speaker. To do this, double-click Mail in Control Panel. Click Microsoft Fax on the MS Windows Messaging Settings Properties sheet and click the Properties button. Select the Modems page and click the Properties button. In the Speaker Volume area, move the slider bar to the Off position.

INSTALLING AND UPDATING WINDOWS 98

In this chapter

PREPARING TO INSTALL WINDOWS 98

Windows 98 performance hinges on the hardware of your computer. The minimum system requirements call for a 486DX processor with at least 4MB of RAM. If you choose to install Windows 98 on a system with these specifications, the following recommendations will speed up installation:

- Run setup from within Windows 95 or Windows 3.x. Try to avoid running the setup from MS-DOS.
- Remove any disk compression from your hard drive.
- If you are installing from floppy disks, extract the floppy disks to your hard drive and run setup from the hard drive instead of the floppy disks.
- If, during setup, you notice that the busy light is flashing on an empty floppy disk drive, insert a blank formatted disk into the drive.

If you have problems during setup, increase the size of your permanent swap file.

Regardless of the system you are installing Windows 98 on, you should follow these steps as well:

1. Perform a thorough scan of your system for viruses. Ensure that the virus detection software you use has the most current update of virus definitions available.
2. Disable any screen savers configured for your system.
3. Disable any antivirus detection software before proceeding with the Windows 98 installation.
4. Run ScanDisk and fix any problems that it finds on your hard drive.

You should also make sure that any components installed on your system are on the Windows 98 Hardware Compatibility List (HCL). The HCL contains components that have been tested to work with Windows 98. The most current version of the HCL can be found on the Microsoft Web site (http://www.microsoft.com).

Although installation on a 386 machine is possible, performance will be poor. A computer running Windows 98 with this type of hardware configuration should be considered only for the most basic of operations, such as simple word processing or sending and receiving electronic mail. For users who plan to use their computers to run more than one application at a time or who often work with large documents, a machine with at least the following specifications is highly recommended.

- A Pentium computer
- At least 16MB of RAM
- At least 100MB of free disk space
- A double-speed CD-ROM drive
- SVGA video capability
- A mouse pointing device

Note

Before beginning, check the Windows 98 installation CD for the SETUP.TXT file. This file contains last-minute setup information and warnings about possible problems that you may encounter during setup with specific pieces of hardware.

The next three sections provide specific information for upgrading from Windows 3.x, upgrading from Windows 95, and installing Windows 98 on a clean hard drive.

UPGRADING FROM WINDOWS 3.X

Windows 3.x users need to take the following additional steps before upgrading:

1. Back up your CONFIG.SYS and AUTOEXEC.BAT files.
2. Make sure that all of your system components (sound cards and so on) are on the Windows 98 HCL.
3. Familiarize yourself with the new Windows 98 interface and basic tasks in Chapter 1.

To begin installation, use File Manager to run SETUP.EXE from the Windows 98 CD-ROM. The menu screens that appear during installation might look slightly different than if you were installing from Windows 95; most notably, the older full-screen version of ScanDisk runs to check your hard drive for errors. Your program groups are migrated to the Programs menu of Windows 98. You might need to manually edit your CONFIG.SYS and AUTOEXEC.BAT files to properly configure legacy devices that are not directly supported under Windows 98.

UPGRADING FROM WINDOWS 95

Upgrading from Windows 95 is fairly straightforward. Insert the Windows 98 CD-ROM into your computer. If AutoRun does not begin installation, go to Explorer and run SETUP.EXE. All program groups are migrated during the installation process.

There have been three releases of Windows 95: Windows 95 Build 950, Windows 95 Build 950A, and Windows 95 Build 950B. Windows 98 will upgrade all three releases.

The original release, Build 950, is identical to the product that has been sold commercially since August 1995. Although there have been service releases since then, no new full installations have been made available to the public. Two original equipment manufacturer (OEM) releases (950A and 950B) have been made available for preinstallation on new personal computers by OEMs. You can check to see which version you have by right-clicking on the My Computer icon and selecting Properties. Figure B.1 shows a typical System Properties dialog box.

These OEM releases include many bug fixes and patches to the original Windows 95. Some of these fixes have been made available to previous owners of Windows 95 through the Microsoft Web site (http://www.microsoft.com/windows95/downloads/), but others are available only preinstalled on new computers. The OEM releases also include various interface modifications. All these fixes are included in Windows 98. In addition, most devices that were supported under Windows 95 are also supported in Windows 98.

PART

VII

APP

B

Figure B.1

You can check the version number in Windows 95 by opening the System Properties dialog box.

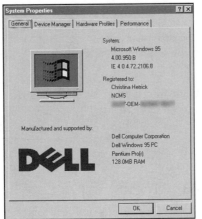

INSTALLING WINDOWS 98 ON A NEWLY FORMATTED HARD DRIVE

If you want (or need) to install Windows 98 on a freshly formatted hard drive follow these steps:

1. Create a new system disk by formatting a new disk and running SYS.COM from the command line. Or, using the Explorer, place a check in the Copy System Files check box.

2. Copy the Fixed Disk utility (FDISK.EXE), FORMAT.COM, and SYS.COM files over to the system disk.

3. Copy your CONFIG.SYS and AUTOEXEC.BAT utilities to your system disk, along with any files referenced in these files (especially those related to your CD-ROM drive).

4. Boot your machine with the floppy disk and make sure you can access your CD-ROM drive.

Caution

FDISK.EXE erases all the information on your hard drive. Make sure you have backed up important data from your hard drive before you use this utility.

5. Run FDISK.EXE, removing the partition from your hard drive and creating a new one.

6. Format your hard drive using FORMAT.COM from the floppy disk and make it bootable by running SYS.COM on it.

7. Copy your CONFIG.SYS and AUTOEXEC.BAT files and your CD-ROM support files to your hard drive.

8. Remove the floppy disk and reboot your machine from your hard drive.

9. Change directories to your CD drive, insert the Windows 98 CD, and run SETUP.EXE to continue with the installation. If you are installing onto a newly formatted hard drive, you also need to choose an installation option during Windows 98 Setup.

Windows 98 Setup offers four installation types:

- Typical—Installs the components that most users find useful (requires 186MB)
- Portable—Is intended for laptop users (requires 175MB)
- Compact—Installs no extra components (requires 159MB)
- Custom—Enables you to pick and choose among components (requires up to 285MB)

You must choose one of these setup options when you install Windows 98 on a new system. If you upgrade, Windows 98 automatically upgrades previous versions of any Windows components that it finds.

COMMON INSTALLATION STEPS

The following steps are common to the installation procedure regardless of whether you are upgrading or installing to an empty hard drive. The Windows 98 installation process is driven by an easy-to-use wizard. The wizard guides you through the necessary steps for a successful upgrade.

To begin the installation of Windows 98 from the CD, follow these steps:

1. Run SETUP.EXE from the Windows 98 CD-ROM. The Windows 98 Setup Wizard appears (see Figure B.2).

The status of the
installation process

Time left in the
installation process

Figure B.2
The Windows 98
Setup Wizard's
welcome screen.

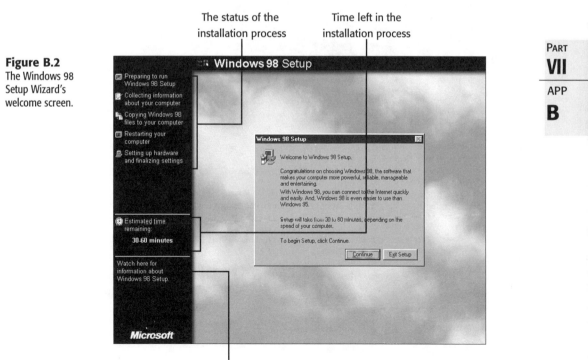

Message window

2. Click Continue to proceed.

3. The Microsoft licensing agreement appears (see Figure B.3). After reading through the licensing agreement, select the I Accept the Agreement option. Then click Next to continue.

Figure B.3
The Microsoft License Agreement screen.

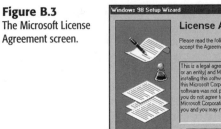

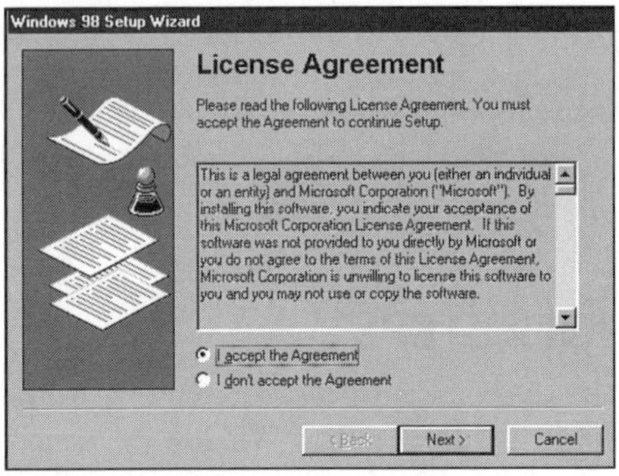

4. The Setup Wizard determines whether you have enough hard drive space to complete the installation. If you don't have enough disk space, the Setup Wizard displays a screen like the one shown in Figure B.4 to let you know how much disk space you need to free up to continue with the installation. Click Next to continue.

Figure B.4
The Not Enough Disk Space notification screen.

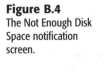

5. The Setup Wizard asks whether you want to save your old system files (see Figure B.5). The system files are saved in a compressed format that takes up approximately 50MB of disk space. You must choose Yes if you think you might want to uninstall Windows 98 in the future. Then click Next.

Because the system files must be saved to a local hard drive (network drives and floppy disks won't work), if you choose Yes, you are prompted to select a disk drive to which the files are saved. At this point, you also need to choose your country so that your Internet Channels can be configured correctly.

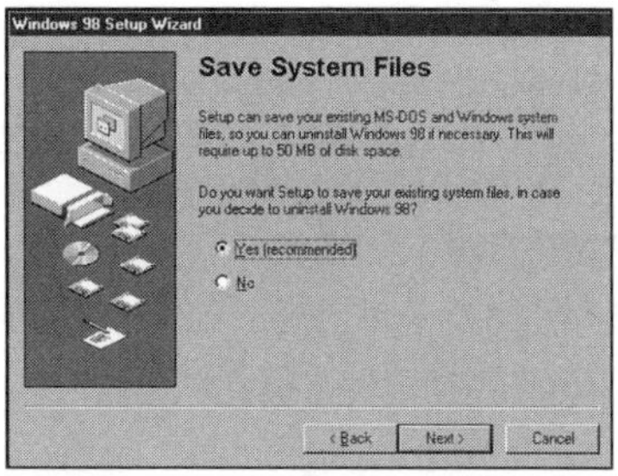

Figure B.5
This is the point of no return if you choose not to save the previous version of your system files.

Note

You are not given the option to save your system files if you are upgrading over an earlier beta version of Windows 98, if you are installing to a new directory, or if you are running a version of MS-DOS earlier than 5.0.

Caution

Any time a new operating system is released, some programs need to be updated to work properly. No matter how sure you are that you do *not* want to go back to Windows 95 or Windows 3.x, you might run into a situation when you have to. (Uninstalling Windows 98 is covered later in this chapter.) Remember, too, that you always have the option of removing the old system files after you're confident with Windows 98.

6. The Windows 98 Setup Wizard begins to automatically detect the hardware that is installed in your computer.

   Next, you're prompted to create a Windows 98 startup disk (see Figure B.6). Click Next, and you get the chance to skip startup disk creation. (You can click Cancel if you don't want to create a backup disk, but that option is not recommended.)

Figure B.6
The Emergency Startup Disk screen.

PART

VII

APP

B

7. When it finishes collecting the necessary information, the Setup Wizard gives you one last chance to change your mind (see Figure B.7). Click Back to go back and change any of your selections or click Next to begin the process of copying files to your hard drive.

Figure B.7
Windows give you a final chance to change your options before proceeding with the file copying portion of the Windows 98 installation.

As the file copy process progresses, the Setup Wizard keeps you updated on how long setup will take.

Your system goes through a cycle of hardware detection, and your computer reboots a number of times until it has detected all legacy and Plug and Play components.

When the Setup Wizard finishes detecting the hardware on your computer, Windows 98 boots again and displays the Welcome screen. The Welcome screen gives you the opportunity to register Windows 98 with Microsoft, provides a tour of new features, helps you configure the system scheduler to automatically fine-tune your Windows 98 system, and lets you read the release notes.

Caution

The first time you run the system tuner after installation, you have the option of upgrading your hard disk to FAT32 format. FAT32 optimizes the way in which Windows 98 stores data on your hard drive. If you choose to upgrade to FAT32, only computers running Windows 98 or Windows NT 5.0 will be able to read the data on your hard drive.

ADVANCED INSTALLATION TECHNIQUES

Windows 98 includes some installation options that most home users can ignore.

USING CUSTOM SETUP MODE

Custom setup mode allows you to preselect options, making installation easier when rolling out Windows 98 to a large number of machines. This feature is most beneficial to companies who want to roll out Windows 98 to numerous machines with a minimum of administrative intervention. By limiting choices, network administrators can automate installation by creating custom setup scripts.

To create a custom setup, follow these steps:

1. Install Windows 98 on a test computer with the configuration you want to replicate.
2. Install the Batch setup from the Windows 98 Resource Kit.
3. From the Start menu, run Microsoft Batch 98.
4. Use the Batch program to create an INF file that will install Windows 98 with options you select. Figure B.8 shows the first Batch screen.

Figure B.8
The Windows 98
Batch setup utility.

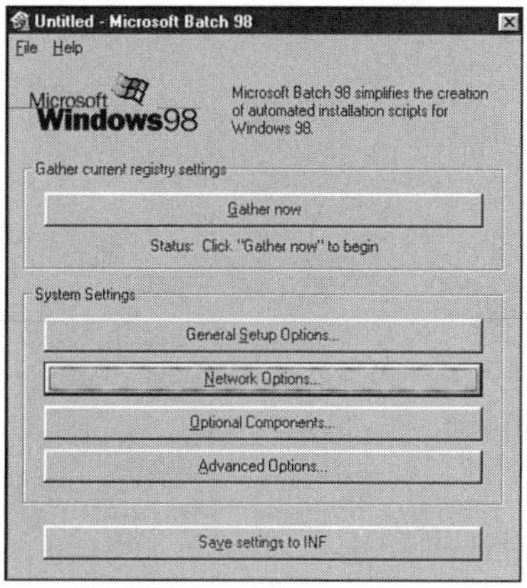

Caution

Microsoft Batch 98 is very involved. Refer to the Windows 98 Resource Kit for specific details regarding custom setup options.

INSTALLING WINDOWS 98 NETWORK FEATURES

Users who will be using Windows 98 in a network environment can install Windows 98 Network components by selecting Start, Settings, Control Panel, Network. Figure B.9 shows the Network dialog box.

Note

You are prompted to install network features if Windows 98 detects a network adapter during setup.

Here, you can select options that enable you to connect to Windows NT servers and NetWare servers. You can also configure network protocols such as Transmission Control Protocol/Internet Protocol (TCP/IP) and internetwork packet exchange (IPX).

The specific options you need to configure depend on your network. Contact your network administrator to find out about options particular to your corporate network.

PART

VII

APP

B

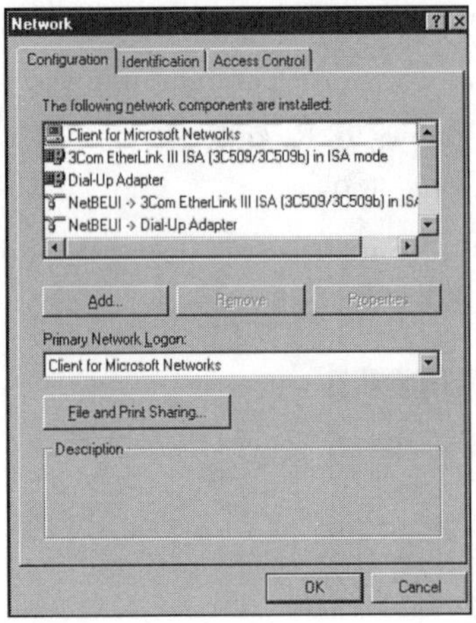

Figure B.9
The Network setup screen in Control Panel.

REMOVING WINDOWS 98

If you selected the Save Old System Files option during installation, you can remove Windows 98 by following these steps:

1. Click the Start button, select Settings, and click the Control Panel icon.

2. Click Add/Remove Programs.

3. Select the Install/Uninstall tab, select Windows 98, and then click Remove. Windows 98 uninstalls itself. When it finishes, you are prompted to reboot your machine, and your previous version of Windows or DOS will have been restored to your computer.

Tip #261

If you have trouble uninstalling Windows 98 from the Control Panel, you can use your Windows 98 startup disk to perform the removal. To do so, boot your computer using the startup disk and run UNINSTALL from the command line. This approach is often the best one to take from the outset.

THE WINDOWS UPDATE WIZARD

In the past, tracking down system patches and updated drivers was difficult. However, Microsoft streamlined the process in Windows 98 by including the Windows Update Wizard directly on the Start menu. If you have Internet access, you can update your installation of Windows 98 by using the Update Wizard, as shown in Figure B.10.

From the Start button, select Windows Update. After connecting to the Windows Update site, select Update Wizard. The Update Wizard scans your Windows 98 installation and displays any updates that are available from Microsoft (refer to Figure B.10).

Figure B.10
The Windows 98
Update Wizard.

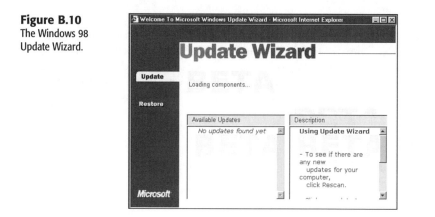

TROUBLESHOOTING WINDOWS 98 INSTALLATION

If you encounter problems during the installation process, follow these suggestions to try to work them out:

1. Most installation problems involve unsupported hardware. The best solution is to remove any problematic system devices in order to complete Windows 98 installation. After installation, reinstall the components one by one, using the Add New Hardware icon in Control Panel.

2. Check the BOOTLOG.TXT, DETLOG.TXT, and SETUPLOG.TXT files for clues to deciphering system problems. Windows 98 creates these files during boot, setup, and device detection. By checking the final entries in these files, you can see what Windows 98 was doing and whether the system crashed during any of these processes.

3. Try using Dr. Watson to diagnose system faults. *Dr. Watson* is a diagnostic tool that takes a snapshot of your system whenever a system fault occurs. Dr. Watson can sometimes identify problems and make recommendations to help you fix them.

> **Note**
>
> Dr. Watson is not loaded by default. To launch Dr. Watson automatically, create a shortcut in your Startup group to \Windows\DrWatson.exe.

4. Try posting a description of your installation problems to a Windows 98 newsgroup. Microsoft provides an interactive NNTP news server (`msnews.microsoft.com`). Netscape and Internet Explorer can easily be configured to attach to multiple news servers; consult your browser documentation. In addition, Microsoft employees monitor the newsgroups and provide limited feedback on problems. Downsides to using newsgroups are that you usually have to wade through many messages, and you are not guaranteed of getting a timely (or any) response.

5. Consult the Knowledge Base on the Microsoft Web site (`http://www.microsoft.com`).

6. If you have a Microsoft TechNet subscription, consult the Knowledge Base.

PART
VII

APP
B

Tip #262

> If you subscribe to Microsoft's TechNet service, every month you will receive several CDs containing information about a wide range of Microsoft products. A CD of updated drivers, a searchable Knowledge Base, and a number of white papers are included. TechNet subscriptions are expensive for an individual user, but any company that has Microsoft software deployed should consider purchasing a subscription. The subscription is especially important to companies that might not have Web access to obtain the free support of Web pages or newsgroups.

7. Call Microsoft support. The final product gives an 800 number to call for support.

USING SAFE RECOVERY

Use the Safe Recovery option if your initial installation of Windows 98 fails. If regular installation fails, turn your computer off and then on again. Run setup, and Windows 98 uses Safe Recovery (see Figure B.11) to pass the point at which the original installation failed.

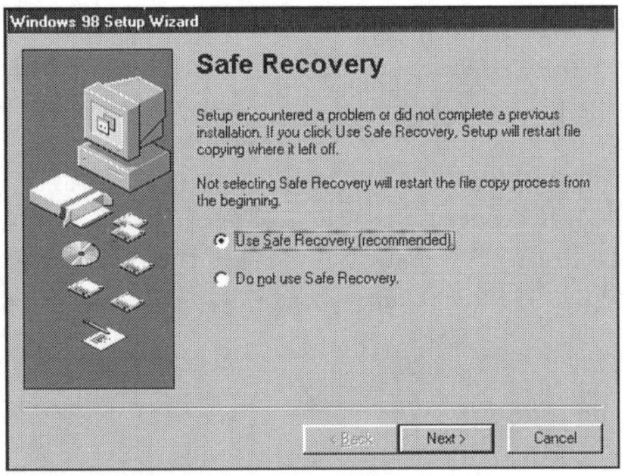

Figure B.11
The Safe Recovery option screen.

Safe Recovery instructs the Setup Wizard to continue copying files from the point of failure instead of starting over from the beginning. If you don't select Safe Recovery, your system might get caught in a loop, continuously failing at the same point during the installation.

Tip #263

> If Windows Setup fails repeatedly even with the Safe Recovery option selected, you need to begin removing hardware such as game cards and sound cards. After you identify the offending piece of equipment, complete Windows 98 installation and then try to install the hardware.

USING SAFE DETECTION

After the initial installation of the operating system, Windows 98 detects Plug and Play devices. Windows 98 prompts you for the installation drivers that have not been installed yet. During Safe Detection, you have the option of using a driver that is included with Windows or a third-party driver from disk.

PERFORMANCE BOTTLENECKS

You must recognize bottlenecks that may be preventing your system from running Windows 98 well. After installation, you should definitely consider which component(s) you may want to upgrade to give you better performance. A lack of disk space is a major bottleneck for systems running either Windows 95 or Windows 98. Windows 9x uses disk space (the swap file) to simulate physical memory or RAM. By using the System Monitor utility (see Figure B.12), you can see how the size of the swap file increases as you open additional programs. If your swap file increases beyond the point of available contiguous disk space, you get an out-of-memory error.

Figure B.12
The Windows 98
System Monitor.

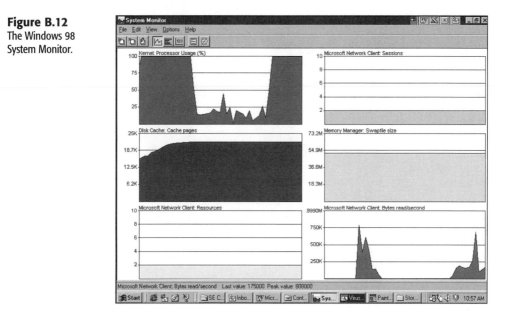

After disk space, the next major bottleneck is physical memory (RAM). In recent years RAM prices have fallen drastically, and it is now relatively economical to upgrade. Other options to consider are 2D/3D video cards and faster CD-ROM drives.

If possible, you should buy only hardware devices and software with the Designed for Windows 98 emblem. This emblem signifies that a product is certified to work optimally with Windows 98. Be wary of devices that are marked "Works with Windows 98." Sometimes, these products use older Real mode drivers that don't perform as well as true native Windows 98 drivers.

PART

VII

APP

B

INDEX

Get **FREE** books and more...when you register this book online for our Personal Bookshelf Program

http://register.quecorp.com/

 Register online and you can sign up for our *FREE Personal Bookshelf Program*...unlimited access to the electronic version of more than 200 complete computer books—immediately! That means you'll have 100,000 pages of valuable information onscreen, at your fingertips!

 Plus, you can access product support, including complimentary downloads, technical support files, book-focused links, companion Web sites, author sites, and more!

 And you'll be automatically registered to receive a *FREE subscription to a weekly email newsletter* to help you stay current with news, announcements, sample book chapters, and special events, including sweepstakes, contests, and various product giveaways!

 We value your comments! Best of all, the entire registration process takes only a few minutes to complete, so go online and get the greatest value going—absolutely FREE!

Don't Miss Out On This Great Opportunity!

Other Related Titles

Special Edition Using Microsoft Office 2000
Ed Bott
ISBN: 0-7897-1842-1
$39.99 US/$59.95 CAN

Special Edition Using ACT! 2000
Curtis Knight
ISBN: 0-7897-2136-8
$29.99 US/$44.95 CAN

Dan Gookin Teaches Windows 98
Dan Gookin
ISBN: 0-7897-1688-7
$19.99 US/$29.95 CAN

Windows 98 User Manual
Jim Boyce
ISBN: 0-7897-1657-7
$19.99 US/$29.95 CAN

Upgrading and Repairing PCs, Eleventh Edition
Scott Mueller
ISBN: 0-7897-1903-7
$59.99 US/$89.95 CAN

Microsoft Windows 98 Quick Reference
Keith Powell
ISBN: 0-7897-2030-2
$9.99 US/$14.95 CAN

Windows 98 Registry Handbook
Jerry Honeycutt
ISBN: 0-7897-1947-9
$19.99 US/$29.95 CAN

Special Edition Using MS-DOS 6.22, Second Edition
Allen L. Wyatt Sr.
ISBN: 0-7897-2040-x
$34.99 US/$52.95 CAN

Special Edition Using Microsoft Windows 2000 Professional
Robert Cowart
ISBN: 0-7897-2125-2
$39.99 US/$59.95 CAN

All prices are subject to change.

CD-ROM Installation

Windows 95/NT Installation Instructions

1. Insert the CD-ROM disc into your CD-ROM drive.

2. From the Windows 95/NT desktop, double-click the My Computer icon.

3. Double-click the icon representing your CD-ROM drive.

4. Double-click the icon titled START.EXE to run the CD-ROM interface.

Note

If Windows 95/NT is installed on your computer and you have the AutoPlay feature enabled, the START.EXE program starts automatically whenever you insert the disc into your CD-ROM drive.

NeoTrace and NeoSpace

Shareware License

License Agreement

You may make copies of the software for backup purposes, as long as all such copies, along with the original, are kept in your possession or control.

You may not make any changes or modifications to the Software, including, but not limited to, de-compiling, disassembling, or otherwise reverse engineering it. You may not rent or lease it to others. You may not use it on a computer network if more than one user can use it on more than one computer during any one twenty-four hour span of time.

NeoWorx hereby disclaims all warranties relating to this software, whether express or implied, including without limitation any implied warranties of merchantability or fitness for a particular purpose. NeoWorx will not be liable for any special, incidental, consequential, indirect or similar damages due to loss of data or any other reason, even if NeoWorx or an agent of NeoWorx has been advised of the possibility of such damages. In no event shall NeoWorx's liability for any damages ever exceed the price paid for the license to use the software, regardless of the form of the claim. The person using the software bears all risk as to the quality and performance of the software.

U.S. GOVERNMENT RESTRICTED RIGHTS

Use, duplication, or disclosure by the Government is subject to standard shrink-wrapped software restrictions.

DISCLAIMER OF WARRANTY